evolve
learning system

To access your Student Resources, visit the web address below:

http://evolve.elsevier.com/Lynch/forensicnursing/

Evolve Student Learning Resources for Lynch: Forensic Nursing Science, Second Edition, include the following:

- ### Key tools and resources for the forensic nurse
  Important information accessible online for your reference:
  - Forensic nursing diagnoses
  - International Association of Forensic Nurses Vision of Ethical Practice
  - Procedures for sexual assault examination in male victims
  - Istanbul Protocol for physical evidence of torture

- ### Essential downloadable forms
  Essential forms for crucial forensic procedures available to you:
  - Body diagrams
  - Operative assessment of organ donors

- ### Web links
  A variety of web links to help you pursue further information and study of key forensic nursing topics

- ### Image Collection
  Complete image collection from the text for closer study of the material

ELSEVIER

SECOND EDITION

FORENSIC NURSING SCIENCE

Virginia A. Lynch
MSN, RN, FAAN, FAAFS
International Consultant in Forensic Nursing
  Science
Fulbright Scholar to India, Punjabi University
Faculty, Beth El College of Nursing and
  Health Sciences
University of Colorado
Colorado Springs, Colorado

with Janet Barber Duval
MSN, RN, FAAFS
Adjunct Associate Professor
Indiana University School of Nursing
Indianapolis, Indiana
Clinical Nurse Consultant
Hill-Rom Company
Batesville, Indiana

ELSEVIER
MOSBY

3251 Riverport Lane
St. Louis, Missouri 63043

FORENSIC NURSING SCIENCE   ISBN: 978-0-323-06637-2

Copyright © 2011, 2006 by Mosby, Inc., an affiliate of Elsevier Inc.

Notices

Knowledge and best practice in this field are constantly changing. As new research and experience broaden our understanding, changes in research methods, professional practices, or medical treatment may become necessary.

Practitioners and researchers must always rely on their own experience and knowledge in evaluating and using any information, methods, compounds, or experiments described herein. In using such information or methods they should be mindful of their own safety and the safety of others, including parties for whom they have a professional responsibility.

With respect to any drug or pharmaceutical products identified, readers are advised to check the most current information provided (i) on procedures featured or (ii) by the manufacturer of each product to be administered, to verify the recommended dose or formula, the method and duration of administration, and contraindications. It is the responsibility of practitioners, relying on their own experience and knowledge of their patients, to make diagnoses, to determine dosages and the best treatment for each individual patient, and to take all appropriate safety precautions.

To the fullest extent of the law, neither the Publisher nor the authors, contributors, or editors, assume any liability for any injury and/or damage to persons or property as a matter of products liability, negligence or otherwise, or from any use or operation of any methods, products, instructions, or ideas contained in the material herein.

Library of Congress Cataloging-in-Publication Data

Lynch, Virginia A. (Virginia Anne)
  Forensic nursing science / Virginia A. Lynch, Janet Barber Duval. – 2nd ed.
    p.; cm.
  Rev. ed. of: Forensic nursing / [edited by] Virginia A. Lynch. c2006.
  Includes bibliographical references and index.
  ISBN 978-0-323-06637-2 (hardcover : alk. paper) 1. Forensic nursing. I. Duval, Janet Barber.
II. Forensic nursing. III. Title.
  [DNLM: 1. Forensic Nursing–methods. 2. Mandatory Reporting. 3. Nurse-Patient Relations.
WY 170 L987f 2011]
  RA1155.F63 2011
  614'.1–dc22

                                                          2010014127

Acquisitions Editor: Maureen Iannuzzi
Associate Developmental Editor: Mary Ann Zimmerman
Publishing Services Manager: Anne Altepeter
Project Manager: Cindy Thoms
Senior Designer: Amy Buxton

Printed in China

Last digit is the print number: 9 8 7 6 5 4 3 2 1

To Ann Wolbert Burgess

A forensic nurse scientist, *even before* the advent of forensic nursing. Dr. Burgess' contributions to research, education, and practice have touched thousands of nurses, igniting their passions for humanitarian care and unselfish public service on behalf of forensic clients.

■

Contributors

Anil Aggrawal, MB, BS, MD
Professor of Forensic Medicine
Department of Forensic Medicine
Maulana Azad Medical College
New Delhi, India

Cliff Akiyama, MA, MPH, CGS, CGP
Assistant Professor of Forensic Medicine
    and Certified Gang Specialist
Department of Pathology, Microbiology, Immunology,
    and Forensic Medicine
Philadelphia College of Osteopathic Medicine
Philadelphia, Pennsylvania

Patrick E. Besant-Matthews, MD
Faculty
Beth El College of Nursing and Health Sciences
University of Colorado
Colorado Springs, Colorado

Ann Wolbert Burgess, DNSc, RNCS, FAAN
Professor of Psychiatry and Mental Health
William F. Connell School of Nursing
Boston College
Chestnut Hill, Massachusetts

Nancy B. Cabelus, DNP, MSN, RN
Senior Law Enforcement Advisor
United States Department of Justice
International Criminal Investigative Training Assistance Program
Nairobi, Kenya

Cari Caruso, RN, SANE-A
Instructor
Law, Science, and Health
University of California, Riverside, Extension
Riverside, California
President/CEO
Forensic Nurse Professionals, Inc.
Pasadena, California

Susan Chasson, MSN, JD
Lecturer
College of Nursing
Assistant Lecturer
J. Reuben Clark Law School
Brigham Young University
Provo, Utah

Paul Thomas Clements, PhD, APRN, BC, CGS, DF-IAFN
Psychiatric Forensic Specialist and Certified Gang
    Specialist
Associate Clinical Professor
Drexel University College of Nursing and Health
    Professions
Philadelphia, Pennsylvania

Patricia A. Crane, PhD, MSN, WHNP-BC, IAFN-DF
Associate Professor
School of Nursing
University of Texas Medical Branch
Galveston, Texas

Sharon Rose Crowley, RN, MN, FCNS
Forensic Clinical Nurse Specialist
Santa Cruz, California
Pediatric SART Examiner, Center for Child Protection
Santa Clara County Valley Medical Center
San Jose, California

Jane Weaver Diedrich, BSN, MN, FNP, JD
United States Air Force, Retired
Fahy, Graduate Student
Washington, District of Columbia

Renae M. Diegel, RN, BBL, CFN, CEN, D-ABMDI, CMI-III, CFC, SANE
Medical Examiner Investigator
Macomb County Medical Examiner's Office
Mount Clemens, Michigan
Forensic Nurse Examiner/Educator
Turning Points Forensic Nurse Examiner Program
Clinton Township, Michigan

Theresa G. Di Maio, BSN, RN
Forensic Nurse Consultant
Forensic Psychiatric Nursing
San Antonio, Texas

Vincent J.M. Di Maio, MD
Forensic Pathologist
San Antonio, Texas

Pamela J. Dole, EdD, MPH, FNP
Consultant
Stonington, Connecticut

Catherine M. Dougherty, MA, RN, FAAFS
Emergency Department
Baylor Medical Center of Waxahachie
Waxahachie, Texas

Alden Fahy
Washington, District of Columbia

Jamie Ferrell, BSN, RN, CFN, SANE-A
Forensic Nursing Clinical Manager
Memorial Hermann Healthcare System
Houston, Texas
Forensic Nursing Consultant
National Forensic Nursing Institute
Oklahoma City, Oklahoma

Cris Finn, PhD, RN, MS, MA, FNP
Assistant Professor
Nursing
Regis University
Denver, Colorado

Bruce A. Goldberger, PhD
Professor and Director of Toxicology
Department of Pathology, Immunology, and Laboratory Medicine
University of Florida College of Medicine
Gainesville, Florida

Gregory S. Golden, DDS, DABFO
Chief Odontologist
County of San Bernadino, California

Rakesh K. Gorea, MD, DNB, PhD, MFFLM
Professor
Head, Department of Forensic Medicine
Gian Sagar Medical College
Ram Nagar, Banur, District Patiala, Punjab, India

Kristine Karcher, RN, BSN, D-AMBDI
Chief Deputy Medical Examiner
Coos County Medical Examiner's Office
Coquille, Oregon

Arlene Kent-Wilkinson, RN, BSN, MN, PhD
Associate Professor
St. Andrew's College
University of Saskatchewan
Saskatoon, Saskatchewan
Canada

Sarah Kerrigan, PhD
Director, Forensic Science Program
College of Criminal Justice
Sam Houston State University
Hunstville, Texas
Laboratory Director
Sam Houston Regional Crime Laboratory
The Woodlands, Texas

Steven A. Koehler, MPH, PhD
Forensic Consultant
Associate Professor of Forensic Science
Point Park University
Pittsburgh, Pennsylvania

Karolina Krysinska, PhD
Center for Suicide Prevention Studies in Young People
School of Medicine
University of Queensland
Brisbane, Queensland, Australia

Linda E. Ledray, RN SANE-A, PhD, FAAN
Director
SANE-SART Resource Service
Minneapolis, Minnesota

Gordon D. MacFarlane, PhD
Senior Research Executive
Hill-Rom, Inc.
St. Paul, Minnesota

Tom Mason, PhD, BSc (Hons), RMN, RNMH, RGN
Professor and Department Head
Mental Health & Learning Disabilities
Faculty of Health and Social Care
University of Chester
Chester, Cheshire
United Kingdom

John R. McPhail, PhD, RN
Forensic Nurse Consultant
Forensic Education Services
Pueblo, Colorado

Stacey A. Mitchell, DNP, RN
Director, Forensic Program
Harris County Hospital District
Houston, Texas

Mary Frances Moorhouse, BSN, RN, CRRN, LNC
Moorhouse Legal Nurse Consultant
Colorado Springs, Colorado

Alice C. Murr, RN, BSN, LNC
Contract Legal Nurse Consultant
Telephone Triage Nurse
Author
Macon, Mississippi

Georgia A. Pasqualone, MSFS, MSFN, RN, CEN, CFN, FABFN
Forensic Nurse Consultant
Adjunct Faculty
Fitchburg State College
Fitchburg, Massachusetts
Boston College
Chestnut Hill, Massachusetts

Susan B. Patton, DNSc, PNP, BC
Associate Professor, Coordinator DNP Forensic Nursing
College of Nursing
University of Tennessee Health Science Center
Memphis, Tennessee
Pediatric Nurse Practitioner, Proprietor
East Arkansas Children's Clinic
Forrest City, Arkansas

Catherine Pearsall, PhD, FNP, RN, CNE
Associate Professor
Nursing Department, St. Joseph's College
Patchogue, New York
Adjunct Faculty
School of Nursing, Duquesne University
Pittsburgh, Pennsylvania

David J. Porta, PhD
Professor of Anatomy
Bellarmine University
Louisville, Kentucky

Robert K. Ressler, BS, MS
Adjunct Assistant Professor
School of Criminal Justice
Michigan State University
East Lansing, Michigan
Adjunct Assistant Professor of Psychiatry
Department of Psychiatry
Georgetown University Hospital
Washington, District of Columbia

Mark E. Safarik, MS, VSM
Supervisory Special Agent (FBI Ret.)
Executive Director
Forensic Behavioral Services International
Fredericksburg, Virginia

Richard Saferstein, PhD
Forensic Science Consultant
Mt. Laurel, New Jersey

Teresa J. Shafer, RN, MSN, CPTC
Executive Vice President and Chief Operating Officer
LifeGift Organ Donation Center
Houston, Texas

Paul D. Shapiro, PhD
Associate Professor of Sociology
Chair, Department of Psychology and Sociology
Georgia Southwestern State University
Americus, Georgia

William S. Smock, MD, FACEP, FAAEM
Emergency Medicine
University of Louisville Hospital
Louisville, Kentucky

Zug G. Standing Bear, MSFS, MPA, MSEd, PhD, FFMed
Consultant and Mentor in Forensic Science and Criminology
Bearhawk Consulting Group
Divide, Colorado
Thomas Edison State College
Trenton, New Jersey

Kent Stewart
Chief Coroner
Office of the Chief Coroner
Ministry of Justice, Province of Saskatchewan
Regina, Saskatchewan
Canada

Deborah Storlie, BSN, RN
Clinical Informaticist
Omaha, Nebraska

Mary K. Sullivan, MSN, RN-BC, CARN, FAAFS
Clinical Forensic Nurse
Mental Health and Behavioral Sciences
Department of Veterans Affairs, Phoenix VA Health
   Care System
Phoenix, Arizona

David Williams, DDS, MPH
Clinical Associate Professor
Endodontics, Prosthetics and Operative Dentistry
University of Maryland School of Dentistry
Baltimore, Maryland

Joyce Williams, DNP, RN, AFN
Clinical Instructor
Acute Care and Public Health
Johns Hopkins University School of Nursing
Baltimore, Maryland

Reviewers

Marie Ann Harris Ahrens, MS, BSN, RN
University of Tulsa School of Nursing
Tulsa, Oklahoma

Eileen M. Allen, MSN, RN, FN-CSA, SANE-A
Freehold, New Jersey

Heidi Bresee, RN, MSN, CRNP, FNEA/P
Shady Grove Adventist Hospital
University of Maryland School of Nursing
Baltimore, Maryland

Rose E. Constantino, PhD, JD, RN, FAAN, FACFE
University of Pittsburgh School of Nursing
Pittsburgh, Pennsylvania

Kim Day, RN, FNE, SANE-A
International Association of Forensic Nurses
Arnold, Maryland

Maria Farmer, MSN, ACNP-BC, EMT-P
Allen College of Nursing
Waterloo, Iowa

Diana Faugno, MSN, RN, CPN, SANE-A, SANE-P, FAAP
Eisenhower Medical Center
Rancho Mirage, California

Joyce Foresman-Capuzzi, BSN, RN, CEN, CCRN, CPN, CTRN, CPEN, SANE-A, EMT-P
Lankenau Hospital
Wynnewood, Pennsylvania

Irma A. Groot, RN, CNOR, DABFN, Fellow ACFEI
Forensic Nurse Consultant
F'NES
Phoenix, Arizona

Joellen W. Hawkins, RN, PhD, WHNP-BC, FAAN, FAANP
Professor Emeritus, William F. Connell School of Nursing
Boston College; writer in residence
Chestnut Hill, Massachusetts
Simmons College, Nursing Department
Boston, Massachusetts

Tara Henry, RN, MSN, SANE-A, SANE-P
Forensic Nurse Services
Anchorage, Alaska

Jane A. Kaminski, DDS
Detroit, Michigan

Arlene Kent-Wilkinson, RN, BSN, MN, PhD
Associate Professor
St. Andrew's College
University of Saskatchewan
Saskatoon, Saskatchewan
Canada

Patricia Pasky McMahon, PhD, CRNP, SANE-A
The Pennsylvania State University
Erie, Pennsylvania

Georgia Pasqualone, MSFS, MSFN, RN, CEN, CFN, FABFN
Forensic Nurse Consultant
Adjunct Faculty
Fitchburg State College
Fitchburg, Massachusetts
Boston College
Chestnut Hill, Massachusetts

David J. Porta, PhD
Professor of Anatomy
Bellarmine University
Louisville, Kentucky

Jaclyn J. Ryujin, RN, SANE, ATCN, EMT-I, EMS Instructor
Salt Lake Sexual Assault Nurse Examiners
Salt Lake City, Utah

Mitchell Spears, BA
Retired Detective
Las Vegas Metropolitan Police Department
Las Vegas, Nevada

Tascha Spears, PhD, RN, SANE-A
Spears + Spears Consulting Services
Loomis, Washington

Foreword

In the foreword to the first edition of *Forensic Nursing*, Dr. Michael Baden emphasized the necessity and timeliness of its production and stated that forensic nursing was a specialty whose time had come. This was certainly both incisive and apposite in 2006, and I am endorsing and reaffirming that statement again in 2010. However, I would also like to emphasize the progress, influence, and transformation of forensic nursing over the interregnum. The march of science has ensured that each of the numerous branches within the wider domain of forensic nursing has developed, refined, and advanced their respective areas of knowledge and expertise. Research inquiry has been central to this enrichment and coupled with the publications and conference debates, as well as the international exchange of ideas, forensic nursing has consolidated its position in modern health care delivery systems. It has now been further embraced by the wider forensic sciences and the criminal justice systems. Through scientific rigor, it has strengthened its wide and diverse range of activities. Forensic nursing in all its applications is built on the foundational pillars of concern for the victims, the perpetrators, and those caught up in the aftermath of the former two: the families, friends, and survivors. Whether children or the elderly, in accidents and emergency departments or high-security psychiatric hospitals, in our homes or on our streets, across the gamut of human behaviors, forensic nursing is in demand. Its sphere of operations is only limited by, and to, the human tragedy that causes harm to others. Its challenge is, as always, to rise to the occasion that we call forensic nursing care.

At the time of writing, we are plagued with the horrors of war with suicide bombers, civilian and soldier victims, and the abuse of the vulnerable in the name of a God, an ideology, or a political creed. First-world and developing countries alike seek strategies of modernity to raise the safety standards for their populations amidst catastrophes, both natural and manmade, and one such tactic in this battle involves the application of forensic nursing scientific principles, across continents and hemispheres, to help alleviate pain and suffering. This is why the second edition, now titled *Forensic Nursing Science*, is as timely as the first edition. The book has grown, changed, adapted, and developed in response to scientific developments and global expansion of the specialty. An examination of the contents reveals a clearer and sharper scientific focus of the chapters and a tighter integration of the units. The second edition updates and upgrades the diverse applications from the particulars of their sciences to their inter-relatedness on a global level.

Virginia A. Lynch has either introduced or influenced the development of forensic nursing in nearly 50 countries over a quarter of a century. She has coalesced contributors from her global network of colleagues, forming an impressive academic group representing diverse disciplines. Each author's clinical experience and academic acumen are matched only by his or her passion of subject and a pioneering spirit. *Forensic Nursing Science* is a seminal work based on the courage, convictions, knowledge, and experience of these hand-picked experts. It is poised to be the most important and central forensic nursing text for the second decade of the twenty-first century.

Tom Mason, PhD
Professor of Mental Health & Learning Disabilities
Faculty of Health and Social Care
University of Chester
Chester, Cheshire
United Kingdom

Preface

The new title for the second edition, *Forensic Nursing Science,* conveys the transition that has taken place in the discipline. Forensic nursing is no longer viewed simply as care for victims of violence, but rather the application of forensic science knowledge and principles to health care. Although the original conceptual model for forensic nursing has not been altered, there has been a metamorphosis among the ranks of forensic nurses and an acknowledgment that the core of practice must have a scientific basis to co-exist and be deemed credible by law enforcement and members of the judicial system.

Fortunately, the popularity of forensic nursing has attracted enlightened practitioners and educators with advanced degrees and broad experiences in dealing with social and legal problems. This new cadre of forensic nurses has begun to use their knowledge and skills for offenders as well as victims. They have reached out for evidence-based "best practices" and encouraged research. New subspecialties have emerged to share the limelight with sexual assault, child and elder maltreatment, domestic violence, forensic psychiatric nursing, and death investigation—the longstanding mainstays of of forensic nursing. For success in today's forensic arena, collaborative practice among several scientific disciplines is required for determining *truth* in a court of law.

The second edition has been designed to be an authoritative text for today's forensic nurses. With its significant content revisions and new chapters, the book offers cutting-edge scientific information that will also support tomorrow's practice. Digital evidence, physics of traumatic injuries, bio-markers of elder and child maltreatment, and analyses of offender behaviors are examples of basic and applied science topics that are introduced in this revision.

The organization of the book has also been redesigned to make the book's information more accessible and its placement more logical.

1. Unit I provides an introduction to forensic nursing science and includes the status of today's nursing education programs and their forensic nursing courses in both undergraduate and graduate curricula.
2. Unit II presents the fundamental principles and techniques of forensic science. It provides the basis for understanding the epidemiology of forensic scenarios, crime scene processing, and techniques for evidence collection and preservation, including photography. Digital evidence, behavioral analysis, and toxicology are also presented as a foundation for forensic nursing practice.
3. The focus of Unit III is human subjects as a source of evidence in various settings ranging from pre-hospital and in-hospital incidents to multi-casualty scenes.
4. Unit IV considers several topics in postmortem science and associated forensic analyses. New chapters include intrafamilial homicide and unexplained childhood deaths, medical evidence recovery at death scenes, as well as the basic information on the role of forensic nursing in death investigation, including postmortem sexual assault evidence recovery, autoerotic incidents, taphonomy, and mass-grave exhumations.
5. Unit V delves into mechanisms of injury and death. In addition to vehicular accident reconstruction, there is essential content on blunt, sharp, bite mark, and firearm injuries. New chapters on physics of fracture and restraint injuries, asphyxia and electrical, thermal, and inhalation injuries provide foundational information for nurse investigators.
6. Unit VI contains core content on child and elder maltreatment, relationship crimes, sexual violence, and exploitation of children. An enlightening chapter on youth gangs and hate crimes has been added to better equip the forensic nurse to detect associated evidence and to understand the behavioral patterns that characterize offenders and their victim targets.
7. Unit VII provides a refreshing new chapter on forensic psychiatric nursing as well as pertinent discussions of suicidal behavior and issues in correctional care. A thorough consideration of sudden death episodes associated with restraints and the excited-delirium syndrome is unique and vital information for nurses who work in any custodial settings where physical restraining techniques are used, including hospital emergency departments.
8. Unit VIII highlights global and cultural crimes. Two international authors discuss sociocultural and sexual deviant behaviors. Female genital mutilation and human trafficking issues are also included in this unit.
9. Unit IX encompasses legal issues in forensic nursing practice such as testifying, malpractice, and negligence. There is a new chapter on ethical decision-making in addition to significant content revisions for the chapters that appeared in the first edition on human subjects in research, organ donation and tissue transplantation, and international law.
10. Unit X addresses credentialing and career planning as well as issues and trends in forensic nursing. An important review outlining the impact of forensic nurses in the military has also been included. The authors reflect on the current status of forensic nursing as a specialty and speculate on the challenges for this discipline within the next decade.

The new edition contains pertinent full-color photographs and other helpful illustrations throughout. Case studies, critical thinking exercises, key points, and best practices—popular features of the original text—have been retained. The availability of all of these features in electronic format should prove to be highly useful to both educators and their students.

Finally, the book showcases several new authors who present refreshing and valuable content on topics that were not included in the original edition. Along with leading educators, practitioners, consultants, and researchers who are well recognized within forensic nursing ranks, there are mavericks who share their novel applications of forensic nursing in the hopes of providing encouragement to those who have found it difficult to find their niche in practice. Opportunities in forensic nursing abound, and new applications are waiting to be discovered.

Virginia A. Lynch, MSN, RN, FAAN, FAAFS
Janet Barber Duval, MSN, RN, FAAFS

Acknowledgment

Forensic Nursing Science is the product of many forensic nurses and other scientists who have contributed chapters, photographs, and other materials. They represent expert practitioners, educators, researchers, and scientists. Some are well-established and their names are widely recognized. Others are pioneers in the sub-specialties, but will be among our future leaders. First and foremost, we acknowledge these contributors who have shared their knowledge and experience within their chapters.

This textbook would be relatively pale without the one-of-a-kind photographs provided from the files of Dr. Patrick Besant-Matthews. As always, he has shared generously to ensure that illustrations are exemplary instructional art. His support of this project and of forensic nursing have been there from the beginning (1982) and is ever-present. From the beginning of the development of forensic nursing, Dr. M.G.F. Gilliland and husband, Gary Gilliland, worked together with Dr. Besant-Matthews to help establish the foundations of forensic nursing science in both medicine and law. They have continued over the decades to assist, promote, and contribute to this field. We are especially grateful that Dr. Besant-Matthews, Dr. Gilliland, and Mr. Gilliland continue to be friends and trusted colleagues.

We recognize and applaud our colleagues within the International Association of Forensic Nurses and the American Academy of Forensic Sciences who have supported forensic nursing and this text. Their expertise, guidance, and direct input into the pages of this book have positively influenced its quality and credibility.

The nurses who have paved the way for forensic nursing in the military and Department of Veterans Affairs deserve a salute for their contributions to this book. They are: Colonel Teresa Parsons, Colonel Heidi Warrington, and Nancy Emma of the U.S. Army Nurse Corps; Commander Lovette Robinson, Lieutenant Commander Cynthia T. Ferguson, and Lieutenant Commander Michelle Ortiz of the U.S. Navy Nurse Corps; Colonel Janet Barber Duval and Colonel Susan L. Hanshaw, U.S. Air Force Nurse Corps; and Mary K. Sullivan, Department of Veterans Affairs. These individuals have made significant impacts within the Department of Defense by introducing new applications of the forensic nursing sciences, affecting the welfare of military personnel on active duty as well as thousands of our veterans.

Our international associates in the forensic sciences have provided a global perspective for the contents of this book and have opened doors for teaching and learning throughout the world. Among those who have provided exceptional opportunities for international endeavors in education and practice include: Dr. Giancarlo DiVella, Michela Stallone, and Luciano Garafono (Italy); Dr. Tom Mason, Dr. Jane Rutty, and Dr. Guy Rutty (United Kingdom); Dr. Anil Aggrawal and Dr. Rakesh Gorea (India); Dr. David Sadler (Scotland); Dr. J.E. Els, MD, and Mohau Maukasani, the first forensic nurse (South Africa); and Arlene Kent-Wilkinson and Sheila Early (Canada).

Certain colleagues continue to illuminate our spirits and influence our practice. Their commitment and dedication to forensic nursing lives on, even though they have retired from their long-standing roles. Colonel Robert K. Ressler (FBI. Ret), Gwendolyn Costello (Forensic Pediatric Nurse), Kenneth Pratley (Scotland Yard, Director of Forensic Medicine, Ret.) and Dr. Joseph H. Davis (Forensic Pathologist, Ret.) deserve special recognition.

Alan Sorkowitz, our agent and professional advisor has been a chief supporter for this project and has been an invaluable resource as we navigate the publishing processes. More authors would be successful if they had the benefit of Alan's expertise and wise counsel.

Finally, we recognize our husbands, Dr. Z.G. Standing Bear and Donald L. Duval, respectively, for their help in writing, creating and transposing artwork, solving computer problems, and simply providing support by listening and understanding.

Virginia A. Lynch
Janet Barber Duval

Contents

UNIT FOUR POSTMORTEM SCIENCE AND FORENSIC ANALYSIS, 179

UNIT FIVE MECHANISMS OF INJURY AND DEATH, 271

UNIT SEVEN FORENSIC MENTAL HEALTH AND CORRECTIONAL ISSUES, 441

CHAPTER 1 Evolution of Forensic Nursing Science

Virginia A. Lynch

Scientific Foundations of Forensic Nursing

The science of nursing has merged with the forensic sciences and the justice system to provide a distinctive discipline: forensic nursing science. This scientific discipline incorporates numerous applications to the major status of the registered nurse at all levels of practice, ranging from the basic or generalist role to advanced practice in forensic nursing. Advances in forensic and nursing science represent a sufficient need identified worldwide by those who understand that the long-range aims of the nursing field would be limited if this need were ignored. Forensic attorneys, nurse scientists, examiners, educators, investigators, administrators, and consultants in local, state, or federal government and nongovernment institutions and organizations fill this need. The forensic nurse is prepared for individual or group interventions and services that will provide a scientific and humanitarian image to those forgotten amid the chaos of a world in crisis. Thus, women and children, the damaged and disabled who represent the most vulnerable populations, will be offered greater protection to shield them from harm.

Forensic nursing science combines the concepts and principles of the traditional forensic sciences and those of nursing in the clinical investigation of trauma and the recovery of medical evidence; it also provides direct services to victims, suspects, perpetrators, and those who witness violence. The forensic nurse scientist identifies, assesses, intervenes, and evaluates trauma, disease, and death while documenting findings, preserves and secures evidence to determine legal outcomes and improve patient care. As interdisciplinary partners in healthcare and law-related agencies, the specialist in forensic nursing science has become a potent influence in the rule of law and provides a collective intelligence for practice and research.

Violence and Healthcare

Violence and its associated trauma are widely recognized as critical health problems throughout the world. Among the challenges that face healthcare providers is protection of the patient's legal, civil, and human rights (Lynch, 1995). Violence is no longer considered solely within the purview of law enforcement but rather is viewed as a mutual responsibility of healthcare and the law.

KEY POINT All trauma patients are considered forensic cases until suspicion of abuse or questions of liability are confirmed or ruled out.

Previously, it was not considered appropriate for nurses to become entangled in a patient's private life, to suspect forces,

motives, and events other than the patient's own statements as representative of the mechanisms of injury that damaged and threatened their lives. It was left to law enforcement agencies to draw out the truth and bring social justice to bear. However, if nurses do not accept these wider truths as a responsibility, they cannot recognize the associated abuse.

In 1979, the U.S. Surgeon General's Report "Healthy People" outlined a strategy for addressing priority areas for improving the health of the nation, which included addressing interpersonal violence, an important contributor to morbidity and premature mortality. One expert noted that public health is in the business of continually redefining the unacceptable, which changes the social norm and eventually changes the problem. Not unlike polio, violence is also a threat to public health (Foege, 1997).

In 1989, U.S. Surgeon General C. Everett Koop challenged healthcare professionals to assume accountability, along with law enforcement, for the problems associated with violence. The surgeon general's workshop on violence and public health addressed domestic violence, child abuse, elder abuse, rape, homicide, murder, and traumatic accidents as pervasive threats to the fundamental public health principle of population exposure. This perspective emphasized that no segment of society can be considered immune from the effects of violence. He remarked that these problems are so pervasive that they can no longer be viewed as acts of individual offenders, rather collectively, a public epidemic of violence. (Koop, 1989). In past decades, the U.S. Department of Health and Human Services has continued to recognize the inevitable outcomes of violence (injury, disability, and death) as the primary benchmarks of public health status.

With the steady increase in reporting interpersonal violence within our society, nurses are recognizing a greater number of victims of criminal acts. These victims, as well as the perpetrators of crime, are often treated in the hospital for injuries and collection of evidence. As perhaps the first point of contact in the immediate posttrauma period, the nurse is in an ideal position to gather information and physical evidence related to the crime. Forensic nurses must be able to identify injuries from weapons or human abuse and to skillfully interview patients and evaluate the nature and scope of these injuries. Nurses interface with law enforcement and the medical examiner/coroner and provide excellent resources for expert testimony when these cases are tried in a court of law. Forensic nursing demands superb assessment skills, second only to a high degree of suspiciousness.

Every injury, illness, or death can have forensic implications. Therefore, a solid forensic education for nurses provides a vital link in the development of clinical acumen required for responding to these forensic circumstances. Forensic nurses represent one

Such physicians also practice in Asia, Latin America, Russia, and Australia, as well as Europe and Great Britain, among others.

The earliest reference in the American medical literature that directly addresses the practice of forensic medicine on living patients is one made by Root and Scott in 1973: frequently, a forensic issue in medicine "is either unrecognized as such, or is consciously or subconsciously evaded" (pg. 68) by practicing clinical physicians (Root & Scott, 1973). Trained as forensic pathologists, these physicians felt that if vital forensic questions were not answered in the living patient, justice would suffer, criminals would go free, and innocent persons could be convicted of crimes they did not commit.

A decade passed until, in 1983, the late William Eckert published "Forensic Sciences: The Clinical or Living Aspects" (Eckert, 1983). Eckert became the driving force behind bringing clinical forensic medicine to the forefront of contemporary American medical practice. This concept, applying forensic techniques to living patients in the U.S., was the basis for a 1986 article by Goldsmith in the *Journal of the American Medical Association (JAMA),* "U.S. Forensic Pathologist on a New Case: Examination of Living Patients" (Goldsmith, 1986).

Cyril Wecht, medical doctor, juris doctor, and former president of the American College of Legal Medicine, in Goldsmith's 1986 *JAMA* article, stated:

> *It's a great shame and a source of much puzzlement why a group similar to police surgeons hasn't developed here. Even within our adversarial judicial system and with our guaranteed civil rights— which are much greater than in many of the countries where forensic clinicians are commonly found—I believe that persons with both medical and forensic training could remove much of the guesswork, speculation, and hypotheses from the disposition of accident or assault cases involving living persons.*

Wecht also supported development of forensic training courses for medical students and residents and eventually came to lend his support and recognition to the developing specialty of forensic nursing.

Clinical forensic concepts or *living forensics* may be attributed to Harry C. McNamara, chief medical examiner for Ulster County, New York. In 1988, McNamara defined clinical forensic medicine as "the application of clinical medicine to victims of trauma involving the proper processing of forensic evidence" (McNamara, 1988) (see Box 1-2 for categories of clinical forensic cases). McNamara was one of the first to recognize and encourage the relationship with nursing to this essential field of healthcare. Although wider in its application, this definition stresses the importance of healthcare providers maintaining an awareness of evidentiary materials and legal issues associated with their patients or clients to preserve national welfare (McNamara, 1988).

Before the evolution of the clinical forensic specialist in the United States, victims or perpetrators of crime who required a forensic evaluation and collection of evidence had to have died from catastrophic circumstances or unknown causes in order to receive a forensic examination. Because few medical schools in the United States offer courses in forensic medicine, the few physicians who are educated in this field rarely practice in clinical medicine. Individuals who survive traumatic events are frequently deprived of quality forensic services, often resulting in a miscarriage of justice. Although forensic medicine is generally a required course of study in other parts of the world, there remains a shortage of forensic physicians and state-of-the-art skills in developing countries. These countries can also benefit from a partnership with forensic nurse examiners in both the clinical environs and death investigation.

Forensic Nursing

Nursing advancements typically parallel those of colleagues in medicine (Box 1-3). The strong foundations of forensic medicine that were well established first in the United Kingdom, on the European mainland, in Asia, and the Orient were obviously influential in the early development of such nursing roles in those countries. See Box 1-4 for the chronology of forensic nursing. Historical documents reveal that before the French Revolution, midwives testified regarding sexual assault and pregnancy (Camp, 1976). Although professional nursing did not yet exist, the inclusion of the midwife was undoubtedly an early prototype of the forensic nurse examiner. In the United Kingdom, forensic psychiatric nurses have been important associates of the clinical forensic team for centuries. As the value of these practitioners was recognized within law enforcement agencies and legal communities, a trend toward the clinical forensic disciplines was ignited in North America as well (Lynch & Standing Bear, 2000).

Forensic nursing was first informally derived from the broad field of forensic medicine in the United Kingdom and in Canada. However, it was first defined as scientific discipline and officially recognized as a nursing specialty in the United States (Lynch, 1995). Forensic nursing is considered an integral component of public health, evolving from the foundation of close association of forensic medicine in public health. Clinical forensic practice focuses on the civil and criminal investigation of traumatic injury or patient treatment with law-related issues. It encompasses living patients: the victims, the accused, and the condemned.

Forensic nurse examiners (FNEs) apply concepts and strategies of the forensic sciences in their specialty practices, which include death investigators, sexual assault nurse examiners, forensic psychiatric nurses, correctional nurse specialists, legal nurse consultants, forensic geriatric and pediatric specialist forensic clinical

---

Box 1-2 Categories of Clinical Forensic Cases

All victims of violence	Automobile trauma
Patients in police custody	Workers' compensation
Sexual assault	Medical malpractice
Drug and alcohol abuse	Food and drug tampering
Child maltreatment	Environmental hazards
Domestic violence	Illegal abortion
Elder abuse	Occult-related injury/death
Survivors of attempted suicide	Cults or religion abuses

Box 1-3 Comparative Practice Model for Forensic Disciplines

THE FORENSIC ASPECTS OF HEALTHCARE PROFESSIONS

MEDICINE	NURSING
Pathology	Death investigation
Psychiatry	Psychiatric nursing
Clinical forensic physician	Clinical forensic nurse
Sexual assault examiner	Sexual assault examiner
Medical jurisprudence	Nursing jurisprudence
Forensic medical examiner	Forensic nurse examiner
Corrections medical officer	Corrections or custody nurse
Legal medical consultants	Legal nurse consultants

Box 1-4 Chronology of Forensic Nursing

18th and 19th centuries	Clinical forensic medical science is developed in Europe, South America, Asia, Russia, and other locations.
1986	Lynch initiates formal curricula for forensic nursing at University of Texas at Arlington with focus on the scientific investigation of death.
1988	McNamara introduces the concept of clinical forensic practice or living forensics.
	Lynch develops forensic nursing model.
	Lynch expands curricula to include clinical forensic nursing.
1989	Lynch introduces forensic nursing as a scientific discipline.
1991	International Association of Forensic Nurses (IAFN) is founded.
	American Academy of Forensic Sciences formally recognizes forensic nursing.
	Clinical Forensic Medical program established at University of Louisville
1995	American Nurses Association's Congress (ANA) of Nursing Practice grants specialty status to forensic nursing.
1997	Scope and Standards of Forensic Nursing Practice is published jointly by IAFN and the ANA.
2000	IAFN celebrates its 10th anniversary with membership of more than 2000.
2010	American Forensic Nurses (AFN) celebrates 18th anniversary with membership of over 3000 and having addressed forensic nursing in more than 50 countries.

nurse specialists, or forensic nurse practitioners. Nonexaminer roles may include those who also practice as forensic nurse attorneys, educators, and managers, among others.

Forensic nursing science is defined as the application of the forensic aspects of healthcare combined with the bio/psycho/social/spiritual education of the registered nurse in the scientific investigation and treatment of the trauma or death of victims and perpetrators of violence, criminal activity, and traumatic accidents. It provides direct services to individual clients and consultation services to nursing, medical, and law-related agencies, and it provides expert court testimony in areas dealing with questioned death investigative processes, adequacy of services delivery, and specialized diagnoses of specific conditions as related to nursing (Lynch, 1990). The International Association of Forensic Nurses (IAFN) further defines forensic nursing as the global practice of nursing where healthcare and legal systems intersect. It has, by its nature, a strong association with both physical and social sciences as they apply to public or legal proceedings. The specialty combines the forensic aspects of heathcare with the scientific investigation and treatment of crime or liability-related cases (IAFN, 2010).

Because of the identified weaknesses in trauma practices addressed in the literature, combined with professional experiences in death investigation, the concept of a clinical forensic specialist in nursing sparked an innovative graduate program at the University of Texas at Arlington (UTA) in 1986. This landmark master's degree program set the pace for further examination and the development of a new discipline in the forensic and clinical sciences and has been replicated across the United States and abroad. In addition to medicolegal concerns (a scientific role), courses focus on sensitivity to victims and families.

SPECIALTY RECOGNITION

To receive specialty status, a practice area must be defined distinctly from other areas of nursing in regard to its purpose and functions. In addition, the rationale for the need for the specialty

must be well outlined, along with supporting data that there is an existing group of nurses devoting themselves to such a practice arena. These background data are described in a written document submitted to the Congress of Nursing Practice of the American Nurses Association (ANA) for approval. A vital component, of course, is graduate education, evidence of a research-based body of knowledge, and a means of disseminating this research to nurses engaged in the specialty. The presence of the IAFN and its code of ethics, along with a network of publications and scientific meetings, were vital preludes to petitioning the Congress of Nursing Practice for formal recognition (IAFN, 1993).

Nursing's Social Policy Statement requires that a specialty delineate a core of practice including roles, responsibilities, functions, and skills of a unique body of knowledge (ANA, 1995). Dimensions, boundaries, and intersections must be outlined to justify the placement of the specialty practice within the broader collegial and collaborative interfaces with other healthcare and social groups related to the discipline. In the case of forensic nursing, the relevant relationships of law enforcement, public policy, and legal standards were illustrated to explain forensic nursing and describe the environment for its practice. Social consciousness, healthcare delivery trends, emerging technology, and the demands of societal organizations are used to confirm the needs for a practice specialty. The Scope and Standards of Forensic Nursing Practice is designed as a living document, subject to revision, because forensic nursing's structural framework is based on dynamic factors that are reactionary to the multiple components of healthcare, social justice, and consumer demands.

The nursing process is likely to be used as a framework for curricula in schools of nursing, and agencies responsible for state licensure and specialty certification use its various components to describe roles and responsibilities of clinicians. The Joint Commission (TJC) has required hospitals and other healthcare facilities seeking accreditation to demonstrate its use of the nursing process. On this basis, the ANA granted specialty status to forensic nursing in 1995.

Forensic nurses care for individuals whose illness, injury, or death stems from acts of violence, maltreatment, abuse, neglect, or exploitation. The forensic nursing process is client centered and establishes a feedback loop that ensures a dynamic mechanism for the reevaluation and revision of care plans. Collaboration is vital to the forensic nursing process. Without strong links to other practitioners within medicine, law enforcement, and the judicial systems, as well as other healthcare and social support personnel, successful forensic nursing interventions could not occur. Although evaluation is multifaceted and may take place at several points throughout the course of forensic case management, the true evaluation occurs when the victim returns to society and functions at a level consistent with preincident functioning. Perpetrators of abuse and violence are also subjects of the forensic nursing process.

Unless there are major efforts to understand and alter the human and social conditions that contribute to abuse, neglect, violence, and exploitation, forensic nursing will fall short of its mission objectives. The major tools and techniques of forensic nursing specialists include forensic assessment and clinical investigative or pathological procedures in both the living and those who die within the clinical environs or the community at large. It is obvious that the forensic nursing process is a collaborative one, encompassing a wide array of physical, psychological, social, and legal interventions from both healthcare and jurisprudence domains.

FRAMEWORK FOR ACCOUNTABILITY

To gain full acceptance as a nursing specialty, forensic nursing was required to analyze its practice and define itself in terms of the nursing process, a goal-directed, dynamic framework for the roles and responsibilities inherent within the discipline. Although nurses had used a systematic approach to nursing problems for well over a century, it was not until 1973 that the American Nurses Association (ANA) Standards of Practice formalized what is now referred to as the nursing process. The nursing process is a scientific method that nurses use to provide care, beginning with an initial patient assessment and the establishment of a nursing diagnosis. Planning, intervention, and evaluation activities complete the nursing process. The steps of the nursing process, coupled with the knowledge and skills inherent within the discipline, have provided both structure and a common nomenclature to the work of nursing.

The ANA Congress of Nursing Practice requires specific criteria to be recognized as a formal specialty of nursing. The core of forensic nursing has been established to support the nursing process, including assessment, analysis, nursing diagnosis, outcome identification, planning, and implementation of interventions and evaluation of responses to its nursing practices. Rules, regulations, and a variety of public policies influence and confirm the validity of forensic nursing as a specialty. The ANA's practice guidelines described in nursing's Social Policy Statement and Standards of Clinical Nursing Practice are vital elements for both justification and framing of a specialty practice. A fundamental requirement for a nursing specialty is that it influences both the processes and the outcomes of nursing care delivery. The Scope and Standards of Forensic Nursing Practice is expected to provide basic direction to educators, researchers, and administrators as well as to forensic nurse practitioners.

KEY POINT All healthcare personnel must be able to use interview skills and physical assessment indicators to detect abuse and neglect.

FRAMEWORK FOR PRACTICE: NURSING PROCESS

Assessment

The first step of the nursing process is patient assessment, which includes a head-to-toe inspection of the body, history taking, and a review of clinical records or other previous documentation. Because a nurse is typically the first professional to encounter a patient in the healthcare setting, initial observations and information, even selected fragments, significantly affect the steps that follow. The systematic assessment should include both objective physical findings and subjective data based on the patient's perceptions about his or her condition. A perceptive nurse is in a key position to note problems that might otherwise be missed. Skilled assessments are essential to evaluate patients and to ensure that they receive the appropriate treatment and follow-up care. All initial assessments must be supplemented by ongoing evaluations and monitoring to test the working nursing diagnosis and to identify a need for revisions of the care plan. The nurse's abilities to elicit, organize, and convey information from the initial screening process are vital to ensure that significant bits of information are not overlooked or undervalued in later forensic analyses of the incident. All data must be precisely documented, steering clear, however, of making interpretive statements in records. The

environment for assessing the forensic patient must ensure that both visual and auditory privacy are assured and that forensic evidence collection is well supported within the space provided.

Planning

Planning to meet the needs of forensic patients encompasses an array of both simple and complex activities and may be directed toward achieving either short-term or long-term objectives. Merely taking steps to provide visual and auditory privacy during a confidential forensic interview and placing a "Do Not Disturb" sign on the room door is a plan, albeit a low level of planning. A more effective option is the special exam suite designated for forensic patients located away from the emergency department (ED) where privacy and accessibility for patients, families, and police officers has become the preferred choice in many hospitals and trauma centers. More typically, when a nursing care plan is outlined, it includes a complex series of activities that extend over days, weeks, or even months. It may involve other nurses, other disciplines, and perhaps an array of outside agencies or resources. Optimum nursing plans not only address the patients' priority needs and problems but also enumerate the activities or processes deemed appropriate to minimize or resolve the problems. Planning mandates the formulation of short- and long-term goals. The ideal forensic examination is carefully implemented to decrease emotional trauma while increasing optimal forensic evidence recovery.

Intervention

Nursing interventions are often described as the core of the nursing process. Interventions encompass providing and directing treatment as well as working with a variety of healthcare workers who also provide care. In past decades, when nursing interventions were described, they typically represented dependent tasks from the medical plan of care, such as giving prescribed medications or doing treatments ordered by the physician. Forensic nurses, however, often function with standing orders, protocols, algorithms, or other directives based on requirements of law enforcement or the judicial processes. As a result, their independence in practice distinguishes them from many other nurses and clearly establishes them in a position of considerable responsibility. Forensic nursing interventions must be continually evaluated and revised based on the response of the patient or the specific legal criteria if the patient dies.

Evaluation

The process of evaluation must take into account all data generated in the nurse-patient encounter. For example, the forensic implications of trauma may not be fully recognized until several days, weeks, or months after the precipitating event. If the patient does not seem to be responding as expected or if unexpected variables or circumstances arise, the forensic nurse must be ready to respond with alternative strategies to achieve the desired outcomes. Feedback must be derived from the patient and from significant associates and other members of the care team, such as advocates, attorneys, therapists, law enforcement officers, and counselors, who maintain relationships with the patient and thus have an opportunity to assess responses to interventional strategies. The standard for measuring patient progress and current status is based on established goals and outcomes.

Nursing goals and outcomes are derived from the nursing process and focus on patient responses, not nursing activities. Standards are stated in concrete, measurable terms and written to ensure that other members of the healthcare team understand and affirm them. Goals and outcomes represent safe, appropriate nursing care strategies and are deemed achievable by the health and justice teams.

Because forensic nurses often encounter patients with the same or similar problems, they may choose to use generic or preformulated care plans. Protocols, policies, procedures, standing orders, computerized care plans, and algorithms reflect practices designed to achieve care plan standardization. Roles of the forensic nurse examiner often overlap and require specific education and cross training in other subspecialties of forensic nursing to effectively evaluate a rape victim who is also the focus of a death investigation inquiry. This patient may be a victim of child abuse, sexual assault, and homicide as well as having survived as a clinical forensic patient for two weeks on artificial ventilation before death. This patient may also be a candidate for organ donation, requiring the examiner to investigate further social and legal interventions while simultaneously managing the grief and anxiety of the family or significant other. All steps of the nursing process are vital to every patient encounter. Even when the situation or time constraints pose limitations, the forensic nurse must not lose vision of the systematic and scientific legal healthcare processes. It should be viewed as a vital problem-solving tool and a way to organize a logical and responsible course of action.

KEY POINT The structure of the entire forensic nursing process is predicated on maintaining a certain state of mind—an investigative, interpretive, dogmatic search for the facts and the truth (NANDA, 1990).

NURSING DIAGNOSIS: BASIS FOR NURSING CARE PLANS

Nursing diagnosis is a clinical judgment about individual, family, or community responses to actual and potential health problems/life processes. In 1990, the North American Nursing Diagnosis Association (NANDA) stated that nursing diagnoses provide the basis for the selection of nursing interventions that will achieve outcomes for which the nurse is accountable. This diagnosis, however, does not include the legal interpretation of rape, homicide, abuse, neglect, etc., which is determined by the judicial process based upon the nurse's (among others) documentation and evaluation of evidence presented in court.

The nursing diagnosis is a statement that evolves from the interpretation and analysis of data. Each represents a problem, a related phenomenon, and specific manifestations with implications for nursing intervention. Domains of nursing diagnoses relate to physiology (basic and complex), behavior, family, health system, and safety. Functional health status, homeostatic regulation, psychological functioning, lifestyle change, family support, the healthcare delivery system use, and safety are all pertinent factors in nursing diagnoses formulation. For example, in instances of domestic violence or human abuse, pertinent diagnoses might include the following:

- Ineffective coping related to an inability to manage situational crises
- Fear related to a perceived inability to control the situation
- Sleep pattern disturbances related to anxiety
- Anxiety related to discussions of intimate information, diagnosis, and concern for partner

The potential for errors related to the establishment of an appropriate nursing diagnosis may include both shortcomings in data collection and interpretation. A broad, sound knowledge base and pertinent clinical experiences are vital for forensic nurses. Having repeated opportunities to deal with the same or similar problems leads to the development of a keen sense of differentiating normal from abnormal based on pattern analysis. Furthermore, critical thinking skills tend to improve with both time and exposure to common problems. The value of a well-formulated forensic nursing diagnosis promotes professional accountability and autonomy by defining and describing the independent area of nursing practice. Diagnostic statements also provide an effective way for nurses to communicate among themselves and with other health professionals and are included in the framework for forensic nursing research (see Appendix B).

PREVENTION OF VIOLENCE

Central to all programs of healthcare delivery and promotion (physical, mental, cultural, and social well being) is the concept of prevention, which includes forensic healthcare. Forensic nursing practice is the nursing care of individuals of all ages with perceived physical or emotional alterations, which may be diagnosed or undiagnosed, and may require immediate or long-term intervention with implicit legal implications. Forensic nursing care is scheduled or unscheduled pertaining to the specific environment in a specific care setting (i.e., a special forensic exam unit, an emergency department (ED), a mobile unit, a child advocacy facility, a suicide prevention center, a forensic mental health institution, a remand center, a correctional setting (jail, prison), or an institute of legal medicine. Thus, forensic nursing practice is episodic (domestic violence, drug abuse) and acute (gunshot wounds, sexual assault), as well as primary, secondary, and tertiary in nature.

As a public service profession, nursing has a responsibility to maintain standards of practice in processing cases involving patients associated with human violence. As a result of the vast number of crime victims presenting in the ED because of trauma or public health considerations, the need for a forensic specialist has been recognized. A historic lack of interagency cooperation involving law and nursing issues, as well as the absence of forensic education available to nurses, has often threatened the patient's legal rights, resulting in miscarriages of justice. There is growing support among those who understand the significant contribution of the role of the clinical forensic specialist in the advocacy and ministration to this plight (Lynch, 1990). The National Victim's Center has recognized forensic nursing as a contemporary movement in forensic advocacy, whether victim or suspect (NOVA, 1988).

Anyone suspected of a crime that the person did not commit becomes a victim of another kind. The forensic nurse must remain an unbiased, objective clinician throughout the scientific evaluation of injury and documentation of evidence in order to refrain from projecting a preconceived opinion or conclusion before the defendant is adjudicated. The problems in society for which this role has been designed to provide solutions are great and multifaceted. These needs require education and expertise that is equally diversified.

Prevention is a key aspect of traditional nursing care and an imperative one for forensic nursing practice. By educating nurses to think more about the legal issues surrounding patient care and to have a working knowledge of forensic responsibilities, the healthcare system will be able to provide a proactive approach. The identification of crime victims, prevention of further injury or death from recurring cyclical violence, and early detection of potentially abusive situations will help stem society's escalating crime patterns and prove to be cost-effective for governments.

Through implementing healthcare policies and practices that address forensic issues in nursing education, critical changes will be effected. These policies will aid law enforcement in meeting the objectives of criminal investigation. Nurse educators must assume the responsibility for establishing formal education programs in this nursing specialty that will assist in confronting violence in our society and alleviate the human suffering that results from global violence and abuse.

Pilot programs to educate nurses and other healthcare professionals to work in synthesis with law enforcement and the forensic sciences must continue to be developed and implemented. To provide adequate education and scope of practice for the forensic nursing specialist, one first must recognize the combination of knowledge required to go beyond mere treatment of symptoms and injuries and to fill a greater role in medicolegal (forensic) expertise. It is also important to consider that TJC has specific guidance that mandate policies and procedures for handling adult and child victims of alleged or suspected abuse or neglect. The 2009 TJC standards emphasize the role of nursing in the identification of victims of abuse and neglect and specify the responsibilities of staff in reporting such cases. They also specify that appropriate reporting and referrals are accomplished for these cases in accordance with hospital policies and procedures.

Future of Forensic Nursing Science

The loss of human life and function due to human violence constitutes a phenomenon that affects the lives of millions of individuals worldwide. These cases represent a major cost in healthcare as well as an increased burden on the criminal justice systems. Previous resources for victims from law enforcement, social services, and the courts have been identified as inadequate in light of the dimension of the problem (NOVA, 1989). Forensic nursing is one example of an expansion of the role nurses will fill in the healthcare delivery system in the twenty-first century. Forensic nurses have initiated positive changes, vis-à-vis mutual responsibility with the legal system, to protect the patient's legal, civil, and human rights. The role of the forensic nurse as a clinical investigator is one approach to aiding law enforcement and the criminal justice system in combating criminal and interpersonal violence through a multidisciplinary approach.

As a new era of nursing practice approaches, forensic nursing has unlimited potential. With the increasing emphasis on forensic nursing services as one strategic step to interrupt cyclical, interpersonal violence, it is perceived that this paradigm will be as essential as infection control. Those who understand the need for a forensic specialist in nursing believe it is realistic to expect that TJC will one day require every hospital or trauma center to have on staff a forensically skilled nurse to ensure that legal mandates are met with reasonable certainty.

Summary

The fact that clinical forensic medicine has been practiced in most other countries in the world for hundreds of years, with the exception of the United States, is a testament to the adage that "nothing is new under the sun." What is comforting is the increasing awareness of a need to acknowledge this phenomenon and approach its management professionally. The inclusion of forensically skilled nurses to the battery of experts doing just that is an important and critical step toward ensuring the comprehensiveness of the services provided and will improve the quality of life and outcomes

in living forensic victims and their cases. It will also provide a greater means of investigating and assessing clinical and community deaths (Smock, 2006).

The primary area of practice and research inquiry for the forensic nurse scientist is human trauma, both physical and psychological. The incorporation of existing bodies of knowledge with new scientific discoveries has provided a sound foundation for evidence-based practice. Thus the integration of forensic and nursing sciences provides unique paradigms pertaining to the investigation of questioned issues concerning healthcare and the law. In this sense, such concerns under investigation are intended to determine the *truth*. Associates in this endeavor include those from the basic health sciences, the biomedical and physical sciences, engineering, and the social and behavioral sciences (Lynch, 2006).

The forensic nurse specialist blends nursing's traditional acumen with those of forensic science and criminal justice. This new specialist, functioning with an interdisciplinary team, will be a valuable resource for the overall public health efforts to combat human conditions that result in disabling physical and psychological injuries or untimely deaths.

BEST PRACTICE Every individual who works in a healthcare facility should receive basic forensic education. This is essential to meet TJC's standards and limit liability in the event of a failure to recognize indications of injuries associated with sexual assault, child or elder abuse, domestic violence, or other forensic trauma.

Resources

BOOKS

American Nurses Association and the International Association of Forensic Nurses. (2009). *Scope and standards of forensic nursing practice.* Washington, DC: Author.

Anderson, W. R. (1998). *Forensic sciences in clinical medicine: A case study approach.* Philadelphia: Lippincott-Raven.

Olshaker, J.S., Jackson, M.C., & Smock, W.S. (2007). *Forensic emergency medicine.* Philadelphia: Lippincott, Williams & Wilkins.

The Joint Commission (TJC). (2009). *Accreditation manual for hospitals, core standards, and guidelines.* Oak Park, IL: Author.

ORGANIZATIONS

Association of Police Surgeons
Clarke House, 18 Mount Parade Harrogate, Yorkshire, UK
American Academy of Forensic Sciences
410 North 21st Street, Colorado Springs, CO 80904; Tel: 719-636-1100
www.aafs.org

JOURNALS

Harcourt Publishers, 32 Jamestown Road, London, England NW1 7BY; Tel: +44 (0) 207-424-4487
Journal of Clinical Forensic Medicine
Journal of Forensic Nursing, Blackwell Wiley Publishers
Journal of Forensic Nursing, International Association of Forensic Nurses, Arnold, MD
Journal of Forensic Sciences, American Academy of Forensic Sciences, Colorado Springs

References

American Academy of Forensic Sciences. (1991). Colorado Springs, CO.

American Academy of Forensic Sciences. (2002). Colorado Springs, CO.

American Nurses Association (ANA). (1997). *Standards and scope of forensic nursing practice.* Silver Spring, MD: Author.

American Nurses Association (ANA). (1995). *Nursing's social policy statement.* Washington, DC: Author.

Camp, F. (1976). *Gradwold's legal medicine.* (3rd ed.). Chicago: Yearbook Medical Publishers.

Eckert, W. (1983). Forensic sciences: The clinical or living aspects. *Inform, 16,* 3.

Eckert, W., Bell, J., Stein, R., et al. (1986). Clinical forensic medicine. *American Journal of Forensic Medicine and Pathology, 7*(3), 182–185.

Eckert, W. G. (1990). Forensic sciences and medicine: The clinical or living aspects. *American Journal of Forensic Medicine and Pathology, 11*(4), 336–341.

Foege, W. (1997). Constructing violence as a public health problem. In L. B. Winett (Ed.), *Public health reports* (vol. 113, issue 6, pp. 498–499). Washington, DC: U.S. Department of Health and Human Services.

Goldsmith, M. F. (1986). U.S. forensic pathologists on a new case: Examination of living patients. *JAMA, 256*(13), 1685.

International Association of Forensic Nurses. (1993). *Codes of ethics for forensic nursing.* Thorofare, NJ: Author.

International Association of Forensic Nurses (IAFN). (1997). *Scope and standards of forensic nursing practice.* Silver Spring, MD: American Nurses Publishing.

International Association of Forensic Nurses (IAFN). (2009). *Scope and standards of forensic nursing practice.* Washington, DC: American Nurses Publishing.

Koop, C. E. (1989). President and surgeon general condemn violence against women, call for new attitudes, programs. *National Organization for Victim Assistance Newsletter, 13.*

Lynch, V. (1990). *Clinical forensic nursing: A descriptive study in role development.* Thesis. Arlington: University of Texas.

Lynch, V. A. (1986). *Forensic nursing: A new field for the profession.* Paper presented at the 38th annual meeting of the American Academy of Forensic Sciences, New Orleans, LA.

Lynch, V. (1991). *Application for new discipline in forensic nursing.* American Academy of Forensic Sciences. Archives of the General Section Annual Scientific Meeting.

Lynch, V. (1995). Clinical forensic nursing: A new perspective in the management of crime victims from trauma to trial. *Critical Care Nursing Clinics of North America, 7*(3), 489–507.

Lynch, V., & Standing Bear, Z. (2000). A global perspective in forensic nursing: Challenges for the 21st century. In D. Robinson, & A. Kettles (Eds.), *Forensic nursing and multidiscipinary care of the mentally disordered offender* (pp. 249–266). Philadelphia: Jessica Kingsley.

McLay, W. D. S. (1990). *Clinical forensic medicine.* London: Pinter.

McNamara, H. (1988). *Living forensics (seminar pamphlet).* Ulster County, NY: Office of the Medical Examiner.

National Organization for Victim Assistance (NOVA). (1988). *Newsletter, 12*(11).

National Organization for Victim Assistance (NOVA). (1989). President and surgeon general condemn violence against women, call for new attitudes, programs. *Newsletter, 13*(6).

North American Nursing Diagnosis Association (NANDA). (1990). *Taxonomy 1.* (rev. ed., pp. 114–117) St. Louis, MO: Author.

Root, I., & Scott, W. (1973, September). The clinician and forensic medicine. *California Medicine, 119,* 68–76.

Smock, W. S. (2002). Forensic emergency medicine. In J. M. Marx (Ed.), *Rosen's emergency medicine: Concepts and clinical practice* (pp. 828–841). St. Louis, MO: Mosby.

Smock, W. S. (2006). Genesis and development. In V. Lynch (Ed.), *Forensic nursing.* St. Louis. MO: Mosby.

The Joint Commission (TJC). (2009). *Accreditation manual for hospitals, core standards, and guidelines.* Oak Park, IL: Author.

CHAPTER 2 Concepts and Theory of Forensic Nursing Science

Virginia A. Lynch

The Science of Forensic Nursing

Among scientific disciplines, *forensic nursing* represents a departure from the traditional foundations of nursing practice while adding a new dimension to the forensic sciences. Forensic nursing science has evolved in response to the needs of a world in crisis. This emerging discipline should be viewed as an integral member of the multisectorial structures that make up a field of inquiry that applies clinical and scientific knowledge to questions of law in both civil and criminal investigations.

The science of forensic nursing has two foci:

1. *The legal principles.* This focus relates to evidence collection and reliability, chain of custody and security, and the healthcare provider role in judicial processes.
2. *The establishment of the manner of injury and cause thereof.* This element includes death, health system documentation, investigation of trauma, care of detainees, and rehabilitation of those who have suffered violence.

Science is defined as an accumulating body of knowledge. A *scientist* is one learned in science, especially one active in some particular field of investigation (*Dorland's Medical Dictionary,* 2005). The *forensic sciences* refer to any aspect of science as it relates to law. *Forensic nursing science* is consistent with these other disciplines. The primary area of practice and research inquiry for the forensic nurse scientist is human trauma, both physical and psychological. The incorporation of existing bodies of knowledge with new scientific discoveries has provided a sound foundation for evidence-based forensic nursing practice.

Among other sciences incorporated in the study of forensic nursing are human anatomy and physiology, physical sciences, engineering, social and behavioral sciences, and biomedical sciences including chemistry and physics. Forensic nursing is a theory-guided and ethics-guided practice that requires an intellectual endeavor within its own distinctive knowledge base, experiences, purposes, and values. Contemporary social conditions involving human violence and abuse have shaped the evolution of forensic nursing education, holistic practice, and scientific research to provide a unique framework for the investigation of issues concerning healthcare and the law.

Violence-related trauma is central to the role of the forensic specialist in nursing (Lynch, 1990). Whether physical, sexual, or psychological, violence remains the single greatest source of loss of life and function worldwide (Reiss & Roth, 1993). Forensic nursing assumes a mutual responsibility with the forensic medical sciences and the criminal justice systems in concern for the loss of life and function because of human violence and liability-related issues.

The forensic nurse, as a clinical investigator, represents one member of an alliance of healthcare providers, law enforcement agencies, and forensic scientists involved in establishing a holistic approach to the evaluation and treatment of crime-related trauma. Forensic nurse investigators address relevant areas in the assessment of criminal violence, abuse, and data collection for establishing hypotheses about the interrelationship between healthcare and the law. Forensic nurses fill voids by accomplishing selected forensic tasks concurrently with other health and justice professionals and by establishing themselves as uniquely qualified clinicians who blend biomedical knowledge with the basic principles of law and human behavior (Lynch, 1991).

Theoretical Foundations

As nursing history delineates the principles and philosophies of nursing in general, it also addresses those of forensic nursing, which parallel traditional nursing care in all specialties within the scope and boundaries of nursing practice. Forensic nursing brings to each nursing specialty specific strategies and considerations for meeting the biological, psychological, social, spiritual, and now legal dimensions of patient care in a humanitarian, holistic, and pragmatic orientation. The theoretical perspectives for forensic nursing practice derive their broad construct from several mainstream nursing theories, including those presented by Paterson and Zderad (1998), Conway and Hardy (1988), Leininger (1995), Giger and Davidhizar (1991), Chinn and Kramer (1995), and Brenner (1984).

These nursing theories become integrated within the theories of sociology and philosophy, such as the theories of Mead (1934), Plato (427-347 B.C.), and those explored by Farrell and Swigert (1982), to design an integrated practice model for forensic nursing, as philosophers, sociologists, and others have focused on the construction of practice theory in nursing. Forensic nursing integrates their theories into a framework that helps to describe and explain phenomena specific to forensic nursing science. This common connectedness unites the philosophies of physical science with the legal dimensions and defines forensic nursing's body of knowledge based on shared theories with other disciplines.

ASSUMPTIONS APPLIED AND DEFINED

Assumptions are statements accepted as given truths without proof. Assumptions set the foundation for the application of a particular theory. Central to the forensic nursing theory is the assumption that integrating disciplines of social science, nursing science, and the legal sciences involves the notion that the multi-skilled forensic nurse benefits the patient, the healthcare institution, society, the law, and human behavior.

TRUTH

Truth is the mantra of the forensic sciences and central to the field of all scientific investigation. Truth explains the objective methodology of forensic sciences applied across a broad base of disciplines and facilitates the collective search for the truth. Reforms in criminal justice systems have come about through advances in DNA technology that have sustained truth and justice in cases where justice had been denied. The Innocence Project was founded in 1992 to determine the truth as it relates to the exoneration of incarcerated prisoners through postconviction DNA testing. It cannot be overemphasized that the forensic nurse is not a victim advocate but rather a patient advocate. The patient, however, may be the accused, a convicted felon, the condemned, or the victim. A forensic nurse is required to remain essentially unbiased and value neutral in all matters—an advocate for truth and justice. Objectivity and neutrality are essential values in the care of forensic patients. The role requires an incisive comprehension of fundamental medicolegal issues as well as the ability to prepare and present testimony in a court of law. It is the search for truth.

Truth, as the central implicit assumption to all forensic investigations, brings enlightenment to unknown, unanswered, and questioned issues related to the origin and manifestations of pathological conditions that affect the person, environment, health, and nursing. The philosophy of forensic nursing practice is based on an ancient philosopher's love of truth (Plato, 347 B.C.). Without the discovery of truth, diagnosis, treatment, evaluation, rehabilitation, recovery, and prevention would be precluded. Without truth, reconciliation and justice are denied.

Research is an essential element for further developing the concepts, theories, and models of care that apply to forensic nursing. Research initiatives and clinical inquiries form the basis of evidence-based practices (Brenner, 1984). Yet research requires appropriate theoretical frameworks for practice, advanced nursing preparation, competency-based training, and experimental work-based academic development to move out of the shadows and forward into the pursuit of truth.

PARADIGMS, THEORIES, AND WAYS OF KNOWING

Central to all nursing theories is the assumption that human beings are made up of various dimensions and that each dimension relates to health and well-being. Forensic nursing theory incorporates the human dimensions pertinent to all nursing theories of care, yet it projects beyond the aspects of bio-psychosocial spiritual and cultural beings to introduce and incorporate a dimension of laws. Laws that portend to govern human behavior and social needs represent the direct correlation among the human dimension, health, and well-being. Culture can advance or limit the human dimension. Cultural change can be seen as social learning. Cultural care and cultural interventions are essential components of the forensic and clinical investigation of trauma.

Forensic nurse examiners utilize Carper's fundamental patterns of knowing in their practice with a variety of models and theories (Carper, 1978). Patterns of fundamental knowing consist of those described as empirical knowledge, aesthetic knowledge, personal knowledge, and ethical knowledge. Other nursing theories and models are symbiotically intertwined and functionally applicable to forensic nursing science.

COMPONENTS OF THEORETICAL CONCEPTS

The following components are typically addressed in any theoretical concept of nursing practice: (1) role clarification, (2) role behavior, and (3) role expectation.

Role clarification identifies shared knowledge and skills. It establishes explicit expectations and boundaries between the role of the self and that of others, and it delineates goals as well as costs and rewards associated with enacting them. Role clarification also demonstrates the extent to which significant others reinforce or validate role behavior via complementary and counter roles.

Role behavior is the performance or enactment of differentiated behavior relevant to a specific position. Role expectation is the obligation or demands placed on the individual in a role position. It encompasses the specific norms associated with the attitudes, behaviors, and cognition required and anticipated for a role occupant.

A major component of the integrated model for forensic nursing is interactionism. The focus of interactionism concerns specific links or associations among persons, environment, concern for persons, social integration, development of meaning, and the integration of persons in a social context, as well as processes engaging persons. Not all social systems generate a sense of community, but those that do create a shared culture and social order among their members. Patient advocacy recognizes healthcare as a primary source of physical and emotional stability to the physically or psychologically traumatized patient. Patient advocacy, an aspect of social behavior that protects and provides patients with an emotionally supportive community, serves as one platform for the forensic nurse examiner role. The understanding and explanation of social order as community is the goal of social sciences. This includes the understanding and explanation of criminal behavior and human violence. It focuses on individuals involved in a reciprocal social interaction as they actively construct and create their environment through a symbiotic interaction. The main focus of this perspective reinforces the need for social order and interdisciplinary coordination in healthcare delivery and the social justice sciences.

Problematic social situations, such as the escalation of trends in criminal violence, demand new interpretations and new lines of action, which reinforce the need to continually redefine the role of the forensic nurse. This parallels the major focus of forensic nursing as it deals with change, dynamics, and the processes by which individuals creatively adapt to a society in flux. The ongoing problems in society and rapid social change place new demands on public service providers. Their role behaviors, in turn, quickly generate new and valid concepts that contribute to safe, effective patient care.

A dynamic role of the forensic nurse examiner has evolved in clinical and community nursing practice; it facilitates specialized and unique behaviors in forensic nursing. This role helps nursing, medical, social, and legal systems to clarify questioned issues in response to the epidemiology and query of murder, suicide, sexual assault, abuse, neglect, intentional trauma, communicable disease, and violent criminal acts that threaten lives. The principle of reciprocal social interaction represents the multifaceted relationships among patient, clinician, and multidisciplinary team members that involve law enforcement agencies, social services, legislative authorities, judicial systems, and healthcare operatives. The reciprocal interaction of interagency coordination and cooperation works to improve the structural and functional management, delivery, and effectiveness of services offered by health and justice institutions.

ASSUMPTIONS OF THE THEORY

This theoretical framework makes the following assumptions:

- Clinical forensic nursing is a relatively new science, and there is limited awareness of this specialty on behalf of health professionals, law enforcement agencies, and forensic science practitioners, as well as healthcare consumers.
- Evolving healthcare systems ultimately require changes in the role of the professional nurse.
- The conception and perception of the clinical forensic nurse is currently evolving and developing and at times is poorly defined.
- The application of clinical forensic science is appropriate for the practice of nursing.
- The registered nurse, qualified by education and experience in a broad range of nursing specialties, is capable of identifying role behaviors of the clinical forensic specialist.
- Human rights are a priority for most members of society.
- Forensic nursing care encompasses a sensitivity to differences among culturally and ethnically diverse populations.
- Truth is the central goal of forensic investigative analysis, which involves patient history, assessment of forensic implications, and correlation with the conditions and circumstances of injury, illness, or death.
- Forensic patients hold equal rights in terms of law and ethics, whether victim, accused, or offender.

PROPOSITIONS

Propositions are ideas brought forward for consideration, acceptance, or adoption. The basic propositions considered in the formation of forensic nursing theory include truth, presence, perceptivity, and regeneration. These propositions are explained as follows:

- *Truth.* The central force in the resolution of questioned issues that involve the physical, psychological, and social health or ills of a human population; includes past and future truths.
- *Presence.* The invisible quality that commands and comforts while directing attention away from one's self and into the being of another, instilling confidence and respect in the self of that being.
- *Perceptivity.* The investigative tool of one who explores human behavior, awareness of the elements of one's environment, and sensory phenomena interpreted in light of lived experiences that guide intuitiveness.
- *Regeneration.* A value and a goal of the advanced forensic praxis in patient healing that affects a victim or offender who has experienced the deepest wounds of the soul; becoming once again as before.

APPLICATION OF PROPOSITIONS

Care that incorporates the nursing process—assessment, planning, intervention, and evaluation, to restore and promote health in the patient throughout the forensic process—is essential. The concepts of truth, presence, perceptivity, and regeneration will guide the forensic practitioner in the ways of knowing, patterns of being, and shared intuition between patient and practitioner.

BEST PRACTICE Forensic nurses should augment their usual nursing assessments and objective documentation with preservation and collection of evidence and steps to prevent the psychophysical, psychosocial, and psychosexual health risks associated with trauma and violence.

The objectives of forensic nursing intervention are injury/illness/death assessment, objective documentation, the collection and preservation of forensic data and evidence, and the prevention of potential psychophysical/psychosocial/psychosexual health risks. Patient empowerment is also a significant issue, consequential to the criminal trauma, healthcare interventions, and the acceptance or rejection by society regarding the circumstances of the criminal act involved, regardless of the patient's legal status.

Theoretical Components of Forensic Nursing

The theoretical support for forensic nursing care involves the biological, psychological, social, spiritual, and legal dimensions of the nursing practice. Forensic nursing is holistic in nature, addressing these concepts individually and collectively. The science of forensic nursing has been recognized by the professional bodies of nursing that direct the development of nursing education, research, and practice. Forensic nursing theory identifies interconnectedness with theories of the legal and physical sciences, which is reflected in The Joint Commission (TJC) guidelines that provide regulatory direction for healthcare practitioners (TJC, 2009).

These guidelines regard the identification of crime victims and the recovery and documentation of evidence, as well as the procedures for reporting abuse or suspicious patient behavior to a legal agency, as the foundations of forensic nursing practice. The legal sciences define and delineate the parameters of the law responsible for the behaviors of the nursing professional. Forensic nursing behaviors involve, among others, the identification of crime-related injury, the collection of evidence, the reporting suspicion of illegal acts to a legal agent, and the abuse or death of patients in custody or that of incarcerated or institutionalized persons. It is, then, the respective dimensions of the health and justice disciplines that integrate a variety of multidimensional theories into nursing practices and define the distinctive conjectures of forensic nursing science.

KEY POINT Forensic nursing is multidimensional, requiring multitheoretical approaches to explain interactions between healthcare and the law.

Descriptive Theory

In the clinical environs, this role is defined as the application of clinical and scientific knowledge to questions of law related to the civil and criminal investigation of survivors of traumatic injury and patient treatment involving court-related issues (Lynch, 1995a). It is further defined as the application of the nursing process to public or legal proceedings, as well as the application of the forensic aspects of healthcare in the scientific investigation of trauma or death-related issues involving abuse, violence, criminal activity, liability concerns, and traumatic accidents (Lynch, 1991).

Prescriptive Theory

Nurses have always been expected to care for crime victims, patients in legal custody, and victims of traumatic accidents and other liability-related injuries. However, in the past, there has been no specialty role or explicit education to ensure that these legal responsibilities were reasonably met as a component of nursing care. The complex legal needs of the patient were often in jeopardy because of the ignorance of forensic issues by the emergency medical response team and the nurse or attending physician. Investigating officers generally depended on the nurse or physician to accurately document injury and to recover evidence. Without specialized knowledge, neither objective was fulfilled. Complex recovery of evidence, specificity in documentation, and managing emotionally traumatized patients concurrently with life-saving intervention require separate roles for those who provide emergency intervention and those who provide forensic services.

The introduction of a forensic clinician in nursing is healthcare's direct response to violence. This new discipline was intrinsic to the role nurses fill in the challenge to address the legal issues pertaining to forensic healthcare and to reduce a previously recognized injustice to society. As nurses acknowledged their role in the health and justice movement, they recognized crime-related issues as justifiable elements for healthcare professionals to integrate into their specialty-oriented practice models. They accepted the challenge to reach beyond the immediate treatment environs into the often-shadowed areas of legal issues surrounding patient care. The concept of an integrated practice model in forensic nursing science has initiated an accomplished clinician, cross-trained in the principles and philosophies of nursing science, forensic science, and criminal justice. The recognition and management of medicolegal cases require healthcare professionals to reconceptualize the nursing practice and its body of knowledge.

KEY POINT Patient care now requires a consideration of legal and human rights as well as an awareness of the greater connection the healthcare delivery system has to other social systems. It is no longer acceptable for the healthcare system to exist in isolation, ignorant of the wider world of interfacing systems.

PRACTICE THEORY

An integrated practice model for forensic nursing science incorporates a synthesis of shared theory from a variety of disciplines including social science, nursing science, and the legal (forensic) sciences. It presents a global perspective on interrelated disciplines and bodies of knowledge that affect forensic nursing practice through social justice. The aspects of a multidimensional theory are activated in the investigation of injury, illness and death, socio-cultural crime, and liability-related questions. An integrated practice model is especially relevant to the applied health sciences.

An Integrated Practice Model

Figure 2-1 illustrates the dynamics symbolized in the following conceptual framework. Forensic nursing science and its humanitarian perspective have the potential to provide new solutions to problems that require a unique multidisciplinary approach. Forensic nursing is a critical component for minimizing the devastating impact of prevalent social and cultural problems in the twenty-first century. It provides a strong theoretical knowledge base for interactional analysis and its prevailing approaches to role development.

DESCRIPTION OF THE INTEGRATED PRACTICE MODEL

The model is described as follows: Three principal components embracing the outer triangle constitute the theoretical basis of forensic nursing. The interlocking circles indicate interconnected,

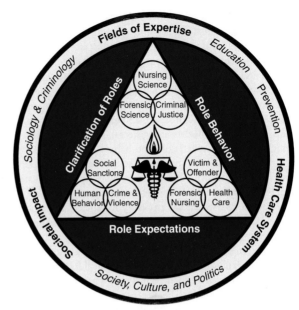

Fig. 2-1 Integrated practice model for forensic nursing science.

interagency coordination, cooperation, and communication essential to public health, safety, and social justice.

- A knowledge base of interrelated disciplines (fields of expertise)–nursing science, forensic science, and the law–use sociological, criminological, and nursing theory to connect role behaviors with the societal consequences of health and human behavior.
- The societal impact components are human behavior (broadly based sociological and psychological notions), social sanctions (legal and institutional sanctions and processes), and crime and violence (both recognized and hidden). Social, cultural, and political factors bring together role expectations within a system of roles.
- A system of roles relates to the victim, the suspected offender or the perpetrator of criminal acts, the significant others of both, forensic nursing science, and the healthcare institution (both its individual and institutional roles). Education, both practical (experiential) and theoretical, brings role behavior and role clarification together.

EXPLANATION OF THE PICTORIAL MODEL

At the center of the internal triangle is the symbol of forensic nursing. This symbol—reflecting the legal, forensic medical, physical, psychosocial, and nursing sciences—is composed of the scales of justice, the bundle of public service, the caduceus, and the eternal flame of nursing. The flame illustrates enlightenment of humanity and perpetuates the challenge in nursing to continue to evolve and expand into new roles as societal trends demand. This enlightenment reflects awareness of the greater connectedness that the healthcare system has to other social systems. The caduceus represents medical science, and enmeshed in this symbol is the interdisciplinary collaboration that integrates nursing into the multitude of highly specialized scientific psychocultural arenas. The bundle of public service represents the complexity and weight of public service obligations in which all modern systems in our society are inextricably involved, including the discipline, punishment, and rehabilitation of those who fail society's laws. Finally, the scales of justice emphasize the notion that patient care must consider legal as well as human rights.

The dynamics of the interlocking circles are omnidirectional. The outer circle, which frames and encompasses these components, symbolizes the environment and underscores the interaction of society, education, prevention, and systems.

The model demonstrates attention to the concepts of person (victim, suspect, offender, human behavior), health (healthcare institutions, nursing science, individuals, and groups), nursing (nursing science, forensic nursing), and environment (experience, societal impact, and healthcare systems), as well as to internal issues (clarification, expectation, and behavior) and external components (sociology and criminology; social, cultural, and political factors; and education). The ultimate evidence of a successful system is an outcome that provides prevention.

The model focuses on the necessity for society to respond to problems that develop among the related fields of nursing, forensic science, and the criminal justice system. These systems of roles are not fixed, precisely defined entities. They have a flexibility that permits open, evolving systems. This theoretical framework allows for the adaptability needed to achieve a dynamic balance in all roles of the forensic nurse. The effectiveness of the forensic nurse is based, in part, on her or his ability to interact with other scientific, legal, medical, and social professionals, as well as victims, suspects, perpetrators, families, and communities. Forensic nursing is not limited to a single context within the definition of a new role. New concepts of forensic nursing will be explored as they continue to emerge within the context of role theory.

This conceptualization embraces an integration of multiple theories derived from other disciplines. As new concepts are integrated into the practice model–such as sociology (sociopolitical impact), criminology (crime, violence, criminal justice, social sanctions, and human rights), clinical and criminal investigation (forensic and nursing science), and education (nursing, medicolegal, staff, patient/clients, and medicolegal specialization)–the cyclic nature of the model speaks to continuance, perpetuation, and balance. Balance is achieved when justice is served–to those who have been victimized, to those accused of crimes they did not commit, to offenders, and to society as a whole. Justice is served when truth is identified, verified, and demonstrated. Thus, the forensic nurse becomes an advocate for justice, an advocate for truth. Truth and justice perpetuate holistic health in the inclusive aspects of the biological, psychological, sociological, spiritual, cultural, and legal dimensions of being human.

Explanatory Theory: Interactionism

The properties and components of the forensic nursing practice function within society and society's institutions (hospitals, necropsy laboratories, jails and other custodial facilities, courts) that provide the framework within which roles are enacted. The interactionist is an individual whose approach focuses on the continual process of interpretation placed on acts and symbols by those interactions with each other (subspecialties within forensic nursing and other forensic specialists) (Conway & Hardy, 1988). From a theoretical perspective, symbolic interactionism can be appropriately applied to the role development of the forensic nurse generalist or specialist as these nurses interact with the living and the dead in medicolegal cases. Role theory as it relates to nursing is approached from the perspective of interactionism between healthcare and the law.

The interactionist concept evolves from the belief that flexibility is critical in the development of a role that remains in constant evolution based on the needs and demands of society.

The dynamic concepts of role theory, as applied to health professions, identify specific characteristics of the role under development. Thus, the role of the forensic nurse will remain flexible and continue to evolve as trends in crime and criminality mutate and transform into new social and cultural crimes. The following concepts are among the variables that influence the characteristics of the forensic nurse interactionist. A synthesis of role clarification, behavior, and expectation provides the forensic nurse examiner with a framework for culturally sensitive care in which the forensic nurse's role includes such skills as the following:

- Identification of trauma (assessment)
- Investigation (planning)
- Documentation (history) pertaining to the incident (intervention)
- Collection of evidence (specimens)
- Postinvestigation review (evaluation)
- Case history (comparative investigation of observation vs. evidence)
- Court presentation (prosecution or defense)

The forensic nurse also provides traditional nursing interventions such as crisis care as they interact with traumatized victims, offenders, and their families. These skills may also be extended to various disciplines and colleagues with whom they interact throughout the investigation of trauma and deaths. Those most frequently subjected to pernicious human behavior in forensic cases, such as law enforcement officers, firefighters, therapists, and paramedics, often suffer from vicarious or secondary trauma. Conversely, forensic nurse examiners must remain alert to the symptoms of this insidious and debilitating condition, as they may become overwhelmed under such circumstances.

Current literature stresses that our social sciences and legal systems must address the ills of social justice and injustice. The offender of social laws and mores brings a different focus into the practice of forensic nursing. Often, offenders are victims of another kind–and of another crime. Forensic psychiatric nurses and forensic correctional nurses, the primary caretaker of those accused of criminal acts and of the offender patient population, find this to be a group with complex healthcare needs. Caring for offenders is nothing new within the clinical environs. Nurses care for patients in custody (prisoners and detainees) in the emergency department, in surgical intensive care, and in the general patient population when physical illness or injuries require medical, surgical, or psychiatric intervention. These patients are often restrained by legal means, generally have armed law enforcement officers in attendance, and are hospitalized in a temporary situation.

Yet caring for the accused, the mentally disordered offender, or the sexual sadist on a long-term basis becomes a formidable task and a challenge to all of a nurse's skills. Although the challenge of caring for this patient population is complex, the duty and responsibility of the forensic nurse remains. Effects of forensic nursing interventions may be hard to assess on an immediate basis, for the psychopathology of the mind is a long-term mystery that requires patience, individualized interventions, reassessment, objective evaluation, and possible changes to more adeptly benefit the client's outcomes or the needs of the social system.

One must remember that just as forensic pathology lays the foundation for all clinical medicine (why people die), forensic psychiatrists, behavioral scientists, and criminologists who study and evaluate crimes and criminal behavior (why people commit crimes) lay the foundation for the prevention of crime. It is difficult, if not impossible, to practice prevention without first knowing the underlying causes of human tragedy, death, disease, or crime. Once forensic pathologists can determine the causes of death, clinical physicians can more readily save lives. Once the forensic behavioral scientist can understand why people commit crimes, she or he can begin to reduce and prevent criminal acts. All forensic intervention must begin with a firm scientific foundation, then explore the unknown, unpredictable regions of the human mind. Forensic nursing science has been recognized as one important component to the solution for today's most serious health and justice problem: Human violence.

Metaparadigms

The dominant constructs of nursing were selected to represent an overriding structure in regard to the role of the forensic nurse. The following constructs are described as metaparadigms applied within the framework of forensic nursing science.

PERSON (PATIENT, VICTIM, SUSPECT, PERPETRATOR, HUMAN BEHAVIOR)

This primary concept represents the nucleus of the humanistic theory of nursing. In specific relationship to forensic nursing, *person* is defined twofold: the victim of crime and the surviving family members (identified as victims by extension) or the suspect or perpetrator, an individual accused or convicted of a criminal act or socially unacceptable behavior. Human behavior guides human social activity by determining the characteristics that distinguish the role of the victim and the offender of justice. The roles of the accused or suspect and the convicted perpetrator of crime provide a particular relevance that further defines the forensic application of nursing practice. Cultural competence and awareness are essential in the forensic management of patients who have immigrated to the United States or seek political refuge. Those who have survived political violence and wars in their countries of origin often experience crime within the boundaries of the United States because of discrimination, racism, hatred, and religious persecution—the same crimes they thought they left behind.

HEALTH (HEALTHCARE INSTITUTIONS, NURSING SCIENCE, INDIVIDUALS OR GROUPS, PHYSICAL OR MENTAL)

The implied definition of health is influenced by the multiple variables related to the subtheories of forensic nursing within the nursing sciences. The loss of life and function result in disabilities derived from societal crime and violence and are consequentially identified conditions for forensic intervention. However, pain involving the violation of the spirit is a phenomenon that challenges health service practitioners' potential to the greatest extent. If life prevails, yet the distress of the human spirit remains impaired, health remains dysfunctional. Sensitivity to victims and families is a fundamental concept that distinguishes forensic nursing care to the emotionally and spiritually compromised patients. Health is not merely a person's physical well-being, but helping that person "become more as humanly possible in a particular life situation" (Paterson & Zderad, 1998, p. 279) describes one core component of forensic nursing praxis. The concern of forensic healthcare provides for needs beyond survival and functioning, assumes responsibilities beyond the immediate treatment environment, and now includes the legal care that may dictate the patient's future well-being.

NURSING (NURSING SCIENCE, FORENSIC NURSING SCIENCE, AND PRACTICE)

For the purpose of this description, the forensic nursing role is based on the concept of a continuously evolving scientific base that challenges health professionals to enhance, reinterpret, and redefine their roles. These roles were designed to face the issues of societies in transition by moving into a social condition that requires nurses to incorporate new knowledge, to reach out to other scientific-based disciplines. There is no stereotype for nurses. Nurses create their own image—based on their responses to others and their compassionate and nonjudgmental intervention to decrease racism, religious or ideological animosity, or economic superiority—without fears or prejudice.

Nurses must affirm a support for community services outside the clinical setting. It is necessary to react to injustices. To gain a new understanding of the phenomenon known as empathy is crucial. The nurse's ability to look directly at the negative human behavior that engenders fear and prejudice in society and implement empathic nurse-patient interactions of coping and accommodation is as essential to recovery as physical intervention when facing degradation of the human spirit.

The forensic nurse is viewed as an integral member of the multidisciplinary investigative team consisting of healthcare professionals, law enforcement agencies, social science advocates, and forensic scientists. The effectiveness of the forensic nurse is based in part on the nurse's ability to interact with other professionals and to view the victim or offender in the humanitarian nursing perspective, a unique kind of nursing. As health is viewed on a continuum, it is essential to provide clients with interventions and resources that will help them reestablish a sense of balance. The forensic nurse examiner strives to facilitate optimum functioning, which begins with objectively assessing the problem, applying the nursing process to achieve mutually established goals, and providing a humane, caring interaction.

ENVIRONMENT (HUMAN EXPERIENCE, SOCIETAL IMPACT, HEALTHCARE SYSTEMS, CORRECTIONAL FACILITIES, COURTS)

The complex milieu of forensic nursing practice incorporates interactions between the healthcare systems and the external social context. This social climate (societal behaviors, laws) dictates role expectations unique to the forensic application of nursing. A more abstract forensic interpretation of the environment may focus on social stress or stressors by viewing the environment as hostile and the human-environment interaction negatively (crime, human abuse, death). Thus, the environment develops characteristics relevant to guide role behaviors appropriate to the treatment and prevention of physical and emotional trauma, psychopathology, unacceptable social behavior, and contamination and violation of the physical world, as well as spiritual degradation of human existence. A more positive symbolic relationship views the environment as one of a contextual space and conditions where forensic nursing intervention is applied and outcomes evaluated on interactions with the life-and-death process.

BEST PRACTICE The forensic nurse must protect the constitutional and human rights of the living, the severely compromised (near-death) individuals, the deceased, and their families during that interval between life and possible death.

The environment of the forensic nurse may reflect ambiguity and conflict. The medicolegal management scenarios vary widely and challenges abound in this new practice area, where the focus is on preventing further injury or death and repairing the lives of those who have suffered indignity. The major components of this environment are sources of stimuli emotionally charged with human conditions, at once nurturing and protective, yet constantly challenged with scientific and legal issues that have the potential to impact standards of nursing practice. This includes improving the quality of life and advancement of humanity.

Relevance and Roles

As healthcare reforms create complex systems for healthcare delivery, the professional nurse must be aware of ethical and legal considerations within those systems. A pattern of accountability revolves around four areas: the public, the patient, the profession, and the law. The forensic practitioner must know the boundaries and circumstances of both autonomy and accountability in order to provide forensically competent care. Issues of autonomy and accountability are subject to either criminal or civil law (equity). The primary care practitioner must adhere to these principles.

Forensic intervention draws on all nursing skills and knowledge to fully address the bio-psycho-socio-spiritual-cultural and legal dimensions of the patient whose health and justice needs require the application of forensic nursing scope and standards of practice (International Association of Forensic Nurses [IAFN], 1997, 2009). This client population is divided equally or unequally, in the social context of victims and offenders; for each victim, there is a perpetrator of criminal acts. However, in many cases, there are multiple victims for each perpetrator.

The role and relevance of forensic nursing practice incorporates the nursing care of individuals of all ages with perceived physical or emotional alterations, which may be diagnosed or undiagnosed and may require immediate or long-term intervention with implicit legal implications. Forensic nursing care is scheduled or unscheduled pertaining to the specific environment in a specific care setting—that is, special forensic exam unit, emergency department, mobile unit, child advocacy facility, suicide prevention center, forensic mental health institution, remand center, correctional setting (jail, prison), or institute of legal medicine. Thus, forensic nursing practice is episodic (domestic violence, drug abuse) and acute (gunshot wounds, sexual assault), as well as primary, secondary, and tertiary in nature.

RELEVANCE

Central to all programs of health delivery and promotion (physical, mental, cultural, and social well-being) is the concept of prevention, which includes forensic healthcare and involves three levels:

- Primary prevention is "pure" prevention, or preventing the health problem from occurring at all, such as determining the cause, manner, and mechanism of death in order to prevent future deaths of a similar nature; providing recommendations for public health and safety (avoidance of tobacco smoking, preventing polio through vaccination); or recommending the elimination of unsafe products or health hazards in the workplace. Clearly, this is the ideal and most cost-effective approach. Primary prevention is often referred to as health promotion, the process of enabling people to increase control over and to improve health through forensic assessment and interventions.
- Secondary prevention involves the prompt detection and successful management or treatment of the health condition to avoid actual damage to the person's health. For example, the early detection and treatment of communicable diseases can prevent epidemics that result from uncontrolled infections; likewise, diagnosing early indicators of domestic violence or child or elder abuse can lead to medicolegal intervention (reporting, etc.), counseling, and shelter placement, which may prevent further injury and death.

- Tertiary prevention seeks to limit the impairment, increase the quality of life, and prolong life. Examples would include forensic interventions in cases that involve serious bodily harm or violent deaths with attention to evidentiary data and removing the offender from the home or the community, thus preventing further threat or death, or rehabilitative services and documentation of evidence for torture victims to help secure political asylum and prevent deportation to country of origin, resulting in summary execution.

ROLES

In introducing practicing nurses to the importance of forensic protocol and tailoring forensic education designed to protect the legal rights of trauma victims in the clinical arena, one must first clarify the roles of a forensic nurse. This constructive action reduces the actual threat associated with uniformed personnel and helps to resolve legal action by and for victims. Role definitions include the following:

- *Clinical forensic nurse.* Provides care for the survivors of crime and liability-related injury and deaths. This specialist has a duty to defend the patient's legal rights through the proper collection and documentation of evidence that represents access to social justice.
- *Forensic nurse investigator.* Employed in the jurisdiction of a medical examiner or coroner; represents the decedent's right to social justice through a scientific investigation of the scene and circumstances of death. This role may also include the investigation of criminal behavior in cases of long-term care, institutionalized care, insurance fraud and abuse, or other aspects of investigative exigency.
- *Forensic nurse examiner.* Provides an incisive analysis of physical and psychological trauma, questioned deaths, or psychopathology evaluations related to forensic cases that involve interpersonal violence (i.e., child abuse, domestic violence, elder abuse, sexual assault, or injury resulting from lethal weapons, torture, police brutality, etc.). The subject of examination (victim or offender) may be living or dead, or the subject of examination may be legal documents in question.
- *Sexual assault nurse examiner.* A registered nurse specially trained to provide the forensic/medical examination and evaluation of sexual trauma while maximizing the collection of biological, trace, and physical evidence and minimizing the patient's emotional trauma.
- *Forensic psychiatric nurse.* Specializes in the assessment and intervention of criminal defendants, patients in legal custody who have been accused of a crime or have been court mandated for psychiatric evaluation.
- *Forensic correctional, institutional, or custody nurse.* Specializes in the care, treatment, and rehabilitation of persons who have been sentenced to prisons or jails for violation of criminal statutes and require medical assessment and intervention as well as detainees held in specific circumstances.
- *Legal nurse consultant.* Provides consultation and education to judicial, criminal justice, and healthcare professionals in areas such as personal injury, product liability, and malpractice, among other legal issues related to civil and criminal cases; investigates questioned documents such as medical records, health histories, or medication instructions pertaining to abuse, neglect, maltreatment, or death; recovers evidence from the context of such documents rather than from the scene of the crime or the body.
- *Nurse attorney.* A registered nurse with a jurist doctorate degree who practices as an attorney at law, generally specializing in civil or criminal cases involving healthcare-related issues.
- *Nurse coroner.* A registered nurse who serves as an elected officiator of death, duly authorized by state and jurisdictional statutes

to provide the investigation and certification of questioned deaths, to determine the cause and manner of death, and to determine the circumstances pertaining to the decedent's identification and notification of next of kin.

Each of these primary roles and other subspecialties of the forensic nurse examiner is investigative in nature, requiring specific knowledge of the law and the skill of expert witness testimony. The prevalence of criminal and negligence-based trauma indicates a growing need for healthcare providers to intercede on behalf of social justice; to require the recognition and reporting of crime-related injury; to ensure accurate documentation and security of evidence; and to evaluate, assess, and treat social offenders.

Prevention and Risk Reduction

The prevention of violence requires a direct response from healthcare professionals. Most perpetrators of crime repeat their criminal acts. To identify risk reduction and preventive measures, one must first identify victims of crime. Preventive measures are provided through forensic interventions, such as the identification of crime-related injuries and the documentation of evidence that will in turn link the victim to the perpetrator or to the crime scene, which assist in identifying criminals and interrupting the cycle of violence. Within the clinical or community environs, forensic nurse examiners apply sound methods of legal and ethical care by providing a crucial role in the clinical investigation of trauma and may determine the outcome of legal decisions or survivor benefits.

BEST PRACTICE It is the obligation of forensic nurses as well as other healthcare workers to suspect that violence has occurred, to inspect the patient for physical signs of abuse or neglect, to protect and respect the patient and family members, and to recover evidence in an objective manner.

If the healthcare professional providing immediate treatment to victims of criminal or liability-related trauma fails to incorporate forensic guidelines, the misinterpretation, omission, or loss of evidence may result in a miscarriage of justice. Moreover, inappropriate evidence recovery in healthcare facilities involving complex situations such as criminal cases may obscure the most important forensic evidence and complicate subsequent investigations. Medical care of the critically ill in the emergency department remains a responsibility that cannot be compromised. Trauma practitioners best serve the needs of society when they can simultaneously recognize and safeguard evidence.

The application of forensic science to clinical nursing reveals a wider role in the legal process that facilitates the medicolegal management of forensic patients from trauma to trial. The forensic psychiatric nursing specialist has been recognized as an asset in the evaluation of criminal suspects through remand evaluations and examination that will impact the adjudication process and patient outcome. As the Scope and Standards of Forensic Nursing Practice (IAFN, 1997, 2009) identifies a significant contemporary phase of healthcare progress, the growing interest among medical and nursing professionals implies a need to further define these roles in terms of forensic specialization and role evolution. Uniquely skilled nurses educated in forensic techniques enhance clinical investigative capabilities and forensic science functions.

Nurses specializing in the care and treatment of victims of pernicious human behavior offer, in addition to traditional nursing care, a composite of skills in the identification of covert and latent patterned injuries, recognition and collection of human

bite mark evidence, photodocumentation, recovery and preservation of genetic evidence, and crucial intervention in emotional trauma. The forensic nurse is equally obligated to protect the constitutional rights of those who have been accused of criminal acts through accurate forensic cognitive assessment as well as the clinical documentation of evidence pertaining to the innocence or guilt of the client.

Predictive Theory

Forensic nursing science has progressed greatly since it was first introduced in 1986 as a formal specialty in nursing at the University of Texas at Arlington, and it continues to do so. Forensic nursing is not only a reflection of society's needs, but it is also a plan for prevention in the future. After centuries of barbarian punishment in an attempt to deter crime without success, these methods were abandoned and society began to approach crime from an intelligent perspective. It was not until the 1830s that society began to fight crime in a positive manner, thinking of solutions to the problem of crime rather than reacting to it. As intellectual foundations of fighting crime with science rather than with brutality were being considered, new concepts were explored. In 1835, the publication of *On Man* by Lambert Que'telet, a criminologist who stated, "society contains within itself the germs of all future crimes," projected a concept that takes one into another dimension of human behavior, one in which the prediction of dangerousness becomes a self-fulfilling prophecy. Crime and criminals will exist. Victims will exist (Que'telet, 1835).

What is the function of forensic nursing science, and what is its future? Futurists who study forensic science predict that in the next century the focus will be on the prevention of crime rather than the detection of crime. With the current innovations in science and technology, the research that led to the development of DNA, lasers, infrared photodocumentation, and other exciting scientific developments will continue. Throughout the twentieth century, the emphasis was on trying to analyze the psychopathology of the criminal mind through various means of scientific and nonscientific methods. Thus far, the criminal mind remains elusive. The one conclusion is that crime is a mental activity; the criminal makes choices, which is not to say that it is a controlled or uncontrolled decision. From the early literature, Dostoyevsky's *Crime and Punishment* became a study not only of the criminal mind but of criminology. In a vivid and impressionistic portrayal of the criminal mind—decisions, retribution, and pride—Dostoyevsky challenged us with a dramatic combination of the mental, physical, and metaphysical description of the mechanics of criminality (Dostoyevsky, 1866).

The mechanics of the criminal mind have not changed, crime has not increased; only trends in crime change with the trends of the time. According to criminologists, those who study the rise and fall of crime statistics as well as the diseases of the mind that result from the germs of societal crime, it is the types of crimes that change, as opposed to the steady increase of crime itself. Therefore, if crime is the outcome of the germs of society resulting in a disease that takes control of the mind and renders it an anomaly, toxic, deviant, or malignant, then forensic nurse professionals must recognize their responsibilities in the identification of the problem: assessment, planning, intervention, and the evaluation of cause, manner, and mechanism of crime-related injury and death.

The roots of crime have been identified. Poverty, aggression, alienation, negativity, hate, lack of structure, lack of identity, revenge, rage, resentment, feelings of inadequacy, greed, power, and other organic and inorganic diseases of the mind: the germs of society. Aggression has been defined as a manifestation of disorganized purpose. Aggression results in extreme forms of behavior. The extremes of human behavior face nurses daily: child abuse, domestic homicide, suicide, sexual criminality, and emotional devastation. There is no simple answer for such complex concerns for a better world. Forensic nurse professionals, however, have been identified as one step in the reduction and prevention of crime.

Awareness, perception, and insight pertaining to the roles and behaviors expected of each respective specialist must become synthesized into one voice: for victims, for the accused, for the offender, and for the health and security of society. Forensic nurses cannot assume the burden of treatment, rehabilitation, and cure for society's ills alone. These are multifaceted problems for which the cause and the cure will require the commitment of each interrelated discipline. If crime is a mechanism of the mind, it stands to reason that the forensic and nursing sciences must focus intellect and energy on the mentally disordered offender, to consider the social and behavioral sciences in addition to the physical and medical sciences as a requirement of forensic nursing education. The need to incorporate the Scope and Standards of Forensic Nursing Practice as essential knowledge in traditional nursing preparation must be addressed in order for nursing students to face the reality of the patients for whom they will care.

Consider, the scene of crime is first in the mind. The mind comprises the body of the crime in as much as the corpus delicti is the essence of the crime. Crime scene investigators, forensic nurse examiners, and forensic medical scientists look to the body of the victim as a primary tool of the investigation of trauma, of crime, and of the criminal. Detectives look for psychological clues as well as the physical evidence at the crime scene. The sexual impulse is primarily a mental process; like murder, it begins inside the mind. The sexual assault nurse examiner also looks for psychological clues as well as physical evidence. The nurse death investigator or coroner evaluates the trauma to determine whether or not the killer was a sexual pervert or a sexual sadist. The mind, then, must be the central organism that bonds each of these disciplines together in health and justice, in the living and the dead. No one role is more or less important than the other. As in the final analysis of the crime, the autopsy of the physical body, the psychological autopsy is equally important in understanding the corpus delicti.

Often, nurses, nursing students, and nurse educators express abhorrence when discussing the role of the forensic nurse examiner who works with offenders—the mentally disordered offender or offenders who remain in control of their minds. Equally, an innate resentment exists for attorneys who defend the criminal at trial. The role of the sexual assault nurse examiner and the nurse death investigator or coroner is often considered with aversion. Society must approach these concerns from a more positive perspective, viewing forensic nurse examiners as those who do not shy away from the reality of crimes involving the degradation of society, who choose not to remain wedged in the archaic philosophy of isolationism and limited capacity but rather move toward more holistic solutions. Serious attempts to eliminate crime must begin with an understanding of the criminal mind and the rehabilitation of the criminal. Most criminals repeat their criminal acts. Statistics indicate that the recidivism rate of the average offender is great. Punishment is a useless expedient; expectation to reform society must be addressed by example and humanness. Forensic nursing science has a role to fill in this attempt to create positive change. The medicolegal management of both victims and offenders in healthcare systems will have a crucial impact on the outcomes of court-related cases.

Deterrent to Crime

Execution has been studied from earliest history; each era has attempted to resolve crime with heinous methods of execution. Generations who have practiced execution as a form of punishment have documented their own opinion and that of statesmen, human rights activists, and criminals themselves that capital punishment is no deterrent to crime. Nor is the swiftness of capital punishment seen as a solution, as pickpockets have been observed working a crowd of spectators as another pickpocket was being hanged, drawn, and quartered (which included disemboweling and placing hot coals in the abdominal cavity). History documents the impact of executions on society (when 10-year-old children and pregnant women were hanged), as well as their impact on the executioners, a number of which went mad or committed suicide. Considering the vast number of those executed in the name of justice, crime should not exist today. Yet crime continues to exist. Only when society is able to understand the mentality of social aggression will true prevention be practiced. To expect society to set the appropriate example, radical changes must emerge.

A learned society recognizes that the most critical aspect in need of change is the parenting and socialization of its children. Studies of the phenomena of serial killers have indicated that the majority of these criminals are physically and psychologically damaged from childhood. It also notes that this human radical wears a "mask of sanity to hide his perverse desires from the world" (Norris, 1991). If hope exists to change the world, to reduce and prevent human violence, it will begin with the protection of the world's children. Diversity in human violence requires diversity in nursing knowledge. To keep pace with the physical and psychological sequelae of the germs of society, a process of multidisciplinary exchange of purpose and shared responsibility must exist. In such a milieu, forensic nurses will contribute, not only to the recovery of the victim or the apprehension of the criminal but also to a new insight into the healing of society.

Summary

Millions are sufficiently injured each year to seek medical assistance in hospitals and clinics for injuries sustained as a result of human violence. An enlightened healthcare system must be oriented toward change: to replace traditional concepts with new philosophies and new specialists to carry out these changes. As a change agent, the forensic nurse is often the crucial link between the untoward events of the real world and the more remote scientific undertaking of the legal sciences. According to criminologists, the lack of forensic knowledge can and will wreak havoc on an otherwise well-functioning system. Historically, these two worlds have not meshed philosophically or practically, which puts the forensic nurse in a unique position that can be both potentially difficult and influential (Standing Bear, 1995).

Forensic science is at the threshold of an explosion of technical advancement. In combating increasingly sophisticated crime, new and improved methods of identification and apprehension of the criminal will revolutionize our ability to bring those who commit violent crime, particularly the serial rapist and murderer, to justice. It is imperative that clinical professionals support law enforcement agencies in this quest to transmit developing knowledge through services that include forensic nursing interventions. Nursing education must engage in inquiry that is not immediately applicable to current clinical practice. It must be continually reevaluated in terms of societal needs and scientific discoveries. This requires nurse researchers to incorporate a variety of approaches to nursing's perspectives. The scope of the forensic nurse goes beyond that required for current clinical praxis.

Nurses are beginning to realize their potential for discovering particular knowledge that is relevant to other disciplines and essential to nursing (Newman, 1979, 1983). There is typically a lag between knowledge discovery and its implementation through practice. Forensic nursing, in its effort to decrease the lag between learning and applying forensic skills and services, has not only a responsibility but also an opportunity to chart new directions. As the spectrum of forensic nursing expands, subspecialties of forensic nursing will continue to evolve where nursing and patient care interface with the law.

Resources

ORGANIZATIONS

American Academy of Forensic Sciences
410 North 21st Street, Colorado Springs, CO 80904; Tel: 719-636-1100; www.aafs.org
American Academy of Nursing
611 East Wells Street, Suite 1100, Milwaukee, WI 53202; Tel: 414-287-0289; www.aannet.org

WEBSITES

University of San Diego, Hahn School of Nursing and Health Science, nursing theory
www.sandiego.edu/nursing/theory
Valdosta State University, College of Nursing, nursing theory
www.valdosta.edu/nursing/history_theory/theory.html

References

Brenner, P. (1984). *From novice to expert: Excellence and power in clinical nursing practice.* Menlo Park, CA: Addison-Wesley.

Carper, B. A. (1978). Fundamental patterns of knowing in nursing. *ANS: Advances in Nursing Science, 4*(1), 253–259.

Chinn, P., & Kramer, M. (1995). *Theory and nursing: A systematic approach.* (4th ed.). St. Louis, MO: Mosby–Year Book.

Conway, D., & Hardy, L. (1988). *The use of knowledge.* Norwalk, CT: Appleton & Lange.

Dorland's Illustrated Medical Dictionary. (2003). Philadelphia, PA: Saunders.

Dostoyevsky, F. (1866, 1980). *Crime and punishment: The Russian messenger.* Norwalk, CT: Easton Press.

Farrell, R., & Swigert, V. (1982). *Deviance and social control.* New York: Random House.

Federal Bureau of Investigation (FBI). (1999). *Uniform crime reports: Crime in the United States* 1998. Washington, DC: U.S. Department of Justice.

Federal Bureau of Investigations (FBI). (2002). *Crime in the United States* 2001. Washington, DC: U.S. Government Printing Office.

Federal Bureau of Investigation (FBI). (2002). *Uniform crime reports: Crime in the United States* 2001. Washington, DC: U.S. Department of Justice.

Federal Bureau of Investigations (FBI). (2003). *Preliminary Uniform Crime Report,* 2002. Retrieved June 28, 2003, from www.fbi.gov/ucr/cius_02/02prelimannual.pdf.

Giger, J., & Davidhizar, R. (1991). *Transcultural nursing: Assessment and intervention.* (2nd ed.). St. Louis, MO: Mosby.

International Association of Forensic Nurses (IAFN). (1997). *Scope and standards of forensic nursing practice.* Washington, DC: American Nurses Publishing.

Leininger, M. (1995). In J. George (Ed.), *Nursing theories: The base for professional nursing practice.* (chap. 20). Norwalk, CT: Appleton & Lange.

Lynch, V. (1990). *Clinical forensic nursing: A descriptive study in role development.* Thesis. Arlington: University of Texas.

Lynch, V. (1991). *Proposal for a new scientific discipline: Forensic nursing.* Anaheim, CA: Presentation to the general section at the annual meeting of the American Academy of Forensic Sciences.

Lynch, V. (1995a). Clinical forensic nursing: A new perspective in the management of crime victims from trauma to trial. *Critical Care Nursing Clinics of North America, 7*(3), 489–507.

Lynch, V. (1995b). Forensic nursing: What's new?. *Journal of Psychosocial Nursing, 33*(9), 1–7.

Lynch, V., & Barber, J. (2006). *Forensic nursing.* St. Louis, MO: Mosby.

Mead, G. H. (1934). *Mind, self, and society.* Chicago: University of Chicago Press.

Newman, M. (1979). *Theory development in nursing.* Philadelphia: F. A. Davis.

Newman, M. (1983). The continuing revolution: A history of nursing science. In N. Chaska (Ed.), *The nursing profession: A time to speak* (pp. 385–393). New York: McGraw-Hill.

Norris, J. (1991). In B. Marriner (Ed.), *On death's bloody trail: Murder and the art of forensic science* (pp. 40–165). New York: St. Martin's Press.

Paterson, J., & Zderad, L. (1998). Nursing theories: The base for professional nursing practice. In J. E. Patterson, & L. T. Zderad (Eds.), *Humanistic nursing* (pp. 287–299). New York: National League for Nursing Press.

Plato (427–347 B.C.). Translated from Greek to English by B. Jowett. *The Republic* (p. 309). Norwalk, CT: Easton Press.

Que'telet, L. (1835). *On man.* In B. Marriner (Ed.), (1991). *On death's bloody trail: Murder and the art of forensic science* (pp. 40–165). New York: St. Martin's Press.

Reiss, A. J., & Roth, J. A. (1993). *Understanding and preventing violence.* Washington, DC: National Academy Press.

Standing Bear, Z. G. (1995). Forensic nursing and death investigation: Will the vision be co-opted? *Journal of Psychosocial Nursing and Mental Health Services, 33*(9), 59–64.

The Joint Commission (TJC). (2009). *Accreditation manual for hospitals.* Oakbrook Terrace, IL.

CHAPTER 3 Forensic Nursing Education

Arlene Kent-Wilkinson

Forensic Nursing Educational Programs

By the end of the twentieth century, forensic nursing educational programs began to appear in the curricula of colleges and universities. The *forensic focus* has been a popular career choice and area of study for many of the health science disciplines. In the mid-1990s, some of the earliest forensic nursing courses were established. Today, courses exist at educational levels that range from certificate to doctoral programs. This chapter provides an overview of the history of forensic nursing educational development and highlights findings from recent research that explored many aspects of forensic nursing education: definitions of forensic nursing and forensic nursing education, factors influencing course development, and benefits of forensic nursing education.

NURSING SPECIALTY EDUCATION

The practice of nursing continues to evolve to meet the changing needs of clients. Like nursing itself, specialized areas of nursing develop in response to needs in society (Cumming, 1995). The need for a medicolegal role was the reason for most of the forensic specialty developments in every discipline, including nursing.

Traditionally, nurses have been trained as generalists, and nurses with extensive clinical experience in a particular area of practice are considered specialists. The view through the knowledge base lens shows that it is impossible to know all aspects of nursing. The 1980s witnessed the early development of a variety of formal and informal nursing specialty educational programs in specific practice areas. For example, specialties such as gerontology, oncology, and perinatology were among the first to seek certification and specialty status. However, it was the mid-1980s before courses and programs for the specialty of forensic nursing began to be established.

FORENSIC NURSING SPECIALTY

Unlike most nursing specialties, forensic nursing is made up of different areas of nursing practice, often identified by the populations served. Subspecialties of forensic nursing are: clinical forensic nursing (which focuses on the victims of interpersonal violence), forensic correctional nurses (offenders), forensic nurse examiners (sexual assault survivors), forensic nurse death investigators (deceased), forensic psychiatric/mental health nurses (mentally ill offenders), and forensic geriatric or pediatric nurses (elderly and pediatric victims of abuse and neglect).

KEY POINT Forensic nursing cares for or serves the populations of victims and perpetrators, living and deceased, and the families of both. Forensic nursing is a combination of not only the nursing process, but also elements of the scientific process and the legal process. Forensic nursing is vital to the assessment, planning, and outcome effectiveness of the nursing care plan. The philosophy of forensic nursing education adheres to the same basic philosophical underpinnings as nursing, which are the nursing process, the nursing paradigm, and the caring paradigm (Kent-Wilkinson, 2008).

Forensic nurses practice in the complex organization of the healthcare system, but they have learned to interface with, and navigate through, many other systems—including the criminal justice system, the child welfare system, the medical examiner/coroner system, and the mental healthcare system—all within which they provide nursing services. Many other disciplines also focus on the forensic aspects of their practice and are identified as forensic specialties (e.g., forensic psychiatry, forensic psychology, forensic social work, and forensic occupational therapists).

KEY POINT Forensic nursing education incorporates concepts from both the forensic sciences and the forensic behavioral sciences to provide students with a repertoire of skills in both domains (Kent-Wilkinson, 2008).

SPECIALTY STATUS

The International Association of Forensic Nurses (IAFN) became the professional association of registered nurses working in the medicolegal nursing arena. Its purpose continues to be to develop, promote, and disseminate information about the science of forensic nursing (IAFN, 1993b). The IAFN was formed in 1992 when 74 forensic nurses, the majority of whom were sexual assault nurses, came together in Minneapolis, Minnesota. Because some of the forensic nurses in attendance also identified themselves as death investigators or practiced with offenders rather than victims, and because some were from Canada, the group decided to create an international association encompassing all areas of forensic nursing globally (Kent-Wilkinson, 2006).

As a result of the efforts of IAFN leaders, in 1995 the American Nurses Association formally recognized forensic nursing as a nursing specialty (ANA, 1995). IAFN members soon after developed their *Forensic Nursing Standards and Scope of Practice,* which the ANA approved and published in 1997 (ANA, 1997).

HISTORY OF FORENSIC NURSING EDUCATIONAL DEVELOPMENT

For many years, forensic nurses in most of the subspecialties learned about their specialty on the job from those who worked with forensic populations of victims, offenders, and the deceased. Information about the specialty was not well communicated to nurses outside the forensic worksite. With the exception of the sexual assault nurse examiner (SANE) subspecialty, many of the forensic nursing subspecialties did not develop concurrently with role development.

Clinical Placements

Historically, students were placed clinically before there was any formal educational development. Until the 1970s, schools of nursing were less than responsive to the health needs of inmate

20

populations (Felton, Parsons, & Satterfield, 1987). "The nursing literature in the 1970s indicated that prisons were not often considered when nursing faculty chose sites for undergraduate clinical experience" (Fontes, 1991, p. 300). Even though the *American Nurses Association's Position Statement on Psychiatric Nursing Practice* in 1967 validated the appropriateness of a prison as a learning laboratory (Bridges, 1981), clinical placements for nursing students in correctional institutions did not commonly occur in Canada and the United States until the 1980s.

Forerunner Courses

Criminology and victimology courses may have been forerunners to forensic nursing course development. Nurses who had electives in basic and advanced programs often took courses like criminology and victimology because of an interest in forensic issues in society and in forensic-specific vulnerable populations (Kent-Wilkinson, 2006). Courses in criminology and victimology became popular options for transfer credits that would contribute to a nursing degree. In the 1980s, victimology and criminology courses were created because of the strong social emphasis on the human rights issues of the 1960-1970s, including victims' rights, women's rights, offenders' rights, and civil rights. Although victimology courses may have been the precursors to clinical forensic and SANE courses, criminology courses were the predecessors to forensic psychiatric/correctional courses. Once forensic nursing became a specialty that covered both victims and perpetrators, formal courses were in demand.

Continuing Nursing Education (CNE) or Continuing Education Units (CEUs)

The continuing education departments (CEDs) of universities were the birthplaces of many specialty educational courses. Packed curricula did not allow room for specialty courses; therefore, a backdoor was created to offer options courses through continuing nursing education. Nursing colleges often had not accepted the idea of developing a separate forensic nursing course or program, and individuals with the expertise frequently were only welcomed and used as guest speakers. Therefore, some of the courses and programs were housed in forensic science facilities rather than in nursing departments (Kent-Wilkinson, 2008). In 1988, a general forensic nursing course was offered for the first time through the Department of Medicine in a continuing education program in the United States (P. Speck, personal communication, March 31, 2006). At that time, forensic nurses taught residents and nurses about sexual assault, domestic violence, and elder abuse. CEDs often provided a foot in the door or an initial home for specialty forensic nursing education. With the successful offerings of forensic nursing courses in the CEDs, similar courses were added to the nursing curriculum in many universities. Later, certificate programs at the postgraduate level and whole tracks at the graduate level were developed.

Sexual Assault Nurse Examiner (SANE) Programs

The development of SANE programs began when healthcare providers realized that the standard of care was inadequate for sexual assault victims admitted into hospital emergency departments. Because victims of sexual assault had to withstand long waiting times before seeing a physician in emergency departments, nurses wanted to provide the necessary examination and follow-up counseling themselves in the emergency departments or in clinics (Kent-Wilkinson, 2006). In 1976, the first SANE program was established in Memphis, Tennessee.

In September 1977, the Sexual Assault Resource Service began in Minneapolis, Minnesota (Ledray, 1992). In 1978, the sexual assault nurse clinician program began in Amarillo, Texas (Ledray & Arndt, 1994).

Formalized Forensic Nursing Education in Colleges and Universities

By the 1980s, various formal and informal educational programs began to be developed for those interested in forensic nursing. However, none if any were sustained. In 1983, the School of Nursing at the Catholic University of America in Washington, D.C., was "awarded a grant from the National Institute of Mental Health to prepare forensic psychiatric nurses as clinical nurse specialists at a graduate level to function in all areas of the correctional system" (Bernier, 1986, p. 21). This may have been the first forensic nursing course offered. Reportedly, it was designed as a subspecialty for psychiatric nursing but survived only one year. Psychiatric programs, although known to be among the first specialties in schools of nursing, have struggled to maintain their important status in the nursing curriculum (D. Shelton, personal communication, January 5, 2004).

In 1986, a forensic nursing graduate program at the University of Texas at Arlington commenced. However, with a change in administration, the new forensic nursing program did not survive (V. Lynch, personal communication, August 5, 1997). In the early years of forensic nursing educational development, both the expertise of clinicians and the support of administrators were needed to maintain programs that were new and not yet recognized as up-and-coming mainstay programs.

Established Programs

In the 1990s, educational programs were established for nurses interested in the specialty of forensic nursing. Forensic nursing education included certificate programs and option courses for credits toward a degree. In the early to mid-1990s, two or three introductory general nursing courses and programs came on the scene in Canada and the United States. They developed into complete programs, addressing all the subspecialties of forensic nurses who worked with victims, offenders, the deceased, and their families (Kent-Wilkinson, 2006). Also in the mid-1990s in the United States, face-to-face postgraduate-level education began with a focus on forensic science and forensic behavioral science at Fitchburg State College in Massachusetts in the east, Beth El College in Colorado in the west, and the University of Calgary, Alberta, Canada, in the north. About the same time, specific forensic mental health and psychiatric courses were launched in the United Kingdom, Australia, and New Zealand (Kent-Wilkinson, 2006).

Online Programs

Considering that the first Web-based course, in California, did not begin until 1995 (Bates & Poole, 2003), forensic nursing education made its online appearance on the global scene relatively quickly. Forensic nursing educators, supported by progressive administrators, used the technology to offer the first online forensic course in January of 1997, at Mount Royal College (MRC) in Calgary, Alberta, Canada (Kent-Wilkinson, Mckeown, Mercer, McCann, & Mason, 2000). By 2001, MRC established a full certificate program of forensic studies with six online courses; a theoretical sexual assault course was added soon thereafter (Kent-Wilkinson, 2006).

In the United States, Bader (2005) noted "four accredited universities offer doctorate level forensic nursing degrees" (p. 23). To date, Canada has well-established forensic certificate programs but does not have forensic nursing graduate or doctoral programs. This could be because fewer forensic nurse educators at the Ph.D. level are required to teach these programs; in addition, a smaller percentage of the country's population has requested this specialized curriculum.

Research to Date on Forensic Nursing Education

Since the 1970s, multiple studies have identified the need for forensic nursing education, but those recommendations did not quickly translate into educational development. The literature shows that educational development did not occur concurrently with role development in all of the subspecialties (Kent-Wilkinson, 2008).

RESEARCH ON THE NEED FOR FORENSIC NURSING

As previously noted, when jails and prisons began to be used as clinical placements in the early 1980s, the concept of correctional healthcare had not transferred into the educational curricula. The findings in a proliferation of studies recommended the need for forensic nursing education, especially in the area of forensic psychiatric and correctional nursing. Educational surveys in the 1980s identified a need for formal courses in forensic nursing (Graham & Gleit, 1981; Gulotta, 1987; Moritz, 1982; Niskala, 1986, 1987; Phillips, 1983; Roell, 1985; Werlin & O'Brien, 1984). However, the research did not lead to sustainable educational programs in the 1980s.

Numerous studies for the next two decades continued to recommend a need for education in every forensic nursing area. Davila (2005) from the University of Michigan's School of Nursing noted that despite the prevalence of domestic violence and its recognition as a priority health issue, the majority of accredited nursing schools in the United States had yet to adequately integrate violence assessment, intervention content, and planned clinical experiences into their curricula. Nurses and the public began to request education to develop their assessment skills and thereby provide better care to domestic violence (DV) patients.

EARLY RESEARCH TO DATE

With the establishment of forensic nursing educational programs in the 1990s, research is beginning to be conducted to explore specific aspects of forensic nursing education. One early study looked at the online delivery of forensic nursing education in Canada, and a few studies have looked at forensic multidisciplinary education in the United Kingdom.

Online Delivery Research

Since 1995, there has been a move toward Web-based learning modalities for nursing education. In an increasingly technology-sophisticated world, it is important for nurse educators to take full advantage of this technology to enhance their learning. A study was commissioned in Canada on the technical and content design characteristics of online forensic nursing courses and the reasons for taking them (Harvey, 1998). The study found that most of the participants surveyed chose to enroll in the courses because of their interest in the forensic subject matter. More than half of the participants chose the courses because of the full online delivery, which was innovative at that time. Personal enrichment and reasons related to career opportunities or enhanced current career status were most often cited as reasons for taking the forensic courses.

Multidisciplinary/Interprofessional Training Research

Research findings on forensic psychiatric nursing and multidisciplinary training done in the United Kingdom offer conceptual guidance or directions for educational course development in this specific focus of forensic nursing. Brooker and Whyte (2000), in a United Kingdom report aimed at multidisciplinary teamwork in secure psychiatric settings, argued that interprofessional training should take place at the clinical interface. They added that it should focus on client-centered, problem-based learning exercises that allowed for reflexive learning.

Mason and Carton (2002), in their effort to determine if common areas of multidisciplinary training in forensic mental health practice existed, reviewed literature and curriculum documents. They found that professional training took a diffused approach, with each profession formulating areas of study for appropriate forensic expertise, usually involving basic training that pertained to the profession followed by postgraduate studies. Mason and Carton advocated that this method of training was unclear and may not be appropriate. Thus, it was necessary to identify what the required skills were to care for or manage this patient population, as well as establish whether the skills were evidence based and to what extent they could be measured. With the trend toward interprofessional education, findings from the multidisciplinary studies are important.

Undergraduate Forensic Nursing Education

The IAFN Education Committee explored how to develop forensic healthcare information for use in undergraduate nursing programs. Typically, undergraduate programs of study were packed with required content that supported the students as they prepared for nursing board examinations. Programs allowed little flexibility for adding new content, despite the fact that the forensic content was in high demand. Forensic nursing was a specialty that students characteristically desired to pursue, but more important, "the information related to all areas of nursing practice, from pediatrics to geriatrics, from psychiatric mental health to the perioperative area" (Crane, 2005, p. 4).

First, the IAFN Education Committee discussed the best approach for integrating forensic content into undergraduate programs and the most efficient method of providing the information to students or to the faculty who taught it. Second, forensic information and case studies in content modules were discussed as potentially useful tools for educators who had the desire but limited time to teach new content. Third, the committee developed and refined a brief survey of IAFN members to determine if nurses were taught general and forensic nursing content and which forensic topics were included in their programs (Crane, 2005). "Of the 534 respondents to the survey, 338 (63.3% of them) were involved in nursing education" (p. 4). The statistical analysis delineated how many educators were teaching general and forensic content. "In addition, 202 faculty members provided continuing nursing education courses with forensic nursing content" (p. 4).

2008 Forensic Nursing Education Study

A study on forensic nursing education (Kent-Wilkinson, 2008) explored forensic nursing knowledge as a specialty area of study and factors influencing educational development from the perspective of forensic nurse educators who had established some of the earliest programs. The motivation for this study came from questions many educators have when developing new specialty educational courses: What concepts need to be included? How do we best organize and deliver this new body of knowledge? And, are we conceptualizing this new specialty area consistently, nationally, and internationally? The rationale for the study was the paucity of research undertaken to identify the constituent parts of this professional practice. The perspective of educators representing all subspecialties of forensic nursing was sought because they had the experience of articulating this knowledge for their forensic nursing courses or programs of study, with the goal of gaining both collective and alternate understandings (Kent-Wilkinson, 2008).

This predominately qualitative study involved interviewing forensic nurse educators who were responsible for developing some of the earliest forensic nursing programs in Canada and the United States. The purposeful sample of 17 participants needed to meet the criteria of having written the content for and taught at least one forensic nursing course. A thematic analysis of the data in comparison to the literature and a constructivist approach allowed the researchers to examine factors that facilitated or impeded the development and sustainability of forensic nursing education (Kent-Wilkinson, 2008).

The forensic nursing educational study was made up of two phases: Phase 1 was an e-mail survey designed to provide demographic statistics about the educators and descriptive information about the courses they developed. Phase 2 was a qualitative phone interview, where findings resulted in constructed definitions of forensic nursing, determined factors that influenced and impeded the development and sustainability of forensic nursing education, and examined reasons why education did not occur sooner or concurrently with role development. The remainder of this chapter will address these findings.

FINDINGS IN THE DESCRIPTIVE STATISTICS

Along with the process of doing a predominately qualitative study, descriptive statistics were collected to elicit demographic data about the nurse educators who participated (see Table 3-1 for a summary of educators' demographics) and to gather basic information about the forensic nursing courses they developed (Table 3-2).

Educators' Demographics

The participants of the forensic nursing educational study in 2008 represented nurse educators from the United States (n = 13/17) and from Canada (n = 4/17); the gender breakdown was female (n = 16/17) and male (n = 01/17). Findings from the descriptive statistics showed that the participants' highest levels of education ranged from baccalaureate to doctorate. All doctoral-level educators in this sample were from the United States (n = 11/17). Most of the participants (n = 14/17) stated that their current position was as a full-time faculty member, and many were currently the directors of their forensic programs (Kent-Wilkinson, 2008).

A significant finding was that most of the earliest forensic nursing programs, 41.2% (n = 7/17), were established by nurses in both countries who were not educated at the doctoral level and were not on the faculty at the time they developed the courses. Instead, these early pioneers were prepared at the baccalaureate and master's levels, and because they were not in full-time faculty positions, it was their passion and determination that drove them to launch forensic courses/programs into the curricula of major colleges and universities; it was something they felt compelled to do (Kent-Wilkinson, 2008).

Course Information

Information about the forensic courses was collected from the participants. The questions involved issues such as whether a needs assessment was completed before developing courses, the types and levels of courses, the types of educational institutions where courses are offered, whether forensic courses are elective or required, years when courses were first delivered, and numbers of students per semester? The analysis of the course information survey showed a consensus among educators about the need for more options in curricula for specialty courses and the need for SANE courses to be recognized for credit at the college/university level.

Table 3-1 Summary of Educators Demographics Survey

1. *Demographics*
   (n = 13/17) United States*
   (n = 04/17) Canada
   (n = 16/17) female*
   (n = 01/17) male
2. *Highest level of education*
   (n = 11/17) doctoral prepared*
   (n = 3/17) doctoral candidate
   (n = 2/17) masters prepared
   (n = 1/17) baccalaureate prepared
3. *Clinical experience in nursing practice* [1-35 yrs]
   Clinical experience forensic nursing practice [0-29 yrs]
4. *Main focus area of nursing*
   (n = 6/17) emergency*
   (n = 3/17) psych/mental health
   (n = 3/17) maternal/women health
   (n = 2/17) forensic nursing only
   (n = 1/17) gerontology
   (n = 1/17) public health
   (n = 1/17) child/pediatric
5. *Main focus area of forensic nursing*
   (n = 7/17) sexual assault nurse examiners*
   (n = 2/17) forensic nursing (multiple areas)
   (n = 2/17) forensic psych/corrections
   (n = 2/17) interpersonal violence
   (n = 1/17) clinical forensic
   (n = 1/17) death investigator
   (n = 1/17) injury prevention
   (n = 1/17) product liability
6. *Forensic related courses taken for credit* (n = 14/17)
7. *Forensic nursing courses taken for credit* (n = 12/17)
8. *Number of forensic courses developed* (each 1-30) (total 88 plus)
9. *Current positions*
   Most full time faculty* (n)= 14/17, many program directors
   N.B. Most significant was that 41.2% (n = 7/17) were not on the faculty initially
10. *Teaching nursing experience* (0-42 years)
    Teaching forensic nursing experience (3-29 years)

Source: Kent-Wilkinson, A. (2008). Forensic nursing education in North America: An exploratory study [doctorial dissertation]. Department of Educational Administration, University of Saskatchewan, Saskatoon, SK. Retrieved September 18, 2008 from http://library2.usask.ca/theses/available/etd-08262008-171000.
*Indicates highest frequency (n = 17); nominal/ordinal data, S = survey.

Table 3-2 Summary of Course Statistics Survey

1. *Type of educational institution*
   (n = 12/23) university*
   (n = 5/23) college
   (n = 5/23) other (SANE) (hospitals)
2. *Needs assessment*
   YES* (n = 12/17) before course development
3. *Educational level of course/program*
   (n = 7/26) certificate level
   (n = 6/26) undergraduate
   (n = 10/26) graduate*
   (n = 2/26) doctoral
   (n = 1/26) other (hospital/non credit).
4. *Prerequisite*
   Yes* (n = 9/17)
5. *Student discipline*
   (n = 10/17) nursing only*
   (n = 7/17) nursing and other disciplines
6. *Mode of delivery*
   (n = 10/24) classroom*
   (n = 9/24) Web based
7. *Clinical component*
   (n = 13/17) YES (SANE*)
8. *Year course started*
   [Range 1977–2005]
   1977–SANE
   1988 Con Ed Medicine
   1994 Nursing
   1995 Con Ed Nursing

9. *Types of forensic nursing courses developed*
   (n = 8/17) introductory course*
   (n = 2/17) both forensic science/forensic behavioral sciences
   (n = 7/17) only forensic science courses*
   (n = 1/17) only forensic behavioral sciences
   (n = 7/17) difficult to determine
10. *Required/elective*
    (n = 9/19) required*
    (n = 7/19) were elective
    (n = 3/19) n/a non credit
11. *Elective options*
    (n = 3/19) had two electives
    (n = 7/19) one elective*
    (n = 7/19) had one elective
    (n = 3/19) had no electives
    (n= 4/19) unsure
    (n = 2/19) n/a (SANE)
12. *Number of semesters offered*
    (n = 7/19) one semester a year*
    (n = 6/19) two semesters a year
    (n = 1/19) three semesters a year
    (n = 5/19) n/a as SANE courses
13. *Average number of students/year registered (range 5-100+)*
14. *Comments*
    Curricula are full–no room for electives
    Needed recognition of SANE for university credit

Source: Kent-Wilkinson, A. (2008). Forensic nursing education in North America: An exploratory study [doctorial dissertation]. Department of Educational Administration, University of Saskatchewan, Saskatoon, SK. Retrieved September 18, 2008 from http://library2.usask.ca/theses/available/etd-08262008-171000.
*Indicates highest frequency (n = 17); nominal/ordinal data, S = survey.

Definitions of Forensic Nursing

Since the inception of forensic nursing, numerous definitions have been written to articulate the knowledge required to practice the specialty. The International Association of Forensic Nurses (IAFN) produced the most commonly cited definitions of forensic nursing in 1993 and more recent definitions in 2006:

- Forensic nursing is the application of the forensic aspects of healthcare combined with the *biopsychosocial* education of the registered nurse in the scientific investigation and treatment of trauma, and/or death of victims and perpetrators of violence, criminal activity, and traumatic accidents within the clinical or community institution (Lynch, 1991, adopted by IAFN, 1993a).
- Forensic nursing provides direct services to individual clients, consultation services to nursing, medical, and law-related agencies, and expert court testimony in areas dealing with trauma and/or questioned death investigative processes, adequacy of services delivery, and specialized diagnoses of specific conditions as related to nursing. Forensic nurses also work with families or significant others and the community (IAFN, 2006a).
- Forensic nursing is defined as the global practice of nursing that results when healthcare and legal systems intersect (Lynch, 2006, adopted by IAFN, 2006b).

RESEARCH DEFINITION OF FORENSIC NURSING

Participants in phase 2 in the qualitative interview of the study on forensic nursing education (Kent-Wilkinson, 2008) were asked broad questions about forensic nursing knowledge. They responded by describing what forensic nursing is, is not, is a combination of, is the same as, and is different from, and they explained what is unique about the knowledge of forensic nursing. Constructivist interpretations were made from a thematic analysis of the data responses and the relevant literature (Tables 3-3 and 3-4). A constructed definition from the analysis of the data from the perceptions of 17 of the early educators on forensic nursing was as follows:

KEY POINT Forensic nursing is a recognized global specialty of nursing, integrating the application of nursing art and science at the clinical/legal interface serving the human health experience as a response to violence in society. Forensic nursing is a specialty in nursing, not a nursing specialty in forensics. Forensic nursing is not just about technical skills or evidence collection; it is also about the person/client (Kent-Wilkinson, 2008).

Unexpected findings from this study resulted in the concept of forensic nursing being described, differentiated, and defined. The constructed definitions of forensic nursing from this study not only validated prior definitions developed by individuals and associations by nonresearchable methods, but they also led to a discussion of what concepts are important to include in definitions of forensic nursing. More research is required to further explore the constituent parts of forensic nursing knowledge.

Table 3-3 Constructed Definitions of Forensic Nursing

Results of the analysis of the study on forensic nursing education were some constructed definitions of forensic nursing as follows:

FORENSIC NURSING IS (DESCRIBED KNOWLEDGE)
- Forensic nursing is a recognized global specialty of nursing, integrating the application of nursing art and science at the clinical/legal interface serving the human health experience as a response to violence in society.

FORENSIC NURSING IS NOT (DESCRIBED KNOWLEDGE—ANTITHESIS)
- Forensic nursing is a specialty in nursing, not a nursing specialty in forensics. Forensic nursing is not just about technical skills or evidence collection; it is also about the person/client.

FORENSIC NURSING IS A COMBINATION OF (BOTH/AND) (MULTIPLE KNOWLEDGE)
- Forensic nursing is a combination of not only the nursing process, but also elements of the scientific process and the legal process. Forensic nursing is vital to the assessment, planning, and outcome effectiveness of the nursing care plan.
- Forensic nursing education incorporates concepts from both the forensic sciences and the forensic behavioral sciences to provide students with a repertoire of skills in both domains.
- Forensic nursing cares for or serves the populations of victims and perpetrators, living and deceased, and the families of both.

FORENSIC NURSING IS THE SAME AS (NURSING KNOWLEDGE)
- The philosophy of forensic nursing adheres to the same basic philosophical underpinnings as nursing, which are the nursing process, the nursing paradigm, and the caring paradigm.

FORENSIC NURSING IS DIFFERENT FROM NURSING (DIFFERENTIAL KNOWLEDGE)
- Forensic nursing is different *from nursing* in general in that forensic nurses are *more likely* to be caring for patients who are victims or offenders on a continual basis; therefore, their practice has a *high likelihood* of interfacing with one of the justice systems. Forensic nurses are *more likely* to rely on the knowledge from law and forensic science, and it is *more likely* that the case and the documentation will end up in court.

FORENSIC NURSING IS DIFFERENT FROM OTHER FORENSIC DISCIPLINES (DIFFERENTIAL KNOWLEDGE)
- Forensic nursing is different from other forensic disciplines in that forensic nursing is *more likely* to have knowledge applied at the clinical/legal interface; *more likely* to provide care and services to both victims and offenders, living and deceased; and *more likely* to be responsible for medication administration, supervision, and evaluation of the impact of medication. Different from other forensic disciplines that also lay claim to a caring paradigm, forensic nursing is *more likely* to include not only therapeutic aspects of caring but also a holistic and objective approach and a social sense of responsibility for the continuous 24/7/365 care across the life span, where care and contact is maintained with the client and care is extended to the family and to the community.

FORENSIC NURSING IS UNIQUE (CORE KNOWLEDGE)
- Forensic nursing truly encompasses the nursing paradigm, with its own unique definitions of person, health, environment, and nursing, resulting in the forensic nursing paradigm.
- The unique aspects of forensic nursing culminate into the forensic nursing process, the forensic nursing paradigm, and the caring paradigm with dual nursing/forensic roles.
- Forensic nursing is a unique area of nursing practice where a dual role with care may be some of the core components of each subspecialty: care and custody, care and collection of evidence, care and chain of custody, care and courtroom testimony, care and collaboration.

Source: Kent-Wilkinson, A. (2008). Forensic nursing education in North America: An exploratory study [doctorial dissertation]. Department of Educational Administration, University of Saskatchewan, Saskatoon, SK. Retrieved September 18, 2008 from http://library2.usask.ca/theses/available/etd-08262008-171000.

Table 3-4 Forensic Nursing Is Dual Roles (Dual Knowledge)

Forensic nursing is a unique area of nursing practice where a dual role with care may be some of the core components of each subspecialty:
- Both care and custody [offender] (forensic psychiatric/correctional nursing)
- Both care and custody [deceased body] (forensic nurse death investigators)
- Both care and collection of evidence (clinical forensic nursing, SANEs)
- Both care and chain of custody (clinical forensic nursing, SANEs)
- Both care and court testimony (forensic nursing, all subspecialties)
- Both care and crisis intervention (forensic nursing, all subspecialties)
- Both care and coordinator/collaborator of care (forensic nursing, all subspecialties)

Source: Kent-Wilkinson, A. (2008). Forensic nursing education in North America: An exploratory study [doctorial dissertation]. Department of Educational Administration, University of Saskatchewan, Saskatoon, SK. Retrieved September 18, 2008 from http://library2.usask.ca/theses/available/etd-08262008-171000.

DIFFERENTIAL FORENSIC NURSING DEFINITIONS

The following differential definitions were constructed from the data of the forensic nursing study and with comparisons to the relevant literature:

Forensic nursing is different from nursing in general in that forensic nurses are more likely to be caring for patients who are victims or offenders on a continual basis; therefore, the practice has a high likelihood of interfacing with one of the justice systems. Forensic nurses are more likely to rely on the knowledge from law and forensic science, and it is more likely that the case and the documentation will end up in court (Kent-Wilkinson, 2008).

Forensic nursing is different from other forensic disciplines in that forensic nurses are more likely to have their knowledge applied at the clinical/legal interface; more likely to provide care and services to both victims and offenders, living and deceased; and more likely to be responsible for administering, supervising, and evaluating the impact of medication. Unlike other forensic disciplines that also lay claim to a caring paradigm, forensic nursing is more likely to include not only the therapeutic aspects of caring but also a holistic and objective approach and a social sense of responsibility for the continuous, 24/7/365 care across the life span where care and contact is maintained with the client, and care is extended to the family and to the community (Kent-Wilkinson, 2008).

IMPLICATIONS FOR INTERPROFESSIONAL EDUCATION

Understanding how knowledge of forensic nursing differs from knowledge of nursing in general and from that of other forensic disciplines has specific implications for interprofessional education (Kent-Wilkinson, in press). A body of forensic knowledge has been developing as specialties in forensic nursing, forensic psychology, forensic psychiatry, forensic medicine, forensic science, and other forensic disciplines evolve. Each discipline has been carving out its unique body of knowledge. With the trend to interprofessional education, specialties that cross disciplinary borders like forensic nursing are well suited. It is important that the different roles and focuses of the different disciplines be demarcated, and it is vital that nurses can articulate how we are different. Research findings in specialty areas that intersect many disciplines may more clearly distinguish the specific knowledge that is similar and different to each specialty and discipline (Kent-Wilkinson, in press).

FORENSIC NURSING MODEL

Forensic nursing educators cited the following as the models or frameworks that have guided their forensic (nursing) educational programs (Kent-Wilkinson, 2008):
- Advanced Practice Forensic Nursing Model
- Expanded Nursing Practice Model
- Multidisciplinary Practice Model
- Nursing Framework with Forensic Science Extension
- Population Health Model
- Public Health Model
- WHEEL (wounding, healing, evidence, ethic, and legal)
- (Forensic) Nursing Process
- (Forensic) Nursing Paradigm

Each of the models and frameworks cited individually and in combination has been effectively applied to forensic nursing. From these findings, the following collective statement can be made about forensic nursing theory:

> *Forensic nursing blends the components of nursing's caring paradigm and a multidisciplinary practice model within a public health framework, under a meta theory (philosophy) of social justice. Forensic nursing is a combination of the nursing process with elements of the scientific process, the legal process, and a public health approach. Forensic nursing encompasses the nursing paradigm with its own unique definitions of person, health, environment and nursing* (Kent-Wilkinson, 2008).

Social Factors Influencing Educational Development

Similar to nursing, specialized areas of nursing have always developed in response to needs in society (Cumming, 1995). Nursing developed because of a social need to care for patients, but the specific need for a medicolegal role was the main reason for the development of most of the forensic specialties in every discipline.

According to the findings of this study, societal factors that positively influenced the educational development of forensic nursing were a social need for a medicolegal role, social awareness of forensic issues in society, and social forensic trends. Social factors that negatively influenced the forensic nursing educational development were educational infrastructures not being in place when the need was realized and the public's fascination with crime (Kent-Wilkinson, 2008; 2009). (See Table 3-5.)

The educators expressed that acknowledgement of the critical need for forensic nursing education was evidenced by the

Table 3-5 Social Influencing Factors (Positive and Negative Influences)

SOCIETAL FACILITATING FACTORS (POSITIVE INFLUENCE)
- Awareness in society
- Forensic trend
- Societal need for role and education
- Acceptance of nursing

SOCIETAL IMPEDING FACTORS (NEGATIVE INFLUENCE)
- Perception of increased violence
- Bandwagon effect
- Fascination with crime
- Physician role sanctioned

MEDIA FACILITATING FACTORS (POSITIVE INFLUENCE)
- Public education by the media/high-profile cases
- Forensic TV shows (such as *CSI*)
- Media help in missing children campaigns
- Increased interest in forensic role

MEDIA IMPEDING FACTORS (NEGATIVE INFLUENCE)
- Sensationalism, forensic roles misrepresented, nurses role hidden, exploitation of victims

ECONOMIC FACILITATING FACTORS (POSITIVE INFLUENCE)
- Government funding/grants
- Cost recovery because of popularity and high enrollment

ECONOMIC IMPEDING FACTORS (NEGATIVE INFLUENCE)
- Inadequate role compensation
- Cost of technology
- Lack of program funding
- More research needed for cost effectiveness

TECHNOLOGY FACILITATING FACTORS (POSITIVE INFLUENCE)
- Advanced technology/DNA
- DNA databases
- Online education

TECHNOLOGY IMPEDING FACTORS (NEGATIVE INFLUENCE)
- Person in trauma is lost in the technology
- CSI phenomenon/CSI effect
- New skills needed to keep up

POLITICAL FACILITATING FACTORS (POSITIVE INFLUENCE)
- Legislation/policy changes
- Specialty status
- Emerging social priorities

POLITICAL IMPEDING FACTORS (NEGATIVE INFLUENCE)
- Generalist versus specialist education
- Societal understanding of traditional roles
- Uphill battles for change

Source: Kent-Wilkinson, A. (2008). Forensic nursing education in North America: An exploratory study [doctorial dissertation]. Department of Educational Administration, University of Saskatchewan, Saskatoon, SK. Retrieved September 18, 2008 from http://library2.usask.ca/theses/available/etd-08262008-171000.

state of the country, terrorism, unrest, and the media focusing on violence, in addition to both man-made tragedies and the natural disasters. Participants stated that healthcare professionals have become increasingly aware that violence is a health issue generally. Nurses have realized that they need to have a better healthcare system response to violence in society. There has been heightened awareness that all kinds of professionals can be involved in forensic applications, and that nurses can have an independent and progressive role in intervening in these areas (Kent-Wilkinson, 2008; 2009).

ORGANIZATIONS'/PROFESSIONAL ASSOCIATIONS' INFLUENCE ON FORENSIC NURSING EDUCATION

When participants were asked how organizations fostered the educational development of forensic nursing courses/programs, their responses identified many types of organizations. Subcategories of organizations evident in the data responses were governmental agencies, healthcare systems, and professional associations (Kent-Wilkinson, 2008; 2009). (See Table 3-6.)

The participants felt that some organizations have done a better job than others, in that some have fostered the visibility of the forensic nursing educational processes (Kent-Wilkinson, 2008; 2009). The IAFN was recognized for its mission to foster and provide leadership in forensic nursing practice by developing, promoting, and disseminating information internationally about forensic nursing science (IAFN, 2008; 2009).

Many of the participants mentioned the IAFN throughout much of the data set. Two participants attributed their first attendance at the IAFN scientific assembly as being the defining moment of change for them, because this is when they were introduced to the broader perspective of all subspecialties of forensic nursing sharing a common identity (Kent-Wilkinson, 2008; 2009).

The Emergency Nursing Association (ENA) was noted as a major influence for publishing a column and articles on forensic nursing. In addition, the American Nurses Association (ANA) was helpful in approving forensic nursing as a specialty (ANA, 1995) when specialty status was proposed by the IAFN members (Kent-Wilkinson, 2008; 2009).

INFLUENCES OF INSTITUTIONS OF HIGHER EDUCATION ON FORENSIC NURSING EDUCATION

Participants were asked how their institutions of higher learning supported new specialty educational development in forensic nursing. Subcategories in the data responses were universities and colleges; nursing departments, colleges, and schools of nursing;

administrators; curriculum/electives; popular trends/market niches; students'/market demand; and educator/resources (Kent-Wilkinson, 2008; 2009). (See Table 3-7.)

Universities and Colleges

More and more nursing departments in colleges and universities were seeing the need for this education and making allowances for new programs and tracks to accommodate it. Forensic tracks were created for advanced practice and doctoral nurse practitioner (DNP) programs. Support or lack of support at the university or college level occurred in the forms of marketing and funding forensic programs. A growing number of universities and colleges are beginning to create forensic nursing programs, especially at the advanced practice or master's level (Kent-Wilkinson, 2008; 2009).

Nursing Departments, Colleges, and Schools of Nursing

Although some nursing departments supported educational development, others did not endorse the idea of a separate forensic nursing course or program being developed, and individuals with the expertise often were welcomed only as guest speakers. In some locations, to gain access to students, forensic nursing courses and programs were housed in forensic-science facilities or started out in continuing education departments (CED) rather than in nursing departments (Kent-Wilkinson, 2008; 2009).

Administrators

Support from administrators was key to programs being initiated. Some of the administrators were supportive and visionary; once they understood the role, they supported it and fostered it a lot more. Other administrators felt it was a trend that would not last (Kent-Wilkinson, 2008; 2009).

Curriculum Limitations/Electives

Forensic nursing educational development was facilitated when curricula had the flexibility to provide elective specialty courses

---

Table 3-6 Organizational Influences

ORGANIZATIONS FOSTER (POSITIVE INFLUENCE)
- Governments grants, policies, funded needed programs
- Forensic systems/services partnerships and agreements
- Healthcare system provided funding, training, tuition, work replacement
- Publications/journals provided widespread dissemination (JEN, JPN, JFN)
- Professional associations fostered (IAFN*, ENA, ANA)
- Community women's groups and agencies fostered
- Other forensic disciplines support for scope of role
- Nursing discipline—forensic nurse leaders, pioneers in professional associations

ORGANIZATIONS DO NOT FOSTER (NEGATIVE INFLUENCE)
- Denial of governments grants/funding
- Forensic systems/services were skeptical
- Healthcare system denied funding, training, tuition, shift replacement
- Employer discourages graduate education as it takes away from the bedside
- Publications/journals could have done more
- Professional associations—many nurses do not participate
- Community skepticism
- Other forensic disciplines barrier to scope of role
- Nursing discipline—a need for leadership

Source: Kent-Wilkinson, A. (2008). Forensic nursing education in North America: An exploratory study [doctorial dissertation]. Department of Educational Administration, University of Saskatchewan, Saskatoon, SK. Retrieved September 18, 2008 from http://library2.usask.ca/theses/available/etd-08262008-171000.

Table 3-7 Institutions of Higher Learning Influences

EDUCATIONAL INSTITUTIONS SUPPORTIVE (POSITIVE INFLUENCE)
- Forensic focus market niche
- Forensic as a societal/educational trend
- Administrators supportive
- Curriculum electives
- Advantages of online education
- Student demand
- Passion and drive of individual educators*

EDUCATIONAL INSTITUTIONS NONSUPPORTIVE (NEGATIVE INFLUENCE)
- Resistance and skepticism from universities, administration, and physicians
- Attitude that trend and popularity will not last
- Online education not supported
- No room in curriculum
- Nursing forensic role misunderstood
- Housed in forensic science, not in nursing
- Nursing shortage
- Shortage of skilled forensic faculty

Source: Kent-Wilkinson, A. (2008). Forensic nursing education in North America: An exploratory study [doctorial dissertation]. Department of Educational Administration, University of Saskatchewan, Saskatoon, SK. Retrieved September 18, 2008 from http://library2.usask.ca/theses/available/etd-08262008-171000.

and when curricula were open to adding full certificate programs or advanced practice forensic nursing tracks at the graduate level. In many cases, however, set curricula at a college or university did not support specialty courses, as there was no flexibility for elective courses (Kent-Wilkinson, 2008; 2009). Crane (2005) noted that "typically, undergraduate programs of study were packed with required content… programs allowed little flexibility for adding new content, despite the fact that the forensic content was in high demand" (p. 4).

Popular Trend/Market Niche

For some educational institutions, the forensic program became the focus niche or flagship for their graduate nursing department or for their university. Other educators felt that some universities had launched forensic nursing programs because of their popularity and the current trend. They questioned the experience of some educators who were being granted the responsibility to develop and teach the programs (Kent-Wilkinson, 2008).

Clinical Qualified Educators/Resources

The data indicated that forensic nursing courses and programs were established at specific colleges or universities where there were nurses with specific clinical forensic nursing experience and the drive to create the programs. Educators felt that in some cases, colleges or administrators wanted to offer the program but did not have qualified faculty to write and teach the programs (Kent-Wilkinson, 2008; 2009).

Students/Market Demand

Students in the behavioral sciences were increasingly requesting practicum experiences in the forensic areas and inclusion of forensic content in their curriculum of study. Factors that supported the impetus for forensic nursing educational development were market demand as evidenced by jobs in the forensic areas and that both students and graduate nurses were calling the university to ask if it had a forensic nursing program (Kent-Wilkinson, 2008; 2009).

Sustainability Factors for Forensic Nursing Educational Development

The participants gave their collective perspectives as to why some of the earliest forensic nursing courses/programs were sustained or not sustained. Reasons given for the sustainability of programs were the faculty resources or qualified faculty with forensic nursing expertise as the key driver, the interest and passion of individual educators, the location of the program, the support from administration, and the availability of needed technical and human resources (e.g., investment in an online mode of delivery that allowed for more accessibility of students and faculty). There were strong indications that the enthusiasm and passion of individual educators had a high correlation with the development and sustainability of programs in both countries. Reasons given for a lack of sustainability for these courses/programs further clarified previous points: lack of qualified faculty; one-person programs (one educator only with a forensic clinical background involved in the development and teaching of programs); lack of administrative support; lack of resources or funding; low compensation for SANEs, their trainers, and nurse death investigators; and the forensic nursing role not being valued (Kent-Wilkinson, 2008; 2009). (See Table 3-8.)

Table 3-8 Factors Influencing Sustainability
SUSTAINABILITY FACTORS (POSITIVE INFLUENCE) • Key driver, significant person with passion and a mission • Administrative support • Resources of online or highly populated location, qualified faculty • Partnerships or affiliations **NONSUSTAINABILITY FACTORS (NEGATIVE INFLUENCE)** • Lack of qualified faculty (one person programs) • Lack of administrative support • Lack of resources, low funding • Low compensation for SANE trainers and examiners

Source: Kent-Wilkinson, A. (2008). Forensic nursing education in North America: An exploratory study [doctorial dissertation]. Department of Educational Administration, University of Saskatchewan, Saskatoon, SK. Retrieved September 18, 2008 from http://library2.usask.ca/theses/available/etd-08262008-171000.

Why Forensic Nursing Education Developed

When asked why forensic nursing courses did develop, respondents provided the following reasons: proactive responses by nurses to the social need for better care and treatment for victims and offenders; significant person(s) in various geographical areas with the expertise and motivation to initiate the programs; government organizations and institutions of higher learning that fostered and funded these specialty programs; curriculum structures that allowed for elective options; increased public awareness of the forensic field through media attention; societal need for the forensic role resulting in market demand and job creation; and administrators who understood the role, were supportive, and were visionary enough to facilitate the process (Kent-Wilkinson, 2008; 2009). (See Table 3-9.)

Why Forensic Nursing Education Did Not Occur Sooner

When asked why forensic nursing courses and programs were not developed sooner, respondents gave the following reasons: lack of qualified experts in the field to develop and teach forensic nursing courses and programs; infrastructures not being in place for specialty education; limited elective options, no room in the undergraduate curriculum, or curriculum competition; forensics not being considered a specialized nursing knowledge but rather a knowledge derived from other disciplines; lack of awareness of the forensic nursing role by the public and by the nurses themselves who did not yet understand the concept of forensic nursing, meaning the time was not right for forensic nursing education; a lack of market demand because related jobs were not available; administrators were not interested, did not understand the role, and were skeptical; and, in many cases, the resistance from other disciplines, especially physicians (Kent-Wilkinson, 2008; 2009).

Role and Responsibility of Educators

In new specialty course development, educators must identify what the unique knowledge is, drawing from whatever resources they have available at the time (i.e., personal clinical experience, educational experience, scholarly publications, and research to

Table 3-9 Historical—Influencing Factors

HISTORICAL—WHY COURSES WERE DEVELOPED (POSITIVE INFLUENCE)

- Need in society for medicolegal role for nursing
- Social awareness, social movements, emerging social priorities
- Infrastructures in place (all of the factors that follow)
- Qualified faculty—passionate person/key driver/educator
- Administration—supportive
- Resources—government grants/program funding
- Curricula—flexible, elective options
- Market demand
- Media—promotion/public education by media
- Forensic trend, market niche/forensic focus
- Role compensation—comparable
- Traditional roles in society—changing
- Physicians and other forensic disciplines—supported
- Technology advancements
- Professional associations—fostered (*IAFN, ANA, ENA)
- Nursing discipline—acceptance

HISTORICAL—WHY COURSES WERE NOT DEVELOPED SOONER (NEGATIVE INFLUENCE)

- Need in society for medicolegal role for nursing—not understood
- Before social movements—vulnerable populations not valued
- Infrastructures not in place—all of the factors that follow (no specialty educational programs in nursing till 1980s)
- Few qualified educators with desire to develop programs
- Administration—not supportive
- Resources and funding—denied
- Curriculum—no room, no elective options
- Market flat—jobs not there
- Media—nursing role hidden/misrepresented, sensationalism
- Forensic trend—will not last
- Role compensation—inadequate
- Traditional roles in society—sanctioned
- Physicians and other forensic disciplines—resistive, nonsupportive
- Technology—high costs, some struggle to keep up
- Professional associations—could have done more
- Nursing discipline—nonaccepting

date on the elements of this developing specialty). Whereas some new specialties are discipline specific or reflect fleeting trends of short duration, others have roles that cross many disciplinary lines and grow over time until they have acquired specialty status with educational courses at all levels.

The responsibility of integrating into an educational curriculum an epistemology that explains the theoretical foundations of the newly formed specialty when one first appears in any discipline is not often acknowledged. This study revealed the important contribution of educators to the forensic nursing specialty and its educational development. The significance of the educator's role in identifying the unique knowledge of forensic nursing and the responsibility of course development had not been previously examined, nor had the important role of educators in the evolvement and advancement of the forensic nursing specialty.

Nurse educators have contributed to the construction of the forensic nursing specialty that is emerging worldwide. Although many factors have influenced educational development, as noted in the study exploring forensic nursing education in 2008, the greatest influence may have been the passion of individual nurses who felt driven by a mission to develop some of the first forensic

nursing educational courses. A significant finding, as previously noted in the descriptive statistics, was that many of the first forensic nursing courses entered into curricula at major colleges and universities were developed by nurses who were not prepared at the doctoral level and were not on faculty at the time. One participant in this study was in fact prepared at the baccalaureate level when she negotiated a forensic program for a major university. This speaks to the passion, drive, and determination of individual nurses who felt compelled to make forensic nursing education a reality (Kent-Wilkinson, 2008).

Benefits of Forensic Nursing Education

Findings from this study and the related literature provide evidence for positive benefits as a direct outcome of forensic nursing education. Some of the benefits were improvements in patient care, changes in attitudes, changes to practice roles, expanded roles, and higher conviction rates.

IMPROVEMENTS TO PATIENT CARE

Educators in this study believed that because of SANE education, patient care has improved. Where they exist, SANE programs have made a profound difference in the quality of care provided to sexual assault victims (Ledray, 1999). SANEs offer victims prompt, compassionate care, and comprehensive forensic evidence collection. Studies consistently indicated that forensic nurses with subspecialty certification in sexual assault examination generally provide better and timelier care and are more competent at collecting evidence that met legal standards (Plichta, Clements, & Houseman, 2004).

CHANGES TO PROFESSIONAL PRACTICE ROLES

There has slowly been a change in society's understanding of conventional professional roles. When the SANE role expanded, the physician was no longer directly involved in providing the sexual assault examination. However, in the case of another model, the sexual assault response team (SART), the physician is still involved as a member of the team. The role of physician in society had been traditionally sanctioned; many believed that certain roles were best performed by a physician without any expectation of additional specialized training. Routinely, emergency physicians, with no forensic training, are those primarily called on to do everyday sexual assault examinations (Kent-Wilkinson, 2008).

EXPANDED ROLES

Recognizing the vital service that SANEs provide in sexual assault cases, some hospitals have expanded the SANE's role to include conducting evidentiary exams on domestic violence victims, accident victims, and other populations where forensic evidence may be useful (Littel, 2001).

CHANGING ATTITUDES AND CHANGES TO PRACTICE ROLES

According to the findings of the recent forensic nursing educational study, education in forensic nursing has encouraged the public, other nurses, and students to not only accept the specialty of forensic nursing but also to change their negative attitudes toward offenders. With knowledge and understanding, the mindsets and approaches have changed. Participants noted and were gratified to see the attitude of the students change toward offenders during the process of taking a forensic nursing course (Kent-Wilkinson, 2008).

HIGHER RATE OF OFFENDER CONVICTION

Studies by Ledray and Simmelink (1997) reported a higher rate of offender conviction due in part to the proper collection of evidence in cases handled by sexual assault nursing services. In addition to helping preserve the victim's dignity and reduce psychological trauma, SANE programs are enhancing evidence collection for more effective investigations and better prosecutions (Littel, 2001).

Summary

To date, forensic nursing educational programs have been developing globally, influenced by similar social factors worldwide. Multiple social factors contributed to why forensic nursing courses were developed and why they were not developed sooner. Social, media, technological, economic, and political factors have influenced educational development in both positive and negative ways. Students in the behavioral sciences are more often requesting practicum experiences in the forensic areas and inclusion of forensic content in their curriculum of study. Forensic courses are beginning to be developed to meet this demand. In the early years of the development of forensic nursing education, it became evident that both the expertise of clinicians and the support of administrators were needed to maintain programs that were new and not yet recognized as future mainstay programs. Forensic nursing education has made a difference in the improvement of care to patients, and forensic nurse educators have played a key leadership role in the advancement of the specialty.

References

American Nurses Association (ANA). (1995). *Nursing's social policy statement*. Washington, DC: Author.

American Nurses Association (ANA). (1997). *Scope & standards of forensic nursing practice*. Washington, DC: Author. (Publication # ST4 2M 12/97).

Bader, D. G. (2005). Forensic nursing: A subspecialty of nursing: The social impact of current forensic science television programs. *Nebraska Nurse, 38*(3), 22–23.

Bates, A. W., & Poole, G. (2003). *Effective teaching with technology in higher education: Foundations for success*. New York: Jossey-Bass/Wiley.

Bernier, S. (1986). Corrections and mental health. *Journal of Psychosocial Nursing and Mental Health Services, 24*(6), 20–25.

Bridges, M. J. (1981). Prison: A learning experience. *American Journal of Nursing, 81*(4), 744–745.

Brooker, C., & Whyte, L. (2000). *Multidisciplinary team working in secure psychiatric environments*. Sheffield, England: University of Sheffield/Sheffield Hallam University.

Crane, P. A. (2005). Survey explores forensic content. *IAFN On the Edge, 11*(4), 4.

Cumming, M. F. (1995). The vision of a nurse-coroner. A "protector of the living through the investigation of death. *Journal of Psychosocial Nursing and Mental Health Services, 33*(5), 29–33.

Davila, Y. R. (2005). Teaching nursing students to assess and intervene for domestic violence. *The International Journal of Nursing Education Scholarship, 2*(1), 1–11.

Felton, G., Parsons, M., & Satterfield, P. (1987). Correctional facilities: A viable community health practice site for students. *Journal of Community Health Nursing, 4*(2), 111–115.

Fontes, H. C. (1991). Prisons: Logical, innovative clinical nursing laboratories. *Nursing and Health Care, 12*(6), 300–303.

Graham, B. A., & Gleit, C. J. (1981). Clinical sites used in baccalaureate programs. *Nursing Outlook, 29*(5), 291–294.

Gulotta, K. C. (1987). Factors affecting nursing practice in a correctional health care system. *Journal of Prison and Jail Health, 6*(1), 3–22.

Harvey, P. (1998). *Innovations in courseware and curriculum: Forensic health studies*. Calgary, AB: Mount Royal College. Retrieved January 11, 2007, from www.mtroyal.ab.ca/olt/main2a.htm

International Association of Forensic Nurses (IAFN). (1993a). *Definition of "forensic nursing." Adopted by the IAFN Board of Directors*. Thorofare, NJ: Author.

International Association of Forensic Nurses (IAFN). Mission statement. (1993b). *On the Edge Newsletter*. Thorofare, NJ: Author.

International Association of Forensic Nurses (IAFN). (2006a). *About IAFN: Forensic nursing*. Arnold, MD: Author.

International Association of Forensic Nurses (IAFN). (2006b). *Definition of "forensic nursing." Definition by V. Lynch and adopted by the IAFN Board of Directors*. Arnold, MD: Author.

International Association of Forensic Nurses (IAFN). (2008). *IAFN mission*. Arnold, MD: Author. Available March 20, 2009 from IAFN website, www.forensicnurse.org

Kent-Wilkinson, A. (2006). Forensic nursing education: Developments, theoretical conceptualizations and practical applications for curriculum. In R. M. Hammer, B. Moynihan, & E. R. Pagliaro (Eds.), *Forensic nursing: Concepts and challenges* (pp. 781–820). Sudbury, MA: Jones and Bartlett.

Kent-Wilkinson, A. (2008). *Forensic nursing education in North America: An exploratory study [doctorial dissertation]*. Saskatoon, SK: Department of Educational Administration, University of Saskatchewan, Retrieved September 18, 2008 from http://library2.usask.ca/theses/available/etd-08262008-171000.

Kent-Wilkinson, A. (in press). An exploratory study of forensic nursing education in North America: Constructed definitions of forensic nursing. *Journal of Forensic Nursing*, [Manuscript accepted Nov 1, 2008 by JFN] (29 pages).

Kent-Wilkinson, A. (2009). Forensic nursing education in North America: Social factors influencing educational development. *Journal of Forensic Nursing, 5*(2), 76–88.

Kent-Wilkinson, A., Mckeown, M., Mercer, D., McCann, G., & Mason, T. (2000). Practitioner training, future directions, and challenges for practice. In D. Mercer, T. Mason, M. Mckeown, G. McCann (Eds.), *Forensic mental health care: A case study approach* (pp. 349–357). Edinburgh, Scotland: Churchill Livingstone.

Ledray, L. E. (1992). The sexual assault nurse clinician: A fifteen-year experience in Minneapolis. *Journal of Emergency Nursing, 18*(3), 217–221.

Ledray, L. E. (1999). *Sexual assault nurse examiner: Development and operation guide*. Washington, DC: U.S. Government Printing Office.

Ledray, L. E., & Arndt, S. (1994). Examining the sexual assault victim: A new model for nursing care. *Journal of Psychosocial Nursing and Mental Health Services, 32*(2), 7–12.

Ledray, L. E., & Simmelink, K. (1997). Efficacy of SANE evidence collection: A Minnesota study. *Journal of Emergency Nursing, 23*(1), 75–77.

Littel, K. (2001, April). Sexual assault nurse examiner (SANE) programs: Improving the community response to sexual assault victims. *OVC Bulletin*, 1–19. Available March 20 2009, from U.S. Department of Justice, Office of Justice Programs, Office for Victims of Crime website, www.ojp.usdoj.gov/ovc/publications/bulletins/sane_4_2001/186366.pdf.

Mason, T., & Carton, G. (2002). Towards a "forensic lens" model of multidisciplinary training. *Journal of Psychiatric and Mental Health Nursing, 9*(5),541–551.

Moritz, P. (1982). Health care in correctional facilities: A nursing challenge. *Nursing Outlook, 30*(4), 253–259.

Niskala, H. (1986). Competencies and skills required by nurses working in forensic areas. *Western Journal of Nursing Research, 8*(4), 400–413.

Niskala, H. (1987). Conflicting convictions: Nurses in forensic settings. *Canadian Journal of Psychiatric Nursing, 28*(2), 10–14.

Phillips, M. (1983). Forensic psychiatry: Nurses' attitudes revealed. *Dimensions in Health Service, 60*(9), 41–43.

Plichta, S., Clements, P. T., & Houseman, C. (2004). Why SANEs matter: Models of care for sexual violence victims in the emergency department. *Journal of Forensic Nursing, 1*(2), 57–64. Available March 20, 2009 from Medscape & eMedicine website, www.medscape.com/viewarticle/5565713.

Roell, S. (1985). Prison practice scores points with student and inmates. *Nursing and Health Care, 6*(2), 103–105.

Werlin, E., & O'Brien, E. (1984). Attitude change and prison health care experience. *Journal of Nursing Education, 23*(9), 393–397.

CHAPTER 4 Forensic Epidemiology and the Forensic Nurse

Steven A. Koehler

A new field of science has emerged that is part forensic science and part epidemiology. It is called forensic epidemiology. This chapter provides an overview of the development of the field; roles within the forensic and public health fields; their functions in different settings; how forensic epidemiologists identify, collect, examine, and present forensic data; and how those within the fields of forensic, law enforcement, nursing, public health, and medical research utilize the data collected by the forensic epidemiologist. This chapter also examines the roles that nurses and forensic nurses play in the identification, collection, and documentation of forensic evidence and how those data are used within the field of forensic epidemiology with emphasis on death investigations conducted by the medical examiner/coroner's (ME/C) office.

Development/Definition of Forensic Epidemiology

In the past, there was not much interaction between the investigations carried out by law enforcement and those conducted by public health authorities. The classic health inspector would examine a restaurant and had the power to fine or even close the establishment without involvement of the police. The risk to the public was mainly from food contamination resulting from improper storage, cross-contamination, or poor hygiene practices. However, in today's society, the deliberate contamination of water, food, air, or land as an act of bioterrorism has become very real. Working alone, law enforcement may not initially recognize these incidences as a bioterrorism threat; the same holds true for public health personnel. The problem is that law enforcement personnel are not trained to spot these types of crimes. On the other hand, public health care personnel are able to detect abnormal or unseasonable increases in illness or types of death but are ill-equipped in the proper protocols in identifying, collecting, and preserving forensic evidence. An unusual or off-season increase in a specific strain of virus would not raise suspicion among police officers, but it would be alarming to those in the public health setting. In turn, public health personnel are not trained in the legal methods and procedures of collecting, preserving, and chain-of custody documentation required to bring a case to trial.

Beginning in the late 1970s, joint investigations involving law enforcement and public health authorities began (Goodman, 2003). These investigations centered on health problems that were suspected to have been intentionally caused or crimes that had potentially significant public health consequences. Examples include foodborne outbreaks caused by intentional contamination of food products (Torok, Tauxem, & Wise, 1997) or, in the

case of the "Angel of Mercy" syndrome, where healthcare providers deliberately assisted patient deaths by administering lethal doses to their patients (Buehler, Smith, & Wallace, 1985; Franks, Sacks, & Smith, 1987; Istre, Gustafson, & Baron 1985; Sacks, Herdon, & Lieb, 1988; Sacks, Stroup, & Will 1988; Stross, Shasby, & Harlan, 1976).

During the late 1990s, the term *forensic epidemiologists* typically referred to traditionally trained epidemiologists who functioned as expert witnesses in civil trials. They testified to issues relating to methodology of the study: number of subjects, subject selection and exclusions, length of the study, methods of analysis, interpretation of the results, and any other limitations. They were also frequently called on to address issues relating to association, such as exposure levels of certain chemicals to certain birth defects or the association of performing a task repeatedly and carpal tunnel syndrome (Last, 1988; Lane, 2004).

The term *forensic epidemiology* was first associated with bioterrorism in 1999 when the former chief deputy of the USSR bioweapon program, Ken Alibek, used the term. Forensic epidemiology was defined then as the activity that would help distinguish natural from manmade epidemics. After the anthrax attacks in September and October of 2001, Dr. Julie Gerberding, a senior official with the Centers for Disease and Control (CDC) National Center for Infectious Disease, defined forensic epidemiology as that practiced by an epidemiologist who would be trained to respond to bioterrorism attacks as well as other public health emergencies.

The events of 2001 underscored the need for law enforcement and public health personnel to work together to conduct joint investigations, especially those centered around a possible bioterrorism event. In 2002, the CDC developed the "The Forensic Epidemiology: Joint Training for Law Enforcement and Public Health Officials on Investigation Reponses to Bioterrorism." A joint collaboration was also conducted between the CDC and the Federal Bureau of Investigation (FBI) that resulted in the "Criminal and Epidemiological Investigation Handbook" (Criminal and Epidemiological Investigation Handbook, 2005). Many states have developed courses specifically designed to help law enforcement officers operate closely and more effectively with public health officers when investigating a public health problem that may have been caused intentionally or with crimes that have a public health consequence. This is accomplished by familiarizing officers with the basic principles of public health and the epidemiological approach to investigation (Forensic Epidemiology, 2007).

In 2002, several definitions of forensic epidemiology emerged. They included (1) the use of epidemiological methods as part of an ongoing investigation of a health problem for which there are

Table 4-2 Number of Deaths by Organ/System, 2000-2005						
TOTAL NUMBER OF DEATHS	2000	2001	2002	2003	2004	2005
Heart-related deaths	312	358	368	412	400	380
Vascular system–related deaths	4	13	—	—	—	—
Respiratory system deaths	45	38	40	35	44	37
Hepatobiliary system deaths	19	13	18	20	24	24
Gastrointestinal tract deaths	9	14	12	17	15	8
Pancreatic disorder–related deaths	1	2	1	—	1	1
Lymphatic system–related deaths	2	1	—	—	—	—
Renal system–related deaths	2	—	2	4	3	4
Female reproductive system–related deaths	6	4	4	1	—	—
Endocrine system–related deaths	5	6	9	8	7	6
Nervous system–related deaths	29	21	33	49	40	20
Congenital deaths	—	1	—	—	—	—
Infectious deaths	—	2	8	11	5	3
Cancer deaths	5	1	3	3	1	2
Immunological disorder–related deaths	1	—	—	—	—	—
Connective tissue disease–related deaths	—	—	—	—	—	—
Psychiatric deaths	—	—	—	—	3	1
Systematic deaths	—	—	—	—	2	1
Blood-related deaths	—	—	—	—	—	2
Sudden infant death syndrome	13	11	8	7	6	9
Total deaths	**510**	**485**	**508**	**568**	**553**	**498**

Data from Allegheny County Coroner's Office statistical report for 2005.

Table 4-3 Methods of Breaking Down Causes of Death into Subcategories among Natural Deaths
CAUSES OF DEATH
TOTAL NUMBER OF RESPIRATORY SYSTEM DEATHS
Pulmonary embolism (PE) and infarction
Pneumonia (acute/bronchopneumonia/hemorrhagic)
Bronchitis
Chronic obstructive pulmonary disease (COPD)
Asthma
Pulmonary thrombosis
Carcinoma of the lungs
Suppurative pleuritis
Invasive squamous cell carcinoma
TOTAL NUMBER OF HEPATOBILIARY SYSTEM DEATHS
Liver cirrhosis
Fatty liver
Steatosis of liver
End-stage liver disease
Liver cancer

The next step would be to create a profile of the demographic features (age, sex, and race), location of death, and level of treatment within each subcategory. For example, what was the average age of victims who died from asthma? Did these individuals die in their residence, in the emergency department, or in the operating room, and was that condition diagnosed correctly on admission?

KEY POINT The forensic epidemiologist's primary role in natural death investigations is to provide a constellation of characteristics that increases an individuals risk of developing a natural disease.

Case Study **4-1**

Natural Death

A psychiatric nurse at the VA hospital calls the medical examiner's office to report the death of Mr. Fox, a 54-year-old patient with a history of schizophrenia. The ME was willing to release the body directly to the funeral home and have the patient's physician sign the death certificate as a natural death due to complications associated with schizophrenia. However, the psychiatric nurse, who has cared for this patient for a number of years, insisted that he was compliant with his medications and showed periods of improvements and did not believe their assessment of the cause of death and strongly asked that a complete autopsy be conducted. The ME's office acquiesced and asked the nurse to make a copy of his medical records and prepare the body for transport to the morgue. The results of the complete autopsy revealed that the heart was cardiomyopathy (583 grams) and there was 90% occlusion to the right coronary artery. Because of the nurses deep understanding of her patient's history and insistence that a complete forensic examination be conducted, the death was correctly classified as a cardiac related death not a psychiatric death. This type of action and involvement ensures the accuracy of death certificates and the national vital statistics that rely on them.

DRUG OVERDOSE

The investigation of accidental drug overdose (OD) begins by an examination of the demographic characteristics (total yearly number, age, sex, and race). This is used to create an epidemiological profile to show the individuals who are at greatest risk of dying from a drug OD. Table 4-4 shows the demographic characteristics of OD death by age, sex, and race among cases examined at the coroner's office in 2005. The analysis revealed that accidental OD was predominant among white males and among individuals between 40 and 49 years old. The analysis also highlights the fact that there were no deaths among individuals younger than

Table 4-4 Drug Overdose Deaths by Age, Sex, and Race in Allegheny County, 2005

AGE	WHITE MALE	WHITE FEMALE	BLACK MALE	BLACK FEMALE	TOTAL
20-24	12	4	—	—	16
25-29	13	8	1	—	22
30-34	7	3	2	—	12
35-39	19	8	3	1	31
40-44	29	10	3	2	44
45-49	26	10	6	4	46
50-54	18	8	5	2	33
55-59	5	1	4	1	11
60-64	—	2	1	—	3
65-70	—	—	1	—	1
>70	1	—	1	—	2
Total (%)	130 (58.3%)	54 (24.2%)	27 (12.1%)	10 (4.5%)	223
					(223 total does not include one 23 year-old Asian male and one white male fetus)

Data from Allegheny County Coroner's Office statistical report for 2005.

20 years old. This type of data provides important information of where to target intervention programs (U.S. Drug Enforcement Administration). Once the basic profile of the victims has been established, the drugs involved are examined. Table 4-5 is a partial list of the drugs detected during the screening of accidental drug deaths. Building on this basic information, the forensic epidemiologist carries out more detailed examinations.

The identified drugs can be evaluated in four ways: (1) by the number of drugs contributing to the death, (2) by the types of drugs, (3) by the concentration of the drugs, and (4) by the grouping into legal and illegal compounds. Table 4-5 shows the number of drugs contributing to the death and the types of drugs involved. Once this listing has been created, the level for each drug is categorized into the following groups: subtherapeutic, therapeutic, lethal, or toxic.

The last analysis is to classify the detected drugs into illegal or legal compounds. Figure 4-2 illustrates the OD deaths by drug type. Today there is a shift away from illegal drugs to the abuse of prescription and over-the-counter medications. The types of drugs responsible for the death should be reclassified as legal, illegal, or a combination of both. Legal drugs are those that were lawfully prescribed to the individual by a physician or, in the cases of alcohol and tobacco, the drug was used by an individual of legal age. An illegal drug–related death occurs when a prescription medication was obtained without a physician's authorization, when it was obtained without a medical or psychological condition requiring that medication, when alcohol or tobacco was used by an individual who was under the legal age requirements, or when the drug had no medical use. During the five-year period, the number of deaths involving only illegal drugs declined, the number of illegal drugs in combination with legal drug-related deaths increased, and deaths from legal drug use alone also increased.

KEY POINT Forensic epidemiologic investigations of drug deaths focuses on the type of drug, the concentration of each drug, the profile of the victim, and trends.

MOTOR VEHICLE ACCIDENTS

The forensic epidemiological investigation of motor vehicle accidents (MVA) involves the examination of the environmental, mechanical, and human factors of the accident. Environmental factors include weather, road conditions, and the characteristics of the road type and contraction. Mechanical factors include types

Case Study 4-2

Drug Death

The Medical Examiner's office was called by paramedics after they had responded to a call of a 24-year-old-white female discovered unresponsive in her bedroom. Unfortunately, the young lady was DOA. Death investigators arrived at the scene and began interviewing the NOK and friends. There was no history of drug abuse or any chronic or acute diseases. On entering the bedroom, the victim was face-up in the middle of a king-size bed on top of a floral colored bedspread. She was dressed in white sweats and a lacey pink tee-shirt. The bed contained several large overstuffed feather pillows, one of them had a small amount of pink sputum. The rest of the room was very neat, clean, and organized. On one shelf was a small collection of stuffed animals, all were facing forward, except for a small white owl that was repositioned at an angle. Upon closer examination, a thin white film was noted just under the bird. The owl was carefully collected and sent to the toxicology laboratory at the crime laboratory. Detailed examination of the owl revealed a small zipper and inside was a small plastic bag containing a white powder. Toxicological analysis of this powder revealed it to be cocaine and the victim's blood also showed a lethal level of cocaine (3.7 mg %). The death was ruled as an accidental drug overdose.

of vehicles, condition of the tires, and the mechanical worthiness of the breaking and steering mechanisms. The human factors would include such things as preexisting medical conditions, level of impairments because of drugs or exhaustion, behavioral actions of the driver, and the physiological response to injury (Spitz & Fisher, 1980).

The forensic epidemiological investigation begins with describing the basic demographic characteristics (age, sex, and race) of the occupants. This is followed by a presented grouping of the fatalities into the following categories: driver in single vehicle accidents (SVAs), drivers involving two vehicles, drivers involved in a three-vehicle accident, and passengers by thenumber of vehicles involved by age (Table 4-6). This type of analysis presents an overview of the profile of individuals killed in MVAs. The majority of the MVAs involved SVAs, with the victim being a white male between 20 and 29 years old.

The data can be further examined by separating the groupings into the specific types of vehicles involved in the accident (Table 4-7).

Table 4-5 Type and Number of Drugs Identified in Accidental Drug Deaths

ONE DRUG: TOTAL 90		THREE DRUGS: TOTAL: 38	
Heroin	25	Heroin + Cocaine + Alcohol	4
Cocaine	28	Heroin + Cocaine + Methadone	1
Alcohol	13	Heroin + Cocaine + Diazepam	1
Morphine	4	Heroin + Cocaine + Paroxetine	1
Fentanyl	3	Heroin + Alcohol + Doxepin	1
Oxycodone	2	Heroin + Alcohol + Benzodiazepines	1
Methadone	4	Heroin + Methadone + Alprazolam	1
Metoprolol	1	Heroin + Propoxyphene + Tramadol	1
Phenobarbital	1	Methadone + Benzodiazepines + Amitriptyline	1
Paroxetine	1	Methadone + Alprazolam + Oxycodone	1
Opiates	7	Methadone + Trazodone + Nortriptyline	1
Salicylate	1	Methadone + Diazepam + Alprazolam	1
		Methadone + Alprazolam + Sertralines	1
		Alcohol + Cocaine + Hydrocodone	1
TWO DRUGS: TOTAL: 77		Alcohol + Cocaine + Amitriptyline	1
Heroin + Alcohol	8	Alcohol + Cocaine + Amoxapine	1
Heroin + Cocaine	28	Alcohol + Cocaine + Methanol	1
Heroin + Methadone	1	Alcohol + Morphine + Trazodone	1
Heroin + Hydrocodone	1	Alcohol + Methadone + Alprazolam	1
Heroin + Fentanyl	1	Alcohol + Codeine + Phenobarbital	1
Alcohol + Zolpidem	1	Alcohol + Oxycodone + Benzodiazepines	1
Alcohol + Opiates	2	Oxycodone + Alprazolam + Methadone	1
Alcohol + Methadone	2	Oxycodone + Hydrocodone + Alprazolam	1
Alcohol + Oxycodone	4	Oxycodone + Methadone + Meprobamate	1
Cocaine + Methadone	4	Cocaine + Fentanyl + Phenobarbital	1
Cocaine + Morphine	3	Cocaine + Fentanyl + Diazepam	1
Cocaine + Opiates	7	Cocaine + Methadone + Opiates	1
Cocaine + Alcohol	1	Cocaine + Opiates + Benzodiazepines	2
Cocaine + Oxycodone	4	Cocaine + Methadone + Alprazolam	1
Cocaine + Fentanyl	1	Cocaine + Meprobamate + Methadone	1
Morphine + Olanzapine	1	Cocaine + Morphine + Methadone	1
Methadone + Morphine	1	Cocaine + Oxycodone + Alprazolam	1
Methadone + Fentanyl	1	Fentanyl + Tramadol + Diazepam	1
Methadone + Alprazolam	1	Hydrocodone + Alprazolam + Cyclobenzaprine	1
Methadone + Nortriptyline	1		
Oxycodone + Hydrocodone	2		
Opiates + Benzodiazepines	1		
Clozapine + Clomipramine	1		

Data from Allegheny County Coroner's Office statistical report for 2005.

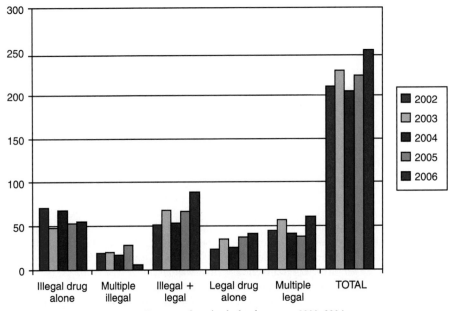

Fig. 4-2 Drug overdose deaths by drug type: 2002–2006.

Table 4-6 Vehicular Fatalities by Occupant and Number of Vehicles Involved by Age

ACCIDENT TYPE	DRIVER (SVA)	DRIVER (TWO VEHICLES)	DRIVER (THREE VEHICLES)	PASSENGER
Total cases	36	29	6	10
AGE				
1–4	—	—	—	1
5–9	—	—	—	1
10–14	—	—	—	—
15–19	—	2	—	1
20–24	7	3	—	—
25–29	7	4	1	2
30–34	3	—	—	—
35–39	4	3	—	3
40–44	2	1	—	—
45–49	3	1	1	—
50–54	3	1	—	—
55–59	2	2	3	—
60–64	2	—	—	—
65–69	—	4	1	—
70–74	1	3	—	—
75–79	1	2	—	1
>80	1	3	—	1

Data from Allegheny County Coroner's Office statistical report for 2005.

Table 4-7 Type and Number of Vehicles Involved in MVAs by Position of the Fatality

POSITION IN VEHICLE / NUMBER OF VEHICLES	DRIVER SVA	DRIVER TWO VEHICLES	DRIVER TWO+ VEHICLES	PASSENGER SVA	PASSENGER TWO+ VEHICLES
TYPE OF VEHICLES					
Car	12	—	—	2	—
Van/light truck	11	—	—	1	—
Jeep	1	—	—	—	—
Motorcycle	9	—	—	1	—
All terrain vehicle	1	—	—	—	—
Bicycle	2	—	—	—	—
Car vs. car	—	7	—	—	6
Car vs. light truck	—	6	—	—	—
Car vs. Pepsi truck	—	1	—	—	—
Car vs. access bus	—	1	—	—	—
Car vs. tractor trailer	—	1	—	—	—
Car vs. van	—	1	—	—	—
Car vs. Blazer	—	1	—	—	—
Car vs. SUV	—	1	—	—	—
Blazer vs. car	—	1	—	—	—
Motorcycle vs. car	—	1	—	—	—
Blazer vs. tractor trailer	—	1	—	—	—
Van vs. car	—	1	—	—	—
Van vs. tractor trailer	—	1	—	—	—
Truck vs. car	—	1	—	—	—
Truck vs. public transportain bus	—	1	—	—	—
Truck vs. tractor trailer	—	1	—	—	—
Scooter vs. car	—	1	—	—	—
Bicycles vs. car	—	1	—	—	—
Car vs. car vs. car	—	—	2	—	—
Car vs. Blazer vs. car	—	—	1	—	—
Car vs. truck vs. tractor trailer	—	—	1	—	—
Car vs. tractor trailer vs. truck	—	—	1	—	—
Blazer vs. tractor trailer vs. tractor trailer	—	—	1	—	—
Total	**36**	**29**	**6**	**4**	**6**

Data from Allegheny County Coroner's Office statistical report for 2005.

These data can be used to answer questions such as the following: Is there a difference in the types of vehicles involved in SVAs among those aged 20 to 24 from those in other age groups? Is one type of vehicle involved in more fatal accidents explained by age? The deaths of those younger than 20 years old should be examined to determine if proper restraint systems were used and their position within the vehicle. The deaths of the elderly, those over 65 years old, should be examined to determine if they were caused by the initial trauma or if they were delayed.

The third element investigated involves the behavioral factors of the driver, which include driving under the influence of alcohol or illegal or legal drugs, the use of safety devices, engaging in unsafe driving behavior, and the natural biological effects of aging. The toxicological analysis specifies the type and concentration of drugs onboard at the time of the accident. The forensic autopsy provides information on the state of health and its role, if any, in contributing to the accident.

Part of the death scene investigation report is noting the use of safety devices—seat belts for motor vehicle accidents and helmets for motorcycle accidents. Table 4-8 presents the analysis of the use of a

Case Study 4-3

Death by Motor Vehicle

A young nursing student was driving her car, a red Corvette, in the eastbound lane. A large white truck hauling furniture suddenly applied its breaks in front of her and attempted to maneuver off the road. She heard a large impact and pulled off the road a few yards behind the truck. A witness, traveling in the westbound lane, a young freelance writer, driving a red Jimmy, noted that the car a few yards in front of him, a late model green 4-door station wagon, suddenly crossed the double yellow lines and hit the truck nearly head-on. After calling 911, the nurse and writer approached the vehicles to asses the condition of the victims. The driver of the truck, a slightly overweight white male appearing to be around 50 years old, was unconscious, but had a strong pulse and regular respirations. The driver of the other vehicle, was an elderly white male appearing to be in his late 80's. He was unrestrained and appeared to have impacted the windshield. The nurse could not palpitate a pulse and did not note any respirations. A large amount of blood was noted on his face. Emergency first responders pulled up to the scene, assessed the two victims, transported the truck driver to the local hospital, and declared the elderly driver DOA. Death investigators from the medical examiner's office arrived at the scene, and immediately closed Route 228 in both directions to conduct their investigation. They begin by photo-documenting the scene. The accident occurred on a two lane paved roadway, at approximately 1:30 PM, the road was dry, and there were no visible defects in the road. After the accident reconstruction was completed the body was transported to the morgue. At this point in the investigation the manner of death could be an accident, suicide, natural, or undetermined. The driver could have been distracted due to a phone call or readjusting the radio causing him to momentarily lose control of the car and resulted in the accident. The driver could have deliberately chosen to end his life by turning directly into the path of the truck. A pre-existing medical condition, typically cardiovascular, could have been the cause of the event. An undetermined manner of death is one where after the complete forensic investigation, the manner of death cannot be ascertained. The result of the forensic investigation, autopsy results, toxicological analysis, police reports, and a review of the medical history indicated that the cause of death was transecting of the aorta. The manner was ruled an accident.

Table 4-8 Seat Belt/Helmet Status among Motor Vehicle Operators and Passengers and by Type of MVA in Allegheny County, 2005

VICTIM AND NUMBER OF VEHICLES AND TYPE OF VEHICLES	SEAT BELT USED/HELMET WORN	SEAT BELT NOT USED/ HELMET WORN	UNKNOWN	TOTAL
DRIVERS IN SVA				34
Driver—car/truck/van	2	17	5	24
Driver—motorcycle	4	4	1	9
Driver—ATV	1	—	—	1
PASSENGER IN SVA				4
Passenger—car/ truck/van	2	1	—	3
Passenger—motorcycle	—	1	—	1
DRIVERS IN MULTIPLE VEHICLE ACCIDENTS				35
Driver—car/truck/van	8	12	12	32
Driver—scooter	—	1	—	1
Driver—motorcycle	—	1	—	1
Driver—bicycle	—	1	—	1
PASSENGERS IN MULTIPLE VEHICLE ACCIDENTS				6
Passenger—car	1	4	1	6
Total	**18**	**40**	**21**	**79**

Data from Allegheny County Coroner's Office statistical report for 2005.

safety device by occupant type and number of vehicles involved in the accident. The table clearly indicates that in SVAs, whether they involved a car, truck, or van, 70.8% of the drivers were not using a seat belt at the time of the accident; only 44% of motorcycle operators were wearing a helmet at the time of their accident.

KEY POINT Forensic epidemiologic investigations of MVAs attempts to ascertain if the cause of death was environmental, biological, or behavioral in nature.

HOMICIDE

Forensic epidemiologists play a major role in the exploration of deaths involving homicide. Aside from providing the important demographic profiles (age, sex, race) of the victims, they present information to justify requests for increased law enforcement personnel, identify locations with emerging criminal activity, and determine where and on whom to target prevention programs.

The profile of the personal characteristics of the victims of homicide is useful and may vary from county to county or even state to state. These profiles are usually presented in terms of age, sex, and race. The separation of age breaking can be narrow, allowing the age range of individuals most at risk to be pinpointed and made the target of intervention programs. Table 4-9 shows a profile of the homicide victim for a one-year period in Allegheny County, Pennsylvania. The table shows that the majority of victims were males, black, and between 20 and 24 years old.

Trend analysis through the examination of deaths over a period of five or more years can highlight if subgroups of a population are at increased or decreased risk of being a victim of a homicide. Figure 4-3 shows that during the eight-year period, there was a steady decline in the number of homicides among white males, a slighter decline among white females, a steady state among black females, but a strong increase among black males.

Table 4-9 All Homicides by Age, Sex, and Race, 2005

AGE	WHITE MALE	WHITE FEMALE	BLACK MALE	BLACK FEMALE	TOTAL
15–19	—	—	17	—	17
20–24	3	1	20	—	24
25–29	—	—	16	—	16
30–34	1	1	7	—	9
35–39	—	—	5	1	6
40–44	1	—	4	1	6
45–49	2	—	3	—	5
50–54	—	—	2	—	2
55–59	1	1	—	—	2
60–64	—	1	1	1	3
Total	**8**	**4**	**75**	**3**	**92**

Data from Allegheny County Coroner's Office statistical report for 2005.

Another feature of major interest, especially to law enforcement, is the activity the victim was engaged in at the time of the event. The activities can be classified as engaged in legal business, leisure-time activity, or illegal activity. For example, suppose a group of teens is hanging out at a corner at 4 a.m. on a Wednesday; a car drives by, and someone from within the car shoots two dead. The deaths might be ruled as drug related, gang related, or the result of a drive-by shooting. Based on the available information contained in a death investigation report, police arrest report, and court transcripts, the forensic epidemiologist will classify each death based on the most probable activity occurring just before the homicide (Table 4-10).

Homicides are also mapped in several ways, including in terms of the exact location where the event occurred; by street address; by the township, borough, or municipality; and by the distance

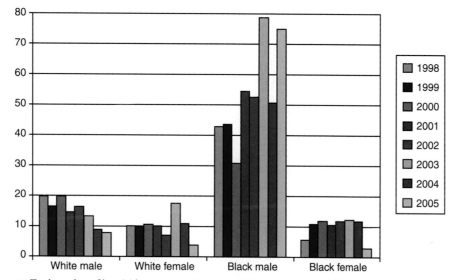

Fig. 4-3 Total number of homicides over an eight-year period by sex and race, Allegheny County, Pennsylvania.

Table 4-10 Activity Before the Homicide in Allegheny County, 1997–2005

ACTIVITY	1997	1998	1999	2000	2001	2002	2003	2004	2005
Drug related	6	15	15	39	10	11	13	24	9
Gang related	6	1	10	—	4	6	3	—	1
Bar fight	—	—	—	1	—	6	—	—	—
At a party	—	—	—	1	—	1	1	—	1
Robbery	13	8	3	4	4	5	4	9	4
Car jacking	—	—	1	—	—	—	—	—	—
Money related	—	—	—	—	1	3	3	—	3
Drive-by shooting	8	8	2	1	4	1	4	3	3
Found on street	—	—	—	—	—	—	—	—	19
Found in car	—	—	—	—	—	—	—	—	9
Neighbor dispute	1	1	—	—	1	—	—	—	—
Law enforcement	1	4	2	2	2	1	1	—	5
Assailant (stranger)	—	20	11	2	—	17	5	14	12
Sexual assault	1	—	1	1	—	—	1	1	—
Arson	1	—	1	5	5	—	2	—	—
Racial killing	—	—	—	7	—	—	—	—	—
Sex related	—	—	—	—	2	—	—	—	—
Argument with friend	—	3	7	—	—	1	6	—	6
Altercation	—	—	—	7	7	—	2	—	—
Shaken-baby syndrome	—	—	—	1	—	—	—	—	—
Overdose	—	—	—	—	2	—	1	—	—
Domestic dispute	15	16	16	12	18	18	26	17	6

(Continued)

Table 4-10 Activity Before the Homicide in Allegheny County, 1997–2005—Cont'd

ACTIVITY	1997	1998	1999	2000	2001	2002	2003	2004	2005
Witness to homicide	1	—	—	—	—	1	—	—	—
Clothing related	1	—	—	—	—	1	—	—	—
Birth by midwife	—	—	—	—	—	1	—	—	—
Babysitter	1	—	—	—	—	1	—	—	—
Structure collapse	1	—	—	—	—	1	—	—	—
Playing with gun	2	—	—	—	—	2	1	1	—
Under investigation	3	3	15	30	31	12	16	14	14
Total	**78**	**79**	**84**	**77**	**91**	**89**	**125**	**83**	**92**

Data from Allegheny County Coroner's Office statistical report for 2005.

between the victim's residence and residence of the perpetrator. This allows the forensic epidemiologist to create detailed maps depicting the spread of different types of homicide over time, types of homicides committed in a particular area, and the distance traveled by the types of homicide committed.

Homicides can be explored in terms of time, day of the week, and month. The goal is to determine if a pattern emerges. Questions to be investigated include the following: Do homicides increase around certain holidays, or is there an association between homicide rates and colder months? More elaborate analyses can compare the type of homicides committed during each month.

Although characteristics of the victims are important, forensic epidemiological investigation also examines the relationship between the personal characteristics of the victim and the perpetrator. The sex of the victim compared to that of the attacker is shown in Table 4-11. Among the cases where the sex of both the victim and perpetrator are known, the majority are both male. An examination of the relationship between the race of the victim and the attacker reveals that the majority of these interactions occur among individuals of similar race (Table 4-12).

KEY POINT The homicide investigation by a forensic epidemiologist focuses on developing characteristic profiles of the victim and the perpetrator, the relationship between the two, and determining the circumstances that lead to the homicide.

Table 4-11 Sex of the Perpetrator Compared to the Sex of the Victim of Homicides, Allegheny County, 1998-2004

VICTIM'S SEX	PERPETRATOR'S SEX	1998	1999	2000	2001	2002	2003	2004
Male	Male	23	12	30	34	29	37	16
Female	Male	9	10	17	11	15	18	16
Male	Female	1	2	2	2	2	5	—
Female	Female	2	1	1	2	—	1	—
Male	Unknown	37	48	19	28	26	50	36
Female	Unknown	4	10	3	6	3	9	3
Unknown	Unknown	—	1	—	—	—	—	—
Unknown	Male	—	—	—	—	—	1	—
Female	Multiple	1	—	1	2	2	3	4
Male	Multiple	2	—	4	6	12	1	8
Total		**79**	**84**	**77**	**91**	**89**	**125**	**83**

Data from Allegheny County Coroner's Office statistical report for 2004.

Table 4-12 Race of the Perpetrator Compared to the Race of the Victim of Homicides, Allegheny County, 1998-2004

VICTIM'S RACE	PERPETRATOR'S RACE	YEAR 1998	1999	2000	2001	2002	2003	2004
White	Asian	—	—	1	—	—	—	1
Black	Black	14	9	28	32	37	36	27
White	Black	6	1	6	5	3	5	4
Hispanic	Hispanic	—	1	—	—	—	—	—
Hispanic	Black	—	—	—	—	—	1	—
White	Hispanic	—	1	—	1	—	—	1
Black	White	2	1	1	1	1	4	—
White	White	13	8	17	16	17	18	9
Asian	White	—	—	3	—	—	—	—
Black	Unknown	33	45	16	33	27	51	36
Unknown	Unknown	—	1	—	—	—	—	—
White	Unknown	11	17	5	3	4	8	4
Black	White/Black	—	—	—	—	—	1	—
White	White/Black	—	—	—	—	—	1	1
Total		**79**	**84**	**77**	**91**	**89**	**125**	**83**

Data from Allegheny County Coroner's Office statistical report for 2004.

Case Study 4-4

Homicide

A young lady was walking back to her car after a day of shopping in the mall. She noticed a middle-age black male slumped over his steering wheel. Being a nurse she attended to obtain a pulse but could not locate one. She immediately called 911. Paramedics shortly arrived and pronounced the individual DOA and contacted the ME's office. The young nurse provided a statement to the police that also reposed to the 911 call. The ME arrived and encircled the death scene with yellow "Do Not Cross" tape. Their search of the scene discovered one shell casing 24 inches from the driver side door. After the victim was photographed, a superficial examination of the body revealed what appeared to be a gunshot wound to the left temporal region of the head. The victim's wallet was searched and a drivers license and credit cards were used to tentatively identify the victim. The body was removed and no weapon or drugs were located inside the vehicle. The police ran the name and the car's license plate and discovered that the victim's ex-wife had obtained a court ordered PFA against her ex-husband. While the body was being transported to the morgue to undergo an autopsy, the police went to the ex-wife's house. The police informed the ex-wife of the events and inquired if she had any firearms in the house. She had a 45 Ruger Automatic and provided it to the police. Examination of the weapon revealed five live rounds in the clip. The weapon was unloaded and transported to the ballistic lab at the crime lab. Back at the morgue an X-ray of the head showed a bullet located on the right temporal lobe. The path of the bullet was left to right, and a slightly downward path. Examination of the entrance wound (left temporal) showed no powder soot, or powder tattooing placing the shooter at a distance from the victim of at least several feet at the time of the shooting. Ballistics was able to match the casing with the bullet recovered from the head and the grooves on the bullet matched those of the 45 recovered from the ex-wife. The homicide detectives were informed of this information and returned to the ex-wife's house. When the police informed her of a match to her gun in the death, she confessed. She called her ex and asked him to meet her in the mall parking lot. She then walked up to his car and shot him once in the head. When asked why, she stated that he had been stalking her and she wanted it to end. She was read her rights and taken into custody.

Role of Nurses and Forensic Nurses in the Forensic Community

Nurses at all levels of training can play a key role in the identification, collection, documentation, and preservation of forensic evidence as well as assist in the review and interpretation of medical data for individuals within the forensic community.

Any form of forensic evidence, be it a piece of hair or a bullet-ridden shirt, is of no forensic value if it is not identified as evidence. Floor nurses, operating room nurses, and sexual assault nurse examiners (SANE) nurses must be able to identify, document, preserve, and ensure the chain of custody of the evidence to guarantee that the item retains its forensic importance and evidentiary admissibility.

Nurses also play a passive role in forensic data collection in the form of their nursing notes. Nurses and forensic nurses may not fully understand the potential importance of the information they observe and note on their charts during the interaction and examination of the patient. Although initially designed to record the patient's daily physical parameters, progression of medical conditions, treatments, and other treatment-related activities, after death this information plays a different role. These nurses'

notes provide an important record of the sequence of events that occurred with that patient from admission through death. Within this vast number of pages lies critical information that can help the forensic pathologist ascertain the cause and manner of death.

BEST PRACTICE Individuals with any type of gun shot wound injuries should be considered a victim of foul play and all measures should be taken to identify, preserve, and ensure the chain of custody of the forensic evidence.

BEST PRACTICE Nurses examining patients admitted with blunt forced trauma should be extensively documenting, with great attention to the number, size, and location of the trauma.

In cases of natural death, the notes may provide a clear picture of the rapid progression of a natural disease that was in the later stage and was beyond medical remission, thereby allowing the forensic pathologist to confidently identify it as a natural death on the death certificate. In situations where the victim has sustained significant trauma, such as in a motor vehicle accident or fall, the nursing notes play a vital role in proving a detailed record of the assessment of the injuries, the lifesaving procedure implemented, the results of the admitting toxicology analysis, and the type and volume of blood, plasma, and drugs administered during treatment. The type and concentration of drugs onboard at the time of the event are important from both a legal and a civil prospective. They are keys to answering questions such as "was the driver intoxicated when the pedestrian was killed?" Or, "was the roofer high on cocaine when he fell off the roof?" However, the results of postmortem toxicological analyses are affected by the infusion of blood, plasma, and medications given during surgery. If antemortem blood was not collected, then observations detailed in the notes–such as *I smelled alcohol on his breath*" or "*His speech was slurred*"–become significant to the death. Nursing notes contain a wealth of data. Forensic epidemiologists who operate as consultants frequently encounter research that involves a large number of nursing notes. Therefore, they often hire nurses to review those notes with specific objectives in mind (e.g., was care of victims within the parameters of standard medical practice) or to abstract key variables.

One of the functions of a forensic epidemiologist is to accurately report the number of deaths by specific disease types, types of injuries, and mechanism. At the state or national level, their number impacts funding allocations, and prevention and intervention programs are derived from information listed on the death certificate. Nurses, because of their intense interaction with the patients and knowledge of patients' past medical history, play a major role in reducing the under- and over-reporting of certain types of death, especially those caused by trauma. Consider the following example.

An elderly female suffers a fall at her residence. She is transported to the local emergency department and admitted with a hip fracture. Her surgery results in extensive bed rest. The lack of activity and position results in positional pneumonia. Several weeks later, she expires. The attending physician issuing the death certificate, in many situations, only focuses on the current pneumonia. The resulting death certificate may be signed out with the immediate cause of death listed as pneumonia and the manner of death listed as natural. The nurse/forensic nurse should play a more active role by ensuring that the physician understands the course of events that led to the development of the pneumonia and, in addition, remind the physician that this death is an ME/C case. The correct death certificate should read pneumonia, due to blunt force trauma, due to a fall, and the manner should be listed as an accident. This level of involvement by the nurse/forensic nurse will have several effects. First, it ensures that the death certificate accurately reflects the true cause of the death. Second, it reduces the likelihood that deaths caused by a traumatic fall are not underreported and that pneumonia deaths are not overreported within the national vital death statistics. Third, the manner and cause of death listed on the death certificate may have implications with regard to insurance benefits.

Nurses and forensic nurses also play a critical role by interacting with family members in cases where the body must undergo an autopsy and explaining the importance and necessity of the procedure. The nurses and forensic nurses can educate the family regarding the significance of and knowledge gained by the autopsy.

Nurses and forensic nurses working in nursing homes and other long-term care facilities also play a vital role in identifying bite marks and, from a forensic prospective, collecting transient evidence such as saliva deposited around the bite mark.

BEST PRACTICE Always remember that nursing notes are presented in criminal/civil trials and all statements and observations noted are closely evaluated.

Within the ME/C's offices, nurses and forensic nurses are playing an increasingly important role. In a number of ME/C offices, the death investigators are nurses who went on to become certified death investigators. Because of their background in human anatomy, pharmacology, and the rapid review of a large number of medical records to extract the most critical sections, they were ideal choices. In addition, some ME/C offices use SANE nurses associated with the office to conduct the examination.

KEY POINT Nurses and forensic nurses are playing an increasing role in the death investigation arena. They are being trained in the identification, methods of processing, documenting, and presenting of forensic evidence in a court of law as expert witnesses.

References

Allegheny County Coroner's Office. (2006). Statistical Report for 2006. Coroner's Office, Pittsburgh, PA.

American Academy of Pediatrics, Task Force on Infant Positioning and SIDS. (1996). Positioning and sudden infant death syndrome (SIDS). *Pediatrics, 98*(6 pt 1), 1216–1218.

American Academy of Pediatrics, Task Force on Infant Sleep Position and SIDS. (2000). Changing concepts of sudden infant death syndrome: Implications for infant sleeping environment and sleep position. *Pediatrics, 105*(3 pt 1), 650–656.

American Academy of Pediatrics, Task Force on Infant Sleep Positioning and SIDS. (1992). *Pediatrics, 89*(6 pt 1), 1120–1126.

Buchholz, U., Mermin, J., & Rios R. (2002). An outbreak of food-borne illness associated with methomyl-contaminated salt. *JAMA, 288*(5), 604–610.

Buehler, J. W., Smith, L. F., & Wallace, E. M. (1985). Unexplained deaths in a children's hospital: A epidemiological assessment. *N Engl J Med, 313*(4), 211–216.

Department of Justice and Federal Bureau of Investigation (2005). *Criminal and Epidemiological Investigation Handbook.* Washington, DC.

Drug Abuse Warming Network: Development of a New Design. (2002 August). Available at www.samhsa.gov. Accessed June 2008.

Forensic Epidemiology. (2007). Kentucky law enforcement. *Fall,* 30–34.

Franks, A., Sacks, J. J., & Smith, J. D. (1987). A cluster of unexplained cardiac arrests in a surgical care unit. *Crit Care Med, 15*(11), 1075–1076.

Goodman, R. A. (2003). Forensic epidemiology: Law at the intersections of public health and criminal investigation. *Journal of Law, Medication & Ethics, 31*(4), 684–700.

Istre, G. R., Gustafson, T. L., & Baron, R. C. (1985). A mystery cluster of deaths and cardio-pulmonary arrests in a pediatric intensive care unit. *N Engl J Med, 313*(4), 205–211.

Koehler, S. A., & Brown, P. A. (2009). *Foundations of forensic epidemiology: Medical examiner/coroner perspective.* Boca Raton: Taylor & Francis Group/CRC Press.

Lane, B. (2004). *The encyclopedia of forensic science.* London: Magpie Books.

Last, J. M. (1988). *A dictionary of epidemiology.* (2nd ed.). New York: Oxford University Press.

Robbins, C. (1989). *Robbins pathologic basis of disease* (4th ed.). Philadelphia: Saunders.

Sacks, J. J., Herdon, J. L., & Lieb, S. H. (1988). A cluster of unexplained deaths in a nursing home in Florida. *Am J Pub Health, 78*(7), 806–808.

Sacks, J. J., Stroup, D. F., & Will, M. W. (1988). A nursing-associated epidemic of cardiac arrests in an intensive care unit. *JAMA, 259*(5), 689–695.

Saferstein, R. (2007). *Criminalistics: An introduction to forensic science.* New Jersey: Pearson Prentice Hall.

Spitz, W. U., & Fisher, R. S. (1980). *Medicolegal investigation of death* (3rd ed.). Springfield Illinois: Charles C Thomas.

Stross, J. K., Shasby, D. M., & Harlan, W. R. (1976). An epidemic of mysterious cardiopulmonary arrest. *N Engl J Med, 295*(20), 1107–1110.

Torok, T. J., Tauxem, R. V., & Wise, P. R. (1997). A large community outbreak of salmonellosis caused by intentional contamination of restaurant salad bars. *JAMA, 278*(5), 389–395.

U.S. Drug Enforcement Administration. Available at www.usdoj.gov/dea/agency/mission.htm.

Wecht, C. H. (2002). Allegheny County Coroner's Office, Statistical Report for 2002. Coroner's Office, Pittsburgh, PA.

Wecht, C. H. (2004). Allegheny County Coroner's Office, Statistical Report for 2004. Coroner's Office, Pittsburgh, PA.

Wecht, C. H. (2004). *Crime scene investigation: Crack the case with real-life experts.* New York: Reader's Digest.

Wecht, C. H. (2005). Allegheny County Coroner's Office, Statistical Report for 2005. Coroner's Office, Pittsburgh, PA.

Willinger, M., James, L. S., & Catz, C. (1991). Defining the sudden infant death syndrome (SIDS): Deliberations of an expert panel convened by the National Institute of Child Health and Human Development. *Pediatric Pathology, 11*(5), 677–684.

CHAPTER 5 Crime Scene Processing

Zug G. Standing Bear

This chapter addresses the proper processing of crime scenes where interpersonal violence, either physical or emotional, is involved, as may be seen in the crimes of murder, manslaughter, negligent homicide, rape and other sexual assaults, maiming, aggravated assault, robbery, and torture. Not detailed in this chapter is the examination of scenes of catastrophic events (such as acts of terrorism in which many persons are killed or disasters such as commercial aircraft crashes), where scene search procedures and protocols are far more extensive and multifaceted than reported here and involve the deployment of specialized teams of investigators. Disaster scene investigation procedures have been meticulously developed by organizations such as the United States National Transportation Safety Board (1999).

The violent crime scene brings together healthcare, emergency service, criminal justice, and forensic science personnel who may have a wide variety of backgrounds, such as police officers, emergency medical technicians and paramedics, forensic nurses, police investigators, firefighters and fire investigators, and possibly highly specialized individuals (such as forensic engineers, forensic entomologists, or forensic anthropologists). Proper care of a victim of violent crime and the professional, careful, and complete processing of the crime scene require that certain tasks be carried out in a specified order. Many adequate publications prescribe and describe proper techniques of searching a crime scene and for collecting, preserving, and identifying physical evidence. Currently, however, only one source, an earlier version of this chapter (Standing Bear, 1999), has spelled out, in succinct fashion, the exact steps to be taken in the thorough examination of a crime scene involving violence. This chapter details an updated protocol for procedures to be followed in responding to a complaint of a crime of violence. It is important that properly skilled personnel, trained in violent crime scene search techniques and the collection/preservation of evidence, be employed in the scene investigation of these offenses. When forensically unskilled officials are first to respond to the incident scene, they should perform steps in this protocol only up to the point at which the scene is secured; then they should arrange for scene security until skilled personnel arrive.

It is important to gauge the experience and expertise of the uniformed law enforcement and investigative personnel one will be working with at crime scenes. If expertise in crime scene processing is lacking, as is often the case, the time to get training is before the scene is examined. Joint training sessions will prepare personnel to work together as a team. Lack of training on the part of any member of a crime scene processing unit invariably leads to interagency disputes and diminished effectiveness.

This chapter details a sequential format to be followed. Performing the scene investigation out of sequence may alter or destroy important evidence. One need review only a few of the recent "celebrity cases," such as the O. J. Simpson investigation or the Jon Benet Ramsey case, to get the picture that all is not well in the conduct of crime scene examinations.

Virtually anyone can discover a crime scene. It is understandable that well-meaning but unskilled citizens may alter a scene to the detriment of solving the case. However, there is no reason why professionals who deal with emergencies and major crimes on a frequent basis—such as emergency medical technicians and paramedical personnel; emergency, flight, or forensic nurses; and police officers and investigators—should not be able to secure and process a crime scene in an effective manner. Although some of the following sequential steps may seem simplistic, they are of utmost importance in the proper processing of a major crime scene. Certain responders, such as emergency medical technicians and paramedical personnel, may have a limited role in the actual processing of a crime scene. Nonetheless, it is important for them to realize the steps that must be followed in order to facilitate the effective processing of the scene, because even their limited role may jeopardize effective evidence collection. The serial killer or rapist who is permitted to remain at large owing to poor evidence collection or crime scene processing will return again to revictimize and tax the resources and emotions of the entire community. Accordingly, good crime scene examination is not solely within the province of the police but is the responsibility of every member of the emergency response team.

KEY POINT Although some of the steps in the sequential crime scene search seem simplistic and intuitive, often crime scenes are irreparably damaged by the failure to observe these procedures.

The scene investigation in a major incident must be undertaken in a systematic, sequential manner by trained and skilled investigators to ensure that all valuable evidence is identified, accurately documented, and effectively recovered, preserved, and secured, so as to permit optimal laboratory or other expert examination. At the same time, the chain of custody must be maintained so that the evidence is admissible. The scene investigation in a major crime is among the most important initial activities in a chain of events that may significantly affect the outcome (successful suspect identification and prosecution, consideration of the victim, public safety, and security) of a serious criminal offense.

Preparation

Investigation of the scene of a violent criminal offense cannot be carried out effectively without adequate preparation before the incident is initially reported. Because timeliness of response to such scenes is of paramount importance in the discovery, security, recovery, and preservation of evidence, the prior possession and maintenance of adequate supplies and equipment are essential.

CRIME SCENE SEARCH EQUIPMENT

In this day of rapidly advancing technology, advancements in various types of equipment specially manufactured for crime scene processing are being made on almost a daily basis. Organizational leaders and policy analysts should develop procedures to explore emerging technologies in such areas as photography, scene protection methods, alternative light sources, trace evidence discovery and collection methods, computerized scene recording and reconstruction software, advanced measurement methods, and improved evidence packaging methods. Resources are available online to explore these emerging advancements through such publications as Evidence Technology Magazine (http://www.evidencemagazine.com).

Scene Security Supplies and Equipment

Adequate scene security supplies and equipment must be maintained. That includes physical barriers, such as sawhorses and crime scene barrier tape, as well as rain protection devices, such as large plastic containers (in the event footprints or tire tracks must be protected from inclement weather) and waterproof tarpaulins.

Scene Documentation Supplies and Equipment

Before notification of a violent incident, scene documentation supplies and equipment must be immediately available to scene investigators, including clipboards, paper, pencils and pens, measuring devices (small inch/centimeter rulers for photographic documentation and 100-foot tape measures for scene measurement), flags and other markers for outdoor scene identification, photographic equipment (high resolution digital camera with photoflash capability), and adequate portable lighting. Contingency plans should be formulated for the rapid replenishment of supplies and equipment should a scene examination require extraordinary resources, such as additional photographic supplies or intensified lighting (available through many large fire departments). Examples of such scenes are a basement during a power outage and a forest at night.

Evidence Recovery Supplies and Equipment

Evidence recovery kits for the investigation should contain sufficient quantities of suitable containers (test tubes, bottles, plastic and paper bags, boxes, rubber gloves, rubber bands, tweezers, print and impression recovery materials, and syringes) to recover a variety of substances. A method must be in place to replenish stock once depleted. In one death case, the host of a party was found dead the next morning in his home, and it was suspected that he had been poisoned. At the scene were 87 drinking glasses containing various levels of liquids and residue, each of which had to be examined.

KEY POINT Gathering of supplies to process a variety of crime scenes requires imagination, and premanufactured crime scene search "kits" usually fall short of what is needed. Stock test tubes for collecting liquids by the gross, not the half-dozen.

MAINTENANCE OF EQUIPMENT AND VEHICLES

All equipment and the vehicles used to transport the investigators and equipment to the scene must be properly maintained and ready to respond to a crime scene 24 hours a day. Equipment and supplies must be adequately stocked on a continuous basis. Written inventory control and replenishment procedures for equipment and supplies should be in place and a specific individual designated as responsible for maintenance and replenishment.

ATTIRE AT THE SCENE

Although suitable field uniforms are commercially available for scene search work, any comfortable and durable clothing that may become soiled or damaged without concerning the wearer and that is suitable to the scene temperature may be adequate in all but the following specialized cases:

- Scenes that contain biohazards, toxic materials, or vapors may require specialized protective clothing for scene investigators.
- Large crime scenes or scenes where several investigating agencies may be working and investigators are not familiar with each other (such as a killing involving drug traffickers or a suspected serial killer) may require special identifying uniform clothing (or other controls such as badges or photo identification) in the interests of operational control.

PORTABLE LIGHTING AND OTHER SPECIALIZED EQUIPMENT

Adequate battery- or generator-powered portable lighting should be available to investigators at all times in the event of outside scenes that must be searched during hours of darkness or indoor scenes that must be searched where electrical lighting is not available, either because of location (cellars, closets, attics) or a power outage. Responsibility for maintaining portable lighting and batteries should be contained in written operating procedures. Also, the appropriation of other specialized equipment and equipment operators (e.g., metal detectors, scaffolding erectors, heavy equipment such as cranes or recovery vehicles, fumigators) should also be written into procedures. Often, memorandums of understanding can be promulgated with fire departments and other specialized organizations for the provision of portable lighting and other special equipment when necessary, as such departments usually maintain lighting and other equipment as a matter of standard practice.

NOTIFICATION AND RESPONSE

In investigating violent crimes, procedures must be in place for an organized and orderly response well in advance of notification of the occurrence of such a crime. Procedures must be in writing and shared among all the agencies that potentially may become involved in an incident. It is as important for each participant to understand what the function and role is of each member responding in an interagency sense as it is for each participant to understand the function and role within a particular agency (intraagency responsibilities).

KEY POINT Know in advance what the special capabilities are of each member of the crime scene search team and capitalize on those capabilities. In the words of General George S. Patton, Jr., "Know what you know and know what you do not know!" (Williamson, 1988 p. 165ff).

These advance understandings will do much to ensure a smooth and effective scene processing and should eliminate much of the on-scene confusion and squabbling too often encountered.

ORGANIZATION FOR RESPONSE

In violent crimes, several investigators should be mobilized if possible. For example, sexual assault investigations generally require a minimum of three responding investigators: at least one to process the crime scene, one to interview the victim and assist the victim through the remainder of the investigative process, and one to locate, apprehend, interview, and process the suspect. Until all initial phases of the investigation (scene searches, interviews, and medical examinations) have been completed, the suspect(s) and victim(s) should be kept separate from one another and should never be transported in the same vehicles or occupy the same treatment, waiting, or interview rooms to avoid cross-contamination of trace evidence, allegations of possible cross-contamination, collusion (such as a possible attempt by the perpetrator to have the victim drop the complaint), and confrontations. Although cross-contamination of evidence is nearly impossible (e.g., from both the victim and the suspect walking across the same hospital parking lot at different times), the perception of the possibility may become very real in court.

Contemporary agencies are implementing a conjoint team approach involving both law enforcement investigators and forensic nurse examiners, specifically in sexual assault, homicide, child abuse, elder abuse, and domestic violence cases. For example, in San Diego, California, police investigators request sexual assault nurse examiners (SANEs) at the scene and at the examination facility to assist in identifying crucial biomedical evidence often unrecognized by investigators without a medical background. Increasingly, investigative agencies prefer that sexual assault examinations be performed by a credentialed SANE nurse following standards set by the International Association of Forensic Nurses (IAFN). SANE Council Standards of Practice (International Association of Forensic Nurses, 1996) and those sexual assault investigation standards are presently developed by the American Society for Testing and Materials (ASTM), Committee E-30 (1998).

PROCEEDING TO THE SCENE

Transport to the crime scene should be done in a safe and lawful manner, with team organization (such as the fixing of responsibility for scene security, scene search, witness interviews, and area check) decided in advance so that the typical confusion present at violent crime scenes will not be exacerbated by an arriving group of disorganized investigators.

INITIAL ACTIONS AT THE SCENE

On arrival at the scene of any violent crime, certain actions must be accomplished quickly and competently so as to gain control of the circumstances and the scene.

Note Time, Date, and Weather Conditions
Immediately on arrival, the investigator(s) should note the time, date, and weather conditions at the scene. This seemingly small detail may become important weeks or months later when alibis of potential suspects are checked and when testifying in court as to the sequence of events at the initiation of the investigation. Attorneys who call into question an investigator's competence by exclaiming, "You mean you do not even remember what day it was?" have embarrassed investigators on the witness stand. Also, weather conditions may contribute to the cause or effect of the incident, and these possibilities may not be realized until some time after the results of the incident have been discovered.

Make Initial Observations of the Scene
Several assessments of a scene must be made simultaneously by arriving investigators to evaluate relative danger, scene scope, control of individuals at the scene, and the coordination of responsibilities.

Nature of Scene (Immediate Danger)
A rapid assessment of the condition of the scene should be made in order to rule out potential danger to the investigator(s) or others. Such dangers may include the presence of dangerous person(s), weather problems, toxic or otherwise dangerous gases or substances, seismic activity, electrical hazards, fire danger, potentially dangerous plants or animals, and possible avalanche, mudslide, or rock slide, or dangerous structures.

Suspects, Victims, and Witnesses
The identification of suspect(s), victim(s), and witnesses at the scene, if any, should immediately be made and decisions reached as to the treatment of each. As a minimum, suspect(s) and victim(s) should be separated and, when possible, witnesses should be separated from each other and interviewed separately so that one does not color another's perception of an incident. As soon as a suspect meets the legal requirements for apprehension, that individual should be placed in police custody. Even though an individual at the scene does not appear, at the moment, to be a suspect, victim, or witness, complete identification (including address and telephone number) is still needed in the event there is a need to recontact that person in the future.

Police
All police officials present at the scene should be identified. If more than one law enforcement agency is present, it should be determined which has primary jurisdiction. The senior official present of the agency or office with primary jurisdiction will take charge of the scene. Often, a crime scene may share primary jurisdiction with several agencies, as when a sexually assaulted dead body is found and the body itself is the responsibility of the medical examiner's investigator while the remainder of the scene is the responsibility of police investigators. In certain cases, specialized agencies may also share jurisdiction, such as the Drug Enforcement Administration (an assault in a drug trafficking case) or the state department of wildlife (an assault in a wild animal poaching case). In these circumstances, it is imperative that both senior officials work in an organized and coordinated way to ensure optimal identification, collection, and preservation of evidence. The senior individual representing the agency with primary jurisdiction at the scene must insist on inspecting the credentials (badges, photo identification, etc.) of other officially authorized persons seeking admission to the investigation or the scene. This inspection is especially important if the senior official does not personally know the individuals. Accordingly, the senior official must be familiar with the authorized credentials issued by other agencies.

Other Agencies
Often, individuals from agencies other than the police with an interest in the crime scene may be represented. Officially authorized agencies, such as coroner or medical examiner's offices, public agency or contracted forensic nurses, emergency medical services, or public safety agencies (fire departments, environmental protection agencies, etc.), may have specific authority and jurisdiction for certain functions at the scene and must be coordinated and cooperated with to the benefit of all concerned. Agencies without official authorization but with an interest in the scene, such the news media, insurance companies, management or labor representatives, various activist/advocacy groups, and property owners, must be controlled and not permitted access to the scene. Such interest groups should be referred to the police

public information officer or the chief of police for information and guidance. Often personnel from unauthorized agencies may use subterfuge or intimidation to gain access to a scene; such practices must be guarded against.

Assure Medical Aid

Any seriously injured or ill persons (at risk of loss of life or limb) at the scene must be provided immediate medical aid, regardless of the necessity to locate, recover, and preserve evidence. Minor illnesses or injuries may be treated at the expense of the loss of identification and recovery of evidence at the discretion of the senior law enforcement official with primary jurisdiction in coordination and consultation with healthcare professionals at the scene.

Although paramedical personnel are primarily concerned with lifesaving interventions, caution to preserve forensically significant evidence should be an important concern as well. Paramedical personnel should be trained in advance in the ability to render emergency treatment swiftly while preserving evidence, such as the rapid removal of clothing when necessary without altering defects or contaminating the clothing at trauma sites.

LOCATE SENIOR POLICE OFFICIAL OR MOST SIGNIFICANT WITNESS

Responding healthcare personnel and investigators should coordinate with the individual possessing the most knowledge about the scene and the incident to prevent interference in the securing and investigation of the crime scene and to establish the physical parameters of the scene. For example, normally in a situation where a sexual assault occurred within a single-family residence, the secured area of the scene would include the house and the adjoining property. However, if a witness saw an individual run from the house in a certain direction, leap a fence, and run through three adjoining vacant lots before getting into a car parked on the next block, the size of the scene to be secured may be greatly expanded.

One important consideration cited by police for the conjoint team approach with forensic nurses concerns the ability of the nurse to elicit often sensitive information from victims and grieving families who may be in shock or may be intimidated by a uniformed officer. This technique may be commonly lacking with officers who may not be skilled in psychosocial intervention.

KEY POINT A crime scene cannot be adequately secured until one is sure about what that scene entails. Careful preparation in advance, although often tedious, pays off in the end.

General Scene Security

The scene should be secured using physical barriers (crime scene/police line tape installed waist high where practical, guarded by uniformed official security personnel) until the scene has been examined and cleared for release to the appropriate owner or tenant.

ENVIRONMENT SECURITY

Nonhuman environmental elements, such as weather, animals, and unnatural elements, may damage or obliterate a crime scene and should be stabilized to the maximum extent possible, not only to preserve evidence but also to provide for the safety of those examining the scene.

WEATHER SECURITY

The scene should be protected from weather elements when necessary. Fragile evidence, such as tire tracks and footprints, should be covered and guarded until the weather clears and recovery efforts can begin.

ANIMAL SECURITY

A crime scene may be destroyed, damaged, or significantly altered by any number of animals in a variety of settings. Scene security procedures should include protection of the scene from not only birds, insects, and other wild animals but domestic animals as well. Also, although some animals may not be particularly dangerous to evidence at the scene itself, they may be quite dangerous to investigators searching the scene. Accordingly, investigators should use extreme caution when working in the unknown habitats of animals such as poisonous snakes, spiders, scorpions, and exotic animals kept as pets.

SECURITY IN EMERGENCIES

In some situations, emergency response personnel, such as firefighters, hazardous materials specialists, and engineers, must make rapid decisions to protect life and property from further danger and destruction. Often this action requires the employment of water, chemicals, explosives, or other interventions. Although evidence discovery and preservation may have to occupy a secondary place in the face of emergency action, continuous coordination and cooperation should be maintained with emergency response personnel to minimize evidence destruction.

Scene Security and the Human Element

Scenes of violent crimes are generally more prone to alteration from human beings than from environmental factors. Although one tends to think of suspects tampering with scene evidence as being the main danger from human involvement with crime scenes, far more evidence is rendered useless or of limited use from the inadvertent contamination or destruction by unknowing witnesses and official investigative personnel.

SECURITY CONCERNING SUSPECTS

Once the scene is secured, a quick check should be made to determine the presence of any suspects or others who are potentially a danger to the scene or the individuals processing it. Places in which a human could escape detection, such as closets, attics, basements, under beds, and outbuildings, should be carefully checked. Occasionally, a suspect is trapped in a scene that has been discovered and is forced to go into hiding. It is rather disconcerting for an investigator, carefully searching the minute details of a crime scene, to come face to face with an armed suspect upon opening the door of a closet. Persons found at the scene who could be considered suspects should be placed in custody.

SECURITY CONCERNING WITNESSES AND VICTIMS

Witnesses, victims, and others ("bystanders") should be identified (correct names, addresses, and telephone numbers noted) and removed from the scene. Even if a person present at the scene may originally appear unconnected with the incident, further investigation may reveal that the individual possesses significant incident-related knowledge. This individual may need to be contacted at a later date. Victims should be initially interviewed to determine what parts of the crime scene should receive particular attention. Beyond the initial interview, victims should be transported to the appropriate healthcare facility for examination and continued investigation. In cases involving all forms of assault, the victim's body is, in and of itself, a crime scene. Thus, victims transported to a treatment or examination facility should be kept separate from others, be they suspects, witnesses, or other victims. In addition, an official member of the investigative team should remain with the victim at all times. Victims should not be permitted to bathe in any way (including washing of the hands) or change clothes until examined.

It is often difficult to ensure that certain scenes be cleared of victims and witnesses, especially if that scene is located at the home of a victim or witness. For example, prudent investigative procedure would have dictated that the wealthy parents of a small girl reportedly kidnapped (whose body was later found in the basement of their home) be immediately required to exit their home and be lodged in a hotel while the scene is examined. There are numerous skillful and diplomatic ways in which such situations may be approached, but prior training in these techniques is required.

KEY POINT Proper crime scene procedures, including the treatment of potential witnesses, should be followed in a uniform manner, regardless of the socioeconomic status of the individuals involved.

SECURITY CONCERNING OFFICIALS

Often, high-ranking officials may wish to visit the scene for a variety of purposes. Ideally, anyone not directly involved in the search of the scene for evidence should be excluded. However, reality dictates that investigators searching a crime scene are occasionally interrupted by officials demanding to inspect the scene. When this occurs, investigators should suspend their search, accompany the inspecting officials, and ensure that officials do not disturb or alter the scene in any way.

SECURITY CONCERNING INVESTIGATORS

Occasionally, a crime scene may be inadvertently altered or contaminated by an investigator who does not recognize the presence or the importance of physical evidence. This evidence then may become obscured, destroyed, or damaged. This precaution is especially germane to sexual assault investigations, in which trace evidence is common and difficult to detect. Investigators must therefore move through crime scenes with utmost caution until the search is complete. It is equally important for investigators to avoid bringing items into the scene and setting them down for convenience, such as clothing items (jackets, etc.) and crime scene equipment containers (evidence collection kits, camera bags, etc.). The scene should be kept "clean," and individual items of equipment and supplies should be brought into the scene only as needed.

Although sometimes irresistibly convenient, investigators must never use any telephone, appliance, or other convenience (such as lights, sink, or toilet) at the scene unless absolutely necessary to process the scene. Even the necessity of turning on or off lights or turning off gas or a motor should be done so that evidence, such as fingerprints, is not disturbed.

SECURITY CONCERNING ADMISSION

Once the scene is secured, it must stay secured. Only one entrance/exit to the scene must be permitted, and that point must be guarded and controlled by a competent official, preferably an experienced police officer. It must be made clear exactly who is to be permitted into the scene and that all others are to be excluded unless the senior official in charge of the scene grants an exception. A detailed log must be maintained of the times, dates, and complete identities of all persons entering and exiting the scene. This log becomes a permanent part of the investigative case file.

WHEN THE TREATMENT ROOM IS A CRIME SCENE

Death or serious injury may occur in the clinical environs: the trauma room, operating room, emergency department, delivery room, and so forth. Consideration must be given to protecting and securing these areas in the same manner as other violent crime scenes. Particular attention should be paid to access, inventory of supplies and medications, and records, including computerized records. It is especially important in these cases that an individual on the investigative team possess medicolegal forensic skills and education in order to minimize conflicts of interest between the institution and the investigation (Lynch, 1991).

Searching the Scene

One may think that once the prior discussed needs have been met, one may begin searching immediately. Such is not the case, however. Until this point, the scene has been prepared for search, but further details must be explored before the physical search can begin.

PREPARATION FOR SEARCH

Before a scene is physically approached with a view toward the search, certain immediate preparatory steps must be undertaken to ensure a complete and orderly search and to document the prior condition of the scene before the physical search began.

Conduct Preliminary Interviews

As previously stated, preliminary interviews of persons with knowledge of the scene and incident should be conducted. Armed with such information, investigators can begin searching the scene with some frames of reference that will permit specific attention to various areas of the scene.

Take Overall Scene Photographs

Overall photographs of the scene should be taken before beginning the search to preserve an image of the scene before the evidence search and recovery process disturbs it. These photographs also help to resolve any future questions concerning the original condition of the scene or if scene reconstruction becomes necessary. It may be appropriate to have aerial photographs taken of the scene, especially if the scene is outdoors and contains many items of physical evidence.

Determine the Method of Search

The search should be conducted using a pattern that accommodates the physical nature of the scene. The criminal investigation literature generally offers at least six crime search patterns. Table 5-1 lists the different search patterns.

- *Line or strip search*. The line or strip search method is used to cover large, open areas and involves personnel who typically form a long line, maintaining an arm's distance between each individual. As the line moves forward as a unit, it essentially creates parallel lanes to search; each member concentrates on one lane. This technique is useful when the scene is long and narrow, such as a roadside area.
- *Grid search*. The grid search involves covering the same area twice, using linear lane patterns (described under line search). In a grid pattern, the group searches along both a horizontal

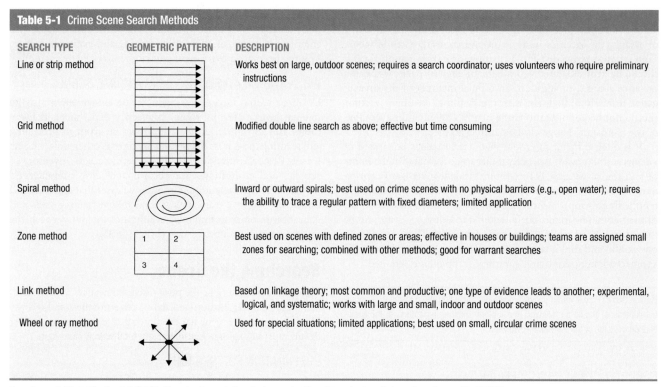

Table 5-1 Crime Scene Search Methods

SEARCH TYPE	GEOMETRIC PATTERN	DESCRIPTION
Line or strip method		Works best on large, outdoor scenes; requires a search coordinator; uses volunteers who require preliminary instructions
Grid method		Modified double line search as above; effective but time consuming
Spiral method		Inward or outward spirals; best used on crime scenes with no physical barriers (e.g., open water); requires the ability to trace a regular pattern with fixed diameters; limited application
Zone method	1 2 / 3 4	Best used on scenes with defined zones or areas; effective in houses or buildings; teams are assigned small zones for searching; combined with other methods; good for warrant searches
Link method		Based on linkage theory; most common and productive; one type of evidence leads to another; experimental, logical, and systematic; works with large and small, indoor and outdoor scenes
Wheel or ray method		Used for special situations; limited applications; best used on small, circular crime scenes

From James S. H., & Nordby, J. J. (2003). *Forensic science: An introduction to scientific and investigative techniques.* Boca Raton, FL: CRC Press.

and a vertical axis. This method is suited to small outdoor crime scenes that do not involve obstructions (such as underbrush) that may pose physical or visual obstructions.

- *Double grid search.* The double grid search is a linear search that involves doubling back upon the original search pattern at 90-degree angles to provide multiple coverage of the same area from different points of view. This search pattern is useful in outdoor scenes where vegetation may obscure vision.
- *Spiral search.* Spiral searches are useful in large outdoor crime scenes. The search usually begins from the "center" of the crime scene (where the principal item of evidence is, such as a dead body, where an assault reportedly took place, or where the majority of the physical evidence is located); however, it may also originate on the periphery (outside limits) and move inward toward principal evidence.
- *Zone search.* Indoor crime scenes are generally approached using the zone search. Specific zones are identified within a crime scene and then individually searched. Close coordination between investigators is needed to ensure that all zones are accounted for and searched.
- *Link method.* In the link method, one piece of evidence leads to another. For example, an empty wallet leads to a knife, a trail of blood-spattered leaves, or a body facedown with stab wounds. This method is not favored among experienced investigators because of its lack of a systematic approach to the scene.
- *Wheel search.* The wheel search, usually advanced as a supplementary search in outdoor areas, is not particularly effective because of the ever-increasing space between search lanes as the searchers move out farther away from the center of the scene.

SCENE SEARCH AND SKETCH

Once the search method has been decided, the scene should be thoroughly searched and sketched simultaneously. At this time, evidence is merely located; it is not further processed unless immediate action is necessary to prevent damaging or destroying the evidence.

Searching

The crime scene should be thoroughly searched, using one of the first five scene search patterns. Particular attention must be paid to the possible existence of trace evidence, such as hairs, fibers, and stains, in very small quantities. This attention to detail requires the use of enhanced lighting, alternative light sources, and magnification devices.

Sketching

A (not-to-scale) sketch of the scene should be prepared simultaneously with the search. The main point at this stage of the search is to locate and document the location of the evidence at the scene, rather than to recover the evidence. Recovery is accomplished after the search is complete and all the evidence is identified. The progress of a crime scene search to locate evidence should be interrupted only in the event of two situations: First, if fragile evidence in danger of immediate destruction or deterioration is located and must be photographed, measured, recovered, and preserved immediately, this should be done at the time of discovery. Second, if intruders such as high-ranking officials invade the scene, they should be dealt with and escorted in such a way that they are not permitted to contaminate the scene.

SPOTTING THE EVIDENCE

As evidence is identified, some mechanism must be in place to mark the location so that the evidence can be recovered. Such a mechanism must also serve as a warning to others working in the scene that this specific location contains evidence. This marking is especially valuable in outdoor scenes where plant growth or other obstacles may obscure the location of the evidentiary material. Small colored flags attached to stiff wires are often useful in achieving this task in outdoor scenes.

BEST PRACTICE Unless discovered evidence is so fragile or so perishable that immediate processing and collection are required, it is best to complete the scene search uninterrupted before evidence is further processed.

EVIDENCE IN NATURAL AND ARTIFICIAL LIGHT

In addition to searching the scene in natural light, using battery-powered, portable artificial lighting in daylight may help to reveal evidence because small objects may reflect light at certain angles. The use of battery-powered artificial light at crime scenes with insufficient natural light (such as at night or in places with inadequate lighting) may be necessary as well, and therefore, such equipment must be available for immediate use.

LOCATING EVIDENCE WITH ALTERNATIVE LIGHT SOURCES

Often, especially in sexual assault cases, portable ultraviolet lighting is useful in detecting articles and stains that may fluoresce under ultraviolet light while remaining invisible in other light sources. For example, semen stains readily fluoresce in ultraviolet light but are often difficult to detect otherwise. The Omnichrome 1000, used on deceased bodies, is now used on living victims of sexual assault (Arndt, 1999). Infrared videography may assist the investigator in the detection of bruises not visible in conventional lighting and is especially useful in the investigation of crimes involving child abuse and battered victims.

Scene Processing

MEASUREMENT AND PHOTOGRAPHY

Once all the evidence is located at the scene, each item of evidence should be photographed in place (before it is moved) both in its natural state and with a measuring device in the photograph. It is also useful for the measuring device to be fitted with a grayscale card (usually preferred by laboratory examiners) or a color card, thus enabling photographic laboratory personnel to ensure that the colors in the evidence photographs are accurate. Color accuracy is especially important when the determination of color is important to the investigation of the case, such as in incidents involving paint chips or dyed fibers. Pasqualone (1996) provided an excellent guide to photographic documentation in the emergency department (see Chapter 7).

> **BEST PRACTICE** All evidence should be documented in regard to its distance from a fixed point in the crime scene to aid in later scene reconstruction.

Fix Locations of Evidence and Measure to Fixed Objects

In the event that the scene may need to be reconstructed, measurements must be taken fixing the location of each piece of physical evidence to stationary objects so that the exact location may again be determined at a later date. Usually this process consists of measurements from three fixed objects (such as the base corner of a building, or the base corner of a room or door, or large nails driven into the base of trees or telephone poles) to three definable points on each piece of evidence. Measurement points should be indicated on the scene sketch, and measurements between points should be recorded in a logbook.

Rephotograph the Entire Scene with Evidence Spotted

Photographs of the entire scene should show where evidence has been spotted to provide an impression of the relationship of each piece of evidence to the other. Again, outdoor scenes and especially large scenes with many items of evidence may benefit greatly from aerial photography.

MARKING THE EVIDENCE

Before recovery, where possible, the evidence should be properly marked for future identification and to assist in the integrity of the chain of custody. Evidence marking is often difficult, and caution

must be exercised so that the process of marking does not obliterate or damage any of its evidentiary features.

Nature of Identifying Mark

Generally it is sufficient to mark evidence with the time and date of recovery, along with the initials of the investigator recovering the evidence. The marks should be applied so that they are difficult to remove, but they must not obscure any potential evidentiary features.

> **BEST PRACTICE** Identifying marks should be placed on an object as far away as possible from surfaces of the object that are going to be examined. When small objects are involved, only the container in which the evidence is placed should be marked.

Location of Identifying Marks

Identifying marks should be placed on an object as far away as possible from surfaces of the objects that are going to be examined. In many situations, especially when small objects are involved, only the container in which the evidence is placed should be marked. Because of the various capabilities of firearms and tool mark examiners in examining cartridges and projectiles under magnification, persons recovering such items at a scene should never mark upon these items. If in doubt, such as in the case of clothing that may harbor latent stains or invisible laundry marks, it is best to avoid marking the individual piece of evidence at all and to simply mark the container into which the evidence is placed. This method should not be problematic if the integrity of the chain of custody is maintained.

EVIDENCE RECOVERY

There is extensive literature pertaining to the recovery of physical evidence at crime scenes. Such procedures fill volumes (Fisher, 1993; Geberth, 1997; Hazelwood & Burgess, 1987; Saferstein, 2003). Although specific directions concerning the recovery of the various types of physical evidence one may find at a crime scene is beyond the scope of this chapter, a few general precautionary notes are germane.

Evidence Preservation and Integrity as the Primary Concern

The key focus in evidence recovery is to ensure preservation of the evidence in order to maximize the capabilities of the forensic laboratory. Achievement of this goal requires not only close attention to the recovery and preservation protocols, but close coordination with laboratory personnel to ascertain the latest preferred methods of recovering and preserving evidence. This collaboration will provide maximum utilization of the instrumentation in the forensic laboratory. An important part of maintaining the integrity of physical evidence is to ensure that the chain of custody is not broken and that the evidence is adequately identifiable from the time of recovery until the disposition of the case. Marking evidence for identification that is fragile or small presents difficult challenges. Improper marking may taint or obliterate important evidentiary materials. Accordingly, it is generally safest to recover the evidence in an uncontaminated state when possible, marking the container in which the evidence is placed with the time, date, and initials of the recovering investigator. For example, a firearm projectile or cartridge casing should be placed in a hard-sided clear plastic container and anchored with cotton so that the item is visible from the outside, and the container is then sealed and marked. Marked in this way, the only person needing to unpack the item will be the laboratory firearm examiner. Others who wish to see the evidence, such as the prosecutor or defense attorney, may view it from the outside of the container. Again, not placing marks directly on the evidence should not pose a problem if the chain of custody is intact.

Recovery of Possible Print Evidence

Evidence that may possibly have fingerprint or other print evidence should be marked as such. Precautions must be taken to prevent abrasions on the surface of an item that may obliterate or obscure print evidence.

Recovery of Trace Evidence

Trace evidence should be recovered as intact as possible. In recovering stains, hairs, or fibers, for example, the material on which the item is found should be recovered along with the item, if practical. For example, in the recovery of a hair adhering to a stain on a garment or a large cardboard box, it would be advisable to recover the entire garment or a portion of the cardboard box.

Recovery of Perishable Biological Evidence

Particular attention should be paid to the recovery of perishable biological evidence to prevent further deterioration. Generally, if wet evidence can be quickly transported to a laboratory, this should be arranged. However, if time or distance precludes immediate transmittal to the laboratory, biological stains (blood, semen, etc.) should be air-dried without heat in as dust-free an atmosphere as possible. Plastic packaging should be avoided due to the possibility of condensation, which might cause evidence deterioration. Commercial evidence packaging materials firms have made great strides recently and should be contacted for advice on new packaging advances.

In many medical facilities, standard operating procedures require that contaminated materials, such as clothing, be placed in biohazard plastic bags. In such a situation, the contaminated garments should first be placed in a paper bag that is then sealed and suitably marked. The paper bag should then be placed in the plastic biohazard bag, leaving the biohazard bag open for air circulation (Lynch, 1991).

Scene Closure

After the rigors of systematically searching a crime scene, often the competent closure of the scene is neglected, frequently resulting in problematic results, such as forgotten materials, security breaches, and lawsuits.

EVIDENCE REMOVAL

All evidence identified and recovered at the scene should be inventoried, logged, and removed, maintaining the preservation and security of the evidence. The inventory and log becomes a permanent part of the case file.

EQUIPMENT REMOVAL

The scene should be resurveyed to ensure that all materials brought into or near the scene have been recovered, such as crime scene search equipment, cameras, and other materials. Although this step sounds simplistic, since this practice was initiated in the 1980s, some rather incredible lapses of judgment have been observed, such as investigators leaving behind cameras, their badges and credentials, their own clothing, and even individual items of evidence.

ARRANGEMENT FOR CONTINUING SECURITY

A completed crime scene cannot simply be abandoned. Significant property loss or vandalism can occur if arrangements are not made for continuing security. At the time a crime scene is searched, it is under the supervision and authority of a public agency. When that agency relinquishes jurisdiction, continuing security must be assured. In some cases, usually major crimes, the scene is sealed for possible later reinvestigation. In these cases, the scene remains in control of a public agency. In other cases, the scene is relinquished to the legal occupier of the property. In these latter cases, assistance and advice should be provided as to how the property owner may resecure the property if, for example, a forced entry had occurred.

Case Study 5-1

Abandoned Vehicle

Responding to an abandoned vehicle notice, Wyoming State patrol officer Vernon Caldwell checked on an old pickup truck that was unoccupied by the side of a dirt road that emptied onto the west side of a paved two-lane, north-south U.S. highway in southern Wyoming. The truck was parked facing the paved highway on the right side of the dirt road about 40 feet from the intersection with the paved road just forward of a cattle guard on the dirt road. The location was on U.S. Highway 285 connecting Laramie, Wyoming, and Fort Collins, Colorado, about 4 miles north of Tie Siding, Wyoming. The truck was unlocked with the key in the ignition and was registered to Melodie Foxx of Casper, Wyoming.

Seeing nothing in the immediate vicinity on the rangeland, the trooper noticed some bird activity over a range fence about 80 yards off the east side of the highway. The trooper climbed over the fence and discovered the body of a male clad in typical rancher clothing. There was some decomposition and evidence of bird scavenging activity, but no signs of trauma were seen on the body. Close by, an empty wooden box lay open in the brush. The box was sturdy, appeared to be handmade, and was about 14 inches square and 8 inches deep with solid sides, top, and bottom. It looked as if the box had been thrown or dropped and had sprung open because the metal latch was broken. On the dead body, the trooper found a wallet with $23 in bills and miscellaneous identification, including a Wyoming driver's license issued to Mitchell Grinsby, age 46, with the address listed as Casper, Wyoming. The body seemed to match the age and weight of the individual described on the license. The trooper also found a key ring on the body containing four keys. Two of the keys were to the pickup truck on the side of the road. There was nothing else remarkable about the truck except that there were six empty chicken cages in its rear bed. Although the cages were old and fairly dirty, they did not contain the minute feathers and fecal matter usually associated with chickens.

SCENE DEPARTURE

The final step, scene departure, marks a formal exit from the scene by investigators, with the intent not to return. If, for any reason, there is doubt as to the finality of this move, the scene should not be released and should stay the subject of continued security until such time as it is considered suitable for release.

Summary

As important as the proper discovery, recovery, and preservation of physical evidence at a crime scene is the necessity to approach and process the scene in a sequential manner. Without invoking the sequential steps described, valuable evidence may be lost or damaged beyond usefulness. Strict adherence to forensic protocol, in the order presented, should help investigators avoid many mistakes made in the past.

Although it may not be the direct responsibility of the healthcare or paramedical personnel, forensic nurses, flight nurses, nurse coroners, and others who may be first on the scene to ensure scene security and integrity, it is a professional responsibility to anticipate the needs of subsequent investigators (police, prosecutors, defenders) and systems (law enforcement, courts) that must invariably be involved in crimes of violence. The better all persons and agencies involved in a major crime coordinate and cooperate with one another, the better the quality of life will become in our communities. The effective examination of major crime scenes brings perpetrators swiftly to justice (and out of circulation) and seeks to free the wrongly suspected or accused. This high level of performance is accomplished only through a coordinated team effort.

Resources

ORGANIZATIONS

American Academy of Forensic Sciences
410 North 21st Street, Colorado Springs, CO 80904; 719-636-1100; www.aafs.org

American College of Forensic Examiners
2750 East Sunshine, Springfield, MO 65804; 800-423-9737; www.acfei.com

Federal Bureau of Investigation
935 Pennsylvania Avenue NW, Room 7350, Washington, DC 20535; 202-324-3000; www.fbi.gov

JOURNALS

Journal of Forensic and Legal Medicine, Elsevier
Journal of Forensic Sciences, John Wiley & Sons, Hoboken, NJ
Journal of the Association of Police Surgeons
Journal Subscription Department, Harcourt Publishers, Foots Cray High Street, Sidcup, Kent DA14 5HP, UK

References

American Society for Testing and Materials. (1998). Standard guide for sexual assault investigation, examination, and evidence collection. *Annual book of ASTM standards* (Vol. 14.02). Standard E 1843-96. Philadelphia: Author.

Arndt, S. (1999, February 15). *Specialized technology in sexual assault investigation.* Workshop in Forensic and Nursing Science: Role of the Forensic Nurse Examiner in Sexual Assault Examination. Annual Meeting of the American Academy of Forensic Sciences, Orlando, FL.

Evidence Technology Magazine. (2009). Wordsmith Publishing. Kearney, MO. http://www.evidencemagazine.com. Accessed November 18, 2009.

Fisher, B. A. J. (1993). *Techniques of crime scene investigation* (5th ed.). Boca Raton, FL: CRC Press.

Geberth, V. J. (1997). *Practical homicide investigation checklist and field guide.* Boca Raton, FL: CRC Press.

Hazelwood, R. R., & Burgess, A. W. (Eds.). (1987). *Practical aspects of rape investigation: A multidisciplinary approach.* New York: Elsevier.

International Association of Forensic Nurses. (1996). *Sexual assault nurse examiner standards of practice.* Thorofare, NJ: Slack.

Lynch, V. A. (1991). Forensic nursing in the emergency department: A new role for the 1990s. *Crit Care Nurs Q , 14*(3), 69–86.

Pasqualone, G. A. (1996). Forensic RNs as photographers: Documentation in the ED. *J Psychosoc Nurs Mental Health Serv, 10*(34).

Saferstein, R. (2003). *Criminalistics: An introduction to forensic science* (8th ed.). Upper Saddle River, NJ: Prentice-Hall.

Standing Bear, Z. G. (1999). Crime scene responders: The imperative sequential steps. *Crit Care Nurs Q, 22*(1), 75–89.

United States National Transportation Safety Board. (1999). *The investigative process.* Washington, DC: US Government Printing Office. Retrieved from www.ntsb.gov/Abt_NTSB/invest.htm. Accessed August 30, 2009.

Williamson, P. B. (1988). *General Patton's principles for life and leadership.* Tucson, AZ: Management and Systems Consultants.

CHAPTER **6** **Principles of Forensic Evidence Collection and Preservation**

Richard Saferstein

Forensic science begins at the crime scene. If evidence cannot be recognized, retrieved, and preserved at the scene, little can be done at the forensic laboratory to salvage the situation. The healthcare professional is in a unique position to facilitate evidence collection. In some situations, the healthcare professional will be in the presence of police personnel at critical moments during the collection and preservation of physical evidence. At other times, the healthcare technician may be the sole determiner of what evidence to collect. The permutations of crime are so varied that one cannot reduce to simple sentences or paragraphs scenarios depicting when the heathcare professional will need to step forward to make critical decisions on evidence preservation. Well-written chapters in this volume already amply depict the basics of crime-scene investigation and the role of DNA profiling in criminal investigation. There is no need to duplicate these efforts. What follows is a short primer on the collection and preservation of key items of physical evidence.

Evidence Sources and the Environment

The conditions under which forensic evidence is gathered are not always ideal, and it may be that the first opportunity to collect evidence will take place in a hospital environment. For this reason, it is imperative that physicians and nurses present in emergency room situations be knowledgeable in recognizing and preserving relevant forensic evidence. This discussion is not designed to mold the healthcare technician into an evidence collector. It is written with the objective of sensitizing the healthcare professional to physical evidence and to an appreciation of how one optimizes the role that science plays in criminal investigation.

BEST PRACTICE The patient's body, hospital supplies and equipment, medical documentation, and the healthcare environment itself can be important sources of evidence in a criminal investigation. Nurses should be prepared to identify, protect, collect, preserve, and transmit certain items of evidentiary value.

LOCARD'S PRINCIPLE

When a person or object comes in contact with another person or object, there exists a possibility that an exchange of materials will take place. This is referred to as **Locard's principle.** This exchange can prove useful when investigating the circumstances surrounding a crime or an accident. The presence or absence of physical evidence can corroborate or disprove a person's recollection of events. Physical evidence can implicate a person to the commission of a crime, or it can exonerate those wrongly suspected or accused of committing a crime. Physical evidence is an invaluable tool that law enforcement authorities utilize for the reconstruction of the circumstances surrounding the incident. However,

evidence is only of value in an investigation or in a court of law if its integrity is upheld through careful handling, proper collection, and a documented chain of custody.

CHAIN OF CUSTODY

Chain-of-custody documents record the link formed between each person who handles a piece of evidence. Transferring evidence from one person or one location to another must be accompanied with written documentation. The end result is a paper trail that records where the evidence was, on what date, and who held responsibility for it from the time it was collected until the time it is presented in court. It is best to use chain-of-custody forms designated by the organization for whom one works. This form should provide a clear and concise presentation for any exchanges of the physical evidence. Once an evidence container is selected, whether it is a box, bag, vial, or can, it also must be marked for identification. A minimum record would show the collector's initials, location of the evidence, and date of collection. If the evidence is turned over to another individual for care or delivery to the laboratory, this transfer must be recorded in notes and on other appropriate forms. In fact, every individual who has occasion to possess the evidence must maintain a written record of its acquisition and disposition. Frequently, all of the individuals involved in the collection and transportation of the evidence may be requested to testify in court. Thus, to avoid confusion and to retain complete control of the evidence at all times, the chain of custody should be kept to a minimum.

Documentation of Evidence

The first step of proper evidence collection is thorough documentation. Descriptive notes and observations should be recorded as soon as possible. The healthcare professional should make note of the condition in which the patient arrived, as well as how and when the patient came into the emergency department. If possible, appropriate personnel should be encouraged to photograph the patient and each specific injured area before the patient receives medical treatment. However, it goes without saying that the foremost concern is with the patient's health and well-being. No forensic protocol must be permitted to inhibit a patient's care. Nevertheless, sensitivity on the part of attending medical personnel to potential forensic investigations may prevent the unnecessary destruction of vital evidence. If photography is a reasonable undertaking, one should avoid cleaning the wound area before it is photographed. A patient's consent should be obtained before the photographs are taken. By doing this, legal complications regarding inadmissibility of evidence can be avoided. When a patient is unable to verbally consent, possibly one can obtain consent from a relative. It is important that whoever gave the consent and that person's relationship to the patient are documented.

BEST PRACTICE A consent form must be obtained before evidentiary photographs are taken. Patient's parents, guardians, or other representatives may provide consent if the patient is unable to do so.

PHOTODOCUMENTATION

Currently there are two methods or approaches to forensic photography: film and digital photography. There are obvious differences between the ways film and digital imaging technology record scenes, notably the methods by which each type of photography converts light into an image. Photographic film consists of a sheet of light-reactive silver halide grains and comes in several varieties. A digital photograph is made when a light-sensitive microchip inside the camera is exposed to light coming from the object or scene you wish to capture. The light is recorded on millions of tiny picture elements, or pixels, as a specific electric charge. The camera reads this charge number as image information, then stores the image as a file on a memory card.

Although the general public is more familiar with digital "point and shoot" cameras, single lens reflex (SLR) or digital single lens reflex (DSLR) cameras are required for photographing a patient. Both kinds of SLR cameras allow for the use of a wide range of lenses, flashes, and filters. Further, SLR and DSLR cameras give photographers the option of manually selecting f-stop, shutter speed, and other variables associated with photography. Digital photography is rapidly becoming the method of choice in the field of forensic science.

The very nature of digital images, however, opens digital photography to important criticisms within forensic science casework. Because the photographs are digital, they can be easily manipulated by using computer software. This manipulation goes beyond traditional photograph enhancement such as adjusting brightness and contrast or color balancing. Because the main function of forensic photography is to provide an accurate depiction, this is a major concern. To ensure that their digital images are admissible, many jurisdictions set guidelines for determining the circumstances under which digital photography may be used and establish and enforce strict protocols for image security and chain of custody.

Photographs of the patient should include the face, along with the injured areas. A photo log should be kept and should include pertinent information such as a patient's name, date, time, photographer's name, type and speed of film, and the specific exposure numbers. Some digital cameras produce an electronic photography log. This log must be submitted along with notes and a handwritten photography log.

When an injured area is photographed, an object of measurement should be included for delineating the size of the injury. For example, placing a quarter next to a bullet hole will allow an investigator to easily interpsret the size of the hole when the photographs are viewed at a later time. More ideally, an American Board of Forensic Odontologists (ABFO) ruler should be employed (see Chapter 7). As the condition of the injured area changes, subsequent photographs should be taken to reflect such changes. Remember that the film and photographs will become part of the chain of custody. Therefore, they should be handled and documented in the appropriate manner. Along with photographs, handwritten notes describing injuries should also be taken.

ANATOMICAL CHARTS AND DIAGRAMS

An anatomical chart is a handy tool to record all of the marks on the body (Fig. 6-1). The description of each mark must include size, shape, color, location, and the characteristics of the edges around the wound. Also, a notation should be made about the presence of any foreign material in or around the wound. Emergency department personnel are often one of the first human contacts a patient will encounter. Verbal statements made by the patient should be recorded using quotations. The value of thorough documentation will prove significant later on during the investigation into what occurred. An inventory list that includes what items were collected, the time and location of collection, the name of the person who performed the collection, and the name and badge number of the officer who received the evidence should be maintained.

BEST PRACTICE Hospital personnel must ensure an accurate inventory of all evidentiary items and observe strict chain–of–custody procedures.

Evidence Kits

Commercial evidence collection kits are a convenient and useful means for assuring the availability of appropriate evidence containers. Commercial evidence containers will also have appropriate chain of custody information printed on the outside of the container. The kit normally includes a variety of small metal cans for the collection of debris, paint chips, glass particles, or metal fragments. Paper envelopes of different sizes are present to package bullets, cartridge cases, or hairs and fibers. Zipper-locked plastic bags provide packaging for soil samples, drugs, or dried plant materials. Evidence seals are an important component of the kit. They allow for the sealing of the various containers within the kit so that evidence tampering is not possible. Any attempt to gain access to the container will require the obvious breaking and disruption of the seal (Fig. 6-2).

Evidence on Clothing

The recognition of physical evidence is not always an easy task. Often, materials that are transferred from one object to another will only exist in trace amounts. However, by learning to recognize where and how such exchanges take place, emergency room personnel can aid in the collection and preservation of potential

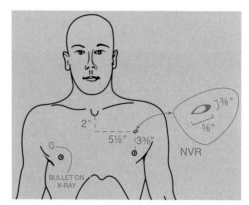

Fig. 6-1 Body map used to document the location of gunshot wounds. Note that specific defects are annotated in relation to easily referenced anatomical landmarks.

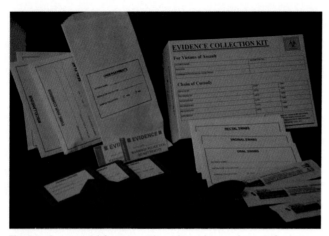

Fig. 6-2 Commercial forensic evidence kit with several types of containers for biological, physical, and trace evidence. The kit also contains tamper-proof tape, labels, and gloves. (Photo courtesy Renae Diegel.)

forensic evidence. In a hospital environment, there probably is no more important an item of physical evidence than the patient's clothing. For example, a shooting victim's clothes may contain a multitude of information. When a bullet penetrates a piece of clothing, characteristic material is usually deposited on the garment. Partially burned and unburned gunpowder particles can be scattered around the bullet hole. The shape and distribution of these particles reveals information about the distance between the firearm and the victim. For example, a shooting victim may claim he or she was intentionally attacked. However, the assailant may claim the shooting was in self-defense and ensued during a struggle. Careful examination of the clothing surrounding the bullet hole may give some important clues. A minute amount of gunpowder residue given off by a firearm may refute the self-defense theory and suggest the weapon was fired at a significant distance between the firer and the target. Even in situations where no gunpowder residue is deposited on the garment, important information can be obtained from a dark ring, known as **bullet wipe,** surrounding the bullet hole. Bullet wipe is composed of material transferred from the surface of the bullet onto the target as the bullet passes through the fabric (Fig. 6-3).

Another piece of significant evidence that can be retrieved from bullet holes in clothing are the rip patterns caused by a penetrating bullet. When a firearm discharges within direct or very close contact with material, a star-shaped rip pattern may characterize the bullet hole. Often, fibers surrounding the hole made by a contact or near-contact shot will be scorched or melted as a result of the heat from the discharge. Cuts in clothing arising from sharp objects such as a knife blade contain important forensic information. Careful laboratory examination may reveal the type of knife blade used or it may reveal whether the assailant hesitated while inflicting the knife wound.

The removal of clothing from a patient must be performed in a careful and conscientious manner. Cutting along seams and away from the injured area will reduce any interference with physical evidence. Whenever possible, cuts should not be made through bullet holes, stab wounds, or any rip or tear caused by a foreign object. If the patient is either dead on arrival or dying while in the emergency room, all clothing, including the shoes and any linen in contact with the patient, are kept with the body when it is turned over to the medical examiner. Whenever possible, any evidence should be left in its original condition on the body. However, if transportation may lead to loss of evidence, the medical professional should properly collect and package those materials.

BEST PRACTICE Clothing should be cut away along seam lines and away from the injured area in order to protect the integrity of physical evidence. All clothing and clothing fragments must be retained as evidence.

PRESERVATION OF CLOTHING-RELATED EVIDENCE

Crimes involving the contact of a victim with another person or object are particularly fertile for the retrieval of physical evidence. In keeping with Locard's principle that every contact leaves a trace, the clothing of the victim of a hit-and-run incident becomes a focus of attention. The blunt force placed on the body by a vehicle will often leave an impression of the material on the car's surface. Therefore, the clothing will be helpful if a suspect vehicle is apprehended. Paint chips and debris could also dislodge during this type of accident. When removing the clothing, be aware of the possible presence of such debris. Anything that is found should be documented in detail as to where it was located (e.g., the left pant leg), properly packaged, and labeled. After each item of clothing is removed, it should be placed in a separate paper bag. As has already been noted, paint chips are most likely to be found on or near persons or objects involved in hit-and-run incidents. The recovery of loose paint chips from a garment must be done with the utmost care to keep the paint chip intact. Paint chips may be picked up with a tweezers or scooped up with a piece of paper. Paper druggist folds and glass or plastic vials make excellent containers for paint. If the paint is smeared or embedded in garments or objects, the investigator should not attempt to remove it; instead, it is best to package the whole item carefully and send it to the laboratory for examination (Figs. 6-4 and 6-5).

BEST PRACTICE Each item of evidence must be packaged separately. The forensic scientist treats all objects placed in the same container as one evidentiary item. Each item of clothing or any physical evidence must be placed in its own separate container to maintain its forensic integrity.

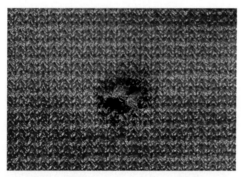

Fig. 6-3 Bullet wipe consisting of soot, carbon, and other soiling materials is noted on the bloody clothing of a shooting victim.

If any article is wet or damp, the healthcare technician should air-dry it in a secured area. Clothing should never be placed in plastic bags. A plastic container can cause moisture to accumulate that may destroy possible evidentiary materials. If possible, the clothing should not be folded. Paper should be placed between any materials that must be folded against each other. Each bag containing a piece of clothing should be labeled with pertinent information, including a detailed description of its contents, the

Fig. 6-4 Blue paint is clearly visible on this pedestrian victim's shoe. The shoe should be photographed before bagging for the crime lab.

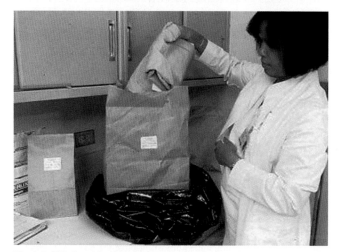

Fig. 6-5 This forensic nurse is ensuring that each evidentiary item is handled carefully and individually packaged in a paper bag.

Fig. 6-6 Victims of firearm injuries should be protected by covering their hands with a paper bag to prevent the accidental loss of vital evidence.

patient's name, the name of person who collected the evidence, as well as the date and time the evidence was collected.

It is important to remember that all objects placed in the same container are treated as one as far as the forensic scientist is concerned. Each item of clothing or any item of physical evidence must be placed in its own separate container to maintain its forensic identity.

BEST PRACTICE All evidentiary items that have become wet or damp must be thoroughly air-dried before placement into a paper evidence bag or other suitable container.

In addition to collecting the clothing of a patient, precautions should be taken to preserve other types of evidence. Washing the hands or rubbing the hands against a foreign object will cause the removal of gunshot residues from the hand's surface. If circumstances permit, persons involved with a shooting, regardless of whether they are alleged victims or assailants, should have their hands placed in paper bags and sealed with tape to the wrist. This procedure prevents the loss of primer residue that may possibly be present, until an appropriate investigator can sample the hands (Fig. 6-6).

PRESERVATION OF FIREARM EVIDENCE

Bullets, cartridge casings, and other types of debris such as glass or metal fragments are sometimes found near or within a patient admitted into an emergency room. All such evidence is fragile,

and necessary precautions need to be taken to ensure all original conditions remain intact as much as possible. When bullets and other types of debris are collected, rubber-tipped forceps or gloved hands should be utilized. Recommended packaging for this type of evidence includes manila-clasped envelopes or zipper-locked plastic bags for each piece collected.

Other Physical and Trace Evidence
GLASS FRAGMENTS

The gathering of glass evidence must be thorough if the examiner is to have any chance to individualize the fragments to a common source. If even the most remote possibility exists that fragments may be pieced together, every effort must be made to collect all glass found. For example, collection of evidence at hit-and-run scenes must include all of the broken parts of the headlight and reflector lenses. This evidence may ultimately prove to be an invaluable means of placing a suspect vehicle at the accident scene, because technicians may actually be able to match the fragments with glass remaining in the headlight or reflector. If the person's shoes or clothing are to be examined for the presence of glass fragments, they should be individually wrapped in paper and transmitted to the laboratory. It is best that the field investigator avoid removing such evidence from garments unless it is thought absolutely necessary for its preservation.

SOIL

Soil found on a victim or suspect must be carefully preserved for analysis. If it is found adhering to an object, as in the case of soil on a shoe, the evidence collector must not remove it. Instead, each object should be individually wrapped in paper bag, with the soil intact, and transmitted to the laboratory. Similarly, no effort should be made to remove loose soil adhering to garments; these items should be carefully wrapped individually in paper bags and sent to the laboratory for analysis. Care must be taken that all particles that may accidentally fall off the garment during transportation will remain within the paper bag. When a lump of soil is found, it should be collected and preserved intact. For example, an automobile tends to collect and build up layers of soil under the fenders, body, and so on. In some situations, the impact of an automobile with another object may jar some of this soil loose. Soil found in this form imparts it with greater variation, and hence greater evidential value, than that which is normally associated with loose soil.

HAIR

When questioned hairs are submitted to a forensic laboratory for examination, they must always be accompanied by an adequate number of control samples from the victim of the crime and from individuals suspected of having deposited hair at the crime scene. Hair from different parts of the body varies significantly in its physical characteristics. Likewise, hair from any one area of the body also can have a wide range of characteristics. For this reason, it is imperative that the questioned and control hairs come from the same area of the body; one cannot, for instance, compare head hair to pubic hair. It is also important that the collection of control hair be carried out in a way to ensure a representative sampling of hair from any one area of the body.

As a general rule, forensic hair comparisons involve either head hair or pubic hair. The collection of 50 full-length hairs from all areas of the scalp will normally ensure a representative sampling of head hair. Likewise, a minimum collection of two dozen full-length pubic hairs should cover the range of characteristics present in this portion of the body. In rape cases, care must first be taken to comb the pubic area with a clean comb to remove all loose foreign hair present before the victim is sampled for control hair. The comb is to be packaged in a separate envelope. Typically, the evidence collector will have an evidence collection kit that has been assembled or approved by the local forensic laboratory. This kit will contain the combs and packaging envelopes necessary to facilitate the collection of evidence at a hospital site. Because a hair may show variation in color and other morphological features over its entire length, the entire hair length is collected. When examining a victim of a sexual assault, this requirement is best accomplished by clipping the hairs at the skin line. This approach is more desirable than pulling hairs out of the skin, as it avoids additional discomfort for the victim. Current laboratory protocols for conducting hair comparisons do not necessitate that hair roots be associated with hair controls **exemplars.**

FIBER

Fiber evidence can be associated with virtually any type of crime. It is the kind of evidence that will not usually be seen with the naked eye, and thus someone not specifically searching for it can easily overlook this evidence. To optimize the laboratory's chances for locating minute strands of fibers, the task becomes one of identifying and preserving potential "carriers" of fiber evidence. Relevant articles of clothing, including shoes, should be packaged carefully in paper bags. Each article must be placed in a separate bag to avoid the cross-contamination of evidence. Scrupulous care must be taken to prevent articles of clothing from different people or from different locations from coming into contact with one another (see Figs. 6-7a and 6-7b). Such articles must not even be placed on the same surface before they are packaged. If a body is thought to have been wrapped at one time in a blanket or carpet, adhesive tape lifts of exposed body areas may reveal fiber strands on examination in the laboratory.

BEST PRACTICE Items of clothing from different individuals should not be permitted to come into contact or to be placed on the same surface. This prevents the accidental transfer of hair, fibers, blood, or other vital evidence.

Occasionally, it may be necessary to remove a fiber from an object, particularly if the possibility exists that loosely adhering fibrous material will be lost in transit to the laboratory. These

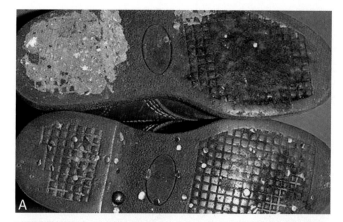

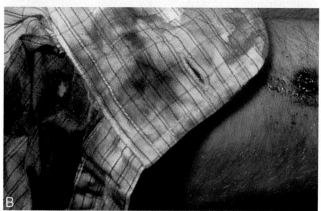

Fig. 6-7 *A*, These shoes must be handled with great care to ensure that important evidence is not altered or lost. *B*, Note the bullet hole and fire soot on this victim's shirt. After photographing the site, the bloody clothing item should be air-dried and packaged in a paper bag to prevent deterioration of evidence.

fibers must be removed with clean forceps and placed on a small sheet of paper, which, after folding and labeling, can be placed inside another container. Again, scrupulous care must be taken to avoid fibers collected from different objects or from different locations from coming into contact with each other.

ARSON EVIDENCE

On occasion, hospital personnel may have to deal with an injured person who is suspected of being involved in the commission of the crime of arson. One important piece of evidence that is not to be overlooked by arson investigators is the clothing of the suspect perpetrator. If this individual is arrested within a few hours of initiating the fire, residual quantities of the accelerant may still be present in the clothing. The forensic laboratory can detect extremely small quantities of accelerate materials, making the examination of a suspect's clothing a feasible investigative approach. Each item of clothing should be placed in a separate airtight container, preferably a new, clean paint can. Paint cans are convenient containers for this type of evidence as they are airtight, unbreakable, and nonreactive with volatile hydrocarbons.

BEST PRACTICE Clothing suspected of containing hydrocarbon residues should never be placed in plastic bags because the plastic will react with the vapors and ultimately consume trace quantities of petroleum residues that may be present on the garment.

SEXUAL ASSAULT EVIDENCE

The finding of seminal constituents in a rape victim is important evidence for substantiating the fact that sexual intercourse has taken place, but their absence does not necessarily mean that a rape did not occur. Physical injuries such as bruises or bleeding tend to confirm the fact that a violent assault did take place. Furthermore, there is a distinct possibility that the forceful physical contact between victim and assailant will result in a transfer of physical evidence–that is, blood, semen, hairs, and fibers. The presence of such physical evidence will help forge a vital link in the chain of circumstances surrounding a sexual crime.

To protect this kind of evidence, all the outer- and undergarments from the involved parties should be carefully removed and packaged separately in paper (not plastic) bags. The packaging of biological evidence in plastic or airtight containers must always be avoided, because the accumulation of residual moisture could contribute to the growth of DNA-destroying bacteria and fungi. Each potentially stained article should be packaged separately in a paper bag or in a well-ventilated box. If the rape victim can stand to disrobe, a number of precautions should be implemented. A clean bed sheet should be placed on the floor and a clean paper sheet placed over it. The victim must remove her shoes before standing on the paper. The person should disrobe while standing on the paper so that the investigator can collect any loose foreign material falling from the clothing. As each piece of clothing is removed, it is collected and placed in its own paper bag to avoid cross-contamination of physical evidence. The paper sheet is then carefully folded so that all foreign materials are contained inside.

Items suspected of containing seminal stains must be handled carefully. Folding an article through the stain may cause it to flake off, as will rubbing the stained area against the surface of the packaging material. If, under unusual circumstances, it is not possible to transport the stained article to the laboratory, the stained area should be cut out and submitted with an unstained piece as a substrate control.

In the laboratory, efforts will be made to link seminal material to a donor(s) using DNA typing. The fact that an individual may transfer his or her DNA types to a stain through the medium of perspiration requires that investigators handle stained articles with care, minimizing direct personal contact. The evidence collector must handle all body fluids and biologically stained materials with minimal personal contact. All body fluids must be assumed to be infectious; hence, wearing disposable latex gloves while handling the evidence is required. Latex gloves will also significantly reduce the possibility that the evidence collector will contaminate the evidence.

The rape victim must be subjected to a medical examination as soon as possible after the assault. At this time, trained personnel collect the appropriate items of physical evidence. It is to be expected that evidence collectors will have an evidence-collection kit that has been disseminated by the local crime laboratory (see Fig. 6-2). Box 6-1 highlights the items of physical evidence that should be collected from a rape victim.

Often during the investigation of a sexual assault, the victim will report that the perpetrator bit, sucked, or licked areas of the victim's body. The high sensitivity associated with DNA technology offers investigators the opportunity to identify a perpetrator's DNA type from saliva residues collected off the skin. The most efficient way to recover saliva residues from the skin is to first swab the suspect area with a rotating motion using a cotton swab moistened with distilled water. A second swab, which is dry, is then rotated over the skin to recover the moist remains on the skin's surface from the wet swab. The swabs are air-dried and packaged together as a single sample (Sweet, 1997).

If a suspect is apprehended, the following items are routinely collected:

- All clothing items believed to have been worn at the time of assault
- Pubic hair combings
- Pulled head and pubic hair controls

Box 6-1 Physical Evidence Collected from Rape Victims

1. *Pubic combings.* Place a paper towel under the buttocks and comb pubic area for loose or foreign hairs.
2. *Pubic hair controls.* Clip two dozen full-length hairs from the pubic area, close to the skin line.
3. *External-genital swabs.* Carefully swab the genital area and inner thighs with two lightly moistened swabs. After the collection is made, the swab must be air-dried for approximately 5 to 10 minutes, then is best placed in a swab box. The swab box has a circular hole, which allows for air circulation. The swab box can then be placed in a paper or manila container.
4. *Vaginal swabs* and *smear.* Using two swabs simultaneously, carefully swab the vaginal area and let the swabs air-dry before packaging. Using two additional swabs, repeat the swabbing procedure, and smear the swabs onto separate microscope slides, allowing them to air-dry before packaging in a swab box. One point is critical: the collected swabs must not be packaged in a wet state.
5. *Cervix swabs.* Using two swabs simultaneously, carefully swab the cervix area and let the swabs air-dry before packaging.
6. *Rectal swabs* and *smear.* To be taken when warranted by case history. Before taking rectal swabs, carefully swab the perianal area with two lightly moistened swabs to prevent contamination of the rectal swabs from vaginal fluid drainage that may be present on the anus. Then using two swabs simultaneously, swab the rectal canal, smearing one of the swabs onto a microscope slide. Allow both samples to air-dry before packaging in a swab box.
7. *Oral swabs* and *smear.* To be taken if oral-genital contact occurred. Use two swabs simultaneously to swab the buccal area and gum line. Using both swabs, prepare one smear slide. Allow both swabs and the one smear to air-dry before packaging in a swab box.
8. *Head hairs.* Clip at the skin line a minimum of five full-length hairs from each of the following scalp locations: center, front, back, left side, and right side. It is recommended that a total of at least 50 hairs be clipped and submitted to the laboratory.
9. *Blood sample.* The blood sample should be collected in a sterile vacuum tube containing the preservative ethylenediamine tetraacetic acid (EDTA). EDTA inhibits the activity of enzymes that act to degrade DNA. The blood sample can be used for DNA typing, as well as for toxicological analysis if it is required. The tubes must be kept refrigerated (do not freeze) while awaiting transportation to the laboratory. Besides blood, there are other options for obtaining control DNA specimens. The least intrusive DNA control and one that can readily be used by nonmedical personnel is the buccal swab. Here, cotton swabs are placed in the subject's mouth, and the inside of the cheek is vigorously swabbed, resulting in the transfer of buccal cells onto the swab (Fig. 6-8).
10. *Fingernail scrapings.* Scrape the undersurface of the nails with a dull object over a piece of clean paper to collect debris. Use separate paper, one for each hand.
11. *Urine specimen.* Thirty milliliters or more of urine should be collected from the victim for the purpose of conducting a drug toxicological analysis for alcohol and drugs.
12. *All clothing.* Package as described in Chapter 13, page 147–148.

Fig. 6-8 A buccal swab can be used to obtain DNA evidence. Two swabs are used to collect cells from inside the cheek and along the gum line. (Photo courtesy Renae Diegel.)

- A blood or buccal swab sample
- A penile swab, to be taken within 24 hours of assault and when appropriate

The persistence of seminal constituents in the vagina may become a factor when trying to ascertain the time of an alleged sexual attack. Whereas the presence of spermatozoa in the vaginal cavity provides evidence of intercourse, important information regarding the time of sexual activity can be obtained from the knowledge that motile or living sperm may generally survive up to four to six hours in the vaginal cavity of a living person. However, a successful search for motile sperm requires that a microscopic examination of a vaginal smear be conducted immediately after it is taken from the victim. A more extensive examination of vaginal collections is later made at a forensic laboratory. Nonmotile sperm may be found in a living female for up to three days after intercourse and occasionally up to six days. However, intact sperm (sperm with tails) are rarely found 16 hours after intercourse but have been found as late as 72 hours after intercourse. The likelihood of finding seminal acid phosphatase in the vaginal cavity markedly decreases with time following intercourse, with little chance of identifying this substance 48 hours after intercourse (Davies, 1974). Hence, taking into consideration the possibility of the prolonged persistence of both spermatozoa and acid phosphatase in the vaginal cavity after intercourse, investigators should seek information to determine when and if voluntary sexual activity last occurred

before the sexual assault. This information will be useful for evaluating the significance of a find of these seminal constituents in the female victim. Blood or buccal swabs for DNA analysis are to be taken from any consensual partner who had sex with the victim within 72 hours of the assault.

Another significant indicator of recent sexual activity is p30 protein. This semen marker is normally not detected in the vaginal cavity beyond 24 hours following intercourse (Kearsey, 2001). (See Chapter 13 for a complete discussion of sexual assault evidence collection.)

BEST PRACTICE It is vital that nurses be familiar with local and state guidelines regarding the collection and packaging of physical evidence.

Summary

An emergency hospital environment is not always controlled and organized. It does require that top priority be given to the immediate care and well-being of the patient. In situations involving the medical treatment of victims and perpetrators of crime, physical evidence must be collected, documented, and preserved properly for subsequent laboratory examination. This book is a testimony to the fact that relevant healthcare personnel are becoming integral participants in the evidence collection process. It is hoped that the material contained within this chapter will provide useful guidance to the proper fulfillment of this objective.

References

Davies, A., & Wilson, E. (1974). Persistence of seminal constituents in the human vagina. *Forensic Science, 3,* 45.

Fisher, B. J. (2000). *Techniques of crime scene investigation* (6th ed.) Boca Raton, FL: CRC Press, Inc.

Kearsey, J., Louie, H., & Poon, H. (2001). Validation study of the Onestep ABAcard® PSA Test Kit for RCMP Casework. *Canadian Society Forensic Science Journal, 34,* 63.

Ogle, R. R. (2007). *Crime scene investigation and reconstruction* (2nd ed.). Upper Saddle River, NJ: Prentice-Hall.

Saferstein, R. (2007). *Criminalistics: An introduction to forensic science* (9th ed.). Upper Saddle River, NJ: Prentice-Hall, Inc.

Sweet, D., Lorente, M., Lorente, J. A., Valenzuela, A., & Villanueva, E. (1997). An improved method to recover saliva from human skin: The double swab technique. *Journal of Forensic Sciences, 42,* 320.

Georgia A. Pasqualone

Historical Background

Alphonse Bertillon (1853-1914) was a French law enforcement officer, biometrics researcher, and criminalist who was the first person to incorporate photography with an identification system called bertillonage. His photograph cards of criminals and suspects, representing the foundations of our present-day "mug shots," contained demographic information suitable for use in criminal investigations. This new concept of using photography in police work spread quickly from Paris throughout the world. In 1859, photographic enlargements were introduced to the court system with a case that involved a dispute about questionable and known handwriting signatures contained within a land grant (Moenssens, Starrs, Henderson, et al., 1995). Finally, in June of 1871, photographs were used for the first time as pieces of crime scene evidence. The consequences of this event resulted in the world bearing witness to incriminating photodocumentation of the Paris police massacring the Communards at the end of the Franco-Prussian War (Sontag, 1977). Since that time, photographs have been utilized by many different types of healthcare professionals around the world.

Nurses, by virtue of their job descriptions, are all occupational photographers. In other words, the camera has become a valuable tool, as serviceable as the stethoscope or syringe. The camera has now become an extension of the nurse's eyes. Through photodocumentation, time can be stopped and history captured. Such a worthwhile and valuable practical tool is crucial to incorporate into the clinical practice of all forensic nurse examiners. Forensic nurse examiners are in the position of being objective scientists, and photography is fast becoming a supplemental form of documentation that must augment our work responsibilities. There is no question that the nurse's first duty is to provide lifesaving treatment for the trauma victim, but the patient and society are ultimately best served when the nurse can also recognize and preserve evidence that may later be used in a forensic investigation.

Exigent Evidence

Along with performing the ABCs of cardiopulmonary resuscitation, forensic nurses must realize that photography should become an automatic function of all trauma protocols. It is not only the trauma victim who needs this instant attention. Certain forensic situations aside from trauma require the immediate responsiveness of photodocumentation. These situations are called "exigent." *Exigent* and *exigency* are terms used within the legal system and translate to mean that, for whatever reasons, information must be obtained now and not at a later time. Exigent evidence can be lost in seconds. It can be washed off, thrown away, flushed down drains, or it may leave with a patient, friend, or family member. Therefore, nurses must realize that evidence is exigent.

One of the foremost examples of exigency and liability is child abuse. Nurses may become suspicious of a parent's or other caretaker's story, wanting to photograph injuries on the child. When consent is requested, parental refusal can create a very uncomfortable and difficult situation. Photographing the injuries is critical because the surface wounds will heal or, worse, the child may die as a result of those wounds. Lack of proper photodocumentation in such circumstances could allow claims that the event never occurred, allowing the perpetrators to go uncharged. For this reason, nurses may have to justify their decision to photodocument without prior consent in court. If the nurse can justify that the photodocumentation of evidence had to be done immediately because the evidence could have been destroyed or lost, no judge should find that nurse liable. Photodocumentation of such injuries can lock events into a proper chronological sequence that can then be used for litigious review. In the past, photographs and x-rays have been the focal point during a child abuse case where the observed injuries and the caretaker's story may not have matched, thus demonstrating the presence of injuries in various stages of healing. If a nurse acts in good faith in photographing a child's injuries, yet the court determines that no exigent circumstances were present, the photographs will usually not be allowed and there should be no repercussions against the nurse.

KEY POINT The principle of exigency of evidence allows the forensic nurse to photograph evidence that would be lost if altered with the passage of time without obtaining prior consent.

Justice is best served by objectivity. When attorneys, judges, and juries can evaluate photographs, along with the proper accompanying written documentation, the entire medical system is better protected from wrongful accusations. Photographing injuries in litigious situations protects healthcare professionals from allegations that patients or clients never received the proper care. For example, if a person claims to have slipped and fallen on a patch of ice or in a tangle of wires, the environment must quickly be photodocumented before changes occur to that primary scene. Photography is capable of capturing moments in time and preserving events for future reference.

Camera Basics

The word *photography* comes from two Greek words meaning "writing *(graphe)* with light *(photos)*." It is the process by which light is used to create a picture. Four basic elements are required in order to make that picture: the camera, lens, film, and light. Today's digital technology can replace film with memory cards and electronic storage devices. Regardless of the technology, all four of these components can be built into one unit in which they are preadjusted to a single setting and activated by pushing the shutter button. However, the four separate entities can also act individually so that every factor can be controlled independently. Therefore, each of these four components will be discussed, as well as some other important photodocumentation concepts, to explain how they all contribute to the taking of a photograph.

THE CAMERA

A camera is nothing more than a light-tight box with a round hole in the front for the lens and a hinged door in the back or bottom for the insertion of either the film or the memory card. Understanding the simplicity of this concept should ward off any fears about handling new photographic equipment. Any further mystery surrounding the camera can be explained by reading the operator's manual and keeping it at hand for ready reference.

Healthcare professionals have the choice of using three distinct camera systems in the forensic setting. These systems are distinguished by their viewing system or by the way in which they visualize the subject. All other systems tend to be too complicated, too large, or otherwise inappropriate for the purpose of medical or crime scene photodocumentation.

The first system is the older, more conventional method, known as a single-lens reflex camera, commonly abbreviated as an "SLR." The SLR allows the photographer to look through the viewfinder to "see" exactly what will be reproduced on the film. It has a "what-you-see-is-what-you-get" viewing system. The second visualization system is referred to as a rangefinder or point-and-shoot (P&S) camera. In this system, the viewfinder is placed near the lens so that the photographer's view and the camera's view are close but not exactly the same. With this system, there is the potential for chopping off the top, bottom, or one side of the subject in the photograph. This situation is commonly referred to as parallax. The problem of parallax becomes worse as the camera gets closer to the subject and becomes actually crucial when photographing close-up images of injuries. For this reason P&S cameras are not preferred for photodocumentation in the emergency department (ED) clinical setting. Unfortunately, most people prefer a P&S camera because of its ease and simplicity of adjustments to whatever is seen in the viewfinder operation. However, with a P&S camera, the necessary adjustments must be made on a specific geometrical plane (e.g., left and right, and top and bottom shifting) while composing the image in the viewfinder. Therefore, in the clinical setting when time is critical, it is desirable to use the SLR viewing systems in which the parameters in one's field of vision are precisely what is captured on film (Fig. 7-1).

The third and most popular system being utilized by the forensic photographer is digital. Digital cameras are one of the most versatile pieces of equipment that the forensic photographer can use today. Digital makes film obsolete, produces more images than a canister of film could ever hold, provides an image preview through the liquid crystal display (LCD) screen, and gives the photographer immediate feedback of what is being visualized. Prices for various models of digital SLRs (DSLRs) are comparably priced with the conventional SLR and P&S equivalents. Also, the more sophisticated the model, the more expensive the camera and lenses are going to be (Fig. 7-2).

The conventional camera systems are further subdivided by the film formats they use. One type is the 35 mm. In this system, the film canister must be removed from the camera to be processed. A negative is produced and any number of prints and enlargements can be made from that negative with further processing. The second type is the "instant," self-developing film. The photograph

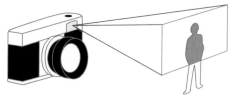

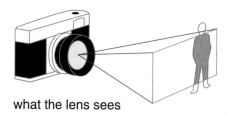

what you see in the viewfinder

what the lens sees

(megapixel.net, 2009)

Fig. 7-1 Parallax view is the difference between what is seen through the viewfinder and what the lens of the camera is actually pointing at. The photograph produced will be composed of what the lens sees, resulting in an unintentional cropping of the top or one side of the subject.

Fig. 7-2 Pentax Optio 450 4.0 megapixel digital camera.

is produced within minutes of exiting the camera. There is no negative, and any copies and enlargements must be created by other means outside the system.

The instant camera system is an almost foolproof method for certain crime scenes and clinical situations. When only a few photographs are needed to document an injury, the instant photograph is a quick solution. Known by its proprietary name, Polaroid, the instant camera system made its debut in 1947. After more than 50 years of innovative improvements, Polaroid provides the closest thing to the P&S camera concept without the parallax error. As of 2008, the Polaroid Corporation ceased manufacturing the instant camera systems as well as the film for these cameras. However, for as long as there continues to be a stockpile of film, there will be institutions that may still incorporate the instant camera systems into their photodocumentation protocols. Until that time, the instant camera system may be considered easy and practical.

THE LENS

The human eye is the equivalent of the lens on a camera. The lens is the window of the camera through which light and the image of the subject travel before imprinting on the film. The quality of the glass and the optics in the lens determine the quality of the resulting photograph. There are two basic types of lenses: fixed and interchangeable.

Fixed Lenses

Fixed lenses are available on all the simpler cameras such as the P&S, the instant camera systems, and the basic digital cameras. They cannot be removed from the camera body, and the photographer has little or no control over how that lens is used. Fixed lenses also have a preset focal plane. This means that the photographer cannot focus on any subject closer than 2½ to 4 feet away. This restricts the capability to take close-up photographs. If the photographer is required to remain 4 feet from the subject, the composition of the photograph changes, and more background is included than desired, thus distracting from the intended subject.

Interchangeable Lenses

Interchangeable lenses are most commonly used on SLR cameras and the higher-end digital cameras (DSLRs) and allow the operator to pick various lenses to suit the situation or need. The ability to choose between different lenses allows the operator to accommodate for changes in focal length, depth of field, and various lighting situations. Interchangeable lenses can be removed or attached to the camera with both a threading and screwing mechanism or with a bayonet system. The bayonet mounting system attaches a lens to the camera by first aligning marks on both, inserting the lens, and then twisting the lens to lock it in place.

Lenses are categorized by a number expressed in millimeters (mm), which represent the lens' focal length. Focal length is the distance measured from the center of the lens to the film plane and determines the field of vision seen through the lens. The most common lens is the 50-mm, or normal lens. The normal lens has a perspective similar to that of the human eye.

Lenses less than 50-mm are known as wide-angle lenses. The 28-mm lens is one of the most common. Wide-angle lenses give a wider view of things than only scanning one's eyes or moving one's head from side to side would provide. Wide groups of people, an entire room with its contents, and greater portions of crime scenes are better photographed with wide-angle lenses.

Lenses greater than 50 mm are known as telephoto lenses. Telephoto lenses work similarly to a telescope, enabling the subject to be closer to the photographer without moving him or her or the camera closer to the subject. They also make certain close-up tasks easier to achieve, especially when photographing injuries on an assault victim. The lens brings the injury closer to the photographer without invading the victim's personal space.

Zoom lenses have variable focal lengths and can adjust to distances by simply moving the telescoping mechanism of the lens forward and back. An excellent choice for a one-lens purchase would be a 24- to 140-mm zoom. This lens would accomplish all wide-angle through telephoto needs in one step. If expense is a major issue, a more economical range would be a 28- to 105-mm lens or a 35- to 70-mm lens.

Close-up and macro lenses are both convenient and necessary for detailed work because they allow the photographer to focus a few inches or centimeters away from the subject. For most forensic nursing applications, the terms *close-up* and *macro* will be synonymous. Close-up photography can mean anything from one-quarter life-size (1:4 or .2×) to a 5× enlargement, depending on the equipment and the available attachments. A 2× enlargement will give a head and shoulders view of the subject (Fig. 7-4). An example of a 5× enlargement would be a photograph of an eye magnified large enough to enable one to count the eyelashes and the blood vessels on the sclera (Fig. 7-5). With colposcopy, the subject matter is magnified up to 30×. (See Chapter 13 for more on colpophotography.)

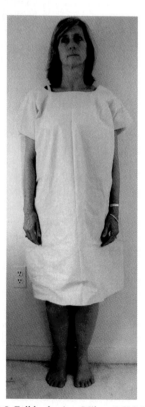

Fig. 7-3 Full-body view (Nikon DSLR D90).

Fig. 7-4 Head and shoulders view (.2×, Nikon DSLR D90).

Fig. 7-5 Close-up (5×, Nikon DSLR D90).

THE FILM

Film is one of the oldest mediums used to record the image of the subject. There are still many film types on the market, and there are specific films for specific functions.

Color negative film has been the most versatile and, therefore, the most popular. There are various sizes and types of film, corresponding to the size of the camera in which it will be used. A forensic nurse will predominantly use 35-mm film in an SLR camera. The number of exposures per canister roll can vary from 8 to 36. The reproduction ratio of pictures is 2:3. This means that the dimensions of the resulting photograph should reflect the same ratio: 4 × 6, 6 × 9, 8 × 12, 16 × 24, and so forth. Before the "jumbo print" phenomenon, the older version of the print size was 3½ × 5 inches. This means that for many years, a good portion of the photo was being trimmed off. Therefore, for the photo to be enlarged to the proper proportions without any of the edges being cropped, the operator needed to request that the negatives be printed "full out" or "full frame." For example, the popularly accepted 8 × 10 loses 2 inches off the 10-inch edge of the photograph. "Full frame" will produce an 8 × 12 print with the subject intact.

All film has an expiration date stamped on the outside of its box. It is vital that an operator not use expired film for photodocumentation of injuries when color is a crucial matter. It is important to store film in a cool, dry place. Personal experience has proved that, if stored correctly, there is a safety net of 6 months to 1 year for most films. If storing film in the refrigerator, maintain humidity at a minimum. Allow the film to stand and attain room temperature before loading it into the camera. Process the film as soon as possible after it is exposed. If this is not possible, simply continue to keep the film cartridge cool and dry. Never store film of any kind in a hot car during the summer months. Heat changes the chemical emulsion and greatly affects color.

LIGHT AND FLASH

There are two physical aspects concerning light that every photographer must remember. The first is that light travels in a straight line. The second is that there are varying intensities of light. Therefore, to use light to the best advantage, it must be provided, controlled, reflected, and bounced. The goal is to produce a photograph that accurately duplicates reality. The photographer must be able to testify that a photograph is a true and accurate depiction of the original scene as it was on the day in question.

There are two basic types of light: available and artificial.

Available Light

Available light, also known as ambient light, is the surrounding, existing light that is illuminating a particular room at a particular time, no matter what the source. It is the lighting inside a room, store, restaurant, train station, tunnel, or examination cubicle. The disadvantage of photodocumenting using only available light is that it is usually much dimmer than outdoor sunlight. Without the use of high-speed, low-light films, the photographer might have to rely on a tripod and slower shutter speeds in order to obtain correct exposure of the subject.

Artificial Light

Artificial lighting, which is illumination produced by other than natural sunlight, may also affect the color quality of the film used. Fluorescent lighting, frequently found in hospitals and medical examiner's offices, tends to give photographs a yellow to green hue. This can be eliminated only with the use of a light source brighter than the fluorescent lighting itself, or the electronic flash. In the majority of contemporary flash units, there are special sensors called thyristors, which are part of the electrical circuitry of the flash unit itself. Thyristors electronically calculate the amount of light that is required to correctly illuminate a subject. For instance, if the subject is close, the flash will not be used to its fullest intensity. This results in a faster recycle time for the next shot and conserves the life of the battery.

Under most circumstances, the photographer must supply artificial lighting. This can be done via a flash unit built into the camera or an external light source. Flash units built into a camera are limited with respect to any photographer control. Most consist of a direct flash that goes from the camera straight toward the subject. In some instances, the flash may be turned away to bounce off another object such as the wall or ceiling. An external flash or light source usually gives the photographer more control of both intensity and direction of the light. With the ability to control the various aspects of lighting, subsequent photographs are usually better exposed. The only drawback is that it also makes the equipment bulkier.

Specialized lighting sources are available to be used with some cameras. Ring-light flashes are utilized with close-up photography to provide even lighting for dimensional subjects as opposed to harsh illumination or washouts. Ring lights are usually standard equipment on the colposcope and are invaluable in lighting anogenital injuries.

Most contemporary autofocus 35-mm SLR cameras have a dedicated flash sensor built into the camera. It is not necessary to set the shutter speed to accommodate the flash because the camera automatically measures the light that reaches the film. On contemporary cameras with liquid crystal displays (LCD), verify that the camera is set for this type of automatic metering. In fact, always check the settings on all manual, digital, and LCD panel cameras before photographing any assignment.

- *Direct flash.* Direct flash can be harsh, especially if it is too close to the subject. The flash can wash out detail, creating a "white out" or "hot spot" in the middle of the photograph. By bouncing the light from the flash, it becomes less harsh and still illuminates the subject adequately. This technique also makes it possible to document fine detail in scars, tool marks, and anything that mandates recording depth or dimension. Most digital cameras have a direct flash capability and the result is a white out if positioned too close to the subject. It is optimal in these circumstances to use the higher-end DSLR, which also has a "hot shoe" for connecting a separate flash unit to the camera and bouncing it off the ceiling. If direct flash is the only option, diminish or "soften" the light source by placing a thin layer of tissue or gauze over the flash on the camera. Be careful not to obstruct the lens during this process.

- *Bouncing flash.* Bouncing a flash means that the light coming from the flash is not aimed directly at the subject but at the ceiling or the wall behind the subject. This technique eliminates harsh shadows and red eye. Bouncing flash relies heavily on the color and height of the ceiling, affecting both subject lighting and color accuracy. There is a simple solution to this problem. Place a white card on the back of the flash so it faces the subject. It can be secured with a rubber band. When light is bounced off the ceiling, the card reflects some of it forward into the dark recesses of shadow, whether on a face, around a fine scar, in a tire impression, or on tool marks made by a screwdriver to pry open a window. This bounce technique will be successful because the autoexposure mode of the flash is still working to determine the correct amount of light necessary for proper exposure (Fig. 7-6).

There are several ways to solve lighting issues in the clinical setting such as using secondary flash units or additional lights to prevent shadows. Use of a faster film speed will also help to accommodate for some lighting problems.

When taking full-length and intermediate photographs of patients in the clinical setting, the availability of equipment may be at a minimum. To increase control of the light from the flash and to eliminate harsh shadows behind the patient, place the patient in a corner. The light will bounce off the two opposing walls and illuminate the sides of the patient's face as well as eliminate the dark shadows behind the head that are created when shooting directly into the patient's face.

"Red eye," which is caused by the reflection of the flash on the blood vessels on the retina, can be prevented by increasing the distance between the flash and the camera lens. This is one of the applications for an off-camera flash unit, synchronized to the opening of the camera's shutter with an extension cord. Two practical ways to diminish "red eye" are to either have the patient look away from the camera lens, or to increase the lighting in the room so that the patient's pupils are more constricted.

SHUTTER SPEED

The shutter of a camera is the mechanism that opens, closes, and determines the amount of time that light is allowed to reach the film. The shutter speeds of P&S cameras are preset at either 1/60th or 1/125th of a second and cannot be changed. DSLRs and conventional SLRs have variable shutter speeds that range in time from 1/1000th second up to 1 second. Setting the camera on "B" for *bulb* will allow the photographer to take a timed exposure. This means that the shutter is left open for any period of time greater than one second, determined by the photographer for the correct exposure. Today, some cameras have an equivalent "T" for *time setting*. The longer the shutter remains open, the longer the subject and the photographer must remain still, as movement will create a blur on the image.

APERTURE

The beam of light that enters the camera and reflects on the film is controlled by an adjustable opening in the lens called the aperture. The aperture is known by many other names, such as lens opening, iris, diaphragm, f-number, or f-stop. The aperture is an iris-like diaphragm, similar to the pupil of the human eye, which provides a variable-sized hole that regulates the amount of light passing through the lens. A lens is identified according to the f-number that corresponds to its widest lens opening. The widest lens opening has the optimal light-admitting capacity. The f-stop is controlled manually by a movable ring surrounding the lens (Figs. 7-7 through 7-9).

DEPTH OF FIELD

Depth of field refers to an area both in front of and behind the subject that is in acceptably sharp focus, usually 7 through 13 feet. The depth of field can be increased by decreasing the size of the lens aperture. By closing the aperture, a longer shutter speed will be required to produce the same amount of light needed to reflect on the film.

Fig. 7-6 A Nikon digital SLR camera with flash attachment and white reflector card pointing upward in order to bounce the light off the ceiling.

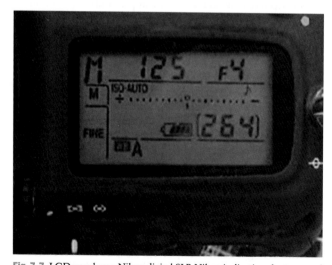

Fig. 7-7 LCD panel on a Nikon digital SLR Nikon indicating shutter speed and aperture (f/11). The number "4" indicates 1/4-second shutter speed.

technical architecture that reduces the area on the chip for capturing light, resulting in less uniformity. Check with the manufacturer specifications for the chip details.

The image, once it is recorded, is then stored inside the camera on a computer disk or storage device. It can then be transferred, or downloaded, at a later time through the use of a computer and electronic technology. One of the storage devices can be the computer's hard drive. If a disk is used for storage, the disk can be removed from the camera, installed into a personal computer (PC) or laptop, and instant images are available. The images themselves can be downloaded to a color printer, e-mailed to other computers, or simply be viewed on the computer screen or a television set in a matter of minutes.

Even without the benefit of a digital camera, traditional photographs and illustrations can be scanned either onto the hard drive of a computer, onto a disk, or onto a photo compact disk (CD). This electronic format can be stored in the computer for future viewing or transmission. When recording an image in the digital camera, the camera stores it. It will continue to store pictures until the storage capacity is filled. Then, the storage device must be cleared by downloading the images onto a computer or replaced with a blank storage device. Other ancillary equipment to support digital photography includes a photoediting program, a scanner, a removable hard drive or CD recorder to store the digital images, and a photo-quality laser or inkjet printer. Also needed is premium picture paper that is compatible with the printer. Laser prints are preferable to inkjet, but both are acceptable. High-gloss, ultrasmooth finish paper produces the greatest detail.

RESOLUTION OF IMAGES

The most important option that the forensic photographer must consider when purchasing a digital camera is the number of megapixels (MP) in the internal hard drive. The digital photograph consists of tiny squares called picture elements, or pixels. A pixel is the basic element that constitutes an image. A megapixel is equal to 1 million pixels. The number of pixels in one photograph can vary from hundreds to millions. The quality, or resolution, of the image depends in part on the number of pixels used to create the image—in other words, how large can you make the image without losing quality? Resolution is one of the most important factors to be considered in digital photography. Resolution is the determining factor when considering an appropriate size of the completed image. As with traditional photographs, the larger they are reproduced, the grainier they become. In other words, with each enlargement, resolution decreases and the photograph loses detail. The greater the number of pixels, the greater the detail within the image.

Resolution is expressed in the numbers of horizontal versus vertical pixels. There should be at least 200 pixels per inch (ppi) in an image to sustain a minimally acceptable standard of quality. For forensic applications, 300 ppi is a better choice. Low resolution is approximately 640 × 480 pixels, which is the resolution of many standard computer monitors and television screens (640 pixels/200 ppi equals 3.2 inches and 480 pixels/200 ppi equals 2.4 inches, or the equivalent of a wallet-sized photograph). An 8 × 10 enlargement from this low resolution would result in a poor quality, degraded image. To obtain an optimal 8 × 10 enlargement, the number of pixels would need to be at least 2000 × 1600. As technology advances, the number of pixels increases significantly, resulting in finer resolution for the maximum amount of enlargement (Box 7-1).

Most computers have the capacity to view only the 2.0 megapixel images on the monitor screen. The entire image appears, but you cannot see it all at once and have to scroll around in order

Box 7-1	Resolution for Maximum Enlargement	
PRINT SIZE	NUMBER OF PIXELS	CAMERA RESOLUTION NEEDED
4 × 6	800 × 1200	1.0 MP
5 × 7	1000 × 1400	2.0 MP
8 × 10	1600 × 2000	3.0 MP
11 × 17	2200 × 3400	6.0 MP
13 × 19	2600 × 3800	10.0 MP

to view it in its entirety. If you are only printing 4 × 6 or 5 × 7 photographs, a 2.0-megapixel camera is adequate and the most economical. The numbers can become very confusing, but the most important thing to remember is that the higher the resolution, the higher the quality of the images. Therefore, the camera, monitor, and color printer must all have high-resolution qualities. The objective is always the perfect photograph, and the perfect photograph still requires good technique and quality equipment. The techniques used with conventional cameras remain the same in digital photography.

The next important option to consider is the memory card. Memory cards are solid-state electronic flash memory data storage devices. The type of memory card you use is dictated by which digital camera you buy. The cards are physically different and are not interchangeable between cameras. Cards come with a memory capacity from 16 megabytes (MB) up to 32 gigabytes (GB). Many cameras will not work with cards larger than 2 GB unless specified by the manufacturer. Be aware of your equipment requirements. For a 2-MP camera, a 16-MB card will hold approximately 16 pictures; 32 MB, 32 pictures; 64 MB, 64 pictures; 128 MB, 128 pictures; 256 MB, 512 pictures; 512 MB, 1024 pictures; and 1 GB, 2048 pictures. With a 5-MP camera, the resolution can be much finer and a 1-GB card will store only 288 pictures. Determine the average number of photographs you take when photodocumenting a case and then purchase your memory cards accordingly. The memory card can be secured without printing the images. The chain of custody will be maintained until that time the card or photographs are required for litigation.

There are great advantages to using digital photography over conventional methods. It saves both time and resources and there is no film to be processed. In addition, the photographer has the benefit of viewing the image, deleting that image if not ideal, and retaking the image to be stored. Chain of custody is simplified because images can be instantaneous. Images can also be transmitted instantly as long as there is an electronic signal and someone with a computer to receive it. The camera and computer combination is now the photo-processing laboratory.

Saving and Storing the Images

Digital photographs take up a tremendous amount of space on the camera as well as on a computer's hard drive. Removable storage media should be utilized to store digital images, and each "case" should be stored on a separate memory data storage device to maintain chain of custody and confidentiality. Compact discs (CDs) are the most archival; however, the computer must be equipped with a CD burner or writing capability software in order to accomplish this task. For much larger files, the digital versatile disc or digital video disc (DVD) is similar to a CD but holds much more data: 4.7 gigabytes compared to 650 to 700 megabytes for a CD. Do not save photographs on a CD that can be written over (CD-RW). The integrity of the discs may come into question in court, and these

CDs are manufactured with thinner layers and can deteriorate over time, causing the images to be degraded or lost. A CD can hold up to 100 good quality photographs. Other types of storage media may be referred to as memory cards, flash drives, thumb drives, or jump drives. The drives are equipped with Universal Serial Bus (USB) ports for easy access to the computer. It is recommended that if hard copies of photographs are not printed, then each case should be dedicated to one storage medium.

The memory cards should be inserted into the camera. Do not photodocument directly onto the camera's own hard drive. This space is limited and it is sometimes cumbersome to transfer the images to the computer. Each memory card has a set memory, which is indicated on the card when it is purchased (Fig. 7-13).

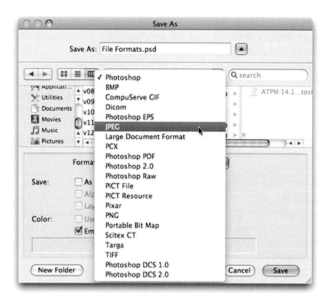

Fig. 7-14 Typical save menu in image editing software indicating the various file formats from which to choose to save the image.

Compression is the way to diminish or shrink the size of a picture so that it takes up less space (Box 7-2). The more the picture is compressed, the more images can be fitted onto a given amount of space on the memory card or USB flash drive. Most digital cameras use a built-in compression system known as Joint Photographic Experts Group (JPEG). JPEG uses a "lossy" compression method to create the final file. Lossy means that the final image is not the pixel-by-pixel equivalent of the original, but an abbreviated data production of the raw subject. Using a lossy method provides more compression capability (Fig. 7-14).

Ultraviolet and Infrared Photography

In the early 1900s, Professor Robert W. Wood, an American physicist, discovered and refined the techniques of ultraviolet, infrared, and ultraviolet fluorescence photography. In fact, in 1903, Wood created the technique for producing a source of ultraviolet light, the Wood's lamp. Ultraviolet (UV) and infrared (IR) light photography, although they cannot be seen in the color spectrum by the human eye, can significantly increase the amount of evidence obtained in child abuse, homicide, sexual assault, and bite mark cases. Injury detail will be enhanced with UV visualization. Likewise, when

Fig. 7-13 Memory cards varying in capacity from 16 MB to 2 GB.

Box 7-2 Compression Formats

GIF (Graphics Interchange Format): Lossless file format designed for Web graphics; not for printed photographs, as color limitation is unsuitable for reproducing color images

JPEG or JPG (Joint Photographers Expert Group): Most desirable and commonly used compression technique for photographic images; can be compressed to about 10% of the original image with only slight loss in quality

PDF (Portable Document Format): Not desirable for photographs; used primarily for documents in Adobe Acrobat

PICT (Personalized Image Capture Technology): Developed for Apple Macintosh computers for on-screen images only; limited resolution; unable to edit

BMP (bitmap): Used to store digital images, especially on Microsoft Windows

PNG (Portable Network Graphics): Provides lossless data compression; designed for transferring images on the Internet; upgrades and replaces GIF

PSD (Photoshop Document): Most popular program for editing; created by and for Adobe Photoshop editing programs; high-quality usage; has storage capability for files over 2 gigabytes

RAW (not an abbreviation): Literally means "raw" or "unprocessed"; files are created in the camera without any in-camera processing affecting the data; all information is captured by the camera's sensors; processing is performed later on a PC with special software

TIFF (Tagged Image File Format): a universal image, lossless format compatible with most image editing and viewing programs; the standard file format to use for saving high quality images ready for printing

PCX (PC Paintbrush Exchange): One of the first widely accepted DOS imaging standards; updated by GIF, JPEG, and PNG viewed with IR, the bruise may actually disappear, because IR penetrates deeper into the skin. IR is more likely to capture severe bruises and incisions such as deep bite marks or knife or gunshot wounds. Digital cameras have made UV/IR photodocumentation techniques faster, easier, and less expensive than conventional film. Instead of film, the CCD collects the incoming light and converts it into an image. However, most digital cameras also may have filtering devices built in to actually inhibit the passage of UV and IR. Therefore, you must contact the manufacturer and inquire as to the camera's UV/IR specifications and capabilities.

ULTRAVIOLET

There are two types of UV photography techniques: fluorescent and reflective. Fluorescent photography will illuminate the phosphates found in semen. By eliminating all other white light sources and shining an alternate light source (ALS), such as an ultraviolet lamp, black light, or Wood's lamp, from the surface in question, the presence of body fluids may be determined. This technique is an investigative tool and presumptive test, allowing establishment of probable cause but not proof of the presence of specific evidence. Laundry detergents also contain phosphates and produce a fluorescence on clothing and linens. A certain degree of skill is required to determine what is evidence and what is not. An even distribution of fluorescence is more than likely detergent, whereas small stains or droplets could indicate the presence of semen or other protein matter.

Reflective UV photodocumentation will produce an image that is otherwise not seen nor photographed by conventional techniques. Reflective UV photography records the reflection and absorption of long-wave UV light by the subject matter, excluding exposure of the film by all other visible light (Krauss & Warlen, 1985). Human skin contains melanin, a substance that absorbs UV radiation. This absorption process protects skin from sunburn. Trauma to the skin and underlying tissues causes a release and spread of melanin throughout the injury area. During the healing process, melanocytes congregate around the edges of the wound, creating an outline of the tissue injury pattern. UV photography is possible because, with the increase of melanin, hemoglobin, and bilirubin around the injury site, absorption of long-wave UV is greater there than in the surrounding area. Injuries have been photodocumented with reflective UV as long as 5 months, posttrauma.

Reflective UV photography can still be accomplished using high-speed black-and-white film. Most applications require hand-held camera situations. Because of the dimness of the light source in combination with the smaller apertures, the high-speed films allow faster shutter speeds. Optimal results are obtained when using a specific UV filter on the camera, which requires a filter frame holder and an adapter ring to secure the filter on the camera lens. But simply adding a UV filter onto the camera does not guarantee that true UV images are recorded. The lens must pass sufficient UV light, and the digital sensor in the camera must be sensitive to UV as well.

The primary light source must be UV lighting (Wood's lamp). Make sure that both the photographer and the person being examined are wearing protective safety goggles. A higher-end digital camera must be set manually to "black and white." Black and white captures more detail and contrast than does color.

Move the UV light source around the site until the best visualization of the injury is achieved. This UV illumination should permit visualization of the injury with the naked eye. Photographs are taken perpendicular, at a 90-degree angle to the subject. In other words, the film plane must be parallel to the injury site. The patient

should remain absolutely still. Stop down to increase the depth of field. The entire injury encompasses areas of tissue below the skin surface. If only the skin surface is focused, the lower levels of injury could be blurry. Use of an American Board of Forensic Odontology (ABFO) No. 2 scale for two-dimensional measurement of the injury will enhance the evidentiary value of the photographs.

INFRARED

Infrared photography can be utilized in cases when victims are found in advanced stages of decomposition. Because infrared light penetrates more deeply than ultraviolet into the skin tissues, the light waves can capture tattoos for identification purposes. There is no simple way for the forensic nurse to produce infrared digital photographs in the clinical setting. Other than using the right conventional film and 35-mm SLR camera, filters, tripods, and various other pieces of equipment would have to be on hand. With digital photography, the UV and IR cutoff filter would have to be removed. The DSLR's autoexposure is not reliable for determining the correct lighting for IR and, therefore, the DSLR is not yet the first choice for IR. In 2006, Fujifilm made this process for photodocumenting with IR incredibly more functional. The manufacturer introduced a camera that is sensitive not only to visible light, but to ultraviolet and infrared as well. With the simple use of filters, the camera can produce UV or IR images.

AUTHENTICITY

One of the primary issues to be considered with regard to digital photography is that of determining authenticity. Testimony must be given that the image entered as evidence accurately portrays the scene as viewed by the photographer at the time the photograph was taken. In view of the ease with which digital photographs can be altered, there must be safeguards in place to uphold the integrity of the images. First, a particularly secure audit trail from the initial image through to the copy produced in court must be established. Two computerized authentication methods are known as encryption and watermarking. Encryption is a way of mathematically breaking an image down, transmitting it, and reconstructing it at the receiving end with the appropriate authorization coding. This does not prevent manipulation, but it does help prevent interception of the transmitted images. Encryption also helps to maintain confidentiality, as well as specifying origins and destinations. A digital watermarking computer software solution will easily address authenticity and ownership issues associated with digital images and photographs. It is an operation that places an arbitrary image imperceptibly in the background of a document or photograph to corroborate its legitimacy, such as the watermarks on finer stationery and paper money.

SAFEGUARDS AGAINST TAMPERING

Digital image forgery and manipulation are growing concerns in criminal cases. Manipulation of photographs can be used to promote a flamboyant news article, defame a defendant, malign a plaintiff, or any number of other objectives. The development of digital image forensic tools is essential to the future of forensic analysis of digital images and the assurance that fraud and manipulation have not taken place. One of the technologies being utilized to safeguard digital photography as legal evidence is called cyclic redundancy checking (CRC). Originally used as a method for tracking errors in data that had been transmitted on a communication link, it is now being used successfully to establish authenticity and ensure the integrity of digital images. The CRC authentication software has three major components: digital signature firmware on the camera, authentication software for the host computer, and a public key management system to enable a trusted third party or third-party proxy to have custody of the public key, ensuring authenticity (Eastman Kodak Company, 2000 and 2009).

The technology behind CRC can be likened to the information found in the genetic codes of DNA's variable number of tandem repeats (VNTRs). Digital color images contain three primary colors: red, green, and blue. There are two bits of information in each pixel. There are 256 levels of color (8 bits) contained within each of the three colors. Eight bits are required for each of the three colors to maintain a continuous "photorealistic" image. Each pixel can contain 256 values for the red component, 256 for the green, and 256 for the blue. Therefore, any one pixel can have 24 bits associated with it, or $256 \times 256 \times 256 \times 224$, or 16,777,216 possible values (Davies & Fennessy, 1999).

CRC technology applies a proprietary algorithm to the data sets that are derived from the pixels. The manufacturer of the image-capturing software usually has the proprietary algorithm, as it is protected for security reasons. The encrypted algorithm is a means of improving the integrity of the validation process. A computation should be performed the moment the photograph is taken into the software. The computation produces a unique, discreet value, a series of numbers and letters. If any discreet value in a pixel is changed, even by one digit, or fraction thereof, which causes an increase or decrease in the number of the red, green, or blue color components, the result is a completely different CRC number when the algorithm is applied (Davies & Fennessy, 1999).

Rather than arguing that an image has not been altered, it is an accepted fact during a trial that an image can be altered to make something more apparent to a juror or trier of fact. The original image, however, can be verified through the CRC numbers. Frye challenges will not arise because an image has been altered but will be based on certain technological disputes regarding the algorithm or the source code or any other aspect of the computerized electronic media and data storage. It has not been questioned as yet, primarily because most states simply have an authentication statement in their rules of evidence.

Attorneys will also attempt to question the authenticity of images transmitted to a forensic professional for review. The challenge would be in the fact that the reviewer is not actually seeing the authentic image due to changes caused by transmission of the image. "What you were looking at was not the actual photograph. Therefore, wouldn't your opinion be different because it wasn't the original?" With CRC technology in place, the image transmitted is the image received and, therefore, the image reviewed. The New Jersey Division of Criminal Justice has been one of the first organizations to accept colposcopic digital imaging capability in its sexual assault cases because of the security of the images, and the CRC method of validating that the image was in fact the one that was taken on a particular date and time. There are other new technologies being developed for fraud detection. Among them are programs that detect anomalous lighting and unusual color distortions.

On October 21, 2002, a ruling in favor of forensic digital imaging was signed into effect in Broward County, Florida, after a Frye hearing was requested in the *State of Florida v. Victor Reyes* case. Digital images had been made of photographs of latent fingerprints. The original fingerprints were unreadable and therefore found to be of "no value." The latent prints were enhanced digitally to make them readable. After extensive evidence and expert witness testimony was presented, the ruling was made to accept the forensic digital imaging as an established discipline in the field of forensic science.

In 2004, in the case of *Connecticut v. Swinton*, challenges were made to digital photographic evidence. The defendant challenged the admissibility of two digitally enhanced submissions. One was a photograph of a bite mark on the victim's body, and the second contained images of the defendant's teeth superimposed on the bite mark. Case law established in *Swinton* provides guidance in how to lay proper foundation when submitting digitally produced evidence. There must be testimony by a person with some degree of computer expertise, who has sufficient knowledge to be examined and cross-examined about the software and its operation. Further, beyond the reliability of the evidence itself, the proponent must establish that (1) the equipment used is accepted as standard equipment in the field, (2) the operator of the equipment was qualified to use the equipment, (3) proper procedures were followed in connection with the input and output of information, and (4) the software used is reliable (Page, 2006/2007). Because the Federal Rules of Evidence still do not set forth admissibility requirements for digital photographs, the traditional rules on relevance and authentication continue to apply. With the acceptance of digital imaging in U.S. courts of law, standards and protocols must be established to govern and validate our practices, as well as build confidence in a new technology. The mission statement of the Scientific Working Group on Imaging Technologies (SWGIT), in conjunction with the Department of Justice and Federal Bureau of Investigation, is "to facilitate the integration of imaging technologies and systems within the Criminal Justice System (CJS) by providing definitions and recommendations for the capture, storage, processing, analysis, transmission, and output of images." SWGIT has written "Definitions and Guidelines for the use of Imaging Technologies in the Criminal Justice System" (Version 2.1–June 8, 1999) and is one of the best sources to reference for standardized policies and procedures acceptable in courts of law. SWGIT has further worked since the 1990s to assist the criminal justice system to transition from a film-based to a digital-based society. Its latest publication is "Recommendations and Guidelines for use of Digital Image Processing in the Criminal Justice System," and it helps ensure that processed images can be successfully introduced in court. Although there is a certain sentimentality regarding 35-mm film and the ways in which we have traditionally captured our past, inevitably digital imaging will dominate our future. SWGIT's position is that any changes to an image made through digital image processing are acceptable in forensic applications provided the following criteria are met:

- The original image is preserved.
- The processing steps are logged when they include techniques other than those used in a traditional photographic darkroom.
- The end result is presented as an enhanced image, which may be reproduced by applying the logged steps to the original image (Page, 2006/2007).

Consent

There is little reason why photography should not be included in the general consent signed by a patient or victim when he or she registers at the hospital or emergency department (ED). After all, the patient consents to treatments, tests, medications, transfusions, x-rays, release of information, and reimbursement. It is reasonably prudent to allow photographic recording of injuries and findings that are likely to help in the evaluation, treatment, and the prosecution of those responsible. As with any medical, surgical, or invasive procedure, the patient must give permission to photograph his or her injuries. The nurse is acting as patient advocate, but it is the patient's body being photographed. After death, a consent is not required to take forensic photographs. Medical examiners and police departments make the decisions and follow their own protocols for accepted procedures with photography. In life, the victim does have control over these procedures, and individuals must give consent for photographs to be taken. If the victim is unconscious, however, and the injuries are linked to a potentially litigious situation, it is advisable to photograph them because one could reasonably assume that the patient would have given consent for this documentation of the trauma.

Most trauma centers and emergency departments in the United States have treatment consent forms that also contain statements such as "patient consents for treatment and documentation of injuries with photography." Consent forms can also be presented to the patient or client when it has been determined that there are forensic issues involved. If the permission is already blanketed in the facility, allow the patient the option of refusing photography. Some patients may be uncomfortable with the concept. Stress that this is part of the advocacy program and can benefit the patient if the case goes to litigation. However, some facilities' permission for treatment forms include a request for permission for photography and use for educational material. This can be most beneficial to the patient if he or she later wishes to file charges or prove extent of injury for insurance or survivor's benefits and to professional educators who are responsible for providing illustrations that reflect exact duplication of injuries and evidence.

A well-thought-out and printed policy and procedure must precede the situation. Get the legal department of the facility involved and discuss the various issues with the hospital attorneys.

Sit down with department managers and local police departments and establish protocols, policies, and procedures regarding photography. Discuss various consent forms. A simple form merely states the patient's name, giving permission to either the institution or the clinician to photograph the injuries listed. Note any objections the patient might have. For example, the patient may only agree to the photographs being used for litigation and not for educational purposes. The patient and the clinician then sign the form, and it is dated, stamped with the patient's plate and identification number, and included in the medical record. Give attention to the "exigent circumstances" that may occur throughout the clinical areas. These are the critical situations when the nurse must have the institution's legal support.

If a consent to photograph is not included in the consent for treatment, Figure 7-15 provides an example of some consent statements for consideration by an institution's legal department.

Guidelines for Photodocumentation in the Clinical Setting

Before initiating any photodocumentation process in the clinical setting, a written photography protocol must be established. Work closely with the nurse manager, medical director, and staff as well as the chief nursing executive, the risk manager, and hospital

---

Consent to Photograph

I authorize_____ Hospital and the staff of the Emergency Department to photograph or permit other persons employed by this facility to photograph

_____ (name of patient) while under the care of this facility. I have been informed and understand that:

Photographs taken for medical purposes will become part of my medical record and will be subject to subpoena with my record.

Photographs in my medical record may be released if they are requested by a person authorized to obtain my medical record. If I do not want photographs released with my medical record, I must specifically exclude them in any authorizations that I sign.

I do not authorize any other use to be made of these photographs.

_____   _____
Patient's Signature   Date
(Parent or guardian if under 18)

_____   _____
Street Address   Witness

_____
City   State   Zip Code

Deposition of Photographs: To be completed by Facility Staff

_____   Photographs were placed in a sealed envelope marked with the patient's name and medical record number and sent to Medical Records

Fig. 7-15 Consent to photograph form.

attorney. It is desirable to have at least one or two nurses on each shift who have been trained in forensic photography and evidentiary documentation.

Simple injuries, such as facial wounds, singular animal or human bites, or injuries not due to multiple trauma, domestic violence (DV), or sexual assault, require only an identifying photograph of the face and of the injury. Multiple trauma, DV, and sexual assault cases require a series of photographs depicting both the presence and absence of injuries.

A full-body photograph of the patient must be taken, with the face included (Refer to Fig. 7-3). Take a full-body photo of the back of the patient to show both the presence and absence of injuries. Have the patient turn his or her face toward the camera for identification purposes. To preserve the patient's modesty, supply a blanket or sheet to use as a robe or cover. Gently maneuver the cover to reveal the injuries that must be photodocumented. The cover will provide the patient with a sense of control over the situation.

Take mid-distance images of each injury (Refer to Fig. 7-4). Include the patient's face in at least one of these photos to establish that the documented injuries were, in fact, found on this patient. Mid-distance photographs provide more detail and relativity than full-body photographs.

Take close-up images of each injury (Refer to Fig. 7-5), one with a standard (ruler) to show injury size and another without to show the standard did not obscure information. Standards get their name from objects that are of a standard size or shape. It is something universal that is recognized by everyone for what it is. Standards are usually rulers, called scales, but can also be a familiar object or coin, such as a quarter. Always place the standard on the same surface level with the injury so that the focus will be sharp and perspective will not be altered. Photograph dimensional injuries by using an ABFO No. 2 reference scale. This scale also serves as a reminder to photograph all injuries parallel to the film plane (i.e., camera at a 90-degree angle to the injury surface). When the injury is parallel to the film, the circles on the scale will appear circular, not elliptical (Fig. 7-16).

***

BEST PRACTICE All forensic photographs should have affixed labels that contain the subject's name or hospital number, the date, the time, and the name of the photographer. Never write directly on the photograph or use paper clips or staples to attach it to other documents.

***

Label all photographs separately. Never write directly on the back of a photograph, as this can create an indentation on the front, altering the image in the photo. Write all information on a self-adhesive

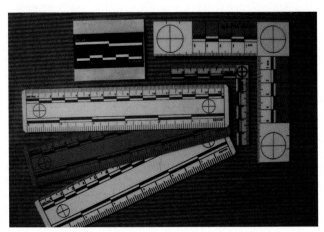

Fig. 7-16 Standards and the ABFO No. 2 scale.

label—patient's name or hospital number, the date, time, name of the photographer, and the type of camera used to photograph the scene. Adhere the label to the back of the photograph. Photographs are a part of the patient record and should be kept in the patient's file at all times. Do not keep photos separate from regular patient records. Photographs can be adhered to special sheets with either self-adhesive strips or slits that have been precut to accommodate a specific size (e.g., 4 × 6 or Polaroid instant). Photographs are to be kept as confidential as the written patient record.

If the patient requests a set of photos and if a color printer is located in the clinical setting, a set may be provided after obtaining the photodocumentation needed. If a Polaroid camera was used, make duplicates with the close-up copy stand provided in the camera kit. Be sure to advise the patient that if she or he is a domestic violence victim, the photos may place the patient in danger if the batterer finds them. If the patient was provided with a set of photographs, note this on the patient's chart. Include the quantity and specify the date the images were provided.

Generally, if patient's photographs are subpoenaed, the medical records department need only provide a copy of the images. The original photographs will require a separate, more specific court order. Check the state laws for further information.

The photographs taken by the forensic nurse or other staff members should not be released to the police but retained with the patient's record to maintain chain of custody. The local police departments are equipped with their own camera systems, and photographs taken by their personnel will include not only physical appearance but also pieces of hard evidence. They will be photographing weapons, such as knives and guns, and bullets and other projectiles removed from the patient by the emergency department physician. It is perfectly acceptable to be asked by the police to take the photographs for them with their own equipment. It is often easier for the nurse to accomplish this task because of the rapport that has been established between the care provider and the patient.

Forensic nurses in the OR should photograph foreign material removed by surgeons in the operating room (OR). These photographs also belong to the permanent patient record. The projectiles will be turned over to the police as evidence, but if not photographed, their existence can be disputed if lost along the way.

When forensic nurse examiners are outside the clinical area in a patient's home or at a crime scene, the geographical location must be established with the initial photographs, called orientation shots. To establish the actual location of the scene, it may be necessary to begin photographing from the street sign inward. Moving from the outside in, photographing from the general to the specific, and indicating the relationship of one object to another are mandatory for reconstruction of the crime scene. After the police release the scene, there is no way to preserve the scene as it was when it was secured.

Photograph "north, east, south, west." In other words, photograph the entire scene in a clockwise manner in order to create 360-degree coverage. Just as the photographer takes full-length, intermediate, and close-up views of the patients, other crime scenes are photographed in the same way. Long views establish geography, location, entrances, exits, and escape routes. Intermediate views establish relationships between people and objects. Close-up views show fine detail, dimensions, and measurements. When taking close-up views of any subject matter, always take one photograph with and one without the standard. Keep the standard on the same plane with the subject. Compose photographs carefully. Be aware of anyone or anything standing in the viewfinder that will distract from the final product. On completion of the photodocumentation,

PHOTO LOG

Photographer	Event or Case
Camera (Make & Model)	Location
Film (Type & ISO)	Date/Time
Other	

Exp	Subject	Lighting	Lens	Notes
1				
2				
3				
4				
5				
6				
7				
8				
9				
10				
11				
12				
13				
14				
15				
16				
17				
18				
19				
20				
21				
22				
23				
24				
25				
26				
27				
28				
29				
30				
31				
32				
33				
34				
35				
36				
37				

Fig. 7-17 Photo log.

rewind the film and process it as quickly as possible. Do not mix more than one crime scene on the same roll. A photographic log should be maintained with each roll of film and for each exposure made (Fig. 7-17).

Remember that photographers tell a story without words through photodocumentation. The full-body and orientation photographs are the introduction. The intermediate and relativity photographs contain the core. The close-up views can be considered the conclusion, the punch line, or the coup de grâce. Combined, the entire set of photographs describes a historical event that cannot be portrayed simply with the written word.

Establish a business relationship with a professional photography lab. Inform the key personnel of the lab that they will be processing crime scene photographs and that the strictest chain of custody and confidentiality must be maintained. Consider the use of a chain-of-custody form with the lab if there is ever a question about the possession of the memory storage device or the film or the length of time either is out of one's possession.

Delegate drop-off and retrieval of the device or film and the photographs to as few individuals as possible. When the photographs are processed, insert them into the patient's record or institutional report immediately. It is important to understand the exact procedure for storage of photographs within the medical records department.

When photodocumenting with either 35-mm film or a digital camera system containing a memory storage device in a hospital setting, it is imperative that all the intricacies of transport concerning the film or memory card are considered in the writing of the policy and procedure. Chain of custody will be scrutinized and the timing of an event may not be convenient for expeditious film processing or photograph downloading and printing. If an event occurs at change of shift, determine where the memory card or film will be secured until it can be processed, who the courier will be, and who will retrieve the memory card, the processed photographs, the negatives, and then the medical record for insertion of the photographs (Fig. 7-18).

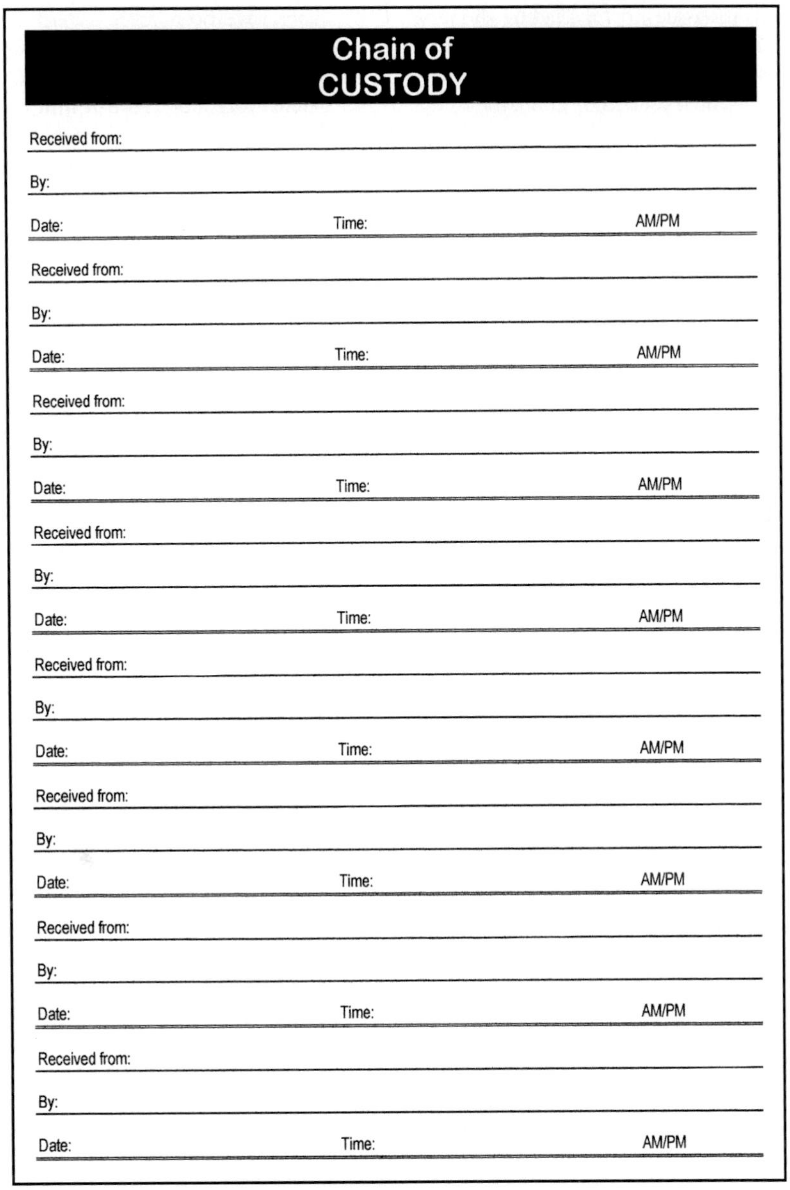

Fig. 7-18 Chain-of-custody form.

Photographs as Legal Documents

In today's litigious society, the more evidence that exists to support the truth, the greater the advantage for healthcare workers who advocate for their patients. Although there are certain concerns about photodocumentation within hospitals, documentation of injuries of abuse, traumatic wounds, and other situations may serve to protect the hospital and its staff members by ensuring precise documentation. There is no simple way to document accurately with written words alone the distribution of 53 stab wounds on a victim's body. The same is true for documenting the existence of bridging in a laceration, blood spatter or body fluid drainage patterns, stippling, or an abrasion ring around a gunshot wound. The completion of the forensic examination of a sexual assault victim includes not only the collection of forensic evidence but also photographs of the evidence, as well as both external and internal trauma.

A forensic photograph is a legal document and must be considered part of the record. In many instances, it completes the record, and, at the very least, it supplements it. Mechanism of injury can often be demonstrated with one photograph. The truth or falsehood of a statement may be proved with a photograph. Photography can capture the tiniest detail that the eye does not see until the photograph is developed. The photograph captures valuable information that may link a victim to the perpetrator, or the perpetrator to the crime scene. Photographs also refresh the memories of victims, law enforcement officials, and witnesses as to the events, conditions, and facts of a matter as they actually existed when the photograph was taken.

Under the Federal Rules of Evidence, a photograph is generally admissible if it demonstrates content and information of value to legal proceedings. Photographs will not be admissible "if their probative value is substantially outweighed by the danger of unfair prejudice, confusion of the issues, or misleading the jury, or by considerations of undue delay, waste of time, or needless presentation of cumulative evidence" (Federal Rules of Evidence, Rule 403). "It has become well settled that color photographs are admissible, provided (1) what they depict is relevant to the issues in the case; (2) they have been shown to be true and accurate representations; and (3) their probative value is not outweighed by gruesomeness or inflammatory character" (Moenssens, Starrs, & Henderson et al., 1995, p. 148).

BEST PRACTICE The forensic photographer should understand the Federal Rules of Evidence and ensure that recorded evidentiary photographs meet the criteria for admissibility for courtroom proceedings.

Photographs are demonstrative evidence. Demonstrative evidence illustrates, demonstrates, or helps explain oral testimony. The Federal Rules of Evidence, Rule 1001, states, "a 'duplicate' is a counterpart produced by the same impression as the original, or from the same matrix, or by means of photography, including enlargements and miniatures…which accurately reproduces the original." Also, the "best evidence rule" can be interpreted as "the best evidence that the nature of the thing will afford." Therefore, because large objects, situations, conditions, or history cannot be brought into the courtroom, the photograph is the next best evidence utilized to demonstrate the original. With digital photography, the original image would more likely than not be interpreted as the one first created and captured by the CCD onto either the camera's hard drive or a memory storage device.

Photographs are not likely to be admitted as evidence if there is no reference to them in the medical record. Nor are they likely to be admitted if there is no reference to the injuries in the medical record that the photographs themselves document. The photographs and medical record supplement and corroborate each other.

If photographs are admitted as evidence, the photographer may be called on to testify to the circumstances under which the photographs were taken. Discuss this situation with the attorney handling the case. When called as a fact witness, remember that photography is a tool that amplifies nursing documentation. The court will not consider the forensic nurse examiner to be an expert witness in photography. Testimony will include verification that the photograph is a fair and accurate depiction of the scene as it appeared at the time it was taken.

ADMISSIBILITY OF DIGITAL PHOTOGRAPHS

The Federal Rules of Evidence define the admissibility of digital photographs. Article X, Rule 1001 (1) addresses "writings and recordings or their equivalent (such as) mechanical or electronic recording, or other form of data compilation." Rule 1001 (3) states, "if data are stored in a computer or similar device, any printout or other output readable by sight, shown to reflect the data accurately, is an 'original.'" Rule 1001 (4) states "a 'duplicate' is a counterpart produced by the same impression as the original, or from the same matrix, or by mechanical or electronic re-recording, or by other equivalent techniques which accurately reproduces the original." Rule 1003 states, "a duplicate is admissible to the same extent as an original unless (1) a genuine question is raised as to the authenticity of the original or (2) in the circumstances it would be unfair to admit the duplicate in lieu of the original." In brief, the existence of digital photographs is acknowledged, the storage of digital images in a computer is acceptable, a digital image stored in a computer is considered an original, and any digital image or duplicate may be admissible as evidence.

There have been several court cases setting precedence with regard to the acceptance of digital imaging as legal evidence in the United States. In the *State of California v. Phillip Lee Jackson*, in 1995, the defense asked for a Frye hearing on the use of digital image processing on a fingerprint in a double homicide case in San Diego. A Frye hearing establishes the general acceptance of a scientific technique by the scientific community. The Frye test must be utilized to guarantee the reliability of any new or novel scientific evidence, and the presiding judge must determine that the basic underlying principles of the scientific evidence have been sufficiently tested and accepted by the relevant scientific community.

The court ruled the hearing to be unnecessary owing to the fact that digital processing is an accepted practice in forensic science and that the integrity of the image had been maintained (Staggs, 2001). In the case of the *State of Washington v. Eric H. Hayden*, also in 1995, a homicide case was taken through a Kelly-Frye hearing in which the defense specifically objected on the grounds that the digital images were manipulated. The court authorized the use of digital imaging, and the defendant was found guilty. In 1998, the appellate court upheld the case on appeal (90 Wash. App. 100, 950 P.2d 1024).

The major objection to digital photography by attorneys and other criminal justice personnel is the fact that the images can be altered or "manipulated" with the assistance of any number of photoediting software computer programs. These programs enable the photographer to enhance and crop the images, change colors, straighten lines or create curves, eliminate scratches or red eye, and even add or eliminate objects or people. This manipulation makes it difficult to rely on the image as an accurate depiction of the crime scene when viewed as photographic evidence in a court of law. In the past, images were controlled in the traditional darkroom with lighting techniques, burning, dodging, and processing chemicals. Essentially, other than the lighting effects, the original subject matter remained unchanged. Today, a simple computer software program can totally change, add, eliminate, or distort an original image.

BEYOND THE MEDICAL SETTING

In addition to assault and trauma cases, photography must be considered for those settings outside the hospital. All nurses must be aware of the opportunities that present themselves in alternative settings and be prepared to photodocument factual information. Industrial injuries, injuries resulting from faulty appliances, the homeowner whose furnace explodes in his face, the facial injuries resulting from motor vehicle crashes, and bruises on the child who makes frequent visits to the school nurse will require adjudication and should be photographed to complete the record.

There are many categories of forensic patients. Any medical incident that the nurse or physician feels will eventually end up in an attorney's office or a court of law is a forensic case and necessitates the gathering of as much evidence as possible. What better way to provide the truth? In addition to those cases already mentioned, there are multiple categories of forensic patients who require photography as part of their documentation and history-taking process: assault and battery; abuse of children, elders, and the disabled; sexual assault; transportation injuries; suicide attempts, that include ligature and hesitation marks; resultant injuries from medical malpractice; product liability including injuries sustained from unsafe products, toys, and tools; physiological abuse from transcultural medical practices, cults, and religious groups; human and animal bites; and any other suspicious, unrecognized, and unidentified trauma. These photos should be taken and retained as part of the medical record.

All healthcare providers in all clinical settings must be alerted that it is to their benefit to use photography as a documentary tool. Forensic nurses are aware of the injuries and trauma inflicted upon the victims of violence. They are becoming astute in recognizing that photodocumentation is one of the prime tools in the pursuit of justice. One does not need to be a professional photographer to photograph injuries. The equipment does not have to be expensive or sophisticated. Cases have been won on the basis of poor quality photographs. If a nurse or physician captures the handprint around a little girl's neck or the bruises on a woman's back, blurry but unmistakably there, the case can be won. Essential equipment is listed in Box 7-3.

Summary

Photography is an essential skill for the forensic nurse examiner. Photodocumentation illustrates and supplements written records and preserves images or injuries and other evidence that can change over time. Photographs also act as an aid to memory, preserving important details of a situation that might have otherwise been overlooked or forgotten. Photos are of great value in the courtroom because they permit the jurors to view injuries and crime scenes, helping them determine if testimony being presented makes sense in context of the documented details. To support intelligent, dispassionate legal deliberations, photographs for the courtroom must accurately depict a scenario without being unduly gruesome or inflammatory (Box 7-4).

Box 7-3 Essential Equipment for the Clinical Setting or Crime Scene

- 35-mm SLR camera, a Polaroid Spectra, a Polaroid Macro 5, or digital camera equipment
- Appropriate film, adequate exposures, extra memory cards for digital cameras
- Thyristor flash unit (as well as a second slave unit if appropriate for the department)
- Ring flash
- Synchronization cord at least 3 feet long (to allow it to be held at arm's length)
- 50-mm lens or a telephoto zoom lens
- Various filters (polarizer, UV, and IR light)
- Scales, standards, ABFO No. 2 scale
- Tripod
- Cable release
- Various appropriate-sized extra batteries for all camera equipment
- Various boxes of film appropriate for camera equipment (12-, 24-, and 36-exposure rolls for 35-mm)
- Securable carrying case or transportable cart for all photographic equipment
- Large flash umbrella (Caution: This does not double for a large rain umbrella, though, if working in precipitation.)
- Slotted pages or manila envelopes for 35-mm negatives and prints and Polaroid photographs (Have necessary forms within easy access, including consent to photograph, chain of custody, and photography log.)
- Appropriate charger for the digital camera battery system; extra AA, AAA, or NiCad batteries and extra rechargeable batteries appropriate for camera being utilized.
- Printer, paper, and color ink available for immediate printing of photographs, preferably 4 × 6

Box 7-4 Suggested Policy for Photodocumentation of Injuries

The staff person who is most competent in photographic technique should be responsible for photodocumentation. When the easiest adherence to chain of custody is an issue, it is recommended that a digital camera system be used for these services. Use a 35-mm SLR or instant camera system only if an appropriate policy ensuring chain of custody of film and photographs is still in place.

POLICY

Photodocumentation of injuries is the accepted standard of care. Photodocumentation is an extremely important service that should be offered to the patient. Photographs require written informed consent and become part of the medical record.

PURPOSE

The purposes of photodocumentation are as follows:
1. To record and communicate that which cannot be communicated with the written word alone
2. To serve as objective witnesses by providing photographic evidence for purposes of adjudication
3. To protect healthcare providers against claims of inappropriate care or failure to accurately document physical appearance, condition, or injuries

PROCEDURE

Follow proper procedures when considering photodocumentation.
1. Determine the need for photodocumentation. Forensic categories of patients potentially requiring photographs include, but are not limited to, the following:
   - Abuse of children, elders, disabled
   - Domestic violence
   - Negligence and malpractice
   - Transcultural medical practices (e.g., cupping, coining, tribal scarring)
   - Environmental and toxic hazards
   - Forensic psychiatric situations (e.g., suicide attempts, hesitation marks, burns, self-mutilation)
   - Transportation injuries (motor vehicle, motorcycle, boating, airplane, railroad)
   - Sexual assault
   - Assault and battery
   - Personal injury
   - Occupation-related injuries
   - Questioned death
   - Product liability
   - Human and animal bites
   - Sharp force injuries (stabbing, puncture)
   - Burns over 5% body surface area
   - Firearm injuries
   - Gang violence
   - Acts of terrorism resulting in mass destruction of property or injuries of victims
   - Any other suspicious, unrecognized, or unidentified trauma
2. Informed consent must be obtained. Signature is required on the consent for photography or in the general consent for treatment, and the signature must be that of the patient, guardian, or caretaker upon arrival to the ED. In emergent cases when a signature is unobtainable, consent will be implied.
3. Steps in photodocumenting injuries:
   - Take "before-" and "after-cleaning" photographs of all injuries. This is most important in recording blood spatter patterns, gunshot residue, and dirt.
   - Some jurisdictions require that essential identifying data, such as the patient's name, date, and case number, be written legibly on a piece of paper and photographed on the first exposure of any given roll of film.
   - Take a full-length photograph that captures both the patient's face and injuries so that it is clear that the trauma was sustained by the victim in the photograph. Also take a full-length photograph of the back of the patient with the head turned toward the camera. This objectively records both presence and absence of injuries. Respect a patient's privacy. Allow the patient to cover up with a blanket or sheet, moving it to expose only the areas and injuries that need to be photographed.

(Continued)

Box 7-4 Suggested Policy for Photodocumentation of Injuries—Cont'd

- The four principal anatomic positions that photodocumentation should consider, but not be limited to, are anterior/posterior, posterior/anterior, right lateral, and left lateral.
- If the location of the injury does not allow for such a photograph, a picture of the face should be included in the set of photographs and an identifying document (e.g., the patient's driver's license) can be included in a picture with the injury.
- Take an intermediate-view photograph, including the patient's face, and a closer view of as many injuries as possible in the same photograph. Have the patient sit in a chair or on a stretcher in a sitting position with a sheet or blanket draped over the patient to maintain modesty, exposing the injuries.
- Take a close-up photo of each of the injuries. The face is not required in these photographs. Identification has already been established with the full-length and intermediate views. Take this view both with and without a standard (ruler) in place. For other than linear injuries, in order to document dimension, photograph both the length and width of the injury.

4. Label each photograph with the date and time taken, the name of the hospital, the medical record number, and the name of the photographer. Do not write on the back of the photograph. Place this information on a self-adhesive label and affix the label to the back of the photograph.
5. Photographs are to be kept in the patient's medical record in a sealed envelope with the written statement "photographs of patient's injuries" or placed in slotted pages specifically for the purpose of inclusion in the medical record. If the prints are obtained from negatives, the negatives are considered the primary evidence. They must be kept with the record along with the prints.
6. If extensive bruising is expected to appear at a later date, and the patient is anticipating litigation, the patient should be advised to return to the emergency department, police department, attorney's office, or insurance company within 72 hours to have additional photographs taken.
7. Assure chain of custody for film processing and retrieval.
8. Assure that final photographs and negatives are placed in the medical record.

Case Study **7-1**

Ted Bundy

During the 1970s, some of the most heinous cases of human violence occurred involving the infamous serial killer Ted Bundy. In one particular scenario during his final rape and murder spree in Tallahassee, Florida, forensic photography provided the most crucial evidence for the prosecution. Because of the number and breadth of atrocities committed by this sexual predator, as well as his ability to escape from high-security detention facilities, the recovery of forensic evidence was essential. Apprehension and identification of Bundy became the priority of all law enforcement agents in Florida and across the United States. There was no doubt that he would kill again.

On January 15, 1978, Bundy struck again, attacking and killing Lisa Levy and Martha Bowman in the same room in their sorority house at Tallahassee's Florida State University. Police stated they had never seen such a brutal attack. Lisa Levy was raped, strangled, and beaten. Margaret Bowman was strangled with a pair of pantyhose and severely beaten. Two other girls in the sorority house had been attacked, and less than an hour and a half later, the man assaulted a fifth victim, who survived. Just a few weeks after that, he abducted, raped, and killed a 12-year-old girl.

No fingerprints were found at the crime scene. The attacker had taken his weapon with him so that item of evidence was also missing from the crime scene collection. Authorities had a blood type, a few print smudges, and sperm samples, but all proved inconclusive. DNA was not yet available. However, a particular piece of evidence became a centerpiece during the trial: an odd bite mark on the left buttock of Lisa Levy. One officer laid a yellow ruler against the patterned abrasion and then stepped back for the photographers. His presence of mind might have made all the difference between conviction and acquittal for Bundy because the tissue specimens were lost by the time of the trial, destroyed in all the analyses. However, the application of forensic photography had memorialized the physical evidence of the bite mark that was to become the world's most famous patterned injury and the crucial evidence needed to convict Ted Bundy.

The forensic nurse examiner does not need to be a professional photographer. However, the nurse must possess basic knowledge and skills of forensic photography to ensure that the resultant images are high quality and can withstand the legal scrutiny for courtroom admissibility. The nurse must be prepared to answer technical questions regarding photodocumentation procedures, maintenance of chain of custody, and authenticity of the images used.

Resources

BOOKS AND ARTICLES

Automated Bounce Flash. (2009). http://forums.dpreview.com/forums/read.asp? forum=1007& message=32424303

Cheng, E. H. (1999). Near Infrared digital photography: A tutorial. http://www.echeng.com/photo/infrared/tutorial Accessed March 13, 2009.

Girardin, B., Faugno, D., Seneski, P., et al. (1997). *Color atlas of sexual assault*. St. Louis: Mosby.

Klingle, C., & Reiter, K. (2008). Ultraviolet and infrared injury photography. *Evidence Technology Magazine*, (September-October).

Krauss, T. (1993). Forensic evidence documentation using reflective ultraviolet photography. *Photo Electronic Imaging*, (February). 7–23.

Miller, L. (1993). *Sansone's police photography* (3rd ed.). Cincinnati: Anderson.

Nice, K., Wilson, T., & Gurevich, G. (2009). *How digital cameras work*. http://www.howstuffworks.com/digital-camera.htm. Accessed February 26, 2009.

Otoupalik, S. (1999). Bringing the crash scene into the emergency department. *Journal of Emergency Nursing: JEN*, 25(5), 388–391.

Pasqualone, G. (1996). Forensic RNs as photographers: Documentation in the ED. *Journal of Psychosocial Nursing and Mental Health Services*, 34(10), 47–51.

Redsicker, D. (1991). *The practical methodology of forensic photography*. New York: Elsevier.

Ricci, L. R. (1994). *Draft guidelines for photographic documentation of child abuse*. Chicago: American Professional Society on the Abuse of Children.

Storrow, A. B., Stack, L. B., & Peterson, P. (1994). An approach to emergency department photography. *Academic Emergency Medicine*, 1(5), 454–462.

Warlen, S. C. (1995). Crime scene photography: The silent witness. *J Forensic Ident*, 45(3), 261–265.

Weiss, S. L. (2008). Forensic photography for SANE and SART practitioners. *Evidence Technology Magazine*, (July-August), 26–29.

Weiss, S. (2009). *Digital low-light photography*. Evidence Technology Magazine, 7(5), 24–27.

References

Davies, A., & Fennessy, P. (1999). *Digital imaging for photographers*. Oxford, England: Focal Press.

Eastman Kodak Company. (2000). Press release: Authentication software for Kodak DC5000 and DC280 digital cameras provide alert when images are manipulated or tampered with.

Eastman Kodak Company. (2009). FIPS 140-2 Security Policy for Eastman Kodak Company® Secure Module 3000, version 0.14. http://csrc.nist.gov/groups/stm/cmvp/documents/140-1/140sp/140sp1226.pdf Accessed September 27, 2009.

Fyffe, J. E. (undated). *Practical crime scene photography. Reference manual.* Public Agency Training Council. Indianapolis, IN.

Krauss, T., & Warlen, S. (1985). The forensic use of reflective ultraviolet photography. *Journal of Forensic Science, 30(1)*, 262–268.

Megapixel.net. (2009). Retrieved April 6, www.megapixel.net/html/articles/articles-gfx3/viewfinders-parallax.gif

Moenssens, A., Starrs, J., Henderson, C., et al. (1995). *Scientific evidence in civil and criminal cases* (4th ed.). New York: The Foundation Press.

Page, D. (2006/2007). www.forensicmag.com/articles.asp?pid=120 Accessed February 26, 2009.

Price, B. (1999). Forensic colposcopy: Getting the most from your equipment. Colposcopy photograph hints. In Proceedings of the International Association of Forensic Nurses, Seventh Annual Scientific Assembly. Scottsdale, AZ.

Sontag, S. (1977). *On photography.* New York: Anchor Doubleday.

Staggs, S. (2001). The admissibility of digital photographs in court. Retrieved from www.crime-scene-investigator.net/admissibilityofdigital.html

State of Washington v. Eric H. Hayden. 90 Wash. App. 100, 950 P.2d 1024. Accessed February 15, 2009.

Teixeira, W. R. (1981). Hymenal colposcopic examination in sexual offenses. *The American Journal of Forensic Medicine and Pathology, 2(3)*, 209–214.

Woodling, B. A., & Heger, A. (1986). The use of the colposcope in the diagnosis of sexual abuse in the pediatric age-group. *Child Abuse Neglect, 10(1)*, 111–114.

CHAPTER 8 Behavioral Analysis

Mark E. Safarik and Robert K. Ressler

Since the 1970s, investigative profilers at the Federal Bureau of Investigation's National Center for the Analysis of Violent Crime have been assisting local, state, and federal agencies in narrowing the focus of an investigation's hunt for the offender by conducting behavioral analyses of all types of violent crimes. Criminal investigative analysis, or criminal profiling as it is popularly known, is a tool that is commonly employed by law enforcement in the investigation of unusual, bizarre, and exceptionally violent crimes (O'Toole, 1999). The types of crimes that lend themselves to this type of analysis include various types of homicide (sexual, serial, and mass murder), serial sexual assault, kidnapping, and extortions. Criminal investigative analysis does not provide the specific identity of the offender. Rather, it focuses on individual level case data, attempts to identify patterns and trends in connected cases, examines the behavior exhibited within each crime scene, and facilitates the identification of the kind of person most likely to have committed a crime by focusing on the major behavioral and personality characteristics of the offender. The criminal investigative analysis process seeks to assist law enforcement's efforts to narrow the focus of violent crime investigations by generating leads relative to the type of person who may have committed the crime.

Criminal Investigative Analysis from Crime Scene Analysis

Criminal profilers and the process of criminal investigative analysis have often been portrayed in sensational manner in the media through such feature films as *Silence of the Lambs*, *Taking Lives*, and *Red Dragon* and the popular current television series *Criminal Minds* and *CSI*. The ability to focus the direction of a criminal investigation, especially one that involves a cold homicide, by describing attributes of the offender is a skill of the expert investigative profiler. Violent crime scenes always tell a story—a story written by the offender, the victim, and the unique circumstances of their interaction. During the crime, the offender acts a certain way as a result of many factors including personality, motivation, criminal sophistication, the influence of drugs or alcohol, and attributes unique to that particular crime including the victim's response. Correctly interpreting the complex dynamics inferred from crime scene behaviors, along with information obtained from the analysis of available forensic evidence, can reveal critical information about how and why the crime occurred (O'Toole, 2006). Special agent profilers in the Behavioral Analysis Unit at the Federal Bureau of Investigation (FBI) Academy have demonstrated expertise in crime and crime scene analysis of a wide array of violent crimes, particularly those involving serial and sexual homicide, mass murder, and serial sexual assault, as well as particularly compelling cases of single or multiple homicides not involving serial killers.

Although commonly associated with unusual homicides and aberrant sex crimes, the methodology used to analyze and interpret behavior has been applied in other types of crimes, such as hostage taking (Reiser, 1982). Law enforcement officers need to learn as much as possible about the hostage taker in order to protect the hostages. In such cases, police are aided by limited verbal contact with the offender and possibly by access to the offender's family and friends. The police must be able to assess the hostage takers in terms of what courses of action they are likely to take and what their reactions to various stimuli might be.

The assessment of terrorists, their culture, religious motivation, and ideology have become a focus of research (Wilson, 2000), especially in light of the attacks on U.S. soil on September 11, 2001. The FBI's Behavioral Analysis Unit added an additional assessment unit in 2002 to specifically address threat assessment and terrorism both nationally and abroad.

Profiling has also been used to identify anonymous letter writers (Casey-Owens, 1984) and persons who make written or spoken threats of violence. In cases of the latter, psycholinguistic techniques have been used to compose a threat dictionary, whereby every word in a message is assigned, by computer, to a specific category. Words used in the threat message are then compared with those used in ordinary speech or writings. The vocabulary usage in the message may yield signature words unique to the offender. In this way, police may be able not only to determine that several letters were written by the same individual, but also to learn about the offender's background and psychological state (Smith & Shuy, 2002).

Bombers and arsonists also lend themselves to profiling. A detailed study was conducted by the FBI's National Center for the Analysis of Violent Crime (Sapp, Huff, Kelm, & Tunkel, 2001) to study causal factors, personality, demographic, and behavioral attributes of bombers. Common characteristics of arsonists have been derived from an analysis of the uniform crime reports. Rapist behavior with victims ranging from young children to the elderly has been carefully studied over the years. Utilizing a careful and detailed interview of the rape victim about the rapist's behavior, law enforcement personnel examine the verbal, physical, and sexual behavior exhibited by the offender during the commission of the crime as well as both pre- and post-offense behavior to build a profile of the offender (Hazelwood & Burgess, 2008). The rationale is that behavior reflects personality, and by examining behavior the investigator may be able to determine what type of person is responsible for the offense. Knowledge of these various crime scene and behavioral attributes can aid the investigator in identifying offender typologies that describe the personality, behavioral, and demographic characteristics of potential suspects. This information can be used to narrow the pool of available suspects and allow for a more focused approach in developing strategies for interviewing these suspects. Studies of the behavioral and forensic dynamics of particular types of crimes have by design focused on particular subgroups of offenders such as those who sexually assault children (Campbell & DeNevi, 2004; Holmes &

Holmes, 2002; Lanning, 2001; Myers, 2002) or the elderly (Burgess, Commons, Safarik, Looper, & Ross, 2007; Safarik, Jarvis, & Nussbaum, 2002). The advances in the forensic evaluation of crime scenes using DNA, fingerprints, and trace evidence as well as research in psychopathy and the behavioral sciences have opened new avenues in cold case investigation.

KEY POINT Criminal investigative analysis does not provide the specific identity of the offender. Rather, it indicates the kind of person most likely to have committed a crime by focusing on analyzing and interpreting crime scene variables and dynamic crime scene interactions to reveal behavioral, personality, and demographic characteristics of the offender(s).

CRIMINAL INVESTIGATIVE ANALYSIS IN SERIAL SEXUAL HOMICIDES

Criminal investigative analysis has been found to be of particular usefulness in investigating the crime of serial sexual homicide. These crimes create a great deal of fear because of their apparently random and motiveless nature, and they are also given significant publicity. Consequently, law enforcement personnel are under great public pressure to apprehend the perpetrator as quickly as possible. At the same time, these crimes may be the most difficult to solve precisely because of their apparent randomness and the observation that no known relationship existed between the victim and the offender before the crime. There has been a considerable upswing in these types of murders. In the 1990s, the rate of serial sexual homicide climbed to an almost epidemic proportion. Estimates of these types of criminals indicate that from 8 to 40 individuals are at large roaming the United States, according to U.S. Department of Justice officials. Some of the more notorious cases have had victims numbering from 48 in the case of Gary Ridgeway, the Green River Killer, to as many as 165 as claimed by Henry Lee Lucas in Texas and his co-conspirator traveling companion Ottis Elwood Toole in Florida. (Author's personal communications with Henry Lee Lucas at Williamson County, Texas, jail and Ottis Elwood Toole, Jacksonville, Florida [c. 1983]).

Offender Motivation

Some of the earliest attempts to capture the types of motives seen in homicides are noted in Boudouris' (1974) study and Lashley's (1929) description of the Chicago Homicide data set. When researchers spoke of motive, they were described as strongly related to the offender-victim relationship. Victim-offender relationships were categorized generally as domestic, friends and acquaintances, business, criminal transactions, noncriminal, and unknown, along with several others. In Lashley's analysis the two categories that dominated the relationship spectrum were gang and criminal related and altercations and fights. Domestic homicides were noted to be infrequent. The conventional designations of motive recognized today were simply not described as such in the early twentieth century research.

In the early 1980s, the FBI's Behavioral Science Unit attempted to develop a motivational model for the classification of homicide. Early work by Hazelwood and Douglas (1980) delineated two categories, the organized nonsocial and the disorganized asocial, to assist in describing offenders who engaged in lust murder. These categories were not meant to explain all sexual homicides or serial homicides but in the ensuing decades have been assimilated into the law enforcement lexicon, representative or not, as an assessment

tool used to categorize all types of homicides, not just lust murders. This work led Ressler, Burgess, and Douglas (1988) to further refine the design for a classification system for serial sexual murder based on crime scene characteristics. This work culminated with the publication of the *Crime Classification Manual* (CCM), now in its second edition. FBI agents in the Investigative Support Unit (the predecessor to the current Behavioral Analysis Unit) and Behavioral Sciences Unit collaborated with numerous law enforcement entities in the development of this classification system using the American Psychiatric Association's *Diagnostic and Statistical Manual* (DSM) as a model. Homicide classification was structured by motive, and as such, four major categories were identified: criminal enterprise homicide, personal cause homicide, sexual homicide, and group cause homicide. Each major category had a number of subcategories, further specifying motive based on crime scene and forensic findings, victim characteristics, and investigative considerations.

Schlesinger (2004) presents a motivational model for understanding sexual homicide based on an analysis of the motivational dynamics of the antisocial act of the homicide itself describing external (sociogenic) factors that stimulate homicide at one end and internal (psychogenic) factors at the other extreme. Other dimensional motivational models have surfaced that look at, among other attributes, instrumental versus expressive violence and impulsive versus ritualistic behavior. These models, although useful, are dimensional in understanding a single aspect of the crime. Interpreting human behavior, especially from a criminal perspective, is a complex and multifaceted endeavor. When criminal behavior is described as homicide and more specifically serial homicide, interpreting the offender's motive based on crime scene behavior has been found to be difficult at best.

Homicides may be interpreted as sexual homicides when sexual activity is observed. The observed sexual activity however, may be the external expression in service of the nonsexual needs of the offender and thus may be misinterpreted (Myers, Husted, Safarik, & O'Toole, 2006). Conversely, many sexual homicides do not have an overtly sexual component to them. When considering homicides without a distinct sexual component, can the method used by the offender to kill the victim, attributes of the crime scene, or characteristics of the victim be used to establish a motive? These same descriptors are more often used when the appropriate classification for the type of homicide is being assigned.

The usefulness of the identification of motive may depend on whether the approach is from the perspective of academic research or an operational interest for case solution. Law enforcement's interest would focus on the usefulness of assessing motive as related to narrowing down a potential pool of suspects or providing investigative direction. Law enforcement investigators are in general agreement on several aspects related to the offender's motive in a serial murder investigation:

- Motive is very difficult to discern and too abstract a concept to definitively identify when examining a violent crime scene.
- Directing investigative effort to discern the motive may cause the investigation to become derailed.
- Analyzing offender behavior and forensic evidence at the crime scene is more useful for determining both what an offender did and why.
- Motive is elusive and may not be helpful even when it can be reasonably determined.
- Complicating attempts to discern the motive in a crime is the fact that there can be more than one motive and they can be reprioritized by the offender, rising and falling in importance as the crime proceeds.

- An offender's motives can evolve both within a particular crime as well as over a series of crimes creating problems during the early stages of an investigation.
- As stated earlier, there can be multiple motives, some of which may be easier to observe in the crime scene behavior than others.
- When considering the level of violence noted in most serial homicides, it may be tempting to differentiate the offender's motives based on the level of injury. However, the motives in serial homicides do not appear as separate and distinct from other violent as well as nonviolent crimes.
- The offender's goal in the crime should not be construed to be synonymous with his motivation.
- External constraints not controlled by the offender can further obfuscate the offender's intended motive.

Collectively, assessing crime scene behavior, the context within which it appears, the temporal and chronological components, and the forensic evaluation of evidence is the key to successfully inferring the motivation(s) of the offender. An offender's affect is often interpreted as the motivation (e.g., anger motivated) when in fact the affect can appear as a subtext for any number of different motivations (Myers et al., 2006). This is a particularly important distinction to make when assessing sexual homicide cases because excessive injury is often misinterpreted as anger related and thus suggestive of a relationship. Although it is not completely accurate to say that these crimes are motiveless, all too often only the perpetrator understands the motive(s), and it is thus unknown to the investigating officers. Lunde (1976) demonstrated this issue in terms of the victims chosen by a particular offender. Although the serial murderer may not know the victims, their selection is rarely random. Rather, it is based on the murderer's perception of certain characteristics of those victims that are of symbolic significance to the perpetrator. An analysis of the similarities and differences among victims of a particular serial murderer may provide important investigative information concerning the "motive" in an apparently motiveless crime. This, in turn, may yield information about the perpetrator. For example, the murder may be the result of a sadistic fantasy or displaced anger in the mind of the murderer and a particular victim may be targeted because of a symbolic aspect of the fantasy (Douglas, Ressler, Burgess, & Hartman, 1986; Safarik, et al., 2002).

In such cases, the investigating officer faces a completely different situation from a case in which a murder occurs as the result of jealousy, domestic violence, or during the commission of another felony (e.g., robbery). In those cases, a readily identifiable motive may provide vital clues about the identity of a perpetrator. In the case of the apparently motiveless crime, the investigative profilers must look to other methods, as well as to conventional investigative techniques, in their effort to identify the perpetrator. In this context, criminal investigative analysis has been productive, particularly in those crimes where the offender has engaged in repeated patterns of behavior at the crime scenes.

Assessment of Murderers

Traditionally, two very different disciplines have used the technique of assessing murderers. The first involves mental health professionals who seek to explain the personality and actions of a criminal through a psychiatric evaluation and diagnosis. This is accomplished through a process often consisting of an interview, testing, and onsite evaluation of the individual in question. The mental health professional usually is in a position to examine the offender and through this examination seeks to explain the offender's behavior. The second discipline involves law enforcement agents who seek to determine the personality, behavioral, and demographic characteristics of the offender through the analysis and interpretation of the behavioral dynamics and forensic examination of evidence left at the crime scene. The behavioral analyst who does not have the offender but only the crime scene behavior works contrary to the mental health professional. Forensic pathologists and law enforcement professionals are utilizing forensic nurse examiners (FNEs) and sexual assault nurse examiners (SANEs) who work with victims and perpetrators of sexual assault to provide rape-homicide examinations in many jurisdictions across the United States. Because FNEs also work with homicide detectives during an investigation and are often requested to accompany law enforcement officers to the scene, it is important for this group of professionals to be knowledgeable of the actions and behaviors of those offenders who engage in a sexual assault of their victims and any evidence that may be useful in assessing and interpreting their criminal behavior.

Psychological Profiling to Criminal Investigative Analysis

As the violent homicide crime rate remains at high levels and criminals become increasingly sophisticated with their crimes, so must the investigative tools of law enforcement be sharpened. One tool that has been providing assistance to law enforcement since the 1970s is criminal investigative analysis. The FBI, and specifically the Behavioral Sciences Unit (BSU) in an effort to assist local police in finding the perpetrator of a homicide, first used the procedure in 1971 when it was known as *psychological profiling*. Though the profiling was done on an informal basis in connection with classroom instruction, the analysis proved to be accurate and the offender was apprehended. In the following years, profiles were informally prepared on a number of cases with a reasonable degree of success, and as a result, requests for the procedure by local authorities increased steadily. Detectives with cases that were unusual, exceptionally violent, or evidenced a significant amount of psychopathology increasingly sought help from agents in the BSU.

In the early 1990s, the operational component of the BSU that was responsible for the "criminal profiling" and traveling on various murder or rape cases was taken out of the BSU and placed in the FBI's Critical Incident Response Group and called the Behavioral Analysis Unit (BAU). Subsequent to the incident at Waco, Texas, the FBI placed all operational components needed during a crisis under one umbrella division. The BSU is still part of the training division but does not engage in operational behavioral crime analysis.

As increasing numbers of cases were sent in for assessment, several of the BSU criminal profilers (Ressler, Hazelwood, & Douglas) began the initial efforts to understand the dynamics of serial murder and sexual homicide and the offenders who perpetrated them. Initially referred to as psychological profiling, it was defined as the process of identifying the gross psychological characteristics of an individual based on an analysis of the crimes he or she committed and providing a general description of the person using those traits. The process normally involved five steps: (1) a comprehensive study of the nature of the criminal act and the type of persons who have committed these offenses, (2) a thorough inspection of the specific crime scene involved in the case, (3) an in-depth examination of the background and activities of the victim(s) and any known suspects, (4) a formulation of the probable motivating factors of all parties involved, and (5) the development of a description of the perpetrator based on the overt characteristics associated with his or her probable psychological makeup.

It is not known who first used this particular process to identify criminals; however, the general technique was used in the 1870s by Dr. Hans Gross, an examining judge in the Upper Styria Region of Austria and, according to some, the first practical criminologist. More recently, Dr. James Brussel, a New York psychiatrist, who provided valuable information in such famous cases as the Mad Bomber and Boston Strangler, popularized a similar approach to criminal investigation. In 1957, the identity of George Metesky, the arsonist in New York City's Mad Bomber case (which spanned 16 years), was aided by psychiatrist-criminologist James Brussel's staccato-style profile: "Look for a heavy man, middle-aged, foreign born, Roman Catholic, single, lives with a brother or sister; when you find him, chances are he'll be wearing a double-breasted suit, buttoned." Indeed, the portrait was extraordinary in that the only variation was that Metesky lived with two single sisters. Brussel, in discussion about the psychiatrist acting as Sherlock Holmes, explained that a psychiatrist usually studies a person and makes some reasonable predictions about how that person may react to a specific situation and about what he or she may do in the future. Profiling, according to Brussel, reverses this process. By studying an individual's deeds, one deduces what kind of person the individual might be (Brussel, 1968).

The idea of constructing a verbal picture of a murderer using psychological terms is not new. In 1960, Palmer published results of a three-year study of 51 murderers who were serving sentences in New England. Palmer's "typical murderer" was 23 years old when he committed murder. Using a gun, this typical killer murdered a male stranger during an argument. He came from a low social class and achieved little in terms of education or occupation. He had a well-meaning but maladjusted mother, and he experienced physical abuse and psychological frustration during his childhood.

Similarly, Rizzo (1981) studied 31 accused murderers during the course of routine referrals for psychiatric examination at a court clinic. His profile of the average murderer listed the offender as a 26-year-old male who most likely knew his victim, with monetary gain the most probable motivation for the crime.

Psychological profiling, a term not currently in use, has given way to the terminology and process of criminal investigative analysis. Techniques used by law enforcement today seek to describe a murderer in terms that provide identifiable characteristics, which are then incorporated into an investigative framework. Investigative behavioral analysts, often referred to by the public and media as profilers, gather their information from the crime scene in order to analyze what it may reveal about the type of person who committed the crime. The criminal investigative analysis process, contrary to the belief by many law enforcement investigators and its portrayal in the media as a method of actually identifying a specific perpetrator, serves to focus a law enforcement investigation's effort to narrow down the pool of potential offenders by identifying certain personality, behavioral, and demographic characteristics of the type of offender who could be responsible for a particular violent homicide or sexual assault. The term *profiling* has many negative connotations, most notably associated with racial and drug profiling. The type of analysis conducted in the behavioral assessment of serial murder and sexual homicide focuses on individual-level case data, attempts to identify patterns and trends in connected cases, examines the behavior exhibited within each crime scene, and facilitates the identification of the major personality and behavioral characteristics of the offender (Douglas,

Burgess, Burgess, & Ressler, 2006). It is because of the case-specific nature of the assessment that it is problematic to engage in gross generalizations about a particular homicide without having intimate knowledge of the details of that crime.

Law enforcement has had a number of outstanding investigators; however, the skills, knowledge, and thought processes of these investigators have rarely been captured in the professional literature. These people were truly the experts of the law enforcement field, and their skills have been so admired that many fictional characters (Wilkie Collins, Sherlock Holmes, Hercule Poirot, Mike Hammer, and Charlie Chan) have been modeled on these experts. Although Lunde (1976) believes that the murders of fiction bear no resemblance to the murders of reality, a connection between fictional detective techniques and modern criminal profiling methods may indeed exist. For example, it is attention to detail that is the hallmark of famous fictional detectives; the smallest item at a crime scene does not escape their attention. This trait is seen in Sergeant Cuff, a character in Wilkie Collins' *The Moonstone*, widely acknowledged as the first full-length detective study. At one end of the inquiry there was a murder, and at the other end there was a spot of ink on a tablecloth that nobody could account for. "In all my experience … I have never met with such a thing as a trifle yet."

However, unlike detective fiction, real cases are not solved by one tiny clue but the analysis of all clue and crime patterns. In fact, one of the fundamental tenants of crime scene analysis is to evaluate variables that explain why this person became the victim of homicide. While conducting an analysis of the behavior that is manifested at violent crime scenes, it is important to avoid becoming too focused on any one aspect of the crime scene and ascribing singular importance to it. The effort is not focused on reconstructing the exact detailed sequence of events. Such an attempt is impractical because of the innumerable possible interactions that could occur between the victim and offender. It is the totality of the circumstances rather than a single crime scene variable that is important in assessing not only what happened but why and how it happened. The most accurate way of assessing the overall victim-offender interaction is to consider the occurrence of various behavioral attributes in conjunction with one another. It is not only important to analyze the crime with respect to what is seen behaviorally but to integrate that analysis with what is factually known through investigative interviews and forensic evaluation of the evidence. Ultimately, assessing the motivation for the murder and placing the variables of the murder into context is paramount to establishing a framework for understanding the dynamics of this crime.

Criminal profiling has been described as a collection of leads; as an educated attempt to provide specific information about a certain type of suspect (Geberth, 2006); and as a biographical sketch of behavior patterns, trends, and tendencies (Vorpagel, 1998). Geberth (2006) has also described the profiling process as particularly useful when the criminal has demonstrated some form of psychopathology. The task of an investigative profiler in developing a criminal profile is similar to the process used by forensic clinicians to make a diagnosis and treatment plan: data are collected and assessed, the situation is reconstructed, hypotheses are formulated, a behavioral assessment is developed and tested, and the results are reported. In many aspects, this method represents the nursing process applied by forensic nurses in their role as associates to forensic pathologists and law enforcement agencies in the investigation of trauma and death. The original behavioral analysts learned profiling through brainstorming, intuition, and educated guesswork. Their expertise was the result of years of accumulated wisdom, extensive experience in the field, and familiarity with a large number of cases. As the discipline came under greater scrutiny both from a research standpoint as well as by the courts, behavioral profilers drew on their vast experience in working literally thousands of these case on their own and in group consultations (the experiential component). These analysts regularly attend postgraduate training courses in forensic pathology, psychopathy, and forensic bloodstain analysis, among many others. As the discipline has grown, so has the base of empirically based research. Analysts of the FBI's Behavioral Analysis Unit have conducted research in such diverse areas as school shootings (O'Toole, 2006), sexual assault and homicide of the elderly (Safarik, et al., 2002, 2005), and the behavioral characteristics of bombers (Sapp, et al., 2001).

An investigative profiler brings to the crime scene the ability to make hypothetical formulations based on his or her previous experience. A formulation is defined here as a concept that organizes, explains, or makes investigative sense out of information and that influences profile hypotheses. These formulations are based on clusters of information emerging from the crime scene information, victimology, and from the investigator's experience in understanding criminal actions. A basic premise of criminal profiling is that the way a person thinks (e.g., his or her patterns of thinking) and his or her personality direct that individual's personal behavior.

BEST PRACTICE Forensic investigators should gather detailed information from the crime scene to assist criminal investigative analysts in determining the type of person who committed the crime. These investigators must be as mindful of the behavioral evidence as of the forensic evidence they collect.

Generating a Criminal Profile

Investigative profilers at the FBI's BAU, National Center for the Analysis of Violent Crimes (NCAVC), have been analyzing crime scenes and generating criminal profiles since the 1970s. Their description of the construction of profiles represents the offsite procedure as it is conducted at the NCAVC, as contrasted with onsite procedure (Douglas, et al., 1986). The criminal profile–generating process is described as five stages with the sixth, the outcome, being the apprehension of a suspect (Fig. 8-1).

The criminal profile-generating process has produced hundreds of profiles. A series of overlapping steps leads to the final goal of apprehension. These steps include:
1. Profiling inputs
2. Decision-process models
3. Crime assessment
4. Criminal profile

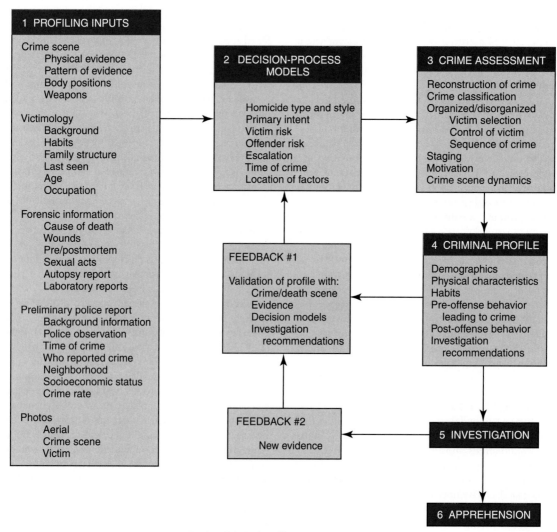

Fig. 8-1 Criminal profile-generating process.

5. Investigation
6. Apprehension

There are two key feedback filters: (1) achieving congruence with the evidence, decision models, and investigation recommendations and (2) adding new evidence.

PROFILING INPUTS

The profiling input stage begins the criminal profile–generating process. Information recorded by local law enforcement officers at the site or location of the crime is gathered and detailed. A thorough inspection of the specific crime scene yields information about physical evidence, patterns of evidence, body positions, number of scenes, weapons, their use and disposition, and other pertinent information.

The focus then moves to factors pertaining to the victim. An in-depth examination of the background and activities of the victim(s) provides information on the victim's background, habits, family structure, and occupation, as well as when the victim was last seen. The cumulative information about the victim, referred to as victimology, is a crucial component to any crime analysis but more so for those homicides that appear motiveless. A decision is made about whether or not the victim was of low or high risk or if his or her risk level had been situationally changed. If low risk is the determination, questions about why the subject targeted the victim are formulated. More information on determining risk is discussed later in the chapter.

Forensic information is compiled about cause and type of death, antemortem and postmortem wounds, and sexual acts committed with the victim. Laboratory and autopsy reports provide a clear picture of the nature and severity of the injuries, which allows the investigator to determine the degree (or lack) of control the offender exhibited over the victim during the crime. For example, stabbings randomly made to the body (as contrasted with stabbings in one part of the body) and identifying defensive wounds may suggest the offender had difficulty controlling the victim. Preliminary police reports and investigative documents that include background information, police observations, time of crime, who reported the crime, socioeconomic status and crime rate of the neighborhood, and photos (aerial, crime scene, and victim [at scene and autopsy]) are sent for evaluation. The personal observations of the officers called to that scene as well as the circumstances under which they were called are all important. These reports do not include suspect information from local law enforcement.

BEST PRACTICE The forensic nurse examiner should use written and photo-documentation to precisely preserve details about the dynamic interaction between the homicide offender, victim, and the scene including the victim's injuries, movement within the scene, sexual acts, and postmortem activity, because such information is essential in order to conduct a behavioral assessment.

DECISION-PROCESS MODELS

The decision process begins the organizing and arranging of the inputs into meaningful patterns. Key decision points, or models, differentiate and organize the information from step 1 and form an underlying decisional structure for profiling.

Homicide: Type and Style

As noted in Table 8-1, type and style classify homicides. A single homicide is one victim, one homicidal event; a double homicide is two victims, one event and in one location; and a triple homicide has three victims in one location during one event. Anything beyond three victims is classified as a mass murder—that is, four or more victims killed during the same incident and usually in one location with no distinctive time element between the murders.

Classic Mass Murderer

There are two types of mass murderers: classic and family. A classic mass murderer involves one person operating in one location at one period of time. That period of time could be minutes or hours and might even be days. Classic mass murderers are usually described as mentally disordered individuals whose problems have increased to the point that they act against groups of people unrelated to these problems. The murderer unleashes this hostility through shootings or stabbings. One classic mass murderer was Charles Whitman, a man who armed himself with boxes of ammunition, weapons, ropes, a radio, and food; barricaded himself in a rooftop tower in Austin, Texas; and opened fire for 90 minutes, killing 16 people and wounding more than 30 others. He was stopped only when he was killed on the roof. James Huberty was another classic mass murderer. With a machine gun, he entered a fast-food restaurant and killed and wounded many people. Responding police also killed him at the site. Pennsylvania mass murderess Sylvia Seegrist (nicknamed Ms. Rambo for her military style clothing) was sentenced to life imprisonment for opening fire with a rifle aimed at shoppers in a mall in October 1985, killing three persons and wounding seven. On April 20, 1999, in a Littleton, Colorado, high school, anger had been building in students Eric Harris and Dylan Klebold. On the 110th anniversary of Adolf Hitler's birth, they swept through their high school corridors in a rampage before committing suicide, leaving 13 dead, 25 injured, and a community in shock. Some mass murderers remain at the scene of the killings and rather than surrendering, engage in behavior that forces the police to kill them in a phenomenon known as "suicide by cop."

Family Member Mass Murderer

A second type of mass murderer is one who kills several family members (family annihilators). If more than three family members are killed and the perpetrator commits suicide, it is classified as a mass murder/suicide. On Christmas Eve 2008, Bruce

Table 8-1 Homicide Classification by Style and Type						
STYLE	SINGLE	DOUBLE	TRIPLE	MASS	SPREE*	SERIAL†
Number of victims	1	2	3	4+	2+	3+ (2+)
Number of events	1	1	1	1	1	3+ (2+)
Number of locations	1	1	1	1	2+	3+ (2+)
Cooling-off period (separate events)	Yes	Yes	Yes	Yes	No	Yes

*Recommendations from the 2005 International Serial Murder Symposium (Morton & Hilts, 2008) advocated that the spree murder classification be discontinued and subsumed into serial murder.

†Numbers in parentheses represent recommendations from the 2005 International Serial Murder Symposium (Morton & Hilts, 2008).

Jeffrey Pardo, went to the home of his ex-wife's relatives where his ex-wife and her family were having a Christmas Eve party. Pardo had come dressed in a Santa suit. Pardo methodically killed his ex-wife, her parents, and five other relatives before setting the house on fire. He then drove to his brother's unoccupied home where he killed himself.

Without the suicide and with four or more victims, the murder is called a family killing. One example involves Vincent Brothers from Bakersfield, California, who shot and killed his wife, mother-in-law, and three young children in 2003. He also stabbed his wife postmortem. He staged the crime to make it appear that they had been killed during a botched break-in robbery. Brothers rented a car in Ohio and drove nonstop to Bakersfield, committed the homicides, and then drove back in order to give himself an alibi that he had been out of state at the time of the murders and therefore could not be responsible. Brothers had been the vice principal of an elementary school in Bakersfield. He was convicted and eventually sentenced to death.

John List, an accountant and employed as an insurance salesman, killed his entire family. In a front room, the bodies of List's wife and three children (ages 16, 15, and 13) were discovered lying side by side and facing up. Each was meticulously covered with a white sheet, and their arms were folded across their bodies. Each had been shot once behind the left ear, except for one son who had been shot 16 times. A further search of the residence revealed the body of List's mother, also shot once behind the left ear. Furthermore, she also had been neatly laid out and covered with a white sheet. Eighteen years after the murder of his family, New Jersey law enforcement approached *America's Most Wanted* to air the case in hopes that List could be identified. Forensic artist Frank Bender created and age-progressed a clay bust that, despite the fact that he had been missing for 18 years, looked remarkably similar to List. Following the airing of the episode, List was identified and subsequently arrested in Richmond, Virginia.

Spree and Serial Murderers

Two additional types of multiple murderers are spree and serial murderers. A spree murder has killings at two or more locations and no emotional cooling-off period. During the 1940s, New Jersey spree murderer Howard Unruh took a loaded German Luger with ammunition and randomly fired his handgun at people, while walking through his neighborhood. Many people were killed. This is not classified as a mass murder because the killer moved to different locations. In 2007 at the Virginia Tech campus in Blacksburg, Virginia, Seung-Hui Cho, using two pistols, killed 32 people in two separate events and then killed himself in the course of about three hours. While technically this is considered a spree killing because of the different locations, most law enforcement professionals would describe it as a mass murder, arguing that the campus was for all intents and purposes a single location and the three hour time frame a single event.

In 2005, the FBI's Behavioral Analysis Unit hosted the first international serial murder symposium in San Antonio, Texas. One hundred thirty-five of the world's experts on serial murder were invited to participate in the five-day event. The validity of spree murder as a separate category was a central topic of discussion (Morton & Hilts, 2008). Many of the attendees had a problem with the current definition of spree murder for which one of the requirements is no cooling-off period between the murders. The lack of a cooling-off period is what differentiates it from a serial murder. There was concern over the definitional problems relating to the concept of a cooling-off period, which creates arbitrary guidelines and is not well defined. Conference attendees advocated the discontinued uses of spree murder as a separate and distinct category. Categorizing a group of homicides as a spree does not provide any operational benefit to law enforcement and for practical purposes would be captured within the parameters of serial murder.

Since the late 1970s, law enforcement, academia, and researchers, among others, have used multiple definitions of serial murder. Although these definitions share common themes, they differ on specific requirements, such as the number of murders involved, the types of motivation, and temporal aspects (Morton & Hilts, 2008). Attendees at the 2005 International Serial Murder Symposium examined these criteria in order to develop a single definition. Depending on the definition being used, the number of victims required ranged from 2 to 10 or more. Most definitions also require a time period between the murders, which, as noted earlier, is commonly referred to as a cooling-off period or a period of emotional downtime.

In 1998, the U.S. Congress passed a federal law titled the Protection of Children from Sexual Predator Act of 1998 (Title 18, U.S. Code, Chapter 51, and Section 1111). This law includes a definition of serial murder that has been universally accepted as the de facto definition and is defined as a series of three or more killings that have common characteristics to suggest the reasonable possibility that the crimes were committed by the same person or persons. This law, however, was not enacted to define serial murder but to set forth criteria establishing when the FBI could assist local law enforcement agencies. During the serial murder symposium, the consensus was to create a simple but broad definition to be used primarily for law enforcement. Researchers wanted the definition of serial murder to have a specific number of murders to facilitate meeting research criteria. From a law enforcement perspective, it was felt that a lower number would allow important resources to be allocated at an earlier point in the investigation. The motivation for committing the murder was also considered as a criterion. Traditionally, serial murder has been considered to be motivated by an emotional or psychological need; and serial murderers were therefore considered different from those who murdered in the course of a criminal enterprise such as contract killers or gang and mob enforcers who are motivated by money or allegiance to a group. The definition of serial murder offered by the symposium attendees is "the unlawful killing of two or more victims by the same offender(s), in separate events" (Morton et al., 2008). The time period between murders is what distinguishes a mass murder from a serial murder. The definition by design has been left broadly described. In serial murder, the killer usually premeditates homicide. The murderer plans and fantasizes, and when the time is right and a period of time has elapsed from the first homicide, the next victim is selected. This time period can be days, weeks, or months.

The mass murderer and the spree murderer are not concerned with who their victims are; they will kill anyone who comes in contact with them. In contrast, a serial murderer selects victims. These murderers think they will never be caught, that they are smarter than the police who hunt them. Serial murderers control the events. They chose the victim, the place, the time, the manner of killing, and oftentimes the disposition of the victim's body, whereas in a spree murder, the events control the killer. The spree murderer can barely control what will happen next. The serial killer is planning, picking, and choosing, and sometimes stopping the act of murder.

A serial murderer may commit spree homicides. In 1984, Christopher Wilder, an Australian racecar driver, went on a murder spree, starting in Florida and traveling across the United States for a period of several months. Wilder would target victims at shopping malls or would abduct them after meeting them in a beauty contest setting or through dating service. While a fugitive as a serial murderer, Wilder was investigated, identified, and tracked by the FBI and almost every police department in the country. Wilder's classification changed from serial to spree murderer because of the multiple murders and the lack of a cooling-off period. The tension caused by his fugitive status and high visibility of his crime gave Wilder (and other noted spree murderers) a sense of desperation. The acts of these murderers are open and public, and this usually means no cooling-off period. They know they will be caught, and the coming confrontation with police becomes an element in their crimes. Often their goal is to have law enforcement take their life as they engage in their last desperate acts.

KEY POINT Mass murderers and spree murderers are not concerned with who their victims are; they will kill anyone who comes in contact with them.

Classifying Homicides

It is important to classify homicides correctly. For example, a single homicide is committed in a city; a week later, a second single homicide is committed; and the third week, a third single homicide. Three seemingly unrelated homicides are reported, but by the time there is a fourth, there is a tie-in, both through forensic evidence and an analysis of the crime scene. These four single homicides now point to one serial offender. It is not mass murder because of the multiple locations and lapse of time that in essence creates separate and distinct events and thus its categorization as a serial homicide. The correct classification not only assists in assessing the crimes from a behavioral and forensic evidence standpoint but may be the catalyst for the release of certain financial resources to assist in the investigation and formation of task force investigations to better cover the various jurisdictions in which related cases have been identified. Similarly, behaviorally assessing a single murder may reveal aspects of the motivation, victim selection, and offender-victim dynamics that might suggest either that may be the first of a coming series or that this offender has likely committed other homicides.

Primary Intent of the Murderer

Murder may have both primary and secondary intentions. The classification of a murder in terms of the killer's primary intent is outlined in Table 8-2. A killer may be acting either on his or her own or as part of a group. The primary intent may involve criminal enterprise. Criminal enterprise includes people who are involved in the business of crime. Criminal enterprise murders

often involve a group (e.g., contract murder, gang murder, competition murder, and political murder). Their livelihood is through criminal business and sometimes murder becomes part of it, even though there is no personal malice. For example, food may be poisoned during an extortion attempt of a business (i.e., extortion notes are written to a company demanding money and threatening the poisoning of products). The primary motive is financial. In 1998 in Los Angeles County, Jennifer Fletcher murdered her husband with the help of her then secret lover. They tried to stage the crime to make it look as if he had been murdered by gang members in the course of a home-invasion robbery. Fletcher planned the killing to collect on several life insurance policies that she had taken out on her husband without his knowledge; the motive was financial gain from the life insurance.

When the primary intent of the murderer involves emotional, selfish, or cause-specific reasons, individuals may kill for self-defense and compassion (e.g., mercy killings where life-support systems are disconnected). Family disputes/violence may lie behind infanticide, matricide, patricide, and spouse and sibling killings. Paranoid reactions may also result in murder, as in the previously described Whitman case (see pg. 84). Mentally disordered murderers may commit a symbolic crime or have a psychotic outburst. Assassinations, such as those committed by John Hinkley and Mark Chapman, also fall into the emotional intent category. Murders in this category involving groups are committed for a variety of reasons: religious (Jim Jones and the Jonestown, Guyana, case), cult (Adolfo Constanzo's Matamoros Cult killings), and fanatical organizations such as the Ku Klux Klan and the Black Panthers Party of the 1970s.

Sexual Homicide

Finally, the murderer may have sexual reasons for killing. Individuals may kill as a result of or to engage in sexual activity, dismemberment, mutilation, evisceration, or other activities that have sexual meaning only for the offender. Sexual homicide results from one person killing another in the context of power, control, sexuality, and aggressive brutality. Those offenders who capture their victims alive with the intention of keeping and torturing them (sexual sadists) are among the most difficult and dangerous sexual predators to identify and capture. The psychiatric diagnosis of sexual sadism states that the essential feature of this deviant behavior (i.e., paraphilia) is the infliction of physical or psychological suffering on another person in order to elicit a response from the victim, and it is this response that facilitates the achievement of sexual arousal. Occasionally two or more murderers commit these homicides together, such as in the case of Lawrence Bittaker and Roy Norris who raped and tortured five women in Los Angeles in a van they called the "Murder Mack."

Table 8-2 Primary Intent of Murderers			
NUMBER MURDERED	CRIMINAL/ENTERPRISE	EMOTIONAL/SELFISH/CAUSE-SPECIFIC	SEXUAL
One	Insurance collection	Self-defense	Rape and other sexual activity
	Contract killing	Compassion (i.e., mercy killings)	Mutilation
		Family violence	Dismemberment
		Paranoid reaction	Evisceration
		Emotional disorder	
		Assassination	
Two or more	Gang	Religious	Same as above
	Competition	Cult	
	Political	Fanatical	

It is difficult to gather dependable statistics on the number of sexual homicide victims for several reasons: (1) the victim is officially reported as a homicide statistic and not as a rape assault; (2) there is a failure to recognize any underlying sexual dynamics in a seemingly "ordinary" murder; (3) those agencies that investigate, apprehend, and assess the murderer often fail to share their findings, curtailing the collective pool of knowledge on the subject; and (4) conventional evidence of the crime's sexual nature may be absent. When law enforcement officials cannot readily determine a motive for murder, they examine its behavioral aspects. In developing techniques for profiling murderers, FBI agents have found that they need to understand the thought patterns of murderers to make sense of crime scene evidence and victim information. Characteristics of evidence and victims can reveal much about the murderer's intensity of planning, preparation, and follow-through. From these observations, the agents begin to uncover the murderer's motivation, recognizing how dependent motivation is to the killer's dominant thinking patterns. In many instances, a hidden, sexual motive emerges, a motive that has its origins in fantasy. The role of fantasy in the motive and behavior of suspects is an important factor in violent crimes, especially sexual murders (Figs. 8-2, 8-3, and 8-4).

Several studies have explored the role of sadistic fantasy (Brittain, 1970; Dietz, Hazelwood & Warren, 1990; Holt, Meloy, & Strack, 1999; Revitch, 1980; Warren, Hazelwood & Dietz, 1996), with MacCulloch and colleagues (1983) suggesting that sadistic acts and fantasy are linked and that fantasy drives the sadistic behavior.

Victim Risk

The concept of the victim's risk is involved at several stages of the behavioral assessment process and provides information about the suspect in terms of not only how he or she operates but the risk the offender is willing to assume in order to commit the murder. Risk is assessed using factors such as age, occupation, lifestyle, and the physical stature of the victim and is classified as high, moderate, low, or situationally elevated. High-risk victims often engage in high-risk behavior such as prostitution, drug use and sales, and other criminal activity. Killers seek high-risk victims at locations where a particular type of victim may be found as well as areas where the isolated nature of the location makes an assault much less risky for the offender. The young and the elderly may have their risk situationally elevated because of their vulnerability and physical inability to resist an attack. Students may be classified as moderate-risk, as it is known that predators may target college-age women because of their naiveté. Low-risk types include those whose occupation and daily lifestyle do not lend themselves to easy targeting or put them in contact with those elements of society who engage in high-risk behavior. Each victim's particular situation must be evaluated individually with care taken not to assign a risk level based strictly on one attribute such as their occupation.

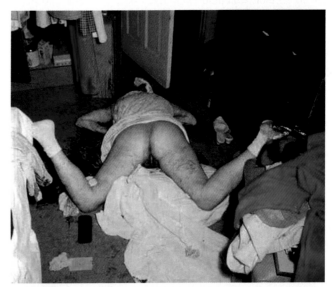

Fig. 8-3 Sexual homicide victim with throat cut and displayed by offender.

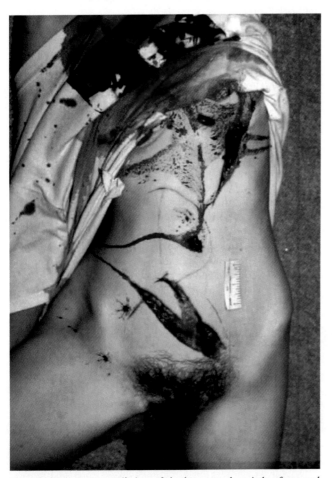

Fig. 8-2 Postmortem mutilation of the breasts and genitals of a sexual homicide victim.

Fig. 8-4 The crime scene will provide the investigator with valuable clues for the behavioral assessment of serial sexual homicide.

An individual's risk level can change from one situation to the next. A prostitute is at a high risk of becoming the victim of a violent crime when she is engaged in her trade. In this environment, she is engaging in one-on-one situations with men she does not know, often under the cover of darkness and in an environment controlled by the customer. In this situation, the risk for the offender is greatly reduced. Contrast this with the same woman when she is not working as a prostitute but instead found within the locked environment of her residence. Her risk level in this environment is significantly reduced. In contrast, not only is the risk for the offender greatly increased, but the fact that he chooses to assault the victim not when she is working and his risk greatly reduced but when she is at home when the risk to him is elevated offers some insight into the relationship dynamic that may exist.

Offender Risk

Data on victim risk integrate with information on offender risk, and the two should not be considered in isolation. The risk the offender assumes in order to commit the homicide is the flip side of the same coin. Assessing both victim risk and offender risk in relation to one another is critical to accurately understanding the size of the potential offender pool and helps to generate an image of the type of perpetrator being sought. For example, abducting a victim at noon from a busy street is a high-risk activity. Thus, a low-risk victim abducted under high-risk circumstances generates ideas about such offenders, such as personal stresses they are operating under, their beliefs that they will not be apprehended, or the excitement or thrill they seek in the commission of the crime.

Escalation

Information about escalation is derived from an analysis of facts and patterns from the prior decision-process models. Investigative crime analysts are able to deduce the sequence of acts committed during the crime. From this deduction, they make determinations about the potential of the criminal, not only to escalate the crimes (for example, from peeping to fondling, to assault, to rape, to murder) but also to repeat the crimes in serial fashion. One case example is David Berkowitz, the Son of Sam killer, who started his criminal career with the nonfatal stabbing of a teenage girl. His killing escalated to the subsequent .44-caliber killings.

Time Factors

There are several time factors that need consideration in generating a criminal profile. These factors include the length of time required (1) to kill the victim, (2) to commit additional acts with the body, and (3) to dispose of the body. The time of day or night that the crime was committed is also important, because it provides information on the lifestyle and occupation of the suspect (and also relates to the offender risk factor). For example, the longer an offender spends with a victim, the more likely it is that the killer will be apprehended at the crime scene. In the case of David Parker Ray, a sexual sadist, he captured and kept his victims for days at a time. Ray chained and tortured his last victim, Cynthia Vigil, for three days at his home in Elephant Butte, New Mexico, before she escaped, nude, wearing only a dog collar and padlock. She alerted authorities, leading to Ray's arrest. A killer who intends to spend time with his victim, whether alive or dead, must select a location to preclude observation. Determining the chronological sequence of events is, of course, important, but assessing how much time elapses between various events at a scene (the temporal component) can also be an important consideration in any behavioral assessment. Temporal consideration can assist in differentiating between antemortem and postmortem activity as well as determining the sequence of injury.

Location Factors

Information about location—where the victim was first approached, abducted, assaulted, murdered, and eventually disposed of—provides yet additional data about the offender. For example, this information provides details about whether the murderer used a vehicle to transport the victim from the death scene or if the victim died at the point of abduction. Rossmo (1999) linked the complexity of the crime and offender to the number of different crime scenes that can be discerned from the crime analysis.

CRIME ASSESSMENT

The crime assessment step in generating a criminal profile involves the reconstruction of the sequence of events both chronologically and temporally and the behavior of both the offender and the victim. Based on the various decisions of the previous steps, this reconstruction of how things happened, how people behaved, and how they planned and organized the encounter provides information about specific characteristics that help generate the criminal behavioral assessment. Assessments are made about the classification of the crime, its organized/disorganized aspects, the offender's selection of a victim, the level of planning and organization, the strategies used to control the victim, the sequence of the crime, the motive, and weapon use, as well as the most commonly identified behavioral manifestations at a violent crime, *modus operandi* (MO), *ritual* behavior, and the less frequently observed *staging* of the crime.

Modus Operandi (MO)

MO behaviors are perceived by the offender as necessary for the successful commission of a crime. There are three purposes for this type of behavior: first, it ensures the success of the crime; second, it protects the offender's identity; and third, it facilitates the offender's escape. MO is dynamic and can change over time for a variety of reasons. An offender develops a successful MO through trial and error and uses that MO over time because it works for the offender's purposes. An offender's MO changes based on, among other things, education, age, the development of criminal sophistication, and having to deal with contingencies of the crime that were unanticipated or beyond the offender's control. The MO may also change as the offender gains more experience and confidence. The offender's MO behaviors are more likely to be intentional and purposeful because they are goal driven.

Ritual

Ritual behaviors are unnecessary for the successful commission of a crime. These behaviors are need driven and engaged in by the offender for a number of reasons. Generally though, in violent homicides, especially those with a sexual component, these behaviors result from psychological and emotional needs. They are both unique and repetitive. These behaviors are manifested through physical actions as well as verbal scripting. In serial offenses, the core of the offender's *ritual* behavior does not change over time. It may, however, evolve as the original *ritual* becomes more fully developed.

Staging

Staging is defined as the intentional and purposeful manipulation of the behavioral or forensic evidence found at the original crime scene. *Staging* at a crime scene is an effort by offenders to create a "new" or different scene and a new motive for the purpose of misdirecting the investigation away from themselves. The offender attempts to overwhelm what would otherwise be a law enforcement investigator's logical deduction regarding what occurred. The offender who *stages* a crime scene perceives that without an attempt to redirect the investigation, law enforcement would quickly focus on the offender as a logical suspect because of a preexisting relationship with the victim, the location, or both. To determine if *staging* has occurred, the "totality of the circumstances" of the crime scene must be considered. In considering the "totality of the circumstances," every observable behavior is analyzed and reconciled with the logic of the available forensic evidence, crime scene reconstruction, and victimology. In addition, logical crime scene attributes, both forensic and behavioral, that are noticeably absent from the scene must also be considered.

The question of whether or not a crime scene has been staged helps direct the investigative profiler to the killer's motivation and relationship with the victim. In one case, a 27-year-old mother of twins was found lying on the living room couch, shot three times in the upper body and head. Her sweat pants and panties had been pulled down below her knees. In one hand she held the battery-operated controls to a sex toy vibrator. The vibrating component was lying next to her thigh. Located in the VCR was a pornographic sex tape. The house appeared to have been ransacked as if the offender were searching for something, although nothing had been taken. On first examination it appeared that the victim had been engaged in autoerotic activity on the couch when the offender broke in and shot her. Both of her young children were reported to have walked through the woods to their grandmother's house. Was this crime staged? The question was answered through both forensic and behavioral evidence. It was determined from blood spatter analysis that the victim had been shot on another part of the couch while sitting up and had been moved to a supine position. It was not possible for her to have moved on her own to the position in which she was found because two of the gunshot wounds were immediately fatal. The position of her sweat pants indicated that she was not the one who had pulled them down. The VCR had not been in the play mode and the vibrator was neither inserted nor turned on. Behaviorally, the victim's response to an unknown offender breaking into her residence (not moving to an upright seated or standing position to confront the threat and pull her pants up) was inconsistent with what was expected. In addition, despite an attempt to make it look like the offender had been searching for valuables, nothing of value had been taken. Investigators determined that the husband and the husband's mother staged the crime. The victim had been planning to divorce the husband and take custody of the children. The husband tried to make it appear that a stranger had killed the victim in the course of a robbery and then tried to taint her image as a good mother by staging the sexual aspect of the crime. The husband could not simply have killed his wife. With a potential divorce pending, law enforcement investigators would have focused on him immediately. With this information, the behavioral crime analyst hypothesized that by staging the autoerotic activity and robbery, the husband had hoped to create a new crime scene with a new motive that would throw the focus onto a stranger who broke into the house and killed his wife.

The classification of the crime is determined through the decision process outlined in the first decision-process model. The classification of a crime as organized or disorganized includes factors such as victim selection, strategies to control the victim, planning and organization, and the sequence of crime. An organized murderer is one who appears to plan the murders, to target victims, to display control at the crime scene, and to act out a sexually violent fantasy against the victim. For example, Robert Yates, the Spokane Serial Killer, successfully abducted young prostitutes in his van and drove them to remote locations. He controlled them using a ruse and then during the course of sexual activity shot them in the head. To prevent blood from leaking into his vehicle and leaving forensic evidence, he covered their heads with plastic bags after shooting them. He drove them to isolated locations and dumped their bodies. He did not care if the bodies were found, only that he had enough time to put distance between himself and the dumpsites. Ted Bundy's planning was noted through his successful abduction of young women from highly visible areas (i.e., beaches, campuses, a ski lodge). He selected victims who were young, attractive, and similar in appearance. He controlled the victims through physical force. These dynamics were important in the development of a desired fantasy victim.

In contrast, the disorganized murderer is less apt to plan the crime in detail, obtains victims by chance, and behaves haphazardly during the crime. For example, Herbert Mullin, who killed 14 people of varying types (e.g., an elderly man, a young girl, a priest) over a four-month period, did not display any specific planning or targeting of victims; rather, the victims were people who happened to cross his path, and their murders were based on impulse as well as on fantasy. There are typically fewer scenes and often everything–including the capture, assault, murder, and body disposition–takes place at a single scene.

CRIME SCENE DYNAMICS AND ANALYSIS

Crime scene dynamics are the numerous circumstances common to every crime scene, which can be misunderstood or misinterpreted by investigating officers. Examples include location of the crime scene, cause of death, method of killing, positioning of body, injury severity, excessive trauma, and location and nature of the injuries. One of the fundamental tenants of crime scene analysis is to evaluate variables that explain why someone became the victim of homicide. While conducting an analysis of the behavior that is manifested at violent crime scenes, it is important to avoid becoming too focused on any one aspect of the crime scene and ascribing singular importance to it. It is often impractical to reconstruct the exact sequence of events because of the innumerable possible interactions that could occur between the victim(s) and offender. However, it is important to consider the totality of the circumstances rather than a single crime scene variable in assessing not only what happened but why and how it happened. This enables the analysis of the crime behaviorally and further integration with what is factually known through investigative interviews and forensic evaluation of the evidence.

The most accurate way of assessing the overall victim-offender interaction is to consider the occurrence of various behavioral attributes in conjunction with one another. Assessing the following variables provides the behavioral analyst with crucial information necessary to accurately interpret the crime scene dynamics:

- The victim's perception or lack thereof of the risk to which she or he were exposed
- The offender's level of risk, intent, degree of organization and planning, presence or absence of displayed anger, and degree of control exercised over the victims, the scene, and him or herself
- The offender's choice of weapons, whether the weapons were brought to the scene or obtained at the scene, and how the offender chose dispose of them

- The significance of the nature, location, and severity of the victim's injuries

Behavioral profilers analyze the dynamics of a crime scene and interpret them based on various criteria. They receive extensive multidisciplinary training in many related fields including death investigation, forensic bloodstain analysis, forensic pathology, wound pathology, psychopathy, threat assessment, group dynamics, personality disorders, and paraphilias, to mention a few. An FBI behavioral crime analyst is an experienced agent who has usually served at least 10 years as a street agent and possesses excellent investigative and analytical skills. These agents also rely on the experiential component—that is, they spend years examining and working these types of cases and following the current research literature. Many of these analysts have conducted empirical research in this and other related disciplines. In-depth interviews with incarcerated felons who have committed such crimes have provided a vast body of knowledge of common threads that link crime scene dynamics to specific criminal personality patterns. It is this training, research, and experience that provide the background for the success and confidence these agents have when assisting state, local, and international agencies with their unusual and complex violent crimes cases.

CRIME PROFILE

The fourth step in generating a criminal profile deals with the type of person who committed the crime and that individual's behavioral orientation with relation to the crime. It is a common misconception that the profiler is trying to identify a particular individual from the analysis and interpretation of the case data. Behavioral analysis is a law enforcement tool not unlike many other types of tools or resources that are employed to bring resolution to a homicide investigation. The interpretation of the case materials assists in constructing a personality, behavioral, and demographic profile of the type of offender who is likely responsible for the crime. This construct helps law enforcement officials narrow the focus of the potential offender pool they may be considering and recommends one investigative direction over another. Once this description is generated, the strategy of investigation can be formulated, because this strategy requires a basic understanding of how an individual will respond to a variety of investigative efforts.

Included in the criminal profile are background information (demographics), physical characteristics, habits, beliefs and values, preoffense behavior leading to the crime, and post-offense behavior. It may also include investigative recommendations for interrogating or interviewing, identifying, and apprehending the offender, as well as role of the media in furthering the investigation.

This fourth stage has an important means of validating the criminal profile; this is called means feedback 1. The profile must fit with the earlier reconstruction of the crime, the evidence, and the key decision-process models. In addition, the investigative procedure developed from the recommendations must make sense in terms of the expected response patterns of the offender. If there is lack of congruence, then profiling investigators must review all available data. This is why it is important that the dynamics of the crime in play before, during, and after are considered in totality rather than in isolation.

Once the congruence of the criminal profile is determined, a report is provided to the requesting agency and added to its ongoing investigation efforts. The investigative recommendations generated in stage 4 are applied, and suspects matching the profile are evaluated. In cases where police have an ongoing effort to identify and arrest a suspect, the investigative recommendations

are applied and suspects matching those criteria are evaluated. If new evidence becomes known (e.g. an additional murder or new witness information), it will be evaluated within the framework of what is already known. Such information may or may not change the information that has already been provided. However, in some case it may in fact provide stronger support for what has been provided. If identification, apprehension, and a confession result, the goal of the profile effort has been met.

APPREHENSION

Once a suspect is apprehended, the agreement between the outcome and the various stages in the profile-generating process are examined. When an apprehended suspect admits guilt, it is important to conduct a detailed interview and to affirm the total profiling process for validity and quality.

QUANTIFYING SUCCESS

In 1981, the Institutional Research and Development Unit of the FBI Training Division was asked to initiate a cost-benefit study to determine the extent to which the service had been of value to the users. Specifically, the analysis was undertaken to examine two questions: (1) what was the nature and extent of any assistance provided by criminal profiling, and (2) what were the actual results of using a criminal profile in terms of offender identification or savings in investigative agent days. A review of the material submitted by the various field divisions for analysis revealed that requests had originated within the jurisdictional areas of 59 field offices located within the United States and two FBI liaison representatives assigned to American embassies abroad. Although the majority of these submissions were from city police (52%), requests came from all levels of law enforcement including county police or sheriffs, FBI officials, state police, state investigators, and state highway patrol. As might be suspected, most of the requests for profiling were submitted in an effort to identify the individual(s) responsible for one or more murders (65%). The second highest offense requested was for rape (8%) with other offenses including kidnapping, extortion, threat/obscene communication, child molestation, hostage situation, accidental death, and suicide. Most of the cases submitted involved a single victim (61%), although 10% involved at least two, and 17 contained six or more victims. Based on the total requests (n = 192), the suspect(s) were identified in a total of 88 or 46% of the cases. In these cases, responding agencies indicated that criminal profiling was useful in the following ways:

- It focused the investigation properly.
- It helped locate possible suspects.
- It identified suspects.
- It assisted in the prosecution of suspect(s).

Only in 15 cases was the profiling stated to be of no assistance. In attempting to document the cost-benefit aspect, the study suggested that the use of profiling resulted in a total saving of 594 investigative agent-days. That number is considered a substantial figure when such matters as salaries, support costs, and availability of personnel for other assignments are considered.

The success of the assistance provided to law enforcement by the FBI served as a catalyst for law enforcement agencies worldwide to start and develop their own behavioral analysis units. The volume of cases submitted to the FBI continued to grow, and because the unit was relatively small, it simply could not address all the requests for behavioral assistance. The cases were triaged to determine where the limited resources of the FBI would be directed. In

1995, the FBI added a child crimes unit as a complement to the adult crimes unit, which had been providing profiling assistance for many years. Although the profilers had always worked on child homicides and abductions, this was the first time that a unit was created to concentrate specifically on child cases and specialize in various aspects of child victimization. That unit is now known as the Behavioral Analysis Unit–Crimes Against Children. After the terror attacks on U.S. soil in 2001, the FBI created an additional behavioral analysis unit to deal specifically with threat and terrorism assessments. The original profiling unit that grew out of the Behavioral Sciences Unit focused its investigative efforts on adult crimes and completes the trio as Behavioral Analysis Unit–Crimes Against Adults.

Case Study **8-1**

Crime Scene Evidence

A young woman's body was discovered by her husband in their second-story apartment when he returned from work around 6 PM. She was nude and tied to the headboard of their bed by two different pieces of cordage. The cordage consisted of the waterbed heater cord, which had been cut with a knife and the cord to a nightstand lamp (lamp still attached). A belt belonging to her husband had initially been used to bind her hands but it broke and was found on the floor between the nightstand and the bed adjacent to where her hands were tied. Her jeans and panties were found turned inside out on the floor and her shirt had been partially cut off. Her bra was pushed up exposing both of her breasts. A washcloth had been used as a gag and had been held in place by one of her husband's neckties, and an article of her clothing had been used as a blindfold. Four wooden spoons from the kitchen had been inserted into her vagina postmortem and left there. Semen was located in the victim orally, vaginally, and anally. The knife used to both stab her and cut the electrical cords used to bind her was found on the floor of the bedroom and had been taken from the kitchen. One of the victim's earrings was found on the bedroom floor and the matching earring on the kitchen floor. Fresh cookie dough was found in a bowl in the kitchen and some of it had been placed onto a cookie sheet in preparation for baking. A spoon with cookie dough was found lying on the floor of the victim's bedroom. The victim was lying on a bare waterbed mattress. Two loads of her clothing and linens were located in the washing machines of the complex laundry room near the victim's apartment. There was no forced entry and nothing was taken by the offender despite the fact that valuables were in plain sight, including jewelry in the bedroom and the victim's purse on the kitchen table.

ELEMENTS OF CASE ANALYSES

Profiling Inputs. In terms of crime scene evidence in the case study, everything the offender used at the crime scene belonged to the victim. The offender apparently did not plan this crime; he had no gun, ropes, or tape for the victim's mouth. He relied on the victim to provide the items that he would use in the course of the rape and murder. He probably did not even plan to encounter her that morning at that location. The crime scene indicated a spontaneous event; in other words, the killer did not stalk or wait for the victim. There is only one scene. The offender captures, assaults, and kills the victim at a single location. When there is only one scene for all the activity, it often indicates a less sophisticated and organized offender.

The victim had a high school education and worked full-time as a secretary for a local company. She was religious and attended church on regular basis. The victim had been married for two years to her high school sweetheart. They were reported to have a good relationship.

She was described as naïve, reserved, and having few friends other than several acquaintances from church, with whom she and her husband associated. Neighbors next to her apartment noted that she and her husband did not appear to entertain people in their home, nor did they associate or socialize with anyone from the apartment complex. Physically, the victim could be described as an attractive young woman, a natural blonde, blue eyes, and of medium build (5'6", 147 pounds at the time of her death). Information solicited from neighbors and friends indicated that the victim lead a conservative lifestyle, guided by church ethics.

Investigation of the victim revealed that her husband left home around 9:30 AM and did not return until 6 PM. Because it was Sunday, the victim did not have to go to work. A receipt was located in the victim's apartment from an automated teller machine (ATM), indicating that she had withdrawn money at 10:12 AM. A grocery receipt was also found in the residence. The time on the receipt revealed that she had departed the store shortly after 10:40 AM. There was nothing to indicate that the victim made any other stops or had interactions with others before returning to her residence. The forensic information in the medical examiner's report was important in determining the extent of the wounds, as well as how the victim was assaulted and whether evidence of sexual assault was present. It was determined that the victim had sustained a small cluster of stab wounds to her neck, one which was fatal as it severed the carotid artery. Another cluster, separate and distinct from the one in the neck, was located center chest with only one of the injuries identified as fatal. Cause of death was identified as exsanguination resulting from the stab wounds. The medical examiner opined that the victim had been dead for several hours before her husband discovered her. This information, coupled with the time-stamped receipts, indicates that the timeframe for the homicide was only a few hours. The fact that the offender used a knife from the victim's kitchen indicates that initially he did not plan to kill the victim and that he saw an opportunity to assault her and acted on that impulse. Despite the fact that it was Sunday and many people were in the apartment complex, no one reported hearing the victim scream. This would indicate that the offender was able to surprise and capture her and that the surprise attack did not provide her the opportunity to resist or scream. The killer used the gag to prevent the victim from screaming and the blindfold in an attempt to prevent her identifying him. If he had originally planned to kill her, then there would have been no need to blindfold her because her ability to identify him would not have made a difference. The offender used the gag because he intended to interact with the victim while she was alive. Semen was identified in the anus, vagina, and mouth of the victim.

Decision-Process Models. This crime's style is a single homicide with the murderer's primary intent making it a sexually motivated type of crime. There was little to no planning, and it appeared that the offender saw an opportunity, when the victim left her apartment to put laundry into the washing machines, to slip into her unlocked apartment and secret himself in the pantry. Because no one would have known when the victim was going to do laundry and the front door of the apartment was difficult to see unless you were in the complex, the offender likely had encountered the victim in the past. The offender was in a position to see her leave the apartment with laundry. The focus of this crime was sexual, and there was no behavior to indicate another motive. Nothing had been taken from the apartment nor the victim.

Victim risk assessment revealed that the victim was naïve and often trusting of those she did not know. She led a church-driven lifestyle and would have tried to reason with her attacker rather than to resist, fight back, scream, or yell. She would have been easily intimidated and controlled. She was not careful about paying attention to her personal security and often forgot to lock the door to her apartment. Based on the information about her occupation and lifestyle, this was a low-risk victim living in an area that was at moderate risk for violent crimes. She and her husband lived in a large apartment complex, containing approximately 1000 units, in a low- to medium-income area. It was reported that the neighborhood was racially diverse. Although there was crime in the area, it was not known to have a history of violent crime.

The crime was considered very high risk for the offender. He committed the crime in broad daylight on a Sunday afternoon, and there was a possibility that people who were walking around the apartments might see him. Because there was no set pattern for the victim to go shopping or do laundry, it appeared that the offender seized on the opportunity, when the victim left her apartment to do laundry, to slip inside the unlocked apartment and wait for the victim to return. The offender secured a knife that he used to capture and intimidate the victim. The offender hid in the pantry closet and surprised the victim as she was making cookies in the kitchen. During the initial struggle to gain control of the victim, one of her earrings was dislodged and fell to the kitchen floor. The offender took the victim to the bedroom in order to sexually assault her.

The time for the crime was considerable. All of the offender's activities with the victim—capturing her; moving her to the bedroom; tying her up; putting on a gag and blindfold; cutting off her shirt; assaulting her vaginally, anally, and orally; stabbing her; and retrieving wooden spoons from the kitchen to insert in her vagina—would have taken a substantial amount of time. The extended amount of time the murderer spent with his victim increased his risk of being apprehended.

The location of the crime suggested that the offender felt comfortable in the area. He had been there before, and he felt that no one would interrupt the murder. He may have questioned the victim about the return of her husband, learning that he had significant time to be alone with her.

Crime Assessment. The crime scene indicated that the murder was one event, not one of a series of events. It also appeared to be a first-time killing, and the subject was not a typical organized offender. The majority of superficial stab wounds suggested that the offender had not killed before and had worked up the nerve to inflict a fatal wound. The offender had not planned the crime but acted opportunistically to sexually assault the victim. He did not bring anything to the crime scene and obtained everything he used from the scene.

A reconstruction of the crime scene provides an overall scenario of what occurred. At some point after returning from the store (approximately 11 AM), the victim prepared cookie dough. During this process, she took two loads of wash to the laundry room in the apartment complex. While she was gone for that short period of time, the offender entered her apartment, secured a knife, and hid in the pantry closet. On her return, she was surprised and captured by the offender. There was an initial struggle, as the victim lost her earring. To carry out his sexual fantasies, the offender needed the victim alive. To prevent her from both resisting and escaping, he bound her to the headboard using electrical cords he cut from items in the bedroom. To prevent her from identifying him, he blindfolded her with an item of her clothing and gagged her with a washcloth from the bathroom. He secured the washcloth with one of her husband's neckties, that he had obtained from the closet.

At some point during the assault, the offender decided that he was going to kill the victim. She may have recognized him in some way. The blindfold may have slipped, or she may have identified his voice. The offender decided that it was too risky to let her live. The offender used a surprise approach rather than a blitz (a blitz being the immediate and overwhelming use of physically injurious force to incapacitate the

victim). As a result, she did not suffer blunt force trauma or defensive injuries because she did not perceive the threat until it was too late. Once the offender gained control of the victim, he moved her from the kitchen to the bedroom. He forcefully removed a spoon from her hand with which she had been making cookies and discarded it on the floor. He proceeded to cut her shirt off and push her bra up exposing her breasts. He sexually assaulted her, leaving semen orally, anally, and vaginally. When he finished sexually assaulting her, he used the same knife that he had cut the electrical cords with to stab her to death. After she died, instead of leaving the apartment quickly in an effort to put time and distance between himself and the crime, the killer returned to the kitchen and removed four wooden spoons from the counter. He returned to the bedroom and inserted the handles of the spoons into her vagina. This last postmortem act served not only to humiliate the victim in death, but to shock and offend those who would ultimately find her. The killer took his time at the scene, and he probably knew that no one would come to the apartment and disturb him. The crime scene was not staged. Ritualistic fantasy generated the sexual motivation for murder. The murderer displayed total domination of the victim. In addition, by inserting the wooden spoons into her vagina and failing to cover her when he left, he intentionally placed the victim in a degrading position, reflecting his lack of remorse for the killing.

The binding of the victim's hands reflected the offender's need to control a living victim and is differentiated from bondage, a ritualized behavior, by the lack of either excessive bindings or the neatness of the bindings and the absence of either symmetry or variety of different positions. Foreign object insertion is more commonly seen with younger offenders who are engaging in the exploration of something unknown for them, the female genitalia, sexual substitution (substituting the insertion of the wooden spoons for the insertion of the penis), or a means to degrade or humiliate the victim even in death. This sexualized imagery of dominance and control had likely been repeated over and over in the offender's mind. On the day of the homicide, the offender crossed from fantasizing about the victim to the reality of putting his fantasy into action when he was presented with the opportunity to act on those fantasies. He took her engagement and wedding ring off her finger. Offenders who remove items of a personal nature can use them to remember the crime; these items are described as souvenirs. They can also serve to remind the offender of the conquest and are then referred to as trophies.

Crime Profile. Based on the information derived during the previous stages, a criminal profile of the offender was generated. First, a physical description of the suspect stated that he would be younger than the victim. Because several hairs of Negroid characteristic were located on the body, the offender was further described as black. The offender would not look out of context in the area. He knew the area and either lived in the complex or had regular access to it. Because the scene suggested a younger offender, it was felt that he would be unemployed and with no military history. He would be of average intelligence.

The lack of sophistication in how the crime was carried out relates to the age factor. The presence or absence of control of the victim would impact on the suspect's age. However, because of the relative lack of a plan or sense of organization, it was felt the offender would be a teenager.

The offender used a surprise attack to gain control over his victim. He failed to bring anything to the crime, instead relying on the victim to provide what items he needed (bindings, gag, blindfold, and weapon). This impulsive act was very risky, because the offender could not be sure he was neither seen nor heard on a Sunday afternoon in broad daylight. He would have some sexual experience, but the youthfulness suggested that he would not be married. The fact that he did ejaculate indicated that he would not be sexually dysfunctional. The subject would have sadistic tendencies; the wooden spoons may represent an act of sexual substitution or an attempt to degrade or humiliate the victim. The sexual acts showed controlled aggression, not unleashed rage. Rage or hatred of women was not observed. The stab wounds were inflicted in a controlled manner in two tightly clustered areas. Most of the stabbing injuries were almost superficial in depth, indicating that this homicide was the offender's first. His stabbing reflected a tenuous quality with only two fatal injuries. The offender killed the victim to eliminate a witness and not as a reaction to rejection from women. In addressing the habits of the murderer, the profile revealed there would be a reason for the offender to be at the crime scene on a Sunday afternoon. He could be employed in the apartment complex, he could be in the complex on personal business such as visiting a friend or relative, or he could reside in the complex. It was felt that the offender had likely interacted with the victim on a prior occasion and it was in this interaction that the fantasy about her began to develop. The offender had a high opinion of himself and his ability to interact with women. He was considered socially competent enough to interact with women; however, his self-inflated opinion would cause others to view his personality as pushy, arrogant, aggressive, and socially inappropriate. The control he exhibited at the scene indicated that alcohol and drugs did not assume a role in this crime. The offender's infliction of sexual sadistic acts, distinct lack of remorse, and postmortem activity to degrade and humiliate the victim indicated that he would likely exhibit psychopathic traits. The killer would have difficulty maintaining any kind of meaningful personal relationships with women. If he dated, he would date women younger than himself, as he would have to be able to exert dominance and control in relationships.

The crime scene reflected that the killer felt justified in his actions and that he felt no remorse. He was not subtle. He left the victim in a provocative, humiliating position, exactly the way he wanted her to be found.

Investigation. The crime received intense coverage by the local media because it was such an extraordinary homicide. The local police responded to a radio call of a homicide. They in turn notified the detective bureau, which notified the forensic crime scene unit, medical examiner's office, and the county district attorney's office. An intensive investigation resulted, which included speaking to and interviewing hundreds of complex residents and their guests. Record checks of known sex offenders in the area proved fruitless. Usable fingerprints of the offender were located on the edge of the bedrail adjacent to the victim's body and on the spoon that the victim had in her hand when she was attacked. She held the spoon in her hand until they reached the bedroom where the offender ripped it from her hand. In the process of pulling the spoon from her grasp, the offender deposited a clear fingerprint on the handle. The FBI's behavioral profilers were contacted to prepare a criminal investigative analysis. The profilers advised that the offender would likely be younger than was currently being considered and that he would have a history of contacts with other females of a similar age that were not reported to police. He would have a high school education but would not have done well. He would be employed in a minimum wage job and have blue-collar skills. If he had a criminal history, it would likely involve nuisance offenses with no arrests for other major crimes except burglaries.

Apprehension. The outcome of the investigation was the apprehension of a suspect over a year after the homicide occurred. After receiving the criminal investigative analysis, police reviewed their files of the interviews that had been conducted at the apartment complex. Several women had reported contacts with several black males in their twenties who had made what they considered to be inappropriate advances toward them. These men became the prime suspects, but fingerprint and DNA evidence ruled them out.

Approximately one year after the crime, a 16-year-old male began to accost women around the swimming pool and laundry rooms of the same apartment complex. This male was visiting a relative in a building in the adjacent apartment complex. He had in fact been visiting the summer before but left the state shortly after the homicide to return home. The parents of the suspect allowed police to take fingerprints from the young male. These prints were ultimately matched to the fingerprints from the crime scene. The suspect had been cooperative with the police until he was matched to the crime scene, at which point he became quite hostile and refused any further cooperation.

The offender had dropped out of the 10th grade and was working at a fast-food restaurant. The relative with whom he was staying lived three apartment complex units away from the victim. The offender had encountered the victim at the community pool where she went to sunbathe, and he targeted her there. His young age precluded military service or having been married, but he did have a girlfriend. He was described a bright youth but he did not apply himself. He was considered cold, arrogant, and very mature for his age. This maturity seemed inconsistent for his age and likely accounted for the sexual assault diversity seen at the scene. The offender did not have any arrests for major crimes. His arrest history consisted of disorderly conduct and drug offenses. The suspect was tried as an adult and found guilty of first-degree murder. He was sentenced to life plus 25 years for the sexual assault.

IMPLICATIONS

Statistics from the FBI Uniform Crime Reports clearly indicate that violent crimes in the United States have been steadily declining since 1992. Many Americans feel society is increasingly violent, most probably due to the speed and drama with which the contemporary media portrays violence. For example, homicide rates in the United States have declined from 9.8 homicides per 100,000 population in 1991 to 5.4 homicides per 100,000 in 2008. However, public pressure is great on law enforcement officials when a community member is victimized by a violent, senseless, apparently "motiveless" crime. In the case of a homicide, a community is generally shocked over the crime and demands swift and positive action from law enforcement in investigating and identifying the suspect. Once a suspect has been arrested and charged, the public then looks to the forensic behavioral sciences for an explanation of the murderer's mental state and motivations. The public often wants to understand how someone from their community—who by all outward appearances of social, financial, and demographic norms and does not appear to be much different than they view themselves—can commit such violent acts.

The advancement of law enforcement techniques requires a knowledge base of the criminal personality. However, there are major hurdles inherent in the study of criminal personality. First, it is difficult to gather sufficient numbers of cases in an unbiased manner. More frequently, single cases are reported often by healthcare clinicians not trained in the forensic sciences. Second, although murder can be classified as an interactional situation involving at least two parties, the literature contains more reports on the murderer than on the victim. Third, before trial as well as after conviction, offenders rarely cooperate in an interview because the material may incriminate them as they continue the appeal process. Fourth, there is a paucity of data from staff who manage offenders in their daily institutional routine that could lend significant understanding to an offender's state of mind. Fifth, archival research of the investigative files pertinent to the homicide cases often lacks the critical data needed with regard to the offender and victim. And sixth, the various disciplines whose work brings them into contact with offenders focus on only one small part of the total picture. They concentrate only on the problem from their specialty perspective.

Interagency cooperation through the sharing of information and collaborating on cases is not practiced to any significant degree, despite the fact that many multiagency task forces such as the Spokane Serial Murder Task Force, which ultimately identified Robert Yates and the BTK (Bind, Torture, Kill) task force that successfully arrested Dennis Rader have gained national recognition conducting successful investigations of high-profile serial and sexual murder cases. Mental health staff members are not knowledgeable about the details of the crime or how the suspect acted during the initial arrest or interrogation. Clinicians see the suspect when the individual's frame of mind is different because the clinical environment is unlike the crime scene, the police station, or prison and the suspect may now be on a drug regimen to address certain behavioral or mental health issues. Similarly, investigators do not see the offender in the structure of a prison or hospital to note adaptive or maladaptive behavior. All of these factors suggest that a systematic multidisciplinary perspective should be applied to the investigation. This would specifically involve the role of the forensic nurse examiner and the forensic psychiatric nurse.

Summary

With agents allowed to specialize in particular types of crime, from rape and murder of the elderly to the sexual exploitation of children to the psychology of female suicide bombers, the behavioral analysis units continue to build on the initial work done by the profilers in the original BSU. As forensic technology has advanced by leaps and bounds, so too has the experience and dedication of those agents tasked with the behavioral analysis and interpretation of some of the most challenging cases in law enforcement, both domestically and abroad. The refinement of these investigative tools means faster suspect identification and apprehension and prevention of additional victims. Further, research efforts by law enforcement agencies are important to the refinement of additional skill in reading the seemingly inert characteristics of crime scene evidence. Understanding the motivational and behavioral matrix of the offender, victimology and victim selection process, and the myriad of multidisciplinary attributes that impact the assessment of the crime dynamics increases law enforcement's use of the connection between patterns of thinking and behaviors.

Law enforcement agencies should take advantage of all the potential tools that are available in the ever-expanding discipline of forensic science and would be wise to develop operational agendas with forensic nurses, especially those trained as sexual assault nurse examiners (SANEs) and who are part of a sexual assault response team. The solution of complex and multijurisdictional serial murder and sexual homicide cases requires outside-the-box thinking and multidisciplinary cooperation to bring clinical and criminal investigation together as partners with a common goal.

Resources

ORGANIZATIONS

Genetest Corporation: Forensic DNA Criminal Profiling
2316 Delaware Avenue, Buffalo, NY 14216; 877-404-4363 or 877-964-2436; www.genetestlabs.com/forensic/forensicscriminalprofiling
National Association of Medical Examiners
430 Pryor Street SW, Atlanta, Georgia 30312; http://thename.org

U.S. Department of Justice
950 Pennsylvania Avenue NW, Washington, DC 20530-0001. www.doj.gov
U.S. Federal Bureau of Investigation: Behavioral Analysis Unit
J. Edgar Hoover Building, 935 Pennsylvania Avenue NW, Washington, DC 20535-0001; www.fbi.gov/hq/isd/cirg/ncavc.htm#bau

WEBSITES

Forensic Behavioral Services International. Mark E. Safarik (ret. FBI) and Robert K. Ressler (ret. FBI), Criminal Profilers. http://FBSInternational.com

References

Boudrouis, J. (1974). A classification of homicides. *Criminology, 11*(4), 524–540.

Brittain, R. P. (1970). The sadistic murderer. *Medicine, Science, and the Law, 10*(4), 198–207.

Brussel, J. A. (1968). *Casebook of a crime psychiatrist.* New York: Grove Press.

Burgess, A. W., Commons, M. L., Safarik, M. E., Looper, R.R., & Ross, S.N. (2007). Sex offenders of the elderly: Classification by motive, typology, and predicators of severity of crime. *Journal of Aggression and Violent Behavior, 12*(5), 582–597.

Campbell, J. H., & DeNevi, D. (Eds.). (2004). *Profilers: leading investigators take you inside the criminal mind.* Amherst, NY: Prometheus Books.

Casey-Owens, M. (1984). The anonymous letter-writer—psychological profile? *Journal of Forensic Science, 29*(3), 816–819.

Dietz, P., Hazelwood, R., & Warren, J. (1990). The sexually sadistic criminal and his offenses. *Bulletin of the American Academy of Psychiatry and the Law, 18*, 163–178.

Douglas, J. E., Burgess, A. W., Burgess, A. G., & Ressler, R.K. (2006). In *Crime classification manual: A standard system for investigating and classifying violent crimes* (2nd ed.). New York: Lexington.

Douglas, J. E., Ressler, R. K., Burgess, A. W., & Hartman, C.R. (1986). Criminal profiling from crime scene analysis. *Behavioral Sciences and the Law, 4*(4), 401–426.

Geberth, V. J. (2006). *Practical homicide investigation: Tactics, procedures, and forensic techniques* (4th ed.). Boca Raton, FL: CRC Press.

Hazelwood, R. R., & Douglas, J. E. (1980). The lust murderer. *The FBI Law Enforcement Bulletin, 49*(4), 18–22.

Hazelwood, R. R., & Burgess, A. W. (Eds.). (2008). *Practical aspects of rape investigation: A multidisciplinary approach* (4th ed.). Boca Raton, FL: CRC Press.

Holmes, R. M., & Holmes, S. T. (2002). Pedophilia and psychological profiling. In R. M. Holmes, & S. T. Holmes (Eds.), *Profiling violent crimes: an investigative tool* (3rd ed., pp. 158–171). Thousand Oaks, CA: Sage.

Holt, S., Meloy, J. R., & Strack, S. (1999). Sadism and Psychopathy in violent and sexually violent offenders. *Journal of American Academy of Psychiatry and the Law, 27*(1), 23–32.

Lanning, K. V. (2001). *Child molesters: A behavioral analysis* (4th ed.). National Center for Missing & Exploited Children.

Lashley, J. V. (1929). Homicide (in Cook County). In J. H. Wigmore (Ed.), *The Illinois crime survey* (pp. 589–640). Chicago: Illinois Association for Criminal Justice and Chicago Crime Commission.

Lunde, D. T. (1976). *Murder and madness.* San Francisco: San Francisco Book Company.

MacCulloch, M. G., Snowden, P. R., Wood, P. J., et al. (1983). Sadistic fantasy, sadistic behavior and offending. *The British Journal of Psychiatry: The Journal of Mental Science, 143*(1), 20–29.

Myers, W. C. (Ed.). (2002). *Juvenile Sexual Homicide.* London: Academic Press.

Morton, R. J., & Hilts, M. A. (Eds.). (2008). *Serial murder: Multidisciplinary perspectives for investigators.* Washington, DC: Federal Bureau of Investigation, U.S. Department of Justice.

Myers, W. C., Husted, M. D., Safarik, M. E., & O'Toole, M.E. (2006). The motivation behind serial sexual homicide: Is it sex, power and control, or anger? *Journal of Forensic Sciences, 51*(4), 900–990.

O'Toole, M. E. (1999). Criminal profiling: The FBI uses criminal investigative analysis to solve crimes. *Corrections Magazine*, *61*, 44.

O'Toole, M. E. (2006). Psychopathy as a behavior classification system for violent and serial crime scenes. In H. Herve, & J. Yuille (Eds.), *The Psychopath: Theory, Research, & Practice* (pp. 301–326). Mahwah, NJ: Lawrence Erlbaum Associates.

Palmer, S. (1960). *A study of murder*. New York: Thomas Crowell.

Reiser, M. (1982). Crime-specific psychological consultation. *The Police Chief*, (March), 53–56.

Ressler, R. K., Burgess, A. W., & Douglas, J. E. (1988). *Sexual homicide: patterns and motives*. Lexington, MA: Lexington Books.

Revitch, F. (1980). Genocide and unprovoked attacks on women. *Correctional and Social Psychiatry*, *26*(3), 6–11.

Rizzo, N. D. (1981). Murder in Boston: Killers and their victims. *International Journal of Offender Therapy and Comparative Criminology*, *26*(1), 36–42.

Rossmo, D. K. (1999). *Geographic Profiling*. Boca Raton, FL: CRC Press.

Safarik, M. E., Jarvis, J. P., & Nussbaum, K. (2002). Sexual homicide of elderly females: Linking offender characteristics to victim and crime scene attributes. *Journal of Interpersonal Violence*, *17*(5), 500–525.

Safarik, M. E., & Jarvis, J. P. (2005). Examining attributes of homicides: Toward quantifying qualitative values of injury severity. *Journal of Homicide Studies*, *9*(3), 183–203.

Sapp, A. D., Huff, T. G., Kelm, K. L., & Tunkel, R.F. (2001). *Behavior and characteristics of bomb related offenders*. USDOJ.

Schlesinger, L. B. (2004). *Sexual murder: Catathymic and compulsive homicides*. Boca Raton, Florida: CRC Press.

Smith, S. S., & Shuy, R. W. (2002). Forensic Psycholinguistics: Using language analysis for identifying and assessing offenders. *FBI Law Enforcement Bulletin*, *71*(4), 16–25.

Vorpagel, R. E. (1998). *Profiles in murder: An FBI legend dissects killers and their crimes*. New York: Dell Publishing.

Warren, J. I., Hazelwood, R. R., & Dietz, P. E. (1996). The sexually sadistic serial killer. *Journal of Forensic Sciences*, *41*(6), 970–974.

Wilson, M. A. (2000). Toward a model of terrorist behavior in hostage-taking Incidents. *Journal of Conflict Resolution*, *44*(4), 403–424. Thousand Oaks, CA: Sage.

CHAPTER 9 Digital Evidence and Forensic Investigations

Janet Barber Duval

The extensive use of computers, voice and video recording devices, surveillance cameras, and a myriad of wireless applications in business and industry have added a new dimension to the realm of evidence that is available for legal proceedings. The use of these devices for forensic surveillance and lawful interception of data is a rapidly growing and specialized field. Hospitals and other healthcare agencies, insurance carriers, law enforcement, and many community services realize the power of forensic evidence in cases involving violent crimes, fraud, and other illegal activities. Forensic nurses and other investigators must have a working knowledge about the access, preservation, and use of digital evidence. This requires a basic identification of digital forensic media, an understanding of the technological features of these various storage devices, including their volatility, as well as the requirements for lawful interception, discovery, and use of digital data in the courtroom.

Introduction to Digital Forensics

Digital forensics is "The application of computer science and investigative procedures for a legal purpose involving the analysis of digital evidence after proper search authority, chain of custody, validation with mathematics, use of validated tools, repeatability, reporting, and possible expert presentation" (Zatyko, 2007, p. 18).

One other expert in digital forensic science defined the content area as "the use of scientifically derived and proven methods toward the preservation, collection, validation, identification, analysis, interpretation, documentation, and presentation of digital evidence derived from digital sources for the purpose of facilitation or furthering the reconstruction of events found to be criminal, or helping to anticipate unauthorized actions shown to be disruptive to planned operations." (Carrier, 2003, p. 1).

In 2008, the American Academy of Forensic Sciences approved a new section, Digital and Multimedia Sciences, in recognition of the essential and rapidly expanding field of computers and their relevance to all disciplines within the forensic sciences. In addition to digital media devices being a prime source of evidence in many cases, digital technology has become a valuable tool in forensic investigations. Shortly after the introduction and proliferation of computers and their supporting networks, it was clear that they could be used to create mischief, incite chaos within business enterprises, and produce harm at the highest levels of government. In 1984, the Federal Bureau of Investigation (FBI) believed that the escalating use of computers and associated problems, such as hacking into networks, transmitting viruses and worms, and using computers for unlawful purposes, required a response. Soon the FBI formed a dedicated computer analysis and response team (CART) as well as regional computer forensics laboratories. Other U.S. entities and many countries throughout the world have followed the FBI's lead and have established similar services to aid law enforcement and the courts in the investigation of forensic cases.

The detection, analysis, and reporting related to evidence found in the physical and virtual memory of computers is termed **computer forensics or cyberforensics**. As in all forensic investigations that are court-worthy, a documented chain of evidence is vital to the processes associated with the discovery, preservation, and use of digital information derived from any digital sources. Computer investigators must follow strict forensic guidelines when accessing a suspect computer. All user actions must be logged with dates, times, and personnel involved. This information will be an important component in validating chain of custody during subsequent litigation.

What Is Digital Evidence?

Digital evidence is any information of probative value that is either stored or transmitted in a binary (digital) form. Digital devices include computer hard drives, scanning devices, compact flash cards, compact discs, digital audio and video devices including answering machines, digital cameras, cell phones, digital fax machines, personal digital assistants (PDAs), and other handheld digital devices. The analysis of data stored in these communication instruments can be recovered and analyzed to assist in determining the facts. Information derived from such sources prove relationships between perpetrators and victims, confirm identification of those involved in a crime, and confirm time lines that support or refute reported information. The motives for certain activity and typical behaviors of offenders can also be appreciated.

Digital Forensic Analysis Processes

The forensic investigation will use both physical and digital evidence, and by using the scientific method, will draw certain conclusions. Three phases are required: (1) acquisition, (2) analysis, and (3) presentation (Carrier, 2003). During the acquisition phase, the digital system is saved and copied, producing an exact image of all allocated and unallocated space on the hard disk. The analysis phase examines files and directories and recovers any deleted content. During these two initial phases, emphasis is on technical issues of salvaging and organizing data. The presentation phase, however, focuses on policy and law. In corporate, military, or healthcare settings, there is representation from human resources, the offices of counsel, and various executives to ensure that privacy standards and organizational policies are followed. To a large extent, these will offer some constraints about what will eventually be made available to a court of law. Judges and juries will examine the evidence only after it has been scrutinized and determined to be admissible. The "Daubert Test," which emerged from a U.S. Supreme Court ruling in *Daubert v. Merrell Dow Pharmaceutical* (1993), will determine admissibility of digital evidence (see p. 547). In regard to procedures related to the recovery and analysis of digital evidence, there are test components that address testing, error rates, publications and peer review, and general acceptance by the scientific community. In regard to the Federal Rules of Evidence, the status of digital evidence is yet to be determined. In accordance with the Daubert guidelines, it is *scientific evidence*, but may be considered *nonscientific technical testimony* according to Rule 901(b)(9).

Dead-Box versus Live-Box Analysis

The conventional technique for computer forensic investigations involves analyses of hard drives, floppy discs, zip drives, and optical media storage (CDs and DVDs). This method is called "dead-box analysis" because the computer system is disconnected before creating an exact copy of the hard drive (Cummings, 2008).

A more recently developed technique for evidence collection is called "live-box analysis" because it relies on the computer's random-access memory (RAM) or volatile memory, giving investigators access to all memory chips. This physical memory must be captured and preserved before the user turns off the computer. When the computer is removed from a power source and shut down, these data are no longer available to investigators. The invaluable information that can be recovered from live-box analysis includes registry data, user names and passwords, instant message or chat exchanges, open documents, and e-mail with addresses. When considering the value of these elements, it is obvious why live-box analysis is vital to help investigators understand a suspect's computer activity over an extended period of time.

Investigators use software utilities, hardware devices, or certain keyboard sequences to create a snapshot of all physical memory within the computer. This is sometimes referred to as a *crash dump*. Common systems such as Windows offer free software designed to capture all physical memory. Once the memory is preserved, special training and software adjuncts are required to reveal all aspects of the memory system. Although live-box techniques are vital to many investigations, they should be used in conjunction with dead-box techniques to ensure a comprehensive approach to computer analysis.

Techniques for Computer Evidence Recovery

Most of the technology regarding the recovery of evidence from computers has been developed by an assortment of investigative agencies. For example, the FBI has identified hackers and intruders, as well as sexual predators who exploit their victims through online communication. The U.S. Secret Service has exposed criminals who engage in financial fraud and identity theft via the Internet. The Departments of Defense and Homeland Security also engage in cyberforensics to uncover networks of international espionage or terrorist plots. Cyber criminals tend to keep one step ahead of technology designed to secure computers from unlawful intrusions into personal and networked computers. Savvy hackers, sometimes sponsored by nation states, have developed specific

malware and modus operandi resulting in intellectual property theft. Much of this sophisticated malware is difficult to detect and to defeat with the traditional computer security systems of business and government.

Lawful Interception of Data

The United States and many other countries have unique prerequisites for lawful surveillance for forensic investigations, including the capture of digital data. In the United States, the legal basis is "probable cause" as defined by the Fifth Amendment of the Constitution for serious crimes such as drug-trafficking, gambling, blackmailing, manslaughter and murder, armed robbery, debt crime and racketeering, bribery, and kidnapping. Prosecutors must establish that the target devices are being used for communications related to the crime, and the order is typically for 30 days or less. The passage of the U.S. Patriot Act has added others. These are the use of chemical weapons and weapons of mass destruction, global terrorism, financial transactions supporting terrorism, and financial support of terrorist and terrorist organizations (Hoffman & Terplan, 2006). Ordinarily, but not in all cases, a U.S. federal or state judge must order surveillance actions. There are some scenarios when alternate legal processes may be employed, such as an administrative or grand jury subpoena, a trial subpoena, a search warrant, or proof of customer consent. The content of unopened mail and electronic communications such as e-mail, voicemail, and text messages is accessible by search warrants in most cases; however, real-time interception of communications or unopened voice messages requires eavesdropping warrants. (Hoffman & Terplan, 2006, p. 340).

There are certain wiretap warrants that involve "real-time" obligations for data handover, and emergency operators represent the highest priority. Numbers such as 911, public-safety, emergency medical service providers and dispatch, fire service, public safety, law enforcement, and hospital emergency or trauma units are among those entities that have immediate access to the caller-identification data, and ordinarily this information is periodically downloaded and archived onto CD-ROMs. Private crisis or suicide-prevention hotlines do not have these same provisions, however (Hoffman & Terplan, 2006, p. 345.) The forensic nurse investigator is often able to use data from such sources to reconstruct communications and activities associated with a victim or suspect.

Digital Data in Healthcare

Within healthcare, there are multiple applications of digital evidence that might become relevant to a forensic investigation. Even before a gunshot victim reaches the hospital, important information has already been captured, which may later prove important to an investigation. The victim may have used a cell phone before or during a robbery attempt, there is the 911 call for assistance at the time of the shooting, police scanners record precise times of units being dispatched, and the conversations of the EMTs and other emergency personnel are being recorded and date/time stamped. In public places, there might be video surveillance of the crime scene. In addition, personal cell phones and digital cameras of bystanders might have been used to document the scene of the shooting. One can readily appreciate that once the patient reaches the hospital, more digital records are being made. The ER ambulance entrance camera records the arrival of the emergency vehicles; a computerized medical record is begun with data streaming to predetermined locales within the hospital; vital signs are automatically monitored, recorded, and sent to the hospital information system; the imbedded computer boards for the ventilator, IV pumps, blood warmer, and internal probes capture details of treatment and the patient's responses to therapy; personnel actions are tracked by pin numbers, passwords, or electronic signatures as they enter and leave the trauma room or access emergency drugs/supplies; digital x-rays are taken and sent to a consulting trauma center; telephonic communications are being recorded; the trauma receiving room is recording all events by audio and video media; and personal digital assistants (PDAs) of physicians and other staff are storing and transmitting data about the patient's condition. These are but a few samples of events in one type of hospital case, but it should be obvious that digital data are rapidly accumulating about the patient's condition and treatment, and such information in retrospect is crucial in reconstructing events within the hospital. Despite the Health Insurance Portability and Accountability Act (HIPAA [Privacy Act]) guidance, there is little or no privacy for the patient or the staff, and most of the information gathered during such incidents is discoverable and can be used later by investigators who suspect that criminal activity has occurred. HIPAA provisions are designed to protect patients from unauthorized or accidental disclosure of medical information during transmission within and among medical facilities, healthcare workers or providers, and third-party payers (Frank-Stromborg, 2006).

Computer Use in Hospital Communications

In today's hospitals, administrators are forced to address efficiencies in patient care and workflow processes. Higher patient acuity, the nursing shortage, and increased demands for documentation have placed new demands on the shrinking workforce, and workers are expected to do more with less. Consumer expectations of healthcare quality are also at an all-time high. In response to the ever-increasing pressures to improve care, contain costs, and operate within a highly competitive environment, hospitals have looked to new technologies for answers. One solution to the dilemma is to provide personnel with connections to data, records, and people that are vital for making the right things happen. Efficiency, expediency, and flawless precision are required for positive outcomes. Since the 1990s, there has been a rapid growth of computer and other digital interfaces at the point of care, which can contribute to these goals and even improve the hospital's "bottom line."

Ready, rapid connectivity through wired and wireless devices offer several advantages to the frustrated nurse who by now has learned to survive in this stressful and complex environment by becoming a genius at multitasking. Hard-wired computer and physiological monitors have contributed immensely to clinical safety and efficiency. Now, in addition, there is an array of sophisticated wireless devices that offer even more opportunities for communication and data access that are vital to prompt clinical decision making.

Wireless Technologies in Healthcare

The widespread use of wireless devices poses multiple challenges for investigators who are attempting to discover all information about a legal scenario. In addition to planned wireless communication connections, personnel bring their own wireless devices and use them liberally during their activities. They initiate and return calls, transmit data, and even take photographs using such devices. PDAs permit the storage and transmission of communications pertaining to patient care, and these devices are often used in public spaces and occasionally become misplaced, potentially compromising sensitive information. The hospital has an impossible job in harnessing and protecting healthcare data. Furthermore, information contained within the memory of such devices is typically discoverable for forensic investigations (Barber, 2007).

Hospitals and physicians have not traditionally permitted interchange between their informational sources and patient records. Federal Medicare regulations do not permit hospitals to share software or other computer services that have the potential for influencing utilization. To prevent hospitals from becoming involved in fraud and abuse investigations, the barriers remain between computer applications of hospitals and physician offices (Goldsmith, 2003). The Internal Revenue code and certain state laws for the nation's 85% of nonprofit hospitals prevent them from giving anything of monetary value to physicians. Sharing software could risk tax-exempt status (Goldsmith, 2003). Although the opportunities exist for improving efficiency through shared computer services and software applications, these real barriers remain until new legislation is enacted.

The most progressive healthcare settings are using wireless connections and Bluetooth technology for many routine communications. In some cases, applications are written into software specifications for the capability of digital recording and archiving of such information, and few personnel are aware of what is being recorded or archived. However, there are safeguards built into most medical devices, permitting the storage of information about the functions of the device, its maintenance history, and often interactions with its users. Although some medical devices such as life-support equipment and critical monitors must be hard-wired to ensure maximum reliability, remote access to bedside monitors and other equipment is often achieved via hard-wired systems that are linked to a remote area such as a nurses' station or telemetry monitoring room. When a patient is moved throughout the hospital, the monitors or other devices must be disconnected and reconnected into receptacles. Wireless connections, however, are managed automatically, making the devices truly mobile. Hospital beds, portable monitors, transport ventilators, and infusion pumps work seamlessly and memory continues, even when unplugged from their power source.

Medical telemetry has been available for several decades and has been widely used to send electrocardiograms (EKGs) from ambulances to the hospital, from one hospital location to another, of from a patient's home phone to a physician's office or telemetry station. Telemetry can also transmit oxygen saturation, blood pressure, respirations, temperature, and other data. Such data transmissions are made possible by radiofrequencies dedicated to medical purposes. These devices operate within low-power bands, 608-614 MHz, 1395-1400 MHz, and 1429-1432 MHz. The Federal Communications Commission (FCC) has restricted the use of these to short, noncontinuous messaging because of bandwidth limitation and issues of interference (Senese, 2003). Another in-building advanced wireless medium (802.11b) has been developed to transmit more complex data and, on demand, to transmit it continuously. This technology uses a broadcast power band centered at 2.4 GHz, which is capable of handling data at a much high rate than earlier telemetric devices.

Bedside portals permit the nurse access to third-party applications and information from the pharmacy or laboratory with just a click of the mouse. In addition, there is ready access to patient test results and immediate feedback of orders placed to dietary or radiology. Hospital personnel have all the resources of the Worldwide Web at their fingertips.

Hospitals who desire to move into the newest age of connectivity adopt wireless local area networks (WLANs). They have been a significant adjunct in the arsenal of approaches to combating medical errors, especially in drug delivery systems. With handheld computer connection to infusion pumps or medication dispensing units, the nurse can verify patient information, track drug delivery in real time, and view any clinical alerts and other actions required for a particular agent. Verification of identity at the point of care is imperative for patient safety, especially when administering medications.

Local area networks serve as transport mechanisms for wireless platforms that enable voice-controlled communications throughout an 802.11b-networked building or location. There is a server that sets up calls between badges of various personnel, effecting instant conversation between two parties or among a group of personnel who may be in various locations at any given time such as an emergency response code team. Calls and data exchanges are secured in several ways and patient privacy is assured within the system and its users. This system can be linked with the facility's PBX system too, permitting prompt connectivity to individuals outside the WLAN. Because this type of communication uses Industrial Scientific Medical (ISM) Wireless Band, it does not impact any other electronic equipment within the facility (Vocera, 2009).

Radio-frequency identification (RFID) is another wireless system that relies on "tags" with information contained within a silicon chip that is antenna mounted. The tags can be on a patient's wrist, worn by a caregiver, or attached to equipment and supplies. The ability to track and locate people, equipment, supplies, and processes is virtually amazing. One advantage over bar coding is that information can be read through and around the human body, clothing, bed linens, and nonmetallic materials. RFID-enabled processes are ideal for ensuring the positive identification of a patient and matching this information with the right drugs and the right equipment. It is also useful in point-of-care testing quality assurance, inventory control procedures, patient billing, and other processes, often making it a high-value proposition within the facility. Forensic investigators can use records stored within these systems to reconstruct events that might have led to serious injury or death or to identify caregivers who misappropriate drugs or hospital supplies. "Footprints" of the interfaces with devices and supplies are left behind with time stamps and event sequences preserved for discovery.

Bluetooth (IEEE 802.15) technology (named after a Danish king who became famous for his ability to unite and merge all of Denmark) is designed to provide wireless local connections between battery-powered devices and peripherals such as a personal computer (PC), a cell phone, or an Internet access point. Because battery power is precious and limited, the application uses little power, thus limiting transmission range capability. Several devices within a small radius (about 30 feet) can be linked, assuming that they have been designed to be Bluetooth compatible. Bluetooth 1.0, the initial version, permitted the user to bind or interface with a single device at a time. However, today's version (Bluetooth 1.1) permits communication with up to eight devices. Bluetooth can be used in conjunction with embedded applications to send serial data to another device for storage and retrieval.

"Plug and play" integration models emphasize the orchestration of people, processes, and technologies. By using a hands-free

wireless device for messaging, alarm notifications are transmitted to the mobile caregiver and can be managed remotely as well, permitting the caregiver to proceed with work, uninterrupted except by a voice message. Prompt notification of critical alarm scenarios improves the safety net for patients, prompting the caregiver to manage alarms at the moment they are generated at the primary source. The wireless phonelike messaging device can be interfaced with many bedside devices, making it extremely valuable for bringing together disparate equipment within the care area.

Global positioning systems (GPSs) and similar systems have been employed in some facilities to support the flow of information by tracking patients during interhospital transfers. Ancillary components to these navigation systems can communicate information including dispatch and arrival times, as well as the patient's clinical status. In addition to a moving map display and alphanumeric paging capabilities, some of these systems have incorporated a wireless PDA for nurses and physicians, to enable them to retrieve information from the server. The "real time" communication of location information and en route progress prevents surprise arrivals by the receiving unit. Although many facilities may not archive this information for extended periods of time during routine operations, the records can be captured and stored, in case there is a sentinel event.

It is now possible to integrate information coming from a wide array of equipment and locations and to make clinical decisions based on the integration of the data. For example, the various physiological monitors, the bed, the infusion pumps, point-of-care testing devices, and other equipment can share data used for clinical decisions. In some cases, decisions can be made by proxy or algorithms, permitting the nurse to engage in other work. The equipment collects the information, analyzes it, automatically initiates action, and precisely documents the events in real time.

KEY POINT Integrated information becomes a valuable resource during investigations of hospital accidents or other sentinel events, and it can validate or refute recalled information of caregivers or details written into the medical records.

Case Study 9-1

Is Technology Replacing Nursing Vigilance and Decision Making?

A postsurgical neurological patient in the intensive care unit (ICU) is experiencing increasing agitation. The bed's mattress senses the restlessness of the patient and validates its finding with the cerebral function monitor. In the meantime, vital signs and oxygen saturation levels are quickly checked to determine if it is appropriate to accelerate the administration of sedation and analgesia via the infusion pumps. Within seconds, the medication is being delivered into the IV line, the monitors confirm that cerebral function and vital signs are within acceptable parameters, the event is recorded for the clinicians, and appropriate notifications are made to the pharmacy to deliver the sedative drugs to the floor earlier than previously scheduled to compensate for the additional administration required by the temporary crisis. Digital information and wireless enabled communication have worked synergistically to effect a positive patient outcome. The typical delays that occur between problem identification and definitive actions are virtually eliminated, and the physicians are reassured that when problems occur, they will be promptly addressed.

(continued)

Case Study 9-1–cont'd

Critical Thinking Questions:

1. What nursing work-related inefficiencies are overcome with the use of digital "smart technology" that provides an integrated database for decision making?
2. In what ways can "smart technology" prevent nursing oversights or errors? In what ways can it contribute to errors?
3. Compare and contrast the automatic digital documentation of the case study events with traditional handwritten chart entries. Do you feel more confident or less confident when relying on digital devices to accurately document nursing interventions?
4. If a networked digital smart system failed and resulted in a disastrous patient outcome, how would you (as the patient's primary nurse), defend yourself in a court of law if you were named in a wrongful death suit?

WIRELESS SECURITY

The security of wireless technology must be protected from unauthorized access and hackers. Bluetooth applications offer several options to maintain security. Identical numbers are established for devices intended to be linked, and thus illegitimate entry attempts from nonidentical numbers are blocked. A second process for security maintenance is authorization in which user access must be approved for a certain set of devices, similar to using a password or personal identification number for computer access. Finally, encryption of data can also be used in some sensitive applications. The privacy of patients and the data can be reliably protected in wireless devices, and thus security concerns can be allayed.

A central database server can maintain records for all users and be accessed at anytime from any place by a radio-enabled PDA or laptop. This type of system ensures the most up-to-date patient information and provides the capability for this information to be updated. In some cases, equipment may have an embedded device that employs both a processor and software running on the device. A PC can be used to download data from the embedded device for storage and access at a later time.

Forensic Value of Hospital Communication and Documentation Systems

In some situations, the medical record is altered after it is known that a case involves a legal action such as suing for damages arising from negligence, malpractice, or failure of the facility, medical equipment, or device. Either the prosecution or the defense may alter documentation in an attempt to improve their chances of winning a lawsuit. This may involve several types of alteration, including adding false statements, changing times or dates, making additional entries or changing those of another provider, removing pages from the medical record, or even completely destroying the medical record by burning or shredding. The hospital or an attorney may retain a nurse to thoroughly investigate all aspects of a medical record, helping to organize and explain the construction, maintenance, and pertinent information in the chart for parties in a legal proceeding.

Often there is an unnatural sequence to a patient's progress notes. The selection of words or descriptions of a disease or condition may be more elaborate than usual, with emphasis about a particular fact or situation. Writing "later entries" in the margin of the paper or inserting additional phrases or sentences is considered

suspicious. Nursing notes that are quite detailed and lengthy (uncharacteristic for a given nurse) should alert the forensic investigator of an unusual circumstance.

A forensic nurse expert or legal nurse consultant who is assisting in preparing a court case will scrutinize the record for unusual entries or for data that prove or disprove certain reported facts or events. Does the hospital invoice support the tests and procedures outlined in the physician's progress notes? Are there charges that cannot be supported by the patient's clinical course? Do medication records from the pharmacy conflict with the medication administration form? Are there entries that appear to be out of chronological order? Do any entries appear to be crowded within a page?

With computerized charting in place at many hospitals, often incorporating some automated documentation, there are more data points to reveal the intentional alteration of records. Computers store precise information about every keystroke, and this information can be extracted from the system's mainframe or one of several backup systems for reconstruction if needed. Changes made at any time can be recovered from the electronic database because all keystrokes are recorded and stored in redundant networks. The stored information reveals removals or changes in information and provides information about the sequence of the associated events. Given today's technology linkage that provides redundancy for various systems, it is difficult (some would say virtually impossible) to defeat or alter automated documentation of medical equipment or devices that generate real-time records of physiological and caregiver events.

Digital Media Devices, First Responders, and the Hospital Staff

First responders and emergency nurses should be aware of any digital media devices that might be in the possession of patients or visitors but might not be obvious, such as a flash drive or a PDA in a pocket or handbag. These could be used to corrupt or download information from the hospital's computers. Many individuals have cell phones with cameras and other mobile storage devices, and when these are brought into the hospital environment, they pose a real threat to patient privacy and overall hospital security. Merely photographing other patients within the setting or capturing images from a computer screen pose significant legal risks. Nurses have reported observations of patients and their visitors taking pictures of the labels on the IV bag, the information from the monitor screens, and even images of patients in the bed or personnel working in the area. Although nurses find this annoying, they do not necessarily appreciate the legal issues that might emerge from such actions. Patients and visitors who use computers or PDAs could become a local intruder or insider threat to the hospital information system (HIS), compromising the medical records of hundreds of patients. Hospitals that link in-room laptops to the HIS or those permitting patients to use their personal computers in environments where there are links to the HIS can be potentially dangerous. Many hospitals have taken these threats seriously and have developed policies and procedures to prevent intrusions. However, others believe that it is the patient's or visitor's rights to retain and use personal computers, cell phones with cameras, and other mobile storage devices within the healthcare complex. Forensic nurses should maintain a high level of awareness about the potential threats that these digital devices pose and should monitor their uses carefully. It is expected that in the future, hospitals may require patients and their visitors to surrender and stow such devices on arrival and use only those provided by the hospital that have built-in protection to safeguard the security of the HIS. Hospitals must ensure patient privacy and the security of hospital information, and drastic changes are indicated when one considers that one unauthorized entry could corrupt important storage or permit the unauthorized download of sensitive medical information.

BEST PRACTICE Emergency nurses and first responders should be educated regarding the potential dangers associated with PDAs, laptops, cell phones, and other digital storage or transmission devices that have the potential to threaten patient privacy or the integrity or security of the hospital's information system. Use of such personal devices should not be permitted in patient treatment areas of the facility.

Cyber Security

Cyber security has recently become a worldwide issue because much sensitive information is stored on computers that are attached to the Internet. The government's initiatives to curb terrorism have accelerated the development of such standards because terrorist threats, plans, and actions have been facilitated via the Internet. Furthermore, identity theft and the needs for protecting proprietary information within business and industry have driven new guidance for cyber security. The most widely used is ISO/IEC 27002, which was initiated in 1995. (See Resources for provisions of ISO/IEC 27002.)

Forensic nurses should understand the elements of maintaining security related to computer and other digital devices. These include choosing and protecting passwords, using antivirus software, and coordinating virus and spyware defenses. Although most nurses are not technophiles, they should appreciate the hidden threats to computers such as corrupted software files, *rootkits* (malware to help intruders gain access to systems without detection), *bots* (remotely controlled software robots that infect a computer with worms or viruses), and *zombies* (criminals who transmit bots to infect networks). *Phishing* is another threat to computers. A perpetrator sends out legitimate-appearing e-mails for the purpose of gaining information to commit identity thefts. To operate safely in today's sophisticated, networked world, it is important for computer users to install and maintain a firewall of integrated security measures to maximize protection against unauthorized access. Because computer threats change dynamically, all firewall components must be regularly updated.

When using the Internet, healthcare users should fully understand the Web browser's security settings and appreciate the meaning of Web site certifications. With the ease of downloading data from the Internet, great care should be exercised to avoid copyright infringement when using such information in presentations and publications. There are also many important factors to know in regard to software licenses, using patches, understanding voice-over Internet protocol (VOIP), and file sharing. It is prudent to limit e-mail communications to friends and colleagues and to open attachments only from trusted individuals. Social networks pose particular vulnerabilities for healthcare workers who may reveal personal information about their job or lifestyle. Even though nurses are engaged in regular networking, they should avoid opening or forwarding "junk e-mail" such as jokes, cartoons, and chain e-mails, which are notorious for being a computer threat. Finally, all computer users should ensure the personal security of their laptops, PDAs, and cell phones, because each of these devices contain important information related to both identity and activities. Carelessly leaving these items unattended in a car, in a locker room, at the hospital, or at the office could have serious consequences including threats to personal safety.

The Medical Record as Evidence

Medical records are considered as *hearsay* because the statements recorded within them were not declared directly to the courts. They are also *prima facie* evidence (i.e., as they seem on first impression.) All medical records must be authenticated or certified to be entered as evidence in a court of law. After it has been accepted as an item of evidence, it can then be discussed in detail in regard to its contents.

The retention and destruction principles for any medical record also apply to electronic records and digital files. It is imperative that hospitals exercise caution to ensure that old backup tapes, instant messages, voicemails, word processing drafts, and other "temporary" files do not become permanent ones. Most organizations have planned "purges" to eliminate these potential sources of surprise during e-discovery processes. If files are no longer considered useful and destroyed within a certain time period according to hospital policies and procedures, this provides a safe harbor for organizations according to the new rule under the Federal Rules of Civil Procedure. Sanctions may be imposed, however, for improper destruction practices.

Legal holds may be placed on digital files as well as paper files. If an attorney or judicial authority believes that a record might be destroyed before its use in current or anticipated litigation, audits, or governmental investigations, these records are placed under a preservation order to prevent their loss. The legal hold order may occur at any time during a potential or actual litigation. Specific authority is granted to one individual, by name as well as job title, to suspend routine purging or destruction of records and, in the event of pending litigation, to ensure the integrity of the preservation order.

BEST PRACTICE In the event that a hospital risk manager believes that any sentinel event or other adverse incident might result in legal action, immediate steps must be taken to suspend any destruction of records related to the scenario.

Spoliation is the intentional destruction, mutilation, alteration, or concealment of evidence. All hospitals must have safeguards in place to prevent tampering, and to ensure backups for digital files in the event of electronic failures that could occur. Even if there is "good faith" and sound procedures have been exercised to prevent accidental losses or utility of files, judges may require hospitals to reconstruct lost data, obviously a costly and tedious process. Nurses should ensure that they understand and follow policies and procedures in regard to all digital information sources and their related files.

Discovery

Discovery is a judicial procedure by which a party in a lawsuit exchanges information with the other party. It is equally valuable to the prosecution and the defense attorneys. The healthcare discovery process usually involves a request for medical records, nursing time schedules, supervisor reports, pharmacy records, telephone operator logs, and personnel performance records. Of course, some cases may extend into the physician office files, cell phone entries, and computers.

E-discovery involves computer communication such as e-mail, instant messaging, and computer-generated medical records.

Discovery is a linear process and encompasses several stages of requesting documents and subsequently more documents as evidence is pieced together and witnesses provide depositions that open new avenues of investigation.

Changes to the Federal Rules of Civil Procedure affect how healthcare facilities manage their electronic data files. These organizations, like other businesses, use e-mail to communicate patient information to internal providers such as nurses, physicians, and other hospital departments and to relay essential data to insurance companies, referral agencies, and to the patients and their families. As you might imagine, much of this information is sensitive and should be treated as confidential. However, when a healthcare facility uses e-communications to improve its operational efficiency, it must engage in rigorous checks and balances to ensure that all patient information is treated as "privileged" and financial records remain confidential.

During e-discovery, scientific methods are used to examine hard drives, servers, and other sources of computer-generated information. PDA files, cell phone records, e-mail, and instant messaging records of key individuals are retrieved and analyzed. To avoid the potential claims of "obstruction of justice," hospital information managers must be fully aware of the locations and types of digital information that may be stored throughout the hospital. Important data may be found on networked computers, laptops, medical devices, and patient care equipment, and these must be readily offered as evidence on request. These multiple sources produce an amazing database pertinent to a legal claim including medical information, financial records, and personnel interactions. However, because of the extensive system of digital information sources, both wired and wireless, it is no longer considered appropriate for attorneys to request "any and all" records pertinent to a legal claim.

KEY POINT HIPAA guidance indicates that any healthcare organization must define its designated record set that includes medical and billing records as well as associated communications pertaining to healthcare management and business operations.

Patient Privacy, Archiving, and Other Dilemmas

Patient privacy is a huge issue in today's medical arena, and to protect the patient's privacy as well as safeguard its staff, institutions must decide whether or not routine e-mail should be stored in archives or routinely discarded, because it can be either an asset or liability during litigation processes. Best practices for all healthcare facilities must include policies and procedures regarding e-communications. Is it best to *keep everything* or routinely *destroy everything* within the e-communication network of a hospital? Nurses, physicians, and other care providers must assume that someone else has access to what is written about patients, their care, or incidents that occur during their hospitalization. E-mails, instant messages, appointment follow-ups, and so on can be very valuable to confirm what is documented in the patient's record. They can also help to validate that what caregivers allege is true. For example, if there is a question about whether or not the patient's laboratory results were communicated to the physician's office, the "sent e-mail" will be a specific way to prove that there was notification. All e-mail is dated and time-stamped, too, so alterations would be obvious. Counterarguments such as "I didn't get the e-mail" could be quickly refuted by experts in

e-communications who can verify all transactions from analyzing network communications. Keeping e-mail in archives could serve many purposes to protect patients and staff. If the facility and its staff are using e-communications for the right reasons, and if the contents contain accurate information, there is a distinct advantage in archiving these messages. Archived "backup" data could be invaluable if other sources of medical records were incomplete or could not be located in the event of a subsequent lawsuit.

Opponents of archiving hospital e-mail and instant message files argue that those involving infants or pediatric patients would need to be held for excessive lengths of time, up to 25 years in some states. An instant message from a nurse on one unit to another nurse within the hospital about an after-work shopping trip to the mall could be used years later by a plaintiff's attorney to prove the nurses' inattention to their workloads at a time when a patient was "coding" or a medication error occurred. Hospitals would potentially be buried in an electronic storage nightmare, and staff might be intimidated and reluctant to use e-mail for sending routine messages regarding a patient admission or a request for a change in a diet order. Most hospitals tend to adopt policies that ensure that all e-communications are treated as temporary documents. These would neither be retained nor archived for a specified period of time. Experts in hospital medical records believe that all essential information should be documented in the patient's medical chart. This should be sufficient for recording actual events occurring on a given day or at a specific time. Multiple places to record data points in patient care could be "setting a trap" for defendants. If there is any incongruity among various sources, plaintiffs could argue about legitimacy and accuracy, casting doubt on the veracity of all documents. The multiple sources of automatically stored data that are regularly transmitted to the hospital information system must also be considered. There is information from the Pyxis®, the monitors, IV pumps, hospital beds, and in-room computers. Any inconsistencies in times, sequencing of events or other data could pose unnecessary liability for the facility. In other words, fewer data sources result in fewer opportunities for discrepancies that could negatively impact a forensic case.

Summary

Forensic nurses must appreciate the sources of digital data within healthcare settings. In addition to the portable and networked computers, cell phones, PDAs, and data recorders, there are many other devices capable of storing or transmitting digital information. Many of these are personally owned and not managed according to the policies and procedures of those devices owned and operated by the hospital. However, when used on duty to augment communication, they may be counterproductive in the event of litigation and its subsequent discovery processes. The risks to patient privacy as well as the evidentiary value of archived information within these devices should be significant deterrents to using personal devices in employment settings to transmit patient information or to use them for patient-centered communications.

The digital forensic scientist is the individual who detects, analyzes, and generates reports about evidence found in the physical memory of computers or within certain applications of wireless devices that store data. These data must be managed with the same chain-of-custody considerations and rules of admissibility as any other evidence. The expert in cyberforensics is rapidly becoming one of the most important expert witnesses in today's courtroom.

Resource

ISO/IEC 27002. Accessed online, 1 April 2009, www.27000.org/iso-27002.htm

References

American Health Information Management Association. *The new electronic discovery civil rule*. Accessed online: 1/18/09, http://library.ahima.org/spedio/groups/public/documents/shima/bok1_031860.hcsp?dDocN

Barber, J. M. (2007). *Wireless connectivity and patient workflow critical care perspectives*. Saxe Communications. (Content used with permission, Saxe Communications, Burlington, VT.).

Carrier, B. (2003). Defining digital forensics examination and analysis tools using abstraction layers. *International Journal of Digital Evidence*, *1*(4), Winter. In Digital Research Workshop II, 2002. 1–12.

Cummings, R. C. (2008). Computer forensics. *Evidence Technology Magazine*, November-December, 12–23.

Frank-Stromborg, M., Burns, K., Morgan, B., & Sierens, D.B. (2006). Health Insurance Portability and Accountability Act (HIPAA). In P. Iyer, B. J Levin, & M. A Shea (Eds.), *Medical Legal Aspects of Medical Records* (Chapter 11). Tucson, AZ: Lawyers and Judges Publishing Co., Inc.

Goldsmith, J. (2003). *Digital medicine, implications for healthcare leaders, ACHE management series*, Chicago: Health Administration Press.

HIPAA Data security and privacy standards for voice communications over a wireless LAN, Vocera Communications, Cupertino, CA 95014 (White Paper, 2005).

Hoffmann, P., & Terplan, K. (2006). *Intelligence support systems: Technology for lawful intercepts*. Boca Raton, FL: Auerbach Publications.

Senese, B. (2003). *Implementing wireless communication in hospital environments with bluetooth, 802.11b, and other technologies*. Los Angeles: Medical Device and Diagnostic Industry Magazine (MDDI), Canon Communications.

Vocera, Inc., San Jose, CA, 2009 (Product Literature).

Zatyko, K. (2007). Defining digital forensics. *Forensic Magazine*, March, 18–22.

10 Forensic Toxicology

Sarah Kerrigan and Bruce A. Goldberger

Toxicological analyses are undertaken in clinical and forensic laboratories to facilitate medical intervention, diagnosis, or treatment, and as part of the criminal justice system. Toxicology also plays a fundamental role in determining the cause and manner of death and is widely utilized in the workplace to deter drug use. *Forensic* comes from the Latin word *forensis,* which means "forum," denoting a court or tribunal. Forensic toxicology is distinct from clinical toxicology in that it is often practiced within a legal domain for the purpose of upholding the law. However, clinicians and medical personnel do play an essential role in forensic toxicology. During medical treatment, they are often the first ones to make observations, diagnoses, and collect biological specimens from injured persons who may be the subject of a legal investigation. Analyses of specimens without the context in which they were collected are generally of limited value. To properly evaluate these tests, the patient's or victim's history of drug usage is needed. Furthermore, improperly collected specimens can yield improper or misleading results. Forensic nurses, because of their unique training, are in a position to aid clinicians, law enforcement officers, and legal personnel with investigations utilizing toxicological testing. They are familiar with the proper collection, storage, and testing of forensic specimens. In addition, they are experienced in conducting interviews and collecting histories, which will aid with the interpretation of the results from the analyses.

Subdisciplines of Forensic Toxicology

The three major subdisciplines of forensic toxicology are human performance toxicology, postmortem toxicology, and forensic urine drug testing. Human performance toxicology has to do with mental and physical effects of drugs that may, for example, impair judgment or coordination. Postmortem toxicology involves the investigation of drugs and poisons in circumstances of death. Forensic urine drug testing has become widespread in the military as well as in public and private sectors of the workplace.

Reasons for Drug Use

Unfortunately, in today's society, the ingestion of a drug or drugs in the absence of medical supervision is commonplace. One common motive for the misuse of drugs includes the pursuit of euphoric or psychedelic effects. Many times these drugs are used to enhance social situations, used as a result of peer pressure, used out of curiosity, or used for "fun" or to "get high."

Alternatively, drugs may be used to enhance mental, emotional, or physical well-being. For example, it is not uncommon for individuals to self-medicate for the relief of anxiety, depression, insomnia, or pain or to increase alertness or relaxation.

Toxicology Investigation

Toxicological findings may provide the necessary insight to explain behavioral or physiological effects (e.g., why a person drives off the road, attempts suicide, or unexpectedly falls unconscious). The use of prescription or over-the-counter (OTC) drugs in a manner inconsistent with accepted medical practice might be of relevance during a criminal investigation, particularly in a case involving driving a motor vehicle, operation of machinery, violent crime, or sexual assault.

As mentioned earlier, the selection, identification, collection, and preservation of biological evidence have a profound impact on the quality of analytical data and the interpretation of toxicological findings. To this end, the toxicologist relies on a variety of analytical techniques, of which some may provide results in minutes or hours, and others may require several days.

There is considerable overlap between the subdisciplines of forensic toxicology, which are largely governed by the natural laws of pharmacology and chemistry. Forensic toxicologists are commonly asked certain questions: Was a drug or chemical involved? If so, what was the drug or chemical? How much was taken and when? Was it responsible for the death or did it affect behavior? The key to answering these questions is an understanding of pharmacokinetics, pharmacodynamics, and analytical techniques.

Trends in Drug Use

The 2007 National Survey on Drug Use and Health (NSDUH), conducted by the Substance Abuse and Mental Health Services Administration (SAMHSA), indicated that an estimated 19.9 million Americans (8% of the population ≥ 12 years old) were illicit drug users, 57.8 million participated in binge drinking, and another 17 million were heavy drinkers. Drug abuse, whether it involves illicit substances or the misuse of therapeutics, is nondiscriminatory in that it has permeated almost every level of society to some degree. Trends in drug use among the young are largely governed by the perceived risk of drug use. As perceived risk decreases, use increases, and vice versa. These findings offer the hope that comprehensive drug prevention efforts, based on drug education and risk assessment, can curb drug use among young people.

In 2007, marijuana was the most commonly used illicit drug in the United States (10.4 million) followed by the nonmedical use of prescription drugs (6.9 million). Of these, an estimated 5.2 million used narcotic pain relievers, 1.8 million used tranquilizers, 1.1 million used stimulants, and 0.3 million used sedatives. In the same year, estimates for cocaine, hallucinogen, methamphetamine, and heroin users were 2.1 million, 1.0 million, 0.5 million, and 0.2 million, respectively (SAMHSA, 2007).

The Drug Abuse Warning Network (DAWN) estimates that in 2006, 1.7 million emergency department (ED) visits were associated with drug misuse or abuse. Of these, 31% involved an illicit drug, 28% involved a pharmaceutical drug, 7% involved alcohol use among minors, and the remainder involved combinations of illicit, pharmaceutical, and alcohol misuse. Over half of the drug-related ED admissions were attributed to illicit drugs, either alone or in combination with other substances. The most frequently reported drugs were cocaine (548,608), marijuana (290,563), heroin (189,780), and stimulants (107,575). Although no significant changes in drug-related ED visits were evident for the major illicit drugs between 2004 and 2006, visits related to the use of nonmedical or pharmaceuticals increased by as much as 38%. Benzodiazepine and opioid-related visits increased 36% and 43%, respectively. In 2006, an estimated 57,550 ED visits involved hydrocodone, 64,888 involved oxycodone, and 45,130 involved methadone.

DRUGS IN THE MILITARY

A Department of Defense survey of substance abuse and health behaviors among military personnel showed that illicit drug use declined dramatically between 1980 (27.6%) and 2002 (3.4%). Substance abuse among military personnel has remained at about 3% since 1995, but it is significantly lower than rates of illicit drug use among the civilian population (5.8%). This downward trend seems to coincide with the 1990 guidelines proposed by the secretary of defense and the secretary of transportation to regulate and implement a comprehensive drug-testing program of military personnel. This deterrent against drug use appears to have been extremely successful and has become widespread in both the public and private sectors. Incentives for a drug-free workplace are improved safety and a reduction in financial losses caused by absenteeism, adverse health consequences, and accidents.

DRUGS AND CRIME

According to a 2002 study by the U.S. Department of Justice, as many as 29% of convicted inmates reported using illegal drugs at the time of the offense. The most common drugs were marijuana (10%), cocaine (11%), stimulants (5%), and heroin or opiates (4%). More than two thirds of jail inmates were found to be dependent on drugs or alcohol, and nearly 70% of probationers report past drug use. The most frequently reported drugs among probationers include marijuana (67%), cocaine (32%), stimulants (24%), hallucinogens (20%), depressants (16%), and heroin or opiates (9%). DWI offenders on probation parallel the overall probation population, which is cause for significant traffic safety concern; they report the use of marijuana (65%), cocaine (28%), stimulants (29%), hallucinogens (20%), depressants (15%), and heroin or opiates (6%).

DRUGS AND DRIVING

According to the Fatality Analysis Reporting System of the National Highway and Transportation Safety Administration (NHTSA, 2002), 41% of the 38,309 fatal traffic crashes in 2002 were alcohol related. The exact number of traffic fatalities involving drugs other than alcohol is not known. However, the NHTSA estimates that drugs are used by approximately 10% to 22% of drivers involved in accidents, often in combination with alcohol. A study of fatally injured drivers from seven states showed that alcohol was present in more than 50% of the drivers, and other drugs were present in 18% of the drivers. An ongoing NHTSA study of nonfatally injured drivers has shown that compared to the general population, the percentage of young drivers (under 21 years old) who test positive for drugs has almost doubled. The

incidence of positive drug findings in injured drivers who receive medical treatment ranges from less than 10% to as high as 40%. The incidence of drug-use among drivers arrested for motor vehicle offenses ranges between 15% and 50%. ED physicians may not have a legal obligation to report impaired drivers to the authorities, and as such, these drivers may not be held accountable for their actions.

In 2007, an estimated 9.9 million people reported driving under the influence of an illicit drug during the past year. This figure corresponds to 4% of the population aged 12 years or older. The highest rates of drug use while driving were reported among 18- to 21-year-olds (12.5%). In 2007, an estimated 31.4 million people in the United States (12.7%) reported driving under the influence of alcohol at least once during the previous year. Highest rates of alcohol-impaired driving were reported among 18- to 25-year-olds (22.8%), and males were nearly twice as likely as females to have driven under the influence of alcohol (SAMHSA, 2007).

DRUGS AND HEALTH

According to the 2007 National Survey on Drug Use and Health, of the 19.9 million Americans who were illicit drug users, an estimated 7.5 million were in need of substance abuse treatment. A further 19.3 million were in need of treatment for alcohol. However, only 1.3 and 1.6 million received treatment for drug- and alcohol-related problems. Dependence and suicide, followed by psychic effects, are the most frequently cited motives for drug use. Common reasons for drug-related admission to the ED are overdose, detoxification, unexpected reaction, chronic effects, or withdrawal. Unexpected reactions and overdoses were the predominant reasons for ED contact in episodes involving gammahydroxybutyrate (GHB), miscellaneous hallucinogens, phencyclidine (PCP), inhalants, methylenedioxymethamphetamine (MDMA, Ecstasy), amphetamines, ketamine, marijuana (THC), lysergic acid diethylamide (LSD), and alcohol in combination with other drugs. Detoxification is a common reason for ED contact for episodes involving heroin and cocaine.

Despite being perceived as a low-risk drug, marijuana is second only to cocaine in drug-related ED visits. Drug use remains somewhat regionalized, accounting for unrepresentative statistics in certain metropolitan areas and states. For example, LSD, GHB, and the designer amphetamines are more prevalent in California, Florida, and New York, where the drug-culture associated with the "rave" scene is popular.

CLUB DRUGS

"Club drugs," which are becoming increasingly popular with young people, are commonly encountered at nightclubs and raves. These include the synthetic designer amphetamine MDMA, GHB, LSD, and methamphetamine, as well as illegally diverted and trafficked therapeutics, such as ketamine and Rohypnol (flunitrazepam). These drugs have been somewhat popularized by the rave culture and the false perception that they are not as harmful as mainstream illicit drugs such as cocaine and heroin. Statistics from DAWN show that ED mentions involving these drugs, notably MDMA and GHB, have increased at an alarming rate since the early 1990s (Fig. 10-1). Legislative efforts to curb this trend have included federal scheduling and inclusion of these drugs into the Controlled Substances Act. These legal efforts will be supported by a $54 million educational campaign, launched by the National Institute on Drug Abuse and partner organizations, to raise awareness of the dangers of GHB and other club drugs.

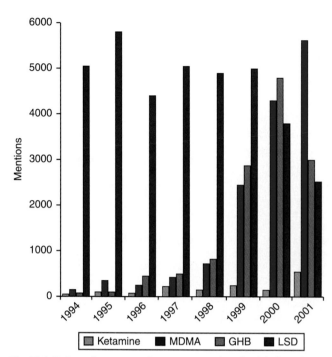

Fig. 10-1 Estimated emergency department mentions for club drugs (1994-2001). (From Drug Abuse Warning Network. (2003). DHHS Publication No. (SMA) 03-3780. Rockville, MD.)

Legend: Ketamine, MDMA, GHB, LSD

Box 10-1 Health Consequences of Intravenous Drug Use

HIV
Viral hepatitis (B and C)
Sexually transmitted infection (gonorrhea, syphilis)
Bone and joint infection
Abscesses and cellulitis
Endocarditis
Tuberculosis
Pneumonia
Septic pulmonary emboli
Septic arthritis
Septic thrombophlebitis
Mycotic aneurysm

Pharmacokinetics

Pharmacokinetics describes the absorption, distribution, metabolism, and excretion of a drug. These factors influence the efficacy of the drug, its concentration at the active site, and the intensity and duration of the drug effect. Pharmacokinetic properties are used by pharmacologists, clinicians, and toxicologists to develop new therapeutics, understand the factors that govern use and abuse, determine how drugs can be detected in the body over time, and interpret their effects on human performance.

ROUTES OF ADMINISTRATION

Onset of action, duration of effects, intensity, and the "quality" of the drug experience may vary, depending on the route of administration. Intravenous (IV) drug administration provides maximum drug delivery and rapid onset of effects. The injection of a drug bypasses the body's natural safeguards. Intravenous administration is complete and not affected by gastrointestinal absorption or intramuscular or subcutaneous absorption. In addition, IV drug administration also avoids the liver (first-pass metabolism) and is transported directly to the site of action without being inactivated by liver enzymes. Complications of intravenous drug use includes the transmission of infectious diseases such as human immunodeficiency virus (HIV) and hepatitis, as well as infection, emboli, blood vessel occlusion, thrombosis, and irritant effects (Box 10-1). For these reasons, inhalation and smoking are popular alternatives because these routes mimic IV administration. When a drug is smoked, it is rapidly absorbed in the lungs and transported to the brain via the arterial blood supply. Smoking is a preferred route of crack cocaine administration because of rapid onset, prolonged duration, intensity, and euphoria. However, pipes and smoking apparatus become hot and may burn the lips. The efficiency and speed of drug delivery increase the reinforcing effect of the drug and its abuse liability. However, not all abused drugs are amenable to all routes. The relative advantages and disadvantages of oral,

inhalation, smoking, intravenous, intranasal, and dermal drug delivery are summarized in Table 10-1.

ABSORPTION

For a drug to exert a pharmacological effect, it must gain entry to the body by absorption and traverse biological membranes to its site of action. The route of entry determines the site of absorption: gastrointestinal, pulmonary, dermal, or parenteral. Unless the drug is administered intravenously, it is unlikely that all of it will be absorbed. The efficiency of this process, known as bioavailability, is the amount of drug that is absorbed relative to the amount that is administered. Physicochemical properties of the drug determine the efficiency of absorption, as well as the concentration of the drug, circulation, and surface area at the absorption site. Physical state, solubility, and formulation of the drug play important roles. Water-soluble liquids are absorbed more rapidly than oils, solids, or sustained-release formulations. Because absorption largely depends on diffusion, the greater the concentration gradient across the membrane (the higher the drug concentration), the faster the drug will be absorbed. A large surface area, such as the capillary-rich surface of the lungs or microvilli of the small intestine, facilitates absorption.

The pH and pK_a of the drug determine how and where the drug gains entry to different compartments of the body. The pK_a is the pH at which the drug is half ionized (Table 10-2). The majority of drugs can be classified as acidic, neutral, or basic. Phospholipid membranes within the body are selectively permeable, depending on size, charge, and lipid solubility of the drug. These membranes are effective barriers against passive diffusion of ionized drugs, which must undergo alternative methods of transport, such as filtration, phagocytosis, pinocytosis, and active or facilitated transport.

Strong acids have low pK_a's (pH 1 through 5), which means that at physiological pH (7.2) they are mostly ionized. This state restricts the mobility of the drug because passive diffusion is not favored (Table 10-3). The pK_a affects absorption and distribution of a drug. For example, the gastrointestinal tract varies widely in pH, from the buccal cavity (pH 7) to the stomach (pH 2), small intestine (pH 6), duodenum (pH 7), ileum and colon (pH 8). As a result, uncharged acidic drugs tend to absorb well in the stomach. Strong bases, however, which have high pK_a values, are predominantly charged at physiological pH values. Even in the most alkaline regions of the gastrointestinal tract (pH 8), basic drugs like methamphetamine (pK_a 9.9) are predominantly charged.

The pK_a of the drug not only determines the absorption, but it also determines where the drug is most likely to reside. For example, when drugs are distributed into the sweat, which is slightly acidic (pH 5), basic drugs like cocaine and methamphetamine become charged and are trapped in the fluid in a process known

Table 10-1 Common Routes of Administration for Abused Drugs

ROUTE	ADVANTAGES	DISADVANTAGES	DRUGS
Oral	Noninvasive	Slow absorption via GI tract First-pass metabolism Variable bioavailability Delayed onset Blunted reaction	Benzodiazepines, cannabinoids, GHB, LSD mescaline, opioids, peyote
Inhalation	Noninvasive Rapid absorption	Limited to drugs with sufficient volatility	Solvents, gases, low boiling-point alkaloids
Intravenous	"Rush" caused by bolus of drug Rapid onset	Invasive Deleterious health effects	Cocaine, methamphetamine, opioids
Smoking	Rapid onset Rapid absorption Noninvasive	Pyrolysis of drug Not all drugs heat stable Reduced bioavailability due to sidestream smoke	Crack cocaine, marijuana, methamphetamine, opioids, PCP
Intranasal	Noninvasive	Irritation of the nasal mucosa Variable absorption	Cocaine, methamphetamine, opioids
Dermal	Noninvasive	Lipid-soluble drugs only Local irritation Delayed onset Blunted reaction, no "rush"	Fentanyl, nicotine

Table 10-2 Pharmacokinetic Properties of Commonly Abused Drugs

DRUG STREET NAME(S)	HALF-LIFE	DURATION OF EFFECT (h)	PROTEIN BINDING (%)	Vd (L/kg)	pK_a	UNCHANGED IN URINE (%)	PRINCIPAL METABOLITE(S)

Cocaine
  Blow, horn, nose candy, jelly beans
  (crack), rooster (crack), tornado
  (crack), moonrock (crack and
  heroin), wicky stick (crack, PCP,
  marijuana), snowball (cocaine and
  heroin)
	0.7-1.5 h	1-2	92	2-3	8.7	<10	Benzoylecgonine, ecgonine
							  methylester, norcocaine

Fentanyl	3-12 h	0.5-1	79	3-8	8.4	1-5	Norfentanyl, hydroxyfentanyl

GHB
  Goop, grievous bodily harm, good
  hormones at bedtime, max, soap
	0.3-1 h	2-5	0	0.4	—	<5	—

Heroin
  Smack, hell dust, big H, thunder,
  nose drops (liquefied heroin),
  crop (low-quality heroin), dragon
  rock (heroin and crack), A-bomb
  (marijuana and heroin)
	2-6 m	3-6	40	25	7.6	<1	6-Acetylmorphine, morphine,
							  glucuronide conjugates

Ketamine
  Cat valium, K, jet, special K, super
  acid
	3-4 h	0.5-2	30	3-5	7.5	2-5	Norketamine,
							  dehydronorketamine,
							  glucuronide conjugates

Lysergic acid diethylamide (LSD)
  Acid, acid cube, backbreaker,
  battery acid, doses, dots, Elvis,
  loony tunes, pane, superman,
  window pane, zen
	3-4 h	8-12	—	0.3	7.8	<1	NorLSD, 2-oxo-3-hydroxy-LSD

Marijuana (cannabinoids)
  Bud, dope, ganja, herb, hydro, indo,
  Mary Jane, shake
	1-3 d (naive)
	3-13 d (chronic)
		2-4	97	4-10	10.6	<1	11-nor-Δ^9-carboxy-THC

Methamphetamine
  Biker's coffee, chalk, chicken feed,
  crank, crystal meth, glass, go fast,
  ice, meth, poor man's cocaine,
  shabu, speed, stove top, trash,
  yellow bam
	6-15 h	2-4	10-20	3-7	9.9	43	p-Hydroxymethamphetamine,
							  amphetamine,
							  p-Hydroxyamphetamine

Table 10-2 Pharmacokinetic Properties of Commonly Abused Drugs—cont'd

DRUG STREET NAME(S)	HALF-LIFE	DURATION OF EFFECT (h)	PROTEIN BINDING (%)	Vd (L/kg)	pK$_a$	UNCHANGED IN URINE (%)	PRINCIPAL METABOLITE(S)
MDMA Disco biscuit, ecstasy, hug drug, go, X, XTC	6-9 h	2-4	—	5-8	—	65	Methylenedioxyamphetamine
Morphine	1.3-6.7 h	3-6	35	2-5	8.1	<10	Glucuronide conjugates, normorphine
Phencyclidine (PCP) Angel dust, busy bee, cadillac, elephant tranquilizer, embalming fluid, hog, jet fuel, killer weed, tick	7-46 h	2-4	65	5-8	8.5	30-50	4-Phenyl-4-piperidinocyclohexanol, 1-(1-phenylcyclohexyl)-4-hydroxypiperidine
Phenobarbital	2-6 d	10-20	50	0.5-0.6	7.2	20-35	p-Hydroxyphenobarbital, dihydrodiol, glucuronide conjugates

Data from Baselt, R. C. (2008). *Disposition of toxic drugs and chemicals in man* (8th ed.). Foster City, CA: Biomedical Publications; Wilson, J. M. (1994). *Abused drugs II.* Washington, DC: AACC Press.

Table 10-3 Effect of pH and pK$_a$ on Acidic, Basic, and Neutral Drugs

DRUG TYPE	PERCENTAGE OF IONIZED DRUG PH UNITS FROM PK$_a$				
	−2	−1	PK$_a$	+1	+2
Acidic drugs (e.g., acetaminophen, ampicillin, barbiturates, non-steroidal anti-inflammatory drugs, phenytoin, probenecid, THC metabolites)	1	9	50	91	99
Neutral drugs (e.g., carbamazepine, glutethimide, meprobamate)	0	0	0	0	0
Basic drugs (e.g., antiarrhythmics, antidepressants, antihistamines, cocaine, narcotic analgesics, PCP, phenothiazines, sympathomimetic amines)	99	91	50	9	1

as "ion trapping." This process becomes important during neonatal drug exposure, which will be discussed later.

DISTRIBUTION

As soon as the drug is absorbed and enters the circulation, the distribution phase begins. Once more, depending on the physicochemical properties of the drug and the surrounding pH, passive diffusion, filtration, or transport mechanisms distribute the drug to surrounding tissues and organs. On entry into the circulation, plasma proteins may bind the drug. This bound state not only limits entry into the tissues, but it also prevents interaction with receptors necessary to produce a pharmacological reaction. Simultaneous administration of multiple, highly bound drugs can inadvertently increase the free concentration of drug, resulting in an acute toxic reaction. Extensively protein bound drugs may have a delayed onset or prolonged duration of action (see Table 10-2). Highly perfused tissues, such as the heart, liver, kidney, and brain, come into contact with the drug much faster than muscle and fat, which are perfused at much slower rates and take much longer to reach equilibrium with circulating drug.

Drugs that are lipid soluble are distributed more readily into the tissues and may penetrate the blood-brain barrier. Tetrahydrocannabinol (THC), the active constituent of marijuana, is lipophilic. It is distributed and stored in tissues and fat depots within the body, accounting for its gradual release and long half-life (see Table 10-2). The extent to which a drug is distributed in the body is given by the volume of distribution (Vd), which is a function of lipophilicity, protein binding, and pK$_a$. Highly water-soluble (hydrophilic) drugs, such as ethanol (Vd 0.5 L/kg), are distributed mainly in the body water and have low volumes of distribution (Vd < 1 L/kg). Conversely, drugs with large volumes of distribution, for example, antidepressants (Vd 10–20 L/kg), are more likely to distribute throughout the body into the tissues. Heroin (Vd 25 L/kg) is capable of penetrating the protective endothelial and glial cells of the blood-brain barrier, whereas morphine (Vd 2–5 L/kg) does not.

METABOLISM

Most drugs are highly metabolized by the body with only relatively small amounts being excreted unchanged (see Table 10-2). To facilitate the process of elimination and to prevent the accumulation of drugs, several different types of biological transformations occur that increase the water solubility of the drugs. Metabolism can affect the pharmacological activity of the drug, sometimes eliminating activity (e.g., cocaine metabolism to benzoylecgonine) or increasing it (e.g., heroin metabolism to 6-acetyl-morphine and morphine).

During phase I metabolism, enzymes, such as cytochrome P450, monoamine oxidase, cholinesterase, and others, oxidize, reduce, hydrolyze, and dealkylate drugs, rendering them more hydrophilic by introducing polar moieties. This process occurs throughout the body, particularly in the liver, but also in the kidneys, blood, lungs, skin, and gastrointestinal tract. During phase II metabolism, water-soluble conjugates are formed between polar functional groups on the drug and endogenous ligands such as glucuronic acid, sulfate, and glutathione. Drugs that undergo extensive conjugation, such as morphine, may require enzyme hydrolysis prior to analysis, which will be discussed later.

Sometimes a drug may undergo biotransformation before entering the circulation. Enzymes in the gastrointestinal tract can metabolize orally administered drugs, reducing their pharmacological activity and clinical utility. When the drug has been absorbed in the lower intestine, the portal circulation transports the drug to the liver, without it ever having reached the general circulation. This "first pass" effect accounts for the reduced bioavailability of some orally administered drugs.

A great many variables can affect drug metabolism, including age, sex, genetic polymorphisms, health, disease, and nutrition. The expanding field of pharmacogenomics is beginning to elucidate the role of genes on drug metabolism. For example, differences in the abundance of certain isoenzymes of cytochrome P450 account for differences in drug metabolism between ethnic populations. These factors are of scientific importance not only for the interpretation of drug findings but also for development of new therapeutic agents.

ELIMINATION

Drugs and their metabolites are eliminated principally via the kidneys and liver, each of which is perfused with more than 1 L of blood every minute. Thus, the efficiency of drug elimination depends on hepatic and renal blood flow. During renal excretion of drugs, glomerular filtration, reabsorption, and secretion occur. The resulting ultrafiltrate accumulates in the bladder via the collecting tubules. The fraction of drug bound to plasma proteins and the glomerular filtration rate determine the amount of drug that enters the tubular lumen of the kidney. Charged species are less likely to permeate the tubular cells and reabsorb, a process that significantly delays elimination of drug. In this way, the rate of elimination is variable, depending on the pH of the urine. The elimination of acidic drugs is enhanced by alkalinization of the urine using sodium bicarbonate. Conversely, basic drugs may be eliminated more readily by acidification of the urine using ammonium chloride. As much as 76% of a methamphetamine dose may be excreted unchanged in acidic urine, compared with only 2% in alkaline urine.

Hepatocytes in the liver secrete bile, which is stored in the gallbladder and is later excreted via the intestines in the feces. Biliary excretion is favored by large polar substances, but when metabolism renders a drug more lipid soluble, the drug may undergo reabsorption, a process known as enterohepatic recirculation.

When a fixed amount of drug is eliminated per unit of time (e.g., ethanol), the elimination is said to be zero order. However, most drugs follow a first-order elimination process, whereby a constant fraction of drug is eliminated over time. Half-life ($T^{1/2}$) is a measure of the rate of elimination. One half-life is the time it takes for the concentration of drug in the plasma to decrease by 50%. These values are dependent on volumes of distribution and clearance rates, which may vary with age, sex, disease state, or drug interactions. The lungs (for elimination of volatile substances) and even sweat, saliva, hair, nails, and breast milk are all relatively minor excretory pathways, but they may be of some forensic importance and will be discussed later.

KEY POINT The link between the amount of drug and its effect over time is the basis for establishing therapeutic and toxic drug concentrations for clinical management and intervention.

Pharmacological Effects

The pharmacological effect of a drug is a result of the drug's interaction at a given receptor site. The concentration of free drug circulating in the blood is in equilibrium with the concentration of drug at the receptor site. An increase in the concentration of free drug modulates the receptor response and enhances the pharmacological effect. The mechanism by which a drug modulates a receptor is described by pharmacodynamics. The link between the amount of drug and its effect over time is the basis for establishing therapeutic and toxic drug concentrations for clinical management and intervention. Such pharmacodynamic responses account for the pharmacological effect of a drug and are known as the dose-response relationship. However, pharmacological effect can be intrinsically dependent on the time passed since the dose was taken, rather than with the concentration of drug in the blood. A given concentration of drug may produce widely variable effects, depending on the time since administration. This phenomenon is referred to as hysteresis. For example, after consuming alcohol, a person tends to feel more excited and euphoric during the initial absorption phase than during the elimination phase, during which time the person may feel sedated and depressed. CNS stimulants such as methamphetamine follow a similar cycle. A concentration of 200 ng/mL methamphetamine in blood may coincide with euphoria, exhilaration, restlessness, and stimulation during the initial absorption phase. However, several hours later during the elimination phase, the same concentration of drug may coincide with confusion, depression, anxiety, dysphoria, and exhaustion.

The pharmacological effect experienced by the user may be apparent from vital signs or involuntary reflexes. For the purpose of determining impairment or acute or chronic toxicity, blood is the matrix of choice. The presence of the drug in the urine is only an indication of drug exposure, over a period of hours, days, or even weeks, rather than an indicator of impairment. With the exception of ethanol, there is no direct correlation between the concentration of a drug in the blood and the level of impairment for legal purposes. Any impairment by drugs is generally inferred by correlating the concentration of the drug with observations made by arresting officers or others involved with the impaired individual. Factors such as tolerance can have a profound effect on the pharmacodynamic response in an individual. A quantity of cocaine sufficient to produce a mild "buzz" in a chronic user could be acutely cardiotoxic in a naïve user, resulting in coma and death.

DRUG RECOGNITION

Drugs may affect normal behavior by enhancing or impairing human performance (e.g., cognition or psychomotor ability), depending on the dose and pattern of drug use. Drug recognition is an important ability for clinicians, toxicologists, and law enforcement personnel. Recognition of abused substances, including illicit drugs and therapeutics, that may have been incorrectly administered or combined with other drugs, is a valuable skill.

Impairment may be observed and documented by either a trained clinician or a drug recognition expert (DRE). The DRE program was developed by the Los Angeles Police Department in the 1980s and is now used throughout the United States and overseas. For law enforcement purposes, a series of physiological and psychomotor tests are used to determine the class of drugs that is likely present: central nervous system (CNS) stimulants,

Table 10-4 Signs and Symptoms of Commonly Abused Substances

	MARIJUANA	NARCOTIC ANALGESICS	HALLUCINOGENS	CNS DEPRESSANTS	CNS STIMULANTS	PHENCYCLIDINE	INHALANTS
Blood pressure	Elevated	Low	Elevated	Low	Elevated	Elevated	Varies
Pulse rate	Elevated	Low	Elevated	Low	Elevated	Elevated	Elevated
Pupils	Dilated/normal	Constricted	Dilated	Normal	Dilated	Normal	Normal/dilated
Pupillary reaction to light	Normal	Slow/none	Normal	Slow	Slow	Normal	Slow
Body temperature	Normal	Low	Elevated	Normal	Elevated	Elevated	Varies
HGN*	Not present	Not present	Not present	Present	Not present	Present	Present
VGN*	Not present	Not present	Not present	Possibly present	Not present	Usually present	Possibly present
Lack of ocular convergence	Present	Not present	Not present	Present	Not present	Present	Present
30-second estimation	Distorted	Slow	Fast	Slow	Fast	Fast	Normal

*HGN, Horizontal gaze nystagmus; VGN, Vertical gaze nystagmus.

Table 10-5 Observable Signs and Symptoms of Commonly Abused Drugs

CNS DEPRESSANTS	CNS STIMULANTS	OPIOIDS	CANNABIS	PHENCYCLIDINE	HALLUCINOGENS
Poor coordination	Anxiety	Constipation	Ataxia	Agitated	Body tremors
Disoriented	Body tremors	Dry mouth	Body tremors	Ataxia	Dazed appearance
Decreased inhibitions	Bruxism	Dysphoria	Disorientation	Blank stare	Diaphoresis
Fumbling	Dry mouth	Euphoria	Eyelid tremors	Confused	Disorientation
Gait ataxia	Excited	Facial itching	Increased appetite	Cyclic behavior	Dysarthria
Ptosis	Euphoric	Low, raspy voice	Odor of marijuana	Diaphoresis	Hallucinations
Sluggish	Hyperreflexia	Poor coordination	Poor time and distance perception	Dissociative	Memory loss
Slowed reflexes	Hypervigilance	Ptosis	Possible paranoia	Anesthesia	Muscle rigidity
Sedated	Insomnia	Puncture marks	Reddened conjunctiva	Dysarthria	Nausea
Slurred speech	Irritability	Mental clouding	Reduced inhibitions	Hallucinations	Paranoia
	Muscle rigidity	Muscle flaccidity	Transient muscle rigidity	"Moon walking"	Poor coordination
	Reduced appetite	Nausea		Muscle rigidity	Poor time and distance perception
	Runny nose	Nodding off			Synesthesia
	Reddening of nasal mucosa	Sedation			
	Talkativeness	Slow reflexes			
		Vomiting			

CNS depressants, narcotic analgesics, hallucinogens, PCP, cannabis, or inhalants. Clinical characteristics such as blood pressure, pulse, respiration, body temperature, nystagmus, ocular convergence, pupil size, and pupillary reaction to light can be useful indicators of drug use (Table 10-4). Other observable effects, such as tremors, coordination, gait, muscle tone, perception, diaphoresis, emesis, lacrimation, and appearance of the conjunctivae, may also provide valuable insight (Table 10-5). Abstinence syndromes resulting from chronic drug use produce effects that vary considerably from those caused by acute drug intoxication. These effects may be impairing and, in some instances, can be life threatening (Table 10-6).

DRUG AND DISEASE INTERACTIONS

Certain disease states can affect the way in which a drug is absorbed, distributed, and eliminated. Clearance rates, protein binding, volume of distribution, and half-life may be affected in some individuals but not in others. Hepatic, renal, gastrointestinal, and respiratory disease have been shown to affect pharmacokinetic parameters in some populations, even though the underlying mechanisms are poorly understood in many cases. Drug interactions

Table 10-6 Withdrawal Symptoms of Commonly Abused Drugs

DRUG	WITHDRAWAL SYMPTOMS
CNS stimulants	Muscular aches, abdominal pain, tremors, anxiety, hypersomnolence, lack of energy, depression, suicidal thoughts, exhaustion
Opioids	Dilated pupils, rapid pulse, piloerection, abdominal cramps, muscle spasms, vomiting, diarrhea, tremulousness, yawning, anxiety
CNS depressants	Tremulousness, insomnia, sweating, fever, anxiety, cardiovascular collapse, agitation, delirium, hallucinations, disorientation, convulsions, shock
Marijuana	Anorexia, nausea, insomnia, restlessness, irritability, anxiety, depression

may occur when more than one drug is administered. The pharmacokinetics of one drug may change the pharmacodynamics of the other, affecting therapeutic effect and toxicity. Although pharmacokinetics and pharmacodynamics of most drugs are relatively well known, few studies have addressed the interactions of

For example, cocaine is a basic drug with two labile ester moieties. In unpreserved samples, benzoylesterases in the blood rapidly convert cocaine to ecgonine methylester after collection and during storage. After 21 days, as much as 100% of the cocaine may be lost at room temperature in the absence of preservative. Despite deactivation of some of the enzymes from using preservative, chemical conversions may occur as a result of the specimen pH. For example, cocaine spontaneously hydrolyzes to benzoylecgonine at physiological pH. Lowering the temperature reduces the rate at which the drug undergoes enzymatic or chemical conversion. Specimens should be refrigerated (4°C or 39°F) for short-term storage for up to two weeks and frozen (−20°C or −4°F) for long-term storage. These temperatures inhibit bacterial growth and reduce reaction kinetics.

PRESERVATION OF SPECIMENS WHILE IN STORAGE

In addition to preservatives, anticoagulant agents such as potassium oxalate, sodium citrate, or EDTA (5 mg/mL) may be added for ease of sample handling. Sodium fluoride may be added to urine, but many postmortem specimens (besides blood) are stored without preservative in tightly sealed containers at low temperature. Some preservatives, such as sodium azide, can interfere with methods of analysis such as immunoassay. Antioxidants such as ascorbic acid or sodium metabisulfite (1% w/v) are sometimes used to prevent oxidative losses, but these agents can act as reducing agents toward some drugs. In a similar fashion, adjusting specimen pH is not generally favored, because just as some drugs are alkaline labile (e.g., cocaine, 6-acetylmorphine), others are acid labile.

Collection of Specimens

Commercial gray-top Vacutainer or Venoject blood tubes that contain sodium fluoride and potassium oxalate should be used for the collection of toxicological specimens. Urine collection should be observed by trained personnel to reduce the likelihood of donor manipulation, such as dilution, adulteration, or substitution. It is particularly easy for females to "dip" the urine container into the toilet bowl during collection. Direct observation and the addition of a coloring agent to the cistern will identify these cases.

Substitution of the urine specimen is less common, but commercial products including lyophilized drug-free urine are readily available for this purpose. In vitro or in vivo adulteration agents are widely available as common household products and OTC medications. In vivo adulteration involves the ingestion of a substance that may enhance elimination of a drug by either diuresis, acidification, or alkalinization of the urine. Commercial adulteration products are readily available, but their use is unlikely unless the subject has some advance notification. In vitro adulterants are added to the urine sample after collection. These substances may interfere with analysis by chemical degradation of the drug. Prevalence of adulterants, particularly in workplace urine drug testing, has led to dipstick tests and other diagnostic assays that can detect some of these agents. Common adulteration agents are listed in Table 10-10.

BEST PRACTICE Specimens for toxicological analyses must be carefully controlled and stored in a secure location. A chain of custody must accompany all forensic specimens.

EVIDENCE SECURITY

The integrity of biological evidence is maintained at all times by tracking the handling and storage from specimen collection to final disposition. A chain-of-custody form is used to document

Table 10-10 Common In Vitro and In Vivo Adulterants

IN VITRO ADULTERANTS	DIURETICS
Ascorbic acid	*Prescription:*
Alcohols	Benzothiadiazines
Amber-13 (hydrochloric acid)	Carbonic anhydrase inhibitors
Ammonia	Loop diuretics
Bleach	Osmotic diuretics
Clear Choice (glutaraldehyde)	
Detergent	*Over the counter (OTC):*
Drano	Aqua-Ban
Ethylene glycol	Diurex
Gasoline	Fem-1
Hydrogen peroxide	Midol
Klear (potassium nitrite)	Pamprin
Lemon juice	Premsyn PMS
Liquid soap	
Lime-a-Way	*Other:*
Mary Jane Super Clean	Alcoholic beverages
13 (detergent)	Caffeine
Salt	Golden seal root
Stealth (peroxidase)	Herbal remedies
THC-free (hydrochloric acid)	Pamabrom
UrinAid (glutaraldehyde)	
Urine luck (pyridinium chlorochromate)	
Vanish	
Vinegar	
Visine	
Water	
Whizzies (sodium nitrite)	

the date, purpose, and name of the person handling the specimen. The four Ws of the chain of custody are as follows:
- Who handled the evidence
- What was handled
- Why it was handled
- Where it was located at all times

Specimen handling and disposition of evidence are scrutinized by the courts. Specimens must be stored in secure locations with limited access where they are not vulnerable to adulteration.

Toxicological Analysis

Typically, toxicological analysis involves a combination of two chemically and analytically distinct methodologies. Most commonly, a rapid screening test such as immunoassay or thin-layer chromatography precedes a more rigorous and labor-intensive confirmatory analysis using gas chromatography–mass spectrometry (GC-MS) or liquid chromatography–mass spectrometry (LC-MS). Immunoassays and GC-MS are the most widely used techniques and will be discussed in more detail.

SCREENING TECHNIQUES

Immunoassays

Immunoassays are antibody-based tests that can provide toxicological results of a presumptive nature in a relatively short period of time (minutes to hours). Generally, these tests are amenable to automation, require very small sample volumes, require limited or no sample pretreatment, and are not technically demanding. Most immunoassays rely on the competitive-binding reaction that takes place between antidrug antibodies and either labeled or unlabeled drug. In an enzyme immunoassay, drug in a donor urine sample competes with enzyme-labeled drug for binding

Table 10-11 Advantages and Disadvantages of Common Immunoassays

IMMUNOASSAY TECHNIQUE	ADVANTAGES	DISADVANTAGES
CEDIA (homogeneous): cloned enzyme donor immunoassay	Highly automated Long shelf-life Wide linear range	Susceptible to interferences Not amenable to all matrices
ELISA (heterogeneous): enzyme-linked immunosorbent assay	Sensitive Minimal matrix effects Potential for automation	Not adaptable to common automated analyzers Expensive
EMIT (homogeneous): enzyme multiplied immunoassay technique	Highly automated Long shelf-life	Matrix effects and interferences False negative results Not amenable to all matrices
FPIA (homogeneous): fluorescence polarization immunoassay	Highly automated More stable than enzyme reagents Highly sensitive	Expensive Endogenous interferences Sample pretreatment for blood
KIMS (homogeneous): kinetic interaction of microparticles in solution	Highly automated Inexpensive More stable than enzyme reagents	Special instrument maintenance Interferences may cause false positives Linear range is small
RIA (heterogeneous): radioimmunoassay	Highly sensitive Minimal matrix effects Amenable to blood and urine	Disposal of radioisotopes Limited shelf-life Limited automation potential

sites on an antibody molecule. If there is no drug in the urine, the enzyme-labeled drug binds to the antibody, unimpeded. However, if the urine sample contains a quantity of drug, the enzyme-labeled drug will not bind as readily; the more drug in the sample, the less enzyme-labeled drug will bind, and vice versa. The amount of enzyme that is bound can be determined colorimetrically and the intensity of the color is related to the concentration of drug in the sample.

A wide variety of immunoassay technologies are commercially available, many of which rely on the use of enzyme-, radioisotope-, or fluorescent-labeled species for detection purposes. Some of these tests are highly automated, allowing high sample throughput on the order of several hundred tests per day, whereas others are more labor intensive and are less readily automated. Many of the highly automated assays are homogeneous in nature and can be performed in one step without the need for separation. Immunoassays that require a separation step to remove unbound from bound drug are called heterogeneous assays. These tests usually take longer to complete, are not readily automated, and are more technically demanding. However, because of the separation step that takes place before detection, heterogeneous immunoassays may be less susceptible to endogenous and exogenous interferences than their homogeneous counterparts. Heterogeneous assays are also less susceptible to matrix effects and are more amenable to blood and alternative fluids, often without sample pretreatment. Several commercial immunoassays used for drugs of abuse testing are summarized in Table 10-11.

Potential Drawbacks of Immunoassay Testing

Because of the nature of the antibody-antigen reaction, immunoassays offer limited specificity. When the antibody recognizes a structural conformation, or epitope, on the drug molecule, it may bind, producing a positive result. Immunoassays are very rarely truly specific for the target drug because structurally similar molecules may also bind to the antibody to varying degrees. However, the degree of specificity may not necessarily limit the usefulness of the test. Some immunoassays are designed to be nonspecific in order to cross-react with several drugs within a given class. In contrast,

Table 10-12 Common Cross-Reacting Substances in Some Immunoassays

ASSAY	COMMON CROSS-REACTING SUBSTANCES
Amphetamine/ methamphetamine	Benzphetamine, ephedrine, methylenedioxyamphetamine, methylenedioxyethylamphetamine, methylenedioxymethamphetamine, phenmetrazine, phentermine, phenylpropanolamine, propylhexedrine, pseudoephedrine
Benzodiazepines	Alprazolam, bromazepam, chlordiazepoxide, clonazepam, clorazepate, demoxepam, diazepam, estazolam, α-hydroxyalprazolam, lorazepam, nitrazepam, nordiazepam, oxazepam, prazepam, temazepam, α-hydroxytriazolam
11-Nor-Δ^9-carboxy-THC	Δ^9-Tetrahydrocannabinol, 11-carboxy-Δ^9-tetrahydrocannabinol, 11-hydroxy-Δ^9-tetrahydrocannabinol
Cocaine metabolite	Cocaine, cocaethylene, ecgonine, ecgonine ethyl ester, ecgonine methylester, norcocaine
Opiates	Codeine, dihydrocodeine, dihydromorphine, hydrocodone, hydromorphone, oxycodone, oxymorphone, morphine-glucuronide, nalorphine, norcodeine, normorphine
Phencyclidine	Diphenhydramine, dextromethorphan, PCP analogs, thiorizadine

the usefulness of a test may be severely limited by its specificity, for example, detection of methamphetamine. Endogenous phenethylamines or OTC decongestants or dietary supplements such as pseudoephedrine, ephedrine, phenylpropanolamine, and other structurally related drugs may cross-react, producing false positive reactions. Common cross-reacting substances are given in Table 10-12. Because of the limitations of immunoassays, these results alone are not forensically defensible. Immunoassay screening tests are excellent tools to indicate which drug or class of drug is present, but a more rigorous and specific test must be performed to unequivocally confirm the presence of a particular drug for forensic purposes.

Effectiveness of Immunoassay Tests

The effectiveness of an immunoassay depends on the cutoff concentration, below which the sample is deemed negative. For the purposes of federal workplace drug testing, the Substance Abuse and Mental Health Services Administration (SAMHSA) has mandated cutoff concentrations for amphetamines, cannabinoids, cocaine metabolite, opiates, and PCP (Table 10-13). These cutoff concentrations are elevated to reduce the number of false positive results and to account for accidental drug exposure from dietary sources (e.g., poppy seeds) or passive smoke inhalation. However, for the purposes of death or criminal investigation, cutoff concentrations are typically much lower to reduce the likelihood of false negative results. Additional drug classes, including therapeutics such as benzodiazepines and barbiturates, are often included. The cutoff concentrations established by the testing facility are set at the lowest concentration of drug that can be reliably confirmed using other techniques (e.g., GC-MS). These low cutoff points are necessary to identify very low concentrations of drug that could be present after a single dose.

Onsite Drug Tests

A number of onsite drug tests now offer immediate results, without the need for sophisticated equipment or highly trained personnel. These tests rely on conventional immunoassay-based principles and use a chromatographic support to provide qualitative drug screen results. When blood or urine is added to one of these devices, capillary action allows any drug in the sample to migrate through the immunochromatographic medium. Unlike the instrument-based immunoassays, which rely on measurement of absorbance, fluorescence, or radioisotopes, the progress of the antibody-antigen reaction can be followed with the naked eye. Antibody molecules are often labeled with colored latex beads or colloidal gold, which may produce a concentrated blue or purple color in the test result window.

Although onsite tests are becoming popular in clinical and private sector toxicology screening, they are not yet widely used in medicolegal drug testing. Onsite assays are largely designed for workplace or emergency room drug testing. These devices are less effective in forensic investigations because of their elevated cutoff concentrations and the limited repertoire of drugs that are detected. However, the increasing popularity of onsite tests together with growing acceptance of alternative specimens, such as saliva, could have an impact on the criminal justice system in such arenas as highway safety and assessment of driving under the influence in the form of roadside drug tests.

CONFIRMATORY ANALYSIS

Because of the inherent uncertainty in immunoassay screening results caused by cross-reactivity and interferences, positive drug screen results must be confirmed using a more rigorous technique. Gas chromatography-mass spectrometry (GC-MS) is the most widely used confirmatory technique in forensic toxicology. It can be used to specifically identify and quantify the drug or drugs present.

Before analysis, the drugs must be extracted from the biological matrix. Common isolation techniques are liquid-liquid extraction (LLE) and solid-phase extraction (SPE). During LLE, organic solvents such as chloroform or ether are used to isolate drugs from biological fluids by manipulation of pH. Partition of the drug between the two immiscible layers (e.g., buffered urine and solvent) depends on polarity, charge, lipophilicity, and the pK_a of the drug. In a manner analogous to the distribution of drugs throughout the body, ionized drugs are more likely to partition into the polar aqueous layer (e.g., blood or urine), whereas uncharged or nonpolar drugs are more likely to partition into the solvent layer. In this fashion, drugs are extracted from biological fluids or tissues using solvents that are subsequently evaporated, concentrated, and analyzed.

Many of the same principles are utilized during SPE whereby the drug is adsorbed onto an immobilized solid support in a cartridge assembly. The affinity of the drug for the solid support allows the drug to bind temporarily. The mechanisms of attraction ("like attracts like") are analogous to those of LLE, with the added benefit of ion exchange, whereby a drug that is positively charged binds to a negatively charged chromatographic support and vice versa. A combination of polar, nonpolar, and ion exchange mechanisms can be used to isolate acidic or basic drugs that contain ionizable functional groups, such as carboxylic acids or amines. Once the drug is bound to the support, interferences are removed by washing. The drug is eluted from the cartridge using an organic solvent or by manipulating the pH to neutralize or reverse the charge.

Additional sample preparation steps may be necessary, depending on the matrix. These may include homogenization, sonication, dilution, centrifugation, protein precipitation, or hydrolysis. The latter of these is particularly important for polar drugs that are highly conjugated (e.g., cannabinoids, benzodiazepines, opiates).

Table 10-13 Screening (Immunoassay) Cutoff Concentrations

		CUTOFF CONCENTRATION (ng/ml)	
DRUG	TARGET ANALYTE	SAMHSA*	FORENSIC†
Amphetamines	Amphetamine, methamphetamine	1000	50-100
Benzodiazepines	Oxazepam, nordiazepam	—	100-300
Barbiturates	Secobarbital	—	200-300
Cannabinoids	11-Nor-9-carboxy-Δ^9-THC	50	20-50
Cocaine	Benzoylecgonine	300	150
Lysergic acid diethylamide	Lysergic acid diethylamide	—	0.5
Methadone	Methadone	—	50-300
Methaqualone	Methaqualone	—	300
Opiates	Morphine	2000	10-100
Phencyclidine	Phencyclidine	25	25-50
Propoxyphene	Propoxyphene	—	300

*Urine.
†Blood or urine.

Chemical or enzymatic methods are used to hydrolyze the sample. Alkaline or acid hydrolysis is commonly used to release glucuronide conjugates of 11-nor-Δ^9-carboxy-THC and morphine, respectively. Chemical hydrolysis is efficient and reproducible, but acid or alkali labile drugs may degrade during the process. Enzymes such as b-glucuronidase can be used to hydrolyze drugs without the need for harsh chemical conditions, but these methods are more expensive, slower, and less reproducible.

Injection of the drug extract onto the GC-MS allows components of the mixture to be separated and identified. On entry to the GC inlet, vaporization occurs and the gaseous sample is transported by a flow of inert carrier gas (e.g., helium). The sample is transported through a heated capillary column, during which time separation takes place. The column, which is typically about 30 m long, is coated with a material that, depending on the physicochemical properties of the drug, allows it to adsorb. Depending on the extent of the interaction between the drug and the column, components of the extract will emerge from the end of the column at different times. The time taken for the drug to elute from the column, known as retention time, is the basis of chromatographic separation.

Drugs or components of the extract then pass through a heated interface and enter the mass spectrometer, where molecular identification takes place. First, the sample enters an ionization chamber. During the ionization process, each drug produces a characteristic selection of ions. Weak bonds in the drug molecule are broken, and the resulting charged fragments are recorded by the mass analyzer. This array of ions, known as the mass spectrum, is like a molecular fingerprint of the drug, allowing it to be identified. GC-MS is a highly specific and reproducible confirmatory technique because identification is based on both the retention time of the drug and its characteristic spectrum.

INTERPRETATION

Negative toxicology sometimes coincides with clinical signs and symptoms or a behavioral response that clearly indicates the presence of an intoxicating substance. These findings are often caused by limitations of the toxicological procedures. Common caveats in immunoassay testing include the inability to detect drugs that may be present below the cutoff concentration or drugs that have low cross-reactivity with the antibody. Conjugated drugs do not always cross-react well in immunoassays, and unless subsequent confirmatory analyses include a hydrolysis step, these drugs may go undetected. Inability to confirm positive immunoassay results may be the result of poor extraction efficiencies or detection limits. Detection of trace quantities of a drug such as THC in blood samples may require highly sensitive and specialized techniques that are not available in all laboratories.

Drug-Facilitated Sexual Assault

The majority of sexual assaults in the United States are reported to be acquaintance rapes, "date rapes," and an increasing number may be drug facilitated. Drug-facilitated sexual assault occurs when a chemical agent is used to assist or procure nonconsensual sexual contact. During a drug-facilitated sexual assault, a victim may be incapacitated or unconscious. Under these circumstances, it may not be possible for a person to resist or consent to sexual contact. The CNS depressant drugs gamma-hydroxybutyrate (GHB) and Rohypnol (flunitrazepam) have received particular attention from the media as "date rape" agents. These reports, however, have not been supported by the scientific literature, which suggests that more than 20 different drugs have been associated with this crime.

Alcohol and marijuana are the most commonly encountered substances in alleged cases of sexual assault, which supports the view that consumption of impairing substances is an important risk factor in sexual assault. The relationship between drug use and sexual assault is complicated: illicit drug use not only increases the risk of sexual assault, but sexual assault increases the risk of subsequent substance abuse. In a study of more than 2000 victims of sexual assault in California, nearly two thirds of the urine specimens contained alcohol or drugs: alcohol (63%) and cannabinoids (30%) accounted for the majority of positive samples, and GHB and flunitrazepam accounted for less than 3%.

In a nationwide study of 1179 alleged victims of sexual assault, flunitrazepam metabolites were detected in only six urine specimens. A review of this study revealed that the prevalence of alcohol was high, followed by cannabinoids, cocaine, benzodiazepines, amphetamines, and GHB (Fig. 10-2). Nationwide, a total of 48 specimens tested positive for GHB (4.1%) compared with 8% in California alone, which highlights the importance of geographical and regional trends in drug use. Multiple drug use was evident in 35% of the cases, frequently in combination with alcohol.

Chemical submission applies to any drug that has the ability to render the victim passive, submissive, or unwilling or unable to resist. Potent, fast-acting depressant drugs that have amnesic properties are effective "knock-out drops." However, a variety of illicit and widely prescribed therapeutic agents, including benzodiazepines, barbiturates, muscle relaxants, hypnotics, and antihistamines, have been associated with drug-facilitated sexual assault (Box 10-2). Typically these agents are CNS depressants that impair consciousness, memory, or lower inhibitions. Others may have an anesthetic-type effect, causing unarousable sleep or produce an "out-of-body experience" whereby the conscious victim is powerless, paralyzed, or unable to move.

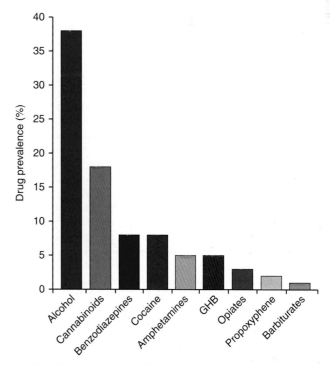

Fig. 10-2 Drugs prevalent in alleged cases of sexual assault. (Data from ElSohly, M.A., & Salamone, S.J. (1999). Prevalence of drugs in alleged cases of sexual assault. *J Anal Tox* 23(3), 141-146.)

Box 10-2 Substances Detected in Alleged Cases of Drug-Facilitated Sexual Assault

Alcohol	Flunitrazepam
Alprazolam	Gamma-hydroxybutyrate (GHB)
Amphetamine	Ketamine
Barbiturates	Lorazepam
1,4-Butanediol (BD)	Marijuana
γ-Butyrolactone (GBL)	Meprobamate
Carisoprodol	Methamphetamine
Chloral hydrate	Methylenedioxymethamphetamine (MDMA)
Chlordiazepoxide	Midazolam
Clonazepam	Opiates
Cocaine	Oxazepam
Cyclobenzaprine	Phencyclidine (PCP)
Diazepam	Scopolamine
Diphenhydramine	Triazolam
Ethanol	Zolpidem
Flurazepam	

GHB AND FLUNITRAZEPAM

GHB and flunitrazepam have received particular attention in light of their rapid onset, extensive biotransformation, and detection difficulties. Flunitrazepam, which is 7 to 10 times more potent than diazepam (Valium), produces onset of actions within 15 to 30 minutes of administration. Disinhibition, passivity, lack of resistance, muscle relaxation, and anterograde amnesia have been reported as effects of flunitrazepam. Not legally available in the United States, flunitrazepam was reformulated to turn blue or hazy in clear or colored beverages. However, illicit sources of flunitrazepam remain odorless, colorless, and tasteless. The effective dose of flunitrazepam is very low (1 to 2 mg) compared to that of GHB (2 to 4 g). Illicit formulations of GHB, which were placed into Schedule I of the Controlled Substances Act in April 2000, can take effect in as little as 15 minutes. This drug, which sometimes has a salty or soapy taste can produce euphoria and disinhibition, as well as nausea, vomiting, respiratory depression, and coma.

SPECIMEN COLLECTION

Delay in specimen collection can profoundly affect the prosecutorial and toxicological outcome of the investigation. Coordination of law enforcement, medical, and scientific personnel is essential. Immediate action must be taken to preserve the evidence by collection of blood and urine by healthcare professionals, such as forensic nurses, with authority to initiate the evidence collection process and chain of custody. The victim should be urged not to urinate until the specimen can be properly collected. The rape/evidentiary examination should include collection of 20 mL of blood preserved with sodium fluoride and potassium oxalate (gray-top tubes). Inadequately preserved blood drawn into yellow- or lavender-top tubes may compromise the toxicological investigation or preclude toxicological analysis altogether. Collection of blood is essential if the ingestion of drug occurred within the last 24 hours. It may also provide valuable interpretive information regarding pharmacological response or impairment. It is possible that positive blood toxicology can be used to corroborate involvement of the drug in the sexual assault, whereas urine toxicology is only indicative of prior exposure to the drug.

BEST PRACTICE Because delays in specimen collection can profoundly affect the prosecutorial and toxicological outcome of the investigation, specimens should be promptly obtained, annotated with a precise time and date of collection, and refrigerated immediately to prevent degradation of the sample.

Samples should be refrigerated immediately and the date and time of specimen collection documented. Chain-of-custody procedure should be initiated. Supplemental information, such as symptoms exhibited by the victim, the suspected date and time of the ingestion, as well as alcohol, drugs, or medications ingested prior to the assault, should be fully documented. Prosecution of drug-facilitated sexual assault and interpretation of toxicological findings can be complicated in cases of multiple drug use by the victim. Incapacitation may be the result of a combination of substances, consumed both voluntarily and involuntarily. For example, voluntary ingestion of alcohol, combined with the surreptitious administration of other CNS depressants, may have a potentiating or synergistic effect that could impair the victim to a far greater extent.

LEGISLATIVE EFFORTS

Legislative efforts to curb the growing trend in drug-facilitated sexual assault have included restricting drug access, federal scheduling, and increased sentencing. In particular, the Drug-Induced Rape Prevention and Punishment Act of 1996 (Public Law 104-305) increases penalties for those who use drugs to assist in the commitment of a violent crime. Under this law, administration of a controlled substance with the intent to commit a sexual assault or other violent crime is a federal felony, punishable by up to 20 years' imprisonment.

For this reason, it is important that the toxicological analysis is conducted by a forensic laboratory familiar with cases of drug-facilitated sexual assault. The use of appropriate cutoff concentrations and sensitive confirmatory testing procedures are required to identify single doses of drugs that may be present at very low concentration. Confirmatory analysis is usually necessitated in these instances, regardless of the screening results. Limitations include the poor cross-reactivity toward conjugated drugs and the absence of effective and reliable screening tests for drugs such as GHB. Drugs administered in low dose (e.g., alprazolam), those with short half-lives (e.g., GHB), or drugs that undergo rapid and extensive biotransformation (e.g., flunitrazepam) pose a particular challenge to drug detection agencies. Urine is advantageous from the standpoint of detection time, although drugs with short half-lives may be undetectable within 96 hours or less (Table 10-14). GHB, which is administered in high doses, is detectable in blood and urine for approximately 6 to 8 hours and 12 hours, respectively. Drug detection times vary considerably, depending on dose, metabolism, and the method of analysis.

EFFECTS EXPERIENCED BY VICTIMS

Victims of drug-facilitated sexual assault may experience confusion, dizziness, psychomotor impairment, drowsiness, impaired judgment, reduced inhibitions, or slurred speech. Victims may lose their ability to ward off attackers, may develop amnesia, and may provide unreliable or confused recall of events. Drug-induced anterograde amnesia, whereby the drug temporarily disables the brain's ability to store information into memory, may cause the victim to be uncertain about the facts surrounding the assault. This uncertainty may procure an unwillingness to report the rape or provide biological samples for forensic testing. Because many of the depressant-type effects of drugs used to incapacitate the victim are similar to the effects of alcohol, it is probable that many incidents of drug-facilitated sexual assault are not recognized.

Table 10-14 Doses and Half-Lives of Selected Depressant Drugs

DRUG	DOSE (mg)	HALF-LIFE
Alprazolam	0.25-1	6-27 h
Barbiturates (short-acting, e.g., pentobarbital)	50-200	15-48 h
Barbiturates (intermediate-acting, e.g., butalbital)	50-100	30-40 h
Barbiturates (long-acting, e.g., phenobarbital)	50-200	48-120 h
Methaqualone	150-500	20-60 h
Chlordiazepoxide	10-25	6-27 h
Clonazepam	0.5-2	19-60 h
Diazepam	5-10	21-37 h
Diphenhydramine	50-100	3-10 h
Flunitrazepam	1-2	9-25 h
Flurazepam	15-30	1-3 h
g-Hydroxybutyrate (GHB)	2000-4000	0.3-1 h
Lorazepam	0.5-2	9-16 h
Nitrazepam	5-10	17-48 h
Propoxyphene	65-400	8-24 h
Temazepam	15-30	3-13 h
Tetrahydrocannabinol	5-20	1-3 d (naïve)
		3-13 d (chronic)
Triazolam	0.25	2-4 h
Zolpidem	5-10	1.4-4.5 h

Data from Baselt, R. C. (2008). *Disposition of toxic drugs and chemicals in man* (8th ed.). Foster City, CA: Biomedical Publications; Wilson, J. M. (1994). *Abused drugs II.* Washington, DC: AACC Press; Tietz, N. W. (1995). *Clinical guide to laboratory tests* (3rd ed.). Philadelphia: Saunders.

WARNING SIGNS

Rape treatment centers provide educational material and tips to help identify and minimize the likelihood of drug-facilitated sexual assault. Women who feel unusually intoxicated and suspect that they may have unknowingly ingested a drug should seek immediate assistance. The following warning signs suggest a possible drug-facilitated sexual assault (Rape Treatment Center, 2004):

- If the victim recalls having a drink, but cannot recall what happened for a period of time after consuming the drink
- If the victim suspects that sexual contact has taken place, but cannot remember any or all of the incident
- If the victim feels more intoxicated than the usual response to the same amount of alcohol
- If the victim wakes up feeling hung over and experiences a memory lapse or cannot account for a period of time

PREVENTION OF DRUG-FACILITATED SEXUAL ASSAULT

Healthcare workers, educators, and public officials have developed a list of "don'ts" to increase awareness of the dangers of unknowingly ingesting substances such as sedating or incapacitating drugs. A national program supports the distribution of educational brochures and posters within high schools, colleges, bars and lounges, and other locations frequented by youth and older singles. The following guidelines have been developed to prevent drug-facilitated sexual assault:

- Don't drink beverages that you did not open yourself.
- Don't share or exchange drinks with anyone.
- Don't drink from a container that is being passed around.
- If someone offers to buy you a drink, accompany that person to the bar, watch the drink being poured, and carry the drink yourself.

- Don't leave your drink unattended.
- If your drink has been left unattended, discard it.
- Don't drink anything that has an unusual taste or appearance (e.g., excess foaming, salty or soapy taste, unexplained residue).

Infant Drug Exposure

Unfortunately, within recent years it has been suggested that as many as one tenth of all infants are exposed to illicit drugs during pregnancy. In a 2002 study of self-reported drug use, 6.8% of pregnant women age 15 to 25 used an illicit drug within the past month (SAMHSA, 2004). The most frequently used drug was marijuana. Binge drinking (defined as five or more drinks on one occasion) was reported in 4.5% of pregnant women in the same age group. Although the American Academy of Pediatrics does not recommend universal screening of infants, it proposes prevention, intervention, and treatment services to pregnant women and their children. Cocaine, heroin, amphetamines, and nicotine are reported to cause impaired fetal growth and acute withdrawal syndromes. Higher rates of fetal distress, growth retardation, and abnormal neurodevelopment have been reported in babies when the pregnant mother commonly abused drugs. A 1997 study of gestational drug exposure in nearly 3000 newborns in Michigan indicated that as many as 44% of neonates tested positive for drugs. Of these, 30.5% tested positive for cocaine, 20.2% for opiates, and 11.4% for cannabinoids.

DRUG USE IN NURSING MOTHERS

Drug use in nursing mothers is also a concern. It is estimated that between 0.4% and 27% of nursing mothers in the United States abuse drugs. Although the developmental effects of drug exposure as a result of nursing are largely unknown, acute toxicity and withdrawal effects are possible. Several difficulties are associated with the study of drug abuse during pregnancy or in nursing mothers:

- It can be difficult to recruit participants for the studies.
- Lifestyle of women abusing drugs may predispose them to adverse pregnancy outcome because of poor nutrition, living conditions, general health, or socioeconomic status.
- Multiple-drug use, particularly in combination with tobacco or alcohol, can complicate assessment.
- Unreliability of subjects is often associated with reporting such factors as drug use, dose, and duration.

EFFECTS OF DRUG EXPOSURE ON THE FETUS OR NEONATE

Exposure of the fetus or neonate to intoxicating substances may cause deleterious effects, including higher rates of fetal distress, demise, abnormal neurodevelopment, and growth retardation. Chronic alcohol use during pregnancy has been long recognized to cause neonatal changes and the effects have been characterized as fetal alcohol syndrome. Cocaine, heroin, amphetamines, and nicotine have been associated with impaired fetal growth and withdrawal syndromes. During normal pregnancy, amniotic fluid is circulated, swallowed, and processed by the fetus at rates of up to 50 mL/hour. Encapsulation of the fetus in this "protective" fluid can actually prolong the exposure to harmful drugs or metabolites that cross the placental barrier. Small lipid-soluble drugs can rapidly diffuse across the placental barrier, yet large, polar drugs are transferred more slowly. The amniotic sac and its contents serve as a deep compartment with restricted, slow equilibrium between adjacent compartments. Basic drugs, such as methamphetamine, may accumulate in amniotic fluid as a result of ion trapping. This phenomenon can produce concentrations of drug that exceed those found in fetal or maternal plasma.

DRUGS IN BREAST MILK

Drugs are also transported by passive diffusion across the mammary epithelium into the breast milk. The slightly acidic pH tends to trap basic drugs and the presence of emulsified fats tends to concentrate lipid-soluble drugs such as THC and PCP. Amphetamines have been detected in breast milk at concentrations three to seven times those of maternal plasma. THC can be eight times higher. In addition, drugs linger in the body; PCP was detected as long as 41 days following cessation of drug use. The transfer and accumulation of drugs in breast milk increases the likelihood of infant toxicity.

DETERMINING PRENATAL OR NEONATAL DRUG EXPOSURE

Prenatal or neonatal drug exposure can be determined using conventional analytical techniques mentioned earlier (e.g., immunoassay, GC-MS). However, interpretation of toxicological findings is often limited because drug dose, route, and time of administration are often unknown. Despite our understanding of the maternal consequences of drug abuse, fetal consequences remain poorly understood. Determining the long-term implications of prenatal drug exposure is a challenging area of maternal-fetal medicine.

Summary

Toxicology is an essential discipline within the forensic sciences. The three major subdisciplines of forensic toxicology are human performance toxicology, postmortem toxicology, and forensic urine drug testing. Because the results of various types of drugs testing are vital elements in the outcomes of many judicial proceedings, there is no room for error in the selection, identification, collection, and preservation of biological evidence.

Forensic nursing personnel have several important responsibilities in ensuring that tests provide precise and accurate data, beginning at the point of deciding which individuals should have toxicological analyses to support their clinical management and to serve as a database for subsequent judicial proceedings.

Case Study **10-1**

Wrong-Way Driver

DISPOSITION. A 23-year-old male driving the wrong way on the highway at 90 miles per hour crashed into oncoming traffic. The driver suffered only superficial injuries, but both passengers in the oncoming vehicle were killed. The driver exhibited muscle twitching and rapid speech. A pipe, an off-white substance, and drug paraphernalia were found in the vehicle. A drug-recognition evaluation revealed blood pressure of 162/111 mmHg, pulse 105 bpm, pupils dilated (9 mm), slow reaction to light, no horizontal or vertical gaze nystagmus, and the time estimation of 30 seconds was only 7 seconds.

FINDINGS/INTERPRETATION. Immunoassay of blood and urine taken from the suspect two hours after the accident indicated the presence of amphetamines. The officer observed symptoms that were consistent with CNS stimulant use. Confirmatory GC-MS analysis revealed a concentration of 730 ng/mL methamphetamine in the blood, which is inconsistent with therapeutic drug use. The concentration of methamphetamine in the blood, which falls into the toxic range, is more consistent with a tolerant or chronic drug user.

Case Study **10-2**

Asleep at the Wheel

DISPOSITION. Drivers on a city street observed a 35-year-old female "nodding off" at the wheel while driving approximately 20 mph. The vehicle eventually stopped at a light post and caused minor property damage. At the hospital, where the driver received treatment for slight injuries, vital signs indicated blood pressure of 112/60 mmHg, pulse 42 bpm, pupils constricted (1.5 mm), unreactive to light, with horizontal gaze nystagmus, and lack of convergence. The driver's eyelids were droopy and her hands felt cold and clammy. The woman stated she had had two glasses of wine with lunch, 30 minutes earlier. Prescriptions for Vicodin and Xanax were found in her purse.

FINDINGS/INTERPRETATION. Blood alcohol concentration at the hospital, one hour after the accident, was only 0.02%. Immunoassay drug screen results were negative, but confirmatory GC-MS analysis revealed therapeutic concentrations of hydrocodone and alprazolam at 10 and 30 ng/mL, respectively. Drug signs and symptoms were consistent with the combined use of three CNS depressant drugs, which have an additive effect.

Case Study **10-3**

Unexplained Coma

DISPOSITION. A 15-year-old girl at a party suffers dizziness, vomiting, and falls unconscious after consuming a nonalcoholic drink. On arrival at the ED, she is comatose, hypothermic, and bradycardic. The girl, who had no history of drug or alcohol use, awoke from the coma several hours later, suffering amnesia. The following day, the girl claimed a sexual assault had taken place at the party.

FINDINGS/INTERPRETATION. In the ED, an immunoassay drug screen for common drugs of abuse was negative. Blood drawn at the hospital was consumed during medical management. Blood and urine collected at the police station 24 hours after the alleged sexual assault was analyzed for "date rape" drugs. GHB was present in the urine (100 mg/L) but not in the blood, consistent with detection times of the drug. Clinical signs and symptoms were consistent with GHB administration.

Resources

BOOKS

Brunton, L. L., Lazo, J. S., & Parker, K. L. (Eds.). (2006). *Goodman & Gilman's the pharmacological basis of therapeutics* (11th ed.)New York: McGraw-Hill.

Flomenbaum, N. E., Goldfrank, L. R., Hoffman, R. S., Howland, M.A., Lewin, N.A., & Nelson, L.S. (Eds.). (2006). *Goldfrank's toxicologic emergencies* (8th ed.). New York: McGraw-Hill.

Haddad, L. M., Shannon, M. W., & Winchester, J. F. (Eds.). (1998). *Clinical management of poisoning and drug overdose* (3rd ed.). Philadelphia: Saunders.

Hawks, R. L., & Chiang, C. N. (Eds.). (1986). *Urine testing for drugs of abuse.* National Institute on Drug Abuse. Research Monograph Series. Number 73. Washington, DC: US Government Printing Office.

Karch, S. (Ed.). (2007). *Drug abuse handbook* (2nd ed.). Boca Raton: CRC Press.

Katzung, B. G. (Ed.). (2006). *Basic and clinical pharmacology* (10th ed.). New York: McGraw-Hill Medical.

LeBeau, M., & Mozayani, A. (Eds.). (2001). *Drug-facilitated sexual assault: A forensic handbook.* San Diego, CA: Academic Press.

Levine, B. (Ed.). (2010). *Principles of forensic toxicology* (3rd ed.). Washington, DC: AACC Press.

Moffat, A. C., Osselton, M. D., & Widdop, B. (Eds.). (2004). *Clarke's analysis of drugs and poisons* (3rd ed.). London: The Pharmaceutical Press.

Physicians' desk reference (63rd ed.). (2009). Williston, VT: Thomson Healthcare.

Ropero-Miller, J. D., & Goldberger, B. A. (Eds.). (2009). *Handbook of workplace drug testing* (2nd ed.). Washington, DC: AACC Press.

Siegel, J. A. (Ed.). (2000). *Encyclopedia of forensic sciences*. London: Academic Press.

References

Baselt, R. C. (2008). *Disposition of toxic drugs and chemicals in man* (8th ed.). Foster City, CA: Biomedical Publications.

Drug Abuse Warning Network (2006). National Estimates of Drug-Related Emergency Department Visits. U.S. Department of Health and Human Services. Substance Abuse and Mental Health Service Administration.

Drugs and Crime Facts. (2002). U.S. Department of Justice. Office of Justice Programs. Bureau of Justice Statistics. NCJ 165148.

National Highway and Transportation Safety Administration (NHSTA). Washington, DC: U.S. Department of Transportation (Website accessed 02/04/2009).

National Survey on Drug Use and Health. (2007). U.S. Department of Health and Human Services. Abuse and Mental Health Service, Administration. Office of Applied Studies.

Pregnancy and Substance Abuse. (2004). The NSDUH Report. U.S. Department of Health and Human Services. Substance Abuse and Mental Health Service Administration. Office of Applied Studies.

Rape Treatment Center. (2004). *Santa Monica-UCLA Medical Center*. Santa Monica, CA Retrieved from www.endrape.org (Website accessed 02/04/2009).

Substance-Abuse and Mental Health Services Administration (SAMHSA). Washington, DC: U.S. Dept. of Health and Human Services.

Wilson, J. M. (1994). *Abused drugs II*. Washington, DC: AACC Press.

Wu, A. (Ed.). (2006). *Tietz clinical guide to laboratory tests* (4th ed.). Philadelphia: Saunders.

CHAPTER 11 Forensic First Response: Approach for Emergency Medical Personnel

Paul D. Shapiro

First Response

Skilled personnel who respond to medical emergencies outside the hospital setting have various titles: emergency medical technicians (EMTs), paramedics, rescue squad members, and search-and-rescue teams are only a few. Whether these personnel work as volunteers or are paid, function otherwise as firefighters, are hospital employees, or work for private emergency medical service companies, these first responders constitute a vital link both in the patient's survival and in the management of any forensic evidence associated with the event. The multiple levels of medical training and experience should not interfere with the education and concepts required to think forensically and preserve evidence.

Forensic evidence is most frequently lost during the interval between the victim's initial injury and death, generally as a result of medical intervention or movement of the body. Preserving forensic evidence is less complicated when a person dies at a residence or in a contained crime scene, rather than in a transportation accident, industrial explosion, or mass disaster. In a more confined accident or death scene, barricade tape can be placed to afford security for medical examiners, detectives, and forensic investigators. Here, in this "controlled" environment, an investigative team can take the time necessary to conduct a thorough crime scene search, ensuring that vital evidence is not overlooked, lost, or altered and that it is collected using proper procedures.

When a person is subjected to life-threatening trauma, forensic evidence moves or becomes unstable in relationship to the victim's body. The crime scene often has only a few bystanders or witnesses initially, but it may quickly become crowded when news of the event is heard. Within minutes, police officers, firefighters, and emergency medical personnel arrive. Because of the number of people interfacing with elements within the crime scene, evidence that could aid in the determination of circumstances before, during, and after the injury or death is frequently lost, destroyed, or simply disappears.

KEY POINT Evidence is often fragile or perishable and can be altered or lost during medical procedures. Once evidence is recognized, it should be documented, collected, and preserved in accordance with established forensic procedures.

Cases of life-threatening injury are not the only situations at risk for loss of critical evidence. Loss of evidence can also occur when patients with minor physical injury, such as sexual assault victims, are transported to an emergency department or other specialized location designated for examination. Highly perishable and fragile evidence used to identify and prosecute a sexual offender successfully requires special handling. Prehospital personnel and others who are among the first to come into contact with these cases must be educated in the recognition, preservation, collection, and transmission of biological evidence (Ryan, 2000).

Many seminars on crime scene preservation focus on the passive role of the first responder. The standard warning in crime scenes, "don't touch anything," is not an option for first responders. However, EMTs and paramedics are often called to crime scenes immediately after the incident occurs. Medical protocols demand that they accomplish physical assessments, control hemorrhage, intubate, defibrillate, perform cardiopulmonary resuscitation, immobilize, and transport patients to the hospital as necessary. To "not touch anything" is impossible. Prehospital personnel focus first on the attempt to save life; recognition and preservation of perishable forensic evidence become secondary. However, these objectives are not mutually exclusive when prehospital personnel are educated and trained in medicolegal protocol and procedures. Rather, basic forensic evidence collection tends to become automatically integrated into practice without creating delays in medical care.

KEY POINT Lifesaving medical care is the top priority for medical personnel and should not be delayed in order to document, collect, or preserve on-scene evidence.

Principles discussed in this chapter are useful not only for EMTs and firefighters but also for emergency nurses who are first responders in the clinical environment or flight nurses at a crime scene. Aeromedical transport has a great impact on criminal investigations. Frequently, patients are injured in a rural setting and must be transported to a trauma center (or other comprehensive care facility) in a distant section of the state or in another state entirely. When a crime is committed in one locale and the patient is transported by ground or air to an institution in a different county or state and subsequently dies, the coroner or medical examiner for the jurisdiction where the death was pronounced will be responsible for the investigation. Such investigators will no longer have access to forensic evidence left at the scene of the traumatic event or crime.

The clinical forensic principles and techniques for first responders that are outlined in this chapter pertain to all scenes, emphasizing the recognition, preservation, collection, and transmission of evidence. This chapter is divided into three sections. The first section discusses death scenes, in which medical intervention is not required; the second section addresses crime scenes in which it is required. The final section presents practical issues (e.g., preservation strategies, chain-of-custody concerns, documentation, and legal testimony).

Forensic Evidence

Courts of law recognize three types of evidence: direct, circumstantial, and real. Direct evidence is an eyewitness account of what happened or statements from witnesses who possess firsthand knowledge of the event in question. Circumstantial evidence is physical evidence or statements that establish circumstances from which one can infer other facts. Real evidence is a physical, tangible object that may prove or disprove a statement in question; such evidence may be direct or circumstantial. Everything from trace physical evidence to eyewitness statements can be considered either direct or circumstantial (indirect) evidence. The difference between direct and circumstantial evidence may best be described in the following example:

Someone looks outside the window and sees that water is falling from the sky and collecting in puddles on the ground. This is good direct evidence that it is raining. Therefore, this person could provide eyewitness testimony that it had rained. Conversely, if someone went outside to find the car covered in beaded droplets and pooling of accumulated water, there is good circumstantial evidence that it had rained. The definition of circumstantial evidence is "indirect evidence by which principal facts may be inferred." This evidence does not result from actual observation or knowledge of the facts in question, but from other facts that can lead to deductions that indirectly confirm the facts being sought (Nash, 1992).

The evidence collected by first responders can be either direct or circumstantial. According to Locard's principle of exchange theory, when a criminal comes into contact with an object or person, a cross-transfer of evidence occurs (Saferstein, 2003). Therefore, if one can link the offender to the scene and the victim to the scene, a conclusion can be drawn that the offender and the victim are linked.

Nonmedical Intervention

DEATH AT HOME

State law regulates the delineation of authority in regard to the declaration of death. Most states allow first responders to declare death when conclusive signs are present. Furthermore, advanced prehospital care providers, such as paramedics, may often declare death when faced with an advanced directive or inability to regain a perfusing rhythm after a set number of interventions. The patient is then classified as dead on arrival (DOA). Often, when first responders reach the scene, they have had advanced information that indicates they should not expect to find a viable patient. The initial 911 call information, scene dynamics, and direct statements from bystanders will provide these clues. In these cases, prehospital teams should approach the body with minimal equipment and supplies and then do a rapid immediate assessment to confirm death while disturbing the scene as little as possible. Personnel and bystanders should enter and leave the death scene by the same route to minimize risks of altering environmental elements at the scene. The first responder team must document all information surrounding the encounter for law enforcement officials and the medical examiner. This documentation should include the times from dispatch, the time the pronouncement of death was made, scene entrance and exit routes, and any disturbances made to the scene by personnel involved in intervention. Physical assessment procedures or other medical care should be noted, including information about any areas of the body that were touched in the process.

Disposable equipment used on the patient (e.g., defibrillator pads) should be left in place for the medical examiner. Gloves or other expendable items used by the care team should be placed in a paper bag, labeled, and left at the scene as well.

RESPONDING TO SUDDEN INFANT DEATH SYNDROME

Sudden infant death syndrome (SIDS) is the leading cause of death among infants age 1 to 12 months and is the third leading cause of infant mortality in the United States averaging more than 4500 deaths a year. Ninety percent of the SIDS deaths occur in infants younger than six months, with a majority dying between two and four months of age (CDC, 2008).

According to Guntheroth and Spiers (2002), SIDS is most likely caused by a combination of three factors. This "triple-risk" model incorporates: (1) biological vulnerabilities, (2) environmental stressors, and (3) a critical development period. Research has shown SIDS to occur more frequently when the baby is male, African American, or Native American. Certain heart and brain abnormalities, as well as certain genetic predispositions have been identified that put some infants at greater risk for SIDS. Additionally, a mother who smokes cigarettes or uses drugs during pregnancy or a baby exposed to secondhand smoke has also been linked to an increased risk of SIDS. Although some of the risks for SIDS can be minimized (for example, by avoiding cigarette smoke and having the baby sleep on his or her back), there is no guarantee that doing so can prevent a SIDS death.

Because EMS personnel are usually the first responders on the scene of a SIDS death, Bledsoe (2008) reported that rescue personnel take on three major roles: (1) providing medical care if needed; (2) offering support and consolation for the family; and (3) observing, assessing, and documenting the scene.

As the first link in the evidence chain, it is extremely important to accurately note the death scene and thoroughly document your findings. First responders need to ask questions about the event and the baby. If possible, the first responder should try to question the parents separately to reduce the likelihood of receiving rehearsed stories. Also, open-ended questions generally provide better information and are recommended.

According to Bledsoe (2008), questions should include the following:

- Can you tell me what happened?
- Where was the baby?
- Who found the baby? When?
- What did you do when you found the baby?
- Has the baby been moved?
- When was the last time the baby was seen alive?
- How did the baby seem today? (Last night? Yesterday?)
- Has the baby been ill recently?

Some families may insist that resuscitation be attempted, whereas others understand that such measures are hopeless. Some parents may simply want to hold the baby. Rescue personnel need to walk a fine line between meeting the family's requests, following medical protocols, and protecting the scene for law enforcement. It is important for first responders to remember that SIDS is often a tragic, innocent, event. But they must always consider the possibility that something criminal may have transpired.

Because most current research shows that SIDS patients have a 0% chance of survival, many scholars suggest that lights and siren responses should not be used and resuscitation (if it has been initiated) be terminated at the scene (Smith, Kaji, Young, Gausche-Hill, 2005). The death of a child is one of the most devastating events that can happen to a family. It is also among the most stressful events that emergency medical services (EMS) personnel encounter. After a SIDS death has been determined, the child's parents and family essentially become the patients. It may be necessary to provide psychological first aid. It is also important to remember that people react to the shock of death in different ways. Rescue personnel must recognize this to remain calm, objective, and professional.

DEATH OUTSIDE THE HOME

Pronouncement of death outside a domestic dwelling produces a different set of challenges for the first responder. Many of these deaths are on major roadways where there may be an increased number of people interacting with the scene of the crime or death. Additionally, wildlife can invade the scene and remove elements that may potentially be considered evidentiary. Because the area is open to the public, the first priority is to isolate the scene. The principles of patient care and scene management are identical to those for "at home" deaths. As soon as death has been confirmed, the immediate area should be sealed with crime scene barrier tape while first responders await law enforcement officers and crime laboratory personnel who will further document and search the scene for evidence. For detailed directions pertaining to large crime scene preservation, see Chapter 5.

Interventions: Life-Threatening Trauma

FIREARM INJURIES

Injuries caused by firearms have altered dramatically since the 1990s, not only in the number of incidents of gun-related violence but also in the increasingly variable population of those using guns and falling victim to gunfire (Perkins, 2003). Without the education of all personnel involved, from first responders through surgeons, evidence needed to properly evaluate and prosecute cases will be lost (Evans & Stagner, 2003).

For example, when the first responder comes into contact with a shooting victim, the responder will normally expose the affected area identified by the loss of continuity of the clothing surface or by the obvious location of hemorrhage. It may seem natural to take trauma shears and cut up to and through the hole in the clothing, or even to use the bullet hole as a starting point in the exposure process. This must not be done, however, because cutting through bullet holes creates the first breach in preserving vital forensic evidence.

When a bullet is fired from a weapon, heated gases emerge, as well as burning and unburned gunpowder. This gunpowder comes to rest on the first surface with which it comes into contact, frequently the victim's clothing. Investigators can use this clothing in several ways. First, the gunpowder itself can be examined and may give an indication about the type of ammunition used. Second, the investigators can take the suspected weapon, along with the suspected ammunition, and test fire it to determine the distance (range of fire) between the perpetrator and the victim when the gun was discharged. Last, the test fire is matched to the victim's shirt. These procedures make it imperative not to cut through the hole caused by the bullet or gases.

Clothing collection is also vital to forensic investigation. Garments should be placed in paper bags, not thrown onto the floor, tossed into a stairwell, left in the ambulance, or crammed into a biohazard bag. If time does not permit proper packaging, clothing should be preserved by hanging it (or placing it) over paper (or on a clean white sheet) to facilitate air-drying. Any clothing that is still wet should be noted as such, packaged, and immediately turned over to law enforcement personnel so that the technical investigative services can complete the drying process. New (nonrecycled) paper bags should be readily available on the ambulance and in the emergency department. Do not place clothing into a plastic biohazard bag. When enclosed in plastic, biological specimens will undergo chemical changes, degrading their value as forensic specimens. Biological evidence must be preserved in a receptacle that permits airflow in and out of the container. However, if clothing is sufficiently saturated with blood or bodily fluids that it cannot be contained in double- or triple-layered paper bags, the entire paper-packaged and sealed garment should be placed in a plastic biohazard bag and left open to air.

BEST PRACTICE Do not discard clothing. Do not cut through bullet holes or other defects mechanically inflicted in clothing. Place articles of clothing in a paper bag to permit air-drying.

Next, in cases involving firearm shootings, first responders should observe and document the characteristics of wounds. Rather than classifying the wound as an entrance or exit wound, first responders should describe in detail the characteristics that would support such a classification. Most important, documentation should consist of location (including measurement from obvious landmarks), the presence or absence of an abrasion ring, the direction of the weighted border of the abrasion ring, and the presence of stippling or soot (Fig. 11-1). Unless absolutely necessary, the first responder should not clean the wound or disturb the patient's or victim's hands. Sophisticated tests may be required to determine whether or not gunshot residue (GSR) is present on the victim's or patient's hands. Paper bags should be placed over the hands and taped at the wrist to prevent any loss of the substance.

Arguments have been made that the hands may be needed for vascular access. However, current standards in trauma care call for large-bore peripheral intravenous lines (IVs) to be placed in the

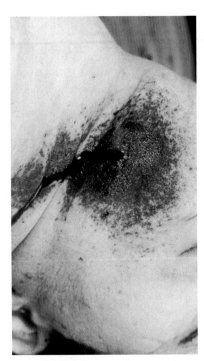

Fig. 11-1 Gunshot wound with stippling.

antecubital fossa. If, in the rare case vascular access can only be obtained in the hand or wrist, cleansing beyond the immediate venipuncture site should be avoided.

BEST PRACTICE Gunshot victims with or without visible or suspected gunpowder residue on their hands should have a paper bag placed over the hands, which is then taped at the wrists to prevent loss of residue. Bullets or bullet fragments must be transferred with gloves or rubber-tipped forceps and placed in a suitable specimen container. Deceased victims of sexual assault should also have paper bags placed over the hands to protect trace evidence.

After the victim arrives at the emergency department, hospital staff should remove bandages covering any wounds and preserve them so that they can be examined for the presence of gunshot residue. Any bullets or bullet fragments should be preserved by picking them up with either a gloved hand or rubber-tipped (shod) forceps and placing them in a small envelope or padded specimen container for transfer to the proper law enforcement authorities (Evans & Stagner, 2003).

SHARP FORCE TRAUMA

First responders encounter several different types of sharp force trauma from which two distinctive categories emerge: incised wounds, including cuts and slashes, or punctures such as stab wounds.

All sharp force trauma produces smooth edges without bridging of tissue. Abraded or contused margins are also usually absent, except when the instrument used is particularly dull or serrated. Incised wounds are classified as such because their length exceeds their depth. Conversely, stab or puncture wounds have a depth that exceeds their surface length. Incised wounds usually give little information about the offending object itself. However, the observation of tailing, which is created when the angle at which the sharp object loses contact with the tissue becomes increasingly shallow, demonstrates the direction of the offending forces (Fig. 11-2). The main objective in preserving evidence of sharp force trauma is accurate documentation of the characteristics of the wounds, as well as their locations on the victim's body.

BLUNT FORCE TRAUMA

There are four primary types of blunt force trauma: abrasions, lacerations, contusions, and fractures. Frequently, a determination can be made from these injuries as to the circumstances that surrounded and caused the injury.

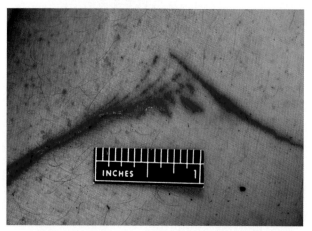

Fig. 11-2 Tailing injury suggesting the direction of force.

Abrasions

These injuries occur when the epidermal layer of the skin is removed secondary to friction against a rough surface. They are subclassified into four categories. First, the scratch abrasion is known for its thin linear formation that resembles that of a cat scratch. Second, graze abrasions are commonly referred to as "road rash." Third, impact abrasions, result when the offending object stamps the skin, thus removing the epidermal layer. Fourth, linear pressure with movement, often seen in cases involving hanging, creates friction abrasions.

Evidence related to abrasion injuries is used to assist investigators in determining the direction of the forces applied to the patient, manifested by linear markings within the wound as well as skin tags seen on the leading edges of the wound. Debris from the offending object or frictional surface can be transferred to the wound. In the prehospital setting, wounds may have been covered or dressed before the first responders have arrived to the scene. If the wound is rebandaged, the original dressings should be saved as evidence. Hospital personnel in the emergency department must also understand the importance of saving all prehospital dressings, which may contain evidence. Trace elements of the offending object or surface may be imbedded in the dressings. These items are placed in a paper bag and law enforcement is notified of their existence.

BEST PRACTICE The characteristics and appearance of wounds should be noted before any cleaning. Wound dressings applied in the field to treat gunshot wounds or blunt force injuries should be collected as forensic evidence.

The appearance of the wound must be documented and forensic evidence collected before cleaning, debridement, or suturing. Failure to do so will result in scrubbing away trace evidence, losing the direction of skin tags, and altering the wound's characteristics.

Lacerations

Lacerations are the results of blunt injury. Healthcare personnel commonly misclassify them. They are characterized by their irregular edges, bridging tissue, localized swelling, and contused margins. They differ greatly from sharp injuries (e.g., slashes and punctures). Although a type of laceration referred to as a split may mimic a sharp injury because of the smoother edges of the wound, bridging of tissue inside the wound will be present.

Contusions or Bruises

These injuries are produced when blood extravasates from the circulating vasculature into the interstitial space. Contrary to popular belief, age determinations cannot be made based on the appearance or colorations of contusions. Contusions with varied color patterns do, however, suggest that the injuries occurred at different times. Of utmost importance to first responders is the presence of a pattern injury that can lead to the identification of the offending object. Whether there are bruises caused by a hand during manual strangulation, or an extension cord impression on the body of a child, all pattern injuries require extensive documentation. Photographic documentation at the emergency department should be conducted at the earliest possibility before healing diminishes the quality of the evidence. Furthermore, follow-up photographs should be taken within 24 hours if the patient is admitted to the hospital.

Fractures

Fracture, the remaining form of blunt force trauma, results in the loss of continuity of the bone and can be direct or indirect (DiMaio & DiMaio, 2001). Direct fractures include focal, crushing, and penetrating types. Focal fractures, such as transverse fractures, result from a force applied to a small area and may be associated with little or no soft tissue damage overlying the fracture site. In contrast, a crush-type fracture occurs when a large amount of force is applied over a larger body surface area, resulting in comminuted fractures and greater soft-tissue damage. Penetrating fractures, the third type of direct fracture, are produced when a large amount of force is applied to a small body surface area. Usually only seen in association with firearm injury, these wounds, while often bone shattering, present with little overlying soft tissue damage.

Indirect fractures caused by forces remote to the fracture site include traction, angulation, rotational, and vertical compression fractures, or combinations thereof. Athletic activity commonly leads to indirect fractures when activities such as jumping, running, and quick turning create linear traction, angular, rotational, or compression forces on the bone. Rotational injury may manifest as spiral fractures in the physical abuse of children. The standard guidelines for fracture management in the prehospital setting work well to preserve fracture characteristics that are vital for forensic investigation regarding the mechanical forces of injury. Short of creating a new fracture or causing a closed fracture to reopen, the fracture evidence should not deteriorate because use of rigid and traction splints preserves the fractures well.

MOTOR VEHICLE COLLISIONS

Motor vehicle collisions (MVCs) are among the most common events that require response from the prehospital care provider. With these collisions comes a host of different circumstances that call for the recognition, preservation, and collection of forensic evidence. The kinematics associated with even low-velocity collisions can still lead to both blunt and sharp injuries. In many instances, the keen first responder can look at the damage of a vehicle and deduce possible injuries sustained by the patients involved.

Some questions regarding patient position before the collision arise when investigating MVCs. Occasionally, however, when a death results from the collision, people still alive at the scene profess to be passengers and not the driver, even when found behind the wheel of the damaged vehicle. Sometimes everyone associated with the vehicle is ejected and unable to explain the positions of the passengers in the car.

Fortunately, clues exist that will give a consistent indication about the position of the occupants when the accident happened. Windshield glass is laminate and composed of two sheets of glass with a plasticized film sandwiched in between. When this type of windshield breaks, it shatters into long slivers of glass that will cause longitudinal sharp injuries on the faces of those sitting in the front seat. In contrast, the side window glass is composed of tempered glass, which shatters into many angular pieces when it breaks (Fig. 11-3), causing angular sharp injuries to the victim on the same side as the window. Therefore, a passenger in the front seat will traditionally have linear cuts down the front of the face and angular cuts—or what forensically are known as dicing injuries—to the right side of the face or even to the shoulder (Fig. 11-4).

Drivers, following the same line of reasoning, would be expected to have dicing injuries on their left sides. Other injuries that suggest the patient's place in the vehicle include pattern contusions or impact abrasions caused by the steering wheel or

Fig. 11-3 Tempered glass pieces revealing characteristic shards in broken automobile windows.

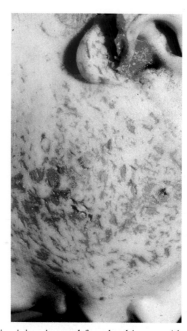

Fig. 11-4 Dicing injury incurred from head impact with tempered automobile glass.

automobile company logos that are frequently found on the dashboard (Fig. 11-5). In the absence of obvious sharp injuries, look for glass fragments that may be caught in the clothing of suspected automobile occupants. Any such glass fragments or shards should be collected and placed in a solid container and preserved as evidence, along with any other debris, such as paint chips, plastic, metal pieces, plant, or grass material.

Clothing should be preserved. Clothing may contain the previously listed forensic evidence, as well as trace evidence from contacts made with the car, street surface, and other objects. Additionally, clothing evidence may also provide key blood-spatter evidence that will allow investigators to determine the

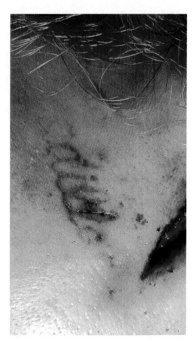

Fig. 11-5 Dashboard impression revealing impact with steering wheel.

direction of force and injury. A frequently overlooked and under-appreciated piece of forensic evidence is the footwear of people involved in serious MVCs. Shoes may be used to determine the occupant's position in the vehicle or even the manner of death, as in the case of suspected vehicular suicide. Impressions on soles from desperate braking attempts, for example, may validate the driver of the car.

Investigations of the scenes of MVCs usually occur long after emergency medical providers have transported the last victim from the area. When occupants are thrown from the vehicle and subsequently transported, the investigating officers frequently lack vital information pertaining to where the patient's body landed, as well as its initial position. If photographic documentation is not available, the conscientious first responder would see to it that detailed references to patient's location and position are made available to investigators. This can be done with tape, chalk, or another method indicating the patient's position. The same method is used when investigating auto-pedestrian injuries.

BEST PRACTICE When managing victims of vehicular collisions, on-scene personnel should document the details regarding the state of the crashed vehicles, the location or apparent position of the occupants at the time of impact, and any other physical factors that could be helpful in predicting the forces of injury.

OVERDOSE OR POISONING

When first responders encounter a patient who may have "overdosed" or may have been a victim of intentional poisoning, care should be taken to recover suspected substances within the immediate environment. Investigators will eventually need to determine whether an elderly person who is admitted to the emergency department was confused, was suicidal and intentionally ingested an overdose of medication, or whether the medication was administered to the patient by another individual with the intent to do harm. Bottles, pill containers, and syringes should be handled carefully to preserve fingerprints or other artifacts that might be important for

the forensic investigating team. Gloves should be worn, and a tool such as a hemostat should be used to move containers or to transfer them to a clear plastic or paper bag. When dealing with cases involving suspected poisoning or overdose by injection, especially if they should become lethal, it is often confusing for the medical examiner to determine which punctures are therapeutic (e.g., missed IV sticks or lab draws) and which were caused by dosing of the illicit substance. To assist these future investigators, forensic first responders can circle the therapeutic puncture sites they created, using ink, to allow investigators to differentiate the two types. Although this method is generally considered acceptable, it should first be cleared with the local medical examiner or coroner. Finally, in preserving evidence of overdose and poisoning, all emesis should be retained and preserved as evidence. If vomiting is going to be induced, first responders should take saline-moistened sterile swabs, swab the inside of each nostril, and preserve the swab as evidence to prevent destruction of any toxic substances that may have been inhaled. The swabs must then be air-dried before packaging in an envelope to prevent cross-contamination.

BEST PRACTICE The containers or delivery device for any toxic substance should be transported with the patient to the hospital along with any emesis produced.

ASPHYXIA

One area in the prehospital setting that has a great impact on criminal investigations is the generic category of asphyxia. Asphyxia is also one topic in which first responders traditionally receive minimal formal education. Without outward signs of trauma, asphyxia can be unidentifiable at autopsy, making well-documented information from the accident or crime scene vital in assuring the proper medicolegal outcome.

First responders should be able to distinguish between the three broad categories of asphyxia—suffocation, strangulation, and chemical asphyxiation—each of which also comprises several subdivisions. Awareness of these classifications provides a knowledgeable first responder with a better conception of the pertinent information needed to adequately document the circumstances surrounding a particular incident.

Suffocation

Suffocation is asphyxiation in which oxygen fails to reach the bloodstream. Inadequate oxygen supply leads to entrapment or environmental asphyxias. Smothering results from obstruction or occlusion of the external airways (e.g., placing a pillow or plastic bag over the victim's face). Choking can occur when air is blocked from entering the airway passages within the throat (choking on an object), whereas external pressure placed on the thorax or trachea is referred to as mechanical asphyxia or strangulation, respectively. One must be clear when documenting choking or strangulation. Choking is generally accidental in nature, whereas strangulation may be either accidental or intentional. Finally, suffocating gases can displace oxygen from the atmospheric air (e.g., carbon dioxide and methane). Combinations of events can occur, such as mechanical asphyxia coupled with smothering, often seen in children sleeping in the same bed as an adult (lying-over deaths). Although mechanisms of suffocation differ, they all involve the failure of oxygen to reach the bloodstream.

Strangulation

This cause of death includes hangings, ligature or manual strangulation, and autoerotic asphyxiation. Hangings are characterized by the use of a noose or constricting band, with asphyxia resulting from compression of the neck vessels by the body's weight. Ligature strangulation also involves the use of a constricting band, although tightened by a force other than the victim's body weight. Use of the hand, forearm, or other limb to compress the neck vessels defines manual strangulation. Autoerotic asphyxia is caused by intentionally inducing hypoxia for intensifying sexual gratification.

Chemical Asphyxia

This type of asphyxia is caused by inhaled substances that prevent oxygen from reaching the cells. Some examples of these potentially lethal chemicals include carbon monoxide, cyanide, and hydrogen sulfide.

Physical findings most common to the asphyxias, in general, are petechial hemorrhages, found in the eyes and on the face, and Tardieu spots (Fig. 11-6), found in the dependent extremities, both of which findings are secondary to vascular congestion. Another important point in documentation is the presence (or absence) of a furrow and its characteristics, because the continuity and track of a furrow may differentiate between homicidal and suicidal asphyxiation. Most cases of hanging involve patients with a furrow that goes around the neck and ends with the point of suspension in an angular position at some point in the track (Fig. 11-7). Ligature strangulation usually produces a furrow that travels circumferentially around the neck. Victims who struggle may create breaks in the continuity of the furrow by placing their fingers between the neck and the constricting implement. With accurate descriptions and documentation of these physical findings, law enforcement officials may access information vital to an investigation that could easily be lost during resuscitative efforts.

OTHER PREHOSPITAL SCENARIOS

Rape and Sexual Assault

Most sexual assaults that occur in the United States are not physically life-threatening to the victims, which makes psychological trauma the primary concern when assisting most patients who have been sexually assaulted or abused. Police or family members usually transport victims of sexual assault to the hospital.

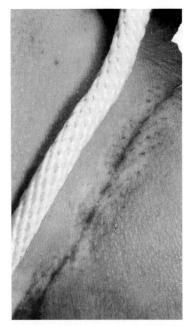

Fig. 11-7 Hanging furrow created by neck ligature.

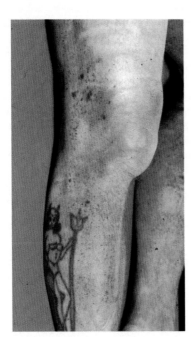

Fig. 11-6 Tardieu spots created from vascular congestion in asphyxia.

Although ambulances may also sometimes transport sexual assault victims, lifesaving prehospital care is rarely required. Several things regarding prehospital care for victims of rape or sexual assault must be mentioned. Foremost, all patients need to be treated with dignity and respect. Whenever possible, allow patients to make decisions about what is going to happen to them. Some controversy exists over the necessity of having female caregivers provide care to female victims of sexual assault. The role of an empathetic male caregiver who returns power to the patient can be very helpful to the female patient and her recovery. It is also important to provide privacy and shelter from public scrutiny or media attention.

For medical treatment and assessment, it is imperative that the first responders touch *only* those areas of the victim's body necessary for stabilization and assessment. Unless absolutely necessary, the first responder should avoid the patient's perineal area. If the victim is at home and has the opportunity to get clean clothing, it is permissible to bring the clothing to the hospital or examination facility. The first responder should explain that the clothing worn during the assault may need to be taken as evidence.

First responders must diligently document any information surrounding the assault volunteered by the victim. The victim's statements should be placed in quotes and in the victim's exact words. These statements may later be used in court as an excited utterance. It is not, however, warranted to interrogate the patient or investigate details of the actual assault other than to obtain information absolutely necessary or openly offered. The victim will appreciate this consideration, if not immediately, then later, after being asked to repeat the details of the attack several times.

Finally, after transferring care of the victim to the hospital or examination facility, provide the medical staff with the linens from the ambulance stretcher, because dirt, hair, and fibers that may have fallen off the patient during the transport to the hospital would otherwise be lost. The linens should be packaged in a paper bag after being folded inward to prevent loss of contents. Ensure that there is a chain-of-custody form and, if possible, turn this evidence over to law enforcement immediately.

Child Abuse

News stories depict the tragedy of child maltreatment that occurs daily across North America and throughout the world. Many children who die at the hands of an abuser have made hospital or clinic visits before the fatal attack. First responders must always be observant for the possibility of child abuse and neglect.

The primary advantage that first responder personnel have in the investigation of child maltreatment and abuse is the ability to observe a child in his or her natural environment. The conditions of the dwelling in which the patient lives can often provide signs of abuse or neglect. First responder's documentation should include objective statements regarding the living conditions and the way the child interacts with the caregiver.

When the least amount of suspicion arises, first responders should attempt to separate caregivers before ascertaining the circumstances surrounding the injury and document their responses accurately and in quotes. Later, their versions may change or become more consistent when they have had the chance (and time) to create an improved story. Parents should be questioned in a nonthreatening manner about feeding difficulties and inconsolable crying of infants, because these are often triggers for abusers with poor self-control. Challenges with toilet training are also a common trigger for abuse.

In addition to the inconsistency of the history, often the appearance of the injury is not consistent with the physical surroundings present. Again, detailed descriptions of suspicious injuries and the possible causative factors are required. First responders occupy a unique position that the physicians and nurses in the hospital rarely do. If parents report the child brushed up against a hot radiator, first responders have the ability to see whether the radiator is actually hot. Are the other radiators on in the house, or was this radiator turned on for some "special" reason? Does the child have pattern marks on his or her skin? Is there anything obvious that could have caused those marks? Only first responders have the opportunity to see the scene immediately after the report of the abuse or injury occurred. Therefore, it is essential that responders document anything that could be used later to either confirm or refute the reported mechanism of injury. The victim and siblings, too, may be potential sources of important and reliable information.

Most states have child welfare laws that require notification to the police or other specified authority if child abuse or maltreatment is suspected. First responders should be familiar with the local jurisdiction's requirements and reporting procedures.

Domestic Abuse or Intimate Partner Violence

As with cases of sexual assault and child maltreatment, first responders can either aid or destroy the patient's ability to escape domestic abuse or intimate partner violence. The first responsibility, of course, is to ensure the safety and protection of the patient by removing them from the situation, either to an ambulance, police car, or neighbor's residence. After the patient is in a safer environment, assessment and treatment of injuries and psychological intervention can begin.

First responders usually enter the scene during the explosion phase, during which fear for one's life or the concern of a family member or neighbor has initiated an emergency response. In the emergency department, abuse becomes even more complicated because many victims of intimate partner violence present with complaints other than battery. In either case, when taking a history, compassionate but straightforward questions will usually prompt the patient to engage in factual conversations regarding his or her abuse (Ellis, 1999). Whether the patient elects to press legal or criminal charges, the best aid for these patients is to document their

history and physical injuries and provide resources quickly if and when they choose to leave the violent situation. Documentation may also be used later if additional attacks prompt legal action. The forensic first responder must also be aware that with currently developing legislation, cases of domestic violence may require mandated prosecution in some jurisdictions. The first responder should always encourage patients to accept transport to a medical facility, not only for the evaluation and treatment of current injuries but also for a more extensive examination and consultation with specialized personnel who are skilled in providing support and assistance to the patients of intimate partner violence.

Responding to Mass Casualty Incidents

Responding to mass casualty incidents (MCIs), especially mass shootings or large-scale bombing events, can be particularly stressful for rescue personnel. It is during these demanding, confusing, and horrifying calls that complete and thorough documentation becomes especially important.

"Documentation during a mass-shooting incident is one of those things you don't think about because you're too busy," noted Kelley (2008, pg. 89). "But having a written record of the incident is more than just creating a timeline." When there are numerous patients, often in multiple locations, with several different law enforcement, fire/rescue, and EMS departments responding, it can become easy for rescue personnel to forget their forensic thinking and proper documentation practices. They must not!

Before the terrorist attacks on September 11, 2001, the April 1995 bombing of the Alfred P. Murrah Federal building in Oklahoma City, Oklahoma, represented the worst terrorist act on U.S. soil. Of the 361 persons in the building at the time of the explosion, 163 died. One hundred thirty-nine other Murrah victims were transported to four different hospitals (Tucker, Pfefferbaum, Vincent, Boehler, & Nixon, 1998). The blast scene also quickly became besieged by volunteers who, although their intentions were to provide help and aid to those injured, created a logistical nightmare for Incident Command.

The phenomenon of serial, spree, and mass murder has become much more pronounced and publicized in the United States over the past few decades (Sewell, 1993). Ever since Charles Whitman killed 14 and wounded 30 at the University of Texas in 1966, school shootings seem to generate intense public emotion and can be particularly unnerving to rescue personnel. Both the immediate incident and the aftermath of the 1998 Jonesboro, Arkansas, shooting, which left 5 dead and 10 injured, and the 1999 Littleton, Colorado, shooting, which left 12 dead and 23 injured, received intense national media coverage.

More recently, on April 16, 2007, a mass shooting occurred on the campus of Virginia Tech University, in Blacksburg, Virginia. Thirty-two students and faculty were killed, and 15 were injured when a mentally disturbed student, Seung-Hui Cho, opened fire. Primarily because of bad weather, air transport of the injured directly to a level 1 trauma center was not possible. The wounded either received their care at three local hospitals or they were stabilized at these local facilities and later transported to level 1 trauma centers (Armstrong & Frykberg, 2007).

One practical concern is that MCI victims are becoming increasingly mobile. Different EMS crews can transport them, sometimes miles away from the incident scene. Occasionally they are even transferred to facilities across county or state lines. As a result, incident specifics, victim statements, and physical evidence can easily become misplaced or lost. It is important not to let the immediate stress and confusion of an MCI response compromise the chain of custody for valuable evidence.

During the initial harried response, it is easy to forget that MCI scenes are frequently crime scenes where criminal evidence needs to be gathered—usually under difficult physical and emotional conditions. In Oklahoma City, rescuers at the Murrah Building worked in four-hour shifts of 200 at a time, with up to 1000 individuals rotating in a 24-hour period (Tucker, et al., 1998). Dan Limmer, a former police officer and paramedic from Colonie, New York, reminds us, "much like a fire scene, it is amazing that any evidence is found among the rubble and ruins. In spite of all the confusion, the basic principles [of forensic thinking] hold true: We are all on the same team and can work together. Saving lives and collecting evidence doesn't have to be mutually exclusive" (Suprun, 2004, p. 65).

Forensic Responsibilities

PREHOSPITAL EVIDENCE PRESERVATION

Methods used for forensic evidence preservation follow some general rules; all specific local and state protocols and their approved guidelines, as well as laboratory specific qualifications, must also be consistently observed. Therefore, it is of paramount importance that before rescue personnel collect any evidence, the local collection methods must be procured and used as a basis for the forensic protocols. From documentation of victim's statements to types of laboratory procedures, all evidence must be preserved with the intention that it will end up in court. All local guidelines and protocols must be followed to ensure admissibility.

First responders have a large supply of equipment that is strategically placed on response vehicles; however, three important items should be added to the equipment list to ensure the proper preservation of forensic evidence:

- Paper bags of various sizes should become standard issue equipment. Rescue personnel can contact the local law enforcement agency for a supply of its recommended collection bags, because the evidence ultimately will be used for law enforcement investigations.
- A small camera with a built-in flash unit should also be added, along with the "one-step" or disposable cameras. Although it is not appropriate for first responders to delay or compromise patient care to photograph evidence, when feasible, it may be beneficial to photograph MVCs, atypical injury situations, and other unusual occurrences. Photography is recognized as the ultimate method of documentation.
- Finally, chain-of-custody forms for evidence should always be among the first responder's basic supplies in order to document evidentiary items and to serve as a record for transfers.

CHAIN OF CUSTODY

Chain-of-custody forms are available through commercial vendors and law enforcement agencies or can be produced by the individual service. Forms should contain the patient's name; other identifying information such as social security number and date of birth; the emergency medical service (or run) number; and a description of the specimen or suspected evidence being preserved. A list of the people who have had control of the evidence at any point of security and transmission should also be included, complete with the date and times of each transfer. The chain of custody starts with the person who initially collected the evidence and continues through the police, the forensic investigators, the laboratory technicians, and anyone else who may have reason to handle or examine the evidence. First

responders who gather evidence in the field should also note on their ambulance call report (or other agency form) that evidence of a particular type was preserved and should list the first transfer that was made. An appropriate notation, for example, would be "white T-shirt with suspected bullet hole was preserved in a paper bag and custody was transferred to Officer Smith at the scene."

Eliminating unnecessary transfers helps preserve the continuity of the chain of custody. Handing evidence to the officer or technical investigator responsible would take the emergency department staff out of that chain, leading to fewer points of attack for attorneys trying to dispute the integrity of the evidence. Finally, when responsible for the evidence, the first responder should be certain that it can be accounted for at all times. If the evidence must be left in the ambulance when the rescue personnel go into the hospital with a patient, the first responder should note where the vehicle was located at that specific time. Preferably, the evidence can be secured in a double-locked cabinet within the locked vehicle itself.

PREHOSPITAL BLOOD SPECIMENS

As previously mentioned, the medical examiner or coroner is ultimately responsible for determining the cause and manner of death. Manner of death may include homicide, suicide, accidental, natural, and undetermined. Forensic laboratories must frequently examine blood specimens that have been diluted by IV fluids, medications, and blood products administered by field responders and emergency department staff. Although these agents are essential in resuscitation efforts, they may complicate accurate forensic analysis. In many jurisdictions, advanced life support personnel are authorized to draw blood samples for in-hospital testing when they initially establish IVs, which are far more representative of the patient's condition just before (or after) death has occurred. Although some hospital emergency departments have policies against using blood samples not drawn by their staff, first responders should not allow their samples to be discarded. The medical examiner's/coroner's office may be interested in having access to them at a later date.

It is imperative that first responders abide by all local protocols regarding the drawing of blood samples. Although in the course of time a nationwide forensic protocol standard will be developed to ensure the proper use of prehospital blood samples, guidelines of individual agencies, county protocols, and statewide regulations must be followed.

DOCUMENTATION

The best way to protect oneself and the rights of patients is to perfect documentation skills, because the emergency response record is at times the only way to preserve forensic evidence. For example, the first responder is often the only one to hear a patient's dying declaration that could implicate a perpetrator of crime. Primarily, however, meticulous documentation provides a legal record that will contain information to reconstruct the circumstances surrounding an emergency response, the condition in which the patient was found, and the treatment provided throughout the encounter. Documentation must be accurate, complete, objective, and legible (Dernocoeur, 1990).

Accuracy involves providing details to prevent uncertainty about what occurred, when, where, and to whom it occurred, and what injuries resulted. When documenting injury, record measurements in relationship to well-known landmarks or from the top of the head and from the sagittal plane separating the right and left halves of the body. Accuracy also requires use of the correct terminology when describing wounds. Labeling a wound caused by the edge of a well-sharpened kitchen knife as a laceration is not only inaccurate but also could have the report and its associated eyewitness testimony disallowed in court. This would be embarrassing as well as tragic if such testimony would reveal that the patient's last words were "Johnny did it."

Further, avoid inaccuracies created by making assumptions, such as classifying gunshot wounds by caliber or as entrance or exit wounds. A .22-caliber gun found at the scene is not necessarily the gun that caused the injury, and entrance and exit wounds should be labeled only after technical investigation and surgical exploration or autopsy. Instead, describe the injury by its shape, length, and the presence or absence of an abrasion ring, stippling, or powder residue. With sharp injury, the presence of tailing or a hilt or guard abrasion should be noted.

Patient and bystander statements should be verbatim, and assessment data should be precise. The first responder should avoid documentation of "within normal limits (WNL)" as assessment data. For example, capillary refill should be "< 2 seconds," and bowel sounds should be "hyperactive," "hypoactive," or "active." Document specific patient behavior and statements as opposed to general statements about the patient's behavior such as "out of control" or "depressed."

The record must be legible because accurate, complete, and objective documentation proves worthless if the investigators are unable to decipher it. In addition, a defense attorney may enlarge a run report to poster size, point out spelling and grammatical errors, and ask the author to read unintelligible scribble, all of which produces a poor perception of the first responder's education, undermines his or her professionalism, and may lead to the discrediting of testimony.

PHOTODOCUMENTATION

An injury can require more than a thousand words to describe it accurately. Therefore, photodocumentation provides a great tool to supplement written documentation. Many first response vehicles are carrying the "one-step" type cameras to bring the kinematics of a MVC to the emergency department physician and to document injury before dressing the wound(s) or surgical intervention. After an initial orientation shot that includes the patient's face in proximity to the wounds for identification purposes, each injury should be photographed twice from the same distance and angle, once with some type of scale, ruler, or standard such as a coin or pencil, and the other without the scale. Without an orientation shot, the wound photograph may not be admissible in court, particularly if it does indicate who the victim was. The patient's name, date, time, and the photographer's name should be placed on the photograph. A policy should be developed to address the disposition of the photographs. Sealing them in an envelope and transferring to the investigating officer with a chain of custody would be ideal. Again, the first responder must not delay or compromise patient care to photograph injuries. Bystanders and other first response personnel are perfect choices for photographers and can be of great assistance when the emergency care providers are busy. (For detailed information on photodocumentation, see Chapter 7.)

LEGAL TESTIMONY

Testifying in court can be a nerve-wracking experience for many first responders. Although experience remains the best way to overcome the apprehension and uneasiness, a courtroom rookie should always consider the following guidelines.

The reputation of one's agency, one's profession, and the criminal justice system are at risk in the courtroom. Rescue personnel should dress conservatively and exhibit exemplary professional behavior. Unless otherwise advised by the attorney, they should not wear uniforms. Both men and women should wear dark or gray business suits. Jeans, sweatshirts, jogging suits, shorts, sneakers, and similar casual attire are not appropriate in the courtroom.

On receiving notice of a pending court appearance, the first responder should contact his or her supervisor and local attorney immediately and should request a copy of the prehospital report. The responder will testify only on what he or she specifically remembers about the case and what is included in the responder's report. He or she should not speculate. When on the witness stand, he or she should listen to the questions carefully, and if unsure, ask for clarification. It is important for the first responder to be calm, stay calm, speak slowly and confidently, and, above all else, be prepared. Knowing in advance the summoning attorney's questions will help alleviate the apprehension associated with appearing in court. If possible, the first responder may review questions and facts of the case with the attorneys before taking the stand. If testifying as an expert witness, he or she should be aware of the state's scientific testimony standards and be prepared with the appropriate materials to support his or her opinions and testimony.

Case Study 11-1

Removing Evidence

Forensic pathologist Milton Helpern (1967) related a story in his book *Where Death Delights,* regarding an interesting case that provides a great example of how first responders can make the pathologist's job difficult.

One morning Helpern was performing an autopsy and he could not determine how the woman had died. After pondering it all morning, he decided to go to lunch. The autopsy laboratory was housed in the basement of the old Bellevue Hospital in New York City, and as he was walking down the hall, a nurse stopped him.

"What did you find out about that suicide?" she asked.

"What suicide?" he replied.

"The one you've been working on all morning."

"What makes you think that it was a suicide?" he asked.

"Well, because of the plastic bag around her head at the scene that was removed for resuscitation."

Although the information was obviously known to the first responder and passed on to the emergency department nurse, it was not placed in the official documentation provided by either one.

Data from Helpern, M. (1967). *Where death delights.* New York: Coward-McCann.

Summary

The nation has focused on improved responses to victims of trauma and violent crime in the new millennium, and prehospital personnel may ensure the first vital link in preservation of key forensic evidence. First responders must remember that any accident or death scene can be the subject of future legal action. It is imperative that they recognize, preserve, collect, and transmit forensic evidence, using proper procedures and techniques. Although medical treatment is always the primary goal of prehospital personnel, it does not preclude secondary and concurrent attention to forensic details on the scene or in the emergency department.

Resources

ORGANIZATIONS

National Registry of Emergency Medical Technicians
Rocco V. Morando Building, 6610 Busch Boulevard, P.O. Box 29233, Columbus, OH 41129; 614-888-4484; www.nremt.org

U.S. Department of Transportation
National Standard Curriculum Emergency Medical Technician Paramedic (EMT-P), NHTSA; www.nhtsa.dot.gov

References

Armstrong, J. H., & Frykberg, E. R. (2007). Lessons from the response to the Virginia Tech shootings. *Disaster Medicine and Public Health Preparedness, 1*(1), 57–58.

Bledsoe, B. E. (2008). SIDS and EMS: What should we do? *JEMS, 11*(2), 66–75.

Centers for Disease Control and Prevention (CDC). (2008). *Sudden infant death syndrome (SIDS) and sudden unexpected infant death (SUID): Bome.* www.cdc.gov/SIDS/index.htm. Accessed April 3, 2009.

Dernocoeur, K. B. (1990). *Streetsense: Communication, safety, and control* (2nd ed.). Englewood Cliffs, NJ: Prentice Hall.

DiMaio, D. J., & DiMaio, V. J. (2001). *Forensic pathology* (2nd ed.). Boca Raton, FL: CRC Press.

Ellis, J. M. (1999). Barriers to effective screening for domestic violence by registered nurses in the emergency department. *Critical Care Nursing Quarterly, 22*(1), 27–41.

Evans, M. M., & Stagner, P. A. (2003). Maintaining the chain of custody: Evidence handling in forensic cases. *AORN J, 78*(4), 563–569.

Guntheroth, W. G., & Spiers, P. S. (2002). The triple risk hypothesis in sudden infant death syndrome. *Pediatrics, 110*(5), p. e64.

Helpern, M. (1967). *Where death delights.* New York: Coward-McCann.

Kelley, R. L. (2008). EMS Response to mass shootings. *EMS Magazine, 37*(10), 86–90.

Nash, J. R. (1992). *Dictionary of crime.* New York: Paragon House.

Perkins, C. (2003). Weapon use in violence crime. In *National Crime Victimization Survey 1993–2001.* Washington, DC: National Center for Victims of Crime.

Ryan, M. T. (2000). Clinical forensic medicine. *Annals of Emergency Medicine, 36*(3), 271–273.

Saferstein, R. E. (2003). *Criminalistics: An introduction to forensic science* (8th ed.). Englewood Cliffs, NJ: Prentice-Hall.

Sewell, J.D. (1993). Traumatic stress of multiple murder investigations. *Journal of Traumatic Stress. 6*(1), 103–118.

Smith, M. P., Kaji, A., Young, K. D., & Gausche-Hill, M. (2005). Presentation and survival of prehospital apparent sudden infant death syndrome. *Prehospital Emergency Care, 9*(2), 181–185.

Suprun, C. (2004). Explosive events: EMS response to a bombing incident. *Emergency Medical Services, 33*(4), 61–65.

Tucker, P., Pfefferbaum, B., Vincent, R., Boehler, S.D., & Nixon, S.J. (1998). Oklahoma City: Disaster challenges mental health and medical administrators. *Journal of Behavioral Health Services and Research, 25*(1), 93–99.

CHAPTER 12 Forensic Investigations in the Hospital

Mary K. Sullivan

This chapter examines the variety of forensic scenarios that occur in healthcare settings on a fairly frequent basis. The forensic roles and responsibilities of forensic nurses and other healthcare providers in the emergency department have gained recognition in recent years, but it is important to note that forensic scenarios are not isolated to this specialty area. There are many areas in a hospital environment in which nurses are in a prime position to identify and collect forensic evidence. Abused individuals may be encountered in hospital clinics or admitted to a nursing unit. During the initial interviews and clinical assessments, signs of abuse or neglect might be noted, such as burns, old scars, abrasions, contusions or musculoskeletal trauma. Elderly patients or individuals with disabilities who cannot protect themselves from aggressive caregivers or environmental neglect may have physical injuries or signs of neglect, such as poor hygiene, scabies, lice, decubitus ulcers and malnutrition. Ligature marks or handprints from restraining procedures might be noted. The operating rooms and special procedures areas are also environments where hidden injuries are often detected. Because pregnant patients are frequently targeted for physical abuse by husbands or boyfriends, nurses in the obstetrics and gynecological departments may detect abrasions, contusions, sprains, strains, or other musculoskeletal trauma. The onset of premature labor is commonly linked to actions of an abusing partner. If the mother or baby has adverse outcomes related to physical abuse, a forensic investigation will be required in order to prosecute the offender.

One goal of this chapter is to reiterate and emphasize the legal responsibilities of all nurses, in accordance with each state board of nursing, to report any suspicious or illegal activity occurring in the hospital, clinic, or any area where patient care in any form is delivered. With the many positive outcomes in healthcare delivery that are a result of the advances made in science and technology comes a negative side: those willing to exploit the weakness of any hospital system or vulnerable patient for personal or criminal gain. It is each nurse's responsibility to become familiar with these weaknesses, at least in one's own area of expertise, and to be able to recognize a forensic scenario if necessary and take appropriate action.

Some criminal activities can be broken down into what investigators label as "white collar" crimes, including computer fraud, medical identity theft, false entry and billing, and drug diversion practices involving the purchase of a discounted product and reselling for a higher price. Data storage within the hospital's computer network and within medical devices can provide a detailed paper trail, which is vital for facilitating such investigations (see Chapter 9).

This chapter addresses criminal activity that occurs in healthcare settings and where forensic nurses can play a prominent role in identifying and collecting evidence as well as helping to resolve the problem. In some instances, obtaining forensic evidence is crucial before a case is even considered viable for investigation. It is absolutely vital that nursing personnel be able to recognize the telltale signs that any of the following may be occurring in a workplace environment: workplace violence among personnel, physical or sexual abuse by hospital personnel of vulnerable patients, illegal use of chemical or physical restraints, drug diversion by healthcare professionals for self-use or street distribution, and suspicious adverse patient events that are linked to negative outcomes or death. In addition, the chapter discusses various patient care scenarios that have medicolegal implications as well as other forensic information of which all healthcare personnel should be aware.

Regulatory and Legal Responsibilities of Hospital Nurses

The Joint Commission (TJC) has the laid the groundwork for the roles of forensic nurse providers and examiners within hospitals in its published scoring guidelines for patient care assessment. Additionally, The Joint Commission includes the review of organization's activities in response to sentinel events in its accreditation process that opens the door for an important role to include the clinical forensic nurse specialist or investigator (Table 12-1).

Joint Commission standard PC.01.02.09 stated: "The hospital has written criteria to identify those patients who may be victims of physical assault, sexual assault, sexual molestation, domestic abuse, or elder or child abuse and neglect." (TJC, 2009). The intent of this standard acknowledges that victims of abuse or neglect arrive at our hospitals in many ways and are often not obvious to the casual observer. It is the responsibility, therefore, of each hospital to have objective criteria for identifying and assessing these patients throughout each department, and all providers are to be trained in the use of these criteria. When the assessment has been made, the provider makes the appropriate decision regarding treatment or referral. The criteria focus on observable evidence and not on allegation alone. The 2009 Joint Commission standards also affirm that hospital patients have "a right to be free from neglect, exploitation, and verbal, mental, physical and sexual abuse" (TJC, 2009, p. RI-10).

KEY POINT Victims of abuse, neglect, and interpersonal violence are more likely to be identified and appropriately managed by nurses who possess specialized skills in forensic assessments, evidentiary management, and reporting/referral processes.

Table 12-1 The Joint Commission Compliance Checklist for Forensic Issues

All personnel are trained in the use of these criteria for detecting abuse or neglect using objective assessments, not allegations alone, to identify cases for further management by the appropriate authorities.

Orientation and annual training programs include information and procedures useful in detecting forensic cases and referring them to appropriate individuals or services for treatment, required interventions, and follow-up.

Personnel are skilled in the appropriate techniques required for identification, collection, preservation, and safeguarding of evidentiary items outlined in the facility's policy and procedure manual.

Patient standards of care include the recognition of forensic patients.

Policy and procedures outline management of sudden, unexpected deaths, sexual assault, and human abuse and neglect.

Personnel training folders incorporate required training and skills validation associated with the management of human abuse and neglect.

The facility has a clear plan for managing victims of sexual assault for all ages and both genders.

The facility has a dedicated space for examining forensic patients, which is equipped with locked units for storage of forensic evidence.

Forensic reference resources are available to providers who may need guidance in identifying signs and symptoms of human abuse and neglect.

The communication and reporting system within the facility is designed to maintain a high degree of patient privacy and discretion when forensic cases are being managed (short chain of reporting, dedicated phone lines, locked files, record security, release of information, etc.).

Mechanisms are in place to accomplish various types of photodocumentation and to manage these photos with a high level of security and flawless chain of custody.

With the influence of forensic science on nursing assessments made by the clinical forensic nurse, it is more likely that a patient who is a victim of domestic abuse or neglect will be discovered. With this discovery, the appropriate assessments, documentation, and referrals will be made in a timely manner. If the assessment uncovers an injury or an admission of physical or sexual abuse in which an evidentiary examination is appropriate and accurate photography is required (i.e., a bite mark on the breast or genital area), the nurse who is conducting the assessment is the ideal candidate for identifying and setting into motion the events that will establish the appropriate treatment and referrals for this patient and, if necessary, activate the justice system.

Patients who are possible victims of alleged or suspected abuse or neglect have special needs relative to the assessment process in any clinical setting. Information and evidentiary materials may be collected during the initial screening and assessment phase that could be used in future actions as part of the legal process. The hospital has specific and unique responsibilities for safeguarding these materials. Therefore, hospitals must have appropriate policies and procedures for collecting, retaining, and safeguarding information and evidentiary materials. Further, the hospital policy must define these activities and specifies who is responsible for carrying them out (TJC, 2009).

The clinical forensic nurse is the ideal person to collect and preserve all evidentiary material in these clinical situations. This nurse is particularly knowledgeable about the safeguarding of evidence and chain-of-custody requirements that are paramount in all cases that involve legal action. Further, this nurse should be involved in writing all policies and procedures that define these activities within the hospital setting.

TJC defines a sentinel event as "an unexpected occurrence involving death or serious physical or psychological injury, or the risk thereof." Serious injury specifically includes loss of limb or function. Such events are called "sentinel" because they signal the need for immediate investigation and response (TJC, 2009, p. SE-1). The Joint Commission emphasizes that not all sentinel events occur because of an error, and not all errors result in sentinel events.

Each hospital should establish mechanisms to identify, report, analyze, and prevent these events and are expected to identify and respond appropriately to all sentinel events. Response includes conducting a timely, thorough, and credible root cause analysis, implementing improvements to reduce risks, and monitoring the effectiveness of those improvements (TJC, 2009). Using the expertise of a clinical forensic nurse will help hospitals fulfill these standards.

Assid and Barber (1999) provided a complete checklist as to what any medical facility needs to do to ensure compliance with the TJC standards noted earlier. These include identified tools that may be used by personnel in clinics, the emergency department (ED), or inpatient, geriatric, or critical care units to identify abuse and neglect as established by the facility.

One forensic nursing subspecialty that is underrepresented and not yet formally recognized within the general hospital setting is that of the clinical forensic nurse. The nurse who fulfills this role must have a broad range of forensic knowledge and skills that may be applied to any patient care area within a healthcare facility. The clinical forensic nurse serves as a role model in clinical situations, increasing staff awareness of the potential for forensic implications in routine patient care, as well as working hand-in-hand with those charged with investigating patient complaints, suspicious patient events, unexpected death, questionable trends, and emergency/traumatic patient admissions. In addition to fulfilling another critical link between the clinical arena and the judicial system, the clinical forensic nurse is in a position to provide vital protection to victims of foul play when they are at their most vulnerable. The importance of evidence recognition, collection, and accurate documentation is a means to an end for giving patients who are victims of violence true holistic care. All of these elements are components of forensic nursing (McCracken, 1999).

The clinical forensic nurse is an essential part of any hospital team with the responsibility to evaluate and perform the root cause analyses (RCA) of adverse patient events. Adverse patient events range from those causing minimal concern to extremely serious action, but the majority of these events are not criminal in nature. Regardless, the precise identification, collection, and management of facts, data and medical evidence are critical, criminal or not. It is the duty of every healthcare provider to ensure a high level of quality patient care and the accurate delivery of such services. This means all healthcare providers must have some level of awareness of what constitutes medicolegal significance. In addition, our patients deserve a safe environment in which to receive healthcare, and healthcare providers deserve a safe place to practice.

In the clinical arena, forensic issues range from trauma and wound pattern evaluation to the proper evidence collection and management and even to the evaluation of the level of care provided and the timeliness of treatment (Anderson, 1998). The role of the clinical forensic nurse is critical in each area of patient care delivery in that the nurse is most often the first to see the patient, whether in triage, as a first responder in a code arrest, before the patient sees the primary care provider in clinic, or before the elderly patient is formally admitted into the nursing home care unit. The nurse is also the one most likely to observe interactions and nonverbal communication between the patient and significant other or parent/guardian.

Recognition of both overt and subclinical abuse and neglect, as well as situations where artificial means are used to create illnesses (Munchausen's syndrome by proxy), is often obscured by the mindset of the healthcare provider, who is focused on "natural" illnesses (Anderson, 1998). The astute forensic nurse practicing in a clinical setting is able to maintain a professional balance between the nursing assessment of "natural" illness and the consideration of all possibilities, no matter how distasteful. Consideration of all angles and maintaining a heightened awareness does not mean the clinical forensic nurse focuses only on the next investigation; instead, this nurses takes a more thorough assessment of any given patient situation.

Winfrey (1999) said it best when describing "the suspiciousness factor" of a forensic nurse: "When an individual nurse masters forensic content and incorporates it into clinical practice, forensic science can also serve as a framework for honing intuition by increasing the suspiciousness factor" (Winfrey & Smith, 1999, p. 3). No individual enters a medical facility diagnosed as either a *victim* or an *offender*. It is the legal system that, after due process, affixes these labels. The nurse must at times help make that identification to activate the justice system. In some cases, it is only a hunch that compels the nurse to act. This hunch or intuition is the suspiciousness factor within the experienced clinician (Winfrey & Smith, 1999). The importance of the rapidity of nursing response inherent in intuition cannot be overlooked or dismissed, especially as it pertains to potential forensic cases. This intuition results in definitive action and timely nursing intervention (Brenner, Tanner, & Chesla, 1992).

Winfrey (1999) acknowledged that critics of this theory question the legitimacy of intuition in the doctrine of nursing. Easen and Wilcockson (1996) concluded that intuition involves the use of a sound, rational, relevant knowledge base in situations that, through experience, are so familiar that the person has learned how to recognize and act on appropriate patterns. Further, Paul and Heaslip (1995) stated that the *thinking nursing practitioner* has learned the art of "critically noticing," and is on the alert for unusual circumstances or deviations from the norm.

Forensic science adds to the cognitive base that supports intuitive nurse actions. If suspiciousness is understood as part of intuition, the resulting actions and interventions are immediate and tailored to the unique features of the clinical situation. The forensically indoctrinated nurse is unique due to a realistic set of responses that assumes the justice system is an established part of the multidisciplinary response to patient needs as reflected in the care in which evidence is collected and how documentation accurately reflects the situation (Winfrey & Smith, 1999).

Role in Hospital Quality/Risk Management Processes

The term *evidence* describes *data* presented to a court or jury to prove or disprove a claim. Evidence is any item or information that may be submitted and accepted by a competent tribunal for the purpose of determining the truth of any matter it is investigating (Federal Bureau of Investigation [FBI], 1993). Evidence may be informational or physical.

When the family or associates of patients file concerns or complaints about the quality or appropriateness of care provided within the hospital, the clinical forensic nurse can provide a valuable link to the patient's experiences on the nursing unit. She or he can apply specific data collected during forensic

processes to assist quality or risk management staffs in conducting a more thorough RCA. What is learned in these processes can contribute directly to process improvements for the healthcare system under scrutiny and potentially would be useful to effect improvements in other facilities with similar problems.

Although the quality management (QM) staff of any medical facility may not play the same role as a court of law or jury, they do share at least one responsibility. QM staff must review a set of data or collection of facts and choose a course of action based on these particular facts. This course of action usually involves a change in process that should improve patient care delivery. It may also entail recommendations to monitor staff competency or to notify appropriate authorities when a suspicious trend of events is identified. Whatever the plan, decisions and recommendations must be based on facts, data, and good evidence.

However, the problem is that attempts to collect the necessary facts and evidence are often made by those without the appropriate training to do so, or the critical information reaches the QM staff long after the event has occurred. Opportunities to capture specific details about the scene and circumstances as well as the immediate recall of those involved no longer exist (i.e., the trail is cold). Further, healthcare providers in all specialties are usually hesitant to admit to or discuss any activities observed that could be viewed as an error in these litigious times.

So how appropriate is the plan of action if the collection of facts on which the decision was made is not accurate or complete?

George Wesley of the Veterans Affairs (VA) Office of Inspector General has pointed out the link between clinical quality management activities and forensic medicine/nursing. In a review conducted by the Office of Healthcare Inspections of more than 1000 cases over 11 years, forensic issues emerged prominently (Christ, Wesley, & Schweitzer, 2000). These forensic issues fall into several major categories including patient abuse/neglect, assault, suicide, homicide, medication or delivery system tampering, improper medication administration/error, and medical equipment or device tampering (Wesley, 2001).

Recognizing the link between forensic nursing and QM may greatly facilitate patient safety activities. The clinical forensic nurse is the crucial link between effective QM activities and the increased recognition of potential forensic cases by healthcare providers. Improved awareness will lead to increased sensitivity to the importance of preserving potential medical evidence for both QM and jurisprudential purposes (Christ, Wesley, & Schweitzer, 2000). Any of the specific roles of the clinical forensic nurse previously described contributes to more effective QM review and investigation efforts by assuring that real-time information/data/evidence is identified, collected, and preserved. This process should result in quicker identification of problem areas via a more thorough RCA.

BEST PRACTICE The clinical forensic nurse investigator and the hospital's quality management team should share roles and responsibilities in performing root cause analyses that can be used to reconstruct sentinel events.

Criminal Behavior: Opportunities in Hospitals

The internal culture of hospitals creates the ideal environment for the commission of criminal acts.

CHANGE OF SHIFT DYNAMICS

Barber (2009) believes that the timeframe between the changes of shifts offers the ideal window of opportunity for the individual who has designs for performing malicious or illegal acts. These acts may include tampering with infusions or life-support equipment or pilfering narcotics or other medications not routinely accounted for. This remains true for any specialty area in any healthcare facility. Several dynamics of both the behavior of the healthcare providers and the overall workplace setting should raise red flags among managers and investigators alike.

For example, staff members who are getting off duty, especially after a busy shift, may disengage from responsibilities too early, leaving loose ends and incomplete reports. Documentation and oral reports often take precedence over hands-on care activities, increasing the risks for omissions or duplications of tasks, medication administration, or specifically timed one-to-one checks on patients in leather restraints or seclusion. There is often a tendency to assume that the next staff will do it or that the previous staff has done it. The oncoming staff will often have the need to "get organized" (e.g., make a fresh pot of coffee) before beginning their shift and will only engage in work duties after the preceding shift has departed. Social interactions may take precedence over professional communications when shift workers merge. Patients as well as visitors are often aware of the confusion and chaos that may occur during a change of shift, and some may take advantage of these opportunities to engage in behavior that is not conducive to the health and welfare of other patients on the unit. Those caregivers who have ideas other than providing healthcare on their minds will also realize that the change of shift provides an optimum time for inappropriate, illegal, or otherwise dangerous behavior (Barber, 2009). Heightened awareness of all staff at these particular times may be encouraged and reinforced by the clinical forensic nurse provider.

A former coworker of a nurse convicted in the serial murder of patients shared this observation:

> She would love to cause all hell to break loose after a very quiet evening shift... always at the change of shift. It seems as if she chose the times when the less experienced staff were on duty, especially if the nurse or doctor was new. She liked one very handsome doctor who worked every Friday night. You could count on a code being called when they were both on and always at the end of a shift. (Rix, March 2007)

KEY POINT The change of shift, with its confusion and ambiguities in roles and responsibilities, is a window of opportunity for visitors and hospital personnel to engage in malfeasance.

Today's reality is that most hospital systems across the country experience huge challenges to ensure that only competent clinicians provide quality hands-on patient care. Hospital inpatient units are filled to capacity with high-acuity patients. There are fewer experienced registered nurses (RNs) to manage the workload and little time to help one another. Supervisory positions have been eliminated in many areas to control costs. Further, many hospitals and medical centers are also teaching environments, which means there may be a mix of experienced and inexperienced staff on duty at any given time (Sullivan, 2009).

The aforementioned former coworker of the nurse convicted for serial murder added:

> Before she was caught, she was very careful about whose patients she chose. If there was a very conscientious physician who stayed on top of details versus the doctor who was not quite as efficient, she would select the patients of the second doctor every time. She knew to look for that kind of thing. (Rix, March 2007)

Case Study **12-1**

A Psychopath Among Us

Kristen Gilbert, 33, former registered nurse, was once described as someone who possessed top nursing skills and excelled during medical emergencies. In 2001, Gilbert was convicted of the murder of four patients and the attempted murder of three others. She was sentenced to four consecutive life terms in prison without the possibility of parole. Investigators believe she was responsible for more than 40 additional deaths.

Gilbert worked at the VA Medical Center in Northampton, Massachusetts, from March 1989 though February 1996. Coworkers began to notice a sharp rise in the number of deaths during her shifts on a 30-bed acute-care medical unit, and three nurses approached their nurse manager with their suspicions. From that point on, the lives of everyone concerned changed forever.

This case exhibits excellent examples of the ripple effect this type of investigation has on frontline care providers, mid-level management, hospital administration, forensic investigators, and the public relations of a hospital system.

The investigation revealed that Gilbert was injecting patients with epinephrine, a heart stimulant that can cause cardiac arrest. After injecting the patients and observing the desired effects, she would then call a code arrest. Many times, the patient would be successfully revived with her full participation on the code team. However, many patients did not survive these resuscitation efforts. There were too many unexplained deaths with her in attendance. The doctors and nurses had given her a nickname behind her back—"Angel of Death." Prosecutors stated that she had been on duty for half of the 350 deaths that had occurred on her ward for the seven years she had worked there. The chance of that being a coincidence, they stated, is 1 in 100 million. The death rate tripled when she came onto that unit on that shift in 1991 compared to the previous three years. When she left that shift, the rates dropped down to 1988 levels once again.

The following incident illustrates Gilbert's cold and calculating behavior. She came on duty one evening to find she had one patient to care for in the unit she was assigned. She then asked her supervisor that if by chance her patient died that night, could she be allowed to leave early. An hour after this request, Gilbert was delivering the patient to the morgue.

There is much speculation on Gilbert's motives with the primary theories being that she was an "adrenalin junkie" and thrived on being the center of attention when saving a life as well as gaining sexual gratification with the increased attention she received from her extramarital relationship, a VA police officer who attended all codes arrests and medical emergencies. However, these acts were among a long list of dysfunctional behaviors that included faking suicide attempts, abusing children in her care, phoning in bomb threats to the hospital, stalking her ex-boyfriend, and attempting to murder her husband.

Office of Inspector General Semiannual Report to Congress, October 1, 2000–March 31, 2001. *VA OIG Case Yield Murder Conviction.* Richard J. Griffin, Inspector General. United States District Court, District of Massachusetts Western Section, *United States of America v. Kristen Gilbert.* Docket No. CR 98–30044-MAP, Springfield, MA, February 22, 2001.

Farragher, T. (October 8, 2000). Death on ward C: Caregiver or killer? *The Boston Globe*, www.bostonglobe.com/globe/metro/packages/nurse/htm. Accessed October 16, 2000.

Reportable Deaths

It is important that all hospital personnel understand their medicolegal responsibilities with regard to certain types of patient death. According to most state or local jurisdictional laws, all citizens, including any hospital employee in any position, have a duty to notify the office of the medical examiner or coroner when possessing knowledge of a death that meets criteria of a reportable death. All known facts are to be provided including time, place, manner, and circumstances of death. Failure to recognize reportable cases may create administrative difficulties and unnecessary distress for bereaved relatives and medical colleagues. Other cases may evade medicolegal investigation altogether because they are not recognized as death due to unnatural causes (Start et al., 1993). In most jurisdictions, not reporting a death is an offense punishable by law. Any institution or individual reporting a death should understand that to provide information is to comply with the law and that failure to do so would place the party in jeopardy of prosecution (St. Louis County Health Medical Examiner Policies and Procedures for Reportable Deaths).

The accurate determination of cause and manner of death in deaths of concern to the public is essential for a variety of reasons, including the proper administration of justice by identifying murders and exonerating the innocent; recognizing and maintaining evidence for use in criminal and civil proceedings; recognizing epidemic threats to the public health; recognizing defective materials, structures, or products; detecting dangerous occupational environments; establishing causes of death in therapeutic intervention; and ensuring that law enforcement officials do not engage in or be unjustly accused of brutality (St. Louis County Health Medical Examiner Policies and Procedures for Reportable Deaths).

Each state contains essentially the same criteria with some exceptions or different verbiage. For example, many states require that a death occurring within 24 hours of admission to a hospital be reported; California and Tennessee do not. There are certain categories of death that are always reported in all states, such as when death occurs by violence of any type. This includes gunshot wounds, stab wounds, blunt trauma, fall-related deaths, fire deaths, drowning, and motor vehicle collisions regardless of the time elapsed from the onset of the incident to the time of death. For example, if a person is shot with an injury to the spinal column resulting in paraplegia then develops a urinary tract infection and sepsis at a later date, the death can be traced back to the injury and this is a reportable medical examiner case. In most states, reportable death criteria are similar (Box 12-1).

Suspicious, Unexpected Patient Death

Since the 1970s, 90 criminal prosecutions of healthcare providers have occurred, with 54 of those actually being convicted of serial murder or attempted murder/assault. The number of patient deaths that resulted in murder conviction is 317, and the number of suspicious deaths attributed to these convicted healthcare providers is 2113 (Yorker et al., 2006). In these cases, nursing personnel comprise the overwhelming majority (86%) of those convicted, along with two physicians and one respiratory technician (Yorker et al., 2007). Injection was the method of murder most widely used, followed by air embolus, oral medications, poisoning, and tampering of medical equipment. The majority of deaths occurred during evening and night shifts in hospital inpatient units and nursing home environments (Yorker et al., 2007).

Box 12-1 Reportable Deaths

- All deaths in which there are unexplained, unusual, or suspicious circumstances.
- All homicides or suicides.
- All deaths caused by poisoning whether homicidal, suicidal, or accidental. This includes alcohol intoxication.
- All deaths following accidents whether the injury was or was not the primary cause of death.
- Any death of a resident or inmate housed in a county or state institution or facility, regardless of where the death occurs.
- Any death of a person in a nursing home or private institution without recent medical attendance. (Some jurisdictions specify how many days must have passed without attendance by a treating practitioner).
- Deaths in the custody of law enforcement officials.
- Deaths alleged to have been caused by malpractice.
- Deaths unattended by a physician.
- Deaths that occur in association with or as a result of diagnostic, therapeutic, or anesthetic procedures.
- Maternal deaths resulting from abortion.
- Any stillbirth of 20 or more weeks of gestation unattended by a physician.
- Any death of infant or child whose medical history does not established a preexisting medical condition.
- Deaths resulting from neglect.
- Death that is possibly, directly or indirectly, attributable to environmental exposure or external workplace factors.
- Any death suspected to be due to an infectious or contagious illness that may represent an epidemic disease (i.e., meningococcal meningitis).
- Some states require a report when cremation of the remains is to be performed.

There are certain types of deaths that may not be listed in state or local law but should be reported. (www.sdcounty.ca.gov/me/hospitals/reporting.html):

- Emergency department deaths: When an individual dies in the ED before a diagnosis can be established.
- Operating room or postoperative deaths: When negligence or accident is suspected, reporting such cases will protect both the hospital and physician and may help in avoiding a malpractice suit.
- Anesthetic deaths: All deaths in which the patient has not fully recovered from anesthetic.
- Therapeutic deaths: Any death that is due directly or indirectly to a diagnostic, therapeutic, or surgical procedure rather than to the disease itself.
- Coma: Any death in which the patient is comatose on arrival to the hospital and remains so throughout the hospital course (unless the cause of the coma has been established as being due to a natural disease).
- Unidentified persons: All deaths of unidentified persons should be reported regardless of the circumstances of death.
- Fetuses: Fetal deaths that result from illegal abortion, unattended deaths, injuries to the fetus, injuries to the mother leading to death under such circumstances as to afford a reasonable ground to suspect that the death was caused by the criminal act of another.

Medications typically chosen for injection were those that were easily available in the hospital and that are difficult to distinguish postmortem from those that are made endogenously (e.g., insulin, potassium, and epinephrine). Neuromuscular blocking agents (e.g., succinylcholine, Pavulon) were used in several of these cases (Yorker et al., 2007). Additionally, some medications used to hasten death remained hidden because they had been prescribed for the patient as part of the treatment regimen (Baden, 2007).

When a patient dies in a hospital, it is assumed that the death is a natural outcome of a disease process or traumatic event and, therefore, it is not suspicious. It is only after a cluster of multiple deaths has been identified under particular circumstances that suspicions are raised. By this time, the challenges for those who must evaluate allegations and proceed with an investigation are significant (Sullivan, 2009). As seen in these cases, suspicious trends and clusters of serious adverse patient events (e.g., high incidence of code arrests on one unit or shift) came to the attention of the quality and risk management (QM and RM) departments in the hospitals involved after the fact. Only in a few cases did this data come to the attention of reviewers before anything was reported. In the vast majority of cases, suspicions had been reported up the supervisory chain and only then were data evaluated to determine if claims were supported before any further action was taken. It is crucial not only that the QM and RM personnel recognize suspicious trends early but that real-time data be available for review on a regular basis, not information collected on random patients days or months after an event (Sullivan, 2009). Yorker et al. 2006 reported that less than routine quality assurance activities are one reason there is an increase in the likelihood of crimes going undetected.

One way to accomplish the goal of identifying suspicious data in real time is to have a forensic nurse respond to every patient death. A thorough evaluation of circumstances surrounding each patient death would be conducted in a systematic manner. This role would be a collateral responsibility similar to being on the rapid response or intravenous (IV) team. The nurse would be paged from her or his routine assignment to the location of the patient death. It is highly recommended that the forensic nurse is someone who neither works on the unit where the patient expired nor participated in the rapid response team efforts to save the patient (Sullivan, 2009).

A collection of facts and other material pertinent to the type of patient care delivered would be identified, gathered, and preserved. A standard set of laboratory work should be collected, and all circumstances surrounding the patient's death should be documented in serial detail. Premortem electrocardiographic tracings and other monitoring data should be downloaded and retained along with other data such as blood gas results and serial vital signs. In some instances, additional specimens may be indicated such as amniotic fluid, vitreous, gastric contents, or nail clippings. All physician orders, medications, treatments, and procedures received in the last 24 hours of the patient's life should be documented as well as those who administered each one. If known, the names of visitors should be recorded as well as any ancillary hospital personnel who had visited that unit during that time period (Sullivan, 2005).

The QM or RM department should then analyze all information as indicated and assuming nothing is suspicious, the information is archived. If a suspicious trend is later identified, more complete information is available for RCA or investigation. In most cases, the death will not be suspicious and this information may be useful for other purposes or analyses for process improvement systems for patients with the same illness or disease process (Sullivan 2005).

BEST PRACTICE When a sudden, unexpected death occurs in the hospital, the clinical nurse should immediately secure the scene, collect baseline laboratory specimens, and preserve all clinical evidence that is associated with the patient.

CHALLENGES FOR INVESTIGATORS

When a suspicious death or deaths are reported weeks, months, or even years after the patient or patients have expired, there are several challenges for investigators who essentially must work a cold case. These specific challenges signal the need for several changes and improvements in response and management of evidence on the part of hospital personnel at all levels (Sullivan, 2009).

First, there is no crime scene to process. Typically in most homicides, there is a body or scene where evidence exists that indicates some criminal action has taken place, and the scene can be processed immediately. However, these suspicious hospital deaths are most often historical investigations as they have been reported after much time has passed and there is nothing to observe, no obvious evidence to collect, and the body of the diseased has long been buried or cremated. Other evidence such as lab specimens, IV lines, syringes, and vials have been destroyed (Sullivan, 2009). Further, for cases like these to be considered viable for investigation and worthy of resources, there must be some type of forensic evidence that suggests there is merit to the allegations. Hospital administrations are cautious when dealing with any issue that may result in a lawsuit or negative publicity that may slow the process and lengthen the amount of time that passes before an official case is opened for investigation.

Second, the need for nontraditional investigative techniques increases significantly. Because the evidence is long gone and bodies have been buried, the investigator will have to develop enough evidence of a crime to have the victim(s) exhumed. Ironically, most of the evidence required may be left in the body to be exhumed. Although postmortem specimens may be the only evidence available to prove this type of murder, it is not foolproof (Baden, 2007). There are specific challenges that are unique to processing this type of evidence; for example, some chemicals cannot be found in exhumed bodies because they are either downgraded or altered by chemicals used in embalming. The quantification of drugs or chemicals varies greatly depending on the degree of dehydration or decomposition of the body after the embalming and burial processes. Donnelly admits that it is typical to look for a drug that was not ordered for the patient than trying to interpret an overdose of a prescribed drug since exhumation toxicology only permits identification of a drug and the quantity of the drug present in a body at the time of death (Donnelly, 2007).

Sullivan (2009) stated that a team of experts will need to complete an exhaustive review of medical records. New or specialized analytical tests will have to be developed or modified for specimens that are ultimately collected at autopsy. Assuming that the case will go to trial, multiple forensic experts will have to be utilized to prove that the patients were, in fact, murdered and did not expire from natural causes.

There is a dearth of expert witnesses such as forensic nurses and other forensically trained clinicians who are able to work between both worlds of complex healthcare environments and law enforcement. For example, medical record verbiage, and other information need to be interpreted or translated for the nonmedically trained investigator. Some omissions would likely be overlooked by someone who is unfamiliar with requirements of any given procedure such as an electrocardiogram. A missing EKG strip after a suspicious code arrest would be a red flag for a forensic nurse, whereas the nonmedical investigator might not even realize this type of documentation exists. Donnelly (2007) professed that the documentation contained in the medical record often provides a road map as to what happened as well as where to look for the evidence. Nonmedical investigators who have had the experience of pouring through volumes of medical records frequently say that the nurse's notes often contain vital details that lead to new avenues of investigation and expose the key to resolving the case. However, as Sullivan (2009) explained, it is a nurse who will most likely be the one to interpret subtle inconsistencies contained in a patient chart with regard to overall patterns of care delivery.

It is also important that reviewing the records remains a team effort and that each expert, from his or her own perspective, sees pertinent information in the same documentation. The forensic pathologist will determine whether the medical records reveal a cause of death or if exhumation will be helpful in determining the manner or cause of death. By combining the nursing assessments of unusual activities or patterns of care delivery and information ascertained by the forensic pathologist, new avenues of investigation may be opened and critical evidence identified (Baden, 2007).

Much of the medical equipment taken for granted in the healthcare setting is capable of tracking and recording information that could be key to investigations like these. In cases when patient death is immediately determined to be suspicious, equipment such as an automated IV pump contains memory that can be interrogated and individual accountability can be confirmed from the software tracking systems. This can be especially useful when allegations of dosing changes are suspected. Any dose changes can be compared to the concentrations of drugs found in the body after autopsy to see if they are consistent with an altered dosing theory (Sullivan, 2009).

Case Study 12-2

Traces of Guilt

Vickie Dawn Jackson, 40, was sentenced to life in prison after pleading no contest to killing 10 patients in her care. The charges state that she murdered these patients by injecting them with Mivacron, a drug used to temporarily halt breathing.

Jackson was employed as a licensed vocational nurse (LVN) at Nocona General Hospital, a small 38-bed hospital located in rural Nocona, Texas. She began working there in November, 1999 and remained employed there until her termination in February 2001. The hospital had two shifts (7 AM to 7 PM and 7 PM to 7 AM) and a regular staff who worked one shift or the other. Consequently, Jackson worked with the same people on a regular basis. Her duties required her to administer medications, including injections, to the patients for whom she cared.

Two unusual events, noticed by staff in the hospital, were occurring during the months of December, 2000 and January, 2001: large amounts of mivacurium chloride, a drug used only by the anesthesiologist in this hospital, began disappearing from the crash cart, and the number of deaths and code arrests began to rise sharply. The death rate for this small hospital had been 3 patients a month. In December, 8 patients died and 3 others experienced sudden respiratory arrests, and they died shortly after being transferred to another hospital. In January, 15 patients died. All of these events were occurring on the night shift when Jackson worked. Additionally, multiple codes and deaths were occurring simultaneously. The vast majority of these deaths were completely unexpected. None of the patients had been admitted for life-threatening diseases or conditions. Even the elderly patients had been improving and there were plans to discharge them the next day.

Jackson's coworkers also noticed that there were some behavior changes in her work routines. She was always eager to be the one to mix medication bags, even for the patients she was not assigned to. She was also more irritable and increasingly resentful of the patients who were more troublesome or those who required a lot of attention by nursing staff. She was also observed on several occasions to underreact to patients who were having extreme difficulty in breathing or were in crisis. She was often hard to find on the unit and would disappear for long periods of time before coming back to work.

During the investigation, it was determined that the Mivacron was the likely cause of death in the patients in question because

the side effects and symptoms were the same as the patients had been experiencing before they died. Jackson actually remained an employee during the investigation and continued to work as a LVN even though she was a suspect. On one last night shift, another staff nurse observed Jackson entering a patient's room with a syringe in her hand. Moments later, the patient coded but survived. He was able to describe what happened and stated that Jackson had come into his room and injected his IV with something. When he began to have difficulty breathing, she merely looked at him and walked out of the room. This time, all IV bags, tubing, and syringes were retrieved and saved. All indicated that Mivacron was present. Further, investigators had obtained a warrant to search Jackson's home. They found a discarded syringe, also positive for Mivacron. Bodies of previous victims were exhumed and all tested positive for Mivacron or its metabolites. Jackson was terminated immediately, and death rates went back to normal.

Jackson eventually pleaded no contest to the volumes of forensic evidence against her, but she never did officially admit to the killings. However, while in jail, she did reveal to her cellmate that she "did kill the patients and never thought they would be able to find traces of Mivacron in the dead bodies." She also told her cellmate that she believed she would never go to heaven now that she killed those people.

The State of Texas v. Vickie Dawn Jackson in the 97th District Court of Montague County, Texas. No. 02–07–0128M-CR. January 3, 2005. *Offer of Proof and Notice of Intent to Introduce Extraneous Offenses.* Tim Cole, District Attorney.

Pressure Ulcers and the Forensic Nurse

Elder neglect and abuse cases often involve the evaluation of pressure ulcers as a key factor in evidence. The absence of pressure ulcers equates to high quality care of the frail, elder patient, whereas the presence of an advanced pressure ulcer is typically linked to inferior and negligent care. In today's healthcare setting, the forensic nurse must consider pressure ulcers as a vital indicator of care quality.

In 2007, a secondary diagnosis of pressure ulcers was reported 257,412 times for Medicare patients. The *additional average charge* for each of these patients was $43,180. Furthermore, approximately 60,000 patient's deaths occur each year as a result of complications associated with pressure ulcers.[1&2]

When elder patients are admitted from a home or nursing care facility, they should receive a head-to-toe inspection and ideally, all body surfaces should be photographed. This documentation

[1]Centers for Medicare & Medicaid Services. Proposed Fiscal Year 2009 Payment, Policy Changes for Inpatient Stays in General Acute Care Hospitals. Available at: http://www.cms.hhs.gov/apps/media/press/factsheet. *Accessed online, 24 July, 2009.*
[2]Centers for Medicare & Medicaid Services. Medicare Program; Proposed Changes to the Hospital Inpatient Prospective Payment Systems and Fiscal Year 2009 rates: Proposed Changes to Disclosure of Physician Ownership in Hospitals and Physician Self-Referral Rules; Proposed Collection of Information Regarding Financial Relationship Between Hospitals and Physicians; Proposed Rule. *Federal Register.* 2008; 73(84):23550. Available at: http://edocket.access.gpo.gov/2008/pdf/08-1135 pdf. *Accessed online, 24 July, 2009.*

verifies either the presence or absence of pressure ulcers and may also reveal other clues to elder maltreatment or neglect such as poor hygiene, lice, scabies, or the use of restraining devices. Occasionally, when doing a thorough physical assessment, indices of other injuries such as bruises, falls, or burns may be noted and documented. It is obvious that a good documentation system for preexisting problems is an important element for a hospital risk management program because liability for causation will be appropriately assigned. Many hospitals continue to place themselves in peril because they underestimate the importance of documented preexisting conditions.

In the United States, third-party payers such as Medicare and Medicaid are reluctant to reimburse care associated with preventable complications such as pressure ulcers, that result from a hospitalization. However, if the complication (i.e., pressure ulcer) was present on admission, the hospital is not penalized for a quality care breach. Payments for any added length of stay as well as the specialized care and treatment for the pressure ulcers are authorized. For specifics regarding Medicare payment rules, go to www.cms.hhs.gov/quarterlyproviderupdates/downloads/cms1533fc.pdf.

The legal issues associated with the development of pressure ulcers typically relate to negligence of providing quality care. In today's "best practices" environments, there are specific guidelines for pressure ulcer prevention, detection, and care. Nursing staff is held accountable for adhering to policies and procedures, including consistent documentation of required components of care.

With the heightened awareness and widespread publicity about the dangers of pressure ulcers, it is easier now for the prosecution to construct a compelling case and to prove that a breach of accountability has occurred when patients experience pressure ulcer complications. Causation examines if the harm to the patient can be reasonably related to a breach of duty of care. Finally, the key factor to prove in negligence is a breach of care standards. Without written evidence of nursing vigilance and flawless documentation of recommended prevention practices, plaintiffs often prevail and are frequently awarded huge settlements. In the United States, awards have ranged from $5,000 to $82,000,000, with a median of $250,000. (Bennett, O'Sullivan, DeVito, & Remsberg, 2000) A study of selected pressure ulcer cases with liability compensations of $14,418,770 could have spared defendants $11,389,989 if documentation could have proved that guidelines had been followed (Goebel & Goebel, 1999). Some hospitals argue that full implementation of pressure ulcer guidelines is costly. However, retrospective studies of the costs of litigations and settlements far outpace implementation of pressure ulcer "best practice" standards.

ROLE OF THE FORENSIC NURSE

The forensic nurse should participate in the education and training of wound care specialists and other care providers regarding liability issues associated with pressure ulcers. Because photography is an expected skill of forensic nurses, they can assist others in using optimum photodocumentation techniques for both overall skin conditions on admission and the development or healing of any pressure ulcer wounds associated with hospitalization. Participation in nursing care conferences, morbidity and mortality reviews, and hospital risk management meetings may also be vital contributions. When considering the expensive outcomes of most litigation related to pressure ulcers, the salary of a forensic nurse could be easily justified in most facilities for limiting the liability in just one case each year!

Restraints

The federal Center for Medicare and Medicaid Services (CMS) has issued requirements for its participating hospitals regarding violation of human rights, including the use of seclusion and restraints. These conditions initially became effective on August 2, 1999. The Joint Commission (TJC) has also created guidance for behavioral health restraint and seclusion, which were effective on January 1, 2001. Unless the rules by CMS are more stringent than those of JCAHO, all Joint Commission–accredited hospitals must be in compliance.

Federal regulations define physical restraints to be "any manual method or physical or mechanical device that restricts freedom of movement or normal access to one's body, material, or equipment, attached or adjacent to the person's body that he or she cannot easily remove" (CMS, 2009). In addition to Posey vests, belts, cuffs, or other devices, this rule also has determined that stationary dining tables that the patient cannot move away, tightly tucked sheets, and deploying all side rails of the bed in the "up" position constitute a restraint. However, nurses may restrain or use protective medical devices for a patient during a procedure or certain therapies to ensure patient and staff safety (e.g., patient may be restrained while the patient is endotracheally intubated to ensure that the tube is not accidentally dislodged). On the other hand, the use of the same type of protective devices may not be used if the patient becomes aggressive or has an angry outburst. Federal standards do not apply to situations in which the staff has applied a restraining device to prevent patient falls or to control wandering of a confused or disoriented individual.

Emergency treatment orders may be obtained to use restraints for a temporary scenario when the patient is endangering him or herself or others. Nursing personnel and physicians must meticulously describe the behavior and conditions that warrant a medical order for temporary restraints. Words such as "violent patient," "dangerous situation," or "behavior directly threatening staff" are insufficient descriptions to justify restraints.

In emergency departments and occasionally on other hospital units, it is tempting for staff to use chemical restraints, including neuromuscular blocking agents, to gain control over a patient who is violent, aggressive, and threatening to the staff or the environment. However, the use of chemical restraints in these scenarios may be viewed as malpractice and therefore are to be emphatically forbidden in the hospital's policies and procedures. If the patient is in a psychiatric or correctional unit and such chemical restraints are an integral part of the patient's treatment plan, other guidance applies. In most facilities, there are provisions for emergency treatment orders for patients who are in imminent danger; actions may be taken without express or informed consent.

In the event that any restraints are used, there are hospital policies and procedures to regularly evaluate the patient and the sites of the restraint application to ensure that no adverse effects are associated with the devices.

Forensic nurses may become involved in patient or family complaints about the application of restraints or may be required to participate in forensic investigations regarding restraint-related injury or even death. They should also be prepared to interpret associated hospital policies and procedures as well as TJC and CMS standards. A thorough understanding of regulatory guidance and the hospital's practices for the application and monitoring of restraints is imperative. Finally, in conjunction with nursing administration and risk management, there must be a program of rigorous auditing for compliance to accepted standards of practice.

Forensic Investigation of Drug Diversion Among Healthcare Workers

Drug diversion occurs at every point in the drug supply chain including at the wholesale level of manufacturing and distribution, through theft of medications in transit, through the use of stolen or forged prescriptions or the sale of controlled substances without a legitimate prescription on the Internet, at the retail level, within hospitals and pharmacies, and finally by clinicians who administer medications.

It is a fact that drug diversion by healthcare professionals has serious outcomes for individuals as well as healthcare systems. Nurses, the largest group of healthcare professionals pilfering opioid analgesics from hospital supplies, represent a group that needs assistance to cease this behavior (Stokowski, 2008). However, data show that physicians, pharmacists, police officers, and other professions with high trust factors are included among those who have been investigated and arrested for drug diversion (Leonard, 2008).

Patients are put at risk or receive substandard care, reputations are damaged, and clinical privileges revoked; there are potential regulatory and insurance liabilities; and often there is negative publicity for the hospital. Clinicians trained in the forensic sciences and the management of medical evidence serve as a valuable resource for healthcare systems in the identification and investigation of these scenarios. Stokowski (2008) stated that the health implications of drug diversion are too important to leave entirely to law enforcement and efforts to prevent drug diversion must be evidence based. Identifying and investigating incidences of drug diversion within the healthcare setting are important responsibilities of the clinical forensic nurse, especially with regard to bridging communication efforts with law enforcement and assisting with capturing data in real time (catching someone in the act) and managing that evidence within the hospital supervisory channels. Leonard (2008) reported that most medical professionals who have stolen medications have likely done so on more than one occasion. One must ask, if individuals are discovered stealing medications at any given time, how many other times has this occurred? Box 12-2 lists some of the most commonly abused and stolen medications.

The Joint Commission has several standards that address prevention strategies to limit drug diversion:

- All orders are reviewed by a pharmacist prior to administration (JC MM4.10)
- Only authorized personnel have access to the drugs (JC MM 2.20)
- Controlled substances are to be stored in secure drawers (JC MM2.20)
- Detailed records of controlled substance activity are maintained (JC MM2.20)

Box 12-2 Commonly Abused/Stolen Medications

Demerol (Meperidine)
Morphine
OxyContin (Oxycodone)
Dilaudid (Hydromorphone)
Phenobarbital
Xanax (Alprazolam)
Klonopin (Clonazepam)
Ativan (Lorazepam)
Valium (Diazepam)
Vicodin (Hydrocodone and Acetaminophen)

Even with the best prevention strategies and proactive workplace environments, this subject is a very sensitive issue for those on both sides of an investigation. It is uncomfortable to be put in the position of discovering that a coworker or otherwise noteworthy employee is suspected of diverting drugs. There are several points to consider when preparing for an investigation an incidence of drug diversion (Cardinal Health Insider, 2009).

A well-defined policy should be in place to minimize the potential for confusion and procrastination if it becomes necessary to take action. A delay in beginning an investigation can jeopardize patient safety, increase liability for the hospital, and decrease the chance of recovery of the healthcare professional in question (Cardinal Health Insider, 2009). Necessary actions to be taken and a time line for investigative processes need to be identified. A multidisciplinary team should be in place that includes a forensically trained clinician in addition to a human resources specialist, appropriate supervisors, hospital police or security, and risk management personnel if patient care delivery has been impacted. A list of what regulatory agencies (e.g., state boards of pharmacy, state boards of nursing, drug enforcement agency, law enforcement) need to be contacted as well as defined communication strategies for staff and how the suspected employee will be confronted must be prepared.

Data should be gathered from all sources including interrogation of those medical devices that record delivery of controlled substances and other pain medication. Medication administration records should be reviewed and compared to staffing patterns and trends occurring on a particular unit, shift, or change of shift timeframe.

Once evidence is gathered and it is time to confront the suspected employee, the multidisciplinary team needs to resolve some issues before the confrontation. For example, how much of the evidence will be shared with each member of the team? Will all have equal knowledge of the facts? What is the plan if the entire team does not agree with the conclusion (e.g., the nurse manager refuses to believe the allegations against one of the hardest working staff members under her supervision)? Who will be the team leader or lead the discussions with the employee? What privacy issues need to be considered? Will drug screens be necessary? Under what circumstances will the individual be placed on leave (Cardinal Health Insider, 2008)?

Communication with the rest of staff is essential and can be difficult. Besides staff morale, there are possible legal ramifications. Human resources will be involved in such cases, but there will constraints on how much detail about any given scenario can be revealed to the staff without violating employee rights. The hospital's legal department and the hospital's policies and procedures provide details about the management of these delicate cases.

Summary

The public continues to view the healthcare systems within the United States with much skepticism. Wrong-site surgeries, fatal medication errors, caregiver-perpetrated homicides, patient neglect and abuse, and drug misuse by healthcare professionals have caused patients and their families to demand answers. Nurses have always been rated very high in regard to public respect and trust, thus placing them in an ideal position to monitor the day-to-day delivery of patient care, both directly and indirectly. Hospital administrators now realize they must take an active role in ensuring a safe environment of care. Investing in and marketing a forensic nursing team may offer the public increased confidence that someone is in place to look after their welfare. Quality-assurance and risk management departments may consider utilizing the skills of a clinical forensic nurse to assist in benchmarking the hospital's performance in regard to medical errors, adverse or sentinel patient events, health insurance or workers' compensation fraud, bomb threats, bioterrorism, theft of narcotics or controlled substances, and physical threats or assaults within the patient care environment (Duval et al., 2008).

Forensic nursing continues to evolve as a nursing specialty, and as with any scientific discipline, its future will depend on the ability of its members to responds to today's needs while concurrently preparing to fill an unknown niche that will emerge tomorrow.

References

Assid, P., & Barber, J. D. (1999). *10th Medical Group*. US Airforce Academy Hospital Checklist.

Anderson, W. R. (1998). Forensic science in clinical medicine: A case study approach. In *Medicolegal implications in clinical patient evaluation and treatment* (pp. 223–234).

Baden, M. (2007). In *The healthcare serial killer: Prevention, investigation, and prosecution strategies*. Paper presented at the American Academy of Forensic Sciences Workshop, Washington, DC.

Barber, J. (2009). *Cause of death: Change of shift*. Paper presented at the University of Bari School of Nursing–Masters in Forensic Nursing Seminar, Bari, Italy.

Bennett, R. G., O'Sullivan, J., DeVito, E. M., & Remsberg, R. (2000). The increasing medical malpractice risk related to pressure ulcer in the United States. *Journal of the American Geriatrics Society, 48*(1), 73–81.

Brenner, P., Tanner, C., & Chesla, C. (1992). From beginner to expert: Gaining a differentiated clinical world in critical care nursing. *Advanced Nursing Science, 14*(3), 13–28.

Cardinal Health Insider. *Drug diversion: Taking action*. Accessed online February 5, 2009. www.cardinalhealth.com/insider/article/insider4/DrugDiversion.asp

Centers for Medicare & Medicaid Services (CMS). (2007). Medicare program; changes to the hospital inpatient prospective payment systems and fiscal year 2008 rates; final rule. *Federal Register, 72*(162), 47130–48175.

Christ, P., Wesley, G., & Schweitzer, A. (2000). *Quality assurance program oversight on a large scale often reveals forensic issues*. Poster session presented at the 107th Annual Meeting of the American Military Surgeons of the United States, Las Vegas, NV (August 2003).

Donnelly, B. (2007). *The healthcare serial killer: Prevention, investigation, and prosecution strategies*. Paper presented at the American Academy of Forensic Sciences Workshop, Washington, DC.

Duval, J. B., Dougherty, C. A., & Sullivan, M. K. (2008). Forensic nursing. In J. Nordby, & S. James (Eds.). *Forensic science: Introduction to scientific & investigative techniques* (3rd ed. pp. 25–41). Boco Raton, FL: CRC Press.

Easen, P., & Wilcockson, J. (1996). Intuition and rational decision making in professional thinking: A false dichotomy? *Journal of Advanced Nursing, 24*(4), 667–673.

Federal Bureau of Investigation. (1993). *Crime in the United States, 1992*. Washington, DC: United States Department of Justice.

Goebel, R. H, & Goebel, M. R (1999). Clinical practice guidelines for pressure ulcer prevention can prevent malpractice lawsuits in older patients. *Journal of Wound, Ostomy, and Continence Nursing, 26*(4), 175–184.

Leonard, R. E. (2008). Drug abuse among health care providers in a rising concern. *The Herald-Journal*, September 7, 2008. www.groupstate.com/apps/pbcs.dii/article?AID=/20080907/NEWS. Accessed online February 5, 2009.

McCracken, L. M. (1999). Living forensics: A natural evolution in emergency care. *Accident and Emergency Nursing, 7*(4), 211–216.

Paul, R. W., & Heaslip, P. (1995). Critical thinking and intuitive nursing practice. *Journal of Advanced Nursing, 22*(1), 44–47.

Rix, K. (2007). *The healthcare serial killer: Prevention, investigation, and prosecution strategies*. Paper presented at the American Academy of Forensic Sciences Workshop, Washington, DC.

St Louis County Health Medical Examiner Policies and Procedures for Reportable Deaths. (2003). *Office of the Medical Examiner*. Accessed online February 5, 2009 www.stlouisco.com

Stokowski, L. A. (2008). *Drug diversion in the United States*. www.medscape.com/viewartilce/572103. Accessed online February 5, 2009.

Start, R. D., Delargy-Aziz, Y., Dorries, C. P., Silcocks, P. B., & Cotton, D. W. (1993). Clinicians and the coronial systems: ability of clinicians to recognize reportable deaths. *Journal of Clinical Pathology, 45*(3), 254–257.

Sullivan, M. K. (2009). Serial murder in healthcare. *Journal of Nursing Management, 40*(6), 32–36.

Sullivan, M. K. (2005). Forensic nursing in the hospital setting. In V. Lynch, & J. Barber (Eds.), *Forensic nursing* (pp. 559–569). St. Louis, MO: Mosby.

The Joint Commission (TJC). (2009). *Accreditation manual for hospitals, core standards, and guidelines*. Oak Park, IL: Author.

Wesley, G. (2001). *Forensic aspects of medical quality assurance: Is "forensic quality assurance" a new medical discipline?* Unpublished manuscript. Washington, DC: VA Office of Healthcare Inspection.

Winfrey, M. E., & Smith, A. R. (1999). The suspiciousness factor: Critical care nursing and forensics. *Critical Care Nursing Quarterly, 22*(1), 1–7.

Yorker, B., Kizer, K., Lampe, P., Forrest, A.R., Lannan, J., & Russell, D. (2006). Serial murder by healthcare professionals. *Journal of Forensic Science, 51*(6), 1362–1371.

CHAPTER 13 Sexual Assault Evidence Recovery

Jamie Ferrell and Cari Caruso

The science of forensic nursing is a distinctive specialty that provides exceedingly skilled healthcare professionals identified as forensic nurse examiners (FNEs) or sexual assault nurse examiners (SANEs) who practice nursing when health and legal systems intersect (Forensic Nursing Scope and Standards, 2009). These professionals are qualified to recognize and preserve the often fragile and perishable biological, trace, and physical evidence from crime scenes, whether in the field or in the hospital environs. The body becomes the identified crime scene as a result of sexual violence in both living and deceased victims. Without forensic clinicians, exceptional education, and specific forensic protocols, critical evidence is commonly lost or destroyed before it is recovered by emergency physicians, police, or forensic pathologists. The investigation of sexual violence requires a complex interplay of physical and testimonial evidence. This evidence is typically collected and interpreted by various professionals in nursing, medicine, law enforcement, mental health, and scientific disciplines.

The Joint Commission requires hospitals to have written criteria to identify those patients who may be victims of sexual assault, sexual molestation, or other forms of abuse. (The Joint Commission, 2009). The Joint Commission guidance also states that hospitals must assist these reported victims by either providing appropriate examinations for the reporting party or referring them to a private or public community agency that can provide these specialized services. In some jurisdictions, patients may be billed for a medical screening examination (MSE) if they initially present to a hospital, and are then transferred to a secondary site for the sexual assault examination.

Role of Sexual Assault Nurse Examiners

Sexual assault describes a wide variety of events, the definition of which varies significantly from state to state. Generally, sexual assaults involve some unwanted (nonconsensual) invasion of the victim, where the mouth, vagina, anus, and/or breast of the female victim and/or the mouth, penis, or anus of the male victim, offender, or both, are involved. In some states the term *sexual battery* is used.

The SANE is a vital member of the health delivery and evidence collection team in sex-related scenarios. SANEs are optimally prepared to assess the physical, emotional, and safety needs while simultaneously gathering evidence from the two most essential components of the crime scene: the bodies and personal effects of the victim and the offender or suspect.

SANEs who care for adult/adolescent patients usually receive the minimum of a 40-hour didactic course followed by a supervised 40- to 45-hour preceptorship. Some states have their own formal courses and their own certifications, which are typically required

for nurses who have designated duties as SANEs. Occasionally, there is confusion between receiving a certificate for completion of a required course of study and the process of certification, which indicates competency. In most states and jurisdictions, one may practice with a certificate of course completion, but sitting for the formal certification examination is typically voluntary and suggests that successful candidates are expert practitioners in the specialty (see Chapter 51).

Advances in technology have enabled forensic scientists to reach far more positive conclusions from minute and seemingly insignificant items. A single hair or fiber, a microscopic particle of pollen, a drop of blood, or a single word in a statement can lead to the identity of a suspect and provide convincing evidence in court (Lynch & Ferrell, 2006). Criminalists and laboratory scientists have the right to expect that the evidence they analyze has been properly collected and preserved. The inclusion of the FNE/SANE as one member of the multidisciplinary investigative unit represents a growing trend in advancing the specifics necessary to reach correct conclusion (Lynch, 2006). This chapter addresses the guidelines developed by sexual assault specialists in the fields of healthcare, law, and forensic science.

Sexual Assault Medical/Forensic Examinations

INITIAL CONSIDERATIONS

There are several ways for sexual assault patients to enter the healthcare system. One way is via the emergency department. Others may be initially encountered in clinics, physicians' offices, or school health systems. Occasionally, law enforcement officers transport suspects or victims to a location staffed with a qualified SANE. Because all medical facilities do not have expert in-house personnel to perform the required examinations, many communities prefer the latter model. Most current sexual assault programs are aware of the Emergency Medical Treatment and Active Labor Act (EMTALA) guidance, which outlines criteria if the sexual assault patient is to bypass the medical screening examination (MSE) and only have evidence collection in the emergency department.

"If an individual presents to a dedicated emergency department and requests services that are not for a medical condition, such as preventive care services (immunizations, allergy shots, flu shots) or the gathering of evidence for criminal law cases (e.g., sexual assault, blood alcohol test), the hospital is not obligated to provide a MSE under EMTALA to this individual." (www.medlaw.com/searchpro/index.php?q=sexual+assault).

However, many facilities require an MSE because of the assaultive mechanism, the patient and clinician being unaware of any injuries until after the assessment is complete, and risk evaluation of pregnancy, STI and HIV exposure. Nevertheless, in the rare case that an individual has incurred obvious serious injuries and is in need of immediate medical attention, this takes priority over the sexual assault examination. Most patients, however, are physically stable and able to complete this voluntary examination process and to discuss the reported event.

Sexual assault patients exhibit diverse and complex needs based on age, gender, and acuity of the circumstance. Physical, psychological, financial, and legal issues are all priorities that must be considered in the plan of care for the patient. It is important to note that the lack of physical injury is not uncommon in the patient who reports a sexual assault. The role of the examiner is that of objectively providing exemplary nursing care and expert, competent evidence collection, and documentation for each patient. Documentation should include the history of the event from the patient, observations, findings, and the samples collected. It should not include opinion-based comments in the summary such as "no injuries consistent with sexual assault are noted".

A stable patient should be placed in a private room as soon as possible, preferably away from the emergency department. Privacy, safety, and confidentiality must be ensured. The Health Insurance Portability and Accountability Act (HIPAA) and other state medical privacy laws permit sharing of information in certain circumstances when the patient provides consent for dissemination or when law enforcement is involved. Covered entities and law enforcement agencies must collaborate to develop concise protocols for protected health information disclosure. State law will dictate whether information must be disclosed and to whom.

It is essential for nurses to have current knowledge of reporting mandates within their jurisdiction and to understand legalities regarding patient rights, consents for evidentiary examinations, and the guidelines for documentation and dissemination of information associated with the event. In most states, the sexually assaulted *adult* patient is not required to report the assault to law enforcement to be provided a medical/forensic examination. However, in all 50 states the sexual abuse of children is a mandated report to police or the child protection agency (Child Abuse Prevention and Treatment Act [CAPTA], 1996).

BEST PRACTICE It is essential for nurses to understand reporting mandates within their jurisdiction and to understand guidance regarding patient rights, consents, and the various provisions for the dissemination of information associated with the sexual assault event.

HISTORY OF THE EVENT

The first step in a medical/forensic examination includes documenting the patient's historical account of the assault. To assure accuracy and avoid misinterpretation, the patient's statements must be documented in his or her precise words, enclosed in quotation marks. This initiates the diagnosis and treatment plan, is one component of the medical record, and is often a critical piece in the courtroom. The detailed physical examination that follows provides an opportunity to assess the body for health issues and as a potential crime scene. Most jurisdictions have a specific form to guide the examiner in obtaining the history of the sexual assault event.

The history of the sexual assault and the assessment provides information that will assist the examiner in collecting the right types of evidence from certain anatomical sites. For example, if the patient reports that he or she was physically restrained, there could be soft tissue defects including contact abrasions and contusions. Adhesive might remain from the use of duct tape, or bite marks might be detectable on

the breasts. Written and photographic documentation should relate to the details provided by the patient history. Reports of oral, vaginal, or anal contact will determine areas of concentration for the detailed examinations of body orifices and the collection of specimens.

KEY POINT The history of events associated with the sexual assault along with the assessment assists the examiner in determining the types of evidence that should be recovered during the medical/forensic examination.

SEXUAL ASSAULT INJURIES

Early in the study of sexual assault, many believed that the examiner could assess the patient and determine whether the intercourse was consensual or nonconsensual. The absence of injury was commonly misinterpreted as a consenting adult. This belief was largely influenced by the 1966 study by Masters and Johnson, which described the body's physiological response to consenting partner's sexual stimulation. The study was used as an attempt to use the body's response to consensual foreplay and stimulation to explain why lack of such stimulation may cause injury in nonconsensual intercourse. The theory was that that the reaction of the body would protect the woman from injury. There is no scientific basis to support the theory in relation to sexual assault cases. *Stephen Johnston v. the Commonwealth of Virginia* (2000) and *Velasquez v. the Commonwealth of Virginia* (2002) challenged the use of this theory for consent cases in court. Recent literature shows that there is little difference in the findings in consensual and nonconsensual intercourse (Anderson, McClain, & Riviello, 2006).

Severe physical injuries or genital trauma associated with sexual assault in an adult are considered to be atypical. However, if sadistic or masochistic tendencies are involved in the sexual act, injuries may be profound. If force has been inflicted, there will usually be evidence of such force on the body or clothes of the victim. Physical injury most commonly includes lacerations, contusions, bite marks, and broken fingernails. It should be noted that the presence of injuries does not necessarily equate to nonconsensual sexual activity or that the absence of injury negates the patient's assertion of rape.

DRUG-FACILITATED SEXUAL ASSAULT

Professionals must also be alert to the prevalence of sexual assaults involving the use of drugs and alcohol. It is imperative that immediate action be taken to preserve evidence because of the rapid speed of the body's metabolism. The most common substance used is alcohol (LeBeau, 1999). Drugs and alcohol can result in a loss of consciousness and an inability to resist. Some drugs cause memory loss and incapacitation even with the use of very unlikely drugs such as in the case of an adult male repeatedly using tetrahydrozoline (Visine) to induce a comatose state in an adult female and four female children for the purposes of sexual assault (Spiller, 2007). The effects of many drugs are enhanced when taken with alcohol. Patients who are impaired from the effects of drugs and alcohol often do not remember the assault. They may be found in public areas partially clothed. There are known cases where the individual is arrested for public intoxication without consideration that a sexual assault may have occurred, initiating the chain of events. Information that this might be a drug/alcohol sexual assault must be given to the forensic laboratory to ensure that the appropriate toxicological analyses are completed (see Chapter 10).

Consent for Examination

When applicable, written, informed consent should be obtained from adult patients before steps are taken to recover forensic evidence. Children under the age of 18 may require consent of parents or a guardian, depending on state law. Other states provide for examination with the consent of the minor only. If the hospital has a qualified pediatric forensic specialist or a certified pediatric sexual assault nurse examiner (SANE-P) on duty, that individual should be contacted for advice about consents, state reporting laws, or other medicolegal nuances associated with the scenario.

Occupational Health and Safety Issues

Alcohol-based hand hygiene products should not be used because these agents are ineffective in the presence of organic materials and degrade DNA on contact (Bjerke, 2004). A clean laboratory coat or disposable gown should be donned for each examination to prevent contamination from previous patients. Long hair should be restrained with a clip or the examiner should wear a disposable head covering (bonnet). Nails should be short to prevent puncturing the gloves. Acrylic wraps, nail polish, and artificial nails are not appropriate in the medical/forensic examination environment. Any rings, other than a smooth band ring, should be removed because they can create tiny, occult defects in the glove that obliterate its value as a protective barrier. Jewelry also tends to harbor soap, debris, and bacteria. Masks and face shields are required for cavity aspirations or any other procedure that could result in splash contamination (OSHA, 2009). Demonstrate precision by handling all evidence with gloved hands (preferably powder-free) and change gloves frequently.

Evidence Recovery Procedures

Evidence is any item, object, event, action, situation, or fact that aids in determining if a crime was or was not committed and who may or may not have committed the crime (National Institute of Justice, 2004a). It is not the role of the FNE to make this determination nor to draw a conclusion as to whether or not rape has occurred. The FNE is only responsible for identifying and documenting injury and recovering potential evidence during the assessment.

Many states have designated evidence collection kits that are used to assist in the collection and preservation but are not intended to dictate or limit what must be collected. Collecting samples for DNA analysis at crime scenes is a critical part of investigating the nature of the crime (National Institute of Justice, 2004b).

A primary goal is to avoid the loss, contamination, or damage of physical evidence. Therefore, any personal items should not be immediately given to the patient's friends or family. Do not bathe the patient or discard, clean, or wash the patient's personal items. Do not cut through holes, stains, or other defects in the patient's clothing. Be careful to collect all evidence individually and maintain items in one's personal possession or secure the area where the evidence will be kept. It is imperative to communicate to appropriate personnel if any item of evidence has been accidentally contaminated during the collection or packaging processes. Potential contamination can be minimized by ensuring that the examination room is meticulously cleaned between patients and is well organized and properly equipped. Wearing appropriate personal protective clothing will also prove to be a valuable safeguard against accidental contamination by the examiner who may disperse saliva by talking, coughing, or sneezing. Obviously, smoking, food, and drinks should not be permitted in the examination room at any time.

It may be necessary to contact police to provide a prompt transfer of evidence from the hospital to the crime laboratory to protect certain evidence from degradation. Custody of the evidence is the responsibility of the FNE/SANE until transfer. Unfortunately, police may fail to provide timely recovery and transfers. During long delays, there may be degradation of certain specimens. Moist or damp articles of clothing should be air-dried in a secure area until the transfer is completed. The hospital is responsible for the custody of evidence and should have a designated evidence custodian. Ideally, this is a FNE who is familiar with policies and procedures regarding the preservation, security, and legal issues pertaining to evidentiary items.

EVIDENCE COLLECTION WITH INJURY

Unique challenges must be considered when bleeding injuries complicate evidence recovery. Collecting the best specimen remains the objective. In clinical practice, cleaning and preparing a wound for a dressing is not evidence recovery, and if the patient is stable, evidence should be collected first. For example, a bite mark causing bleeding should be swabbed where the lips of the suspect made contact with the skin above, below, and in the middle of the injury *before* performing other wound care. This will provide for the best sample to distinguish deposited DNA from the patient's blood. When extreme genital injuries are present, evidence recovery is complicated. If a severe vaginal tear exists in certain anatomical locations, the optimum ejaculate specimen may have been washed out of the vaginal vault with the flushing of the blood. In this type of scenario, one might consider collecting the entire blood trail beginning from the end of the trail and proceeding upward with a 4-by-4-inch gauze moistened with sterile water. This can be repeated for each anatomical structure such as foot, lower leg, or thigh until collection is complete to the vaginal vault. These gauze wipes will need to air-dry and be packaged individually, sealed, and labeled as noted in later sections. Unusual circumstances affecting evidence collection and preservation will occur. It is sensible in these situations to consult a law enforcement evidence technician or a crime laboratory analyst for suggestions.

EVIDENCE RECOVERY DURING MENSTRUATION

If patients are menstruating, collect tampons and sanitary napkins. Air-dry them as much as possible and then place them in a separate paper collection bag. Wet evidence that cannot be dried thoroughly at the exam site should then be packaged in leak-proof containers and separated from other evidence. This must be communicated when being signed over to law enforcement.

PHYSICAL EVIDENCE

Tangible evidence has a collective significance in the criminal and civil investigation of sexual violence. The nature of trace or "transfer" evidence is highly variable and can be found at almost every crime scene. Trace evidence can include hair, fiber, glass, soil, and other particulate matter. The media has highly influenced the public's perception about crime scene investigations and the role of evidence in legal proceedings. This immersion in crime scene investigations through television programs such as *CSI* has also raised expectations of those who identify, collect, and process evidence. Most states have patterned their policies and procedures for consistency with the laboratory standards of the Federal Bureau of Investigation (FBI). However, the SANE must be aware of variations within the state or local jurisdiction.

BIOLOGICAL EVIDENCE

Sources of potential biological or genetic evidence are continually expanding with advances in scientific analysis and testing of materials that might be suitable for DNA typing. DNA is contained in all body tissue fluid and cells, with the exception of white blood cells (McClintock, 2008). FNEs are not mandated to collect DNA evidence but rather obtain body fluids or tissues that might contain DNA. Among these are blood and blood stains, semen, saliva, hair roots, bone, teeth, and tissue. Similar to perspiration or sebaceous secretions, urine also contains enough epithelial material to generate a DNA profile (McClintock, 2008). Swabbings of the oral or vaginal cavity as well as bite marks (see Chapter 26) can be used to recover DNA. Certain items of physical evidence collected at the scene of the crime may also contain DNA. Examples are cigarettes, toothpicks, bottles or cans, bullets, condoms, ligatures, clothing, knives, and other weapons.

Biological evidence possesses its greatest value in investigations where DNA types can be compared to known profiles obtained from either the victim or the suspect. The investigation efforts may occur over several years, so precise documentation, record keeping, and specimen management are imperatives. It is important, therefore, to collect the samples on a medium that can stabilize the genetic material. The use of an FTA collection card permits both short- and long-term storage of biological specimens at room temperature (FTA is a registered trademark of Flinders Technologies, Pty. Ltd.). This card is made from an absorbent cellulose-based paper that contains chemical substances to inhibit bacterial growth and to protect the DNA from enzymatic degradation. Samples such as blood and saliva can be "spotted" onto this collection card for storage up to 17 years (McClintock, 2008). These cards are preferred for collecting offender DNA samples for inclusion into forensic databases.

Certain biological materials such as semen and urine require refrigeration or freezing. The local crime laboratory will provide guidance for these and other specimens such as hair, bone, teeth, and body tissue. To avoid cross-contamination of evidence that may contain DNA, the forensic examiner must take precautions to wear a mask and to do frequent handwashing and glove changes throughout the examination.

KEY POINT Crime scene investigations may take years to complete. Biological evidence specimens must be collected using processes that ensure long-term preservation without enzymatic degradation of DNA.

Photographic Documentation

Forensic photography is an essential method for documenting evidence and injury. Evidence must be photographed in situ before it is recovered from a crime scene or from the body. Digital photography is the preferred method for recording evidentiary photographs because the images can be reviewed immediately and retaken if necessary to ensure that important details are captured. The images can be downloaded onto a computer and reproduced for use in the courtroom.

Distant range photos showing the location of apparent injuries should be taken as an orientation shot. Next, midrange and finally, close-up photos should be taken with an American Board of Forensic Odontology (ABFO) #2 Grey Scale in place. This is the preferred scale and is valuable for use in bite mark and other injury/evidence documentation (Olshaker, 2007). A coin or another object of a known size may be used if the examiner does not have access to the specified photographic scale. Many photographs may be required to fully document injuries over the body surfaces and to record precise findings within the mouth and the genital/anal areas. Colposcope-mounted cameras may be employed to magnify

and document certain findings but the above forensic photography principles would not be applicable due to the magnification and sensitivity of the genital images (see Chapter 7, Fig. 7-11).

Alternate Light Source (ALS)

Forensic nurse examiners may employ ultraviolet (UV) and infrared (IR) technology to document injuries that are not easily seen by the naked eye. Hidden details of a deep bruise may be revealed using UV technology, whereas details of an incised wound can be better appreciated with IR technology (Klingle & Reiter, 2008). Hospitals or law enforcement agencies may supply these helpful adjuncts to aid the FNE in detection and documentation of bruises, fingerprints, and soft tissue defects. Before using any ALS, the forensic examiner should be well versed in the techniques for using these devices, including assets and limitations of the various UV or IR technologies. Both the examiner and the patient must wear a suitable type of safety goggles if these ALS adjuncts are used to document injuries during the course of a forensic examination (Klingle & Reiter, 2008). The use of eye protection should be annotated in the patient's record to protect the nurse and the hospital from liability-associated eye injuries. (See Chapter 7 for a complete discussion of forensic photography and alternate light sources.)

Methods of Evidence Recovery

Sexual assault evidence collection will vary depending on local crime laboratory testing methodologies, protocol, and the choice of kits. The kit itself should never be the predictor or limiting hindrance of appropriate evidence collection for any victim of sexual assault. The collection kit is provided as a tool to assist the FNE with packaging the best specimens. When collecting evidence onto paper, use a clean piece of paper and fold into a bindle (Fig. 13-1).

CLOTHING

A vital part of evidence collection is the patient's clothing. Clothing worn by the victim at the time of the sexual assault is often found to have physical or biological evidence that needs to be preserved. If clothes have been changed, collect the clothing items that remain next to the body areas affected. This is most commonly the underwear and in many cases the bra or undershirt. Case studies are demonstrating significant value with DNA results from the bra because of saliva on the breasts. Look briefly at the clothing and describe the presence of any stains or tears. A more detailed inspection will be done in the forensic laboratory. Clothing preservation can be facilitated by first placing a clean sheet or piece of table paper on the floor to act as a barrier. Then place a second sheet or layer of table paper on top of the barrier and have the patient disrobe over it. Carefully drop each item of clothing at a separate location on the sheet/paper, making sure to not to commingle clothing items in a single pile (Ferrell, 2007).

Also, if indicated, maintain and package any hospital linen used during the transport, care, and treatment of the patient. Proceed by labeling each clothing item with the patient's name and the collector's initials, being careful to avoid any rip, stain, or affected area. Next, place individual clothing items in separate, clean paper bags. Optimally, multiple items should never be placed together in the same bag. Next, fold and place the top sheet/table paper in a separate clean paper bag, double-fold the open edge of the paper bag, and apply tape from one end of the fold all the way across to the other end to provide a complete seal (never use staples).

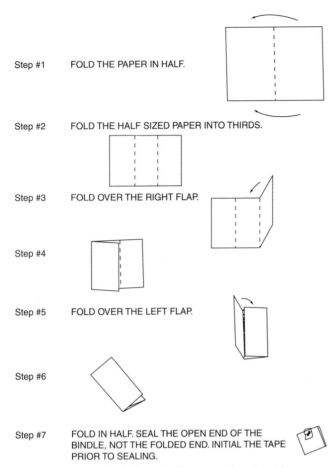

Step #1   FOLD THE PAPER IN HALF.

Step #2   FOLD THE HALF SIZED PAPER INTO THIRDS.

Step #3   FOLD OVER THE RIGHT FLAP.

Step #4

Step #5   FOLD OVER THE LEFT FLAP.

Step #6

Step #7   FOLD IN HALF. SEAL THE OPEN END OF THE
           BINDLE, NOT THE FOLDED END. INITIAL THE TAPE
           PRIOR TO SEALING.

Fig. 13-1 Technique for folding a bindle to secure forensic evidence.

After the seal is complete, write the collector's initials across the tape and onto the bag to provide a tamper-resistant seal. Then complete and attach a chain-of-custody label to the outside of each bag. If stains are present, place clean paper over the stains before folding, to avoid cross-contamination. If any items are wet, leave the paper bag open to allow the contents to continue to air-dry until given to law enforcement, identify the paper bag as wet, and immediately notify law enforcement of the situation. Always package the clothing in paper containers or bags; avoid using any plastic bags, plastic containers, or airtight containers because they retain moisture, which hastens degradation of organic materials. Avoid handling the clothing excessively, and change gloves frequently (Hochmesiter, 1998; National Institute of Justice, 2004).

The practitioner must also be alert to the dispersal of debris or objects as the patient disrobes. Hair, fiber, rocks, sand, mud, or other foreign materials from the scene may be noted. These items should be handled as little as possible and collected onto paper. The paper bindle should be deposited into an envelope and labeled with the patient's name, the site from where debris was collected, the person collecting, and the date and time of collection.

SWABBING FOR BIOLOGICAL MATERIALS

When a fluid deposit is identified, each secretion should be collected by the double-swab technique. Moisten a swab lightly with sterile water and swab the indicated area; swab the same area again with a dry swab (this is referred to as the wet-to-dry swab technique). Dry the swabs end place the two swabs in an envelope. Use different swabs for each location where a secretion has been

identified and collected. Control swabs should also be obtained from a nonaffected area.

If crusted material is identified, scrape the area over a paper bindle sheet, place the bindle in an envelope, and label it by specifying which site of the body the material was collected from. Preserve any dried blood or debris identified on the patient's body. It may be necessary to lift pieces of evidence by using the adhesive lift or "tape lift" method (described in Chapter 19) or by using forceps with plastic-coated tips (Hazelwood & Burgess, 2009).

Preservation can be accomplished by swab, paper bindle, or another approved technique. The collected item is then placed in an envelope, sealed, and labeled appropriately. Debris evidence optimally should be packaged in separate envelopes to prevent cross-contamination and avoid labeling confusion. It is helpful to use a packaging envelope that provides a body diagram on which to indicate the anatomical site from where the debris was collected. Sterile water is used to provide best evidence preservation and circumvent potential DNA degradation during long periods of storage. As DNA testing and sensitivity improves, more research will be needed to categorize the impact of various chemicals and minerals present in local tap water.

Fingernails

Fingernail swabbing, now a preferred method by criminalists, can often provide valuable information depending on the action taken by the victim during the attack. Swabbing under each fingernail has proven to be a more effective method of evidence preservation than fingernail scraping, as demonstrated in case studies (Hochmeister, 1998). Begin by moistening one swab and swab under the fingernails of one hand; repeat the process with another swab for the other hand, then place the swabs separately in swab dry boxes and label the left and right hand accordingly. Complete the collection by placing the boxes in an envelope, seal it, and label it. If fingernail scrapings are to be done, place one hand at a time over a clean paper and allow evidence to fall onto the paper. Use separate papers for each hand, and then fold the paper, place in an envelope, seal, and label.

Oral Cavity

If history or assessment indicates oral penetration, evidence preservation should be done. The nurse should swab the mouth with four swabs, paying attention to the underside of the tongue and rear crevices of the oral cavity. Some jurisdictions no longer request smears. However, if the examiner elects to make a smear, this should be done at this time by rolling one applicator over a ½-inch spot in the center of a clean glass slide. Mark the slide with an "O" to indicate the source of the smear. All swabs and slides should be air-dried before placing them into boxes, which will be finally inserted into envelopes, sealed, and labeled. The gingival tissue has been shown to be an excellent area for obtaining smears of foreign biological materials. Smears from around the lips and periorbital areas may contain semen or other DNA evidence. In one case of fellatio reported by Lynch, the subject was not examined until 17 hours after the attack. The victim had brushed his teeth, eaten supper and breakfast, and washed his face. Cotton swabs moistened with saline were passed through his mustache and found to be positive for spermatozoa (Lynch, 2000).

An alternate technique is to request that the victim rinse her or his mouth with sterile water, which is then expectorated into a cup and an aliquot is preserved in a test tube. If the sample cannot be processed promptly, it can be frozen for later processing.

Dental Tape

Currently, many programs continue to use dental tape (or floss), as a new approach to oral evidence recovery. The Anchorage SART program is one example of successful case studies when routine oral swabs and smears were negative (Tara Henry 2003). The procedure is to take 16 inches of unwaxed dental tape/floss, in the middle tie 2 knots approximately 2 inches apart and either the patient or nurse examiner will floss between his or her teeth (Tara Henry 2003). Indiana evidence recovery kit has recently been updated to include an envelope specifically for dental floss, serving as a reminder of the evidentiary value. Nurses must use caution to not disrupt the gum barrier because a break in the tissue, causing bleeding, can expose the patient to the offender's body fluids.

Human Bite Marks

Reported/suspected bite mark swabbing provides valuable information when a sexual assault has occurred. Collection of saliva from the suspected bite mark should be made before the cleansing or dressing of a wound. If the skin is broken, swabbing of the actual punctures should be avoided when collecting dried saliva. Instead, use the double-swab technique to swab the area directly surrounding the center of the bite marks. Collect saliva from the bite mark by slightly moistening a swab with sterile water and gently swabbing the surrounding area. Repeat the swabbing with a dry swab. Dry the swabs, and place them in a swab box. Indicate on the "Debris" envelope the location of the suspected bite mark. Place swabs in the "Debris" envelope, seal, and label.

KEY POINT The role of the examiner in trial is to have no stake in the case, tell the truth, and accurately describe the findings whether she or he is appearing for the prosecution or for the defense.

Controversial Techniques

BODY PIERCING

Contemporary body piercing is a common practice often overlooked when evaluating for trace evidence. Piercing trends vary from ear lobe to genital structures. Forensic nurse examiners must carefully consider if the piercing was involved in a trace transfer to obtain and preserve best specimen. Prior to handling a piercing, lightly moisten a swab with sterile water and swab the indicated piercing. Air dry the swab and place in an envelope. Use different swabs for each location where a transfer has been identified. If possible, allow the patient to remove the item, place in a bindle and then in an envelope marked with the site of the piercing. Retaining this item requires the patient's consent (Fig. 13-2).

PLUCKED HAIR

Since the 1990s, most SANE programs across the country no longer collect pulled head hair or plucked pubic hair from victims. Although this can be an issue of local debate, it has seldom been useful evidence and the collection can be painful. This recovery can be obtained at a later time if necessary. The idea that DNA could be obtained from the bulb of the hair follicle has been far surpassed by the current DNA methods. There are few reasons to collect pubic or head hair from the victim unless there is some significant substance in the hair, and even then, the hair can be removed without plucking.

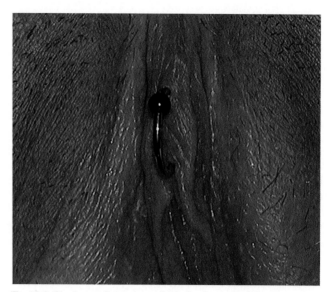

Fig. 13-2 Piercing to the prepuce of the clitoris on an adult. As visualized here there is protrusion of the piercing that should be considered for presence of trace evidence.

DETERMINING THE AGE OF BRUISES

Several decades ago, it was believed that clinicians could accurately predict the age of a bruise based on its color and other characteristics. However, ongoing research and clinical observations have refuted that idea. There are many factors which impact the color of bruises, which include the patient's age and state of health, the amount of blood released in association with the trauma, and even characteristics of skin pigmentation. Bruising can be masked in individuals who are heavily tanned or naturally dark. The location of the bruise will be instrumental in its appearance and characteristics, as well. If traumatic force impacts a bony prominence, the bruise will most likely appear rather quickly and have sharp margins with deep red and purple coloration. If the bruise is on a fatty area it may not appear for several days. At late stages, long after injury, discoloration may remain. However, this remaining discoloration may well be more of a response to injury (scar formation, breakdown products of blood pigments, and melanin) than true bruising. As a rule, older bruises experiencing absorption will most likely appear to be yellowish/greenish/grayish/and brownish with fading margins. One noted forensic pathology text states, "every human being has his or her own spectrum of unique physiologic responses. Because heating is a physiologic process it is not possible to precisely determine age of contusions (bruises)" (Dolinak, 2005, p. 128). The forensic examiner should take high resolution photographs and document the appearance of the bruise in the narrative record, carefully describing any pattern, coloration, or sharp margins that might be discernable during the examination. Avoid any references to the possible age of the bruise in nursing documentation (see also Chapter 25).

Evidence Recovery Procedures for Females

ANAL AND GENITAL INSPECTION AND EVIDENCE RECOVERY

Inspection of the anus and collection of evidence should be done before vaginal instrumentation to prevent secretions from seeping into the anal folds after the speculum has been removed. When there is no history of anal penetration and positive results are obtained from the collection, it is often assumed that the victim is too embarrassed to communicate this or does not recall. Consideration must be given to the natural gravitational flow of secretions from the vaginal vault to the anal folds. Anal dilatation utilizing the prone knee-chest position should be utilized when there is a history of penetration, pain, or injury to provide optimum visualization. This position, coupled with a lifting of the buttocks, allows for the external and internal sphincter to relax and open. Positioning and effective relaxation allows for the SANE to complete the anal examination without the need of instrumentation. Collection site identification should be differentiated accurately by documenting the anal folds, anus, or rectum.

For a premenarchal child, the assessment is completed by performing an initial inspection using gross visualization, varying positions, and magnification. Intravaginal instrumentation (speculum, vaginal swabs) is rarely warranted but if needed, sedation should be considered (ACEP, 1999).

Any medical condition should be treated during the initial visit; however, in the case of children, cultures must be obtained before initiating antibiotic therapy. Failure to do so may result in the loss of valuable diagnostic information, and forensic evidence will be permanently lost. Children who are suspected of being sexually abused or are symptomatic should have cultures as indicated of the vulva, penis, anus, and pharynx for gonorrhea and chlamydia (ACEP, 1999).

A gross visual inspection, preferably with an ALS, should be accomplished to identify secretions on the body and genital surfaces. If any area fluoresces, the examiner should swab the area using the standard procedure.

Pubic hair combings can be completed by placing a clean paper under the patient's buttocks and combing through the pubic hair (collecting all foreign material) into the paper. Fold the comb into the paper and place both into an envelope that will then be labeled and sealed. If indicated, cut any matted pubic hair and place it into a separate paper bindle, into another envelope, and seal and label envelope as previously discussed.

In many states the case law has clarified "penetration" of the female genitalia as "penetration however slight." This means that breaking the plane of the labia majora will then constitute penetration. It is not the purpose of the forensic nurse examiner to interpret the law but to appreciate the critical points that impact the precise interpretation of the information. This is imperative in the evaluation of the pediatric patient.

LABIAL INSPECTION AND EVIDENCE COLLECTION

Labia majora assessment and evidence collection begins by gross visualization of the outer labia majora. If swabbing the outer labia majora, the specimen should be labeled using this description. Then separation of the labia majora assists in evaluating the inner aspects of the structures for collection and injury documentation. Swabs should be collected by using four cotton tip applicators, moistened with sterile water if needed to ease collection. One slide should be made to identify seminal fluid and spermatozoa. The swab is made by rolling one applicator over a ½ inch of the center of a clean glass slide. All swabs should be air-dried before placing in swab box. The envelopes should be labeled "OLMJ" (outer labia majora) or "ILMJ" (inner labia majora) before sealing and labeling.

The assessment of the labia minora is done by gross visualization. Labia minora structures are inside the female genitalia, negating the need for differentiating the outer versus the inner.

Labia minora swabs should be collected by using four cotton tip applicators, following the same procedure as previously described for the labia majora. The examiner should proceed by inspecting the clitoral hood, collecting evidence as indicated. The urethral and hymen structures and the posterior fourchette area of the labia minora are best visualized by the use of the traction technique. In adult/adolescent patients, this is accomplished by tunneling the labia minora tissue bilaterally. Prepubescent females are benefited by tunneling the labia majora for best visualization.

VAGINAL EXAMINATION AND EVIDENCE COLLECTION

The speculum exam (menarche and older) is completed using appropriate size and design. The FNE should avoid placing any object on or through the prepubertal nonestrogenized hymen. Sterile water can be used to lubricate the speculum. A water-soluble lubricant jelly should be avoided, because it is considered to be an added contaminant to the crime scene prior to evidence collection. If using a plastic speculum, test the speculum for imperfections by running the preceding edge over the gloved hand. Note any dragging or snags, which could indicate burrs or other defects that could scrated the genital tissue. After inserting the speculum, the cervix and vaginal walls should be inspected, noting any trauma. Four swabs should be used at this site. The examiner should make a vaginal slide, using the technique described earlier. The slide should be marked with a "V" to indicate the site of collection.

A binocular optic colposcope can be used as an adjunctive examination tool providing a three-dimensional magnified view with precision of tissue color and depth. Examination of the genital and anal areas for the presence of injury and debris are enhanced with illumination and various magnification capabilities.

BEST PRACTICE   The forensic nurse examiner should use adjuncts to the examination, which will enhance the assessment and collection of certain evidence. These include the colposcope-mounted camera, alternate light sources, toluidine blue dye, and the Foley catheter technique.

Special Techniques to Enhance Evidentiary Examinations

USE OF TOLUIDINE BLUE DYE

Toluidine blue dye (TBD) can be used to identify trauma not visible with the naked eye or magnification. If TBD is going to be used, proceed to the anal inspection and evidence collection before TBD application (Box 13-1).

Forensic nurse examiner Russell Rooms, director of the National Forensic Nursing Institute, initiated the use of the single-dose forensic blue swab, which minimizes cross-contamination and improves application technique. TBD is a nuclear stain that with a positive effect merely indicates that the skin has been broken. It is unable to either prove or disprove nonconsensual intercourse or identify the penetrating source. Application of TBD is done before the insertion of a speculum or examining fingers. A 1% aqueous solution of TBD is applied with a cotton swab applicator or the forensic blue swab on the posterior genital area, perineum, or anal folds. Do not apply the dye to mucosal surfaces (the hymen structures and beyond) because results are difficult to interpret (Fig. 13-3) (McCauley, 1986).

Box 13-1 Toluidine Blue Dye (TBD) Application in the Sexual Assault Forensic Examination

PURPOSE

To aid in the detection and visualization of minor injury to the genital area that is not readily identified on inspection. This is a procedure for use to the anal folds, perineum, and vulva (up to the hymen tissue) only. TBD does not stain the surface layers of the skin but will dye nucleated squamous cells in the deeper layers of epidermis exposed by even superficial lacerations.

SUPPLIES

- Toluidine blue dye, 1% aqueous solution
- Squirt bottle containing 1% acetic acid
- Lubricating jelly
- Cotton swabs
- 4-by-4-inch gauze

PROCEDURE

- Collect all external genital specimens as indicated by history or examination before the application of TBD, and consider photodocumentation.
- Before speculum examination or instrumentation to area, apply TB dye by using a sterile cotton swab to genital area in question (avoid inserting dye into the vaginal vault).
- Dye application may be used on the labia majora, labia minora, posterior fourchette, hymen, perineal body, and perianal area.
- Allow to dry for approximately one minute.
- Using spray bottle, gently, with broad spray, flood the area until excess TBD is flushed away.
- Gently blot the area with a 4-by-4-inch gauze. Do not rub the area.
- Consider photodocumentation of the area following TB dye application.

PATIENT TEACHING

Advise the living patient that small traces of TBD may shed in the clothing over the next two days.

After drying for approximately one minute, the area is cleaned with 1% acetic acid to remove the excess stain from all non-nucleated areas (ACEP, 1999). If needed, a swab moistened with 1% acetic acid can be used to remove residual dye trapped in crevices. A negative result is indicated by no uptake or a light diffusely stippled uptake of dye. A positive result is indicated by deep, royal blue staining in skin defects (Jones, et al. 2004).

HYMENAL ASSESSMENT AND THE FOLEY CATHETER TECHNIQUE

Providing a detailed assessment of the hymen will vary dependent on the sexual maturity of the patient. In the nonestrogenized prepubescent hymen, avoid placing anything on or through it because of the heightened sensitivity in the living patient. Supine frog-leg, labial traction, prone knee-chest, and various other positioning techniques should be used for adequate visualization. Any hymenal concern for well-healed injury in the nonestrogenized prepubescent child should be confirmed in the supine and prone-knee chest positions (McCann, 1999).

To aid in the examination of the estrogenized hymen, a large cotton swab can be inserted into the vaginal vault to assess the edge. The cotton swab technique does not facilitate circumferential visualization. The use of the Foley catheter will improve the evaluation. The Foley technique should always be done after the collection of vaginal specimens to avoid altering evidence that might be present and to ensure that the best specimens are preserved. When assessing the need for the Foley catheter technique, note that the chronological age of a patient does not accurately reflect the developmental changes seen in the female genitalia. Most of these changes are influenced by various levels of estrogen found in the female at varying life stages of infancy, childhood, and adolescence.

Estrogen is present at birth in the female infant because of maternal estrogen effects and can continue to be present in the genital tissue up to two to four years of age. This is demonstrated most often by small amounts of mucus and blood being secreted vaginally into the diaper as maternal estrogen dissipates. Estrogen then returns at puberty and is demonstrated with the onset of menses. The effect of estrogen on the female genitalia has tremendous impact in the evaluation of sexual assault. With estrogen present, the tissue is more elastic, redundant, and not painful to touch. The redundancy or excessive folds make evaluation of the hymen at this stage challenging.

In clinical forensic nursing practice, the Foley catheter technique is reserved for patients who are of menarche age and older (Ferrell, 1995). It is *not* used in the living infant. The stage of menarche fluctuates by age and is further influenced by a range of variables. The onset of menses can begin at age 10 or earlier. In this patient population, the Foley catheter technique can prove

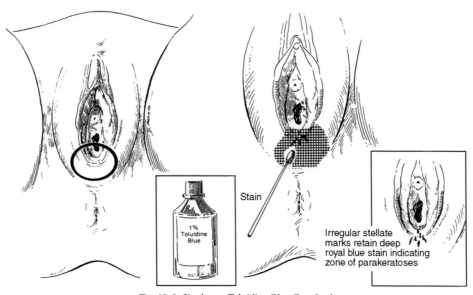

Fig. 13-3 Single-use Toluidine Blue Dye Swab.

to be beneficial for injury evaluation and precise documentation. Answers to the questions "Is there injury present?" and if so "to what extent?" are best derived by use of the Foley catheter technique.

Case Study **13-1**

The Foley Catheter in Use

In the deceased patient, the Foley catheter balloon technique also serves as a valuable tool to assess the hymen of the infant and young child where estrogen is present (a residual of maternal estrogen) before autopsy (Lynch, 2006).

HISTORY. A three-month-old female patient presented with no pulse or respirations. Full resuscitation efforts were in progress by the paramedics. No history was presented other than that the infant was found lifeless in its crib. On arrival to the emergency department, the infant was pronounced dead. One of several concerns on examination was the ecchymotic labia minora. After consultation with the medical examiner's office, the FNE was requested to perform a sexual assault evaluation before autopsy.

EXAMINATION. During the postmortem evaluation, after specimen collection, the Foley catheter balloon technique is demonstrated on this three-month-old infant (Fig. 13-4a). In a nonestrogenized deceased infant or child, this technique is not necessary because of the absence of estrogen and the tissue tension that occurs with application of the traction technique. Under these conditions, a clear view of the hymenal edge is readily observed.

Once again, the steps of evaluation begin with inspection of external female genitalia, progressing to separation of the labia majora, then separation of the labia minora (Fig. 13-4b). Oftentimes, the examination would end at this point because of the "closed" or "intact" appearance of the hymen as perceived by the inexperienced or ineffectual practitioner. The examination should continue with the traction technique in order to evaluate the edge of the hymen or rim of the hymen tissue. In the evaluation of a child, traction is accomplished by gently tunneling the tissue of the labia majora outward toward the clinician. As Figure 13-4c shows, the rim of the hymen has pronounced projections with an obvious opening.

The postmortem state of the infant provides the opportunity to use the Foley catheter balloon technique to clearly answer the questions "Is there presence of well-healed tears?" or "Because of estrogen, is this a hymen with prominent projections whose appearance will smooth out with stretching?"

A 12 French Foley catheter is then inserted just past the hymen and inflated with 30 cc of air. Visualized in Figure 13-4d, the projections smooth out, and the examiners unquestionably conclude that the projections were not caused by injury. The hymen viewed has no injury present.

The forensic nurse should exercise care when documenting information about the hymen. For example, avoid describing the hymen as *intact*. Use of this term implies that no injuries are present, however, it is often misinterpreted as no penetration has occurred.

IMPERFORATE HYMEN

Accurate description of the morphology and integrity of the hymen is critical in the diagnosis of female sexual abuse. When no hymenal opening is present, a membrane covers the area of the vaginal opening, and this condition is termed an *imperforate hymen*. In these cases, surgery is required to facilitate menstrual flow.

Forensic Evidence Recovery for Males

PENILE/SCROTUM INSPECTION AND COLLECTION OF EVIDENCE

The penis and scrotum require careful inspection, augmented by swabs and smears. The proper method of collecting a skin surface penile smear is to use two moistened cotton swabs to thoroughly swab the external surface of the penile shaft and glans. All outer areas of the penis and scrotum where contact is suspected should be swabbed. These swabs are not, however, for use in the medical diagnosis of sexually transmitted infections; therefore, they should not be used to swab inside the penile opening. The urethral meatus should also be avoided. A slide is only required when the potential for sperm/semen of suspect is collected. Proceed by rolling one swab on ½ inch in the center of a clean slide and label the frosted area of the slide with "P"; the evidentiary specimens should be air-dried and packaged as previously described. If bite marks are present on the penis or scrotum, they should be managed in the usual way. (See Chapter 26.)

ANAL INSPECTION AND EVIDENCE COLLECTION

Anal dilatation utilizing prone knee-chest position should be utilized when there is a history of penetration, pain, or injury to provide optimum visualization. This position, coupled with a lifting of the buttocks, allows for the external and internal sphincter to relax and open. Positioning and effective relaxation allow the SANE to complete the anal examination without the need for instrumentation. Collection site identification should be differentiated accurately by documenting the anal folds, anus, or rectum. In consideration of patient comfort, swabs should be moistened with sterile water and collected one at a time. Swab the anus with four swabs. Make an anal slide according to local protocol using the first swab, before drying. Label the slide "A" to indicate the source. Air-dry all swabs before placing them in swab boxes and inserting into an envelope for sealing and labeling.

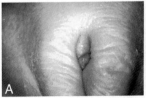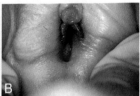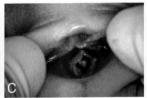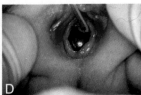

Fig. 13-4 *A*, 3-month-old postmortem infant evaluation; inspection of external female genitalia. *B*, 3-month-old postmortem infant evaluation; separation of the *labia majora* and *minora* providing visualization of the hymen tissue. *C*, 3-month-old postmortem infant evaluation demonstrating use of the traction technique by gently tunneling the *labia majora* tissue in order to provide evaluation of the rim of the hymen tissue. As visualized, the rim of the hymen has very pronounced projections with an obvious opening. *D*, 3-month-old postmortem infant evaluation. An uninflated 12 French Foley catheter inserted past the hymen and inflated with 30 cc of air. As visualized here, the projections smooth out and the hymen has no injury present. The Foley technique is only to be used in the living child after menarche age.

Security of Evidence

Chain of custody may be defined as the identity of the individuals having control or custody over evidentiary, potentially evidentiary, or other property. The chain of custody always begins with the first to come in contact with the evidence. As an evidence custodian, this is the responsibility of the FNE/SANE from the time the evidence is recovered until it is transferred to the proper legal agency. Consideration of evidentiary items that require refrigeration (not frozen) must also be locked in a protected environment-controlled unit with one key or combination in the same manner narcotics are protected. This key should not be turned over to any other person without a signature for custody. Agencies that are seasoned in interface with the courts generally require, as a matter of policy, that the chain of custody be in the form of a written documentation. For example, most hospitals and police agencies have printed forms for this purpose. These actions are the responsibility of the evidence custodian (Lynch, 2000).

Accurate documentation of the transfer of all evidence will establish and safeguard the integrity and competence of every specimen or piece of evidence. When there is a failure to maintain a complete chain of custody, evidence is rendered worthless for presentation in court. Begin by placing a label on the outside of every package that would include the patient's name, a description of the item in the package, and the name of the agency assigned to the case with the case/report number if applicable. Also include the name of the person sealing the item with date and time, the name of the person releasing the item with date and time, and the names of the person and agency receiving the item with date and time. In addition, limit the number of people in the chain of custody to avoid complications at trial.

Evidence Disbursement Sheet

When multiple items are released to law enforcement, consider using an evidence disbursement sheet. This can be placed in the patient's chart for later review and provides a check and balance should there be questions at a later date. This sheet does not take the place of the chain-of-custody labeling that should be on the outside of every package, but it provides written documentation for review. This sheet should contain the patient's name, the name of the agency accepting item, a list of each packaged item to be released, the name of the person who collected the item with date and time, the name of the person releasing the item with date and time, and the name of the person receiving the item with date and time. A copy should be placed in the patient's chart and one provided to the law enforcement agency.

Role of the Victim Advocate

No discussion of the sexual assault examination would be complete without discussing the role of the victim advocate member of the team in regard to the medical/forensic examination. In some jurisdictions, the advocate is present during the examination; in others, the advocate is not present. Many SANEs believe that the presence of an additional individual in the room during the assessment and evidence collection process increases the risk for distractions and heightens the potential for cross-contamination of evidence. At the least, it changes the intimate relationship between the examiner and the patient.

It is well recognized that the advocate serves an important role in providing emotional support for the psychologically impaired or traumatized patient. However, advocates should never be permitted to participate in the evidentiary collection processes in any way. Nonforensic volunteers, if present during the examination, may be subject to subpoena for court testimony when issues arise regarding chain of custody, examination techniques, and the psychological status of the patient. Generally, victim advocates are not prepared to respond to such interrogatives that might occur during court proceedings. This can have serious implications for the advocate, the nurse examiner, and the patient, as well as for the outcome at trial. It is preferable, unless the patient requests the advocate's presence during the examination, for the advocate to use this time to support and educate families and friends of the victim. On occasions in which the advocate may enter the examination room, strict instructions regarding forensic protocol should be followed. Some examiners also relate that the presence of another person at this time has interfered with the history of the event (such as when an advocate answers questions directed to the patient), reduced the ability of nurse-patient bonding, and failed to maintain confidentiality. In Adelaide, South Australia, all victim advocates are required to hold a bachelor's degree as well as special training that pertains to their role. It is recommended that any rape crisis or victim advocacy agency require extensive training for volunteer personnel before allowing victim assistance in any role.

BEST PRACTICE The forensic nurse examiner should ensure that the victim advocate does not participate in any way during the assessment and evidentiary processes except within a direct role to support the patient emotionally.

Summary

All clinical nurses should have knowledge of the various elements of the sexual assault examination, even when they may not have the primary responsibility for conducting them. In addition to ensuring that patients who report sexual assault are identified and receive proper medical and forensic care and follow-up, there must be the keen awareness of the legal implications for documentation, reporting, and referrals. The forensic nurse will not be able to conclude whether a sexual assault occurred, but the documentation and photography can be invaluable to the investigation. The FNE should always remember that her or his role is to be objective and nonbiased. The role of the examiner in trial is to have no stake in the case, to tell the truth, and to accurately describe the findings whether appearing for the prosecution or for the defense.

The ultimate goal of healthcare systems and victim services is to positively affect patient outcomes by increasing the capability of designated professionals providing sexual assault examinations and to help the criminal justice system successfully resolve sexual assault complaints. By providing specially educated clinicians and state-of-the-art methods and technology to detect, recover, preserve, and analyze physical and testimonial evidence on a nationwide basis, we will begin to combat the epidemic of sexual violence in the United States.

Providing proven and reliable methods of simultaneous health assessment and evidence collection are vital in a program sensitive to traumatized victims. This will not only encourage reporting, but reliable evidentiary methods tend to discourage acts of sexual violence as successful prosecutions are increased (Hazelwood & Burgess, 2009, p. 48). Sexual offenders are aware of the frequent failure to report or prosecute these crimes; they realize that without the physical and/or biological evidence to corroborate the circumstances, the courts will not be able to obtain a conviction. Equally important is that meticulous evidence collection can ensure that suspects are not falsely accused of a crime they did not commit.

As the public demands more conclusive evidence than oral testimony in cases of sexual violence, the succinct recovery and preservation of evidence will protect the legal, civil, and human rights of both the victim and the accused. Forensic evidence is needed to substantiate and support the prosecutor's claim, to exonerate a defendant who has been falsely accused, to aid the defendant against jury sentiment in favor of the prosecution, and to establish public confidence in the courts to accurately determine the guilt or innocence of the defendant.

Resources

WEBSITES

American Institute of Forensic Education
www.taife.com
International Association of Forensic Nurses
www.iafn.org
University of California, Riverside
Forensic Nursing Certificate Program
www.ilearn.ucr.edu

References

American College of Emergency Physicians (ACEP). (1999). *Evaluation and management of the sexually assaulted or sexually abused patient.* Dallas, TX: Author.

American Nurses Association. (2009). *Forensic nursing scope and standards.* Washington, DC: American Nurses Publishing. Silver Spring, MD.

Anderson, S., McClain, N., & Riviello, R.J. (2006). Genital findings of women after consensual and nonconsensual intercourse. *Journal of Forensic Nursing, 2*(2), 59–65.

Bjerke, N. B. (2004). The evolution: Handwashing to hand hygiene guidance. *Crit Care Nurs Q 27*(3), 295–307.

Child Abuse Prevention and Treatment Act. (CAPTA, Revised, 1996), 42 U.S.C. 5101, et.seq. (P.L. 104-235.)

Dolinak, D., Matshes, E., & Lew, E. (2005). *Forensic pathology, principles and practice.* pg. 128.

Ferrell, J. (1995). Foley catheter balloon technique for visualizing the hymen in female adolescent sexual abuse victims. *Journal of Emergency Nursing, 21*(6), 585–586.

Ferrell, J. (2007). *Forensic aspects of emergency nursing, emergency nursing core curriculum* (6th ed., pp. 1025–1032). St Louis, Saunders.

Finch, S. (2007). *The times picayune.* New Orleans, LA (http://nl.newsbank.com/sites/tp/ Viewed July 10, 2009.)

Gilson, J. A., (2002). The Virginia Supreme Court Case: Forensic Nursing Comes of Age. *On the Edge.* 8(2), Summer.

Hazelwood, R., & Burgess, A. (2009). *Practical aspects of rape investigation* (4th ed.). Boca Raton, FL: CRC Press.

Henry, T. (2003). *Lip swabs, floss, effective for collecting DNA evidence.* On the edge. International Association of Forensic Nurses. 9(1).

Hochmeister, M., & Ferrell, J. (1998). *Sexual assault: The health care response A complete guide to the forensic examination and evidence collection of the adult sexual assault patient (video tape).* Institute of Legal Medicine University of Bern.

International Association Forensic Nurses. (2009). *Forensic nursing scope and standards of practice.* Arnold, MD: American Nurses Publishing. Silver Spring, MD.

Jones, J., Dunnuck, C., Rossman, L., Wynn, B., & Nelson-Horan, C. (2004). Significance of toluidine blue positive findings after speculum examination for sexual assault. *American Journal of Emergency Medicine, 2*(3), 201–203.

Klingle, C. & Reiter, K. (2008). *Evidence Technology Magazine.* 4(2), 34–37.

LeBeau, M., Andollo, W., Hearn, W. L., et al. (1999). Recommendations for toxicological investigations of drug-facilitated sexual assaults. *J Forensic Science, 44*(1), 227–230.

Le Beau, M., Mozayani, A., et al. (2001). *Drug-facilitated sexual assault a forensic handbook.* Academic Press. London UK.

Lee, H., & Harris, H. (2000). *Physical evidence in forensic science.* Tucson, AZ: Lawyers & Judges Publishing.

Lynch, V., & Duval, J. (2006). *Forensic nursing.* St. Louis: Mosby.

Lynch, V., & Ferrell, J. (2006). *Forensic medical records. Medical legal aspects of medical records* (pp. 807–843) Tucson, AZ: Lawyers & Judges Publishing.

Lynch, V. (2000). *Clinical forensic nursing: A new perspective in trauma.* Bearhawk Consulting Group. Ft. Collins, CO.

McCann, J., & Kerns, D. (1999). *The anatomy of child and adolescent sexual abuse.* CD-ROM Atlas: Intercorp. St. Louis.

McCauley, J., Gorman, R. L., & Guzinski, G. (1986). Toluidine blue in the detection of perineal lacerations in pediatric and adolescent sexual abuse victims. *Pediatrics, 78*(6), 1039–1043.

McClintock, J. T. (2008). *Forensic DNA analysis: A laboratory manual,* Boca Raton, FL: CRC Press, pp. 3–6.

National Institute of Justice. (2004a). *Crime scene investigation: A reference for law enforcement training.* Washington, DC: US Department of Justice, Office of Justice Programs.

National Institute of Justice. (2004b). *What every law enforcement officer should know about DNA.* Washington, DC: National Commission on the Future of DNA Evidence.

Occupational Safety and Health Administration (OSHA). (2008). *Bloodborne pathogens.* Washington, DC: United States Department of Labor Regulations -29 CFR, 1910–1030.

Olshaker, J., Jackson, M., & Smock, W. (2007). *Forensic emergency medicine.* (2nd ed.). Philadelphia: Lippincott Williams & Wilkins.

Spiller, H.A., Rogers, J., and Sawyer, T.S. (2007). Drug facilitated sexual assault using an over-the-counter ocular solution containing tetrahydrozoline (Visine®). *Legal medicine, 45,* 782–786.

Spitz, W. U., Spitz, D. J., and Fisher, R. S. (2006). *Medicolegal investigation of death.* 4th ed. Charles C. Thomas: Springfield, IL.

The Joint Commission. (2009). *Comprehensive accreditation manual for hospitals (CAMH): The official handbook.* Oakbrook Terrace, IL.

Velasquez v. the Commonwealth of Virginia, (2002) 35 Va. App. 189, 196, 543 S.E.2d 631, 635 (2001).

Catherine M. Dougherty

Forensic Focus in the Emergency Department

The first article to appear in U.S. emergency medicine literature regarding forensic medicine in the emergency department came in 1983 (Smialek, 1983). In *Emergency Medicine Clinics of North America,* Smialek stated, "medical care of the critically ill in the emergency department has a significant impact on the practice of forensic medicine. Many victims of homicide or accidents receive some degree of medical or surgical treatment prior to expiration." Smialek recognized that evidence, necessary to accurately reconstruct the event, prove guilt, or establish innocence, was disappearing in the emergency department. This evidence was being destroyed, either by commission or omission, in the provision of patient care. That same year, Roger Mittleman, a medical examiner for Dade County; Hollace Goldberg, an emergency nurse; and David Waksman, a state attorney for Florida, published "Preserving Evidence in the Emergency Department" in the *American Journal of Nursing* (Mittleman, 1983). This article emphasized the importance of recognizing and preserving evidence on patients presenting to the emergency department.

The need for nurses to be involved in evidence collection in the emergency department was first mentioned in literature in 1986. Harry C. MacNamara, the chief medical examiner for Ulster County, New York, proposed to provide forensic training to emergency nurses and physicians. Principally, MacNamara recognized that evidence was being destroyed or discarded; wounds were being cleaned, repaired, and surgically altered without adequate description or documentation; and statements in records were being recorded without factual basis (MacNamara, 1986). These factors often complicated the work of the medical examiner and created ambiguity and confusion within courts of law. Richard Carmona, a trauma surgeon and U.S. Surgeon General, reported that a review of 100 charts of trauma patients who presented to a level 1 trauma center in California revealed poor, improper, or inadequate documentation in 70% of the cases. Additionally, in 38% of cases potential evidence was improperly secured, improperly documented, or inadvertently discarded (Carmona & Prince, 1989). The message from the medical and law enforcement communities was clear: a patient's evaluation must be adequately documented narratively, diagrammatically, and photographically, in the patient's chart for possible use in future legal actions. The failure to do so may have far-ranging consequences for the hospital, the patient, the accused, and potentially the treating physician. The Emergency Nurses Association (ENA) acted promptly to formally define the role of nurses in evidence collection and initiated special education and training for its members. However, even now, the American College of Emergency Physicians (ACEP) has not issued a position statement regarding the role of forensic physicians or police surgeons in emergency departments (EDs) in the United States. Even so, the organization has issued forensic policy statements and training guidelines related to evidence collection in cases of sexual assault and has recommended that residency curricula include training in the recognition, assessment, and interventions in child abuse (ACEP, 2000). The ACEP also acknowledges the benefits of sexual assault nurse examiners (SANEs) and strongly supports their use in the emergency department for the benefit of patient care.

EMERGENCY NURSING ADOPTS FORENSIC ROLE

An article titled "Forensic Nursing in the Emergency Department: A New Role for the 1990s" charted the course for forensic nursing during the 1990s (Lynch, 1991). Lynch recommended the inclusion of forensic nurse examiners (FNEs) as a functional component of emergency department care. In addition to performing sexual assault examinations, these nursing specialists would provide other services such as formal assessments for abuse and neglect, forensic photography, wound identification, evidence collection, and expert testimony.

In October 1998, the U.S. ENA initially issued its position statement that clearly outlined the responsibilities of ED nurses in evidence collection. The most recent revision of this document was approved by the ENA board of directors in 2003. The position statement clearly states that performance of forensic procedures is a component of emergency nursing practice (ENA, 2003).

By the time that the ANA's Congress of Nursing Practice recognized forensic nursing as a unique and specialized area of nursing in 1995, many emergency nurses had already been expressing their interest in this new specialty and were seeking ways to educate themselves in forensic theory and practice. They were enrolling in postgraduate courses, participating in online offerings, and attending workshops and professional meetings to learn more about forensic nursing. Motivated by personal goals and enticed by a desire to participate in an exciting, challenging new area of clinical practice, nurses pursued forensic education.

In some states, forensic nursing practice is being driven by local, state, or federal agencies, and sometimes pressure or support from advocacy groups. The state of Texas recently passed legislation with provisions for mandatory forensic education for nurses working in the ED as well as for medical students. In 2007, Connecticut considered legislation that would require the state's 31 acute care hospitals to make forensic nursing services available to patients. Additionally, The Joint Commission (TJC) also has established guidance that states that hospitals must educate their staff regarding the identification of forensic patients and have policies and procedures in place to ensure that they are properly managed and referred to ensure their human rights. This includes the collection and preservation of forensic evidence (TJC, 2009)

KEY POINT The Joint Commission guidelines emphasize that patient assessment must be conducted within the context of the requirements of the law to preserve evidentiary materials and support future legal actions (TJC, 2009).

A study published in the *National Institute of Justice Journal* (NIJ, 2009) demonstrated that jurors sitting on criminal cases fed nightly on both fictional and reality television shows about forensic science have developed an awareness and
- 46% expected to see some kind of scientific evidence in *every* criminal case.
- 22% expected to see DNA in *every* criminal case.
- 36% expected to see fingerprint evidence in *every* criminal case.
- 32% expected to see ballistics or other firearms laboratory evidence in *every* criminal case.

In forensic nursing literature, you will find many experts advocating the use of specially trained and educated nurses, commonly referred to as FNEs, to do the work of identifying, collecting, and preserving forensic evidence. This is a sound proposal, but in reality, it is not always practical. When human resources and economic resources are constrained, hospital administration is reluctant to create new positions and expand services within the facility. As a consequence, all nurses are expected to have basic understandings about forensic patients and the issues related to the recognition and preservation of evidence. The Joint Commission, the legal system, and the public have affirmed their expectations that healthcare personnel must behave in a responsible manner when caring for victims and suspects of crime. The explosion in "*CSI*" media has fueled the public's expectation of forensic science's role in the outcome of legal proceedings. The criminal cases presented emphasize that successes and failures for both the prosecution and the defense rest squarely on the shoulders of those responsible for the collection and custody of forensic evidence.

Forensic Patients in the Emergency Department

The ED is the portal that funnels victims and perpetrators of violent crimes into the healthcare system. These and many others who enter for care are, by definition, *forensic patients.* Hoyt (1999) suggested that a forensic patient is any client or that person's significant others whose nursing problems bring him or her into actual or potential interaction with the legal system. Further, according to Pasqualone's research, a large number of emergency department patients require collection and preservation of evidence (Pasqualone, 1998).

KEY POINT Transitory and sometimes crucial evidence may be overlooked, lost, or destroyed if caregivers fail to recognize those individuals who are *forensic patients.*

Pasqualone determined that there were at least 24 types of forensic categories among patients seen in one community hospital ED. Pasqualone's 60-day survey of 914 patients presenting to that hospital's ED revealed that 27% were forensic patients. She identified the following categories of patients:

1. *Occupational injuries.* Typically, at a minimum, patients referred to the ED for treatment of occupational injuries are required to provide a urine specimen for toxicology. These specimens must be handled using strict chain of custody to protect both the injured employee and the employer.
2. *Transportation injuries.* Transportation injuries can run the gamut from a pedestrian struck to the mass disaster scene of a derailed train, all of which will undoubtedly have interaction with the law.
3. *Substance abuse.* Substance abuse with all its inherent medical complications also carries with it potential for legal involvement secondary to the illegal use of scheduled drugs or buying and selling of these drugs.
4. *Personal injury.* Attempts at or succeeding in taking one's life is not illegal but is often considered to be a criminal case.
5. *Child abuse and neglect.* Any suspicion of these acts is reportable by law.
6. *Forensic psychiatric admission.* Psychiatric patients who may be sent to psychiatric facilities by order of protection or otherwise involuntarily must have their rights protected.
7. *Environmental hazards.* Cases of environmental hazards such as exposure to hazardous waste may result in the endangerment of an individual or community's health and may be subject to jurisdiction according to the U.S. Environmental Protection Agency's Resource Conservation and Recovery Act.
8. *Assault and battery.* Interpersonal violence is familiar to ED personnel and often requires police involvement. Knowledge of local and state laws is of paramount importance in dealing with these patients.
9. *Abuse of the disabled.* Abuse or neglect of any disabled individual may necessitate legal intervention.
10. *Human and animal bites.* Human bites often constitute a form of interpersonal violence, and animal bites may require public health surveillance as well as involve animal control.
11. *Questioned death cases.* Any death within less than 24 hours of hospitalization becomes a medical examiner case and will require special handling of the body.
12. *Elder abuse and neglect.* Many states have mandatory reporting requirements that protect the elderly.
13. *Domestic violence.* Laws vary from state to state as to how domestic violence is handled and reported.
14. *Clients in police custody.* Patients in custody requiring restraint provide a challenge for the practitioner. Consider the effects that stressors, legal medication, and drugs of abuse have on the cardiovascular system, which puts these patients at risk for death by excited delirium syndrome.
15. *Sexual assault.* Forensic nurses have been identifying, collecting, and preserving evidence from sexual assault victims for years.
16. *Sharp force injuries.* Sharp force injuries can range from the stab wounds of interpersonal injuries to impalement by a javelin at a high school track meet.
17. *Product liability.* Products representing a potential public health hazard may be subject to multiple federal statutes.
18. *Transcultural medical practices.* Many cultures in the United States use methods of healing that may mimic abuse, such as cupping or coining. Use of these practices may, in fact, constitute abuse in some states.
19. *Organ and tissue donation.* All deaths in hospitals must be reported to local or regional organ/tissue banks to ensure that

survivors have the right to donate organs or tissues if that is their wish.

20. *Burns over 5% body surface area.* Burns involving 5% or more of body surface area must be investigated thoroughly to determine if there was intentional harm or possibly product liability.

21. *Firearm injuries.* In many states every firearm injury, even accidental, must be reported to local police.

22. *Food and drug tampering.* Any threat to the general public may be considered a federal offense as well as a public health issue.

23. *Gang violence.* Any incident of gang violence may be treated as organized crime.

24. *Malpractice or negligence.* An obvious legal term with legal consequences, any findings of malpractice or neglect must be carefully handled.

Although this is by no means an exhaustive list, it highlights the most common forensic presentations to the ED. It is imperative that the emergency nurse understands the various classifications of forensic patients to ensure that forensic evidence is identified and properly managed. For a complete summary of Pasqualone's quantitative findings, see Table 14-1.

Table 14-1 Percentages of Forensic Categories Seen at a Community Hospital Emergency Department

SAMPLE POPULATION BASED ON A 60-DAY SURVEY (N = 3436)		
914 PATIENTS (27%) QUALIFIED AS FORENSIC CASES		
FORENSIC CATEGORY	**FREQUENCY**	**PERCENTAGE (%)**
Occupation-related injuries	289	8.41
Transportation injuries	193	5.62
Substance abuse	160	4.66
Personal injury	125	3.64
Child abuse and neglect	464 per year	2.06*
Forensic psychology	49	1.43
Environmental hazards	25	0.73
Assault and battery	22	0.64
Abuse of the disabled	130 per year	0.58*
Human and animal bites	90 per year	0.40*
Questioned death cases	10	0.29
Elder abuse and neglect	56 per year	0.25*
Domestic violence	6	0.17
Clients in police custody	2	0.06
Sexual assault	2	0.06
Sharp force injuries	7 per year	0.03*
Product liability	1	0.03
Transcultural medical practices	1	0.03
Organ and tissue donation	6 per year	0.03*
Burns >5% BSA (body surface area)	3 per year	0.01*
Firearm injuries	7 per 3 years	0.01*
Food and drug tampering	0	
Gang violence	0	
Malpractice and/or negligence	0	

*Data based on a yearly ED population of 22,500.
From Pasqualone, G. (1998). An examination of forensic categories among patients seen at a community hospital emergency department. Unpublished master's thesis, Fitchburg State College, Fitchburg, MA.

Evidence Recovery Processes

Once the nurse has identified a forensic patient, directions for a systematic approach to the identification, collection, and preservation of evidence must be in place. Any shortsightedness can usually be avoided if the nurse follows established hospital policies and protocols, which are based on the principles of forensic science as well as the recommendations of law enforcement, legal counsel, and the medical examiner or coroner.

EVIDENCE DEFINED

What is evidence? The word *evidence* can have many meanings. In the usual everyday use of the word, it is something that tends to prove, that which makes another thing evident. It is facts and data. In relation to the law, evidence may be the statement of a witness, the testimony of an ED nurse, or an object that bears on or establishes a point in question. There are several distinct types of evidence. Examples include admissible, circumstantial, documentary, and real evidence. For the purposes of this section, the discussion will be limited to physical evidence. Physical evidence is any matter, material, or condition, large or small, solid, liquid, or gas, that may be used to determine facts in a given situation. Therefore, items such as clothing, hair, nails, bullets, contusions, lacerations, and other wounds are classified as physical evidence. What is critical in medicolegal cases is to ensure that any and all evidence is appropriately managed using precise forensic procedures. Physical evidence is the concern of the criminalist who will identify and analyze the materials submitted to the crime laboratory. For the evidence to be used, it is imperative that it has been properly collected and preserved. It is hoped that the evidence will link a victim to a suspect, link a suspect to a crime scene, identify an assailant, establish an element of a crime, or corroborate or disprove an alibi.

Emergency personnel need to understand the legal procedures required in handling physical evidence, the types of physical evidence, and the value of that evidence. They must also know proper methods for collecting, documenting, and preserving forensic evidence. Education should include the identification of specific wounds and how their interpretation may provide critical information regarding the type of weapon and circumstances surrounding the injury. In the absence of a specially educated forensic physician or nurse clinician, potential liability exists. Search and seizure become complex. It is recommended that healthcare professionals seek legal counsel or information about forensic procedures when questions arise concerning the legality of evidence recovery. Once medical personnel are taught the value of physical evidence and the proper procedures for handling it, they generally support police requests for assistance and do not inadvertently hinder progress of the investigation.

Most trauma EDs have some type of cooperative program established with the local police when evidence collection is required. However, many rural or smaller EDs do not handle evidence collection often and therefore may not be aware of the specifics regarding recovery and documentation. Forensically trained nurses can assist patients and other ED personnel by sharing their education and training and by assisting in the development of policies, procedures, and protocols for other facilities. It is recommended that the forensically trained nurse work in conjunction with the local crime lab and district attorney's office to ensure strict compliance to guidelines within the jurisdiction.

KEY POINT The emergency nurse must ensure that lifesaving care is the first priority; resuscitation can usually be accomplished with minimal compromise of forensic evidence.

Establishing Priorities

A forensic patient is first and foremost a patient, and caring for the physiological and psychological needs of the patient are paramount. Airway, breathing, and circulation are the first order of business but can usually be addressed with minimal loss of evidence. Being prepared and equipped to identify, collect, and preserve evidence will enable the nurse to act quickly and efficiently and to provide nursing care while maintaining medicolegal standards protecting the patient's civil and human rights.

Forensic Examinations in the Emergency Department

SPACE AND EQUIPMENT CONSIDERATIONS

Unfortunately, few emergency departments have a dedicated room for forensic examinations and evidence collection. Obviously when other nonforensic patients share the space with those requiring evidentiary examinations, there is a risk of "foreign" biological materials that could potentially confuse findings in evidentiary specimens. Hair, clothes fibers, body fluids on surfaces of an exam table, or any materials left behind by previous patients could be problematic. To avoid concerns about cross-contamination of evidence, the nurse ensures that all items from a previous patient's care and treatment are removed from the room. This includes the emptying of all trash containers and linen receptacles (Barber Duval, 2006).

Efficiency demands that all supplies needed for forensic patients be easily available to the nurse. See item 12 in Box 14-1 (Eisert, et al., 2009).

EVIDENCE COLLECTION GUIDELINES

Patients who are victims of violent crime must be protected and made to feel secure. Access to the patient must be controlled. Policies and procedures should ensure that visitors are required to check in with the primary nurse or law enforcement officer, and all visitations must be documented. Some EDs have sophisticated airport-like screening procedures and devices to ensure a safe environment. Assigning a Jane or John Doe name to the patient may also protect the patient from information being given out inadvertently.

Evaluate all potential physical evidence. Remember to initially focus on any evidence that could be lost or altered with time or treatment and collect the least transient evidence later. Informed consent may be required for evidence collection. Explain the procedures and the associated rationale before requesting signatures from patients or their representative.

When all necessary supplies are assembled, the nurse should don a gown, gloves, and any other protective equipment deemed necessary to prevent occupational exposure and evidence contamination. Gloves should be changed frequently during the evidence collection processes to prevent cross-contamination.

If the patient is physically able and can cooperate, place two sheets on the floor, one on top of the other. Instruct the patient to stand in the center of the sheet and remove clothing, one article at a time. During this process, in addition to assessing for injuries, certain observations can be made about the patient's mental status, physical coordination, and functional capabilities. For example, is the patient moving reported injured body parts without distress?

Each article of clothing should be placed on a distinct part of the sheet, avoiding any overlap of garments. Bag each article separately, if deemed necessary. After the clothing is secured, fold the top sheet inward on itself and package in a separate bag. The sheet beneath merely protects the top sheet from any debris on the floor that may contaminate the clothing.

If the patient is unconscious or severely ill or injured and cannot assist in removing clothing, the nurse must remove clothing from the patient, maintaining as much garment integrity as possible. Do not shake the clothing. When cutting garments from a patient, do not cut through defects in the clothing such as bullet holes, tears, or stab entry areas. Package and label as appropriate any linen that has come in direct content with the patient (e.g., top and bottom sheets, emergency medical services [EMS] stretcher covers, pillowcases). The greatest universal error made by ED staff during treatment of a trauma case is throwing clothing on the floor in the trauma room. This egregious error results in the cross-contamination of critical evidence as it comes in contact with debris such as hair, fibers, dust, drops of solutions, soil, and other contaminants, as well as blood and bodily fluids, commonly present during emergency trauma treatment. Consider what may be tracked into the hospital and into the trauma unit on the soles of the paramedics directly from the crime scene. Is the evidence adhering to the clothing from the victim, the perpetrator, from the first responders or the doctors and nurses within the trauma environs?

Observe patient for general hygiene, posture, eye contact, and demeanor. Accept any offered explanation about causation of marks, injuries, or general condition and record without further discussion.

Begin a systematic head-to-toe exam of the patient. Have forensic supplies nearby including body diagrams, ABFO ruler, and camera equipment if consent for photographs has been obtained.

At this point, if it is appropriate, use a Wood's lamp or other alternate light source (ALS) to look for body fluids. If the light source reveals organic material on the body, these areas should be swabbed for the potential recovery of biological sources of DNA. Under ideal situations, the ultraviolet or other light source will pick up both wet and dried secretions; however, swab any specific areas that the patient has suggested as having contact with foreign fluids such as semen, blood, saliva, urine, or excrement. Document all identified evidence and collection sites on the body diagram as well as within the narrative notes. The forensic examination is invasive to personal privacy and may be embarrassing for some patients. The nurse should provide the patient with a sheet or towels to drape individual body parts during the examination. A forensic examination typically requires examination of the body, head to toe. If any area or part is not addressed in the examination, the rationale should be annotated in the clinical chart.

HEAD-TO-TOE EXAMINATION PROCESS

Take your time and begin the exam with the head and neck, then extremities, trunk, and finally genitalia. Document each physical finding on the body diagram and in narrative notes, giving precise descriptions of the size, orientation, and characteristics of soft-tissue defects. Record the presence of old scars, tattoos, or piercings. Use descriptive language such as "3-centimeter laceration lateral to, and 1 centimeter inferior to, the left nipple." Avoid use of any terminology with which you are not absolutely familiar. If you do not know the distinctions between Battle's sign and raccoon's eyes, merely describe what is visualized. The inclusion of improper terms can create unnecessary controversy in courtroom proceedings and may even undermine the credibility of the forensic examination. Do not attempt to "age" bruises. Again, describe

Box 14-1 Forensic Evidence Collection Guidelines

Model "Forensic Evidence Collection Guidelines for the Emergency Department" were developed for the York Hospital WellSpan Health System, York, Pennsylvania, by Eisert, P. (PI), Eldredge, K., Hartlaub, T., Huggins, E., Keirn, G., O'Brien, P., Rozzi, H., Pugh, L., & March, K.

I. Purpose
   A. To establish guidelines in the collection and handling of forensic evidence from patients who have gunshot or stab wounds, or were assaulted, requiring treatment in the emergency department.
II. Guideline Statement
   A. The medical needs of the patient are paramount. The next concern, however, must be the recognition, collection, and proper handling of forensic evidence from patients that received gunshot or stab wounds, or were severely assaulted. These are guidelines for the collection and handling of forensic evidence.
III. Equipment
   A. Forensic Evidence Collection Kit
   B. Containers for Clothing
IV. Procedure
   1. Evidence Collection
      A. General Recommendations
         a. Always wear gloves and other personal protective equipment, as appropriate, when handling evidence.[1,4,8,9,10,12,15,16,22]
         b. Change gloves frequently (when possible) to prevent cross contamination.[10]
         c. Clothing/ personal items should not be given to family or friends.[3,11,16]
         d. Place each piece of evidence in separate paper bag or bindle (piece of folded paper) and label with patient's name, collector's name, date/time of collection, contents and where it came from.
         e. Dry all specimens before sealing the package.[4,12]
         f. Do not lick envelopes to seal. Moisten them with a gloved finger or use patient label.[12]
         g. Bags/envelopes/containers should be sealed with evidence tape and labeled with patient's name, the date and time, and printed name and signature of person collecting and securing evidence.[14]
         h. Do not staple bags closed.[16]
         i. Body cavity searches, if requested by law enforcement, should be done by physicians and must be fully documented with the signature of the physician and accomplished in front of a witness the same gender of the patient.[16]
   2. Assessment
      A. All patients who are victims of violence, or suspected victims of violence, should be completely undressed and all body surfaces assessed.[1]
         a. Wear personal protective equipment.
         b. Assess the patient head-to-toe.[1]
         c. Collect evidence and document per the below guidelines.
   3. Body Fluids
      A. Blood
         a. Wear personal protective equipment.
         b. Draw red-,[16] purple-,[1,16,20] and gray-[1,16,20] topped blood tubes and label with patient's name, collector's name, date/time of collection. Blood tubes are to be placed in an envelope labeled with patient's name, collector's name, date/time of collection, sealed, and chain of custody followed as it is transferred to the lab. This blood work should be drawn on all gunshot and stabbing victims, and assaults that are life threatening.
            i. Draw labs prior to transfusion of blood products, because it alters DNA for several months post-transfusion.[24]
         c. Use Povidone-iodine to prepare the venipuncture site; do not use alcohol.[16]
         d. Circle venipuncture sites.[11]
         e. Follow the chain of custody.
   4. Bullets
      A. General
         a. Wear personal protective equipment.
         b. Handle bullets, pellets, wadding, or casings with rubber-tipped forceps or regular forceps with gauze over ends to prevent marking.[1,4,9,11,12,15,16,17,24] Do not mark any bullet fragments.[1,4,9,11,12]

c. Do not place in metal container.[15]
d. Store in a plastic specimen cup with gauze. If wet, allow to air-dry before sealing lid, then close and seal with evidence tape, printed name and signature of collector, and date. Place patient identifier on container. Document location of the recovered bullet (e.g., left shoulder) on container. One bullet per container.
e. If any trace evidence exists around the wound, follow the trace evidence recommendations (section #10).
f. Follow the chain of custody.
   5. Chain of Custody/Evidence
      A. General
         a. Use the chain-of-custody/evidence form when handling any evidence.[1-4,6-13,17] This procedure ensures that evidence is always accounted for.
         b. Keep the chain of custody as short as possible.[1,2,7,12]
         c. Patient Information
            i. Name
            ii. Patient medical record number and/or trauma identification number
         d. Name of person collecting evidence (printed and signature)
         e. Transferring of evidence
            i. Name of person releasing and receiving evidence (printed and signature).[2,7,8,11]
            ii. If law enforcement is receiving the evidence, they must also include their badge number.[2,7,8,11]
         f. Evidence cannot be left unattended and must be in plain view of the collector. If it cannot be observed, it must be secured in a locked area.[4,7,9]
         g. If evidence is secured, it must be reflected on the chain-of-custody/ evidence form.
         h. The chain-of-custody/evidence form must follow the evidence.
            i. The original copy (white sheet) accompanies the evidence when transferred to law enforcement.
            ii. The second sheet (yellow) is to be maintained in the patient's medical record.
            iii. The third sheet (pink) is to be sent to Hospital Security. (When evidence is transferred directly to Hospital Security, keep the white and pink sheets together.)
   6. Clothing
      A. General
         a. Clothing can be of critical importance in the investigation of a crime.
      B. Handling and Collection
         a. Wear personal protective equipment.
         b. Cut clothing along the seams if possible. Avoid cutting through holes, tears, or stains.[1-5,7,8,11,15,16]
         c. Do NOT place clothing on floor because it will become cross-contaminated.[3,11,15,17]
         d. Place two clean sheets on the floor to place clothing until it can be bagged.[3,9,12,9,16] The top clean sheet is submitted into evidence, as debris may have fallen onto it.[3,9,12,16] The bottom sheet can be placed in hospital laundry. Due to space limitations, a sheet-lined cardboard box or paper bag can be substituted for the sheet method (described above) until it can be bagged.
         e. Include sheet under patient (gurney sheet) as evidence.[3,9,16]
         f. Do not shake clothing out.[1,3,16]
         g. DRY: Place each piece of clothing in separate PAPER bags and seal with evidence tape.[1-12,15,16,17,22] Document the patient's name and hospital identification number (patient sticker), content, signature and printed name of collector, date and time.
         h. WET: Place each piece of clothing in separate PAPER bags and then place in plastic biohazard bag. Do NOT close the plastic bag, because moisture will cause fungal growth. Leave the plastic bag OPEN, notify the police as soon as possible and inform them the clothing is wet.[1,7,9,15,16,17] Document the patient's name and hospital identification number (Patient sticker), content, signature and printed name of collector, date and time.

(Continued)

Box 14-1 Forensic Evidence Collection Guidelines—cont'd

    i. Footwear can be valuable evidence and each shoe is to be placed in separate paper bags and handled like clothing.[7]

    j. Follow the chain of custody.

7. Documentation

  A. Patient History

    a. Use exact words, quotations.[4,7-9,11-13,16,17] "Excited utterances" can be admitted to court.[7]

    b. The patient's statements should be accurately reproduced, unedited, and unsanitized.[7,8]

    c. Use the name of the alleged perpetrator, if named by patient.[7]

    d. When documenting the patient history, use terms such as patient "states" or "reports," opposed to "patient alleges." Avoid phrases such as "patient refuses," instead, use "patient declines."

  B. Physical Assessment

    a. Wear personal protective equipment.

    b. All documentation needs to be legible![4,7]

    c. If body maps are used they should convey location and type of injury.[1,3,12]

    d. Document location, size, and appearance of defects before they are altered by time or medical intervention.[1,3,10,17] If a medical intervention altered a wound, document it.[9]

    e. Use landmarks to note location, not other wounds.[1]

    f. Do not document "entrance" or "exit" wound.[1,4,9,12,13,17]

    g. Document observable patterns.[2]

    h. If the patient is a victim of a gunshot, note the presence/absence of gunshot residue (powder, soot, particles, and/or small punctuate hemorrhages.)[3,5,6,11]

    i. Document appearance of patient on arrival (e.g., tearful, makes no eye contact, clothes torn).[3,8]

    j. Note any unusual odors.[8]

    k. Note patient's behavior, attitude, preoccupation with items or persons.[8,17]

    l. Follow the chain of custody.

8. Gunshot Residue (GSR)

  A. General

    a. Documentation should note the presence/absence of gunshot residue (powder, soot, particles, and/or small punctuate hemorrhages). [3,5,6,11]

    b. If a dressing was applied in the field, save it as evidence.

    c. If possible, photograph GSR before/after intervention.[4,5]

    d. Do not wash away GSR until photographed, unless absolutely necessary.[5]

    e. Follow the chain of custody.

9. Photography

  A. Obtain consent for photography.[1,4,7,12,14,16]

  B. Take photos as soon as patient is medically stable[1,4,15] or as treatment allows.

    a. Photograph patient's ID (patient sticker)[7] and photographer's ID badge.

    b. Get picture of patient (face and body shot).[1,12]

    c. If possible, photograph each individual wound. First, take an orientation photo (identifying body part), followed by a close-up of the injury with and without a scale.[1,4,7,8,12,15,16] An ABFO scale or tape measure are ideal, but anything that can be used to determine size comparison, e.g., coin, or syringe without needle, may be utilized. It may not be possible to use a scale in every case.

    d. Photograph injuries before/after intervention.[2,4,7,11,16]

    e. Photographs are best if they are taken at a 90 degree angle.[4]

    f. Photograph any evidence that can be destroyed or changed.[14]

    g. Photographs are part of the medical record and should not go with police.[16]

    h. After photographing the injuries, remove the memory card and place in an envelope with the name of the photographer, the patient's name and medical number, date and time. Notify the SAFE Team and

SAFE Team member will download the pictures to a CD and maintain it with their forensic records.

    i. The camera and extra memory cards are kept in the trauma bay pyxis.

    ii. Follow the chain of custody.

10. Trace Evidence

  A. General

    a. The skin is the most important organ of the body for forensic evidence.[4]

    b. Evidence should be collected before medical intervention if possible.[4]

  B. Collection

    a. Wear personal protective equipment.

    b. Assess patient head-to-toe.[1]

    c. Examine the patient for any trace evidence (e.g., vegetation, paint chips).

    d. Evidence should be placed in a paper bindle, then sealed in an envelope with patient name and ID (patient sticker), collector's name and signature, date and time.[2,4,12,17]

    e. Trace evidence, such as hair, fiber, or paint chips, can be lifted with transparent tape and then taped directly to the bindle, then sealed in an envelope with patient name and ID (patient sticker), collector's name and signature, date and time.[2,4,12,17]

    f. Include sheet under patient (gurney sheet) as evidence.[3,9,16]

    g. Document where trace evidence was found.

    h. Dried secretions, such as saliva, can be obtained with a moistened swab (sterile water).[4,12]

    i. Swab any area that has body secretions not obviously explained by the patient's injuries.[9]

    j. Dry swabs at room temperature,[2,4,10] then seal in an envelope with patient name and ID (patient sticker), collector's name and signature, date and time.[2,4,12,17]

    k. Follow the chain of custody.

11. Weapons

  A. General

    a. Use care when handling any weapons.

    b. Give weapons to police. If they are not immediately available, transfer to a security officer until police are available. Use a chain-of-custody form with any transfers. (If a weapon is legally registered to a patient and not related to a crime, security retains until they are discharged.)[11]

  B. Collection

    a. Wear personal protective equipment.

    b. Weapons should be placed in a large rigid specimen container or get police to receive it immediately.[11]

    c. Follow the chain of custody.

12. Forensic Kit

  A. Four forensic kits are to be maintained, one for each trauma bay and a fourth in reserve.

  B. Contents

    a. ABFO scale (1)

    b. Bindles (2)

    c. Blank labels (12)

    d. Box (appropriate size for knife or handgun)

    e. Chain-of-Custody forms (2)

    f. Cotton swabs (4)

    g. Envelopes (8, one for each bindle and cotton swabs)

    h. Evidence tape (1 roll)

    i. Gauze, 2×2 (4)

    j. Marker (1, for labeling bags)

    k. Paper bags, large, grocery style (2)

    l. Paper bags, small, lunch style (4)

    m. Purple-top blood collection tubes (2)

    n. Specimen cups (2)

    o. Sterile water (1, for moistening swabs for dried secretions)

    p. Styrofoam cups (4, can be used to hold swabs while drying)

    q. Transparent tape (1 roll)

Box 14-1 Forensic Evidence Collection Guidelines—cont'd

Chain of Custody/Evidence

Patient Name _____

Medical Record Number and/or Trauma ID_____

Check YES or NO for all items (if no, explain)

Photographs:	☐ YES	☐ NO_____
Clothing (list): Shirt/Blouse	☐ YES	☐ NO_____
Pants/Slacks	☐ YES	☐ NO_____
Bra	☐ YES	☐ NO_____
Underpants	☐ YES	☐ NO_____
Jacket/Coat	☐ YES	☐ NO_____
Shoes	☐ YES	☐ NO_____
Socks	☐ YES	☐ NO_____
Other	☐ YES	☐ NO_____

Other Evidence: _____

_____

Collector: Printed name & signature   Date   Time

Transferred to (print)_____

Signature of receiving person/badge number   Date   Time
Transferred to (print)_____

Signature of receiving person/badge number   Date   Time
Transferred to (print)_____

Signature of receiving person/badge number   Date   Time
Transferred to (print)_____

Signature of receiving person/badge number   Date   Time

Patient Label

White copy—Law Enforcement Yellow copy—Patient Medical Record Pink Copy—Hospital Security

Courtesy York Hospital, York, PA.

Guideline References

[1] Assid, PA. (2005). Evidence collection and documentation: Are you prepared to be a medical detective? *Topics in Emergency Medicine*, 27:15–26.

[2] Meserve, KL. (1992). Preserving medicolegal evidence: A guide for emergency care providers. *Journal of Emergency Nursing*, 18:120–123.

[3] Lynch, VA. (1995). Clinical Forensic Nursing: A new perspective in the management of crime victims from trauma to trial. *Critical Care Nursing Clinics of North America*, 7:489–507.

[4] Brown, K. Evidence collection and preservation in a healthcare setting. Nursing Spectrum Continuing Education. Available at: http//:nurse.com/ce/print.html?CCID=4249. Accessed January 29, 2008.

[5] Pavlik, KA. The importance of gunshot residue. Forensic Nurse Magazine. Available at: http//:forensicnursemag.com/FNCategories/ClinicalForensicNursing/511feat1.html. Accessed February 2, 2008.

[6] Sharma, BR. (2003). Clinical forensic medicine-management of crime victims from trauma to trial. *Journal of Clinical Forensic Medicine*, 10:267–73.

[7] Sheridan, DJ. (1996). Forensic documentation of battered pregnant women. *Journal of Nurse-Midwifery*, 41:467–472.

[8] Carrington, M, Collington, P, Tyndall, J. (2000). Forensic Perioperative Nursing: Advocates for justice. *Canadian Operating Room Nursing Journal*, December:12–16.

[9] McCans, JP. (2006). Forensic evidence: Preserving the clinical picture. *RN*, 69:28ac1–28ac4.

[10] McGillivray, B. (2004). The role of Victorian emergency nurses in the collection and preservation of forensic evidence: a review of the literature. *Accident and Emergency Nursing*, 13:95–100.

[11] Wick, JM. (2000). "Don't destroy the evidence!" *AORN Journal*, 72:807–827.

[12] Hoyt, CA. (1999). Evidence recognition and collection in the clinical setting. *Critical Care Nursing Quarterly*, 22:19–26.

[13] McCracken, L. (2001). The forensic ABCs of trauma care. *Canadian Nurse*, 97:30–33.

[14] Pasqualone, GA. (1995). Forensic nursing: the importance of forensic photography in the emergency department. *Journal of Emergency Nursing*, 21:566–567.

[15] Evans, MM., Stagner, PA. (2003). Maintaining the chain of custody: evidence handling in forensic cases. *AORN Journal*, 78:563–9.

[16] Fulton, DR, Assid, P. (2006). Evidence collection in the emergency department. In VA Lynch, editor. *Forensic nursing*. St. Louis: Elsevier Mosby, pp. 570–577.

[17] Muro, GA, Easter, CR. (1994). Clinical forensics for perioperative nurses. *AORN Journal*, 60:585–593.

[18] Carmona, R, Prince, K. (1989). Trauma and Forensic Medicine. *The Journal of Trauma*, 29:1222–1225.

[19] Sievers, V, Murphy, S, Miller, J. (2003). Sexual assault evidence collection more accurate when completed by sexual assault nurse examiners: Colorado's experience. *Journal of Emergency Medicine*, 29:511–514.

[20] Federal Bureau of Investigation: *Handbook of Forensic Services*. Colleen Wade, Editor. Quantico: FBI Laboratory Publication, 2003.

[21] Crandall, C, Helitzer, D. (2003). Impact Evaluation of a Sexual Assault Nurse Examiner (SANE) Program: U.S. Department of Justice.

[22] American College of Emergency Physicians. Evaluation and Management of the Sexually Assaulted or Sexually Abused Patient. Available at: www.acep.org/workarea/downloadasset.aspx?id=8984. Accessed February 5, 2008.

[23] Ledray, L, Simmelink, K. (1997). Efficacy of Sexual Assault Nurse Examiner evidence collection: A Minnesota study. *Journal of Emergency Nursing*, 23:75–77.

[24] Forensics: Protocols for evidence collection. Central Washington Hospital Protocol. Personal communication with Laura Gaukroger-Holland, March 8, 2008.

Acknowledgement

The Chain-of-Custody/Evidence form adapted from the Pennsylvania Sexual Assault Evidence Collection (SAEC) Committee, 2008.

what you see: "elliptical-shaped 4-centimeter greenish discoloration over the left antecubital area." Do not attempt to make forensic interpretations of wounds. Avoid documenting gunshot wound descriptions such as "entrance wound" or "exit wound." If trace evidence is revealed during the examination, it should be documented and collected in accordance with jurisdictional and procedural guidelines. After examining individual marks and injuries, step back and examine any defects that are in groups or patterns. Determine the need for additional photographs.

All wounds, marks, or evidence of medical procedures, no matter how minor, should be carefully documented. After days, weeks, and months of elapsed time, these may be indistinguishable from the wounds associated with the accident or assault in question. Remember to rely on all senses of sight, touch, hearing, and smell during the exam. A patient may present with a particular odor, such as an accelerant, a chemical, or wood fire smoke. These will quickly dissipate, and such details may be overlooked during the subsequent analysis.

DNA can be recovered from body fluids, tissues, and stains on clothing. It may also be recovered from certain physical evidence such as a used condom, a bullet, a toothpick, or a cigarette butt (McClintock, 2008). The results of DNA analysis of questioned biological samples are then compared with the results of known DNA samples. This type of analysis can associate victims or suspects with each other and a crime scene. Two sources of DNA are used in the analysis of forensic evidence. Nuclear DNA is typically found in evidence that contains blood, semen, saliva, body tissues, and hairs that have tissue at the roots. Mitochondrial DNA will be found in evidence containing naturally shed hair, hair fragments, bones, and teeth.

When specimens for DNA recovery are not properly documented, collected, packaged, and preserved, they will not meet legal and scientific requirements for admissibility in court. For illustration, if they are not properly documented, the origin of the specimen can be questioned; if not properly collected, biological activity can be lost; if not properly packaged, the specimen could be contaminated; finally, if not properly preserved, useful biological components might decompose and deteriorate, making the specimens useless for DNA recovery (Box 14-2).

When collecting routine blood specimens for analysis, at least two samples in 5-ml purple-top tubes should be obtained. Toxicological blood specimens for drugs or alcohol should be collected in gray-top tubes containing sodium fluoride. Identify each tube with the date, time, subject's name, location, collector's name, and case or evidence number if available.

If it is necessary to provide body fluids other than blood such as gastric contents, chest tube drainage, peritoneal tap fluid, or urine for analysis, place fluids in clean plastic or glass containers. It is essential to seal the neck of the containers with a waterproof tape such as parafilm. The evidence tape should be affixed, extending over the parafilm, and a patient label should be placed on the specimen. The collector should initial both the tape and the label. Each specimen should be placed in a separate bag and then sealed with evidence tape and a patient label. The name of the specimen (type of body fluid) should be noted on the chain-of-custody/evidence form along with other pertinent information, including the precise time of collection.

If there is nondried blood, semen, urine, or other body fluid on the patient, suspected to be from an external source, the substance should be absorbed onto a sterile 2 × 2 gauze pad or swab. A second unused 2 × 2 gauze pad or swab should be maintained as a control specimen. After the cloth or swab is air-dried, it should be

---

Box 14-2 Blood Alcohol Specimens for Legal Purposes

- A written request from law enforcement must be submitted to the ED. For the evidence to be admissible, a qualified laboratory duly authorized by the state jurisdiction must do the blood alcohol determination.
- The blood test must be related to a lawful arrest with probable cause that a crime was committed while the offender was under the influence of alcohol or while intoxicated.
- ED personnel should provide necessary medical care and treatment without consideration of the forensic laboratory specimen that has been or will be ordered.
- Usual laboratory collection procedures are followed. Alcohol is typically not used to cleanse the skin, however. Povidone-iodine or other agents are preferred. The nurse who obtains the sample should document on the label that alcohol was not used to clean the skin. Note: Offenders who are on anticoagulant therapy or who are hemophiliacs are typically exempt from an ordered phlebotomy.
- Hospital policy should clearly articulate the procedure for obtaining blood alcohol samplings and the conditions of consent. The consent of the patient is necessary, and it should be informed consent.
- Blood should be drawn in the police officer's presence so that he or she can so testify, eliminating the need for other witnesses to appear and testify.
- Blood drawn must be given to the officer requesting it, who then takes it to an authorized laboratory, preserving the chain of evidence.
- A notation of blood drawn, by whom, and the time must be documented in the ED record of the patient, and the blood so labeled before it is sealed with tape, cross-initialed, and given to the officer.
- If a blood alcohol determination is needed for medical purposes, separate samples must be drawn.
- The skin preparation for drawing a blood-alcohol sample should be done with aqueous benzalkonium (aqueous Zephiran) rather than alcohol.
- Draw 10 mL, and label with the name, date, time drawn, and initial. If it is a case of negligent homicide, draw two samples, one hour apart, to demonstrate the curve as firm legal evidence. Either the blood-alcohol level will have peaked and started down or it will be higher, indicating that the subject took more alcohol immediately before the incident. It is estimated that the blood level will fall 15 to 20 mg/100 mL per hour, so if, for instance, a blood alcohol is drawn four hours after an arrest and tests at 0.18% (180 mg/100 mL), it can be assumed that the subject's blood level at the time of arrest was 0.26%, or 260 mg/100 mL (Lanros & Barber, 1997, pgs. 496–497).

---

placed in a clean paper bag or an envelope with sealed corners. Plastic containers should not be used.

Dried specimens of these same substances should be collected using a sterile 2 × 2 gauze pad or a swab lightly moistened with sterile water. The swab should be rolled over the surface of the dried substance. A moistened 2 × 2 can also be placed over the dried area, allowing for absorption. An unused 2 × 2 must be preserved as a control. Specimens should be air-dried and packaged in a clean paper bag or envelope with sealed corners.

Other Evidence

There are other forms of valuable forensic evidence that might be found on, or removed from, the victim during examination and treatment, including bullets, glass, fibers, paint chips, hair, grass, or rocks. Each of these can be analyzed for forensic details, providing links to the crime scene, weapon, or the suspect. (See Chapters 6 and 24.)

Although GSR deposited on clothing may be useful as evidence when collected by medical personnel, residue on hands must be collected by law enforcement using a collection kit designed to be analyzed by scanning electron microscopy.

photography and evidence gathering, she acts to preserve this transient evidence. The nurse retrieves the camera from the ED's forensic supplies, places a 4×6 index card with patient identification and an ABFO scale above the bundles, and takes a series of photos to document the duct-taped packages. She then photographs the patterned injury on the chest. Team members then remove the bundles to adequately assess the patient. When tape is pulled away from the patient, the bundles are revealed to be multiple small plastic bags filled with a white substance. One team member calls internal security as specified by the hospital's policies and procedures and requests that they take receipt of the bundles. The bundles are placed in another unused paper bag, sealed, dated, identified, and initialed appropriately. When a security officer arrives, the nurse provides him with the bagged bundles and requests that he sign a chain-of-custody form.

Continually changing gloves to prevent transfer of trace or biological evidence, the team continues to examine the patient. When the blue jeans have been fully removed they, too, are placed on disposable incontinence pads, spread out to avoid transfer of bloodstain to other parts of the jeans. After covering the patient's genitals to provide modesty, the nurse photographs the leg wounds and the bilateral open tibia-fibular fractures, including the 4×6 patient ID card and ABFO scale. While the patient is receiving fluids and the vital signs are stabilizing, the nurse takes time to measure and document the bruising as well as lacerations, abrasions, and other wounds. She uses anatomical landmarks to describe the location and characteristics of all injuries and other markings on the body, including several old scars and tattoos on the arms, face, chest, and back. Additionally, she draws a sketch of the wounds on a body diagram.

Team members at the head of the bed examine the head wound and find a gaping 7-cm laceration to the right temple. There are currently no signs of active bleeding. Bits of dirt and grass are stuck in the laceration. Photographs are taken of the laceration with appropriate identification and scale provided in the photo. A team member carefully removes larger pieces of grass and dirt with rubber-tipped forceps and places them in a rigid plastic container. The container is labeled with the patient name, date, time, location from which the debris came, and the collector's name and initials. The container is then placed in an unused brown paper bag, which is sealed and identified with the same information.

While attempting to start an additional IV line in anticipation of a trip to the operating room, a team member discovers there is a phone number written in ink on the patient's palm. Pictures are taken of the palm with the numbers clearly in focus and identifiers in place.

A decision has been made to transport the patient to the operating room for an exploratory laparotomy and for stabilization and fixation of the open fractures. Shortly after the patient has left the ED, state police officers arrive, and in compliance with previously established agreements with local law enforcement, physical evidence is transferred to the officers. The team has packed all clothing and trace evidence appropriately, and the officers have been informed that some items of clothing are still wet. Photographs taken by the nurse will become a part of the patient's permanent medical record. The nurse reviews and completes all written documentation before exiting the trauma room.

BODY SEARCHES

Emergency personnel may be requested to participate in body cavity searches for contraband. These searches must be court-ordered or done with the written consent of the offender.

Exceptions may be made for contraband that might be immediately life-threatening to a patient (Mallon & Perez, 1999). Cavity searches must be fully documented with the signatures of two physicians and accomplished in the presence of a witness of the same gender as the patient. Recovered items or contraband must be accounted for, using the ordinary chain-of-custody procedure. Depending on the law in individual state statutes, the forensic nurse must either turn contraband over to the police or have the destruction of the materials witnessed according to hospital policy. This is important information that may protect the patient's constitutional rights or protect the forensic nurse from being sued by the patient for giving away his or her personal property. A hospital forensic protocol should address this situation according to the legal statutes that will indicate when to act and when not to act. This forensic protocol should also include rules of evidence applicable to the specific state regarding search and seizure in the ED.

Mandatory Reporting Laws

The forensic nurse should be aware of the mandatory reporting laws for forensic patients: the Emergency Medical Treatment and Active Labor Act (EMTALA) or the Consolidated Omnibus Budget Reconciliation Act (COBRA), coroner's cases, infectious diseases, adverse drug reactions, sexual assault, child and elder abuse, domestic violence, workplace violence, and impaired physicians or nurses (Mallon & Kassinove, 1999). In some states or jurisdictions, additional reportable cases may exist. It is essential that specific provisions of these laws are immediately available for staff reference if reportable cases are encountered. In some areas there are additional reportable events such as seat belt violations, medical device failures, foodborne illness, and acute lapses in consciousness. The failure to report is usually the result of lack of knowledge that a report is required, or personnel making the assumption that someone else will take the responsibility to initiate the report. Neither of these reasons for nonreporting reduces the responsibility of any staff member to make reports or negates legal actions for failing to report. Forensic nurses in the ED must understand and respect mandatory reporting laws. When there are doubts about reporting any event or condition, consult hospital administration or its legal team for guidance.

The Body as Evidence

If, despite all efforts, a patient is dead on arrival at the ED or dies in the ED, the nurse must be aware of death reporting criteria in the particular state. Although at the onset of care a patient may not be identified as a forensic patient with actual or potential interaction with the legal system, upon death many may subsequently be classified as forensic patients. In these cases, the body becomes a potential crime scene and becomes evidence from which a cause of death will be determined. (See Chapters 16 and 19.)

In Collin County, Texas, deaths that affect the public interest are reportable to the medical examiner and include, but are not limited to, those in Box 14-5. The body of the deceased and all personal property of the patient whose death is reported are under the sole custody and jurisdiction of the medical examiner. IV lines, tubes, traction devices, IV fluids, Foley bags and

---

Box 14-5 Reportable Deaths

1. All deaths occurring within 24 hours of entry into the hospital
2. All trauma deaths, even those that may be remotely related to trauma (this includes all deaths in which a fractured hip has occurred and injury during hospitalization; it would naturally include homicides, accidents, and suicides)
3. All deaths under anesthesia and immediate post-anesthesia period
4. All deaths occurring as a result of operative or diagnostic procedure
5. When the suspected cause of death is work related, whether traumatic or natural, or related to environmental or occupational hazards
6. When the attending physician has no reasonable, proximate cause of death
7. Stillbirths when the delivery took place outside, not inside, the hospital, or if the stillbirth is related to trauma
8. Maternal deaths before, during, or after delivery where abortion is suspected
9. All prescription drugs or illicit drug use–related deaths, without exception
10. Unexpected death of a child or newborn less that 6 years of age
11. All nursing home deaths without exception

Source: Collin County Texas Office of the Medical Examiner.

their contents, and any therapeutic medical paraphernalia are not to be removed until the medical examiner gives authorization. IV puncture sites, minor procedure marks, or surgical wounds made during resuscitation should be circled with an indelible marker and annotated. These wounds may be covered with a dry sterile dressing and taped in place. If there is suspicion of any trace evidence remaining on hands or under fingernails of victims of violent death, the hands should be bagged and securely taped. The medical examiner becomes the immediate custodian of all clothing and personal belongings. ED staff should never give these to the family. They should be collected and managed in accordance with procedures for forensic evidence.

BEST PRACTICE When a patient has received medical care and subsequently dies in the emergency department, the body and all related property is within the jurisdiction of the medical examiner. All lines, tubes, or other evidence of medical therapies must be annotated and left in place.

In the event that the patient has died under suspicious circumstances, the nurse will ensure that the body is not viewed by family members without the attendance of ED personnel to prevent any opportunity of accidentally or intentionally altering potential sources of evidence.

Summary

Nurses in the ED daily treat victims and perpetrators of sexual assault, victims and perpetrators of interpersonal violence, victims of child abuse, victims of elder abuse, victims of blunt and sharp trauma, and patients in custody. In the provision of nursing care and the practice of nursing science the nurse assumes responsibility to partner with law enforcement to protect the human, civil, and legal rights of anyone under her or his care. The concept of forensic nursing incorporates this new dimension into the holistic approach to patients seen in the ED. The ability to accurately and efficiently identify, collect, and preserve forensic evidence demonstrates clearly the ED nurse's commitment to high-quality healthcare in the primary care setting.

KEY POINT The failure to incorporate forensic guidelines into the clinical assessment and management of patients may result in far-reaching consequences for the patient, the accused suspect, and, potentially, the hospital and its personnel.

Case Study 14-2

Accidental Injury or Child Abuse?

At 0300, a young father presents to the triage nurse with toddler son stating that his son cannot sleep because his right arm hurts. The child is solemn and makes no eye contact. It is summer and he has on shorts and a T-shirt. His right arm is not in the sleeve of the T-shirt. The arm is rotated slightly forward and is held at an odd angle. The child is placed on a chair and the triage nurse begins to take vital signs and assess the child. Vital signs are normal with the exception of an elevated heart rate. When asked what happened, the child continues to be silent and puts his head down. When the dad is asked, he states that early in the evening his children were kicking a ball around. He further states that the ball was kicked into the boy's arm. The father explained he was not at home at the time of the injury and that his girlfriend was watching the boy. The triage nurse evaluates the arm and finds that the upper arm is tender and the boy will not move it. There are no neurovascular abnormalities. She tells the father that she suspects that the upper arm is broken. She documents her findings and quotes the father directly as to the mechanism of injury.

The triage nurse is suspicious that the injury is one of abuse because the story the father has told is inconsistent with the type of presenting injury. She places the child in an exam room and speaks confidentially with the primary care nurse to express her concerns.

The primary nurse documents the child's demeanor, his silence despite obvious pain, and generally notes hygiene, clothing, and nutritional status. She attempts to get him to talk.

The x-ray reveals a greenstick fracture of the midshaft of the humerus. With children younger than 3 years of age, the nurse knows that abuse must be considered. The doctor orders a second x-ray called a "babygram," which will reveal the entire skeletal system. The x-ray may be analyzed to determine if there are other new or old fractures present. No other fractures are noted. The child is given a sling, medicated for pain, and given an orthopedic referral. Both nurse and doctor speak to the father and ask him to again describe how his son came to have the injury. He again repeats that children close to his son in age were kicking a ball and the ball struck his son in the arm. He says he did not personally see the incident but is repeating what his girlfriend told him.

Both nurse and doctor explain to the father that his child's injury does not appear to be caused by a ball kicked by another small child. They explain that the injury is more consistent with a stronger force and could represent child abuse. They further explain that they are obligated by state law to refer the case to the child protective services (CPS) division of the state's attorney general's office. The father acknowledges this statement and is told he may expect a visit from someone from the CPS office. The nurse then calls the CPS office and gives all necessary information. She receives a case number, which she documents in the child's ED record.

Resources

WEBSITES

American College of Emergency Physicians, Dallas, TX; www.acep.org
Emergency Nurses Association, Des Plaines, IL; www.ena.org
International Association of Forensic Nurses, Arnold, MD; www.iafn.org

References

American College of Emergency Physicians. (2000). *Child abuse. ACEP Policy Statement, no. 400279.* Dallas, TX.

Barber Duval, J. (2006). Occupational health and safety issues. In V. A. Lynch (Ed.). *Forensic Nursing* (Ch 54, p. 579). St. Louis: Mosby.

Carmona, R., & Prince, K. (1989). Trauma and forensic medicine. *The Journal of Trauma, 29*(9), 1222.

Emergency Nurses Association. (2003). *Position statement: Forensic evidence collection.* Des Plaines, IL.

Hoyt, C. (1999). Evidence recognition and collection in the clinical setting. *Critical Care Nursing Quarterly, 22*(1), 19.

Lynch, V. (1991). Forensic nursing in the emergency department: A new role for the 1990s. *Critical Care Nursing Quarterly, 14*(3), 69–86.

Mallon, W. K., & Perez, J. F. (1999). Weapons fabrication from medical supplies. *Topics in Emergency Medicine, 21*(3), 55–62.

MacNamara, H. (1986). *Living forensics (seminar proceedings).* Ulster County, NY: Office of the Medical Examiner.

McCarron, M. M., & Challoner, K. R. (1999). Emergency department treatment of patients in custody. *Topics in Emergency Medicine, 21*(3), 39–48.

McClintock, J. T. (2008). *Forensic DNA Analysis* (p.4). Boca Raton: CRC Press, Taylor-Francis Group.

Mittleman, R. E., Goldberg, H. S., & Waksman, D. M. (1983). Preserving evidence in the emergency department. *The American Journal of Nursing, 83*(12), 1652–1656.

National Institute of Justice Journal, No. 259, pp. 1–8.

Pasqualone, G. (1998). *An examination of forensic categories among patient seen at a community hospital emergency department.* Fitchburg MA: Fitchburg State Unpublished Master's Thesis.

Smialek, J. E. (1983). Forensic medicine in the emergency department. *Emergency Medical Clinics of North America, 1*(93), 693–704.

Smock, W. S. (1994). Development of a clinical forensic medicine curriculum for emergency physicians in the USA. *Journal of Clinical Forensic Medicine, 1*(1), 27–30.

Smock, W. S. (2002). Forensic emergency medicine. In J. M. Mark (Ed.), *Rosen's emergency medicine: Concepts and clinical practice* (pp. 828–841). St. Louis, MO: Mosby.

Smock, W. S., & Besant-Matthews, P. (2007). Forensic photography in the emergency department. In J. D. Olshaker, M. C. Jackson, & W. S. Smock (Eds.), *Forensic emergency medicine* (chapter 17, pp. 268–291). Philadelphia: Lippincott Williams & Wilkins.

The Joint Commission Standards on Hospital Accreditation. (2009). Oak Park, IL.

York Hospital, WellSpan Health System. (2009). *Forensic evidence collection guidelines for the emergency department* York, Pennsylvania. Guidelines developed by Eisert, P., Eldredge, K., Hartlaub, T., Huggins, E., Keirn, G., O'Brien, P., Rozzi, H., Shue, N., Wilkerson, H., Pugh L., & March, K. (Eds.).

CHAPTER 15 Multi-Casualty Scenes

Joyce Williams and David Williams

Forensic nurses are likely to be involved in the aftermath of disasters resulting from natural phenomena as well as from acts of terrorism. Dense population centers, the widespread use of mass transportation, and social-cultural conflicts are factors that increase the probability for any of these events to generate hundreds or even thousands of victims. Disaster prevention and risk reduction strategies have been receiving increasing attention. Local communities, states, countries, and international organizations are networking to raise public awareness of specific threats and vulnerabilities, as well as to create response plans (McGlown, 2004).

In this new era, the focus has become comprehensive emergency management including pre-event (preparedness and mitigation) and post-event (response and recovery) activities (McGlown, 2004). It is no longer a question of whether another catastrophic event will happen; it is a matter of when it will occur and what type it will be. Where will the next mass homicide or suicide, terrorist bombing, building collapse, plane crash, or tornado take place? How many people will be injured and or killed? What will be the extent of property loss, and how will the incident be handled as a medicolegal event?

With today's sophisticated communications technology and global media coverage, disasters that affect lives in one area are exposed within minutes to concerned populations around the world. To control and diminish feelings of helplessness, there has been an increasing emphasis on proactive elements such as risk management and threat assessments (McGlown, 2004). A risk assessment matrix can be developed for a community, its infrastructure, and utilities; for a business; or for a dedicated facility such as a school, sports arena, or hospital. For example, the airlines have identified operational vulnerabilities that weaken their defenses and threaten the safety of both passengers and cargo. They have responded with countermeasures such as increased passenger screening and operating with a cockpit lockdown. Although such initiatives do not eliminate the threat of hijacking or other acts of terror, they are ways of reassuring the public that we have some control over catastrophe.

Role of Forensic Nursing in Disasters

History demonstrates nursing involvement in the frontline attention to casualties of war and palliative care of victims of natural catastrophe. As early as the days of Florence Nightingale, nurses have been a vital clinical and humanitarian resource in times of emergent need. Military nursing in wartime is among the first documented disaster responses to a man-made event; of late, the disaster nursing response has been developing quickly, adapting and reacting to threats of environmental terrorism and other criminal incidents. This adaptation continues as research is initiated and personal accounts of nurses' experiences are shared. An understanding of past disasters and their management is an initial step in preventing or ameliorating the effects of future disasters (Illing, 2000).

With some highlights of past man-made events one can certainly grasp the nature of role development of the forensic nurse responding to disasters. Threat assessment is imperative across communities to determine what vulnerabilities exist that could endanger the population and the infrastructure. The creation of a plan must include all hazards and contain comprehensive data to support the needs assessment. By using a plan that details multiple vulnerabilities, a community can embrace a return to functionality more readily in spite of the threat.

Preparedness is defined as readiness capability. The Federal Emergency Management Agency (FEMA) takes it a step further: "the leadership, training, readiness, and exercise support, and technical and financial assistance to strengthen citizens, communities, state, local and tribal governments, and provisional emergency workers as they prepare for disasters, mitigate the effects of disasters, respond to community needs after a disaster and launch effective recovery efforts" (pp. 3-4) (Haddow & Bullock, 2003). Forensic nurses possess knowledge and skills that can be applied to strengthen individuals and populations.

Overview of the Disaster Response System

The Robert T. Stafford Disaster Relief and Emergency Assistance Act, PL 93-288, was enacted in 1974 and provides "federal assistance to states to manage the consequences of domestic disasters by expediting aid, assistance, and emergency services" (McGlown, 2004). On gubernatorial request and declaration by the president that there is a disaster, the FEMA disaster assistance programs are launched.

To achieve a coordinated response, the Government Accounting Organization (GAO) has identified nine key items that ensure "a coordinated response" (McGlown, 2004). (See Box 15-1.)

When a disaster occurs, a joint preliminary damage and needs assessment is done. The local emergency operations center (EOC) is activated, and a command center is set up in a secure location. The local area immediately puts into motion mitigation for the prioritized and identified hazards. The state emergency management agency (EMA) is contacted to respond and also calls in assistance from other states as predetermined through mutual aid agreements. State assets may well be overwhelmed thus requiring a call for assistance from the governor to the president (McGlown, 2004). A presidential declaration of a federal emergency or major disaster provides assistance to the event as specified in the Federal Response Plan (FRP). Before the actual authorization of federal assistance, FEMA can "authorize critical supplies and equipment such as food, water, generators, or emergency medical teams" (p. 161) (McGlown, 2004) in situations of imminent damage.

Fig. 15-1 The devastation associated with the World Trade Center bombing in 2001 was a stimulus for governmental agencies to analyze and upgrade their disaster response plans.

Box 15-1 GAO Elements of Coordinated Disaster Response

- Emergency medical services
- Fire services
- Hazardous materials teams
- Law enforcement
- Hospitals
- Laboratories
- State and local government agencies
- Public and private utilities
- Public health

From McGlown, K. J. (Ed). (2004). Terrorism and disaster management: *Preparing healthcare leaders for the new reality.* Chicago, IL: Health Administration Press.

In the early 1980s, the U.S. government recognized the need to improve emergency preparedness by establishing the Emergency Mobilization Preparedness Board. The eleven working groups within the board provided the precursors for our present system of emergency support functions (ESFs) allocating functional responsibilities to specific cabinet departments and the American Presidency Project (The American Presidency Project).

Its response to the presidential mandate for health program development resulted in the creation of a single system charged with the responsibility to care for large numbers of casualties from either a domestic, natural, or man-made disaster or a conventional overseas war. Services are expanded to include health and medical assessment, surveillance, surge capabilities, evacuation, definitive care, food, drug and device safety, veterinary services, medical personnel, worker health and safety, weapons of mass effect (WME), mental health, public information, vector control, potable water and solid waste disposal, and mortuary services.

The National Response Framework (NRF) is the basis on which state and local plans are constructed. It is built on scalable, flexible, and adaptable coordinating structures to align key roles and responsibilities across the nation, linking all levels of government, nongovernmental organizations, and the private sector. It is intended to capture specific activities and best practices for managing incidents that range from serious but purely local, to large-scale terrorist attacks, to catastrophic natural disasters (Fig. 15-1). This is the basis of the "all hazards" strategy.

Preparedness planning is lead by the Office of Preparedness Planning (OPP) in order to fulfill Health and Human Services (HHS) responsibilities under ESF8 of the NRF and Homeland Security Presidential Directive (HSPD) 10. The Office of Preparedness and Emergency Operations OPEO leads the HHS and interagency planning and response activities required to fulfill HHS responsibilities under ESF 8 of the NRF and HSPD 10 OPP works to integrate mass casualty preparedness activities, through its surge capacity efforts, across local, state, and federal levels consistent with the National Incident Management System (NIMS). NIMS provides a consistent nationwide template to enable all government, private-sector, and nongovernmental organizations to work together during domestic incidents. It goes beyond the incident command structure by providing a common and universal framework for maximum response regardless of the size of the event.

The National Disaster Medical System (NDMS) is a cooperative asset-sharing partnership of four federal departments and agencies including the Department of HHS, Department of Defense (DoD), Department of Veterans Affairs (VA), and FEMA (Twomey & Goll-McGee, 1999).

One essential element of any disaster response plan is implementing the Emergency Management Assistance Compact (EMAC).

This compact provides form and structure to interstate mutual aid crucial to states when local and state services become overwhelmed from a disaster. EMAC is administered by the National Emergency Management Agency (NEMA) and administers liability and reimbursement issues when finances are already strained. Equally important is the inclusion of memorandums of agreement among regional agencies that may have not been affected by the impact of the event and can respond immediately to assist with the response and return to normalcy. Advanced arrangements are not only smart but bring in coordinated interagency support to a damaged infrastructure.

KEY POINT All healthcare facilities, whether acute or long-term, are required to establish an emergency response plan to mitigate common and uncommon events.

Healthcare disaster response expertise is found globally. In the United States, specialty teams have been formed regionally under the auspices of the Department of Homeland Security (DHS). The Disaster Medical Assistance Team (DMAT) is a group of "volunteers and support personnel with the ability to quickly move into a disaster area and provide emergency medical care or augment the efforts of overloaded local care organizations" (p. 47) (Langan & James, 2005). Deployment conditions may be hazardous and harsh with medical care rendered in field hospitals, tents, or abandoned buildings. These teams are fully equipped and self-sufficient, enabling their immediate response to an austere environment or to augment the response of previously deployed teams and to support overwhelmed local and state resources as necessary. The dynamic response is dictated by need with specific pediatric, burn, trauma, critical care, and international specialty teams augmenting the efforts of a responding DMAT.

"Care and identification of the dead in a Mass Casualty Incident (MCI) can overwhelm a medical examiner/coroner system. Disaster Mortuary Operational Response Teams (DMORTs) were originally formed to support a national level response, enhancing the original unit conceived by the National Funeral Directors Association (NFDA). DMORT also is charged with victim identification and mortuary services in the event of a mass disaster" (p. 32) (Williams, personal communication). These teams have been integrated into the federal system and now fall under NDMS.

DMORT serves to provide the "establishment of mobile morgue operations, forensic examination, DNA acquisition, remains identification, and search and recovery. In addition, DMORT can provide scene documentation, records data entry, embalming and casketing, antemortem data collection, and postmortem data collection, and establish family assistance centers" (p. 48) (Ibid, p. 4) or care teams. Teams may be predeployed for consequence management of planned events (Olympics) or high-profile events.

It is paramount for the forensic nurse to be involved in the disaster management system before a critical incident occurs. This affiliation will provide essential indoctrination to mass casualty responses and establish opportunities for leadership. Preparedness is what unlocks opportunities to respond with other medical relief organizations. Connecting among and within one's community ideally positions the forensic nurse to contribute effectively to the team of stakeholders.

Roles of the forensic nurse include identifying the dead, recognizing medicolegal issues, supplying information and education, providing direct patient care, and conducting disaster research. There is definite opportunity for specialized role negoti-

ation and role development with the evolving threat of domestic and foreign disasters. The forensic nursing specialty is not limited within or restricted to any practice areas. The role of the clinician is elastic for a forensic nurse specialist responding to disasters. The dimensions of the clinical forensic nurse specialist embrace research, the experience of peers, and consults with those in other disciplines. Forensic nurse leaders manage clinical staff and advise in protocols and response, adhering to the scope and standards of forensic nursing at each practice effort. The scope and standards of forensic nursing practice state that "the victim can be the client, the family, the perpetrator and the public in general" (IAFN, ANA, 2007). Disaster response satisfies advocacy to all these areas serving "the client and the family" affected by the catastrophic event, and the "public in general" with a security focus for reasons to which the forensic nurse specialist must be knowledgeable.

In light of the medicolegal aspects and potential of man-made and natural disasters, forensic nurses bring to these teams the ideal cross training, versatility, and expertise on which the team's success, specificity, and efficiency rely. The legal aspects of various man-made disasters call for the recognition, collection, and preservation of evidence at the scene, when possible, concurrently with treatment to the individual. The medicolegal aspect of any disaster extends itself from the inception of the event through the recovery phase for cause and manner to support and adjudicate the findings as presented throughout the legal process. The timely and efficient identification of disaster victims satisfies the natural inclination and emotional strain of loved ones to give remains a proper burial. The scientific identification of a victim provides the basis for the issuance of the death certificate. This legal document is required for the settlement of estates and wills, payment of life insurance benefits, and other legal actions such as the remarriage of survivors.

Those affected by natural catastrophes may be aggravated by the human error or carelessness underlying the medicolegal aspects from substandard construction codes. Other areas of concern are nuclear reactors built without sufficient infrastructure to guard against radiation hazards, improper engineering and construction of dams and levees, and design flaws in transportation systems. The forensic nurse aware of the link between the primary and secondary impact does not understate this type of secondary victimization.

Another focus that the forensic nurse specialist involved in disaster response ponders, predicts, and addresses involves current and future public needs for information, education, and guidance about health and environmental threats or concerns as a direct result from the disaster. The forensic nurse clinician improves clinical skills through an extensive knowledge base augmented with experience expanding the professional capabilities into advanced practice nursing capacities. These include, but are not limited to, clinical response, family assistance, and forensic processing.

Clinical Response

The forensic nurse specialist serving disasters provides direct care services that are quantitatively and qualitatively different from those provided by other responders. Clinical experience in emergency/trauma or critical care settings is the basis for the development of expertise in clinical forensic nursing disaster management. The forensic nurse specialist prepares for this expanded role by involvement in community disaster planning, state emergency management, and hospital disaster protocols. The extent of involvement in disaster medical response depends on active membership in teams and the specialties, which the clinical forensic nurse specialist fosters.

BEST PRACTICE Involvement in the disaster management system before a critical incident occurs is paramount for the forensic nurse specialist interested in responding to those affected by a disaster. These activities yield essential responsibility and result in an ideal leadership role for forensic nurses preparing to concentrate in this advanced practice arena.

Mass casualty response comprises four basic elements, which include "search and rescue, triage and initial stabilization, definitive medical care and evacuation" (p. 71) (Briggs & Leong, 1990) (Fig. 15-2). Search and rescue teams render aid to individuals to minimize loss of life and injury and assist in the recovery of human remains from a mass casualty incident. The intent of triage to do the greatest good for the greatest number of people functions as "an analytical sorting process in classic MCIs of limited scope" (p. 73) (Briggs & Leong, 1990) (Fig. 15-3). "Adequate triage and casualty distribution is more difficult to achieve in disasters such as tornadoes, floods, hurricanes, and earthquakes, that cause injury and destruction over a wide area"(Chapter 8) (American Red Cross, 1997). The American Nurses Association (ANA) and the Centers for Disease Control and Prevention (CDC) have developed altered standards of care in which modifications to protocols are used in times of limited resources. The clinical forensic nurse specialist provides proficient care as a registered nurse for victims in various stressful, fast-paced, and often demanding clinical situations by assessing vital signs, managing pain and wounds, and maintaining the patient's homeostasis and hemodynamic stability. "The medicolegal patient population, however, require that these same goals *plus* forensic concerns be addressed" (p. 9) (Goll-McGee, 1999).

Expert clinical care is vital, as disaster nursing and other healthcare roles are often expanded to meet the acute demands of the situation. Included in the assessment of disaster patients is vigilance concerning the index of suspicion to uncover the how and why of their mechanisms of injury or illness that placed them under the care of the specific disaster team.

The single most important aspect must be detailed documentation of all injuries, comorbidities, and resulting conditions in addi-

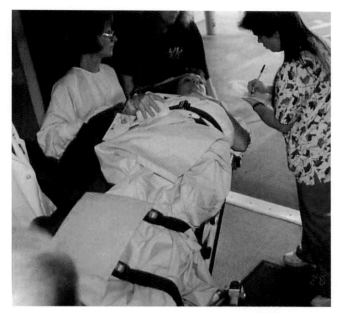

Fig. 15-3 Forensic nurse specialist triages casualty upon arrival at a trauma center.

tion to resultant deaths from the incident for future data collection and research. This is accomplished to satisfy the medicolegal management of disaster victims and to promote research, furthering the basis for evidence-based practice to satisfy the continued education of healthcare professionals and the public in general regarding a critical incident or disaster. Each disaster contributes to the knowledge by the evaluative process and "lessons learned." What is learned from one disaster must be shared in order to establish more effective responses and to avoid the pitfalls in future events. What is acquired knowledge in one event may lead to the early detection in future events and improved medical management affecting mortality and morbidity and quality assurance.

"Substantial efforts in training, monitoring, and review of actions in the field now take place in all agencies and units set up for disaster response" (p. 78) (Briggs & Leong, 1990).

BEST PRACTICE The nurse ensures thorough documentation of all aspects of disaster-related injuries and deaths, because this information is vital for public education and other aspects of morbidity/mortality prevention.

Family Assistance

The Aviation Disaster Family Assistance Act (ADFAA) of 1996 requires the National Transportation Safety Board (NTSB) and all American air carriers provide integrated family assistance and support to families of mass casualties. The ADFAA created the family assistance care team (FACT). The intent of the team is to provide relatives and friends of victims with "information and access to services they may need in the days following the incident; to protect families from the media and curiosity seekers" (p. 22) (Emergency Management Institute National Emergency Training Center, 1996).

The team is comprised of investigators, forensic nurses, and funeral directors who liaison with the families and the NTSB to obtain information necessary to provide scientific identification of the deceased. This response to the federal mandate challenges

Fig. 15-2 Evacuees from the Southern California wildfires are registered and processed at a local high school where healthcare and social services are managed by Red Cross volunteers. (Courtesy Talia Frenkel/American Red Cross.)

forensic nurses to integrate advanced practice professional standards of forensic nursing care while working as members of the multidisciplinary team. This is accomplished by identifying the needs, rights, and obligations of individuals. Forensic nursing provides care for grieving families of those involved in a catastrophic event and addresses the needs of suffering families by participation and cooperation among interagency organizations. In situations where the mass fatality incident is widespread, as in Hurricane Katrina, the State Department was effective in locating family and records from abroad.

The airline is the agency that connects the team to the families. Throughout the identification process, antemortem data is collected consisting of personal and medical information that will assist in the timely and efficient identification of the deceased or missing individual, using guidelines established by the team of professionals, with the forensic nurse as part of that team. The interviews with the family members take place at the designated site determined by the initial assessment team with staggered appointment times to allow for sufficient time spent with the family.

A useful tool developed through DMORT is the victim identification profile (VIP). The VIP consists of an eight-page document that elicits comprehensive data about the potential deceased. Included in this interview is a description of the physical characteristics, such as hair and eye color, scars, implants, and tattoos, which will yield information useful in the identification process. Additional data valuable to this approach include historical information such as jobs where fingerprinting would be part of the hiring process, past military service or incarceration, and the location of medical and dental records. These personal attributes along with the descriptive traits of the individual are critical elements to aid in the antemortem data collection that will be used along with the postmortem comparison, with the goal of rendering a positive identification of the person.

Manifests of commercial air crashes limit the universe of potential victims, particularly in this day of multiple ID checks before boarding an airliner. Disasters are not always associated with a manifest where a list of potential persons is available such as a public forum or an event housing large groups. Examples are the 1996 Olympics in Atlanta, Georgia, the 2003 Station Nightclub Fire in Rhode Island, and those affected by the 2004 tsunami in Southeast Asia. "The World Health Organization (WHO) through PANEL 2.16 identified four factors that characterized MFI's [mass fatality incidents] with the objective that proper resource allocation can be made. These factors include (1) existence of a manifest; (2) the condition of the remains; (3) the rate of recovery of the remains; and (4) the number of victims" (p. 455) (Tun et al., 2005). The forensic nurse forwards the compiled data for entry into software programs, which begin systematic identification efforts. The forensic nurse interviewer identifies areas of missing information and obtains pictures, original dental records, medical records, and other types of evidence. She or he may also obtain DNA swabs from next of kin to be used in the comparison with that sampled from human remains.

In addition to the request for information to aid in the identification of the human remains (HR), the team is sensitive to the needs of those who have experienced a great loss in their lives. The forensic nurse on the team provides emotional support in this time of grief. The site of the FACT is selected in a quiet, convenient location with accommodations as part of the facility when possible. On completion of the meeting, the airline returns to continue next steps while waiting for evidence that the identification has been determined. The team remains available for any additional questions or information that should become available. Accommodations should generally be provided at the same location if it has been established at a hotel; if not, accommodations are desirable that are located away from, but convenient to the disaster site. Mortuary services can be offered, when necessary, with assistance from experienced staff and should be mediated with state association. Flexibility aids in optimal outcomes in every effort to meet individual needs. Forensic nurses and others working within the center determine the priorities and work collaboratively to achieve the designated goal of providing the families with sensitivity, compassion, and peace of mind.

Forensic nurses use a rapid needs assessment in an effort to "obtain a small amount of relevant information quickly in order to plan and implement immediate or prolonged response" (p. 1) (Goll-McGee, 1999). Incident command system (ICS) structure is the most efficient method in disaster-type scenarios. Assessment, diagnosis, outcome identification, planning, and implementation do not always designate a restricted order of activity but act as an integrated approach between standards, an ever-changing dynamic approach used by the forensic nurse specialist to meet the demands of the care team. The outcome of the FACT is to serve families and those affected by a disaster by providing positive identification in a timely manner through a working association with the medical examiner's or coroner's office, DMORT teams, and healthcare institutions, to provide victim identification using proper resource allocation and scientific methodology in mass-fatality management.

Forensic nurses may specialize in ongoing education, collaboration, and research to be leaders in disaster management at the local, regional, and federal level and be members of think tanks in professional nursing organizations (ANA, IAFN, International Council of Nurses [ICN]), as well as universities with the goal of steering practitioners in evidence-based practice issues.

Annual team training and mock disaster scenarios with participation by healthcare facilities, death investigation offices, the American Red Cross (ARC), airport staff, law enforcement, and national disaster response teams not only educate, but familiarize all with best practice and provide critique opportunities to evaluate areas requiring further development (Fig. 15-4). Regular training also provides opportunities for reviewing protocols and updating procedures in concordance with research for best practices. This also allows team building opportunities rather than meeting for the first time at an MCI. Every incident will be unique; however, our attempts to understand and deal with each respective incident may identify trends and give lessons to response efforts. The response for aviation disasters, the formation of the care team, and the role of the forensic nurse are important for response to various other disaster events.

Forensic Processing

When a mass fatality incident (MFI) occurs, human remains are recovered onsite and transported to a permanent or temporary morgue. To augment these buildings, temporary units may house the equipment needed to provide the processing of the human remains. DMORT has this type of unit known as the disaster portable mobile unit (DPMU, 2009) (Fig. 15-5). The actual recovery process requires a methodical, efficient, and scientific manner to process large numbers of human remains, thereby expediting victim identification. A temporary morgue facility is utilized when

Fig. 15-4 Red Cross volunteer nurse checks on a young patient at a shelter set up during the California wildfires. (Courtesy Talia Frenkel/American Red Cross.)

Fig. 15-5 DMORT facility set-up following aviation accident near Wilkes-Barre, PA.

the regular morgue is insufficient to accommodate the large volume of victims of an incident or whose location is not conducive to immediate transport of remains to the facility. "Requirements for a temporary morgue" include convenience "to the scene, but removed enough to be out of harm's way," "adequate capacity for the number of bodies expected," complete security, "easy access to the facility" by vehicles, "adequate ventilation, hot and cold water, drainage, electrical capacity for necessary equipment, communications office space, rest and debriefing area, refreshments area and restrooms" (pp. 14-15) (Emergency Management Institute National Emergency Training Center, 1996). Temporary morgues may be located in an airplane hangar, on an ice skating or hockey rink, or in an armory or a field tent.

The actual recovery of human remains is coordinated depending on the specific circumstances. In the case of an authorized transportation incident, the NTSB will collaborate with the local medical examiner (ME), to determine how the recovery will be executed. DMORT may be employed in other than transportation incidents where mortuary and identification services are needed such as the Hardin Cemetery flood of 1993 and the Noble, Georgia, incident of 2002. DMORT may be the outsourced agency for foreign events

through the Office of Foreign Disaster Assistance (OFDA) of the U.S. Agency for International Development (USAID). When the cause of the MFI appears to be terrorist or crime related, federal agencies such as the Federal Bureau of Investigation (FBI) and the Alcohol Tobacco and Firearms (ATF) take the lead in managing the recovery of all evidence, including human remains. "When a catastrophe occurs, identification is always difficult due to the large numbers of bodies and injury to the person and requires the involvement of multidisciplinary teams" (p. 428) (Martin-de las Heras et al., 1999).

The morgue may use DMORT team members depending on the magnitude of the incident and the resources of the local response. When activated, DMORT teams provide local authorities with personnel to recover and provide scientific identification of HR. Teams are composed of forensic pathologists, forensic anthropologists, forensic odontologists, fingerprint experts, dental assistants, radiology technicians, funeral directors, medical records personnel and mental health debriefers (for the team only), forensic nurses, law enforcement officers, secretaries, logisticians, and computer experts dispatched in whole or in part depending on scope of the disaster. Regardless of the actual position, each DMORT member must be flexible and have sufficient cross training to assume a team position that will expedite the goal of forensic identification of the dead.

The role of the forensic nurse functioning within the temporary morgue is as varied and diverse as the individual's training and experience. These nurses are challenged with developing strategies to promote advanced practice standards of forensic nursing care and evidence-based practice. "Identification of human remains is dependent on two factors—first, the availability of sufficient antemortem information obtained from records and relatives, and second, the existence of sufficient postmortem material for the recording of identification data" (p. 428) (Martin-de las Heras et al., 1999).

"When processing is completed, the manner and cause of death are determined and recorded and the remains are then released to the family" (p. 239) (Wright et al., 1999). From both a humanitarian and a religious point of view, the identification of victims of a mass disaster is considered essential. Identification is also important for judicial reasons (Martin-de las Heras et al., 1999).

Standard reception areas for morgues are a secure entrance where transported remains from the disaster site arrive in body bags. Recovered remains are provided with identification numbers in the admitting station. A packet of worksheets accompanies the HR for all of the forensic processing stations. The flow of operations within the morgue is flexible; however, there is a recommended protocol that ensures safety to the staff and the completeness of the forensic investigation. It is imperative that the human remains are radiographed early in the process to ensure that there are no sharp or concealed weapons or explosives that could harm any member of the team, to sort out debris, and for comparison with antemortem medical records of orthopedic injuries, other patterned injuries, implanted surgical devices, projectiles, and other anomalies.

The stations that follow have some adaptability, but often pathologists prefer to examine the HR before fingerprinting and anthropology. Each event dictates slight changes in the processing and is dependent on the type of incident and conditions of the remains. The other stations vital to the scientific identification process are dental, autopsy (as indicated), fingerprinting, and DNA. Documentation is initiated as the bag is opened, its contents triaged and photographed, and personal affects such as clothing and jewelry are removed and logged; once initial documentation is complete, an appropriate number is assigned. Remains may be intact or not. Regardless of the condition, the processing protocols are the same. The HR are now ready to continue through the processing workstations. A tracker accompanies all remains.

Fingerprints are part of the scientific process essential in the identification process. Advanced forensic nurses with extensive training in fingerprinting technique, often affiliated with a law enforcement office, may augment resources in obtaining fingerprints. Designated law enforcement personnel will conduct postmortem fingerprinting using various examination techniques, but they first obtain exemplars from the deceased. The FBI fingerprinting team is generally called to mass fatalities incidents to assist with this task. Fingerprints are then compared to those available on file for confirmation of identity. Because many individuals do not have antemortem fingerprints, investigators may request personal items from the victim's home to obtain fingerprints for comparison. This occurs only if sufficient cause exists, because the process also includes dental records, medical devices, and DNA as other positive means of identification.

Comparing antemortem and postmortem radiographs is a widely accepted method in forensic dental identification. Lists of potential victims are compiled, and information on the victim's dentists are obtained from victims family and or friends. Complete dental records including the dental chart, original radiographs, and models are requested. These materials are then compared to postmortem data to determine a medical positive identification. Restorations, prosthesis, missing teeth, pathology, and even bone trabeculations can be used in the antemortem-postmortem matching procedure (Williams, personal communication). The importance of dental evidence in the identification of burn victims has been emphasized in numerous case reports and in papers regarding mass disasters. The teeth are the most resistant tissue in the body and may sometimes be the only thing that avoids total decomposition and survives severe fire (Knight, 1997).

The ME or coroner maintains legal custody of the body until it is released from jurisdiction and is required by jurisdiction statutes to perform autopsies on certain classifications of deceased individuals (Hoyt & Spangler, 1996). "The medico-legal autopsy functions to discover some or all of the following facts: the identity of the body, the cause of death, the nature and number of injuries, the time of death, the presence of poisons, the expectation of duration of life for insurance purposes, the presence of natural disease and its contribution to death, especially where there is also trauma, the interpretation of the injuries, either criminal, suicidal or accidental and the interpretation of any other unnatural conditions, including those associated with surgical or medical procedures" (p. 16) (Knight, 1997). The initial examination of the body begins with photography and trace evidence collection. The appearance and any medical interventions are meticulously recorded. Various bloods, body fluid, and tissue samples are taken for blood grouping, toxicology, and DNA testing. Cytological smears have been reported to be a potential source of DNA reference samples, which can be compared to DNA recovered from found human remains (Sweet et al., 1999). Forensic nurses trained in death investigation can assist in the autopsies performed on the victims of catastrophic events. The ME or coroner may also waive the autopsy or inspect the remains after the initial investigation of the death and release the body to the next of kin (Hoyt & Spangler, 1996). The number and extent of autopsies depends on

the situation and type of mass fatality. Because of the medicolegal nature of aviation disasters, for example, the NTSB requires autopsy of crew members. Common tissue or human tissue that is not identified because of comingling or sheer amount is buried in a common grave.

Forensic Aspects of Disaster Response

The forensic nurse practices in accordance with the established standards of care. These include scientific process, evidence collection, documentation, and crisis intervention. Disaster events may challenge the advanced practice forensic nurse; however, education and collaboration among forensic practitioners allows the forensic nurse to provide a necessary function within the multidisciplinary team.

KEY POINT The forensic nurse's ability to discover, identify, and collect physical and nonphysical evidence may play an important role in the investigation of a disaster. It is imperative for the forensic nurse to discern what may be evidence and how and if it should be collected.

Competency education is a necessary aspect of the preparedness of healthcare providers across the spectrum. Forensic nurses are no exception and require expertise in scientific knowledge to support their ability to respond to MCIs. A set of core emergency preparedness competencies exists for public health workers, created by Dr. Gebbie. These core competencies were used as the model for the core emergency and disaster preparedness competencies outlined for nurses in general (Williams, 2003). In 2003, the International Nursing Coalition for Mass Casualty Education (INCME) published the *Educational Competencies for Registered Nurses Related to Mass Casualty Incidents* (Educational Competencies for Registered Nurses Responding to Mass Casualty Incidents). In clinical disaster response, the forensic nurse may be the most familiar with physical and nonphysical evidence collection and may be required to instruct the healthcare team why and how to collect it. Chain of custody must also be taught and maintained. Physical evidence collection occurs with the assistance from the forensic nurse during the autopsy in the morgue and in the emergency/trauma bay once resuscitation efforts stabilize the victim. Wound debris, projectiles and clothing are among the most commonly found physical evidence on individuals; however, forensic nurses in clinical response may work in concert with law enforcement agencies to collect bomb residue swabbings from injured victims of a building explosion or package bomb. Perhaps the evidence may be a sputum sample of those involved in the confined noxious gas inhalation of a terrorist attack. Life-threatening conditions may compromise the opportunity for physical evidence collection in the clinical environment as decontamination efforts destroy physical evidence.

"In disasters of sudden onset, whether natural disasters such as earthquakes or terrorist bombings, the absence of warning and the potential for the event to cause immediate injury or death to large numbers of people can at best evoke only a reactive medical response, not only among the first responders but also among the professionals who are first at the scene" (p. 75) (Briggs & Leong, 1990). Physical evidence collection occurs with the assistance from the forensic nurse during the autopsy in the morgue and in the emergency/trauma bay once resuscitation efforts stabilize the victim.

Documentation throughout a disaster event is central with forensic nurses functioning in a fast-paced, high-stress, and demanding environment. Scrupulous documentation provides evidence for a victim and testimony for the court, and it is best achieved with timely and efficient methods such as photography, diagrams, and written and electronic records.

"Crisis intervention may be the most challenging experience for nurses to endure and practice because it relates to issues that require a personal, professional, and frequently an emotional commitment" (p. 5) (The American Presidency Project). Examples include expertise of the forensic nurse as a notifier of death or a resource for family viewing deceased disaster victims. Those forensic nurses providing crisis intervention require critical incident stress management training to be sensitive as well as effective during these times of misfortune.

The forensic nurse in the clinical trauma setting must use caution in treating patients as victims when indeed they may be perpetrators. Working with remains that may be contaminated necessitates caution and diligent use of personal protective equipment.

Confidentiality in disaster response is crucial to protect the dignity of the responders, the hope of the families, and the safety of the victims. The public may have a high degree of interest in the incident. "If an emergency or disaster is declared by the President or if a public health emergency is declared by the secretary of HHS, certain sanctions and penalties may be waived by the secretary against a covered hospital that does not comply with certain provisions of the HIPAA Privacy Rule." On presidential or secretarial declaration termination, all hospitals must comply with all requirements of the Privacy Rule for any patient still under its care. HIPAA waivers in case of declared emergency or disasters. (Retrieved August 12, 2009 from www.hipaacompliancejournal.com/2009/07/hipaa-waivers-in-case-of-declared-emergency-or-disasters/)

Incomplete or erroneous reporting can lead to complications later, so it is imperative that there is a standardized media response given only by a designated individual, typically the public information officer (PIO), and the forensic nurse should not disclose any information without proper authority.

Disaster-Related Conditions

The forensic nurse responding to disasters will see, think, and do things beyond ordinary assessment and treatment of traumatic, medical, and psychological disaster-related conditions. A disaster is not outside the scope of a responding level I trauma center, for example. It is important for the forensic nurse to recognize this and teach other healthcare professionals in disaster response the methods and dimension of thought that support medicolegal management of the disaster population.

Clinical forensic nursing practice on a daily basis can only enhance the efficiency and likelihood of the response in matters of larger-scale disasters. "When an explosion occurs, the explosive material is suddenly converted into a large volume of gas with the release of a tremendous amount of energy" (p. 612) (Marshall, 1977). A person in the vicinity can experience an isolated blast injury, dismemberment, or complete annihilation and dissemination. The person can also "be injured by the wave of pressure, called the shock wave, which spreads concentrically from the blast center" (p. 612) (Marshall, 1977). The organs most likely to be affected are the tympanic membranes of the ears, lungs, bowel, cardiovascular, and central nervous system. The resulting blast injury may help to ascertain proximity

to the explosive device. "In the outer, or injury zone there is no immediate mortality from primary injuries and secondary or tertiary blast injuries accompanying them" (p. 893) (Mellor, 1992). The secondary blast injury may also contain evidentiary material such as "fragments of burned safety fuse, torn and twisted pieces of clock mechanism, parts of batteries, short bits of wire, parts of switches, electrical tape and or container pieces" (p. 602) (Marshall, 1977).

At the scene, wounds may be wrapped or left unwrapped. Until the wound can be irrigated, a pressure bandage is likely to be applied. If the wound is dressed, the forensic nurse will examine the bandage and the wound for particulate evidence, which may be removed and then the nurse will irrigate the wound. A basin can be placed under the blast injury during irrigation. The irrigant may be saved and later strained further for collection of any debris that may be useful in determining which type of incendiary device was used.

When unsure if material is evidence, it should be collected. Obvious rules for evidence collection and handling apply, and under no circumstances should the condition of the patient be compromised to collect evidence. Of particular importance is what the patient may have heard or seen before an explosion. This is carefully documented and shared with investigative personnel.

Sometimes a perpetrator may have been injured in the handling of the device. Burn injuries often accompany miscellaneous blast injuries and may be of varying depths. The most common type of burn during an explosion includes the flash burn, an often-superficial burn that may be patterned to illustrate position during the explosion. A photograph of this type of burn injury and other patterned burns is the best documentation of any injury, as well as diagrams and written documentation, which may later reveal proximity and the location of a patient involved in a blast. Deeper burns may also be present in varying degrees and surface area disguising the presence of flash burns. The location of an individual with this type of burn may be more important in explosions of smaller scale such as a pipe or letter bomb in a closed environment. The presence of accelerant may also give insight into the origin of a burn.

Also, chemicals and radiation passing through tissue may cause burns. Blunt force injury is sustained by absorbing energy and can fall into four categories, which are "abrasions, contusions, lacerations and fractures" (p. 91) (DiMaio & DiMaio, 2001). "Tertiary blast injury" is blunt force trauma "due to the victim being thrown against an object" (p. 536) (DiMaio & DiMaio, 2001). The forensic nurse examining blunt force injury will again use the techniques of forensic wound identification, described in previous chapters, to photograph and collect evidence from the wound. Documentation of injuries during disasters is of particular importance for later data comparison to similar events. For instance, at the 1992 Hurricane Andrew in Florida, blunt trauma was the foremost cause of accidental death responsible for 8 of the 15 reported as a "direct result of its physical forces on land and on the water" (p. 449) (Lew & Wetli, 1996). Blunt force from flying debris and crush injury are commonly seen together also in tornadoes, earthquakes where buildings collapse, and other natural and man-made disaster scenarios. Documentation of injuries during a disaster gives disaster healthcare responders an idea of what they might potentially face during future emergencies of similar type. Also it may provide testimony to the court when victims seek justice and restitution.

"The management of patients contaminated externally with radioactive materials is directed toward early recognition of the problem, avoidance of a secondary spread of contamination within a hospital, and skin decontamination by washing or showering" (p. 1553) (McGlown, 2004). Under no circumstances is loose radioactive material collected for evidentiary value. Because of the delayed effect of radiation exposure, a forensic nurse may be suspicious of populations that present with immunosufficiency, "cataracts, acute radiation syndrome, chromosomal aberrations, genetic mutations, or cancer" (p. 1553) (Everly & Mitchell, 1993) and have a history to corroborate the diagnosis.

Medical disaster-related conditions may involve toxic inhalation, poisoning, bacterial, or viral infection. "The pulmonary route of entry generally involves a volatile substance, gas, dust, smoke, or aerosol" (p. 1570) (Winek, 1977). Poisoning and bacterial or viral infections are generally inhaled, aspirated, or ingested.

Evidence collection may include sputum samples and bronchial washings, or "specimens of blood, urine, and stomach contents" (p. 209) (Smialek & Schwartz, 1999). Forensic nurses are also aware of the reportable requirements to the CDC. Bacterial and viral infection reminds caregivers to avoid contagion and contamination. Again, scrupulous documentation of the circumstances is inherently important to the medicolegal disaster population.

Disaster-related psychological effects are profound not only to the injured victims of a disaster but to those secondary victims who experience a loss of loved ones or possessions, a sense of violation, and a question of safety. "Critical Incident Stress Management (CISM) spans a continuum of services from pre-crisis preparedness to acute care services to post-intervention procedures that address the psychological aftermath of critical incidents and prevent or mitigate the potential onset of Posttraumatic Stress Disorder" (p. 1) (Everly & Mitchell, 1993). Trained forensic nurses are aware of the acute and delayed sequelae experienced by survivors and the resource they pose to provide CISM debriefing sessions "within the first 24 to 72 hours following a critical incident" (p. 40) (Martin, 1993). "A majority of victims experience acute stress disorder with disruptions in reasonable mastery, caring attachments, and meaningful purpose in life, the three domains associated with good physical and mental health" (p. 238) (Flannery, 2000). The forensic nurse trained in CISM recognizes the "three stages of ambiguity, depression and posttraumatic stress disorder" (p. 40) (Martin, 1993). These nurses are also aware of the potential of their own "role conflict during a disaster situation," their own "emotional reactions," (p. 16) (Stanley, 1990) and the need to recover "a sense of control" in their own lives.

Summary

Disasters, both technological and natural, have increased in frequency and severity since the introduction of formal disaster management in the U.S. government in the 1950s. Changes in climate and population increases and shifts portend this pattern continuing in the future.

Box 15-2 Nursing Diagnoses Related to Disasters

Coping due to stress, individual, ineffective
Preparedness and readiness conflict
Infection, risk for
Injury, risk for
Safety, altered
Skin integrity, impaired, risk for
Trauma, risk for
Role performance, altered

The role of the forensic nurse in disasters will continue to unfold as the research and body of knowledge expands. Many of the forensic functions that are demanded in a disaster are natural extension of the services that are provided to patients on a day-to-day basis, but others are unique to the disaster field. Forensic nurses can bring their unique perspective through all phases of the disaster cycle, ultimately improving care and services to their clients.

Case Study 15-1
Working Together

The shifts caring for the burn victims of the World Trade Center were busy and long, but after work, concerns of medical personnel rapidly moved to management issues and plans for replacement, as physicians knew the long-term nature of caring for burn trauma patients. It became evident that burn intensive care unit (ICU) nurses who could take the place of the disaster nurses already deployed over the next six to eight weeks were needed. At the time, only 30 burn ICU nurses were registered within the NDMS, 7 of which were already there. An urgent call went out through the American Burn Association and to ICU nurses. Rapid applications were processed as nurses from around the country continued to respond to this demand. This is a real-life occurrence in which interagency cooperation and the disaster nurse's advance practice disaster management skills directly affected the mortality and morbidity of living forensic patients and resulted in an improved and enlarged pool of disaster nursing resources for use in future events. Substantial efforts in training, monitoring, and reviewing actions in the field now take place in all agencies set up for disaster response (Briggs & Leong, 1990).

References

The American Presidency Project. Retrieved April 15, 2009, from www.presidency.ucsb.edu/ws/index.php?pid=433889.

American Red Cross. (1997). *Plan for implementation of the federal family assistance act for aviation disasters*. Washington, DC: American Red Cross. Chapter 8.

Briggs, S., & Leong, M. (1990). Classic concepts in disaster medical response. In J. Leaning (Ed.). *Humanitarian Crises: The medical and public health response* (pp. 73, 75, 78). Boston: Harvard Publishing.

DiMaio, D., & DiMaio, V. (2001). *Forensic pathology* (pp.91, 536). Boca Raton, FL: CRC Press.

Disaster Portable Mobile Unit. Retrieved April 15, 2009, from www.dmort.org/DNPages/DMORTDPMU.htm

Educational Competencies for Registered Nurses Responding to Mass Casualty Incidents. www.nursing.vanderbilt.edu/incmce/competencies.html

Emergency Management Institute National Emergency Training Center. (1996). *Mass fatalities incident response course manual SM-386* (pp.132, 22, 14–15, 19). Washington, DC: United States Government Printing Office.

Everly, Jr., G. S., Flannery, Jr., R. B., & Mitchell, J. T. (1999). Critical Incident Stress Management (CISM): A review of the literature. *Aggression and Violent Behavior: A Review Journal, 5*, 23–40.

Flannery, R. (2000). Treating family survivors of mass casualties: A CISM crisis intervention approach. *International Journal of Emergency Mental Health*, 238.

Goll-McGee, B. (1999). The role of the clinical forensic nurse in critical care. *Critical Care Nursing Quarterly, 22*(1), 8–18 pp. 1, 9.

Haddow, & Bullock. (2003). In K. J. McGlown (Ed.), *Terrorism and disaster management: Preparing healthcare leaders for the new reality*(p. 116). Chicago, IL: Health Administration Press.

Hoyt, C., & Spangler, K. (1996). Forensic nursing implications and the forensic autopsy. *Journal of Psychosocial Nursing, 34*(10), 24–31. pp. 25, 26.

Ibid. p. 4.

Illing, P. (2000). Toxicology and disasters. In B. Ballantyne, T. Marrs, & T. Syversen (Eds.). *General and applied toxicology* (2nd ed., p. 1837). United Kingdom: Macmillan Reference Limited.

International Association of Forensic Nurses, American Nurses Association. (2007). *Scope and standards of forensic nursing practice* Washington, DC: American Nurses Publishing.

Knight, B. (1997). *Simpson's forensic medicine* (11th ed., pp. 16, 34). New York: Oxford University Press, Inc.

Langan, J., & James, D. (2005). *Preparing nurses for disaster management* (pp.3, 47). Upper Saddle River, NJ: Pearson Prentice Hall.

Lew, E., & Wetli, C. (1996). Mortality from hurricane Andrew. *Journal of Forensic Sciences, 41*(3), 449–452.

Marshall, T. (1977). Explosion injuries. In C. Tedeschi, W. Eckert, L. Tedeschi (Eds.). *Forensic Medicine: A study in trauma and environmental hazards* (pp. 612, 602). Philadelphia, Saunders.

Martin, K. (1993). Critical incidents: Pulling together to cope with the stress. Nursing, 39–43.

Martin-de las Heras, S., Valenzuela, A., Villanueva, E., et al. (1999). Methods for identification of 28 burn victims following a 1996 bus accident in Spain. *Journal of Forensic Sciences, 44*(2), 428–431.

McGlown, K. J. (Ed.). (2004). *Terrorism and disaster management: Preparing healthcare leaders for the new reality* (pp. 12, 41, 51, 151, 159, 161, 1553). Chicago, IL: Health Administration Press.

Mellor, S. (1992). The relationship of blast loading to death and injury from explosion. *World of Surgery, 16,* 893–898.

Smialek, J., & Schwartz, G. (1999). Forensic emergency medicine. In G. Schwartz (Ed.). *Principles and practice of emergency medicine* (4th ed., p. 209). Philadelphia, Williams and Wilkins.

Stanley, S. (1990). When the disaster is over: Helping the healers to mend. *Journal of Psychosocial Nursing, 28*(5), 12–16.

Sweet, D., Hildebrand, D., Phillips, D. (1999). Identification of a skeleton using DNA from teeth and a AP smear. *Journal of Forensic Sciences, 44*(3), 630–633.

Tun, K., et al. (2005). Panel 2.16: Forensic aspects fo disaster fatality management. *Prehospital and Disaster Management, 20*(6), 455–458.

Twomey, J., & Goll-McGee, B. (1999). Answering the call when disaster strikes. *Nursing Spectrum, 3*(13), 5.

Williams, D. Personal communication.

Williams, J. (2003). DMORTs meet the forensic needs of mass-disaster incidents. *Forensic Nurse, 2*(1), 32–33.

Winek, C. (1977). Injury by chemical agents. In C. Tedeschi, W. Eckert, & L. Tedeschi (Eds.). *Forensic medicine: A study in trauma and environmental hazards* (pp. 1570). Philadelphia, Saunders.

Wright, R., Peters, C., & Flannery, R. (1999). Victim identification and family support in mass casualties: The Massachusetts Model. *International Journal of Emergency Mental Health, 1*(4), 237–242.

CHAPTER 16 Forensic Investigation of Death

Virginia A. Lynch and Steven A. Koehler

Health and Justice

Society's need to understand the disease mechanisms and biomechanical factors associated with various forms of death is essential to systems of public health and the administration of justice. These processes, which help to determine the precise precipitating factors and causes of death, not only benefit medical science but also serve the public's general welfare by ensuring that natural, accidental, and crime-related fatalities are systematically identified and investigated in regard to cause, manner, and mechanism of death.

Regardless of the circumstances of death, there are usually acute emotional reactions of significant others as well as inherent legal consequences. For example, the precise way individuals die and the events that surround the dying process can determine the execution of last wills and testaments, life insurance distributions, rights of survivorship, and more.

In a typical social structure, the loss of a loved one is a disruptive and often devastating experience. In addition, if death comes suddenly or unexpectedly or involves a violent act, it now becomes a forensic case, demanding a systematic legal inquiry. Historically, nurses have been among the key individuals to care for both the dying patient and the bereaved in that delicate period before and after death. They often participate in lifesaving intervention or resuscitation efforts and perhaps later prepare the deceased for postmortem procedures or release to a funeral home. Furthermore, contemporary nursing practice mandates forensic accountability as a priority in sudden, unexpected, and questioned deaths, a duty deemed second only to lifesaving interventions or resuscitation efforts. With these factors in mind, one can readily appreciate the appeal of death investigation as a forensic nursing career choice.

Historical Perspective of Forensic Death

Death is the permanent cessation of all vital bodily functions: the end of life (*Dorland's*, 2000). The causal factors of death establish the principal foundation of medical science: sustaining and improving the quality of life. Without knowledge regarding *why* people die, it would be virtually impossible to establish preventive healthcare practices. From the beginning of civilization, death roused the interest and curiosity of the public to determine what separated the living from the dead. Because of human deaths, medical science and the law initiated a search that has lasted from antiquity until the present. The question of why people die has unfolded criteria for both natural and unnatural death, yet even now there remains a requisite mystery surrounding unexplained deaths. The need for absolute accuracy is compelling. Forensic medicine becomes the "application of clinical and scientific knowledge that provides answers to questions of law and/or patient treatment involving court related issues" (American Academy of Forensic Science [AAFS], 2002).

In the United States, *forensic pathology* is a subspecialty of anatomical pathology and forensic medicine charged with the responsibility of determining the cause and manner of questioned deaths. The manner of death will determine whether a crime has been committed. This is an important area where the forensic nurse examiner (FNE) can bring clinical management skills and expertise to the grieving and bereaved.

A Multidisciplinary Task

Justice Blackmun referred to the circumstances of death investigation as the *unavoidable intersection* between law and medicine that requires cooperation and understanding, rather than distance and isolation between investigating agencies (*Law & Politics Book Review*, 1998). Accordingly, nurses must be aware of the circumstances of death and the legal statutes that unite them with law enforcement agencies in the role of a clinical investigator. The universal application of nursing accountability includes the scientific investigation of death.

The earliest application of forensic medicine dealt with suicide, generally regarded as a crime against public interest since classical times (Baden, 1989). The criminality of suicide and the penalty involved included condemnation of the offender by the Roman Catholic Church. For the violation of canon law by suicide to be confirmed, the investigation of death evolved from the need to determine the accurate cause of suicidal deaths (Spitz & Fisher, 1993). During these times, the investigation relied solely on the circumstances of death without a specific examination of the body.

Not until the thirteenth century did the autopsy become a standard of practice in the postmortem evaluation of death. China is the first country known to have developed extensive, detailed instructions on necropsy pathology and the autopsy. The Chinese handbook *Hsi Yuan Lu* specified precise protocols addressing the types of wounds inflicted by sharp versus blunt instruments, death by drowning versus submersion in water after death, and death by fire versus burning after death (*Hsi Yuan Lu* in Camps, Robinson, & Lucas, 1976).

Since these earliest beginnings, there has been an intense and ever-expanding interest in death investigation, specifically as it relates to solving crimes. New technologies have emerged to complement the examination and dissection of the body.

Contemporary death investigation incorporates the application of infrared video-graphic, ultraviolet lights, lasers, spectrographs, neutron activation analysis, computer software, scanning electron microscopes, and DNA analysis. However, the contribution of the autopsy has remained unchanged and irreplaceable.

Death Investigation and the Law

Every death has actual or potential legal implications. Health or disability insurance payments, survivor benefits, transfer of estates, anatomical tissue or organ donations, and criminal charges all depend on information that emerges from the death scene investigation and the results of the forensic autopsy. Data that suggest suicide, evidence of torture, presence of toxicological residue, or the discovery of an unknown pregnancy can significantly affect subsequent judicial proceedings, as well as determining the corpus delicti in criminal liability. *Corpus delicti* refers to the substantial and fundamental fact necessary to prove the commission of a crime (*Dorland's*, 2000). This term is often used erroneously to designate the physical body of the homicide. For example, the corpus delicti of homicide is the *fact* that a person died from unlawful violence (Adelson, 1974). This legal term literally refers to the body of the crime or offense, not the corpse of the decedent, and must be determined for successful prosecution of a criminal death.

KEY POINT The cause of death is the factor that initiated the sequence of events that culminated in death, such as cancer or multiple injuries from a vehicle incident.

The manner of death refers to the circumstances from which the cause of death emerged—that is, natural, accidental, homicidal, suicidal, or undetermined.

Fundamentals of Death Investigation

Death investigation is a process that involves the identification, collection, analysis, interpretation of physical evidence, and the circumstances of the event from which conclusions are derived or hypothesized. The investigation process is systematic and ongoing. The actual conduct of an investigation, evaluation of data obtained during the investigation, and the reinvestigation and reevaluation of new data as necessary is part of the medicolegal investigation of death.

Death is the actual state of nonbeing. Death investigators should possess a deep understanding of the medical process of death, the signs of death, the sequence of physiological events surrounding death, and the laws governing determination of death. This responsibility demands knowledge of the presumptive signs of death as well as laws governing determination of death. The ability of an individual to declare an individual dead varies from state to state and even from county to county within the same state. In some states while lay individuals can pronounce someone dead, emergency medical services (EMS) personnel typically conduct this task. In other jurisdictions, the forensic nurse death investigator (FNDI) or registered nurse deputy coroner (RNDC) pronounces the death at the time of their arrival at the scene. Consequently, the time of their arrival at the scene is noted as the estimated time of death unless it has been witnessed. Pronouncements made by EMS involve placing three electrocardiogram (EKG) patches to determine if any electrical activity can be detected in the heart. A flat line indicates no cardiac activity and death. In cases of obvious deaths such as those seen in

decapitation or decomposition, firefighter or police officers at the scene can make the pronouncement. Although most legal rights are suspended at death, certain laws pertain to an inquiry into the circumstances of death, security of personal property, and disposition of the body, as well as individual human rights, which remain in death. The rights of the decedents and their families become legal issues once the processes of death are complete.

The forensic medical investigation of deaths includes has two main objectives:

1. Determining the positive identity of the individual
2. Determining the cause and manner of death

Classic questions are asked:

- *Who* is/was the person? (confirm the identity beyond any doubt)
- *What* happened? (stabbing, beating, fall, collision, or exsanguination)
- *When* did the person die? (the best estimate of the time of death)
- *Where* did it happen? Where did the person die? (e.g., in the street and then in the hospital)
- *Why* did it happen? (argument, lost consciousness, defective product)
- *How* did it happen? (a car spun on ice, rotated, glanced off a building, then struck a pedestrian)

The initial issue in the investigation is to determine *who* the decedent is. The methods used to determine the positive identity range from low-tech methods of visual identification to highly sophisticated techniques such as facial reconstruction. The method used to determine identification is dictated by the level of decomposition or extent of trauma.

The next phase is to determine *what* events happened to cause the death. A detailed examination of the surroundings often provides a clue to what precipitated the death. Did the victim fall out the window? Was he pushed out the window? Did he deliberately jump out the window in an act of suicide?

When the death occurred is often essential information to help determine the circumstances and manner of death. Methods used to ascertain the time of death begins by a detailed examination of the body for stages of livor mortis, rigor mortis, and algor mortis. Other methods used to determine time of death include stomach content analysis and entomological evaluation.

Where represents the location of the body when it was found. Was the individual killed elsewhere and then moved? Did the person walk to her or his death, or was the body transported to this particular place?

Why refers to the series of sequential circumstances pertaining to events that occurred before death, at the time of death, and immediately afterward.

How refers to a descriptive account of the circumstances of *why* in an investigator's report.

Answers to these questions will help establish the cause of death and the manner of death. Although *what* is often the most controversial issue in the investigative process and courtroom debate, each aspect of the investigation must interface with the others to provide a precise conclusion. Determining what occurred depends on the quality of scene investigation, recovery and preservation of evidence, the autopsy, and toxicology evaluation.

The final diagnoses are based on the answers to these issues. The issue of *what* occurred is of paramount importance in determining whether a crime has been committed. The need for absolute accuracy is vital for establishing the cause of death (Besant-Matthews, personal communication, April 2004). These questions and their answers will guide the investigator through a plan of action and provide an evaluation of outcomes.

CAUSES OF DEATH

The cause of death is the event or condition that resulted in death due to natural or traumatic conditions.

Natural deaths are a result of disease processes such as the occlusion of a coronary artery resulting from plaque, cirrhosis of the liver resulting from chronic alcohol use, or hemorrhage resulting from an aneurysm of an artery in the brain. A death is deemed occurring from a natural cause if it stems from congenital anomalies or involves a degenerative disease, an infection, or is the result of a metabolic or neoplastic disease that interferes or disables vital organ functions.

A death can be the result of injury from trauma that is sufficient enough to affect a vital organ or system. Trauma can result from an intentional or nonintentional act as in the case of a gunshot wound, indicating a homicide, suicide (self-inflicted), or accident. Nonintentional trauma can include injuries received during a motor vehicle collision (blunt force trauma), falling down steps, being injured on a construction site, or from being hit by a baseball during a game.

A cause of death can also occur without trauma but not be natural. Deaths from drug overdose (accident or suicide) typically show no external signs of trauma. Drowning and certain types of asphyxiation also leave no external detectable signs of trauma.

Basic knowledge regarding the scientific investigation of death involves the following:

- Identification of trauma, natural disease processes, self-inflicted wounds versus those inflicted by another, pharmacology, toxicology, entomology, anthropology, anatomy and physiology, risk factors, statistics, and human behavior
- Recognition of wound characteristics related to injuries resulting from weapons used to inflict death range from the subtle, innocuous signs of abuse or neglect to catastrophic fatal injuries or mutilation of bodies before and after death
- Recovery and documentation of evidence, collection and preservation of highly perishable and fragile specimens, and the security of such materials (related to the cause of death) are primary responsibilities of the medical death scene investigator.
- Notification of next of kin in a personal, timely, compassionate, and sensitive approach

At the scene of death, the responding investigator assesses the circumstances of death, observing for indicators of violence, poisoning, homicide, suicide, or accident. The investigator interviews the decedent's family or significant others at the scene to determine if the person has a notable medical history, obtains the name of the attending physician, and documents any medications or other clues at the scene that might reveal an associated medical condition. The investigator may request the family to contact a mortuary and inform them that the body will be sent to a morgue for further assessment. In the latter case, the investigator is responsible for arranging legally secure transportation of the body to the medical examiner's or coroner's (ME/Cs) facility. Emergency medical personnel on the scene will rarely assume this role because they must be immediately available to respond to calls involving living persons. If the death is deemed a natural death, and if the decedent's physician has agreed to sign the death certificate, the medical examiner or coroner may permit the body to be taken to the funeral home while awaiting certification.

The body should not be embalmed prior to a postmortem examination. It is vital to ensure that the death is not a forensic case before any mortuary procedures are initiated, because embalming may introduce artifacts or destroy evidence, especially in cases of poisoning.

BEST PRACTICE Forensic autopsy should precede embalming procedures, because body alterations and use of embalming fluids affect the appearance and characteristics of body surfaces, organs, tissues, and the blood.

Although embalming temporarily preserves the condition of the body and significantly reduces the risk of infection from the corpse, it is essential that any investigative procedures are accomplished first. When the body is released for burial, the mortician will obtain permission to proceed with embalming techniques according to the wishes of the family (Adelson, 1974).

Forensic Pathologist/Medical Examiner/Coroner at the Scene

The ME/C may not be required by law to go to the death scene and may decide to send a designee, either a death investigator or a deputy coroner (such as the FNDI or RNDC), to oversee the death scene investigation. The presence of these professionals enhances the understanding of the case. Although it would be ideal to have a forensic pathologist at all scenes of death, these professionals may only go to the most complicated scenes because of their low numbers, limited time, and limited opportunity.

The majority of deaths are expected, caused by natural diseases, and are well documented within the medical history. These cases do not require the involvement of the ME/Cs office and are commonly reported by a physician or next-of-kin (NOK) to the ME/C office by phone providing a detailed past medical history. In most jurisdictions, the deputy coroner or the death investigator can authorize the transfer of the body from the scene directly to the funeral home if he or she is satisfied that the death was the result of a natural process and that there was no foul play or signs of trauma.

When the presence of a death investigator or deputy coroner is required at a scene, this individual is notified by either the responding police office or emergency medical responder once it has been determined a death has occurred. The ME/C or the investigator has the authority by local or state law to conduct an inquiry and a death scene investigation. The ME/C will determine if a forensic autopsy will be performed to determine the decedent's identity and the cause and manner of death.

The ME/C or designee has the authority to take custody and control of the body, respond to and investigate the scene, take possession of evidence, and obtain and review medical records. Only the ME or coroner, however, is authorized to certify the cause and manner of death under independent authority, unfettered by political or other influences.

The forensic nurse, medical investigator, or deputy coroner who is representing the ME/C collects information that may be used to confirm the identification of the decedent and establish an approximate date and time of death. These data will assist the forensic pathologist at the time of autopsy and contribute to the determination of cause, manner, and mechanism of death.

Death Scene Control and Processing

BODY AT THE SCENE

Once the person is declared dead, the body, the area surrounding the death scene (crime scene), and the associated medical forensic evidence comes under the jurisdiction of the ME/C office investigating the death. The law enforcement officials are responsible for ensuring the security of the crime scene, the safety of the investigators, conducting detailed interviews with family, friends, and witnesses and begin to create a list of possible suspects. Securing and protecting the death scene are the initial roles of the law enforcement personnel.

The forensic investigation of a crime scene involves interagency cooperation, scene examination, and preservation as well as photography and field notes. Law enforcement is present to accomplish a criminal investigation; however, the coroner or medical investigator achieves a separate and concurrent medical investigation. The two entities must function as a team. Both may perform interviews of witnesses and next of kin. The objectives of each agency are different, as are the responsibilities.

BEST PRACTICE Essential steps in managing a body at a scene include identification, photography, creation of a scene diagram, documentation of the condition of the body and clothing, preservation of trace evidence, and bagging of the hands and the body of the deceased.

Before the processing of the scene, the body and its surroundings must be photodocumented. This is typically conducted by a forensic crime-scene photographer employed by a ME office or associated with a coroner's office. The forensic nurse death investigator (FDNI) or deputy coroner may also be highly skilled in scene photography and assume this responsibility for the ME/C. These individuals photograph the scene in a specific sequence starting from a distance and working their way toward the body. The body and evidence cannot be touched or moved until it has been photographed and the scene forensic photographer grants permission. Photographs are important in that they present the state of the scene at the time of the death, the position of the body, its relationship to other objects, and a general layout of the scene. These photographs allow those not at the scene to gain an overview of the scene without being there. The images are also viewed by the forensic pathologist before conducting the autopsy, as well as homicide detectives, lawyers, and possibly juries in a court of law.

Once the scene has been photodocumented, the next step is to identify, photograph, and collect trace evidence from the body and the surrounding scene that may be lost or destroyed during the transport of the body. The identification and collection of forensic evidence is handled by the FDNI, RNDC, or forensic scientists trained in varies subspecialties such as fingerprinting, blood splatter, trace evidence, and ballistics from the ME/C office. After the body has been processed at the scene, it is placed onto a white sheet and then into a body bag for transport to the morgue.

PLACE OF DEATH

Because 60% to 75% of reportable deaths occur without an attendant physician, it is reasonable to expect death to transpire in a residence. When the decedent has not been admitted to the hospital before death or when the individual lives alone, a significant amount of time may lapse before the body is discovered. Without prior arrangements with legal and medical authorities, such as hospice cases, the investigators must proceed to the residence to pronounce and examine the scene of death.

When death occurs in a public area, prompt removal of the body from the scene or from public view may be in the best interest of the family, bystanders, or traffic. However, a thorough investigation is time consuming, and related legal statutes are specific regarding the protection of the body and scene. Generally, it is a violation of the law to remove a body from the scene of death or to remove any items from the body before the scene investigation

has been completed. There are a few exceptions. For instance, if the body is in an unsafe location or is blocking traffic, it maybe removed to a site near the place of death until the investigation is complete. If the death occurs in a hospital, all medical devices such as central IV lines, dressings, or other paraphernalia should remain intact and be transported to the morgue.

Death Investigation Systems

Within the United States, there are two primary types of death investigation systems: the medical examiner's system and the coroner's system. There may also be a combination of the two known as a mixed system, as well as a law enforcement/coroner system such as a sheriff coroner.

MEDICAL EXAMINER SYSTEM

In a medical examiner's office, the chief ME is a forensic pathologist certified by the American Board of Forensic Pathology and is an appointed position. These examiners often operate with several deputy medical examiners (also forensic pathologists) under their command. In the United States and Canada, there is a significant lack of board-certified forensic pathologists (fewer than 400); the distribution is uneven, and smaller states may have far fewer than needed to cover the number of deaths in their jurisdiction. The ME's death investigators can include laypersons, paramedics, and forensic nurses who have received extensive training in death investigation. These investigators represent the authority of the chief ME at the scene of death.

CORONER'S SYSTEM

The current U.S. coroner's system can trace its origins back to the year 1194 in England. The coroner is an elected public officer with the requirements dictated by state laws; however, coroners typically are not physicians and have minimal or no medical experience. The title of coroner is also dictated by law and may become a dual title if the coroner is also a forensic pathologist. In this case, the correct title is coroner/medical examiner to differentiate from the lay coroner. The coroner typically appoints deputies, whose qualifications are also set by each state. According to Marion Cumming, a forensic nurse coroner for 17 years, "The coroner is a public official who is primarily charged with the duty of determining how and why people under the coroner's jurisdiction die" (Cumming, 1995).

Forensic nurse examiners have functioned as elected coroners, investigators for forensic pathologists, or deputy coroners, and have conducted external postmortem examinations, exhumations, and site recovery during disasters, as well as documentation of torture in cases of political asylum. Efficient, well-equipped, well-trained investigators contribute significantly to a successful investigation and removal of remains in catastrophic, unexpected, or unattended natural deaths. Smooth functioning and close cooperation between the first responders, police agencies, fire department officials, emergency services, mortuary personnel, and death scene investigators demonstrate a high level of confidence to the community in medicolegal matters.

Systems structured for the investigation of death are organized to conduct a professional practice within the framework of standards developed and approved by the discipline's governing body and within the parameters of legislative authorities.

Governing statutes, administrative rules, and professional performance standards define the duties and responsibilities of those who are appointed to conduct a forensic death investigation.

Medical examiner's or coroner's systems are responsible for determining the cause and manner of questioned deaths.

Where the law provides for a system of death investigation under the jurisdiction of the medical examiner's, coroner's, or mixed system, the death will become a point of legal inquiry from both a medical and a legal perspective. The law states that certain categories of deaths are to be reported to the county or state death authority for its participation in the investigation.

Types of Deaths That Require a Forensic Investigation

Not all deaths require a forensic investigation. Although each individual medical examiner's and corner's office determines the types of cases it can legally accept, the following categories of deaths are typically investigated:

1. All sudden deaths when the cause of death cannot be properly certified by a physician based on prior (recent) medical attendance
2. All deaths occurring under suspicious circumstances, including but not limited to those in which alcohol, drugs, or other toxic substances may have had a direct bearing on the outcome
3. All deaths occurring because of violence or trauma, whether apparently homicidal, suicidal, or accidental, including but not limited to those resulting from mechanical, thermal, chemical, electrical, or radiation injuries, drowning, cave-ins, or subsidence, regardless of the time elapsed between the time of the injury and death
4. Natural deaths in which the decedent does not have a personal physician familiar with the patient's medical history, social or environmental situation, or the circumstances of the terminal event
5. Any stillbirth or infant death occurring within 24 hours of birth where the mother has not been under the care of a physician or where the mother has suffered trauma at the hand of another person
6. Deaths suspected to be a result of sudden infant death syndrome (SIDS)
7. All criminal abortions, regardless of the gestational age of the fetus
8. All hospital deaths that occur as a result of accidental injury during diagnostic or therapeutic procedures, including but not limited to surgical procedures, and all deaths following the accidental administration of excessive amounts of a drug, including but not limited to blood or blood products; in addition, all operative, perioperative, and postoperative deaths in which the death is not readily and clearly explainable based on prior disease
9. Deaths of all persons while in legal detention, jails, or police custody, including any prisoner who is a patient in a hospital, regardless of the duration of hospital confinement
10. Deaths resulting from disease, injury, or a toxic agent that occurs during active employment
11. Any death wherein the body is unidentified or unclaimed.
12. Any death in which there is uncertainty as to whether it should be reported

KEY POINT All trauma deaths are categorized as forensic cases and require investigation.

Intuitively, it appears to be a better choice to have someone with a healthcare background and clinical expertise fill this important role. Nurses are particularly prepared to recognize signs and symptoms of natural disease processes, to interact with physicians or other healthcare professionals, and to interact with grieving families. The nurse investigator or nurse coroner must also collaborate with scientific and legal personnel, law enforcement agents, and other investigative agencies involved in the medicolegal investigative process.

Jurisdiction of Death

Legislative statutes of the state, province, or country of residence establish jurisdiction and authority for the medical examiner's, medical investigator's, and coroner's systems in forensic deaths. Legal statutes defining jurisdiction differ according to the local, state, federal, or provincial levels, and they vary in different countries; however, the categories of death generally remain the same or similar in nature.

State or provincial statutes define jurisdiction over the body of any person who dies as a result of trauma, violence, accident, suicide, or homicide, or whose death is unattended or involves any suspicion of foul play. The ME or coroner may also be notified depending on the circumstances of death of persons who have no known pertinent medical history. This category of death is intended to include those about whom nothing medical can be found—for instance, a traveler passing through the state who dies at the bus station. It does not include a person who is found dead under nonsuspicious circumstances whose regular attending physician or other clinical physician is unwilling to certify death simply because the physician was not present to observe the death. Certification of death is based on the physician's ability to determine the cause of death based on reasonable medical certainty. The ME or coroner can assume jurisdiction over the body of a person who has died of an obvious natural disease (no trauma or foul play) if the decedent's private physician is temporarily unavailable or unwilling to sign the death certificate. In these deaths, the ME/C office will release the body to the funeral home, determine the cause of death from information contained within the patient's medical records, and issue the death certificate. Some jurisdictions do not include nursing home deaths, as all patients have attending physicians, unless suspicious circumstances are reported or suspected.

KEY POINT Certification of death is based on the physician's ability to determine the cause of death based on reasonable medical certainty.

Furthermore, it is necessary to eliminate natural deaths from being sent to the forensic pathologist when possible. This is an important consideration in situations in which forensic nurse investigators or nurse coroners can examine and evaluate the death from a medical perspective and then release the body directly to the funeral facilities. The ability to divert the natural deaths from the forensic facility helps by reducing the workload on the forensic pathologist, lessening the emotional trauma to the family, and decreasing the operating cost to the office.

Death Defined

The diagnosis of death is traditionally made using the *Triad of Bichat*, which states that death is "the failure of the body as an integrated system associated with the irreversible loss of circulation, respiration and innervation." This is also known as somatic death or clinical death (University of Dundee, 2003). The American College of Legal Medicine defines legal death as "a human body with irreversible cessation of total brain functions, according to usual and customary standards of medical practice, shall be considered dead" (Liang & Snyder, 2004).

BRAIN DEATH

Brain death is a state in which that organ is incapable of sustaining spontaneous respiration and circulation as a result of severe and irreversible injury (American Bar Association and the National Conference of Commissioners of Uniform State Laws 1968, cited in Spitz & Fisher, 1993). Brain death was further defined by the Iowa State-wide Organ Procurement Organization as the irreversible loss of all functions of the brain. The criteria for brain death includes the following: (1) no electrical activity occurring within the brain as demonstrated by an electroencephalogram (EEG), (2) no blood flowing to the brain, and (3) an absence of functioning in all parts of the brain as determined by clinical assessment (no movement, no response to stimulation, no breathing, no brain reflexes).

Brain death can occur as a result of anoxia, ischemia, intracranial hematoma, gunshot wound to the head, intracranial aneurysm, or tumor mass. These conditions cause the brain to swell. Because the brain is enclosed in the skull, it cannot expand, thus increasing intracranial pressure. This can stop blood flow to the brain, kill brain cells, and cause herniation of the brain. When brain cells die, they do not regenerate; thus, any damage caused is permanent and irreversible (Emory, 2003).

KEY POINT A person who is declared brain dead is legally dead.

In spite of some differences in legal definitions of brain death in various states, physicians can meet the requirements of all by using commonly accepted criteria of brain death or by having two physicians, one of whom is a neurologist, make the determination. To avoid any appearance of impropriety when the death of an organ or tissue donor is being certified, physicians should not be members of the recipient's transplant team. Brain death must be declared before artificial ventilation is disconnected and before any organs or tubes are removed (Spitz & Fisher, 1993).

MOLECULAR DEATH

Molecular or cellular death is a definitive sign of death. It is the death of individual organs and tissues of the body consequent on the circulation. Different tissues die at different rates depending on their oxygen requirements. Thus, within four minutes of the blood supply to the brain ceasing, the central nervous system is irreversibly damaged (University of Dundee, 2003).

Postmortem Interval Determination

Estimation of the time of death is based on a determination of the postmortem interval, that period between death and the time the body was found. Clues of value to the death investigator are the presence of biochemical changes as well as circumstantial evidence (clothes and belongings, extent of digested food, urine and fecal matter, the crime scene) (Gorea, 2004).

Certification of Death

Death certification is the accurate determination of the cause, manner, and mechanism of death. Certification is essential to differenti-

ate a homicidal death from a death resulting from suicide, accident, or natural causes. Appropriate assessment and investigative analysis are based on data collected, evidence recovered, and physical findings obtained during the investigation and autopsy examination.

In spite of scientific advances in forensic pathology and the investigation of death, some things remain unchanged. Lester Adelson, one of the pioneering *greats* in the annals of forensic pathology, emphasizes the importance of both the medical and legal aspects of evidence to determine cause and manner of death. The cause and mechanism of death are derived from the assessment data obtained during research and exploration of the death. These data are supported by investigative findings and are validated by the examination of the remains and review of appropriate medical and other documents. The manner of death is consistent with the cause of death and is corroborated by investigative findings.

The most significant concern in validating the death certificate is the accuracy of terms used. A clear understanding of following terms is essential: the *cause* is defined as that which initiates the series of events ending in death; the *manner* is defined by those circumstances in which the cause arose. The five manners of death include *natural, accidental, homicide, suicide, or undetermined* (NAHSU). The mechanism (or mode) refers to the physiological or biochemical disturbance as a result of the cause. This terminology is essential knowledge to the individual responsible for the investigation as well as for the certification of death (Adelson, 1974).

TERMINOLOGY OF INJURY

Accurate medical terminology is essential in documentation of wound characteristics, injury patterns, and the cause and manner of death, whether in legal proceedings or in a public health setting. In addition, knowledge of various types of weapons (firearm or blunt object) is critical. The accurate and correct use of terminology is critical in the education of medicolegal investigators of death. The certification of death becomes the foundation for the many national statistics used in the prevention of crime, violence, communicable diseases, and death by unnatural causes. The National Centers for Health Statistics (NCHS) compiles data from death certificates. In contrast, the Federal Bureau of Investigation (FBI) Uniform Crime Reports are based on police reports (National Committee for Injury Prevention and Control, 1989).

SPECIAL ASPECTS OF CERTIFICATION OF DEATH

A certification of death is required before the body is disposed by either burial or cremation. The procedure to cremate human remains, though it varies from state to state, generally requires an application by relatives for cremation and the signature of the registered medical practitioner in attendance at the time of death who has also signed a death certificate. Finally, the authority to cremate is issued by the medical referee, medical examiner, or coroner. A record of the cremation and disposition of the remains is noted (Gresham & Turner, 1979).

DEATH CERTIFICATE

The death certificate provides legal proof that an individual is deceased; it is prima facie evidence of the fact of death. Accurate certification of death is one of our most important vital statistics (Fig. 16-1).

Implications for the persons immediately concerned and for society as a whole are addressed on the official death certificate. Viewing the perceived value of this document and the inferred outcomes of death reflected in this document, one would assume that all medical personnel authorized to certify death would be required by law to demonstrate a command of knowledge pertaining to

The cause of death means the disease, abnormality, injury, or poisoning that caused the death, <u>not</u> the mode of dying, such as cardiac or respiratory arrest, shock, or heart failure.

In <u>Part 1</u>, the <u>immediate</u> cause of death is reported in line (a). Antecedent conditions, if any, which gave rise to the cause are reported on lines (b), (c), and (d). The <u>underlying</u> cause should be reported on the last line used in Part 1. No entry is necessary on lines (b), (c), and (d) if the immediate cause of death on line (a) describes completely the train of events. ONLY ONE CAUSE SHOULD BE ENTERED ON A LINE. Additional lines may be added if necessary. Provide the best estimate of the interval between the onset of each condition and death. Do not leave the interval blank, if unknown, so specify.

In <u>Part 2</u> enter other important diseases or conditions that may have contributed to death but did not result in the underlying cause of death given in Part 1.

See examples below.

35. PART 1 ENTER THE DISEASES, INJURIES OR COMPLICATIONS THAT CAUSED THE DEATH. DO NOT ENTER THE MODE OF DYING SUCH AS CARDIAC OR RESPIRATORY ARREST, SHOCK, OR HEART FAILURE. LIST ONLY ONE CAUSE ON EACH LINE.	Approximate Interval Between Onset and Death
IMMEDIATE CAUSE (Final disease or condition resulting in death) → a. **Rupture of Myocardium**	Mins.
b. **Acute Myocardial Infarction**	6 days
Sequentially list conditions, if any, leading to immediate cause. Enter UNDERLYING CAUSE *(disease or injury that initiated events resulting in death)* LAST c. **Chronic Ischemic Heart Disease**	5 years
d.	

PART 2 OTHER SIGNIFICANT CONDITIONS CONTRIBUTING TO DEATH BUT NOT RESULTING IN THE UNDERLYING CAUSE GIVEN IN PART 1 (i.e., substance abuse, diabetes, smoking, etc.) **Diabetes, Chronic Obstructive Pulmonary Disease, Smoking**	36a. AUTOPSY? [X] YES [ ] NO	36b. AUTOPSY FINDINGS AVAILABLE PRIOR TO COMPLETION OF CAUSE OF DEATH? [X] YES [ ] NO

37. DID TOBACCO USE CONTRIBUTE TO DEATH [X] YES [ ] PROBABLY [ ] NO [ ] UNKNOWN	38. DID ALCOHOL USE CONTRIBUTE TO DEATH [ ] YES [ ] PROBABLY [X] NO [ ] UNKNOWN	39. WAS DECEDENT PREGNANT AT TIME OF DEATH [ ] YES [X] NO [ ] UNK WITHIN LAST 12 MO [ ] YES [X] NO [ ] UNK

35. PART 1 ENTER THE DISEASES, INJURIES OR COMPLICATIONS THAT CAUSED THE DEATH. DO NOT ENTER THE MODE OF DYING SUCH AS CARDIAC OR RESPIRATORY ARREST, SHOCK, OR HEART FAILURE. LIST ONLY ONE CAUSE ON EACH LINE.	Approximate Interval Between Onset and Death
IMMEDIATE CAUSE (Final disease or condition resulting in death) → a. **Cerebral Laceration**	10 mins.
b. **Open Skull Fracture**	10 mins.
Sequentially list conditions, if any, leading to immediate cause. Enter UNDERLYING CAUSE *(disease or injury that initiated events resulting in death)* LAST c. **Automobile Accident**	10 mins.
d.	

PART 2 OTHER SIGNIFICANT CONDITIONS CONTRIBUTING TO DEATH BUT NOT RESULTING IN THE UNDERLYING CAUSE GIVEN IN PART 1 (i.e., substance abuse, diabetes, smoking, etc.)	36a. AUTOPSY? [X] YES [ ] NO	36b. AUTOPSY FINDINGS AVAILABLE PRIOR TO COMPLETION OF CAUSE OF DEATH? [X] YES [ ] NO

37. DID TOBACCO USE CONTRIBUTE TO DEATH [ ] YES [ ] PROBABLY [X] NO [ ] UNKNOWN	38. DID ALCOHOL USE CONTRIBUTE TO DEATH [ ] YES [X] PROBABLY [ ] NO [ ] UNKNOWN	39. WAS DECEDENT PREGNANT AT TIME OF DEATH [ ] YES [X] NO [ ] UNK WITHIN LAST 12 MO [ ] YES [X] NO [ ] UNK

Fig. 16-1 Death certificate.

the cause, manner, and mechanism of death. This is not the case. Failure to correctly identify the cause of death is a consistent problem for the Department of Vital Statistics and law enforcement agencies. Nonforensic physicians and nonmedical coroners have historically been at fault in determining the precise cause of death and entering it correctly on the death certification document.

In the United States, only general physicians are, by law, permitted to complete death certificates that involve natural conditions. If the death was caused by unnatural conditions, the death certificate must be completed by either a medical examiner or a coroner. Nurses can play a key role in assuring that physicians do not attempt to sign death certificates that are not for natural deaths.

The death certificate is written and certified using standard nomenclature for classification of diseases and injuries and conforms to established guidelines in the country of death. Some countries subscribe to the World Health Organization's (WHO) universal definition of death, which includes guidelines for the terminology to be used on the death certificate. These guidelines also specify "do not enter the mode (mechanism) of death such as cardiac arrest, cardiorespiratory arrest, shock, or heart failure below," referring to the circumstances under which the death occurred as the cause of death. These circumstances are known as the mechanism of death, therefore, cannot be the cause. Unfortunately, this error in documentation continues to occur, resulting in a misinterpretation of statistical data used to allocate public health funds as well as researchers that identify persons and conditions of high risk for death.

Pronouncement of Death

Pronouncement of death is a confirmation that the individual has met the criteria of death. The time and day of pronouncement is documented on the death certificate along with the signature of the physician who certified the death. Although nurse pronouncement laws have been enacted in the United States, nurses in this country do not sign death certificates. In South Africa, however, the death certificate identifies the *professional nurse* as one who is authorized to sign for the certification of death. With advanced practice, forensic nurse examiners are certifying natural deaths in certain jurisdictions as independent practitioners who are licensed healthcare professionals. Although U.S. law varies from state to state, the elected coroner (nurse or otherwise) may certify death. Note that time of death is not necessarily the same as time of pronounced death.

Time of Death

Determining the exact time of death is an inexact science and represents a major challenge to death investigators. Precise techniques for accurately determining the exact *time of death* are highly desirable but have not yet been achieved despite extensive research (Evans, 1996). The basis of methods for the estimation of time of death are greatly influenced by external and internal factors affecting the level of accuracy of determination of the time of death.

Signs of Death: Postmortem Changes to the Body

Nurses are familiar with early signs of death that include changes in the eyes and skin as well as a general cooling of the body. Upon death, the pupils dilate and there is no reaction to light. Corneal reflexes are absent and the cornea gradually becomes cloudy. A thin film of cornea cloudiness may be observed within two to three hours if eyes remain open; if eyes are closed, it may take up to 24 hours. In the postmortem period in a dry environment, there is a blackish-brown discoloration on the exposed area of the eyes between the eyelids called *taches noires* (Fig. 16-2). Other changes include a loss of pressure in eyeballs and the *railroad* or *boxcar phenomenon*. This common phenomenon induced by the settling of red blood cells in a boxcar pattern within the fundi of the eyes is an immediate sign of death. The absence of respiration and electrical and mechanical heart action for five minutes or more also constitutes death.

Generally, the principle of sequential postmortem changes following death can be used in the estimation of time of death and the related destructive and or artifactual changes that may simulate premortem injury or modify toxicological findings (Spitz & Fisher, 1993). Physical changes that occur after death such as livor mortis, rigor mortis, body temperature degree of decomposition, and stomach contents is used to help determine the time of death. Unfortunately, these indictors of postmortem interval can be affected by environmental factors and features of the individual (body mass index, health, type of injuries, and drugs in the system). Without witnessing the event of death, it is all but impossible to indicate the precise time death occurred. When deaths are witnessed, the time of death is the time that resuscitation efforts were stopped and the pronouncement of death is recorded.

Several methods are used to estimate the time of death.

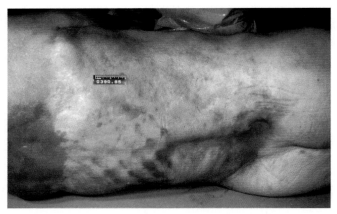

Fig. 16-3 Livor mortis (also termed *postmortem lividity*) is the purplish-red discoloration noted on these dependent areas of the body as a result of the gravitational pooling of blood after circulation ceases.

Livor Mortis

Upon death, the skin tends to lighten in color, and loses tone and translucency. *Livor mortis* (Fig. 16-3) (also termed *postmortem lividity*) is a purplish-red discoloration noted on dependent areas of the body as a result of the gravitational pooling of blood after circulation ceases. This process typically starts as early as 30 minutes after death. The process begins as mottled patches of color, but over the next few hours gradually spreads, affecting larger areas. Livor mortis can be used as an indicator of the postmortem interval (i.e., the time between death and discovery of the body). During the first two hours after death, the livor mortis is called "nonfixed." During this early stage, if the body is repositioned from a face-up to a face-down position, the blood will redistribute to the lower portions of the body. Between 8 and 12 hours after death, the pooled blood becomes "fixed," meaning that if the body is repositioned, the blood will not redistribute to the dependent area. Livor mortis can be used as an indictor that the body was repositioned after the blood had become fixed.

Rigor Mortis

After death, the muscles display a process called rigor mortis (Fig. 16-4). Muscles become flaccid soon after death, but beginning within 2 to 4 hours after death, the muscles begin to stiffen. At about 6 to 12 hours after death, the entire body is at its maximum state of rigor mortis. About 36 hours after death, the rigor

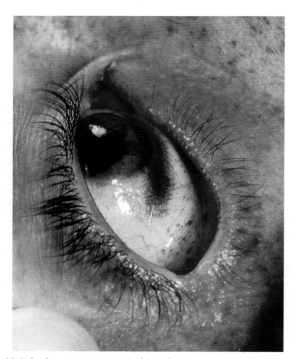

Fig. 16-2 In the postmortem period in a dry environment, blackish brown discoloration of the exposed eyeball, termed *taches noires*, occurs.

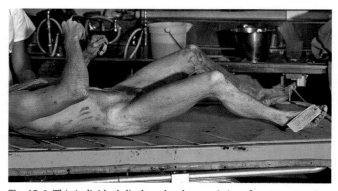

Fig. 16-4 This individual displays the characteristics of postmortem rigor mortis.

mortis disappears. These stages can be affected by external factors such as environmental conditions and internal factors such as strychnine poisoning or exertion immediately before death.

This condition is induced by a stiffening and shortening of muscles after death as a result of loss of adenosine triphosphate (ATP). Actin and myosin form a stiff gel in both involuntary and voluntary muscles and affect the body from head to toe. Along with livor mortis, the presence of rigor mortis helps to define the postmortem interval for estimating the time of death.

BODY TEMPERATURE

During life, the normal body temperature is 98.6°F. Soon after death, the body loses heat through conduction, convection, and radiation. During the first 12 hours after death, the body cools at the rate of 1½°F per hour. The rate then slows to about 1°F for 12 to 18 hours after death. Factors that affect the rate of body cooling include layers of clothing, type of surface the body is in contact with, body surface area, type of trauma, and the environmental conditions. The current method for obtaining core body temperature is to first place a long thermometer through the lower abdomen region into the liver and then take an ambient air temperature reading.

DECOMPOSITION

Later signs of death include changes in the color and composition of body tissues. After death, two processes take place: autolysis and putrefaction. **Autolysis** is the breakdown of cells and internal organs caused by enzymes. **Putrefaction** is caused by the activity of bacteria and fermentation. After death, the normal bacteria floras of the gastrointernal tract invade the body. Putrefaction is accompanied by discoloration and a foul smell caused by accumulating gases. Ammonia, hydrogen sulfide, carbon dioxide, methane, phosphorated hydrogen, indole, skatole, and mercaptan are among these foul-smelling substances. At this point, the body surfaces appear taut and the face, abdomen, and genitalia are bloated due to escalating gaseous pressures in body tissue and cavities. The presence of sulfmethemoglobin creates a greenish discoloration over the sacrum, flanks, abdomen, genitalia, and other body parts. Certain skin surfaces may develop blisters and appear denuded. There may be an evacuation of dark body fluids of decomposition through the nose and mouth as a result of increased pressures within the body. This phenomenon is termed *purging* (Fig. 16-5).

Maggots may also be evident at this stage. The climate and ambient tissue as well as the predeath health status of the individual often influence the rate and amount of putrefaction. The earliest

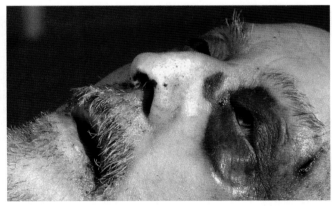

Fig. 16-5 Note the dark drainage from the nostril induced by increased gaseous pressures within the body during decomposition. This is referred to as *purging*.

external manifestations of decomposition (24 to 48 hours after death) affect the lower abdominal wall, which presents as a greenish discoloration over the bowels. The internal manifestation of early decomposition occurs in the stomach, intestine, spleen, liver, omentum, mesentery, larynx, trachea, and brain. Later decomposition, which occurs over a two- to three-day period, affects the heart, lungs, kidneys, urinary bladder, esophagus, pancreas, diaphragm, blood vessels, testes, prostate, and uterus. Several other changes also occur, each helping to identify the postmortem interval. Teeth are loosened in three to seven days, skeletonization occurs in one to three months, and bones are typically destroyed in 25 years. In the postmortem period, three weeks to one year, under conditions of high temperature and diminished airflow, a waxy substance called *adipocere* may form. Adipocere creates a waxy appearance of fatty tissue in the face, extremities, buttocks, and female breasts. In rare instances of high environmental temperature, low humidity, and good ventilation, mummification rather than adipocere will result.

ENTOMOLOGY AND TIME OF DEATH

Forensic entomology is the analysis of insects and their offspring that inhabit decomposing remains. Several hours after death, the body begins to attract insects such as flies, beetles, wasps, moths, and eventually small rodents. The study of the succession the order of arrival and the life cycles of these insects can be used to estimate the minimal time of death.

It is important for investigators to recognize the importance of identifying and collecting the flying, crawling, and burrowing insects at the scene and on the body. Note that some insects burrow themselves under the corpse or into the soil; therefore several soil samples should be collected. Insects should also be collected during the autopsy of the body and from the clothing. Maggots and other insects such as blowflies and beetles on the body are regularly used in determining an approximate time of death. Forensic entomologists study the stages of insect growth and coordinate the insect's growth stages from the egg to the adult to establish the approximate timeframe of death (Box 16-1).

Detailed descriptions of the techniques of proper collection, preservation, and rearing entomological specimens are available through the forensic science literature on forensic entomology. Problems arise when relying solely on these criteria, and major problems result because of variations in the environmental and individual factors on the magnitude and kinetics of postmortem phenomena (Knight, 1996; Rodriguez & Lord, 1997; Spitz & Fisher, 1993).

OTHER METHODS OF ESTIMATING TIME OF DEATH

Other methods used to estimate time of death include an examination of stomach contents, gastric emptying, the potassium concentration of vitreous fluid, and the postmortem residual reactivity of muscles to electrical or chemical stimuli (e.g., electrical stimulation of the masseter muscle and reaction of the iris to chemicals); these approaches may be limited to Europe and are uncommon in the United States. These methods are used in conjunction with

Box 16-1	Cycles of Growth
Ova	18-36 hours
Maggots	24 hours
Pupa	4-5 days
Adults	4-5 days

the circumstances of the death scene and witness statements. It is important to note that these methods are used to estimate the time of death and can be affected by many factors such as environment, the decedent's features, and the type of injuries and preexisting medical conditions.

Cause of Death

One primary objective of the postmortem evaluation is to determine the *cause of death*. The cause of death is the injury, disease, or the combination of the two responsible for initiating the train of physiological disturbances, brief or prolonged, that produces the fatal termination. When trauma results in immediate death, the injury is both the proximate and the immediate cause of death (i.e., gunshot wound to the head). If the sequence of events leading to death is sufficiently prolonged to develop pneumonia, peritonitis, or a massive pulmonary embolism, these sequelae would become the immediate cause of death (complications of underlying cause). The original injury would become the proximate (initiating event) or underlying cause of death. Thus, the cause of death must be etiologically specific.

In addition to inquiring into sudden and unexpected deaths, the determination of *jurisdiction* must be considered because of the possibility of delayed effects of injury. There is no statute of limitations for fatal injuries in certifying the cause of death (Adelson, 1974; Gorea, 2004). For example, if an individual is hospitalized for smoke inhalation as a result of an accidental fire, develops pneumonia, and dies six months or a year later, then the death certificate will read: Immediate Cause of Death: Pneumonia; Due to: Smoke inhalation. Manner of death: Accident.

The following sections discuss some examples of causes of death.

ASPHYXIA

Mechanical (Traumatic)

Asphyxia encompasses a variety of conditions that results in the interference with the uptake or use of oxygen with failure to eliminate carbon dioxide. Subnormal oxygen in the blood supply to the brain causes rapid unconsciousness. Microscopic evidence of central nervous system damage occurs as early as 30 to 40 seconds after oxygen deprivation. One category, mechanical or compression asphyxia, results from an external weight (i.e., car) placed on the chest or neck that prevents normal expansion of the chest and respiration (Spitz & Fisher, 1993).

Drowning

Cause of death in drowning is a complex combination of asphyxia (10% to 12%) and inhalation of large amounts of water. However, drowning is a complicated diagnosis that requires extensive evaluation of the scene and the drowning medium, whether fresh water, brackish water, or sea (salt) water. Recovery of a corpse from water raises two critical questions (Adelson, 1974; Spitz & Fisher, 1993):

1. Was death a result of drowning or from some other cause, natural or unnatural?
2. If death was caused by drowning, was it accidental, suicidal, or homicidal?

GUNSHOT WOUNDS

Firearms are involved in approximately two thirds of all homicides in the United States. The majority involves handguns (automatic or revolvers) with a smaller number involving long rifles (or shot-

guns). Gunshot wounds of the brain will frequently show signs of intracranial pressure where the vital centers were not injured, but pressure causing deformation toward the foramen magnum still occurs. Pressure secondary to the deformation may be the fatal mechanism in these cases (DiMaio, 1985). A detailed explanation of injury associated with firearms is covered in Chapter 25.

Manner of Death

The second role of the medical examiner's or coroner's office is to determine the *manner of death*. The manner of death refers to the circumstances in which the cause of death occurred. There are only five possibilities: homicide, suicide, accident, natural, or undetermined (cannot be determined). The manner of death should be given when there is a preponderance of evidence based on all available knowledge of the case. The manner of death is an opinion that can change with the presentation of substantive additional information. The manner of death influences the direction of future civil or criminal investigation.

HOMICIDE

Homicide is a neutral term. It merely describes the act and does not pronounce a judgment as to its moral or legal quality. There are instances when homicide may be committed without any criminal intent and without criminal consequences. Execution is homicide, carried out as a lawful judicial sentence. Other noncriminal or justifiable homicides may include a homicide committed in self-defense or a police officer causing a homicide as the only possible means of arresting an escaping felon.

In his book *Pathology of Homicide*, Adelson wrote:

> *Until the pathologist has demonstrated that death was produced directly or indirectly by some kind of violence or culpable negligence, there is no homicide to investigate ... if he misdiagnoses a nonexistent homicide, he may place an innocent person in jeopardy.... Conversely, if he fails to give adequate weight to the part played by violence and concludes that the death resulted entirely from natural causes, a murderer goes free and a crime goes unpunished. (1974, p. 15)*

Types of Homicide

Homicide can be classified in one of four ways: justifiable, excusable, felonious, or sexual.

Justifiable homicide or **noncriminal homicide** is committed intentionally but without any evil design or motive. It is also committed under such circumstances of necessity or duty as to render the act proper and relieve the party from any blame whatsoever. Justifiable homicides include self-defense, a killing to prevent the commission of a felony, or an execution carried out by the state.

Excusable homicide is the killing of another by misadventure or also by self-defense. There may be an element of fault, error, or omission, but that element is so trivial that it is excused from the guilt of a felony. Excusable homicide is best defined as the unfortunate killing of another during the commission of a lawful act without any intention to hurt.

Felonious homicide is criminal homicide. It is the wrongful killing of a human being without justification or excuse. There are two degrees of criminal homicide: murder and manslaughter.

In **sexual homicide,** the sexual element provides a basis for the sequence of acts leading to murder. The performance and significance of this sexual element vary with the offender. The act may range from rape (either before or after death) to a symbolic sexual assault. This category is divided into organized sexual homicide, disorganized sexual homicide, mixed sexual homicide, and sadistic murder (Olshaker, Jackson, & Smock, 2001).

Murder can be subdivided into first-, second-, and third-degree murder and two degrees of manslaughter: voluntary and involuntary.

First-degree murder is the intentional killing of a human being. It is characterized by a plan or lying in wait. First-degree murder lacks spontaneity.

Second-degree murder is committed when the slayer is the principal or an accomplice in the perpetration of a felony. It is commonly known as "felony murder." There exists an intention to carry out the felony, but not the intention to commit the murder. Examples include the killing of another human during a bank robbery or the death of a person as the result of arson.

Third-degree murder is simply all other kinds of homicides that cannot be categorized as intentional or as having been committed during the commission of a felony.

Voluntary manslaughter is the killing of a person without lawful justification while acting under sudden and intense passion resulting from a serious provocation by the individual killed. A person may also be guilty of voluntary manslaughter if another is killed with the unreasonable belief that the killing is justified. For example, a person may kill another while under the mistaken and unreasonable belief that self-defense is necessary to protect themselves.

Involuntary manslaughter is the death of another as the direct result of an unlawful act in a reckless and grossly negligent manner. Additionally, a lawful act in a reckless or grossly negligent manner that results in the death of another may give rise to the determination of involuntary manslaughter.

Role of the Medical Examiner/Coroner in a Homicide

It should be noted that the role of the ME/C is only to determine if the victim died from homicide. It is the responsibility of the legal system to determine if the death was first-, second,- or third-degree homicide, justifiable homicide, or manslaughter.

SUICIDE

Suicide is defined as an intentional death inflicted by one's own action. As proof of suicide, it must be demonstrated that the individual could have carried out the act alone. The most common methods of suicide include self-inflicted gunshot wounds, hanging, and drug overdosing. Methods such as self-stabbing, wrist cutting, or throat cutting are rarely used and rarely result in death. The method chosen is dictated by the ease of availability, familiarity with the methods or devises, and methods used on prior attempts. In all cases of suspected suicide, the scene, the victim's computer files, e-mails, and text messages should be forensically searched for a possible suicide note. Note, however, that only about 20% of individuals who kill themselves leave a suicide note (Omalu, 2005).

ACCIDENT

To determine an accidental death, it is essential to rule out intent by self or others or natural causes. An unintentional death resulting from a chance event or carelessness not due to any fault or misconduct by the individual but from the consequences of such entity or circumstance is categorized as accidental. The main types of accidental deaths investigated by the ME/C office include the following: motor vehicle accidents, drug overdose deaths, falls, fires, drowning, medical misadventures, and industrials accidents.

NATURAL

The majority of reported and investigated deaths in medical examiner's or coroner's jurisdictions are natural deaths. Natural deaths are due to disease pathology of the internal organs or due to the degenerative aging processes. Death due to natural conditions involves the forensic system when the death is unattended by a physician or if physician will not sign the death certificate for a variety of reasons. However, each death must be approached with an index of suspicion until any suggestion of foul play, however slight, has been ruled out and the cause of death has been clearly determined.

UNDETERMINED

The cause of death is designated as undetermined if (1) there are insufficient physical findings at autopsy, (2) toxicology and microscopic examinations yield nonspecific or insignificant results, (3) the level of injuries or state of decomposition prevents identification of a specific cause, or (4) a final case review concludes that circumstances surrounding the death are elusive or impossible to confirm with a degree of medical certainty. Undetermined cases may result from trauma or violence or from natural causes.

Mechanism of Death

The mechanism of death is defined as the physiological derangement or biochemical disturbance incompatible with life, which is initiated by the cause of death. It may also be referred to as the mode of death as often seen on the death certificate. Mechanisms of death (not causes) include hemorrhagic (hypovolemic) shock, metabolic disturbances (acidosis and alkalosis), cardiac asystole and ventricular fibrillation, respiratory depression and paralysis, cardiac tamponade, sepsis with profound bacterial toxemia, and so on (Adelson, 1974). The mechanism of death is distinct from the cause, which initiates the mechanistic sequence of factors incompatible with life. For example, a stab wound (cause) may lead to blood loss and collapse of the lung, resulting in hemorrhagic shock (mechanism).

A mechanism may be included in part 1 of the death certificate where clinical clarification of a specific etiology is appropriate, provided both the mechanism and the underlying etiology are listed.

Clinical Autopsy versus Forensic Autopsy

There are significant differences between the clinical (hospital) autopsy and the forensic autopsy:
- The clinician is mainly concerned with the inside of the body and with the processes of nature, as well as the location/presence/absence of natural disease.
- The forensic autopsy is mainly concerned with the exterior of the body, vectors, forces, directions, body positions, physical capabilities, and the cause and manner of death.

When a death occurs during hospitalization and is deemed a natural death, it can be referred to the clinical/anatomical pathologist. The attending physician typically signs the death certificate. Hospital autopsies are generally performed at the request of the physician or the family to determine the origin or extent of a disease process or the effectiveness of treatment regimen. This procedure requires the permission of the family and is a primary resource for medical research.

The purpose of a forensic autopsy is to determine the cause, manner, mechanism of death, identification of the body, time and place of death, and reconstruction of the fatal episode.

The forensic autopsy is accomplished to investigate suspected criminal cases or to determine the cause of death. Any death other than natural death falls within the medical examiner's/coroner's jurisdiction.

BEST PRACTICE Autopsies should be performed only by physicians solidly grounded in gross and microscopic anatomy and pathology to avoid errors in procedures or analyses of derived findings (Adelson, 1974).

Necropsy Pathology: The Autopsy

The examination of the body after death is most often referred to as the autopsy (Greek: *autopisa*, to see for one's self; *opsesthai*, with one's own eyes). A more technically correct term for the evisceration and dissection is necropsy, or looking at the dead. The objective of the autopsy is to identify the body and the medical cause of death (Wright, 2003). *Autopsy* and *postmortem* are the terms most commonly used in the United States, *morbid anatomy* is a British term, and *necropsy* is most commonly used in Latin America and European countries.

The autopsy provides valuable information through postmortem analysis such as cause of death, mechanism of injury, multiorgan system failure, communicable diseases, and so forth. Because the forensic examination is directed mainly toward the cause and manner of death, it is a mistake to assume that all bodies handled in a ME/C setting will undergo a complete forensics examination. In fact, a significant proportion will only receive an external examination.

Anatomy and Physiology of the Autopsy

Understanding the anatomy and physiology of the body is fundamental in relation to the autopsy dissection and determination of cause of death. This includes the classification of the organs that comprise the systems as well as the precise terminology. The relationship between cause, manner, and mechanism of death requires in-depth inductive and deductive reasoning to assure an accurate investigation of why people die. An astute understanding of these processes begins with the three major systems of the body: the nervous system, cardiovascular system, and respiratory system. Other body systems include the gastrointestinal, genitourinary, endocrine, musculoskeletal, integumentary, and lymphoreticular.

Momentary interruption of any one of these three main systems may commence an irreversible, potentially fatal process (e.g., interruption of circulation for four minutes causes irreversible brain damage). The only other mechanism that leads to irreversible damage quickly is hemorrhage. Rapid hemorrhage would involve blood loss through a breach of artery.

PREREQUISITES TO AUTOPSY

Before examining the body, the forensic pathologist will review all available information about the death. He or she will review the incisive report of circumstances of death and documentation

of the scene of death as observed by the medical investigator, coroner, or deputy coroner; the police reports; other first responder's reports; and medical records. An insightful investigator will collect reports from other agents at the scene, compile, recover, and review medical records from the hospital, interview the family physician, and review statements from witnesses in order to compile a complete and comprehensive evaluation of information pertaining to the possible cause and manner of death. Police reports may contain valuable information regarding the criminal investigation of death, yet they may be unrelated to the medical cause of death. In the same sense, shared information related to the medical investigation of death may be invaluable in helping the criminal investigator confirm or rule out whether or not a crime has been committed.

In addition, the forensic pathologist will review all the photographic documentary of the body, the scene, and the evidence. Based on this information, the pathologist will determine the type of autopsy to be performed on the body.

Postmortem Evaluations

EXTERNAL EXAMINATION VERSUS COMPLETE EXAMINATION FORENSIC AUTOPSY

A body can undergo either an external-only examination or a complete examination. The factors that determine which type of examination the body will receive include the type of case, the past medical history, and the circumstance surrounding the death.

An external (view) examination refers to a postmortem examination limited to external examination of the clothing and the body, and a review of medical records and investigative information to arrive at the cause and manner of death without evisceration of the body. Cases that typically undergo an external-only examination include well-documented deaths by suicide with a through-and-through gunshot wound to the head or an elderly individual with significant past medical history.

A complete forensic examination indicates that in addition to the external examination, the body is opened and the internal organs and structures are examined. These autopsies are required by law and do not require the permission of the family. Forensic autopsies focus on the external body and are a primary resource for public health and law enforcement agencies.

Autopsy Procedure

All forensic autopsies begin with a detailed visual inspection of the body as it arrives at the morgue. The body is described and photographed. The clothing is described by type and condition. The layers of clothing are removed and photographs are taken as each layer is removed. When the body is nude, it is photographed head to toe, front and back, and close-up images are taken where trauma or injuries are noted. Forensic trace evidence should be identified and collected before the body is autopsied.

The dissection of the human body generally entails the removal of all the internal organs through a Y-shaped incision, beginning at the top of each shoulder. The incisions are extended downward at an angle, meeting at the xyphoid process, and then extending through the midline of the abdomen to the top of the pubic bone. The T incision has been adopted to facilitate the examination of the tongue and neck (Wright, 2003). After removal of the chest plate, the heart and lungs are exposed. At this point in the examination, blood, bile, and urine samples are collected and sent to the crime lab for toxicological analysis. Next, the lung, pancreas, spleen, kidneys, gastrointestinal tract, and small and large intestines are removed. Examination of the brain requires an incision from behind one ear to the other, reflecting the scalp backward and sawing the skull in a circular cut followed by the removal of the skullcap.

After removal, each organ is weighed and then dissected to determine disease or injury. Information derived from the medical history, witness statements, scene examination, and autopsy will determine further dissection or analysis of tissue that may be performed following the routine procedures just described (Wright, 2003).

Documentation of each step of the autopsy procedures is essential to ensure relevant and ultimately admissible evidence in court. The forensic nurse examiner must remain aware that any involvement in death investigation—from the scene, the hospital, the residence, interviews, evaluation or examination of injuries, and so on—may or may not result in legal testimony. All forensic professionals consider testifying as a requisite of their position and must be prepared to explain actions or opinions to the court.

Autopsy examination may determine what type of weapon caused injury and death, determine whether injuries are antemortem or postmortem in nature, and determine if a single injury or multiple injuries are responsible for death. Determination of the postmortem interval, the lapse of time between death and discovery of the body, and the probable duration between injuries or incapacitation or death is essential for understanding the circumstances of death.

SPECIAL CASES

When infant, fetus, or maternal deaths occur, documenting evidence of trauma and history of abuse is essential. These deaths are all forensic cases, necessitating an adaptation of routine autopsy procedures. Special procedures are required in newborn or stillborn infant deaths. The investigation requires obtaining detailed information regarding the prenatal history, birth records, postbirth checkups, and a detailed death scene investigation.

Generally, the autopsy procedures are similar to those used on adults, with a few notable exceptions. Modifications may be required in the removal of specific organs such as the heart, thymus, and brain. In the case of a fetus, determining the actual age of the fetus in relation to the duration of the pregnancy is important. Fetal age is generally determined by the weight and measurements of the body, specifically the circumference of the head. The presence of lanugo, a fine delicate hair over the shoulders of a fetus, indicates immaturity, as does the lack of fingernail growth. The centers of bone growth also indicate the state of maturation at the end stage of a normal pregnancy. Postmortem examination of a stillborn infant must include an examination of the placenta. Placental abnormality is frequently a cause of fetal death, and without it, a diagnosis is often impossible (Gresham & Turner, 1979).

Epidemiological data suggest that 50% of American women are in violent relationships and ~33% of all emergency department visits by women are related to domestic violence. Of these visits, only 5% are recorded as battering or maltreatment on the hospital record. In addition, 37% of pregnant women have a history of physical abuse, which is considered to be the leading cause of infant mortality and birth defects. Battering by an intimate partner may be the single most common cause of injury to women worldwide and the cause of traumatic death in pregnancy.

Findings from various studies indicate the incidence of abuse occurs in 10% to 26% of all pregnancies. Despite the fact that battered women are frequently seen in the emergency department setting, the diagnosis of abuse is often missed. Historically, healthcare professionals have not been trained to recognize, identify, or intervene for the battered woman. The number of women who have experienced domestic violence has not been routinely detected or reported by emergency department physicians and nurses. Before these women can be offered help, they must first be identified in the healthcare setting.

The Joint Commission (TJC) has established guidelines requiring routine assessments for abuse in emergency and ambulatory settings, as well as education for healthcare providers who come into contact with such victims. Because many women seek medical assistance in acute care settings and only a small percentage of domestic violence cases are detected, it has become a mandate that all women presenting to an emergency department or prenatal clinic undergo routine screening for interpersonal violence. Forensic nurse examiners assigned to urgent care and mother-baby units have proved to be beneficial in reducing and preventing the number of deaths of mothers and the unborn. This futuristic approach to case management of the forensic patient is being developed in contemporary healthcare institutions worldwide (Lynch, 2003).

KEY POINT Trauma is noted to be the leading cause of maternal death during pregnancy.

Identification of the Body
METHODS AND MEANS

On arrival at the scene, determining the positive identification of the body is a priority, as it is one of the main roles of the medical examiner's or coroner's office. The investigator's first question should be, "Has the body been positively identified?" The methods to establish identification include the following: visual methods, clothing recognition, document matching, tattoos, scars, fingerprints, dental comparisons, medical and surgical implants, DNA comparisons, computer or video identification, and facial reconstruction (Fierro, 1993).

Visual

Identification of the decedent by a close family member or companion is the most readily used method of positive identification. Typically, visual identification is conducted at the scene in direct presence of the body. On occasion, positive visual identification is conducted at the morgue by way of closed-circuit television or through a glass partition. Direct contact with the body must be avoided to ensure the chain of evidence and secure the body. Another method of visual identification is to compare the victim with a photoidentification card such as a driver's license, employment card, or other government issued ID card.

In certain cases, the NOK or significant others may not recognize the individual because of the emotionally traumatic effect of the death or the condition of the body. Visual identification is often unreliable and frequently leads to misidentification if the victim was burned, submerged in water, decomposed, or exposed to toxic chemicals.

Fingerprints

The first book on fingerprints as a method of identification was published as early as 1892. When the body is unclaimed, visual methods cannot be used because no known relation or other individual is available to identify the decedent; therefore, the method of fingerprint comparison is employed. No two individuals have the same fingerprints; even identical twins have different ridge patterns. The process involves fingerprints of the deceased collected on a standard fingerprint card and attempts to match those prints with those on file with the FBI and other government agencies. Assuredly, many citizens remain outside the list of millions of fingerprints, but because there is a significant likelihood of fingerprint identification, the effort is worthwhile (Evans, 1996). Other than fingerprints, scientists have found footprints and lip prints to be suitable for identification as well. Footprints of children under age 14 have become routine in identification comparisons. One forensic task that may be considered for the forensic nurse consultant is fingerprinting. One California police department inquired if forensic nurses could be trained to take fingerprints, stating that because of its overwhelming workload, the department was considering contracting this job to civilians.

Forensic Odontology

If no fingerprints are available and no visual identification can be made, identification is attempted through dental identification. Forensic odontology is the application of the arts and sciences of dentistry to the legal system (Glass, 2003) and refers to the specialized science of dental identification. No part of the human body outlasts the teeth after death, so they provide an ideal means of identification. Often the teeth may be the only means of identification, specifically for severely burned or decomposed bodies. Teeth are also useful for determining the decedent's age at death. However, dental comparison cannot be used if the identity of the body is unknown. It is imperative to have both antemortem and postmortem dental records; without known dental records, there is nothing to compare. Forensic odontologists can also confirm a crime suspect's identification through the interpretation of human bite marks. Human dentition provides irrefutable evidence when compared to the bite mark on tissue, based on the individual class characteristics of the accused (Evans, 1996).

DNA

Deoxyribonucleic acid (DNA) forms the building blocks of life. DNA provides powerful, compelling evidence. For the past century, science has been trying to identify what makes each living thing unique. Each individual has the potential to be identified by his or her biological fluids or trace evidence. As in dental identification, however, if the identity of the decedent is not known or suspected, a confirmation is not possible. DNA evaluation is time consuming and expensive, generally out of the reach of most budgets in routine death investigations. In a criminal investigation, the specimens are generally blood, hair, bloodstained clothing, semen, saliva, or any cell of human tissue. The likelihood that two individuals would have the same DNA is estimated to be about one in the billions. There is nothing to suggest at this time that DNA is anything other than the most significant forensic breakthrough since the discovery of the forensic application of fingerprints (Evans, 1996).

Computer or Video Identification

The use of computer-enhanced imagery is a rapidly growing method of identification. This is a revolutionary computer program that simulates aging. When criminals or victims have been missing for a number of years, this program can simulate the appearance of the individual based on a psychosocial profile of lifestyle and project a likely current appearance. Such features as sags, wrinkles, or receding hairline help to produce the suspected appearance concurrently with the number of years the individual has been missing. Equipment designed to manipulate photo images to remove blemishes has been used to create a likeness of how a battered corpse had looked when alive. Video superimposition is another method of identification in which a high-resolution video image or photograph is placed over an image of a skull to determine whether the two are images of the same person. Follow-up with fingerprints or DNA for further confirmation is used with both computer-enhanced imagery and video superimposition (Evans, 1996).

Facial Reconstruction

The art of reconstructing a face from a skull has been used since as early as 1895, when anatomists began creating human likenesses for the purpose of identification. Modern practitioners of facial reconstruction work with various art forms to create likenesses that are remarkably similar to the subjects in question. The initial evaluation of unidentified skulls begins with establishing skin thickness at strategic points over bone. Modeling clay is then applied in accordance with carefully delineated measurements of the mouth and cheeks. However, because cartilage decomposes quickly after death, the nose poses one of the most difficult aspects of reconstruction. Prosthetic eyes and the appropriate color of wigs (where hair is found with the body) produce amazing results and often provide an accurate identification of the unknown dead (Evans, 1996).

EXHUMATION

Circumstances in an investigation may come to light after the burial of an individual that requires an exhumation of the body for further evaluation to clarify the cause and manner of death. An autopsy on an exhumed body is rare. The legal removal of a body from the burial site requires permission of the family or by a court order. An exhumation involves disinterment of the body to investigate a suspected homicide, to establish doubtful identity, or to answer claims for compensation or charges of malpractice. The disinterred body is within the jurisdiction of the ME/C until the remains are reburied. The pathologist must be present at the scene of exhumation and document every step of the procedure with photography (Knight, 1996).

RECOVERY OF SKELETAL REMAINS

Occasionally, all that remains of a body are bones—generally dry, brown, fragile, and sometimes clearly ancient. These bones are often discovered during construction, hiking, or after a heavy rain and are reported to law enforcement agencies, which notify the ME/C. Before any removal, determination of human or animal origin is preferred.

Precise guidelines for the removal of skeletal remains must be outlined before investigators enter the scene of death. Homicide detectives lead the investigation at the scene with an initial evaluation of the location. Measurements must first be taken of the distances involved from the central mass of the body to each item of evidence, and next, to three stationary objects for scene reconstruction purposes. Each item of evidence must be located, staked with an identifying flag, photographed, and measured before the remains are removed. The removal procedures are strictly the responsibility of the medical examiner's or coroner's office. It is not exceptional for a rural scene investigation to take two to three days before the skeletal remains are transported to the autopsy laboratory.

FORENSIC ANTHROPOLOGY

Forensic anthropology can be broadly defined as the application of the theory and methods of anthropology to forensic problems. This subspecialty of physical anthropology, the study of human biological functions and variations, particularly skeletal biology (Sorg, 2009).

Several basic questions arise with the discovery of any skeletal remains. Forensic anthropologists are trained to evaluate the conditions and circumstances of how a person lived and died through an incisive examination of the structure of the human body. The age at the time of death, sex, race, and height of the person remain the most forensically significant observations when determining the identification of the decedent or the cause of death. Whether the remains are of the ancient or recently dead, whether they are those of active-duty military personnel killed in action or the passengers of airline disasters, skeletal remains can unfold the history of debilitating diseases, healed fractures, handedness, and even possibly the occupation of the person in life. This information may be invaluable to the evaluation of the quality and quantity of forensic evidence made available through forensic anthropology.

Case Study **16-1**

Death Investigation

A 62-year-old white male is reported dead at his residence by his spouse. Law enforcement officers arrive and notify the forensic nurse examiner on duty. The decedent's wife identifies him as L.B.D. Death is pronounced at 0900 hours. There are no weapons or obvious signs of breaking and entering, and there is no evidence of a struggle. The doors were locked from the inside when the wife returned home. Evidence at the scene includes copious amounts of blood on the floor, ceiling, walls, and furniture. Bloody footprints from the central area of the house to the location of the body are observed. Blood is pooled underneath the decedent's head. The body is on the floor in the bedroom in a supine position; it is cold to the touch and in full rigor, and early stages of decomposition are noted. The decedent is wearing black, knee-length shorts only. The body presents with a pale yellow discoloration, consistent throughout, with numerous irregular patches of bruising. Blood is exuding from the nose and mouth. No open wounds are observed. Severe distention of the abdomen is present. Aspirin and cigarettes are located on the bedside table. A large bottle of vodka on the bed is noted. Police suspect foul play. This case is being investigated as a homicide until proven otherwise (Figs. 16-6, 16-7, and 16-8).

Medical history: The decedent is known to have been under the care of a family physician for several years. His wife states that the decedent has not been compliant with medication or medical appointments for the past year until he was recently treated for alcohol withdrawal. Complaints include hallucinations, flapping tremors, abdominal pain (acute pancreatitis), and shortness of breath (postural asphyxia).

Signs and symptoms: Jaundice, ecchymosis, ascites, projectile vomiting of blood

Diagnosis: End-stage cirrhosis of the liver

Cause of death: Exsanguinating hemorrhage from ruptured esophageal varices
- due to cirrhosis of the liver
- due to chronic alcoholism

Manner of death: Natural

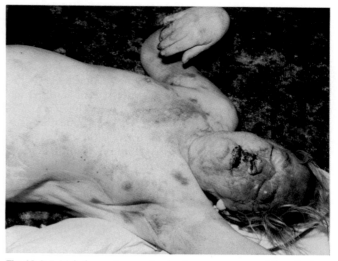

Fig. 16-6 Initial observations at the death scene suggest a violent death.

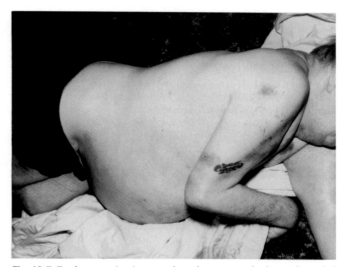

Fig. 16-7 Further examination reveals ecchymoses and a large, distended abdomen.

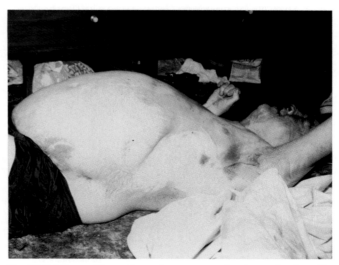

Fig. 16-8 Side profile confirms the presence of ascites and other skin changes consistent with cirrhosis.

Summary

Death investigation is an essential part of the forensic sciences because every death has actual or potential legal implications. Detailed procedures are required to determine the cause of death, aid medical science, and contribute to the administration of justice. The forensic autopsy is a vital part of the death investigation process, which is systematic and ongoing. It involves the collection and analysis of data and physical evidence from which certain assumptions and conclusions are derived. These data serve as a basis for further investigations to establish the identification of the decedent, the approximate interval of time since death, and the cause, manner, and mechanism of death.

Resources

BOOKS

DiMaio, V. J., & DiMaio, D. J. (2001). *Forensic pathology.* (2nd ed.). Boca Raton, FL: CRC Press.

Dix, J. (1999). *Color atlas of forensic pathology.* Boca Raton, FL: CRC Press.

Haglund, W. H., & Sorg, M. H (Eds.). (1997). *Forensic taphonomy: The postmortem fate of human remains.* Boca Raton, FL: CRC Press.

Spitz, W. U. (Ed.). (1993). *Medicolegal investigation of death* (3rd ed.). Springfield, IL: Charles C Thomas.

JOURNALS

American Journal of Forensic Medicine and Pathology. Lippincott Williams & Wilkins, Philadelphia, PA; www.amjforensicmedicine.com

Journal of Forensic Sciences. American Academy of Forensic Sciences, ASTM International, 100 Bar Harbor Drive, PO Box C700, West Conshohocken, PA 19428; 610-832-9585

WEBSITES

Armed Forces Institute of Pathology
www.afip.org.

National Association of Medical Examiners, Writing Cause of Death Statements
www.thename.org/CauseDeath/COD_main_page.htm.

References

Adelson, L. (1974). *Pathology of homicide.* Springfield, IL: Charles C Thomas.

American Academy of Forensic Sciences. (2002). *Informational brochure.* Colorado Springs, CO: Author.

Baden, M. (1989). *Unnatural deaths: Confession of a medical examiner.* New York: Random House.

Cumming, M. F. (1995). The vision of a nurse-coroner: A "protector of the living through the investigation of death." *J Psychosoc Nurs Ment Health Serv, 31*(11), 7–14.

DiMaio, V. (1985). *Gunshot wounds.* New York: Elsevier.

(2000). *Dorland's illustrated medical dictionary.* (29th ed.). Philadelphia: Saunders.

Emory, S. (2003, December). *What is brain death?* Iowa Statewide Organ Procurement Organization. Retrieved from www.transweb.org/faq/q6.shtml.Accessed September 3, 2009 .

Evans, C. (1996). *Forensic detection.* New York: John Wiley and Sons.

Fierro, M. (1993). Identification of human remains. In W. Spitz, & R. Fisher (Eds.), *Medicolegal investigation of death*, (3rd ed., pp. 71–117). Springfield, IL: Charles C Thomas.

Glass, T. (2003). Forensic odontology. In S. James, & J. Nordby, *Forensic science* (pp. 61–62). Boca Raton, FL: CRC Press.

Gorea, R. (2004). *Adapted from course outline, signs of death.* Punjab, India: Government Medical College Patiala.

Gresham, G., & Turner, A. (1979). *Post-mortem procedures.* (An illustrated textbook). Chicago: Year Book Medical.

Hsi Yuan, Lu. (1976). Instructions to coroners. As cited In F. Camps, A. Robinson, & B. Lucas (Eds.), *Gradwohl's legal medicine* (3rd ed., p. 7). Chicago: Year Book Medical.

Koehler, S. A., & Brown, P. A. (2009). *Foundations of forensic epidemiology: Medical examiner/coroners perspective.* Boca Raton, FL: CRC Press.

Knight, B. (1996). *Simpson's forensic medicine* (11th ed., chap. 3). Bedfordshire, UK: Arnold.

(1998, December). *Law & politics book review.* American Political Science Foundation. University of Maryland, 8(2), 447–449.

Liang, J. W., & Snyder, J. W. (2004). *Legal medicine.* (6th ed.). American College of Legal Medicine. St. Louis, MO: Mosby.

Lynch, V. (2003, September 6). *Domestic violence in pregnancy.* Paper presented at 6th World Congress on Perinatal Medicine, Osaka, Japan.

National Committee for Injury Prevention and Control. (1989). *Injury prevention: Meeting the challenge.* New York: Oxford University Press.

Olshaker, J., Jackson, M. C., & Smock, W. (2001). *Emergency forensic medicine.* Philadelphia: Lippincott.

Omalu, B., Macurdy, K., Koehler, S. A., Nnebe-Agumadu, U. H., Shakir, A. M., Rozin, L., et al. (2005). Forensic pathology and forensic epidemiology of suicides in Allegheny County, Pennsylvania: A 10-year retrospective review (1990–1999). *Forensic Science Medical Pathology*, 1(2), 125–137.

Rodriguez, W. C., & Lord, W. D. (1997). *Other means of estimating time of death* (11th ed., pp. 25). Oxford: Oxford University Press.

Sorg, M. (2003). Forensic anthropology. In S. James, & J. Nordby, *Forensic science* (3rd ed., pp. 101–120). Boca Raton, FL: CRC Press.

Spitz, W., & Fisher, R. (Eds.), (1993). *Medicolegal investigation of death* (3rd ed.) Springfield, IL: Charles C Thomas.

University of Dundee. (2003). *Brain stem death and organ transplantation (molecular death defined).* Retrieved from www.dundee.ac.uk/forensic-medicine/notes/brstem.pdf. Accessed September 3, 2009.

Wright, R. (2003). Role of the forensic pathologist. In S. James, & J. Nordby (Eds.), *Forensic Science* (pp. 19, 20). Boca Raton, FL: CRC Press.

CHAPTER 17 Forensic Nurse Examiners in Death Investigation

Virginia A. Lynch

The Culture of Death

"The fundamental law of the social order is the progressive control of life and death."

—JEAN BAUDRILLARD, 1976

Death was once considered to be due to invisible vectors and forces. It was remote, but it was familiar. Care of the dead involved a personal commitment, and the community marked it with funerary rituals and long periods of mourning. Variable attitudes, customs, and beliefs relating to death and dying, as well as the care of the dead impacted the behavior of people from all levels of society. In recent years, as death and dying are better understood in terms of scientific explanations, many of the longstanding rituals surrounding death, dying, funerals, and mouring have been abandoned, especially in certain social classes and within some religions."Life for the living" took center stage, and the business of dying became less fashionable. In a fast-paced society, long days of mourning, elaborate funeral rites and the funeral cortege to the gravesite became obstacles to the existing pace of life. Slowly moving funeral processions could no longer be tolerated where impatient drivers move rapidly to their next venue. The current economy prohibits costly funeral details when considering the casket, the flowers, the vault, the gravestones and more. Drive-by visitations, email condolences, prompt disposal of the bodies by cremation or donation to science are contemporary practices that seem to be more appropriate for this century.

A new culture of death is seeping into our new social order. Alternatives to grief-laden funerals embrace the celebration of life instead of death. Rather than flowers to honor the deceased, we give donations to charities that benefit the living. Environmentalists are concerned about the impact of human remains, cemeteries, and gravestones consuming the landscape. With body parts needed for transplantation, the recovery of implanted medical devices and hardware for re-use, the dead have become a valuable commodity. The criminal element of our society has seized the opportunity to profit from certain aspects of death, such as the preparation for burial or cremation. There have been cases where the body has not been buried properly or buried at all! The re-use of expensive caskets and gravesites is not unheard of. Cremations and burials which have not been carried out in accordance with social, religious and legal expectations occur with some regularity. The news media reports all too often about incidents of commingled cremains, organ thefts, and confiscation of the deceased's personal property.

The rise of science and technology brought a death-rich culture into our visible environments through mass media documentaries and entertainment. Death in the twenty-first century is no longer a remote concept. Death is no longer invisible. War, mass destruction, gang bloodshed, interfamilial violence and aggression have become death denial in the contemporary world of disposable and replaceable lives. The younger generation considers violent death a fact of contemporary life or the exponential number of acts of violent fatalities witnessed daily through the media, videos, or films to be artificial, unreal, and certainly unrelated to them. The older generation perceives death as fear related to abuse, abandonment, isolation, institutionalization, disease, or violent home invasions, but there is no denial of genuine death. Thus, in the broad scheme of things, we are left with the perspective that individuals' lives and deaths are commercial and, by extension, inconsequential. There have been profound changes in the demographics of developing societies that indicate a new role in who dies, how we die and why we die, as well as the quality of death. Yet, increasing privatization of death and the institutionalization of the dying has removed the socialization and personal management of death from our culture leaving questions of how and why we die to the medical and legal processes and systems of society.

Death as a Phenomenon

Death is considered one of the great rites of passage in human existence. Death involves more than the physical medical sciences that require attention to postmortem procedures and burial practices. Death is one factor that defines each culture and the theological concepts surrounding the bioanthropology of its people. Regardless of any given society's belief—that life continues beyond death, or that it ends at that moment of death, or that existence after death is unknown—death is a shared phenomenon of the human experience. As nurse scientists, skilled in the forensic investigation of death, each of these societal beliefs are to be considered as one ventures into the realm of questioned deaths. It is the forensic nurse examiner's duty, then, to tread cautiously as interpretations are made, taking particular care to avoid judgmental reactions toward attitudes of death that may differ from one's own (Lipson, 1996). The scientific and social phenomenon of death represents the two primary aspects of death investigation on which the practice and philosophy of forensic nursing science is founded. These principles will guide the forensic nurse examiner (FNE) toward the expected outcomes of holistic forensic care, which include body, mind, spirit, and the law.

The medicolegal aspects of death investigation are defined by forensic thanatology (*thanatos* meaning "death" and *logos* meaning "science," or simply the study of death). It is a known phenomenon that death occurs in two stages: (1) somatic, systemic, or clinical death and (2) cellular or molecular death. The term *death* as commonly employed refers to somatic death, which is due to complete and irreversible cessation of vital functions of the brain, followed by the heart and lungs. Previously, cessation of the beating heart and respirations were used as the criteria for death.

Now, with the advent of cardiac transplantation, the emphasis has shifted to irreversible cessation of brain function (Parikh, 1999).

Among death's phenomena, perhaps the most difficult for families to understand is the beating-heart cadaver. What emotional trauma could be greater than having to make the ultimate decision to remove someone from a perceived life source: artificial ventilation. It is often confusing to the family and to the nursing staff to accept that death exists while oxygen still infuses the lungs, the blood still circulates, and the body is soft and warm. These phenomena reflect centuries of confusion over how, exactly, to define death, that precise moment when the intangible life force ceases to exist. Before brain activity could be measured, the absence of a beating heart had long been considered the defining moment. Yet the brain survives for 6 to 10 minutes after the heart has failed. Considerable fears surround the family while contemplating these issues: Could there be hope? What if we make the wrong decision? How can we live with the anxiety and doubt once the decision is made?

When emotional support is needed at times such as this, who is up to the task? Who can explain brain death with clarity, but nonetheless in a way that a person in denial can understand? What about the need for compassion, for empathy? Or what if the bereaved is a suspect in the death of the patient? Of all the issues involved, this circumstance presents the most difficult professional responsibility while, at the same time, requiring the necessary psychosocial intervention in case the suspicion is invalid. Experience in forensic nursing and guidelines in death investigation help provide the ways of knowing and critical thinking that determine the basis on which accurate case management of questioned deaths can be provided.

Science of Death Investigation

Death has become a respectable field of inquiry, particularly in the social and behavioral sciences, as well as an acceptable topic of study in the curricula of institutions of higher learning. The science of death investigation joins with nursing science to address the physiological, psychological, and legal aspects of death and dying. Certainly, the most refreshing change is the emphasis on a human caring. This approach to the scientific investigation of death seems to parallel trends in other sectors of society, which are attuned to the advancement of humanity. Previously the emphasis on mechanism of injury, cause, and manner of death and knowledge of the law stood alone within the forensic arena of death investigation.

Death brings with it innocent, living victims by extension, those who survive the loss of lives they cherished. According to those who work with individuals, families, and communities that suffer from the catastrophic impact of tragic death, the forensic response alone is not enough. Grief psychologist Jerry Harris in Fort Worth, Texas, stated, "In a science which stresses the careful collection and accurate documentation of evidence, it is interesting that the psychological impact of traumatic death on survivors receives little attention in actual practice" (personal communication, Jerry Harris, February 11, 1989). Recognition of this concept reflects the distinction between normal and pathological mourning, unresolved grief, and mental illness, and it calls for a complete reexamination of the premise on which views of death and dying are traditionally based. There is definitely a place in nursing and other health sciences for the recognition and application of a more empathic discipline pertaining to questioned death than has existed in the past. Intervention in grief must be seen and supported as a means toward adaptation and health (Lynch, 1993).

Historically, an acknowledged deficit has existed in the U.S. death investigation system, one that has often resulted in miscarriages of justice because of the insufficient, ineffective, and often insensitive investigation of questioned deaths. Traditionally, persons who performed this role have an extensive background in law enforcement or are laypersons without sufficient professional training. Advances in the medical and legal sciences indicate a greater need for biomedical requirements to prepare investigators in the medical cause of deaths. Criminal investigators are present at such scenes, providing a duplication of services where police-trained death investigators are used, rather than providing a medically trained investigator in the endeavor of medical investigation.

Art and Science of Forensic Nursing

One solution to these concerns has been identified in the development of a forensic specialist in nursing. This discipline, known as *forensic nursing science* (FNS), represents a mutual responsibility between medical science, forensic science, and criminal justice. It pertains to the medical investigation of death, the forensic management of medical evidence, and a professional concern for the families of the deceased. This science defines the role of the *forensic nurse death investigator* (FNDI) in both basic and advanced preparation of the *forensic nurse examiner* (FNE) whose practice addresses crime-related trauma, death from natural disease processes, catastrophic deaths, abuse, violence, sexual assault, liability concerns, traumatic accidents, mechanism of injury, multiorgan system failure, cause and manner of death, basic chemistry and physics, human psychology, knowledge of the law, and other pertinent medicolegal issues. The FNE with a specialty practice in the science of death is considered an expert in this field. This involves a broad acumen of knowledge, skills, and attention to justice concerns that has previously been unavailable in most nonmedical jurisdictions.

Significance of the Role

In most jurisdictions throughout the United States, the medical examiner/coroner (ME/C) has the responsibility of investigating all violent, suspicious, and sudden deaths as well as natural deaths in certain categories. It is the dramatic intrusion of the unexpected that is so often responsible for arousing suspicion. Every unexpected death has actual or potential medicolegal aspects. Medical interest lies in accurately establishing the nature of a fatal disease or injury. The legal importance derives from the availability of objective data for the administration of justice, whether civil or criminal. In all such situations, the forensic nurse in the role of medicolegal investigator can make an important contribution to the investigation process for the family and the community at large. The nurse's knowledge and experience can be invaluable in recognizing signs and symptoms of unexplained deaths (such as fatal infectious diseases and unnatural, unknown, or unattended deaths) where the signs are so subtle that the untrained eye would overlook or misinterpret valuable medical evidence.

Death under any circumstance is difficult to accept, especially if it is sudden and unexpected. It is most common to insulate oneself until other defenses are marshaled. Denial is the first response to unanticipated death and permits hope to exist but it is short lived. The next most common expression is anger. The nurse investigator can expect this response and not take it personally. It is better to permit the bereaved to express their anger, their

The Forensic Nurse Death Investigator (FNDI) or other medicolegal investigator is responsible for items that may include, but are not necessarily limited to, the following:

1. Collecting medical, physical, and other evidence that pertains to the cause and manner of death
2. Collecting information on the circumstances before, at the time of, and following the person's death, as well as the decedent's medical history or hospital records
3. Preparing an investigative report detailing all necessary biographical data, as well as summarizing all the information relevant to the time of death and the immediate precedent and subsequent events
4. Notifying the next of kin
5. Maintaining appropriate confidentiality of records while ensuring that all relevant records are promptly and properly delivered to appropriate designated persons
6. Managing dialogue with the media in cases attracting media attention (protecting both the public's right to know and the privacy rights of the victim and significant others)
7. Educating law enforcement professionals regarding aspects of unexplained or unidentified deaths such as evidence recovery, confidentiality issues, public relations—especially vis-à-vis the media and relevant community resources (e.g., hospitals)—and relating to the deceased's family and friends
8. Assisting in autopsy/medicolegal examination as appropriate; not as an official function, but adducing to the investigator's knowledge base regarding cause, manner, and mechanism of death while providing the forensic pathologist with direct on-the-scene information
9. Testifying in court, at inquests, at civil law hearings, or at criminal law trials
10. Counseling the deceased's family/significant others or reviewing/explaining the autopsy report/death certificate

sense of helplessness, and their outrage. By doing this, their feelings will have been vented, allowing them to move more rapidly into a stage where they can begin the unfinished business of their own lives, including helping to complete the investigation and funeral arrangements. Nurses are regularly and effectively used as medicolegal investigators, thus clearly revealing that the forensic nurse can establish a significant role in the scientific investigation of death and make important contributions (Box 17-1).

Unique to Nursing

As health and justice systems enter the twenty-first century, forensic nursing provides the partnership that has historically existed in every medical specialty with the exception of one: forensic medicine. In 1975, John Butts, chief medical examiner in Alberta, Canada, was the first to recognize that the registered nurse represented a valuable resource to the field of death investigation. After conducting a five-year study to determine the ideal professional related to medical investigation, he concluded that it was the registered nurse who provided the qualities and professionalism essential to a scientific, social, and cultural investigation of death. Butts established a program using nurses as medical examiners' investigators, citing the nurses' biomedical education and emphasizing their knowledge of natural disease processes, medical terminology, and pharmacology, as well as their ability to empathize as their most important qualifications. The nurse's experience in public relations is also a major priority in representing the medical examiner at the scene of death, handling confidential material and being comfortable relaying sensitive information to family members (Lynch, 1993).

Butts stressed the importance of coordination and cooperation between the criminal and biomedical investigative personnel. He expressed concern that medically untrained officers often disregarded medical evidence, maintained poor sensitivity, and were noncommunicative with grieving families. Conversely, healthcare professionals recognize the integrity of criminal evidence, the suspect interview, and the investigation of leads.

The ability to review health histories and medical records; understand medical terminology; interpret medical abbreviations; communicate with physicians and paramedical personnel; evaluate the impact of surgical or chemical interventions prescribed and performed before death; and relate social, financial, and interpersonal relationship factors of a psychological autopsy must also be included in the armamentarium of the investigator of forensic deaths. These skills are unique to nursing. Essential knowledge regarding the investigation of sudden and unexpected death or the clarification of suspicious or natural deaths across the life span must begin with an incisive understanding of the phenomenon of death. An elucidation of these issues may become a point of contention in a court of law.

Forensic Intervention

Medical professionals, criminalists, and police officers alike recognize the strategic benefits of the forensic nursing role. Nurses recognize this as an opportunity to expand their professional horizons and promote their professional goals. The concept of forensic nursing, which embraces a multidisciplinary approach to abuse detection and community mental health, enhances the quality of community life through effective systems coordination. The tri-care systems approach, involving healthcare, forensic science, and the law, provides an interdisciplinary team technique as the nurse death investigator works closely with the crime laboratory, law enforcement operatives, and community legal service agencies to identify possibilities of human abuse in questioned deaths. A comprehensive total health and justice program in any progressive community will provide the three major components of forensic intervention: (1) prevention of death, (2) intervention at the time of death, and (3) postdeath care (post-vention) for the decedent's significant others. To recognize these essential elements of dying as a life process, with a greater shift toward human caring, is to provide an insightful contribution to nursing science and to humanity.

Related research has sought to identify behavioral responses to death, both physiological and psychological, in an attempt to categorize significant etiological factors that promote or inhibit change in the public health status. Forensic nurses are in a position to make primary contributions to the long process of restoring homeostasis to the bereaved. These strategies are supported by what seems to be of paramount importance as new perspectives arise for considering the familiar phenomena of health, illness, and death in relation to human life.

FORENSIC NURSE INVESTIGATOR

Nurses are exceptionally capable of interacting with police, physicians, and grieving families and collaborating with other professionals in forensic investigations. In the initial phases of establishing a forensic nurse investigative team, however, police, prosecutors, or physicians without awareness of the accomplishments forensic nurses have attained will often express objections and fail to fully support the integration of a nurse into their investigative agenda.

Forensic nurses do not participate as criminal investigators but rather as clinical investigators, though the interface and assistance to criminal investigation is extensive. It has been noted, however, that the interface between clinical nurses and law enforcement officers has often been characterized by strife and resentment in hospital scenarios. This is not limited to nurses and police in the emergency department setting; it also arises between forensic nurses and criminal investigators at scenes of crime or death. Law enforcement officers have, at times, resented the idea of working with nurses, of having to share responsibility, or communicating with a discipline so foreign to their own. Frequently, this professional friction is based on suspicion of the unknown, untested, or simply untried. Although the benefits of forensic nursing are well documented and increasingly accepted, arguments against the concept have been raised in the fields of medicine and justice. The significance of FNEs in death investigation and the unique qualifications they contribute to a field often lacking in biomedical professionals is primarily based on a lack of understanding—or funding. This can create professional jealousy, rejection, and lack of acceptance.

However, according to Z. G. Standing Bear, retired federal agent and criminologist, "Forensic nursing brings together the necessarily neutral, detached and suspicious arena of the law enforcement investigator with the empathic, involved and accepting dimensions of psychosocial nursing" (Standing Bear, 1987, p. 7). He further advised:

Forensic nurse examiners and forensic nursing services are a revolutionary concept for utilizing nursing abilities in an arena of human services not previously explored by nurses. Nurses can make significant contributions to the area of death investigation as well as services to survivors. In a world where academic camps are alienated from and even hostile toward one another, this idea speaks to a refreshing blend of energy and cooperation. Breaking down these old barriers of competition and building up new cooperative programs cannot help but benefit humankind. The obvious benefits of this new idea contribute to the quality of community life, as well as bringing together of two historically different disciplines with a common and worthwhile purpose. (Standing Bear, 1995, p. 63)

Other arguments oppose the use of registered nurses in death investigation because nursing education is primarily based on the common assumption that the goal of nursing is the preservation of life. This view holds that using nurse death investigators is inappropriate or even a waste of resources, that nurses would do well to disregard the carnage and loss of human life and rather focus on the needs of the living. Countering this argument are those who assert that death and dying are as much a part of the life cycle as birth and that those who die leave the living in need of care as a result of their deaths (Lynch, 1993). Further arguments are that the forensic pathologist, medical examiner, or medical coroner are first physicians whose fundamental education and training are also perceived to simply focus on those who endure and survive life—not those who die.

Until now, a limited number of job opportunities posed the greatest argument in preparing nurses for professional roles in this field. Because of the existing medicolegal systems, there is little demand or opportunity for nurses to become involved in the death investigation field. Although interest in the field remains high, without hope of employment, there is limited motivation to pursue advanced practice for those not already in the system. There are, however, numerous archaic death investigation systems in the United States and abroad that are, albeit slowly, converting toward biomedical professional models. As this occurs, the potential for the employment of nurses in greater numbers appears promising. Because this is a pioneering arena for nurses, salaries are typically low in contrast to clinical nursing. Conversely, with the emerging emphasis placed on higher standards in death investigation, forensic nurse examiners in enlightened jurisdictions are receiving competitive salaries, commensurate with advanced education and clinical forensic experience.

Previously, forensic investigative staff generally consisted of nonbiomedical personnel, often retired law enforcement officers or morticians. On being interviewed, one forensic pathologist, when asked why police officers without education in the physical and psychosocial sciences were used to investigate traumatic death and interface with grief-afflicted families, stated that "retired homicide detectives were more economically budgeted because they receive a retirement salary and can subsist on the low-salary position created for nonmedical personnel." As forensic nurses pursue advanced education in the forensic and nursing sciences, attaining postgraduate degrees as well as doctoral studies in the forensic investigation of death and specializing in a variety of related fields such as forensic anthropology, bioterrorism, and disaster management, government agencies and scientific institutions are investing in these professionals to enhance the medicolegal management of death investigation.

Workforce development has become a critical challenge across all federal departments, and justice is facing an increasing challenge with demographics (caused by the current world financial crisis), new advances in technology, and new threats of terrorism. Previously employed ME/C law enforcement investigators who worked for an extra income to supplement retirement cannot be replaced at the current salary. Now is the time for nurses seeking training/instruction on the scientific methodology of medicolegal death investigation to pursue their education so they are prepared as new positions become available. This recession will recede, new jobs will become available, and death investigation agencies will begin to hire forensic nurse investigators. With attention to the success of ME programs in Texas and Michigan, replication of these innovative roles combining nurses and police death investigation units will become one of the future forensic trends (see Chapter 19). The existing training/information/education programs will also be of benefit to current nurse educators, who can adopt/adapt these courses to meet their needs as required to teach forensic nursing science.

One of the most significant contributions to nurses in death investigation was initiated in Canada as early as 1975. At the insistence of John Butts, who initiated the first formal position for FNDIs, the salary and benefits were established to be equivalent to that of clinical nurses with equal education and experience. These pioneering nurses were also required to maintain their nursing licensure and national nursing association membership. These requirements should be incorporated into any forensic nurse investigator or nurse coroner program. Failing to do so was the single greatest mistake made by those employing nurses in medicolegal investigation as this concept moved from Canada into the United States. Although many clinical nurses have chosen to work in this field, they were unable to do so without sufficient financial compensation. This alone would have moved FNEs forward into the realm of forensic pathology and the investigation of death decades ago.

CARING FOR THE DEAD

Although nurses have traditionally been recognized as the primary caretakers of the living, it must be recognized that nurses throughout history have also been the caretakers of the dead. In addition, as a component of the caregiver role, nurses comfort or console those who survive, including other members of the healthcare team who share in the grief and mourning process. Hospice nurses become experts in death and dying. Oncology nurses are prepared to provide terminal patients and their families with insightful perspectives on the stages of death and essential emotional support during those last moments of life. Neonatal nurses are exceedingly familiar with loss of life in the neonatal intensive care unit and the impact of grief that undermines the traditional joy accompanying birth. No department in the hospital faces the trauma of death and dying more frequently than the emergency department, as those who are admitted suddenly and unexpectedly because of random violence, catastrophic mass disasters, and natural or unknown causes often fail to survive.

To identify and recover microscopic bomb fragments while debriding a wound and to relate them to a detonator associated with known criminals, to relate wound characteristics to distinctive weaponry from crimes of this century and the last (such as the Unabomber, the World Trade Towers, Guantanamo Prison, and other incidents of custodial torture and more), is to acknowledge healthcare's accountability in combating crime. The United States has displayed great national sensitivity in the recovery, identification, and memorial of the public, private, national dead. So, too, have other nations where civility and respect for death has brought together governments and families in mourning. The forensic sciences are responsible for the primary identification and repatriation of the war dead. Military nurses have launched initiatives in forensic nursing and Veterans Administration hospitals have established specific procedures to guide the clinical investigations of suspicious deaths among their patient populations.

William Gladstone, a nineteenth-century British prime minister, spoke of the value of caring for the dead as a reflection of the morals and ethics of a society when he wrote one of his most famous statements, one that has memorialized the dead of wars over the centuries: "Show me the manner in which a Nation cares for its dead and I will measure with mathematical exactness, the tender mercies of its people" (Jalland, 1996). (Cited at the dedication of the Vietnam Veterans Memorial in Washington, D.C., in 1986). This statement has specific meaning for those who have lost loved ones in war or in peace.

Gladstone addressed death from a diverse perspective, as both good and bad. He stated that "death is an inevitable experience for us all, but the manner of dying varies greatly, as do individual and family responses to death and their mourning rituals" (Jalland, 1996). The French historian Michel Vovellehas observed that death "in the human adventure stands as an ideal and essential constant" (Jalland, 1996). Though it remains a constant in the reality of death, it is relative in relationship to the times of the social and religious perspectives of death. As times of social change continue to evolve, so does the manner in which people die. Pierre Chaunu further emphasized this concept by observing that every society gauges and assesses itself in some way by its system of death resolution. In the same manner, the study of death and bereavement in the past has helped people to understand the

present; the study of medicolegal death investigation, historical or in the recent past, helps people to evaluate and improve a systems approach to the scientific investigation of death. Cumulative experience with death and dying and the social interaction derived from helping grief-stricken survivors combine to shape the beliefs and behaviors that the FNDI brings into practice. It should not be surprising that the forensic nurse examiner has been found to be an ideal clinician to fulfill the requirements of the death investigator role.

Death investigation is an essential part of the healthcare and judicial systems. However, clinical physicians are typically ill prepared to assume the responsibility inherent to the medicolegal management of questioned death cases. In North America, few medical schools provide curricula that include forensic medicine; even fewer address the psychosocial interventions associated with death. These two topics are essential aspects of developing a socially appropriate death investigation system. Furthermore, many physicians are not attracted by the prospect of becoming a public governmental employee with fixed income, continuing public scrutiny, and bureaucratic constraints. This has led to a dearth of qualified forensic medicine practitioners to work within the death investigation systems at a point in history when the need for this role is expanding exponentially. These circumstances have resulted in an increased opportunity for nurses to fulfill forensic roles in death investigation and clinical forensic practice. FNEs are stepping forward to assume these responsibilities in hospitals, clinics, and the community at large.

FORENSIC NURSE EXAMINER

Nurses are serving as the officiator of death in numerous areas throughout the United States. The FNE specializing in death investigation as an elected coroner (an independent authority) or medical investigator (under the direction of a forensic pathologist) has brought a higher standard of administration and case management to questioned deaths than has existed in the past. Titles vary from one jurisdiction to another depending on the role and preference designated by the chief medical examiner or coroner. These titles evolve as nurses fill existing roles or as new roles are developed for nurses in the forensic investigation of death.

As an elected or appointed official, the title of coroner or deputy coroner is used in South Carolina, Wisconsin, Georgia, Colorado, and California, among others. In some states (e.g., in North Carolina), the forensic nurse has replaced the non-forensic physician. This nurse holds the title of district medical examiner and serves under the authority of the state medical examiner. In certain settings, such as the military or international death investigation systems, titles such as special investigator or chief forensic nursing officer may be appropriate. Among other titles assumed by nurse investigators in medical examiner systems are field investigator, field agent, forensic investigator, forensic nurse investigator, medical investigator, medicolegal investigator, medicolegal death investigator, and FNDI. Where nurses fill a supervisory role, titles may include chief investigator, senior investigator, or coordinator of the investigative team. Regardless of the title, authority and jurisdiction over the body at the scene of death remain the same. FNEs present the requisite skills and knowledge acquired as a natural extension of their nursing assessment proficiency and healthcare education. Nurses are valued components of the medicolegal death investigation team in jurisdictions of both coroners and medical examiners (Allert & Becker, 2002).

The title *forensic nurse examiner (FNE)* is appropriate for any of the subspecialties of forensic nursing where forensic examinations are performed. The FNE conducts an investigation of trauma or death; provides an examination of physical, psychological, or sexual assault trauma; and examines the questioned analysis of medical records (e.g. legal nurse consultant) or court-ordered evaluation of mental status, provided the education, experience, and other qualifications of a forensic nurse are met. It is important to recognize that FNE is a title and does not designate certification.

NURSE CORONER

Where the law does not require the coroner to be a physician, this position often remains open to anyone who has reached the minimum age of 18 years, can provide proof of county residency for the past one or two years, and obtains the majority of votes. Although the statutes regulating this position vary from state to state, it remains accessible to the unskilled, untrained, nonmedically oriented, and politically driven elected official known as a lay-coroner. However, according to Cumming, "This person must possess medical knowledge in order to be able to make critical judgments based on symptoms, medical history, postmortem appearance, toxicology and other diagnostic studies, combined with evidence revealed by other aspects of the investigation" (Cumming, 1995, pp. 29-33).

Contemporary communities recognize that the expectations and qualifications for an officiator or investigator of questioned deaths must incorporate medical, psychological, and environmental acumen in a scientific and accurate determination of cause and manner of death. These communities elect and employ forensically skilled nurses who are well qualified to differentiate between postmortem changes and signs of victimization, understand interpretative toxicology, correlate mechanism of injury to cause of death, associate psychosocial histories with manner of death, comfort survivors, and provide appropriate referrals and support (Cumming, 1995).

A Nurse Coroner's Perspective

Charles E. Kiessling Jr., RN, BSN, CEN, Lycoming County coroner in Williamsport, Pennsylvania, is one example of an FNE who exemplifies quality death investigation. According to Kiessling, nurses are well qualified to fill the role of an officiator of death. Kiessling describes his role and experiences as typical of those who serve as the elected official in a growing number of U.S. jurisdictions (Kiessling, no date):

Nurse coroners have a thorough understanding of the pathophysiology necessary in determining the cause of death. In most counties across Pennsylvania the coroner is called to the scene to investigate the cause and manner of death. Registered Nurses, through their nursing education and clinical experience, make excellent medical legal death investigators. Nurses also have significant experience in dealing with death and dying, frequently helping patients and families during some of the most difficult times of their lives. Who better to serve as an advocate for injury and death prevention than nurses who have experienced firsthand the catastrophic loss of life in their communities?

The nurse coroner has the ability to monitor causes of death in the community and effect changes through such organizations as: SAFE KIDS, Child Fatality Review Teams, DUI Advisory Boards, Emergency Medical Services, Health Improvement Coalition and Driver Safety Task Force. Nurse coroners are also well versed on community resources to not only deal with the investigation of the death scene, but also to assist families deal with the

aftermath of sudden deaths including such services as grief counselors and support groups as necessary. As elected officials, nurse coroners are generally well positioned with political contacts to recommend legislative changes when necessary.

Law enforcement personnel in Lycoming County generally perceive most nurses as fellow professionals. As long as nurses recognize their limited knowledge regarding processing of crime scenes and legal procedures and remain willing to work cooperatively with law enforcement personnel, they will work well as nurse coroners. Conversely, law enforcement personnel will generally look to the nurse coroner for their expertise in medical pathophysiology, pharmacology, toxicology and mechanisms of injury in traumatic deaths.

Kiessling is presently working to change hospital policy and procedures regarding the retention of specimens pertaining to critically ill and or injured patients that may eventually end up as coroner's investigations. Presently the local hospitals hold blood and urine specimens for three days and then discard these specimens unless directed to do otherwise. In 2003, a drug trafficking case resulting in death was nearly lost because of the loss of these initial specimens. Fortunately, autopsy findings were consistent with a methadone overdose, witnesses identified the suspect, and he then confessed. In the future these specimens will be retained until the patient is discharged or dies and the coroner clears these specimens for disposition. This change will assure that specimens are available to develop the prosecution's case against illegal drug dealers who deliver drugs that result in deaths. Specimens are now retained for at least one year or more on all cases that may involve criminal charges.

Kiessling knew firsthand that no matter how small or rural a county was, such incidents could bring the focus of the entire world on their operations, for example, Somerset County, PA on 9/11/01. Kiessling served as a regional vice president for the Pennsylvania State Coroner's Association and as a liaison to the Pennsylvania State Coroner's Education Board. One of the State Coroner's Association's four disaster assistance trailers is housed in Lycoming County and is ready to respond to any requesting county whenever a disaster exceeds local resources. The trailer contains digital dental x-ray equipment, portable autopsy tables, personal protective equipment including masks, gowns, gloves, respirators, body bags, and evidence collection and scene processing equipment.

Because of an increasing number of possible overlaying asphyxiation deaths in Lycoming County, Kiessling utilized his position as chair of the Lycoming County Child Fatality Review Team and the Lycoming County Coroner's Office to initiate a Cribs for Kids Program in Lycoming County to ensure that all newborns go home to a safe sleeping environment. The program is cooperatively run by representatives from the Williamsport Hospital Labor and Delivery Unit, the Pennsylvania Department of Health Nurses, the Lycoming County Coroner's Office, and Lycoming County Safe Kids.

Implications for Forensic Nursing

Most laws have relegated medical-forensic tasks strictly to physicians within clinical and community environs. Exceptions were made, however, to include paramedical personnel, law enforcement officers, and elected officials to activate death investigation procedures. Currently in the United States, many physicians and nonphysician professionals who hold these positions are not

Case Study **17-1**

Homicide, Suicide, or Accident?

In May of 2000, a 62-year-old psychiatric patient assaulted his psychiatrist and nursing staff on the Outpatient Behavioral Health Unit where he went for a regular examination. Based on these assaults against healthcare providers, a felony warrant was issued for his arrest. Because the patient lived in a rural part of Lycoming County in Williamsport, Pennsylvania, and was known to have many firearms in his home, law enforcement personnel decided to avoid executing an arrest at the patient's home to prevent the increased risks associated with firearms in the home. Instead, law enforcement personnel chose to execute the arrest while the patient was taking his wife to her physical therapy appointment at the Williamsport Hospital. The patient drove his pickup truck into the drop-off area at the Williamsport Hospital Rehabilitation Center, allowing his wife to exit the vehicle. As officers attempted to block the patient from driving away, he sped through flowerbeds, down the sidewalk across the roadway and into the hospital parking lot. The patient nearly struck persons waiting at the bus stop, employees traveling to and from the hospital at shift change. He was then blocked in by police officers. The patient exited his truck, and when approached by police he assaulted the officers, fracturing the nose of officer 1 and then struggling with officer 2 on the ground. During the scuffle, officer 2's knee became dislocated. The patient was sprayed with pepper spray in effort to bring him under control. Additional officers and hospital security personnel arrived on the scene, and the patient was then handcuffed and placed in custody. As officers were assessing the injuries of officers 1 and 2, they noticed the patient was no longer struggling and appeared to have stopped breathing. Closer evaluation found him to be pulseless and apneic. He was quickly loaded into a police vehicle and transported to the emergency department on the back side of the hospital.

The patient was pulled from the police vehicle and transferred into the emergency department where he was found to be in ventricular fibrillation. Defibrillation and resuscitation efforts were continued with return of a perfusing cardiac rhythm and normal vital signs. Once stabilized, he was transported to the intensive care unit (ICU) where his condition remained unchanged for five days. After five days, he died. A forensic autopsy determined that the cause of death was complications of restraint asphyxiation.

The Lycoming County coroner's office continued the investigation in an effort to determine the manner of the patient's death. The decision to be made was whether the manner of death was accidental or a homicide. Family members felt that the law enforcement had killed their father/husband. Interviews with law enforcement personnel who executed the arrest determined that there was no evidence of excessive force, which would have been necessary to rule the manner of death as homicide (the death of an individual at the hands of another).

Although not common, an additional consideration is *suicide by cop*. This may occur when a depressed or desperate individual wants to end their own life, but, for various reasons (cowardice, a desire to make a point, insurance, moral aversion to suicide), is not willing to do it himself. Instead, the unstable individual engineers a situation in which someone else will be forced to do it for him. The "classic" scenario involves a criminal indiscriminately attacking innocent bystanders or police so that they will be forced to shoot him. Less violent characters, however, will simply pull an unloaded gun or realistic toy gun on a police officer and hopes the officer panics. This scenario could be broadly applied to any situation where an individual attacks specifically because the expected reaction from authorities will cause the desired outcome.

The hostage-taker, for example, lacking courage to inflict the usual fatal mode, may rely on law enforcement officers, snipers, or other special forces such as a *Special Weapons And Tactics* (SWAT) team to cause their death. (tvtropes.org/pmwiki/pmwiki.php/Main/SuicideByCop).

Because of the possibility of law enforcement personnel being charged with homicide, the decision was made to hold a coroner's inquest. Coroner Kiessling issued subpoenas to 33 persons including the patient's psychiatrist, nursing staff, law enforcement, hospital security, emergency room nurses, physicians, ICU physicians, nurses, the forensic pathologist, a restraint expert, and the deceased's family members to appear at the coroner's inquest, which was held in September of 2000. The eight-member coroner's jury heard all testimony over four days and then ruled the manner of death as accidental. Kiessling then ruled the manner of death as accidental, and no criminal charges were filed against law enforcement personnel.

Case Study **17-2**

World Events, Rural County

On April 7, 2003, one of the worst highway tragedies in Lycoming County (Pennsylvania) occurred. Nine college vice presidents from Beijing, China, were traveling from Niagara Falls to Washington, D.C., in an 11-passenger van when the vehicle suddenly spun out of control during a freak snow storm, left the roadway, and struck a tree; seven of the occupants were killed on impact. The Lycoming County coroner's office personnel were called to the scene, along with local and state police, to investigate the crash. Law enforcement and coroner's office personnel photographed the scene; all personal items were collected and retained with the decedents.

The next task was to identify each of the deceased and to notify their widows in Beijing, China. Representatives from the Chinese Consulate in New York were contacted, and they responded to Lycoming County officials. These representatives examined the crash site and the decedents to verify that the incident was accidental in nature. One survivor who spoke English was taken into the morgue to assist with the identification process by comparative exams of the decedents' passports. Coroner Charles Kiessling, a forensic nurse examiner, through the Williamsport Hospital's list of local translators, was able to make contact with a Lycoming County resident who spoke Chinese and agreed to assist with the translation of communications between the two survivors and the widows in Beijing.

Because one funeral home was inadequately sized to handle all seven decedents, Kiessling contacted three local funeral homes and coordinated the arrangement of the decedents' final disposition, holding the decedents until the widows could travel from Beijing to Williamsport, Pennsylvania. The widows requested to view their husbands. The decedents were then cremated, and the cremains were returned to China with the widows.

required to have forensic expertise. This role is often filled by laypersons (nonmedical and nonforensic personnel) who wish to run for public office. Their responsibility is to determine the cause and circumstances of death, provide a comprehensive scene investigation, request a postmortem evaluation as required, and notify the next of kin. This requires a systematic and methodical approach to confirm or rule out events disclosed before, during, and immediately after death occurs. A miscarriage of justice often results in cases where specific knowledge related to the medical, legal, and social aspects of death investigation does not exist.

Until recent times, neither clinical nor community agencies nor institutions extended nurses the authority to pronounce death. Exception was extended to the nurse who was an elected or appointed official in the county's medicolegal jurisdiction—not because the person was a nurse, but because she or he was an official or forensic investigator. Excluding clinical nurses appears to be an oversight that is incongruent with the education, experience, and professionalism of nurses when compared with that of paramedics and police or the local lay-coroner. Since the late 1980s, however, nurse pronouncement laws have changed significantly. Where these laws exist, they provide nurses with the authority to pronounce death. Families no longer have to await the arrival of a physician to pronounce a terminal patient dead and can proceed with rites of passage and funeral arrangements without the anxiety of unnecessary delay.

In these jurisdictions, the attending physician no longer has to come to the hospital or nursing home to pronounce an expected death for the family to release the body to mortuary services. Law enforcement officers at the scene of death or at the hospital appreciate the timeliness of nurse pronouncements and the reduction of time required to remain with the body. Physicians find that this is an appropriate responsibility for nurses to assume and that it reduces the unnecessary pressure of being on call.

Laws continue to be updated, and some nurses can pronounce death; however, only a physician may sign a death certificate in the United States. One exception is the nonphysician coroner who may be authorized to certify death in certain states. This exception, however, can present a series of problems when the nonmedical coroner may fail to require an autopsy or recognize the accurate cause of death. Other common problems include the hesitation to release transplantable organs, inaccurate documentation, or the lack of important information regarding the circumstances of death.

As in any field of practice, all coroners cannot be judged by the same failures to practice satisfactory death investigation. In many jurisdictions, the elected coroner may be a general medical practitioner, a nurse, a paramedical professional, or a veterinarian. Others may be lawyers, muffler repairmen, tow-truck operators, or sheriffs—who have no medical or nursing proficiency. Some 500 counties in the United States employ morticians as coroners in spite of the fact that this is considered to be a conflict of interest in certain states. The California attorney general's opinion—which is next to law—considers this conflict of interest to be unethical when there is more than one mortician practice in a single jurisdiction. In Washington State, morticians are prohibited from seeking the elected position of coroner. However, one cannot determine the qualifications of an official by the title; in some states, the coroner may be a board-certified forensic pathologist. The law determines the title of the officiator of death as well as the term limits.

The Forensic Science Foundation in Colorado Springs, Colorado, estimates that when lay-coroners rule in questioned deaths, 10% to 50% of felonious deaths go unrecognized and unreported. These statistics also estimate that lay-coroners rule 40% more heart attacks than medically oriented officiators do, because of the lack of glaring evidence of foul play (such as gunshot or stab wounds) (Fields, 2004). For example, in Texas, the lay-coroner is known as a justice of the peace, an antiquated system practiced over a century ago (since 1869) that still prevails. Qualifications for justice of the peace require the candidate to be at least 18 years old and to have resided in the county for 12 months, yet justices of the peace have the authority to certify death, to initiate murder charges, and to influence life insurance claims, malpractice suits, and other important proceedings.

Critics state that homicides go undetected, accidental deaths are mistakenly ruled natural, life-threatening occupational and environmental hazards are missed, and child abuse deaths and suicides are underreported. Because the nonmedical, nonnursing coroner (or justice of the peace) does not have the necessary training to determine the exact cause of death, such as fatal infectious diseases, communities may be at peril when such cases go unrecognized and unreported. The lay-coroner may fail to recognize the subtle signs and symptoms of natural disease processes that generate concern when one considers that 65% to 75% of reportable deaths in the United States are natural deaths, such as the complications of a diabetic coma, a gastrointestinal bleed, end-stage cirrhosis of the liver, or status epilepticus. These are frequent causes of deaths of individuals who die alone or unattended by a physician (Lynch, 1993). The 2002 U.S. census estimated that 2,537,000 deaths occurred. Of that number, 20% were certified by U.S. coroners and medical examiners. The remaining 80% were certified by attending physicians. Thus, more than half a million people, approximately 507,400, constitute the number of ME/C cases each year that require an investigation of death.

Why Nurses?

The criminal investigator's responsibility is to determine if a crime was committed and, if so, who committed the crime. Medical investigators are charged with the determination of death and, if so, what caused the death based on medical evidence. The medical investigator must include medical science when determining the precise precipitating factors and causes of death; doing so not only benefits medical science but also serves the public's general welfare by ensuring that natural, accidental, and crime-related facilities are systematically identified and investigated regarding the cause, manner, and mechanism of death. Wherever nonmedical coroners/justice of the peace/lay investigators are employed, professionalism, serious liability, and ethical problems are common, including but not limited to those listed in Box 17-2.

Traditionally, individuals hired as death investigators have had an extensive background in law enforcement, although advances in forensic and nursing science indicate the need for investigators with a stronger background in anatomy and physiology, psychology, pharmacology, medical terminology, and a comprehensive

---

Box 17-2 Nonmedical Officiators of Death

- Poor scene investigation
- Failure to recognize medical evidence
- Improper evidence preservation/chain of custody
- Hesitant to release organs for transplantation
- Failure to order autopsies because of budget restraints
- Conflict of interest (involving personal or political gain)
- No requirement to report unidentified bodies (UIBs)
- Not aggressive in identifying UIBs (some kept on premise for 10 to 20 years)
- Insensitive notification of death
- Inappropriate or failure to make death notification
- Unethical practices
- Unwilling to increase educational standards (current attempts to lower standards)
- Incorrect cause of death
- Unfamiliar with natural disease processes (majority of reported deaths)
- Unavailable in crisis to police or families
- Poor documentation/writing skills
- Unable to communicate in medical language
- Incapable of interpreting medical records/prescriptions

knowledge of communicable and natural diseases (Lynch, 1986). Medical examiners and coroner systems that employ forensic nurse investigators find that the nurse who is cross-trained in forensic science and legal issues provides a collaborative practice approach, which benefits forensic science professionals. A forensic specialist in nursing represents an innovative concept in an area of human services not previously explored by nurses but ideally suited for the forensic nurse examiner.

Forensic analysis provides data to develop trauma care systems and clinical practice standards. Thus, a hospital trauma care system's program for quality assessment helps to identify preventable deaths in order to modify care protocols and outcomes in subsequent cases. Clinical and community health nurses should also include clinical history and documentation of evidence. These components are critical elements in the administration of justice.

Forensic Nursing Services

The unexpected death is most often responsible for arousing suspicion. The presence of the FNE initiates an investigation based on the Scope and Standards of Forensic Nursing Practice approved by the American Nurses Association Congress of Nursing Practice and the International Association of Forensic Nurses. The application of the nursing process forms the basis for the investigation of injury, illness, disease, disorder, or death in all human health conditions. Whether the individual at the center of the investigation is a patient in the hospital or dies at the scene of a crime, in a residence or in police custody, the evaluation of circumstances surrounding the death requires a systematic, scientific approach, which is applicable through the nursing process.

The duties of a nurse death investigator are carried out in accordance with the performance standards and procedures established under the medical examiner's or coroner's system of death investigation and the jurisdictional regulations. The standards established by the National Association of Medical Examiners, State Coroners Associations, the International Association of Forensic Nurses, and the American Nurses Association conform to legislation and professional policies and procedures, administrative rules, and standards for professional practice. Coping with death-related grief is a manifested problem. Grief is seen as a social role, not only a "condition," and treatment plans are designed to help alleviate this problem.

The nurse investigator works as one member of the multidisciplinary team in the scene investigation process requiring an in-depth evaluation of cases such as homicides, suicides, accidents, and cases of unknown or unrecognized trauma. In jurisdictions where the majority of the ME's caseload is composed of natural deaths, which do not require a high investigative profile involving law enforcement officials, the forensic nurse assumes legal custody of the body until mortuary services arrive. This prevents police officers from being unnecessarily detained because of a natural death and allows them to devote more time to criminal investigation. Forensic nurses do not compete with, replace, or supplant other practitioners—rather, they fill voids by accomplishing selected forensic tasks concurrently with law enforcement agencies.

Although both law enforcement agents and the forensic nurse death investigator (FNDI) are present at the scene of death, two distinct jurisdictions prevail. In most ME/C jurisdictions, the crime scene belongs to the police, and the body belongs to the medical investigator. Each must recognize boundaries and coordinate specific aspects of the investigation, clearly designating individual

and mutual responsibility. Failure to clarify roles and authority can result in unnecessary friction, territoriality, and even liability when matters go wrong (Lynch & Weaver, 1998).

BEST PRACTICE Respect boundaries. The law enforcement agent's jurisdiction is the crime scene; the agent's objective is to determine if a crime has been committed and who committed the crime. The medical examiner/coroner's jurisdiction is the body, and the objective is to determine the cause and manner of death (i.e., why and how death occurred).

DEATH IN THE CLINICAL ENVIRONS

The priority to save lives is obvious to emergency department nurses in catastrophic near-death treatment. Yet the importance of properly identifying, securing, and preserving items that can later be considered as evidence may be forgotten as the patient dies. The ME and the crime laboratory rely on the attending staff to provide an accurate and detailed description of wounds, to collect and preserve admission or postmortem blood and body fluids, and to recognize and recover trace evidence. The FNE on duty will be responsible for gathering essential documents, contacting appropriate authorities and agencies, ensuring notification of death, and intervening with the decedent's family.

The dead on arrival (DOA), or those who die during trauma treatment, in the operating room, delivery room, or other area of the hospital, require specific considerations when certifying the place of death. The pronouncement of death will determine the place of death, even if the initial trauma or end stage of the disease process responsible for death occurred elsewhere. If the decedent's body is removed from the site of death or dies during transport and is pronounced DOA, the hospital becomes the place of death and is documented as such on the death certificate. Thus, the trauma room, for example, becomes a scene of death and should be protected as a crime scene until the body is removed and final evidence collection and documentation are completed.

When identification of the decedent is not in doubt, as with most individuals who die in the hospital, the investigation is simplified to a certain extent. When the cause of death is not in doubt and is not a traumatic or suspicious but is required to be reported by law, the attending physician generally signs the certificate of death and the medical examiner's jurisdiction is waived. The body is released to the funeral home and the investigation is completed. Yet each death must be considered on the merits of the individual case. Under known or unknown circumstances, it is beneficial to have a death investigator with a biomedical background and who has the ability to review medical records and to interpret medical abbreviations and nurses' notes, natural disease processes, and surgical interventions. The death investigator should also be familiar with pharmacology to eliminate or confirm medication errors. Clinical nurses must recognize the ME/C jurisdiction of the case and maintain chain of custody over the body, scene, and evidence while awaiting the arrival of the death investigator. The FNDI will interview clinical personnel, family or friends, and police at the hospital; collect evidence; document the condition of the decedent; and assume chain of custody before transferring the body to the forensic pathology laboratory.

Generally, information not readily available at the scene of death is available on the admission note or medical records. Medical history, diagnosis, time of death, and names of the next of kin and attending physician are available to the death investigator on request. Laws in the United States provide for access to this information involving forensic cases of death. The ME/C has no jurisdiction over living persons but has ultimate authority over all questioned deaths within his or her jurisdiction. The exception would be in states where the coroner has jurisdiction over mental health–related issues.

Nurses who decline to divulge information related to a patient's death can be considered to be obstructing justice by failing to cooperate with the ME/C. Medical investigators generally carry documents that provide the authority to access medical records. If the healthcare professional refuses to comply, a special warrant is required to obtain the documents (primarily because of complications in health privacy laws). When a person dies in the hospital and there are no relatives, generally, the health authority is lawfully in charge of the body.

Under a ME/C system, the body is transferred to the investigative facility for a reasonable length of time so that the relatives can be located. After approximately 48 hours, if no relation can be traced, the health authority can authorize an autopsy. The health authority is equally responsible for the disposal of the body by burial or cremation. The health authority must bear the cost of the disposal of the body (see Box 17-3).

Clinical nurses are continuously required to contact the ME/C's office to report deaths that occur in hospitals and nursing homes. Frequently, nurses are unaware of the specifics of death-reporting procedures or the laws that govern which deaths must be reported to the medicolegal system. Failure to report a forensic death and insufficient or erroneous information may cause investigation procedures to be hampered, and interagency relations may be jeopardized.

KEY POINT Nurses and other medical professionals, law enforcement agencies, forensic scientists, and public health authorities must engage in interagency cooperation for optimum death investigation processes to succeed.

Death-Reporting Initiatives

The clinical forensic nurse educator on the hospital staff should incorporate the following information in a death-reporting orientation for emergency services personnel and other departments. Ideally, nurses should know the law before they face legal issues in sudden and unexpected death. Nurses should keep a laminated copy of the law and of the information required for reporting to the ME/C in the desk or ambulance for ready reference and create a death information checklist. Nurses should also know what to report (anything other than natural death or a natural death that falls within the parameters of the law), what number to call (the ME/C office), who to ask for (medical investigator or deputy coroner), and what information that person will request. The forensic nurse should not release personal property to the next of kin without the permission of the police, the coroner, or the medical examiner. A patient's personal belongings often constitute

---

Box 17-3 Procedures for Handling a Body at the Hospital

- Clothing: Recover, dry, and pack in paper container (not plastic)
- Hair: Recover and package.
- Treatment records: Obtain necessary copies and information.
- Hardware: Do not remove; rather tie off or clamp.
- Bag hands: Any patient that died of sexual assault or gunshot injuries.
- Preserve evidence in general.

---

forensically significant evidence. This includes clothing, valuables, or other property. Once the property has been released, the chain of custody has been severed and it is no longer admissible in court.

PROPER BODY HANDLING

When a person dies in the hospital, nurses are typically instructed to follow the clinical protocol for preparing the body, which is generally outlined in the nursing procedure manual. If the decedent is to be sent to the ME/C office, routine postmortem care is no longer appropriate. Although contrary to general procedure, the wrists and ankles should not be tied together. Binding limbs with gauze or other material will leave marks that can be confused with ligature or handcuff marks or may destroy any such impressions that preexist. Although limbs have traditionally been tied to assist those who are handling the body after death, it is preferable to wrap the body in a clean white sheet, tying each end together to protect the body and extremities.

SUSPICIOUS DEATHS

When a traumatic death is pronounced on arrival or shortly after the patient was admitted, or when any suspicion of circumstances has been reported to the police or ME/C, routine postmortem care is no longer appropriate. Do not remove clothing or treatment paraphernalia, and do not wash the body. In the final documentation, the FNE should distinguish those features caused by injury from those caused by lifesaving intervention or medical treatment. It is important that the FNE documents these features on the patient's chart or uses a skin marker on the body with ME/C approval. This should be cleared by contacting the local ME/C for preferences in procedures, and it should be written in the hospital's forensic protocol.

NOTIFICATION OF DEATH

The consequences of violence and other unnatural causes of death take a tremendous toll on individuals, families, and communities. These consequences are not only legal issues but also add difficulty to times of great personal crisis. The immediate aftermath of a sudden, unexpected, and unexplained death requires direct and intimate communication. Notification of death is one of the most traumatic moments in the lives of individuals closely related or intimately involved with someone who has died suddenly or unexpectedly, whether a result of catastrophic events or casualties common to community lives. A family's immediate response to the news of a death is often unpredictable. Death is a difficult topic to discuss, both personally and professionally. With the death of a child or parent, or the anticipatory grief of family elders for those closest to them, for that moment, the living experience is a distortion of reality.

KEY POINT Violent deaths are more stigmatizing and traumatic. Violent deaths trigger feelings of guilt, hatred, perplexity, resentment, panic, confusion, and rage.

The office of the ME/C is ultimately responsible for the notification of deaths within its jurisdiction. Because nurse coroners generally employ nurses as deputy coroners, the staff is well prepared to intervene with the unknown and unexpected emotional reactions to death notification.

The use of FNDIs is growing in the United States and becoming preferred in many medical examiners' jurisdictions. Forensic pathologists who employ nurse investigators stress the importance of teamwork between criminal and biomedical investigative personnel. They have expressed concern that medically untrained officers often disregard medical evidence, maintain poor sensitivity, and are not communicative with bereaved families (Butt, 1993). FNEs who fill the role of death investigator or coroner contribute holistically by bringing together clinical expertise, forensic technique, and empathy.

Vernon McCarty, (retired) coroner, Washoe County, Nevada, has employed nurses in his office since the 1980s and is an advocate for using nurses in death investigations. He stated:

The medical investigator will often play a key role in notification of the next of kin, advisement as to death related events, and grief counseling. The investigator should never overlook this opportunity to provide social support. The investigator should be acquainted with grief related responses. In doing so it is realized that not only will the investigative function be much simplified and that an important human need will be fulfilled. Medical examiner's investigators are required to make judgments and solve problems on their own initiative and in liaison with other disciplines. The consequences of error are great, with effects that could lead to aggravation of grief or litigation. (Handbook for Death Reporting, no date)

When a sudden and unexpected death occurs, the first responders are generally the police, emergency services, and the death investigator or coroner. They usually share in the responsibility of interviewing the survivor and documenting the evidence. The task of communicating with the decedent's survivors requires tact and human caring. When the shock of the loved one's death is compounded by violence, the death notification is frequently an overwhelming scenario of grief, despair, and anguish. Whether the interface with the next of kin or significant other is at the scene of death or in the emergency department, the alleviation of human suffering remains to be an important objective of the empathetic health and justice professional.

Social scientists have studied the survivors of traumatic grief. These individuals display signs and symptoms of posttraumatic stress disorder resulting not only from the death trauma but from "secondary wounds" caused by the circumstances surrounding the aftermath. This begins with the notification of death.

How can the FNDI help the survivors of catastrophic death trauma? The relatives and friends of the victim are recognized as victims by extension, often requiring crisis intervention and grief therapy. Shneidman (1984) indicated that "post-vention" (i.e., appropriate and helpful acts after the tragedy) will render immediate and on-the-scene crisis intervention. Post-vention reduces the aftereffects of a traumatic event for the victim-survivors.

Defense Mechanisms

As healthcare professionals, FNEs have a responsibility to the family to understand the verbal and nonverbal clues and to determine how to help them. The most common defense mechanisms often present are one's reactions to the notification of a sudden death and include shock, panic, guilt, confusion, rage, and resentment.

As an immediate source of support, the death investigator making the notification provides the opportunity for the bereaved to vent their feelings. The FNE cannot prevent the primary injury and emotional trauma caused to the victim-survivors by death. However, the FNE's responsibility is to prevent the secondary wounds from an insensitive or inappropriate notification of death.

BEST PRACTICE The forensic nurse should develop a flexible system of death notification before approaching the family and should be prepared to manage a wide range of reactionary emotional outbursts.

Death notification is a sensitive and delicate message that needs to be delivered in person and as soon as possible. The investigator responsible for making the announcement should have developed a flexible system of notification, interviewing, and questioning before approaching the family. Because emotional defense mechanisms are unique to each individual, one must understand that any reaction from the next of kin is their way of coping under stress. Often the bearer of sad news is the first to receive the brunt of an emotional outburst of anger, rage, or grief. This should not be taken personally; rather the FNE should adjust to the reactions of the adult or child in a way that offers assistance in this difficult time.

KEY POINT An important part of the work of the coroner or medical examiner is to serve as a liaison with the next of kin. This facilitates the grieving process, assists families in expressing emotion, and decreases guilt by ensuring families that grief is a natural reaction.

A historic lack of comprehensive training for investigators or officiators with criminal investigative backgrounds has resulted in definitive problems related to notification of death. Police have been cited as lacking sensitivity and the ability to display empathy. Families state they perceive this interaction with law enforcement officers to be cold, callous, and indifferent. This lack of emotion most often negatively affects the mental health of grieving relations (Lynch, 1995). It is difficult for a staff without appropriate education to understand the basic needs of the bereaved as well as to provide the necessary cooperation from the standpoint of interagency and interpersonal communication. The educational preparation of a death investigator must include psychosocial skills in order to reduce and prevent further emotional trauma or the negative issues often associated with law enforcement investigators in notification of death procedures.

Human consolation is not the objective of criminal investigation. Officers often state that they find it necessary to operate according to unstated rules to remain objective and maintain control. These unstated rules include the following:

- Don't get too close.
- Don't ask unnecessary questions.
- Don't focus on feelings of the survivors.
- Don't get personally involved.

This is without criticism of law enforcement officers. In regard to criminal investigation, they are trained to display traits necessary to gain their objectives. In the same sense that professionals in any field cannot be judged alike, all law enforcement agents cannot be judged by the negative behavior of some. Empathy is a learned behavior as well as a personality trait. Many officers are sincerely concerned with the impact of sudden death on parents, children, or significant others and provide a sensitive and perceptive approach when addressing those who are victims by extension.

Conversely, a chief complaint often accorded to nurses addresses their failure to be objective, suspicious, or remain alert to potential indicators of criminality when families express sentiments of emotion and shock. The forensic nurse, however, is taught to maintain a strong sense of suspicion in behavioral evaluation, while at the same time providing a perceptive and observant assessment. Based on their cross training in criminal justice and forensic science technique, forensic nurses are cautioned to approach each death as if it were a homicide until proved otherwise. In the same manner, clinical FNEs are taught to consider unrecognized or unidentified injuries as abuse until confirmed or ruled out.

Current nursing theories and practices emphasize a caring response to the complex and sensitive issues surrounding death and dying. Emotional trauma resulting from abnormal grief or inappropriate adaptation to stress directly affects health and disease orientation. Intervention in grief must be seen and supported as a means toward adaptation and health. Forensic nursing is a part of an essential shift in human consciousness that represents a much needed and long overdue concern for survivors.

Proper Notification of Death Techniques

The National Organization for Victims Assistance Bulletin 110 (NOVA, no date) advises the following notification procedures:
- Never make a notification by telephone. This can generally be avoided by contacting a local chaplain that works with the police department or other agency skilled in the notification of death in a different city or country and request personal notification.
- Arrange a personal contact.
- Project warmth and compassion.
- Convey the information simply and directly.
- Be aware of the survivors' medical history.
- Use concise terms, such as *dead, died,* or *was killed.* Avoid ambiguous terms such as *passed on, expired,* or *is gone.* These terms are easily misunderstood and create false hope.
- Never refer to the decedent as "the body"; instead use the decedent's name or familial status.
- Don't fear emotional involvement; don't be afraid to join the survivors in their grief.
- Be empathic and let the survivors know you care about them and their loss.
- Encourage them to cry freely, expressing their grief in whatever way they wish and for as long as they wish.

Forensic nurse death investigators are often the first to come in contact with the next of kin in the immediate postdeath period. A sensitive approach should include the application of psychosocial interventions among those listed here:
- Consoling the survivors
- Listening
- Talking about the decedent
- Evaluating the emotional status of the survivors
- Offering referral information
- Sharing strength and concern through touch
- Not being in a rush to leave
- Never leaving them alone
- Encouraging them to express other emotions; anger and guilt need to be ventilated/shared
- Reassuring them that the death was not their fault
- Maintaining a policy of availability to relatives who often have no place to turn with their questions about the most delicate circumstances of the death
- Giving them as much information as possible
- Supporting their need to repeat questions
- Encouraging them to seek additional support
- Never saying, "I understand," "It was God's will," or "At least you have other children"

Psychosocial Intervention

Post-vention is described as appropriate and helpful acts after a tragedy and provides immediate and on-scene crisis intervention. It also helps to reduce the aftereffects of a traumatic event in the lives of the survivors. Three psychological stages of post-ventive care include the following:
1. Resuscitation: Working with the initial shock and grief in the first 24 hours
2. Rehabilitation: Consultations with family members from the first to the sixth month
3. Renewal: Healthy tapering off of mourning process from the sixth month on (Shneidman, 1984)

Caution: Although the nurse investigator must not let emotions interfere with professionalism, the family's loss must always be recognized. This requires a balance of objectivity and empathy, never becoming so insensitive that their loss cannot be felt. The nurse investigator should always say, "I'm sorry," and let the next of kin know he or she is sincere.

Guidelines for Approaching the Family

- Do not make death notifications from the doorstep!
- Identify yourself and ask to come inside. Tell them your position. Ask for their names.
- Make eye contact. Eye contact and a quiet voice convey caring and establish some rapport.
- Offer to find a place where everyone can be seated. Never stand when a victim-survivor is seated.
- It is appropriate to "anchor" the family member with a touch—hold a hand, touch a shoulder. Brief physical contact conveys compassion.
- Start with, "I have very difficult news to bring you" or "It's about your son, it is very serious," then "Your son was killed today."
- Never draw out the point of the notification—the longer the news is drawn out, the greater the stress.
- Never give the family members too much information at one time. Wait until they ask the next question before continuing with the information. Hesitate between each sentence, giving them the time to react and absorb what they are being told.
- Speak slowly. Slowing down helps the family to gradually grasp the news. They will be in shock and will not want to believe what they are hearing. They will have an immediate onset of physical symptoms from the rush of adrenaline. Their hands will be cold, respirations rapid, and heartbeats fast.
- Explain what the next sequence of events will be. Leave written information. They may not remember later what you said. Include instructions regarding the investigation, the coroner, the autopsy, the mortician, and so on.
- Activate at least one source of support. Contact a family member, clergy, neighbor, or victim advocate. It is not appropriate to leave someone in acute grief alone. The person is vulnerable, in shock, and fragile. Newly bereaved individuals are often at risk for serious accidents.
- Follow up with a phone call, letter, or visit (some ME/C offices have specially prepared letters). The FNE will be remembered with gratitude and respect and will not be forgotten. The FNE will become part of their healing process (adapted from Monroe, 2003).

VIEWING OF THE BODY

Whenever possible, allow the family or significant others to see their loved one. With rare exception, it is essential that they be allowed to view the body if they have requested to do so. Prepare them for what they may see. Explain the condition of the body and give them the opportunity to change their minds. If they are confident this is what they wish, give them a moment to organize their thoughts while the body is arranged for viewing.

In a forensic case, any treatment paraphernalia from the body should not be removed and the face should not be washed. Cover any injured body parts and drape the body with a clean white sheet. If the head is injured, wrap a clean white towel around the hair and lower the room lights. Be prepared to support them both emotionally and physically as the situation demands. However, they should never be alone with the body. Explain that they cannot touch the body. This is a precaution for the security of evidence in a forensic case. The FNE has custody of the chain of evidence initiated with the body. It is not uncommon for the spouse, parent, or others close to the decedent to be the primary suspect. The nurse investigator or coroner should supervise the entire viewing process as well as protect the body and evidence from any disturbance throughout.

This supervision should be of particular consideration in child deaths. Children are most frequently killed by their parents or primary caretakers. Until the autopsy has been completed and suspicion of abuse or murder has been eliminated, no one should be allowed to touch, to hold, or to be alone with the body. Within the nursery (neonatal or infant class of deaths), significant concern has been expressed by nurses who are requested by the ME or coroner not to allow the parents to hold the baby's body before releasing it for autopsy. Although the hospital's intention is to allow the parents to initiate some extent of closure, one must also consider the risk that a suspected sudden infant death syndrome case might actually be a homicide. If the body is to be autopsied, no one should come in contact with the body or evidence. The nurse investigator should explain that the death is now an ME/C case, and contact is not allowed. The reason for this precaution is to prevent loss or cross-contamination of evidence. The explanation should be kept simple, brief, and firm (it is not necessary to explain that the parent may be considered a suspect). Generally parents are considerate of this request. If the death is not an ME/C case and is of natural causes, parents should always be allowed the opportunity to hold, touch, and share last moments with the infant or child.

Attempts to lessen traumatic shock when viewing the body or making visual identification during the initial postdeath period is an important responsibility of the forensic nurse. Medical examiners and coroners recognize this need and often provide special viewing rooms for privacy and security of the body. A small, quiet, comfortable room with a plate-glass window or closed-circuit television visualization to observe the body is beneficial to the one making identification. This helps to distance the impact of trauma, eliminates smells, and provides for security of the body. Some facilities have a chapel that also serves as a viewing room. Digital photographs have proved to be a significant visual identification method in mass disasters, eliminating the need for an actual viewing of the body. This reduces the time management and emotional trauma of families when dealing with mass disasters. These bodies are removed directly from the scene to the forensic pathology facilities for identification and autopsy, and they are often stored in refrigerated transportation units. The next of kin, in these cases, would likely prefer to make identification from the photographs. However, it is the special presence of the forensic nurse that provides the physical and psychological support that often helps to stabilize the

family members in this difficult experience. How they are treated is significant post-vention care—something they will remember always.

As a clinical nurse cares for the dying and counsels their families during the hospital stay, the FNDI is able to continue in the role of a nurse. In a very real way, the planning is continued as originated in the clinical setting. The nurse sees to the needs of those left behind and is a visible part of the community care system. The position description of the FNE in death investigation falls within the parameters of the standards of nursing care and meets the criteria of the nursing process. There is ongoing evaluation of the position description as FNEs work with other members of the profession.

The Question

It is not uncommon to be asked why a nurse would want to perform the duties of an investigator of death. Generally, peer professionals in the clinical setting (even some nurse educators) or in the public eye cannot imagine why anyone would choose this role. They cannot conceive the scenarios faced by the nurse investigator and the risk of vicarious trauma that can, and may, affect the psychological well-being of those who most often are to first come in contact with the family, to bear the brunt of sudden shock and grief. It must be remembered that the decedents, regardless of the circumstances of death or the condition of the body, are the same individuals often treated in the emergency department, only they are no longer breathing.

Each person is our patient. Whether someone dies on the trauma table or on an interstate highway, of a natural death or violent causes, FNEs have a responsibility to treat the individual as if the victim were a member of his or her own family. Who wants to think that when the time of death comes anyone should be afraid or repulsed to tend to our last needs? There was a time when each family was responsible for the care of their own dead. Although it must have been difficult, it was surely done with love and tenderness. That no one would want to do this job—with care—is a reflection on our lack of humanness. It should be considered an honor to become the deceased's last friend, to represent the deceased as one would the disabled, to speak for the dead, with the deceased's family or in a court of law.

The ultimate goal of death investigation, to determine why one dies, is to save lives of a similar nature in the future. To make recommendations for public health and safety is one vital aspect of health and justice objectives. Death investigation is intellectually stimulating; each case is a challenge, an anticipation of the unknown. One must consider the contribution to society—the reduction and prevention of injury, illness, and death. To know you have performed a job that few others would want, to diminish human suffering in some small way, and to care when others do not—these acts bring their own reward.

The Future

Forensic nursing science has contributed significantly to both the forensic sciences and to traditional nursing practice. The forensic nurse continues to be of assistance in the evolution of a health and justice-oriented system of care based on society's values and needs. This continuing evolution will require varying degrees of assistance in stabilizing and advancing forensic nursing as a discipline and as a science. Society demands a specific kind of help from persons specially qualified to care for the situations and circumstances often called for in human death.

Consider, now, another turning point in the ever-expanding role of the forensic nurse. FNEs and the future of death science are clearly interrelated. Scientifically, nurses are prepared to participate in and to assist with all aspects of the investigation of death, from the scene of death to the autopsy laboratory, from the hospital and the community setting to a court of law. The FNE serves as a liaison between the ME/C's office and the police, news media, governmental agencies, families, and other individuals. For families, the FNE extends a more sensitive approach to death investigation. For the pathologist, the forensic nurse is the natural protégé. The various components of the proposed training program are intended to be adopted or adapted by ME/C's offices, forensic nursing boards and associations, law enforcement agencies, and crime laboratories in cooperation with National Center for Forensic Sciences/ Institute for Simulation Training (NCFS/IST).

ADVANCING THE SCOPE OF FORENSIC SCIENCE

After the implementation of the first graduate program to prepare nurses as medicolegal investigators at the University of Texas at Arlington, the question was "Where will we go?" In 1988, Charles Petty, chief medical examiner in Dallas County, Texas, when queried regarding the status of nurses in death investigation, replied in a personal letter to Lynch:

> The basic premise is that death investigation is better carried out by individuals with medical training. This was recognized over 100 years ago, first in Massachusetts when the first medical examiner system was established. Gradually since then, more and more death investigation systems have incorporated physicians as medical examiners, supplanting the old lay-coroner system. In many large metropolitan areas, the physician medical examiner does not have the time to conduct the basic death investigation in person. Individuals who are trained by the medical examiner to visit scenes and to carry out telephonic investigations do this. Until recently, nurses were not engaged in this type of investigation. However, in this office, we have now, and have had in the past, registered nurses who proved to be excellent death investigators because of the past medical training possessed by them (personal communication, Charles Petty, January 27, 1988).

As forensic pathology became the preferred method of death investigation and was considered the standard by which all questioned deaths were to be evaluated, a significant limitation was recognized because of the shortage of those qualified to practice as medical examiners. Forensic medicine remains the second smallest specialty in the practice of U.S. medicine. Inevitably, this leaves a serious deficit of specialists to manage the multitude of forensic cases reported in North America.

One solution to this shortage is to use FNEs. This approach utilizes a preexisting resource, one who is educated and skilled as a forensic professional for the role of coroner, deputy coroner, or FNDI in adjunct to a forensic pathologist. Where the law does not require this position to be filled by a physician, the FNE provides an ideal solution to existing problems within the system of death investigation.

Petty further stated, "This is a new field for nurses and I believe will become one that will be most acceptable to both nurses and medical examiners. I can foresee the time when in metropolitan

areas nurses will be involved as death investigators, possibly supplanting others" (personal communication, Charles Petty, January 27, 1988). Petty explained the rationale for a preference to nurses or lay-investigators, as opposed to the use of police officers as field agents in medical investigation. He stated that it was more advantageous to take an individual with a medical background and train him or her in investigative technique than it was to teach a criminal investigator about medical knowledge and technique.

This has become the principle on which nurse coroners and nurse death investigators have been recognized as uniquely qualified to serve as officiators of death and to represent the forensic pathologists at the scene. This principle, originating with John Butt in 1975, has been embraced by many U.S. jurisdictions and has reached into the distant areas of Africa and Asia. Butt believes that forensic nurses fill a multifaceted role beyond scene investigation, expanding their nursing skills to touch the lives of the grieving and bereaved in a manner that has brought a new respect to the field of death investigation.

Figures 17-1 through 17-3 illustrate the activities of Judy Cook, Dallas County Forensic Nurse Death Investigator, during the initial investigation at an apparent homicide scene.

Fig. 17-1 A FNE makes an initial assessment while investigating an apparent homicide scene in conjunction with law enforcement officers.

Fig. 17-2 Bags have been placed over the victim's hands to preserve trace evidence.

Fig. 17-3 A law enforcement officer and FNE scrutinize another potential evidentiary item at the scene.

ADVANCED PRACTICE IN DEATH INVESTIGATION

Forensic nursing has come of age. A viable conceptual system has been established, one that provides comprehensive, relevant guidelines for theory building and research. No longer are FNEs overly concerned with status as forensic nurse scientists; instead they are concerned with the phenomena of life and death as equal counterparts in human care. FNEs are beginning to realize their potential for discovering a particular kind of knowledge that is relevant to other disciplines and essential to nursing. The problem of the past has been the dearth of forensic nursing knowledge. The problem of the future will be the acceleration of that knowledge into every aspect of each nursing specialty, for there is no nursing specialty that cannot benefit from the application of this knowledge. There is no nursing specialty that does not come in contact with the realities of human violence as a public health concern.

Although our charge was clear more than 100 years ago, Florence Nightingale envisioned a better world for humankind through nursing. Nurses have always cared for victims of crime—and for the dead. Yet because of the direction nurses have taken in search of nursing knowledge, only recently have they begun to discover that truth and justice also lie within the nucleus of nursing care. Nursing is on the threshold of an exciting venture into new domains of knowledge, science, and the law. Its application to traditional nursing practice will be enhanced by forensic nursing as a tool for preventing human abuse, premature deaths, and social injustice. Forensic nursing is at a new juncture of development and has led this emerging discipline toward a new image and profile. At the same time, it has lent a new level of sophistication and prestige to forensic medicine through the acceptance of highly skilled and competent counterparts in forensic nursing. This collegial relationship and association represents a value that is seen as both necessary and desirable in reinforcing a degree of security within both professions as FNEs work together to conduct mutual research and outcomes nonexistent in the past.

To join with other health professionals in expanding concepts that cross the barriers of tradition for tradition's sake is invigorating. Nursing has long recognized the need to focus on topics such as the right to die, children and death, youth suicide, grief and bereavement, sudden death trauma, and defining death. Perspectives on death emphasize quality of life issues that cannot be quantified in psychosocial and scientific research. Theories and practices share caring responses to the complex and sensitive issues surrounding death and dying. The social services available to those facing death, dying, and grief are reported in a complex intermingling of disciplines that include nursing, medicine,

law, genetics, philosophy, psychology, religion, sociology, anthropology, political science, economics, and education. Such complexity affects the role of every professional concerned with the quality of life for humankind. Considering the increasing effects of the life span of humankind, the greater number of elderly will have a significant impact on healthcare and on death investigation where the prevention of exploitation and abuse and the improvement of the quality of life interface with health, peace, and quantification of years.

FNE/FNDI Duties

1. *Forensic nurse death investigator.* Provide highly trained death scene investigators with a medical perspective pertaining to cause, manner, and mechanism of death
2. *Forensic nurse examiner.* Develop their role at an advanced practice level to assist the forensic pathologist in selected responsibilities in the autopsy laboratory, provide external examination in natural deaths, provide rape/homicide examination, intercede on behalf of the ME/C in the scientific investigation of death, and reduce an unnecessary workload on the forensic pathologist
3. Participate in the national and international development of forensic nursing education, research, and practice for the advancement of death investigation systems, the identification of preventable deaths, and increase the number of positive identifications in the unidentified dead (UND)

The continual evolution of forensic nursing practice is being considered for more advanced roles as associates in forensic pathology, in scientific research, and in clinical trials with goal-directed outcomes involving education, publications, supervisory positions in large institutional facilities, and as direct service providers in medical examiner and coroner systems. Advanced specialists in forensic nursing will provide an enhanced image to the complex field of death investigation, a field once viewed with disdain by clinical professionals, families of the dead, and the public at large. Considering that the major status of the forensic nurse is, foremost, nursing, it is the nursing process and nursing ingenuity that guides the investigative actions of the forensic nurse. As nursing becomes more independent, the nurse investigator's level of practice will be subjected to greater scrutiny, requiring more sophisticated education, qualifications, and skills.

In the United States and increasingly in other countries, governments and nongovernment organizations (NGOs) are turning to FNEs with expectations to fill a void where a deficient number of forensically skilled physicians have resulted in inadequate prosecutions, loss of evidence, long delays in response time, and the loss of human lives. Forensic nursing services can assist law enforcement and emergency physicians in meeting the expectations of victims and their families through accessible and cost-effective programs. The expectations are as follows:

1. Utilize nursing principles and skills in communication, interviewing, and physical assessment through appropriate nursing interventions with the decedent, the decedent's family, and other relevant persons in the community.
2. Synthesize and apply skills of physical assessment and knowledge of biomedical investigation to assess, plan, provide, and evaluate nursing interventions, with and on behalf of the deceased, the family, and the community.
3. Participate effectively on the multidisciplinary ME/C team to plan and provide direct and supportive nursing care; to assess needs for and make referrals to other healthcare services and to counsel individuals and families through periods of stress.
4. Participate in investigations under the direction of the ME/C to determine circumstances surrounding sudden death.

5. Plan and implement forensic educational programs for nurses, other healthcare providers, and the community, such as in child abuse, child safety, grief counseling, and health maintenance promotion, and prevention programs for people at risk for major health problems.
6. Assume accountability as a FNE by accepting responsibility as a nurse clinician, recognizing one's own abilities and limitations, and consistently seeking guidance, counseling, direction, and learning experiences that promote professional and personal development.
7. Demonstrate a leadership role in forensic nursing—including innovation, consultation, advocacy, accountability, and responsibility—to improve services to the family, the community, and, as appropriate, the criminal justice system in cases of sudden death.

It is interesting to note that since the 1970s, FNEs have stayed the course. From the Canadian model to the worldview of forensic nursing, the foundation of practice has been maintained with clarity. Forensic nurse Laynese Guay, a pioneer in death investigation, addressed the essence of forensic nursing from the twofold perspective: physical intervention in death and psychological intervention in society. In introducing the role of the nurse in death investigation to the Canadian Nurses Association in 1985, Guay noted that medicolegal investigation is a relatively new role for nurses, but it is neither a shadowy occupation nor a morbid experience. Rather it is a role that can make considerable contributions to important aspects of social justice, public service, and community mental health. Indeed, helping establish the exact cause of sudden death can, in itself, provide for adjudication of criminal cases, instill confidence in public administration, and be a way of helping survivors work through their grief. The future progress of the profession of nursing will display many facets in an increasingly demanding society. The opportunity to be a part of the development of a new specialization is an exciting challenge. We expanded our role during the previous century, and we will continue to break new ground as nurses. The role of the caregiver continues.

Summary

The need for a new generation of medical investigators blending biomedical training with the investigation of death indicates a new trend in the forensic sciences. Advances in medical and forensic science indicate a need for individuals with a background in anatomy, physiology, and pharmacology, along with an emphasis on grief and crisis intervention. Forensic pathologists and criminalists alike recognize forensic nurses as professionals who can make diverse contributions to the scientific investigation of death (Lynch 1986).

The forensic nurse examiner is well prepared to meet the scientific demands of death investigation by assisting law enforcement officers in the recovery of medical evidence while meeting the needs of grieving and bereaved families. The forensic nurse can provide an immediate support system and play a key role in the tragic and traumatic environment of sudden and unexpected death. The opportunity to provide adequate social support should never be overlooked, although the investigator's primary mandate remains (Lynch, 1995).

The education of the forensic nurse is exceptionally extensive, ranging from on-the-scene management of the decedent and medical evidence, incorporating legal authority and jurisdiction, to a wide range of concepts and procedures pertaining to death and dying. The ability to maintain an index of suspicion while providing a sensitive yet probing interview with family members takes tact and skill. Such an incisive education also prepares the forensic

nurse to identify aspects of academic research involving the epidemiology of death, to apply deductive reasoning in evaluating potential prevention analysis, and to make concluding assessments of the agents and forces that result in the loss of human life. "Whether those vectors be physical, environmental, chemical, microbiological or unknown, the knowledge between survivable injury and death is simply a matter of degree—the pattern of injury is the same" (Anderson & Gay, 1996). Clinical knowledge and nursing experience remain the basis for expertise in the medical investigation of death, separating the FNE from the lay-investigator and from the criminal investigation of death.

When criminal or civil issues are involved in the death assessment of traumatic injuries or the subtle indications of abuse and neglect, nurses have a professional and ethical responsibility to address the decedent's legal rights through the recovery and proper documentation of evidence. Through the implementation of healthcare policies that address forensic issues, the biomedical investigation of a vast number of cases of child abuse and crimes against women and the elderly will aid law enforcement agencies in meeting the objectives of criminal investigation. Nurses who provide a forensic assessment share common interests and role behaviors with social and justice advocates in the medicolegal management of the dead, the dying, and their families. This includes the assessment, case management, intervention, and evaluation of death scene investigation, as well as a forensic holistic concern for body, mind, spirit, and the law. As the science of death investigation joins with nursing science today to address the physiological, psychological, and legal aspects of death and dying, the holistic collaboration of personnel, public prosecution, and prevention emerge as one.

Resources
ORGANIZATIONS

American Board of Medicolegal Death Investigators
c/o Division of Forensic Pathology, St. Louis University School of Medicine, 1402 South Grand Boulevard, St. Louis, MO 63104-1028; 314-977-5970; www.slu.edu/organizations/abmdi
Forensic Medical Death Investigation Course
Dr. Mary Dudley, Chief Medical Examiner, Sedgwick County Kansas; www.forensicmi.com/Course%20Description.htm
Harris County Medical Examiner Office
1885 Old Spanish Trail, Houston, TX 77054; 713-796-9292; www.co.harris.tx.us/me
International Association of Forensic Nurses 1517 Ritchie Highway, Suite 208, Arnold, MD, 21012-2323; (410)626-7805; http://www.iafn.org
Beth El College of Nursing, University of Colorado, Colorado Springs, CO; Undergraduate, Graduate, and Certificate Programs; http://web.uccs.edu/bethel

TRAINING PROGRAMS

Introduction to Medicolegal Death Investigation: A Nursing Internship; for more information on this program, contact South Charleston coroner Rae Wooten at rwotten@charlestoncounty.org
Injuries and Death Investigation through the Eyes of the Forensic Nurse; Metropolitan Dade County, Medical Examiner Department, One Bob Hope Road, Miami, FL 33136-1133

References

Allert, L., & Becker, M. (2002). Death investigation. In *The Forensic Nurse* (pp. 16–18) premiere issue.
Anderson, W., & Gay, R. (1996, February). *The Forensic Sciences in Clinical Medicine,* workshop presented at the American Academy of Forensic Sciences, Nashville, TN.

Baudrillard, J. (1976). *Symbolic Exchange and Death* (p. 172). Ann Arbor: University of Michigan Press.

Butt, J. (1993). Forensic nursing: Diversity in education and practice. Cited in V. Lynch, *J Psychosoc Nurs Ment Health Serv, 31*(11), 7–14.

Cumming, M. F. (1995). The vision of a nurse-coroner: A "protector of the living through the investigation of death." *J Psychosoc Nurs Ment Health Serv, 33*(5), 29–33.

Fields, K. (2004). *Cause of death uncertain.* Colorado Springs, CO: Historical Archives, American Academy of Forensic Sciences.

Handbook for Death Reporting, Office of the Coroner, Washoe County, Reno, NV (n.d.)

Hirtz, S. (2001). *The forensic nurse coroner.* Unpublished manuscript.

Jalland, P. (1996). *Death in the Victorian family.* Oxford: Oxford University Press.

Kiessling, C. (no date). *A nurse coroner's perspective.* Unpublished manuscript.

Lipson, J., Dibble, S., & Minarik, P.A. (1996). *Culture and nursing care.* San Francisco: University of California at San Francisco Nursing Press.

Lynch, V. (1986, February). *The registered nurse functioning as an investigator of death: A new field for the profession.* Paper presented at the American Academy of Forensic Sciences. New Orleans, LA.

Lynch, V. (1993). Forensic nursing: Diversity in education and practice. *J Psychosoc Nurs Ment Health Serv,* 31(11), 7–14.

Lynch, V. (1995, November). Forensic nursing: Management of crime victims from trauma to trial. *Crit Care Nurs Clin North Am,* 7(1), 497–501.

Lynch, V., & Weaver, J. (1998). Forensic nursing: Unique contributions to international law. *J Nurs Law, 5*(4), 23–34.

Monroe, A. (2003). How to deliver tragic news. Workshop brochure.

National Organization for Victims Assistance (NOVA). (no date). *Network information bulletin* (Vol. 110, Issue 2–3), Washington, DC: Author.

Parikh, C. (1999). *Textbook of medical jurisprudence, forensic medicine and toxicology.* (6th ed., Section 3, p. 1). New Delhi: Ministry of Law, Justice and Company Affairs, Government of India, CBS Publishers and Distributors.

Shneidman, E. (1984). *Death: Current perspectives.* Palo Alto, CA: Mayfield.

Standing Bear, Z. G. (1987, April). *Interview in the Valdosta Daily Times* Valdosta, GA.

Standing Bear, Z. G. (1995). Forensic nursing and death investigation: Will the vision be co-opted? *J Psychosoc Nurs Ment Health Serv, 33*(5), 59–64.

CHAPTER 18

Intrafamilial Homicide and Unexplained Childhood Deaths

Stacey A. Mitchell

The death of a child is tragic whether it results from a natural disease process or from inflicted trauma. Although healthcare providers and law enforcement are exposed almost daily to childhood death, the death of a child seems to take more of a toll when it is due to child maltreatment. The Centers for Disease Control and Prevention (CDC) reported that in 2006, more than 1500 children died from abuse and neglect. That is a rate of 2 per 100,000 children. Approximately 78%, occurred among children younger than four years old (CDC, 2008b). Between ages 4 to 7 years old, 12% died from abuse and neglect (CDC, 2008b). The National Child Abuse and Neglect Data System (NCANDS) defines child fatality as the death of a child caused by an injury resulting from some form of abuse and neglect or in a situation where abuse and neglect was a factor (U.S. Department of Health and Human Services [USDHHS], 2009). Most statistics are reported through state welfare agencies. However, information may also be obtained from state child fatality review teams and state health departments. Nonetheless, many researchers and healthcare practitioners believe that the numbers of child fatalities resulting from abuse and neglect are grossly underreported (USDHHS, 2009). Factors that contribute to this include the following:

- Variation in state child fatality review processes
- Differences in death investigation systems and training of investigators
- The ease with which circumstances surrounding the death may be concealed
- Inaccurate determination of cause and manner of death (USDHHS, 2009)

Mercy et al. (2006) discussed the impact that the National Violent Death Reporting System may have on alleviating some of these discrepancies. By linking several reporting systems, police reports, death certificates, and child protective services reports, a more accurate account of intentional childhood deaths may be identified. The information learned will also influence prevention strategies and serve as a means of evaluating those efforts (CDC, 2008a, National Violent Death Reporting System).

KEY POINT By linking several reporting systems, police reports, death certificates, and child protective services reports, a more accurate account of intentional childhood deaths may be identified.

Although an understanding of the statistics and their impact on screening for abuse and the many prevention efforts in communities is critical, it is the death investigation that lays the foundation for the determination of cause and manner of death. Thus, the death investigation affects the way law enforcement agencies and child protective services approach a case, the family, and others who may be involved in the death. Without a proper death investigation, an accurate cause and manner of death cannot be identified, resulting in inaccurate statistics from which to base all future interventions.

The forensic nurse examiner (FNE) is an important member of the infant and child death investigation team. These cases are medically and socially complicated investigations. A forensic nurse is equipped with the knowledge and expertise to assist in gathering the appropriate information to enable the forensic pathologist to determine the cause and manner of death. This chapter discusses child homicide and unexplained deaths. The role of the FNE and its bearing on the investigation are also explored. Although this is a difficult category of death to investigate, it must be done thoroughly and in a timely manner so perpetrators may be brought to justice.

Types of Intrafamilial Homicides

To appropriately investigate an infant or child death, forensic nurse death investigators (FNDIs) must first understand the type of death that they have been called to investigate. The type of death will guide the investigation from a medical and social standpoint.

NEONATICIDE

Neonaticide is defined as the killing of a neonate shortly after birth. In most cases, the death occurs on the first day of life (Jenny & Isaac, 2006). The practice of neonaticide has been observed since ancient times. Evidence of ritual killings of infants with deformities has been documented in Aztec, ancient Chinese, and some African cultures. Weak or deformed infants were killed so that they would not become a burden on society. This was also seen in ancient Greece and Rome. Other evidence indicates that males were often preferred over females, and neonaticide was an effective means of birth control (Craig, 2004). Neonaticide is more common in teenage mothers than in older mothers (Craig, 2004). Today, the perpetrator is often the mother (Jenny & Isaac, 2006). She has denied the existence of the pregnancy and often has psychotic or dissociative disorders (Jenny & Isaac, 2006).

A connection to poverty has not been established, nor has a presence of congenital anomalies been identified. However, two factors for neonaticide in today's society have been postulated: these are failed pregnancy concealment and a means for late-term abortion (Craig, 2004). Other areas are being studied, but research is limited. Although neonaticide is almost exclusively a "female crime," infanticide is commonly committed by either the mother or the father or stepfather (Jenny & Isaac, 2006).

INFANTICIDE AND FILICIDE

The intentional killing of an infant aged one day to one year has been identified as **infanticide** (Stone, Steinmeyer, Dreher, & Krischer, 2005). One out of four of all infant homicides occur by two months of age, whereas 50% of infanticide cases occur by age four months (Jenny & Isaac, 2006).

There are many definitions of **filicide**. It has been described as the murder of a child or the murder of a child by the mother (Friedman & Resnick, 2007; Rouge-Maillart, Jousset, Gaudin, Bouju, & Penneau, 2005). These older children are often the victims of physical abuse. One study shows that the some of the most frequent mechanisms of filicide include head trauma, strangulation, suffocation, and drowning (Rouge-Maillart, 2005). Firearms may be used, but not in many cases. Reasons for filicide vary throughout history. They may encompass one or many of the following factors: disability, questionable paternity, gender, and a lack of resources (West, Hatters Friedman, & Resnick, 2009). Researchers developed a classification system that categorized the death based on the motives or circumstances:

- *Altruistic.* The child is killed because it is perceived to be in the child's best interests (parental reasoning may be due to psychotic or nonpsychotic factors).
- *Acutely psychotic filicide.* The parent is psychotic and there is no rational motive.
- *Unwanted child.* The child is regarded as a hindrance.
- *Accidental or fatal maltreatment.* The child is unintentionally killed as the result of abuse or neglect.
- *Spousal revenge.* One spouse kills the child in an effort to get back at the other (West, et al. 2009).

No matter the motive, a thorough investigation must be conducted for every infant and child death.

Victims

The victims in these cases are obvious. They are the youngest and the most vulnerable. Children are dependent on adults for everything. This makes them susceptible to injury and death. The risk of a child becoming a victim of homicide is highest during the first year of life (Friedman & Resnick, 2007). The Centers for Disease Control and Prevention has reported the most current statistics regarding demographics of fatal child abuse victims. Females are at a higher risk than males. Caucasian children are murdered the most, with African Americans being second, and Hispanics ranking third (CDC, 2006). However, the true incidence is not known. Murders may be hidden and signs are misinterpreted, as investigations are often substandard. Many of these deaths are medically complicated, and law enforcement investigators are not educated in medical topics (American Academy of Pediatrics [AAP], 1999; CDC, 2008c). Thus the data gathered do not accurately reflect the true numbers.

Perpetrators

It is difficult to comprehend that a parent would kill his or her own child. But it does happen and happens often. In neonaticide, the mother is often young and is attempting to conceal the pregnancy (Craig, 2004). The child is killed shortly after birth as the final act in disguising the pregnancy. It is difficult to identify women who are at risk to abuse or kill their child. Many mothers who have killed have a significant history of trauma. This past trauma may affect how they bond and approach the maternal role (Mugavin, 2008). Mental illness has also been found to play a part in infanticide and filicide. Mothers with schizophrenia and severe depression are at risk for killing their children (Levene & Bacon, 2004). These mothers may be in their twenties or thirties and unable to care for their children. The mothers are often described as being immature. Some have been found to be unemployed; some are suicidal and some are not suicidal (Rouge-Maillart, et al. 2005).

Unfortunately, attempting to determine the motive is often difficult when the parent describes the act as senseless (Rouge-Maillart, et al. 2005). Mugavin (2008) surmised that when there is a predisposition to mental illness or a traumatic history or substance abuse, one of these will possibly trigger the fatal event. That trigger may be the result of faulty thought processes in connection to revenge, sometimes against the other parent, the effects of substance abuse, desperation, or a mercy killing (Mugavin, 2008; Rouge-Maillart, 2005). The peak lifetime prevalence for psychiatric disorders is within the first three months after childbirth (Spinelli, 2004). This has important implications for prevention efforts. Physicians should be involved in screening for mental illness. The possibility for homicidal tendencies should not be underestimated (Rouge-Maillart, et al. 2005; Spinelli, 2004). Child homicide may be prevented, but it involves diligence on the part of the healthcare system to identify the signs and symptoms so that the mother may be treated.

Although the literature focuses on maternal filicide, studies have shown that paternal filicide occurs in approximately half of the cases (West, et al. 2009). Fathers are the most frequent perpetrators in the deaths of older children, whereas mothers are more likely to kill younger children (Adinkrah, 2003). In comparison to biological fathers, stepfathers are more likely to kill the stepchild (West, et al. 2009). Many of these deaths are the result of physical abuse. The father or stepfather did not intentionally set out to kill the child (West, et al. 2009). The child is often left in the care of the father or stepfather and over the course of beating the child for whatever reason, the child is fatally injured. Other factors associated with paternal filicide include unemployment, substance abuse, mental illness, and other situations such as the possibility of spousal separation (Marleau, Poulin, Webanck, Roy, & Laporte, 1999). Common methods used to kill include beatings, strangulation, suffocation, and drowning (West, et al. 2009). The literature is sparse, but the studies show many of the same circumstances are consistent in paternal filicide as in maternal filicide, meaning that prevention strategies for fathers or stepfathers are important and should be implemented.

Role of the Forensic Nurse in the Death Investigation

In the child death investigation, the FNE's knowledge and expertise may impact the outcome of the medicolegal investigation. Forensic nurses may be employed in medical examiner's offices as death investigators or elected as coroners or appointed as deputy coroners. Regardless of the title, the forensic nurse conducting the death investigation utilizes the nursing process. This type of investigation is especially complicated as homicides are often mistakenly classified as natural. The forensic nurse possesses a depth of knowledge that allows her or him to thoroughly navigate these complex issues. Knowledge of pathophysiology, toxicology, pharmacology, anatomy, physiology, and child development are critical. In addition, the forensic nurse has the ability to interact with sensitivity to the family to obtain critical medical and social information.

The forensic nurse performs the duties that are outlined in medical examiner law, coroner law, and the State Nurse Practice Act. Medical examiner (ME) and coroner law each delineate which deaths are reportable and provide the statutory authority to investigate. The Nurse Practice Act discusses where the nurse's scope of practice begins and ends. It is in combining these laws and regulations that the forensic nurse is able to function in the death investigator role.

Whether the child died in a hospital, at a residence, at the daycare or babysitter's residence, or at some other location, the evaluation of circumstances surrounding the death requires a systematic, scientific approach, which is applied through the use of the nursing process (Lynch, 2006). In approaching each death investigation in this manner, the forensic nurse is able to systematically and consistently obtain the necessary information for the pathologist to determine the cause and manner of death:

- *Assessment.* This involves observing all findings concerning the scene and the decedent. The forensic nurse obtains information from the responding law enforcement officials, the family, and any healthcare providers who cared for the child. Medical records are reviewed for ongoing medical issues that may have impacted the death.
- *Planning.* In this step, the forensic nurse outlines a plan of action that includes the location of the initial investigative efforts. For example, if the infant was found unresponsive at the residence but later died in the hospital, the forensic nurse must decide which of these two locations should be investigated first. If the family is still at the hospital, for example, it would make the most sense to go there to speak with them and the healthcare providers.
- *Intervention.* The scene and the decedent are documented. Documentation includes narrative descriptions of what is observed at the scene and the physical assessment of the deceased. Medical evidence is also recovered. The forensic nurse may notify relatives of the death, if needed, and make appropriate referrals to community support agencies as well.
- *Evaluation.* The forensic nurse discusses the scene investigation with the pathologist. Supplemental information is obtained as required. In addition, the pathologist shares the autopsy and toxicology results with the nurse. This may lead to further investigation (California State University, 2006; Lynch, 2006).

Nurses functioning in this role must be skilled in both forensic science and nursing science. This is what makes them unique and invaluable to the forensic pathologist. The forensic nurse becomes the eyes and ears of the pathologist and ensures that a complete scene investigation is conducted. In particular to the child death investigation, the forensic nurse is able to speak with the family, obtain the medical and social history, and educate the family as to the medical examiner or coroner procedures. The FNE is also able to explain the cause and manner of death and their implications once determined.

As part of the multidisciplinary team, the forensic nurse is able to work closely with law enforcement and child protective services. Important information is shared and then relayed to the examining pathologist by the forensic nurse. Each agency is required to conduct a separate, parallel investigation into the child's death. However, collaboration among the agencies is crucial for ensuring an appropriate outcome of the case. The FNE is a key member of the team.

Medicolegal Death Investigation

A child death investigation is emotionally charged. Each death must be examined thoroughly and appropriate testing completed. This type of investigation includes the scene investigation, autopsy examination, and laboratory studies (Corey, Hanzlick, Howard,

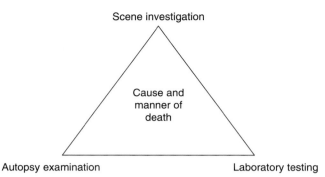

Fig. 18-1 The infant/child death investigation. Each component must be thoroughly performed in order for an accurate cause and manner of death to be determined.

Nelson, & Krous, 2007). Each component is dependent on the others, and missteps may negatively impact the determination of cause and manner of death (Fig. 18-1).

Time is critical. Therefore, the child death investigation must begin as soon as possible because scenes may change and potential evidence may be lost or destroyed (O'Neal, 2007). The forensic nurse must quickly choose which scene, if more than one, requires the immediate response. Communication between the FNDI and law enforcement is essential if the investigation is to run smoothly. The forensic nurse should never arrive at an unsecured scene without law enforcement. Safety is always the priority and must be considered first (CDC, 2007; U.S. Department of Justice [USDOJ], 1999).

The FNDI should first organize the scene response equipment and make sure all is in working order. Digital camera batteries should be fully charged. New batteries for the camera flash should be installed. All paperwork and any agency informational brochures should be packed in the scene response kit. Other adjuncts such as rulers, paper, gloves, and thermometer, both ambient and body, should be clean and functional (Box 18-1). Agency policy should dictate the specifics of the investigative procedure.

SCENE INVESTIGATION

The scene investigation is a dual investigation conducted by the law enforcement agency and the medical examiner/coroner. The scene may be in multiple locations. Therefore, it is imperative that the forensic nurse death investigator respond and fully document each one. Examples of scene locations include the following:

- Hospital
- Daycare center
- Babysitter location
- Residence

If the terminal events occurred at, for example, the child's residence but the death was pronounced at a healthcare facility, the FNDI should respond to both. One method for a multidisciplinary investigation is for the forensic nurse to meet the law enforcement investigators at one scene and process it. Then she or he can follow them to the next scene and continue documenting observations.

On arrival at the scene, forensic nurses identify themselves to the investigating officers. They must obtain information and communicate with people who have different roles and responsibilities. Emergency medical technicians and hospital and daycare employees are valuable resources and must not be dismissed. These scenes may be chaotic as grieving family members and other

Box 18-1 Contents of the Scene Investigation Kit

Forensic nurses who investigate deaths should have a scene kit that contains all but not limited to the following items:

- Scene kit (should be sturdy enough to withstand adverse weather conditions but allow the nurse to be organized; should have a handle or wheels)
- Camera
- Camera flash
- Extra batteries for camera and flash
- Gloves
- Rulers of varying sizes
- Tape measure
- Ambient thermometer
- Body thermometer
- Paper bags
- Evidence tape
- Envelopes (for small pieces of evidence)
- Containers with screw tops
- Flashlight
- Tape
- Markers
- Pens/pencils
- Report
- Business cards and any agency brochures
- Scissors
- Hemostats
- Protective eyewear
- Masks
- Foot covers
- Body bag
- Insect repellent

official personnel will be present. Therefore, introductions to all those present will establish a collaborative investigative environment (CDC, 2007). Information required from law enforcement includes the following:

- Demographics of decedent and family members
- Date and time of injury
- Date and time of death
- Police report number
- Investigating officer's contact information
- Overview of the circumstances
- Description of any evidence that has been collected prior to medical examiner/coroner arrival
- Which emergency medical services (EMS) personnel responded (O'Neal, 2007)

Next, the forensic nurse conducts a "walk-thru" at the scene with the police investigator. This will establish scene parameters and allow the forensic nurse to become familiar with the environment (CDC, 2007). During this phase, the location of the infant/child is identified and the physical living space is assessed. Once the scene walk-thru is completed, the entire scene should be photographed, beginning with the exterior of the residence (Corey, 2007). Images of each room are taken from a variety of angles. Cabinets, closets, and refrigerators must be opened and photographed. This will allow for documentation of food, clothing, and items used to care for the infant or child. A complete social assessment is performed, confirming if the child's basic needs are being met.

BEST PRACTICE The entire death scene should be systematically photographed, beginning with the exterior of the residence and including all interior rooms, cabinets, closets, drawers, the refrigerator, and the medicine chest.

If family members are present, they should be interviewed by the forensic nurse, but only with the permission of the police investigators. Detectives may wish to be present while the nurse obtains vital information such as the infant's or child's medical history, last pediatrician appointment, any signs or symptoms of infection or sickness, deviations from the normal routine or changes in behavior over the previous 24 hours, circumstances of death, the mother's birth history, medical history, the names and birth dates of everyone who resides in the residence, and social history (CDC, 2007; O'Neal, 2007). The forensic nurse must keep in mind that the family members are grieving and reactions to questions will vary. Assuring the family that their assistance is vital to determining why the infant or child died is crucial. Explaining that even the most mundane of information may be important to the pathologist who will determine the cause and manner of death often elicits the parent's or caregiver's active participation. Additional information may be gathered using prompts from tools that have been developed for this purpose. The CDC spearheaded a project that developed the Sudden Unexpected Infant Death Initiative Reporting Form. This form is a detailed tool that documents all information necessary to conduct a thorough investigation, such as the following:

- When the infant was last known to be alive, where and in what position
- Who found the child
- What was around or on the child (blankets, pillows, toys, etc.)
- Resuscitation efforts
- Medical history
- Birth information
- Dietary information
- Mother's pregnancy information
- Scene observations

The forms may be downloaded from www.cdc.gov/SIDS/PDF/SUIDIforms.pdf. Other agencies have developed their own documentation tools to gather the supplemental information required for the investigation. For example, forensic nurses at the Harris County Medical Examiner's Office in Houston, Texas, created a document that meets the pathologist's needs and is similar to the CDC form. (Fig. 18-2.)

Once all information has been gathered, a physical assessment is completed, if the child was pronounced at the residence. A complete head-to-toe assessment is necessary. All findings or lack of physical findings must be documented in the report. Body diagrams may be used, but only within guidelines established by individual medical examiner/coroner offices. Photographs of the decedent must be taken. The infant or child should then be placed in a body bag and removed from the scene as quickly as possible. The forensic nurse should accompany the medical examiner/coroner transport service personnel all the way to the vehicle, as grieving family members may attempt to impede the removal.

HEALTHCARE FACILITY INVESTIGATION

If the infant or child was transported to the hospital, the forensic nurse should respond to that location. This will provide the opportunity for the forensic nurse to speak to the attending physician and nursing staff who have provided care. Detailed information about resuscitative measures, lab results, and physical assessment findings should be documented in the nurse's report (O'Neal, 2007).

If the family is present, the history may be obtained at that time. Delay in obtaining the history of the event, medical history, social history, and terminal event information may delay determination

Infant Death Supplement

Harris County Medical Examiner's Office
Forensic Investigative Division
Supplemental Report: Infant Death

ML Case Number _____

Investigator _____   Police Agency _____

Detective _____   Police Case Number _____

CPS reference number & individual spoken to _____

Any previous CPS referrals __ yes __ no. Explain _____

A. Decedent Information

1. a. Decedent's Name _____ b. Sex__ Male __ Female c. Age ___ d. Date of Birth _____

2. a. Date of Death _____ b. Time of Death _____   c. Place of death (if different from home address)

_____

3. a. Home address & telephone number_____

B. Decedent's Mother Information

1. a. Mother's Name _____ b. Age & DOB _____ c. Occupation _____

2. a. Tobacco (frequency & inside/outside) __ yes __ no. Explain _____

3. a. Alcohol (type, frequency & inside/outside) __ yes __ no. Explain _____

4. a. Drug Usage (type, frequency & inside/outside) __ yes __ no. Explain _____

5. a. Previous Pregnancies _____ b. Live Births _____ c. Stillborn _____ d. Abortions _____

6. a. Any SIDS death in the immediate family __ yes __ no. Explain _____

_____

7. a. Any recent blood relative death __ yes __ no. Explain _____

C. Decedent's Father Information

1. a. Father's Name _____ b. Age & DOB _____ c. Occupation _____

2. a. Tobacco (frequency & inside/outside) __ yes __ no. Explain _____

3. a. Alcohol (type, frequency & inside/outside) __ yes __ no. Explain _____

4. a. Drug Usage (type, frequency & inside/outside) __ yes __ no. Explain _____

D. Social History

1. a. Primary language spoken by the family _____

2. a. Decedent lives with ___ mother ___ father ___ both parents ___ other, explain _____

3. a. Who resides at the residence

Name	Age & DOB	Relationship to deceased	General health condition
_____	_____	_____	_____
_____	_____	_____	_____
_____	_____	_____	_____
_____	_____	_____	_____
_____	_____	_____	_____
_____	_____	_____	_____

Infant Death Supplement

4. a. Previous Addresses (include length of residency and date moved) _____

_____

_____

5. a. Current or Previous Foster Care _____

_____

6. a. Does the decedent attend daycare __ yes __ no. List name of daycare & telephone number, length of time at daycare

_____

E. Prenatal History

1. a. Name of Doctor or Clinic, Address & Telephone Number_____

_____

2. a. Number of Prenatal Care Visits _____ b. Maternal complications during pregnancy __ yes __ no. Explain _____

_____ c. Prenatal complications __ yes __ no. Explain _____

3. a. During pregnancy, did the mother smoke __ yes __ no b. use drugs __ yes __ no, if yes, what type _____

c. use alcohol __ yes __ no d. prescription medications __ yes __ no. Explain any yes responses _____

_____

F. Birth History

1. a. Name of Hospital _____ b. Obstetrician & Telephone Number _____

c. If transferred to another hospital after birth, list hospital & reason for transfer _____

_____

2. a. Gestational Age _____ b. Multiple Birth _____ c. Birth Weight _____ d. Birth Length _____

3. a. Prematurity __ yes __ no. b. Any difficulty at birth, labor & delivery complications __ yes __ no. Please explain

_____

_____

4. a. Type of Delivery _____ Vaginal _____ C-Section

5. a. Maternal complications during pregnancy __ yes __ no. Explain _____

_____

6. a. Maternal health problems prior to pregnancy __ yes __ no. Explain _____

7. a. Newborn Course (include length of stay at hospital, any complications during stay, NICU, etc.) _____

_____

_____

G. Medical History

1. a. Pediatrician (or family physician) _____ b. Telephone Number _____

2. a. Date of last doctor visit, reason & outcome _____

3. a. Last known weight & height _____

4. a. Have any of the following ever been noted

_____ heavy snoring   _____ breath holding spells   _____ seizures/convulsion   _____ cyanosis (turning blue)

_____ anything unusual about sleeping habits or breathing.

If any of the above is checked, please explain _____

Infant Death Supplement

5. a. Has decedent ever required hospitalization or emergency care since birth __ yes __ no. If yes, explain why, when & where _____

_____

6. a. Has the decedent have any minor or major illnesses since birth __ yes __ no. If yes, explain why, when & where

_____

_____

7. a. Has the decedent received any kind of medical treatment recently __ yes __ no. If yes, explain why, when & where

_____

_____

8. a. Has the decedent been immunized within the last 72 hours __ yes __ no. If yes, type of immunizations _____

_____ b. Did the decedent have any reaction to the shots _____

9. a. Has the decedent been given any recent medications (prescribed/OTC/home remedies) __ yes __ no. If yes, what, amount & time _____

H. Familial Disease

1. a. Maternal family diseases _____

2. a. Paternal family diseases _____

3. a. Any childhood diseases _____

I. Recent History

1. a. Last seen alive (date & time) _____ b. Decedent is __ breast-fed __ bottle fed __ both c. Last feeding, time & what _____

2. a. If bottle fed list type of formula, amount and how prepared _____

_____

3. a. Recent illness __ yes __ no b. If yes, what _____ sniffles _____ cold _____ fever _____ diarrhea _____ cough

_____ wheezing _____ irritability/colic _____ vomiting _____ appetite change _____ weakness/"floppy-ness"

Please explain _____

_____

4. a. Is anyone in the house ill __ yes __ no. If yes, who & illness _____

5. a. Are there any pets in the house __ yes __ no. Explain _____

6. a. Recent exposure to chemicals __ yes __ no. Explain _____

7. a. Recent fall or injury __ yes __ no. Explain _____

8. a. Are any monitoring devices used __ yes __ no. Explain (type, why, when, etc.) _____

_____

J. Scene Investigation

1. a. Who discovered the decedent _____ b. Relationship _____

2. a. Who last saw the decedent alive _____ b. Relationship _____

3. a. Precise location of decedent when last seen alive _____

4. a. Precise position of decedent when last seen alive __ abdomen __ back __ side

Infant Death Supplement

5. a. Precise location of decedent when found _____

6. a. Precise position decedent was in when found __ abdomen __ back __ side

7. a. Which way was the decedent's head facing when found __ face down __ face up __ left side __ right side

8. a. Were the nose & mouth obstructed __ yes __ no. If yes, with/by what _____

9. a. Describe decedent's clothing, bedding, covering and items in the area (include # of blankets, sleeping surface, ie. waterbed, pillow, cushion, etc...and any unusual items in the area) _____

_____

_____

10. Describe items located in the bed – if crib, see below (toys, stuffed animals, etc.)_____

_____

Continued

11. a. Was the sleeping alone __ yes __ no. If no, who with _____ b. Was this person under the influence of medications, drugs or alcohol __ yes __ no. Explain _____
c. List the height & weight of all persons in bed with decedent _____
_____

12. a. List persons that stay in the same room as the decedent _____
_____

13. a. Did the decedent feel hot/sweaty when found__ yes __ no.
14. a. Type of Heating/Cooling and Proximity of decedent to source _____
_____

15. a. Temperature of Room _____ b. Humidity of Room _____ c. Temperature Outside _____
16. a. Explain attempts to revive the decedent _____
_____
_____

K. Scene Description
1. a. General description of dwelling/area _____
_____
_____

2. a. Condition of room/area where decedent was found _____
_____
_____

3. a. Type – Construction - Condition of Crib/Bed – Area where decedent was found _____
_____
_____

4. a. Obvious CO Source_____
5. a. Changes to scene from time of discovery _____
_____
_____

Infant Death Supplement
L. Crib Assessment
1. a. Dimensions of crib _____
1. a. Height from floor to top of railing with rail up _____ b. rail down _____
2. a. Type of mattress _____ b. Does the mattress properly fit the crib __ yes __ no. If not, list dimensions of mattress _____ c. Measure distance from mattress to railing _____
3. a. Is the railing functional __ yes __ no
4. a. What type of bedding in crib (number of blankets, pillows, etc.) _____
_____

5. a. Describe items located in crib (toys, stuffed animals, etc.) _____
_____

M. Assessment of Decedent – Preliminary Examination by Investigator at Scene
1. a. Position of decedent _____
2. a. Description of decedent _____
3. a. Axillary temperature of decedent (date & time) _____
4. a. Lividity present __ yes __ no. Explain _____
_____

5. a. Rigidity present __ yes __ no. Explain _____
_____

6. a. Presence of Vomitus _____ Froth _____ Blood _____
7. a. Any visual trauma noted _____
_____
_____

N. Additional Pertinent Information
_____
_____
_____
_____

O. Narrative

Fig. 18-2 Supplemental Report for Infant Death Used by Harris County Medical Examiner's Office, Houston, Texas.

of the cause and manner of death. The forensic nurse then may return to the residence or secondary scene location to document the social assessment and conduct a doll reenactment.

DOLL REENACTMENT

When the decedent's body has been removed from the scene, a doll reenactment will allow for the visualization and documentation of the infant's initial place position and then the discovered position (CDC, 2007). This information will provide valuable information that may assist in determining the cause and manner of death (O'Neal, 2007). The parent or caregiver may have difficulty describing the positions but may be better able to demonstrate them. Each step should be photographed. This enables for a more complete evaluation of the relationship between the infant, objects, and people in the immediate vicinity (Pasquale-Styles, 2007). The forensic nurse should explain the reenactment to the parent or caregiver. The parent or caregiver will then be asked to demonstrate placing the infant or child in the position when last seen alive. The forensic nurse photographs the position of the doll. Then the caregiver or parent will reposition the doll to show the exact position in which the infant or child was found. Images are obtained of this as well (O'Neal, 2007). Consideration should be given to the presence of blankets, toys, and other items during the demonstration (CDC, 2007). If the infant was found unresponsive while sleeping with the caregiver, then ask the caregiver to demonstrate the position and photograph with the doll in place.

Doll reenactments are not widely used by many investigators. There is the fear that further emotional damage to the parent or caregiver will occur (O'Neal, 2007). However, there are clear benefits to utilizing the doll reenactment during the death investigation:

- Provides the caregiver or parent the opportunity to demonstrate the location and position in which the infant or child was found
- Provides the opportunity for the forensic nurse to clarify previous descriptions of the events
- Helps to identify inconsistencies between verbal statements and doll demonstration
- Provides a permanent record of the event through photographic documentation (O'Neal, 2007)

Doll reenactments are an important tool that, if done correctly, will provide a multitude of information. The forensic nurse must ensure that the reenactment is performed compassionately. The parent or caregiver must be fully informed of the process and be allowed to ask any questions. Stuffed animals or dolls that are part of the scene should never be used, as that item will become a visual reminder of the loss (O'Neal, 2007). The forensic nurse should bring a doll that is about the size of a three- to five-month-old infant. The limbs should move and the head should turn. This will allow the appropriate demonstration of positions. Doll reenactment will enable critical preautopsy data to be relayed to the pathologist (CDC, 2007). A thorough scene investigation, which includes responding to one or more locations, obtaining a detailed history, conducting an external physical examination, and carrying out a doll reenactment, is the critical first step in determining the cause and manner of death.

KEY POINT Scene investigations, detailed historical accounts, external physical examinations, and doll reenactments of the death scene are inherent steps in determining the cause and manner of a child's death.

AUTOPSY EXAMINATION

When the sudden and unexpected death of an infant or child occurs, the pathologist performs a complete autopsy examination. It will provide additional information that is correlated with the scene investigation and laboratory studies. Without the autopsy, there is not enough information for the determination of cause and manner of death (Krous, 2006). The National Association of Medical Examiners recommends the following: radiograph studies, an autopsy examination that includes an in situ assessment of the brain and heart as well as subsequent removal and dissection of all organs, microscopic studies if there is no obvious cause of death, collection and retention of tissue samples, and the performance of appropriate laboratory tests (Corey, 2007; O'Neal, 2007).

The forensic nurse should communicate the scene findings to the examining pathologist. This will provide the foundation to which the autopsy findings will be compared. Inconsistencies may be identified, which will require additional investigation on the part of either law enforcement or the forensic nurse (O'Neal, 2007). The forensic nurse should also take time to explain the procedure to the family and notify them once the examination is complete so the decedent may be released for burial.

Religious considerations may be taken into account during the autopsy. For example, in the Muslim faith, the deceased must be buried within 24 hours after death. The pathologist may elect to conduct the postmortem examination immediately upon the decedent's arrival to the morgue. However, medical examiners and coroners have the authority to override religious objections and to complete the autopsy without permission (O'Neal, 2007).

The cause and manner of death may be determined immediately after the postmortem examination in some cases of homicide. Physical findings of trauma, such as skull fractures, epidural and subdural hematomas, cerebral edema, and optic nerve sheath hemorrhage, are often associated with inflicted head trauma and therefore the manner is classified as homicide (Fiske & Hall, 2008). These findings are identified with the clinical manifestations of shaken baby syndrome (Altimier, 2008). In these cases, there may be injury to the eyes because of the repetitive acceleration-deceleration injury. The pathologist will most likely remove the eyes and dissect them once fixed in formalin. The ocular examination may demonstrate retinal hemorrhages not seen on funduscopic examination (Gilliland, Levin, Enzenauer, Smith, Parsons, & Rorke-Adams, 2007). Strict protocols are followed as to the appropriateness and procedure for ocular removal during autopsy.

Petechial hemorrhages in the conjunctiva, abrasions around the nose and mouth, bruises and lacerations to the lips or gums, and cerebral edema may be signs of intentional suffocation (Sharma, 2007). Rib fractures and visceral injuries may indicate inflicted trauma as well. All findings or lack of findings will be documented in the autopsy report.

LABORATORY TESTING

The third component of a complete infant and child death investigation is the laboratory testing. In many instances, the postmortem examination will reveal no physical findings or findings associated with infection or congenital disease. In these cases, laboratory studies would be appropriate and may identify issues that could explain the death.

If the scene, history, or autopsy findings suggest there was exposure to illicit drugs, prescription drugs, over-the-counter medications, or herbal remedies, toxicology studies should be performed (Corey, 2007). Toxicology studies should also be ordered if the cause of death is not readily apparent at autopsy (Krous et al., 2005). Metabolic screening should be considered if birth screening results are not available and the liver appears fatty (Corey, 2007). For any history of fever or signs of infection, cultures from blood, urine, and cerebral spinal fluid should be obtained (Krous et al., 2005).

BEST PRACTICE Toxicology studies should be ordered if the cause of a child's death is not readily apparent at autopsy.

The FNE will be able to assist the pathologist by obtaining all medical records and any antemortem test results. This may provide clues and guide the pathologist's decision making when requesting laboratory studies.

Other Considerations for Cause of Death

ACCIDENTAL OVERLAY DUE TO CO-SLEEPING

Many infant deaths that were once considered to be the result of sudden infant death syndrome (SIDS) are now being placed in a different category. With improved scene investigation methods and diagnostic testing, cases of accidental overlay of an infant due to a co-sleeping adult are now being identified (Knight, Hunsaker, & Corey, 2005). Co-sleeping, also known as bed sharing, occurs when the infant and the parents sleep in the same bed or location (Thompson, 2005). Various mechanisms of death where co-sleeping was a factor have been argued, including accidental overlay and rebreathing of carbon dioxide (Knight, et al. 2005). Despite the opposition, there is much support for bed sharing as it promotes breast feeding, parental attachment, and prevents SIDS by affecting infant sleep patterns promoting arousal (Thompson, 2005). Nonetheless, deaths where co-sleeping was described must be investigated in order to rule out other causes and manners of death.

ASPHYXIAL DEATHS

Infants and children are also at risk for suffocation when sleeping in unsafe environments (Payne-James, Busuttil, & Smock, 2003). When placed in adult beds, the potential for suffocation and entrapment is present. Infants, especially those younger than two years of age, may become wedged between the bed and the wall, a parent and the sofa, or any other location where they may become pressed up against something else (Payne-James, et al. 2003; Person, Lavezzi, & Wolf, 2002). Plush bedding may also contribute to the rebreathing of carbon dioxide and obstruct the nose and mouth (Person, et al. 2002). Infants and young children may also become wedged in cribs. Parent and caregiver statements and doll reenacts will provide critical information for the pathologist to use when determining the cause and manner of death (O'Neal, 2007). The forensic nurse should measure crib railings and the space between the bars and should assess if the mattress is appropriate for that type of crib. In addition, photographic documentation and possible retention of the bedding will be useful to the pathologist.

SUDDEN INFANT DEATH SYNDROME

Sudden infant death syndrome (SIDS) is defined as "the sudden death of an infant younger than one year that remains unexplained after thorough case investigation, including performance of a complete autopsy, examination of the death scene and review of the clinical history" (Hymel, 2006). The incidence for SIDS in the United States is 1.2 per 100,000. A diagnosis of exclusion, SIDS is found to be most common in infants younger than six months of age (Sharma, 2007). The infant is previously healthy and apparently dies during sleep (Hymel, 2006). An exact cause of death in these cases is not known. Organic disease, accident, and inflicted injury must be ruled out before the diagnosis of SIDS is made (Payne-James, et al. 2003). It has been theorized that SIDS may be caused by some type of autoimmune disorder (Staines, 2004). However, this is only theory and more research is needed in this area.

Because of the ambiguity, a meticulous death investigation must occur. All aspects of the scene must be documented. Any medical records and birth records are reviewed. The postmortem examination must include a complete autopsy with organ inspection and dissection, tissue retention, radiographs, and laboratory testing (Corey, et al. 2007). The major challenge for the forensic pathologist is to rule out all unnatural and other natural causes of death. The FNE is an important part of the investigating team.

Summary

Investigating the death of an infant or child is an extraordinarily emotional task. It is a devastating loss to family and friends. Unfortunately, infants and children do not always die from natural causes. In some cases, the death is due to inflicted trauma, most often at the hands of a parent or caregiver. Physical findings may be obvious or not so obvious. Nonetheless, the death must receive the full attention of law enforcement, child protective services, and the medical examiner or coroner.

For an appropriate cause and manner of death to be determined, information must be correlated from the scene investigation, medical record review, autopsy examination, and laboratory studies. From the medicolegal death investigation perspective, a knowledge base in anatomy, physiology, pathophysiology, pharmacology, child growth and development, and grief are necessary requirements for the medical examiner's/coroner's investigator. The FNE who possesses these qualities will contribute greatly to this investigation. The information shared by the nurse with the forensic pathologist before autopsy will enable a more accurate interpretation of postmortem physical findings and appropriately order ancillary laboratory testing.

In cases where inflicted trauma is ruled out, the forensic nurse assists the pathologist with investigating alternate natural or accidental causes of death. Congenital anomalies and sudden infant death syndrome must be considered over the course of the investigation. The forensic nurse is a key team member in the infant and child death investigation.

References

Adinkrah, M. (2003). Men who kill their own children: Paternal filicide incidents in contemporary Fiji. *Child Abuse and Neglect*, *27*(5), 557–568.

Altimier, L. (2008). Shaken baby syndrome. *Journal of Perinatal and Neonatal Nursing*, *22*(1), 68–76.

American Academy of Pediatrics (AAP). (1999). Investigation and review of unexpected infant and child death. *Pediatrics*, *104*(5), 1158–1160.

California State University. (2006). *Steps of the nursing process*. Retrieved March 14, 2008, from www.csub.edu/nursing/nrs_process.shtml.

Centers for Disease Control and Prevention. (2007). *Sudden, unexplained infant death investigation*. Retrieved March 15, 2008, from: www.cdc.gov/SIDS/PDF/508SUIDIGuidelinesSingles.pdf.

Centers for Disease Control and Prevention. (2008a). *National violent death reporting system.* Retrieved March 7, 2009, from: www.cdc.gov/ncipc/profiles/nvdrs/default.htm.

Centers for Disease Control and Prevention. (2008b). *Child maltreatment: Facts at a glance.* Retrieved March 7, 2009, from: www.cdc.gov/ViolencePrevention/pdf/CM-DataSheet-a.pdf.

Centers for Disease Control and Prevention. (2008c). *Sudden infant death syndrome (SIDS) and sudden unexpected infant death (SUID): Sudden, unexpected infant death initiative.* Retrieved on March 14, 2009, from: www.cdc.gov/SIDS/SUID.htm.

Corey, T. S., Hanzlick, R., Howard, J., Nelson, C., & Krous, H. (2007). A functional approach to sudden unexplained infant deaths. *The American Journal of Forensic Medicine and Pathology, 28*(3), 271–277.

Craig, M. (2004). Perinatal risk factors for neonaticide and infant homicide: Can we identify those at risk? *Journal of the Royal Society of Medicine, 97*(2), 57–61.

Fiske, E. A., & Hall, J. M. (2008). Inflicted childhood neurotrauma. *Advances in Nursing Science, 31*(2), E1–E8.

Friedman, S., & Resnick, P. (2007). Child murder by mothers: Patterns and prevention. *World Psychiatry, 6*(3), 137–141.

Gilliland, M. G. F., Levin, A. V., Enzenauer, R. W., Smith, C., Parsons, A., Rorke-Adams, L. B., et al. (2007). Guidelines for postmortem protocol for ocular investigation in sudden unexplained infant death and suspect child physical abuse. *American Journal of Forensic Medicine and Pathology, 28*(4), 323–329.

Hymel, K. (2006). Distinguishing sudden infant death syndrome from child abuse fatalities. *Pediatrics, 118*(1), 421–427.

Jenny, C., & Isaac, R. (2006). The relation between child death and child maltreatment. *Archives of Diseases in Childhood, 91*(3), 265–269.

Knight, L. D., Hunsaker, D. M., & Corey, T. S. (2005). Cosleeping and sudden unexpected infant deaths in Kentucky. *American Journal of Forensic Medicine and Pathology, 26*(1), 28–32.

Krous, H. (2006). Why is a postmortem examination important when an infant or child dies suddenly? *Pediatric and Developmental Pathology, 9*(2), 168–169.

Krous, H., Chadwick, A. E., Crandall, L., & Nadeau-Manning, J. M. (2005). Sudden unexpected death in childhood: A report of 50 cases. *Pediatric and Developmental Pathology, 8*(3), 307–319.

Levene, S., & Bacon, C. J. (2004). Sudden unexpected death and covert homicide in infancy. *Archives of Diseases in Childhood, 89*(5), 443–447.

Lynch, V. (2006). Forensic nursing. St. Louis: Mosby.

Marleau, J. D., Poulin, B., Webanck, T., Roy, R., & Laporte, L. (1999). Paternal filicide: A study of 10 men. *Canadian Journal of Psychiatry, 44*(1), 57–63.

Mercy, J. A., Barker, L., & Frazier, L. (2006). The secrets of the National Violent Death Reporting System. *Injury Prevention, 12*(Suppl 2), ii1–ii2. Retrieved on: March 7, 2009, from: http://dx.doi.org/10.1136/ip.2006.012542.

Mugavin, M. (2008). Maternal filicide theoretical framework. *Journal of Forensic Nursing, 4,* 68–79.

O'Neal, B. J. (2007). *Investigating infant deaths.* Boca Raton. FL: CRC Press.

Pasquale-Styles, M. A., Tackitt, P. L., & Schmidt, C. J. (2007). Infant death scene investigations: The assessment of potential risk factors for asphyxia: A review of 209 sudden unexpected infant deaths. *Journal of Forensic Science, 52*(4), 924–929.

Payne-James, J., Busuttil, A., & Smock, W. (2003). *Forensic medicine: Clinical and pathological aspects.* San Francisco. Greenwich Medical Media: Ltd.

Person, T. L. A., Lavezzi, W. A., & Wolf, B. C. (2002). Cosleeping and sudden unexpected death in infancy. *Archives of Pathology and Laboratory Medicine, 126*(3), 343–345.

Rouge-Maillart, C., Jousset, N., Gaudin, A., Bouju, B., & Penneau, M. (2005). Women who kill their children. *The American Journal of Forensic Medicine and Pathology, 26*(4), 320–326.

Sharma, B. R. (2007). Sudden infant death syndrome: A subject of medicolegal research. *American Journal of Forensic Medicine and Pathology, 28*(1), 69–72.

Spinelli, M. G. (2004). Maternal infanticide associated with mental illness: Prevention and the promise of saved lives. *American Journal of Psychiatry, 161*(6), 1548–1557.

Staines, D. R. (2004). Is sudden infant death syndrome (SIDS) an autoimmune disorder of endogenous vasoactive neuropeptides? *Medical Hypothesis, 62*(5), 653–657.

Stone, M. H., Steinmeyer, E., Dreher, J., & Krischer, M. (2005). Infanticide in female forensic patients: The view from the evolutionary standpoint. *Journal of Psychiatric Practice, 11*(1), 35–45.

Thompson, D. G. (2005). Safe sleep practices for hospitalized infants. *Pediatric Nursing, 31*(5), 400–409.

United States Department of Health and Human Services (USDHHS). (2009). *Child abuse and neglect fatalities: Statistics and interventions.* Retrieved March 7, 2009, from: www.childwelfare.gov/pubs/factsheets/fatality.cfm#children.

United States Department of Justice (USDOJ). (1999). *Death investigation: A guide for the scene investigator.* Office of Justice Programs. Retrieved March 15, 2009, from: www.ncjrs.gov/pdfiles/167568.pdf.

West, S. G., Hatters Friedman, S., & Resnick, P. J. (2009). Fathers who kill their children: An analysis of the literature. *Journal of Forensic Science, 54*(2), 462–467.

CHAPTER 19 Medical Evidence Recovery at the Death Scene

Renae M. Diegel

In forensic science, tangible items and recorded materials that are pertinent to the legal proceedings of the court are defined as evidence (Venes, 2009). Evidence is central to the outcome of a trial in which a suspect is granted freedom, incarcerated, or executed according to the laws of the jurisdiction. The evidence collected, along with precise documentation of on-scene observations, are vital elements in the legal deliberations. Traditionally, forensic evidence collected at crime scenes involving death has been the responsibility of law enforcement officers skilled in homicide investigation. However, with the escalating scientific impact of DNA evidentiary materials, greater consideration is given to recovery of this fragile evidence from the body. Medically oriented personnel are ideally suited to collect DNA sources such as blood and bloodstains, semen and seminal stains, tissues and cells, bone and organ fragments, and teeth (Lynch, 2000).

DNA analysis and other scientific advances have required changes in police department evidence collection protocols and policies. The police department administration in Macomb County, Michigan, has responded by using teams of both forensic nurse examiners (FNEs) and law enforcement evidence technician teams. The FNEs are civilian specialists, qualified as experts in the collection of forensic evidence from surviving patients and suspects of sexual violence, human abuse, and questioned deaths. The FNEs provide a service in death investigation under the direction of Dr. Daniel Spitz, Chief Medical Examiner of Macomb County, who is perpetuating the program initiated by his father, Dr. Werner Spitz.

Community Relationships

In Macomb County, Michigan, a unique and effective relationship was established that provided an immense benefit to the entire community (Betzold, 2004; Kirschke, 2005). In 1999, Turning Point (a provider of sexual assault, domestic violence, and shelter services) established the Forensic Nurse Examiner (FNE) Program in Macomb County and employs a full-time forensic nursing team. This program provides forensic examinations to adult, adolescent, and pediatric patients, free of charge to community members. In 2000, the team was expanded to provide services to law enforcement agencies for suspect examinations. In 2004, Dr. Werner Spitz, Chief Medical Examiner of Macomb County at that time, requested that the FNEs provide consultation services on a case involving a suspicious death.

This case involved the body of a female, found naked, indicating to a high suspicion of sexual assault. The FNE unit responded to the morgue where a thorough forensic evaluation, examination, and evidence collection process was completed. From that incident, the late David Woodford, head of the Serology and Trace Evidence Unit of the Michigan State Police Forensic Science Division at that time, contended that if nurses could collect such valuable evidence for cases in the morgue, the team could be used even more effectively at the scene of a crime. It was then recommended that the FNE team should be used in all suspicious deaths (not just known homicides) to collect trace evidence from the body before it is removed from the scene.

This author, the initial and current program director of the Forensic Nurse Examiner Unit, and Woodford joined with Dr. W. U. (Werner) Spitz to create and operate a joint forensic investigation team. Spitz required that the nursing team complete the Wayne State University/Michigan State Police Medicolegal Death Investigation course before responding to suspicious death scenes. The original vision was becoming a reality because of the support of all key players in the forensic science community.

In his proposal to law enforcement administrators, Spitz stated,

Forensic nurses can give you more information with the potential trace evidence they remove from the body than I can. For example, if a child is hit by car and there is a paint chip on the child's body that the nurse collects at the scene, you will have more information from that paint chip than I can give you at the autopsy. Furthermore, if it is not immediately recovered it will most likely be lost in transport to the morgue.

Woodford addressed the quality of evidence collected by the forensic nursing unit and stressed that nurses are "trained to examine a body, they do it every day; they are the ones who should be doing this." He also stressed, "The nurses are not there to take over the crime scene; they are strictly responding to examine the body... nothing else." The fact that evidence has been lost under these and similar circumstances captured the attention of these law enforcement agents. The evidentiary value of paint chips or paint swipes alone has resolved vast numbers of such cases.

Crime laboratories are capable of comparing the layers of paint applied to vehicles and matching them to fragments of paint from the clothing or soft tissue lacerations resulting from pedestrian/motor vehicle collisions. Transfer evidence from the vehicle to the victim may allow the identification of the make, model, and color, as well as the year of manufacture. Forensic scientists may also determine if the headlights were on or off at the time of impact from filaments recovered from clothing or tissue. Likewise, the precise point of impact on the body from the colliding vehicle will indicate if the decedent was walking, running, or standing still at the time. Therefore, observation and recovery of evidence with identifiable forensic characteristics may be critical in discovering the unknown vehicle and driver (Saferstein, 2007). The opportunity to consider a new approach to preventing the lost of critical evidence was persuasive. With full support and official endorsement of the Macomb County prosecutor, forensic nurses were formally sanctioned and accepted for their designated roles in collecting on-scene evidence and providing courtroom testimony. In coordination with the Michigan State Police Forensic Science Division and the Macomb County Sheriff's Department Evidence Technician Unit, the forensic nursing and law enforcement teams trained together to better understand one another's role at the scene. When classes began, there was an obvious social and cultural divide among the classroom teams, with nursing on one side and law enforcement on the other. However, the environment soon changed. Mock crime scene scenario assignments required the teams to work together to recover all essential evidence. This innovative investigative program established through a joint health and justice endeavor has already improved the rate of successful prosecutions of suspicious death cases in one community.

Before actual on-scene investigation, an intense training period for the joint units included mock crime scenes requiring both medical and criminal investigations. One scenario involved a convenience store robbery where the victim was stabbed multiple times and was pronounced dead at the scene. Law enforcement officers processed their portion of the scene for fingerprints and footprints while the nurses processed the body for trace and physical evidence. In another mock crime scenario, a female victim was found dead at the scene, partially clothed, with obvious bite marks on the body. Law enforcement officers promptly realized the potential value of the FNE observing their skillful collection of evidence from a body. They agreed that they could and should work together to improve the on-scene evidence-gathering processes (Fig. 19-1). The forensic pathologist, however, maintains the responsibility for the identification and documentation of precise injuries during the autopsy.

Science of Evidence Recovery: Education and Training

The FNE's induction into the realm of law enforcement crime scenes began with instructions based on the foundation of evidence collection as a scientific method. This theoretical concept developed by the French pioneer, Dr. Edmond Locard (1877–1966), formulated the basic principle of forensic science in the recovery of evidence. This method is founded on Locard's exchange principle, which states, "Whenever two surfaces come in contact with one another, there is a mutual exchange of matter across the contact boundary" (Lee, 2001, pg. 115). In brief, every contact leaves a trace (Box 19-1).

Nurses who provide forensic services must have appropriate skills and credentials to ensure that medicolegal evidence recovery is being accomplished in accordance with practice standards and expectations of the crime laboratory. Appropriate education, training, and certifications also help to establish credibility when providing courtroom testimony. Attesting to these requirements, the nurses who work with the Macomb County's Medical Examiner Office, Sheriff's Department, and Office of the Prosecutor are

Fig. 19-1 Michigan State Police supervisor of the Serology and Trace Evidence Unit, the late David Woodford, and FNE program director Renae Diegel.

Box 19-1 Locard's Principle

This process is recognized as an ideal method, which provides a systematic approach to identification, recovery, preservation, security, and presentation of evidence that will provide the basis for determining the truth:

Wherever he steps, whatever he touches, whatever he leaves, even unconsciously, will serve as a silent witness against him. Not only his fingerprints or his footprints, but his hair, the fibers from his clothes, the glass he breaks, the tool mark he leaves, the paint he scratches, the blood or semen he deposits or collects. All of these and more bear mute witness against him. This is evidence that does not forget. It is not confused by the excitement of the moment. It is not absent because human witnesses are. It is factual evidence. Physical evidence cannot be wrong, it cannot perjure itself, it cannot be wholly absent. Only human failure to find it, study and understand it… can diminish its value. (Kirk, 1953)

---

expected to meet such requirements. For example, the FNE director is certified in emergency nursing, forensic nursing, and medical investigation. She also holds additional certification from the American Board of Medicolegal Death Investigation (ABMDI) and is a certified sexual assault nurse examiner (SANE).

General Purpose of the Forensic Nurse Examiner Evidence Recovery Unit

The purpose of the FNE evidence collection team is to help law enforcement agencies in Macomb County develop proof that a crime has been committed, to corroborate or disprove an alibi, to establish that a certain person committed a crime, or to ascertain that a certain person did not commit a crime. Such evidence is also used to connect a victim to a suspect and to associate the suspect to a crime scene. Evidence is often able to reflect the *modus operandi* (MO), or pattern of behavior, such as how the crime was committed, which may help identify an assailant. These elements of crime can also be established by evidence recovered from the crime scene (Lynch, 2000).

Since the FNE must be prepared to testify in court, an understanding of the various classes of evidence must be well understood. Evidence may be any type of admissible proof that can be presented during a legal proceeding in an attempt to influence a judge, attorney, or jurors about a particular point (Garner, 2004). Types of evidence are: direct evidence, eyewitness evidence, witness statements, and circumstantial evidence. Physical evidence, or statements that establish circumstances from which other facts at issue can be inferred, is often called "real evidence." This can be either direct or circumstantial evidence. Medical evidence differs from criminal evidence in the sense that its purpose is to provide proof regarding the mechanism of injury or cause and manner of death. This evidence is the responsibility of the medical investigator, not the criminal investigator. On the other hand, the focal purpose of the law enforcement investigation is to prove that a crime has been committed and, if so, to establish who committed the crime (Lynch, 2006).

The objective of medicolegal death investigation is to identify, collect, document, preserve and secure medical/forensic evidence. "Physical evidence encompasses any and all objects that can establish that a crime has been committed or can provide a link between a crime and its victim or a crime and its perpetrator" (Saferstein, 2007, p. 33). Physical evidence is generally located at the crime scene or it may be found on the body of the victim or suspect (Box 19-2). Evidence from *both* sources is equally important in a medicolegal death investigation. In some jurisdictions, evidence recovered from the suspect in custody has also become a responsibility of the FNE. Accompanied by a police officer, the FNE responds to the place of custody (jail, prison, or hospital) and performs a thorough evidence collection process (www.nursetv.com/visit profiles; Waddell, 2009).

California law enforcement units report that they now obtain grants from the state to maintain checkpoints for offenders driving under the influence (DUI). They are able to request funding for the cost of a registered nurse to be assigned to the checkpoint and draw blood, rather than the police having to transport a DUI suspect to the nearest hospital. The checkpoint duty is performed by forensic nursing personnel who possess skills and credibility in evidence collection, preservation, and chain of custody. Formerly, DUI suspects and their apprehending officers were required to wait for hours until there was someone available to perform the phlebotomy. Now, officers can be patrolling for other offenders rather than waiting in emergency departments. Certainly, the police departments favor the use of dedicated FNE and strongly support

the employment of nurses with forensic skills (www.nursetv.com/visit profiles; Waddell, 2009).

Forensic nursing personnel may be required to collect numerous types of evidence. Physical evidence is subdivided into five categories: transient evidence, conditional evidence, pattern evidence, transfer evidence, and associative evidence (Coyle, Ladd, & Lee, 2006, p. 45).

1. *Transient evidence* "is physical evidence that is temporary in nature and can be easily changed" (Coyle, Ladd, & Lee, 2006, p. 45). Examples of transient evidence are odors (e.g., alcohol, acetone), the presence of moisture, and the color characteristics of stains or bruises.

2. *Conditional evidence* "is a type of physical evidence that results from an event or action" (Coyle, Ladd, & Lee, 2006, p. 45.) This is the condition of the body and what is attached to the body. What is the condition of the clothing? Is it present, how is it on the body, is wet or dry, is it appropriate for situation, is it torn or intact? What is the condition of the body? Is livor mortis present? What is its description and what is the state of rigor or decomposition? What defects can be observed on the body such as gunshot/stab wounds, amputations, deformities, or tattoos?

3. *Pattern evidence* "is generally produced by physical contact between person, vehicles, weapons, and other objects" (Coyle, Ladd, & Lee, 2006, p. 45). The pattern that is found takes the shape of an offending object, which may not always be identifiable at the scene as to what the object causing the pattern is, but it is important to note that it is characterized by a distinct pattern. Patterns that can be found on the body can be from tire impressions, shoe marks, bloodstains, burn marks, bite marks, or weapon impressions, as well as an infinite variety of other objects and events.

4. *Transfer evidence*. According to Locard's principle, when two objects come in contact, an exchange of material may occur. Common items detected during the inspection of the body include blood, semen, saliva, foreign body, hairs, tissue, paint, and soil. Transfer evidence is sometimes confused with trace evidence; however, there is a distinct difference. Trace evidence is something so minute it can be easily overlooked or contaminated. It is evaluated by a microscope, staining, or light technique and not just the human eye. Paint chips from a vehicle found on a pant leg are categorized as transfer evidence but not trace evidence. DNA from a drop of sweat found on the floor near the scene of a sexual assault would be considered trace evidence (Rooms, R., personal communication, January 7, 2009).

5. *Associative evidence* is defined as evidence that can associate a victim or suspect with the crime scene (Coyle, Ladd, & Lee, 2006). This can consist of notes, money, jewelry, wallets, and similar items.

Time alone can be a great factor in how a crime scene can change. The necessity for timely collection of forensic evidence is the key in any medical legal investigation of death. Evidence collected from the body at the crime scene can be crucial to the facts of the case. The potential for disturbance of evidence is significantly increased during the transfer process of packaging and storing of the body. (Coyle, Ladd, & Lee, 2006, p. 46)

Recovery of trace and physical evidence should be accomplished before the body has been initially disturbed. After this point, the potential to lose evidence from the body increases

---

Box 19-2 Potential Sources for DNA

Hair with follicles	Clothing
Bite marks	Chewing gum
Dental floss	Tampons
Condoms	Toothpicks
Cigarette butts	Hair
Bed linens	Hats, bandanas
Fingernails	Washcloths
Rims of bottles/cans	Ears/breasts
Urine and saliva (contain sloughed nucleated cells)	

exponentially. With concern for the high priority of medical/forensic evidence collection from a decedent, one must consider who is most familiar with human anatomy, identification of trauma, mechanism of injury, multiorgan system failure, or the natural disease processes most often responsible for death. Indeed, the crime scene investigator with education and experience in healthcare has become recognized as the most appropriate professional to fill this role. The skilled FNE or medical death investigator (MDI) has been brought from the clinical environs to the scene of crime and death. This discipline is well acquainted and comfortable with the examination of the human body, inspecting it for microscopic or catastrophic injury while concurrently collecting, preserving, and photodocumenting critical evidence.

Roles and Responsibilities

Forensic examinations for patients of sexual violence should be performed by a healthcare professional with medical/forensic expertise. The FNE who holds a certification as a SANE is highly skilled in the physical and emotional care of rape patients as well as the accused. The FNE can be certified in the examination of pediatric or adult sexual assault patients. Prosecutors, police, and patients concur that the FNE provides medical/forensic services that are superior to those that have been previously provided. Emergency physicians and forensic pathologists, with rare exception, are not board certified in sexual assault evaluation and examination or are not aware of the most recent advances in sexual assault evidence recovery. The availability of improved services has led to a quality standard of care for sexual assault patients and an increase in prosecution rates (Campbell, Bybee, Ford, & Patterson, 2009).

The employment of forensic nurses in this field has significantly improved and yielded a greater number of successful prosecutions than before. As early as 1996, the U.S. Federal Bureau of Investigation (FBI) identified the FNE as the "ideal clinician" to provide sexual assault evaluations, documentation of injury, recovery of genetic evidence such as DNA, and to facilitate entry of such data into the Combined DNA Index System (CODIS) project for the identification of unknown perpetrators (Lynch, V., & Miller, J., personal communication, 1996). Information compiled by the National Institute of Justice indicates that the use of the FNE for sexual assault examinations has increased positive prosecution rates by 20% (Campbell, et al., 2009).

The ideal method of providing a systematic forensic approach to evidence collection in the clinical milieu is to designate the FNE as a hospital-evidence custodian and a clinical forensic liaison to the police. This FNE is responsible for retaining evidentiary/personal property items, which would then be receipted to the appropriate law enforcement agencies. The nurse with forensic skills, whose education prepares her or him for gathering the forensic patient's history and preserving evidence, will assist police in reconstructing the circumstances of injury or death. It is in the best interests of public health and safety to provide forensic standards that guide the practice of healthcare professionals.

The primary responsibility of the FNE is to provide care and support to the survivor of violent criminal acts or the patient's family. If the victim dies or is found dead, the responsibility is to focus on the body, liaison with police, and interface with decedent's family. Secondary to lifesaving intervention, foremost forensic actions include the (1) identification of injury and (2) recovery of evidence whether the victim is living or dead. These two forensic actions lay the foundation for all additional forensic intervention-

tions. The utilization of FNEs assists hospitals in ensuring that The Joint Commission's standards regarding the medical needs of forensic patients, while protecting their legal and human rights (The Joint Commission [TJC], 2009). (See Guideline PC.3.10 for specific TJC guidelines.)

Elements of a Crime

The central issues that determine whether a sexually related crime has occurred relate to *consent* and *use of force*. The presence or absence of internal or external injury often provides evidence of force but not necessarily lack of consent; the patient's statements are usually the only proof of this factor. The FNE must employ critical thinking processes in addition to meticulous evidence management when accomplishing this type of evaluation. Comprehension of the physical forces involved in an assault is an essential skill, because some injuries may not be easily detected with a routine inspection. The ability to differentiate between normal and abnormal human conditions of body tissue is essential for the recognition and evaluation of force as one element of the crime. Evidence enhancement techniques, such as the Wood's lamp or other alternate light source (ALS) should be available to augment forensic examinations. Cameras and other forms of equipment are also necessary to photograph evidence before and after medical treatment.

The discovery of a specific injury may require not only observation skills but a high index of suspicion of where an injury might be, based on the description of an accident or other scenario. Nurses must understand that the historical accounts often do not reflect actual events because victims are likely to be too intimidated to speak openly. Family members or witnesses often distort facts to protect offenders.

In a homicide case, little or no history may be available. Without credible witnesses, the scene, the body, an injury, a weapon, evidence of a natural disease process or prescription medication may be the only clues available to help investigators reconstruct the probable events surrounding the death. Case Study 19-1 illustrates the value of a medically skilled and experienced nurse examiner who is capable of evaluating and relating the significance of certain evidence found at the scene.

The FNE is also responsible for the security of the body and the evidence until it is turned over to the proper legal authorities. A flawless chain-of-custody process must be maintained to ensure the integrity of all evidence during transport, examination, and storage until presentation in court. Failure to maintain an intact chain of custody renders evidence unacceptable for analysis or presentation in court. The primary responsibilities of the FNE/medical death investigator are presented in Box 19-3.

Clothing is the most valuable category of evidence to pass through the hands of physicians, nurses, or paramedics that is most often lost or destroyed by nonforensic personnel. Destruction generally occurs as clothing is removed with scissors, cutting through rips, tears, or defects from projectiles. Loss of clothing generally occurs when it is discarded in containers for medical waste or cross-contaminated when thrown onto the emergency department floor. Garments are second *only* to the body in terms of evidentiary value. They become even more important after the body has been handled, moved, wrapped, or washed.

BEST PRACTICE Personal property should never be returned to the family in medicolegal cases without the permission of police or the medical examiner.

Case Study **19-1**

Till Death Do Us Part

A 78-year-old woman was found dead at home by a social worker (Fig. 19-2). The decedent's husband was discovered near-death with multiple stab wounds and transferred to the local hospital for emergency medical treatment. The Macomb County's FNE unit was notified to respond to the crime scene for evidence recovery. Medical evidence at the scene indicated the husband had been prescribed drugs to treat psychiatric disorders. At this point, the husband became a person of interest. The FNE team proceeded to the hospital where a forensic examination was performed. He later became a suspect.

In this case, the husband is identified as crime scene 1. Since he was being prepared for surgery his body had the potential to change first. Next, the deceased female, identified as crime scene 2, was examined at the scene of death. When a person is found nude or partially nude, sexual assault is presumed to have occurred. The decedent was nude at the time the body was discovered and a sexual assault examination was performed on-scene. The examination was initiated with an ALS light, followed by the tape-lift procedure. How did the husband get injured? Further investigation revealed that the husband actually tried to take his own life; after killing his wife, he stabbed himself multiple times, resulting in a collapsed lung.

Outcome: The *weapon of opportunity*, a kitchen "butcher" type knife, was discovered in the dishdrainer; it had traces of blood from both the victim and the suspect (Fig. 19-3). The evidence collection kits were not processed in this case because the husband confessed after surgery. He stated, "I was trying to cut the *devil* out of her." He had developed psychiatric issues later in life and was sentenced to spend the rest of his life in a long-term mental health facility.

Fig. 19-2 Death scene of a 78-year-old woman, possibly raped and murdered by husband who was determined to be mentally ill.

Fig. 19-3 This butcher knife was the murder weapon recovered from the dishdrainer at the scene.

Box 19-3 Primary Roles of the Forensic Nurse Examiner/Medical Death Investigator

- Independently identifying and developing health details and collecting medical evidence related to the cause of death in both criminal and noncriminal cases
- Interpreting the patient's health history and circumstances before death
- Researching health records and preparing case history summaries to facilitate death investigation
- Interviewing physicians and other healthcare providers to help establish cause and manner of death
- Providing direction in handling the body and personal effects of the deceased
- Arranging transportation of the body when necessary
- Conducting interviews with persons reporting deaths and with other persons as appropriate
- Conducting follow-up interviews with the family members and assessing for unresolved grief and stress-related diseases, with referral to appropriate agencies (Lynch, 1990, 2008)

Dr. Ivor E. Doney, a forensic medical examiner (FME) and United Kingdom Police Surgeon, has cautioned healthcare providers to recognize and preserve vital trace evidence before "washing it away in a sea of wound cleansing antiseptic." He further stated, "the forensic scientist who analyzes the evidence is entitled to know that other members of the multidisciplinary team have provided competent service and that the specimens they are examining are indeed accurate" (Doney, 1988, pp. 15-20).

Preparation to Enter the Crime Scene

FNEs and forensic nurse death investigators (FNDIs), also titled medical death investigators (MDI), must possess formal education and hands-on training before they enter a crime scene to assist law enforcement with evidence collection. Many courses and technical institutes offer curricula designed to prepare evidence-recovery technicians. It is also recommended that the FNE, FNDI, or MDI complete a basic SANE's training program to acquire essential knowledge and skills for managing a sexual homicide. It is equally important for law enforcement officers to know the components of a thorough sexual assault examination to appreciate the extensive time required to complete all details associated with evidence collection.

Developing a professional relationship with key community members is essential. Nurses, for example, might obtain an internship with the community crime laboratory, office of the district attorney, county sheriff's department, or local law enforcement agencies. However, an FNE should not be permitted to recover evidence from the body without formal permission of the medical examiner or coroner of the jurisdiction. Unauthorized evidence recovery is against the law in many jurisdictions and could result in criminal charges. However, when permission is given, the legal community must establish a jurisdictional protocol with approved policies and procedures.

Role Delineation

Before the FNE responds to a crime scene, she or he must determine what equipment and supplies will be necessary to manage a particular scenario. It is also imperative to predict the human resources needed to meet the expectations of the medical examiner/coroner. Local law enforcement personnel must work with the medical examiner to resolve issues such as regulations for evidence collection from the body and the scene.

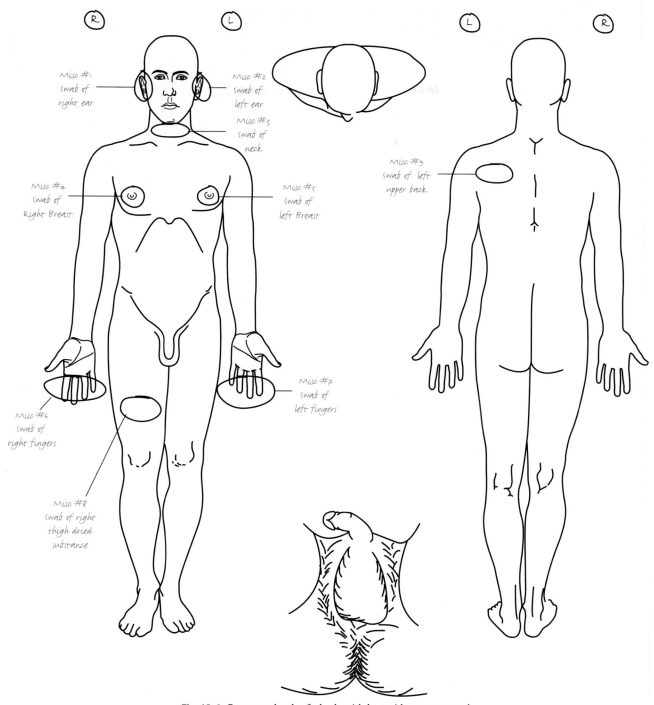

Fig. 19-4 On scene sketch of a body with key evidence annotated.

Documentation forms should consist of demographic information, the name of the agency requesting the FNE services, multiple body maps with different views of the body and, if possible, infant, child, and adult illustrations (see Evolve website), an evidence collection log, documentation of photography, names of team members that responded, and a chain-of-custody sheet. When responding to crime scenes, the body map is not used for injury documentation but as a "crime scene sketch" to document where the evidence was taken from the body (Fig. 19-4).

KEY POINT Exchanged physical evidence of such a small size that it is referred to as *trace* can be overlooked or contaminated.

Physicians and nurses who lack forensic indoctrination might not recognize that the patient's personal property could be dangerous, hazardous, or illegal and considered contraband. Many of these questionable items have evidentiary value in a civil or criminal case. If healthcare personnel fail to collect and report this type of evidence, they are obstructing justice and essentially protecting the criminal in cases of violent crimes. For examples of some types of evidence recovered from patients, see Box 19-4.

Under ideal circumstances, a team of three FNEs can efficiently manage on-scene investigations and complete evidence collection in a timely manner. Before entering the scene, the FNE team should identify a leader and assign individual roles. It is important to formally designate the team leader, who will present

Box 19-4 Trace and Physical Evidence Recovered from Clinical Patients

Clothing	Bullets
Gunshot residue	Weapons: Knives
Hair	Body fluids (semen)
Wood	Paper
Soil	Bloodstain pattern
Tool marks	Fingerprints
Teeth	Chemicals (fires)
Paint chips	Fibers

Fig. 19-5 FNE swabs hands and fingernails of victim at the crime scene to recover trace evidence.

the medical/forensic evidence in court, if the case is subject to subpoena. This will lessen the probability that all members would need to be present for courtroom testimony.

The team leader is routinely assigned to collect evidence from the body. This FNE is the only one who will inspect the body and gather evidence. This procedure minimizes the possibility of cross-contamination of evidence during the recovery process. The second FNE role is to provide documentation. This includes completion of all required forms and the annotations on body diagrams illustrating the location where each piece of evidence was recovered. Because the body is considered to be the medical crime scene, these diagrams become the anatomical scene sketch (see Fig. 19-4). This second FNE, "the scribe," also records the time the evidence was collected and notes the number of each item in the evidence collection log. The third FNE organizes and arranges all supplies for the examination and assists the nurse recovering evidence. This individual is also known as the "supplier"; he or she provides the extra pair of hands that will be needed on the scene, similar to the surgical nurse who "circulates" during surgery. Any one of the FNEs can take photographs of the body; however, this role should also be designated before arriving at the scene. There must be continuous communication between all three FNEs during the examination process to prevent errors and to ensure thoroughness and efficiency at the scene.

Another issue to consider at the scene regards the documentation of body surface injuries. It is recommended that this is not accomplished at the death site. Proper lighting is rarely available at the scene of death, particularly in the outdoors or in remote locations. Removing the decedent's clothing is essential so that no injury is overlooked; however, removal of clothing at the scene is not appropriate. This process needs to be determined beforehand and an acceptable process should be in place. The forensic pathologist will identify and record the precise injuries during the autopsy.

Crime Scene Evidence Techniques

No two crime scenes are ever the same. No precise algorithm can be written on how to collect evidence from the body. It is a critical thinking process. The nursing process is fundamental to understanding the principles and techniques of forensic evidence recovery, the equivalent of what is taught in evidence technician programs.

When approaching the scene, the FNE must determine which item of evidence holds the greatest potential for being lost or altered. This evidence is collected first. Preliminary steps of evidence collection include taking initial photographs, inspecting the body with an alternate light source (luminescent areas must be swabbed immediately), then tape-lifting the body surface for trace and physical evidence (Fig. 19-5). Specific techniques and the use of designated containers are mandatory for effective preservation of evidentiary items.

Essential equipment includes portable evidence collection supplies. Certain processes will be drastically different when processing a body at a crime scene as opposed to collecting evidence in a hospital or clinical setting. The FNE will need ready access to water for frequent handwashing and disposable garbage bags for supplies or medical waste. These supplies should be routinely organized and brought to the scene. Equipment essential to evidence recovery and examination of the decedent are listed in Box 19-5.

Tampering is a concern that cannot be disregarded. A proper seal provides physical proof that item integrity has not been compromised by access. Evidence must be stored properly to ensure that evidence does not degrade in the storage process, possibly contaminating the results. The primary requisite of a good seal is that it will readily reveal any tampering. Accurate labeling is essential to security as well as to the chain of custody. All packages should be sealed with evidence tape and the container should be annotated with the collector's initials, as shown in Figure 19-6. Because policies and procedures may vary by jurisdiction, it is advisable to determine the precise protocol for the agency in question and to coordinate procedural details with the crime laboratory or medical examiner or coroner.

Tape-Lifting Technique

Tape-lifting is a process that is applied by the FNE/MDI in the recovery of minute or microscopic trace evidence from a body and its environment. This technique requires the use of wide, clear, one-sided adhesive tape (either a 2- or 4-inch piece

Box 19-5 FNE Tools of the Crime Scene

Large bag/suitcase on wheels	Powder-free gloves
Sterile swabs	Sterile water bottles
Plastic bags	Paper bags (multiple sizes)
Evidence tape	Swab rack/dryer
Extension cords	Outlet adapters
Sterile urine cups	Garbage bags
Evidence collection kits	Vaginal speculum/speculum light
Foley catheters	Flashlights
Alternate light source (ALS)	Digital camera
Clear packaging tape	Clear sheet protectors
Scissors	Nail clippers
Roll of butcher paper/exam table paper	

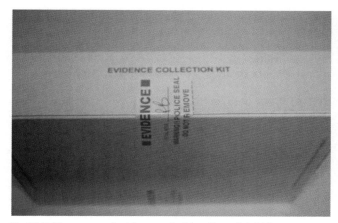

Fig. 19-6 Tamper-proof evidence seal with collector's initials across tape.

Fig. 19-7 An FNE is using the tape-lifting technique to recover trace evidence from a body.

Fig. 19-8 State crime lab personnel conduct microscopic analysis of trace evidence obtained by the tape-lifting method.

of packaging tape works well) in sections approximately 10 to 12 inches long that is placed directly on the skin or clothing to recover any potential trace materials such as hairs or fibers (Fig. 19-7). This technique is referred to as *tape-lifting or taping*. The body is usually taped in four different sections; one piece of tape can be used to tape the top front half of the body, a second piece of tape is used on the lower front half of the body, a third piece is used on the back top half on the body, and a final piece is used on the lower back half of the body. Each individual piece is placed on a clear piece of plastic (paper or plastic sheet protectors work well, but the FNE should check with the local crime laboratory for recommendation) (Fig. 19-8). Each piece of tape must be correctly labeled to identify from which half of the body it was collected (U.S. Department of Justice, 2003). After completion of the tape-lifting procedure, a head-to-toe examination is performed. The position of the body will differ from scene to scene. The body should be examined in the position it is first found, without exception. After all possible evidence is recovered, only then should the body be moved. The jurisdictional forensic laboratory will examine and analyze the specimens.

BEST PRACTICE The FNE should thoroughly inspect the body and collect all evidence before it is moved to a secondary location.

Investigation at the Public Scene

Occasionally, a protective environment must be created within the crime scene because of privacy issues, security concerns, and climate or other environmental circumstances. Material to construct a barrier or tent should be considered and made available. The following case study provides one example of securing a scene from public view.

KEY POINT If ever in doubt regarding the collection of a piece of evidence or not, you should always collect it! You cannot go back later.

Once the on-scene examination is completed, the body should be rolled on to a large, clean sheet or sterile white paper, placed into the body bag, sealed with a tamper-resistant seal, and transported to the anatomical pathology department. One member of the FNE team also responds to the morgue for other possible evidence items that may be needed to be collected during autopsy. This can include clothing, a noose or ligature from the neck, or duct tape used on the body related to the crime. Although a buccal swab (see Chapter 6) is typically collected, the FNE must

also collect one tube of blood for DNA purposes. This blood tube should be packaged in a plastic bag and padded to prevent breakage (the FNE will check with the crime laboratory for its requirements). Contents of the evidence collection kit should be identified that it contains a blood specimen to alert the next agency to refrigerate the evidence immediately after transfer.

Case Study 19-2

A Case of Privacy Please

A 43-year-old female was found dead in an alleyway in a business and residential area. The decedent was fully clothed with no obvious external trauma noted (Fig. 19-9). The FNE team responded to the scene to provide trace evidence collection.

Curious crowds soon flooded the area, climbing onto rooftops of nearby houses to observe the officers and medical investigators at work. A tent was quickly constructed to maintain the victim's privacy, and the crime scene was secured (Fig. 19-10).

Outcome: Physical examination revealed a bite mark to the victim's breast, and an unknown pubic hair was found in the victim's teeth. The bite mark impression and dried saliva on the breast and the unknown hair (along with multiple other specimens) were recovered. The cause of death was asphyxiation from manual strangulation.

Because the victim had not been sexually penetrated and no semen was found, the bite mark and pubic hair were two primary items that provided a positive link to the suspect. These small but crucial items could have easily been lost if not collected at the initial crime scene. However, it was this evidence that convicted the murderer.

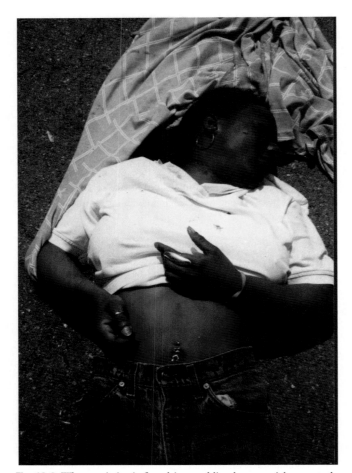

Fig. 19-9 When a victim is found in a public place, special scene techniques are often required.

Fig. 19-10 Tent erected at crime scene to protect the privacy of the victim and the investigators, and to secure the crime scene.

Because an exact history of the event is unknown, the possibility exists that the oral cavity could include mixed or multiple specimens containing semen from more than one source. The body will likely be buried or cremated shortly after death, making it difficult or impossible to obtain another specimen. Most laboratories prefer buccal swabs to analyze for DNA instead of the former practice of using gauze squares that have been saturated with saliva. Although current protocols suggest that the sexual

assault examination on living patients be performed within a 72- or 96-hour window, there is no timeframe for cases that are examined at the scene of death. All guidelines should be deliberated on an individual basis with considerations for the history of the assault as well as local forensic laboratory recommendations.

BEST PRACTICE When crime victims die in the hospital, all forensic evidence should be collected before permitting the family to view the body. The FNE should remain with the body at all times to ensure the integrity of evidence and the security of the deceased.

Hospital as Scene of Death

When forensic patients are admitted to the hospital, it is not only appropriate but often legally required that evidence be identified, recovered, and preserved. The Emergency Nurses Association (ENA), under its Forensic Evidence Collection Position Statement, now identifies forensic evidence collection from patients in the hospital setting as a standard of care. The ENA recognizes the value of evidence recovery and suggests that healthcare professionals work with local law enforcement agencies to become familiar with essential forensic procedures. It is recommended that hospital administrators seek legal counsel or information about forensic procedures when questions arise concerning the legality of evidence collection. Once medical personnel are taught the value of physical evidence and the proper procedures for handling it, they generally support police requests for assistance and do not inadvertently hinder the progress of the investigation.

If the decedent was transferred from the crime scene to the hospital, an initial examination, including recovery of evidence, should be performed before the body is transferred to the morgue. The hospital staff should be notified that no one, not even family members, are allowed access to the body until the FNE team has completed the evidence collection process. This includes cases involving children. Parents often want to hold the child after a death; however, this risks the contamination of evidence. The body, which is now a potential crime scene, should not be touched. The family may be allowed to grieve over the body afterward. If a known suspect is in custody, a suspect examination should be performed as soon as possible. This is *not* just for sexual assault cases. Any time there is a potential for evidence on a suspect's body, regardless of the crime, evidence collection should be considered.

In the absence of an FNE investigative team in the hospital trauma center, potential liability exists. Search and seizure is a complex legal issue. When ambulance or emergency department personnel treat the near-death victim of violent crime, valuable forensic evidence is often lost or destroyed. Medical personnel are generally not aware of its presence or potential value. Studies indicate the causes of this deficiency are poor communication between medical and law enforcement personnel and a lack of forensic education for physicians, nurses, and prehospital workers. The FNE can effectively serve as a liaison between the hospital and law enforcement, facilitating communication and reducing the potential for interpersonal conflict between hospital personnel and law enforcement officers (Lynch, 2000).

The problem of gathering evidence in the clinical setting is not restricted to the failure to recognize or collect evidence, but the failure to properly preserve perishable evidence. Accurate documentation of medicolegal evidence is essential. Digitalized, photo documentation is the current preferred method used to memorialize the evidentiary item, its location, and its condition, as well as its volume or dimension. A measurement scale should be photographed within range of the evidence (see Chapter 7). Descriptive documentation, body maps, scene diagrams, and photographs are mandatory for confirming or explaining evidence and will serve as backup in the event that any items are lost or destroyed.

Cold Case Evidence Recovery

Although it is not a frequent experience, the Macomb County FNE team was called to recover evidence from a cold case in which the decedent was murdered in 1978. Exhumation was approved based on the possibility of recovering evidence for DNA analysis, a procedure not available at the time of the murder.

Case Study **19-3**

After All These Years

The cold case decedent was a 27-year-old female who was murdered 25 years earlier. The cause of death was hemorrhage resulting from 42 stab wounds to her back. DNA profiling had now become accessible. The decedent's family initiated contact with the prosecutor about the possibility of exhuming the body to obtain DNA specimens from the victim. During the funeral, the family had remembered noticing that her fingernails were painted, an unusual habit for her. The family had asked the funeral director to remove the nail polish at the time and were told "there was too much stuff" underneath her nails so they would not come clean. The nails were painted to cover this debris.

The body was exhumed and transferred to the medical examiner's office for examination and evidence collection. The remains were in exceptional condition because of a meticulous embalming process, a superior vault and casket, and the near ideal environmental conditions of the burial site (Figs. 19-11 and 19-12). Dr. Werner Spitz, the Macomb County medical examiner at the time, requested that the FNE unit collect medical/forensic evidence from the body. A complete sexual assault evidentiary examination was performed. Specimens recovered included head and pubic hair, fingernails, toenails, body cavity packing from the vaginal vault, and vaginal and anal samples for DNA analysis.

Outcome: Although evidence recovered from the body was analyzed, no DNA was found. The case remains an open homicide. However, the primary suspect's DNA was later entered in the CODIS system (DNA data bank) for future reference. He is currently incarcerated for another crime.

Fig. 19-11 Michigan police at an exhumation scene.

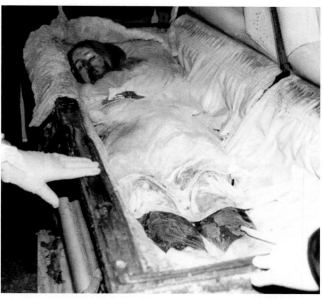

Fig. 19-12 The body, buried since 1978, had endured 25 years of snowstorms.

Some cases are more complicated than others and require extensive evidence recovery and documentation techniques. Case Study 19-4 demonstrates a tedious process of evidence collection on the body of a murder victim.

Case Study **19-4**

Bizarre Case of Stolen Identity

The police were notified to provide a welfare check on a young couple after their family could not reach them. Law enforcement officers responded to the couple's residence and discovered that the man and his wife were dead. Both were found wrapped in a plastic sheet, bound with duct tape (Fig. 19-13). Once the wrappings were removed, the male presented multiple injuries from a violent struggle. The body displayed massive blunt force trauma to the head (inflicted with the butt of a gun).

The male victim's feet were injected with bleach (needle marks were present on the sole of the feet). His hands and arms were tied with an electrical cord and duct tape. A sock was inserted into his mouth and forced down his throat and duct tape covered his mouth (Figs. 19-14 through 19-16). His teeth were missing as a result of blunt forces.

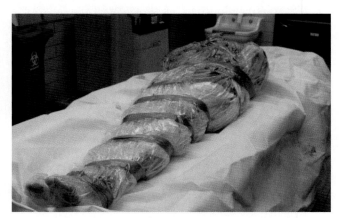

Fig. 19-13 The victim was murdered and wrapped in plastic and duct tape in an effort to hide evidence from police.

Fig. 19-14 The victim's upper torso, showing the massive amounts of evidence to collect from the body: plastic, duct tape, plastic bags, belt from neck, and electrical cord.

Fig. 19-15 Close-up of the victim's upper torso.

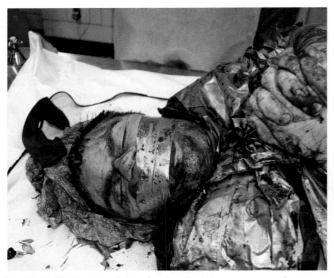

Fig. 19-16 Head of the victim after the plastic bag was removed.

A plastic bag was placed over his head and tied with a belt around his neck. His cause of death was asphyxia by suffocation. The autopsy revealed the female victim was three months pregnant. Her cause of death was asphyxia by strangulation.

Outcome: The man and woman were murdered by Patrick Selepak and Samatha Bachynski, a couple who wanted to steal their identity.

Selepak and Bachynski had previously murdered another man in a neighboring county. The murdered couple was marginally mentally impaired. The female victim worked at a local grocery store where the murderer, Patrick Selepak, had befriended her and knew the couple would be an easy target. Selepak confessed to murder one, and his case never went to trial.

Afterwards, Selepak continued to emotionally torment the family from his jail cell. He alleged an affair with the female victim and claimed he was the father of her baby. However, this was not possible because Selepak was incarcerated for a different crime during the time he claimed the affair had happened. Samatha Bachynski claimed that she was in fear of her life and maintained that this was the reason that she participated in the crimes with Selepak. She was found guilty of first-degree murder. Both will serve life in prison with no chance of parole (Case number 06002570-FC [Macomb]). (*The Macomb Daily*, April 4, 2006).

Success Achieved

In August 2004, all planning and education preparing the joint FNE/Law Enforcement Evidence Recovery Unit was tested when Detective Thomas McMullen of the Sterling Heights Police Department recommended that the FNE team be requested to provide evidence recovery in the following case.

Case Study **19-5**

Case of the Missing Shoestring

The decedent is a 34-year-old female who failed to show up for work. Her employer called the police to request a welfare check. When police entered the home, the decedent was found dead on the floor of the living room. Her home was unkempt and in disarray, but this was reported to be its normal state. Although she was wearing a shirt and bra, it had been pulled up to expose her breast, and she was nude from the waist down. The FNE unit responded to the scene and a complete head-to-toe examination and sexual assault evidence collection was performed, A ligature tied tightly around her neck was later identified as a shoestring from the suspect's sports shoe, which the prosecutor labeled as proof of premeditation (Fig. 19-17). A search warrant was issued for evidence recovery as required for a living suspect. The FNEs were also requested to respond to the jail to provided the suspect examination and evidence collection.

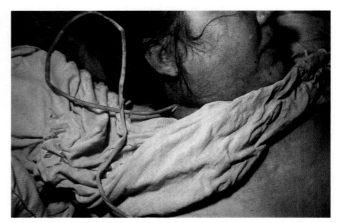

Fig. 19-17 Shoestring ligature from the victim's shoe.

Outcome: Results from the Michigan State Crime Laboratory revealed a positive DNA match between the victim and the suspect and on the ligature removed from the victim at the time of the autopsy. Cause of death was asphyxia due to ligature strangulation. The lead nurse testified at the trial regarding the forensic examination process. The suspect, a neighbor next door, was found guilty of murder and was convicted to life in prison with no chance of parole.

The forensic evidence analysis revealed these results: (1) the suspect's DNA on the victim's genital swabs, (2) positive results of the victim's DNA on the suspect's penile swabs, and (3) positive results of the suspect's DNA on the ligature that was around the victim's neck. This pivotal case changed the forensic community's perspective and established the precedence for this innovative concept of including the FNE team in the criminal investigation process. Macomb County has since elected a new prosecutor, Eric Smith, and has a newly appointed chief medical examiner, Dr. Daniel Spitz, who has now signed the protocol formalizing this joint crime scene investigative team.

Detective Lieutenant Elizabeth Darga of the Macomb County Sheriff's Department emphasizes the success of the joint evidence recovery unit:

The working relationship we have developed with the forensic nurse examiner program is invaluable. There had always been the possibility of uncollected evidence at crime scenes prior to initiating this program. Now that there is a cooperative working relationship between our department and the forensic nurse examiners, it would be rare that any evidence is overlooked. The nurses are highly trained, and our department has an extreme level of respect for their team. (Darga, E., personal communication, 2009)

Summary

These forensic nurse examiners have overcome incredible challenges in making this process a reality in Macomb County, Michigan. It could not have come about without the intense dedication and trust of all disciplines involved. The FNE team is usually the silent participant, not recognized in the media or thanked by family members, but recognition is not their purpose. Their reward is in knowing that they have fulfilled their duty—to ensure that the guilty are prosecuted and the innocent are exonerated. Since the inception of this team, the FNEs are now called for all homicides or other suspicious deaths that occur within the county. The entire forensic investigation community, along with the nurse examiners, share the positive outcomes of this success. These coordinated efforts have provided this one community with immense benefits. However, a genuine success story will recount that other legal agencies across the country have replicated the Macomb County model and are also reaping benefits from this unique approach to medical/legal investigations.

References

Betzold, M. (2004). Collection and detection. *Detroit HOUR Magazine.*

Campbell, R., Bybee, D., Ford, J. K., & Patterson, D. (2009). *A systems change analysis of SANE programs: Identifying the mediating mechanisms of criminal justice impact.* (NIJ Publication No. 2005 WG-BX-003). Washington, DC: National Institute of Justice.

Coyle, H. M., Ladd, C., & Lee, H. (2006). Biological Evidence in the Human Body (Chapter 2). In *Spitz and Fisher's medicolegal investigation of death* (4th ed.). Springfield, IL: Charles C Thomas.

Doney, I. (1988). Who is first at the scene? London. *Forensic Science International, 369*(2), 15–20, Elsevier.

Garner, B. A. (Ed.), (2004). *Black's law dictionary* (8th ed.). Madison, WI: West Group.

Kirk, P. A. (1953). Crime investigation: Physical evidence and the police laboratory. Interscience Publishers, Inc. New York.

Kirschke, J. (2005). Florence Nightingale meets Sherlock Holmes. *Metro Times Magazine.*

Lee, H. (2001). *Crime scene handbook.* New York: Academic Press.

Lynch, V. (2000). *Clinical forensic nursing and death investigation.* Colorado Springs, CO: Bearhawk Consulting Group.

Lynch, V. (2006). *Forensic nursing.* St. Louis: Elsevier.

Saferstein, R. (2007). Criminalistics: An introduction to Forensic Science (College Edition) Prentice Hall, Upper Saddle River, NJ.

U.S. Department of Justice. (2003). *Handbook of forensic sciences.* Washington D.C.: Federal Bureau of Investigation Laboratory Division.

Venes, D. (Ed.), (2009). *Taber's cyclopedic medical dictionary* (21st ed.). Philadelphia: F. A. Davis.

Waddell, M. (2009). Profiles. www.nursetv.com. Viewed May 1.

CHAPTER 20

Postmortem Sexual Assault Evaluation

Sharon Rose Crowley

This chapter explores a segment of the medicolegal examination of the deceased victim wherein the unique skills and expertise of the forensic nurse examiner (FNE) may be invaluable. It is vital to emphasize the importance of *teamwork*. In an ideal situation, the forensic nurse functions as an interactive member of a homicide investigation team and can be asked to participate in the postmortem anogenital evaluation. In most cases, the purpose is to facilitate the determination of concomitant sexual assault in cases of homicide. There is no living victim to recount details of the event or behaviors of the offender; thus, this information is crucial to the investigation as a whole. Wide variance may exist in the expertise of the FNE, both in antemortem case experience and death investigation skills specific to sexual assault. Collaboration is pivotal.

The mobile system for these examinations, previously described in 2004, was based on the Sexual Assault Response Team (SART) model, with adaptation to the autopsy milieu (Crowley, AAFS, 1998 & 2001, Crowley, 2004). The role of the FNE is one with a defined scope of expertise (i.e., expertise in the medicolegal evaluation of the sexual assault victim). If the nurse examiner's previous expertise is limited to the antemortem arena, normal postmortem artifact may be misinterpreted as traumatic. Ongoing education and collaboration is essential.

The usual method of case referral is from a forensic pathologist, detective, or coroner. The interpretation of genital findings in the deceased is both vital and timely. Until recently, little information was available on the nature and appearance of the anogenital tissues during the postmortem interval. Ongoing, normative, baseline studies are yielding useful data on postmortem genital anatomy (Crowley, 2002-2009).

The sequential methodology for the examination of sexual homicide victims was developed to respond to the need for a systematic protocol. The mobile system grew out of a need to bring the examiner to the patient, such as in jurisdictions that lack a centralized morgue. This protocol incorporates colposcopy. Aspects of the initial protocol were refined and expanded (Crowley, 1998; Crowley, 2004).

The deceased victim of sexual assault presents both special challenges and unique opportunities for the forensic nurse. During the autopsy, traditional methods of examination, such as gross visualization, may have precluded detection of the more subtle findings that may constitute genital trauma during sexual assault. The colposcope affords magnification and photographic capability. This modality enhances visualization and facilitates peer review. It also provides the opportunity to study the effects of the postmortem interval and other factors on the anogenital tissues.

Theoretical Framework: Sexual Murderers

Hazelwood, Dietz, and Burgess defined sexual fatalities as deaths that occur as a result of or in association with sexual activity (Hazelwood et al., 1982). These activities span a broad range, including deaths from natural causes during coitus, masturbation, autoerotic asphyxia deaths, and lust murder. Suicidal sexual fatalities are extremely rare; usually autoerotic fatalities are accidental. In the United States, sexual murders outnumber autoerotic fatalities. The latter, in turn, outnumber sexual manslaughter. After all efforts at resolution, in a small number of cases, the manner of death remains elusive; thus, a small number of equivocal cases remain (Hazelwood et al., 1982).

HISTORICAL PERSPECTIVE

Against Our Will: Men, Women and Rape (Brownmiller, 1975) provided a historical perspective and discourse on the nature, breadth, and scope of sexual assault. Later articles on motivational models for sexual homicide were consistent in their discussions related to the dearth of information on the number of rape-murders committed. This is due to the fact that these are treated solely as homicides by both law enforcement and the courts.

An epic example of the complex issues involved in sexual homicide was the 1964 murder of Kitty Genovese. Kitty was stalked, raped, and murdered in Queens, New York City. Thirty-eight people heard her cries or witnessed some part of her death. While in court, the defendant, 29-year-old Winston Moseley, calmly announced, "I just set out to find any girl that was unattended and I was going to kill her" (Brownmiller, 1975, p. 199).

The famed Boston Strangler, Albert DeSalvo, strangled and stabbed 11 women between June 1962 and January 1964, including elderly victims. DeSalvo left their sexually mutilated bodies posed garishly, with a nylon stocking around the victim's neck (Brownmiller, 1975, p. 200). The murders stopped in 1964, when DeSalvo was hospitalized in Bridgewater State Hospital for observation. DeSalvo also operated as the "Cambridge Measuring Man" and "Green Man". As "Measuring Man," he gained entrance to young girls' apartments by posing as the representative of a model agency. DeSalvo would "measure" their breasts and hips. As "Green Man," he tied his victims to the bed; he then either raped or sodomized them or attempted to do so. DeSalvo gave indications of the sexual dysfunction of premature ejaculation. The charge that sent him to prison was breaking and entering (Brownmiller, 1975, p. 201). When later asked about a 75-year-old female victim, he replied, "Attractiveness has nothing to do with it. She was a woman. When this certain time comes on me, it's a very immediate thing" (Brownmiller, 1975, p. 205).

Research on sexual murderers suggests that these crimes are based on persistent, violent sexualized thoughts and fantasies (Ressler, Burgess, & Douglas, 1988). Therefore, the meaning and performance of acts committed during a murder vary with the offender. The sexual acts may vary from actual rape (with penetration before, during, or after death) to symbolic acts, which may include the insertion of foreign objects into body orifices of the victim (Douglas, Burgess, Burgess, & Ressler, 1992).

TYPOLOGIES OF RAPISTS

Following are typologies of rapists from the perspective of criminal investigative analysis, a program of the National Center for the Analysis of Violent Crime (NCAVC) of the Federal Bureau of Investigation (FBI).

Impulsive Offenders

Impulsive offenders are reactive rapists; they are criminally unsophisticated, use a significant level of physical force, and often have a diverse criminal history. In general, impulsive rapists and molesters do not kill their victims. Their anger is undifferentiated, and they are prone to "stupid" mistakes.

Ritualistic Offenders

Ritualistic offenders are more criminally sophisticated; they devote time and effort to planning, rehearsing, and execution of the crime. The level of force used in commission of the crime may increase over time. Fantasies are pervasive and defining. Paraphilic interests are diverse.

Power Reassurance Rapists

Power reassurance rapists are the least violent of the typologies. This rapist is a ritualistic offender. He is typically a low achiever, single, and with low self-esteem. His intent is *not* to physically harm the victim. The level of force used during the rape is minimal; he usually preselects a victim, either his own age or slightly older. The victim is either alone or solely in the company of a small child. The element of surprise is employed to approach the victim. He may take a souvenir and keep records. Like many other rapists, he manifests sexual paraphilias. He has a history of prior sex crimes and confidence increases with experience.

Power Assertive Rapist

The **power assertive rapist** is the most common of the typologies and more often uses greater physical force. He is impulsive, with a sense of entitlement. He utilizes the con approach and selects age-mate victims in public places. He often assaults women he has some connection to, for example, dates, girlfriends, wives, associates, or coworkers (Prodan, Michael, Lt. [Supervisory Special Agent], personal communication, 2009). This rapist is macho, has a history of alcohol use, is self-centered, and flashy in dress and vehicle. He has been married and divorced, has a male-oriented job, and has a history of arrests for fighting.

Anger Rapist

The **anger rapist** is impulsive, angry, and the one most recognizable to the general public. His victims are most likely to report; thus, he is more often apprehended. Most prevention programs address this type of rape. This rapist tends to be criminally unsophisticated. His *modus operandi* is to spend a short time with his victims; preoffense

acting out may have been with wives, girlfriends, or prostitutes. He tends to assault outside, using a *blitz* approach. He is verbally degrading and may experience retarded ejaculation. His victims are usually his own age or slightly older. He uses both drugs and alcohol, and his explosive temper predisposes him to use violence to control his victims. This rapist has a sense of entitlement; he is macho, married, and divorced. He likely has a history of child and spousal abuse. He presents as a flashy dresser and often drives a flashy, stereotypically macho car. He is self-centered and works in a male-oriented job (Prodan, Michael, Lt. [SSA], personal communication, 2009).

Sadistic Rapist

The **sadistic rapist** engages in ritualistic fantasy and derives pleasure and excitement from the suffering of his victim(s). His goal is to inflict physical or emotional suffering, in addition to exerting power and control over his victims. The sexual sadist is usually a white male of average to high intelligence. His crimes have been fantasized for years; they are premeditated. The approach to the victim is a con and the level of force is brutal. As long as the victims are not too young, age is not a factor. Often, the victims of sexual sadists are wives, girlfriends, or other female acquaintances. This factor may preclude recognition as the work of a sexual sadist. The crime may instead be incorrectly written off as the product of an "angry" assailant or as domestic violence (Prodan, Michael, Lt. [SSA], personal communication, 2009). Victims may be taken to preselected locations and may be kept for hours or days (Crowley, 1999). Most sexual sadists (77%) employ bondage (Dietz, Hazelwood, and Warren, 1990).

Like other paraphiliacs, the sexual sadist may freely engage consenting or paid partners to play the submissive role. Some sexual sadists cultivate compliant victims. These individuals initially enter into a consensual relationship, but become progressively more caught in the web of manipulated activities of a sadomasochistic nature. Compliant victims differ from consensual partners; most are wives or girlfriends. The sexual sadist may progress to animals, consenting/paid partners, compliant victims, and finally, sexually homicide victims (Prodan, Michael, Lt. [SSA], personal communication, 2009).

Bondage is the restriction of movements, or use of the senses to enhance the sexual arousal of the offender. It differs from *binding*, which is done solely for purposes of victim restriction or restraint. *Bondage* includes four characteristics:
- The binding has symmetry, neatness, and balance.
- The victim is bound in a variety of positions; he or she is often photographed in those positions.
- The binding is more than necessary to control or secure the movement of the victim.
- The binding is elaborate and excessive.

When evaluating behaviors that may be manifested at the crime scene or on the body of the victim, it is important to differentiate other behaviors, that might be confused with sexual sadism. These include institutional or politically sanctioned cruelty, mob mentality, revenge, interrogative behaviors, ritual abuse, and postmortem mutilation (Prodan, Michael, Lt. [SSA], personal communication, 2009).

According to Dietz (1990), there may be evidence of severe torture, even mutilation, without true representation of sexual sadism. Pain cannot be inflicted on a dead or unconscious person; thus, postmortem mutilation or necrophilia is *not* motivated by the same set of desires.

In an uncontrolled, descriptive study of 30 sexual sadists, 22 were responsible for 187 murders. This study included characteristics of both the sexual sadist and his crime(s). Of note, there was a greater incidence of forcible penetration of the anus and mouth versus the vagina. Anal rape was the most common sexual activity (occurring in 22 of the 30 rapists. This was followed by fellatio, vaginal rape, and foreign object penetration. Most of the victims (two out of three) were subjected to at least three of the four acts (Hazelwood et al., 1992).

All but one assailant in the sexual sadist study group was white. Forty-three percent were married at the time of the offense; some sadists repeatedly used the same torture methods. This suggests that it was the offender's signature, or calling card. The study confirmed the association of sexual deviations in this group of paraphiliacs. Over 50% kept detailed documentation (written, photographic, video) of their exploits. Sexual sadists' crimes were extremely well planned and executed (Dietz, et al., 1990). Other characteristics of sexual sadists included the following:

- Demographic specificity in his victims
- Con approach; selfish and brutal
- High IQ; paranoid/psychopath
- Theme-oriented pornography
- Gun/knife collection; Nazi collections
- Detective magazines
- Suicidal ideation
- Big dogs
- Able to hide sexual behaviors well; little to no arrest history (Prodan, Michael, Lt. [SSA], personal communication, 2009)

Forensic implications for this typology of rapist include bondage, cutting of clothes, recording of activities, and retarded ejaculation. Because the victim may be kept and tortured over a period of hours to days, there may be wounds in various stages of healing (Crowley, 2004).

To identify an offender's sexual motivation for a particular homicide, information is gleaned from the following sources
- Accurate assessment of information regarding the victim
- Crime scene(s)
- Forensic reports
- Nature of the behavioral exchange between the victim and offender (Hagan, S., in Crowley, 2004):

Collaboration of a forensic clinical nurse specialist (FCNS) with a criminal investigative analyst illustrated the complimentary nature of the two disciplines during the investigation of a sexual homicide (Crowley & Prodan, 1996).

Sequential Methodology for the Evaluation of the Sexual Homicide Victim

Even within state borders, jurisdictions and programs may vary in how they implement a particular protocol. This holds true for a methodology that has been designed to capture all facets of the examination process and ensure that the myriad aspects will be completed. The following methodology and protocol is largely derived from "A Mobile System for Postmortem Genital Examinations with Colposcopy: SART-TO-GO" (Crowley, 2004).

ROLES AND RESPONSIBILITIES

Before the actual autopsy, the clarification of individual roles and responsibilities is essential. There are unavoidable areas of potential overlap, including the collection of clothing, photography, documentation of nongenital trauma, and the collection of samples from potential bite marks (Crowley, AAFS, 1998). Although a FNE may routinely collect, examine, package, and document clothing for a living sexual assault victim, this may or may not be the routine for a particular medical examiner's/coroner's (ME/C's)

office. For the postmortem milieu, creation of checklists for team members is a pragmatic way to ensure that someone with the appropriate skill level is attending to all the tasks at hand. Unlike the procedure followed with the antemortem patient, the opportunity to reexamine (i.e., return for an additional follow-up examination) is rare. The forensic nurse may be in an advantageous position to provide overview of this process or at least ensure that the role she or he has undertaken is symbiotic and efficacious with other members of the homicide team.

As an example of potential role overlap, if a forensic odontologist is not readily available, the FNE may collect saliva samples or provide castings of a potential bite mark. If at all possible, the FNE will conduct the genital examination and collect biological specimens before the forensic pathologist conducts the general autopsy. However, there are instances where the autopsy has already been performed and the nurse examiner is consulted afterward. Flexibility is essential.

The anogenital examination should be preceded by a preliminary overview of the body by the forensic pathologist, with notation of gross features, such as clothing, general physical status, grossly apparent nongenital trauma, and other findings. The genital examination can then include prompt collection of biological specimens. It also avoids obscuring the genital area "field" by leakage of body fluids through the vaginal opening (Crowley, AAFS, 2003).

Set up a work area before the examination begins. Although this step seems obvious, some jurisdictions do not have a centralized morgue. In some cases, private mortuaries are used to conduct the actual autopsy. Space may be limited. If sufficient counter space is not available, a spare gurney may be covered with paper drapes or even personal protective gowns to use as a workstation. In addition to the usual, customary supplies used during an antemortem examination, the postmortem milieu brings to the stage a new set of ubiquitous factors and considerations (Table 20-1).

Open a sealed **sexual assault evidence kit** (Fig. 20-1). Arrange items in the anticipated order of collection. If a Lucite air-drying box is available, swabs and slides can be lined up, in slots prelabeled or marked with a pencil/slide marker to indicate each body cavity or anatomical site of collection. A 10% bleach solution should be available to disinfect the swab-drying box between patients, to avoid cross-contamination of DNA.

SALIENT CASE DATA

Note both on the form and on the evidence kit which law enforcement agency is investigating the case. This case number often serves as the case identifier for evidentiary samples, photographs, and documentation forms. Some case data, such as the cause and manner of death, should always be verified with the forensic pathologist, and this information can be completed after it is available.

In the process of documentation, the following items should be indicated:
- The number of victims (and suspects, if known)
- The manner (type) of case (natural, suicide, accident, homicide)
- The date/time/location that the body was discovered
- The general interval to examination (defined as interval from the time of body discovery to the postmortem genital examination):
  ≤ 24 hours
  24 to 48 hours
  48 to 72 hours
  72 to 96 hours
  ≥ 5 days
  Unknown

Table 20-1 Components of the Mobile System: "SART-TO-GO"

COLPOSCOPE & CAMERA	EXAM EQUIPMENT	EVIDENCE KIT & SUPPLIES	OTHER	DOCUMENTATION
Colposcope	Vaginal specula, various sizes, individually wrapped	Sealed sexual assault evidence kit	Wood's lamp	Medical-legal forms
Rolling base	Alternate light source (optional)		Autopsy diagrams/ traumagrams	
Colposcope mount system	Anoscopes-individually wrapped	Extra Dacron/cotton swabs, slides	Film for fluorescent & reflective imaging (optional)	
Travel case	Rubber-bulb syringe	Extra bindles & paper bags	Bitemark impression material (optional)	Dictation format
Folding ramp for loading colposcope	Balloon-covered swabs		Gloves	
Food pedal (optional)	Procto/rectal swabs	Sterile water: bottle or single-use plastic vials	Scrubs	Photographs, prints, slides
Autowinder for 35 mm SLR 33 mm SLR Camera: Databack or unique ID system	Sterile scalpels, slides		Personal protective equipment	Videos, CDs
Colposcope ID Tag; Various lenses, macrolens		Post-its; Suture removal kits (with scissors), Pipettes, syringes	10% bleach solution Disinfectant solution/ wipes	Supplemental medical records
Flash system, optional ringflash, 35 mm film (slides or prints)	Body positioning aides: Headrests		Protective coverings for camera/colposcope*	
L-shaped ABFO-scale	Sandbags (vinyl-covered; at least 4.5 kg each)	Lucite swab-drying box		
Optional camera systems: Digital, video; Tripod (optional)	Urine specimen cup			

*Cut fingers off of powder-free exam gloves. Stretch over camera, lenses, colposcope handles, etc., to keep clean. Disposable shower caps can also be used.
(Crowley, Sharon Rose. "Postmortem Genital Examinations with Colposcopy: SART-TO-GO." Reprinted with permission, from the *Journal of Forensic Sciences*, Vol. 49, No. 6, copyright ASTM International. 100 Barr Harbor Drive, West Conshohocken, PA 19428).

Fig. 20-1 Sexual assault evidence kit: Los Angeles County/City Sexual Assault Evidence (includes urine specimen cup and envelope for medicolegal form). *(Courtesy Los Angeles County Sheriff's Department Crime Laboratory).*

DEMOGRAPHIC DATA

Document any identifying information available at the time of the postmortem anogenital examination. Also describe the general appearance of the body at the time of the discovery of the decedent. There is often a scarcity of information available at the initial point in the investigation. However, the FNE can document the need to review the medical history, when available (Crowley, 2004). Where information is missing or unknown, indicate as such. Examiners should try to record the following:

- Name (alias, nicknames)
- D.O.B., age or apparent age (if apparent, per forensic pathologist)
- Gender (male/female)
- Ethnicity
- Race
- Address
- Social Security/driver's license/passport/other identification number
- Note if the individual was institutionalized.
- Name of the person who found the body
- Last known time the decedent was seen and by whom
- Position of the body when it was discovered (Was it openly displayed, concealed/hidden, or unknown?)
- Staging: the body is intentionally placed in an unnatural or unusual position (staging is alteration of the crime scene before the arrival of police, either by the offender to redirect the investigation away from the most likely suspect, or by family and friends of the victim to protect the victim or victim's family)
- Ligatures or other restraints
- Type of binding material: gag, blindfold, other
- Location of the restraint on the body (Was it left on the victim or found at the scene?)
- Weapon use? (If known, document, the type of weapon that the assailant used. Was the weapon left at the scene?)
- Condition/disarray of clothing on the victim's body or at the scene (Was the victim fully/partially dressed, completely nude, redressed, cut/torn? Were there obvious items missing, unknown? Were the clothing and bed linens removed from the crime scene?)

HISTORY

If information and records are available, the examiner should glean as much as possible about the victim's prior health and lifestyle. Document the source of the data.

- Past medical history, surgeries; known significant (recent) weight loss or gain
- Psychiatric illnesses
- Medications (over-the-counter or prescription), supplements, herbs, hormones, other
- Any physical disabilities, use of assistive devices, amputations, skeletal remains
- Was the victim pregnant? (If yes, note estimated day of delivery [EDD] or number of weeks. Also note if this EDD was determined by history, examination by the forensic pathologist, or both.)
- Known gynecological conditions; number of children
- Last medical/gynecological examination
- Last menstrual period (LMP)
- Consensual sexual activity (≤ 5 days), or last known consensual sexual activity
- Occupation or visible means of support

- Lifestyle (e.g., homemaker, student, professional, technical/trade, homeless, runaway, prostitute, hitchhiker, drug user/seller, other, unknown)
- Sexual orientation: heterosexual, homosexual, bisexual, transgender, unknown, transsexual (male to female), transsexual (female to male)
- Relationship of the victim to the offender (stranger, acquaintance, relative, spouse/ex-spouse, boyfriend/ex-boyfriend, employee, coworker, neighbor, other, unknown) (Crowley, 2004)

GENERAL PHYSICAL EXAMINATION

Document the physical condition in which the body was found. After consultation with the forensic pathologist, note the following:

- Presence of rigor mortis, livor mortis, algor mortis
- Insect activity
- Rodent/animal activity
- Height, weight (note whether estimated or measured)
- Hair (color/length/style)
- Eye color
- Glasses, contact lenses, eye prosthesis
- Teeth: condition (e.g., absent, dental work, braces, dentures)
- Vomitus, feces, or apparent urine that may be on the body or clothing; describe
- Scars, tattoos, birthmarks, moles, piercings, any other marks (e.g., writing/drawing on the victim's body)

CLOTHING

The examiner may assist or collect any clothing found on or with the body. Items of clothing may be evaluated relative to particular features of the crime. Examples are tears in clothing that may correspond to wounds on the victim's body, weapon use, or undergarments that are on backward/inside out. Observe for tears, rips, stains, and overt foreign matter. Backlighting of clothing items can also be incorporated.

If the clothing is still on the patient at the time of the nurse examiner's arrival, the nurse should place two sheets of examination paper on the floor. This will permit collection of bits/particles of trace evidence or debris, which may fall out when the clothing is removed from the body. Avoid shaking clothing items or folding garments across a stain. Collect debris, fibers, and any foreign material; inspect and package the clothing *over* the protective sheets of paper, reviewing each clothing item. It may be helpful to *scan* items, especially underpants, with a light source (e.g., a Wood's lamp or an alternate light source). Salient items may be photographed.

Using paper bags, package items of clothing separately. Ascertain if any bed linens/bedding were collected from the scene, if appropriate. Itemize and provide a brief description of the items on the outside of the paper bag; this should ideally be done before inserting them into the bag. Note obvious tears, stains, or other marks on the paper evidence bag and label accordingly. The top sheet of paper used for protection from contamination by the floor should be packaged into a separate, labeled bag/bindle. The bottom sheet(s), directly in contact with the morgue floor, should be discarded.

TOXICOLOGY, SEROLOGY, AND URINE SPECIMENS

Depending on local protocol, the nurse examiner may either assist with collection of these specimens or simply note that they were collected by the ME/C staff. All of the vitreous humor and urine are collected with a clean needle and new syringe.

In some cases, and depending on local protocol, the HIV status of the decedent may be requested. The local public health department may request serology after accidental exposure to blood or body fluids by emergency first responders. To satisfy this request, an extra red-top tube of peripheral blood can be obtained during the autopsy. This tube can be spun down in the morgue laboratory; the decanted serum is saved. This serum would then be submitted to the pubic health laboratory for HIV testing (Peterson, 2009).

Any wounds and body cavities should be inspected for obvious signs of debris, trace evidence, or body fluids. The entire body can be scanned for suspicious stains or fluorescence. Darken the room and scan the entire body using either a Wood's lamp or alternate light source. If an alternate light source is not available, a Wood's lamp is still considered a useful adjunct for general scanning to help discern potential stains and guide the collection of evidentiary swabs (Golden, 2008).

Check for stains and areas of positive (+) fluorescence. To collect a sample of fluorescent areas or those with visible stains or dried secretions, use Sweet's double-swab technique (Sweet, 1997). Saturate the tip of the first swab with sterile distilled water. Roll the swab's long axis along the skin surface. Use moderate pressure and circular motions. This ensures maximum contact between the swab and skin and washes dried saliva from the surface. The second swab is collected with the same technique, but with a dry swab. The second swab should be rotated so that the dry tip goes over the skin to recover moisture that still remains on the surface from the first swab. Roll the second swab over the entire area to ensure the removal of all moisture.

Each secretion should be swabbed with a separate pair of swabs (e.g., bite marks for recovery of saliva, dried bloodstains, or possible semen) (Sweet, 1997). Dried blood may be scraped off with a sterile scalpel. While using sterile, distilled water, collect a control swab from an unstained area of the body, preferably an area adjacent to the stain; if not adjacent, then use a contralateral body part. A single-body-surface control swab should be sufficient for comparison. No slide is needed. Air-dry, package as for other specimens, and document findings on the traumagrams.

EVALUATION OF NONGENITAL TRAUMA

The forensic nurse may take limited photographs of the injuries. An American Board of Forensic Odontology (ABFO) scale should be used; both orienting and close-up photographs should be taken. Appropriate documentation on the medicolegal form can be a short, succinct description of the injuries, validated by the forensic pathologist, and accompanied by "Defer to M.E.'s Report" (Crowley, 1998, 2003, 2004).

TOUCH DNA

The FNE should consider touch DNA samples and low-copy-number (trace) samples when evaluating the deceased victim's body. Consider areas of the body where there may have been skin-to-skin contact with an assailant during a struggle. It may be useful to collect samples from the victim's body, in areas such as the neck, breasts, forearms, wrists, hands, waist, and forehead, if not obscured by blood or other body fluids. Significant technology advances have been made in the analysis of these samples (Johnson, 2009).

It is difficult, if not impossible, to see evidence of trace biological samples with the unaided eye. If there is not a visible stain or one visualized by an alternate light source, consider swabbing the areas of the body that the assailant likely touched during the commission of the crime. Try to consider the circumstances of the case; consult with the criminalist.

Conventional forensic terminology should be used to describe the nature and appearance of both nongenital and genital trauma (Crowley, 2001, 2004). In addition to the customary wounds and injuries and defense injuries that are often found on homicide victims, the following nongenital findings may be present in sexual homicide victims:

- Evidence of sexual bondage
- Wounds in various stages of healing; the sexual sadist may keep and torture the victim(s) over several days or longer
- Bite marks

Bite marks should be photographed with an L-shaped ABFO scale. At least one photograph should be taken without the scale. Both orienting and close-up photographs should be taken. A colposcope may also be used for detailed, magnified photographs of nongenital findings (e.g., at 5×, 7.5× magnification). Bite marks should be measured and carefully swabbed, using the double-swab technique (Sweet, 1997). If a forensic odontologist is not immediately available and casts of the bite mark are recommended, ABFO protocol should be followed (Bowers, 1995).

Photograph other nongenital injuries in the same way as described for bite marks. Protocols vary by jurisdiction. Photographs may be taken by a forensic odontologist, law enforcement, evidence technician, pathology assistant, or the forensic nurse. Any ligatures that remain on the victim should be photographed in situ. Knots should not be untied. When the ligature is removed for submission to the criminalist, the ligature should be cut away from any knots; the cut should be indicated. The ligature should then be placed in an appropriate paper bag or envelope (Devine, personal communication, 1999; Johnson, 2009).

FACE, HAIR, AND NECK

The face should be photographed with an ID tag and ABFO scale. At least one photograph should be taken without the scale. In examining the face, hair, and neck, collect foreign matter, debris, and fibers and place them in bindle or paper envelope; label and seal.

Perioral swabs may be collected for potential seminal fluid. Any suspicious stains in the perioral area should be swabbed. Dried secretions should be collected using the double-swab technique (Sweet, 1997). Moist secretions can be collected with dry swabs to avoid dilution.

The oral cavity should be inspected, along with the frenulum, inside of the lower lip, and the pharynx. Inspect for exudates, lacerations, ecchymoses, or petechiae. Note damaged or missing teeth. Thorough inspection may be hampered by anatomical or other considerations; defer to the pathologist. Collect two swabs from the oral cavity, and make one or two dry-mount slides using the following technique:

- Holding two swabs together, swab the area from the gums to the tonsillar fossae, the upper and second molars, behind the incisors, and the fold of the cheek.
- Prepare one or two dry mount slides from these swabs by smearing the swabs onto the slides; label each slide to correlate to the swab from which it was made.

To collect a hair reference sample, tug and collect 20 to 30 hair samples, representative of different areas of the head (front, top, sides, and back). For males, collect samples of facial hair, if present. Package, label, and seal.

Depending on crime laboratory preference, saliva reference samples may be either of the following: two dry swabs inserted into the mouth, swept between the cheek and gum until saturated, or a cotton gauze/pledget placed under tongue until saturated. Use clean forceps and gloves to handle all items.

Use the tool provided in the sexual assault evidence kit to collect fingernail scrapings (toothpick or wooden manicure stick). Scrape underneath nails, one hand at a time. Place all scrapings from one hand into a separate container (bindle/bag). Label and seal both containers. Mark "R hand" or "L hand" on container.

If nail clippings are requested, use a clean fingernail cutter that has been disinfected and handled only with gloves. Place the cuttings from each hand into separate containers or bindles. Package and label; mark "R hand" or "L hand" on container.

Some jurisdictions or agencies may prefer collection of swabs under the fingernails.

GENITAL AND ANAL EXAMINATION

For a child or adolescent victim, assess and document the Tanner Stage. (See page 000.) Perform the initial inspection using gross visualization. Document any of the following findings that may be present:

- Insect activity (maggots)
- Skin slip
- Blood
- Prolapse
- Other postmortem artifact
- Visible injury that is seen upon gross inspection

Note any concomitant gynecological conditions that may be present (e.g., lichen sclerosis or labial adhesions). Use a Wood's lamp or alternate light source to scan the anogenital area and the surrounding skin (anterior and posterior body surfaces, thighs, and buttocks). Collect swabs of any suspicious areas. These swabs should be labeled "W.L. #___," or "A.L.S. #___" to denote the anatomical site of collection as well as the screening tool used (Figs. 20-2 and 20-3).

To obtain an external genital sample, moisten two cotton swabs with sterile water. Swab the external genital area with the two swabs together. Smear swabs on two slides and label. If a control swab has not already been made, collect one now. Collect/cut any matted pubic hair, and package it in designated bindles or envelopes.

To collect pubic hair combings, place clean examination paper or paper towels underneath the patient's buttocks. If the area is very wet, simply spread the decedent's legs enough to position the paper between the legs so that the paper catches the combings. The pubic hair should be combed or brushed toward the paper to collect any debris or loose hairs. Fold or package the comb/brush with the debris into the paper and place into a bindle. The folded paper or towel should go in a separate bindle.

Pubic reference samples can be obtained by tugging 20 to 30 pubic hairs from different areas. Place these into a labeled bindle/envelope.

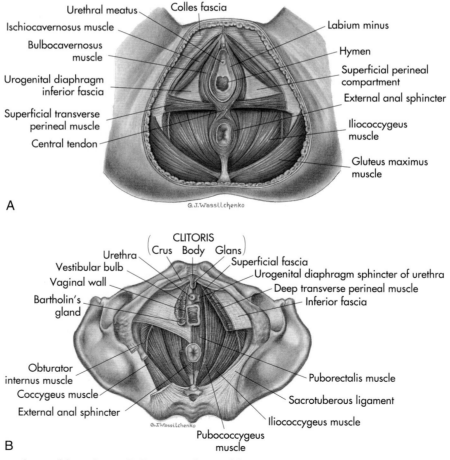

Fig. 20-2 A, Superficial musculature of the perineum. **B,** Deep musculature of the perineum. *(From Thompson et al, [2002]. Mosby's Clinical Nursing, 5th ed. Mosby, Inc. St. Louis, MO).*

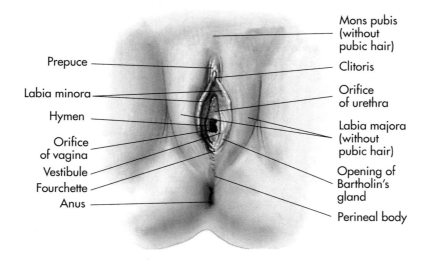

Fig. 20-3 External female genitalia. *(From Lowdermilk and Perry [2005]. Maternal Child Nursing Care, 3rd ed. Mosby, Inc. St. Louis, MO).*

COLPOSCOPE EXAMINATION

Colposcopy is well established for the evaluation of both adult and child antemortem sexual assault patients. During the author's early foray into sexual homicide investigations, colposcopy was not available in the autopsy setting. It soon became apparent that a system was needed that would facilitate detailed scrutiny of the anogenital tissues at various postmortem intervals. Colposcopy was chosen because of its magnification potential, photodocumentation, and capacity for peer review.

Technique

First, inspect the vulva using only gross visualization. Begin with a lower magnification, if possible, for orientation; proceed to greater magnifications to capture the more subtle presentation of the postmortem anatomy. Remember, only a small amount of information exists on this population of patients.

Record the magnification setting(s) on the colposcope (if a fixed magnification system).

Initial the colposcope tag. In older systems, a tag with relevant case data was incorporated into the camera/colposcope system. Newer systems may have camera databanks for entry of the case identifier. A separate ID tag may be completed for each case and used with all photographic systems (e.g., stand-alone digital and colposcopic setups).

The unique case identifier may be the medical record number or law enforcement case number. Chain of custody must be maintained for colposcopic photographs, as for all physical evidence.

Labial Separation

Labial separation exposes the introitus. Separate the labia majora laterally and aim slightly downward; use fingertips of one or both hands. Using the colposcope, inspect and photograph the following anatomical structures (see Fig. 20-4):

- Labia majora
- Clitoris, clitoral hood, and periurethral area
- Labia minora (inner and outer aspects of each labium minus)
- Fossa navicularis
- Posterior fourchette
- Perineum
- Hymen and distal portions of the vaginal barrel

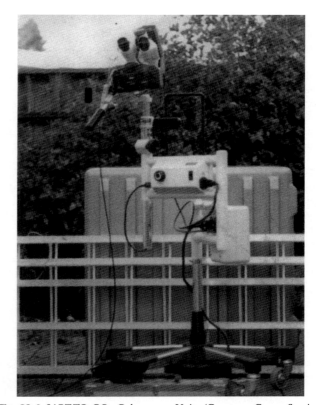

Fig. 20-4 SART-TO-GO, Colposcopy Unit. (Courtesy, CooperSurgical Leisegang, Inc. Reprinted with permission, from the *Journal of Forensic Sciences*, Vol. 49, No. 6, copyright ASTM International, 100 Barr Harbor Drive, West Conshohocken, PA 19428.)

Labial Traction

Grasp each labium minus between the thumb and index finger or the thumb, index, and middle fingers. Gently pull both labial edges outward and slightly upward, in a direction toward the examiner. Use slight lateral traction on both labial edges. This technique opens and widens the vaginal orifice; it exposes most of the hymenal rim, as well as the distal vagina. In the young child, the examiner may be able to visualize the cervix because of postmortem dilatation.

Colposcopic magnification may aid in the visualization of minute particles of foreign materials or debris. These can be collected by "catching" the particle on the tip of a swab while simultaneously viewing through the colposcope eyepieces. Moistening the swab slightly with sterile water may facilitate the adherence of the particle. The particle and swab can be placed onto the sticky part of a clean Post-it. Select the Post-it from the middle of a new pad of Post-its, while wearing gloves. Place the Post-it carefully into paper or bindle; avoid placing in air-dryer, because minute particle(s) may become dislodged and lost.

Collect external genital swabs by moistening the preselected cotton swabs with sterile, distilled water. Swab the labia and the vulva, using two swabs held together. Smear the swabs on one or two slides.

SPECULUM EXAMINATION

Select an individually wrapped speculum of appropriate size. Using the colposcope, carefully photograph areas that may stretch during initial insertion of the vaginal speculum (labia minora, hymen, fossa, posterior fourchette, and perineum). Use as large a magnification as possible; this provides a baseline to establish the initial integrity or appearance of the tissues in the event of iatrogenic trauma (e.g., insertion of the speculum).

Strive to simulate the lithotomy position as closely as possible. This ensures good visualization without requiring excessive manipulation of tissues. Standard autopsy head blocks or vinyl-covered sandbags can be used to position the legs open or to elevate the upper thighs above the level of the buttocks. The sandbags should weigh at least 4.5 kg each. Most of these cases are done without benefit of a gynecological table (Crowley, 2004).

Use only sterile water if it is necessary to lubricate the speculum. While holding the speculum in one hand, spread the labia majora from above. Use gross visualization, followed by colposcopy. Before collecting any samples, inspect the following landmarks:
• Vaginal walls
• Cervix
• Cervical os

Evaluate the integrity of the vaginal mucosa. Note the appearance of the vaginal rugae. The earliest signs of estrogen loss during menopause occur here. Atrophic changes to the vaginal epithelium include flattening of the rugae and a smoother, more tubular contour of the interior of the vagina.

COLLECTION OF VAGINAL SWABS

Collect four vaginal swabs simultaneously, from the vaginal pool, located in the posterior fornix of the vagina (Fig. 20-5). The swabs are arbitrarily designated as #1, #2, #3, and #4. From swabs #1 and #2, make one or two dry-mount slides; these must correspond to swabs #1 and #2. Designate the #3 swab and as the "vaginal wet-mount" slide. Swab #4 is extra. All slides should be labeled to correspond to the swab from which they were prepared.

Place a drop of normal saline or buffered nutrient onto the #3 vaginal slide to preserve any sperm motility that may be present. Roll this swab back and forth in the drop to transfer any cellular debris to the drop. Place a cover slip on the slide; examine within 5 to 10 minutes using a biological microscope, if available.

Scan first at 100 power (10×) to discern sperm. Examine more closely at 400 power (40↔) to determine if sperm are present. Note that nonmotile sperm are best visualized after fixing and staining by the criminalist (Crowley, 1999).

Collect two swabs from the cervix, and make one or two dry-mount slides. If the crime laboratory requests a vaginal lavage or aspirate, instill 3 mL of sterile saline or water through the speculum blades. Aspirate the contents, using a pipette; place the contents into an appropriately labeled tube or vial, ensuring that the material is carefully sealed (Crowley, 1999).

ANAL AND RECTAL EXAMINATION

Inspect and photograph the perianal area and anus, using first gross visualization followed by colposcopy (Fig. 20-6). Note the presence of normal postmortem dilation and lividity. If dilation is present, it is vital that the examiner recognizes it as a normal postmortem artifact. Postmortem relaxation of the anal sphincters has been mistaken as a traumatic finding. When in doubt, consult the forensic pathologist, either in person or via good-quality case photographs.

Check for the presence of an abnormal mass within or on the anal orifice. Carefully apply gentle lateral traction around the entire perianal area; this separates and flattens the anal folds. It

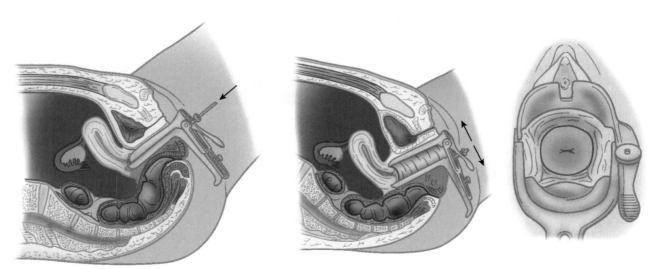

Fig. 20-5 Speculum examination. *(From Seidel, Ball, Dains, and Benedict [2006]. Mosby's Guide to Physical Examination, 6th ed. Mosby, Inc. St. Louis, MO).*

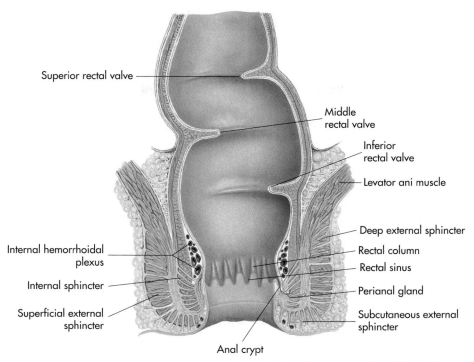

Fig. 20-6 Anatomy of the anus and rectum. *(From Seidel, Ball, Dains, and Benedict [2006]. Mosby's Guide to Physical Examination, 6th ed. Mosby, Inc. St. Louis, MO).*

also permits visualization of the anal verge and anus. For consistency in one's approach, proceed from 12 o'clock, to 3 o'clock, to 6, to 9, and back to the 12 o'clock position. Tears can easily be obscured within the perianal folds of tissue.

Collect any dried secretions. These may be seen grossly or with the aid of a Wood's lamp or alternate light source. Distilled water should be used to moisten the swabs, which should be labeled "perianal" to differentiate them from the rectal samples.

The perianal area should then be gently cleansed, using only sterile water. This will avoid contamination of the rectal swabs from any runoff vaginal drainage that is already present on the perianal skin. Do not rub vigorously, as friction should be avoided and friable tissues may be denuded in the process.

If anoscopy is unavailable, two rectal swabs should be slightly moistened with sterile water. Insert one swab at a time through the rectal sphincter to a distance of about 2 cm. Prepare two dry-mount slides.

ANOSCOPIC EXAMINATION

To conduct an anoscopic examination, insert the anoscope gently into the anal canal. Direct the anoscope toward the umbilicus. Remove the blunt-tipped obturator (Fig. 20-7).

Use the colposcope to inspect the rectum for any injuries or bleeding. Photograph the rectal mucosa. Hold two swabs together; insert through the lumen of the anoscope and collect the rectal samples. Make one or two dry-mount slides, labeled to correspond to each rectal swab. As the anoscope is withdrawn, observe and photograph the rectal mucosa at different levels.

At this point in the examination process, samples have already been collected for biological evidence. If desired, adjuncts may now be employed to reexamine and more thoroughly explore the hymenal borders. Microtrauma may be obscured within the hymenal folds of a redundant hymen. Balloon-covered swabs

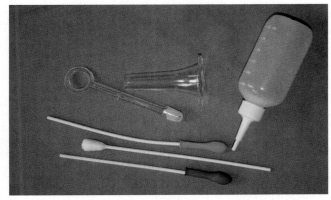

Fig. 20-7 Examination adjuncts: Disposable anoscope with obturator, rubber bulb syringe, and balloon-covered procto/rectal swabs. (Reprinted with permission from Sharon Rose Crowley, RN, Forensic CNS, Santa Cruz, CA.)

"splay" the hymenal rim. This enhances photographic contrast of partial or complete hymenal transections. A rubber-bulb syringe can be used to squirt water from directly above the vaginal opening of a prepuberal female. As the hymenal tissue "floats" inward and outward, the margins can be inspected and photographed (Crowley, 1999).

POSTMORTEM GENITAL EXAMINATION OF THE MALE VICTIM

1. Open a sealed evidence kit. Prepare and prelabel swabs and slides (Table 20-2).
2. Obtain salient case data. Include the exam date/time/site, investigating agency and case ID, examining pathologist, number of victims, type of case, and interval since discovery of body.

Table 20-2   Orifices and Swabs

SITE	ADULT	CHILD	REFERENCE
Oral	2 swabs; 1-2 dry mount slides	Same as for adult	Saliva: Gauze square or 2 saturated swabs
Vagina	4 swabs from vaginal pool; 1-2 dry mount slides; 1 wet mount slide	2 vestibular swabs (inside labia minora, over hymenal surface); 2 dry-mount slides; Pubertal: same as for female adult	Blood Head hair: 20-30 tugged hairs Chest/facial hairs: representative samples Pubic hair: 20-30 tugged hairs.
Vaginal Lavage	3 cc sterile saline or water; collect with pipette or syringe into sealed tube/vial.		
Cervix	2 swabs; no slides		
Male Genital	2 penile swabs (1 shaft, 1 glans); No slides 2 scrotal swabs, held together; No slides	Same as for adult	
External Genital	2 swabs held together; 2 slides (over surface of labia majora, fossa, fourchette)	Vulvar: 2 swabs (external surface of labia majora)	
Anal	2 swabs (inserted 2 cm, or through anoscope); 1-2 dry mount slides	2 swabs 1-2 dry mount slides	
Dried Secretions or Areas of Positive (+) Fluorescence	2 swabs (separate pair of swabs of each stain), e.g., bitemark for saliva, dried blood, semen. Smear swabs on 2 slides.	Same as for adult.	Body control swab: Moisten swab with sterile distilled water. Collect 1 sample from unstained or contralateral area of body. Label as "W.L. control," (No slides).
Debris	Collect all debris (grass, sand, loose hairs, fibers, etc), found upon gross examination. Place debris into sheet of paper; fold into bindle to minimize loss. If debris is in more than one location, collect each into separate bindle. Place bindle(s) into larger envelope.	Same as for adult	
Fingernail Scrapings	Carefully place material and scraping tool (wooden applicator, toothpick) into bindle. Collect and package each hand separately. Return evidence envelope to outer envelope.	Same as for adult.	
Pubic combings	Place bindle under buttocks; comb pubic hair toward paper to collect debris. Fold comb/brush with debris, into paper. Place folded paper into evidence envelope.		
Crusted Stains (may be semen or blood)	Collect by gently scraping with edge of clean glass slide or back of sterile scalpel blade into appropriate bindle or envelope. If material is in pubic hair, the matted hairs should be cut out and packaged separately.	Same as for adult	
Condoms	Collect the entire item. The criminalist will collect separate samples from the external and internal surfaces of the condom. Minimal handling is essential. Place condom in a paper bag/envelope. If visible liquid is present in the condom, and it cannot be sampled right away, package in an airtight container and freeze.		

*Preparation and packaging of biological evidence for criminalistics laboratory: Swabs and slides should be individually labeled and coded to show which slides were prepared from which swabs, with a notation of the date/time collected. All swabs and slides should be air-dried for 60 min in a stream of cool air. Containers for individual items (tubes, bindles, envelopes, bags) should be labeled with the patient's name, contents, anatomic site, exam facility, date/time, and the initials of the collector. A copy of the medical-legal examination form should be included in the sexual assault evidence kid. The kit should be sealed with tamper-resitant seal that includes date, time, and initials. Staples alone are an insufficient seal. (Personal Communication: E. Devine.)

(Crowley, Sharon Rose. "Postmortem Genital Examinations with Colposcopy: SART-TO-GO." Reprinted with permission, from the *Journal of Forensic Sciences*, Vol. 49, No. 6, copyright ASTM, International. 100 Barr Harbor Drive, West Conshohocken, PA 19428).

3. Record the disposition of the body at the scene. Include when, where, how the body was found; staging, ligatures.
4. Record the history. Consider past medical history, medications, lifestyle, sexual orientation, victim/suspect relationship.
5. Examine the clothing. Collect more than two sheets of paper. Note tears, stains, debris. Inspect, scan, photograph, as appropriate. Package items separately.
6. Scan the entire body for suspicious stains/fluorescence. Use a Wood's lamp or an alternate light source. Collect dried secretions and areas of positive fluorescence. Collect one body control swab. Note this information on the traumagram.
7. Evaluate for nongenital trauma. Measure, document, and photograph defense wounds, bruises, lacerations, abrasions, and bite marks. Use an L-shaped ABFO scale. Using the double-swab technique and distilled water, swab bite marks for saliva. Refer to forensic odontologist and cast per local protocol and ABFO guidelines.
8. Inspect the head/oral. Collect foreign matter/debris in the hair. Collect hair reference samples (20 to 30 representative samples). Add samples of facial hair and chest/body hair to standard reference samples. Inspect and scan the perioral area: swab if positive fluorescence. Inspect the oral cavity, frenulum, and inside lower lip for signs of trauma and petechiae. If appropriate, photograph (can use magnification with colposcope 5× or 7.5×). Collect two oral swabs and prepare one or two dry-mount slides. Collect a saliva reference sample (gauze square or two swabs).

9. Collect fingernail scrapings/cuttings. Package the left and right hand separately.

10. Examine the genital area. Evaluate and record the Tanner stage if adolescent or child victim. Inspect and scan the inner thighs, perineum, buttocks, and perianal area. Collect foreign material or matted pubic hair. Collect any dried/moist secretions.

11. Comb pubic hair, and package comb/brush into envelope. Collect 20 to 30 pubic reference samples.

12. Inspect the penis (glans, foreskin, and shaft) and the scrotum for signs of trauma (Fig. 20-8). Check the glans for injuries, abrasions, or tearing of the urethral meatus. Photograph injuries. If the victim is uncircumcised, collect any retained foreign matter or secretions underneath the foreskin. Collect two penile swabs, one from the glans and one from the shaft. Moisten the swabs slightly with distilled water. Collect two scrotal swabs but no slides (individual crime labs may request slides in addition to swabs). Moisten the swabs, and hold both together during collection. Focus on the areas of the scrotum that are in closest proximity to the shaft of the penis.

13. Inspect for anal and perianal trauma. Photograph with colposcope. Collect any dried perianal secretions using Sweet's technique. Insert the anoscope. Inspect and photograph the rectal mucosa. Collect two rectal swabs through the anoscope. Prepare one to two dry-mount slides to correspond to each rectal swab.

14. Ensure that all laboratory information has been obtained. Verify collection of urine specimen, serology, and toxicology by medical examiner.

15. Summarize the findings. Document on medicolegal forms, traumagrams; supplemental narrative dictation; document the nature and pattern of the anogenital tissues; note concomitant postmortem tissue changes (Crowley, JFS, 2004).

DOCUMENTATION OF THE POSTMORTEM GENITAL EXAMINATION

The postmortem sexual assault examination forms the framework for all medicolegal reports related to the case. This includes the following:
- Medicolegal forms
- Summary of findings
- Any supplemental narrative reports

Include a copy of the medicolegal examination form within the sealed sexual assault evidence kit for submission to the criminalist. Existing SART or medicolegal examination forms that have been designed for living sexual assault victims need to be adapted/modified for use in the postmortem venue (Crowley, JFS, 2004). A large portion of existing antemortem SART forms is usually allocated to the history of the assault, as related by a living victim who can recount details of the assault. These details include specific sexual acts, threats, and other behaviors that are salient to the assault. Other gaps in the postmortem forms are past and current medical history, medications, postassault hygiene, clothing changes, positions used during assault, and the order of sexual acts, to name a few.

Clarify in the documentation any areas where roles may have overlapped. Document on the form and narrative the "need for further review" (e.g., of additional records/reports), need to consult with forensic pathologist, or review photographs in detail. After completion of the follow-up, summarize results in a succinct addendum to the original report.

Document all examination methods utilized, including the following:
- Gross visualization
- Colposcopy
- Handheld magnifier
- Speculum examination

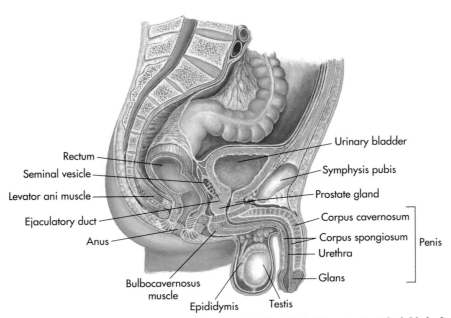

Fig. 20-8 Male pelvic anatomy. *(From Seidel, Ball, Dains, and Benedict [2006]. Mosby's Guide to Physical Examination, 6th ed. Mosby, Inc. St. Louis, MO).*

- Anoscopy
- Use of video/35-mm photos/other photographic capture method(s)

Specify adjuncts to the examination that were employed:

- Balloon-covered swabs
- Rubber-bulb syringe
- Wood's lamp or alternate light source
- Reflective photography

The items of clothing that the FNE collected should be documented. A separate section should be devoted to meticulous documentation of the evidence that was collected, packaged, and submitted to the crime laboratory, in conjunction with this evaluation (Crowley, 2004).

SUMMARY OF FINDINGS

This section of the medicolegal documentation is both a key source of information for other members of the team and a final summation of the examination process:

- Describe the nature and pattern/location of any injuries. Use conventional terminology (i.e., blunt versus sharp force trauma) to describe any findings.
- Distinguish single versus multiple sites of injury to the anogenital tissues.
- Describe the overall integrity and appearance of the anogenital tissues. This may include concomitant postmortem tissue changes (e.g., lividity, dilatation, skin slippage, or mucosal shedding) (Crowley, 2004).

DEVELOPMENT OF A TAXONOMY FOR POSTMORTEM GENITAL EXAMINATIONS

Ongoing, baseline studies of genital anatomy and the nature of postmortem tissue changes have generated a taxonomy, or classification system, to facilitate an ordered arrangement of terms. These will more accurately describe the clinical findings of the postmortem genital examination (Crowley & Peterson, AAFS, 2004).

Case Study **20-1**

Collaboration between Forensic Nurse Examiner and Criminal Investigative Profiler

The forensic clinical nurse specialist was asked by the lead detective of the coroner's division of the sheriff's department to respond to the mortuary for the autopsy of a 75-year-old, non-Hispanic, white female. Neighbors had reported that they had not seen her during routine daily activities. After peering in the window, one neighbor saw her lying on the floor. Someone called 911, and the paramedics and fire department responded, along with law enforcement.

After being pronounced dead at the scene, the victim was transported to the designated mortuary. Of note, the county had no centralized morgue at the time. Autopsies were conducted at participating private mortuaries; the homicide team responded to these sites.

The forensic clinical nurse specialist conducted the entire genital examination, including the collection of all biological specimens and reference samples for the sexual assault victim evidence kit. The genital examination was done using gross visualization. An alternate light source was also employed to facilitate visualization of the genital area. Photodocumentation via colposcopy was unavailable for this examination. Subsequent to arrest, another forensic nurse examiner conducted a suspect medicological examination at the SART facility.

Nongenital injuries to the decedent consisted of a 25-mm incised wound of the right neck, which incompletely severed the right carotid artery. Minor defense wounds were also present. A postmortem 35-mm photograph, taken by the FNE, illustrated an ecchymotic area on the victim's left inner thigh. The bruise was not located over a bony prominence; the medical examiner concurred that this injury could be consistent with forced abduction of the victim's legs by the assailant.

Genital injuries were present; these consisted of linear lacerations to the posterior fourchette, between 5 and 7 o'clock. Also present was a vaginal tear at 6:30 to 7 o'clock and hymenal ecchymosis at 6 o'clock. A subsequent analysis of biological swabs from the sexual assault evidence kit was nonconclusive.

The victim—an elderly, obese female—weighed approximately 250 pounds. The suspect—a non-Hispanic/white male in his thirties of short stature and slight build—presented a quiet, cooperative, almost meek demeanor.

Criminal investigative analysis based on the model by the FBI National Center for the Analysis of Violent Crime involves a behavioral approach to the offense from a law enforcement perspective, focusing on identification and apprehension of the offender. Salient aspects of this case were victimology, the medical examiner's report, the forensic clinical nurse specialist's report, results of crime scene analysis, and all other law enforcement reports. The significant contribution by the behavioral analyst was to provide the entire multidisciplinary team with a unique perspective that combines an overview of all facets of the crime with a repertoire of experience from similar crimes committed around the country. The victim was felt to be at moderate risk because she was elderly, alone, and suffering from physical limitations (adult-onset diabetes, hypertension, and limited mobility secondary to weight and age). The suspect targeted her as vulnerable and available. Analysis of other elements of the crime scene suggested that the motive for the crime was sexual in nature. Because the drama did not unfold in the manner envisioned by the offender, he silenced the victim by murdering her to keep his only witness from reporting him for the sexual assault.

The California medical protocol makes it succinctly clear that a significant role of the physical examiner in the evaluation of adult sexual assault victims is to obtain a clear patient history, document all sex acts, note the identify of the suspect, and record threats or use of force and any postassault activity. Subsequent to the medical examination, the examiner must determine if the physical findings are consistent/inconsistent with the history provided. Obviously, this entire facet is missing in the case of an unwitnessed homicide. The nurse examiner found physical findings that could be consistent with blunt force trauma sustained in a sexual assault. The "meek" demeanor of the assailant during the SART suspect examination and other proceedings seemed incongruous with the intensity of the sexual assault and murder of an elderly victim. The forensic clinical nurse specialist suggested that inclusion of a criminal investigative profiler might be highly efficacious to help clarify the entire homicide scenario. The collaboration of the two professional entities provided the missing link for both.

(Crowley, S., & Prodan, M. (1996). Presented at the American Academy of Forensic Sciences, Nashville, TN.)

Fraser et al. modified a 1966 World Health Organization classification system. The authors undertook a multicenter study using colposcopy to look for changes in the vaginal and cervical appearance related to sexual intercourse and other factors. They cited 'appearances' or 'conditions' in their classification of the findings of the vagina and cervix after colposcope examinations were performed on healthy sexually active females (Fraser, Lahteenmaki, Elomaa, Lacarra, Mishel, & Alvarez, 1999, p. 1974). Their classification was a useful method to describe findings in living subjects. Sommers et al. (2001 p. 256) noted that "standardized classification systems to organize severity and location of injury need to be developed and tested." Slaughter and colleagues found that the typical pattern of injury and types of genital trauma in female rape victims consisted of tears, ecchymoses, abrasions, redness, and swelling (TEARS); these were characteristic of blunt force trauma. The authors noted that the development of a taxonomy of genital trauma can help "establish a more reliable basis for forensic analysis" (Slaughter, Brown, Crowley, Peck, 1997, p. 616). A taxonomy germane to the postmortem genital examination should incorporate salient terms, such as TEARS, or other easily recognizable terms, that could be consistent and universally acceptable in the forensic community (Crowley & Peterson, AAFS, 2004).

During the evaluation of living victims, the examiner assesses the nature and pattern of wounds and injuries in living tissues. The astute examiner must also consider various factors that may influence the appearance of findings. Normal anatomical variations, nonspecific findings such as tags and adhesions, various gynecological conditions, and postmenopausal changes to the genital anatomy are all part of the differential evaluation.

The same 11 anatomical structures in the female that are the most frequent sites of trauma in living rape victims must be equally scrutinized in postmortem cases. These sites are the periurethra, labia majora, labia minora, hymen, vagina, cervix, posterior fourchette, fossa navicularis, perineum, anus, and rectum.

Factors such as lividity, rigor, postmortem interval, skin slippage, mucosal autolysis, and normal postmortem dilatation versus antemortem prolapse of the vagina, urethra, cervix, or rectum will affect the appearance of the tissues. Concomitant with this postmortem artifact may be findings consistent with injuries resulting from blunt force.

The forensic pathologist is well familiar with postmortem factors; however, the skin and mucous membranes of the anogenital area have received less specific scrutiny. Attention to detail of the anogenital sites has only recently been studied (Crowley, AAFS, 2000-2008). The utilization of colposcopy (Fig. 20-9) has further augmented the precision of evaluation (Crowley, AAFS, 2004).

This taxonomy continues to be refined through the clinical evaluation of a normative, core group of baseline cases (Crowley, AAFS, 2008, 2009). It is hoped that a taxonomy or classification system will do the following:
- Improve the diagnostic acumen of the examiner.
- Provide a theoretical framework for documentation.
- Avoid ambiguity.
- Promote consistency and reliability among examiners.

The ultimate goal of this research is to better visualize, in order to improve our understanding of what is normal and what is not in anogenital anatomy during the postmortem interval. This will allow us to more reliably compare fatal sexual violence

Fig. 20-9 Leisegang Optik2 Colposcope, with Canon Rebel Camera. (Photo courtesy CooperSurgical, Inc., 2009.

trauma to the types of injuries seen in living sexual assault victims (Crowley, 2007). To this end, careful scrutiny and meticulous documentation will both add to individual case yield and enhance our overall body of knowledge within this area (Crowley, 2008, 2009).

References

Bowers, M., & Bell, G. (1995). *Manual of forensic odontology.* (3rd ed.). Montpelier, VT: ASFO.

Brownmiller, S. (1975). *Against our will: Men, women and rape.* New York: Simon & Schuster.

Burgess, A. W., Hartman, C. R., Ressler, R. K., Douglas, J. E., & McCormack, A. (1986). Sexual homicide: A motivational model. *Journal of Interpersonal Violence, 1*(3), 251–272.

Crowley, S. R. (1998, February). *Genital exam of the sexual homicide victim by forensic nurse examiners.* Proceedings of the 50th Anniversary Meeting of the American Academy of Forensic Sciences. San Francisco, CA and Colorado Springs, CO: McCormick-Armstrong Co.

Crowley, S. R. (1999). *Sexual assault: The medical-legal examination.* Stamford, CT: Appleton & Lange.

Crowley, S. R. (2001, February). *Postmortem Genital Examinations with Colposcopy: SART-TO-GO.* Abstract/Workshort. Proceedings of the 53rd Annual Meeting of the American Academy of Forensic Sciences Annual Meeting. Seattle, WA and Denver, CO: Publication Printers.

Crowley, S. R. (2002, February). *Postmortem genital examinations.* Atlanta, GA: American Academy of Forensic Sciences (AAFS).

Crowley, S. R. (2003, February). *Postmortem genital examinations and evidentiary protocol with colposcopy.* Abstract. Proceedings of the 55th Annual Meeting of the American Academy of Forensic Sciences, Chicago, IL and Denver, CO: Publication Printers, Corp. *49*(4):18–22.

Crowley, S. R. (2003, September). *Postmortem genital examination protocol with colposcopy.* (Vol. 136). Proceedings of the 3rd European Academy of Forensic Sciences Meeting. Istanbul, Turkey and Shannon, Ireland: Elsevier.

Crowley, S. R., & Peterson, B. (2004, February) *A proposed taxonomy for postmortem genital examinations with colposcopy.* Dallas, TX: American Academy of Forensic Sciences (AAFS).

Crowley, S. R., & Prodan, M. J. (1996). *Correlation of genital findings to offender typology: Collaboration between forensic nurse examiner and criminal investigative analyst.* Nashville, TN: American Academy of Forensic Sciences (AAFS).

Crowley, S. (2004, November). A Mobile System for Postmortem Genital Examinations with Colposcopy: SART-TO-GO. *Journal of Forensic Sciences, 49*(6), 1299–1307.

Crowley, S. R. (2005, February). *To dye or not to dye: A tale of the blues.* New Orleans, LA: American Academy of Forensic Sciences (AAFS).

Crowley, S. R. (2005, June). *Colposcopy for the genital examination of victims of rape homicide.* Monastir, Tunisia: Mediterranean Academy of Forensic Sciences (MAFS).

Crowley, S. R. (2006, February). *Anogenital anatomy: Colposcopy to study the appearance and changes during the postmortem interval.* Seattle, WA: American Academy of Forensic Sciences (AAFS).

Crowley, S. R. (2006, September). *Anogenital anatomy: Use of colposcopy to study postmortem interval changes for comparison to sexual homicide.* Qawra, Malta: Mediterranean Academy of Forensic Sciences (MAFS).

Crowley, S. R. (2007, February). *To dye or magnify! A proposal to study the efficacy of toluidine blue dye vs. colposcopy in the postmortem anogenital examination.* Dallas, TX: American Academy of Forensic Sciences (AAFS).

Crowley, S. R. (2008, February). *Postmortem genital examinations with colposcopy in the evaluation of fatal sexual violence against women.* Washington, DC: American Academy of Forensic Sciences.

Crowley, S. R., & Wacker, C. (2008, February). *Evaluation of fatal sexual violence against women: Collaboration between forensic clinical nurse specialist and body donation program.* Washington, DC: American Academy of Forensic Sciences.

Crowley, S. R. (2009, February). *Evidence-based, medical-legal documentation of the postmortem anogenital examination.* Denver, CO: American Academy of Forensic Sciences.

Devine, E. M. S. (1999). Personal communication.

Dietz, P. E., Hazelwood, R., & Warren, J. (1990). The sexual sadistic criminal and his offenses. *Bull Am Acad Psychiatry Law, 18*(2), 163–178.

DiMaio, V. J., & DiMaio, D. (2001). *Forensic pathology.* (2nd ed.). Boca Raton, FL: CRC Press.

Douglas, J., Burgess, A. W., Burgess, A. G., & Ressler, R. (Eds.). (1992). *Crime classification manual* New York: Lexington Books, pp. 259–268.

Fisher, B. A. M.S., M.P.H. (2009). Los Angeles, California: Director, Los Angeles County Sheriff's Crime Laboratory, Personal communication.

Fraser, I. S., Lahteenmaki, P., Elomaa, K., Lacarra, M., Mishel, D.R., Jr., Alvarez, F., et al. (1999). Variations in vaginal epithelium surface appearance determined by colposcopic inspection in healthy, sexually active women. *Human Reproduction, 14*(8), 1974–1978.

Golden, G, D.D.S. (2008). Personal communication.

Groth, A. N., Burgess, A. W., & Holmstrom, L. L. (1977). Rape: Power, anger, and sexuality. *American Journal of Psychiatry, 134*(11), 1239–1243.

Groth, A. N. (1978). The older rape victim and her assailant. *Journal of Geriatric Psychiatry, 2*(11), 203–215.

Hagan, S. (2004). Personal communication.

Hazelwood, R. R., & Douglas, J. E. (1980). The lust murderer. *FBI Law Enforcement Bulletin, 49*(4), 18–22.

Hazelwood, R. R., & Warren, J. (1990). The criminal behavior of the serial rapist. *FBI Law Enforcement Bulletin, 59*(2), 1–17.

Hazelwood, R. R., Dietz, P. E., & Burgess, A. W. (1982, October). Sexual fatalities: Behavioral reconstruction in equivocal cases. *Journal of Forensic Science, JFSCA, 27*(4), 763–773.

Hazelwood, R. R., & Warren, J. (2000). The sexually violent offender: Impulsive or ritualistic? *Aggression and Violent Behavior, 5*(3), 267–279.

Johnson, D. J. M.S. (2009). *Assistant Professor School of Criminal Justice and Criminalistics.* Los Angeles: California State University.

National Center for the Analysis of Violent Crime. (1993). *Deviant and Criminal Sexuality* (2nd ed.) Quantico, VA.

National Center for the Analysis of Violent Crime. *VICAP (Violent Criminal Apprehension Program Crime Analysis Report).* U.S. Department of Justice. Federal Bureau of Investigation. FD-676 (Rev 4-1-98). OMB No. 1110-0011.

Peterson, B., M.D (2008, 2009). Deputy Chief Medical Examiner, Milwaukee, Wisconsin: Personal communication.

Prodan, M., Lt. (SSA). (2008, 2009). South Carolina Law Enforcement Division. Behavioral Science Unit, Columbia, South Carolina. *Profiling the Crime Scene-Behavioral Aspects of Death Investigation, and Criminal Sexuality.* North Carolina: Justice Academy.

Prodan, M., Lt. (SSA). (2009). *South Carolina Law Enforcement Division (SLED).* Columbia, South Carolina: Behavioral Science Unit, Personal communication.

Ressler, R. K., Burgess, A. W., & Douglas, J. E. (1988). *Sexual violence: Patterns and motives.* New York: Lexington Books.

Royal Canadian Mounted Police. *VICLAS (Violent Crime Linkage Analysis System).* Canada: 3364-1 (1998-12). V 1.0.

Slaughter, L., Brown, C., Crowley, S., & Peck, R. (1997). Patterns of genital injury in female sexual assault victims. *Am J Obstet Gynecol, 176*(3), 609–616.

Smerick, P. (1992). Crime scene photography. In J. Douglas, A. W. Burgess, A. G. Burgess, & R. Ressler (Eds.), *Crime classification manual* (pp. 269–298). New York: Macmillan.

Sommers, M. S., Schafter, J., Zink, T., Hutson, L., & Hillard, P. (2001). Injury patterns in women resulting from sexual assault. *Trauma, Violence & Abuse, 2*(3), pp. 240–258.

Sweet, D., Lorente, M., Lorente, J., Valenzuela, A., & Villanueva, E. (1997). An improved method to recover saliva from human skin: The double swab technique. *Journal Forensic Science, 42*(2), 320–322.

Safarik, M. E., Jarvis, J. P., & Nussbaum, K. E. (2000). Elderly female serial sexual homicide: A limited empirical test of criminal investigative analysis. *Homicide Studies, 4*(3), 294–307.

Warren, J., Reboussin, R., Hazelwood, R. R., Cummings, A., Gibbs, N. A., & Trumbetta, S. L. (1998). Crime scene and distance correlates of serial rape. *Journal of Quantitative Criminology, 14*(1), 35–59.

Warren, J., Reboussin, R., Hazelwood, R. R., Cummings, A., Gibbs, N. A., & Trumbetta, S. L. (1998). The distance correlates of serial rape. *Journal of Quantitative Criminology, 14*(1), 35–59.

ADDITIONAL REFERENCES

Brownmiller, S. (1993, January 4). Making female bodies the battlefield. *Newsweek*, 37.

Bureau of Justice Statistics. (1994). *Elderly crime victims: National Crime Victimization Survey.* Washington, DC: U.S. Department of Justice, Office of Justice Programs.

Dresang, L. (2005). Colposcopy: an evidence-based update. *J Am Board Fam Pract, 18*(5), 383–392.

Falzon, A. L., & Davis, G. G. (1998). A 15-year retrospective review of homicide in the elderly. *Journal of Forensic Sciences, 43*(2), 371–374.

Federal Bureau of Investigation. (2000). *Crime in the United States.* Washington, DC: Government Printing Office.

Kaufman, R., Faro, S., Friedrich, E., & Gardner, H. (1994). *Benign diseases of the vulva and vagina* (4th ed.). St. Louis: Mosby.

Post, T., Stiglmayer, A., Lane, C., et al. (1993, January 4). A pattern of rape: War crimes in Bosnia. *Newsweek*, 32–37.

Muram, D., Miller, K., & Cutler, A. (1992). Sexual assault of the elderly victim. *Journal of Interpersonal Violence, 7*(1), 70–76.

Sommers, M. S., Fisher, B., & Karjane, H. (2005, Spring). Using colposcopy in the rape exam: Health care, forensic, and criminal justice issues. *Journal of Forensic Nursing, 1*(1), 28–34.

CHAPTER 21 Analysis of Autoerotic Death Scenes

Mary K. Sullivan and Ann Wolbert Burgess

This chapter concerns deaths occurring in the course of auto-erotic activities in which a potentially injurious agent was used to heighten sexual arousal. Autoerotic fatalities are deaths that occur as the result of, or in association with, masturbation or other self-stimulating activity.

The majority of autoerotic fatalities involving injurious agents are accidental, but scene characteristics can lead to mistaken impressions of suicide or homicide. The fact that many autoerotic fatalities share common elements with suicide, such as finding the victim alone in a locked room or dead as a result of hanging, sometimes leads to an incorrect classification of these deaths. Other features, such as the presence of a blindfold, a gag, or physical restraints, have led to mistaken suspicions of homicide. Causes of death in these cases have included strangulation by compression of the neck, hanging, asphyxiation, smothering, choking, chest compression, and gas inhalation.

It is important for forensic nurses who assist in death investigation cases of this nature to have an understanding of the unique features of the autoerotic death scene as well as the importance of the correct classification of such fatalities. Family response to the untimely death of the victim will also be discussed.

Definition

Autoerotic death has been defined as an accidental death occurring during solitary sexual activity in which some type of apparatus, material, or substance that was used to enhance the sexual stimulation of the deceased caused unintended death. Autoerotic asphyxial death then refers to the subset of cases where hypoxia is used to enhance orgasm (Byard, 2005).

The term *asphyxia* has a variety of meanings, but in this chapter it is used synonymously with *hypoxia,* a decrease in the availability of oxygen to the tissues of the body, particularly the brain. A mild degree of asphyxia results in the familiar feeling of being out of breath, causing an increase in the frequency and depth of respiration in an unconsciously controlled effort to restore the normal levels of oxygen and carbon dioxide in the blood. Greater degrees of asphyxia produce cyanosis, loss of consciousness, convulsions, brain damage, and death. Relief from asphyxia and prompt intervention may interrupt this process at any stage before death and may be lifesaving. It is important to note that carotid arteries are occluded by a pressure of 3.5 kg, jugular veins by 2 kg, trachea by 15 kg, and the vertebral artery by 16.6 kg (Parikh, 1990).

Incidence

The precise incidence of this type of behavior has been difficult to determine, mostly because law enforcement and forensic pathologists become aware of these cases only when there has been the unexpected fatal outcome. In the United States alone, it is estimated that the death rate from these circumstances is between two and four cases per million of the population per year. Rates vary among regions and tend to be underreported (Byard, 2005).

In the spring of 1978, the Federal Bureau of Investigation (FBI) issued a mandate that original in-depth research be conducted on matters relevant to the law enforcement community. In response to this mandate, Supervisory Special Agent Robert Hazelwood requested that students at the FBI Academy submit cases for the study; 157 suspected cases were submitted to the Behavioral Science Unit over a three-year period.

The materials submitted varied somewhat between cases. In all instances, investigative reports were submitted along with either a description or photographs of the scene of death. Additional information was obtained related to interviews with the person who found the body and statements made by relatives. Writings, drawings, photographs, or notes that had been made by the victim were submitted in a number of cases. Although this collection of cases cannot be said to be a probability sample, it appears to be the largest collection of thoroughly investigated reported cases. The 157 cases were classified into four types of autoerotic death: asphyxial, atypical, partner involved, and suicide.

BEST PRACTICE The forensic nurse investigator should carefully analyze all circumstances to differentiate autoerotic death scenes from those of suicide.

Asphyxial Autoerotic Death

Asphyxial autoerotic activity was the most common form of death among those studied, accounting for 132 deaths or 84% of the sample. The asphyxial techniques most commonly recognized are compression of the neck through hanging or strangulation, exclusion of oxygen with a plastic bag or other material covering the head, obstruction of the airway through suffocation or choking, compression of the chest preventing respiratory movements, and replacement of oxygen with anesthetic agents.

It is important to note the distinction between autoerotic or sexual asphyxia on the one hand and asphyxia as a cause of death on the other. Autoerotic or sexual asphyxia refers to the use of asphyxia to heighten sexual arousal, more often than not with a nonfatal outcome.

Although not necessarily fatal, sexual asphyxial practices are clearly dangerous. The autoerotic-asphyxia practitioner who dies while engaged in autoerotic asphyxiation most often dies from an unexpected overdose of asphyxiation when, for one reason or another, the person becomes unable to terminate this means of enjoyment. From time to time, however, someone engaged in autoerotic asphyxia may die a nonasphyxial death (for example, from a heart attack, stroke, or exposure) during this activity. Conversely, it is theoretically possible that someone engaged in nonasphyxial autoerotic activities might die an asphyxial death (for example, carbon monoxide poisoning from a faulty heater or automobile exhaust system).

The overwhelming majority of victims in this sample were male and white. Of 132 persons who died by asphyxiation, 5 were female. There were 4 black males, 1 black female, 1 Native American male, 1 Hispanic male, and 1 Hispanic female. The mean age of decedents was 26.5 years. Four victims were preadolescent, 37 were teenagers, 46 were in their twenties, 28 in their thirties, 8 in their forties, 6 in their fifties, 2 in their sixties, and 1 in his seventies. Although 76 (67.9%) of the 112 decedents for whom marital data was known were single, 41 of the 132 decedents were under age 20. Available data on social class suggest that the decedents were more often middle class than upper, working, or lower class. This is an unusual observation for cases coming to the attention of medical examiners and law enforcement agencies, for members of the lowest social strata usually are disproportionately represented among traumatic deaths.

Atypical Autoerotic Fatalities

There are forms of dangerous autoerotic activity that do not involve the purposeful use of asphyxia. These activities involve a wide variety of potentially dangerous activities, such as the use of nonasphyxial sexual bondage, infibulation, electricity, insertion of foreign bodies in the urethra, vagina, or rectum, and life-threatening games.

Although it cannot be said with certainty whether these nonasphyxial dangerous practices are more widely practiced than sexual asphyxia, with the exception of electricity they seem less likely to result in death. Deaths from such activities are less prevalent than deaths during autoerotic asphyxia, and they are therefore referred to as atypical autoerotic fatalities.

Nonasphyxial autoerotic practices can result in a variety of causes of death. There were 16 such cases submitted, including death by electrocution (6), heart attack (4), poisoning (4), exposure (1), and undetermined cause (1). In two other atypical cases, autoerotic asphyxia resulted indirectly in an asphyxial death as a result of aspiration of vomitus. These 18 decedents were made up of 16 white males and 2 black females.

Sexual Asphyxial Fatalities Including a Partner

Sexual asphyxial deaths also occur in the presence of a partner. Most often, these are homicides in which a male assailant strangles, smothers, or otherwise asphyxiates a rape victim (male or female). Cases in which it was obvious that this is what occurred were not requested for this study, and none was submitted. A less common occurrence is the death by asphyxia of an individual who apparently consented to engage in sexual activity. In such instances, it is likely that there will be considerable difficulty in determining willful murder from negligent manslaughter. In addition, under certain circumstances, there may be difficulty in determining whether a sexual partner was present at the time of death.

It is also possible that a person engaged in autoerotic activity may incidentally become a homicide victim. The autoerotic activity may have nothing to do with the homicide. For example, an individual may be engaged in autoerotic activity when a burglar enters his home and kills him. The autoerotic activity may have some bearing on the homicide. In one case (not from the study sample), a wife shot and killed her husband in his bed, believing him to be her husband's lover. What she did not know at the time of the shooting was that her husband was a transvestite and had fallen asleep dressed in his female clothing after engaging in autoerotic activity.

A remote possibility that must always be borne in mind is that of a homicide scene staged to appear to be accidental autoerotic death. In one unusual case from the study, the decedent's wife, who had previously observed him engaging in autoerotic asphyxia, altered the death scene to make it appear like a homicide. Her effort was singularly unsuccessful, for she left the noose within sight and inflicted a minor stab wound that was readily shown to have been inflicted after death by asphyxia.

Autoerotic Suicides

True autoerotic suicides are rare. Over the years, many autoerotic fatalities have been mistaken for suicide, largely because the investigators were unaware of the phenomenon of autoerotic asphyxia. Thus, cases described as a suicide by unusual methods or a bizarre form of suicide are scattered throughout the literature.

In addition, some cases are factitious suicides in which family members or others have removed evidence of sexual activity to make the manner of death appear to be suicide. In one study case, for example, the decedent's wife removed the female clothing he had been wearing at death and dressed his body in a suit before calling the police.

Two study cases were autoerotic suicides that could be documented as such on the basis of antemortem behavioral indicators, such as a suicide note. There is no possible means by which to determine with certainty how often other cases may have involved clear suicidal intent. It is certainly feasible that an individual fond of dangerous autoerotic activity will include that behavior in a purposeful suicide. It is conceivable that a suicidal individual, having heard of sexual asphyxia, might choose an asphyxial method of suicide over other options in order to lessen discomfort, but this possibility remains highly speculative. Also, an individual who repetitively engages in dangerous autoerotic practices might decide to end his or her life, although there is no proof of this ever having occurred. More likely, individuals fond of sexual risk taking might escalate the risk to their lives purposefully with full knowledge that death might ensue, but without formulating a conscious intent to die on one particular occasion. Courts deciding whether to award accidental-death benefits in asphyxial autoerotic fatalities have presumed the intent of the decedent, ruling that the fact of the insured's having engaged in an obviously life-threatening act is sufficient evidence of the intent to bring about "the natural and probable consequences of the act," quite apart from whether any particular consequence was consciously intended in a given instance.

BEST PRACTICE The forensic nurse should follow these rules in a suspected autoerotic death investigation: (1) always keep an open mind because what you think you see is not always what you think you see, (2) never make a threshold diagnosis, (3) never go against what the forensic evidence indicates, and (4) never allow the seriousness of the injury to determine the manner of death (Hazelwood, June 2007).

The Autoerotic-Death Scene

As in all death investigations, the autoerotic death scene should be preserved through photographs and sketches to complement the written record. The scene will vary according to age, resources, sexual interests, and level of fantasy. The possibility of a victim's parent or spouse legally challenging the cause or manner of death listed on the death certificate should be anticipated. There have been situations in which parents have litigated cases believing their child was murdered or pressuring a local coroner to change a ruling from accident during autoerotic acts to accident due to physical exertion. Furthermore, the decedent's insurance company may also contest the manner of death when accidental-death benefits are at stake. Thus, a careful investigation and documentation of the death scene is of utmost concern.

ROLE OF FANTASY

It is important to note that fantasy and sexual preferences are key factors in autoerotic death investigations. Fantasies are the mental representations of sights, feelings, and other sensations and are a universal component of sexual arousal. These individuals attempt to duplicate the fantasy in real life as much as physically possible. The most effective fantasies vary widely among individuals.

Sexual preferences are as varied as the persons themselves. The individuality of sexual preference is such that activities abhorrent to most people are sexually arousing to others (Hazelwood, 2007, course lecture).

LOCATION

Sexual fantasies precede and accompany an autoerotic act. Thus, the individual preparing to act out fantasies typically selects a secluded or isolated location. The selection and location itself play a significant role in the victim's fantasy, and preparation is part of the arousal. The locations involved in the FBI study sample included locked rooms; isolated areas of the victim's residence such as attics, basements, garages, or workshops; motel rooms; places of employment during nonbusiness hours; summer residences; and wooded areas. The victim's desire for privacy is paramount in that all future concentration can be devoted to the minute details of the fantasy itself. The fantasy scenario depends on the use of props and may require considerable preparation time. Thus, the individual takes all precautions to avoid disruption.

Case Study **21-1**

Location of the Body

A 28-year-old repairman was discovered dead by coworkers when he failed to return to the office. His repair truck was located on a rural road approximately 2 miles from his last service call. The body was located in a heavily wooded area 250 feet from the roadway. The victim was lying facedown with the upper portion of his body resting on his forearms. Around his neck was a ⅜-inch hemp rope secured by a slipknot. The rope extended from his neck to a tree limb approximately 6 feet overhead. To the left front of the victim were four magazines depicting nude females. The victim's pants were undone, and his underwear had been lowered sufficiently to expose the penis and scrotum. Medical authorities recorded the cause of death as asphyxiation due to constricted carotid arteries.

VICTIM POSITION

Most commonly, the victim's body is partially supported by the ground, floor, or other surface. Occasionally, the victim is totally suspended. The most common position noted in the study was one in which the deceased was suspended upright with only the feet touching the surface. In most such cases, some type of ligature was around the neck and affixed to a suspension point within the reach of the victim. Accidental-death victims have been found sitting, kneeling, lying face upward or downward, or suspended by their hands.

THE INJURIOUS AGENT

The forensic nurse death investigator at the death scene is charged with the responsibility of gathering information that will allow determination of any action or lack thereof that contributed to the victim's death. That includes that the injurious agent be studied in great detail, including a careful search for and analysis of possible malfunctioning.

In the study, the most common injurious agent was a ligature of some sort that compressed the neck. Other injurious agents included devices for passing electrical current through the body; restrictive containers; obstruction of the breathing passages with gags; and the inhalation of toxic gases or chemicals through masks, hoses, and plastic bags.

In the construction or use of these devices, the individual risks miscalculation. Depending on the mechanism used, the individual may misjudge the amount of time, substance, pressure, or current.

THE SELF-RESCUE MECHANISM

The self-rescue mechanism is *any* provision that the victim has made to reduce or remove the effects of the injurious agent. This may appear insignificant to the investigator or even overlooked at first. The self-rescue mechanism may be nothing more than the victim's ability to stand up straight, thereby lessening the pressure about his neck, or it may be as involved as an interconnection between ligatures on the extremities and a ligature around the neck, thereby allowing the victim to control pressure on his neck by moving his body in a particular way or pulling on a key point. Any of a wide variety of items or potential actions that the practitioner had available may have been intended as a self-rescue mechanism. If the injurious agent is a ligature, a slipknot or knife may be involved; if locks are involved, a key may be present; if chains are involved, a pair of pliers may be nearby. As with the injurious agent itself, the possibility of a malfunction of the self-rescue mechanism must be carefully considered.

BONDAGE

The terms *bondage* and *domination* are used to describe a range of sexual behaviors closely related to the features commonly associated with autoerotic deaths. Bondage refers to the physical restraining materials or devices that have sexual significance for the user. This factor is important, for its involvement is most often responsible for the misinterpretation of these deaths as homicidal rather than accidental (Fig. 21-1). In one case, a man covered himself entirely with mud before placing a ligature around his neck. As the mud dried, it caked and constricted the skin. Examples of restrictions on the organs of sensation and expression identified in this study include hoods, blindfolds, and gags. In addition, belts, decorative chains, and other features have been observed that were presumed to be elements of symbolic bondage for the victim, as they often are for individuals who engage in other forms of sexual bondage behavior.

Fig. 21-1 Evidence of bondage using locked wrist restraints.

Case Study **21-2**

Injurious Agent: Ligature

A 32-year-old fully clothed man was found lying on his stomach on his floor. A handkerchief was over his mouth and tied behind his head. A length of rope was wound around his neck and tied with a slipknot. The rope ran down his back and was attached to a brown leather belt, which held his ankles together. His feet were pulled toward his head by the rope connecting his neck and feet. Blood had trickled from his nose and ears. The responding officers initially thought the death to be a homicide. An examination of the decedent's head revealed no blunt force trauma, and the ear and nose bleeding was properly attributed to asphyxiation. They also noted the victim's arms were free: had he not lost consciousness, he could have released the ligature by the slipknot at his neck or by cutting the rope with the serrated steak knife found on the floor nearby. On a table beside the body were two similar pieces of rope that had been tied with slipknots. He had probably practiced with those two pieces of rope before engaging in the lethal act.

Case Study **21-3**

Injurious Agent: Chloroform

A 23-year-old single white male college student was found dead, clad in a pair of shorts in his apartment that he shared with another male. His hands were secured in a pillory that rested across his shoulders. This restraining device consisted of two pieces of wood secured at one extreme by a spring-loaded hinge. Two holes, lined with gray rubber, held his wrists, and a 6-inch hole had been cut to fit the neck. Situated between the neck and one wrist aperture was a padlock. Approximately 2 feet from the victim's body was a set of keys, one of which fit the padlock securing the pillory. He was wearing a full-face gas mask with a hose leading from the mask to a metal canister, which contained 13 cotton balls saturated with chloroform, a wadded washcloth, two sheets of toilet paper, and a small bottle containing chloroform. He apparently dropped the keys, was unable to retrieve them, and lost consciousness. He died from chloroform inhalation.

Case Study **21-4**

Self-Rescue: Slipknot

A 23-year-old white female died as a result of ligature strangulation. The woman had used an extension cord to interconnect her ankles with her neck. She had used a slipknot as a self-rescue mechanism. Examination of the slipknot revealed that in tying it, her hair had become entangled in the knot, thereby preventing her from disengaging it.

KEY POINT The presence of physical restraining or bondage devices is the most common reason that autoerotic fatalities are misclassified as homicide rather than accidental.

Physical restraints in the study included ropes, chains, handcuffs, and similar devices that restricted the victim's movement. Even in obvious cases, the death investigator needs to prove it was physically possible for the victim to have placed the restraints as they were discovered. It may be necessary to duplicate bindings or knots, and for that reason, the knots should not be cut or undone before they are scrutinized.

SEXUALLY MASOCHISTIC BEHAVIOR

It will sometimes be observed that the decedent had inflicted pain upon his genitals, nipples, or other areas of the body. In addition to whatever pain may be associated with bondage restraints or constrictive materials, pain may have been induced mechanically, electrically, or through self-induced burns, piercing, or frank mutilation. Cases in the study have included a belt tightened around the scrotum, clothespins affixed to the nipples, electrical wire inserted into the penis or anus, an electrified brassiere, and cigarette burns to the scrotum. The term *infibulation* is used to describe the passing of needles or pins through the body, most often through the scrotum, penis, or nipples, but sometimes through an earlobe or the nose (Fig. 21-2). In one case, pins had been passed through each of the decedent's nipples.

ATTIRE

Sometimes the victim is attired in one or more articles of female clothing, especially undergarments. Nylon, lace, leather, rubber,

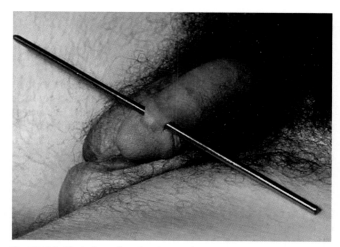

Fig. 21-2 Infibulation of penis using steel pin.

Case Study 21-5

Constriction and Restriction

A 40-year-old man was discovered dead by his wife in the basement of their home. He was totally suspended by a rope that had been wrapped several times around an overhead beam. Around his neck was a hangman's noose that had been meticulously prepared. The body was dressed in a white T-shirt, a white panty girdle with nylons, and a pair of women's open-toed shoes. His hands were bound in handcuff fashion with the wrists approximately 10 inches apart. Over his head was another girdle, and his ankles were bound with a brown leather belt. On discovering the body, the wife assumed her husband had been murdered.

The investigators correctly assessed the death as accidental and attributed the bound wrists, ankles, and covered head to sexual bondage. They recognized that the girdle covering his head was a bondage-related feature. Bodily restraint through bondage includes not only restrictions in the movement of the body but also constriction of the body and restriction of the organs of sensation and expression. Constrictive materials identified in this study included elastic garments (for example, girdles, support hose, and tight underwear) and other materials such as ace bandages.

Case Study 21-6

Masochistic Behavior

A 31-year-old white male was found suspended from a beam by a hangman's noose around his neck. His feet were touching the floor. He was nude except for a black leather belt around his waist. Handcuffs secured his wrists in front, and a key to the handcuffs was found in his right hand. Examination of his penis revealed a surgery-like incision around the circumference of the shaft. Inserted and tightened into the incision was a metal washer. The outer edge of the washer was flush with the penis shaft.

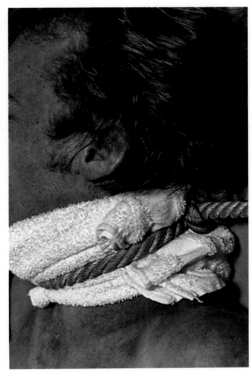

Fig. 21-3 Padded ligature mechanism used by victim in autoerotic sexual acts.

Case Study 21-7

Attire

A 16-year-old white male was discovered dead in his room by his father. When the police arrived, they found the victim lying on his back and wearing blue jeans, a T-shirt, jockey shorts, and wool socks. A belt looped on one end was near his head, as were his glasses. His father informed the officers that when originally found, his son was wearing only his T-shirt and socks. The victim's underwear and pants were on the floor at the end of the bed. The father said that he did not know why his son had been undressed when first found and that he had dressed his son without thinking.

Had the adjustment in attire not been discovered, the death might have been ruled a suicide. Close examination of the body and its lividity may reveal that attire or restraints have been adjusted, altered, or completely changed, or that the body has been moved since death.

or other materials that hold sexual significance for the victim are commonly part of his attire. The investigator needs to be aware that the attire may have been adjusted, altered, or completely changed by family members before the arrival of the investigative team. In the instances where this had been done, family members said they attributed their alterations to shame, embarrassment, or impulse. Careful examination of the body and its lividity may reveal such alterations.

PROTECTIVE PADDING

Frequently, the victim will be found with soft material between a ligature and the adjacent body surface. The purpose of this protective padding is to prevent abrasions or discoloration that might prompt inquiries from family or friends. In one case, the parents had no idea their son was involved in such dangerous activities. His mother, however, recalled that some months before her son's death she had noted burn marks on both sides of his neck. When she inquired as to their cause, he explained that the marks occurred when he had been grabbed by his jersey while playing football. When he was discovered dead, no protective padding was in place (Fig. 21-3).

SEXUAL PARAPHERNALIA

Sexual paraphernalia was found on or near the victim in many cases in the study sample. These paraphernalia included vibrators, dildos, and fetish items such as female garments, leather, and rubber items. Often materials that are present are not recognized as having a sexual meaning for the victim because they do not appeal sexually to the investigator and are dismissed as inconsequential. All items at the scene and their proximity to the body should be noted and photographed in their original positions for later interpretation. In the case of a 51-year-old single male victim, discovered fully dressed with the exception of wearing two leather jackets, and suspended by a rope around his neck and attached to a tree limb, a search of his residence revealed the following: more than 50 leather coats; ropes, chains, and handcuffs; leg irons; a penis vice; scrotum weights; electrical shock devices; discipline masks; traffic cones with fecal material on them; 107 pairs of leather gloves of which 29 were determined to have seminal stains inside; a mace with chain and spiked ball; canes; whips; and assorted padlocks.

PROPS

Items found at the death scene may have been used as fantasy props. Items so identified in this study included mirrors, commercial erotica, photographs, films, and fetish items. One wife volunteered that the bondage magazine found by her husband's body was open to his favorite bondage picture. She said he would replicate to exact detail every knot and tie in the picture. Magazines about women's fashions and hairstyles were also found in the possession of some cross-dressers. In one case, a movie projector threaded with a pornographic film was found, indicating the victim had been watching the film before or during his final autoerotic act. One man found bound and hanging, with mirrors arranged such that he could view himself, had been watching an explicitly sexual movie on cable television.

MASTURBATORY ACTIVITY

The victim may or may not have been engaged in manual masturbation during the fatal autoerotic activity. The presence of seminal discharge is not a useful clue in determining whether a death is due to sexual misadventure. Seminal discharge frequently occurs at death, irrespective of the cause or manner of death. To be sure, the existence of seminal stains on the victim or nearby surfaces should be noted, photographed, and collected for possible blood-type determination and comparison to the victim, but the mere presence of seminal staining is not evidence of sexual activity.

Manual masturbation may be suggested by finding the victim's hand on or near the genitals, but it is to be remembered that the extremities may twitch or move in the final movement of life. Other indicators of sexual activity include such findings as a dildo or vibrator in or near the body, the penis wrapped in cloth to prevent staining of garments, or exposure of the genitals of a victim who is otherwise dressed. Individuals committing suicide by hanging avoid nudity (except for prisoners). Complete nudity in death is presumptive evidence of an autoerotic death.

Frequently no direct evidence of manual masturbation exists. Indeed, some living practitioners of autoerotic asphyxia have reported that they did not manually masturbate while asphyxiating themselves but rather used asphyxiation to arouse themselves sexually, after which they would manually masturbate.

EVIDENCE OF PREVIOUS EXPERIENCE

Five types of information were found in the study that are useful in judging the extent of the victim's prior experience: information from relatives and associates, permanently affixed protective padding, suspension-point abrasions, complexity of the injurious agent, and collected materials.

Information from Relatives and Associates

Although family members, sexual partners, and friends sometimes have no awareness of the victim's dangerous autoerotic practices, they may nonetheless have observed behavior that gains meaning in retrospect. One father noted that his son was always tying knots. Another father knew that his son occasionally put a belt around his neck and tightened it until he became weak.

Permanently Affixed Protective Padding

One factor indicative of prior practice is the permanent affixing of protective padding to ligatures or devices used in the activity. This suggests that the victim has engaged in similar acts in the past and intended to do so in the future. The padding indicates the victim's intent to prevent leaving marks on the body.

Suspension Point Abrasions

If the victim's death involved the use of ligatures over or around suspension points, the forensic specialist should examine those areas and others like them for abrasions or grooves caused by similar use in the past. A young white male died while suspended from a braided leather whip that went around his neck and over the top of a closet door. The whip was secured to a wheel and tire on the opposite side of the door. His hands were free, but his ankles were loosely bound with leather thongs. The door top revealed several grooves and abrasions from previous use.

Complexity of the Injurious Agent

When the injurious agent is highly complex, it is likely that the apparatus became complex through repetitive experience and elaboration over time. One 26-year-old victim was discovered dead wearing a commercially produced discipline mask and had a bit in his mouth. A length of rope was attached to each end of the bit and ran over his shoulders, going through an eyelet at the back of a specially designed belt he was wearing. The pieces of rope ran to eyelets on both sides of his body and were connected to wooden dowels that extended the length of his legs. The ropes were attached to two plastic water bottles, one on each ankle. The bottles were filled with water and each weighed 7 pounds. The victim's ankles had leather restraints about them. A clothespin was affixed to each of the victim's nipples. The victim's belt had a leather device that ran between his buttocks and was attached to the rear and front of the belt. This belt device included a dildo that was inserted into his anus and an aperture through which his penis protruded. His penis was encased in a piece of pantyhose and a toilet-paper cylinder. A small red ribbon was tied in a bow at the base of his penis.

Collected Materials

The type, quantity, complexity, and cost of sexual materials collected by the victim provide indirect evidence of the duration of these activities. Although in most instances the victim will be found in close proximity to this collection of sexual materials, the forensic specialist should assess other areas that are known to be under the control of the victim for additional materials.

FAMILY RESPONSE

Although the forensic and law enforcement literature describes the investigative and medical components of autoerotic deaths, little exists in the behavioral or social science literature that describes this type of fatality or the response of family members and others. This absence may be attributed largely to (1) misdiagnosis of suicide or homicide rather than accident, and thus an underreporting of this manner of death, (2) a general acceptance and encouragement of all types of consenting sexual activity and a concomitant reluctance to acknowledge or emphasize the dangerous component in certain sexual activities (e.g., sexual bondage), and (3) the social stigma surrounding sexually motivated death.

With regard to the investigator's communication with the victim's family, Vernon Geberth (2003) said it best:

As professional investigators we are entrusted with a professional duty and responsibility not only to the deceased but also to the surviving family. It is imperative that by our professional and nonjudgmental demeanor that we do all in our power to assist the surviving family members. After considering the family's ability to cope with the facts of the case, it is imperative to note that each case and set of circumstances will dictate the proper course of action with regards to notification. (Geberth, p. 154, 2003)

Clearly there is a need to alert forensic nurses and mental health professionals about young people who engage in this type of activity so that they and their families can be counseled. This need has been heightened through the study, as researchers learned of parents of young victims who had been shocked at the sudden death of their children and who had known nothing about the manner of these deaths. If parents who have lost children to this type of death believe it is timely to talk about the subject, not only to investigators but to the news media, then forensic nurses whose work may bring them into contact with these families need accurate information also.

TRAUMATIC NEWS

There is no news that has so great a psychological effect on survivors as the death of a family member or close associate. Although many factors influence the severity of a stress reaction to a traumatic grief event, the emotional response is particularly devastating when a family member or friend discovers the body, when the death is untimely, when the decedent is young, and when the death is sexual in nature. These are the factors generally present in autoerotic fatalities.

The discovery of the body can occur in several ways. In the majority of cases in this sample, the victim was found dead by a family member or friend. Of the 34 cases with data from the teenage group, 25 parents discovered their son dead. Of the 17 cases with data on married victims, 11 were found dead by their wives. In the unmarried group, out of 59 cases with data, 10 parents and 9 relatives found the decedent. More frequently in this group, the victim was found dead by friends, roommates, landlords, janitors, maids, employers, colleagues, police, or search parties.

On learning of the victim's death, friends and family were invariably stunned and shocked. The victim was usually described as having been in good spirits and physical health, as active, and having a future orientation. There was rarely any suspicion of suicidal ideation.

A sexual death resulting from the use of an injurious agent during a masturbatory ritual is considered an unusual type of death because many people, professionals included, have never heard of it. Although many people are familiar with autoerotic practices using manual stimulation, it appears that a significantly smaller number of people are aware of techniques for reducing oxygen to the brain to achieve an altered state of consciousness and to enhance erotic sensations and fantasy. The sexually associated features of this type of death puzzle and confuse family members.

Family members often helped investigators to determine if the victim had prior experience with autoerotic asphyxia. Some associates or relatives reported no prior awareness of the victim's activity. In other cases, relatives made pertinent observations but, lacking the knowledge of dangerous autoerotic activity, failed to attach significance to the victim's preoccupation with tying knots, signs of red marks on the victim's neck, bloodshot eyes, or confused behavior for short time periods.

Case Study 21-8

Accident or Suicide?

A 30-year-old married man had stayed home alone for three hours while his wife, who was eight months pregnant, and their two children went to a church-related activity. On her return, she discovered him dead in an upstairs bedroom that he was converting to a nursery. The victim was suspended from a rope that encompassed his neck and was attached to a pulley. A second rope passed over the pulley and ended in his left hand. The pulley was hooked to a metal bar, which extended between two beams in the roof. His feet were touching the floor, his pants were around his ankles, his underwear was semen-stained in front, and his shirt had been rolled up to expose his chest. The cause of death, as determined by the medical examiner, was asphyxiation due to hanging.

This case was submitted for opinion by the attorney for the executrix of the decedent's estate. His widow was involved in litigation with her husband's insurance company concerning the accidental-death-benefits clause of his life insurance policy.

The evidence in this case is consistent with accidental death. The victim used a pulley apparatus with two ropes. One rope went over the pulley and attached to his neck with a hangman's noose; the second rope served a control or braking function. By maintaining pressure on a braking rope, he could prevent the pulley from turning. This, in turn, would allow the noose to compress his neck and alter the flow of blood to his brain, producing a transient hypoxia, the extent of which he could control, at least while conscious. He could then loosen the ligature by allowing the control rope to slip or, should he lose consciousness, the control rope would slip from his grasp, automatically slackening the rope attached to his neck: a dead man's release. On this occasion, one rope had slipped off the track and jammed the pulley, preventing its rotation and resulting in his body weight being suspended from the rope, thereby causing his death.

The victim hid this sexual activity from his family and friends. At the time he died, his family had been at church, and he had removed the telephone from its cradle to prevent calls from interrupting his autoerotic activity.

The hangman's noose used for the ligature had symbolic value to the victim, who probably had an execution fantasy. His history also suggested a fascination with bondage activities in that he collected handcuffs, ropes, and locks and was very knowledgeable about the various types of knots.

The complexity of the apparatus he used strongly suggests prior practice. Rather than simply hanging himself, he used a sophisticated pulley system as part of his autoerotic ritual. On prior occasions, he was apparently able to engage in this activity without serious consequences.

The victim was described as being in excellent spirits, oriented toward the future, enjoying good physical health, and being interested in his work and family. His recent weight reduction was said to have improved his self-image. No precipitating stresses were identified, and there was no history of psychiatric disorder. His wife reported their life together as being at its highest point, with good prospects both financially and personally. If he had intended suicide, he would not have required an elaborate pulley system to achieve this aim.

KEY POINT When investigating asphyxial deaths, "Do not get bogged down in theory and hypothetical speculation. In death investigation, there are no absolutes." (Geberth, p. 152, 2003)

The families' reactions to the manner of death depended on how, when, and what they were told. There were cases in which the manner of death was quickly determined to be accidental and reported to the family. In others, the death was initially labeled a suicide or homicide and later reversed to accidental. Thus, the family members may have to deal with a change in their conception of the manner of death or with uncertainty for a time.

Families were noted to respond in several ways to the manner of death. In some cases, the families accepted the victim's death because they had strong feelings about alternative manners of death, with one mother commenting this type of death was "just a shade below suicide." There are some families who accepted that the victim had died accidentally but would not accept the nature of the death as sexual. Parents of a 21-year-old college student were successful in having the cause of death changed on the death certificate. And there were a few cases in which the family would not accept the determination that the death was accidental. Most often these families believed the death was a homicide and became angry with investigating officers for closing the case prematurely. Some families were upset and angry with the victim and refused to believe anything. One family refused to bury a son after learning that his death was sex related.

FORENSIC ISSUES

The most frequent question that arises in the death investigation of sexual fatalities is whether an individual who was alone committed suicide or died accidentally. Less often, the question posed is whether another person had been present and, if so, whether the death was intended or not. These questions involve complex issues of fact, behavior, and intent and are not always answerable. Opinions should not be rendered in such cases without detailed information about both the death scene and the victim's history.

Summary

There are problems for the person engaging in autoerotic activity, because the stigma and secrecy surrounding the behavior prevent him or her from disclosing. There are problems for families in dealing with this type of sexual activity, because they may not know about it, know how to look for signs, or what to do if they do discover their child with sexually oriented equipment. There are problems for therapists, because there is no specific psychiatric diagnosis or appropriate discussion of this behavior.

Attention has been called to autoerotic activity because of the awareness of the sizable number of deaths resulting from it, such that mental health clinicians cannot ignore it. Forensic nurse specialists can educate others about the type of activity and warn of its lethality. The study emphasized that families want basic information about the manner in which they have lost their loved ones, as well as emotional support through their grieving process.

Resources

ORGANIZATIONS

American Academy of Forensic Sciences
410 North 21st Street, Colorado Springs, CO 80904-2798; 719-636-1100; www.aafs.org
American Foundation for Suicide Prevention
120 Wall Street, 22nd Floor, New York, New York 10005; 212-363-3500 or 888-333-AFSP; www.afsp.org
National Association of Medical Examiners
430 Pryor Street SW, Atlanta, GA 30312; 404-730-4781 www.thename.org

WEBSITES

Law-Forensic.com
www.law-forensic.com/autoerotic_2.htm
Literature review of autoerotic asphyxia and fatalities
Silent Victims
www.silentvictims.org

References

Byard, R. W. (2005). Autoerotic death. In J. Payne James, R. W. Byard, T. Corey, C. Henderson (Ed.), *Encyclopedia of forensic and legal medicine* (Vol I). Oxford, England: Elsevier, Academic Press.

Geberth, V. (2003). Sexual asphyxia and autoerotic fatalities. In *Sex-related homicide and death investigation: Practical and clinical perspectives*. New York: CRC Press.

Hazelwood, R. (2007). *Lecture presented in the Violent Behavior Program.* Manassas, VA: Academy Group, Inc., Equivocal Deaths Lecture.

Hazelwood, R. R., Dietz, P. E., & Burgess, A. W. (1997). *Autoerotic fatalities*. West Newton, MA: Awab.

Kinsey, A. C., Pomeroy, W. B., Martin, C. E., et al. (1948). *Sexual behavior in the human male*. Philadelphia: Saunders.

Kinsey, A. C., Pomeroy, W. B., Martin, C. E., et al. (1953). *Sexual behavior in the human female*. Philadelphia: Saunders.

Masters, W. H., & Johnson, V. E. (1966). *Human sexual response*. Boston: Little, Brown.

Mendelson, J. H., Dietz, P. E., & Ellingboe, J. (1982). Postmortem plasma luteinizing hormone levels and antemortem violence. *Pharmacol Biochem Behav, 17*(1), 171–173.

Money, J., & Ehrhardt, A. A. (1972). *Man & woman, boy & girl: The differentiation and dimorphism of gender identity from conception to maturity*. Baltimore: Johns Hopkins University Press.

Parikh. (1990). Parikh's Textbook of Medical Jurisprudence. *Forensic medicine and toxicology for classroom and courtrooms. Violent asphyxial deaths* (6th ed.). Delhi, India: CBS Publishers and Distributions

Paulos, M. A., & Tessel, R. E. (1982). Excretion of B-phenethylamine is elevated in humans after profound stress. *Science, 215*(4536), 1127–1129.

Walker, A., Milroy, C. M., Payne-James, J. (2005). In J. Payne James, R. W. Byard, T. Corey, C. Henderson (Ed.), *Encyclopedia of forensic and legal medicine* (Vol. I). Oxford, England: Elsevier, Academic Press.

CHAPTER 22 Taphonomy, NecroSearch, and Mass Grave Exhumation

Deborah Storlie and John R. McPhail

This chapter explores how the application of taphonomy principles helps investigators to discover the truth about the events leading to the suspicious death of victims found in clandestine graves. Throughout the international community, there are reported incidents of human atrocities. These atrocities range from single-victim crimes to mass genocides. Often victims and evidence related to the human rights violations are buried in a clandestine grave. A clandestine grave "represents an intrusion into the natural and/or ambient environment" (www.necrosearch.org, 2009).

Science of Taphonomy

Taphonomy is the study of the fate of human remains after death (Haglund & Sorg, 1997). A vivid imagination is required to entertain all of the physical, environmental, and circumstantial possibilities that might alter a body that has been hastily abandoned in the woods or buried in a shallow grave as opposed to one that received a contemporary burial when the body is carefully prepared, perhaps embalmed, protected in a sealed casket and vault, and placed into the ground or mausoleum crypt. As Haglund noted, at clandestine gravesites, the body influences the surroundings as much as the surroundings influence what happens to the body (James & Nordby, 2005). This dynamic interaction can assist medical death investigators in determining when the body was deposited at a given location and whether or not it has been moved, be it by criminal design or by the acts of nature, animal scavengers, or other natural forces.

TAPHONOMY IN THE FORENSIC CONTEXT

Taphonomy was developed within the disciplines of paleontology, archaeology, and paleoanthropology (Haglund & Sorg, 1997). Forensic taphonomy focuses on reconstructing events at and following death. This is done through collection and analysis of data, distinguishing perimortem and postmortem alteration of remains, estimating how long the remains have been at the site, and estimating time of death.

GRAVE LOCATIONS

Human remains may be encountered in mountains, glaciers, deserts, rain forests, and farm fields, and it is imperative to answer questions about what happened to the body before death, at the time of death, and after the remains ultimately reached a final resting place. Each of these sites is likely to produce important information regarding the length of time since death and how body decomposition and dispersal has been affected by the unique environmental characteristics of each locale. The taphonomist, working with other

forensic investigators, is better able to answer these questions after having studied similar scenarios where known characteristics can be matched. However, some of these case findings are so unique that little or no prior information is known about the normal processes of decomposition and disarticulation in that given location.

The increasing importance of such knowledge was the stimulus for the origination of NecroSearch International, Inc., a nonprofit, volunteer organization dedicated to research, education, and investigation in the location of clandestine graves, the recovery of the remains, and the investigation of associated evidence in and around the graves (France, Griffin, Swanburg, et al., 1997). Volunteers consist of individuals from law enforcement, investigations, serology and chemistry, forensic nursing, forensic anthropology, archaeology, entomology, geology, pedology, geophysics, geochemistry, petrology, photography and aerial photography, thermal imagery, meteorology, botany, wildlife biology, and criminal psychology. Naturalists and computer data analysts are the other valuable personnel associated with the project. Scent-detecting dogs and their handlers, as well as other outside resources, may be obtained as needed in certain phases of the project studies.

HISTORY OF TAPHONOMY

The concept of utilizing scientific techniques in locating clandestine graves originated in 1987 by a group of law enforcement investigators and scientists who were frustrated by conventional grave location methods such as large-scale ground searches and trial-and-error excavations employing heavy equipment (France, Griffin, & Swanburg, et al., 1992; Haglund, Reichert, & Reay, 1990; Imaizumi, 1974). In 1986, law enforcement originated a search on a 2200-acre ranch located approximately 30 miles west of the Kansas border near Stratton, Colorado. According to information provided by an informant, up to a dozen bodies had been buried in an area of several square kilometers over the course of several years. Three bodies were unearthed and recovered through the use of backhoes, which unfortunately destroyed not only the crime scene but also much of the evidence. The remaining area was then arbitrarily trenched and plowed as investigators searched for further remains but turned up none. Because of the destructive and intrusive methods used in the search, further detection utilizing scientific methods proved ineffective. It was then and is still believed that additional bodies remain undiscovered on the property.

Because of the limitations found with traditional methods in the location and excavation of clandestine graves, the basis of the NecroSearch research began with Project PIG ("Pigs in Ground"). In 1988, a study of the relationships between buried pig carcasses and their surroundings was implemented using various techniques from the scientific community and applying the results to actual cases of buried human remains. The multidisciplinary project involved law enforcement agencies, scientists, private businesses, and academicians (France, et al., 1992). The information gained in this research had traditionally been obtained separately if at all. It should be noted that there is no singular technology that can determine if a body is buried beneath the surface; however, a compilation of all the techniques can identify a particular site or number of sites that are the most likely to be the location of a clandestine grave. In the same vein, compiling these techniques may also determine that there are no disturbances beneath the surface in a given area, saving time and unnecessary excavations (Hoving, 1986; Killam, 1989). Success is not always measured in recovery of remains, but sometimes in knowing where not to dig.

RESEARCH STRATEGY

Pigs were originally used for burial at the research site, and they continue to be used for the following reasons. First, Colorado law does not allow human cadavers to be used for these types of studies. Second, pigs have a fat-to-muscle ratio similar to humans, and their skin is not heavily haired. The pigs used in this research were similar to humans in weight (70 kg/154 pounds), although some smaller pigs were included to simulate bodies of different ages or sizes. Third, pigs have been previously used in studies of patterns and rates of decay and scavenging because they have been considered to be similar to humans biochemically as well as physiologically.

The site of the original NecroSearch project was approximately 20 miles south of Denver, Colorado, on the Highlands Ranch Law Enforcement Training Facility property (Fig. 22-1). The site was selected because it offered proximity to human and physical resources and yet had strict operating procedures and security barriers to control public access. Baseline data, including a series of black-and-white aerial photographs, geophysical measurements, and environmental observations of the site, were carefully recorded before the burial of the first pig. Aerial photography is the least destructive method, because it is virtually nonintrusive. It provides an excellent characterization of a particular site, including the access, culture, drainage, and topography. In addition, an extremely large area can be covered in a relatively short time. Preburial photographs may be available from a variety of sources including the U.S. Geological Survey (USGS), county planning boards, utility companies, and railroads.

Fig. 22-2 A pig ready for burial at the research site.

BASELINE DATA

Near-field factors (i.e., interacting with the burial system) and far-field factors (i.e., uninfluenced by the burial system) were recorded before and after the burial of each pig carcass to appreciate physical site disturbances associated with the burial processes (Fig. 22-2). Other research components included calibration pits (graves without an interred pig) and a control site (undisturbed at both the surface and the subsurface). The latter site is necessarily remote from where pigs have been interred. The back dirt (i.e., excess soil deposited near the perimeter of the grave or calibration pit) serves as a valuable marker of gravesites, useful even with aerial photography used to identify near-field characteristics. Vegetation growth patterns, soil markings associated with excavational boundaries, and snow settled in grave depressions were phenomena visible from the air. Because an extended period must elapse before the gravesite returns to its original state, pig burial sites continue to be monitored and photographed on a regular basis. Climatic conditions, seasonal changes, and freezing/thawing cycles affect soil properties and change the land's appearance when viewed from the air (Fig. 22-3). The best aerial photographs result from using a large film format, which allow investigators to fully appreciate the details of vegetative or terrain changes.

Fig. 22-1 View of the Project PIG site at Highlands Ranch Law Enforcement Training Facility located south of Denver, Colorado.

Fig. 22-3 Gravesite after a fresh snowfall. Note the high visibility because of the contrast. Using aerial photography with the photographs taken in early morning or late afternoon also makes depressions and backfill more visible because of the shadows created.

ENVIRONMENTAL MARKERS

Researchers prepared a list of all plants within the law enforcement training site including all plants growing on graves, calibration pits, and back dirt areas. When a grave has been created and a body buried, certain vegetation is destroyed and secondary successions are set into motion (Bass & Birkby, 1978). Five years after the pig burials, it was noted that undisturbed plots contained the greatest diversity in plant species, both weeds and wild flowers. After burials, the plots showed little species diversity. Although eventually other species invaded from the surrounding undisturbed areas, plots did not recover the plant mixture that they originally possessed. It should be noted, however, that even in graves that no longer contained pigs because of intentional disinterment or animal scavenging, revegetation characteristics were identical to those that still contained a pig. Warmth associated with a decaying pig in the ground and the presence of certain nutrients added to the soil did not seem to support or inhibit plant growth. It is evident from the NecroSearch findings that knowledge of native plants in an area can provide valuable clues to the site of a clandestine grave, particularly where the vegetation is largely otherwise undisturbed.

Burial of a corpse hinders the normal faunal succession of arthropods, many of which are useful as forensic indicators (Smith, 1983). Control sites with traps were created to study airborne and surface insects at 1, 2, 4, 7, 12, 25, and 30 days post-pig burial. There were no readily visible entomological indicators of the buried pigs, such as surface stains from saponification or liquefaction 30 days after the burial. The blowfly (*Calliphora vomitoria*) was noted in the Malaise trap within 24 hours of burial, and *Phormia regina* arrived 48 hours postburial. In two weeks, significant numbers of blowflies were trapped at the active graves compared to control sites. Pit traps did not capture any arthropods, typically considered to be forensic indicators (Payne, King, & Beinhart, 1968).

ASSETS AND LIMITATIONS OF DETECTION TOOLS

When searching for clandestine graves, the team must consider many factors when choosing tools and other resources to aid in their work. The place, weather, and season are just a few of the factors that must be carefully considered. Methods used to detect clandestine graves include aerial photography, geology, botany, entomology, geophysics and magnetics, electromagnetics, ground penetrating radar, self-potential, soil gas, metal detection, thermal imagery, decomposition dogs, naturalists, archaeologists, and forensic physical anthropologists. The methods selected to aid in the search efforts maximize the team's efforts and minimize any impact on the environment.

Many methods are considered advantageous because they are nonintrusive; however, often these methods can also be limiting. For example, ground-penetrating radar is nonintrusive, yet it is limited because the equipment is difficult to obtain. In the same way, a metal detector is relatively nondestructive and nonintrusive and can easily detect bullets, jewelry, and other metallic objects (Fig. 22-4). However, this method assumes there is metal on the body.

Mass Graves

NecroSearch International has combined scientific research and the science of taphonomy to provide the international community with tools to utilize in locating clandestine graves. These pressure tested methods are becoming increasingly beneficial as the search and discovery of mass graves gains global attention.

Fig. 22-4 A metal detector in excavation is useful for the detection and recovery of metal objects such as bullets, belt buckles, or jewelry.

Bodies are buried in mass graves for a number of reasons. Governments may use mass graves following natural disasters out of necessity to contain disease. Other mass graves contain victims and evidence of human rights abuses. Per the United Nations (UN), around the globe, extralegal, arbitrary, and summary executions include (1) political assassinations, (b) deaths resulting from torture or ill-treatment in prison or detention, (3) deaths resulting from enforced "disappearances, (4) deaths resulting from the excessive use of force by law-enforcement personnel, (5) executions without due process, and (6) acts of genocide. In the majority of cases, mass graves are a method used to dispose of and hide remains. Forensic experts are often called on to exhume the bodies and to make positive identifications. In cases of human rights abuses, forensic experts are also solicited to determine the chronology of events leading to death for the purpose of bringing the perpetrators to justice and preventing similar events from occurring. Often these killings are deliberate, unlawful, and politically motivated. These deaths are considered homicides (Kirschner & Hannibal, 1994).

The United Nations has accepted the definition of mass graves as "locations where three or more victims of extra-judicial, summary or arbitrary executions were buried, not having died in combat or armed confrontations." (United Nations: ICTY) The intent of conducting mass grave exhumations is to corroborate witness testimony, to recover evidence related to reported events of wrongful death, to document injuries, and to recover human remains.

Mass gravesites can support witness testimony and provide irrefutable evidence that crimes such as summary executions were committed. John Gerns, forensic expert of the United Nations' International Crime Tribunal for the former Yugoslavia (ICTY), stated, "Regardless of the reliability of the witness, testimonial evidence without corroborating physical evidence can be the most contentious and weak form of evidence in an investigation or during the subsequent trial" (United Nations: ICTY).

KEY POINT Postmortem examinations are generally done for the purpose of determining the cause and manner of death and to collect and record data to aid in the identification of mortal remains. (Skinner, Alempijevic, & Djuric-Srejic, 2003).

Mass grave exhumations have been called "a milestone in the rendering of international justice" (United Nations: ICTY, no date). Before the 1980s, documentation of human rights abuses was almost entirely through witness and victim testimony. From 1984 to 1985, forensic scientists from the United States, working under the auspices of the American Association for the Advancement of Science, exhumed skeletal remains for identification of disappeared persons in Argentina. "It became apparent that medical and forensic verification of torture and extra-judicial executions could provide irrefutable evidence that such activities had taken place" (United Nations: ICTY, no date). Such missions have been conducted in more than 30 countries including Bosnia-Herzegovina, Kosovo, El Salvador, and Guatemala, to name only a few.

Consulting Scientists in Death Investigation

Several types of scientists may be enlisted to assist the forensic medical examiner in determining the cause and manner of death when the death has been recent and the identity of the individual is known. However, when a partially decomposed body or skeletal remains are discovered in a remote area or at a clandestine gravesite, new questions arise that mandate the use of additional experts, including forensic anthropologists, archaeologists, botanists, naturalists, and climatologists. Anthropologists can be very helpful in answering certain questions, such as the following:

• Are the bones from an animal or a human?
• If human, what is the approximate age, race, gender, and stature of the individual?
• Have scavenging animals disarticulated the body or damaged bones?
• If there are defects in the body assemblage, were they caused by premortem or postmortem events?
• What effects have plants, animals, weather, and climate had on the body over time?

In some instances, archaeologists will be involved in distinguishing contemporary burials from ancient ones. When the geological period of the burial site is in question, paleontologists are consulted. Botanists, naturalists, climatologists, and geologists can also help to answer many questions for forensic death investigators.

Stages of Exhumation

Mass grave exhumations involve many partitioned activities that can be grouped into four stages. Each calls on the skills of the experts described earlier. Forensic nurse examiners (FNEs) offer knowledge and skills that complement or expand on those of other forensic professionals. Forensic nurses can be utilized in the field and can be a valuable asset throughout the entire exhumation process and postexhumation analysis. Therefore, forensic nurses interested in this activity should present their skills and

training to groups such as Physicians for Human Rights and make a place for themselves in the exhumation process.

The first stage is the identification and exhumation of a gravesite using forensic recovery methods. Following the careful, well-planned exhumation of the remains, the second stage, postmortem identification, is attempted using a variety of techniques. Autopsy and laboratory results, along with investigation reports, then allow for reconstruction of the crime scene and the criminal activities leading to death. This is the third stage. The ultimate goal, and final stage, is the identification and prosecution of the perpetrator(s). This chapter discusses the primary issues encountered at each stage, emphasizing the role of the FNE in contributing to the success of the mission. The four stages allow the forensic investigation team to discover the truth about the events leading to the suspicious death of victims in mass graves by seeking to answer, at a minimum, the set of questions outlined in Table 22-1, as defined in the United Nations Manual on the Effective Prevention and Investigation of Extra-Legal, Arbitrary and Summary Executions, U.N. Doc. E/ST/CSDHA/.12 (1991).

Regardless of the circumstances of exhumation, a chain of custody must be followed for recovered evidence to be admissible at trial. Clyde Snow, the world-renowned forensic anthropologist, emphasized the gravity of the forensic examiner role while exhuming a mass grave in Vukovar, Croatia: "Lose one tooth or even a foot bone and you're an accomplice to the crime" (Stover, p. 14, 1997).

The greatest injustice that can be done to the wrongfully executed and their family, second only to ignoring evidence, is the improper collection of evidence so as to make it inadmissible in court. Mass graves exhumed by formal forensic teams are exhumed for forensic reasons relating to prosecution charges. Additionally, local governments may conduct exhumations for the primary purpose of identification of missing and disappeared persons. The importance of standards for proper investigation into all cases of suspicious deaths has been formally recognized since 1988.

The physical exhumation usually takes about a month, depending on the number of bodies to be exhumed and extraneous circumstances. According to Federal Bureau of Investigation (FBI) special agent Tom O'Conner, who worked with teams in Kosovo to exhume mass graves, "on average a team of 8 or 9 investigators can exhume 5 or 6 bodies a day" (Lumpkin & Chang, 2002). The forensic and pathological examinations require considerably more time.

KEY POINT The very existence of mass graves, alone, does not provide proof of criminality because many possible explanations may exist for their creation. Plagues, famine, and mass disaster in Third World countries all produce dangerous health situations that demand the rapid mass burial of victims to prevent further deaths from disease.

Table 22-1 Purpose of Inquiry at Each Stage of Mass Grave Exhumation*

PURPOSE OF AN INQUIRY	RELATED STAGE OF MASS GRAVE EXHUMATION
To recover and preserve evidentiary material related to the death to aid in any potential prosecution of those responsible	Stage 1
To identify possible witnesses and obtain statements from them concerning the death	Stage 1
To identify the victim	Stage 2
To determine the cause, manner, location, and time of death, as well as any pattern or practice that may have brought about the death	Stage 3
To distinguish between natural death, accidental death, suicide, and homicide	Stage 3
To identify and apprehend the person(s) involved in the death	Stage 4
To bring the suspected perpetrator(s) before a competent court established by law	Stage 4

*United Nations Manual on the Effective Prevention and Investigation of Extra-Legal Arbitrary and Summary Executions, U.N. Doc. E/ST/CSDHA/.12 (1991)

STAGE 1: EXHUMATION STRATEGIES AND FORENSIC RECOVERY METHODS

Primary Issues

Before beginning exhumation, preparatory work must be completed. This involves two stages: (1) searching for the site, and then (2) preparing the site for exhumation. Searching for the site is often the first of many challenges. Investigation begins before exhumation is started through interviews with witnesses and a detailed survey of the area. The crime scene investigators incorporate witness statements, previous investigative and casualty data reports, alterations to the landscape, and evidence distribution to determine the area most likely to contain human remains (Hoshower, 1998). At times, the local government is asked to inform investigators of mass grave locations. Satellite photographs are also used to locate areas of disturbed earth and vegetation (Hoshower, 1998). Those trying to locate a mass burial site also rely on infrared film to detect heat emitted from a decomposing body as tissue begins to rot. The gravesite should be identified and treated as a crime scene where homicides took place. This includes any location where physical or trace evidence may be found. Electronic mapping procedures precisely measure and map the entire grave area.

KEY POINT The crime scene begins where the suspect(s) changed intent into action and continues through the escape route.

Searching for the Site: Evaluation Tools

Many methods, strategies, and resources are used to assist in detecting clandestine graves. They include photography; interpretation of the environment through geological, geophysical, botanical, and entomological sciences; and thermal imagery (Figs. 22-5, 22-6, and 22-7). Additional evaluation strategies include team augmentation using decomposition or scent-detecting dogs and the consultation of additional personnel, such as naturalists, archaeologists, and forensic physical anthropologists.

Geophysical

Three specific geophysical tools have been proven most useful to identify the location of a clandestine gravesite: magnetics (MAG), electromagnetics (EM), and ground-penetrating radar (GPR). These geophysical tools can be efficiently run using portable equipment (Davenport, Lindemann, Griffin, et al., 1998). Portable computers in the field can be used to gather and store MAG and EM survey data for presentation as contour maps or individual profiles. Real-time GPR data are acquired in real-time formats and can be used immediately by field investigators. EM surveys have proven to be more useful than MAG surveys because the ground conductivity changes over graves as a result of the increased porosity of the backfill materials. EM surveys may be used to determine changes in ground conductivity and to detect ferrous and nonferrous metals in the soil. A GPR survey, however, seems to be the most useful method for finding and delineating gravesites because expert GPR technicians can readily identify soil changes and excavation patterns. Enhancements provided by color monitoring of the GPR systems allow investigators to easily identify changes in soil horizons over actual gravesites (Sheriff, 1983).

BEST PRACTICE Utility records for existing buried power lines, sewer lines, gas lines, and water lines should be obtained because they may produce artifacts and reduce the specificity of geophysical magnetic field readings.

Fig. 22-5 Field study personnel on case site using ground penetrating radar (GPR). (The box is the antenna of the GPR.)

Fig. 22-6 Researcher preparing remote-controlled helicopter for flight. Attached underneath the helicopter is a 35-mm camera, also remote controlled.

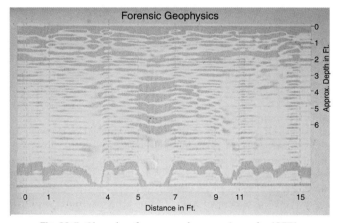

Fig. 22-7 Chart data from ground-penetrating radar (GPR).

Soil Gas

A soil gas survey performed at the research site can be a useful technique for locating graves. However, this technique is labor intensive. Background levels of methane and other volatile compounds must be determined for the entire research site, and near-field readings must be taken directly over graves and calibration pits. Certain soil types and above-freezing temperatures provide the most favorable results when using gas surveys (Kelly, 1989).

Thermal Imagery

Far-field thermal imagery of steady-state and dynamic scenes can be obtained by panning the camera across the terrain of the research site; aiming the camera toward and fixing it on each grave and calibration pit provides near-field information for researchers. Aerial photography combined with infrared photography (forward-looking infrared, or FLIR) has been successfully used in searches for buried bodies (Dickinson, 1977). A FLIR system offers high resolution but requires a truck mount. Experts believe that the use of infrared should not be limited to detecting heat-related changes associated with decomposition. It is also valuable for detecting compaction or density differences between the disturbed and undisturbed ground, and therefore it can be used to detect gravesites, even years after heat-generating decomposition has ceased (McLaughlin, 1974).

Scent-Detecting Dogs

The use of scent-detecting dogs or decomposition dogs, more commonly known as "cadaver dogs," is relatively nondestructive. Dogs can be effective over water as well as on land. Bloodhounds are often used because of their keen sense of smell. They are an excellent resource for locating bodies, whether above ground, buried, or even underwater. The dogs are tethered to a 15-foot lead, working over zigzag patterns downwind from a suspected area until the animal "alerts" to a scent. At this point, the dog is allowed to work its own search pattern to the source. Note that the parameters for far-field and near-field investigations are essentially defined by the animal itself.

The utility of scent-detecting or decomposition dogs is limited by high temperatures (temperatures above approximately 29°C, or 85°F) because of general animal discomfort; limitations are also imposed by extremely low temperatures, and in such conditions the dog must be within one meter to locate the source. Optimal conditions for the successful use of scent-detecting dogs include temperatures between approximately 4° and 16°C (40° to 60°F), 20% or higher humidity, moist or very moist ground, and a wind speed of at least 8 km (5 miles) per hour (Galloway, Birkby, Jones, et al., 1988). No upper limit for wind speeds has been established, although the scent cone becomes quite narrow and more difficult to detect with higher wind speeds. Meteorologists are helpful members of the team in determining optimum times for the dogs to be used.

Based on prior experience using scent-detecting dogs, researchers have found the trained animal will indicate the presence of decayed human scent when human blood, feces, urine, and other organic compounds are noted. Other materials that have been handled or worn by humans will also give rise to a false positive indication.

Tests are being devised to determine the maximum time since death in which dogs can detect decomposition scents, because some decomposition dogs have identified archaeological remains that are 1400 years old. Ordinarily, they have been recognized as successful in locating decomposed human tissue scents more than 170 years postburial (Hunter, 1994).

Upon recognition of a possible mass grave, aerial photographs should be taken of the area before disturbing the landscape (similar photographs should be taken at the completion of exhuma-

tion for comparison). Using a T-shaped steel rod and a probe to detect methane gas and measure temperature is useful when a possible gravesite is discovered. The use of these techniques prevents unnecessary excavation at all suspected sites, which can be costly and time consuming (Boyd, 1979). Additionally, investigators must differentiate mass graves related to conflicts from those dating back to conflicts in the same territories during previous periods of violence (e.g., World War II). It is also important to distinguish between graves of combatants or civilians who were buried collectively for the purpose of sanitation or for logistical reasons.

BEST PRACTICE The forensic death investigator should arrange all logistical details before starting groundbreaking associated with exhumation.

Preparing the Site for Exhumation

A temporary autopsy site and forensic laboratory must be set up. Vehicles to transport the bodies and evidence should be arranged. Other details focus on funding and time constraints—funding is usually limited and deadlines are often restrictive. Time constraints often create a challenge in utilizing proper scientific procedures, in recovering optimal data, and in closing the site in a timely manner. Time constraints include cultural pressures to rebury the bodies within a given period of time.

The gravesite is now ready to prepare for exhumation. First, the scene must be secured from weather, wild animals, and people. The crime scene is most likely to be disturbed by suspects, witnesses, high-ranking officials, and investigators. The physical security of the exhumation team must also be considered at this time.

KEY POINT When an item of evidence has been moved or altered, it is impossible to restore it to its original position or condition.

Complicating factors include heavily scavenged sites, unexploded ordnances, environmental and physical hazards, and time and budget constraints as well as demands made by foreign governments, cultural barriers, and a politically and emotionally charged atmosphere (Hoshower, 1998). It is not unusual for international incident scenes to be subjected to concomitant cultural and natural transformations (Webster, 1998).

Because each situation is unique, so must be the excavation strategies for each investigation. The situation includes physical, cultural, and resource limitations and is usually logistically complicated. Often, detecting and removing land mines are the first safety measures undertaken. Such mines are often buried with the bodies or on top of and around the site. De-mining and booby trap disposal is an activity that takes place throughout the exhumation process. During the reburial of victims from the Srebrinica massacre in the Bosnian War in August 1995, the Bosnian Serbs buried grenades and booby traps at multiple levels with the victims to deter exhumation efforts.

An excavation grid is placed around the area and excavation proceeds in gridded units. On initiation of exhumation, investigators will begin documenting evidence and remains, noting the condition and relative position of each. Measuring distances to fixed objects that will remain long after the search ends is the best practice. Nearly all evidence is fragile and susceptible to contamination, breakage, or deterioration, so precautions should be taken to prevent such damage.

BEST PRACTICE Never mark directly on the evidence; always mark on the container. Record specific information on each photographic exposure including date, time, and personnel involved.

After exhumation efforts have begun, collection, preservation, and analysis of evidence become the focus of the investigation (Fig. 22-8). Soil is carefully removed in increments of whatever levels had been determined to allow the maintenance of three-dimensional control throughout the excavation. Three-dimensional control of artifact provenance is required to reconstruct the sequence of events (the focus of stage 3) in a mass grave with bodies superimposed over one another with shell casings and wadding scattered in, around, or between bodies (Hoshower, 1998). Throughout the investigation, several forensic experts from various disciplines are used. This group includes at least one forensic pathologist, archaeologist, anthropologist, odontologist, toxicologist, psychiatrist, entomologist, and botanist, along with the crime scene technician, detectives, and criminalistics laboratory personnel. At the gravesite, forensic pathologists, forensic anthropologists, and forensic archaeologists are present along with workers. There may also be an investigating judge provided by the host government.

Physical evidence may be divided into three types: objects, body materials, and impressions. Objects include weapons, notes, letters, bullets, and cigarette/cigar butts. Body materials include blood, hair, tissue, urine, feces, and vomitus. Impressions can be in the form of fingerprints, tire tracks, footprints, bullet holes, and palm prints. Relevant evidence generally includes shell casings and bullets, and nonburied evidence (e.g., bullet hole patterns on nearby trees). It is important to remember that recovered items could bear latent fingerprints (Boyd, 1979). Plant and insect remains are also removed and studied to help identify the time of death more accurately.

The location and position of the bodies on exhumation can be central to establishing how the victims were killed and their remains disposed. The positions can reveal whether victims were lined up and shot, and from what angle, and whether they were bulldozed into the site after being executed. The spatial distribution of items such as bones and teeth recovered in surface finds can help in determining the original position and location of the body (Hoshower, 1998). An electronic locator, called a surveying station, has begun to be used to provide exact coordinates for recovered remains and evidence. If such technology is not available, a detailed diagram should be used. This diagram provides a record of the three-dimensional relationship between objects.

One of the golden rules of forensic investigations has been stated time and again in articles published on this subject: Never replace, for the purpose of photographing, any evidence that has been moved even it it was moved accidentally or by mistake. Items should be photographed with and without identifying numbers, a scale, and an arrow pointing to magnetic north. All removed material should be sifted through two screens: the first with quarter-inch squares and the second with a standard window screen (Boyd, 1979). The condition of evidence depends on the presence of water and insects, as well as the pH of the soil. These factors can act to destroy or preserve evidence (Webster, 1998). Therefore, samples of the soil and water in the grave should be taken (Fig. 22-9). This will allow forensic specialists to estimate the expected timing of degradation of evidence, including bodies, and therefore determine an approximate time of death.

Role of the Forensic Nurse Examiner

Some forensic nurses are affiliated with multinational military units who are highly trained in de-mining pertinent areas. These nurses bring this expertise, along with forensic skills, into human rights missions. Captain Baldiv Adjula Singh is a FNE and a specialist in removing land mines as well as other engineering skills with the Singapore Armed Forces. FNEs such as Singh would be an excellent addition to the human rights mission in the exhumation of human remains.

Fig. 22-9 Screening fill dirt from an excavation site allows recovery of evidential items that may have been missed during the excavation.

Fig. 22-8 A researcher sits in grave pit with remains that are being recovered.

Case Study **22-1**

Missing Person—Homicide (Search)

Robert A. Madison was reported missing in mid-May 2000. He was last seen on the afternoon of April 24, 2000. The police department detectives conducted numerous interviews and located an individual who became an informant. According to the information gathered, the victim was shot near where the body was hidden and covered in the tumbleweeds for one to two days before the offenders arrived to move it. The informant assisted the suspect in loading the body in the bed of a pickup truck, transporting the body to a location on the west edge of the city limits, and dumping the body in a hole. They filled in the hole with the dirt that the suspect had previously removed with a backhoe, which was still at the scene. They dumped the body off the back of the truck where it "crumpled" at the bottom of the hole, then threw the white cotton blanket that had covered the body on top and filled the hole with the dirt the subject had removed with the backhoe. The informant described the hole as being about 12 feet deep. He stated the hole was approximately two bucket widths at the bottom and flared out toward the top. He stated a mound of dirt was on his left and a tree was behind and off the side, which he was able to see in the lights of the backhoe.

The detectives took the informant to the described site on several occasions, and he picked an area that he thought was the location of the grave. Because a housing development had been started the previous year about the time of the burial and the area had seven new homes, the informant stated the area looked much different than when he had been there the previous year. The location he picked seemed about the right distance to the best of his recollection. Aerial photographs, taken before April 2000 and between May 2000 and the time the area had been leveled for development, were acquired. After review of the photographs, a mound or depression was visualized about 100 feet east of the trees, which correlated with the site described by the informant.

Two bloodhounds were brought to the chosen sight and gave a positive indication for decomposing human tissue. The areas indicated were marked and documented. This area was just north of the arroyo. The marked area was wet, and there had been no rain in the area for more than 48 hours. This was the only spot located that remained wet. According to the precipitation records, during the time period surrounding the burial the area received less than 0.5 inches of rain.

An employee with the construction company working in the area at the time of the burial stated that a backhoe matching the specifications had been moved and was tangled with barbed wire. The employee stated that he followed the tracks in the wet ground to an area where the backhoe had been used. Upon arrival at the site, investigators noted obvious evidence that the ground had been disturbed. There was a slight berm at the edges, and it was readily visible where old growth vegetation had ceased. Additional aerial photographs were reviewed, and the newest photograph showed the possible primary burial site.

At this time this area, which was west of the area where the dogs indicated, was considered the primary location because of the additional information acquired. The area indicating a disturbance was outlined with pin flags. A botanical survey was the first priority before using other more invasive techniques. A survey was also taken of the secondary area. Ground penetrating radar (GPR) was used to search the outside of the disturbed area. The area was cleaned of vegetation and leveled approximately 2 meters past the edges of the disturbed area, to attempt to visualize the backfilled trench through color or texture changes in the soil. Next, the area

was hand excavated in a series of shallow, narrow test trenches, which were shovel width and approximately 2 meters apart. Near the southern end of the marked area, a locality with less consolidated fill was discovered. However, the size or shape of the area could not be visualized. The GPR was utilized again within the marked area, but no anomalies were noted, even after several passes. A cone penetrometer was used in an attempt to measure the approximate degree of compaction of the soil, and two separate areas of less compacted soil were found. This, coupled with shovel testing, led to probing using a surveyor's pin and actual excavation using a trowel. Through these methods, the north wall of the filled trench was located. Once the approximate limits of the grave trench were located, the trench was then excavated using shovels and trowels and passed through a quarter-inch mesh screen to allow recovery of any evidence missed in the excavation process.

Because of the available information indicating the victim was buried at a depth of 10 to 12 feet, limited personnel, and a vehicle observed circling the area that was thought to be associated with the suspect, it was decided that a backhoe would be used to dig approximately 5 to 6 feet into the trench before proceeding with hand excavation. The backhoe was used to excavate the material until a patch of dark color was observed in the trench. The backhoe was removed from the immediate site and hand excavation again resumed. The distal portion of the right humerus of a buried human body was located. The right ulna was located near the distal end of the humerus, but the right radius and hand could not be located. During the screening process, the left side of the mandible (with teeth intact) and several teeth were recovered. The left hand and arm were found to be intact and unharmed. Continued hand excavation revealed the remains were intact and were partially mummified, with the victim lying prone on a steeply sloping trench with the arms outstretched. The feet were lowest in the trench with the remains at approximately a 45-degree angle. The cranium was located in the spill dirt along with the right radius, right hand, and an earring. The remains were completely uncovered, and the coroner's office was contacted to complete its investigation and to remove the remains. The area was screened for additional evidence, and a final mapping was completed. The site was then secured.

The victim had been missing for 14 months before his remains were located, and it took another 18 months for the perpetrator to be brought before a jury. That jury took only six hours to find him guilty, and he is currently serving 26 years in prison for murder in the second degree.

Critical thinking questions for Case Study 22-1
1) What makes the site of this buried body a clandestine grave?
2) What detection tools and strategies were used to locate the clandestine grave?
3) What similarities exist between the excavation of this body and the excavation of bodies in mass graves that resulted from human rights abuses?

The proper collection and preservation of evidence from the crime scene, in this case the grave, serves several purposes. Primarily, the evidence is used to establish that a crime has been committed, that a certain person has committed a crime, and to determine how the crime was committed. Most evidence collected in buried body cases is physical in nature, defined as any matter, material, or condition that may be used to determine the facts in a given situation. For each type of physical evidence, there is an appropriate collection technique that is to be followed by an appropriate preservation technique.

During this stage of investigation, the FNE can be of assistance in documenting the location, condition, and removal of evidence. The forensic nurse may also be in charge of regulating the systematic numbering and tagging of remains and keeping the evidence and associated remains correlated. The FNE may participate in the photographic documentation of the crime scene, both before and after the removal of objects. A chain-of-custody (evidence) form should be provided for each single piece of evidence and remains. The forensic nurse can take charge of this as part of the tagging system. A solid chain of evidence must be maintained to ensure the integrity of every specimen or piece of evidence seized. Failure to establish or maintain the chain of custody will prevent admissibility of the evidence in court (Fig. 22-10).

During this stage, interviews may be conducted. Sexual assault investigation and examinations involving the documentation of evidence is one area of the FNE's expertise. Many victims, especially women, are more comfortable talking to other women about the crime, especially if rape is involved. This makes the FNE essential during all phases of the investigation of the crime when interviews are conducted.

Although several agencies and many people are involved, remember that everyone is working as a team and each participant is a vital link in the process. This is the first step in bringing closure and justice to survivors of the victims. It also allows the truth to be known.

FNEs have been trained in the exhumation of human remains at the Dade County Medical Examiner Metro Dade Police Department course in Miami, Florida. Other specialized courses in exhumation are available and are recommended for forensic nurses interested in working with human rights organizations. Greater numbers of nurses are becoming involved in forensic science and human rights organizations than ever before. This group of professionals represents a previously untapped resource to the forensic pathologist, anthropologist, and death investigative team. As the need for forensic services expands in the military forces, new roles and new responsibilities will be assigned to FNEs in death investigation, documentation of torture and abuse, and sexual assault of both living and deceased victims.

All forensic nurse death investigative (FNDI) personnel can be prepared with minimal training in minimal time to contribute to mass grave exhumation teams because of their extensive background in death investigation and experience. This includes the postmortem examination of rape/homicide victims. The need for such personnel is at an all time high because of greater human

rights investigations, the investigation of war crimes and crimes against humanity, and the number of prosecutions in the World Court, which require forensic specialists in these areas. The FNE is a well-recognized expert in many areas of consequence where healthcare, forensic science, and the law intersect.

STAGE 2: POSTMORTEM IDENTIFICATION OF REMAINS
Primary Issues
Bodies and remains are transported to the lab where they are first radiographed before forensic autopsy. The goals of the autopsy are identification, documentation of injury, and determination of cause and manner of death. Primary identification is based on the estimated stature of the deceased, the gender, age, and whether the deceased was right- or left-hand dominant. These characteristics are based on the forensic examination of bones. Bones can also indicate the cause of death. Entry and exit wounds or a pattern of bullet holes can show the manner of death and are often indicative of mass execution rather than death in combat. When there is commingling of skeletal remains, bones should be examined with shortwave ultraviolet light to segregate them (Kahana, 1999). After segregation, the bones should be arranged in anatomical order.

Buried body cases are complicated by mass numbers of bodies to compare with mass numbers of missing individuals. This makes a quick match nearly impossible. Personal effects are often recovered and can be returned to family members at the conclusion of the investigation. Clothing, dentures, and eyeglasses can aid identification if they have inscriptions or writing on them or if the eyeglass prescription is known for missing people. If complete decomposition has not occurred, tattoos or other skin markings are of considerable importance. Of course, fingerprints are useful, but only if fingerprints are available with which to compare them. In many countries where mass grave exhumation takes place, fingerprints are not often available.

No two sets of teeth are identical. Even if direct identification is not available, dentition can offer information on age, gender, racial affinity, and possibly socioeconomic status. In many cases of mass casualties such as disasters, dental identification is often the employed method of identification. However, the successful use of dentition for positive identification of remains can occur only when antemortem records are available for comparison (Weedn, 1998). Along the same lines, medical records reveal a history of illness, injury, or surgical procedures. This is most useful in ruling out an identity or confirming whether a unique characteristic is noted.

Radiology is a common tool used to identify foreign matter in a body or the presence of illness. Sinus films provide good comparison tools, as they are highly variable between individual people. In cases of mass grave exhumation, anthropological examination is one of the most powerful tools available to determine what happened, how it happened, and also to narrow the possible identities of the various remains. For example, hair is analyzed for characteristics such as color, length, and texture for the purpose of excluding identity and for investigative purposes. However, forensic anthropology alone should not be relied on for conclusive identification but can contribute to presumptive conclusions (Weedn, 1998).

Given that the absence of dental and fingerprint records is common in these situations, DNA analytical methods are generally employed. Most tissue or fluid, including hair and bone, will permit DNA testing. Polymerase chain reaction (PCR)-based genetic testing allows analysis of old, severely decomposed, and small samples. The advantages of DNA are that it is the same throughout the body

Fig. 22-10 A law enforcement officer and a forensic nurse collect evidence at a mass gravesite.

(in all cells), throughout life, and it is unique in each person (with the exception of identical twins). Each cell contains the same DNA, which in humans contains 3 billion base pairs. Sets of thousands of base pairs code for one gene and generally each gene codes for a protein. Although proteins tend to be indistinguishable among most individuals, there are many regions on the DNA that do not code for proteins and vary considerably among people. These variations are exploited in the identification of individuals. All the genes in the body are passed on from the parents of the person. For this reason, if DNA from both the mother and the father can be collected and sequenced, then the identity of the individual can be confirmed or ruled out with a high degree of reliability. The type of DNA used for this process called fingerprinting is chromosomal DNA.

Another type of genetic testing is mitochondrial DNA (mtDNA) testing. There are thousands of copies of mitochondrial DNA for every copy of chromosomal DNA. Thus, when insufficient quantities of chromosomal DNA are available, an alternative exists. Mitochondrial DNA is more variable among individual people than chromosomal DNA. Additionally, because mitochondrial DNA is passed on only from the maternal contribution, an exact DNA sequence match can be found in a sibling, mother, aunt, or even distant maternal relatives.

Mitochondrial DNA is limited in its applications, however, because it cannot distinguish individuals from the same maternal line from each other, such as two siblings. Therefore, mtDNA should be used to confirm findings based on other clues such as height, gender, and medical history (Skolnick, 1993).

Teeth are optimal sources of DNA because the exterior surface of a tooth surrounds and protects soft pulp, which is composed of living cells. This DNA is therefore protected from the external environment and thus biological degradation (Weedn, 1998).

Evidence such as bullets, shell casings, and bullet fragments are also analyzed at the laboratory. These are compared with data on types of firearms and tool-mark analysis of suspected weapons, specifically those well recognized as being associated with a specific group of military or paramilitary organizations suspected of committing the crime.

If the remains are to be reburied before obtaining a positive identification, the United Nations has published recommendations regarding samples to retain for further analysis in the UN Manual on the Effective Prevention and Investigation of Extra-Legal, Arbitrary and Summary Executions, U.N. Doc. E/ST/CSDHA/.12 (1991). Samples to be retained include midshaft cross sections from either femur and either fibula (minimum of 2 cm in height), a section of the sternal end of a rib, a tooth, several molar teeth and a cast of the skull for possible facial reconstruction.

Role of the Forensic Nurse Examiner

The FNE may be called on to assist in the autopsy, especially in situations of mass body exhumation. Here the forensic nurse may need to rely on his or her forensic training and experience to identify trauma characteristics. For instance, the examining physician may request the forensic nurse to assist in distinguishing between blunt and sharp trauma or entrance and exit wounds from bullets. The forensic nurse may also be requested to make incisions or assist in specimen collection. The most common types of specimens to be collected in such situations are tissue and hair to be used for the purpose of assisting in identification of remains as well as identifying time of death and possibly means of death (if identifiable through toxicology).

When investigating human rights abuse cases, the FNE may also be called on to interview living survivors. In this case, the nurse will employ interviewing, documenting, and examination techniques to collect evidence and witness testimony. Forensic pathologists,

forensic anthropologists, and other forensic specialists, as well as laboratory technicians, do most of the work at this stage.

Forensic expertise helps families learn the fate of their loved ones (Kirschner & Hannibal, 1994). Emotional healing can finally be initiated for loved ones and family members at this time (Webster, 1998).

Case Study 22-2

Preserved Remains

A 35- to 45-year-old female's remains were sent to the National Museum of Health and Medicine in July 1992. The remains were found at a flea market entrance on August 20, 1989. The suspect was a man who was a rival in the flea market business. Following the suspect's death in 1990, friends and relatives provided information on the remains.

The body had supposedly been stored in a copper coffin in a funeral home for many years. After the sale of the funeral home, the body was placed on the rafters of what became a hardware outlet. A local historian remembered viewing the remains in 1993.

When the remains were examined, the ligaments, tendons, and muscle tissues were all preserved and evident in the legs, arms, and head. However, the tissue appearance differed from mummified remains. Internal organs had been injected with a red clay suspension in a paraffin base and a talc derivative comprised largely of carbonate. These hardened inside the organs and the organ tissues were dried and paperlike in texture. The appearance of the soft tissues and presence of organs represented an anatomical preparation similar to those done in the late 19th and early 20th centuries.

Modified from Sledxik, P. S., & Micozzi, M. S. (1997). Autopsied, embalmed, and preserved human remains: Distinguishing features in forensic & historic context. In W. D. Haglund and M. H. Sorg, *Forensic taphonomy: The postmortem fate of human remains.* Boca Raton, FL: CRC Press.

Critical thinking questions for Case Study 22-2

1) How was the science of taphonomy used in this case?
2) What would be considered the clandestine grave site(s) in this case?

STAGE 3: RECONSTRUCTING CRIME SCENE AND CRIMINAL EVENTS LEADING TO DEATH

Primary Issues

A medicolegal autopsy will assist in identifying remains and also in determining the cause, manner, and mechanism of death. One of the challenges for the forensic pathologist is distinguishing between antemortem and postmortem injuries. As such, the forensic pathologist will rely on information collected by the exhumation team to aid in determining the potential causes of injuries. Table 22-2 provides the physical finding descriptions related to known torture techniques as published in the United Nations Manual in 1991.

The cause of death is based on knowledge of the circumstances, history of the victim, and environmental factors. Circumstances are based on witness statements and physical evidence at the crime scene. If identification is made, the social, political, and medical background of the victim is considered. The investigation also includes an analysis of the environment where the body is found.

It must be determined whether the assault took place at the grave or if the bodies had been moved to the gravesite after death occurred. This is generally easy to determine based on the presence of shell casings and the position of the bodies. If bodies are found

Table 22-2 Postmortem Detection of Torture

TORTURE TECHNIQUE	PHYSICAL FINDINGS
BEATING	
1. General	Scars; bruises; lacerations; multiple fractures at different stages of healing, especially in unusual locations, which have not been medically treated
2. To the soles of the feet ("falanga," "falaka," "bastinado"), or fractures of the bones of the feet	Hemorrhage in the soft tissues of the soles of the feet and ankles, aseptic necrosis
3. With the palms on both ears simultaneously ("el telephone")	Ruptured or scarred tympani membranes, injuries to external ear
4. On the abdomen, while lying on a table with the upper half of the body unsupported ("operating table," "el quirofano")	Bruises on the abdomen, back injuries, ruptured abdominal viscera
5. To the head	Cerebral cortical atrophy, scars, skull fractures, bruises, hematomas
SUSPENSION	
6. By the wrists ("la bandera")	Bruises or scars about the wrists, joint injuries
7. By the arms or neck	Bruises or scars at the site of binding, prominent lividity in the lower extremities
8. By the ankles ("murcielago")	
9. Head down, from a horizontal pole placed under the knees with the wrists bound to the ankles ("parrot perch," "Jack," "pau de arara")	Bruises or scars on the anterior forearms and backs of the knees/marks on the wrists and ankles
NEAR SUFFOCATION	
10. Forced immersion of head in water, often contaminated ("wet submarine," "pileta," "Latina")	Fecal material or other debris in the mouth, pharynx, trachea, esophagus, or lungs; intrathoracic petechiae; intrathoracic petechiae
11. Tying of a plastic bag over the head ("dry submarine")	Intrathoracic petechiae
SEXUAL ABUSE	
12. Sexual abuse	Sexually transmitted diseases; pregnancy; injuries to breasts, external genitalia, vagina, anus, or rectum
13. Prolonged standing ("el planton")	Dependent edema, petechiae in lower extremities
14. Forced straddling of a bar ("saw horse," "el cabellete")	
15. Cattle prod ("la picana")	Burns: appearance depends on the age of the injury—immediately: red spots, vesicles, and/or black exudates; within a few weeks: circular, reddish, macular scars; at several months: small, white, reddish, or brown spots resembling telangiectasias
16. Wires connected to a source of electricity	
17. Heated metal skewer inserted into the anus ("black slave")	Perianal or rectal burns
MISCELLANEOUS	
18. Dehydration (spiders, insects, rats, mice, dogs)	Vitreous humor electrolyte abnormalities

From the United Nations Manual (1991) on the Effective Prevention and Investigation of Extra-Legal, Arbitrary and Summary Executions, U.N. Doc. E/ST/CSDHA/.12 (1991)Annex II. Postmortem detection of torture.

wrapped around others, as though clinging to each other in their last moments or life, then they were probably killed at that site.

Forensic entomology aids in determination of manner of death, movement of a cadaver from one site to another, and the length of the postmortem interval (Lord & Burger, 1983). Insects on, in, and below the corpse are collected. The insects should be kept in containers with the collection date and time, location of remains, area of body infested, and name of the collector on the container. Insects are helpful in determining time since death occurred, as well as the movement of bodies from other locations (Lord & Burger, 1983).

There are three stages of change after death: early, late, and tissue changes. Cessation of respiration, cessation of circulation, skin pallor, muscle relaxation, eye changes, and blood coagulation and fluidity characterize the early stage. The late changes after death are algor mortis, livor mortis, and rigor mortis. Algor mortis is the cooling of the body after death. Clothing, body size, and activity before death affect the rate of cooling. Livor mortis is a bluish red discoloration of the dependent portions of the external surface of the body as a result of the postmortem stasis of blood. These spots are generally 4 to 5 mm or larger. Livor mortis indicates the position of the body soon after death. It can be used to indicate that the body was moved since initial burial. Rigor mortis is cadaveric

stiffness. In the case of mass grave excavation, many postmortem markers have subsided as the death usually occurred months or years prior. Most important to such investigations are postmortem tissue changes. Decomposition occurs as the body degenerates as a result of natural cell enzymes and bacterial action. Box 22-1 outlines the order of tissue decomposition.

Over time, insects migrate to the body and lead to skeletonization or removal of the soft tissue. Mummification is the drying of the body or its parts with leather-like changes, generally a finding that occurs in dry climates. Adipocere is the formation of a waxy

Box 22-1 Order of Tissue Decomposition

1. Intestines, stomach, accessory organs of digestion, heart, blood and circulation, heart muscle
2. Air passages and lungs
3. Kidneys and bladder
4. Brain and nervous tissue
5. Skeletal muscles
6. Connective tissues and integument

Data from Gill-King, H. (1997). Chemical and ultrastructural aspects of decomposition. In W. D. Haglund and M. H. Sorg, *Forensic taphonomy: The postmortem fate of human remains* (pp. 97–98). Boca Raton, FL: CRC Press.

substance as a result of the hydrogenation of body fats. This occurs in moist environments. These stages of death are good indicators of the time of death, but time of death is always an estimate. Plant life (flora) is examined by forensic botanists to indicate a range of time of burial and location change of bodies. Plants, seeds, or bark that grow in one area often do not grow in a neighboring area. Therefore, evidence of a plant foreign to an area of a grave indicates that it was brought there with the body from a different location (Lane, Anderson, Barkley, et al., 1990). This indicates that the body was moved from its original location. It is not uncommon for bodies in mass graves to be moved one or more times before discovery. Often bodies are moved for the discrete purpose of preventing their discovery, as they are evidence of a crime. Therefore, revealing that the bodies have been moved is an important finding.

Different fabrics decompose at different rates. Clothes worn by a deceased person generally last two years or longer before total decomposition. Therefore, the level of decomposition of clothing can also indicate the length of time a body has been buried. The clothing can also indicate the social class and lifestyle of the victims (hospital workers versus farmers).

Role of the Forensic Nurse Examiner

The FNE has been an integral part of evidence collection and therefore has much to contribute to the reconstruction of criminal events. Forensic investigation into human rights–related casualties serves as documentation to set the historical record straight. Therefore, it is important that all forensic experts be included in identifying the criminal events that led to the death casualties.

STAGE 4: IDENTIFYING AND PROSECUTING THE CRIMINAL

Primary Issues

In cases of human rights abuses, the persons responsible for the abuses are generally known. Prosecutors require physical evidence in addition to eyewitness testimony to pursue justice. The numerous bodies exhumed and the manner of death determined for these people are used to construct the case against the suspected criminal(s). At the conclusion of the investigation, indictments for the arrest of suspected war criminals are issued. In Bosnia and Rwanda, the international community had to conduct extensive exhumation and crime scene investigations before issuing indictments for the arrest of war criminals.

Role of the Forensic Nurse Examiner

At this point, the FNE may become an expert witness and testify in grand jury or trial proceedings. The nurse may be called on to verify the chain of custody, initial collection, and location of evidence, and to describe exhumation methods used by the forensic team. The FNE may be called on to give his or her expert opinion on trauma types, specimen collection procedures, and how the crime most likely occurred. This nurse may also be put on the stand to defend or explain his or her documentation during the investigation.

The primary purpose in the courtroom is to establish the corpus delicti, which is composed of three parts: identifying the deceased, determining that the death is not natural, and verifying that the death resulted from a criminal act and is thus not accidental or suicidal. Therefore, the FNE may participate in any or all of these efforts. It is hoped that such investigations will prevent such violations from occurring in the future by holding those responsible for the atrocities accountable for their actions.

Forensic missions to investigate deaths following human rights violations have traveled to Argentina, Bolivia, Bosnia, Afghanistan, Iraq, and many other countries. Legal obstacles often hamper these investigations. In addition, eyewitnesses are reluctant to testify because they fear reprisals or because the only living witnesses were those conducting executions themselves (United Nations, 1991). Sometimes the lives of investigators are subject to threats. The ultimate goal is to re-create as accurately as possible the circumstances of the crime committed, to identify and apprehend the perpetrator(s), and to guide the case successfully through the criminal justice system (Boyd, 1979).

Vukovar is a town on Croatia's eastern border. During the Balkan War of the 1990s, the Yugoslav National Army (Joint National Army [JNA]), composed primarily of Serbs, attacked Vukovar, a Croatian stronghold. That city quickly fell to the Serbs after an intense attack. The JNA soldiers took 200 patients and staff from the hospital and drove them to a farm complex called Ovcara. The JNA soldiers then brutalized these individuals by beating and mentally torturing them. At the time this grave was excavated, the Serbs held the territory and made claims that the bodies were related to the fighting that took place and not the result of human rights abuses. UN troops stood guard for the excavation.

It was determined that the Ovcara grave was not related to the battlefield casualties (Stover, 1997). Seventy-five spent cartridges of a caliber consistent with a standard JNA weapon were found mixed in with the bodies. Shortly after a forensic team visited the site for an initial analysis, the Serbs governing the area passed a resolution prohibiting work at the grave. This is an example of the tremendous influence local governments have on international exhumation efforts. There is potential for the FNE to have a vital and important role in the exhumation of mass graves.

Summary

Taphonomy, or the science of decomposition and dispersion of the body after death, is extremely important in the investigation of clandestine gravesites and other areas where the identity of the body, circumstances of death, and elapsed time since death are unknown. This relatively new subspecialty of forensic sciences and death investigation is dependent on an improved understanding of events that shape the fate of human remains in various locations and conditions. Unfortunately, research into this topic is influenced by the many factors that limit cadaver-related research. Fortunately, the ability to study certain elements using animal specimens has been facilitated by NecroSearch International. In addition to a research role, the organization has been beneficial in the investigation of more than 255 cases in 30 states and six countries. NecroSearch has grown from 15 members at its incorporation in 1992 to 41 members as of November 2009.

The NecroSearch membership has remained relatively low, as members are admitted by invitation only, and then only after a thorough background check and a presentation by the prospective member outlining additional skills that may be brought to the organization. It is not the number of persons in the organization but the quality of the individuals and their expertise that are paramount. Forensic nurses bring unique perspectives to the team by using knowledge from a professional acumen that includes medical, legal, and scientific education and training. Nurses have been invited to participate in NecroSearch endeavors, representing another opportunity for individuals interested in death investigation.

The exhumation of clandestine mass graves entails attention to detail, patience, cultural awareness, and an ability to extract the precise details of the criminal event. These are qualities innate in the forensic nurse through specialized education and training. This role is awaiting further development by forensic nursing pioneers and the exhumation teams who will benefit from inclusion of the FNE. The consequences of ignoring this area are not only a loss of scientific professional development but, more important, a loss to the greater cause of justice in the resolution of crimes against humanity.

Critical thinking questions for Case Study 22-3

1) What forensic specialties would have been employed to locate and identify the bodies of the "disappeared" and to reconstruct the events that led to their deaths?

2) What contributions can the forensic nurse examiner make in this scenario?

3) What barriers did forensic professionals face in successfully reconstructing the activities that led to the death of these men in Argentina?

Case Study 22-3

In Search of Clandestine Graves

During years of political strife and civil war in developing countries, mass executions are common where powerful groups attempt to persecute weaker, less organized groups or individuals of one country or a neighboring country. At the time of the "disappeared" in Argentina, men, both young and old, were taken from the streets never to be seen again. Thousands of these individuals simply disappeared. It is well known that the political powers use unnecessary and lethal force to reduce the number of potential soldiers who may one day fight for the opposing rebels. Those who had lost family members, friends, and loved ones sought help from the police, yet it is often the police who are used as an arm of the government to carry out mass murder as a means of instilling fear and threats among the population of minorities or noncombatants. The police did not assist in locating the "disappeared," nor did they assist in identifying any discovered human remains, which were brought out of shallow graves by the families.

The next cry for help went to the scientists at the universities in the departments of legal medicine. The scientists were afraid to get involved—knowing if they did, they would be next. However, a visitor to the university happened to be a forensic anthropologist from the United States, Dr. Claude Snow. A mother of a young boy who had been missing was searching for help in identifying the remains of a small body suspected to be her son. Snow stated it was not his place to get involved in cases outside his country, but seeing the depth of grief in the mother, he agreed to identify this one case, which turned out to be her son. All the mothers and wives began to beg Snow to identify other remains, to relieve them of the ultimate question of life or death. He could not reject their pleas, but he needed help at a time when local forensic professionals feared for their lives. The students at the university volunteered to help and became forensic professionals under pressure. They soon identified hundreds of bodies buried in clandestine graves, 200 to 400 at a time. When Snow made his final visit, these impromptu forensic specialists had become the genuine specialists, unearthing remains alone and relying on the expertise they had learned. Ultimately, the numbers of bodies are documented for the prevention of such crimes against humanity, and identification of the remains helps to reduce human suffering among the survivors. Truth as the mantra of the forensic sciences has served both health and justice.

Resources

ORGANIZATIONS

American Academy of Forensic Sciences (AAFS)
400 North 21st Street, Colorado Springs, CO 80904; 719-636-1100; www.aafs.org

Amnesty International, USA
5 Penn Plaza, 14th Floor, New York, NY 10001; 212-463-9193; www.amnesty.org

Armed Forces Institute of Pathology
6825 16th Street NW, Washington DC 20306-6000; 800-577-3749; www.afip.org

NecroSearch International, Inc.
Box D, 9008 Highway 85, Littleton, CO 80125; 303-663-7205; www.necrosearch.org

Physicians for Human Rights
2 Arrow Street, Suite 301, Cambridge, MA 02138; 617-301-4200; www.phrusa.org

PUBLICATIONS

Boyd, R. M. (1979). Buried body cases. *FBI Law Enforcement Bulletin, 48*(2), 1–7.

Haglund, W. D. (1991). *Applications of taphonomic models to forensic investigations.* PhD dissertation, University of Washington, Seattle, Ann Arbor, MI: University Microfilms.

Jackson, S. (2002). *No stone unturned: The true story of NecroSearch International.* New York: Kensington Books.

Mayo, K. (2004). Recovering human remains from clandestine graves. *Evidence Technology Magazine, 2*(3), 18–21. www.evidencemagazine.com. Accessed February 2009.

Rodriguez, W. C., III, & Bass, W. M. (1985). Decomposition of buried bodies and methods that may aid in their location. *Journal of Forensic Sciences, 30*(3), 836–852.

Smith, K. G. (1972). *Insects and other arthropods of medical importance.* London: British Museum of Natural History.

References

Bass, W. M., & Birkby, W. H. (1978). Exhumation: The method could make the difference. *FBI Law Enforcement Bulletin*, 6–11.

Boyd, R. M. (1979). *Buried body cases.* Published by the Federal Bureau of Investigation, U.S. Department of Justice, FBI Academy Quantico, VA. Reprinted from the *FBI Law Enforcement Bulletin, 48*(2), 113–118

Davenport, G. C., Griffin, T. J., Lindemann, J. W., et al. (1988). Geoscientists and law enforcement professionals work together in Colorado. *Geotimes, 35*(6), 13–15.

Davenport, G. C., Lindemann, J. W., Griffin, T. J., et al. (1998). Geotechnical Application 3: Crime scene investigating techniques. *Geophysics: The Leading Edge of Exploration, 7*(8), 64–66.

Dickinson, D. J. (1977). The aerial use of an infrared camera in a police search for the body of a missing person in New Zealand. *Journal - Forensic Science Society, 16*(3), 205–211.

France, D. L., Griffin, T. J., Swanburg, J. G., et al. (1992). A multidisciplinary approach to the detection of clandestine graves. *Journal of Forensic Sciences, 37*(6), 1445–1458.

France, D. L., Griffin, T. J., Swanburg, J. G., et al. (1997). NecroSearch revisited: Further multidisciplinary approaches to the detection of clandestine graves. In W. D. Haglund, & M. H. Sorg (Eds.), *Forensic taphonomy: The postmortem fate of human remains* (Chapter 32). Boca Raton, FL: CRC Press.

Galloway, A., Birkby, W. H., Jones, A. M., et al. (1988). Decay rates of human remains in an arid environment. *Journal of Forensic Sciences, 34*, 607–616.

Haglund, W. D., Reay, D. T., & Swindler, D. R. (1989). Canid scavenging/disarticulation sequence of human remains in the Pacific Northwest. *Journal of Forensic Sciences, 34*(3), 587–606.

Haglund, W. D., Reichert, D. G., & Reay, D. T. (1990). Recovery of decomposed and skeletal human remains in the Green River murder investigation: Implications for medical examiner/coroner and police. *The American Journal of Forensic Medicine and Pathology*, *11*(1), 35–43.

Haglund, W. D., & Sorg, M. H. (1997). *Forensic taphonomy: The postmortem fate of human remains*. Boca Raton, FL: CRC Press.

Hoshower, L. M. (1998). Forensic archeology and the need for flexible excavation strategies: A case study. *Journal of Forensic Sciences*, *43*(1), 53–56.

Hoving, G. L. (1986). Buried body search technology. *Identification News*, 3, 15.

Hunter, J. R. (1994). Forensic archaeology in Britain. *Antiquity*, *68*(261), 758–769.

Imaizumi, M. (1974). Locating buried bodies. *FBI Law Enforcement Bulletin*, *2*(3), 2–5.

James, S. H., & Nordby, J. J. (2005). *Forensic science: An introduction to scientific and investigative techniques* (2nd ed.). Boca Raton, FL: CRC Press.

Kahana, T. (1999). Forensic radiology. *The British Journal of Radiology*, *72*(854), 129–133.

Kelly, D. P. (1989). *Postmortem gastrointestinal gas production in submerged Yucatan micro-pigs*. Fort Collins, CO: Colorado State University. Unpublished MA thesis.

Killam, E. W. (1989). *The detection of human remains*. Springfield, IL: Charles C Thomas.

Kirschner, R. H., & Hannibal, K. E. (1994). The application of the forensic sciences to human rights investigations. *Medicine and law*, *13*(5–6), 451–460.

Lane, M. S., Anderson, L. C., Barkley, T. M., et al. (1990). Forensic botany: Plants, perpetrators, pests, poisons, and pot. *BioScience*, *40*(1), 34–39.

Lord, W. D., & Burger, J. F. (1983). Collection and preservation of forensically important entomological materials. *Journal of Forensic Sciences*, *28*(4), 936–944.

Lumpkin, B., & Chang, A. (2002). *Old skills, new uses: Investigators in Mexico use techniques developed in Kosovo*. Retrieved from http://abcnews.go.com/sections/world/DailyNews/mexicojob991201.html. Accessed January 2003.

McLaughlin, J. E. (1974). *The detection of buried bodies*. Yuba City, CA: Study of Andermac.

Payne, J. D., King, E. W., & Beinhart, G. (1968). Arthropod succession and decomposition of buried pigs. *Nature*, *219*, 1180–1181.

Sheriff, R. E. (Ed.), (1983). *Encyclopedic dictionary of exploration geophysics* (2nd ed.). Tulsa, OK: Society of Exploration Geophysicists.

Skinner, M., Alempijevic, D., & Djuric-Srejic, M. (2003). Guidelines for international forensic bio-archaeology monitors of mass grave exhumations. *Forensic Science International*, *134*(2), 81–92.

Skolnick, A. A. (1993). Mitochondrial DNA studies help identify lost victims of human rights abuses. *Med News Perspect*, *269*(15), 1911–1913.

Smith, K. (1983). *A manual of forensic entomology*. Ithaca, NY: British Museum (Natural History) and Cornell University Press.

Stover, E. (1997). The grave at Vukovar. *The Smithsonian*, *27*(12), 7–25.

United Nations: International Criminal Tribunal for the Former Yugoslavia (ICTY). (no date). *Bulletin: Exhumations*. Retrieved from www.un.org/icty/BL/08art1e.htm. Accessed January 10, 2009.

United Nations Manual on the Effective Prevention and Investigation of Extra-Legal Arbitrary and Summary Executions, U.N. Doc. E/ST/CSDHA/.12. (1991). Washington, DC.

Webster, A. D. (1998). Excavation of a Vietnam-era aircraft crash site: Use of cross-cultural understanding and dual forensic recovery methods. *Forensic Science*, *43*(2), 277–283.

Weedn, V. (1998). (W). Postmortem identification of remains. *Clinics in Laboratory Medicine*, *18*(1), 115–137.

CHAPTER 23 Physics, Restraints, and Fractures

David J. Porta and William S. Smock

In many forensic cases, injury reconstruction is a critical component. Whereas engineers and specially trained police officers are skilled at reconstructing the motion of vehicles in an accident, it usually takes a person with intimate knowledge of anatomy as well as a basic understanding of physics to reconstruct how a particular occupant motion led to a specific injury. Much of the physics can be found in a general college physics course, but there are numerous reference texts worth exploring (e.g., Brach & Brach, 2005; Rivers, 2006).

Physics

Injuries involve motion. To understand motion, it is important to begin with some principles of basic physics. The simplest measurements are scalar quantities—that is, they can be described by a single number (and appropriate units) with no mention of direction and other such factors. These include mass (M), temperature (T), time (t), and distance (D) (e.g., length, height, width, and circumference). These scalar quantities can be combined to give us a more detailed manner of describing motion. Velocity (V) and speed (S) are often used interchangeably, and it usually makes no difference in forensic cases. However, using the strict definitions in engineering or physics, velocity is a vector quantity; that is, it should have both magnitude and direction (e.g., 30 mph south). When we ignore the direction, we are simply referring to speed (e.g., 30 mph). Please note that most of the following descriptions are vector quantities. This means they should technically include a magnitude and direction. Another way of looking at this is to note that it is not just a number describing a motion, but how this motion occurs. Speed is a measure of how fast or slowly something moves. That, in and of itself, is not enough information to show that something is or is not injurious. A basketball moving at 25 mph is not injurious if it does not hit you. In fact, even if it does hit you, it might not cause an injury, depending on the angle of impact and how your body responds. When dealing with humans, it is important to include considerations of anatomy and physiology. That 25-mph basketball might be easily caught by a pair of skilled hands. But if the same ball, moving at the same speed, were to strike a single finger at the tip of the long axis of the digit, it could result in a fracture or at least a soft tissue injury.

VELOCITY = DISTANCE/TIME

Velocity equals the distance traveled over a period of time (V = D/t) in a particular direction and is often measured in miles per hour (mph), feet per second (fps), kilometers per hour (kph), or meters per second (m/s). Velocity is an important consideration in assessing injury potential as well as other factors (Box 23-1). If forced to choose between being struck by a baseball traveling at 20 mph or a baseball traveling at 100 mph, all but our masochistic readers would choose the 20 mph impact. The reason is simple; it will hurt less. At very low velocities, one would not expect serious injuries, but at higher velocities, injury severity will generally increase. At some point, injury will be maximal and even higher velocities will be irrelevant. For example, a pedestrian run over by a large truck going 50 mph will be just as dead as the pedestrian run over by the same truck at 100 mph. The only difference will likely be how far the pieces are scattered at the accident scene.

DELTA V

In the study of accidents, one often hears discussion of the "change in velocity" or "delta V" (a.k.a. ΔV). Occasionally it is noted that a higher delta V indicates greater injury potential. As used in the engineering literature, this is generally true. However, one must keep in mind that the engineers and accident reconstructionists are assuming this delta V occurs over a very short period of time.

BEST PRACTICE When evaluating biomechanics and injury potential, the forensic nurse should study the forces of deceleration, including how deceleration occurred and over what distance.

When traveling to work in a car, bus, or train, a person may zoom along at 45 mph and at some point slow to a stop for a traffic light or a stopped vehicle. If we contrast this with the force generated by someone who falls 68 feet from a sixth-story window, that person will reach a velocity of 45 mph just before striking the concrete below (Box 23-2). Both people will have changed their velocity from 45 mph to 0 mph, so they each experienced a delta V of 45 mph. In the first, virtually any member of our society would be able to bear this delta V with no problem. However, the change in velocity during the second scenario would certainly be injurious, if not fatal for most people. Obviously the difference is the amount of time it took for this change in velocity to occur. In the latter example, the change in velocity occurred over a very short period of time with disastrous consequences. Our body simply cannot maintain its structure when asked to change speed so quickly. When we look at a change in velocity over time, we call this *acceleration* (when the velocity is increasing) or *deceleration* (when the velocity is decreasing). Engineers may also refer to these as positive or negative acceleration, respectively.

TERMINAL VELOCITY

In falls from great heights, wind/atmosphere resistance (drag) plays a much greater role in determining the speed at which we strike the ground. When skydivers jump from a plane, they accelerate toward the earth. However, after a short time, they reach a point during

---

Box 23-1 Example of the Use of the Velocity Equation

Consider that a human eye blinks in approximately 0.4 second. If one is driving on the interstate at 70 mph, how much of the roadway is missed with each blink?

$$Velocity = Distance/time$$

This can be rearranged to solve for D, such that D = Vt. Also, mph may be converted to feet per second (fps) by multiplying it by 1.46667, thus 70 mph is equivalent to 102.7 fps. When we solve for D, we see that 102.7 ft/s × 0.4 s = 41 ft. Therefore, with each blink of the eye, your vehicle travels 41 feet down the road. Imagine how much of the roadway is missed while adjusting the music, tending to passengers, or dialing a cell phone!

Box 23-2 Calculating Velocity Achieved from a Particular Drop Height

APPROXIMATE DROP HEIGHT IN FEET	APPROXIMATE VELOCITY AT IMPACT IN MPH
10	17.3
15	21.2
20	24.5
25	27.4
30	30.0
40	34.6
50	38.7
60	42.4
70	45.8

V = square root of 2 gh, where g (gravity) = 32.2 ft/s² and h = drop height in ft. Note that this results in a velocity expressed as ft/s. To convert this to mph, simply multiply ft/s by 0.6818. For those more interested in metrics, g is expressed as 9.8 m/s² and h is drop height as measured in meters. The result would be a velocity in m/s. These calculations do not take into account resistance encountered by wind/atmosphere, but the effect is negligible at low drop heights. Note that mass is also not a concern. If one were to drop an 8-lb bowling ball from 20 feet, and a 16-lb bowling ball from 20 feet at the same time, they would both hit the ground at the same time and both would be traveling 24.5 mph. However, if one dropped an 8-lb bowling ball and a loosely wadded piece paper, the bowling ball would hit first because the paper would be affected by wind resistance. Fortunately, when examining the fall of a person from a relatively short height, resistance (a.k.a. drag) is negligible.

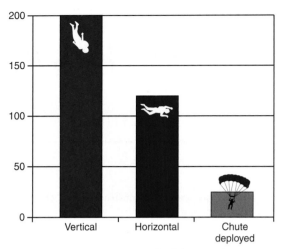

Fig. 23-1 Terminal velocity for falling parachutist.

potential for injury would exist. A small blood vessel might have been stretched too quickly, resulting in a rupture, and blood would leak into the surrounding tissues creating a hematoma or bruise. Inside the mouth, there might be a tear of the *labial frenulum*.

Acceleration and deceleration injuries both relate to *inertia*. Sir Isaac Newton (1643–1727) taught us that a body in motion wants to stay in motion until acted on by an external force. The opposite is also true; a body at rest will tend to stay at rest until acted on by an external force. The human body is fairly well equipped to deal with changes in inertia. In fact, some publications have even attempted to document a human's ability to cope with everyday accelerations (Allen et al., 1994; Funk et al., 2007; Ng et al., 2006).

KEY POINT It is when the acceleration or deceleration tolerance levels of our body or body part are exceeded that injuries occur.

Although it is difficult to assess the relative incidence of acceleration versus deceleration injuries, it is not difficult to illustrate examples of each. Acceleration injuries include the following: (1) A person is stopped in her car when her vehicle is violently impacted by a truck. Her body might accelerate faster than her head and neck, and this might result in a cervical or head injury. (2) A pedestrian crossing the street is struck on the leg by a passing car. The impacted portion of the tibia is accelerated faster than the bone can handle and a fracture results. (3) A boxer punches his opponent's head. This accelerates the cranium more quickly than the cervical vertebrae. The result is a pinching of the brain stem near the foramen magnum, which temporarily affects the reticular formation and causes the loss of consciousness. (4) Lastly, a gunshot wound is a horrible example of an acceleration injury. If we took a bullet and tossed it at a person's abdomen, it would bounce off harmlessly. The skin would tolerate the impact of a low mass bullet traveling at very low speed. The abdominal skin in the area of impact, with no initial velocity, would be able to deform or dimple as it accelerated while absorbing the energy of impact. However, the same low mass bullet, when fired from a gun, now has tremendous velocity. As the fired bullet contacts the skin, the skin cannot accelerate quickly enough to accommodate the force and it tears along with the deeper tissues that are penetrated.

Examples of deceleration injuries are also easily conjured. Falls have been mentioned previously, but it would be wise to remember

the fall when velocity no longer changes. This is called *terminal velocity*. The reason is that the wind resistance encountered during the fall will not permit the skydiver to go any faster. As Figure 23-1 shows, a skydiver falling horizontal to the ground with arms and legs outstretched will achieve a terminal velocity of about 120 mph. However, if he decreases drag by angling head first toward the ground with all extremities adducted, he can increase the speed to about 200 mph before wind resistance stops the acceleration. The skydiver does not stop, of course; he stops going faster and faster and maintains a constant velocity until reaching the ground—assuming that the parachute is not opened. Deployment of a parachute greatly increases the drag and the terminal velocity will fall to a level that is far more tolerable to the body.

ACCELERATION/DECELERATION

Injuries may occur when a body, or body part, is accelerated or decelerated more rapidly than our tissues can accommodate. For instance, if a hand is slowly rubbed across someone's face in the area of the mouth, the skin might be stretched a bit, but the elastic nature of the skin and hypodermis will accommodate this action with no untoward consequences. However, if there were a more rapid acceleration of this same skin (i.e., a violent slap), greater the cliché "It's not the fall that kills you–it's the sudden stop!" Sporting accidents are probably responsible for producing the greatest *number* of deceleration injuries–for example, a skier striking a tree, a volleyball player rolling an ankle while landing on another player's foot, or a tackler compressing his spine while spearing an opponent. Athletes certainly experience a large number of deceleration injuries, but the really serious ones are rare. Motor vehicle accidents likely give rise to the greatest number of *serious* deceleration injuries (head-on collision, rollover, ejection, underride, etc.).

FORCE = MASS × ACCELERATION

Often when a person is injured, one of the questions for a forensic investigator is "How much *force* was involved?" It seems attorneys and perhaps juries would like a simple number on which to make judgments. Such simplifications should be avoided. A thorough understanding of force is necessary before attempting to use it in the description of a mechanism of injury. Quantifying a force is often not nearly as important as describing *how* the force was applied. Remember, force is a vector, not a scalar quantity. Force involves mass. It was previously noted that mass typically has no significant effect on the velocity of a human body falling from short heights. However, when the victim strikes the ground with an abrupt deceleration, mass does come into play. The cliché "The bigger they are, the harder they fall" is completely true. Why can an insect fall the equivalent of 20 times its body height with no apparent injury, but a person falling 20 times his or her height will almost surely die? The difference is related to the mass (weight). Falling occurs at a constant acceleration (gravity). Force is the result of mass × acceleration, so a creature or object with more mass will strike the earth with more force and thus there is more potential for injury.

It is obvious that a falling mass will cause more damage if it falls or is dropped from a higher distance. Occasionally, one hears of the supposed fact that if a 200-lb person falls or jumps from a certain height, the effective weight is doubled or tripled. As with most popular misuses of physics, there is a hint of truth behind this, but critical details never seem to be included. It is true that the potential energy varies with both mass and drop height. *Potential energy* is defined as *mass × gravity × height* of the drop and yields energy values (e.g., foot-pounds in U.S. units, or Joules in metric units, not pounds force). The *impacting force* is highly dependent on the *give* of the impacter and/or impacted surface. If a 200-lb man stands on someone's foot, he exerts 200 lbs of force on it. If he jumps off a 6-inch curb landing with both feet on the same foot, it will be perceived by the victim to be much more than 200 lbs. The *give* is the important detail that is often missing when one is asked "how much more force does a 200-lb man exert when he jumps 6 inches onto a surface?" There is a simple formula for figuring this out, but there are important assumptions that need to be clearly stated: (1) To maximize the effect, the man must keep his joints very rigid (i.e., no bending at the knee, hip, or spine)! (2) The amount of *give* is the deformation of the foot from soft tissue compression and the like, plus the *give* in the soft tissues or shoes worn by the jumper. It would be estimated to be about 2 inches in this case illustration. Therefore, if a 200-lb man rigidly jumps 6 inches onto another person's foot, it would result in about 1200 in pounds of force. However, this must be divided by the *give*, so 1200/2 = 600 lbs of force. Thus, under these conditions/assumptions, the man's impacting force tripled his weight when he jumped 6 inches. It is very important to note that had the man flexed his ankle, his knee, his hip, and his spine, the effective force would have been much lower. Consider the high-flying maneuvers in the wrestling entertainment arena (Fig. 23-2). A 200-lb man may jump off the ropes

Fig. 23-2 Ten thousand pounds of impact force? (Photo compliments of the Christian Wrestling Federation of FI).

and fly 100 inches down to land on his opponent. His impact force is never 10,000 lbs [(200 lb × 100 inches) / 2 inches]. There are several reasons why there is no major injury: (1) He does not land with all his weight on one relatively small area (e.g., his feet planted on his opponent's head); (2) he maximizes the amount of give in his body by flexing at multiple joints; (3) his opponent also maximizes his give by flexing several joints and collapsing his body at impact; and (4) the wrestling mat is designed to provide several inches of *give* as well. But even understanding force from falls is insufficient when studying a mechanism of injury.

STRESS = FORCE PER UNIT AREA

As noted earlier, it is a common mistake to make generalizations about a supposedly injurious force without defining how it is applied. Recall that force is mass × acceleration. Once again, using a dropped object as an example, it is easy to understand the importance of *how* a force is applied. If a 2-lb knife is dropped 4 feet from one's hand, it will have a certain force. If it lands horizontally on a foot, it will bounce off harmlessly. If it lands on the point of the blade, it will quite likely penetrate the foot and cause an injury. The force in these two examples is the same (same knife mass, same drop height, same gravity, and same amount of *give* in the foot). The difference here is in the area on which the falling force was allowed to act. If force is applied to a small area, it has much greater injury potential than if it is were applied over a larger area. This is the engineering concept of stress. *Stress* is force per unit area (e.g., pounds per square inch or psi in U.S. units, Paschals in metric).

KEY POINT When trying to understand trauma, it is critical that one takes into account the shape of the surface that impacts or is impacted on as well as its *give*.

Design engineers know all too well the value of these factors. A relatively tiny amount of padding can make huge differences in the injury potential of a dashboard, shin guard, or helmet. Even better than padding is the control of deceleration. If one lengthens the time of deceleration, a great number of injuries may be mitigated. This is the basis for the development of seat belts, air bags, collapsible steering columns, laminated glass, energy-absorbing bumpers, crumple zones, and other features (Holt, 2005). All of these are designed to allow a moving person to slow down over a longer period of time (sometimes referred to as *ride down* time in motor vehicle collisions). A relatively tiny increase in ride down can mean the difference between life and death.

ENGINEERING DESIGN CHALLENGES

If one merely wanted to stop an object, it is relatively easy to accomplish this through design. For example, let us imagine that a vandal has been throwing eggs and breaking a window of a residence. If the homeowner wanted to design a window that would be break resistant, a few assumptions would be needed about the dimensions and mass of a typical egg as well as the speed at which it could be thrown. To simply stop the egg, a break-resistant window could be installed that would resist the stress of the thrown egg. However, even with this new window in place, the homeowner would still be required to clean up the mess from the shattered eggs on the window. To get an idea of the challenges that design engineers face, assume the egg is your head and it is hurled at the windshield of the car you are driving as you crash into another vehicle. It would be easy to design a windshield that keeps your head in the car, but the trick is to also keep your head from shattering. This is why biomechanics researchers will often subject cadavers or cadaver parts to impact studies (Fig. 23-3). The idea is to develop an understanding of how bodies or body parts move when subjected to injurious forces and try to establish tolerance curves. This data may ultimately be used to design

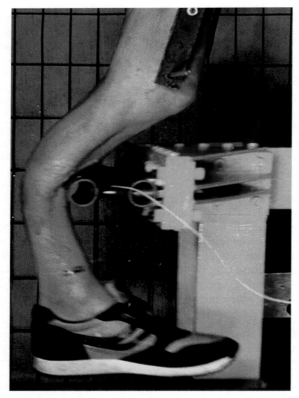

Fig. 23-3 Example of cadaver research test investigating pedestrian impact force.

crash test dummies or computer modeling programs, which, it is hoped, will translate into producing safer vehicles, sporting gear, and work environments.

It should be noted that design engineers in virtually all arenas continually attempt to improve safety, and a major way to accomplish this is to try to control acceleration/deceleration, force, and/or stress in predictable situations. For example, shin guards are designed to keep the force of an impact from being transmitted to a small portion of the leg. A small amount of padding, covered by a relatively impact-resistant shell, works very well. This spreading of the load is a key method of engineering safety. Spreading the load effectively decreases stress.

In an automotive environment, the challenge to incorporate occupant protection is quite a bit greater than designing to protect a shin from being injured by a kick in a soccer game. Crash injuries may occur because of factors such as acceleration, deceleration, rotation, intrusion, crush, and rollover, and these may occur individually, in multiples, and repeatedly.

Restraints
SEAT BELTS

Seat belts are still the primary safety feature of motor vehicles. Although initially their design was rather simple (but still fairly effective), seat belts have evolved with advances in technology and understanding of crash forces. Modern seat belts incorporate high-tech retractors with pyrotechnic pretensioners and the latest webbing materials. The combination of spool out and belt stretch allows for a more controlled ride down of a crash. The seat belt also keeps occupants in position to take advantage of other safety designs within the vehicle (padding, air bags, etc). The only area where seat belt technology has not sufficiently improved is in the area of marketing. Seat belt use is still only approximately 83% in this country according to data available on the website of the National Highway Traffic Safety Administration (NHTSA). Seat belts may cause injuries (abrasions, lacerations, and even fractures), but safety experts agree that in the overwhelming majority of cases, the restrained occupant is trading catastrophic injuries for relatively minor ones. Here are the most common arguments made to this author by consumers *not* wanting to use their seat belts: (1) "I'm afraid I won't be able to get out of the seat belt if the crash involves a fire or water submersion." (2) "I know a guy who was in a wreck, and he wouldn't have survived if he'd been wearing his seat belt because he was ejected from a massively crumpled car." (3) "I rarely drive very far or on the expressway and I'm a great driver so I won't be in an accident." (4) "It's uncomfortable and restricts my movement within my car." There is insufficient space in this chapter to list all the facts from voluminous research to counter these arguments, but briefly here are some:

1. *Fires and water.* Crashes involving fires and submersions are extremely rare, and a belted person is far more likely to survive the accident and maintain consciousness. Conscious people have a much better chance of unbuckling themselves than unconscious people! Also, a restrained driver is more likely to maintain a decent driving position during an accident and thus perhaps brake or steer away from a more severe accident (such as from driving into a pond).

2. *"I know a guy..."* I know a guy who won the lottery, but that is a one in a million chance. Time and time again, research shows that people are far more likely to be injured or killed when ejected from their vehicles. Also, the crumpling of a car is by design. There are weak spots engineered into certain parts of

the vehicle so that metal will crumple rather than intrude into the occupant space (e.g., a hood will crumple in a characteristic manner during a frontal collision so that it is not thrust through the windshield).

3. *Short trip on local roads.* This is part of the invincibility argument. Short trips and lower speed do not preclude the possibility of a serious accident. It can happen to you. Why not be prepared?

4. *Uncomfortable and restrictive.* Comfort is a poor argument, especially given that we often subject our bodies to painful actions for the simple sake of making ourselves more attractive (e.g., wearing high-heeled shoes or neck ties, getting piercings or tattoos). We accommodate to all these painful actions, and people who get in the habit of buckling up will also accommodate to the point that it is not noticeable or uncomfortable. As for restricting movement, that's the whole idea. We and our other passengers are far better protected when we are restricted from flailing around the cabin during an accident. A single unrestrained person in a vehicle with other occupants may actually *become* an injurious force. It is not uncommon for an unrestrained passenger to impact fellow passengers with injurious consequences for both.

AIR BAGS

One other argument for not wearing a seat belt is "I've got an air bag, so I don't need to wear a seat belt." Advanced air bags are an excellent safety feature, but it should be stressed up front that these are "supplemental restraint systems" designed to be used in conjunction with a seat belt. A belted person is more likely to be in proper position to take advantage of a deploying air bag. Also, air bags are limited to a single deployment (e.g., a frontal air bag will typically deploy in a frontal or near frontal impact of greater than 14 mph delta V). Accidents often involve multiple impacts, and a seat belt is a more durable restraint mechanism that is far more beneficial in multivehicle accidents and rollovers.

There is no question that air bags have saved lives. The NHTSA (2009) has estimated that from 1990 through 2008, 28,244, lives were saved by frontal air bag deployments. However, given that air bags are an explosive form of restraint, they deserve further comment. Air bag prototypes were developed in the 1950s, and their lifesaving potential (as well as injury-producing potential) were evident early on. Air bags were first required for all cars beginning in 1987 and all light trucks in 1988 per Federal Motor Vehicle Safety Standard 208. From 1987 to 1997, the automobile industry voluntarily installed 56 million driver air bags and 26 million front passenger air bags in cars destined for America's roadways. Different manufacturers chose different designs, but they all have critical components in common. The air bag is a canvas bag housed in a module that is constructed of a variety of materials. These materials include plastics, foams, and metals covered with vinyl to match the interior. Sensors at the front of a vehicle trigger deployment when a significant deceleration is registered. Air bags deploy due to pyrotechnics. An explosion is necessary in order for them to deploy quickly enough to be completely inflated during an accident and before an occupant contacts them. At the moment of deployment, the air bag module cover (with manufactured seams designed to split) peels into the occupant compartment as the inflating air bag escapes the module to occupy the space that a driver or passenger will enter a fraction of a second later during the crash event.

Sodium azide is the propellant used to initiate the deployment cycle in most air bag designs today. When it is ignited, the gaseous by-products of combustion fill the bag. The module cover

and deploying air bag have produced injuries and even deaths. The NHTSA has confirmed 296 deaths from air bag deployments since 1990. Of these, 93 were adult drivers, 13 were adult passengers, and 185 were children. First-generation bags would be propelled toward the occupant at up to 210 mph. Second-generation bags deployed with 25% to 30% less power. Advanced air bags installed in cars since 2007 now take advantage of an array of sensors designed to let the computer estimate the position or weight of the occupant and determine if and how violently the air bag should deploy for the given crash circumstances. The combination of technological advances and a better informed consumer (don't sit closer than 10 inches to the air bag module cover; don't let small children sit near an air bag; wear your seat belt, etc.) has led to a dramatic decrease in the number of deaths due to air bag deployments (Fig. 23-4). Although deaths are now rare, it is important to note there are still many injuries from air bag deployments.

INJURIES FROM THE MODULE COVER

The violently moving module cover is potentially a significant injury-producing factor. The driver's side cover is generally made of a rubberized plastic material that blends with the rest of the steering wheel. A major problem with steering wheel–mounted air bags is their proximity to various controls for the horn, cruise control, and radio, which are often mounted inside the rim of the steering wheel and thus they are close to the deploying air bag and module cover. Hand and arm injuries observed in individuals whose extremities were in contact or close proximity to the module at the moment of its rupture include degloving, fracture dislocations, and amputation (partial and complete) of digits and forearms (Fig. 23-5) (Huelke, Moore, Comptom, et al., 1994; Smock, 1992, 2000; Smock & Nichols, 1995).

If the module cover impacts the occupant's face, head, or neck, skull fractures and severe and fatal head injuries have been observed (NHTSA, 2004; Smock & Nichols, 1995). The passenger module cover often has a large metal housing, which adds even more potential for producing injuries (Figs. 23-6 to 23-8).

INJURIES FROM AN AIR BAG INTERACTION

In the initial phase of deployment, wounds may be produced as the air bag punches out from the module cover, especially in persons seated too close. Rapid acceleration of the head may lead to atlanto-occipital dislocations; skull fractures, cervical spine fractures, and brain stem transection; cardiac, hepatic, and splenic lacerations; diffuse axonal injuries; cortical contusions, subdural, and epidural hematomas (Fig. 23-9) (Horsch, Lau, Andrzejak, et al., 1990; Mertz & Weber, 1982; NHTSA, 2003; Prasad & Daniel, 1984).

Catapult-type injuries are seen when occupants impact the air bag during the midstage of its deployment. They are injuries consistent with the head and neck having been driven rapidly upward and rearward. Severe cervical spine hyperextension occurs with energy sufficient to rupture blood vessels and ligaments and to fracture cervical vertebrae. The cervical spine injuries more commonly seen from this kind of movement are atlanto-occipital dislocation, comminuted fractures of one or more vertebrae, rupture of the anterior and posterior longitudinal spinal ligaments, and cervical spine disarticulation with transection of the cervical cord (Horsch, Lau, Andrzejak, et al., 1990; Mertz & Weber, 1982; NHTSA, 2004; Prasad & Daniel, 1984). The airway is also susceptible to direct trauma. Blows to the trachea or larynx from the module cover or air bag can fracture the hyoid bone and laryngeal

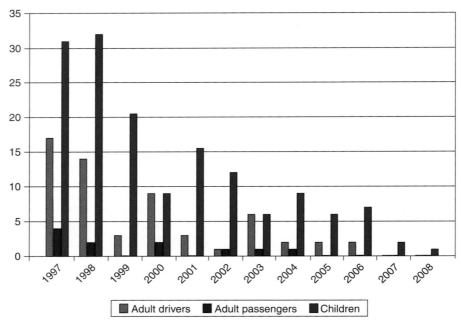

Fig. 23-4 Confirmed frontal air bag–related fatalities in the past 12 years (NHTSA, 2009).

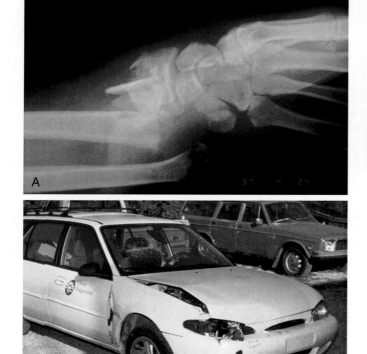

Fig. 23-5 *A,* This victim sustained a partial hand amputation from placement of a hand on the passenger module cover while bracing for a minor impact. *B,* The 1995 Ford Escort displays minor damage, yet the restrained passenger sustained a permanently disabling hand injury.

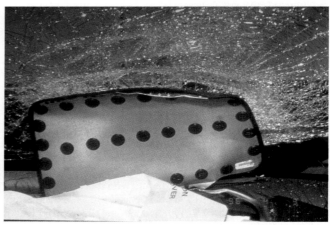

Fig. 23-6 Passenger-side air bag module covers may contain a metal housing. Placement of any extremity on the module cover, to brace oneself, will result in severe traumatic injuries including amputations of hands, arms, fingers, and feet.

structures and thus may compromise respiratory efforts (Perdikis, Schmitt, Chait, et al., 2000). Air bag–induced retropharyngeal hematomas have been noted to result in fatal airway compromise (Tenofsky, Porter, & Shaw, 2000).

Bag slap–type injuries are incurred during the latter stage of deployment when the bag is at the peak of its excursion. When the canvas bag slaps the occupant's face, abrasions commonly result (Figs. 23-10 and 23-11).

Eye injuries from air bags range in severity from corneal abrasions and chemical burns–basic (high pH) caused by contact with unburned sodium azide–to retinal detachment and globe rupture (Fig. 23-12) (Baker, Flowers, Singh, et al., 1996; Bhavasar, Chen, & Goldstein, 1997; Duma, Kress, Porta, et al., 1996; Gault, Vichnin,

Fig. 23-7 The placement of a horn activation button on the module cover is an invitation to a traumatic upper extremity injury. Many severe air bag–induced hand injuries have occurred because drivers were attempting to blow the horn when the air bag detonated.

Jaeger, et al., 1995; Ghafouri, Burgess, Hrdlicka, et al., 1997; Han, 1993; Kuhn, Morris, Witherspoon, et al., 1993; Larkin, 1991; Lesher, Durrie, & Stiles, 1993; Manche, Goldberg, & Mondino, 1997; Rosenblatt, Freilich, & Kirsch, 1993; Scott, Greenfield, & Parrish, 1996; Scott, John, & Stark, 1993; Vichnin, Jaeger, Gault, et al., 1995; Walz, Mackay, & Gloor, 1995; Whitacre & Pilchard, 1993). In some cases, eyeglasses appear to have afforded the wearer an appreciable degree of protection from these sequelae.

Shortly after the air bag begins inflating, it begins to deflate. Exhaust ports typically located on the surface facing away from the occupants allow the escape of the gaseous by-products of the combustion of the sodium azide propellant, as well as other inert materials like cornstarch and talc (Gross, Haidar, Basha, et al., 1994; Gross, Koets, D'Arcy, et al., 1995; Weiss, 1996). Chemical pneumonitis and asthma-type symptoms have been observed in individuals who have inhaled the gases. Air bag deployment is often associated with the simultaneous presence of a whitish cloud of these products that occupants frequently mistake for smoke

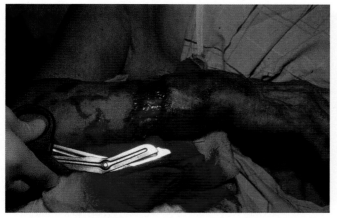

Fig. 23-8 A severe degloving, open fracture of the radius and ulna from forearm contact with the module cover of a 1989 Lincoln Continental.

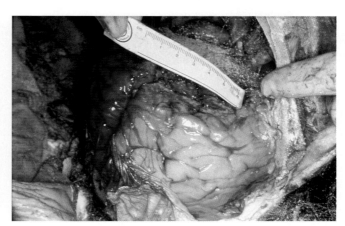

Fig 23-9 Air bag deployment rapidly accelerated the victim's head rearward, causing bridging veins to tear and this resultant subdural hematoma.

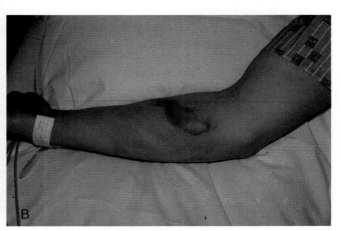

Fig. 23-10 Abrasions to the face *(A)* and arms *(B)* are common injuries and are typically sustained during the final or "bag-slap" state of deployment.

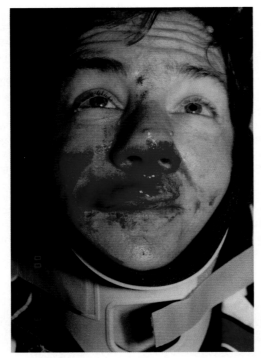

Fig. 23-11 Facial abrasions are the most common air bag–induced injury seen in the emergency department. This 34-year-old restrained driver estimated that her face was approximately 12 inches from the module cover at the time of deployment.

from a vehicle fire. The gaseous products may also cause chemical irritation to eyes and open wounds.

Examination of the air bag and the module cover may reveal evidence of impact with the injured occupant (Smock, 2000). Trace and gross evidence may give investigators valuable clues

regarding an occupant's position at the time of the collision and the configuration of the steering wheel at the moment of the bag's deployment. Evidence transferred from occupant to air bag may take various forms. Of course, blood and epithelial tissue are the most common transfers, but lipstick, blush, and mascara are also common.

Fractures

The preceding review of physics and restraints is certainly applicable to the discussions on sharp and blunt injuries, as well as motor vehicle–collision reconstruction later in this unit. But much of this can also be applied to the study of bone fractures. Bone tends to fracture in fairly consistent patterns when subjected to particular forces. It should, however, be noted that these patterns are often obscured or obliterated when the energy of impact is great and bone fragmentation is prominent. In medical terms, we say that the patterns may be difficult to discern because of comminution. It is generally accepted that greater input force results in greater potential energy, and this can lead to greater comminution, but one must be careful not to jump to this conclusion until bone integrity is also considered. Weakened bones (as a result of osteoporosis, *osteogenesis imperfecta*, rickets, etc.) will tend to fragment with far less force than normal healthy bones. Likewise, smaller bones will fracture with less force than larger bones.

Any break in a bone is termed a *fracture*. Fractures may be described by a number of eponyms, but basic anatomical descriptions are preferable. First, is the skin broken over the

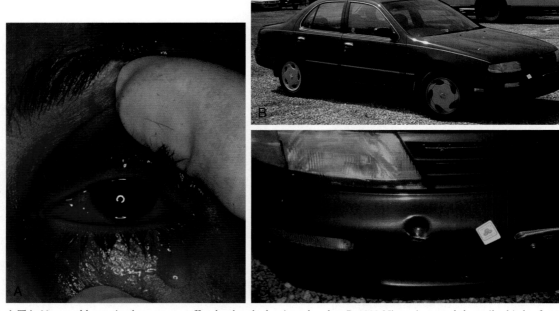

Fig. 23-12 *A,* This 33-year-old restrained passenger suffered a detached retina when her *B,* 1993 Nissan impacted the trailer hitch of a stopped truck at very low speed. *C,* Note minor damage on bumper from trailer hitch.

fracture? If so, it is termed an *open fracture*; if not, it is a *closed fracture*. How many fragments are seen? If none, then the fracture is considered *incomplete*. If the bone is broken into two or more pieces, it is a *complete fracture*. Finally, if the bone is fractured into more than two fragments, it is termed *comminuted*. These descriptive terms merely give a clue about the magnitude of force applied to a bone and/or the structural integrity of the bone. A fracture pattern, if distinguished, tells much more about how a bone was broken.

IMPACT FORCE

When a body part is hit or a body part hits something, this is generally referred to as an impact fracture. When viewed in a laboratory setting, it is clear that bone will attempt to bend before it breaks (except in cases like gunshot wounds where the soft and hard tissues in the local bullet impact area accelerate so quickly that the entire bone organ is unable to bend). Bending fractures result in the struck part of the bone (the concave part of the bend) being subjected to compressive forces. The bone begins to fail (fracture) on the opposite side. This is because the tissue on the convex side of the bending bone is in tension (being stretched). When periosteum is removed, it often becomes clear that a bending bone shows multiple signs of failure emanating from the tensile side. Figure 23-13 shows the lateral view of a tested human femur (Porta, 1996). Notice the tension lines emanating from the posterior edge of the bone (on the left side of the image). This bone was hit on the anterior surface. As it bent, tension lines

radiated back toward the hit surface. From this image, one can see that transverse, oblique, and wedge-type fracture patterns are all manifestations of bending failure. In this case, an oblique fracture resulted. It is not currently clear what determines which of the three patterns will appear, but it may be as simple as the precise angle of impact or the line with the least amount of bone tissue because of the presence of Haversian canals and so on. Note that a wedge fracture is usually a telltale sign for the direction of impact because the base of the wedge is the side that was struck. Likewise, if tension lines are visible on medical imaging or at autopsy, the direction of impact may be determined for a transverse or oblique fracture pattern, because the lines emanate from the opposite side of the impact (Kress, Porta, Snider, et al., 1995). The shape of the impactor or impacted site must not be ignored. If sufficient force is transmitted through a broad surface, then a segmental fracture may result.

TWISTING FORCE

The oblique pattern is one that has probably caused more discussion than any other. Some authors assume that transverse fractures were due to bending/impact and oblique fractures were due to some combination of bending and twisting. It is now clear that oblique fractures need no twisting force whatsoever. However, in the event that twisting and bending are combined, oblique patterns may result if the bending force is more prevalent than the twisting force (Frick, 2003). If twisting is the predominant force, a distinct and elegant fracture pattern known as a spiral is seen (Fig. 23-14). In a single radiograph, of low quality, this is sometimes confused with an oblique pattern. But good-quality orthogonal x-rays will almost always show the definitive signs of the spiral—the presence of a helical fracture line connected by a vertically oriented hinge (so called because it often retains the periosteal connections across the vertical fracture component).

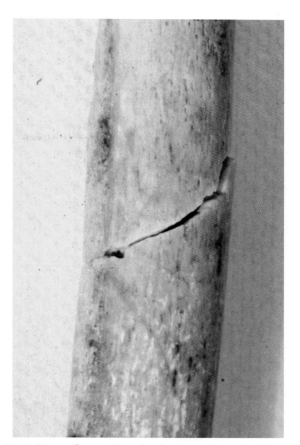

Fig. 23-13 Human femur subjected to bending or impact loading on the anterior surface. Tension lines radiate from a point on the posterior surface toward the anterior (Porta, 1996).

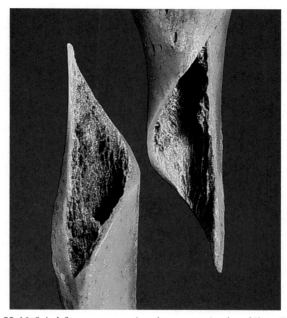

Fig. 23-14 Spiral fracture pattern in a humerus twisted to failure (Porta, 1996). (Photo courtesy Patrick Besant-Matthews, M.D.)

COMPRESSIVE FORCE

When a compressive force is applied to a bone along its long axis, and that force is relatively pure, then an impacted fracture can be expected—that is, the diaphysis will be driven into the epiphyseal spongy bone. But it should be known that our bones are designed to support our body weight and thus are considerably stronger in axial loading than in bending. For example, when the knee of an unrestrained motor vehicle occupant strikes the dashboard during a frontal crash, acetabular or pelvic fractures may result before the femur fails. When the femur does fracture, it is often at the epiphyseal bone—femoral neck proximally or in the area of the condyles distally (Box 23-3).

Summary

An understanding of basic physics, and especially the nuances of acceleration, force, and stress, is critical if one is to attempt to reconstruct accidents or the injuries that occur in them. This knowledge should be helpful in understanding the design of restraints and the potential injuries that may result from their use. The manner by which forces are applied to bones will often result in a distinct fracture pattern, which may be important in a forensic case. In addition to aiding in motor vehicle accident reconstruction, a knowledge of the cause of particular fracture patterns may also be useful when, for example, attempting to corroborate the story of caregiver suspected of physically abusing a child. If the story indicates a bending type of force but the fracture pattern is a spiral (a result of twisting), there should be an elevated level of suspicion.

Box 23-3 Fracture Patterns and Mechanism of Injury

FRACTURE PATTERN	LIKELY MECHANISM OF INJURY
Transverse	Bending
Oblique	Bending
Wedge	Bending
Spiral	Twisting
Impacted	Compression
Segmental	Impact by broad surface
Comminuted	Difficult to determine

References

Allen, M. E., Weir-Jones, I., Motiuk, D. R, Flewin, K. R., Goring, R. D., Kobetitch, A., et al. (1994). Acceleration perturbations in everyday living. A comparison to whiplash. *Spine, 19*(11), 1285–1290.

Baker, R. S., Flowers, C. W., Singh, P., et al. (1996). Corneoscleral laceration caused by air-bag trauma. *American Journal of Ophthalmology, 121*(6), 709–711.

Bhavasar, A. R., Chen, T. C., & Goldstein, D. A. (1997). Corneoscleral laceration associated with passenger-side airbag inflation (Letter to the Editor). *The British Journal of Ophthalmology, 81*(6), 514–515.

Brach, R. M., & Brach, R. M. (2005). Vehicle accident analysis and reconstruction methods. Warrendale, PA: Society of Automotive Engineers (SAE).

Duma, S. M., Kress, T. A., Porta, D. J., et al. (1996). Airbag-induced eye injuries: A report of 25 cases. *The Journal of Trauma, 41*(1), 114–119.

Frick, S. (2003). *The Effects of Combined Torsion and Bending Loads on Fresh Human Cadaver Femurs*. [master's thesis]. Louisville, KY: University of Louisville School of Medicine.

Funk, J. R., Cormier, J. M., Bain, C. E., Guzman, H., & Bonugli, E. (2007). An evaluation of various neck injury criteria in vigorous activities. 2007. In *Proceedings of the International Research Council on the Biomechanics of Impact (IRCOBI)*. (pp. 233–248).

Gault, J. A., Vichnin, M. C., Jaeger, E. A., et al. (1995). Ocular injuries associated with eyeglass wear and airbag inflation. *The Journal of Trauma, 38*(4), 494–497.

Ghafouri, A., Burgess, S. K., Hrdlicka, Z. K., et al. (1997). Airbag–related ocular trauma. *The American Journal of Emergency Medicine, 15*(4), 389–392.

Gross, K. B., Haidar, A. H., Basha, M. A., et al. (1994). Acute pulmonary response of asthmatics to aerosols and gases generated by airbag deployment. *American Journal of Respiratory and Critical Care Medicine, 150*(2), 408–414.

Gross, K. B., Koets, M. H., D'Arcy, J. B., et al. (1995). Mechanism of induction of asthmatic attacks by the inhalation of particles generated by airbag system deployment. *The Journal of Trauma, 38*(4), 521–527.

Han, D. P. (1993). Retinal detachment caused by air bag injury (case report). *Archives of Ophthalmology, 111*(10), 1317–1318.

Holt, J. (2005). *100 Years of Vehicle Safety Developments*. Warrendale, PA: Society of Automotive Engineers (SAE).

Horsch, J., Lau, I., Andrzejak, D., et al. (1990). *Assessment of air bag deployment loads*. SAE Paper No. 902324. Detroit: Society of Automotive Engineers.

Huelke, D. F., Moore, J. L., Comptom, T. W., et al. (1994). *Upper extremity injuries related to air bag deployments*. SAE Publication No. 940716. Detroit: Society of Automotive Engineers.

Kress, T. A., Porta, D. J., Snider, J., & Fuller, P. M. (1995). Fracture patterns of human cadaver long bones. In *Proceedings of the International Research Council on the Biomechanics of Impact (IRCOBI)*. (pp. 155–169).

Kuhn, F., Morris, R., Witherspoon, C. D., et al. (1993). Air bag: Friend or foe? (editorial). *Archives of Ophthalmology, 111*(10), 1333–1334.

Larkin, G. L. (1991). Airbag-mediated corneal injury. *The American Journal of Emergency Medicine, 9*(5), 444–446.

Lesher, M. P., Durrie, D. S., & Stiles, M. C. (1993). Corneal edema, hyphema, and angle recession after air bag inflation (case report). *Archives of Ophthalmology, 111*(10), 1320–1322.

Manche, E. E., Goldberg, R. A., & Mondino, B. J. (1997). Airbag–related ocular injuries. *Ophthalmic Surgery and Lasers, 28*(3), 246–250.

Mertz, H. J., & Weber, D. A. (1982). *Interpretations of impact response to a three year old child dummy relative to child injury potential*. SAE Paper No. 826048. Detroit: General Motors.

National Highway Transportation Safety Administration (NHTSA). (2003). *The Third Report to Congress on the Effectiveness of Occupant Protection Systems and Their Use and Air Bag Related Fatalities and Serious Injuries*. Retrieved from www.nhtsa.dot.gov/airbags. Accessed December 2, 2009.

National Highway Traffic Safety Administration (NHTSA). (2009). *NHTSA Special Crash Investigations–Counts of Frontal Airbag Related Fatalities and Seriously Injured Persons*. Report dated January 2009. Washington, D.C.: U.S. Department of Transportation, National Center for Statistics and Analysis, Crash Investigation Division. Available at http://www-nrd.nhtsa.dot.gov/pubs/811104.pdf. Accessed December 2, 2009.

National Highway Transportation Safety Administration (NHTSA). (2004). *Sensible Solutions*. Retrieved from www.airbagonoff.com.

Ng, T. P., Bussone, W. R., Duma, S. M., & Kress, T. A. (2006). Thoracic and lumbar spine accelerations in everyday activities. *Biomedical Sciences Instrumentation, 42*, 410–415.

Perdikis, G., Schmitt, T., Chait, D., & Richards, A. T. (2000). Blunt laryngeal fracture: Another airbag injury. *The Journal of Trauma, 48*(3), 544–546.

Porta, D. J. (1996). *Anatomy and biomechanics of experimentally traumatized human cadaver lower extremity components [dissertation]*. Louisville, KY: University of Louisville School of Medicine.

Porta, D. J. (2005). Biomechanics of impact. In J. Rich, D. Dean, & R. Powers (Ed.), *Forensic medicine of the lower extremity* (pp. 279–310). Totowa, NJ: Human Press.

Prasad, P., & Daniel, R. P. (1984). *A biomechanical analysis of head, neck and torso injuries to child surrogates due to sudden torso acceleration*. SAE Paper No. 841656. Detroit: Society of Automotive Engineers.

Rivers, R. W. (2006). Speed analysis. In R. W. Rivers (Ed.), *Evidence in traffic crash investigation and reconstruction* (pp. 183–229). Springfield IL: Charles C Thomas Publisher.

Rosenblatt, M. A., Freilich, B., & Kirsch, D. (1993). Air bag–associated ocular injury (case report). *Archives of Ophthalmology, 111*(10), 1318.

Scott, I. U., Greenfield, D. S., & Parrish, R. K. (1996). Airbag-associated injury producing cyclodialysis cleft and ocular hypotony. *Ophthalmic Surgery and Lasers, 27*(11), 955–957.

Scott, I., John, G. R., & Stark, W. J. (1993). Air bag–associated ocular injury (case report reply). *Archives of Ophthalmology, 111*(10), 1318.

Smock, W. S. (1992). Traumatic avulsion of the first digit, secondary to air bag deployment. In Proceedings (Vol. 36, p. 44). Des Plains, IL: Association for the Advancement of Automotive Medicine.

Smock, W. S. (2000). Airbag related injuries & deaths. In J. A. Siegel, P. J. Saukko, & G. C. Knupfer (Eds.), *Encyclopedia of forensic science.* London: Academic Press.

Smock, W. S., & Nichols, G. N. (1995). Air bag module cover injuries. *The Journal of Trauma, 38*(4), 489–492.

Tenofsky, P., Porter, S. W., & Shaw, J. W. (2000). Fatal airway compromise due to retropharyngeal hematoma after airbag deployment. *The American Surgeon, 66*(7), 692–694.

Vichnin, M. C., Jaeger, E. A., Gault, J. A., et al. (1995). Ocular injuries related to air bag inflation. *Ophthalmic Surgery and Lasers, 26*(6), 542–548.

Walz, F. H., Mackay, M., & Gloor, B. (1995). Airbag deployment and eye perforation by a tobacco pipe. *The Journal of Trauma, 38*(4), 498–501.

Weiss, J. S. (1996). Reactive airway dysfunction syndrome due to sodium azide inhalation. *International Archives of Occupational and Environmental Health, 68*(6), 469–471.

Whitacre, M. M., & Pilchard, W. A. (1993). Air bag injury producing retinal dialysis and detachment (case report). *Archives of Ophthalmology, 111*(10), 1320.

CHAPTER 24 Motor Vehicle Collision Reconstruction

Kristine Karcher

Motor vehicle collisions are considered a medicolegal event. The accurate investigation and reconstruction of motor vehicle collisions are important for determining the cause and events involved in a crash and provide valuable information and statistics that are used to produce safety changes. These include improvements in vehicle and roadway engineering, as well as information that may be useful in criminal or civil prosecutions. The annual production of vehicles continually integrates new features to improve the safety of occupants based on the information obtained. Roadway engineers will improve dangerous sections of highway based on the frequency and cause of crashes at a certain location. The importance of a thorough investigation and collision reconstruction cannot be underestimated. The forensic nurse examiner can contribute significantly in the investigation through knowledge of injuries, injury causation, and the understanding of the **biomechanics** of impact.

KEY POINT The analysis of motor vehicle collisions by the accident reconstructionist contributes to improved automotive and roadway design and develops evidence for criminal or civil prosecutions.

Laws of Motion

It is important to have an understanding of the basic physics that govern the behavior of all moving objects, including vehicles. **Newton's first law of motion** states that if you are in rest you tend to remain in rest, whereas if you are in motion you tend to remain in motion, unless you are acted upon by an unbalanced external force. This describes inertia. If you are an occupant of a vehicle and it suddenly stops, the inertia of your body will tend to resist the stopping, and you will slide forward against your seat belt. **Newton's second law of motion** states that the acceleration of any body is directly proportional to the force acting on the body, whereas it is inversely proportional to the mass or weight of the body. If you are an occupant in a vehicle and it is traveling 50 miles per hour (mph), your body within the vehicle will also be traveling at the same rate of speed. **Newton's third law of motion** states that for every force exerted on a body by another body, there is an equal but opposite force reacting on the first body by the second. In other words, for every action there is an equal but opposite reaction. In the field of motor vehicle collision investigation, acting and reacting forces are found when a vehicle skids to a stop.

Biomechanics of Impact

The science that assists us in understanding the mechanism of injury and the tolerance of the human body is known as the *biomechanics of impact* and links medicine with science. In vehicle crashes, the injuries generated are related to both the speed of the vehicle and how suddenly it stops. This sudden change in velocity is known as **delta V** and measures the severity of the crash or impact. This change in velocity may occur to the occupant's entire body or specific blows to certain areas. It is dependent on the varying deceleration that occurs to anatomical structures, such as the head (for example, impacting the windshield), chest (impacting the steering wheel), or lower extremities (striking the dashboard) within the vehicle. The human response to these various forces and the change in vehicle velocity contributes to the science of biomechanics (Association for the Advancement of Automotive Medicine (AAAM) 1992).

Vehicle collision investigators describe a collision as a series of four impacts:
1. When the vehicle impacts something that changes or stops its speed
2. When the occupant is thrust toward the direction of the impact, striking the interior of the vehicle
3. When the occupant's various body parts collide within the person's body. (Besant-Matthews, 1998)
4. When objects (pets, groceries, aluminum cans, etc.) being carried within the vehicle impact the body.

The human body, observing the laws of motion, continues to move forward at the same rate of speed that the vehicle was traveling. The shorter the time and distance to stop, the greater the force required to bring motion to a halt. The opposite is true when the time and distance to stop deceleration is delayed—the force is reduced. Consequently, if a person decelerates more gradually, this will improve the chance that less bodily injury will occur (Besant-Matthews, 1998). The slower the deceleration, sometimes by just a few feet or a fraction of a second, the greater chance there is for positive occupant outcome.

Automotive Engineering Improvements

Automotive engineering improvements include seat belts, air bags, auto safety glass, and changes in dashboards.

SEAT BELTS

The development and implementation of seat belt use has proved the most effective advancement in the prevention of serious injuries and fatalities. Seat belts were designed to provide a longer ride down (deceleration) within the vehicle, allowing occupants to avoid impact with the interior of the car. The longer the ride down, the less chance there is of injury. This is accomplished by the actual stretching of the seat belt, as much as 6% to 14%, to allow the occupant to decelerate slower and ride down the collision. Seat belts also prevent ejection from the vehicle by holding the occupants in their seats and distributing the force more evenly over the body surfaces (Besant-Matthews, 1998).

The force in a serious crash is such that parts of the human body are still going to contact the steering wheel, dashboard, or windshield. The average forward motion in an abrupt collision at 34.2 mph can result in forward movement of the head 22 inches, forward movement of the chest 15¾ inches, and forward movement of the pelvis 14½ inches. This forward motion is due to seat belt stretch, seat belt slack, improper use of the seat belt (i.e., wearing it too loose or in the wrong position) (Besant-Matthews, 1998), and, finally, momentary flexing of vehicle parts. The ride down of properly worn seat belts has reduced death and injury by 45% (AAAM, 1992) (Fig. 24-1).

Injuries associated with seat belt use range from superficial abrasions in minor collisions to major internal injuries in high-impact collisions. Lap belts may cause lacerations or injury to the liver, spleen, omentum, and mesentery, whereas shoulder belts are often the cause of injuries such as fractures to the spine, clavicle, sternum, and rib cage.

AIR BAGS

To improve and supplement seat belts, air bags were developed. Not only do they protect the chest from the steering wheel and column, they provide gradual deceleration of the head and neck, preventing the whiplash motion of frontal impact. The use of air bags has significantly decreased injuries to the neck, face, and head that only a few years ago were commonly seen when drivers impacted steering wheels. As with seat belts, air bags also have associated injuries (see Chapter 23).

Commonly made of a nylon-type material, air bags are kept folded in a container until sensors detect a frontal collision of sufficient force, causing them to deploy. Air bags deploy at speeds of up to 150 to 200 mph in 24 to 45 milliseconds. Bursting through the flaps that cover them, air bags deploy with enough force to dislocate, fracture, and even amputate thumbs (Spitz, 2006). They are capable of causing an array of injuries including fractures to the forearms, abrasions and contusions to the face, corneal abrasions, and head injuries (Spitz, 2006). With the increased use of side air bags, related injuries including rib fractures and related contusions and abrasions will be observed. In spite of associated injuries, air

bags and seat belts have played a major role in decreasing the fatalities associated with motor vehicle collisions.

AUTO SAFETY GLASS

Another safety improvement to vehicles is to the material content of windshields. They are made of two layers of glass, separated by a thicker interlayer of polyvinyl butyryl. This allows the windshield to absorb more energy and freely bulge (as much as 5 inches) before the plastic interlayer tears. In a high-speed collision, the body is thrust forward and the head arches forward and downward, making contact with the windshield and often resulting in large, deep cuts. These cuts may be horizontal, diagonal, or parallel to the face and neck because of head bobbing after impact. In less severe impacts, the incisions to the face will be more superficial. These injuries can be seen on the nose and forehead and result as the head slides down the sharp edges of broken glass (Spitz, 2006) (Fig. 24-2).

Side windows differ in construction and are not laminated, as are the windshields. Injuries associated with impact to the side windows are very identifiable. When side glass is broken, it disintegrates into numerous ¼-inch cubes with sharp edges. These produce right-angled superficial cuts to the skin and are referred to as dicing injuries (Spitz, 2006). Dicing injuries are easily recognized and are usually located on the side of the face, shoulder, or arm nearest the involved side window. The presence of dicing injuries can assist in determining where an occupant was seated in the vehicle at the time of impact. In the clinical setting (hospital, emergency department), pieces of glass that remain embedded in the wound would be secured as evidence (Figs. 24-3a and b).

DASHBOARDS

Change of dashboard contour is another safety feature development that is worth discussion. Dashboards have the capability of changing form up to 3 inches, contributing to a slower deceleration. The knees commonly contact the dashboard in frontal, head-on collisions. The severity of injuries to the knees depends on the amount of contact that occurs with the dash and may range from a bruise or minor abrasion to a large laceration or dislocation/fracture. It is important to examine both knees for even subtle injury. The steering wheel column has undergone safety features as well and is constructed to collapse when impacted by an occupant, allowing for a slower ride down.

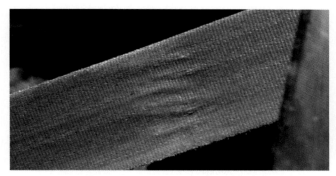

Fig. 24-1 Characteristic appearance of "stretched" seat belt.

Fig. 24-2 Safety windshield glass is fractured and stretched from force of impact, but it retains its integrity because of a shatterproof design.

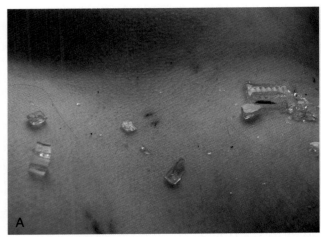 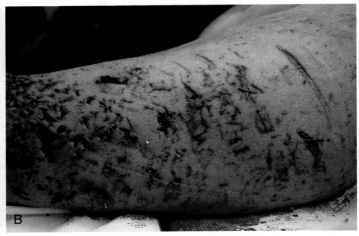

Fig. 24-3 A, Characteristic of vehicle side windows in which the glass disintegrated into cubes when impacted. **B,** Dicing injury pattern from glass cubes.

Probably the most overlooked piece of evidence on the body at a collision scene is patterned injuries. These usually arise from contact with something within the vehicle, such as a knob or handle, and may be subtle or very impressive. As with other injuries, they may help investigators determine the position of the occupant, as well as the direction of impact.

Collisions

Types of collisions to consider include frontal, side-angled, motorcycle, and automobile versus pedestrian crashes.

FRONTAL

Frontal collisions account for 50% of all motor vehicle crashes. The force to a unrestrained occupant in a frontal crash of a vehicle traveling 30 mph and impacting a rigid object resulting in a 2-foot intrusion to the bumper is equivalent to falling out a third-story window onto concrete. This intrusion to the front of the vehicle occurs in 90 to 100 milliseconds or one tenth of the time it takes to blink (AAAM, 1992). Vehicles do not have structures that crush uniformly. Front structures such as the bumper or grill are much less rigid and do not actually slow a vehicle as much as contact with more rigid structures such as the vehicle frame, engine, or suspension. As previously mentioned, an unrestrained front seat occupant of a vehicle traveling 30 mph would strike the dashboard, steering wheel, or windshield with different parts of the body. The injuries would then relate to the structures within the front of the vehicle that were impacted and the amount of localized deceleration of each. For instance, was the occupant's head experiencing a slower ride down because of windshield bulge, or were chest injuries lessened because the steering wheel column collapsed?

SIDE OR ANGLED

Side or angled collisions account for approximately 20% of motor vehicle crashes (Fig. 24-4). The occupants move toward the point of impact and often make contact with the windows, A-pillars (roof supporters between the windshield and front door), or roof. Even in 90-degree side impacts, lap belts will restrain the occupant. The rotation of vehicles after impact will often complicate the injuries observed to the occupant. Common injuries that result from lateral or side impacts include rib fractures, lung contusions, hemothorax, pericardial damage, and aortic rupture or tears. If the

Fig. 24-4 Side-impact crash. Note the bulging of the windshield as a result of the massive forces applied during the collision.

vehicle rolls over and makes no contact with a solid object, the injuries observed may be minor, but if the vehicle strikes a solid object, the injuries will be more severe. Ejection of occupants through the doors or windows of a vehicle are not uncommon in rollovers. Ejected occupants often have severe neck, head, or brain injury, and research has shown that most injuries to occupants are sustained before they are ejected.

MOTORCYCLE

Motorcycle collisions account for about 8% of motor vehicle crashes, and the rider is 10% to 25% more likely to be killed or injured based on a comparison of miles traveled. Helmets have decreased the incidence of head injury. The injuries sustained by the rider of a motorcycle usually involve the head, chest, and lower extremities. The lower limbs are usually in direct contact with bumpers or the objects they are impacting.

AUTO VERSUS PEDESTRIAN

Pedestrians account for 16% of road deaths, which usually occur in urban areas at speeds less then 22 mph. An adult is impacted at knee level and may sustain fractures as well as ligament and joint injury. These are commonly referred to as bumper injuries and increase with severity as the vehicle speed/impact increase. Bumper injury results when impact occurs at the level of the most protuberant section of the bumper, and the pattern of the bumper may be evident on the pedestrian (a patterned injury). If the vehicle was braking, the bumper will be at a lower level when it contacts the pedestrian. On impact, the pedestrian is rotated onto the hood of the vehicle, frequently fracturing the femur. As the pedestrian continues onto the hood of the vehicle, his or her body is accelerated to the speed of the vehicle and will be thrown onto the roadway where rolling and sliding injuries will be sustained. At this point, the pedestrian may actually be run over by the vehicle. There is tremendous potential for injuries to pedestrians struck by vehicles. Injuries are often extensive and may include fractures to the skull, spine, pelvis, ribs, or extremities, as well as multiple contusions, abrasions and lacerations.

The higher bumper, such as that on a truck, impacting an adult pedestrian, usually results in the pedestrian being thrown directly down onto the roadway. The person may be carried on the front of the vehicle and dropped to the ground as a result of inertia as the vehicle slows down. It is not unusual for the pedestrian to be run over by the vehicle if the brakes are not applied. A child struck by a car is comparable to an adult being struck by the height of a bumper on a truck. However, as one might imagine, injuries are most often to the head and pelvis.

Bumper injuries provide valuable information about the position and movement of the pedestrian at the time of impact. Questions regarding standing, walking, running, or being struck from behind must be in the foreground of the investigator's thoughts. Comparison measurements must be made between the height of the bumper injury and the height of the bumper of the vehicle in determining whether or not the driver was braking. Tire tread marks may be evident on the clothing or skin, and glass or paint transfer should not be overlooked.

Motor Vehicle Collision Reconstruction

The reconstruction of a motor vehicle collision determines how the crash occurred and is based on evidence gathered at the scene. The absence of a thorough investigation will limit *and* compromise the outcome of the reconstruction. The evidence collected combined with the thoroughness of the investigation is critical to a reconstruction.

SCENE AND VEHICLE

The scene of the collision provides additional roadway evidence that the reconstructionist will measure and examine, including skid marks, yaw tire marks (markings from a sliding vehicle), gouges or scrapes in the pavement, the final positions of the vehicles, and debris from the vehicles themselves. The area of the initial impact will be determined. Damage to the vehicles is examined for the amount and direction of intrusion or crumple, and secondary impact. Secondary impact occurs when several vehicles are involved or if the vehicle impacted a roadway object, such as a road sign, before or after the initial collision. The amount of intrusion is measured and will help investigators determine the rate of vehicle speed at the point of impact. Vehicles crush differently; for example, newer vehicles have safety features such as crumple zones that are designed to slow deceleration. Engineers have designed engines to collapse down and back during a collision, which increases the amount of visible distortion to the front of

the vehicle. The damage may appear severe when in actuality the vehicle was responding the way it was designed to, by providing a slower deceleration to the occupants (Fig. 24-5). The amounts of tire tread, tire pressure, brakes, steering, and the overall mechanical wellness of the vehicle should be assessed. If there is a question as to whether vehicle lights were in use at the time of impact or if a vehicle was braking, light filaments will be examined. If the light were in use, the filament would be hot on impact causing it to stretch. If the lights were off, the filament would be cool on impact and would break easily. The reconstructionist must also consider obstructions, such as weather or a dirty windshield, that would have interfered with the driver's view when determining additional details of the collision.

WITNESS ACCOUNTS

Information should be obtained surrounding the drivers of the vehicles, including witness statements regarding the collision and observations of the vehicles before the collision. Were the drivers observed driving erratically or otherwise unsafely? The investigators will seek information about the driver's driving experience, where and when the driver started traveling, where the driver was traveling to, whether the driver stopped to eat, and whether he or she was fatigued, under stress, emotionally upset, preoccupied (e.g., using a cell phone), or under the influence of alcohol or drugs (illegal or prescription). The forensic nurse examiner (FNE) can assist in collecting blood or urine from the drivers following the guidelines of the state or hospital. Every attempt should be made to gather as much information as possible.

BEST PRACTICE Witness accounts of the accident and statements regarding the driver's behavior before the crash will be invaluable for determining why and how the collision occurred.

VEHICLE INTERIOR DETAILS

The interior of the vehicles will be examined for evidence, such as seat belt use and air bag deployment. Seat belts are examined for stretch, as well as for transfer from the clothing of the occupants. If the air bag deployed, DNA evidence should be available from saliva or blood. The brake pedal is examined for the possible imprint of the driver's shoe, and the entire interior—especially the interior windshield, dashboard, A-pillars, roof, and steering wheel—is carefully checked for blood, tissue, and hair transfer. Any evidence found within the interior of the vehicle is to be collected, preserved, and placed into evidence.

Role of the Forensic Nurse Examiner

The FNE is a member of the investigative team and works closely with the multidisciplinary members. At the scene of a motor vehicle collision, the FNE should make contact with the reconstructionist to gather as much detail surrounding the dynamics of the crash as possible to determine where and how the occupants rode down the collision. The direction of impact is information that will assist the FNE in assessing and predicting occupant injuries. The FNE will take several photographs including the overall scene from a distance first, and then she or he will continue to take pictures while walking toward the collision. This should be done from both directions. Photos of each vehicle should be taken individually, including shots from the middle, all four sides, and including the license plates of the vehicles involved. Pictures should include

Fig. 24-5 These two photos are from the same crash and illustrate the different effects of vehicular design. The pickup has an engine that has dropped on impact and spared the driver's compartment. The other vehicle is an older, big car, but the engine was shoved into the driver's compartment. The driver of the pickup walked away, but the injuries to the driver of the car were fatal.

roadway evidence, debris, and numerous photos of the intrusion and damage to the vehicles.

BEST PRACTICE The forensic nurse investigator should take a series of photographs that will document the entire accident scene from multiple directions. The license plates and conditions of all vehicles and the roadway should be documented.

INJURY ASSESSMENT AND DOCUMENTATION

With the information that has been obtained from the scene, the FNE can better assess injuries of all the vehicle occupants. By knowing the direction of impact, the FNE should first assess for injuries that would be expected. For example, if the collision sustained frontal impact, associated injuries might include lap and shoulder restraints, air bag deployments, knees contacting the dashboard, or windshield and dicing injuries. The shoulders of the occupants should be examined carefully. Contusions or abrasions from the shoulder restraint may be subtle and difficult to visualize, but there is usually at least a small area of erythema over the anterior shoulder or clavicle.

The FNE should assess for patterned injuries by carefully documenting every visual injury observed (Figs. 24-6 and 24-7), either with photographs or by completing a **traumagram**. Also, examine the shoes of the known drivers for possible imprints of the vehicle pedals on the soles, as well as the clothes worn by the occupants when the collision occurred. These should be described and documented, and in some cases they may need to be seized as evidence.

Any glass or other foreign bodies found on victims' clothing or bodies, such as in hair or on wounds, should be documented

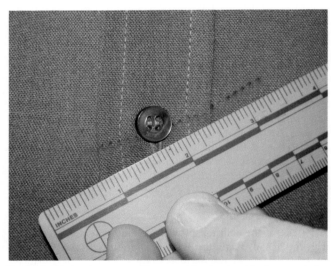

Fig. 24-6 Friction burn on a shirt caused by the shoulder harness during the crash.

and seized. All evidence that is seized must maintain a chain of custody.

VEHICLE INSPECTIONS

With the injuries of all known occupants, it will be most beneficial to then perform vehicle inspections. This will be the most important assessment to determine the biomechanics of impact. This is when all injuries are known and the interior of the vehicle can be examined to identify the direction of forces and structures that caused each specific injury. It is the role of the FNE to

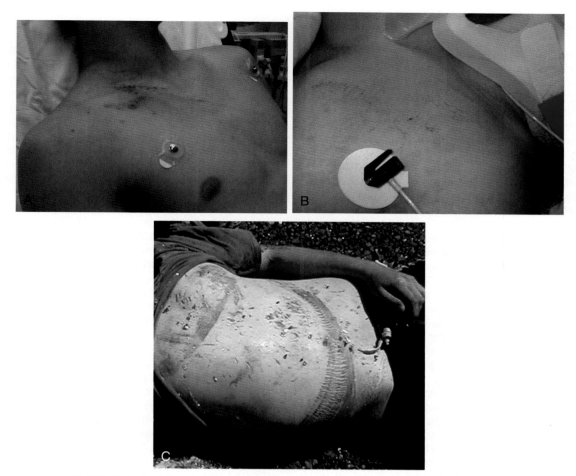

Fig. 24-7 Typical soft tissue injuries from the shoulder harness and lap belts of restrained passengers.

understand and describe the mechanism of all injuries that were sustained. The interior of the vehicle should also be examined for evidence, such as clothes, hair, blood, or tissue transfer. The location of such evidence will be made much easier because of the knowledge of injuries sustained and the expected location based on that knowledge. For example, if the driver has a large facial laceration located on the left side of his forehead, the FNE would examine and expect to find evidence of impact on the steering wheel, door, or A-pillar.

KEY POINT A thorough inspection of the vehicle involved in a collision provides the most important information for determining the type and extent of occupant injuries.

The results of the information, evidence, and findings of the FNE's investigation must then be written in report form. The report will include all times, dates, locations, names of the individuals contacted, a list of the evidence seized, including photographs or traumagrams, and, most important, a narrative of the entire investigation. The report includes the FNE's findings and the biomechanics of impact. It should describe the mechanism for every injury to every occupant, as well as identifying their seating positions. It should be complete and thorough. A copy of this report will go to the investigative officer, and in cases that are to be prosecuted, a copy will go to the district attorney.

Summary

The FNE provides an ideal addition to the multidisciplinary investigation of motor vehicle collisions. As discussed earlier, it is critical for the FNE to conduct a thorough investigation that includes documentation, photos of injuries, injury causation, and relevant evidence that will assist the reconstructionist in determining the cause and series of events during a motor vehicle collision. The FNE brings a knowledge that enhances the science of the biomechanics of impact and can act as a liaison that connects law enforcement, district attorneys, and the medical profession.

Resources

Crash Injury Research and Engineering Network

The Crash Injury Research and Engineering Network (CIREN) is a multicenter research program involving a collaboration of clinicians and engineers in academia, industry, and government. Together, they are pursuing in-depth studies of crashes, injuries, and treatments to improve processes and outcomes. CIREN's mission is to improve the prevention, treatment, and rehabilitation of motor vehicle crash injuries to reduce deaths, disabilities, and human and economic costs. See the NHTSA site below for contact information.

National Highway Traffic Safety Administration (NHTSA)

400 7th Street, NW, Washington, DC 20590 www.nhtsa.dot.gov.

Case Study **24-1**

A two-vehicle, frontal collision occurred on a rural highway in Coos County, Oregon and resulted in the fatality of one of the passengers in vehicle one, a new Toyota Tundra pickup. The occupants were two friends, A.C. and L.Y., who were driving to the coast to spend the day, stopping on the way at the river for a swim and a few beers. Back on the road, with L.Y. driving, the vehicle was witnessed to be traveling at a high rate of speed, recklessly passing other vehicles. As they emerged from a long, straight stretch of a two-lane highway into a sweeping "S" curve marked with a double yellow line, L.Y. lost control of the vehicle, sliding into the oncoming traffic and began rolling over, impacting vehicle two, a Ford van containing two occupants (Fig. 24-8).

POST-COLLISION SCENE DETAILS Vehicle one, the Toyota pickup, rested upside down in the middle of the eastbound lane, facing north. It had extensive damage to the entire vehicle and the cab was completely crushed. The passenger compartment was not visible due to the intrusion of the roof. The driver's compartment was open, and the door had been removed with the use of Hurst Tools ("jaws-of-life" spreaders and cutters). Vehicle extrication was provided by the firefighters and emergency medical professionals. The air bag had deployed, and it appeared the seat belt had been in use. The left front tire and wheel were lying in a field off the south shoulder, approximately 75 feet from the vehicle. The Ford van rested facing east, off the north shoulder of the highway with intrusion into the front grill, hood, and roof.

Occupants: Details Of Injuries. The body of A.C., the passenger in the pickup, was located in the eastbound lane, halfway between the two vehicles, clothed in a black nylon swimsuit, a green T-shirt, and white ankle-high socks. Visible injuries included a shoulder belt abrasion across the upper chest, approximately 8 inches in length, higher on the right side. A large abrasion across the lower abdomen, slightly wider on the right side, was consistent with a lap belt restraint sliding upward upon impact. Fabric transfer from the green T-shirt was visible within the abrasion. A linear abrasion and contusion was noted over A.C.'s right shoulder with numerous other abrasions, contusions and areas of *road rash* over the entire body. A large portion of windshield was lying on his chest, partially covering his face. The nares had been completely avulsed, exposing the nasal septum. A large laceration was noted over the occipital area.

The forensic nurse examiner (FNE) was on the scene approximately 2 hours before proceeding to the hospital. She was informed that L. Y.,

Fig. 24-8 The analysis of a highway crash scene by accident reconstructionist was used to decipher the biomechanics of the collision.

the driver of the pickup was in surgery for repair of a dislocated right knee, and a fractured right tibia and fibula. Hospital staff reported his blood alcohol level was .09% (90 mg/dL). The FNE contacted and interviewed the nurse in charge of L.Y.'s care who recounted the injuries. In addition to numerous lacerations, there were extensive injuries of the right leg, including the lower leg fractures and a knee dislocation. The nurse also described facial cuts, a right elbow laceration, and abrasions to the left knee, right cheek, and chin. According to this nurse, a 3-inch-wide abrasion with contusion was noted over the right flank area extending around the hip and periumbilical area. This contusion appeared to be spreading and worsening since admission. This patient was air-lifted shortly after midnight to a trauma center in Portland for specialized care for his severely injured right leg.

The driver of vehicle two, the Ford van, sustained a concussion, and exhibited contusions, and abrasions as well as symptoms of an existing cervical spine problem which had been aggravated by the collision. The FNE was informed that the child passenger who had sustained severe facial injuries and a closed head injury had also been transferred to the trauma center in Portland. The FNE then proceeded to the funeral home to perform a secondary examination and to photograph A.C.'s body. She also collected blood, vitreous humor, and urine, as well as buccal swabs and head hair standards.

Follow-up. The day following the crash, the FNE met with Oregon State Police at the wrecking yard where the Toyota pickup was secured. Closer examination revealed extensive damage to the entire vehicle. The passenger side of vehicle had completely collapsed, with the passenger seat extending out the small rear window where the roof had folded over. The passenger air bag had deployed, and the seat belt had been torn and ripped apart. This seat belt also contained fiber transfer from the decedent's green T-shirt. Green fibers were removed and collected from the passenger doorframe. There was little to no space available on the passenger side, and no blood was noted. The intrusion into the driver's compartment came from the passenger side. There were blood smears and black hair on the ceiling of the driver compartment. A sample of black hair was collected and tape lifts were pulled off the steering wheel and air bag.

The Ford van was later located and examined. There was extensive damage to upper portion of the grill, near the hood, and considerable damage to the front bumper. There was also evidence that the pickup had rolled onto the top of the van and slid off the rear passenger side roof. There was intrusion of the roof into the front passenger seat, as well as from the A-pillar. Little damage or intrusion into the driver's compartment existed.

Autopsy Findings. An autopsy was performed on the decedent. The results indicated A.C. had multiple rib fractures, a complete mid-cervical spine transection, a right clavicle fracture, multiple bilateral lower extremity fractures, avulsion of the esophagus and the trachea, laceration and pulpifaction of the liver and spleen, bilateral hemithoraces, and multiple lacerations and abrasions to the face, body, and extremities.

Survivor Outcomes. Within two weeks, the FNE received and reviewed the medical records of the crash survivors. L.Y. had suffered severe right lower leg fractures and a right knee dislocation that resulted in occlusion of the popliteal artery. This injury required numerous surgical repairs. The FNE also reviewed digital photographs of L.Y. taken after his admission to the trauma center in Portland. These photos revealed a large open wound over his right lower leg, as well as surgical incisions of the knee. There were linear abrasions over the lateral left elbow which had resulted from the shoulder restraint as it slipped off the shoulder during the rollover. A circular abrasion was noted on the right cheek, approximately 2 cm by 1 cm, and there appeared to be a friction burn. An abrasion due to the lap belt restraint was noted over the lower abdomen and right hip, extending to his posterior hip.

According to medical records, injuries involving the driver of vehicle two included a concussion; neck, right shoulder, and arm pain; abrasions to the left temple and left upper eyebrow; and multiple small lacerations to the right arm, as well as bilateral pulmonary contusions. Injuries to the female child passenger of the van included a temporal skull fracture, facial fractures and lacerations, and a left compressed facial nerve with paralysis, requiring surgical repair.

SUMMARY. The impact to the second vehicle, the Ford van, occurred while the Toyota pickup was rolling and airborne. This is evidenced by the lack of damage to the front bumper of the van, as well as blood on the hood and outer windshield frame, most likely deposited by A.C., the passenger in the pickup.

The female child on the front passenger seat of the van was thrust forward toward the direction of impact. Her chest, face, and head made contact with the intruding roof or A-pillar as well as with the pickup as it impacted the windshield, climbed onto the roof and slid down the passenger side of the vehicle. The driver of the van made little contact with the interior of the vehicle; her injuries and complaints were from the severe motion of impact. The deceased passenger in the pickup had green-tinged abrasions on his chest and abdomen consistent with wearing lap and shoulder restraints. The abrasions to his chest were in an upward direction toward his right clavicle, and he had an abrasion on the top/back of his right shoulder. The right clavicle was severely fractured from the force applied by the restraint. A.C.'s belt was caught in jagged metal at the point of impact, placing an enormous strain on it and causing it to rip apart, allowing him to be ejected onto the pavement.

The surviving driver, L.Y., also had abrasions resulting from the shoulder restraints and the seat belt, but they remained intact. His abdominal abrasions, as well as the abrasions to his left arm, resulted from the initial impact thrusting him toward the passenger side of the vehicle in an upward direction. This motion caused the shoulder strap to slip down on his left arm, resulting in the linear abrasions to his left elbow. The majority of L.Y.'s injuries were primarily on the right side of his body, consistent with the intrusion of the passenger side into the driver's compartment.

L.Y. was charged with first-degree manslaughter and two counts of second-degree assault. He absconded the morning of his trial but was eventually located and arrested three years later. He insisted that he was innocent and that A.C. had been driving. Witnesses and forensic evidence clearly placed L.Y. in the driver's seat. He was found guilty and was sentenced to 120 months for the manslaughter conviction and 140 months for two counts of second degree assault. He is now serving 260 months in prison.

National Institute for Occupation Safety and Health, The Centers for Disease Control and Prevention
1600 Clifton Road, Atlanta, GA 30333; 404-639-3311 www.cdc.gov.
"NIOSH Alert: Preventing Worker Injuries and Deaths from Traffic-Related Motor Vehicle Crashes." DHHS (NIOSH) Publication No. 98–142, is available from the NIOSH toll-free information number, 1-800-35-NIOSH (1-800-356-4674). Copies also available on the NIOSH Home Pagenorhmpg.htmlwww.cdc.gov/niosh. Further information on NIOSH research is also available from the toll-free number and on the home page.

References

Anderson, W. (1998). *Forensic sciences in clinical medicine. A case study approach*. New York: Lippincott-Raven Publishers.
Association for the Advancement of Automotive Medicine. (AAAM). (1992). *Traffic injury: The medicine-engineering link* [Video].

Besant-Matthews, M. D. (1998). *Injury and death investigation*. Colorado Springs, CO: Beth-El College of Nursing.
Daily, J. (1988). *Fundamentals of traffic accident reconstruction*. Institute of Police Technology and Management, University of North Florida.
Rivers, R. (1997). *Technical traffic accident investigators' handbook* (2nd ed.). Springfield, IL: Charles C Thomas.
Spitz, W. (2006). *Medicolegal investigation of death; Guidelines for the application of pathology to crime investigation* (4th ed.). Springfield, IL: Charles C. Thomas.

CHAPTER 25 Blunt, Sharp, and Firearm Injuries

Patrick E. Besant-Matthews

The forensic nurse examiner must thoroughly understand the multiple characteristics of blunt and sharp force injuries or wounds and be able to predict the types of mechanical forces that might have caused them. This includes, in some cases, a specific weapon or wounding instrument. To make accurate annotations in the medical records or to convey pertinent information to members of law enforcement or the judicial system, it is essential that precise, nonambiguous descriptive terms are used in both oral and written communications. In addition, for known or potential forensic cases, photodocumentation is a vital element to record the size, location, and nature of blunt or sharp force injuries. The ability to relate this information to accident or crime scene reconstruction can assist in the identification of the wounding instrument and eventually the perpetrator.

This chapter introduces wound identification, classification, and documentation by focusing on the details that will contribute to appropriate medical care and later to a credible forensic investigation.

Wound Terminology

In the English language, many words have multiple meanings, which gives rise to the misuse of words, even common ones. A good example is the word *fire,* which has at least nine common meanings:

1. The phenomenon of combustion manifested in heat and light
2. To inspire a person
3. Liveliness of imagination
4. Brilliancy, luminosity
5. To discharge or let off
6. To discharge from a position, dismiss from employment
7. To process by applying heat
8. To fuel or tend a boiler or furnace
9. To eject or launch a projectile

Almost any large, unabridged dictionary will list several other less common meanings.

In the healthcare and law enforcement fields, doctors, nurses, paramedics, emergency medical technicians, and police officers devote considerable time during training to mastering necessary technical phrases. Failure to continue this education into description of injury often reduces the quality of documentation, even though reports may be lengthy. The surgeon's report after an operation may contain numerous statements about an injury and what was done to it, yet this report often fails to specify where on the body surface the wound was located or to include other characteristics such as its size and appearance, which may be of great importance when a lawsuit is filed.

Anyone working in the medical or law enforcement fields may be called on to interpret injury patterns; to write reports concerning the condition of someone, dead or alive; and sometimes to testify concerning the appearance of an injured party. Proper use of descriptive terms greatly enhances one's ability to write effective reports and to provide meaningful information in depositions or testimony. This also applies to day-to-day progress notes. Skill and effort are wasted if descriptions are not absolutely clear and meaningful.

DOCUMENTING WOUND CHARACTERISTICS

A common failing of treatment and surgical reports is that they do not mention the specific place, depth, and direction of force related to the identified injuries. After a critical surgery, the location of wounds should be included in the dictated report. For example, in the case of a single stab wound, failure to note that it entered the abdomen at a point located about 3 inches diagonally above and to the patient's right of the umbilicus, penetrated for a maximum depth of about 3 inches, and was directed from front to back and slightly downward is a significant omission. What was injured and repaired will almost always be mentioned, but without a location this information will not be much use. Courtroom questions are inevitably centered on the location, depth, and direction, because these are the features that will fit or discredit the allegations and circumstances.

Body Diagrams

Outline diagrams of the human body and body parts can be useful. Simply draw the findings on these outlines and add notations. It is fast, accurate, helps to prevent right/left errors, and makes it easier to document angles and patterns. Body diagrams are excellent supplements to other documentation.

Clock Face Orientation

The clock face is sometimes used to document the angulation or inclination of a feature or wound. For instance, if a person is standing at attention (in the standard anatomical position) and has a streak of dirty material running from the inner part of the left eyebrow to the lower right corner of the mouth, then this might be described as being oriented from 1 to 7 o'clock when viewed from the front. If the standard anatomical position is not used, additional documentation is needed, such as "when viewed from the right, with the patient lying face up, the wound is angled from 10 to 4 o'clock."

Track and Tract

A *track* (spelled with a "k") is detectable evidence that something has passed, a vestige or trace, or the course along which something has moved. Note that the word *tracks* is also used to describe the linear scars overlying veins resulting from repeated intravenous injections associated with drug abuse.

A *tract* (spelled with a "t") is a series of bodily parts that collectively serve a combined anatomical purpose. There are more than 50 tracts within the body.

So unless someone swallows or inhales a bullet, it will pass down a track, not a tract. Failure to distinguish between track and tract is a reliable indicator of the amount and quality of training received, as well as the care, or lack of it, in producing reports.

Instrument and Weapon

An instrument is something with, or through which, something is done or effected (i.e., a tool, implement, or utensil). Namely, it is an object with a primary function other than use as an offensive or defensive weapon. A weapon is an instrument of offensive or defensive combat, something to fight with, or an object of any kind used in combat to attack or overcome others. A weapon is essentially an object whose primary function is as an offensive or defensive device. An object such as a kitchen knife, although manufactured as an instrument, can be used as a weapon. Proper use of these terms will depend on the circumstances and fashion of use (e.g., to cut bread or to cause injury).

In this chapter there are many of the terms used to describe injuries. It is suggested that anyone who treats patients, evaluates injuries, or works in the fields of law or law enforcement be exposed to and be aware of these terms, not only for personal benefit but also to protect the interests of the institutions and individuals they serve.

KEY POINT Forensic nurse examiners may be requested to testify or to give a deposition; therefore, it is important to use appropriate and precise terms when describing injuries or wounds in forensic cases. The failure of a report to be completely accurate may cast doubt on one's credibility as a witness or testifying expert.

DOCUMENTATION AND LEGAL PROCEEDINGS

An injury that is of little consequence medically may be extremely important to family members, investigators, insurance companies, attorneys, and the courts. For example, suppose there's an L-shape abrasion (graze), about 1¼-inches in greatest dimension, on the inner aspect of the left lower leg near the bony prominence of the ankle joint. The wound is reported to be the result of an automobile collision, is not life threatening, and will soon heal. Later it turns out that both occupants of the vehicle are unconscious, the brake pedal is bent, and the main issue is determining who was driving. If the leg is in a cast, and nothing was noted in the chart, the wrong person may be charged with negligent driving, manslaughter, or even vehicular homicide.

There are several routes to good documentation. Here are some points to ponder:

- Describe wounds in logical sequence, such as from head to foot, or from front to back, or from wrist to elbow. Organization is important in court.
- Use landmarks that cannot easily be challenged by a skilled attorney. Good landmarks include the midline of the body, the notch at the top of the breastbone, the centerline of a limb, the base of a heel (provided the ankle is at 90 degrees), the top of the head, the external ear canals, or the Frankfort plane (the horizontal line between the bottom of the eye socket and the top of the external ear canal). The best choice depends on the case and even on the direction of force.

- When dealing with stab wounds (and bullet holes), measure from the body landmark to the center of each. This is important when there are many irregular wounds, or else the distances between them will not add up.
- If measurements are made around a body curvature, make it clear in the description. Failure to do so will cause a wound that's recorded as 12 cm to the left of the front midline of the face to sound as though it is out in space somewhere, instead of 5 cm in front of the ear canal.
- Do not locate one injury and then say that another was at a certain distance from it. Doing this will accumulate measurement errors. This rule does not apply if injuries are obviously paired (e.g., carving fork) or grouped (e.g., dinner fork).
- Do not split up or disperse parts of a single injury within the notes. If there is no choice but to examine the outside before the inside, then "Subsequent examination of …" will get the narrative back on track.
- When describing marks that encircle or partly encircle the wrists, ankles, or neck, pick a starting point, and begin with "For descriptive purposes, the marking commences at a point," continue on, until returning to the starting point.
- Use national standard or internationally accepted abbreviations. A common error is to use *cc* for fluid volumes, when fluids are measured in liters not centimeters. Thus, *ml* is technically correct. In many important cases, consultants will read the report, note minor errors, and bring them to the attention of the defense.
- If someone misinterpreted a birthmark as a bruise, but injuries were not substantiated, it will help to make notations such as "Not found—evidence of injury to the face" or "Incidental findings—birthmark ("port wine" stain) on face."

Good forms and a notation system (using arrows and lines with clock face numbers at each end) make notes easier to read during a deposition or courtroom testimony.

Blunt and Sharp Injuries

From a medical perspective, the ability to distinguish between the various types of injuries is extremely important because it provides valuable information about causation and, in some cases, will determine treatment. For example, a confused young female patient is admitted to the emergency department with a linear injury to her upper forehead. If this injury has been caused by a sharp instrument such as a straight razor, there is little to be done except to suture the wound and then explore how it was incurred. Did it occur as an accident? Was it the result of interpersonal violence? Was it self-inflicted? Answers to these questions will be extremely important to the healthcare team and to law enforcement. Perhaps the patient had been drinking or taking drugs? However, if the linear injury was caused by being struck forcefully by the edge of a coffee table or a piece of angle iron, then the clinical problem is quite different and involves wound contamination, blunt force injury, potential for skull fracture, and neck injury, plus the need to consider brain injury with or without intracranial bleeding. Sharp force injury rarely contains trace evidence.

Proceeding appropriately requires distinguishing a sharp injury from a blunt injury. However, these are the two most frequently mistaken for one another in those areas of the body surface that have bone beneath them, including the skull.

The forensic nurse examiner must actively be involved as an investigator when providing wound care in a clinic or within the hospital emergency department. If the wound occurred as an industrial accident (on the job) rather than while the individual was engaged in recreation, workers' compensation and other insurance coverage may be relevant. If the victim of injury subsequently has extended complications or dies from the wound, there may be issues of liability and criminal negligence. The cause of death or permanent disability also impacts the payment of claims on disability policies or life insurance. If the wound was self-inflicted, there are important mental health implications to explore. If an assailant caused the wound, there is the need for law enforcement to find the perpetrator. Forensic responsibilities cannot be taken lightly because they may make a huge impact on law enforcement, the judicial system, and the overall economy. Taking time to carefully remove clothing, to photograph and measure the wounds, and to precisely document the patient's statements regarding how the wound was incurred will become extremely important if there are subsequent judicial proceedings.

Symmetry of abrasion, bruising, and undermining of tissue is consistent with a more perpendicular application of force. An example would be on the scalp, over the curved surfaces of the skull, if an individual were struck with the flat surface of a 2-by-6-inch piece of wood. Because lacerations result from blunt impact, shearing, or tearing, they are likely to be contaminated with foreign material such as road gravel and dirt, headlight glass and paint chips, or clothing fibers indicating the kind of surface that was contacted. For example, examination of a traffic accident victim may reveal the presence of small fragments of paint within a tear on the side of the head, indicating that the head contacted part of a vehicle; or it might contain gravel and greasy dirt, which is more in keeping with contact with the underside of a vehicle.

Improper description and interpretation of injuries may lead the police on a lengthy search for a knife or sharpened object when in fact they should be looking for a brick, angle iron, or other such angular object with a definite edge to it. Experience shows that sharp injuries (cuts and stabs) are better understood than blunt injuries (scrapes, bruises, tears, and fractures).

PATTERN OF INJURY

A pattern of injury is a combination or distribution of external or internal injuries that suggest a causative mechanism or sequence of events, indicating infliction of wounds over a period of time versus those occurring simultaneously. A pattern of injury may indicate repetitive abuse, whereas injuries occurring from a single incident are generally associated with nonintentional injury.

PATTERN INJURY

A pattern injury is one that possesses features or configuration indicative of the object(s) or surface(s) that produced it (Smock, 2007). For instance, it may bear the imprint of clothing, an object such as the radiator grill of a car, or the head of a specific type of hammer.

PENETRATING AND PERFORATING

A penetrating injury is one that enters but does not exit, whereas a perforating injury passes through and through. Thus, confusion may arise because a knife that entered the front of a thigh and stopped just short of the bone represents not only a penetrating injury of the thigh as a whole but also a perforating, through-and-through wound of the skin. It is necessary therefore to specify what was or is penetrated or perforated. Use *penetration* as the common term for the majority of injuries that enter and do not exit, and refer to all others as through-and-through injuries.

Blunt Force Injury

There are four main subdivisions of blunt injury:
1. Scratches and grazes—abrasions
2. Bruises—contusions
3. Tears—lacerations
4. Fractures of bone

These types of injury often occur in combination, but each will be reviewed separately.

ABRASIONS

An abrasion represents the removal of the outermost layer of the skin by a compressive or sliding force. Usually the skin is not perforated, but this can occur if the force and severity are sufficient or if the injury is great enough for areas to be physically worn away. Abrasions are seldom life threatening, but they are of great importance in interpreting what happened because they must, by their very nature, mark the exact point at which contact occurred (Fig. 25-1). Thus, the presence, form, and distribution of abrasions may need to be recorded in considerable detail. As blunt force is applied to the surface of the body, two vectors of force come into play. One is directed primarily inward and the other primarily longitudinally or parallel to the skin surface. The magnitude of each may differ, producing characteristics that allow subdivision into pressure or sliding types. It is well to consider abrasions in these terms, because it makes one think about the mechanism of injury and direction of force. The

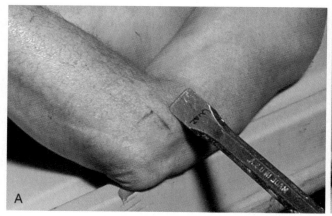 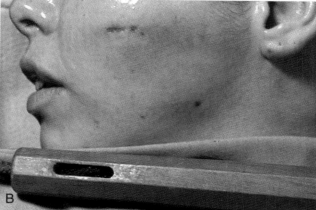

Fig. 25-1 *A,* Patterned abrasion. Note the contact point and the mirror image of the pry bar. *B,* Wounding instrument and resultant pattern abrasion and slight contusion.

surface tissues may be pushed toward one end of a sliding abrasion, like dirt moved to the far end of the "push" by a bulldozer or road grader, in which case tags and tissue fragments frequently indicate the direction toward which the force was applied (Fig. 25-2).

Similar to most wounds, abrasions tend to darken as the tissues dry. In most instances, this is noted first at the edges of the wound or in more shallow areas of the abrasion. After death, when there is no longer circulation or body movement to keep them moist, abrasions will dry and darken. This may lead to the false interpretation that the injury resulted from burning, bruising, or even that a hot object contacted the tissues.

Abrasions are sometimes classified according to their shape. If long and narrow, as from contact with thorns, they are called scratches. If wider areas are involved, they can be called grazes. The claws of a cat will leave scratches. The knee of a child who fell from a tricycle onto blacktop will be described as grazed. The direction of force is useful in evaluating the patient's statement of how the injury occurred. For instance, are the abrasions due to being struck on the thigh or buttock by the front of a car or due to the victim's sliding along the road surface after being knocked down? The form and appearance of the injury should be noted because it may help interpret the mechanism and circumstances of injury.

In summary, abrasions have the following characteristics:
- Indicate contact with a rough surface or object
- Indicate the exact site of contact or impact
- Will eventually crust over or scab (i.e., dry and darken)
- May reveal the direction of the force of injury
- May exhibit characteristic patterns (e.g., knurled tool handles, motorcycle drive chains)
- May be seen in conjunction with bruises and lacerations because forces sufficient to produce scraping may distort the underlying soft tissues enough to tear vessels

CONTUSIONS

A contusion, or bruise, results from leakage of blood from vessels into the tissues after sufficient force has been applied to distort the soft tissues and tear one or more vessels—hence the term

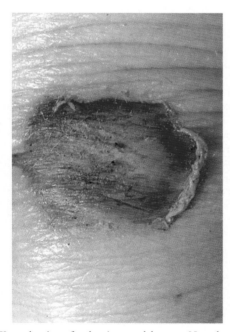

Fig. 25-2 Knee abrasion of pedestrian struck by auto. Note the skin roll on bottom wound edge that indicates the direction of the impact force.

extravasation (*extra* = outside; *vasa* = vessel). The vessels involved are usually small (such as capillaries), but they may be larger and on occasion, when a larger vessel is involved, leakage can occur quite rapidly. An abrasion may be observed nearby, and if present, it may signify the exact point of contact or application of force. Fresh bruises may be slightly raised above the adjacent surfaces if enough blood escapes, and even when a large bruise is deeply seated, swelling may be apparent when the size of a limb or body part is compared to its opposite member.

Contusions result when blunt forces distort the soft tissues to an extent sufficient to result in disruption and leakage of blood vessels. Escape of blood from the blood vessels is what produces the discoloration. The amount of blood that escapes from the vessels will depend on features such as the size of the contusion and the pressure within it, the ability to clot, the space available for blood to leak into, and so on.

The subcategories of contusions include the following:
- Deep seated, such as in the internal organs, often in the form of hematomas
- Beneath the skin, where contusions give the discolorations commonly know as bruises
- In the skin itself, where the contusions give rise to patterned bruises
There are two other meanings of the word *contusion*, both of which relate to the brain:
1. The clinical meaning of contusion describes a somewhat imprecise clinical diagnosis of a patient who, after a blow to the head, suffers prolonged loss of consciousness with appearance of clinical signs of brain injury. Note that the expression "contusion of the brain" is not typically used in the presence of dramatic and definite clinical signs such as paralysis. In such circumstances, the description becomes "head injury with hemiplegia."
2. Contusion of the brain substance occurs when forces are exerted on the head, sufficient to cause the crests of the gyri (surface ridges of the brain) to contact the inner surface of the skull. This results, in the early stages, in small linear hemorrhages resembling splinters of wood under a fingernail. These hemorrhages may become larger and more confluent if injury is more severe.

Fresh Bruises and Color of Bruises
A fresh bruise usually begins with the reddish color of oxygenated blood, from the arterial side of the circulation, but like superficial vessels these bruises may appear blue. This is because blue light bounces (e.g., blue light bouncing off dust particles in the atmosphere gives blue skies) and red penetrates more deeply (e.g., restaurants use infrared lights over the food to keep it warm). Also think in terms of varying depths of skin and yellow fat. Later bruises turn a more purplish hue and ultimately, as the blood pigments break down, the sequence of colors passes through those of a ripening banana, through greens, yellows, and browns, at which point the coloration fades. A closed bruise with only a scrape on the skin above it will not behave the same as a bruise forming in distorted or torn fat, or one that can leak out through a defect in the skin.

The persistence of discoloration varies with age, location of the bruising on the body (circulatory efficiency), and the amount of blood released. Some individuals bruise more easily than do others of the same age and sex; others seldom bruise. Bruising can be masked by natural coloration of the overlying skin and may be almost invisible if the skin is heavily tanned or naturally dark. At late stages, long after injury, discoloration may remain. However, this remaining discoloration may well be more of a response to injury (scar formation, breakdown products of blood pigments, and melanin) than true bruising.

Estimating the Age of a Bruise

The rate at which a bruise appears and disappears depends on many factors, including the quantity of blood originally released, the effectiveness of the local circulation, age, location of the bruised area on the body, and the general physical activity and condition of the individual. Some textbooks and journal articles suggest the rate at which bruises fade is fairly predictable; however, the various authors disagree on the rate. Any opinion concerning the age of a bruise based on its color is extremely difficult and should be attained and stated with the greatest caution and circumspection (Smock, 2007).

Estimating the age of bruises based on appearance or coloration is difficult, both before and after death. To prove the difficulty during life, simply observe bruises of known age. In postmortem tissues, age estimation is difficult with both the unaided eye and the microscope. The pathologist should obtain a set of tissue sections to ensure a truly average and representative sampling. During testimony, it is prudent to admit that there is every reason to be both cautious and skeptical when trying to match changes in injured soft tissues in a person who may have been in shock and organ failure or undergone treatment (including advanced life support, transfusions, antibiotics, and dialysis), and then try to draw a parallel with results from studies in humans and experimental animals taken in the days before modern-day techniques were even thought of.

The forensic nurse examiner should make detailed annotations about the size and appearance of the bruise rather than attempt to estimate the age of the bruise based on literature. Photographs of bruises taken immediately upon examination are also helpful as a means of documentation because the characteristics of the affected area change gradually over hours and days.

Distribution of Bruises

The distribution of bruises may be important. Small bruises around the neck or on a limb may be the only external signs of violence. Indeed, it is possible to have massive internal injury with very little evidence on the body surface, and on occasion there may be no evidence whatsoever. Sometimes superficial patterned bruising may be of value in identifying a particular instrument or weapon such as a whip or cane in which the bruises may have a linear or double-line configuration. When called on to examine the victim of an alleged assault, remember that bruises may not become visible immediately and therefore may not be visible at the time of an examination performed soon after the event. Advances in technology using alternate light sources aid in detecting bruised tissue, even before the skin reveals any type of discoloration. Later on, even without special adjuncts, bruises are likely to become visible on the body surfaces. Reexamination of a victim, updated annotations in the medical record, and careful photodocumentation may provide helpful comparisons with the original observations. This is particularly true with cases of alleged abuse of an elderly person in a nursing home. Bruising may be found in the areas around the eyes and within the soft tissue of the eyelids themselves, particularly in the elderly who sustain minor impacts to these regions when they collapse or fall. Discolorations do not necessarily appear at the place(s) at which force was applied because the coloration may result from blood that has tracked around muscles and flowed in the tissue fluids on route to the surface. For example, hitting the ankle sometimes results in discoloration of the toes. Only an abrasion or a pattern in or near the bruising itself will indicate the actual point of contact.

Bruiselike discoloration can appear many inches away from the point at which force was applied and look just like bruising when it was not involved in the force and remains the same color until it fades. Bruises of many colors are seen simultaneously as a result of a single episode of injury. This should confirm that bruises do not develop at the same speed or progress and resolve in a uniform fashion. In addition, there are cases in which several bruises result from accidents such as a fall or walking into a door. Yet these bruises disappear at different rates, some taking far longer than others. The forensic nurse examiner should consider that one or more bruises of different ages may be adjacent to or overlapping one another, confusing the assessment.

Advanced Assessment Techniques

Because color tends to be an unreliable indicator for the age of the bruise, the forensic pathologist may need to use advanced techniques of tissue study to determine the timing or duration of the injury that caused the bruising. Subspecialists may also be used to provide additional information about certain body tissues such as the heart, brain, or liver. It is imperative, however, that representative tissue samples are obtained and that reference tissues from other body parts are used for comparison, especially when there are complicating factors such as cardiopulmonary resuscitation procedures, blood administration, or the use of mechanical ventilation.

Patient Populations with Easy Bruising

Bruising is accentuated in the presence of blood dyscrasias such as leukemia or any impairment of the blood-clotting processes, including hemophilia. Bruising is also commonly noted in patients who are on anticoagulants or antiplatelet drugs. Selective serotonin reuptake inhibitors, a class of antidepressants (e.g., Zoloft), inhibit blood platelet activity and may be associated with bruising in unusual locations.

It is generally easier for blood to escape into loose tissues and fat; therefore, bruising is more common in the following circumstances:

- In certain parts of the body
- At the extremes of age
- After weight loss
- In obesity
- If there is disease of the blood vessels

Relationship between Blunt Forces and Bruising

The intensity and duration of forces associated with bruising are difficult or impossible factors to estimate unless other features such as abrasions or lacerations are also present. Significant blunt forces do not necessarily result in the formation of bruises. Not every blow a boxer strikes results in a bruise, and many such blows are forceful. Tissues exposed to repeated trauma may firm up and scar, making it harder for blood to enter and for bruising to occur. The forceful distortion of tissues necessary to result in bruising may itself selectively alter the ability of blood to make its way through injured tissue, such as fat, to the body surface to produce discoloration. If a vessel is lacerated, any blood that escapes will tend to depart through the open wound rather than permeate into the adjacent tissues. Thus, a laceration may have less bruising adjacent to it, not more, even though the force was greater. Likewise, if fat is slightly torn beneath a closed wound, the blood will pass more easily into some parts than others.

In the living, a bruise may appear more or less prominent, according to the amount of peripheral vasoconstriction (standing out in the cold) or vasodilatation (just after a hot bath) of adjacent and overlying skin.

Postmortem Bruising

The question often arises as to whether it is possible to produce bruising at and around the time of death or even after death. Limited bruising can be produced immediately following death if the body is mishandled or struck, assuming enough blood is present and is free to move (not set, sludged, fixed, clotted, or otherwise altered) under the influence of gravity. Therefore, everyone who handles the recently deceased should be cautious.

Postmortem bruises are, however, usually small, few in number, and localized, and they do not usually pose much of a problem. Bruises are easily overlooked in areas into which blood has been forced or has settled (including postmortem lividity) or in areas in which circulation is failing. In some instances of severe injury accompanied by rapidly falling blood pressure, bruises that are still forming at the time circulation ceases may assume colors that are more commonly associated with greater age. These often have a subtle, almost grayish appearance.

After death, it may be necessary to cut into the skin to demonstrate subtle or concealed bruising, especially if there is any significant degree of natural coloration of the overlying skin. In some European countries, where open-casket funerals are relatively rare, it is not uncommon to demonstrate the presence of bruising at autopsy by completely removing selected areas of skin. In the United States, where open-casket funerals are common, only the minimum number of incisions necessary to properly define the nature and extent of bruising are made.

Focal bleeding within the soft tissues of decomposed or decomposing bodies is difficult to interpret, requiring considerable experience on the part of the forensic specialist. Decomposition makes it much harder to tell antemortem from postmortem bruising. Bruising is harder to see in areas of postmortem lividity.

Case Study 25-1

Postmortem Bruising

A body (following death from head injuries) was first examined in the autopsy room and had a normal color, normal face, and unswollen eyelids. Photographs that included the face were taken of injuries on the front of the body, and other photos were taken for identification purposes. After the examination of the front was completed, the body was turned facedown for examination, documentation, and photography of injuries on the back. By the time the body was once again turned faceup for opening and internal examination, both upper eyelids had swollen and turned blue-gray from leakage of blood from fractures of the supraorbital plates, the thin bone between the frontal lobes of the brain and eyes. Although uncommon, under the right circumstances, if blood is present and free to move, such effects can and do occur.

Keep these points in mind when assessing bruising:
- Bruises may not become visible for minutes, hours, or even a few days. This is possible because it may take time for blood leaking from vessels located beneath fat or behind other structures such as fascial planes to wend its way to the surface. Furthermore, in the presence of shock, the extravasation of blood may be retarded until adequate perfusion pressure has been restored.
- Bruises are often larger than the area of impact or the causative object because of the flowing and spreading of blood as it makes its way to the body surface (Box 25-1).

Box 25-1 Studying Bruising Patterns

To learn more about the practical aspects of bruising, use 3 × 5-inch file cards or make forms on a computer. Put the following headings on the cards or forms, and fill in the data whenever bruises of exact known age are observed. Be extremely selective, and include only those cases in which the time of injury is absolutely known and is therefore the true time since injury.
- Identifying information, such as hospital, ambulance, or dispatch number
- Date and time of observation
- Ambient/prevailing lighting
- Age, sex, skin color
- Location and size of bruise/bruises
- Bruise color in your own words
- Cause of the injuries and bruising (e.g., motor vehicle collision, bar fight, fall)
- Ambient/prevailing temperature and prior activity (vasoconstriction or vasodilatation)
- Any medications or conditions that would affect the clotting process

Look for injuries that occurred at the same time but that developed different colors (for instance, if someone falls and the bruise on the person's face is yellow whereas another bruise on the trunk is purple).

Another worthwhile study is to make a note of the date and minute when you accidentally hit yourself hard enough to notice it. If a bruise appears, you will know the time of injury to a minute and be able to record discolorations that result. If you do not bruise, you will be able to state that when you hurt yourself to the point of discomfort you only get a bruise a certain percentage of the time. Whether you do or do not bruise easily, the results may surprise you.

ECCHYMOSIS

Ecchymosis is a term that is often misused by clinical personnel. Ecchymoses (plural) are not the same as contusions or bruises. They are small, nonelevated, painless hemorrhagic spots that tend to be somewhat larger than petechiae. Typically they are irregular and appear as blue or purplish patches. These ecchymotic spots are induced by bleeding of a hematological nature, not trauma. They are found in both skin and mucous membrane. Capillary fragility in older adults often leads to ecchymotic areas from slight to moderate pressure from an outside force. When described in forensic or medical documentation, they are often termed *senile ecchymosis* (Fig. 25-3) (Beutler, et al. 2001).

LACERATIONS OR TEARS

The term *laceration* is commonly misused when describing injuries. Blunt objects produce lacerations, and sharp objects produce cuts, incisions, or incised wounds (Wright, 2003). A surgeon may make an incision with a surgical knife (scalpel) and call it an incision, then walk into the emergency department, examine a knife cut on a patient's face, and call it a laceration. This misuse is not only incorrect, but it can also cause confusion with legal implications.

KEY POINT Lacerations are *blunt force* injuries resulting from tearing, ripping, crushing, overstretching, pulling apart, bending, and shearing of soft tissues.

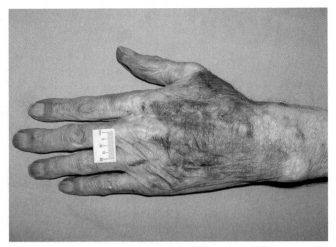

Fig. 25-3 Senile ecchymosis induced by a thinning of the perivascular connective tissue.

Strictly speaking, lacerations are defects in soft tissues resulting from tearing, ripping, crushing, overstretching, and shearing. Soft tissue defects should be described as tears (lacerations) or cuts (incised wounds) to indicate if an injury was from a blunt or sharp object when a medical record is reviewed.

In the boxing community, a tear near a boxer's eyebrow is referred to as a cut. The tear in the skin near the eye occurs when the heads of the two boxers collide so that the soft tissues between the bony ridges and surfaces are forced aside. To illustrate, lay a line of toothpaste along the edge of a bathroom sink and then press a finger into it. The paste will escape from either side of one's finger. So it often is with soft tissues and, to be technically correct, lacerations do not result from sharp objects. Use of the term *laceration* should be strictly reserved to those wounds that result from blunt force.

Compressive shearing force applied to a tissue or organ may cause an internal tear without external tearing; the impact site in such instances may only be denoted by an abrasion or nearby bruise. Because overstretching of tissue is an important factor in the production of lacerations, the plasticity or potential mobility of the tissues influences the occurrence of this type of blunt injury. Therefore, skin lacerations are frequently found overlying bony prominences of the body where the skin is relatively fixed and less able to move when stressed. Similarly, laceration of the aorta or other organs occurs most frequently at points of relative immobility or mechanical disadvantage, particularly if the energy of impact is conducted to a point at which the vessel or organ is fixed to an adjacent structure.

Typical Skin Lacerations

The typical skin laceration has an irregular margin that may be scraped or bruised, especially if there was an impact with an object or rough surface. Because the tissue is torn apart, there is frequently an incomplete separation with stronger tissue elements (such as little blood vessels, nerves, and connective tissue strands) surviving to bridge or span the gap from one part or side of the wound to the other. This bridging of tissue is particularly evident deep within a wound or at its corners and is helpful in accurately differentiating blunt from sharp force injury. Closer inspection of lacerations may reveal characteristics that are useful in interpreting the mechanism of wound production. For example, if one side is scraped/abraded and the opposite margin undermined, partly

crushed, or pushed aside, these findings suggest that the force was directed at an angle over the surface, which was scraped and directed toward the side that is crushed, undermined, or pushed back (Figs. 25-4 and 25-5).

Internal Organ Lacerations

Lacerations of internal organs are a relatively common result of blunt force or impact applied to the exterior of the body. Classical injuries involve the liver, spleen, and kidneys, all of which tear with relative ease if the force is sufficient. The lungs may be torn by inwardly displaced ends of broken ribs or result from severe forces. It is noteworthy that it is possible to have serious internal blunt injures without surface manifestations such as abrasions and bruises. If this were not so, surgeons would never have to undertake exploratory procedures to rule out injury. Surface indications are often present, but they do not have to be, and their absence does not rule out the possibility of internal injury. The following list identifies key points to remember when assessing lacerations:

- Lacerations result from blunt force, crushing, tearing, ripping, shearing, overstretching, bending, and pulling apart of soft tissues.
- They have ragged, variably irregular margins.
- They will, in most cases, have scraping and bruising of the wound margins.
- They may bleed less and become infected in crushed tissues (especially if the victim survives).

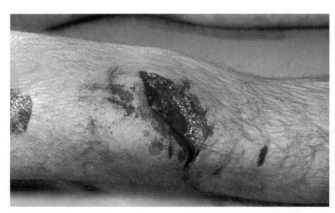

Fig. 25-4 Laceration from blunt force trauma incurred by the knee of an unrestrained passenger hitting the dashboard in a motor vehicle crash. Note the grazes, which illustrate the direction of the forces of impact.

Fig. 25-5 Homicide victim with multiple stab wounds and a large laceration with tissue bridging.

- Lacerated tissue may survive the force and be observed "bridging" or "spanning" within parts of a wound if it is a stronger tissue component, such as blood vessels, nerves, tendons, and connective elements. Hair roots and other skin structures may be seen protruding from the margins, having been torn out of their supporting tissues.
- They frequently contain foreign materials including trace evidence such as glass, paint chips, bark, fibers, and grease.
- Their overall size and shape vary widely by virtue of their blunt, tearing, shearing, or crushing origin. When attempting to reapproximate the edges of a blunt torn injury, the examiner may notice that the wound still looks ragged, whereas most sharp injuries are more easily restored for suturing.
- Tears resulting from forceful contact with angular objects can, if there is underlying bone, lead to the formation of linear injuries, which may be mistaken for cuts from sharp objects.
- Lacerations may indicate direction of force when, for instance, the bent knee of a vehicle occupant hits the lower part of the dash in a frontal collision. Some people use the expression "trapdoor laceration" to describe the directional nature of such an evulsion injury, an inverted U- or V-shaped flap of skin that remains attached at its upper margin.

FRACTURES

The fourth major variant of blunt injury is bone fracture. Bone may fracture in different ways according to the amount of force and the fashion in which it is applied. The classical transverse or V-like fracture of the lower leg as a result of being hit by a car bumper is likely to be different from the spiral twisting of the fracture sustained by a falling skier. Most of the time it is not easy to tell what happened because most of the bones are covered by tissue and the fracture sites may have been dressed to prevent infection. An observant, well-trained orthopedic surgeon, nurse, or paramedic may see features at the time of treatment that can help solve the classic "hit from the front, back, or side" question. It may be easier at autopsy because tissue can be removed and there is less blood to impede the examination, but even then detection may not be possible.

SUMMARY

The four major varieties of blunt injuries have been reviewed. The principal points to note are the following:
- Abrasions, although not life threatening, can be of great assistance in working out what happened.
- Assessing the age or duration of bruises is difficult and unreliable.
- Laceration is a term that is widely misunderstood and misused. Lacerations result from blunt injuries and may be contaminated with foreign material or contain trace evidence. Lacerations of soft tissue, brought about by contact with angular objects in areas that overlie bone, may be mistaken for cuts.
- Directional characteristics are frequently present in abrasions and lacerations, and occasionally in fractures, although broken ends of bone are seldom examined with direction of force in mind (with the exception of bullet wounds).

Sharp Force Injuries

There are two main subdivisions of sharp injuries: cuts (which include slashes and slices) and stab wounds.

CUTS

In cuts, a sharp object comes against the skin with sufficient pressure to divide it. The force is usually directed mainly along the surface while some inward pressure is applied. Thus, such wounds are, by definition, longer than they are deep. Cuts may tail off at one end and be more superficial at one end than the other. The characteristics of the cutting instrument are usually not well reflected by a cut. After all, did a cut result from the last inch of a long blade or most of a short one? If only one edge did any cutting, how can one possibly tell anything about the edge that never made contact? It is also difficult to assess the amount of force required because this largely depends on the sharpness and configuration of the instrument and the resistance offered by clothing, if any (Fig. 25-6).

Two similar terms that refer to sharp injury are *slash* and *slice*. Slash means cutting or wounding with strokes or in a sweeping fashion with a sharp instrument or weapon: to gash, to strike violently or at random, to move rapidly or violently, to cut slits in, or to deliver cutting blows. A slice is a relatively thin, flat, broad piece cut from the primary object, or it means a sharp cut or to cut cleanly.

Thus, these terms are commonly used in two circumstances:
1. When describing cuts on the wrists, neck, and other body parts of a person attempting suicide and as a descriptive term (e.g., "she slashed her wrists")
2. In reference to reckless savage cutting, with overtly malicious intent, often forcefully and in a sweeping manner without careful aim. Such injuries are associated with gang wars, vendettas, crimes of passion, sex murders, control of prostitutes, and retaliation against suspected informants.

A slash, or slice, is a special variant of cut. Keep the following factors in mind when evaluating cuts:
- Cuts result from sharp objects coming against the skin with pressure to cause an injury.
- Cuts are longer than they are deep (in contrast to stab wounds).
- Cuts have clean-cut edges, usually without abrasion or bruising.
- In cuts, there is no bridging, spanning, or selective sparing of tissues.
- Overlying hair, the hair roots, and other small structures within the skin will be cut if the object is sufficiently sharp.
- There is scarcity or total absence of foreign material and trace evidence unless something such as glass is present.
- Cuts tend to bleed freely unless vessels are completely divided and able to retract. There is no scraping or bruising at the edges.

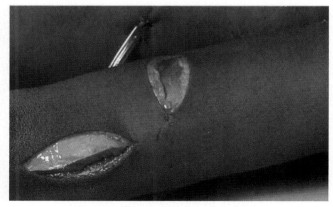
Fig. 25-6 Characteristic sharp force injury.

- Cuts may be irregular if the skin was creased, wrinkled, or affected by clothing at the moment of cutting.
- Cuts may be deeper at one end than the other. This can give rise to questions of right- or left-handedness.
- A cut can be irregular if the skin was moved between the time of injury and examination.

STAB WOUNDS

Stab wounds result whenever a sufficiently sharp and narrow object is forced inward. This is not necessarily the result of a thrust but can occasionally result when one falls onto something sharp. Relative motion and enough force to cause the object to pass through the skin are conditions that are required for stabbing to result. The skin does offer most of the resistance, and once it has been penetrated, the amount of force required will diminish unless tissues such as cartilage or bone are encountered. Although there is a great deal of deliberate stabbing with knives, other less sharp objects such as metal rods, ice picks, and screwdrivers may be used. If a penetrating object is not truly sharp or if it tapers and becomes thicker as it enters, then it is possible to see some stretching of the wound margins with resulting abrasion; however, stab wounds are primarily sharp in character. Occasionally, force is so great that really blunt objects are driven into the body, in which case these injuries are best classified and described as lacerations.

Stab wounds are more likely to reflect information of forensic importance—such as the causative instrument or weapon—than are cuts, because a rounded object tends to cause a rounded hole, a square object a squarer hole, and so forth. For example, a fairly thick knife blade that is sharpened only on one of its two edges will tend to leave a defect that has a cleanly cut acute angle at one end and a more squared-off or slightly torn, angular appearance at the other. A cross-shaped Phillips screwdriver may produce wounds, which have a subtle, but definite cross-shaped configuration when examined carefully. Unless a known stabbing object is present for examination, the exact depth of penetration must remain unknown until the body is opened at surgery or autopsy. For this reason, many surgeons elect to explore the internal situation following stab wounds. Occasionally stabbing instruments (tips of cast blades or big pieces of glass) may break off in the depths of a wound, especially if bone is encountered. Recovery and retention of such fragments may be vital to effective prosecution of a criminal case or even to prove the cause of an accidental injury. Always look for evidence that a knife or tool was forced in as far as its handle (Smock, 2007). Areas of abrasion

near the entry defect may signify this. Regardless of the length of the blade, such features indicate that it went in all the way, and generally this is not favorable to the patient as it increases the potential for deep-seated injury.

This classification into cuts and stabs is simplified for clarity and instructional purposes. Classic stabs and cuts represent opposite ends of a spectrum of injuries. For example, one may wonder what to call a wound that is about as deep as it is long. The important thing is to recognize it as a sharp injury and be able to separate it from the results of a blow (blunt injury). Stabs and cuts are often seen together in a single patient or victim. Decide if the force was primarily inward or transverse with respect to the skin, and describe the injuries as best as possible. Photography remains the best method of documentation.

If criminal activity is involved, try to document the surface dimension, depth, and direction of wounds. Cuts that are inflicted across the natural lines of tension (Langor lines) in the skin tend to gape open. Those inflicted parallel to the lines of tension tend to remain closed and relatively undistorted (i.e., the "zipper-locked bag effect"). Surgeons are familiar with these lines of tension and endeavor to make their incisions parallel to them. Members of the street scene do not worry about such subtleties, so the injuries inflicted are often distorted by the effects of tension in the skin combined with body movement. This means one must consider how the injury looked before skin tension and body movement led to a change of shape. Beveling or shelving of wound margins are again clues to the internal direction of a wound track. Tracks should never be probed indiscriminately. In the event a chest tube or other device should be placed through a fortuitously located injury, this should be clearly indicated in the treatment or operative report. Otherwise, if the victim dies, the pathologist may not be in a position to properly interpret the features and wounds inflicted by an assailant (Figs. 25-7, 25-8, 25-9, and 25-10). However, it is preferable to never insert a chest tube into a bullet wound or stab wound.

Not infrequently, autopsy or surgical exploration reveals a wound track that extends inward for a distance greater than the length of the weapon alleged to have caused it. This is because when someone is struck with a blow, the body wall may compress with momentary indentation of the tissues, which may even be combined with a subsequent change in the position of the body by the time the internal examination takes place. Even the chest wall can be compressed. This is why modern cardiopulmonary resuscitation (CPR) can effectively squeeze the heart between the momentarily depressed sternum and the forward projection of the

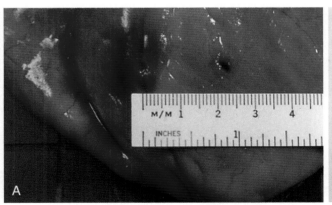

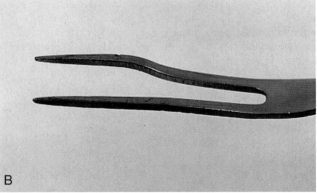

Fig. 25-7 *A,* Stab wound of heart with a meat fork. *B,* Meat fork used in the stabbing episode.

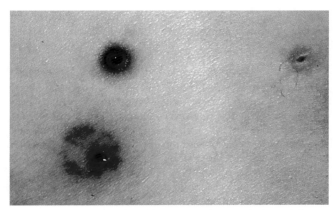

Fig. 25-8 Stab wounds inflicted by an ice pick. Note the lower left entry illustrating the contusion from the ringed collar of the pick's handle.

Fig. 25-9 Stab wound involving a rib that reveals a multilinear pattern, suggesting the type of knife used in the assault.

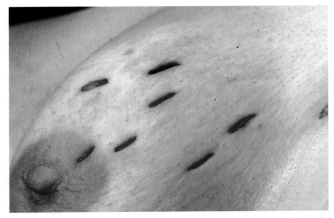

Fig. 25-10 Multiple stab wounds of the chest clearly distinguishing the sharp *(left)* and dull *(right)* edges of the knife.

vertebral bodies and overlying structures. A short, stubby knife is certainly capable of inflicting a wound an inch or two longer than its greatest dimension, especially in the abdomen or when there is little muscle to resist momentary indentation.

Exactly how much increase is possible in these cases is not clear because of a lack of controlled circumstances. By the time of surgical exploration, the living patient has been repositioned, the bowel

has gone completely or partially into a state of ileus (mechanical or adynamic obstruction), blood and gas have collected, and the intestine has rearranged itself. This leads to estimates of weapon size that are often significantly in error. In an elderly person with reduced abdominal musculature and a sagging, relaxed abdominal wall, a relatively short blade can easily reach the aorta and inferior vena cava if a forceful blow is struck. In addition, tangential injuries may appear larger at the surface than those directed radially inward.

SUMMARY

Keep the following points in mind when evaluating sharp force injuries:

- Stab wounds result from variably sharp or pointed objects forced inward by a thrust, movement, or fall.
- Depth exceeds width in stab wounds.
- With stab wounds, there is danger to vital internal structures and the risk of delayed incapacitation, exemplified by cardiac tamponade (blood in the sac surrounding the heart) or tension pneumothorax (air trapping between a lung and the chest wall).
- Stab wounds may begin with internal bleeding, then later blood may appear when the victim "overflows" or collapses. This often confuses inexperienced or untrained individuals.
- Stab wounds may reflect the causative instrument or weapon (single edge, double edge, square, round, etc.).
- There is relatively little abrasion of stab wound margins unless the weapon is tapering and wedges/stretches the skin on its way in.
- Occasionally fragments of a penetrating object will break off in a stab wound. Remnants should be recovered and retained whenever practicable and handled as potential evidence.

Other Wounds

There are other wounds with characteristics that do not necessarily fit well into either blunt or sharp force injuries. The weapon or instrument, as well as the forces involved, will determine the type of resultant injury.

MIXED BLUNT AND SHARP INJURIES

Mixed blunt and sharp injuries exist and are frequently observed because people are attacked and injured by semisharp, semiblunt objects. Examples include old axes, machetes, meat cleavers, roofing hatchets, being ejected onto crushed rock, or falling onto scrap metal. However, understating the basic subtypes of blunt and sharp injury will allow one to recognize a mixture of injuries.

Chop Wounds

Chop wounds are deep, gaping wounds often involving major structures and resulting from the use of relatively heavy and sharp objects such as meat cleavers, axes, machetes, and brush hooks. If the instrument is fairly sharp, wounds may show a mixture of both sharp and blunt characteristics. One key to recognizing them is the combination of force and depth.

Blister or Friction Blister

The friction blister is not usually of medicolegal significance, but blisters may be observed on the feet of those who have been walking a lot. This is especially true if the person is not used to much walking or has new, unsuitable, or ill-fitting footwear. Blisters cause high rates of disability in the military services, especially during training and on the march. Occasionally, the associated ulceration (when the surface layer separates) and secondary infection can be significant and may even become life threatening, especially in diabetics and the elderly when there is poor circulation to the area. Research has shown that dry and extremely wet skin affords less friction than slightly moistened surfaces.

The friction blister is not due to heat and does not represent second-degree burns, even though it may feel hot. Research has never shown a temperature rise of more than a few degrees, even under extreme experimental conditions. Blisters are formed by a shearing between the more superficial and deeper skin structures, resulting eventually in a split or cleft into which fluid flows or transudes. Blisters are most frequent in the skin of the hands (palms) and feet (soles, heels, sides of the feet, and tops of the toes). The cleft almost invariably occurs above the basal cells, in or below the granular layer of the skin. The fluid within blisters contains most of the proteins of blood serum, but in lesser concentration and usually with little or no fibrinogen. It is important to remember that there are other possible causes of skin blistering, including burns, exposure to chemicals, prolonged immersion, and decomposition.

DEFENSIVE INJURIES

Defensive injuries are incurred in attempts to ward off blows of a weapon or assailant or in trying to grasp a sharp weapon. Injuries resulting from blunt attack can be in the form of scrapes, bruises, tears, and even fractures. In the case of a sharp attack, defensive injuries could be cuts and stabs. Defensive injuries are likely to be found on the arms and hands, but they may be seen elsewhere. They are usually found on those parts of the body that a victim tends to interpose between himself or herself and the assailant and including the backs of the hands, wrists, forearms, and to a lesser extent the shoulders and elbows (Sheridan, 2007).

Defense wounds are helpful because they indicate that the victim was, regardless of drugs and alcohol, aware, conscious, and able to resist. They also indicate if the weapon was sharp or blunt. On occasion, the type of weapon may be evident and the sequence of events apparent (Fig. 25-11).

Diversionary Wounds

Although not a common a term, the phrase *diversionary wounds* is sometimes used to describe those wounds inflicted in the course of an attack, to promote a response that will facilitate the exposure of previously guarded, less exposed, or more vital areas. Diversionary wounds merge into, and may be indistinguishable from, defensive injuries.

FACTITIOUS INJURIES

Factitious injuries (i.e., injuries that have been fabricated, forged, or invented) are self-inflicted, not with the intent of suicide but with the intent of accusing or blaming someone else, obtaining money or reward by false pretenses, or avoiding unpleasant duty. They are not particularly common in North America but are more common elsewhere; nevertheless, factitious injuries occur often enough that the possibility should not be ignored. Factitious injuries are often superficial or relatively minor in nature, usually located on readily accessible parts of the body, and they may be encountered in disturbed or mentally ill persons or in those who bear a grudge. These injuries are usually superficial, blunt, not too painful, and usually located in those areas where self-infliction is easy. Injuries on the face are likely to be vertical and more oblique on the left in a right-handed individual, and they do not show the irregularity associated with a fight or the movement in struggle. Another clue is often that the person with self-inflicted wounds is open about them and wants them to be noticed. To experiment with possible angles and marks, have a nonmedically trained person inflict imaginary injuries using a marker or water-soluble dye on a swab.

HESITATION MARKS

Hesitation marks (trial, tentative, decision cuts) are the superficial, often somewhat parallel cuts made in the course of attempting suicide, in an attempt to gain courage or attention, or arising from vacillation. For instance, a person bent on self-destruction by cutting may try the blade on the wrists and neck to see how painful it is before inflicting deeper wounds. The significance is that these wounds strongly support the conclusion that they are self-inflicted and help to separate suicide from homicide. In any suspected suicide it is always worth looking for well-healed, faint, and barely visible parallel cuts on the wrists, arms, and neck (from a previous episode of self-inflicted injury).

PAIRED OR GROUPED INJURIES

It is essential to keep in mind the possibility that instruments such as scissors, shears, and forks may be used to inflict more than one injury simultaneously. Some medieval weapons also produced injuries in this fashion. The same thinking applies today with irregularly shaped objects such as tools and gear wheels. Some of these injuries may have an obvious pattern to them. An important aspect is that the number of wounds observed may exceed the alleged/reported number of thrusts or blows.

SCRIMMAGE WOUNDS

Scrimmage wound or *scrimmage enlargement* are terms that have been used to describe the enlargement by tearing of a wound as a consequence of relative motion between the tissues and a weapon before it is completely withdrawn. Sometimes these terms are used to refer to a partial double track, for instance, when a stab wound was inflicted, the victim moved, and the assailant promptly pressed the knife in again to its fullest extent. This usually applies when the penetrating weapon enters and is then withdrawn in a forceful manner to one or the other side of the plane in which it entered. Such wounds show features of both the initial stab and the subsequent reinsertion component.

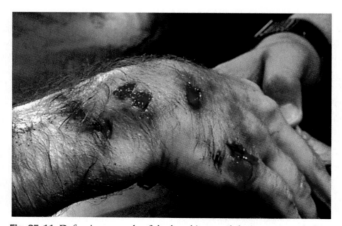

Fig. 25-11 Defensive wounds of the hand incurred during an assault from an offender who was using a wrecking bar or claw hammer as a weapon.

WRINKLE WOUNDS

The term *wrinkle wound* is sometimes used to describe a situation wherein a single sweeping cut or motion of a sharp instrument contacts the skin several locations in sequence as it passes by. This may occur if the skin is folded or deeply creased, if the individual is obese, or if clothing intervenes, produces folds, or offers a variable amount of resistance.

The importance of identifying wrinkle wounds is that the number of cuts, slashes, or thrusts reported by witnesses may not match the number of wounds on the body. A similar result may occur in relation to anatomical landmarks or positions. For instance, two cuts sustained when the arm was bent at the elbow may appear distinct and separate when the patient or victim later comes to assume the arms-at-the-side position during treatment or autopsy examination.

Gunshot Injuries

FIREARMS

Ever since gunpowder was invented, firearms have operated faster than the eye can readily see. This has led to misleading statements and mystique, which confuses healthcare providers and hinders the evaluation of injuries. In addition, the entertainment industry often portrays people being thrown several feet and through windows by a single bullet, while the person shooting them does not move, which defies the laws of physics. The general level of understanding of missile-tissue interaction is poor.

Although there may seem to be an immense variety of weapons, for practical purposes, they can be divided, more or less, into three types: (1) handguns and submachine guns, (2) shotguns, and (3) rifles and machine guns. All firearms use gunpowder, which propels one or more missiles at a high rate of speed.

Handguns and Submachine Guns

Handguns include revolvers, semiautomatic pistols, derringers, and single-shot weapons (which accept only one cartridge at a time). Submachine guns use handgun ammunition but do so in a fully automatic fashion rather than firing once for each pull of the trigger.

Shotguns

Shotguns require a separate review because of the many wads, shot metals, shot sizes, filler materials, and components within their cartridges.

Forensic personnel must understand the basics of firearm injuries if they expect to participate in crime scene documentation and associated evidence collection. When there is a small, well-demarcated area of powder markings on the skin and the suspect says the victim was shot from the other side of the street, one should know that the suspect is wrong or not telling the truth. Conversely, if a man comes in for treatment of a bullet graze wound on one side of the chest and has a few small stipple marks scattered over the adjacent skin after he dropped his gun on the floor, his story is believable.

BULLET CHARACTERISTICS

A cartridge consists of a formed metal cylinder (commonly of a brass alloy) that is more or less closed at one end with primer mixture at the rim of the base (rimfire cartridge) or a primer cap in a recess in the center of the base (centerfire cartridge). A specified weight or charge of gunpowder is introduced through the open end. Finally, a bullet is inserted to close the opening, preventing the powder from falling out, and rendering the cartridge a self-contained unit.

When a firing pin strikes the rim of a rimfire cartridge or the centrally located primer of a centerfire cartridge, the primer mixture explodes, resulting in a small burst of flame, hot gas, and particles; this causes the main powder charge to undergo chemical change, thereby generating the gas pressure necessary to force the bullet down the barrel. It is doubtful that any normal smokeless powder charge ever burns completely. Therefore, a small, and somewhat variable, but significant percentage of the powder charge in any given cartridge is not consumed. These unburned grains, and remnants of others in various stages of consumption, follow the bullet out of the barrel, accompanied by the gray, sooty products resulting from the gunpowder that was consumed in the process of making gas.

Therefore, what an observer sees on the body surface and clothing will depend on the range of fire unless objects such as doors, furnishings, and clothing are interposed.

Following injury or death by firearms, three main items need to be evaluated and documented:
1. Range of fire
2. Relative angle of impact
3. Interposed factors (between the firearm and tissue)

RANGE OF FIRE

Range of fire is the factor that considers the distance from the barrel or muzzle of a firearm to the target. It can be considered contact (or near contact), close/short range, medium range, or long range.

The estimation of range depends on reproducing the diameter, distribution, and density of the powder marks or soot observed and described at the start of the case. Exact distances do not need to be known.

Near Contact and Contact Range

In a near contact or contact range, the weapon is close to touching or makes actual contact with the skin and clothing. In addition to the bullet hole, powder, and soot, other features may be seen, such as the following:
- Evidence of transient heating
- Tearing of soft tissues by the gases escaping behind the bullet under pressure
- A marking to indicate that the barrel itself touched the skin as the tissues, expanded by in-rushing gases, came back on to the muzzle of the weapon. Such barrel markings may be complete enough to indicate or characterize a type of weapon (e.g., revolver versus pistol) and on rare occasions a specific make or model of weapon. Exactly what one finds will depend on a multitude of factors including barrel length, muzzle configuration, type of weapon, amount of gas (itself a function of caliber and load), and presence or absence of bone just beneath the skin (Smock, 2007) (Fig. 25-12).

KEY POINT The presence of powder or soot, in addition to a bullet hole, indicates a near-contact or contact-range injury.

Short or Close Range

When the muzzle of the weapon comes within a few inches of the skin or clothing, one will find the bullet wound, the powder grains or powder markings called fouling, and an additional feature, namely the powder soot (or simply soot) produced by combustion of the gunpowder itself. The powder that was consumed in the process of producing gas gave rise to a gray, sooty residue.

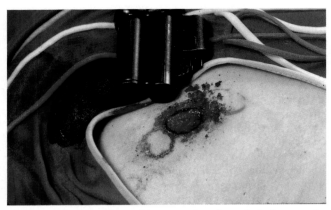

Fig. 25-12 Muzzle marking with soot and outline of tubular magazine and foresight cover, indicating that the weapon was in direct contact with the skin.

Just as powder grains vary in size and shape, so do they also vary in their burning characteristics. Some give rise to very little soot and others to far more. So it is not possible to state the exact range from an examination of soot near a wound. One can only say that it was a few or several inches, or soot would not be found. Once again, additional information and a test firing are usually required (Fig. 25-13).

Medium Range

Within the medium range, the weapon is within a few feet of the victim and not only is the bullet wound found, but there is also evidence that some gunpowder grains struck the skin or clothing with sufficient force to leave small impact marks, or even driven partly or completely into the surface if they strike with sufficient force. Although gunpowder grains are capable of traveling many feet from a gun after firing, it is only for the first 2, 3, or sometimes 4 feet that these particles retain sufficient energy to mark the skin or stick in the weave of clothing materials. The marks will be varied but dependent on the size and shape of the individual particles. When the gunpowder grains strike the skin with sufficient force to make marks, the aggregation of impact markings is usually called tattooing or stippling. *Speckling* and *peppering* are less frequently used but acceptable terms. Those who are detail minded may elect to use the term *stippling* for impact marks and *tattooing*

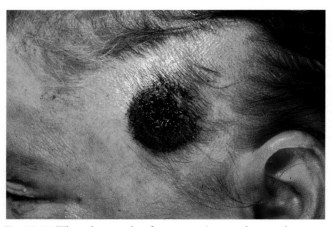

Fig. 25-13 When the muzzle of a weapon is very close to the target, a sooty residue from burned gunpowder will be deposited.

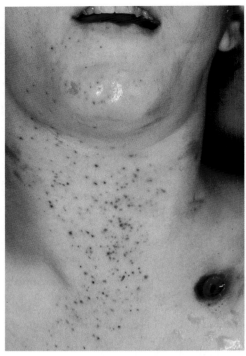

Fig. 25-14 This wound is consistent with a range of fire that is greater than 8 inches but less than 18 to 36 inches, characterized by stippling (small abrasions and hemorrhages) created when unburned or partially burned gunpowder strikes the skin.

for actual indriving of grains. Although either term is understood, it may be an important distinction when it comes to deciding if an injury was the result of an attempted homicide or suicide (Fig. 25-14).

KEY POINTS Stippling or tattooing of the skin by gunpowder residue is characteristic of medium-range firearm injuries.

Modern single-base (nitrocellulose) and double-base (nitrocellulose with nitroglycerin) smokeless gunpowders are manufactured in discrete grains of various shapes and sizes (Rowe, 2003). There are many shapes, but for any given size and weight of grain, some will have better aerodynamic properties than others and fly more readily through the air as they leave a barrel behind a bullet. Flake powders were common until the early to mid-1930s when ball powders were developed. With several different shapes on the market, it is desirable to know which are prevalent within a specific area. One reason is that older textbooks inaccurately state that powder from handguns is incapable of marking skin beyond about 18 to 24 inches. Generally, flake powder is still unlikely to mark skin at distances greater than about 2 feet, but ball powders may do so out to about 4 feet, with the maximum distance for flattened ball falling somewhere between. A second reason is that one must look critically at the shape and size of the markings on the skin, as they generally reflect the size and shape of the grains that made them. It is a simple mirror image or impression phenomenon. Small, more or less spherical grains leave rather numerous, uniform rounded markings, whereas larger flakes give rise to fewer, larger, and more variable markings. Some grains, especially from the 22-caliber rimfire cartridges, may be small enough that the distances at which they will mark are less than might be predicted from their shape alone. Size, shape, and weight are the major determinants of their ability to fly and to strike with sufficient force to leave marks (Rowe, 2003).

Long or Distant Range

At this range, only the bullet will reach the skin and clothing. As the bullet makes contact with the skin, it causes a momentary indentation, like pressing the tip of the little finger into the soft, fleshy front part of the forearm. This is important because, for an instant, there is friction between the front and side of the bullet and those parts of the skin that are going to constitute the margins of the entrance wound. Thus, when the bullet continues inward and the surface returns to the former, nonindented position, one should anticipate a hole, slightly smaller than the bullet, because of inherent tissue elasticity, surrounded by a narrow rim of superficial abrasion or scraping commonly called the *abrasion ring* or *margin*. The abrasion margin is due to the forward, pushing motion of the bullet—it does not result from rotation of the bullet about its longitudinal axis imparted by rifling, nor does it result from the bullet being red hot. Bullets are warm after firing, but they can be picked from the floor of a range with the fingers and they are regularly recovered by shooting into cotton wool, which is only occasionally set on fire, and even then, only by friction.

Another myth is that bullets enter with a rotary, screwlike, drilling motion. In fact, the average handgun bullet makes about one turn in 10, 12, 14, or 16 inches of forward movement, so even if a bullet is making one turn in 10 inches it will only complete $\frac{1}{10} \times \frac{1}{16}$ or $\frac{1}{160}$ th of a turn while passing through skin that is $\frac{1}{16}$ th of an inch thick. If an entry wound happens to lie in skin that has bone closely underlying it, the abrasion margin may be narrower and harder to see, especially with certain shapes of bullets, because the skin is not so easily indented as the bullet enters.

If the bullet is made of lead alloy, if it has lubricant on its surface, or if it picked up any sooty dirt as it passed down the barrel, then an additional feature known as bullet wipe or bullet wipe-off (particularly if the bullet enters through light color clothing) may be seen (Fig. 25-15). A detailed examination of skin wounds occasionally reveals the presence of traces of such dark foreign material toward the periphery of the abrasion margin where it may be known as gray ring or gray rim, but obviously *bullet wipe* or *bullet wipe-off* are sound, descriptive terms. Naturally such remnants are far less commonly present if a bullet has a clean, hard metallic jacket and came from an unsoiled barrel.

Presence of an abrasion margin or bullet wipe-off indicates that a wound is one of entry until proven otherwise. If a bullet enters a surface at right angles, then the zone of abrasion will be more or less symmetrically developed around the wound; but if it should enter at an angle, there will be far more abrasion on the side where the bullet first made contact. This knowledge is useful because unless a victim was very obese or is in a different position than when injured, the abrasion margin gives a useful preliminary and generally reliable indication of the direction in which the bullet was traveling.

Therefore, healthcare personnel should appreciate that the estimation of range depends on reproducing the diameter, distribution, and density of the powder marks observed and described at the start of the case.

Case Study 25-2

Determining Range of Fire

An individual, under the influence of crack cocaine, starts a fight with two law enforcement officers and ends up being shot in the back. Questions are asked, an inquiry held, and someone asks that his shirt be examined for gunshot residues. Both visible (gunpowder and soot) and invisible (primer) residues should be examined to estimate the range of fire. One version of events was that he was shot deliberately from about 8 feet after he had given up and had raised his hands above his head. The other story is that he was just getting up off the ground holding a gun wrested from one officer when the other officer shot him at close range. If his arms were raised in surrender, the hole should be relatively lower in the shirt than in his back.

RELATIVE ANGLE OF IMPACT

The relative angle of impact refers to the relative angular directions from/at which the bullet entered the body. Direction is best described with respect to the standard body position: standing at attention with hands open, palms to the front, and thumbs to the outside. The relative angle can be influenced by many factors, including the position of the weapon, the type of ammunition, interposed objects, and protective clothing. A wider margin of abrasion usually indicates the direction of travel from the firearm (Spitz, 1993) (Fig. 25-16).

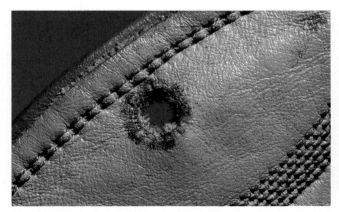

Fig. 25-15 This defect is characterized by bullet wipe or wipe-off, which appears as a grayish discoloration surrounding the perforation on the shaft of a boot.

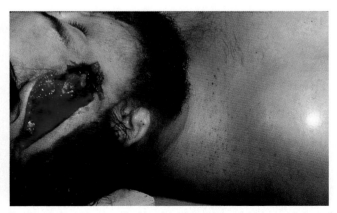

Fig. 25-16 Contact wound of head (with revolver suicide); angulation of weapon and injection of gas created scalp laceration and irregular clavicular stippling.

INTERPOSED FACTORS

Interposed factors refer to any observations or evidence that provides information about the weapon and the ammunition or about any objects that may have been interposed between the gun and the victim at the time of shooting. Some are surprisingly easy to see—such as bits of clothing, wood, plaster, or metal—indicating that the bullet hit some other object before reaching the intended target.

MYTHS AND REALITIES

There are many examples of inaccurate and poorly documented accounts of shooting incidents. To put things into perspective, it is important to understand the basics of the energy forces involved in firing a weapon, the bullet's travel to the target, and the ultimate impact on the victim's body.

Ballistic experts and enthusiasts usually think and speak in units such as feet per second, grains of weight, and foot-pounds of energy. Unfortunately, most healthcare workers are unfamiliar with these measurements. To appreciate the basic concept of velocity and impact force, here are some examples. Across a street or room, bullets from handguns and 22-caliber rimfire weapons typically travel about the speed of, and up to about a third faster, than a jet airliner at cruise. The kinetic energy they possess, roughly equating to two to four "ace" serves by a top tennis professional.

Clearly such bullets do not have what it takes in terms of potential to throw people off their feet, into walls, or cause individuals to behave as depicted in motion pictures. This is important because these images give false expectations, particularly if gunshot wounds are relatively uncommon in a given jurisdiction or unfamiliar to the jurors.

In general, when hit by commonplace "street" bullets, the victim will do one of the following three things:

1. Continue in the direction in which he or she was previously moving, less a small fraction of a foot per second
2. Fall in the direction in which he or she was leaning, until such time that the victim's legs give way or muscular action of any kind, deliberate or not deliberate, causes the victim to do otherwise
3. Go down immediately and perhaps exhibit some transient muscular twitching if struck in the spinal cord or most parts of the brain

WOUNDS: ASSESSMENT AND DOCUMENTATION

When watching movies, people often get a false impression of what happens when a firearm hits someone. This fact can be demonstrated in several ways. Let's look at some contrived and actual scenarios of what might happen when a bullet impacts a person to appreciate how the human body responds to the forces generated by the weapon being fired.

Some real-world examples follow:

- If a researcher were to place approximately 170 pounds of sand (the equivalent of average adult weight) into a bag, cover it with body armor, and suspend it from a rope or coil spring so that it could swing free when struck by a missile, one would be unlikely to see much action. In actuality, after the firearm is discharged and contacts the sandbag target, very little happens, perhaps a slight swinging motion of about ½ to 1 inch.
- An average-sized man floating in microgravity within an orbiting spacecraft will take about seven to eight seconds to drift backward 1 foot, should he absorb the entire energy of a medium-caliber handgun bullet such as from a 9-mm semiautomatic pistol. If he

is heavier, it will take longer. One can calculate the momentum involved: mass × velocity = mass × velocity.

- If action and reaction are indeed equal and opposite, as taught in school, a victim should no more be thrown about or propelled by the bullet striking him or her than the person who was holding the weapon.
- When debriefing personnel who have shot others in the course of military or police duties, nearly all express surprise at how little effect their bullets often seemed to have, unless they have struck the brain or spinal cord.
- One needs to merely watch what happens when actual shootings are recorded on videotape during times of war and in terrorist incidents. For example, soldiers storming the beaches of Normandy on D-day were not thrown back into the English Channel by rifle and machinegun bullets. They continued to walk or run up the beach or stumble forward before they collapsed. The bullets that struck them carried far more energy of motion than the bullets commonly dealt with today.

Other false impressions perpetuated by motion pictures include the following:

- Excessive damage produced at the time of bullet impact, such as doors and walls falling down, when the usual is a small hole.
- Too much blood too soon and over too big an area. Many shooting victims have less blood on them 15 minutes after injury than in the next frame following a motion picture "shooting."
- Bullets causing great showers of sparks on impact when, in fact, production of sparks is a rarity in average circumstances. Most bullets are made of lead and copper alloys, which do not give rise to sparks.
- Incorrect relationships between the sounds of weapons discharging and the arriving bullet. For instance, a military rifle is shown being fired some distance away, but the sound is heard before the bullet arrives, when in real life it is the reverse. Wouldn't it be interesting if a hunter shot at an animal, the animal heard the sound of the rifle, and moved before the bullet arrived; or if an infantryman could take cover after he heard a shot! The reality is that the speed of sound in air at sea level standard temperature is about 1116.45 feet per second (1120.27 feet per second is used for ballistic calculations), so rifle bullets at 2800 feet per second are moving 2 to 2½ times faster than sound!

Learning to evaluate gunshot wounds means first seeing through the layer of misinformation that covers and surrounds them, blocking clear vision. Blunt injuries on a gunshot victim resulted from the fight that preceded the shooting, or from the fall, vehicle crash, or blows that followed the shooting, not from the bullet physically throwing the victim around. Other things can occur with heavy weapons in military combat, but that is not the ordinary course of events.

These facts offer several lessons:

- Books written before the 1940s are outdated when it comes to the maximum distances at which gunpowder from handguns and similar weapons is capable of marking skin. Two feet was about the maximum when powder was only made in flakes, but today one is likely to encounter newer and more aerodynamic shapes with better flight characteristics. These may mark the skin or get stuck in the clothing at distances up to 3 or 4 feet.
- Careful examination of the markings on the skin may help determine the shape of the grains that were involved. The situation is much the same as the sliding scraping marks of bulged, laminated windshield glass, and the small cuboid,

dicelike fragments from the tempered side and rear windows that produce the markings often referred to as dicing.

- With any powder grains or particles on the skin or clothing, a sample should be collected and retained. One way to do this is to hold a strip of self-adhesive masking tape, adhesive side out, over the thumbs, and use this to pick up grains. Then, these grains should be placed over a glass slide to assist experts in subsequent range determination and other tests.
- If there were two assailants, both or several bullets exited, and the assailants used different cartridges loaded with different powders, the powder remnants may help distinguish one type of ammunition from another.
- The 2- to 4-foot range is a distance at which people struggle for control and possession of weapons.
- Something must be known about the caliber before making range estimates because there may be an associated change in grain size, especially in some of the small calibers.
- It is not possible simply to look at a zone of powder markings and estimate the exact range of fire until one has considerable experience. Even experts who are familiar with the many variables usually require more information or a test firing.

Entrance Wounds

A number of unfamiliar terms, although they may appear complicated, are simply an attempt on the part of a prior observer to convey the perceived relationship between the barrel and the skin or clothing at the moment of discharge. If it was concluded that the muzzle was very close to, but not actually touching, then words such as *near, close,* or *impending contact* may be used. If the barrel actually made contact, then the terms *full, tight, firm, hard,* or *press(ed) contact* are appropriate. If the barrel was not held at right angles but was inclined to the surface, words such as *angled* may appear. It is the combination of these expressions (e.g., angled near contact or inclined hard contact) that generates the apparent complexity, but in practical terms they all mean that the gun was so close to the skin and clothing that the details become largely a matter for the forensic expert. The care provider deals with a bullet traveling at top speed, plus some residues and gas under pressure.

If a partial or complete outline of the muzzle is present, this may be called *muzzle stamp, muzzle imprint, barrel abrasion,* and similar terms. It is often relatively easy to distinguish a contact wound caused by a revolver from one caused by a semiautomatic (auto loading) pistol. Outlines of foresights, ejector rods, slides, and similar gun parts may be clearly visible at the margins of the entry wound, either continuous with or adjacent to the barrel marking itself. Obviously such findings are highly significant and should be recorded with care, commonly by means of a diagram or sketch. They may be overlooked beneath blood and dressings.

So although the features one may see are subject to considerable variation in terms of the distance at which they occur, and not all authors use this simple system of range classification, the fundamental issue is to understand the sequence of events: at a distance, bullet only; at a few feet, bullet and powder; at a few inches, bullet powder and soot; then finally the realm of contact. For instance, a bullet hole surrounded by a slightly enlarged and irregular abrasion with slivers of wood on the overlying shirt is in keeping with the victim standing next to a wooden door when a bullet came through it. Absence of residues on the skin combined with absence of clothing during the cold season means that the whereabouts of the clothing must be determined before any conclusions concerning range can be drawn. A gray zone resembling soot on a white T-shirt, but without a trace of gunpowder, may in fact be lead dust because a lead bullet passed through a car door as the victim stood behind it and became sprinkled with lead particles. Some bullets emitting particles or small metal fragments (e.g., copper-jacketed bullets) may be mistaken for powder particles and their impact marks.

It is not particularly significant if an investigator prefers to use a given number of inches as the dividing line between medium and close range or to subdivide the range into all sorts of complicated zones provided the proposed system makes sense and is applicable to the weapon and situation. In real life, the weapon is often unknown at the time a patient is examined or an autopsy performed, which is why a general system, that makes allowance for variation from weapons to weapon, is so practical.

If a weapon is in contact with soft tissues when it is discharged, there may be actual tearing by the propulsive gases as they leave the barrel and enter the tissues behind the bullet. How much tearing occurs will vary according to powder charge, gas volumes, gas pressure, caliber, elasticity of the tissues, how much soft tissue there is to cushion the shock, presence or absence of underlying bone, and similar factors (Smock, 2007). Contact wounds may not be torn at all or may be the width of a hand. Parts of the head may even come away if the weapon is powerful enough and the conditions are right. Exact figures for the gas pressures behind bullets as they exit the muzzle are not readily available for handguns but certainly many hundred to a few thousand pounds per square inch are reasonably common figures according to caliber, barrel length, type of powder, and powder load. Wildly exaggerated figures are often quoted for gas volumes, such as "thousands of gallons." If such fantasies were true, (1) elite naval personnel would not be able to fire their weapons under water without emptying the swimming pool, dying of blast injuries, and causing great spouts of water during training exercises, and (2) firing a gun in a room would result in departure of the windows, doors torn off their hinges, and eardrums ruptured by overpressure. These phenomena do not usually occur.

Suppose a person commits suicide by means of a powerful handgun (such as a .357-Magnum revolver with a relatively short barrel and one of the higher-pressure cartridges). Suppose further that the barrel is held just in front of and slightly above the right external ear canal and the gun is aimed from right to left, and upward about 30° with respect to the horizontal axis—what should one expect to see? Probably a hole in the soft tissues at the entry site about 1 to 1¼ inches in diameter and extending upward from this, a somewhat Y-shaped laceration of the skin extending into the scalp, measuring as much as 3 to 4 inches vertically. Sooty residues and powder grains will be visible in the entry wound with some focal pink coloration resulting from carbon monoxide. On the left side of the head, the exit wound will be located about 3 inches higher than the corresponding point of entry but will appear sharp edged and about ¾ inch to 1 inch in greatest dimension. Such observations are very important because this is a case in which the gas-torn wound of entry is far larger than the wound of exit, and many people wrongly believe that exit wounds are always larger than entry wounds.

Indeed, an entry wound may be larger than an exit wound for several reasons:

- Situations, such as the one discussed earlier, in which the soft tissues at the entry are torn by in-rushing gases and the exit wound is of average size, relatively far smaller
- When a bullet is yawing as it enters, perhaps because of striking something en route to the target, or very occasionally, because of insufficient longitudinal rotation imparted by rifling

- When an entire bullet enters but only a portion of it exits
- Tangential entry wounds with focal avulsion of tissue and bone
- Bullets entering through folded or creased skin but exiting through a less complicated surface
- Tangential entry wounds but less angled exits
- Combinations of these factors

KEY POINT Wound size should never be used as the sole determinant of entry or exit.

Wound size should never be used as the sole determinant of entry or exit. Size alone is totally unreliable and very misleading. Size is just one of many features that should be considered. Record the size of wounds, but decide if they are entries or exits based on their characteristics and by the "company they keep."

Entrance wounds vary widely and should be described in terms of location and appearance (Figs. 25-17 and 25-18). From a clinical standpoint, the important factors are the type of bullet and how that bullet interacts with the tissue it encounters (Silva, 1999).

Exit Wounds

Assume that a bullet is coming through the tissues and approaches a body surface. As it reaches the skin, it pushes from within and, if it has the necessary energy of motion, it will burst the skin outward producing a sharp-edged, slightly irregular wound. Such wounds are sometimes called stellate because many have a somewhat star-shaped configuration. There will be no marginal abrasion because the bullet pushed its way out, not in. The majority of simple handgun and submachine gun exit wounds are less than 1 inch in greatest dimension, some a little larger. Rotation of bullets about their longitudinal axes, induced by rifling, is only

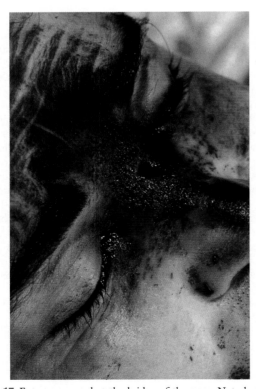

Fig. 25-17 Entrance wound at the bridge of the nose. Note heavy soot deposits and indriving of gunpowder, indicative of an entrance wound.

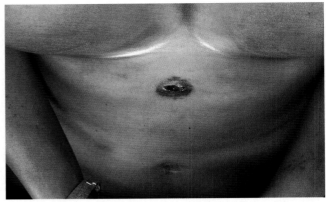

Fig. 25-18 Suicide victim with entrance wound between breasts. Notice the cylinder flare evident on both forearms.

sufficient to make them stable in air, and unless the bullet hits something or the circumstances are exceptional, bullets remain pointed forward and do not tumble in flight. However, it would require about 25 to 35 times (the square root of the density ratio between tissue and air) more axial/longitudinal twist to stabilize bullets in tissue, which is impractical. This means that most bullets are potentially unstable in tissue, and they will yaw and tumble eventually unless they exit before doing so or unless the distribution of weight or their shape prevents it from happening.

If (1) an exit wound is produced by a bullet that was tumbling or (2) for any reason the bullet is coming sideways through the tissues, or (3) the exit wound happened to be in a part of the body in which the skin has a fold or change of direction (buttock crease, parts of the face, underarm, groin, or umbilical areas), then the exit wound may appear elongated and slitlike. After examining gunshot wounds on a regular basis, it will only take a few weeks before one encounters an exit that appears remarkably like a stab or incised wound. This resemblance occasionally gives rise to mistaken impressions during clinical care.

Skin is tough, resilient, and equivalent in resistance to a greater thickness, perhaps a few inches, of muscle or liver, so it is not uncommon to find bullets beneath the skin, more or less on the opposite side of the body from which they entered. It is always worth scrutinizing and actually making a point of feeling the body surface for any signs of slight bulging, fluctuant bleeding into the subcutaneous tissues, or a hard lump that may represent a bullet. This can be helpful both during clinical treatment and in making initial assessments before x-rays have been taken because the majority of "street" bullets pass through the body in a slightly curved or more or less straight line path unless they ricochet after striking bone or other obstructions in their pathway.

A typical entry wound, then, is rounded or elliptical with marginal abrasion, sometimes with bullet wipe, whereas a typical exit wound has sharp edges, is outwardly bursting in nature, and is sometimes elongated (Fig. 25-19).

Shored or Supported Exit Wounds

There are circumstances and conditions that can cause confusion and are exceptions to these guidelines—for example, whenever a bullet emerges through an area of skin that is sufficiently supported by something. Chairs, car seats, mattresses and bedding, clothing, articles in pockets, floors, walls, and doors are common supporting objects. In such circumstances, the skin surrounding the exit wound is apt to be forced outward, in effect squeezed

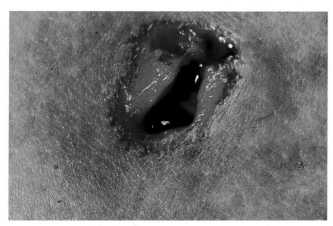

Fig. 25-19 Atypical "shored up" exit wound. Note the irregular pattern abrasion and elongated wound.

or slapped against the supporting surface by the emerging bullet, which often leads to the formation of a zone of abrasion at the margins of the exit. Any such abrasion results from a cause totally unrelated to a bullet having forced its way inward; however, such features may be mistaken for wounds of entry. In fact, when such wounds are examined critically, many will exhibit a mixture of entry and exit characteristics with entry often appearing to predominate at first glance.

Identification

The usual indication that the wound was a shored (as in shored-up or supported) exit is that the abrasion is irregular at its edges, lopsided, too large, or simply does not make sense because it is not in keeping with the shape of an entering bullet (even one that is distorted or tumbling). Such features help forensic experts and other skilled observers ascertain that a victim was on or adjacent to a surface such as a floor or seat when shot. Occasional shored exits can be difficult to distinguish from entry wounds, for instance, when it is cold and many layers of clothing are being worn, but then the situation should immediately be clarified by examining the clothing. It is possible to have more than one exit defect associated with a single bullet entry because of fragmentation, separation of bullet jacket from core, displacement of bone fragments, and so on.

Fortunately there is yet another directional characteristic—the fashion in which bone chips or breaks when struck by a bullet. The appearance is similar to the behavior of glass when a bullet or small stone chips it. If glass remains sufficiently intact to examine, the entry side will appear sharp edged and relatively small whereas the exit side will be sloping and larger. That is, a cone-shaped chip is produced and the defect tapers, becoming larger in the direction in which the bullet was traveling (the apex or point of the cone points back to the origin of the bullet). There are many areas within the body where this works consistently and well, including the skull, sternum, pelvis, ribs, and almost any relatively flat bone of sufficient thickness. Unfortunately, there are some locations (including parts of the facial bones, supraorbital plates, metacarpals, and metatarsals) where it may not prove helpful because the bone in these locations is so thin that it is often impossible to read the bevel even with the aid of a dissecting microscope. The same chipping, beveling effect may also be observed in teeth, dentures, thumbnails, and other items of suitable consistency on and about the body (Rowe, 2003).

The Skull

There are, as is so often true, a few initially perplexing situations such as when a bullet makes tangential contact with a curved surface such as the skull. If this occurs, one may observe chipping in both directions because the bone that is struck first chips inward, then the surface subsequently contacted chips outward, producing what some refer to as a keyhole wound. Likewise, when a bullet passes through windshield glass, separation of fragments at the margin of the outer or inner glass layer can simulate reverse beveling. One must look closely and correlate all the findings.

Unusual Situations

In addition to these basic rules, the occasional difficult or unusual situation may crop up. For instance, a bullet might pass through something substantial (window, vehicle, door, crate, plywood, drywall, furniture, thick shoe sole) en route to the body or exit one body part and reenter another that was in contact with it. In such circumstances, the usual guidelines may appear to have failed, even if they have not. In the latter case, the slapping of skin against skin can produce abrasions around the primary exit and the reentry, or one or other may appear like a slit. However, as soon as the basics are understood, one knows when something does not look right.

It is also possible to encounter cases in which a surgeon altered bone at the entry or exit wounds while trying to save the victim's life. Most surgeons will not notice, and therefore fail to document the direction of chipping. Generally, however, bone is very helpful. Fractures propagate through bone much faster than all common bullets travel, therefore it is occasionally possible to determine which of two holes was made first (or if the victim was struck and then shot in contradistinction to shot and then struck) because of the way in which the fractures associated with each injury intersect.

BEST PRACTICE Do not determine that wounds are entrance wounds or exit wounds. Confine the description to the location and characteristics of the wound.

EXAMINATION AND DOCUMENTATION OF CLOTHING

Preservation, examination, and retention of the clothing must be emphasized and regarded as a priority in all gunshot cases. Without clothing, it may not be possible to ascertain the range of fire. If a weapon is discharged in the vicinity of thick clothing during cold weather, the residues are most likely to be on the outermost clothing, not on the skin (in the course of which it is common for clothing to be indiscriminately cut off or torn away). Clothing should not be cut away or torn through the bullet hole if it can be avoided; instead clothing should be cut between, around, or at a distance from the bullet hole. Improper handling makes subsequent examinations in the crime laboratory that much more difficult. Likewise, if part of the head hair adjacent to a wound is removed during treatment, it should be preserved for gunshot residue analysis.

BEST PRACTICE Save all body tissue fragments, hair, clothing, and physical debris associated with gunshot wounds and preserve them in the same manner as other forensic evidence.

GUNSHOT RESIDUES

The previous discussion brings us to the various residues and how they are used in range determination. Firearm or gunshot residues fall into two main categories: those normally visible and those that are not. The basic understanding of visible residues associated with gunpowder was discussed earlier. If nothing can be seen with the unaided eye or with a magnifier, then state so. It does not mean that the police laboratory cannot, by means of sophisticated instrumentation or methodology, find some minute traces of something at a later time. The statement "absence of visible residues" means to the best of one's ability, in the prevailing circumstances, no residue was discernable. If powder grains, grain markings, or a combination of these with soot were found, then they should be documented by the character, distribution, and size of the areas involved in relation to the point at which the bullet entered. Only then (perhaps weeks, months, or even years later) will it be possible for the laboratory staff to compare their test patterns to these findings and thereby estimate the range of fire. The better and more informative the description, the more accurate the conclusion can be.

As distances increase, the grains lose their ability to strike with sufficient force and they may just remain capable of marking skin but not the paper, cardboard, or other target substituted for skin in the laboratory. Thus, there is a danger that, if there is insufficient mutual understanding and communication between the examining clinician or pathologist and the lab personnel, significant and potentially embarrassing differences of interpretation can arise, which may not become apparent until trial. If a person is shot into a certain type of clothing, an identical material is tested; however, skin cannot be tested the same way. So testers resort to target enhancement, using carbon paper, thin layers of plastic, or other such means, in selected cases. Gunpowder grains can mark skin through clothing in certain instances. For example, when heavier weapons are fired at fairly short distances (up to a foot or so) with certain powders, grains may be driven through thin clothing (e.g., a single layer of a blouse or a shirt) or mark the skin through it.

Primer Mixture

Important but invisible residues are derived from the primer mixture, not from the gunpowder. Modern primers contain a number of substances, and in the momentary intense heat of detonation, minute particles containing lead, barium, and antimony are formed, resolidify, and come to rest on the skin or clothing. These can be seen and photographed, even analyzed, with a scanning electron microscope. Most of these minute particles only travel short distances in the gas cloud and beyond about 3 to 6 inches are seldom present in sufficient numbers for anything but a scanning electron microscope to detect. They may be removed from the skin by any action or process that would remove talcum powder, such as wiping, rubbing, washing, putting the hands in pockets, or doing ordinary things for a few hours. It is for this reason that a paper bag (not plastic because of subsequent internal condensation of skin moisture) should be carefully placed over the hands of any victim of a recent gunshot wound to protect them until the police or a forensic scientist can obtain specimens for primer residue tests by whatever method is in use.

Because scanning electron microscopy is relatively time consuming and expensive, other methods may be used whenever large numbers of gunshot cases are being processed. For instance, one effective technique is swabbing the appropriate portions of the backs and palms of both hands with 5% analytical grade nitric acid and then quantitating the trace metals by means of flameless atomic absorption spectrophotometry. Firearm examiners must use special techniques to visualize gunshot residue on dark, bloodstained clothing (Rowe, 2003).

The methods vary according to needs, budgets, demands, skills, and available technology. A positive finding is meaningful, but a negative finding only means that no metals characteristic of

primer residues were detected. Absence of primer residues may imply the following:

- Residues might never have been present.
- Residues might have been present but then removed or reduced below the critical threshold of methodology.
- Residues were not sought out in timely fashion.
- The cartridge primer might not have contained all three metals, especially in the case of some 22-caliber rimfire primers. Because of attempts to reduce the amount of lead in the environment, other metals such as zinc and manganese may be found in some primer mixtures.
- Residues might have been deliberately removed.
- Not all those who fire a weapon will test positive for primer residues even if tested immediately after firing. The type of weapon has considerable bearing on the probability. In lab tests, only about half of those firing handguns might be negative for residues by flameless atomic absorption spectrophotometry (FAAS). All things being equal, those who shot revolvers should test positive more often than those who operated pistols because of cylinder flare (gases leaking between the cylinder and barrel of a revolver). With rifles and shotguns, only a few might test positive according to the condition of the weapons and the methods used.

For these and other reasons, gunshot residue tests may not be performed as often or in the way they once were. However, prompt, careful examination of the hands is essential in any case of injury by firearms because the circumstances of injury are often unknown at the time of treatment.

Other chemical and physical tests are used to detect invisible metal particles and nitrogen compounds on clothing, bedding, and other objects. Most good books on criminalistics are likely to contain information about them with their practical applications and limitations.

Powder Burns

A potential source of misunderstanding is the expression *powder burns*. In fact, the term is outdated and should not be used on a regular basis. From the time of its invention until about 1890, gunpowder was made of entirely different ingredients than it is today. Black powder, as the old kind is commonly known, is a mechanical mixture of about 15 parts charcoal, 75 parts potassium nitrate, and 10 parts sulfur. It is still used in punt guns, line throwers, signaling flares, blank rounds, and antique weapons, but it is almost never used in modern cartridges and firearms of the kind used on the street. When a weapon charged with black powder is fired, there is considerable muzzle flash and large amounts of white smoke appear.

In the days when clothing consisted entirely of natural fibers, it was not unusual to sear or focally ignite the clothing at shorter distances. This is how the term *powder burns* originated. Today, small arms are usually loaded with single (about 90% to 99% nitrocellulose), double (about 50% to 85% nitrocellulose plus 20% to 45% nitroglycerin), or even triple base smokeless powders.

BULLET DESIGN AND TYPES OF GUNS

Bullet Design

Weapons generally discharge bullets that are made of lead or of a lead core partially or completely covered by a jacket that is almost always made of a harder metal than the core itself. Jackets are often made of a copper alloy, but many other alloys and materials have been used ranging from aluminum to steel and plastic. Some bullets that appear jacketed are not made by forcing a lead core into separately formed jackets but instead are made of lead that is then plated with quite a thick layer of copper or brass material known as a "wash" or "coat," which serves the same function. Many designs and types of bullet exist, and therefore the type of bullet recovered is potentially meaningful to the firearm expert and to the disposition of justice. It is important to keep bullets from different wounds separated from one another, unless this is impossible by virtue of two bullets coming to rest side by side in the same location, perhaps in an accumulation of blood in part of a body cavity.

Centerfire Rifles

Centerfire rifles operate in the same general fashion as rifles but are more powerful. The numbers, including gas pressures, bullet weights, and velocities, are significantly greater, and rifles are effective at far greater distances than are handguns and submachine guns. Accurate shooting at several hundred yards is commonplace. Muzzle velocities in a few commercial calibers are as much as 4000 feet per second from the muzzle, but initial velocities in the range of 2100 to 3700 feet per second are more usual. Bullet weights range between about 0.05 to 1.15 ounces with a few even greater. Exit pressures are often approximately several thousand pounds per square inch and sometimes far more. The momentum and kinetic energy of a bullet varies according to its mass (weight in our daily terms) and velocity, so a higher velocity means that rifle bullets possess considerably more energy of motion than do bullets from handguns and submachine guns, therefore inflicting more injury.

Intermediate Weapons

Between handguns and submachine guns, there are weapons that are intermediate in terms of their power and performance. Some are known as carbines, a rifle of short length and lightweight originally designed for mounted troops. A modern example of such a weapon is the U.S. 30-caliber M1 carbine, which was developed in World War II as a combat improvement to the 45-caliber semi-automatic pistol. There are also a few special-purpose, single-shot handguns, some of which are chambered for a variety of large handgun and rifle cartridges, which fall into this intermediate group. Although firearms and their injuries tend to fall into categories according to type and caliber, there is a continuum from the smallest to the largest, and injuries do not increase in a stepwise fashion.

Rifle injuries are not radically different from other gunshot wounds. In fact, it is the different wounding mechanisms and the addition of features such as a considerable amount of bullet fragmentation that make the difference.

FIREARM WOUNDS: MECHANICS AND CHARACTERISTICS

The internal effects of bullets are frequently misunderstood. The potential of a bullet goes into many factors including the following:

- Crushing, punching, and tearing
- Stretching and splashing
- Friction
- Heating
- Various combinations of bullet distortion, expansion, and fragmentation
- Imparting slight motion to the target
- Generation of sound waves
- Exiting and striking something else
- Rotation about the longitudinal axis

Therefore, most of the energy eventually ends up as heat and the potential of a bullet cannot all be devoted to producing injury. This simple fact is all too often ignored.

In practical terms, there are two major interactions between the bullet and the body:

1. *Crushing, punching, and tearing of tissue because of the physical passage of the bullet itself.* This corresponds approximately to the size, configuration, and attitude of the bullet as it penetrates. The inherent elasticity of some tissues results in some measure of restitution of the walls of the track along which a bullet passed, but it is the crush/punch/tear combination that produces most of the so-called permanent cavity seen at the time of surgery or autopsy.

2. *Stretching or splashing.* As a bullet passes through tissue, it leaves a momentary wake or splash, akin to a boat speeding across, or a stone thrown into, water. This effect is also known as temporary cavitation.

Water closes in behind a boat or a stone as the ripples spread. Tissue behind a bullet behaves in similar fashion; however, tissues are not perfectly elastic and the end result of momentary stretching depends largely on the nature of the tissue involved. Momentarily stretch a loop of small intestine containing only gas and the result is usually a hole about the size of the bullet, but stretch a congested friable spleen and the result will be a zone of shattered, mushy tissue. Other tissues behave in accordance with their structure and consistency. Lung and muscle often exhibit bullet holes surrounded by zones of bruising and hemorrhage.

Therefore, when looking at a wound, two factors should be kept in mind: (1) the path along which the bullet passed and (2) the variable amount of splashing and stretching along the tissue margins where the bullet is passing. Wound ballistics (a part of terminal ballistics) is the study of the combination of these two effects—in other words, a study of the missile-tissue interaction.

Sonic Pressure Waves

When a bullet strikes tissue, a sonic pressure (sound) wave travels ahead of the bullet in the tissues. Various ill effects have been ascribed to this reaction, but the duration is exceedingly short, so short that there is no time for significant tissue displacement to occur. It has not, to the knowledge or satisfaction of many experts, been proven that this produces any significant ill effects. After all, medical science uses concentrated sound waves for diagnosis (ultrasound) and many minutes of focused shock waves (from a lithotriptor) to break up kidney and gallstones without soft tissue damage. Part of this disagreement may be because some articles confuse and fail to distinguish between (1) splash/stretch, known as temporary cavitation, and (2) sonic pressure/sound waves.

Correlation between Type of Gun and Injury Caused

Then, of course, differences in injuries are brought about by bullet behavior and in particular by the occurrence or nonoccurrence of fragmentation. The damage caused by a bullet is directly associated with its intended purpose. For example, most military bullets are intended to remain intact and cause casualties. These bullets are better able to pass through doors, windows, and vehicles. Casualties are desirable from the standpoint of an opponent. Civilian hunting ammunition, however, is intended to stay within the game animal, not only for safety, but to induce maximum damage and kill the animal.

There are exceptions both ways—for instance, the M-193 bullets from the U.S. M-16A1 combat rifle, which often fragment, and bullets for elephant and cape buffalo, which must remain relatively undistorted if they are to penetrate deeply enough. The fact that some bullets fragment in tissue and others do not is the source of part of the confusion and is potentially hazardous in the ballistic and medical literature in the last quarter of the twentieth century. The forensic nurse should remain skeptical and apply strict scientific methodology.

Classic Errors and Myths
Some classic errors are summarized as follows:
- *Believing that velocity is the sole determinant of injury.* If this were true, the initial portions of wounds would be larger and more significant than the parts produced after bullets have slowed down.
- *Relying on scientific articles that have been centered around loss of bullet energy, based on the difference between velocity at entry and exit, but that ignored loss of weight resulting from bullet fragmentation.* Thus, the presumed weight(s) at exit and the calculations based on them are invalid.
- *Drawing conclusions concerning fragment behavior and position based on studies using x-rays taken only in a single plane.* Fragments were assumed to lie in one part of a wound when in fact they were somewhere else altogether.
- *Concluding that bullets above a certain speed are unstable in flight and tumble end over end.* If this were so, weapons would lack accuracy, many military bullets would be unable to enter their targets, streamlining bullets by making them pointed would be a total waste of time, and thin "witness" sheets placed along their flight paths would show elongated as opposed to rounded holes.
- *Assuming that energy delivery equates to severity of injury.* It cannot because the specified amount of bullet energy might be delivered into clothing, a thick layer of body wall fat, or muscle, with a far lesser amount to vital areas such as the heart and great vessels.
- *Expecting the human body to react the same way other objects would react to impact.* Shooting bullets into watermelons and cans of water may look impressive, but neither relate to, or constitute part of, the human body. The body does not contain as high a percentage of water as do melons, and does contain a large amount of connective tissue, which prevents the human body from splattering all over the floor.
- *Forgetting that terms often have different meanings in parts of the world.* For instance, "high velocity" may mean faster than sound in one country but imply 2000 feet per second elsewhere. Simply stating the velocity in feet or meters per second avoids the problems arising from nonscientific terms.

Unfortunately, the dissemination of such erroneous information can also be to the disadvantage of injured patients. A victim may be brought in saying he has been shot with a rifle whereupon a surgeon, largely unfamiliar with such wounds, immediately envisions dire internal consequences and proceeds to remove more tissue than is actually justified. Fortunately, medical and surgical treatments are well covered elsewhere in the literature.

Bullet-Tissue Interaction
The injuries found in a patient or a victim at autopsy depend largely on the bullet-tissue interaction. Therefore, the particular combination of crush/punch/tear (permanent cavity) and splash/stretch (temporary cavity)—unless propulsive gases happen also to be involved—is crucial for correctly understanding injuries. All bullets tear a track, but some, by virtue of different energy of motion, construction, and behavior after impact, produce more

temporary cavitation than others. Most handgun and submachine gun bullets cause injury mainly by crush/punch/tear with some stretch/splash. Rifle bullets also crush/punch/tear but often have significantly more splashing/stretching, plus fragmentation to take into account. This is why some rifle calibers have at times been regarded as unduly injurious. Indeed, when the effects of cavitation were first encountered, some armed forces were even accused of using exploding bullets (Fig. 25-20).

To be effective for law enforcement or combat purposes, there must be the following:
- Sufficient depth of penetration to reach a vital organ
- A large enough hole in a vital organ
- Suitable placement of the shot

Guns Fired into the Air
Guns fired into the air constitute yet another cause of speculation and source of misinformation. The key is to distinguish clearly between two situations:
1. Guns are fired upward at very steep angles, so that the bullets eventually come to a halt and then fall back to earth. Common handgun bullets take about 9 to 14 seconds to go up and about 16 to 26 seconds to fall. When they approach the ground, they are only falling about 130 to 250 feet per second, which is close to the speed at which bullets are able to penetrate skin. Thus, some will bounce off and others will cause a superficial wound. Serious injury seldom results from shooting handguns into the air. Rifle bullets, however, fall faster and thus stand a slightly greater chance of causing injury, but they are not particular threatening.
2. Guns are fired at high angles but at an elevation such that the bullets move in a high arcing trajectory and retain some of their forward velocity. This can and sometimes does cause serious injury or death.

RADIOLOGICAL EXAMINATION
Always x-ray gunshot victims if equipment and circumstances permit because x-rays diminish chances of error in wound assessment and prediction of resultant organ and tissue injury. X-rays constitute part of the documentation and show the situation existing before the victim was opened or altered surgically. At least one lateral view is needed to show depth of penetration and distribution of fragments if there are any (Fig. 25-21). X-rays are vital adjuncts to wound evaluation because they demonstrate the following:

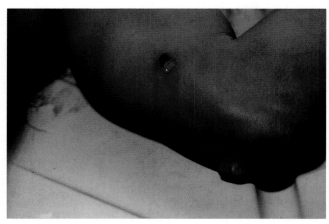
Fig. 25-20 Wadcutter bullet lodged just under the skin at the elbow.

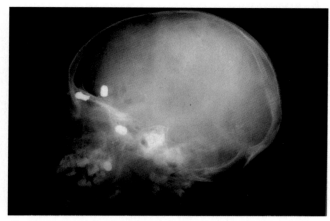

Fig. 25-21 X-ray of a skull showing bullets lodged in the frontal region.

• How many bullets or fragments there are
• Where bullets and fragments came to rest
• The nature and extent of injuries

By accurately showing the exact site of a resting bullet, x-rays reduce inadvertent and further tissue damage induced by probing for a bullet that may have been lodged in deep tissue or have impacted bone. X-rays also locate bullets, or parts thereof, that may have traveled in the flow of blood and lodged at a different location (bullet emboli).

X-rays also reveal any separation of jackets from cores. Taking x-rays is particularly important if something exited. It could have been a core by itself, meaning that the jacket, which bears the land and groove impressions from the rifling, can still be present inside the victim. Radiographic films also characterize some types of bullets by their terminal behavior. About 10 to 20 types of ammunition have fairly typical appearances, and in some instances, x-rays may also characterize or suggest certain weapons.

Other benefits of x-rays are that they help to do the following:
• Reveal unsuspected ("old") bullets from previous shooting episodes, both wartime and civilian.
• Locate occult or unsuspected wounds if, for instance, a bullet should enter through the open mouth or ear canal.
• Reveal injuries when the body surface is altered or obscured. It is not unusual for criminals to kill, rob, and then set fire to a building. If the body surface is hard to examine for any reason, be sure to take x-rays.
• Reveal the presence of intervening objects when bullets enter through objects such as zip fasteners, jewelry, and spectacle frames, or drive small coins into the tissues.
• Locate bullets and bullet fragments in bloody clothing.
• Disclose how many significant fragments are present if a bullet is no longer intact.

There are rare instances when a bullet is almost stopped by the edge of body armor and produces a superficial wound that looks serious enough, but then some remaining strands of Kevlar may pull out the bullet. A small piece of metal in the x-ray, on the underlying bone or in the tissue, proves how the injury was produced, even though the treating physician may be unable to explain what happened.

Simple x-rays, however, will not permit immediate determination of caliber (because of projection distortion or possible bullet deformation) and will not prove the direction of travel of a bullet (because of possible internal deflection without fragmentation). In addition, certain alloys such as aluminum bullet jackets may show

up poorly or not at all. Likewise, the direction in which a bullet is pointing after it has come to rest is not a reliable indication of its initial direction because of the inherent instability of most bullets in tissues and the tendency of many to come to rest in the reversed position.

In the autopsy setting, if getting x-rays proves difficult (for instance, because of an inability to take a decomposed body into the local hospital), do not overlook local veterinarians. They are highly skilled and often equipped to x-ray large animals in difficult circumstances.

Healthcare personnel should do the following:
• Always look carefully at the hands of any shooting victim for features such as abrasions, visible gunpowder, or soot.
• Be sure to maintain a legally sufficient chain of custody, possession, or evidence for all bullets.
• Always glance at bullets before packaging them in case they show something helpful. For example, if one appears to have struck bone and the preliminary examination only disclosed a flesh wound of the thigh, something was overlooked.
• When removing bullets from tissues, use only gloved fingertips or forceps with tips protected by rubber tubing or pads to prevent making any marks on the bullet that might interfere with crime lab procedures. Metal on metal can unintentionally leave markings that can confuse ballistic specialists when they attempt to determine the exact weapon used in the crime under investigation. Bullets should be placed in a padded, clean receptacle to avoid additional defects. Do not wash the bullet or place it into formalin or other fluids because this is likely to displace any hair, fiber, or other evidence from the bullet's surface.
• If the patient dies soon after being injured, cover the hands with paper bags to protect any primer residues or other evidence that might be present.
• Be sure to save the clothing for the medical examiner, coroner, or police, as the case may be. If it is wet or bloody, air-dry it before packaging. Obtain packing instructions from the medical examiner, coroner, or police laboratory.
• Do not cut away clothing through the gunshot holes unless absolutely necessary. Doing so makes the job of the forensic pathologist and criminalist more difficult.

BEST PRACTICE Care of the living always comes first, but while attempting to save life, see to it that a minimum of damage is done to the evidence that other care providers and agencies (state and local police, medical examiner/coroner, federal agency) will need if they are to do their jobs effectively.

WOUND DOCUMENTATION

The documentation of wounds is a vital detail for the forensic nurse to understand. Following are key points, if properly addressed, should ensure the gathering of all necessary information. More details are included in the documentation of an autopsy than for a living patient. Nevertheless, this is what information experts will require if they are to help make interpretations or back up the findings when legal action or a trial begins. The fact is that much of the information can be obtained in the course of treatment or during surgery. Do not worry if one or more of the following items must be omitted in a living person. Simply do the best in the prevailing circumstances. At the very least, for each wound, note the following:

- Location
- Dimension
- Character

Location and Dimension of Wound

Note the location of the center of the entry wound with respect to fixed landmarks such as the midline, the top of the head, the base of the heels, the external ear canal, and so on. Report these dimensions in whichever units are most familiar to police, judges, and jurors. Some countries use centimeters and others inches. If in doubt, consider using both. If measuring around any curvature of the body, be sure to make this clear or else a wound reported as being 5.5 inches to the left of the front midline of the face may sound as if it is somewhere in space to the left side of the head. Measure to the center of wounds, not to their edges because as soon as more than one wound is present the distances from one to another will not add up without extraordinary organizational and mathematical effort. It is also easier to calculate angles.

Character of Wound

The size and description of the entrance wound and any adjacent features other than stippling and powder soot must be recorded. Make annotations regarding the condition of clothing at the site. Note any visible gunshot residues, stippling, and soot on the skin or clothing. If there is none, state this in the documentation. If present, specify the character, overall dimensions, and distribution in relation to the line along which the bullet entered. If powder particles are seen, they can be picked up with an adhesive aid such as a Post-It note and placed in a sealed envelope.

The x-ray appearance of the involved body parts should be documented, noting bullets or significant fragments. To appreciate anything beyond simply the location of an intact bullet, obtain x-rays in two or more planes.

The track and resulting injuries, best described in the direction and sequence in which the bullet traveled, are vital factors to be recorded. Include the amount of blood evacuated from cavities and other findings that will inevitably be relevant, such as major nerve damage and the size of holes in critical organs such as the heart and great vessels. Without these data, it will be difficult, if not impossible, to answer questions at a later date concerning incapacitation, rate of loss of consciousness, pain and suffering, chances of survival if treated sooner, and so forth. Be sure to integrate the description into a coherent whole. Avoid making classic errors such as putting parts of injuries elsewhere under some other description. For instance, putting the entry wound at the beginning of a report and the injury to the liver elsewhere allows easier comprehension if there are several wounds in a single victim. Fragmented description also creates problems when testifying. Having the wound description in proper order in one part of the report, under a heading such as "Evidence of Injury" or simply "Injury," makes things easy when asked to describe the findings. Another error in simple cases is to assign different numbers to each entry and exit wound or to call the first bullet recovered "number one" even though it was recovered from the second wound described. A few such organizational errors and nobody will understand. The essence of good report writing is to recognize that almost no one who reads it will have medical training. Therefore, the clearer the report is, the fewer phone calls and requests for clarification there will be.

In the early stages of documenting internal features of injury, it is preferable to err a little on the side of detail because this will help an expert assist with wound interpretation at a later date

should the need arise. This usually occurs when the prosecution claims a deliberate shooting and the defense an accidental stray shot. With good reporting, the details of injury permit evaluation of bullet behavior, from which velocity and thereby estimates of probable range can be derived. If in doubt, draw the wound profile on a piece of squared paper (in approximate diameters and features along the length of the wound track).

The place(s) at which the bullet or its major parts were recovered and the greatest depth of penetration should be documented too. Be certain to mention any fragments that were recovered, their appearance, and how they were preserved or conveyed to the police or responsible agency. Do not state an exact caliber or manufacturer. Simply measure, weigh, or photograph the bullet for documentation. Do look at the bullet for the possible presence of foreign material or unusual markings such as evidence of ricochet before handing it over. Learn how to mark and package a bullet. Establish and preserve legal chain of custody/possession of the evidence, noting the date and time and obtaining a signature with each transfer. Any failure or procedural error or omission will be brought out in court, in almost theatrical fashion, with impressive flourish.

Annotate the location and description of the exit wound, if any, and the approximate distance, if it can be measured, from entry to exit. Indicate the condition of the clothing at the exit.

Check for the possibility of residues in, on, or adjacent to the exit wound and clothing. Occasionally residues are blown from a contact wound along the entire length of a wound track, especially in smaller body parts and in children. It is also possible for the entry of another wound to be located near the exit being described, when a comment to ensure clarity and separation of unrelated features is called for.

The direction from which the bullet entered and traveled is vital to investigations. This is best recorded with respect to the standard anatomical position in all three axes. If a bullet entered the front of the right shoulder and continued in virtually a straight line to exit the back of the left shoulder, the trajectory would be described as being from right to left, slightly from front to back and horizontal. In the event the bullet should have entered in one direction and then after some distance deviated for any reason, the initial angle of entry should be noted and distinguished from the subsequent direction.

Forensic examiners seldom know what position a person was in at the moment of injury and it is only later, perhaps in court, that counsel will propose various possibilities and scenarios. Good notes allow the examiner to state if the findings are consistent with theories or otherwise.

Add any other notes that are necessary. For instance, if numerous spotty skin lesions or petechial hemorrhages (or, on the dead victim, marks made by insects) are found adjacent to an entry wound, a comment regarding their presence and specifically that they do not represent powder grain impact markings is essential. Such information is easy to document at the time; otherwise, in the event that the photographs do not turn out too well or that the color film was inadvertently developed as black and white, there could be a problem explaining the markings at trial. Mark the various wounds on an outline diagram of a body, and it is a good idea to make a simplified diagram part of the chart. In this way, police, attorneys, judges, and jurors will be able to understand the essentials of the case at a glance. If unskilled with a camera, see to it that photographs are taken for the record.

If unsure whether the wound was one of entry or exit, or if it is not necessary to make such a determination, simply call each a "wound" or "perforation" of the skin, and record its location, dimension, and appearance, leaving the direction unspecified (Smock, 2007). Good notes provide the data for someone who understands the subject.

Summary

The preservation of evidence in the clinical setting requires planning, attention to detail, and precise adherence to established policies and procedures (Hoyt, 1999). Because everyone makes mistakes, the aim is to make as few as possible and become proficient as soon as possible. Documentation failure usually has a variety of causes, including inadequate training, excessive workloads by personnel, a lack of photographic resources, and inattention to detail.

The location, size, and appearance/character of injuries must be documented before they are altered by treatment, passage of time, inflammation, and the healing process. Usually there is only one chance for accurate documentation. By the time of trial, there will probably be nothing except scars on living victims, the records relating to the case, and perhaps an autopsy report reflecting postmortem findings.

Forensic personnel must realize that oversimplification and assumptions regarding ballistics may compromise legal proceedings. Preservation of evidence and documentation are vital responsibilities of healthcare personnel (Russell & Noguchi, 1999). It may not be possible to obtain every item of information, even when the clinician is highly trained and experienced. The forensic nurse must simply do the best job possible, following guidelines for assessment and documentation of all forensic evidence, with considerable attention paid to the wound itself, noting the location, dimensions, and characteristics.

Resources

VIDEOS

Blunt force, sharp force and pattern injuries, examination, interpretation, documentation (video instruction). ANITE Group, P.O. Box 375, Pinole, CA 94564; www.projectile.com.
Deadly effects (wound ballistics), deadly weapons (firearms and firepower), gunshot wounds (examination, interpretation, documentation) and forensic firearms evidence (video instruction). ANITE Group, P.O. Box 375, Pinole, CA 94564.

WEB SITES

www.pediatrics.wisc.edu/education/derm/tutb/petechiae.html
Definition/explanation of ecchymosis

References

Anderson, W. R. (1998). *Forensic sciences in clinical medicine: A case study approach*. Philadelphia-New York: Lippincott-Raven.
Beutler, E., Lichtman, M. A., Coller, B. S., Kipp, T. J., & Seligsohn, U. (2001). *William's hematology* (6th ed.). Clinical evaluation of the patient. New York: McGraw-Hill.
DiMaio, V. J. M. (1999). *Gunshot wounds: Practical aspects of firearms, ballistics, and forensic techniques* (2nd ed.). Boca Raton, FL: CRC Press.
Dolinak, D., Matshes, E., & Lew, E. (2005). *Forensic pathology, principles and practice*. Burlington, MA: Elsevier Academic Press.
Hoyt, C. A. (1999). Evidence recognition and collection in the clinical setting. *Critical Care Nursing Quarterly, 22*(1), 19–26.
Knight, B. (1997). *Simpson's forensic medicine* (11th ed.). New York: Oxford University Press.
Olshaker, J., Jackson, C., & Smock, W. (2007). *Emergency forensic medicine* (2nd ed.). Philadelphia: Lippincott Williams & Wilkins.
Rowe, W. F. (2003). *Firearm and tool mark examinations in forensic science: An introduction to scientific and investigative techniques*. Boca Raton, FL: CRC Press.
Russell, M. A., & Noguchi, T. T. (1999). Gunshot wounds and ballistics: Forensic concerns. *Topics in Emergency Medicine, 21*(3), 1–10.
Sheridan, D. J. (2007). Treating survivors of intimate partner abuse: Forensic identification and documentation. In J. S. Olshaker, M. C. Jackson, & W. S. Smock (Ed.), *Forensic emergency medicine* (pp. 202–222) (2nd ed.). Philadelphia: Lippincott Williams & Wilkins.
Silva, A. J. (1999). Mechanism of injury in gunshot wounds: Myths and reality. *Critical Care Nursing Quarterly, 22*(1), 69–74.
Smock, W. S. (2007). Forensic emergency medicine. In J. S. Olshaker, M. C. Jackson, & W. S. Smock (Eds.), *Forensic emergency medicine* (Chaps. 4 and 9, pp. 63–84, 160–161). Philadelphia: Lippincott Williams & Wilkins.
Spitz, W. U. (1993). *Spitz and Fisher's medicolegal investigation of death*. Springfield, IL: Charles C Thomas.
Wright, R. K. (2003). Investigation of traumatic deaths. In *Forensic science: An introduction to scientific and investigative techniques* (pp. 27–44). Boca Raton, FL: CRC Press.

CHAPTER 26 Bite Mark Injuries

Gregory S. Golden

Forensic odontology is the branch of dentistry that deals with the collection, evaluation, and proper handling of dental evidence to assist law enforcement as well as civil and criminal judicial proceedings. Three main areas encompass the scope of forensic dentistry:

- Identification of unknown deceased
- Documentation and analysis of bite mark evidence
- Examination of oral-facial structures for determination of injury, possible malpractice, or insurance fraud

Certainly in the field of nursing, healthcare personnel occasionally find themselves providing medical care for the recipient of single or multiple bites that have been inflicted by another individual, animal, or, on rare occasion, self-inflicted. The practical aspects of collecting evidence from bites and documenting bite mark injuries falls under the purview of forensic nursing because many of these injuries become important as evidence later in judicial settings. For this reason, recognizing bite marks and applying the clinical protocol for documenting and handling bite mark evidence are essential components for the forensic nurse examiner.

Psychological Aspects of Biting

Crimes with an element of violence (rape, homicide, battery, child and elder abuse) have been identified as those most associated with biting events (Pretty, 2000). The psychological factors that motivate perpetrators of bites have been identified as varying themes of power, control, potency, and anger. The emotional overload and catharsis that occur can block any memory of the biting event and can suspend logical, rational behavior (Walter, 1985). Emerging research on domestic violence offenders who are prone to biting has identified numerous additional behavioral factors correlated with battery, abuse, alcohol use, emotional insecurity, and features of antisocial and borderline personality disorders (Murphy, 1994). In contrast to the previous situation is the event wherein the victim of the abuse bites the perpetrator. Although there are certainly fewer psychological implications in this situation, the act of biting nevertheless occurs as a response to motivational stimuli, especially in defending one's own life. Whatever the circumstances or the crime, bite mark evidence can contribute an integral part of the forensic investigation.

Animal Bites versus Human Bites

The Centers for Disease Control reports that more than 4 million dog bites occur every year in the United States (Sacks, 1996). Treatment for nearly 368,000 bitten victims occurs annually under the supervision of nurses in urgent care facilities and emergency departments (MMWR, 2003). At first glance, animal and human bites can appear similar, but a closer evaluation will reveal some fundamental differences in their appearance.

BITE CHARACTERISTICS

The prototypical human bite is generally an ovoid or circular bruise pattern that consists of two opposing U-shaped arches separated at their bases by open space (Fig. 26-1). Frequently there is a central area of ecchymosis or contusion between the opposing arches (Fig. 26-2). In many bite marks, individual tooth patterns or the dental signature left by the anterior teeth can be seen. If the injury meets these criteria, chances are excellent that it is, in fact, a bite mark. Many factors affect bite mark dynamics and appearance, with both the victim and the biter. Age and race of the victim play an important role in the variation of wound healing and visibility of bites (Wilkes, 1973). The location of the bite will affect its manifestation. Bite marks can be distorted due to the biomechanical properties of skin and underlying tissue (Bush, 2009). Bites on unsupported tissue such as the breast usually are more diffused than bites on tissue that is well supported by muscle or bone. Thin skin such as one finds on the face will generally produce more classic characteristics and individualizing characteristics of the biter's teeth than the thick skin found on the palms and soles of feet. The actual size of the bite mark will vary with the type of tissue and area where sustained. Unsupported tissue typically produces larger-than-life–sized bite marks. Thin, supported tissue generally produces bite marks smaller in size than the actual dentition that created it.

Factors linked with the perpetrator include the number of teeth, the strength of the biter, and movement during the act of biting. Bites made through clothing sometimes may result in a diffused bruise pattern. Additional variables to consider are time elapsed before the bite is documented and environmental factors such as temperature, humidity, and contamination.

It must be said at this point that there are other blunt force injuries from a variety of instruments that can mimic the appearance of a bite mark; however, this chapter only shows examples of known bites. Ultimately the final determination should be made using the assistance of a qualified forensic odontologist.

Dog bites vary in degree of severity and can be more oblong and even V-shaped. In their least aggressive form, they can appear as a superficial bruise (Fig. 26-3). Similarly, human bites seen and analyzed are often limited to damage of the surface epithelium, dermis, and muscle tissue; or they can appear to be only superficial or predominantly contusions and abrasions. In contrast, the more severe dog bites typically involve punctures and laceration of the skin. Figure 26-4 shows an adult male who was fatally attacked by eight pit bull terriers. Even though there were

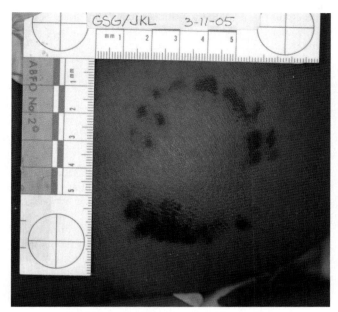

Fig. 26-1 Typical two-dimensional human bite.

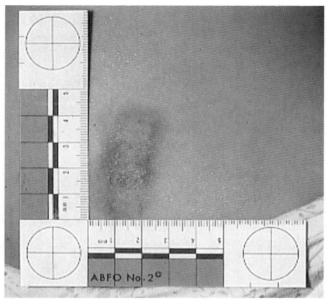

Fig. 26-3 Two-dimensional dog bite.

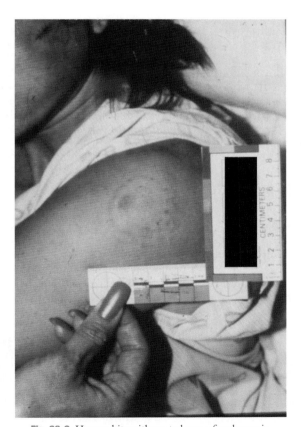

Fig. 26-2 Human bite with central area of ecchymosis.

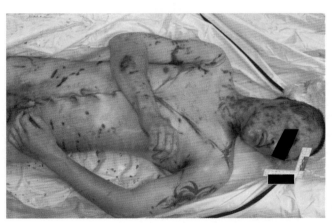

Fig. 26-4 Male victim of fatal multiple pit bull attack.

demonstrates the obvious size difference between the canines and anterior incisors in domestic dogs. Similar conditions exist in cougars, bears, and many other animals known to have bitten people. As the longest teeth, the canines create the most damage to the bitten victim. Animal canines typically produce telltale punctures and parallel linear abrasions or lacerations caused by movement of these teeth over the surface of the tissue as the bite occurs. Human canines, also typically the longest of the anterior teeth, do not usually inflict the same extent of damage or leave the same pattern as animal canines.

Both animal bites and human bites can take place either as single or multiple injuries. Some lacerations can be fatal, particularly in areas where large vessels are near the surface of the skin, such as in the neck. The crushing power of even a medium-sized dog's jaws has also been documented to cause multiple fractures in infant skulls and adult bones as well.

Whatever the severity of the bite, in any emergency department setting, concern for the patient is most important and preempts collection of the bite mark evidence. Only after the victim is stabilized and out of danger is attention to be directed to collecting evidence from the bite mark injury.

numerous punctures and lacerations noted at autopsy, the cause of death was asphyxiation, not exsanguination.

The most noticeable difference between animal and human bites occurs as a result of the canine teeth. An examination of canine teeth in most domestic animals reveals that they are proportionally much longer, relative to the other anterior teeth, than are human canines to their adjacent anterior teeth. Figure 26-5

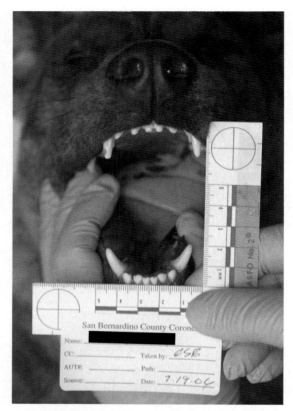

Fig. 26-5 Dentition of dogs showing long canine teeth.

KEY POINT Penetrating bite wounds pose a serious risk for infection. After swabbing for DNA and photographic documentation, the bite mark wound should be thoroughly cleansed with a professional-grade antimicrobial agent, and antibiotic therapy should be initiated.

PATHOGENIC CONSIDERATIONS

The most critical determinant for any animal bite, wild or domestic, is the possibility of rabies transmission. Although studies on maternal periparturient grooming and in licking wounds have shown dog saliva to have bactericidal effects against certain pathogens (*Escherichia coli* and *Streptococcus canis*) (Hart & Powell, 1990), other research has shown canine salivary bacterial content to often contain levels of *Pasturella multocida* and *Staphylococcus aureus*, both known human pathogens (Bailie, Stowe, & Schmitt, 1978). In any event, particularly deep bites contaminated by animal saliva frequently require antibiotic therapy (Peeples, Boswick, & Scott, 1980).

The human oral environment can support more than 250 known gram-positive and gram-negative bacteria as well as viral components at any particular time (Leon Levy Center for Oral Health Research 2002). A bite by a human is a much more serious injury than an animal bite from an infective standpoint. Likelihood of infection is virtually guaranteed if penetration of the skin has occurred and was left untreated. In the hospital emergency department or trauma care facility, after DNA sample collection and photographic documentation of a human bite have been completed, thorough cleansing of the wound with a professional-grade antimicrobial detergent should be performed and antibiotic therapy should be initiated. Suturing is typically

unnecessary in the majority of human bites, but the opposite is true in animal bites and in the most severe human bites. If left untreated, a penetrative bite to the hand or foot will often ultimately require surgical debridement, parenteral and oral antibiotics, and continued monitoring for cessation of infection.

Bite Mark Recognition

For a bite mark to be recognized as a bite, the injury should first meet the criteria previously mentioned that establish its validity as a bite pattern injury. Occasionally only a single arch is represented, such as in the case of a bite to a finger, hand, or foot (Fig. 26-6). If a nurse examiner is unsure whether or not an injury is in fact a bite mark, the assistance of a qualified forensic odontologist should be requested.

Within the classic bite pattern are individual "tooth prints" generally created by the incisal or cutting edges of the six upper and six lower front teeth. Characteristics that may be used to individualize the dental signature to a particular suspect, or rule out others, are most important. Positional relationships of adjacent teeth, rotations, chips and fractures, spacing, and relative height in the dental plane of occlusion are all features that assist the forensic odontologist in the analysis of the bite mark. Some terms generally used to describe the extent of a bite mark injury are *petechial hemorrhage, abrasion, contusion, erythema, ecchymosis, indentation,* and *laceration.*

KEY POINT The size, shape, and appearance of a bite mark injury may vary according to the location on the body, skin support, and dynamics of motion during the act of biting. Bite mark analysis is based primarily on correlation of the bruise pattern to the arrangement of the teeth that caused the injury, giving less weight to the relative size of the injury to the teeth.

Types of Human Bites
TWO-DIMENSIONAL BITE

A two-dimensional bite is the predominant type of injury that occurs during confrontational episodes. The typical two-dimensional bite has width and breadth but no penetration of the epidermis (see Figs. 26-1 and 26-2). Although one might misconstrue the pressure necessary to create such an injury to be minimal, usually the forces associated with the average human bite are significant and exceed

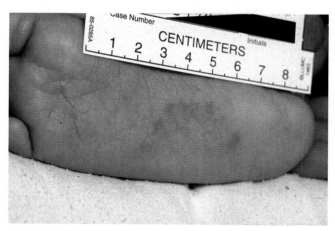

Fig. 26-6 Single upper arch bite on sole of foot.

normal pain threshold tolerances. The degree of subsequent bruising depends on a combination of factors, such as the age of the victim, elasticity of the skin, location of the bite including underlying structures, force applied, and morphology of the dentition.

THREE-DIMENSIONAL BITE

A three-dimensional bite has all the components of the two-dimensional bite plus depth of penetration (Fig. 26-7). When appropriate and useful as evidence, and when the skin surface has been broken during the act of biting, a reproduction of the injury may be obtained utilizing impression materials common to dentistry (Fig. 26-8). The impression should be taken by trained personnel and should be collected soon after the injury and before any long-term healing response occurs. The subsequent imprint of the damaged skin surface can then be used to create either a flexible or hard model of the injury that accurately represents the actual dimensions and depth of the bite. The replica of the injury may then be employed for comparison to suspects' teeth and later introduced as evidence or used as an exemplar in court.

AVULSED BITE

An avulsed bite is one that is so severe in force that the bitten tissue has been completely separated from the victim. Generally, avulsed bites result more frequently from large animals, although in rare instances humans have produced avulsed bites (Fig. 26-9). The avulsed bite is rarely useful as evidence because the actual dental information is lost in the process of forcible tissue removal. If recovered, the piece of tissue might be reattached surgically, but typically, no dental information exists after the suturing or surgical repair. For those people who are unfortunate enough to not survive an attack by animals such as bears, large cats and dogs, and sharks, supplementary information is usually available to confirm

Fig. 26-8 Plaster cast of breast demonstrating three-dimensional bite with depth and penetration of tissue.

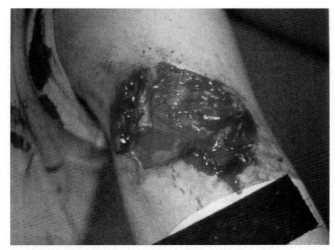

Fig. 26-9 Avulsed human bite on upper arm. (Photo courtesy Colton Police Department, Colton, California.)

the source of the victim's demise. On some occasions, measurements of the teeth will be taken and DNA samples collected if a suspected animal is located so that a comparison for consistency can be made to the bite mark pattern injuries.

Bite Mark Analysis

A comparison of a suspect's teeth to the dental signature left on the skin of the victim can be accomplished by a variety of methods. For several decades, the accepted protocol has included using transparent acetate overlays that indicate the biting edges of the six maxillary and six mandibular anterior teeth (Fig. 26-10). A 1-to-1 (life-sized) photographic print is then created from either a slide, negative, or digital image. The overlay created from the biting edges of the suspect's teeth is then compared to the pattern injury for consistent features or concordant points (Fig. 26-11). Some odontologists prefer to work at even larger magnifications such as 2-to-1 or even a 3-to-1 for better visualization.

Technological advances have popularized the use of computers for bite mark analysis. Imaging software programs such as Adobe Photoshop allow the contemporary odontologist to employ a computer for all phases of bite mark comparison, especially the generation of the overlays (Sweet, Parhar, & Wood,

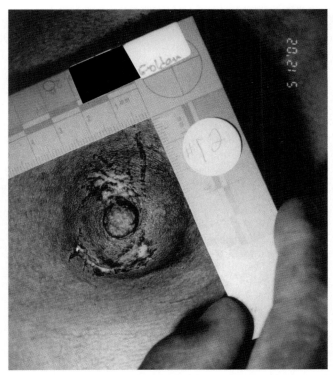

Fig. 26-7 Three-dimensional (penetrative) bite to breast. Reflective UVA photo.

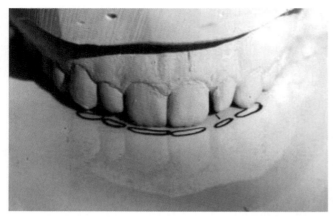

Fig. 26-10 Acetate overlay below model indicating outline of biting edges of maxillary teeth.

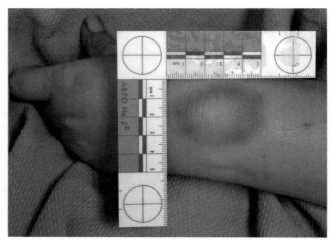

Fig. 26-12 Aging wrist bite demonstrating the "smoke ring" phase of healing.

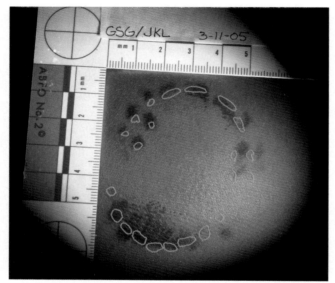

Fig. 26-11 Digital overlay compared to life-sized photograph of bite mark.

1998), the correction of photographic distortion of the bite mark (Johansen & Bowers, 2000), and the actual comparison of the suspect's teeth to the bite.

It is of utmost importance to collect photographic evidence of the bite mark as soon as possible. As a bite mark ages and heals in the living victim, the intradental and interdental characteristics of individual teeth fade as the subcutaneous bruising diffuses into the surrounding tissues. The resultant amorphous bruise often looks like a **smoke ring** (Sperber, N., personal communication, February 1994) (Fig. 26-12). Extremely diffused bite marks usually contain minimal evidentiary value unless some measurement or determination can be made on gross features alone that would either rule out or implicate a suspect.

Collection of Evidence

SWABBING THE BITE

The first and most important phase of evidence collection should be swabbing the bite for salivary residue. Research has confirmed that bite marks frequently contain a salivary component and accompanying DNA microquantities that can be

collected and identified through polymerase chain reaction (PCR) technique (Sweet & Lorente, 1997). Any secretory residue should be collected by employing the method proposed by Sweet and colleagues (1998). Care should be taken not to touch the area of the bite before gloving to avoid cross-contamination. It is also important to refrain from washing the bite mark before this procedure is completed. In most instances, a crime scene technician or other qualified law enforcement investigator conducts the DNA swabbing. If no criminalist is immediately available, the forensic nurse examiner should swab the injury. Before swabbing, the responsive victim should be asked whether or not the bite injury has been contaminated or disturbed in any way and whether or not the victim remembers biting the assailant. In this case, any suspects apprehended should also be examined for bite marks that can later be compared to the victim's dentition.

BEST PRACTICE Suspected bite mark wounds should not be cleansed until they have been swabbed for DNA evidence and photodocumented. The moistened, double-swab technique should be used and samples should be permitted to air-dry.

The first swab, usually consisting of a cotton-tipped swab (Q-tip) moistened with distilled or sterile water, is lightly rolled (not scrubbed) over the bite mark, working from the outer area inward to the central portion of the bite. This moistened tip rehydrolizes the salivary sample. A second dry swab is then used to collect the moisture left from the first swab, moving in the same pattern from the outer edge of the bite to the central area where generally the tongue has left most of the salivary sample. The second swab routinely contains most of the biological specimen, although both should be submitted together.

Both swabs should be allowed to air-dry without coming into contact with anything before being offered for laboratory analysis. Heat-assisted drying is contraindicated, and the swabs should also be kept out of sunlight because heat and ultraviolet light degrade the DNA. If the samples are to be kept overnight before submission to an appropriate laboratory for analysis, they can be refrigerated but not frozen. Ideally if long-term storage is anticipated, the dried swabs should be maintained at cryogenic temperatures –20° C.

PHOTOGRAPHY

The second and next important phase of evidence collection of bite marks is obtaining an accurate photographic image of the injury. Orientation and close-up photographs are routinely taken to document the pattern of the bite mark so that a record of the injury is obtained and the resultant photo can be used for indirect comparison to suspects at a later date. The photographic evidence is crucial to the investigation and judicial proceedings. Photographic accuracy in the documentation of evidence is exceedingly important for providing reliability in the forensic odontological evaluation process. Although numerous methods can be used to photograph injury patterns (digital, video, film), methods described herein will apply to the conventional film and digital techniques.

In the past decade, the Scientific Working Group on Imaging and Technology (SWGIT) has published numerous documents describing best practices for forensic imaging. Several of these documents have become the standard for admissibility of digital images and digitally processed images in court. The primary PDF document can be viewed online and downloaded at www.fdiai.org/images/SWGIT%20guidelines.pdf. As a part of compliance with the Forensics Standards and Accreditation Board (FSAB), the American Board of Forensic Odontology adopted the SWGIT guidelines for evidence collection and image management.

Photographic techniques have been standardized and a protocol established to ensure reliable, predictable results that will be acceptable as evidence (Stimson & Mertz, 1997; Dorion, 2005).

Cameras and photographic equipment vary in their features, advantages, and benefits to the user, and all come with different price tags. Individual needs and the limits of one's budget usually determine the equipment one ultimately procures. If new equipment is out of financial reach, excellent used and reconditioned camera bodies and close-up lenses are frequently available from pawnshops and camera stores. With some basic knowledge of the requisites and a little professional help, one can find an acceptable outfit that fills all the requirements necessary for capturing a satisfactory close-up image on a slide, print film negative, or digital photo at a reasonable price.

With recent advances in and competition among manufacturers of digital cameras, these instruments have become very affordable. Digital cameras provide a distinct advantage in that most of them have a liquid crystal viewing screen that enables the photographer to either preview the image or immediately see the image just taken. Another advantage of digital equipment is the ability to download images immediately to a computer and, if necessary, transmit them to other locations via electronic mail. The speed and ease of capturing and seeing the digital image immediately, combined with the elimination of additional costs for chemical photo processing and enlargement, will undoubtedly eventually bring an end to traditional film photography for practical purposes (Dorion, 2005).

BASIC EQUIPMENT
Film (35-mm) Photography

If the photographer elects to employ traditional film photography, the 35-mm format is recommended for most forensic applications. A single lens reflex (SLR) camera body with through-the-lens metering is preferable. A continuous focusing macro lens with a 60- to 105-mm focal length and good optical quality should provide excellent pictures. A point flash with a guide number of 40 to 45 should be mounted at the end of the lens via a mounting bracket. Ring flashes are also acceptable in most close-up applications, but they often leave reflective ghosts on wet surface specimens, and they are inappropriate for oblique, off-camera lighting angles. A sturdy tripod is also necessary. Several photographic equipment manufacturers make excellent tripods that have telescopic legs and three-axis tilt adjustment levers.

Instruction on basic camera familiarization and fundamentals of photography can be found through photographic supply stores, in books (*Kodak Guide*, 1989), and at universities throughout the country, as well as in numerous independent photography courses. Ultimately, the goal of the photographer should be to get to know the camera and exposure settings well enough to be able to produce reliable and predictable results consistently and under any conditions. This level of expertise generally takes some practice, particularly because the fundamental principles of close-up photography are not always easily absorbed.

Digital Cameras

The forensic investigator or forensic nurse examiner who opts for digital format should make certain that the camera and lens are capable of taking close-up photographs (macrophotography) without any parallax or other distortion. Several midpriced digital cameras are now manufactured with interchangeable lenses that allow the user to select the desired format under varying conditions.

The digital photographer who anticipates self-processing his or her images should have more than a basic understanding of how to download an image from the camera to a computer. One should also be able to open the file in an image management software program, print it life-size, and save it to storage media such as a disk, hard drive, or CD (compact disk). Numerous professional photo processing labs will provide these services if one prefers to use them instead, but this service is sometimes more expensive than straight film processing. Outsourcing forensic digital images also opens the window of opportunity for viewing what may be highly sensitive material to the public domain and may also present chain-of-evidence concerns.

Digital photography involves numerous other factors that should be discussed with a knowledgeable person who can provide not only input about the hardware and software that goes with the camera but also technical support when problems arise.

Orientation Photos

Before close-up (macrophotographic) exposures, orientation photos should be taken to typically demonstrate exactly in what area of the body the bite exists. They are taken from a distance, usually without a scale, and are self-explanatory for information about the bite mark location. The camera need not be on a tripod, and there is little concern for angular distortion.

SHOOTING CLOSE-UP PHOTOGRAPHS

Some basic requirements apply for taking close-up pictures of bite marks. Use an appropriate scale with accurate millimeter markings. The scale should be placed adjacent to the bite mark without covering up the bite. The scale should also be positioned in the same plane as the injury to maximize the depth of field and to minimize photographic distortion. The scale can also be used to include information about the particular case. Data such as the case number, photographer's name, date, time, and agency can all be written on a label and placed on the scale at one end. One highly recommended scale is the ABFO No. 2, which fulfills all the requirements for photographic accuracy (Fig. 26-13).

Camera positioning relative to the injury should be perpendicular to minimize the angular distortion (Fig. 26-14). Pictures taken at incorrect angles introduce errors in size and shape of the pattern injury. One way to determine whether or not the image coming through the lens of an SLR camera is at 90 degrees to the plane of the bite mark is to use a small mirror placed immediately in front of the bite in the same plane as the injury. The photographer can then look through the viewfinder of the tripod-mounted camera and should be able to see his or her own eye looking back through the lens as it is reflected from the mirror. When bites or injuries are located on curved surfaces such as the arm or leg, where the entire pattern cannot be visualized, each arch of the bite injury should be photographed separately at 90 degrees.

A detachable flash with a coiled connecting cord will permit multiple shots at different angles of lighting (Fig. 26-15). The location of the incident illumination can be varied from directly over the bite mark to low angles. Additionally, the flash may be positioned at different reference points from the bite, as though moving around the face of a clock. Sometimes the depth of a three-dimensional bite can be highlighted at low-incident illumination and shadows can be made to delineate individual teeth or spacing (Fig. 26-16). The low-incident lighting angle image may look completely different than one taken from directly overhead (Fig. 26-17).

Digital cameras and armamentaria that are appropriate for bite mark and close-up photography differ with each technique. Advanced photographic techniques such as alternate

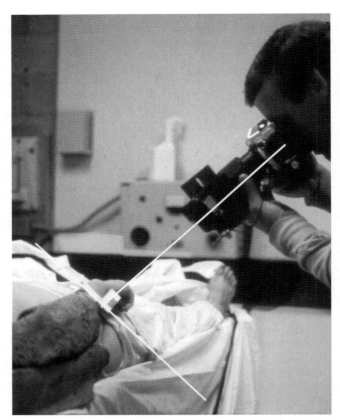

Fig. 26-14 Depiction of correct (perpendicular) angle position for close-up photography of bite marks.

Fig. 26-15 Digital SLR camera demonstrating detachable flash for off-angle lighting.

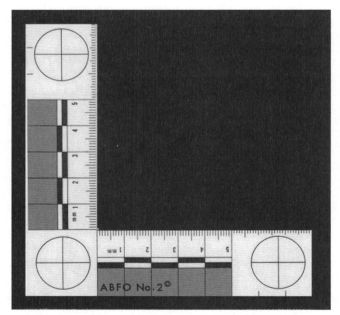

Fig. 26-13 ABFO No. 2 scale. (Courtesy Armor Forensics Co. Available from Lightning Powder Company, 1230 Hoyt Street SE, Salem, Oregon 97302.)

light imaging, reflective ultraviolet, and infrared photography are available and typically conducted by experts who know the protocols for these techniques. For most situations applicable to photography in nursing care settings, digital cameras can be set at 100 to 400 ISO for most flash-accompanied forensic documentation. Remember to take multiple shots and use the whole roll if using film, bracketing for varied exposures. If employing the aforementioned advanced photographic techniques, a specially modified digital camera and filters will be required,

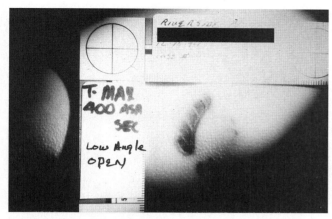

Fig. 26-16 Low-incident angle of illumination showing injured tissue geography. Note raised areas where tissue was pinched between teeth.

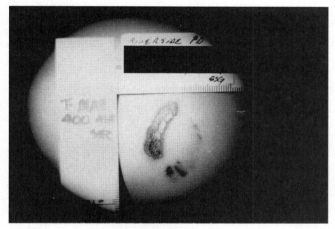

Fig. 26-17 Same bite mark shown in Figure 26-16, taken with overhead lighting angle. Note outlines of incisal edges of lower teeth.

along with proper training. Typically for UVA photography, a panchromatic film such as Kodak T-Max 400 is appropriate. Infrared photography requires specific film and special handling characteristics as well. Several additional equipment and training requirements apply for these advanced and nonvisible light techniques. Periodic courses can be found in forensic continuing education venues where instruction on advanced photographic techniques are given. Two of these courses are the International Forensic Photography Course, given twice yearly in Miami through the Dade County Medical Examiner, and the Advanced Forensic Photography Seminar, sponsored by the University of Texas Health Sciences Center at San Antonio School of Dentistry.

Summary

Forensic odontology can play an important role in identifying those suspected of committing violent crimes, specifically by the inclusion of bite mark evidence. For the bite mark evidence to become a useful part of the judicial process, serological swabs must be properly obtained for salivary deposition so that laboratory analysis for blood typing and DNA assessment can be performed. The bite must then be documented photographically with the scale and camera positioned correctly to eliminate angular distortion. An accurate image of the injury is mandatory for comparison to suspects and demonstration of findings during court proceedings and depositions.

The bridge between forensic odontology and forensic nursing crosses paths at bite mark recognition and documentation. It is imperative that the forensic nurse examiner has the ability to recognize bite marks and accurately document them as useful evidence. Meeting these requirements ensures competency that is vital to the leading role nurses perform as caregivers to the victims of violent crimes.

Case Study **26-1**

Child Abuse/Homicide with Multiple Bite Marks

Karen Culuko and her boyfriend, Leslie Garcia, brought her seven-month-old infant, Jose Galindo Jr., to a family health center for respiratory distress. Following their arrival, the infant went into respiratory and cardiac arrest and expired, despite vigorous resuscitation efforts. Forensic nursing personnel noted extensive bruising on the infant and notified law enforcement officials.

A forensic expert in the field of child abuse examined the child and noted that the injuries were indicative of battering. There were numerous contusions, including hematomas to the forehead, left temporal area, cheek, lips, chest, lower abdominal area above the genitals, scrotum, arms, and legs.

The infant's mother, Culuko, stated that the injuries occurred as a result of the infant rolling off a bed onto the floor at the motel where they lived. Both Culuko and Garcia denied any involvement with the injuries. Homicide detectives were notified, and an autopsy was conducted.

The actual cause of death was found to be internal bleeding from a ruptured artery within the posterior abdomen. The investigating pathologist stated that it would have taken a "major force, like a violent punch," to rupture this artery. There was also intracranial subdural bleeding, typically noted when infants have been violently shaken. Neither injury could have been caused by a fall from a bed. Examination of other injuries revealed human bite marks to the right forearm, genitalia, and both feet (Figs. 26-18 through 26-22).

Search warrants for dental impressions and photographs of the teeth of both of the child's custodians were obtained, and this evidence was collected (Figs. 26-23 and 26-24). One can observe from Garcia's teeth that he had significant canine wear, chipping, fractures, and rampant decay. Culuko's teeth on the other hand, exhibited sharp edges with no apparent wear, no abnormalities, and a smaller arch width.

A comparison of dentitions to the bite mark injuries was conducted using life-sized prints of the injuries and revealed consistencies with the child's mother (Figs. 26-25 and 26-26). A significant aspect about this trial was that this was the first California case wherein alternate light imaging photos and reflective ultraviolet photos of bite marks were entered and accepted as evidence.

The two defendants were tried together in the Superior Court of Riverside County and convicted of second-degree murder, felony child endangerment, and aiding and abetting felony child endangerment.

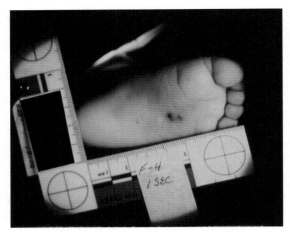

Fig. 26-18 Alternate light image revealing one arch of a bite mark on sole of left foot.

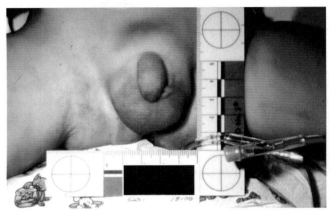

Fig. 26-19 Bite mark injury on genitalia of infant.

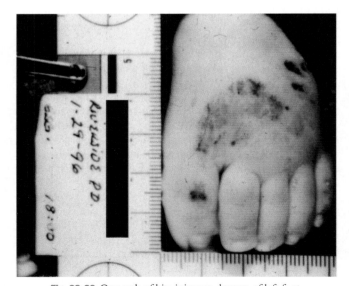

Fig. 26-20 One arch of bite injury to dorsum of left foot.

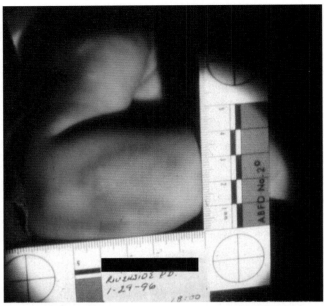

Fig. 26-21 Alternate light image of bite mark on right forearm.

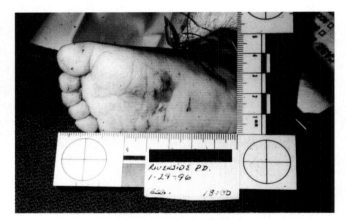

Fig. 26-22 Injury to sole of right foot.

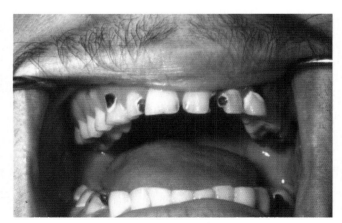

Fig. 26-23 Dentition of Garcia.

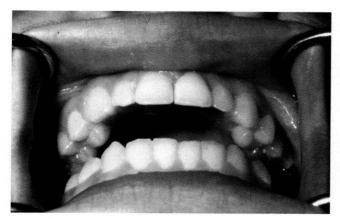

Fig. 26-24 Dentition of Culuko.

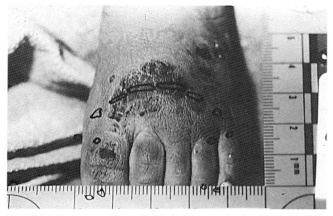

Fig. 26-25 Acetate overlay of Culuko's upper teeth placed on ultraviolet photo of bite injury to dorsum of left foot. Note consistent tooth width to abrasions on surface of tissue.

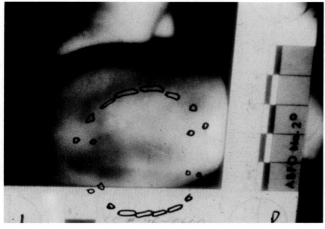

Fig. 26-26 Acetate overlay of Culuko's upper teeth placed immediately below bite mark on right forearm (alternate light image). Note consistency of arch shape and tooth position compared to bruise pattern.

Case Study **26-2**

Dental Evidence

On October 30, 2005 (Halloween eve), several fishermen found severed body parts on Highway 138 on their way to Lake Silverwood, California. The parts consisted of two arms, two lower legs, and the head of an elderly man (Fig. 26-27). Seventeen miles south of this location, a torso was found a few hours later in a public park in San Bernardino (Fig. 26-28). After all the evidence was collected and delivered to the forensic science center, it was determined to be from the same individual. He had been washed with bleach after he was killed and dismembered. Investigators from the San Bernardino Police Department discovered what appeared to be several human bite marks on the decedent. One particular bite on the left buttock was of evidentiary value (Fig. 26-29).

From a missing person's report to the local authorities, the identity of the 73-year-old man was determined through dental records. The reporting party was the man's caretaker, a 54-year-old woman who stated that he suffered from mental retardation, schizophrenia, paranoia, and was prone to impromptu unsupervised walks, thereby getting lost in the process. She had been appointed his conservator in 1989, and he had moved in with her in 2004. On the evening of his disappearance, she stated that she heard voices from people she did not know who were outside her house. There were no witnesses to his disappearance or encounters from people walking through the neighborhood during the Halloween festivities.

During an initial search of the caretaker's house, blood spatter was found on the screen of a television. Once a search warrant was issued, investigators reported finding an "extensive crime scene" including drag marks in blood from the victim's bed to the backyard. DNA results showed the victim's blood was found in the caretaker's car and on a hacksaw in her kitchen.

This author was contacted to collect dental impressions from the caretaker and to perform a comparison of her dental signature to the bite mark injury. After analysis, it was determined that the caretaker's teeth did, in fact, have a pattern of consistency with the bite mark on the buttock (Fig. 26-30). After a lengthy argument by the defense, challenging the reliability of dental evidence, the caretaker was found guilty of murder.

Fig. 26-27 Dismembered body parts on shoulder of State Route 138, California.

Fig. 26-28 Torso found in public park, San Bernardino, California.

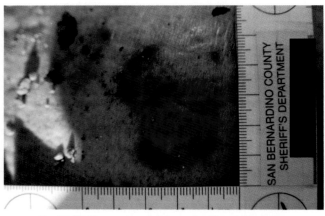

Fig. 26-29 Bite mark on left buttock of homicide victim.

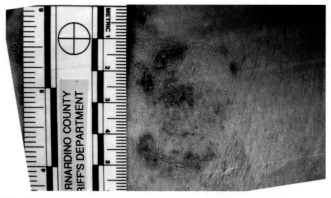

Fig. 26-30 Digital overlay of suspect's dental signature on bite pattern injury. Note consistent locations of tooth prints to individual bruises. It was speculated that this bite was made through clothing.

References

Bailie, W. E., Stowe, E. C., & Schmitt, A. M. (1978). Aerobic bacterial flora of oral and nasal fluids of canines with reference to bacteria associated with bites. *Journal of Clinical Microbiology, 7*(2), 223–231.

Bush, M. A. et al. (2009). Biomechanical factors in human dermal bitemarks in a cadaver model. *Journal of Forensic Sciences, 54*(1), p. 167.

Dorion, R. (2005). *Bitemark evidence*. New York: Marcel Dekker.

Golden, G., & Wright, F. (2005). Photography: Noninvasive analyses. In R. B. J. Dorion (Ed.), *Bitemark evidence* (pp. 87–307). New York: Marcel Dekker.

Hart, B., & Powell, K. (1990). Antibacterial properties of saliva: Role in maternal periparturient grooming and in licking wounds. *Physiology & Behavior, 48*(3), 383–386.

Johansen, R., & Bowers, C. M. (2000). *Digital analysis of bite mark evidence using Adobe Photoshop*. Santa Barbara, CA: Forensic Imaging Services.

Kodak guide to 35mm photography. (6th ed.). Rochester, NY: Eastman Kodak Co.

Leon Levy Center for Oral Health Research, University of Pennsylvania, School of Dental Medicine. Retrieved from http://biochem.dental.upenn.edu.

MMWR. (2003). (52). pp. 605–610.

Murphy, C. (1994). Treating perpetrators of adult domestic violence. *Maryland Medical Journal (Baltimore, Md.: 1985), 43*(10), 877–883.

Peeples, E., Boswick, J. A., Jr., & Scott, F. A. (1980). Wounds of the hand contaminated by human or animal saliva. *The Journal of Trauma, 20*(5), 383–389.

Pretty, J. A., & Sweet, D. (2000). Anatomical location of bitemarks and associated findings in 101 cases from the United States. *Journal of Forensic Sciences, 45*, p. 812.

Sacks, J. J. (1996). Dogbites: How big a problem? *Injury prev, (2)*, pp. 52–54.

Stimson, P., & Mertz, C. (1997). *Forensic dentistry*. CRC Press.

Sweet, D., & Lorente, J. (1997). PCR based typing of DNA from saliva recovered from human skin. *Journal of Forensic Sciences, 42*(3), 447–451.

Sweet, D., Parhar, M., & Wood, R. E. (1998). Computer-based production of bite mark comparison overlays. *Journal of Forensic Sciences, 43*(5), 1050–1055.

Walter, R. (1985). Anger biting. The hidden impulse. *The American Journal of Forensic Medicine and Pathology: Official Publication of the National Association of Medical Examiners, 6*(3), 219–221.

Wilkes, G. I., Brown, J. A., & Wildnauer, R. H. (1973). The biochemical properties of skin. *Crit Rev Bioeng, 1*(4), pp. 453–495.

Wright, F., & Golden, G. (1997). Forensic photography. In P. Stimson, & C. Mertz (Eds.), *Forensic dentistry* (pp. 101–136). Boca Raton, FL: CRC Press.

CHAPTER 27 Asphyxia

Kent Stewart

Asphyxia is a broad term used to describe conditions of inadequate cellular oxygenation. It can be caused by lack of oxygen in the blood, a failure of cells to use oxygen, or the failure of the body to eliminate carbon dioxide (Dolinak, Matshes, & Lew, 2005). Death investigators must recognize that asphyxia is used to describe many conditions in which there is a decrease in the concentration of oxygen in the body accompanied by an increase in the concentration of carbon dioxide. Lack of oxygen, either partial (hypoxia) or total (anoxia), can lead to unconsciousness and death. Asphyxia can occur rapidly or gradually, but death investigators often encounter victims in which this event is sudden in onset and precipitated by trauma or an act of violence.

Suffocation is an often misused word that actually means asphyxia caused by failure of oxygen to reach the blood. It is used to describe cases of entrapment, gaseous inhalations, smothering, and choking as well as mechanical and traumatic asphyxia. Because it is such a broad term, forensic personnel are urged to use precise terms to describe asphyxial phenomena when writing reports or explaining a scenario to jurors, attorneys, and judges.

Asphyxia can be categorized in physiological terms such as anoxic, hypoxic, anemic, stagnant, and histotoxic. However, this type of classification is typically not used in the courtroom because it would be difficult to explain to laypersons. Consequently, death investigators typically explain asphyxia in terms of its underlying causes. This approach facilitates explanations when several interacting causes have combined to cause injury or death.

BEST PRACTICE Use precise terms to describe asphyxial phenomena. Asphyxia is best explained in terms of underlying causes.

Before pursuing the various causes of asphyxia, it is important to recall the distinction between the *cause* and *manner* of death. The *cause* of death is defined as the injury, disease, or combination of the two, responsible for initiating the sequence of disturbances, brief or prolonged, that produced the fatal termination. The *manner* of death is the fashion or circumstances in which the cause of death arose. There are five options in the United States: natural, accident, homicide, suicide, and undetermined. Other countries list additional manners of death such as open verdict, misadventure, and unclassified.

KEY POINT Petechiae are commonly noted in asphyxial death; however they are not always *diagnostic* of an asphyxial death.

The most common and relatively consistent finding in asphyxial death is the presence of pinpoint bleeding sites, which are called *petechiae* (Fig. 27-1). Equally important to remember, this finding may be absent in asphyxial deaths (Ely & Hirsch, 2000). Petechiae can occur in many types of deaths including anyone who is found in the prone position, especially those who have died from coagulopathy or cardiovascular disease. They have also been noted in some burn victims (Dolinak, et al., 2005). Petechiae tend to be prominent in most asphyxial deaths and can be seen in the sclera, eyelids, cheeks, and the forehead, as well as other parts of the body. Other characteristic findings of asphyxial deaths include visceral congestion, cyanosis, and fluidity of blood.

Hanging

In hanging, asphyxia is caused by compression or constriction of the structures of the neck by the weight of the body. Hanging can be caused by complete or incomplete suspension of the body. It is not uncommon to come across hangings where the body is in a sitting position or where the feet, toes, or knees are in contact with the ground. The only requirement is that sufficient sustained pressure is applied to the neck. Death is caused by occlusion of the jugular veins and carotid arteries causing insufficient oxygen supply to the brain. Less commonly, obstruction of the airway can occur by obstruction of the trachea or when the ligature causes displacement of the tongue, obstructing air entry.

Examination of the scene of death is important. The best examination occurs if the body is still suspended; however, commonly the body is cut down before the arrival of police and the death investigator. Ideally, the body should be photographed in situ before any disturbance. The body should then be secured (lowered) where additional close-up photographs can be taken. The ligature should always remain in place until the autopsy. If for some reason the ligature has been removed or cut, or if there is a need to remove the ligature, this should be done carefully. If the ligature has been cut, the examiner should tie a string between the ends of the ligature illustrating the original configuration.

The posture, position, and method of hanging and the ligature used must all be examined. Injuries, other than those associated with hanging, require careful assessment and interpretation. Ligatures are most commonly towels, ropes, electrical cords, bed sheets, chains, or clothing (Fig. 27-2). Most hangings are suicidal or

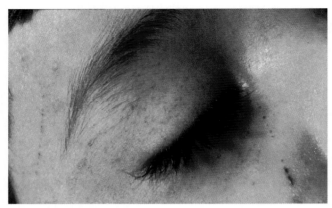

Fig. 27-1 Petechial hemorrhages commonly associated with asphyxia.

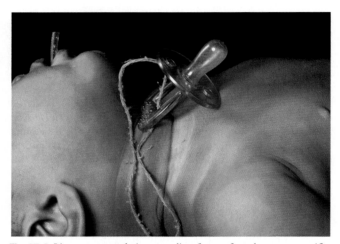

Fig. 27-2 Ligature strangulation revealing furrow from long-term pacifier wear.

accidental, whereas homicidal hangings are rare. Accidental hangings more commonly involve children caught in drawstrings of clothing or exposed curtain drawstrings. In one case investigated by the author, a child was found hanging from the drawstring of a blind that hung into the crib.

As weight is applied, there is upward movement of the noose or loop, which increases constriction about the neck. This often produces surface abrasions, which eventually dry and darken, taking on a parchment-like appearance. There is frequently an inverted V-shaped furrow extending toward the point of suspension. If the noose is not tightly fitting or if the head leans away from the point of suspension, the suspending object may pull away from the neck on one side, leaving a mark that does not completely encircle the neck. In most circumstances, the marks are usually higher on the side of suspension. The characteristics of the marks on the neck are dependent on the ligature used; therefore, they are deep and narrow if the result of a wire but are nearly nonexistent if a towel or soft material is used. Natural attempts to release the ligature prior to unconsciousness occasionally may result in claw-type abrasions or even fingers entrapped under the ligature, leaving similar indentations. It is important to carefully examine and document the ligature mark.

After complete pressure is applied to the neck structures, loss of consciousness occurs quickly, usually in seconds. However, cessation of cardiac activity may not occur for as much as 15 to 20 minutes. The face may appear cyanosed or congested because

of the overfilling of blood, but in some circumstances, it may be pale. Pressure on the base of the neck and areas in which the tongue is attached frequently causes the lower jaw to drop and the tongue to protrude from the mouth; with time, it dries and becomes blackened. As circulation ceases, blood drains to the dependent parts of the body. The combination of pressure and decreased oxygen can cause rupture of small vessels with the development of petechiae or *Tardieu's spots* (ecchymotic hemorrhages) (Fig. 27-3) beneath the skin.

Fractures of the vertebrae are uncommon in hangings unless there is considerable force, as is seen in judicial hangings that are a common form of execution in many parts of the world. Fractures can also occur when the victim has jumped from a significant height. If fractures do occur, they are usually located in the upper cervical spine. The classic hanging fractures occur at C3 or C4, although this should not be confused to what has been called the "hangman's fracture of C2" (Besant-Matthews, 2009).

The autopsy findings include the ligature mark, which is usually abraded and parchment-like and may show a specific pattern associated with the ligature. The deepest furrow is opposite the point of suspension and fades as it approaches the knot. Petechial hemorrhages are usually absent when the full weight acts on the body but may be present in varying degrees when the victim is only partially suspended. There is usually little focal bleeding into or between the soft tissues and muscles of the neck. Small fractures of the cartilage of the larynx or fracture of the hyoid bone may be observed. Frequently, postmortem lividity is a deep purple color because of complete oxygen depletion in the venous system.

Ligature Strangulation

Strangulation is a form of asphyxia caused by occlusion of the blood vessels of the neck as a result of external pressure on the neck causing cerebral anoxia. In ligature strangulation, pressure is applied to the neck by a ligature tightened by a force other than the weight of the body. Death is due to occlusion of the carotid arteries and jugular veins with resultant cerebral anoxia. Most ligature strangulations are due to assault or homicide, and suicides are very uncommon. Easily concealable weapons are often used as a ligature in combination with sudden attack. Certain victims, including children, the elderly, smaller individuals, the mentally or physically debilitated, and those intoxicated by drugs or alcohol, are more vulnerable and less capable of fending off the attack. Accidental ligature strangulations are rare and usually involve

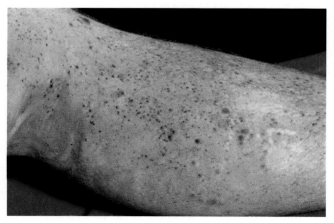

Fig. 27-3 Characteristic Tardieu's spots.

pieces of clothing becoming entangled in machinery. Children may also snag their clothing while climbing and playing on slides and become a victim of ligature strangulation.

Manual Strangulation

Manual strangulation, sometimes referred to as throttling, is asphyxia caused by pressure of the hands, forearm, or other limb on the neck, which compresses the internal structures causing occlusion vessels supplying blood to the brain. It is important to recognize that suicide is not possible by manual strangulation given that as unconsciousness occurs, the grip relaxes, blood flow is restored and consciousness returns. Again, certain victims such as children, the elderly, smaller individuals, the mentally or physically debilitated, and those intoxicated by drugs or alcohol are generally more vulnerable to and less capable of fending off such an attack. Injury or death by manual strangulation is always associated with violent assault and homicide.

At autopsy, the face appears congested in a large proportion of such deaths, and petechiae can be identified in the sclerae and conjunctivae as well as around the eyes and, at times, the cheeks. Abrasions and contusions can be seen on the neck and under the jaw. Fingernail marks may be identified on the neck. Hemorrhages may be seen in the strap (short) muscles of the neck and in the area of the thyroid gland. There may be fractures of the hyoid bone or thyroid cartilage depending on the amount of force used, such fractures being more common among elderly victims.

Law enforcement agencies have been known to use neck holds, including chokeholds or carotid sleeper holds, to restrain violent individuals. The arm or forearm is used to compress the structures of the neck, producing hypoxia and unconsciousness. In the "sleeper hold," the forearm and upper arm are placed around the neck with the antecubital fossa sparing the midline of the neck. The carotid arteries and jugular veins are compressed. The free hand then grips the wrist of the arm creating a vicelike effect. If applied appropriately, decreased blood flow to the brain causes unconsciousness. When the hold is released, consciousness is restored within seconds (Dolinak, et al., 2005). It is important to recognize that the hold is used in violent and uncontrolled situations and, as such, death can occur from inadvertent compression of the airway or from prolonged use of the hold past unconsciousness, which can result in death from manual strangulation.

In chokeholds or bar-arm holds, the forearm or sometimes a flashlight or nightstick is placed across the neck while the other hand grips the wrist, pulling it back and causing collapse of the airway and displacement of the tongue to the back of the throat, occluding the hypopharynx. Airway and carotid artery obstruction causes decreased oxygen to the brain and unconsciousness. In some cases, injury such as fracture to the larynx or hyoid bone can occur. If the hold is held too long, death can occur as in manual strangulation.

Surviving victims occasionally are admitted to the emergency department after being manually strangulated. The eyes may appear bloodshot because of capillary hemorrhages. Petechiae on the sclera and conjunctiva, a mild cough, hoarseness or aphonia, respiratory distress with stridor, and, in some cases, changes in the victim's mental status may be noted. Swallowing may be difficult or painful. Patients often experience hyperventilation and difficulty breathing, either as a result of anxiety or the underlying injuries to the structures of the neck, which may include scratches, abrasions, scrapes, fingernail marks, and subtle or obvious ligature marks.

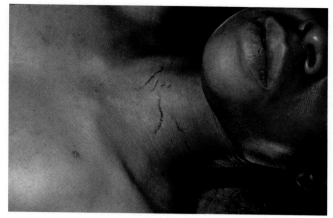

Fig. 27-4 Soft-tissue neck injuries from manual strangulation.

KEY POINT Soft tissue injuries of the neck (Fig. 27-4), bloodshot eyes or petechiae of the *sclera* or *conjunctiva*, hoarseness, difficulty swallowing, and respiratory distress are findings that require careful analyses because they are commonly associated with a manual strangulation event.

Choking

Lay individuals typically think of choking as grabbing someone by the neck. However, the term *choking* refers to an obstruction of the internal airways. Asphyxia from choking is caused by internal blockage of the inner air passages, usually by foreign material. The manner of death may be natural or the result of an accident or a homicide. Obstruction of the airways can also result from natural disease such as acute epiglottitis caused by a bacterial infection.

Most choking deaths are accidental and involve blockage of the posterior pharynx and larynx by food (Fig. 27-5) or foreign material. Accidental choking deaths in adults commonly involve food and are often referred to as "café coronary." Typically, while eating, the individual stops talking, stands up, and collapses suddenly. Coughing is not associated with asphyxia, because the act of coughing depends on air entry. These types of deaths in adults are usually associated with some type of underlying condition such as alcohol/drug intoxication, neurological disorder, dementia, psychiatric disorder, bad teeth, or absence of dentures. In children, accidental choking often is caused by a hot dog, toy, ball, balloon, or candy, all entirely preventable. Children often

Fig. 27-5 Airway occlusion from food obstruction in the airway.

rush while eating, taking large bites and failing to chew and swallow before running or playing. If they slip and fall, or gasp or talk with a mouthful of food, it can "go down the wrong way" and cause death.

At autopsy there are no specific signs of asphyxia, and the diagnosis is only made when the airway is found completely occluded or if the clinical circumstances indicate that the airway was completely occluded before removal of the foreign body during resuscitation. It is not unusual to find some material from the stomach in the back of the mouth and near the opening into the larynx in the unconscious or deceased person. The finding of small amounts of food material in the airway does not indicate that the individual choked to death. There is, however, a tendency for physicians who have limited forensic knowledge to ascribe the cause of death as "aspiration of gastric contents" when in reality this may be a common agonal feature and not associated with choking and death.

Case Study **27-1**

Hot dog Obstructs Child's Airway

A two-year-old female routinely attended a daycare facility. At lunchtime, the child was eating a whole hot dog when she inadvertently aspirated it into her airway. Daycare personnel recognized the problem immediately, and although they were trained in basic first aid, they were unable to dislodge the obstruction and cardiopulmonary resuscitation was ineffective. Paramedics responded; however, on arrival, the child was obviously dead. The investigation revealed that hot dogs were routinely fed to the children. At autopsy, there was no indication of natural disease or trauma. A 2-inch portion of hot dog located in the laryngopharynx, completely obstructing the airway.

Smothering

Asphyxia by smothering results from mechanical obstruction of the nose and mouth. This can be caused by gagging, holding a pillow over the face, placing a plastic bag over the head, or simply obstructing the nose and mouth with a hand. Smothering deaths may be accidental or the result of suicide or homicide. The most common type of suicidal smothering is accomplished by securing a plastic bag over the head. Accidental asphyxia can occur in young children in cribs/beds with plastic mattress or pillow covers. In some circumstances, smothering may be combined with compression asphyxia. *Overlaying* is when an adult accidentally rolls over on an infant during co-sleeping, which often goes unnoticed and may mistakenly be thought to be sudden infant death syndrome.

It is important to recognize that at autopsy, there are typically no signs of asphyxia; therefore it is critical that the investigation includes a thorough examination of the circumstances and the scene. In homicidal smothering, a pillow is most commonly used to obstruct the airways. Although there are usually no physical findings, adults may resist vigorously and there may be bruising around the mouth or nose and scratches may be apparent.

Traumatic, Crush

Mechanical/crush/traumatic asphyxia occurs when there is pressure on the chest and abdomen restricting respiratory movements or the ability to breathe. These deaths are almost always acciden-

tal and occur in situations such as pinning of the victim beneath an overturned vehicle or when an individual working in a trench or tunnel is caught in a cave-in. Most commonly this occurs in rollover motor vehicle collisions in which an unbelted occupant is thrown from the vehicle and the vehicle comes to rest on the person. In these circumstances, the head may remain completely exposed; however, pressure on the chest and abdomen may prevent adequate respiration.

In these situations, trauma may be minimal or nonexistent. There may be evidence of severe congestion and cyanosis above the level of the compression, frequently with a sharp line of separation, and there may be small areas of bleeding in and around the eyes and eyelids. Petechial hemorrhages are prominent and are typically seen above the point of compression. If force is applied rapidly to the chest, there may be evidence of forceful redistribution of air in the lungs, some of which is forced into the margins of the various lobes of the lung, causing a bubbly appearance that can be felt on palpation. There may be associated skeletal injury.

Postural, Positional, Situational

Positional or postural asphyxia is a form of asphyxia that occurs entirely because the person's position impedes or prevents him or her from breathing. These are virtually always accidental and associated with alcohol or drug impairment or in some circumstances may occur as a result of seizures associated with epilepsy. The victim is found in a position that interferes with pulmonary exchange. In making the determination that death was caused from positional asphyxia, it is important for the healthcare professional to satisfy him or herself that there is a reasonable explanation for why the victim was unable to extricate from the position. Other potential causes of death must be thoroughly explored and excluded. In these situations, there is usually obvious congestion, cyanosis, and petechial hemorrhages.

Case Study **27-2**

Positional Asphyxia

A 27-year-old male had a 10-year history of epilepsy as a result of a brain injury sustained in a motor vehicle collision. He suffered grand mal seizures for which he was prescribed phenytoin. Family members reported that if taking the medication regularly, his seizures were well controlled; however, on occasion he neglected to take his medications, which occasionally resulted in seizure activity, approximately once per month. Unable to contact him for several days, a friend went to his apartment to investigate. After gaining entry, he located his friend, deceased in a bedroom. He was lying partially suspended head first between the bed and a dresser. His head was hyperflexed forward so that his chin rested securely on his chest. His face and head were severely congested and cyanosed, and there were florid petechiae in the sclera, around the eyes, and on the cheeks. An autopsy was completed, which showed no acute disease or injury and severe visceral congestion. Toxicological analysis showed subtherapeutic levels of phenytoin. Death was attributed to positional asphyxia as a result of epileptic seizure.

Wedging is a term which describes a mechanism of positional asphyxia, particularly in infants. Essentially, there are circumstances where the infant is placed on a bed, sofa or other makeshift sleep surface, allowing them to become entrapped between mattress sections, cushions, pillows or other items which lead to suffocation.

Beds placed against furniture or walls can create a similar condition. Chest excursions required for normal ventilation are impaired, and eventually compromised breathing leads to hypoventilation and asphyxia death. This condition is common in 3-6 month-old infants when they have developed the abilities to move and turn over, but unfortunately, do not have the strength to extricate themselves from tight spaces. Forensic nurses who investigate such deaths should suspect wedging when small infants sleep with older children or adults, or if they fall asleep on laps or chests and are likely to slip into a "wedged" position on a sofa or chair. There have been reports of children dying in the arms of their mothers while breast-feeding since they often turn slightly and fall asleep in the crook of the supporting arm. (Dolinak, et al., 2005).

DROWNING

No review of asphyxia would be complete without a discussion of drowning. It is a common form of asphyxia caused by immersion or submersion in a fluid. The fluid is usually water, because of its abundance, but people do drown in oils and vats of other liquids. One- and two-year-old toddlers are particularly at risk, and there is a second risk phase in the late teens and young adult years.

Drowning is often associated with concurrent accidents in which traumatic injuries render the victim unable to swim or otherwise stay afloat. Contributory factors include alcohol, drugs, and risk-taking behaviors. Medical conditions such as heart attacks, asthmatic attacks, seizures, and suicidal ideations may be underlying factors in many of the statistical deaths from drowning. Good swimmers often hyperventilate to blow off carbon dioxide and to enrich their body with oxygen to support longer underwater swimming. The absence of sufficient carbon dioxide, the normal chemical stimulant for breathing, may reduce the respiratory drive, inducing hypoxia and loss of consciousness.

When an individual in water realizes that safety is in peril, she or he will begin a struggle to stay afloat and to breathe air without water. Panic often ensues, and the individual begins to bob up and down in the water. During this phase of gasping for air, water is aspirated into the airways and may be swallowed into the stomach. As water is inhaled into the trachea, laryngospasm occurs and the airway is further obstructed. Hypoxia and unconsciousness quickly follow. The laryngospasm may protect the individual's lungs from being saturated with water because the airway spasm prevents further entry of both air and water into the lower airways. This phenomenon accounts for the fact that some victims of drowning have only small amounts of water in their airways or lungs (Lanros & Barber, 1997). In near drowning scenarios, laryngospasm may actually contribute positively to pulmonary recovery. If the individual succumbs during the immersion, the contributory mechanisms of death include hypoxia, ischemia, hypothermia, and neurological injury. Cervical spine trauma, often linked to diving accidents, induces prompt paralysis of muscles, which support the mechanics of respiratory excursions.

Forensically oriented healthcare providers and investigators should also be aware of the four possible phases of exposure to cold water, which may lead to death. These are; (1) initial immersion/cold shock, (2) short-term immersion/swimming failure, (3) long-term immersion/hypothermia, and (4) postrescue, or circum-recovery, collapse. Today, these are well recognized and familiar to those who teach ocean survival and lifesaving skills, but they still seem unknown to many who handle and evaluate cases that just seem to involve "drowning."

Forensic investigators should suspect drowning if the body is found in the water. There are no objective findings that confirm that drowning has occurred. It is usually diagnosed by excluding other apparent causes of death such as natural causes or traumatic injuries. Authorities agree that autopsies are required in these cases. Although there are common findings in drowning deaths, without corroborative information, they are not considered to be conclusive. These include white foam exuding from the nose and mouth, wrinkling of the skin as a result of water saturation, and water in the stomach (Wagner, 2009).

If an individual drowns and the body is not recovered shortly after death, gases eventually collect within the decomposing body, causing it to rise to the surface, unless the body has been intentionally weighted (e.g., homicide case). However, if the water the individual sinks into is seasonally cold, he or she may not surface until the water warms up enough for putrefactive gases to form.

Containment, Entrapment, Environmental

Asphyxia by entrapment occurs when an individual or individuals enter an oxygen-restricted environment. These deaths are almost always accidental although they can occasionally be suicidal or homicidal. This type of death was more common some years ago when children would become trapped in discarded refrigerators. Given changes in manufacturing (magnetic strips instead of mechanical latches), this is rarely seen now. Children, however, can suffocate in airtight containers such as toy boxes, luggage, or, more recently, beanbag chairs. Initially, they may be able to breathe with small amounts of residual oxygen. However, the supply of oxygen is gradually depleted.

In other instances, asphyxia can occur when someone mistakenly enters an area where there is a shortage, or absence, of oxygen. In theses circumstances, oxygen may be displaced by carbon dioxide or nitrogen without any involvement of poisons or toxic chemicals. In both of these situations, the autopsy will show few or no specific findings, and investigators will ultimately determine the cause of death by completing a thorough investigation of the circumstances and eliminating other potential causes.

Case Study **27-3**

Entrapment with Asphyxia

Two eight-year-old boys were playing in the driveway of a residence on a cold, wintery day. There was a large snowfall the previous night in addition to the large amounts of snow that had accumulated throughout the winter. The resident routinely shoveled the snow, piling it carefully on one side of the driveway. The boys had been playing in the snow much of the day and eventually decided to build a snow cave. After several hours, they had dug a crater large enough that both easily sat upright into the accumulated mound of snow. The snow from above collapsed and completely covered the 3-foot entrance leading to the outside air. Both boys were located approximately one hour later, one deeply unconscious and the other obviously dead. The investigation revealed that initially both boys attempted to dig their way out; however, both eventually succumbed in an airtight environment of snow.

Chemical, Poisonous, Toxic

There are two categories of gaseous suffocation. The first group are scenarios in which gas displaces oxygen, leading to a hypoxic air mixture; the second group involves cases in which gases prevent cells from using oxygen (Dolinak, et al., 2005). One example of the first category is asphyxia by inhalation of helium. When the concentration of helium is sufficient enough to displace most of the oxygen, the resultant hypoxic air mixture leads to death.

Certain gaseous compounds can prevent the effective use of oxygen at the cellular level. The most common asphyxiants are carbon monoxide, carbon dioxide, hydrogen cyanide, and hydrogen sulfide. Chemical asphyxia is most commonly encountered in relation to industrial accidents and fire scenes (see Chapter 28).

Case Study 27-4

Suicidal Carbon Monoxide Poisoning

A 47-year-old male was found dead in a closed garage. His vehicle ignition was in the on position, but the vehicle was not running and the gas tank was empty. The body was located prone beside the vehicle. Examination of the body showed characteristic cherry-pink coloration of the tissues consistent with carbon monoxide poisoning. He was dressed in casual clothing and his hands were clean. The vehicle hood was up and tools were located carefully on a nearby workbench. He was found by his wife, who indicated that he went out to the garage to work on the car at approximately 9 PM, which was not uncommon. She went to bed at approximately 11 PM. She indicated that her husband had no medical problems. An autopsy was completed, which confirmed carbon monoxide poisoning as the cause of death. Toxicological analysis showed therapeutic levels of paroxetine. There was no indication of natural disease or trauma. Further investigation revealed that the deceased had a significant history of depression and suicidal ideation and was taking antidepressant medication. There were indications of significant financial problems with his business in addition to ongoing marital problems. Despite the assertions from the wife that it was accidental, the death was ruled suicide.

Cerebral Hypoxia and Euphoria

When the brain is deprived of oxygen and cerebral hypoxia occurs, there is an associated period of euphoria. There are several common scenarios in which the victim intentionally evokes this response by using an alternate gas to replace oxygen, physically occluding the carotid arteries with a ligature or compression of the chest to minimize the ability to breathe. Regardless of the mechanism, the effects are the same.

One form of intentional cerebral hypoxia is accomplished in privacy for sexual gratification. The individual may use an elaborate scheme of devices to induce or escape from the hypoxia event. Occasionally, the escape mechanism is poorly designed or fails, which results in death from hanging, or the victim suffers an unexpected toxicological gas exposure or positional asphyxia. The death scene may be confused with a suicide. However, death investigators are trained to look for paraphernalia at the scene which offers clues to a sexually-oriented event such as sex toys, pornographic visual materials, or cross-dressing (See Chapter 36).

Recently, the media has addressed a similar recreational activity among teenagers that involves the induction of hypoxia to achieve euphoria. This so-called "choking game," often involves manual strangulation or the use of a noose to effect hypoxia. These activities occur in groups and they are not associated with the quest for sexual gratification. Although there is little empirical data to clearly identify the number of such injuries or deaths, in a recent study of media reports between 1995 and 2007, the Centers for Disease Control and Prevention identified 82 probable deaths among youths aged 6 to 19 years; 71 of those were male, and the average age was 13.3 years (CDC, MMWR, 2008).

BEST PRACTICE Nurses and other forensic personnel should be alert to the injury and death potential of autoerotic asphyxia practices. In addition to the identification of physical findings on the body, scene searches are vital for revealing the presence of paraphernalia that might distinguish autoerotic events from those of recreational nature, or to suggest an act of suicide.

Summary

Asphyxia can result from multiple circumstances. These deaths are classified as natural, accidental, homicidal, suicidal, or undetermined. In some situations, the role of asphyxia may be obvious, whereas in others, it may be elusive and indeed very subtle. Death investigators strive to understand the sequence of events that directly cause or contribute to death. As a result, it is important that the investigation of such deaths includes a thorough examination of the history, the scene, the circumstances, and the body to identify the potential role and significance asphyxia may have played in the death. The challenge becomes to incisively investigate suspected asphyxial deaths at the scene, in the autopsy suite, under the microscope, and in the toxicology laboratory. As in many death investigation situations, things may not be as they seem. The apparent suicide by carbon monoxide poisoning, where the decedent is sitting in a car in an enclosed garage, may, in fact, be a homicidal cyanide poisoning rigged to look like a suicide. In such a case, only the toxicologist will have the answer. Cutting corners in any phase of such inquiries may lead to false conclusions and a resultant miscarriage of justice.

References

Bell, M. D., Rao, V. J., Wetli, C. V., & Rodriguez, R. N. (1992). Positional asphyxia in adults. *The American Journal of Forensic Medicine and Pathology*, 13(2), 101–107.

Besant-Matthews, P. (2009). (Personal communication), 30 July.

Centers for Disease Control (CDC), MMWR weekly, February 15, (2008). Unintentional Strangulation Deaths from the "Choking Game" Among Youths 6-19 Years–United States, 1995–2007. pp. 141–144.

DiMaio, V. J., & DiMaio, D. (2001). *Forensic pathology* (2nd ed.). Boca Raton, FL: CRC Press.

DiMaio, V. J. M., & Dana, S. E. (2007). *Handbook of forensic pathology*. (2nd ed.). Boca Raton, FL: CRC Press.

Dolinak, D., Matshes, E. W., & Lew, E. O. (2005). *Forensic pathology: Principles and practice*. Burlington, MA: Elsevier Academic Press (Chapter 8).

Ely, S. F., & Hirsch, C. S. (2000). Asphyxial deaths and petechiae: A review. *Journal of Forensic Sciences*, 45(6), 1274–1277.

Lanros, N., & Barber, J. (1997). *Emergency nursing* (4th ed.). Stamford CT: Appleton & Lange.

Spitz, W. U., Spitz, D. J., & Fisher, R. S. (2006). *Medicolegal investigation of death: Guidelines for the application of pathology to crime investigation* (2nd ed.). Springfield, IL: Charles C Thomas.

Wagner, S. A. (2009). *Death scene investigation: A field guide*. Boca Raton, FL: CRC Press.

CHAPTER 28 Electrical, Thermal, and Inhalation Injuries

Janet Barber Duval with contributions by Patrick E. Besant-Matthews

Electrical and thermal injuries are capable of causing extensive tissue trauma and death. Forensic nurses must understand the various types of burns and their effects on human tissue. This information is vital for forensic investigators who must gather the physical evidence required to reconstruct the forensic scenario and to help law enforcement and judicial teams in deciding whether the injuries or death were results of accidents, suicidal intentions, or malfeasance. The sources of thermal agents, chemical agents, or electrical energy must be considered in context of the history of injury. An important part of the forensic analysis is determining whether or not the history of the incident and the resulting tissue injury seems to logically coincide.

Electrical burns and lightning strikes pose unique problems at either the accident or death scene. The pathophysiology of electrical injuries and their associated wounds will be considered, along with the characteristic wounds they produce. On-scene safety, of course, is a major concern for the forensic team.

Thermal Burn Wounds

CLASSIFICATIONS

Burn wounds are typically classified according to the damage they create to tissue. Formerly the classifications related to degrees of burned tissue. First-degree burns affect only the epidermis and the patient experiences redness and pain; second-degree burns impact the dermis, too, and are additionally characterized by the formation of blisters. Third-degree burns involve the subcutaneous tissue. A fourth-degree burn is associated with deep tissue loss. The current, more popular burn classification refers only to partial thickness or superficial burns (first and second degree) or full thickness (third degree) associated with whitish skin changes, charring, or, ultimately, deep tissue loss (fourth degree).

Direct skin contact with hot objects such as curling irons, cigarettes, radiators, or hair dryers easily results in full-thickness burns. Differentiation of accidental burns from those intentionally induced by caretakers is based on the pattern of the burn. Accidental burns have uneven patterns of contact as the victim quickly pulls away from the hot object; a regular, even pattern of injury typically indicates that the individual was purposefully pressed again the object for an extended period of time (Olshaker, Jackson, & Smock, 2007).

SCALDING BURNS

These hot liquid–related burns are divided into three classifications: immersion, splash or spill, and exposure to steam. These can be either accidental or deliberately induced (e.g., human abuse or torture). It takes up to six hours of continuous contact to produce a burn with low water temperatures at 111°F; however, at 130°F water can cause full-thickness burns in only 10 seconds. At 140°F, burns may occur after only a second (Olshaker, et al., 2007). Patterned burn injuries are easily detectable by experienced forensic personnel (Geberth, 2006). Scalding and immersion are commonly associated with child abuse. These are characterized by burns of the lower extremities, the buttocks, or perineal areas from dipping the child into hot water. There may be irregularities at the demarcation zone from splashing actions of the victim in an attempt to escape the scalding water. Although circumferential burns are invariably associated with intentional acts of abuse, elderly individuals or those with altered sensory perception may accidentally suffer immersion burns from scalding water in a sink or bathtub. There is a uniform degree of burn, the margins are distinct, and there are seldom any related satellite splash marks (Fig. 28-1).

Burns with Inhalation

Even though the patient's visible burns may be dramatic, it is imperative that forensic nurses in the prehospital and emergency department settings perform a thorough assessment for signs and symptoms of inhalation injury, because its contribution to morbidity and mortality may be greater than the burn wounds on other parts of the body. All clothing, even though it may have been extensively damaged in the fire or explosion, should be salvaged. It often provides valuable clues about the nature of the fire and the presence of any accelerants or volatile chemicals that might have been present at the scene. Any burn victim should have all body surfaces thoroughly inspected, and photographs should be obtained initially and periodically postburn to record evidence about the burn wounds. Other evidentiary specimens may include blood, sputum, bronchial washings, and swabs from the nasal and oral cavities.

It is vital to determine the exact environment where the burn occurred. Many victims of smoke inhalation are firefighters and industrial workers who are exposed to products of combustion in confined or poorly ventilated spaces. The upper airway is damaged from toxic fumes, superheated gases, and irritating substances, both dry and moist. Facial burns, singed nasal hair, and carbonaceous deposits in the airway and sputum are hallmarks of inhalation injury, but the absence of these does not rule out inhalation injury. Factors such as blistering, edema, thick saliva accumulation, and glottic closure can lead to partial or complete airway obstruction. In living victims of inhalation injury, stridor, hoarseness, difficulty speaking, and chest retractions point to upper airway injury. Laryngospasm and sloughing of tissue may be present with severe exposures (Fig. 28-2).

Fig. 28-1 Elderly nursing home patient with immersion thermal burns. Note the uniformity of the diagonal "high water mark" on the chest caused by leaning back in the bathtub.

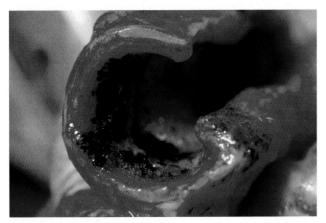

Fig. 28-2 Cross-section of trachea with accumulation of soot. Note also the classical pink coloration associated with a high carbon monoxide saturation.

The nose and mouth should be examined for soot and singed hairs. Sputum may be sooty; the patient may be hoarse and subjectively complain of difficulty swallowing and shortness of breath. A chest x-ray should be obtained as a baseline, but the initial film may be normal. Positive findings such as lung infiltrates, pulmonary edema, and other indications of inhalation damage do not become obvious for a day or two. If the victim becomes cyanotic, upper airway obstruction resulting from chemical insults and edema should be suspected (Lanros & Barber, 1997). Circumferential burns of the neck and chest with edema and eschar will also contribute to respiratory compromise by mechanically obstructing airflow and limiting chest excursions, respectively. If there is prolonged exposure to high concentrations of toxic fumes or irritating substances, the lower airways are also damaged.

In living fire victims, such conditions as tracheobronchitis, bronchospasm, bronchorrhea, and pulmonary edema can be observed if irritation has extended deep into the tracheobronchial structures. Bronchial blood flow will intensify, and the edema in the airways and alveolar tissue may be aggravated. Other problems include surfactant dysfunction, increased lung water, decreased lung compliance, increased airway resistance, and increased pulmonary vascular resistance leading to ventilation-perfusion (V/Q) mismatching and an increase in physiological dead space, which decreases the PaO_2, increases the $P(A-a)O_2$, and increases the necessary minute ventilation to normalize the $PaCO_2$. The central nervous system and myocardium respond to reductions in oxygen transport and its use at the cellular level; oxygen cannot exit readily from the hemoglobin, and the oxyhemoglobin dissociation curve shifts to the left. The anemia and hypoxia persist despite favorable plasma PaO_2. Cerebral edema occurs from hypotension and the impaired oxygen transport. In some cases, there is cell death resulting from the presence of certain toxins.

If the individual is encountered in an unconscious state, there is a high likelihood of carbon monoxide and hydrogen cyanide poisoning. First responders, forensic personnel, and emergency department staff must be able to promptly recognize the classic indices of these two life-threatening inhalation-related poisonings.

CARBON MONOXIDE POISONING

This toxic inhalation injury occurs when individuals breathe the products of incomplete carbon combustion. Examples of where such fumes may be present include automobile exhaust and confined areas where gas-flame heating units and charcoal grills are used. Because carbon monoxide (CO) has a 200 times greater affinity for hemoglobin than oxygen, it will preferentially bind, thus limiting oxygen availability. Furthermore, studies indicate that CO may also bind to myoglobin and cytochrome oxidase, thus interfering with intracellular respiration (Ayres, Grenvik, Holbrook, & Shoemaker, 1995). If a fire or smoke-inhalation victim is pregnant, it is important to recall that carbon monoxide is readily taken up by a fetus because the fetal hemoglobin has even more affinity for CO than does the typical child or adult. Even at low levels of exposure to carbon monoxide, pregnant patients and their unborn are at significant risk. Blood should be drawn to determine carboxyhemoglobin levels (the normal level is 0 to 5 ppm). In living patients, arterial blood gases may reveal a low partial pressure of oxygen (PO_2) and a high partial pressure of carbon dioxide (PCO_2) in the blood (Levine & Fromm, 1995).

The patient with CO poisoning cannot be properly evaluated with a pulse oximeter because oxyhemoglobin and carboxyhemoglobin have similar light absorption spectra. The documented pulse oximetry reading will be falsely elevated in carbon monoxide poisoning. Arterial blood gases are also unreliable because PO_2 is a measurement of the partial pressure of oxygen in millimeters of mercury, *not* of the oxygen saturation of hemoglobin (Ayres, et al., 1995). Carboxyhemoglobin spectrophotometry is the standard measurement for CO poisoning. Handheld carbon monoxide breath analyzers have also been shown to be highly reliable (Cunnington & Hormbrey, 2002).

KEY POINT Blood levels of carbon monoxide must be evaluated using carboxyhemoglobin spectrophotometry or a handheld CO breath analyzer. Pulse oximeters and arterial blood gases are unreliable measures.

The clinical manifestations of CO poisoning are obscure until the blood level reaches 20% to 40%. Up to that point, only mild headache and exercise-induced angina (in susceptible individuals) occur. However, at higher levels, these symptoms worsen and vomiting, muscular weakness, visual disturbances, dizziness, and impaired judgment are noted. Tachypnea, tachycardia, seizures, syncope, and irregular breathing follow when levels reach 40% to 60%. Above 60%, shock, coma, apnea, and death occur. The classic "cherry-red skin" sign of CO poisoning is an unreliable determinant of this life-threatening condition.

Burn victims, rescuers, and forensic personnel with suspected smoke inhalation injury should promptly receive 100% oxygen. Accumulated CO is eliminated through the lungs. The half-life of CO in room air is three to five hours; with 100% oxygen administration, it is 30 to 90 minutes. Hyperbaric therapy is used in some severe cases, but no controlled studies confirm its superiority to regular modes of oxygen therapy for the majority of patients. Considerations for its use include coma, cardiovascular involvement, pregnancy, and carboxyhemoglobin levels >40%.

CYANIDE POISONING

Cyanide is extensively used in industrial and agricultural applications and is liberated in fires by the burning of wool, silk, nylon, and polyurethanes. It also occurs naturally in some plants and in fruit pits. Hydrogen cyanide gas has been associated with suicides, judicial executions, and mass executions (e.g., Nazi extermination camps, Jonestown massacre). Because cyanide can be inhaled, injected, ingested, or absorbed through intact skin and mucous membranes, it is of great concern in any extensive fire or a terrorist-related event such as the World Trade Center bombing in 2001.

Detection of the presence of cyanide is usually swift by noting the smell of bitter almonds, a hallmark of cyanide poisoning. However, only about 65% of all humans can detect this scent (Ayres, et al., 1995). On contact, it produces eye irritation and a burning sensation. Exposed individuals should be removed from any confined space and placed in fresh air. Mouth-to-mouth respiration should *not* be attempted because of risks to the rescuer. Cyanide is readily absorbed, so unprotected skin and mucous membranes must be flooded immediately with copious amounts of water to minimize systemic effects. Clothing should be placed in impervious containers and distinctively marked "hazardous" to prevent accidental exposure by other forensic investigators. Prompt emergency care at the hospital is essential to minimize cyanide's potentially lethal effects (Haddad, Shannon, & Winchester, 1998).

Effects from cyanide poisoning can be immediate in confined spaces; in low-level exposures where fresh air is abundant, symptoms are usually delayed. Initially, the patient with cyanide poisoning exhibits nonspecific signs and symptoms including anxiety, agitation, flushing, tachycardia, tachypnea, and dizziness. Seizures, metabolic acidosis, coma, and death will rapidly ensue without specific emergency interventions. Definitive treatment includes respiratory support with supplemental oxygen and prompt use of the agents contained in a typical emergency "cyanide kit," which includes nitrite, sodium nitrite, and sodium thiosulfate.

BEST PRACTICE First responders, forensic investigators, and hospital personnel should wear protective clothes when dealing with suspected cyanide poisoning cases because skin, pulmonary structures, stomach contents, and other body fluids can contain the agent. This caution applies to both living and deceased victims.

Case Study 28-1

Cyanide Emergency in Hospital

A routine hospital autopsy sparked a hospital alert and a hazardous materials response when the stomach of the deceased was incised to facilitate examination of the contents. Potassium cyanide gas was released into the room. Personnel immediately experienced the agent's classic bitter almond odor, along with headache, dizziness, and respiratory distress. Personnel took immediate action to ensure that airflow in the autopsy area was isolated and then reported promptly to the emergency department for further assessment. No personnel suffered serious injuries from the brief exposure. It was later learned that the deceased individual had intentionally ingested the potassium cyanide to commit suicide.

HYDROGEN SULFIDE

This is a cellular asphyxiant, and although carboxyhemoglobin from carbon monoxide inhalation and cyanide are the most classic examples associated with fires, hydrogen sulfide can also produce rapid morbidity and death, depending on the concentration and duration of exposure. This gas has a specific gravity of 1.19, and like cyanide, hydrogen sulfide produces cytotoxic anoxia by binding with ferric iron in cytochrome oxidase. It is a natural product generated by putrefaction of sewage and animal waste products, and has a characteristic rotten-egg odor. Encounters with a high concentration of hydrogen sulfide are possible in certain types of fires, especially in small, confined spaces. Exposures can be rapidly fatal. Too frequently, unsuspecting rescuers and forensic personnel have also become victims of this deadly inhalation. In living victims, signs and symptoms include several ocular phenomena including blepharospasm, pain, conjunctival injection, and blurred, iridescent vision. Confusion, dyspnea, stupor, cyanosis, coma, and respiratory arrest soon follow (Haddad, et al., 1998).

Forensic pathologists can often identify hydrogen sulfide victims during autopsy by a greenish discoloration on the thorax muscles and well as on the surface of the stomach. This discoloration may also be noted in the eyes, cervical region, and precordia. Extensive pulmonary edema and generalized congestion of the head, neck, and shoulders have also been observed. Other findings include massive hemorrhagic edemas in body organs (Solarino, 2009).

If victims are promptly identified, hydrogen sulfide inhalation victims respond to almost the same treatment as used in cyanide toxicity. In addition to oxygen, the immediate administration of the amyl nitrite and sodium nitrite contained in the cyanide kit will rapidly reverse the profound metabolic acidosis of the cytotoxic anoxia caused by hydrogen sulfide. (Sodium thiosulfate should not be administered, however.)

DEATH INVESTIGATION CONSIDERATIONS

Forensic death investigators should understand that the majority of fire deaths result from smoke inhalation, not thermal injury. Carbon monoxide can be fatal within minutes, with little or no burns to body tissue. The heat of the fire is less important than the length of time that an individual might have been exposed to flames and how close one was to the fire (Wagner, 2009). Death investigators are expected to determine if the individual was dead before the fire was started or if the individual died as a result of the fire. Evidence of smoke inhalation and CO content of the blood are key pieces of evidence that will be sought during the forensic autopsy. CO is typically associated with a cherry-red livor mortis. However, when the victim is killed in an explosion or rapidly dies in very hot fire scene, the CO may not be necessarily high.

Fire-associated burns range from partial to full thickness, including charring and incineration. Death investigators should appreciate that the height and weight of the body will be dramatically changed, and skin splits may occur with evisceration. Intense heat can create thermal fractures, which are difficult to differentiate from antemortem fractures. It is important to x-ray the remains, to document their characteristics, and to detect foreign objects such as impaled metal fragments or bullets. Hair color, other than black, may change dramatically and confuse victim identification. Brown hair may become red and blond hair may become gray when exposed to fire and intense heat (Wagner, 2009).

Forensic death investigators often work with skilled arson investigators. Arsonists set fires to conceal another crime, for profit or fraud, or to convey messages of hate and spite. Fires are also deliberately started as acts of social protest or terrorism. Although there are juvenile fire-setters and thrill seekers, pyromania is believed to be uncommon. If arson is suspected, a special investigating team will use a variety of sniffers and detecting devices to identify accelerants and other evidentiary material (Lee, Palmbach, & Miller, 2001).

Chemical Burns

It is rare that chemical burns result in death. However, there are incidents where individuals are targeted and intentionally assaulted with chemicals in an attempt to maim or kill. The forensic investigator must search for historical details about the incident and the scene to determine if foul play is a factor to be considered. It is rare that chemicals alone are used to commit homicide. However, some cultures use chemicals as a form of punishment, and most of these cases involve the face, hands, or genitalia.

Caustic materials continue to burn until they are removed or neutralized. They produce different pathophysiological changes than do thermal burns. The chemical reaction may be oxidizing or a reduction reaction, or a protoplasmic poison, desiccant, vesicant, or corrosive (Stewart, 1990). The skin destruction is a product of the extent and nature of the exposed skin surface. Delicate areas such as the face, eyes, and genitalia are often the targets in cultural crimes aimed at disfiguring the victim.

The eschar provides some clues to the chemical used. Sulfuric acid causes green black to dark brown discoloration, nitric acid produces yellow eschar and tissue staining, hydrochloric acid creates yellow-brown eschar and tissue staining, and hydrofluoric acid produces a grayish to brown eschar (Stewart, 1990).

BEST PRACTICE The on-scene management of chemical burns and the collection of associated evidence require considerable caution. Forensic nurses should consult experts in hazardous materials before making physical contact with chemical burn victims, either living or deceased.

Electrical Burns

Electrical burns are typically incurred by construction workers and electricians. They are the combined result of direct tissue heating, contact burns, arc burns, and thermal burns from the ignition of clothing (Stewart, 1990). Electrical burns are usually the result of accidents or intentional acts of homicide (Fig. 28-3). However, there are rare reports of suicide involving electricity.

However, there are many cases among "do-it-yourselfers" who fail to observe prudent practices associated with electrical wiring, appliances, and tools (Figs. 28-4 and 28-5). Burns from these causes differ significantly from those induced by lightning. Electrical burns create extensive local burn wounds as well as a range of systemic effects, dependent on the intensity of current flow and duration of contact. Skin and tissue resistance, grounding, and current pathway are also determining factors in the electrical injury and the resultant burn wounds. Factors that increase

Fig. 28-4 The ground pin of a three-conductor electrical plug that was modified for use in a two-pin outlet. Without the ground in place, the operator was electrocuted.

Fig. 28-5 A conductor inside an electric tool associated with an accidental 120-V electrical death. Note the resolidified ball-like mass of copper. A faulty repair led to a strand of copper wire touching the inside of the housing. A sudden passage of current killed the unsuspecting user. The copper wire then melted, breaking the contact.

current density include perspiration, low tissue resistance, a small contact area, and high voltage (more than 1000 V).

Tissue damage is largely due to heat, which induces vascular spasms, thrombosis, neurological injury, and muscle necrosis. Certain body organs and tissues are more subject to electrical

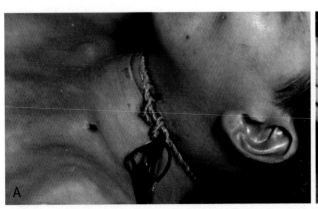

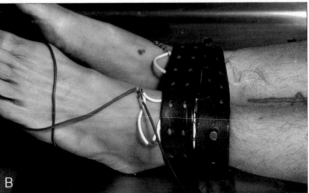

Fig. 28-3 Young adult male with a history of mental health problems committed suicide by using a two-wire electrical cord, dividing the ends, and passing wire around his neck *(A)* and both ankles *(B)*. He connected the plug to a time switch and waited for it to activate.

energy than others because of their physiological properties, which contribute to low resistance. For example, central nervous system tissue that is specifically designed to carry electrical signals has exceptionally low resistance. Cardiovascular and respiratory systems also have low resistances because of the high composition of electrolytes within these organs. Skin, tendon, fat, and bone have higher resistances, but if the voltage is high, the heating becomes greatest in the most resistant tissues. During prolonged contact with electrical energy, fat and tendons actually melt and bone incurs significant periosteal damage (Stewart, 1990). Other damage includes muscle necrosis and rhabdomyolysis. Rhabdomyolysis can be detected by massive amounts of hemoglobin in the urine, but without red cells or red cell fragments. Assays for myoglobin should also be done along with creatinine phosphokinase (CPK) levels. Levels range up to 20,000 units for victims of severe electrical injuries.

ELECTRICAL BURN WOUNDS

Contact wounds may appear benign, but there may be extensive subfascial tissue damage when there is little skin resistance of the current passage. Low voltage usually produces small burns that may be overlooked, especially if they occur on the feet or hands. The peripheral area is typically red, black, or white, with a depressed firm white center. If there is high resistance at contact points, the local injury may be extensive with loss of digits or even extremities (Feliciano, Moore, & Mattox, 1996). High-voltage deaths are easily confirmed because there are deeply charred areas of entry and exit lesions. These typically have a charred, blackened center, a central zone of grayish white coagulation necrosis, and a periphery of partial tissue damage (Figs. 28-6 and 28-7) (Stewart, 1990). Exit or entry points may not be detectable if the current source impacted a wide area of the body (e.g., the victim was standing in a pool of water when energized). In conjunction

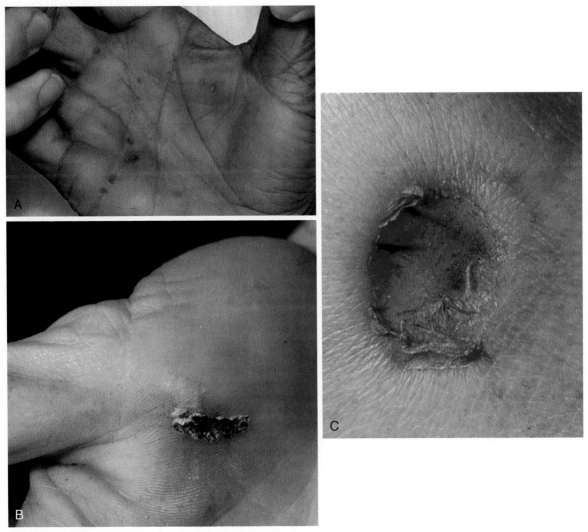

Fig. 28-6 *A,* Subtle 120-V electrocution mark on the hand near the base of the index and middle fingers. Marks are often subtle and difficult to detect. *B,* A more obvious 120-V electrical burn with a central pale depressed area of thermal coagulation, about ¼-inch across. The surrounding area is characterized by blistering, focal redness, and puckering. *C,* Electrocution mark near the base of the thumb of a utility worker who was accidentally electrocuted while pulling electrical cable. The high-voltage charge was approximately 7600 V AC.

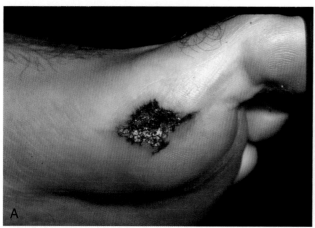

Fig. 28-7 *A,* High-voltage electrical burn near the right great toe of a utility worker who accidentally contacted a source of 7200 V AC. *B,* Tiny holes in the exterior surface of the boot that he wore. The interior of shoes, boots, and gloves should be inspected for defects because moisture and heat accumulations contribute to ease of conduction.

with any electrocution or severe electrical injury, a qualified expert should test the electrical equipment. When a body is found near electrical wires, electrocution should be suspected, and investigators should ensure that the source of energy has been identified and neutralized before entering the scene (Wagner, 2009).

Forensic nurses should be alert to lip or mouth burns in toddlers who bite or suck on electrical cords or sockets. The electrolyte content of saliva rapidly conducts the electricity, and an oral burn occurs. There are seldom serious sequelae from these burns, but they deserve management by a surgical specialist to prevent lip contractures and to ensure optimum cosmetic results with healing.

Electrical Damage to Vital Organs

Alternating current (AC) electrical energy below 1000 V produces ventricular fibrillation at a rate of 3600 times per minute. The human heart can tolerate rates only up to 300 beats per minute, and therefore the patient promptly expires. With high-voltage electrical energy, however, the heart essentially is defibrillated. After a sustained tetanic contraction, assuming that the electrical flow has been interrupted, the heart will resume a normal rhythm (James & Nordby, 2009). The forensic death investigator must often determine whether or not a death has been caused by electrocution. Of course, the environment and historical accounts of witnesses are important. Low-voltage deaths may produce no evident physical injury. High-voltage deaths produce obvious burn injuries. The death scene should be carefully photographed, and all clothing should be saved. Remember that burns to the skin can also result from ignited apparel (Fig. 28-8).

Lightning Injuries and Death

Lightning can cause a high-current electrical injury and can kill by direct or indirect strikes. Indirect lighting strikes are associated with arching (i.e., the current is conducted by a metallic object). Direct lightning strikes often result in immediate unresponsiveness and death from cardiac arrest or motor paralysis involving the respiratory centers. In these cases, thousands of amperes flow through the body. The cardiovascular system is immediately compromised by massive vasomotor spasm that causes loss of peripheral pulses, loss of sensation and color in the extremities, and the sequelae of peripheral arterial thrombosis. However, other victims

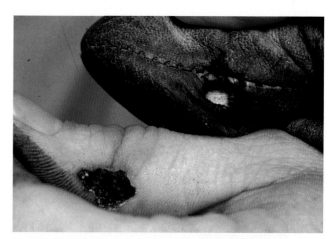

Fig. 28-8 Example of association between clothing (leather glove) and the location of a high voltage (7200 V AC) electrical burn.

are merely stunned or have retrograde amnesia. Motor paralysis and hyporeflexia that correspond to spinal cord levels may be noted, and it is not uncommon for victims to be unable to speak or to hear. Hysteria, personality changes, and visual impairment have also been reported. Typically if the individual survives, he or she may suffer less brain damage than other arrested individuals because cell metabolism is halted as electrical forces pass through the body. There is a period of relative "cellular arrest," which may actually be useful in preventing brain damage. Myoglobinuria is common with lightning-related injuries, and this may often be the evidence that helps to confirm that that an injured individual has been struck by lightning or suffered a similar electrical energy incident (Lanros & Barber, 1997)

KEY POINT The feather-like, arborescent imprints associated with lightning injuries must be photographed promptly because these skin manifestations are transient findings.

Lightning should be considered as a cause of death when an individual is found outside and there is, or has been, a thunderstorm in the area. Forensic death nurse investigators must thoroughly examine potential victims of lightning strikes for feather-like imprints that are characteristic of these incidents. As electrical current spreads over the skin, it produces linear, spidery arborescent and erythematous skin imprints and discolorations. This is a hallmark of electrocution. These wounds should be promptly photographed because this characteristic pattern may disappear within hours of the death (Wagner, 2009). If exposure to lightning is suspected, there should be a thorough body search for exit wounds, paying particular attention to obscure areas such as the bottom of the feet or the anus. The presence of lens injuries and perforated tympanic membranes also suggest lightning injury. Because lightning strikes ordinarily result in rapidly developing cerebral edema, it is important to search for this phenomenon during the autopsy.

Case Study 28-2

Lightning Strike Death

An elderly man returned home after a grocery-shopping trip. While he was unloading his car during a thunderstorm, lightning struck a tree that was adjacent to the driveway and house. The lightning strike melted part of his belt buckle, tore his clothing, and singed his pelvic region. The strike left its classical arborescent markings (Fig. 28-9) (Besant-Matthews, 2009).

Cold-Related Tissue Injury

Forensic personnel assess the bodies of both living and deceased individuals for tissue injury. Many burns and electrical injuries have characteristics that facilitate easy identification. However, it is imperative to consider cold-related thermal injuries as well,

because the resultant characteristics may mimic thermal or electrical burns (Fig. 28-10).

The pathophysiology of local, cold-related tissue injury occurs at the arteriole, capillary, and venule levels of the circulatory system. When the body is chilled, the arterioles constrict to conserve body heat. This is tolerated well for a brief period. After prolonged vasoconstriction and flow redirection, however, the microvasculature becomes occluded, and the capillary bed becomes inactive. Eventually, the associated cells become compromised as aerobic metabolism ceases. Furthermore, the shunted blood returning to the heart is chilled by the cold surrounding tissue, contributing to a gradual cooling of the core. The involved tissue is compromised in terms of its vital processes, and if the temperature is below freezing, ice crystals begin to form and expand extracellularly at the expense of adjacent tissue that may yet be functioning normally. Dehydration occurs promptly, and surrounding cells are adversely affected. Muscles, nerves, and blood vessels are initially insulted, followed later by the more resistant tissue, such as ligaments, tendons, and bones. It is important to note that critical tissue injury can occur in temperatures above the freezing point. Any prolonged exposure to cold that results in significant vasoconstriction and sluggish circulation can create injury to exposed areas of flesh.

FROSTNIP

Frostnip occurs in cold weather and primarily affects exposed areas of the body farthest from the trunk, such as the nose, ears, cheeks, chin, hands, and feet. Initially the nipped area blanches, and the victim experiences a burning, tingling sensation that eventually

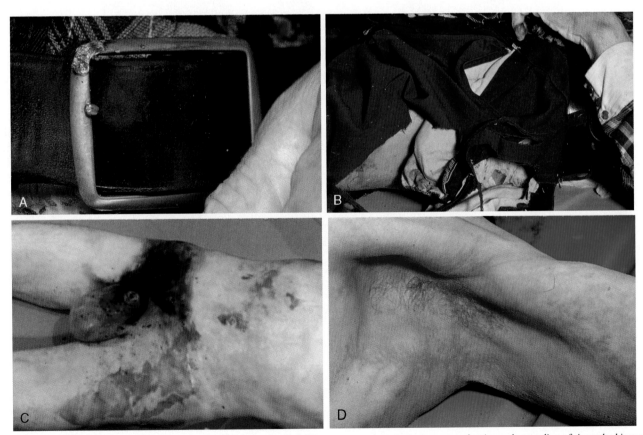

Fig. 28-9 *A,* Belt buckle showing focal conduction of lightning charge. *B,* Heat converts rainwater to steam; superheating and expanding of air resulted in torn clothing. *C,* Pelvic burns that occurred as a direct result of lightning source. *D,* Transient finding of arborescent or feather-like pattern produced by lightning.

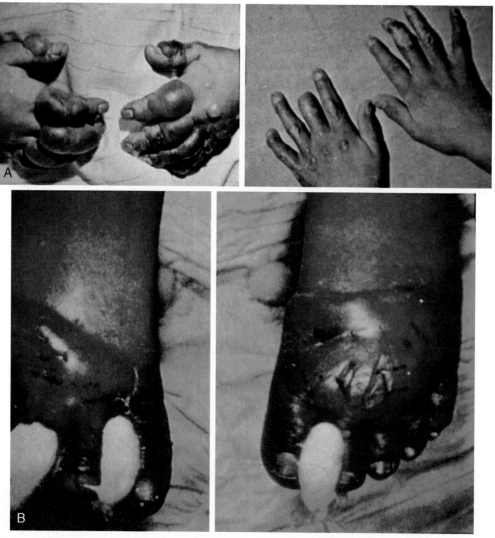

Fig. 28-10 *A,* Variations of devitalized tissue from frostbite. *B,* Extensive tissue leakage, edema, and discoloration may mimic burn injuries.

evolves to numbness. The condition comes on gradually, and active persons may be oblivious to its early warning signs.

FROSTBITE

Frostnip, if not treated promptly, progresses to frostbite. In superficial frostbite, the skin and superficial tissue layers become solid from freezing, but the deeper tissues remain resilient. The skin has a waxy, white appearance and is numb. After rewarming, the area becomes mottled and purplish, but the numbness persists. Edema and burning and stinging sensations follow. The damaged tissue is often marked by blisters that dry up and become hard and black within 10 to 14 days. Resting the part encourages the early resolution of edema, but the throbbing and burning may last for weeks. Eventually, the skin peels away, and the underlying red, tender area retains its sensitivity to the cold and tends to perspire abnormally for an extended time.

Deep frostbite includes damage to the skin, the subcutaneous tissue, muscle, and blood vessels. The area is hard and cannot be depressed when touched; its color is pale or gray. Tremendous swelling that may last for weeks occurs after rewarming. Blisters form within three days, and a blue-violet or blue-gray discoloration persists. A sharp, throbbing pain is typical, and this may be present for several weeks. The blisters dry, turn black, and slough,

leaving a new red layer of tender skin that is sensitive to the cold and perspires and itches for up to six months. In rare instances in which rewarming has not been promptly executed, gangrene of the affected part may occur and amputation is ultimately required.

Death investigators may encounter an individual who died as a result of extremely cold conditions. The elderly, chronically ill, or neurologically impaired or those under the influence of drugs or alcohol are likely victims of accidental death from hypothermia. Typically, there are no signs of external trauma unless there was a predisposing circumstance that rendered the victim helpless, such as a fall or a blow to the head. Wagner cautioned about "paradoxical undressing," as victims of hypothermia tend to feel warm as their body temperature drops and they remove their clothes in response. When such individuals are found partially clothed or naked, the assumption may be that a sexual assault has occurred (Wagner, 2009). First responders who encounter a rigid, cold body within a cold ambient environment should suspect hypothermia and attempt resuscitation and rewarming procedures before declaring the death. Successful clinical recoveries have been reported two or three hours after clinical death in such cases. In states of extreme hypothermia, the brain and other vital organs are protected from the devastating effects of anoxia that ordinarily occur after cardiopulmonary arrest. Some authorities have advocated that no hypothermic patient be declared dead until rewarming has taken place and resuscitation has been attempted with the warm body (Lanros & Barber, 1997) Obviously, this observation should serve to alert first responders and morgue personnel to exercise caution with hypothermic bodies before presuming death has occurred.

Summary

The forensic nurse must have an appreciation of the basic issues regarding burns and fire-related and electrical injuries, including lightning strikes. Cold-related injuries, especially of the limbs and extremities, often mimic burns. These thermal injuries, as well as hypothermia, pose special challenges for forensic personnel.

First responders, clinical personnel, and death investigators must carefully assess patients to distinguish accidental injuries from intentional abuse or violent acts of offenders. Identification of non-accidental injuries and other forensic cases is a vital process, ensuring that victims of abuse are identified and protected. Additionally, precise collection of evidence and prompt reporting of forensic cases will facilitate the apprehension of violent offenders.

References

Ayres, S. M., Grenvik, A., Holbrook, P. R., & Shoemaker, W. C. (1995). *Textbook of critical care.* Philadelphia: Saunders.

Besant-Matthews, P. E. (2009). *Burns, fire and arson deaths and injuries.* (Unpublished papers).

Cunnington, A., & Hormbrey, P. (2002). Breath analysis to detect recent exposure to carbon monoxide. *Post-Graduate Medicine Journal, 78*(918), 233–237.

Feliciano, D. V., Moore, E. E., & Mattox, K. L. (1996). *Trauma* (3rd ed.). Stamford, CT: Appleton & Lange.

Geberth, V. J. (2006). *Practical homicide investigation.* (4th ed.). Boca Raton, FL: CRC Press, Taylor & Francis.

Haddad, L. M., Shannon, M. W., & Winchester, J. F. (1998). *Clinical management of poisoning and drug overdose* (3rd ed.). Philadelphia: Saunders.

James, S. H., & Nordby, J. J. (2009). *Forensic science* (3rd ed.). Boca Raton: CRC Press, Taylor & Francis.

Lanros, N. E., & Barber, J. M. (1997). *Emergency nursing* (4th ed.). Stamford, CT: Appleton & Lange.

Lee, H. C., Palmbach, T., & Miller, M. T. (2001). *Henry Lee's crime scene handbook.* San Diego, CA: Academic Press.

Levine, R. L., & Fromm, R. E., Jr. (1995). *Critical care monitoring from pre-hospital to the ICU.* St. Louis, MO: Mosby-Yearbook.

Olshaker, J. S., Jackson, M. C., & Smock, W. S. (2007). *Forensic emergency medicine* (2nd ed.). Philadelphia: Lippincott, Williams & Wilkins.

Solarino, B. (2009). *Worker Fatalities by Hydrogen Sulfide Poisoning: Autopsy and Toxicological Findings, (Abstract: G105: page 289).* Proceeding of the American Academy of Forensic Sciences (Denver, CO).

Stewart, C. E. (1990). *Environmental emergencies.* Baltimore: Williams & Wilkins.

Wagner, S. A. (2009). *Death scene investigation: A field guide.* Boca Raton, FL: CRC Press, Taylor & Francis.

CHAPTER 29 Child Maltreatment: Forensic Biomarkers

Cris Finn

Child abuse and neglect have occurred throughout history, but for many years no laws existed to protect young victims or to ensure their human rights. In the late 1800s, a group of church workers in New York State had to use laws written by the Society for the Prevention of Cruelty to Animals to protect a young child from an abusive home situation (Holter, 1979). In 1961, Dr. Henry C. Kempe spoke of the child abuse problem to the American Academy of Pediatrics, providing clear data on what he termed the battered child syndrome (Kempe, Silverman, & Steele, 1962). Kempe's presentation significantly impacted attendees, and legislation to protect the battered child was developed in all 50 states within the next four years. In 1973, a Senate hearing resulted in the Child Abuse Prevention and Treatment Act (CAPTA).

Carol Bellamy, executive director of UNICEF, stated in the United Nations Conventions on the Rights of the Child, "A century that began with children having virtually no rights is ending with them having the most powerful legal instrument that not only recognizes but protects their human rights" (Moorhead, 1997, p. 51).

The role of the pediatric forensic nurse examiner (PFNE) in child abuse and neglect cases is to ensure child abuse and neglect are promptly identified and appropriate interventions and referrals are initiated to ensure the child's welfare and safety. Detailed written and photographic documentation of the child's appearance and behavioral interactions with parents or other caregivers is imperative. All evidence should be obtained according to standard procedures of the PFNE.

BEST PRACTICE Infants and children encountered in any healthcare setting should be assessed for indications of abuse and neglect; documentation, reporting, and referrals should be promptly accomplished.

This is a summary of the recent knowledge regarding the common biomarkers of child maltreatment. Biomarkers are characteristics that can be objectively measured and evaluated, and such features assist healthcare professionals and others who come in contact with children, in the early identification of the physical and behavioral signs of child abuse and neglect.

Child abuse crosses all socioeconomic and ethnic boundaries. It is rarely the result of a single factor. More typically it is a complex interplay of societal, familial, and individual characteristics.

Child abuse and neglect is a national problem that has increased to epidemic proportions. An estimated 905,000 children were determined to be fatal victims of child abuse or neglect in 2007 alone (U.S. Department of Health and

Human Services, 2009, [USDHHS]). Abuse is found in all socioeconomic groups and in all cultures (Hamby & Finkelhor, 2000; Hammer, Moynihan, & Pagliaro, 2006; Herman-Giddens, et al., 1999; Lerman, 2002; Penn, Schoen, & Berland, 1999). According to the National Clearinghouse on Child Abuse and Neglect Information (2004), nearly 3 million children were found to have been abused in the United States in 2002. Fourteen percent had been victims of sexual abuse, and 29% had been physically abused. Sadly, research indicates that although many child victims had been treated for previous injuries, the majority had no prior contact with child protective services (CPS) at the time of their death (Hamby & Finkelhor, 2000; NCANDS, 2004; Stower, 2000). Thus, healthcare professionals did not adequately identify and report these abuse victims. Trokel, Wadimmba, Griffith, and Sege (2006) concluded 29% of infant cases were diagnosed as abuse at children's hospitals compared with 13% at general hospitals. Trokel et al. could not explain the discrepancy.

The problem of child sexual abuse is not a new crisis of the twenty-first century; children have experienced sexual abuse throughout history. Yet it was only during the late 1970s that the first reports of child sexual abuse began appearing in the psychological, medical, and nursing journals (Burgess, Holstorn, & McCausland, 1977). Since that time, interest has grown in attempting to understand the effects of childhood sexual abuse.

Children are being hurt every day. The National Child Abuse and Neglect Data System (NCANDS, 2004) reported an estimated 1400 child fatalities in 2002. NCANDS defines "child fatality" as the death of a child caused by an injury resulting from abuse or neglect, or where abuse or neglect were contributing factors. This translates to a rate of 1.98 deaths per 100,000 children in the general population. Types of maltreatment reported by the of Health and Human Services (2009) included the following: neglect, 59%; physical abuse, 19%; sexual abuse, 10%; psychological maltreatment, 7%; and other, 19.5% (percentages total more than 100% because children often are victims of more than one type of abuse).

The U.S. Child Abuse Prevention and Treatment Act (2003) defines child abuse to include physical abuse, child neglect, sexual abuse, and emotional abuse.

- *Physical abuse.* Infliction of physical injury as a result of punching, kicking, beating, biting, burning, shaking, or otherwise physically harming a child.
- *Child neglect.* Failure to provide a child's basic needs, physically, emotionally, medically, and educationally.

- *Sexual abuse.* Includes fondling a child's genitals, intercourse, incest, rape, sodomy, exhibitionism, and commercial exploitation through prostitution or the production of pornographic materials.
- *Emotional abuse.* Acts or omissions by the parents or other caregivers that have caused, or could cause, serious behavioral, cognitive, emotional, or mental disorders.

Child abuse is a highly complex issue and is not easily identified. Identification of abuse requires establishing a clear history of abuse events and circumstances, along with clearly visible physical signs of abuse (e.g., wounds, fractures, bruising, emotional traumatization (Corby, 1993; Elliott & Briere, 1994; Hamby & Finkelhor, 2000; Herman-Giddens, Brown, Verbiest, Carlson, Hooten, Howell, & Butts, 1999; Marshall & Lock, 1997; Stower, 2000; Trokel, et al., 2006; U.S. Child Abuse Prevention and Treatment Act, 2003).

Healthcare professionals are not identifying and reporting child abuse consistently. Admittedly, this is not easy; however, some emergency departments do it better than others. Child abuse victims usually find their way into the healthcare system through the emergency departments (Pyrek, 2006). Flaherty, Sege, and Binns (2000) found that providers who saw children with suspected abuse did not report to child protective services, stating they were not confident they knew what injuries or signs to evaluate for abuse. Additionally, Trokel et al. (2006) concluded 29% of infant cases were diagnosed as abuse at children's hospitals, compared with 13% at general hospitals. Thus, one might conclude that healthcare professionals did not adequately identify and report these child abuse victims.

In a time of receding social services, it increasingly falls upon healthcare professionals to recognize, manage, and triage families of victimized children into the social service system. Assessment of the level of a child's risk for abuse, or the risk for reinjury, is one of the more troublesome challenges that healthcare providers face. The encounter with a suspected victim of child abuse and her or his family is suffused with layers of ethical, diagnostic, and emotional tensions that must be given serious consideration by the healthcare provider.

Many hospitals and medical centers have established an interdisciplinary team approach to child abuse. Such teams may include nursing, medical, psychological, legal, social work, and other child abuse experts, and they may have an ongoing liaison with a local child protective service agency. Members of such teams are available to provide consultation to the community at all times. Thus, professionals unfamiliar with child abuse should consider seeking consultation from such a team when a child presents with ambiguous signs of suspected child abuse.

Definitions

Child abuse and neglect are defined at both U.S. federal and state levels. The federal Child Abuse Prevention and Treatment Act (CAPTA) is the federal legislation and outlines minimal guidelines the states must follow (National Clearinghouse on Child Abuse and Neglect, 2004). CAPTA defines the term *child abuse and neglect* to mean the physical or mental injury, sexual abuse, negligent treatment, or maltreatment of a child under the age of 18 by a person who is responsible for the child's welfare under circumstances that indicate that the child's health or welfare is harmed.

State statutes of what is considered abuse may vary in terms of "harm or threatened harm" in a child's health (National Clearinghouse on Child Abuse and Neglect, 2003a). In addition, the states

may differ on exemptions, which may include, for instance, a religious exemption, cultural practice, corporal punishment, and poverty. Many states include the terms *abandonment* and *intentional harm* versus *unintentional harm* in their definitions of child abuse and neglect.

Although statutory laws and definitions vary from state to state, there are concrete areas of agreement (Giardino, Christian, & Giardino, 1997; National Clearinghouse on Child Abuse and Neglect, 2003b). Child abuse may include acts of omission or commission, usually found to be on a continuum rather than an isolated incident. Although each state has its own precise delineations and definitions for various types of neglect and abuse, laws typically consider four broad categories: neglect, emotional abuse, sexual abuse, and physical abuse. For example, the Commonwealth of Virginia includes abandonment in its definition of maltreatment; Rhode Island defines mental injury to include failure to thrive, loss of ability to think or reason, loss of control of aggressive or self-destructive impulses, acting out or misbehavior, including incorrigibility, ungovernability, or habitual truancy. Each state's unique definitions and interpretations of what constitutes abuse and neglect dictate the reporting requirements for the state.

An epidemic of global violence, the effects of recent changes to the U.S. Citizenship and Immigration Services (USCIS) law, and the need to review state laws governing crime and victimization are bringing forensic patients from each corner of the world into nursing practice. Immigrants and refugees bring with them their traditional and cultural healthcare practices, which are often misunderstood, misinterpreted as abuse or neglect, and thus impact healthcare delivery. The expected results include developing models, tools, best practices, culturally sensitive, and ethical guidelines for global planning and interventions.

INCIDENCE

In 2007, according to the NCANDS annual report of reported child maltreatment cases in the United States, an estimated 2.9 million referrals alleging child abuse or neglect were reported and accepted by the state and local child protection agencies (USDHHS, 2009). Of these cases, approximately 906,000 children were identified as actual victims of child abuse and neglect. Childhood neglect was responsible for 60% of the cases, physical abuse equated 20%, sexual abuse accounted for 10%, and the remaining 5% were emotional maltreatment cases. Data reveal that infants and children age birth to three years old are the most common victims of maltreatment, and females are slightly more likely to be abused than males (USDHHS, 2009). In addition, race and ethnicity studies showed the highest rates in Pacific Islanders (21.4 per 1000 children), American Indian or Alaska Natives (21.3 per 1000), African Americans (20.4 per 1000 children), and whites (11.0 per 1000 children). In 2003, an estimated 1500 child fatalities were the result of maltreatment, a rate of 2 deaths per 100,000 U.S. children. Documentation of specific cases remains difficult to quantify because of various reporting criteria and definitions among states, as well as underreporting.

Of the documented NCANDS cases in 2007, approximately 57% of the victims received some sort of services following the assessment and investigation (USDHHS, 2009). Services included in-home and foster care services. Child victims of multiple types of maltreatment were more likely to receive treatment than those with physical abuse alone.

In 2007, NCANDS reported approximately 80% of the perpetrators were parents, 16% were other family members or unmarried partners of parents, and the remaining 4% were "others" (USDHHS, 2009). Women were more common perpetrators than men (58% to 42%, respectively) and were generally younger than male perpetrators. For sexual assault, approximately 76% of the perpetrators were friends or neighbors, with the remaining 30% being family members (only 3% of these were parents).

Theory, Assessment, and History: Gathering Information

MODELS AND THEORY

Over the past few decades, several child maltreatment models (Cowen, 1999; De Paul & Guibert, 2008) have presented the multiple facets involved in the intentional harm and maltreatment issue, including the model that examines the complex nature of the interactions between the parent and the child, the stressors within and outside the family, and the broader social and cultural system (Howze & Kotch, 1984). This model expanded on earlier models to include familial, social, and cultural aspects, as well as the impact of these relationships with stress, social support systems, and child maltreatment. These authors recognized that stress in the maladaptive abusive family may be situational, acute, or chronic. Milner (1993) worked to develop a physical child abuse risk assessment tool that could be used to assess demographic, social, cognitive/affective, and behavioral risk factors. He based his work on Belsky's (1980, 1993) organizational model that described four ecological levels found in other models of child abuse: (1) the ontogenic level (individual factors in the child), (2) the microsystem (refers to family factors), (3) the ecosystem (reflecting the community), and (4) the macrosystem (identified as the culture). Belsky (1993) emphasized that his model and assessment tool helps predict the risk of maltreatment behaviors, but not actually maltreatment. Additional models and theories are developing, which have similar concepts. Milner (1993) has refined his own work to include sociocultural, family system, and learning paradigms and sublevels of understanding of each concept, including such details as understanding the social information processing in the abusive parent. The review of literature reveals a complex etiology for child abuse and neglect.

DYNAMICS OF CHILD MALTREATMENT

Experts in child maltreatment have identified a dynamic interrelationship of three types of characteristics that must exist for child abuse to evolve (Belsky, 1980; Milner, 1993). These three characteristics involve the parent or adult (perpetrator), the child (victim), and the environmental context. The interaction of all three groups is deemed necessary for predicting high risk for abuse.

Parental or Adult Characteristics (Perpetrator)

Parental characteristics associated with child abuse include parents who had serious difficulties in the parent-child interactions when the parents were children; for example, they were either abused themselves or observed abuse in their family. The parent may have poor social contacts, be isolated, and have little social support. These parents often have inappropriate expectations of the child, with a poor understanding of normal growth and development, intellectual status, and physical abilities of the child. They may lack necessary parenting skills or be unaware of the physical and emotional needs of the child, as with adolescent parents and low-income parents (Houxley & Warner, 1993). In their own relationships, their dependency needs have not been met, and they are frequently unable to develop close, trusting relationships with others. Perpetrators generally display a low self-esteem with poor impulse control and poor coping mechanisms. Other risk factors include adolescent parents, single parents, and military personnel. Less than 10% of these adults have severe mental disorders such as psychosis.

Child Characteristics (Victim)

Characteristics of the abused child include being considered "special" or "different." For example, the child may be the result of an unwanted pregnancy, may be the "wrong" sex, or may simply look like a "wrong" person. The intensity of the "special child" or "different" characteristics is defined in the parent's eyes. In more obvious cases, the child may have an acute or chronic illness or a limiting disability (mental or physical) or be preterm, requiring a great deal of time and attention (Hobbs, Hanks, & Wynne, 1993). Poor mother-infant attachment or bonding has been associated with prolonged separation at birth (high-risk infants) and even with multiple births (Sachs & Hall, 1991). Theorists assert it is difficult for a mother to bond or attach with more than one infant at a time; therefore, one or more children in a multiple birth are left with potential delayed bonding and potential tendencies toward child maltreatment.

Environmental Characteristics

Environmental characteristics associated with child abuse include a family that is in stress. This may be acute, chronic, or situational stress, or a series of crises such as serious illness, death, divorce, extramarital affairs, financial problems, and unemployment. Inadequate housing or substandard living conditions characterized by crowding, lack of privacy, and disrepair are also contributing elements. Repeated relocations may mean social isolation and a lack of support systems, which leaves the adult with no one to turn to for help, advice, or caregiving relief from the child (Ricci & Botash, 2002). Children who witness domestic violence can suffer severe emotional and developmental issues similar to those who have been direct victims (National Clearinghouse on Child Abuse and Neglect Information, 2004; Walton-Moss, Manganello, Frye, & Campbell, 2005).

Parent-Child Interaction

Parent-child interactions may present themselves in a parent not comforting a child or being detached from the child. The parent may demonstrate a lack of control or impulsive behaviors. A child or parent may have inappropriate expectations of the child based on age and developmental stage. Some clinicians report observing conflicts that more closely resemble parent-parent (adult-adult) interactions than child-parent.

KEY POINT Nurses need to be knowledgeable of possible indicators of abuse and neglect, especially those that are manifested before a child suffers a serious injury, emotional impairment, or developmental delay. Early recognition and intervention are the keys to preventing subsequent abuse and negative sequelae.

Categories of Child Abuse and Neglect

PHYSICAL ABUSE

Physical abuse is defined as a situation in which a person inflicts physical injury to the child, ranging from bruises to multiple fractures and brain damage. Physical abuse is not usually a controlled, planned action. It is generally an impulsive reaction to stress that involves a cycle of stages, including a tension-building stage, the actual abusive act, and periods of nurturing in between. As with other forms of abuse, it is considered a family problem and reflects a dysfunctional family. All family members suffer when abuse occurs, even those not being physically harmed. Physical child abuse is seldom an isolated incident.

EMOTIONAL ABUSE

Emotional abuse is defined as a maladaptive parent-child interaction. In emotional neglect, there is a failure to meet the affection, attention, and nurturing needs of the child (Hockenbery, Wilson, Winkelstein, et al., 2002). An additional form of emotional abuse occurs when the adult purposely attempts to destroy or hamper the child's self-esteem (Nester, 1998). This form of abuse is seen when a parent rejects, isolates, terrorizes, or verbally assaults the child. Frequently in emotional abuse, inappropriate expectations or demands are placed on the child. For example, toilet training may be expected too early. A child may also be expected to carry out more adult functions, such as childcare for siblings, cooking, and cleaning. A parent may place a heavy emotional burden on the child or have adult expectations that result in a reversal of the child-adult roles.

SEXUAL ABUSE

Sexual exploitation can range from noncontact indecent exposure to fondling and genital contact to actual adult-child sexual intercourse (National Clearinghouse on Child Abuse and Neglect, 2004). The Child Abuse and Prevention Act states sexual abuse is the "use of persuasion or coercion of any child to engage in sexually explicit conduct, or the producing of visual depiction of such conduct, or rape, molestation, prostitution, or incest with children." A child does not have the knowledge, emotional maturity, or social skills necessary to enter into a sexual relationship of any nature on an equal basis with an adult. Therefore, it is legally concluded a child cannot be held responsible for a sexual relationship with an adult.

There are two primary forms of sexual abuse. The first is when an adult initially pressures a child into a nonsexual liaison based on a long-term trusted relationship. As the relationship grows, the child eventually participates in the sexual activity to maintain the rewards, attention, approval, or recognition provided by the adult who essentially uses the child to meet his or her unfulfilled needs. The second type of sexual abuse is the forced relationship in which the offender intimidates the child by threatening harm or actually harming the child or someone else the child cares about. The adult has no emotional investment in the child but rather uses the victim to meet short-term sexual needs. Authorities believe most offenders do not actually desire to harm the child; however, a few of the perpetrators seem to obtain vicarious pleasure from harming the child (Hockenbery, et al., 2002).

NEGLECT

Child neglect is defined as the failure to provide adequate care. Neglect is considered an act of omission and accounts for over half of the reported child maltreatment (Cowen, 1999; Helfer, 1990; Hockenbery, et al., 2002). Situations of neglect may include inadequate supervision, which may lead to accidents and injury. Overall lack of attention to food, shelter, and medical needs are also considered neglect and can quickly endanger the well-being of a child. In addition, the lack of providing education at both the grade school and high school levels is deemed neglect. Many of these factors are closely related to poverty, single parenthood, and unemployment, leading to a multifaceted social problem. The 1974 Child Abuse Prevention and Treatment Act deemed neglect a form of abuse and required medical attention. Although reporting has improved, actual cases of neglect remain high.

Neglect can result in malnutrition, poor dental care, and a generally poor health status. Children left unattended are at a high risk for injury. Over 75% of neglect victims were reported to have a serious injury or illness within three years of documented neglect (Green & Kilili, 1998). Neglected children can be extremely passive, withdrawn, undisciplined, or disabled (Cowen, 1997). More extreme neglect can lead to Failure to Thrive Syndrome (FTT). Manifestations of FTT include withdrawn effect, decreased and aggressive social interactions, and fewer positive play behaviors such as offering, sharing, accepting, and following (Peterson & Urquiza, 1993). Additionally, the child may experience impaired or delayed growth, delayed language development, and maturational and behavioral difficulties in achieving developmental milestones (Schmitt & Mauro, 1989). It is not uncommon for a child with FTT to die from secondary metabolic defects or other illnesses. Their deaths may also be the result of intentional or unintentional trauma and neglect. The differential diagnosis of FTT may include a wide range of possible organic conditions (inborn metabolic disorders, congenital viral infections, chromosomal syndromes) and external factors including criminal acts.

Forensic pathologists determine if a child's death is natural or unnatural. If abuse and neglect are the determined cause or contribute to the cause of death, criminal charges can be filed. Because there are important consequences, the diagnosis must be confirmed. This may be difficult when there may be several underlying causes such as organic FTT, cystic fibrosis, abuse, and neglect. A detailed forensic investigation is required.

Case Study 29-1

Power Windows

A three-year-old girl became trapped in a power window of her mother's car and was killed. She was left in the car while her mother went inside a friend's house. The girl apparently removed her seat belt and lowered the window of the running car. The mother told investigators she found the girl caught in the window when she returned after about five minutes. Emergency crews found the girl was not breathing when they arrived at the scene. She was pronounced dead about an hour later at the medical center.

Other Abuse and Neglect Issues
SIBLING ABUSE

Sibling abuse, when one sibling abuses another, is among the most overlooked forms of child abuse. Sibling abuse takes the form of physical, sexual, and emotional abuse and has devastating consequences to victims. Sibling abuse victims often suffer long-term social and psychological disturbances and propagate cycles of family violence. Numerous familial and environmental factors have been identified as predicted risk factors for sibling abuse (Walton-Moss et al., 2005). Forensic investigation of suspicious circumstances concerning child injury, behavior, or death is paramount to facilitate the elimination of historical cultural neglect of child abuse cases and to initiate prevention strategies to help eradicate sibling abuse in society.

The murder of a child by his or her sibling is categorized as *siblicide*. From Doug Mock's animal research on killing of siblings, one can hypothesize sibling abuse occurs as a result of a deficiency in the family or parental structure that will cause children to exhibit abusive behaviors toward siblings to gain more resources. However, not enough is known about sibling abuse to draw firm conclusions. Despite the lack of attention that sibling abuse receives from parents and society at large, it can have detrimental long-term effects in children and can result in premature death in some cases (Smith & Smith, 2001).

Statistical information reveals that child abuse committed by siblings is a prevalent social problem previously ignored. In a Canadian study (2001), siblings were perpetrators of 28% of sexual offenses and 24% of physical assaults in child victims less than 12 years of age (Johnson & Au Coin, 2003). Research results are particularly shocking when examining incidences of sexual abuse. The National Society for the Prevention of Cruelty to Children indicates siblings are twice as likely to be abused by brothers than by fathers or stepfathers (Spenser, 2000). Incidences of sibling abuse differs somewhat from adult abusers. Unlike parental child abuse where the most vulnerable age for maltreatment is 12 months to 5 years, children of any age can be targets of sibling abuse. Younger children have a higher mortality rate whether the perpetrator is an adult or a sibling.

Physical and emotional neglect is commonly associated with parental child abuse, whereas phenomena such as bullying are more often related to sibling abuse. Dominance and control appear to be a common link among most types of child abuse and are especially apparent in different forms of sibling abuse.

Sibling abuse is often mistaken as "sibling rivalry," a seemingly harmless and playful interaction, which parents tend to ignore or join in with the supposed playfulness. However, survivors of this type of abuse report their parent's reaction to sibling violence as one of nonchalance, denial, or blame (Wiehe, 1997). Parents commonly trivialize the event or do not believe such reports, and they often accuse victims of deserving or enabling maltreatment. For example, when a child is verbally degraded, the parent may see retaliatory self-defense as the initial cause of the child being teased. Unfortunately, if parents do not address sibling abuse, they are essentially condoning abusive behaviors.

TEASING

Teasing is a common form of emotional abuse. Emotional abuse has been found to be the most destructive force among all types of abuse with the most damaging long-term effects (Keltner, Capps, Kring, Young, & Heerey, 2001; Wiehe, 1997). Teasing and other forms of emotional abuse often accompany physical and sexual abuse. According to Wiehe, 7% of his sample indicated emotional abuse alone, compared to 71% indicated experiencing emotional, physical, and sexual abuse.

It may be difficult to distinguish abuse from playful interaction between siblings, parents, or other adults or children. Social interaction that revolves around negative verbal communications directed at a child can be considered emotionally abusive. This differs from joking because emotional abuse is conducted at the victim's expense (Wiehe, 1991). Fear and intimidation are often used against victims as a means of control and dominance. Older siblings may be able to inflict more emotional damage because they are often idolized by the younger siblings and have developed more hurtful behaviors (Simonelli, Mullis,

Elliott et al., 2002). Victims often internalize hurtful comments, which produce feelings of low self-worth. Conversely, some victims externalize emotional abuse, which manifests itself as negative behaviors (Hart & Brassard, 1987).

BULLYING

A prime example of the integration of emotional abuse with other forms of sibling abuse is bullying. Bullying is primarily emotional but can also lead to physical intimidation and violence. Bullying is emotional intimidation perpetrated by a person who is stronger than or in a position of power over the victim. The bully child often has high dominance needs, lacks empathy, and has a positive view of aggression. Bullying can take on many forms and often occurs between peers or siblings (Nansel, Overpeck, Pilla, Ruan, Simons-Morton, & Scheidt, 2001).

Research reveals children involved in sibling bullying are more likely bullies or victims at school (Duncan, 1999). According to Duncan, 53% of 210 college freshmen reported bully victimization during their childhood. Yet society continues to underestimate the potential emotional damage of bullying. Research statistics indicated 22% of participants who were bullied were pushed, hit, or shoved, and 81% reported being "beaten up" (Duncan, 1999). Bully victimization has been linked to psychological difficulties such as depression, anxiety, and low self-esteem.

HUMAN TRAFFICKING

A multibillion-dollar industry, human trafficking generally is a hidden problem. Periodically, a few cases appear in the mainstream media. It is important to understand the breadth of the problem as an individual and public health issue and to know how to identify and effectively intervene in these cases.

In a June 2008 Trafficking in Persons Report, the U.S. government noted it is difficult to precisely determine the magnitude of human trafficking both nationally and globally because of the underground nature of the problem. This report quoted estimates by the United Nations' International Labor Organization that at any given time, some 12.3 million people are in forced labor or bonded labor, forced child labor, or sexual servitude. It is unclear how many of these persons are children.

Federally sponsored research found roughly 800,000 persons are trafficked across national borders annually; about 80% of transnational victims are women and girls, and up to 50% are minors. Typically, victims are promised a better life through employment, educational opportunities, or marriage. Instead, they find themselves entrenched in modern-day slavery, working as domestics, laborers, sweatshop workers, nail salon employees, or commercial sex workers. Victims generally do not identify themselves because many traffickers use physical, sexual, or emotional abuse to control them, according to a background brief distributed at the September 2008 National Symposium on the Health Needs of Human Trafficking Victims held by the U.S. Department of Health and Human Services. Trafficking victims experience many social and health problems, including sexually transmitted infections (STIs), malnutrition, substance abuse, and mental illness (USDHHS, 2008).

Nurses need to understand that human trafficking touches all communities. As nurses, we are supposed to promote the humane treatment of all human beings. Therefore, we need to be more aware of this issue because human trafficking is not just a public health issue but an ethical moral issue. It is not just the responsibility of the emergency department, forensic nurses, or public health nurses. All nurses must be adept at recognizing and assisting trafficking victims. We all need to be working on this together because it is part of our professional obligation to the public.

METHAMPHETAMINE EXPOSURE TO CHILDREN

Parental drug use can have a devastating impact on children. Although many illegal drugs impact a person's ability to parent, methamphetamine (also called "meth") use is now epidemic. Many people who become addicted to meth or other drugs often lose track of their priorities and present as disorganized and increasingly violent, in addition to experiencing many other problems. The silent victims of drug addiction are too often the children. If a caregiver is getting "high" and "crashing" for days at a time, his or her ability to safely parent is compromised.

There has been a lot of attention in the media given to meth abuse and manufacturing because it is such an addictive and dangerous substance. The U.S. Drug Enforcement Agency (U.S. DEA) documents that the use of this substance has been consistently high for many years. According to the U.S. DEA web site, "methamphetamine is one of the most widely abused controlled substances…and availability is high." Meth is cheaper than most drugs, easily accessible, somewhat easy to manufacture, and creates an intense feeling of euphoria or "high." Because of this intense feeling and other effects, it is *extremely* easy for a person to become addicted, sometimes after only one use. The negative effects of meth can be uncomfortable and can include depression, irritability, paranoia, fatigue, and anxiety. A person may binge on meth to avoid these feelings. The tolerance for the drug builds up quickly, which requires a person to use more at a faster rate to get the same high.

Unfortunately, children and youths are often lost in the drug addiction of their parents. The risk of children being neglected or physically and sexually abused is high because their parent/caregiver has lost the ability to attend to their physical and emotional needs. Risks to children include exposure to toxic fumes and the danger of explosions or fires; drugs and drug paraphernalia within easy reach; loaded weapons and booby traps in the home; exposure to sexual abusers and violent drug users, leading to possible physical and sexual abuse of the child; neglect, including lack of food and inappropriate sleeping conditions; exposure to pornography; and a greater risk of becoming an addict.

Some people who are addicted to meth are irritable, become agitated much easier, and their decision-making process is compromised. This can lead to an increased risk for physical and emotional abuse. If a child does something the parent does not want him or her to do, the child could be yelled at and called names. These parents may spank their children to discipline without realizing how hard they spanked; a bruise could be left on the child's skin. In severe cases of abuse, a parent could become frustrated with an infant's crying and shake the infant, causing brain damage and death.

U.S. Congress House of Representatives Bill 5842 mandates that exposing a child to meth is child abuse and neglect. (www. legislature.mi.gov/documents/2005-2006/billanalysis/House/ htm/2005-HLA-5842-1.htm). More and more children are being taken into protective custody by law enforcement and child welfare caseworks as a result of their exposure to caregiver meth use.

Case Study 29-2

A Life with Methamphetamine

Josh, Annie, and Hannah are six months, three years, and seven years old, respectively. They live with both parents in a nice neighborhood in a medium-sized city. Their parents are routine users of methamphetamine. They have several "friends" who live with them on and off. When their parents crash on meth and temporarily stop taking the drug, they can sleep for up to 48 hours, and it is very difficult to wake them. Therefore, the children are left unattended, alone, and unsupervised or with unsafe people who take advantage of the situation and offend all three children sexually; "friends" of the parents scold and harshly discipline the children for making noise. These children often must fend for themselves, including feeding and meeting basic needs for themselves and their siblings. Various safety hazards such as getting burned while cooking and toxic contamination as a result of unsanitary conditions, in addition to the typical safety hazards present in all homes where water, electricity, and heat are present. Hannah, the oldest, feels the burden of caring for and protecting her younger siblings. The children are also left in the care of the parents' friends who may be fellow users or "cooks" themselves. When the children are in the homes of the "cooks," they are exposed to the toxic chemicals, fumes, and by-products present during the cooking process. The meth is cooked over a period of time during which certain stages of the process require storage in the refrigerator. The children may mistake these stored drugs for drinks or other food and ingest it, not only potentially poisoning themselves but also risking retaliation from the adults because of the loss of their product.

MUNCHAUSEN SYNDROME BY PROXY (MSBP)

A curious category of child abuse, known as Munchausen Syndrome by Proxy (MSBP) (a term coined by Roy Meadow in 1977), is rarely recognized and uncommonly seen. MSBP, also known as factitious illness by proxy, is a dangerous form of child abuse in which a parent or caregiver induces or fabricates numerous illnesses and falsifies medical history that results in unnecessary medical evaluation and treatment leading to prolonged or repeated contact with the healthcare system. The deception is usually repeated on numerous occasions, resulting in hospitalizations, morbidity, and death. The perpetrator usually injures the victims to gain sympathy or attention for herself or himself (Feldman, 2004).

It is not uncommon for the abuse to continue during periods of hospitalization. Pediatric forensic nurse examiners (FNEs) can provide an important role in the observation and surveillance with video cameras to monitor and document the abuse. The use of covert video surveillance (CVS) has been tied to some legal issues involving the Fourth Amendment of the U.S. Constitution and is subject to some controversy. However, visual evidence is often required to convince the courts that parents could do such things to their own children (Brown, 1997).

ABUSIVE HEAD TRAUMA/SHAKEN BABY SYNDROME

Abusive head trauma or shaken baby syndrome (SBS) is a significant cause of infant morbidity and mortality, most often involving children younger than two years, but it may be seen in children up to five years of age. The hallmark finding of abusive head trauma is the absence of any external trauma to the head, face, and neck, along with massive intracranial or retinal hemorrhages (National Institute of Health, 2008). Because the child is most often nonverbal or unable to tell what occurred, one must be aware of the signs and symptoms associated with abusive head trauma. In less severe cases, there is typically a history of poor feeding, vomiting, lethargy or irritability, hypothermia, failure to thrive, and increased sleeping with difficulty arousing. In more severe cases, there may be seizures, a full or bulging fontanel, bradycardia, respiratory distress, decreased responsiveness of the pupils, and eventually coma and cardiovascular collapse. This type of abuse is the most often missed in the emergency departments (Trokel, et al., 2006). Magnetic resonance imaging (MRI) and computed tomography (CT) imaging are required to substantiate repeated abusive head trauma injuries that point to abuse.

SUDDEN INFANT DEATH SYNDROME (SIDS)

Sudden infant death syndrome (SIDS) is defined as a sudden, unexpected death of an infant less than one year of age, which remains unexplained after an autopsy, toxicological studies, and a thorough investigation of the scene and the circumstances surrounding the death. This term is used to describe a deceased infant and not a condition or disease. Most SIDS deaths occur in infants between two and four months old. Although intensive studies have been implemented to ascertain the causes of SIDS, the etiology is still unknown (Bowman, Hargrove, 2007; National Infant Sleep Position Household Survey, Summary Data, 2006). There is no test for SIDS. The campaign to place a baby "back to sleep" appears to be helpful (National Infant Sleep Position Household Survey, 2007). Conditions that may be associated with child abuse such as facial fractures and vertebral artery compression must be thoroughly considered. Without evidence of underlying trauma, however, suffocation is indistinguishable from SIDS at autopsy. Emergency physicians or pediatricians cannot legally diagnose SIDS, which constitutes a medical examiner's/coroner's (ME/C) case and is only determined after the exclusion of any other possible cause.

SEAT BELTS AND CHILD RESTRAINTS

The law requires the use of vehicular seat belts and child restraints because they are considered among the most protective devices for infants and children in the event of vehicular collisions. Children up to four years old or 40 pounds in weight are required to use a child safety seat (Insurance Institute, 2009).

By current laws, the adult driving is responsible for the safety of the child and will be charged with negligence or vehicular homicide if the child is killed under the specific circumstances of the law related to child safety. Adults have the right to choose whether they will be in violation of state seat belt laws; children do not. The child's fate is partly decided by the adults who care for him or her. Experts in the investigation of transportation collisions are responsible for the accurate interpretation of evidence and accident reconstruction, which may determine the outcome of charges filed.

CHILD PROSTITUTION

Throughout history, children have been sexually victimized and child prostitution remains one of the most ignored forms of child abuse. Although prevalent across centuries, the United States documented an increase in child prostitution in the late 1970s as a result of the Juvenile Justice Delinquency Prevention Act passed in 1974 that forbade law enforcement to detain runaway children, therefore allowing them to exist on the street. A study released in 2001 reported that between 300,000 and 400,000 U.S. children are victims of some type of sexual exploitation each year (Estes, 2001;

Willis & Levy, 2003). According to Estes, child exploitation is the most hidden form of child abuse in North America. It is estimated that 75% of the child sex trade victims are white and from middle-class families; boys are victimized as often as girls.

Identification of Abuse and Neglect

The FNE with pediatric expertise, working with other members of a multidisciplinary team, provides an effective strategy for identifying, confirming, and confronting child abuse and neglect. This requires a planned, objective, and coordinated response with defined policies and procedures that can be put into effect the moment abuse or neglect is suspected (Pasqualone & Fitzgerald, 1999). If these are in place, the child's safety is assured and staff can promptly involve other healthcare services, community agencies, and systems of advocacy.

Intervening on the child's behalf may prevent further injury or death. Some hospitals and long-term institutions for children are developing positions for advanced practice nurses such as the forensic pediatric nurse practitioner (FPNP) or forensic clinical nurse specialist (FCNS). As in-house forensic clinicians, these specialists are considered an essential part of the multidisciplinary team who are qualified to detect, assess, and manage cases of child abuse and neglect.

CREATING A SAFE ENVIRONMENT

A child's self-disclosure of abuse is a critical component in initiating intervention to stop the abuse, address its effects, and decrease the likelihood of long-term negative outcomes. It is not yet clearly understood why some children disclose their abuse while others remain silent (Finn, 2008). Reported cases of child sexual abuse reached epidemic proportions with a reported 322% increase from 1980 to 1990 (Sorensen & Snow, 1991). To make the national crisis of sex crimes against youth even more alarming, Janssen (1984) contended there may be at least ten times as many cases that go unreported. According to USDHHS (2009) most experts agree that many, if not most cases go unreported. As Janssen (1984) suggested, "Only the tip of the iceberg has been touched concerning the incidence of child sexual abuse."

The forensic nurse is in a position to create a "safe" environment from which the children can disclose their abuse to authorities and receive help. Finn (2008) suggested that the forensic nurse is the environment for the child; she or he must hear and believe the unbelievable horrors many children will share when *allowed* to share.

HISTORY

Obtaining and documenting a thorough history is a critical step in the assessment of child abuse. The child may be accompanied by a nonabusive parent or adult, the abusive offender, or a child protection services worker (Ricci & Botash, 2002). It is important to interview the child and the adult separately. If an adult tries to prevent the child's privacy, the nurse may need to intervene on the child's behalf. The pediatric FNE should use open-ended questions that do not lead the child. The interview should include questions not only about actual abuse (physical, sexual, emotional, or neglect) but also about domestic violence and witnessing abuse (Ricci & Botash, 2002).

Red-flag findings in the history include the absence of an adult, poorly explained histories, or conflicting histories from different sources. Histories inconsistent with physical findings or inconsistent with the child's growth and development stage may reflect a false story or an inappropriate expectation for the child (Lynch, 1997). The caregiver may be reluctant to explain, may blame others for the injury, or may refuse additional tests or treatments. Sometimes the caregiver reflects an inappropriate level of concern or is absent altogether. When there are delays in seeking medical treatment and a history of repeated injury or unmet medical, physical, and emotional needs, child abuse should be considered.

Often, adults will bring the child in for complaints other than those directly related to the abuse, or they may have either an increased or a decreased level of concern related to the actual problem presented. The child or adult may be reluctant to explain the injury, may blame someone else, or may refuse additional tests or treatments. In sexual abuse, the child may refer to a "special relationship" or a "secret" they have with an adult. These children should be specifically asked about sexual issues. If they are threatened and scared, disclosure may be very difficult (Finn, 2008).

Occasionally the historian will be an eyewitness to the abuse; however, in the absence of a witness, the nurse should never ignore subtle or overt "cries for help" from either the child or the adult. Child abuse is seldom an isolated event (Finn, 2008). The history should be compared to the physical findings as well, including the child's appearance and behavior, parent-child interactions, and physical clues. Laboratory, radiographic, and body scan testing may be necessary, and careful documentation through charting and forensic photography is essential (see Appendix D for sexual abuse forms).

CHILD'S APPEARANCE AND BEHAVIOR

A child may display hostility, insincerity, or appear to be fearful of the adult. In other cases, the child may actually cling to or go to the abusive person for protection or comforting. Other typical behaviors displayed by the child include social withdrawal, hypersocial aggression, depression, and helplessness. Some children may demonstrate inappropriate infantile-type or adult behaviors inconsistent with their age, growth, and development. With older children, some of the sequelae of child abuse may already begin to exhibit themselves in such behaviors as poor school performance, poor social interactions with peers, fantasies, phobias, eating and sleeping problems, drug and alcohol abuse, sexual promiscuity, running away from home, suicidal thoughts and attempts, and specific psychiatric disorders (Green & Kilili, 1998; Hockenbery, et al., 2002).

Physical Evidence of Abuse and Neglect

Children of abuse often will present with physical clues that are well defined and others that are more vague or hidden. Signs of neglect and emotional abuse are less clearly presented than those of physical abuse. Sexual abuse may be completely missed if a sexual history or examination is not performed as part of routine assessment.

Some signs of neglect include poor skin care, grooming, oral hygiene, or malnutrition and dehydration without a medical cause (Helpguide, 2008; Hockenbery, et al., 2002). Repeated accidents reflecting improper supervision, poor health maintenance (e.g., no immunizations), and failure to thrive symptoms, which improve with hospitalizations, all reflect potential neglect. Emotional

abuse is more difficult to pinpoint; it may result in FTT, feeding disorders, neurosis, sleep disorders, and developmental delays.

Sexual abuse indicators can be found in any genital, rectal, oral, or buttocks trauma, bleeding, or discharge. Sexually transmitted infections, pregnancy, recurrent urinary tract infections, or general somatic complaints are commonly associated with sexual abuse (Helpguide, 2008), although there are cases where no physical evidence of sexual abuse is found. Physical abuse should be suspected in any injury to a child less than 12 months old. Other suspicious injuries include injuries of the soft tissue, such as hematomas, bruises, lesions, and scars in different stages of healing or injuries reflective of an inflicting implement (e.g., ropes, buckles, cigarettes). Multiple fractures, bleeding (including retinal bleeds), burns, neurological damage, convulsions resulting from poisoning, coma, and abdominal distention or injury may be seen in child abuse and warrant investigation (Helpguide, 2008).

Patterned Injuries Suspicious for Abuse

IMMERSION BURNS

Immersion burns result from a child being forced into scalding liquid, most often domestic hot water. These first-, second-, and third-degree burns are identified as "forced immersion" burns. With most forms of burn injuries, a pattern is present or develops, enabling medical and investigative personnel to determine how the injury may have occurred. Significant patterns are recognized in forced immersion burns. For instance, the face and neck are generally spared. When the child is held, dipped, or plunged into hot liquid, the child will react by flexing that portion of the body contacting the hot liquid, thus sparing the flexion crease areas. Clinically, three characteristic burn patterns result from immersion:

- "Donut" pattern (central sparing), produced when the body is held against the bottom of a heated container such as a large metal pan or porcelain tub of hot water
- "Stocking or Glove" pattern, produced by the waterline when the child's feet, hands, or legs are held in hot liquid (Fig. 29-1)
- "Tripod" pattern, induced by a child raising up on his hands and feet to protect his buttocks and perineum from burning in a shallow-filled container of hot water

On the other hand, the child who is accidentally burned by falling or climbing into or turning on hot water presents a burn injury consistent with the action. The waterline may be blurred and there are likely to be splash burns. A splash pattern injury, however, cannot be used as a single factor in determining whether the burn is accidental or intentional, since they are sometimes noted in association with forced immersion.

BEST PRACTICE It is essential that nurses gain an understanding of the immersion burn as a form of physical child abuse and be able to differentiate accidental from intentional burns.

PATTERNED BURNS

Intentional burns occur primarily in the high-risk child age range of 12 months to 5 years of age (Lowell, Quinlan, & Gottlieb, 2008). There are more male victims than female, and when extensive burns occur, younger children have a higher mortality rate than older children. The majority of burn injuries associated with

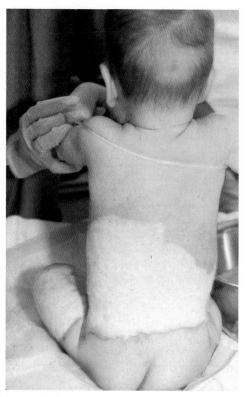

Fig. 29-1 Immersion burn. Note sparing in diaper area and bald area on head, which sometimes indicates prolonged lying in one position.

BITE MARKS

The FNE may note wound characteristics of a bite on any body surface and must differentiate human bites from animal bites. Because both adults and children can inflict bites, the wound must be photographed, diagrammed, and precisely measured for evidentiary purposes (Fig. 29-3). Distances of greater than 3 cm between canine teeth typically indicate an adult bite (Suggs, Lichenstein, McCarthy, et al., 2001; Thali, 2003). Because human bite marks most frequently indicate sexual abuse, wounds should also be swabbed for DNA to assist in identification of the perpetrator. Serial photographs may be required on one or more subsequent days postinjury to fully appreciate the wound characteristics, as redness and edema can interfere with visualization of subtle marks useful in pinpointing the individual who inflicted the bite.

Sequelae of Child Abuse and Neglect

The physical, psychosocial, and economic sequelae of child abuse and neglect can potentially damage generations. Results may include physical disfigurement, neurological damage, and major emotional and psychological trauma (Cowen, 1999; Finkelhor, 1998; Green & Kilili, 1998; Ricci & Botash, 2002; U.S. DHHS, 2004). The abuse teaches violence in the family and society, resulting in victimization and future potential abuse cycles. Child maltreatment can interrupt the physical and emotional development potential of a child, resulting in a lack of trust, feelings of helplessness, poor peer

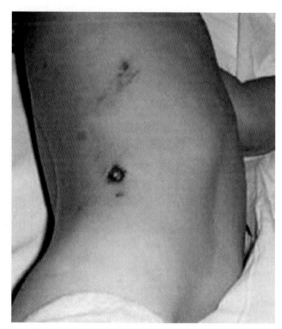

Fig. 29-2 Cigarette burn. The location strongly supports an intentional injury by a perpetrator.

abuse resemble the pattern of the object involved. Common patterns noted by forensic experts have been inflicted by hairdryers, irons, cigarettes, a car cigarette lighter, or hot cooking or eating utensils (Fig. 29-2). Patterned burns commonly are seen on the dorsum of the feet or hands and occasionally on the face or neck (Lowell, Quinlan, & Gottlieb, 2008).

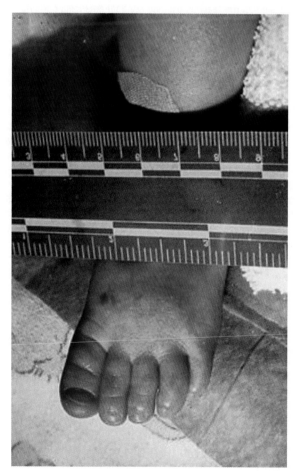

Fig. 29-3 Bite mark on foot of an infant.

relationships, sexual promiscuity, and potential alcohol and drug use (Finkelhor, 1998; National Center of Child Abuse and Neglect Data, 1997). Children also manifest with frequent complaints of illness and discomfort, sleep and eating disorders, and an inability to concentrate or a short attention span, delaying their potential cognitive and emotional development (Schuster, Wood, Duan, et al., 1998). McCauley, Kem, and Kolonder (1997) agreed with the previous problems and identify, in addition, anxiety disorders, depression, interpersonal sensitivity, and suicidal thoughts and attempts.

Case Study 29-3

A Lifetime of Abuse

Long before Lydia was old enough to start school, she was a victim of both physical and psychological abuse by an alcoholic father as well as a dependent and frustrated mother. Lydia was the youngest of five children and the only girl. Her family lived far from town in an isolated rural area with no neighbors within sight. During the day, her mother assigned chores beyond Lydia's physical and mental development, punishing her at any opportunity to maintain power and control. Her father tied her to a tree in the front of the house and left her there through the night. This terrorized Lydia and instilled an unnatural fear of the dark as well as fear of both parents and a fear of being punished. Because her three older brothers were gone from home, Lydia also became the target of teasing, bullying, and sexual abuse by the one older brother who remained at home.

Lydia looked forward to starting school and escaping the continued abuse. On her first day at school, she carefully prepared to make a good impression on her teacher, wearing her best dress and carrying wildflowers as a gift. Her mother had given Lydia a stick of chewing gum as a favor on this day, telling her to behave and learn well. When Lydia approached the teacher with the flowers, the teacher suddenly reached up, slapped her face so hard the gum flew from her mouth, and said, "Don't you ever come into my room chewing gum again!" Lydia never recovered emotionally from this day and subsequently felt that there was no place where she was safe.

Over the next years, she submitted to various abuses with expectation. As an adolescent, she became promiscuous. As a young adult, she married a dominant man who controlled her just as her parents had. She continued to reach out to men for attention. As she inadvertently sought conversation, her best friend's husband raped her. Afterward, she became the victim of numerous incidents and sexual assaults in various settings. Depression, guilt, and hopelessness led to suicide ideations. Lydia never escaped her childhood abuse and those who victimized her.

Laws and Regulations

LAWS REQUIRING REPORT OF SUSPICION

All 50 states have laws that require the reporting of suspected child abuse or neglect by all healthcare professionals practicing in their profession. Others mandated to report include school personnel, childcare providers, social workers, law enforcement officers, and mental health professionals. All 50 states have passed some form of a mandatory child abuse and neglect reporting law to qualify for funding under the Child Abuse Prevention and Treatment Act (CAPTA) (Jan. 1996 version), 42 U.S.C. 5101, et seq. The act was originally passed in 1974, has been amended several times, and was most recently amended and reauthorized on October 3, 1996, by the Child Abuse Prevention and Treatment and Adoption Act

Amendments of 1996. Healthcare professionals must be knowledgeable of the laws governing their state practice, as each state has its own definitions and particular reporting protocols. The extent of the knowledge triggering the duty to report varies. Some statutes call for reporting on a mere "reasonable cause to believe" or a "reasonable suspicion." Other statutes require the reporter to "know or suspect," which is a higher degree of knowledge. Generally states require that the practitioners report directly to the local health department child protection services.

Purpose of the Report

Despite mandatory reporting laws in all 50 states, some professionals assert reasons for not reporting, such as patient-provider confidentiality protection. All states have eliminated the right of confidentiality when child abuse is suspected (National Clearinghouse on Child Abuse and Neglect Information, 2003b, 2003c). The report helps protect the child and society from any future harm and initiates the process. Other providers are concerned about alienating or angering the parent. The provider must recognize the report is the beginning step to helping the child and family and should tell the accused that a report will be submitted, not an allegation of abuse. The decision to wait and see or give the abuser another chance places the child in jeopardy for additional harm. Additionally, a failure to report can result in civil liability for the healthcare provider.

Content of the Report

An oral report of the suspected child abuse or neglect is made in person or by telephone within 24 hours to the appropriate agency. A written report follows within 72 hours. Reports should be as objective and as complete as possible, including but not limited to the description and nature including the extent of the injury or condition and any evidence to support the findings. Most state laws allow the reporter to photograph (color and black-and-white recommended) and prepare radiographic studies (to rule out unsuspected old and recent fractures) without the consent of the parent or persons responsible for the child when abuse or neglect is suspected.

A thorough examination by a trained sexual assault nurse examiner (SANE) should be done in the case of suspected sexual assault, including objective data collection of gonorrhea cultures, serological tests for syphilis and DNA samples, the application of Wood's light exam to detect seminal fluid, and pregnancy testing. Other testing may be necessary to rule out abuse, such as coagulation studies to test for clotting disorders and neurological examinations.

Descriptions of the child and parent behaviors and interactions are strongly recommended. Documentation must focus on objective observations rather than drawing conclusions. Hearsay literally means information gathered by the first person from a second person concerning some event, condition, or thing of which the first person had no direct experience. When submitted as evidence, such statements are called hearsay evidence. As a legal term, *hearsay* can also have the narrower meaning of the use of such information as evidence to prove the truth of what is asserted. Such use of hearsay evidence in court is generally not allowed. If a child's statements are properly documented as part of a medical examination, they may be admissible in a court proceeding. Experts recommend documenting the questions asked, the direct verbal responses (quotations), and any nonverbal communication and body language. Most states have an exception to the hearsay rule for statements provided to healthcare professionals during diagnostic and treatment sessions.

Documentation is essential from the beginning of any contact with the child or parent. Each visit or event should be documented carefully during and immediately following the contact. Medical records are approved in court as admissible evidence only if they are recorded at or near the time of the contact. These records must describe behaviors, rather than label them. Inconsistencies in facts must be documented to allow the system to determine the facts.

BEST PRACTICE Nurses need to describe behaviors; for example "the child avoided direct eye contact when describing the abuse" versus "the child was circumspect in his description of the event."

FNEs are in a leading position to help other healthcare professionals discover what data may be necessary for collection and how to best document the findings. Documentation of the findings is a critical component of the process and in cases handled out of court, because it provides a baseline for the child protective agency work.

Penalty for Failure to Report

All but five states have laws that include penalties for failure to report suspected child abuse and neglect (National Clearinghouse on Child Abuse and Neglect, 2003b). Currently the criminal liability affixed to mandatory reporting statutes for healthcare providers is hardly more than window dressing, or a vague, unrealized threat. Although the threat of criminal liability has dramatically increased reporting levels, reporting has not nearly maximized its potential. This situation contributes or at least does little to prevent children from suffering at the hands of those entrusted with their care. Increasing the number of prosecutions, however, would help the statutes do what they are meant to do—protect children from the hands of their abusers. Penalties are a criminal offense with fines up to $1000 and can evoke prison sentences up to one year. Criminal charges are basically nonenforceable; however, there are exemplars where it was proved a conscious choice by the reporter to break the law.

Under civil law, two California cases have supported the right of the victim or parents to sue and receive awards for damages resulting from the practitioner's negligence to report. In *Landeros v. Flood* (1976), an eleven-month-old child was taken to a hospital for diagnosis and treatment of a leg fracture and presented with other injuries including multiple bruises and a skull fracture. The child was treated and released home to her mother, with no explanation provided. Later the child was seen again for nonaccidental injuries. The child's subsequent guardian sued the doctor for negligent failure to diagnose and report battered child syndrome. The guardian won the case, and the mother and common-law husband were convicted in a criminal action of child abuse.

In the second California case, *Robinson v. Wical, M.D. et al.* (1970), a young boy was brought to a hospital twice with severe injuries by his mother and her boyfriend. In neither incident did the hospital report suspicion of abuse. A day later, the child was diagnosed at a different hospital with permanent brain damage. The father, who was divorced from the mother, sued the first hospital and doctors for negligence in failure to report suspected abuse. The case was settled out of court for $600,000 awarded to the father.

In an Arkansas case, *Cooper Clinic v. Barnes, (2006)*, the father brought his three-year-old to the walk-in clinic for treatment of a bump on the boy's head. The father said another child had hit him on his head with a golf club. The physician examined the boy. In addition to the large lump on his forehead, his body was covered in bruises and his teeth were chipped and decaying. The physician realized the boy was a battered child. However, she relied on the father's statements that his mother, from whom he was separated, had abused the boy and he, the father, was going to report her to the authorities in the state where she lived. The boy was brought back in for stomach pains, nausea, and vomiting. The same physician did a blood glucose test but did not ask or follow up on the abuse issues. Ten months after his first visit, the boy died from blunt force trauma to his abdomen for which his father and stepmother were convicted of negligent homicide. A civil lawsuit followed against the clinic based on the inaction of the clinic's physician and nurse in the face of their legal duties as mandatory reporters of child abuse. The jury's verdict was $2,500,000.

KEY POINT The nurse should be familiar with the mandatory reporting requirements independent of the patient's consent.

Laws That Provide Immunity Protection

All states provide some type of immunity, if only qualified immunity for protection from legal liability for those who file a report of suspected child abuse (National Clearinghouse on Child Abuse and Neglect, 2003b). Most states provide immunity to those reports submitted in good faith, meaning the reporter believed there were reasonable grounds to suspect child abuse or neglect. It is important to remember the law does not require proof of abuse; reporting is required when a professional has evidence that would lead a reasonable professional to suspect abuse or neglect. Delaying a report until all doubt is eliminated violates the intent of the law.

Approximately half the states have a clause in the law that presumes good faith. In the case of immunity, the plaintiff would have to prove the child abuse report was filed with malicious intent, or possibly with gross negligence (National Clearinghouse on Child Abuse and Neglect, 2003b). This immunity clause generally covers health professionals who take the child into temporary custody.

TEMPORARY HOLDING CUSTODY

State laws provide the right for a physician, nurse practitioner, child protective service personnel, or law enforcement official to take a child into custody for up to 72 hours without prior approval of the parents or guardians, when it is believed the continued residence or care by the child puts the child's life or health in imminent danger.

THE INVESTIGATION

Except in specific cases, the local child protection services agency is responsible for receiving and investigating complaints and reports. The investigation, viewed as a fact-finding mission, is to be initiated within 72 hours of the complaint (National Clearinghouse on Child Abuse and Neglect, 2003b).

DeShaney v. Winnebago County Department of Social Services (1989) questioned whether aggravated negligence by the state in failing to protect a child from physical abuse can amount to an unconstitutional deprivation of liberty for that child under protection of the 14th Amendment (Reidinger, 1989). The lower courts were questioned regarding the state's duty to protect a four-year-old child from his abusive father; even though the state had not assumed custody of the child (a caseworker was closely following the case but had not removed the child from the home). The U.S. Supreme Court ruled in 1990 the state agency's failure to protect the child from the violence did not violate the child's rights under substantive component of the due process clause.

At the time of investigation, the child protection service is not required by law to inform the accused perpetrator of the charges being made, and no state law requires that the investigation be limited to the reported charge (National Clearinghouse on Child Abuse and Neglect, 2003b). However, if an individual has been placed under criminal arrest for charges of child abuse or neglect, no information gathered (including statements or evidence) can be used in a court of law unless the individual has been advised of his or her rights. The members of the military are an exception, since information can be shared.

TESTIMONY AND JUDICIAL HEARINGS

Forensic nurses and other healthcare professionals can best prepare themselves for court with an accurate understanding of the state and federal laws associated with child abuse and neglect. Proper collection and documentation of evidence is essential. Healthcare professionals are frequently called to testify as expert witnesses because they have special skills and education to assess and work with children and families. Thorough review of documents, as well as guidance of an attorney, is recommended before these individuals testify.

In the Pennsylvania case *Commonwealth v. Haber* (1989), the court deemed that judicial creation of the tender years hearsay exception, which provided for the admission of hearsay testimony of sexually abused children, is unjustified on evidentiary and constitutional grounds. The courts may order psychological, psychiatric, and physical examination of a child or parent/guardian.

The U.S. Supreme Court ruled in the case *Coy v. Iowa* (1989) that a defendant has a constitutional right in the Sixth Amendment to confrontation with the accuser (the case specifically dealt with sexual assault). Several other cases have been related to the *Coy v. Iowa* case, including *Kenteek v. Stiner* (1986), in which the U.S. Supreme Court held that a defendant suffered no confrontation clause violation when excluded from in-chambers competency hearings of two minor witnesses. In *Louisiana State v. Murphy* (1989), the court ruled the state's statute, which generalized the presumption that a child victim or sexual abuse victim would suffer trauma as a result of testifying in the presence of the accused, does not outweigh the criminal defendant's right to confrontation.

In civil cases, the preponderance of evidence must establish that the abuse was the fault, by either omission or commission, of the accused at the time the injuries occurred. In criminal cases, the law requires evidence to support the abuse allegation beyond a reasonable doubt. The forensic nurse must recognize the types of evidence required and be clear regarding the standard of care.

Mimicking Injuries

The PFNE makes vital assessments that help to determine if the child requires specific healthcare, protective custody, or other interventions. The evaluation of physical injury in children requires a team approach, and common sense must be used when evaluating the injury and correlating it with the history. The following phenomena may be confused with child abuse.

Mongolian spots are benign flat congenital birthmarks with wavy borders and irregular shape, most common among East Asians and Turks. They are also extremely prevalent among East Africans and Native Americans. They normally disappear three to five years after birth and almost always by puberty. The most common color is blue, although they can be blue-gray, blue-black, or even deep brown. Approximately 90% of African Americans have such spots. These spots can also be found in Asian, Hispanic, and other children with pigmented skin. These darkened areas are congenital and commonly found on the lower back and buttocks but may occur anywhere. They do not sequentially change colors as bruises tend to, but they often are mistaken to be the result of trauma when initially observed.

Impetigo contagiosa is a bacterial, inflammatory skin disease characterized by the appearance of pustules in which the developing vesicles do not rupture but progress to form bullae, which collapse and become covered with crusts. Sometimes occurring epidemically in hospital nurseries and schools, the disease may mimic cigarette burns and be suspected as abuse (Bays, 1994).

Osteogenesis imperfecta (OI, and sometimes known as *brittle bone disease*) is a genetic bone disorder. People with OI are born without the proper protein (collagen) or the ability to make it. People with OI either have less collagen than normal or the quality is poorer than normal. As collagen is an important protein in bone structure, this impairment causes those with the condition to have weak or fragile bones. This disease is often misunderstood and misdiagnosed as child abuse. Signs may include a tendency to bruise easily; hearing impairment; excessive laxity of joints (Silence, 1988); sclera with a blue, purple, or gray tint; and a tendency toward spinal curvature. A punch biopsy of the skin for analysis of collagen synthesis is an important test to rule out or confirm OI (Bays, 1994).

Coining and spooning is a Southeast Asian healthcare practice that is commonly misinterpreted as child abuse. It is a cultural healing method where warmed oil or ointment is applied and then rubbed with the edge of a coin or spoon in a linear/streaking fashion, usually on the chest or back. The repetitive rubbing causes multiple erythematous/petechial bruise marks or welts (Nielsen, 2009).

KEY POINT There are conditions that mimic abuse, and these must be carefully differentiated during the examination processes to prevent false accusations of child abuse.

Summary

The United Nations Convention on the Rights of Children (1989) stated, "Mankind owes to the child the best it has to give." Without early identification and intervention to interrupt the cyclical nature of abuse, the surviving child will be most often damaged in the overt or covert results of human abuse. Often, this cyclical behavior is referred to as the three-generational pattern of abuse: perpetuating abuse of one generation onto the next, from child abuse to intimate partner abuse and into the most recent phase of interpersonal crime, abuse of the elderly. Forensic specialists in nursing will promote the necessary expert skills and insight to the eradication of maltreatment and abuse against children. The sequelae of childhood abuse incorporate a variety of consequent symptoms in the living and validation of suspected overt or covert violence in the deceased.

Health professionals must understand federal and state laws in order to protect children and avoid negligence charges against themselves. Forensic experts are in a key position to educate healthcare providers on creating a safe environment where appropriate assessment, collection, and documentation techniques routinely occur. Nurses need to be prepared when a child is ready to disclose. As continued research is conducted and investigators analyze their findings in an attempt to reach statistical significance, it is important to remember that providing protection and safety for even one child is significant.

Resources

CHILD ABUSE HOTLINES: WHERE TO CALL TO GET HELP OR REPORT ABUSE

If you suspect a child is in immediate danger contact law enforcement as soon as possible.

To get help in the United States, call:

1-800-4-A-CHILD (1-800-422-4453)–Childhelp National Child Abuse Hotline

To get help for child sexual abuse, call:

1-888-PREVENT (1-888-773-8368) –Stop It Now

1-800-656-HOPE Rape, Abuse & Incest National Network (RAINN)

ORGANIZATIONS

National Center for Missing and Exploited Children

Charles B. Wang International Children's Building, 699 Prince Street, Alexandria, VA 22914-3175; 703-295-3900, 800-THE-LOST www.missingkids.com.

References

Bays, J. (1994). Conditions mistaken for child abuse. In R. M. Reece (Ed.), *Child abuse: Medical diagnosis and management* (pp. 358–385). Philadelphia: Lea and Febiger.

Belsky, J. (1980). Child maltreatment: An ecological integration. *American Psychologist, 35*, 320–335.

Belsky, J. (1993). Etiology of child maltreatment: A developmental-ecological analysis. *Psychological Bulletin, 114*, 413–434.

Bowman, L., & Hargrove, T. (2007). *Exposing sudden infant death in America.* Scripps Howard News Service. retrieved Aug, 4, 2009, www./dailycamera.com/news/2007/oct/08/saving-babies-exposing-sudden-infant-death-in.

Brown, M. (1997). Dilemmas facing nurses who care for Munchausen syndrome by proxy patients. *Pediatric Nursing, 29*(4), 416–421.

Burgess, A., Holstorn, C., & McCausland, M. (1977). Child sexual assault by a family member: Decisions following disclosure. *Victimology, 2*(2), 296–1250.

Cooper Clinic V Barnes. (2006). S.W. 3d, WL 1644635. Arkansas.

Corby, B. (1993). *Child abuse: Towards a knowledge base.* Buckingham: Open University Press.

Cowen, P. (1999). Child neglect: Injuries of omission. *Pediatric Nursing, 25*(4), 401–430.

De Paul, J., & Guibert, M. (2008). Empathy and child neglect: A theoretical model. *Child Abuse & Neglect, 32*(11), 1058–1062.

DeShanney, v. Winnebago County Department of Social Services. (1989). (109 S. Ct. 998).

Duncan, R. D. (1999). Peer and sibling aggression. An investigation of intra- and extra-family bullying. *Journal of Interpersonal Violence, 14*(8), 871–886.

Elliott, D. M., & Briere, J. (1994). Forensic sexual abuse evaluations of older children: Disclosures and symptomatology. *Behavioral Sciences and the Law, 12*, 261–277.

Estes, R. J. (2001). *The sexual exploitation of children: A working guide to the empirical literature.* Philadelphia: University of Pennsylvania, School of Social Work.

Feldman, M. (2004). *Playing sick?: Untangling the web of Münchausen syndrome, Münchausen by proxy, malingering & factitious disorder.* Philadelphia: Brunner-Routledge.

Finkelhor, D. (1998). Improving research, policy, and practice to understand child sexual abuse. *JAMA, 280*(21), 1864–1865.

Finn, C. K. (2008). *Forensic nurses' experience of receiving child abuse disclosure* (Doctoral dissertation, University of Colorado Denver, 2008).

Flaherty, E., Sege, R., & Binns, H. J. (2000). Healthcare providers' experience reporting child abuse in the primary care setting. *Arch Pediatric Add Medicine, 154*(5), 489–493.

Giardino, A. P., Christian, C. V., & Giardino, E. R. (1997). *A practical guide to the evaluation of child physical abuse and neglect.* Thousand Oaks, CA: Sage Publications.

Green, B. F., & Kilili, S. (1998). How good does a parent have to be? Issues and examples associated with empirical assessments of parental adequacy in cases of child abuse and neglect. In J. R. Lutzker (Ed.), *Handbook of child abuse research and treatment.* New York: Plenum Press.

Hamby, S., & Finkelhor, D. (2000). The victimization of children: Recommendations for assessment and instrument development. *Journal of the American Academy of Child & Adolescent Psychiatry, 39*(7), 829–840.

Hammer, R. M., Moynihan, B., & Pagliaro, E. M. (2006). *Forensic Nursing: A Handbook For Practice.* Sudbury, MA: Jones and Bartlett Publishers.

Hart, S. N., & Brassard, M. R. (1987). A major threat to children's mental health: Psychological maltreatment. *American Psychologist, 42*, 160–165.

Helfer, R. (1990). The neglect of our children. *Pediatric Clinics of North America, 37*(4), 929–942.

Helpguide. (2008). retrieved Aug 4, 2009 . www.helpguide.org/mental/child_abuse_physical_emotional_sexual_neglect.htm.

Herman-Giddens, M., Brown, G., Verbiest, S., Carlson, P., Hooten, E., Howell, E., et al. (1999). Under ascertainment of child abuse mortality in the United States. *JAMA, 282*(5), 463–467.

Hobbs, C. J., Hanks, H. G. I., & Wynne, J. M.(Eds). (1993). *Child abuse and neglect: A clinician's handbook.* Edinburgh, Scotland: Churchill Livingston.

Hockenbery, M. J., Wilson, D., Winkelstein, M. L., et al. (2002). *Wong's nursing care of infants and children.* St. Louis: Mosby Company.

Holter, J. C. (1979). Child Abuse. *Nurse Clin North Am, 14*(3), 417–429.

Houxley, P., & Warner, R. (1993). Primary prevention of parenting dysfunction in high risk cases. *American Journal of Orthopsychiatry, 63*(4), 582–588.

Howze, D. C., & Kotch, J. B. (1984). Disentangling life events, stress and social support: Implications for the primary prevention of child abuse and neglect. *Child abuse and neglect, 8*(4), 401–409.

Insurance Institute for Highway Safety. (2009). *Child restraint laws.* Retrieved January 4, 2009, from www.iihs.org/laws/ChildRestraint.aspx.

Janssen, M. R. (1984). Incest: Exploitive child abuse. *The Police Chief, 51*, 46–47.

Johnson, H., & Au Coin, C. (Eds). (2004). Statistics Canadian Center for Justice Statistics, Family Violence in Canada: A statistical profile, 2003.. Published by the authority of the minister responsible for statistics in Canada. Minister of Industry 2003. June 2003. Ottawa

Keltner, D., Capps, L., Kring, A. M., Young, R. C., & Heerey, E. A. (2001). Just teasing: A conceptual analysis and empirical review. *Psychological Bulletin, 129*(2), 229–248.

Kempe, C. H., Silverman, F. N., & Steele, B. P. (1962). The battered-child syndrome. *JAMA*, (1), 105–112.

Landeros, v. Flood. (1976). (51 P. 2nd 3889).

Lerman, R. (2002). Wedding bells ring in stability and economic gains for mothers and children. Retrieved August, 4, 2009, www.urban.org/Template.cfm?NavMenualD=24&template+TaggerCotent/ViewPublication.cfm&Publication ID-7858.

Lowell, G., Quinlan, K., & Gottlieb, L. J. (2008). Preventing unintentional scald burns: Moving beyond tap water. *Pediatrics, 122*(4), 799–804.

Lynch, V. A. (1997). *Clinical forensic nursing: A new perspective in trauma and medicolegal investigation of death.* Fort Collins, CO: Bearhawk Consulting Group.

Marshall, W., & Locke, C. (1997). Statewide survey of physician attitudes to controversies about child abuse. *Child Abuse and Neglect, 21*(2), 171–179.

McCauley, J., Kem, D. E., & Kolonder, K. (1997). Clinical characteristics of women with a history of childhood abuse: Unhealed wounds. *JAMA, 277*(17), 1362–1368.

Milner, J. (1993). Social information processing and physical child abuse. *Clinical Psychology Review, 13*, 295–1294.

Moorhead, C. (1997). All the world's children. *Index on Censorship, 2*, 51–160.

Nansel, T. R., Overpeck, M., Pilla, R. S., Ruan, W. J., Simons-Morton, B., & Scheidt, P. (2001). Bullying behaviors among US youth. *JAMA, 285*(16), 2094–2100.

National Child Abuse and Neglect Data System. (2003). *Services to prevent child maltreatment.* Retrieved April 18, 2005, from www.acf.dhhs.gov/programs/cb/ststs/ncands97/s11.htm.

National Clearinghouse on Child Abuse and Neglect. (2003a). *Definitions of child abuse.* U.S. Department of Health and Human Services. Retrieved August 3, 2009, from http://nccanch.acf.hhs.gov/general/legal/statutes/define.cfm.

National Clearinghouse on Child Abuse and Neglect. (2003b). *2003 Child abuse and neglect state statute series statutes at a glance: Mandatory reporters of child abuse and neglect.* Retrieved August 3, 2009 http://www.acf.dhhs.gov/programs/cb/ststs/ncands97/s11.htm.

National Clearinghouse on Child Abuse and Neglect. (2003c). *2003 Child abuse and neglect state statute series ready reference: Reporting laws: Immunity for reporters.* U.S. Department of Health and Human Services. Retrieved August 3, 2009 http://nccanch.acf.hhs.gov.

National Clearinghouse on Child Abuse and Neglect. (2004). *Children and domestic violence.* Retrieved August 3, 2009 http://nccanch.acf.hhs.gov/general/legal/statutes/domviol.cfm

National Infant Sleep Position Household Survey. (2007). *Summary Data 2006.* Retrieved August 3, 2009 http://dccwww.bumc.bu.edu/ChimeNisp/NISP_Data.asp

National Institute of Neurological Disorders and Stroke [NINDS]. (2008). *Shaken Baby Information Page.* Retrieved August 3, 2009 www.ninds.nih.gov/disorders/shakenbaby/shakenbaby.htm

National Institutes of Health. (2008). *NINDS Shaken Baby Syndrome Information Page.* Retrieved January 4, 2009, from www.nidnds.hih.gov/disorders/shakenbaby/shakenbaby.htm.

Nester, C. (1998). Prevention of child abuse and neglect in the primary care setting. *The Nurse Practitioner, 29*(9), 61–73.

Nielsen, A. (2009). Guasha research and the language of integrative medicine. *Journal of Bodywork and Movement Therapies, 13*(1), 63–72.

O'Keefe, v. Osoui. (Cook County Circuit Court, N. 70L-14884).

Pasqualone, G., & Fitzgerald, S. (1999). Munchausen by Proxy Syndrome: The forensic challenge of recognition, diagnosis, and reporting. *Critical Care Nursing Quarterly, 22*(1), 52–64.

Penn, Schoen, Berland (1999). *How America defines child abuse.* National survey for Los Angeles-based Children's Institute International. Retrieved August 3, 2009 www.childreninstitute.org/publications.html.

Peterson, M., & Urquiza, A. (1993). *The role of mental health professionals in the prevention and treatment of child abuse and neglect.* Washington, DC: US Department of Health and Human Services.

Pyrek, K. M. (2006). *Forensic nursing.* Boca Raton, FL: CRC Press.

Reidinger, V., DeShaney (1989). Winnebago County Department of Social Services 489 U.S. 189. 812 F.2d 298 (7th Cir., 1987).

Ricci, L. R., & Botash, A. S. (2002). Pediatrics, child abuse. *eMedicine, 3*(4). Retrieved April 17, 2005, from www.emedicine.com/emerg/topics368.htm.

Robinson, v. Wical. (1970). (3 Cal. S.Ct.).

Sachs, B., & Hall, L. (1991). Maladaptive mother-child relationships: A pilot study. *Pub Health Nurs, 8*, 226–293.

Schmitt, B., & Mauro, R. (1989). Nonorganic failure to thrive: An outpatient approach. *Child Abuse & Neglect, 13*(4), 248–295.

Schuster, M., Wood, D. L., Duan, N., et al. (1998). Utilization of well-child services for African-American infants in a low-income community. *Pediatrics, 101*(6), 999–1005.

Silence, D. (1988). Osteogenesis Imperfecta nosology and genetics. *Annals of the New York Academy of Science, 543*, 1–15.

Simonelli, C. J., Mullis, T., Elliott, A. N., et al. (2002). Abuse by siblings and subsequent experiences of violence within the dating relationship. *J Interpersonal Violence, 17*(2), 103–121.

Smith, R. L., & Smith, T. M. (2001). *Ecology and Field Biology.* (6th ed.). New York: Benjamin Cummings.

Sorenson, T., & Snow, B. (1991). How children tell: The process of disclosure in child sexual abuse. *Child welfare, LXX*, 3–15.

Spenser, D. (2000). Sibling abuse. *Times Educational Supplement*, (4405), 20.

Stower, S. (2000). The principles and practice of child protection. *Nursing Standard, 14*(17), 48–56.

Suggs, A., Lichenstein, C., McCarthy, et al. (2001). Child Abuse/Assault. In J. S. Olshaker, et al. (Eds.), *Forensic emergency medicine* (pp. 161). Philadelphia: Lippincott Williams & Wilkins.

Thali, M. (2003). Bite mark documentation and analysis: the forensic 3D/CAD supported photogrammetry approach. *Forensic Science International, 135*(2), 115–121.

Trokel, M., Wadimmba, A., Griffith, J., & Sege, R. (2006). Variation in the diagnosis of child abuse in severely injured infants. *Pediatrics, 117*(3), 1–7.

U. S. Department of Health & Human Services (USDHHS), Administration on Children, Youth and Families. (2009). *Child maltreatment 2007.* Washington, DC: U.S. Government Printing Office.

U. S. Department of Health and Human Services. (2008). *National Symposium on the Health Needs of Human Trafficking Victims.* Retrieved August 3, 2009 www.acf.hhs.gov/trafficking/campaign_kits/index.html.

Walton-Moss, B. J., Manganello, J., Frye, V., & Campbell, J. C. (2005). Risk factors for intimate partner violence and associated injury among women. *Journal of Community Health, 30*(5), 377–389.

Wiehe, V. (1997). *Sibling Abuse: Hidden, Physical, Emotional, and Sexual Trauma.* (2nd ed.). Thousand Oaks, CA: Sage Publications.

Willis, B., & Levy, B. (2003). Child prostitution: Global health burden, research needs, and interventions. *Lancet, 359*(5), 1417–1422.

CHAPTER 30 Elder Maltreatment: Forensic Biomarkers

Catherine Pearsall

Background

Elder maltreatment is one of the most underdiagnosed and under-reported problems in society, and as such it presents as an integral challenge for the forensic nurse. Although there has been some attention and research directed toward elder maltreatment in recent years, relatively little is known about its characteristics, causes, or consequences or about effective means of management and prevention. Little information is available regarding the true extent of elder abuse, in large part because surveillance is limited and the problem remains hidden (National Center on Elder Abuse, 2005). Victims are often reluctant to reveal abuse due to shame, self-blame, denial, fear of reprisal, or a desire for privacy (Hirsch, Strattan, & Loewy, 1999). Discussion of elder abuse first appeared in the literature in the 1960s (Lachs & Pillemer,1995). Researchers have attempted to determine the prevalence and clinical scope of this phenomenon since that time.

Elder Maltreatment Statistics

The National Center on Elder Abuse (2005) has reported that, annually, between 1 million and 2 million Americans aged 65 and older have been the victims of abuse or mistreatment by someone on whom they depend for their care or protection. The frequency estimates vary between 2% to 10% and are based on diverse sampling, methodologies, and case definitions. In domestic settings, data suggest that only one in fourteen incidents, excluding self-neglect cases, are brought to the attention of authorities. It is further estimated that for every case of elder maltreatment reported to authorities, approximately five more go unreported (National Center on Elder Abuse, 2005). This problem will most likely increase in magnitude, as the elderly population increases (Bonnie & Wallace, 2003).

According to the Department of Health and Human Services, the population identified as persons 65 years or older numbered 37.3 million in 2006, an increase of 10% since 1996. This represents 12.4% of the total population of the United States and equals approximately one in every eight Americans (Administration on Aging, 2008). The United States Census Bureau population statistics project that by the year 2050, this population will number approximately 80 million. The highest percentage of population growth is projected to be for those 85 and older as it is estimated that this population will more than triple from the 5.4 million in 2008 to 19 million in 2050 (U.S. Census Bureau, 2008). Unfortunately, those 85 years or more suffer abuse and neglect two to three times their proportion of the total elder population (National Center on Elder Abuse, 1998). Life expectancy of people born in the United States has been rising throughout the past century, and as the population ages, so does the incidence of age-related diseases and disabilities (Bonnie & Wallace, 2003). The risks of experiencing abuse and mistreatment increase as individuals age and become frail (Lachs, Williams, O'Brien, Pillemer, & Charlson, 1998); as such, forensic nurses should anticipate an increase in the number of cases of elder maltreatment.

BEST PRACTICE The forensic nurse should assess all elderly patients for signs and symptoms of maltreatment, neglect, self-neglect, and financial exploitation.

The first ever National Elder Abuse Incidence Study (NEAIS) reported that based on a national estimate, 449,924 elderly persons aged 60 and over, experienced abuse and/or neglect in domestic settings in 1996 (National Center on Elder Abuse, 1998). Of this total, 70,942 (16%) were reported to and substantiated by adult protective services (APS); however, the remaining 378,982 (84%) were not reported to APS. The estimated number rises to 551,011 elderly individuals, ages 60 and over, when self-neglect is added to the equation. Of this total, 115,110 (21%) were reported and substantiated by APS, and the remaining 435,901 (79%) were not reported to APS. These results confirmed the "tip of the iceberg" theory of elder abuse. According to this theory, official reporting agencies such as APS are alerted to the most visible cases of abuse and neglect. However, large numbers of incidents remain unidentified and unreported. In the NEAIS, community sentinels were solicited for information on their professional encounters with elderly clients and contacts (National Center on Elder Abuse, 1998). Case information was obtained from local adult protective service agencies as well as from specifically trained groups of individuals known as "sentinels" who were drawn from agencies such as law enforcement agencies, senior citizen programs, banking institutions, hospitals, and clinics that serve the elderly. The "sentinel" approach has been employed in three federally sponsored child abuse surveys. The assumption that underlies this approach is that reported cases reveal the proverbial tip of the iceberg and that many community cases are never reported. Yet even this estimate is considered to be low, as many abused elderly are homebound and isolated and not seen in settings such as banks, senior centers, hospitals, or police stations where sentinels would identify them (Wolf, 2000).

KEY POINT Elder maltreatment is one of the most underdiagnosed and under-reported problems in society.

Elder Maltreatment Definition Controversy

The greatest impediment to epidemiological research in elder abuse is the differing definitions of elder abuse and maltreatment itself (Lachs & Pillemer, 1995). Definitions and legal terms vary from state to state. Many states, for example, include self-neglect in their statutes and reporting statistics when describing the elderly who are living alone in the community and are unable to provide for themselves that which is necessary for physical or mental well-being. Some argue that these individuals should not be included in epidemiological studies of abuse of elderly persons; however, they account for a substantial proportion of the APS caseload (Lachs & Pillemer, 1995). Researchers have used various definitions of elder abuse and maltreatment. Many estimates of the frequency of elder abuse involve prevalence studies, and they are difficult to compare because of the differences in definitions, sample characteristics, and methodologies used (Kleinschmidt, 1997). Even the age of an "elder" is in question, as some researchers identify age 60 and above as elderly, whereas others include only those individuals over the age of 65.

Literature indicates that the prevalence and perception of elder abuse, and thus how one defines abuse, may differ by ethnic and cultural group. Limited inquiry has been made into this research arena, which further influences statistical analysis (Wieland, 2000). Wieland listed two reasons for this knowledge gap: most studies include predominately or exclusively white samples, and ethnic group identity has not typically been viewed as a variable in elder abuse research. The United States is a multicultural society, so definitions for what constitutes elder mistreatment may differ drastically among various cultural groups.

One of the foremost challenges confronting forensic nurses is the need to develop an objective definition of what characterizes elder maltreatment.

Categories of Elder Maltreatment

Kleinschmidt reviewed 21 studies and identified four general types or categories of elder abuse identified in the literature: physical, emotional, financial, and neglect. Some researchers included sexual abuse in the physical abuse category, whereas others expanded the category list and included a separate category for sexual abuse. In addition, some researchers added yet another separate category for self-neglect (Kleinschmidt, 1997).

PHYSICAL ABUSE

Physical violence or abuse is an act that is carried out with the intent of causing physical pain or injury such as hitting, grabbing, slapping, pushing, or other bodily injury and that may result in sprains, bruises, abrasions, skeletal fractures, burns, and other wounds (Lachs & Pillemer, 1995). Some researchers also include sexual abuse within their definitions of physical abuse (Kleinschmidt, 1997).

PSYCHOLOGICAL/EMOTIONAL ABUSE

Psychological or emotional abuse is commonly listed as a category of mistreatment (Lachs & Pillemer, 1995). This includes verbal or nonverbal insults, humiliation, or infantilization (Kleinschmidt, 1997) and is often defined as an act carried out with the intention of causing emotional pain or injury. Psychological abuse often accompanies physical abuse (Lachs & Pillemer, 1995).

FINANCIAL ABUSE

Material exploitation or the misappropriation of money or property is the third category identified in the literature. This would include the theft of social security or pension checks, coercion in financial matters, and threats to enforce the signing or changing of legal documents such as wills or deeds (Lachs & Pillemer, 1995). Some researchers restrict this definition to only illegal or improper use of only specific government benefits, and often this form of elder mistreatment is not addressed in studies on elder abuse (Kleinschmidt, 1997). It is estimated that only 1 in 25 cases of financial exploitation is reported, which suggests that annually there may be as many as 5 million financial abuse victims (National Center on Elder Abuse, 2005).

NEGLECT

Neglect is often defined as the failure of a designated caregiver to meet the needs of an elder who depends on that individual's care. Neglect may be further divided into intentional neglect, where there is a deliberate failure in caregiving responsibilities with the intent to harm or punish an elder, or unintentional, which may be the result of ignorance or incapability to provide care (Lachs & Pillemer, 1995). Intent is a difficult concept to prove. This presents a problem in the literature, as intent-based definitions may technically not exist because intent may not be proved (Kleinschmidt, 1997). Some researchers consider abandonment a form of neglect (Kleinschmidt, 1997). Much of the controversy that surrounds the conceptual definition of elder abuse focuses on the issue of neglect. Cases of neglect raise difficult questions regarding who the responsible caregiver is, what the specific responsibilities are to the neglected individual, and whether this neglect was intentional or unintentional (Lachs & Pillemer, 1995).

SELF-NEGLECT

The area of self-neglect is occasionally discussed in elder abuse research as a category of elder abuse. This is often defined as an act being conducted by an elder that threatens that individual's health or safety as in an individual who has difficulty performing activities of daily living and refuses assistance despite resulting problems (Kleinschmidt, 1997).

SEXUAL ABUSE

Sexual abuse is defined as nonconsensual intimate contact. Elderly are at particular risk for sexual maltreatment as they may be too weak to resist assaults or they may be unable to recognize or report the abuse because of cognitive deficiencies (Kleinschmidt, 1997).

OTHER

The National Aging Resource Center on Elder Abuse (NARCEA) has suggested that states use a separate category called "all other types." This would include violation of rights, medical abuse, and abandonment (Kleinschmidt, 1997).

An argument exists that in our attempt to subdivide elder abuse into categories to assign blame, we are ignoring the needs of the victims themselves and that emphasis and resources should be directed to improving functions and quality of life. In response to this argument, many researchers choose to avoid the terms *abuse* and *neglect* and instead refer to the problem as the *mistreatment of the elderly* or the *inadequate care of the elderly,* which includes both the acts of omission and commission (Lachs & Pillemer, 1995).

Cause of Elder Abuse and Maltreatment

No one explanation for the cause of elder abuse exists. Abuse is a complex problem that is rooted in multiple factors. Fulmer, Guadagno, Bitondo, Dyer, and Connolly identified five theories worthy of further exploration:

- The situational theory adopts the belief that increasing caregiver overburden and demands creates the environment for mistreatment.
- The exchange theory speaks to the long-term dynamics between an elder and the perpetrator.
- The social learning theory espouses that mistreatment is a learned behavior and is influenced by environment.
- Political economic theory concentrates on the challenges of role changes as one ages.
- The psychopathology of the caregiver theory explores the caregiver's mental health status and how that places an elder at risk for maltreatment.

Unfortunately, few studies have tested these theories (Fulmer et al., 2004).

Despite the popular image of elder abuse occurring in a setting of a dependent victim and an overstressed caregiver, there is accumulating evidence that it is neither caregiver stress levels nor the dependence level of the victim that are the core factors leading to elder abuse. It is now felt that stress may be a contributing factor in abuse cases, but this does not explain the phenomenon. Recent studies on the relationships between caregiver stress, Alzheimer's disease, and elder abuse suggest that it is the long-term or preabuse nature of the relationships that is the important factor in predicting instances of maltreatment. The mental status of the perpetrator (which includes emotional, psychiatric, and substance abuse problems), the dependency of the perpetrator on the victim, and the lack of outside-the-home external support for the victim continue to emerge as elder abuse risk factors (Wolf, 2000).

Anetzberger discussed the complexity of elder abuse and the results of prior studies, which suggest that the etiology of elder abuse is multifaceted and that caregiver stress and burden is not the only dominant risk factor. She stressed that the reality of elder abuse demands the development of new explanatory and intervention models (Anetzberger, 2000). A number of sociodemographic factors have been identified as possible contributors to elder abuse. Levine (2003) listed the following factors: intrafamily stressors (including separation, divorce, and financial strain), ageism, increased life expectancy, and medical advances that have prolonged years lived with chronic disease.

Elders are abused in homes, hospitals, nursing homes, and in other institutions. Prevalence or incidence data on elder abuse in institutional settings are lacking despite the vast existing literature on issues of quality of care. A survey conducted in one U.S. state reported that 36% of nursing and support staff reported had witnessed at least one incident of physical abuse by another staff member during the prior year, and 10% admitted to having committed at least one act of physical abuse themselves (Wolf, 2000). A cross-sectional retrospective chart review of new in- and outpatients conducted by a Montreal General Hospital Division of Geriatric Psychiatry in one calendar year studied the prevalence and correlates of four types of elder abuse and neglect in a geriatric psychiatry service (Vida, Monks, & Des Rosiers, 2002) Although this study was limited by a clinically derived and a relatively small sample size of 126 patients, it was reported that elder abuse and neglect was suspected or confirmed in 16% of patients studied.

Living with nonspouse family, friends, or other persons in a nonsupervised setting, along with a history of family disruptions by widowhood, divorce, or separation were significantly correlated with abuse, whereas statistically nonsignificant yet potentially important identifiers included female gender, alcohol abuse, and low functional status.

Most elder abuse and neglect takes place in the home and is inflicted by family, household members, and paid caregivers (Smith, 2002). Elders are most at risk from family members. The perpetrator is a family member in two thirds of known cases of abuse and neglect, and these family members were identified as adult children or spouses (National Center on Elder Abuse, 1998).

A cohort of 2812 community-dwelling adults over the age of 65 from the New Haven Established Population for Epidemiologic Studies in the Elderly were studied to determine the risk factors and prevalence of APS utilization by older adults in an 11-year longitudinal study (Lachs, Williams, O'Brien, Hurst, & Horwitz, 1996). Referral to the state ombudsman on aging for protective services was the main outcome measure. The prevalence of APS use was 6.4% over the 11-year period. Self-neglect was the main indicator for referral, accounting for 73% of the cases. Elder mistreatment, poverty, minority status, functional disability, and worsening cognitive impairment were found to be risk factors for reported elder abuse.

A case-controlled study conducted in Baylor College of Medicine Geriatrics Clinic in Texas sought to describe the characteristics of abused or neglected patients and to compare the prevalence of depression and dementia in those referred because of neglect with that of those referred for other reasons (Dyer, Pavlik, Murphy, & Hyman, 2000). This institution provides interdisciplinary geriatric assessment and intervention to older people in Harris County. Forty-seven elders in this survey were referred to the clinic because of neglect, whereas 97 were referred for other reasons. A total of 45 cases of abuse or neglect were identified of which 37 (82%) were diagnosed with self-neglect and 7 experienced multiple types of abuse and neglect (2 cases of caregiver neglect with self-neglect, 2 cases of abuse with self-neglect, 2 cases of caregiver neglect and abuse, and 1 case of all three forms of abuse and neglect). A statistically significant higher prevalence of depression (62% versus 12%) and dementia (51% versus 30%) was reported in victims of self-neglect compared to patients referred for other reasons, which suggests that geriatric clinicians should assess for neglect or abuse in their depressed or demented elder patients (Dyer et al., 2000).

One study investigated community characteristics associated with elder abuse by analyzing county level data, which included county-level population adjusted numbers of abused elderly, abused children, children in poverty, high school dropouts, physicians and other healthcare providers, hospital beds, social workers, and caseworkers in the Department of Human Services; subjects from 99 counties in Iowa between 1984 and 1993 were studied to identify the relationship between elder abuse rates and county demographics (Jogerst, Dawson, Hartz, Ely, & Schweitzer, 2000). The study concluded that county demographics such as population density, children in poverty, and reported child abuse were the community characteristics associated with an increased rate of elder abuse. Reported incidence of child abuse was identified as having the strongest correlation.

There is a dire need to further explore and empirically test existing theories and to create tested theoretical models that can be utilized in clinical practice.

Elder Abuse Detection

Elder abuse is difficult to detect, as some elderly experience social isolation. However, even the most isolated elderly individuals may come in contact with the healthcare system at some point in time. Elderly patients visit their primary care providers an average of five times per year, yet primary care providers constitute only a small percentage of the cases reported to APS (Harrell, Toronjo, McLaughlin, Pavlik, Hyman, & Bitondo Dyer, 2002). For a dependent elder, the primary care provider may be the only opportunity for abuse detection, yet, unfortunately, many primary care providers attribute the medical findings that may, in fact, signal abuse to aging or an underlying disease (Hirsch et al., 1999). An analysis of the state of Michigan's records of reported cases of suspected adult abuse for the years 1989–1993 revealed that physicians reported an average of only 2% of all reports of suspected elder abuse and that physician reporting rates were highest in small counties with low physician-to-population ratios (Rosenblatt, Cho, & Durance, 1996). It was suggested that increasing physician awareness of the problem of elder abuse could increase the number of cases screened for potential abuse and, as such, increase the number of elder abuse reports to responsible agencies (Rosenblatt et al., 1996).

Few studies have specifically examined the barriers to elder abuse detection and reporting by primary care providers. Krueger and Patterson surveyed family physicians to determine their perceptions of barriers and strategies in the effective detection and appropriate management of abused elders. A lack of knowledge about the prevalence and definition of elder abuse, denial of abuse, resistance to intervention, lack of protocols, and lack of guidelines regarding confidentiality were identified as important barriers to detection (Krueger & Patterson, 1997).

FORENSIC BIOMARKERS

Healthcare or legal professionals are often not witnesses to elder abuse. Therefore, the legal system relies on other reporters and evidence to identify the existence of abuse. Most extreme and heinous cases of mistreatment can be easily identified as abuse, for example, gunshot wounds, knife wounds, bite marks, and rope burns. The majority of cases, however, are not as clear cut because they may mimic or be mistaken for physiological and psychological changes that occur with age (Dyer, Connolly, & McFeeley, 2003), as elders respond differently from younger individuals in their response to injury (Centers for Disease Control and Prevention, 2001). In addition, elders recover at a slower rate from even minor injuries because of the age effect on the body's ability to respond to injury and the disruption of physiological balance (Brown, Streubert, & Burgess, 2004). A research gap exists in the literature, as there is a paucity of primary research data regarding forensic markers of elder abuse (Dyer et al., 2003). The use of forensic markers may help evaluate elder abuse (Pearsall, 2005). Forensic markers include abrasions, lacerations, bruising, fractures, restraints, decutiti, weight loss, dehydration, burns, cognitive and mental health problems, hygiene issues, burns, and sexual abuse (Bonnie & Wallace, 2003). A discussion regarding potential forensic markers in each of the categories of elder abuse follows (Pearsall, 2005).

PHYSICAL ABUSE

Numerous forensic markers have been identified through research that may signal the occurrence of elder physical abuse and maltreatment. These may include bruises, abrasions, lacerations, and fractures.

Blunt force trauma with associated rupture of small blood vessels under the skin without breaking the skin, results in the superficial discoloration of the skin commonly known as a bruise (Dyer et al., 2003) or a contusion (Brown, Streubert, & Burgess 2004). Blood escapes into the surrounding tissues and can track through fascial planes, resulting in bruising apart from the site of injury. Generally, with age, the blood vessels become easier to rupture (Dix, 2000). A bruise can become noticeable hours or days after an initial trauma. Eyelids, neck, and scrotum are very susceptible to enduring a bruise. In the elderly, bruises occur more frequently and resolve more slowly than in a younger person and can last for months rather then weeks (Dyer et al., 2003). Elder skin is fragile because with age it becomes thin, loose, and transparent with a decreased vascularity and atrophy. In addition, elders bruise under less force than do younger individuals (Brown et al., 2004). There is currently no way to determine exactly the amount of force needed to produce a bruise (Dix, 2000).

KEY POINT Normal changes of the skin such as capillary fragility and friability are associated with aging, and illness may mimic trauma of abuse. Bilateral bruising on the upper arms often indicates abuse involving shaking, pushing, or restraining.

A classic study that was inspired by a case of child abuse looked at the question of the aging of a bruise (Langlois & Gresham, 1991). The goal was to determine whether it was possible to establish the age of a bruise by its appearance. Photographs were obtained of bruises using high-definition color film from three sources: patients presenting to the emergency department, inpatients, and staff. Only bruises where case and age were known were used. Photographs were obtained in sequence from the time of appearance to resolution whenever possible. These were then assessed for the presence of particular colors, and data were collected. A total of 369 photographs were obtained from 89 subjects with an age range of 10 to 100 years spanning a five-month period of time. The main colors that were noted were blue, red, yellow, and purple/black. Frequency of occurrence of each color was determined within each time interval for the two age groups and for the two age groups combined. Red was found to be commonly present in all age groups, whereas purple/black was less commonly seen. Yellow was found not to be present in bruises within the first two time intervals (0 to 6 hours and 7 to 18 hours), whereas it was observed with increasing frequency in the 157- to 288-hour time frame. The appearance of a yellow coloration was found to be highly significant, as a yellow bruise was very likely to be more than 18 hours old. Elders (individuals over the age of 65), showed a slower development of yellow color. Bilirubin, which is the result of hemoglobin metabolism, has been attributed to the yellow coloration in a bruise. Red, blue, and purple/black appeared anytime from within one hour of bruising to resolution of up to 21 days (Langlois & Gresham, 1991). The issue of whether a bruise on an elderly victim can be accurately aged by appearance remains controversial. This issue is currently under investigation. An accurate description of observed bruising should include the location, shape, and color of the bruise using appropriate terminology (Brown et al., 2004).

Bruises alone do not necessarily indicate abuse; however, they do necessitate further assessment. The size, shape, and appearance of all bruises, patterns of injury, injuries in unusual locations, and burns must be carefully and thoroughly documented including as much objective information as possible. Photographs of the injuries are helpful, and any suspicious injuries require further investigation (Humphries Lynch, 1997).

The pattern of bruising may suggest the cause of the injury, as a bruise can possess the shape of knuckles or fingers and parallel discoloration marks can demonstrate injury from a linear cylindrical object (Dyer et al., 2003). Brown et al. stressed the importance of a comprehensive assessment of the entire body of an elderly assault victim for bruising. The neck, arms, and legs may manifest fingertip bruising from restraint. The face, breast, chest, abdomen, and extremities may manifest bruises from punches and may resemble the shape of a fist with a central clear area, which is created when the punch trauma forces capillary blood away from the targeted location (Brown et al., 2004).

One study sought to develop a scoring system for bruise patterns as a tool for identifying abuse in children (Dunstan, Guildea, Kontos, Kemp, & Sibert, 2002). The aim was to determine whether abused and nonabused children differed in the extent and pattern of bruising and whether existing differences were sufficient to develop a score to assist in the diagnosis. The total length of bruising in 12 areas of the body (anterior chest and abdomen, back, buttocks, left and right arms, left and right face, left and right ears, other areas of the head, and neck) was determined in 133 physically abused and 189 control children ages 1 to 14. Abuse cases were identified via a child protection database, whereas the bruising patterns of control children were obtained from presentation to an ambulatory outpatient consultation for reasons other than abuse. Bruises were measured, and details of bruises were recorded together with the maximum dimension of each bruise and whether or not each bruise had a specific shape. Differences were noted between cases and controls in the total length of bruises. A scoring system was developed using logistic regression analysis using total duration of bruising. The authors concluded that a scoring system can provide a measure that discriminates between abused and nonabused children. However, it is noted that this score should not replace the complex analysis of abuse that includes a thorough history and physical examination (Dunstan et al., 2002). A review of the literature did not produce similar data regarding elder maltreatment.

Falls are the most common cause of injury in an adult and are often associated with bruising (Dyer et al., 2003). Falls have numerous causes such as decreased vision, accidents, and chronic medical conditions and are not always preventable. However, abusive or neglectful caregivers can accredit intentional bruises to an accidental fall. Falls alone are not indicative of elder abuse, as 30% of community-dwelling elderly and 50% of nursing home residents fall, and most elders who experience falls will have one to three falls annually (Dyer et al., 2003). However, complaints associated with a history of a fall require further questioning, assessment, and awareness on the part of the healthcare professional in terms of the potential for elder maltreatment.

Abrasions are exposed skin caused by friction, whereas lacerations are noted to be tears of the skin resulting from blunt trauma (Dix, 2000). Skin thickness, elasticity, and tensile strength decreases with age, and abrasions can result even from minor trauma. Abrasions may occur if an elder victim is pulled or dragged across a surface (Brown et al., 2004). Abrasions are vital for diagnostic purposes, because they retain the pattern of the causative agent better than any other form of injury, making careful documentation essential in identification of the mode of injury. Skin tears are a common form of lacerations in the elderly and can present on the forearms and occasionally on the lower extremities when the epidermis separates from the underlying connective tissue resulting in a skin flap (Dyer et al., 2003). The forensic nurse must be aware that an elder's skin will often tear, causing a laceration if the victim is punched, pulled, or restrained (Pearsall, 2005).

Fractures are often the by-product of trauma and include a severing, splintering, or compression of the bone. The hip and distal wrist are the most common sites of fracture. Bones become thinner and less dense with age, exposing the elder to an increased risk for fractures. In addition, conditions such as osteoporosis, chronic steroid use, cancer, osteomalacia, Paget's disease, poor nutrition, alcoholism, and age-related sex hormone deficiencies debilitate the bone and escalate the risk for fracture. In addition, elders heal at a much slower rate, and little or no data are available on the fracture resolution rate in the elderly population. Forensic nurses must conduct a detailed history and a comprehensive examination, as well as a complete assessment of medical records, to determine if a fracture should raise the suspicion of an abusive situation. Fractures of the the head, spine, and trunk are more indicative of abuse injuries than are fractures of the limbs, sprains, or musculoskeletal injuries. However, extremity fractures may occur in the struggle of an attacker to restrain an extremity during an attack, and arm fractures may be the result of an attempt to break a fall or by raising the arms as a means of protection against an attacker's assault. Rib and thoracic cage fractures may occur when force is exerted to the chest wall when a victim is forced to the ground and sustains blows from the perpetrator's arms, legs, or by other means of assault (Brown et al., 2004). In addition, fractures that exhibit a rotational component and spiral fractures of large bones absent of history of gross injury may also be indicators of abuse (Dyer et al., 2003).

PSYCHOLOGICAL/EMOTIONAL ABUSE

Most physical abuse is accompanied by a psychological component, or psychological abuse may occur alone and may be difficult to recognize unless examples of verbal threats, insults, or humiliation are observed (Humphries Lynch, 1997). Subtle signs such as depression, change in behavior, fear, anxiety, or withdrawal, under careful assessment, may reveal that the elder is experiencing intimidation and maltreatment from the perpetrator (Wieland, 2000). Assessment or psychological maltreatment presents as a challenge, because the forensic nurse needs to search for concealed indicators in the dynamics presented by the elder and the caregiver (Pearsall, 2005). The importance of early identification is key because a forensic nurse can intervene early when signs of psychological abuse are subtle. In doing so, it may be possible to not only halt the abusive psychological behavior but also prevent the escalation to physical mistreatment (Humphries Lynch, 1997).

FINANCIAL ABUSE

The inappropriate use of an elderly individual's resources for personal gain is termed financial exploitation. This category includes credit card and telemarketing fraud, predatory lending, and theft or extortion, and it is accompanied by psychological abuse. These activities are often targeted at vulnerable elders who have cognitive impairment and are thus more vulnerable to trusting caregivers, relatives, and acquaintances. Financial exploitation is often unrecognized despite the devastating emotional and financial losses experienced by the elder. Up to one half of all categories of elder maltreatment in the United States is attributed to financial abuse. In the United States, an annual conservative estimate of elder maltreatment in individuals 65 years old and over is 3%

to 4%. When financial abuse is included as an option in calculation of those figures, the prevalence rate may be closer to 12% (Tueth, 2000).

Financial abuse can present in three common situations (Tueth, 2000):

• Caregiver, relative, or acquaintance abuse is often viewed as the most prevalent, egregious, and predatory. This may occur when perpetrators find themselves in an opportune situation where they are caring for a disabled elder or when a perpetrator actively searches for vulnerable elders with the intent of financial exploitation.

• Door-to-door scam operations where a perpetrator identifies him or herself as a skilled worker, repairman, and the like and bills for services that are not provided, double-bills, or otherwise falsely collects funds.

• Business professionals, either professional or imposters, such as investment and insurance agents who target vulnerable elders in schemes (Tueth, 2000).

Financial abuse can be devastating to the victim and is often traced to family members, trusted friends, and caregivers. It is likely to occur with the tacit acknowledgment and consent of the elder person. The manifestations of financial abuse generally are not immediately evident and discoverable (Bonnie & Wallace, 2003).

Potential clinical indicators of financial abuse include observable changes in behavior related to the abuser and the elder, excessive interest in an elder's personal assets, demonstration of excessive control, controlling phone use, unusual degree of fear exhibited by the elder, unexplained bank account withdrawals, and credit card activities (Tueth, 2000). A coercion to change a will or transfer assets abruptly and without forethought may also be a warning sign (Wieland, 2000).

NEGLECT

Dehydration is a potential forensic **biomarker** for neglect. Dehydration is caused by intentional fluid withholding or if inadequate water intake persists for a long period of time. A lack of staff or family support may also lead to dehydration. Decreased fluid intake or excessive water loss can cause an inadequate level of body fluid, which results in dehydration. The elderly are much more prone to dehydration. Often elderly have decreased body fluid reserves, impaired thirst drives, and the central nervous system fluid regulation may be compromised. Medical illness is the most common cause of dehydration; however, indicators of dehydration can be used as forensic markers for abuse or neglect when fluid withholding or neglect of care is identified during a comprehensive examination (Dyer et al., 2003).

Malnutrition is often used as a forensic marker for neglect. Malnutrition refers to an inadequate health status resulting from a diminished intake of necessary nutrients. An age-related decrease in smell and taste may contribute to a decrease in appetite. In addition, illness, poor dentition, mental status changes, malabsorption syndromes, cancer, and other disorders can lead to malnutrition. Potential adverse effects of pharmacological agents, such as mental impairment and appetite suppression, can also contribute to malnutrition. The loss of 40% of body weight can cause death. The most frequent cause of malnutrition due to neglect in the institutional setting is often attributed to an inadequate staffing to assist individuals who require eating assistance. In addition, improper feeding techniques may contribute to choking, aspiration, pneumonia, or death (Dyer et al., 2003).

Use and abuse of medications may be forensic markers for abuse and neglect, as abusive or neglectful caregivers may withhold required medications, consume the prescriptions themselves, or overdose an elder (Dyer et al., 2003). Careful assessment of medication and treatment regimens, prescription renewal history, as well as appropriate laboratory medication levels may be helpful in ensuring that therapeutic medication levels are maintained (Pearsall, 2005).

Deep decubiti in multiple sites may indicate an abusive situation. A decubitus, or pressure ulcer, results from circulatory failure secondary to pressure and shearing forces that causes thrombosis of the microcirculation and leads to tissue necrosis. The elderly are more likely to obtain decubiti, not simply based on their age but because of disease states and lack of mobility. Assessing whether decubiti are due to illness or due to abuse or neglect maybe difficult (Dyer et al., 2003).

Burns may be a forensic marker for elder maltreatment and self-neglect. Individuals over the age of 65 incur twice the national average death rate resulting from burns, and this rate triples at age 75 and quadruples at age 85. Burn tissue injury results from exposure to heat above 50°C and is classified by the affected body surface and the depth of tissue destruction (Dyer et al., 2003). Bowden and colleagues explored the relationship of elder maltreatment and neglect to burns in the University of Michigan Burn Center and reported that 70% of the cases were due to neglect and abuse (Bowden, Grant, Vogel, & Prasad, 1988). Another study found that 40% of burn cases in individuals over the age of 60 were the result of abuse or neglect and 36% of the cases were attributed to negligence (Bird, Harrington, Barillo, McSweeney, Shirani, & Goodwin 1998).

SELF-NEGLECT

The area of self-neglect is occasionally discussed in elder abuse research as a category of elder abuse. This is often defined as an act being conducted by an elder that threatens that individual's own health or safety, as in an individual who has difficulty performing activities of daily living and refuses assistance despite resulting problems. Self-neglect presents as an ethical dilemma of patient autonomy versus beneficence, and some believe that this reflects more a failure of society than an issue of elder abuse (Kleinschmidt, 1997). When elders neglect themselves by choice so that their home environment and personal cleanliness falls drastically below the societal acceptable standards, the results present a challenge to health and social service professionals (Adams & Johnson, 1998).

One study examined nurses' perception of self-neglect in people living in the community by the administration of a semistructured questionnaire to a convenience sample of nurses to ascertain if the concept held any meaning for them in their clinical practice and what they considered its key characteristics to be (Adams & Johnson, 1998). The researchers reported that all the nurses were able to identify patients who had shown features of "gross self-neglect." Poor nutrition was identified as a key identifying factor. The relationship between poor nutrition and resulting weight loss representing an important sign of self-neglect was stressed as a suggested venue for further research. This area has not received due prominence in medical research, yet the establishment of a "failure to thrive" diagnosis as a possible diagnostic-related grouping for self-neglect may provide a scope for future nursing intervention (Adams & Johnson, 1998).

Lauder (1999) explored how the medical construction of self-neglect came to dominate the self-neglect literature. He presented the argument that although nurses frequently encounter patients who neglect their personal hygiene and household cleanliness, self-neglect is often identified within the parameters of the medical model where objectification and categorization is emphasized. According to the author, the medical model's development of the construct of self-neglect operates under the assumption that there is a self-neglect medical syndrome that can be objectified and measured. This may obscure the fact that patients and professionals have differing ideas about what self-neglect is and what it is not. Different professional groups and those individuals who are categorized as self-neglecting may differ in their objective and subjective perception of self-neglect. Lauder has challenged the notion of self-neglect on the basis that it is a normative judgment that involves the norms of cleanliness and hygiene. Nurses are encouraged to challenge the notion of self-neglect as a medical syndrome, and nurses must be aware that there may be a number of differing constructions of self-neglect. Nurses should explore the patient's own construction (Lauder, 1999).

Research and practice in the self-neglect arena have been hampered by a lack of theoretical development, and it is felt that self-neglect is underconceptualized and needs to be studied within a broader theoretical context. Lauder et al. theorized that sociological and psychological theories offer radically different venues for looking at this phenomenon than does the medical model. They seek to explain, understand, and place emphasis on the dynamic and interpretative nature of self-neglect rather than simply classifying it as a medical disorder (Lauder, Anderson, & Barclay, 2002).

Dementia involves an advancing decline in cognition that may result in a reduced ability to care for oneself. Elderly patients who suffer from early stages of dementia often experience anxiety and depression and in later stages of the disease process they may suffer from delusions and hallucinations. In the elderly, dementia is often a risk factor for maltreatments as it is often associated with self-neglect and mental health concerns. This makes the elder more vulnerable to and less able to defend him or herself from perpetrators. The ability to care for oneself decreases as dependence on others increases, which in itself increases the risk for maltreatment and neglect by caregivers who may be unable or unwilling to deliver assistance. In addition, self-neglect may be a forensic marker that maltreatment has occurred, as the elder victim may become depressed and then may lose the desire or ability for self-care (Dyer et al., 2003). Forensic interviewing of elderly patients with dementia or cognitive deficits presents unique challenges, because obtaining a reliable and accurate report of the injuries and location of pain may be difficult (Burgess, Dowdell, & Brown, 2000).

A decline in hygiene has also been suggested as a marker of neglect (Lachs & Pillemer, 1995). The capacity and ability to maintain cleanliness and hygiene is an important component of health, well-being, and disease prevention. If cognition remains normal, elders are generally able to perform the activities of daily living and maintain proper hygiene. Impaired eyesight may hinder the ability to maintain a clean home and clean clothing. Mental illness or dementia may contribute to a lack of ability for self-care, and depressed elders may be less inclined to provide self-care. However, poor personal care may be a matter of personal choice and individual lifestyle and should not be blamed on age or on cognitive changes (Dyer et al., 2003).

Often, it is difficult to ascertain and distinguish declining capacity from eccentricity, especially when the elder has lived by his or her own rules for many years and may have rejected a traditional lifestyle early on (Humphries Lynch, 1997). The decision to intervene may be more difficult in self-neglect than in cases of physical, psychological, or caregiver neglect. While trying to ensure the elder's personal safety, one must also respect the legal right to self-determination (Humphries Lynch, 1997). Patient education plays a valuable role in persuading the elder to accept assistance, while on some occasions needing to respect the right to decline services (Humphries Lynch, 1997). An effective intervention includes the assessment of functionality, informational, and motivational needs in addition to awareness of what services are available to the elder while being sensitive to self-esteem matters of lifestyle and independence (Humphries Lynch, 1997).

SEXUAL ABUSE

Sexual abuse is rarely discussed in the literature, and few prevalence estimates exist (Kleinschmidt, 1997). Sexual contact or exposure without consent is categorized as sexual abuse and includes those individuals who are not able to consent (Dyer et al., 2003). No reliable incidence data are available regarding the degree of elder sexual assaults (Burgess, Prentky, & Dowdell, 2000). In one study, aggregate data from APS case files in the state of Virginia yielded 42 substantiated cases of sexually abused adults aged 60 years and older during a three-year collection period (Teaster, Roberto, Duke, & Kim, 2000). The majority of the adults who experienced sexual abuse reported to APS were female, typically over 70 years old, and resided in facilities such as nursing homes. The majority of the abusers were men who were either staff members or residents. The majority of the cases were not prosecuted either because of insufficient evidence or the elders were not able to participate in the prosecution.

Burgess, Prentky, and Dowdell (2000) explored the nature of perpetrators who target highly vulnerable individuals in nursing homes for sexual assault by reviewing files that included employee reports, in-service records, depositions of nursing home personnel, reports of abuse to human service agencies, expert evaluations, police reports, and trial testimony and criminal justice depositions of cases reported to law enforcement. Twenty case files were reviewed with 18 perpetrators identified who ranged in age from 16 to 82 and included 15 employees and 3 male residents of the nursing home categorizing two separate groups of offenders. This descriptive study was limited by a relatively small sample; however, it raised two principal areas of concern: the issue of victimology and fundamental liability issues because the majority of perpetrators were employees, leading to questions related to the issue of negligent hiring practices. The victims of these nursing home sexual assaults were advanced in age and suffered from some degree of dementia, which complicated the assessment and examination process and compounded the treatment and recovery. According to this source, the impact of the trauma on the very frail constitutions of these victims resulted in the death of 11 of the 20 victims within 12 months of the rape. Alternative methods of examination and treatment must be developed and incorporated into nursing home policy and procedures as well as proper training of nursing/medical personnel in effective, humane methods of examination (Burgess et al., 2000). Discussion of the sexual abuse of an elderly individual remains a taboo in our society; however, victims remain unprotected when society refuses to acknowledge this issue (Heath, 1999).

A study comparing 53 sexual assault victims aged 55 and older with 53 victims aged 18 to 45 found that older victims (53%) were significantly more likely to sustain genital injury than the younger women (13%) (Muram, Miller, & Cutler, 1992). Elder women may experience physiological changes because of decreased estrogen levels that may alter vaginal wall thinning and shape, increase vaginal dryness, create pain and bleeding during intercourse, and may increase the rate of vaginal or bladder infections (Dyer et al., 2003). An elder individual's skin is atrophic, making it more fragile. An elder's skin in general may become thin, loose, and transparent (Brown et al., 2004). As such, elder sexual assault victims may exhibit greater skin and mucous membrane injury than younger victims. Extremities are more vulnerable to bruising in an elder.

Forensic markers, such as inner thigh bruising, are common findings in elder sexual assault victims (Brown et al., 2004). The presence of oral venereal lesions, bruising of the uvula and palate, bleeding and bruising of the anogenital area as well as difficulty in sitting and walking may be indicators of maltreatment (Dyer et al., 2003). A new diagnosis of a sexually transmitted disease may also indicate sexual abuse. In addition, behavioral changes such as anger, depression, fear, withdrawal, difficulty sleeping, an increased interest in sex, or sexual or aggressive behavior could also indicate elder sexual abuse (Dyer et al., 2003).

The elderly rape victims are often a neglected group, because they represent a vulnerable and poorly understood population (Burgess et al., 2000). Even the most experienced and skilled clinicians may feel emotionally uncomfortable, uninformed, and lack confidence in their ability to intervene and manage suspected elder sexual abuse cases. Knowledge of what to assess and how to appropriately intervene can avert a potentially tragic consequence (Teitelman & Copolillo, 2002).

Teitelman and Copolillo presented guidelines for recognition and intervention of sexual abuse among persons with Alzheimer's disease. They identified four avenues for screening for the presence of possible sexual abuse: being sensitive to the observable signs and symptoms associated with sexual abuse, determining the individual's capacity to consent to sexual activity, using appropriate interviewing techniques and questions, and using more formal assessment tools when needed to determine the likelihood that sexual abuse occurred (Teitelman & Copolillo, 2002).

Safarik, Jarvis, and Nussbaum (2000) examined the degree of empirical validity that criminal investigative analysis brings to the investigation and apprehension of offenders that perpetrate elder female sexual homicide. Data were collected by the Federal Bureau of Investigation's National Center for the Analysis of Violent Crime (NCAVC) via numerous sources and consisted of 33 solved cases of females identified as 60 years of age and older who were victims of serial sexual homicide. The offenders in these cases were arrested, convicted, and deemed responsible for at least two sexual homicides each of elderly females. Four dependent variables—offender race, offender age, the relationship of offender to victim, and the distance of offender's residence from that of the victim—were addressed. Of specific note were the following:

- Elder white female serial sexual homicides may be perpetrated by offenders that are of dissimilar race, as it was noted that 82% of the black offenders in this study victimized white females.
- The majority of offenders were found to be significantly younger (ages 20 to 35) than their elderly victims.

- It is highly improbable that the offenders repeatedly came in physical contact with the elderly females whom they subsequently raped and murdered in the course of other criminal activity such as burglary or robbery.
- Oftentimes the theft of items from the victim was an afterthought for the offender (Safarik, Jarvis, & Nussbaum, 2000).

EDUCATION

The National Aging Resource Center on Elder Abuse (NARCEA) conducted a study that sought to investigate the degree to which elder abuse and neglect course content is a part of higher education curricula in aging, to determine which specific elder abuse and neglect course content is or is not included in required and elective coursework, and to describe the attitudes of instructors toward including elder abuse and neglect course content in the overall curriculum. This study utilized a questionnaire, which was sent to 319 contact persons who represented gerontology instructional program members of the Association for Gerontology in Higher Education and yielded 211 usable responses. Only slightly over one quarter of all courses offered within the undergraduate instructional units included content on aging, whereas approximately one third of all courses offered within the graduate instructional units include content on aging, and an extremely small number included course content on elder abuse and neglect. Approximately 95% of both the undergraduate and graduate curriculums do not require courses with primary content in elder abuse and neglect; however, 76% of undergraduate curriculums and 68% of graduate curriculums include elective courses in this area as a segment or component of the course content (NARCEA, 1992). It has been suggested that increasing physician awareness of the problem of elder abuse will increase the number of cases screened for potential abuse and, as such, increase the number of elder abuse reports to responsible agencies (Rosenblatt et al., 1996).

A randomized controlled trial was conducted using nurses, care assistants, and social workers who worked with elders; it compared the effectiveness of attending an educational course to printed educational material in improving management of elder abuse. Eligible participants were randomly assigned to either group 1, which attended an educational course, or to group 2, whose members were given reading material with the same content as the course and asked to complete a pre- and postintervention questionnaire. The main findings of this study included information that there was a lack of knowledge of good management in dealing with elder abuse and that educational coursework was superior to printed material in increasing elder abuse knowledge and interventional management (Richardson, Kitchen, & Livingston, 2002).

A lack of knowledge in the area of elder abuse interferes with awareness and alertness to elder abuse among healthcare professionals (Meeks-Sjostrom, 2004). A major gap in nursing knowledge exists in the area of elder abuse educational preparation, and this holds great implications for nursing education.

SCREENING TOOLS

There have been few screening tools to identify potential elderly victims or perpetrators of abuse. Although these instruments performed fairly well in studies, they have not been tested in healthcare settings and there have been no identified studies of interventions in the elderly individuals (Nelson, Nygren, McInerney, & Klein, 2004). A review of some of the most widely used screening tools follows.

Indicators of Abuse Screen

Reis and Nahmiash (1998) designed and validated the 29-item Indicators of Abuse (IOA) Screen to identify elder abuse cases based on previous risk factor research (Bonnie & Wallace, 2003). The majority of the validated elder abuse screens have been designed to be completed by the potentially abused elder himself or herself or by a caregiver. This may present a concern related to accuracy as both the caregiver and the recipient could be concealing the abuse (Reis, 2000).

The IOA screen is designed to be administered by a professional instead of the caregiver or recipient. Even though this is a screening tool, it requires knowledge of the caregiver's and recipient's characteristics obtained via interview (Bonnie & Wallace, 2003). A 60-item preliminary checklist was initially developed that included 48 possible indicators of abuse in addition to 12 background and demographic items, such as age and gender. These initial 60 items have been identified in prior research as being associated with abuse and involved mostly with problems of either the caregivers or the care recipients. The researchers felt that the problem-oriented view of abuse etiology was well supported by a number of theories. These problems included items such as a caregiver's substance abuse, high degree of stress, or a recipient's increased dependency or physical impairment. The purpose of this preliminary measure was to test the 60 items of concern, which had previously only been studied individually or only a few at a time. The initial goal was to identify which items presented a valid measure to reliability and which items would prove to be "myths" or unimportant in screening (Reis, 2000). This study was part of an extensive three-year initiative called PROJECT CARE and was supported by Health Canada (Reis & Nahmiash, 1998). There were 301 participants in the IOA validation study. Inclusionary criteria included those care recipients over 55 years of age who had unpaid caregivers, either a friend or relative, who provided regular assistance. Each case required an initial two- to three-hour home interview by a professional agency employee, usually a nurse or social worker. The purpose of the home visit was to complete an overall assessment that included a review of the recipient's biological, psychological, and social problems. The preliminary IOA screen was then completed in approximately 20 minutes. From the 60-item initial checklist, a smaller 29-item subset was developed that was designed to predict whether abuse was likely to be present and reported rather impressive results. Sensitivity and specificity results indicated that these 29 items could predict whether abuse was likely to be present 78% to 84.4% of the time, and nonabuse cases were successfully identified 99.2% of the time (Reis, 2000).

The overall findings indicated that abuse is strongly associated with the caregiver's personal and emotional problems and that the caregiver's risk factors rather than the receiver's were most important in predicting abuse and neglect (Reis, 2000). In addition, it was found that several issues that were assumed to be important factors in risk identification, such as the physical or emotional impairment of the care recipient or an increased need for help with activities of daily living, did not signal abuse, nor does a situation where the caregiver is under much stress or is socially isolated (Reis, 2000). These issues may certainly be important and may need intervention; however, they were not found to be abuse markers (Reis, 2000).

The typical abuse case profile was characterized by "a troubled caregiver, who has difficultly getting along with others and a situation in which the care recipient has been abused in the past and in which there is inadequate social support" (Reis, 2000, p.15).

A strength to this tool is that it assesses both the caregiver and the care recipient and that it assesses multiple forms of abuse. A high false negative rate, limited applicability of the tool to assesses elder marital relationship, causes of domestic violence, and the need for in-depth knowledge of the participants are considered this tool's major weaknesses (Bonnie & Wallace, 2003).

ELDER ASSESSMENT INSTRUMENT

The Elder Assessment Instrument (EAI) has been discussed in the research and used in clinical practice since 1984 (Fulmer, 2003). This tool uses a 41-item Likert scale, which consists of seven subscales that review the signs, symptoms, and subjective complaints of elder abuse, neglect, exploitation, and abandonment. It is designed to identify elders at high risk of mistreatment and those who should be referred for further assessment if the following exists: evidence of mistreatment without sufficient clinical explanation, a subjective complaint by the elder of mistreatment, or the clinician believes there is high risk or probable abuse, neglect, or exploitation. The EAI is appropriate for usage in all clinical settings and is completed by clinicians responsible for elder mistreatment screening (Fulmer, 2003). It is comprehensive and can be utilized for serial assessments (Bonnie & Wallace, 2003). The tool requires approximately 12 to 15 minutes to complete. Psychometrical studies identify a content validity index of 0.83, interrater agreement of 0.83, sensitivity of 71%, and specificity of 93% (Fulmer et. al, 2004).

HWALEK-SENGSTOCK ELDER ABUSE SCREENING TEST

Hwalek and Sengstock originally pooled more than 1000 items from existing elder abuse assessment protocols to develop a 15-item instrument that measured three abuse aspects: direct abuse or violation of personal right, vulnerability characteristics, and potential abuse. The goal of the original study was to identify a set of items that would differentiate those elderly who were abused from those in a control group who were known not to be abused in the hope of creating a screening tool (Hwalek & Sengstock, 1986). Over time and with use of discriminate analysis, the original 15-item tool was validated (Neale, Hwalek, Scott, & Stahl, 1991), and it was found that a six-item tool effectively discriminated between abuse and nonabuse as well as the original 15-item tool. This is a self-reporting measure that is designed to be completed by the individuals themselves and was the only self-reporting tool identified in this literature search. This screen is designed to be followed by a more in-depth interview by a clinician if the scores warrant (Wolf, 2000).

CAREGIVER ABUSE SCREEN

The Caregiver Abuse Screen (CASE) is designed to be completed by the caregivers and is a relatively quick and short eight-item tool that assesses abuse and neglect (Bonnie & Wallace, 2003). Direct questions about mistreatment are avoided; the authors use wording that is designed to be nonblaming. This tool is designed for community use to screen for current physical, psychosocial, or financial abuse and neglect and is based on the larger elder abuse intervention and research project, PROJECT CARE. The tool's authors stress the importance of caregiver screening based on studies reporting that care receivers report less abuse than caregivers and that caregiver's characteristics such as substance abuse and a problem history more than care-receiver characteristics are felt to be of primary importance in abuse (Reis, 1995).

Kottwitz and Bowling (2003) piloted the Elder Abuse Questionnaire (EAQ) that is designed to measure the perception of elder abuse within a described population. The Betty Neuman systems model was used as a framework for the study. The EAQ contains 25 items that were derived from Neuman's variables related to physiological, psychological, sociocultural, developmental, and spiritual stages of the multidimensional person. A descriptive study design was selected for the instrument development, and the Likert scale was chosen as a method of data measurement. The population included the power of attorneys (POA) for 40 residents and 40 employees of a long-term care facility. The questionnaire was mailed to 40 residents' POAs and was included in 40 employees' pay envelopes with a self-addressed stamped envelope; it resulted in a 61.25% participation rate (N = 49). Results of the pilot indicate that the EAQ has strong to moderate reliability as an instrument based on a one-factor solution and was measured using Cronbach's coefficient alpha to compute the internal consistency of the questionnaire. The authors acknowledge that the population was narrowly focused and recommend that the EAQ be repeated in numerous populations for reliability comparison (Kottwitz & Bowling, 2003).

Elder Abuse Management

LEGISLATIVE HISTORY

Elder abuse was brought from behind closed doors and onto the national stage when in the mid-1970s testimony about "parent battering" was presented at a U.S. congressional subcommittee hearing on family violence (Wolf, 2000). Linked to family violence, elder abuse became a topic in the media when horrific case reports were uncovered by the U.S. House of Representatives Select Committee on Aging requiring state policy makers to react by pressing for special elder abuse legislation (Wolf, 2000).

In 1962, Congress passed the Public Welfare Amendments to the Social Security Act, which authorized payments to the states to establish protective services for individuals with physical or mental limitations who were unable to manage their own affairs or who were neglected or exploited. The Title XX amendment to the 1974 Social Security Act was adopted 12 years later, and adult protective services (APS) became a state-mandated program covering all adults 18 years and older (Wolf, 2000).

Since the APS system for reporting and investigating cases was already in place by the time elder abuse became a public concern, legislators were permitted to support action on elder abuse without having to call for additional state expenditures, and in a few years time, most states followed by passing elder abuse laws or making amendments to existing adult protective services legislation to address this concern (Wolf, 2000). Congressional hearings in the 1980s led to the creation of an Elder Abuse Task Force, and in 1990 the U.S. Department of Health and Human Services established the National Institute on Elder Abuse (Wieland, 2000). Child abuse laws became the prototype for legislation in over three quarters of the states, since a model statue on elder abuse did not exist. However, the inadequacies of this application of child abuse legislation to the elder abuse legislation soon became apparent. The potential for violating civil rights by infantilizing elders along with new findings on the prevalence of spouse abuse, which suggested that a domestic violence model might be a more appropriate fit, necessitated policy makers to expand interventions and treatment possibilities to include the methods and instruments of the public health and criminal justice systems. Laws answering the multifaceted nature of elder abuse and incorporating new conceptualizations on the state and federal levels are continually being amended (Wolf, 2000).

In an attempt to address the phenomenon of elder abuse, states have drafted protective measures in identifying and combating elder mistreatment and have enacted statutes that require mandatory reporting, civil and criminal penalties, and emergency interventions (Smith, 2002). All states and the District of Columbia include provisions governing the reporting of suspected elder mistreatment, with all but a few of those jurisdictions mandating reports by specified categories of persons (Bonnie & Wallace, 2003).

ELDER ABUSE REPORTING CONTROVERSY

Elder abuse laws are designed and intended to protect vulnerable citizens and to punish violators, yet they may be in conflict with the principles of medicine, raising doubts among clinical professionals about appropriateness and feasibility of reporting. Although mandatory reporting is in place for child abuse, it has not been established in reporting for elder abuse. Reporting potentially violates provider-patient trust and confidentiality and may threaten the therapeutic alliance between the provider and the caregiver/abuser (Hirsch , Strattan, & Loewy, 1999). Reporting is the most common and yet the most controversial intervention (Bonnie & Wallace, 2003). Supporters of mandatory reporting argue that by legally requiring reporting, those individuals who may initially be hesitant to report elder abuse, fearing error or interference in another family's personal affairs, may be more forthcoming in identification. Opponents to mandatory reporting stress that an involuntary intervention into an elder's life will only encourage ageism in society and deter elders from confiding in clinicians or seeking medical assistance for fear that they will be a subject of investigation (Smith, 2002). The concept of mandatory reporting of suspected abuse was borrowed from the child abuse laws without the benefit of research data to demonstrate applicability to the older population. The ongoing debate surrounding mandatory reporting raises numerous empirical questions regarding the effectiveness of these laws on the behavior of mandated reporters and the consequences of reporting on the lives of those affected by them (Bonnie & Wallace, 2003). Forensic nurses interface with elders and are in a unique position to address the issue of elder abuse reporting.

RESEARCH RELATED TO CLINICIAN ELDER MALTREATMENT DETECTION AND MANAGEMENT

The following literature review was conducted to identify existing research that sought to identify a healthcare provider's knowledge of elder abuse, screening methods used, elder maltreatment reporting practices, and perceived barriers to reporting. The retrieval process resulted in the identification of the following five studies:

- Harrell, et al. (2002) interviewed 10 geriatricians using a standardized set of open-ended questions to identify how practicing geriatricians define, diagnose, and address elder abuse and neglect. The subjects were asked to identify what points in the history and physical led them to diagnose elder abuse. The purpose of this study was to obtain descriptive data regarding the diagnosis of abuse and neglect, signs and symptoms obtained from the history and physical examination, differences between how geriatricians define caregiver neglect and self-neglect, and how suspicion for neglect is addressed to advance elder abuse knowledge and assist primary care physicians in making a diagnosis of elder abuse. Rapport between the patient and caregiver, medical noncompliance, assessment of activities of daily living, and instrumental activities were the most commonly reported identifying clues in the history. Bruising/trauma, general appearance, hygiene, malnutrition, and dehydration were noted as the most common identifying clues on physical examination. When asked to indicate the most important history and physical finding that alerted them to a diagnosis of elder abuse or neglect, the majority of geriatricians reported the need to assess the totality of the bio-psycho-social issues rather than focusing on a single part. Geriatricians presented a diversity of responses regarding interventions utilized in suspected abuse and neglect cases. Some reported the need to immediately notify APS, whereas others, feeling that they had an established relationship with the patient, often attempted their own intervention as a first step before contacting APS. This diversity in treatment methodology requires further exploration (Harrell et al., 2002).

- In another study, all general medical practitioners working in an inner London borough in the United Kingdom (UK) were asked to complete a questionnaire that asked about their knowledge and experience of elder abuse (McCreadie, Bennett, & Tinker, 1998). Seventy-three practitioners responded (68% response rate) to questions regarding 20 situations where it would be reasonable to hold a suspicion of elder abuse. Five main types of abuse were grouped for analysis: physical, psychological, sexual, financial, and neglect. Forty-nine percent of general practitioners (GPs) reported having known or suspected a case of an elder who sustained one or more types of abuse. Respondents were then asked about 20 "at-risk" situations that covered five types of abuse and asked to check appropriate boxes while responding to the following question: "With regard to the care of older people living in the community, during the last twelve months have you had any patients who are or might be in any of these situations?" (McCreadie et al., 1998). The response to these scenarios does not refer to the prevalence rate; rather it highlights the range of situations encountered by GPs and how common those scenarios are in GPs' experience. The key findings of this study in regard to GPs' knowledge and experience of elder abuse were as follows: 84% reported having had an older patient in at least one of these situations, 75% were aware of a patient in a situation involving risk of psychological abuse, 52% were aware of a risk of neglect, and 47% were aware of a risk of physical abuse. This study raises two important questions: Are GPs failing to recognize abuse or failing to define situations as being abusive? How are they responding to these situations?

- A Swedish study congruent with this UK study used the same questionnaire, which was translated into Swedish to describe the awareness among Swedish general practitioners of elderly patients at risk of or suffering from abuse during a 12-month period (Saveman & Sanvide, 2001). The questionnaire was sent to 110 physicians and yielded a 59% response rate. In this study, 25% of the responding GPs reported being aware of patients who were subjected to verified or suspected elder abuse when responding to the first question directly inquiring about the physicians experience with a case of abuse during the past 12 months, which is only half the percentage reported in the UK study. In this study, a large proportion of GPs (77%) reported having elder patients in situations where there is risk of abuse or neglect. This is very similar to the 84% reported in the UK study and once again raised the question, are GPs failing to recognize abuse?

- A self-administered four-page national survey composed of 44 questions focusing on the magnitude of elder abuse was used to determine physician awareness of applicable state laws and the barriers to reporting suspected cases (Jones, Veenstra,

Seamon, & Krohmer, 1997). A random sample of 3000 members of the American College of Emergency Physicians yielded 705 completed surveys (response rate of 24%) that answered questions that included practice characteristics, number and type of suspected cases of elder mistreatment seen in the emergency department, number of cases reported, reasoning for not reporting cases, the availability of elder mistreatment protocols, and familiarity with local laws and reporting requirements. In this study, 52% of the respondents identified elder mistreatment as prevalent yet less so than spousal or child abuse, approximately 50% of suspected cases of elder mistreatment were reported, 31% reported having a written protocol for reporting suspected cases and they were generally unaware about applicable state laws, 25% were able to recall educational content regarding elder abuse, 74% did not believe that there was a clear-cut medical definition of elder abuse or neglect, 58% were uncertain that emergency physicians can accurately identify cases of abuse, and 92% reported that states did not have sufficient resources to meet the needs of victims. The results suggest that practicing emergency physicians are not confident in identifying or reporting elder abuse, and this lack of confidence may reflect inadequacies of training, research, and continuing education.

- Lastly, a questionnaire survey developed for the Research Subcommittee of the Elder Abuse and Self-Neglect Task Force of Hamilton-Wentworth was used in Krueger and Patterson's (1997) study to determine family physician's perceptions of barriers and strategies in the effective detection and appropriate management of abused elderly people. A total of 189 eligible physicians were randomly selected from the Canadian Medical Directory with 122 responding. The following barriers were identified: family/patient denial of abuse, resistance to intervention, not knowing where to call for help, lack of protocols to assess and respond to abuse, lack of guidelines about confidentiality, fear of reprisal, and lack of knowledge of the prevalence and definition of elder abuse. The following strategies were noted to be helpful: a single agency to call, a directory of services, a list of resource people, an educational package, guidelines for detection and management, reimbursement for time spent on legal matters, continuing education, revision of the fee structure, and a central library of resources on elder abuse.

These studies highlight the dire need for awareness and educational interventions and further research and exploration as to potential dynamics surrounding the underdiagnosis and underreporting of elder maltreatment.

Forensic Nurse's Role

It is a forensic nurse's professional responsibility to identify and appropriately intervene in elder maltreatment cases. Forensic nurses must be aware of the statutes in the state where they practice. In addition, forensic nurses must review the protocols of their institutions in regard to the identification and intervention in elder maltreatment and must seek appropriate screening tools. They must also be instrumental in the development and revision of these protocols to best meet the needs of the population they serve. Intervention requires a multidisciplinary approach. The following guidelines may be helpful as the forensic nurse prepares for this vital role (Pearsall, 2005).

BEST PRACTICE A multidisciplinary approach utilizing social workers, healthcare providers, lawyers, the police, and coordinated by the forensic nurse examiner is the optimal approach to intervention in elder maltreatment cases.

History and Interview

- Interview the elder and caregiver separately, as many elders are ashamed of maltreatment and fear that exposure may lead to litigation and potential institution.
- Be aware of discrepancies that may be red flags that maltreatment is occurring.
- Begin discussion with nonthreatening questions regarding the elder's perception of home safety, and then progress to more specific questions as needed.
- Avoid confrontation, and use a nonjudgmental approach throughout the process.
- Keep questions simple and direct; the less the forensic nurse speaks, the more information she or he will obtain.
- Be alert to inconsistencies regarding the history of injury and illness.
- Ensure that interview documentation is accurate, detailed, and objective, noting in quotations the exact wording used by the elder and the caregiver.
- Be aware of the risks of financial abuse, and be alerted to the potential markers such as behavior changes between the elder and the caregiver, excessive controlling behavior, control over phone use, unexplained bank account or credit card transactions, and abrupt changes to wills or transfer of assets.
- Listen and be aware.

Physical Assessment

- Assess the elder's overall appearance for hygiene, grooming, and appropriate seasonal dress.
- Examine the skin for hydration, abrasions, lacerations, contusions, burns, bites, decubiti, poor wound healing, and excoriations from incontinence.
- Assess the entire body.
- Carefully and thoroughly document the size, shape, and appearance of all findings, including patterns of injury and injuries in all unusual locations, including as much objective information as possible.
- Assess the neck, arms, and legs for fingertip bruising from restraint.
- Carefully examine the face, breast, chest, abdomen, and extremities for punch bruises that resemble the shape of a fist with a clear area in the center.
- Assess for malnutrition.
- Be aware of the risk of sexual abuse in vulnerable elders and be vigilant to potential signs such as bruising to the inner thighs, difficulty sitting or walking, bloody or stained undergarments, oral venereal lesions, bruising to the uvula and palate, newly diagnosed sexually transmitted disease, and reddened ecchymosed, itching, or a painful genital area.
- If sexual abuse is suspected, remember that it is important to preserve potential evidence; the victim should not be bathed and the victim should be referred to a forensic professional for a post-assault examination.
- Obtain photographs of injuries, as this is often a helpful tool.
- Assess the elder's neurological status for slurred speech and potential signs of overmedication.
- Review all available medical records for patterns, inconsistencies, and evidence of healthcare "hopping," missed appointments, and so on.
- Conduct a careful psychological assessment to uncover subtle signs of depression, changes in behavior, fear, anxiety, or withdrawal, or an increased interest in sexual or aggressive behavior.

- Be aware that assessing for psychological maltreatment is challenging and often requires a search for hidden clues in the dynamics presented by the elder and the caregiver.
- Assess for potential inadequate levels of care.

Intervention

- Listen to your "inner voice."
- Remember that the elder's decision-making capacity and current safety should guide team management.
- Be aware that intervention requires a multidisciplinary approach.
- Remember that law enforcement or adult protective services should be alerted as per state statues and institutional policies.
- Be aware of services available to the elder and the resources available to the forensic nurse.
- Be aware that the decision to intervene in self-neglect may be a difficult one. The forensic nurse must respect the legal right to self-determination. Patient education may help the elder to accept assistance, which on some occasions may mean respecting the elder's right to decline services.
- Assess the elder's functionality and informational and motivational needs.
- Encourage elderly patients to alert 911 should they find themselves in a dangerous situation, and ensure that they are educated on available services in their area.
- Seek educational opportunities to expand one's knowledge in elder maltreatment.

Case Study 30-1

Elizabeth Morgan, age 88, has been admitted to the hospital. On examination you observe bruising on her upper extremities and to her inner thighs. The patient states that she does not remember how she sustained these bruises and adds that she "bruises easily: "I am always bumping into things." She lives with her daughter and son-in-law. You question the daughter, who states that she is unaware of any recent falls and has not noted any bruising on her mother.

- What are your initial thoughts?
- How might you proceed?
- Describe the assessment process.
- Are interventions indicated? If so, how would you intervene?

Case Study 30-2

Jack Smith, age 78, suffers from hearing difficulties, disabling rheumatoid arthritis, and depression. He lives alone since being widowed 8 years ago. His family was concerned for his safety since he has sustained numerous falls and has exhibited signs of dementia. The family recently hired an experienced live-in caregiver. The caregiver accompanies the elder on his clinic appointments, appears attentive, and answers many questions for the patient, so much so that instead of answering questions himself, the patient refers them all to the caregiver.

- What are your initial thoughts?
- How might you proceed in this situation?
- Describe the assessment process.
- Are interventions indicated? If so, how would you intervene?

Case Study **30-3**

Caregiver Abuse of an Elder

This 79-year-old female suffered a cardiac arrest and EMS personnel were summoned. Despite attempts at resuscitation, the patient was pronounced dead in the emergency department. The family practice resident who had treated her as an outpatient signed the death certificate, annotating "Cardiac Arrest due to Alzheimer's Disease." The body was transferred to the morgue awaiting pick-up by a funeral home. In the meantime, a hospital morgue employee noticed the suspicious wounds on the patient's body and brought the case to the attention of a forensic pathologist. At that point, the medical examiner assumed jurisdiction of the body and performed a forensic investigation.

During an extensive investigation, it was revealed that reports of suspected abuse had been filed with the Department of Social Services (DSS) five months earlier, but on a visit the month prior to the patient's death; the social worker was not allowed to see the patient. Although the resident physician had been made aware of the DSS concern at that time, he had written a letter to convey that he saw nothing to confirm the suspicion. However, during the death investigation, law enforcement officers learned that the caregiver would beat the patient when she would lose control of her bladder or bowels. Weapons included a broom stick and the caregiver's hands.

The autopsy findings revealed multiple lacerations and contusions in varying stages of healing on the head and extremities. The nose was fractured, two teeth were avulsed, and radiographs identified fractures of the hands and forearms (Figs. 30-1 through 30-3). Although the examination of the brain confirmed the presence of Alzheimer's disease, and there was evidence of heart disease and osteoporosis, the death was eventually certified as "Blunt Force Injuries of Head, Trunk, and Extremities." The manner of death was ruled "homicide." The caregiver pled guilty and served three years in prison.

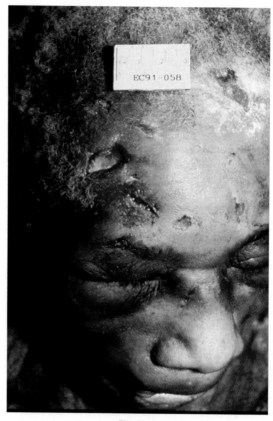

Fig. 30-1

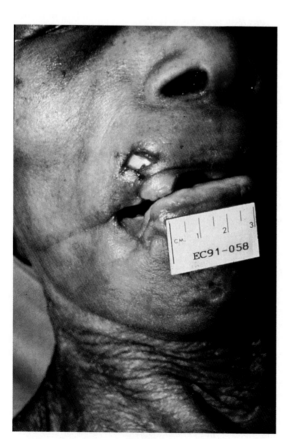

Fig. 30-2

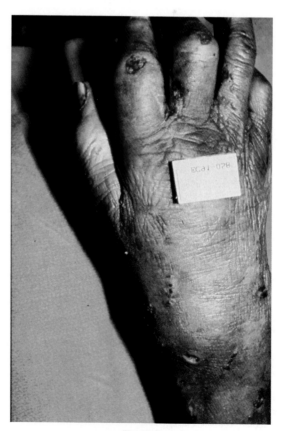

Fig. 30-3

Summary

Individuals are living longer than ever before. However, as the elderly population grows, so does the incidence of elder maltreatment. We are only aware of the tip of the iceberg, as many cases are unrecognized and unreported. It is vital for forensic nurses to be knowledgeable about the prevalence of elder abuse and the potential markers of abuse to be instrumental in its prevention and early intervention.

A forensic nurse must first reflect and ask the following questions: How do I define elder maltreatment? How has education prepared or influenced me in my knowledge of elder maltreatment? What influences me to report elder maltreatment? What assessment tools, if any, do I use to measure elder maltreatment risk, potential, and occurrence? What forensic markers alert me to elder maltreatment? How often do I encounter suspected cases of elder maltreatment? What are my reporting practices and protocols? What barriers exist to my reporting suspected cases?

Elder maltreatment and neglect is dangerously underdiagnosed and underreported. All too often the signs of abuse imitates those of chronic disease and accidental injury. Many common complaints among the elderly may be the result of mistreatment, yet those signs are missed. The vital key to interpreting these signs is not simply noting their presence but also identifying their characteristics. The characteristics will assist in differentiating between a natural or an intentional occurrence. A gold standard forensic marker for maltreatment does not yet exist; however, certain symptoms should alert suspicion (Pearsall, 2005). Forensic nurses play a crucial role in the identification of elder abuse, as they are especially well placed to detect and potentially prevent instances of maltreatment because even the most frail and elderly individuals come in contact with their care. There is much work yet to be done to progress our knowledge in this challenging field. So many questions remain.

References

Adams, J., & Johnson, J. (1998). Nurses' perceptions of gross self-neglect amongst older people living in the community. *Journal of Clinical Nursing, 7*(6), 547–552.

Administration of Aging. (2008). *A statistical profile of older Americans aged 65+*. Retrieved January 10, 2009, from www.aoa.gov

Anetzberger, G. J. (2000). Caregiving: Primary cause of elder abuse?. *Generations, 24*(2), 46–51.

Bird, P. E., Harrington, D. T., Barillo, D. J., McSweeney, A., Shirani, K. Z., & Goodwin, C. W. (1998). Elder abuse: A call to action. *The Journal of Burn Care & Rehabilitation, 19*(6), 522–527.

Bonnie, R., & Wallace, R. (Eds.), (2003). *Elder mistreatment: Abuse, neglect, and exploitation in an aging America. Panel to review risk and prevalence of elder abuse and neglect*. Washington, DC: National Academies Press.

Bowden, M. L., Grant, S. T., Vogel, B., & Prasad, J. K. (1988). The elderly, disabled and handicapped adult burned through abuse and neglect. *Burns, Including Thermal Injury, 14*(6), 447–450.

Brown, K., Streubert, G., & Burgess, A. (2004). Effectively detect and manage elder abuse. *The Nurse Practitioner, 29*(8), 22–43.

Burgess, A. W., Prentky, R. A., & Dowdell, E. B. (2000). Sexual predators in nursing homes. *Journal of Psychosocial Nursing & Mental Health Services, 38*(8), 26–35.

Burgess, A., Dowdell, E., & Brown, K. (2000). The elderly rape victim: Stereotypes, perpetrators, and implications for practice. *Journal of Emergency Nursing, 26*(5), 516–518.

Centers for Disease Control and Prevention. (2001). *The effects of unintentional injury*. Retrieved November 3, 2005, from www.cdc.gov/ncipc/pubres/unintentional_activity/02_effects.htm

Dix, J. (2000). *The color atlas of forensic pathology*. New York: CRC Press.

Dunstan, F., Guildea, Z., Kontos, K., Kemp, A., & Sibert, J. (2002). A scoring system for bruise patterns: a tool for identifying abuse. *Archives of Disease in Childhood, 86*(5), 330–333.

Dyer, C., Pavlik, V., Murphy, K., & Hyman, D. (2000). The high prevalence of depression and dementia in elder abuse or neglect. *American Geriatrics Society, 48*(2), 205–208.

Dyer, C. B., Connolly, M. T., & McFeeley, P. (2003). The clinical and medical forensics of elder abuse and neglect. In R. J. Bonnie, & R. B. Wallace (Eds.), *Elder Mistreatment: Abuse, neglect and exploitation in an Aging America* (pp. 339–381). Washington, DC: The National Academies Press.

Fulmer, T., Firpo, A., Guadagno, L., Easter, T., Kahan, F., & Paris, B. (2003). Themes from a grounded theory analysis of elder neglect assessment by experts. *The Gerontologist, 43*(5), 745–752.

Fulmer, T. T. (2003). Elder abuse and neglect assessment. *Journal of Gerontological Nursing, 29*(6), 4–5.

Fulmer, T., Guadagno, L., Bitondo Dyer, C., & Connolly, M. T. (2004). Progress in elder abuse screening and assessment instruments. *Journal of the American Geriatric Society, 52*(2), 297–304.

Harrell, R. M., Toronjo, C. H. C., McLaughlin, J. B., Pavlik, V. N. P., Hyman, D. J. M., & Bitondo Dyer, C. M. (2002). How geriatricians identify elder abuse and neglect. *The American Journal of Medical Sciences, 303*(1), 30–38.

Heath, H. (1999). Sexual abuse of older people. *Elderly Care, 11*(9), 4.

Hirsch, C. H., Strattan, S., & Loewy, R. (1999). The primary care of elder mistreatment. *Western Journal of Medicine, 170*(6), 353–358.

Humphries Lynch, S. (1997). Elder abuse: What to look for, how to intervene. *American Journal of Nursing, 97*(1), 27–30.

Hwalek, M. A., & Sengstock, M. C. (1986). Assessing the probability of abuse of the elderly: Toward development of a clinical screening instrument. *The Journal of Applied Gerontology, 5*(2), 153–173.

Jogerst, G. J. M., Dawson, J. D. P., Hartz, A. J. M., Ely, J. W. M., & Schweitzer, L. A. M. (2000). Community Characteristics Associated with Elder Abuse. *Journal of the American Geriatrics Society, 48*(5), 513–518.

Jones, J. S., Veenstra, T., Seamon, J., & Krohmer, J. (1997). Elder mistreatment: National survey of emergency physicians. *Annals of Emergency Medicine, 30*(4), 473–479.

Kleinschmidt, K. C. M. (1997). Elder abuse: A review. *Annals of Emergency Medicine, 30*(4), 463–472.

Kottwitz, D., & Bowling, S. (2003). A pilot study of the elder abuse questionnaire. *Kansas Nurse, 78*(7), 4.

Krueger, P., & Patterson, C. (1997). Detecting and managing elder abuse: Challenges in primary care. *CMAJ, 157*(8), 1095.

Lachs, M., & Pillemer, K. A. (1995). Current concepts: Abuse and neglect of elderly persons. *The New England Journal of Medicine, 330*(7), 437–443.

Lachs, M., Williams, C., O'Brien, S., Hurst, L., & Horwitz, R. (1996). Older adults: An 11-year longitudinal study of adult protective service use. *Archives of Internal Medicine, 156*(4), 449–453.

Lachs, M., Williams, C. S., O'Brien, S., Pillemer, K. A., & Charlson, M. E. (1998). The mortality of elder mistreatment. *JAMA, 280*(5), 428–430.

Langlois, N., & Gresham, G. (1991). The ageing of bruises: A review and study of the colour changes with time. *Forensic Science International, 50*(2), 227–238.

Lauder, W. (1999). The medical model and other constructions of self-neglect. *International Journal of Nursing Practice, 5*(2), 58–63.

Lauder, W., Anderson, I., & Barclay, A. (2002). Sociological and psychological theories of self-neglect. *Journal of Advanced Nursing, 40*(3), 331–338.

Levine, J. (2003). A primer for primary care physicians. *Geriatrics, 58*(10), 37–44.

McCreadie, C., Bennett, G., & Tinker, A. (1998). Investigating British general practitioners' knowledge and experience of elder abuse: Report of a research study in an inner London borough. *Journal of Elder Abuse and Neglect, 9*(3), 23–39.

Meeks-Sjostrom, D. (2004). A comparison of three measure of elder abuse. *Journal of Nursing Scholarship, 36*(3), 247–250.

Muram, D., Miller, K., & Cutler, A. (1992). Sexual assault of the elderly victim. *Journal of Interpersonal Violence, 7*(1), 70–76.

National Aging Resource Center on Elder Abuse (NARCEA). (1992). Elder abuse and neglect content in higher education programs on aging. In *United States Administration on Aging*. Washington, DC: Clearinghouse on Abuse and Neglect of the Elderly.

National Center on Elder Abuse. (1998). *National elder abuse incidence study (NEAIS): Final report*. Retrieved January 10, 2008, from www.aoa.gov/eldfam/Elder_Abuse/AbuseReport_Full.pdf

National Center on Elder Abuse. (2005). *Elder abuse information series*. Retrieved January 10, 2009, from www.elderabusecenter.org

Neale, A. V., Hwalek, M. A., Scott, R. O., & Stahl, C. (1991). Validation of the Hwalek-Sengstock elder abuse screening test. *The Journal of Applied Gerontology, 10*(4), 406–418.

Nelson, H., Nygren, P., McInerney, Y., & Klein, J. (2004). Screening women and elderly adults for family and intimate partner violence: A review of the evidence for the U.S. preventive services task force. *Annals of Internal Medicine, 140*(5), 387–396.

Pearsall, C. (2005). Forensic biomarkers of elder abuse: What clinicians need to know. *Journal of Forensic Nursing, 1*(4), 182–186.

Reis, M. (1995). Validation of the caregiver abuse screen (CASE). *Canadian Journal on Aging, 14*(Suppl. 2), 45–60.

Reis, M. (2000). The IOA screen: An abuse-alert measure that dispels myths. *Generations, 24*(2), 13–16.

Reis, M., & Nahmiash, D. (1998). Validation of the indicators of abuse (IOA) screen. *The Gerontologist, 38*(4), 471–480.

Richardson, B., Kitchen, G., & Livingston, G. (2002). The effect of education on knowledge and management of elder abuse: A randomized controlled trial. *Age and Ageing, 31*(5), 335–1301.

Rosenblatt, D. E., Cho, K.-H.M., & Durance, P. W. P. (1996). Reporting Mistreatment of Older Abuse: The Role of Physicians. *Journal of the American Geriatrics Society, 44*(1), 65–70.

Safarik, M., Jarvis, J., & Nussbaum, K. (2000). Elderly female serial sexual homicide. *Homicide Studies, 4*(3), 294–301.

Saveman, B., & Sanvide, A. (2001). Swedish general practitioners' awareness of elderly patients at risk of or actually suffering from elder abuse. *Scandinavian Journal of Caring Sciences, 15*(3), 244.

Smith, W. (2002). Adult Protective Service Statutes: Are the States Doing Enough to Protect Their Elderly? *Juris, Spring*, 37–40.

Teaster, P. B., Roberto, K. A., Duke, J. O., & Kim, M. (2000). Sexual abuse of older adults: Preliminary findings of cases in Virginia. *Journal of Elder Abuse and Neglect, 12*(3/4), 1–16.

Teitelman, J., & Copolillo, A. (2002). Sexual abuse among persons with Alzheimer's disease: Guidelines for recognition and intervention. *Alzheimer's Care Quarterly, 3*(3), 252.

Tueth, M. J. (2000). Exposing financial exploitation of impaired elderly persons. *American Journal of Geriatric Psychiatry, 8*(2), 104–111.

U.S. Census Bureau. (2008). *U.S. Census Bureau*. Retrieved January 14, 2009, from www.census.gov

Vida, S., Monks, R., & Des Rosiers, P. (2002). Prevalence and correlates of elder abuse and neglect in a geriatric psychiatry service. *Canadian Journal of Psychiatry, 47*(5), 459–467.

Wieland, D. (2000). Abuse of older persons: An overview. *Holistic Nursing Practice, 14*(4), 40.

Wolf, R. S. (2000). The nature and scope of elder abuse. *Generations, 24*(2), 6–12.

CHAPTER 31 Relationship Crimes

Cris Finn

This chapter highlights and explores the various considerations integral to the holistic care of the victim of relationship crimes of violence. This is a summary of the recent knowledge; as such, it is not intended to be a comprehensive review of the literature. It is written to assist forensic nurses, healthcare professionals, and others who come in contact with relationship violence victims. To ensure optimum management of victims of violence, The Joint Commission has advocated some practice guidelines.

> **BEST PRACTICE** Possible victims of abuse are identified using specific criteria. Staff members are trained in the use of these criteria, which must focus on observable evidence and not on allegations alone. Staff members are also able to make appropriate referrals for victims of abuse and neglect. Patient care assessment standards include the recognition of forensic patients and mandate that evidence is collected and preserved.

Violence against another person is illegal as well as contrary to the moral and ethical standards that guide human behavior. Relationships are nothing short of complicated. Relationships are unions between two individuals or more that are established on mutual agreements that are formal or informal. Relationships can vary based on many external factors; however, the preceding definition is the most widely accepted. Mutual emotional attachments may or may not be obligatory in relationships.

The topics to be explored in this chapter include domestic violence, acquaintance violence, stalking, escort/prostitution violence, violence against men, elder abuse, workplace violence, mentor-teacher student abuse, and crimes against homeless people.

Domestic Violence

Domestic violence (DV) encompasses all acts of violence against persons within the context of family or intimate relationships. Violence in the home has many names: domestic violence, intimate partner violence, spousal abuse, interpersonal violence, and family violence, in addition to battery, partner abuse, or spousal abuse. It is an issue of increasing concern because it has a negative effect on all family members, especially children. Domestic violence occurs in every culture, country, and age group. It affects people from all socioeconomic, educational, and religious backgrounds and takes place in same-sex as well as heterosexual relationships. Women with fewer resources or greater perceived vulnerability, girls, and those experiencing physical or psychiatric disability or living below the poverty line are at even greater risk for domestic violence and lifetime abuse. Children are also affected by domestic violence, even if they do not witness it directly. Although both men and woman can be victims, it is the leading cause of injury to women in the United States, where they are more likely to be assaulted, injured, raped, or killed by a male partner than by any other type of assailant. Statistics indicate that 29% of all violence against women by a single offender is committed by an intimate: a husband, ex-husband, boyfriend, or ex-boyfriend (Centers for Disease Control [CDC], 2008). Accurate information on the extent of domestic violence is difficult to obtain because of extensive underreporting. However, it is estimated that as many as 4 million instances of domestic abuse against women occur annually in the United States (CDC, 2008).

> **KEY POINT** Domestic violence has become one of the primary areas of interest for forensic nurses. Early screening, identification, and treatment of intimate partner violence patients can help break often serious and deadly cycles of violence.

SCOPE OF THE PROBLEM

According to a National Violence Against Women Survey (2008), 22% of women are physically assaulted by a partner or date during their lifetime, and nearly 5.3 million partner victimizations occur each year among U.S. women ages 18 and older, resulting in 2 million injuries and 1300 deaths. Further findings include the following: nearly 25% of women have been raped or physically assaulted by an intimate partner during their lives; 15.4% of gay men, 11.4% of lesbians, and 7.7% of heterosexual men are assaulted by a date or intimate partner during their lives; and more than 1 million women and 371,000 men are stalked by partners each year (American Medical Association [AMA], 2008). Each year it is estimated that expenses for domestic violence total at least $5 million; businesses forfeit an additional $100 million in lost wages, sick leave, absenteeism, and nonproductive time (Domestic Violence for Health Providers, 1991). It is estimated that only about 10% of all domestic violence incidents are reported. Each year more than 1 million women seek medical treatment for injuries inflicted by their significant other. The Federal Bureau of Investigation (FBI) has reported that approximately one third of all female homicide victims are killed by husbands, ex-husbands, boyfriends, or ex-boyfriends (1992). Between 8% and 11% of pregnant women are abused by their partners (AMA, 2008).

In the mid-1980s, the U.S. attorney general began drawing attention to domestic violence and the act of victimizing an intimate partner. Men are the perpetrators in approximately 90% of all reported domestic assaults, and women are ten times as likely as men to be injured in episodes of domestic abuse. Among female murder victims in the United States, about one third are killed by their partner each year, whereas only 4% of all male victims are killed by their partners (Campbell, 1995).

RISK FACTORS

The risk factors that place women at risk for abuse are as broad and unique as is the population. Simply based on their gender, women are at risk (Stark & Flitcraft, 1996). Abusers use many ways to isolate, intimidate, and control their partners. It starts insidiously and may be difficult to recognize. Early on, the partner seems attentive, generous, and protective in ways that later turn out to be frightening and controlling. Initially the abuse is isolated incidents for which the partner expresses remorse and promises never to do again or rationalizes as being due to stress or caused by something the woman did or did not do.

A number of studies have looked into identifying individuals who are most at risk for domestic violence. The most common feature is an imbalance of power and control. However, neither those who experience domestic violence nor the partners who abuse them fall into distinct categories. They can be of any age, ethnicity, income level, or level of education. The following are examples of situations that are common among people who experience domestic violence. It is important to understand that anyone can be abused.

Some common themes among individuals at risk are as follows:
- Planning to leave or has recently left an abusive relationship
- Previously in an abusive relationship
- Poverty or poor living situations
- Unemployed
- Physical or mental disability
- Recently separated or divorced
- Isolated socially from family and friends
- Abused as a child
- Witnessed domestic violence as a child
- Pregnancy, especially if unplanned
- Younger than 30 years
- Stalked by a partner

Although the abusers also share some common characteristics, it is important to note that abusers choose violence to get what they want in a relationship. Risk factors may point to an increased likelihood of violence in a relationship, but the person is not destined to become violent because of the presence of certain risk factors. Nor is the violence justifiable because it happened while the abuser was in a rage that he or she was powerless to control.

The following factors may indicate an increased likelihood that a person may choose violence:
- Abuses alcohol or drugs
- Witnessed abuse as a child
- Was a victim of abuse as a child
- Abused former partners
- Is unemployed or underemployed
- Abuses pets

CLINICAL PRESENTATIONS

Domestic violence may lead to both physical and psychological signs and symptoms in the victim. Victims may have obvious physical signs of traumatic injury, but they may also complain of non-injury signs and symptoms, such as chronic abdominal pain, that may seem unrelated to an abusive relationship. Family and friends, even coworkers, may see the following signs and symptoms. These are also signs that forensic nurses and all healthcare providers look for in assessing potential victims of domestic abuse.

PSYCHOLOGICAL SIGNS AND SYMPTOMS

Recognizing the signs and symptoms of domestic violence begins by observing the behavior of both the abuser and the person being abused. The abuser may appear overly controlling or coercive, attempting to answer all questions for the victim or isolating him or her from others. This type of behavior may occur in the context of a visit to the healthcare provider where the abuser refuses to let the victim out of his or her sight and attempts to answer all questions for the victim. In stark contrast, the person being abused may appear quiet and passive. He or she may show outward signs of depression such as crying and poor eye contact. Other psychological signs of domestic violence range from anxiety, depression, and chronic fatigue to suicidal tendencies and the battered woman syndrome—a syndrome similar to the posttraumatic stress disorder seen in people threatened with death or serious injury in extremely stressful situations (such as war). Substance abuse is also more common in the person enduring domestic violence than in the general adult population. The abuse of alcohol, prescription drugs, and illicit drugs may occur as a result of the violent relationship rather than being the cause of the violence.

BIOMARKERS

Domestic violence assault may lead to specific injury types and distributions. These injury types and patterns may result from things other than domestic violence but should raise suspicion of abuse when present. Injury types seen more commonly in domestic-violence injuries than in injuries caused by other means are tympanic membrane (eardrum) rupture; rectal or genital injury; facial scrapes, bruises, cuts, or fractures; neck scrapes or bruises; abdominal cuts or bruises; loose or broken teeth; head scrapes or bruises; body scrapes or bruises; and arm scrapes or bruises.

Physical signs and symptoms of domestic violence that result from traumatic injury may seem similar to injuries resulting from other causes. But some injury types and locations may increase the suspicion of assault violence. The distribution of injuries on the body that typically occurs in the domestic-violence assault may follow certain patterns. Some frequently seen patterns of injury are as follows:
- *Centrally located injuries.* Injury distribution is in a bathing-suit pattern, primarily involving the breasts, body, buttocks, and genitals. These areas are usually covered by clothing, concealing obvious signs of injury. Another central location is the head and neck, which is the site of up to 50% of abusive injuries.
- *Characteristic domestic violence injuries.* These include cigarette burns, bite marks, rope burns, bruises, and welts with the outline of a recognizable weapon (such as a belt buckle).
- *Bilateral injuries.* Injuries involving both sides of the body, usually the arms and legs.
- *Defensive posture injuries.* Injuries to the parts of the body used by the woman to fend off an attack: the small finger side of the forearm or the palms when used to block blows to the head and chest; the bottoms of the feet when used to kick away an assailant; and the back, legs, buttocks, and back of the head when the victim is crouched on the floor.
- *Injuries inconsistent with the explanation given.* The injury type or severity does not fit with the reported cause; the mechanism of injury reported would not produce the signs of injury found on physical examination.
- *Injuries in various stages of healing.* Signs of both recent and old injuries may represent a history of ongoing abuse, and a delay in seeking medical attention for injuries may indicate either the

victim's reluctance to involve doctors or his or her inability to leave home to seek needed care.

- *Non-injury physical signs and symptoms.* Individuals experiencing ongoing abuse and stress in their lives may develop medical complaints as a direct or indirect result. Often the person enduring domestic violence goes to the emergency department or clinic on multiple occasions with no physical examination findings to account for his or her symptoms. Some typical medical complaints may include headache, neck pain, chest pain, heart beating too fast, choking sensations, numbness and tingling, painful sexual intercourse, pelvic pain, urinary tract infection, vaginal pain, HIV/AIDS, and dysmenorrhea resulting from forced and unprotected sex.

SCREENING AND ASSESSMENT

There are several published, reliable, and valid screening tools used in healthcare settings. Among the best known are the three-question Partner Violence Screen (PVS) (Feldhaus, Koziol-McLain, Amsbury, Norton, Lowenstein, & Abbott, 1997) and the Abuse Assessment Screen (AAS) (Helton, 1986; McFarlane, Parker, Soeken, & Bullock, 1992); versions of varying lengths are available. Early screening, identification, and treatment of domestic violence can help break often serious and deadly cycles of violence. Each time a battered woman presents for care, a window of opportunity is opened. Abuse escalates and increases in severity over time, thus the cycle of violence continues. The key to comprehensive assessments includes insight and knowledge of the various presentations consistent with domestic violence. Persons who present with a history of trauma should be carefully assessed for injuries consistent with the history or the injury. Injuries to the face, head, and trunk are consistent with battering and abuse. Nontrauma-related presentations such as vague somatic complaints, depression, suicide attempts, and gynecological problems may be related to abuse by a partner.

The health provider or forensic nurse must conduct the interview in a private area, which affords the patient the opportunity to disclose the precipitating factors resulting in the symptoms. Emergent and urgent medical needs can be precipitated by trauma and injury, as well as pre- or postpartum complications. Sensitive and direct questions validate and confirm the seriousness of the situation and the availability of help and education. Assessing for domestic violence with a reliable and valid screening tool is now considered a nursing standard of care. With any positive finding of abuse, the forensic nurse should have immediate access to the Danger Assessment and HARASS tools to further explore for risk of domestic homicide.

The evidence reviewed in this chapter suggests that sanctions against partner beating or battering (and some form of sanctuary for women when they were first beaten) are important in keeping levels of violence against women somewhat contained. Experience has shown that the immediate posttrauma period is both the most dangerous time for the woman to leave their home, but it is also the most teachable moment for forensic nurses to help them to make positive changes. Interventions at this point are vital. Nurses, as healthcare professionals (and in some states as mandatory reporters), have ethical, legal, and moral obligations to report abuse to appropriate agencies and to provide understanding; considerate, competent, and supportive nursing interventions that safeguard personal dignity and respect cultural, spiritual, and psychosocial values to the diverse populations seen in their practices. The Emergency Nurses Association position statement on DV and approaching diversity in healthcare addresses this issue for emergency nurses (ENA, www.ena.org, 2009).

CHILDREN AS VICTIMS AND WITNESSES

The risk of child abuse is extremely high in families where domestic violence occurs. In the United States, at least 3.3 million children between the ages of 2 and 18 witness parental violence annually (CDC, 2008). Children of abused women are much more aware of the violence than their parents realize (Nettleton, 2001). Strategies must be considered by the forensic nurse to make a difference in the lives of these vulnerable children through identification, access to services, and coordination for protection.

Acquaintance Violence (Date Rape)

Acquaintance rape, which is also referred to as "date rape," has been increasingly recognized as a real and relatively common problem within society. Much of the attention that has been focused on this issue has emerged as part of the growing willingness to acknowledge and address issues associated with domestic violence and the rights of women in general since the 1970s. Although the early and mid-1970s saw the emergence of education and mobilization to combat rape, it was not until the early 1980s that acquaintance rape began to assume a more distinct form in the public consciousness. The scholarly research done by psychologist Mary Koss and her colleagues is widely recognized as the primary impetus for raising awareness to a new level.

When people think of rape, they might think of a stranger jumping out of a shadowy place and sexually attacking someone. But it is not only strangers who rape. In fact, about half of all people who are raped know the person who attacked them. Girls and women are most often raped, but boys and men also can be raped. Most friendships, acquaintances, and dates never lead to violence, of course. But, sadly, sometimes it happens. When forced sex occurs between two people who already know each other, it is known as date rape or acquaintance rape. According to Dictionary.com, date rape is "Rape perpetrated by the victim's social escort." Wikipedia defines it as "Rape or non-consensual sexual activity between people who are already acquainted, or who know each other socially–friends, acquaintances, people on a date, or even people in an existing romantic relationship–where it is alleged that consent for sexual activity was not given, or was given under duress. In most jurisdictions, there is no legal distinction between rape committed by a stranger, or by an acquaintance, friend or lover." The term *date rape,* also *called contact rape, acquaintance rape,* or *sleep rape,* refers to nonconsensual sexual activity between people who are already acquainted, whose consent for sexual activity was not given or was given under duress. Date rape and acquaintance rape are forms of sexual assault involving coercive sexual activities perpetrated by an acquaintance of the rape survivor. The perpetrator is almost always a man, and though both men and women can be raped, women are most often the targets of this violence. It is difficult, because of a lack of research on the subject and the tendency for rape survivors not to report attacks, to come up with precise statistics on male survivors. However, men are raped by other men and are also victims of sexual violence. Date and acquaintance rape can happen to or be perpetrated by anyone. Incidences are very high: this form of rape comprises from 50% to 75% of all reported rapes. However, even these figures are not reliable. According to conservative FBI statistics, only 3½% to 10% of all forms of rape are even reported.

SCOPE OF THE PROBLEM

According to the National Studies of College Women (National Institutes of Health, 2005), 84% of women who were raped knew their assailants; 57% of rapes occurred on a date; 25% of men surveyed believed that rape was acceptable if the women asks the man out, if the man pays for the date, or the woman goes back to the man's room after the date; 33% of males surveyed said they would commit rape if they definitely could escape detection; 84% of male students who had committed acts that clearly met the legal definition of rape said what they had done was definitely not rape; 75% of male and 55% of female students in an occurrence of date rape had been drinking or using drugs; only a quarter to a third of women whose sexual assaults met the legal definition of rape considered themselves rape victims; many women do not report or characterize their victimization as a crime for reasons such as embarrassment, because they do not want to define someone who assaulted them as a rapist, or because they do not know the legal definition of rape. Many women blame themselves. Nearly 5% of college women are victimized in any given year, meaning over a four-year period, one fifth to one quarter of a cohort of women may be assaulted. Similar numbers experienced attempted rape. The majority of rapes occur in living quarters: 60% in the victim's residence, 10% in a fraternity, and 31% in other living quarters. Off-campus victimizations also took place in bars, dance clubs, and work settings. Fifty percent of high school boys and 42% of girls said there were times it was acceptable for a male to hold a female down and physically force her to engage in intercourse.

Even if the two people know each other well, and even if they were intimate or had sex before, no one has the right to force a sexual act on another person against his or her will. Although it involves forced sex, rape is not about sex or passion. Rape has nothing to do with love. Rape is an act of aggression and violence. Some people say those who have been raped were somehow "asking for it" because of the clothes they wore or the way they acted. The person who is raped is not to blame. Rape is always the fault of the rapist. Healthy relationships involve respect, including respect for the feelings of others.

ASPECTS

1. Date rape is forced or coerced sex between partners, dates, friends, friends of friends, or general acquaintances.
2. Date rape can be coerced both physically and emotionally. Some emotional tactics include threats to reputation, threats to not like the person, name calling, saying the person "brought it on" or "really wants it," and threats to break up.
3. If a person has had too much to drink or is on drugs, she or he cannot consent to sex and having sex with this person is legally rape.
4. There are certain date rape drugs that render the victim unconscious and limit memory; using these drugs on somebody carries harsher penalties than date rape and is a federal crime with a possible 20-year sentence (1996 Drug-Induced Rape Prevention and Punishment Act).
5. Date rape drugs may be difficult to trace, but evidence of intercourse is not, and in cases where use of these drugs is suspected, evidence of rape standards are lower.
6. Date rape is the most common form of rape (78%) with one in four girls expected to fall victim to rape or attempted rape before they reach 25, and three out of five rapes occur before a woman reaches age 18.
7. Although girls and women are more often victims of rape, boys and men can be raped too.
8. *No means no!* If a person says no to sex (no matter how quietly or unconvincingly) and sexual relations occur, that is rape.

Date-rape drugs are drugs that are sometimes used to assist in committing a sexual assault. Sexual assault is any type of sexual activity that a person does not agree to. Because of the effects of these drugs, victims may be physically helpless, unable to refuse sex, and unable to remember what happened. The drugs often have no color, odor, or taste and are easily added to flavored drinks without the victim's knowledge. Despite the attention given to these so-called date rape drugs, alcohol, marijuana, cocaine, and benzodiazepines are far more frequently associated with sexual assault. For a complete discussion of "club drugs" and drug-facilitated sexual assault, see Chapter 10.

SCREENING AND ASSESSMENT

Physical harm may include fractures, bruises, cuts, and other injuries from violent acts, injuries to the genitals or anus, exposure to sexually transmitted diseases (including AIDS, herpes, gonorrhea, and syphilis), and unwanted pregnancy.

Emotional harm may include feeling ashamed, embarrassed, guilty, and worthless. Other issues may include fear, depression, anger, trust issues, attraction to men (if the attacker was a man), problems with consensual sex later in life (inability to enjoy sex without intrusive recollections of the abuse), flashbacks (reliving the rape in your mind), nightmares, falling and staying asleep, and hypervigilance (Table 31-1).

PREVENTION

The following section has been adapted from *I Never Called It Rape*, by Robin Warshaw (Warshaw, 1994). Prevention is not just the responsibility of the potential victims, that is, of women. Men may try to use acquaintance rape myths and false stereotypes about "what women really want" to rationalize or excuse sexually aggressive behavior. The most widely used defense is to blame the victim. Education and awareness programs, however, can have a positive effect in encouraging men to take increased responsibility for their behavior. Despite this optimistic statement, there will always be some individuals who will not get the message. Although it may be difficult, if not impossible, to detect someone who will commit acquaintance rape, there are some characteristics that can signal trouble. Emotional intimidation in the form of belittling comments, ignoring, sulking, and dictating friends or style of dress may indicate high levels of hostility. Projecting an overt air of superiority or acting as if one knows another much better than the one actually does may also be associated with coercive tendencies. Body posturing such as blocking a doorway or deriving pleasure from physically startling or scaring are forms of physical intimidation.

Harboring negative attitudes toward women in general can be detected in the need to speak derisively of previous girlfriends. Extreme jealousy and an inability to handle sexual or emotional frustration without anger may reflect potentially dangerous volatility. Taking offense at not consenting to activities that could limit resistance, such as drinking or going to a private or isolated place, should serve as a warning.

Many of these characteristics are similar and contain themes of hostility and intimidation. Maintaining an awareness of such a profile may facilitate quicker, clearer, and more resolute decision making in problematic situations. Practical guidelines that may

Table 31-1 Myth versus Reality

MYTH	REALITY
A woman who gets raped usually deserves it, especially if she has agreed to go to a man's house or park with him.	No one deserves to be raped. Being in a man's house or car does not mean that a woman has agreed to have sex with him.
If a woman agrees to allow a man to pay for dinner, drinks, and the like, then it means she owes him sex.	Sex is not an implied payback for dinner or other expense no matter how much money has been spent.
Acquaintance rape is committed by men who are easy to identify as rapists.	Women are often raped by "normal" acquaintances who resemble "regular guys."
Women who don't fight back haven't been raped.	Rape occurs when one is forced to have sex against their will, whether or not the person has decided to fight back.
Intimate kissing or certain kinds of touching means that intercourse is inevitable.	Everyone's right to say no should be honored, regardless of the activity that preceded it.
Once a man reaches a certain point of arousal, sex is inevitable and they can't help forcing themselves upon a woman.	Men are capable of exercising restraint in acting on sexual urges.
Most women lie about acquaintance rape because they have regrets after consensual sex.	Acquaintance rape really happens—to people you know, by people you know.
Women who say no really mean yes.	This notion is based on rigid and outdated sexual stereotypes.
Certain behaviors such as drinking or dressing in a sexually appealing way make rape a woman's responsibility.	Drinking or dressing in a sexually appealing way are not invitations for sex.

decrease the risk of acquaintance rape are available. Expanded versions, as well as suggestions about what to do if rape occurs, may be found in *Intimate Betrayal: Understanding and Responding to the Trauma of Acquaintance Rape* (Wiehe & Richards, 1995) and *I Never Called It Rape* (Warshaw, 1994).

Stalking

Among the common crimes against women, stalking remains relatively unidentified in legal statutes. Stalking is the willful, malicious, and repeated following and harassing of another person, affecting approximately 1.4 million Americans. Stalking crimes are motivated by interpersonal aggression rather than by material gain or sex. The purpose of stalking resides in the mind of stalkers who are compulsive individuals with a misperceived fixation (Wright, 1995).

The attention of a stalker, victims find themselves the object of an unsolicited focus of unwanted attention. When the target fails to respond positively, the stalker accepts negative attention because it is still misinterpreted as making the stalker a part of the victim's life. Although most stalking does not escalate to violence, the threat of violence is a serious potential. Before any action can be taken in a stalking case, it is imperative that a threat analysis be validated by law enforcement agents. Conflict comes when the stalker comes to accept the fact he or she is not part of the victim's life and is being rejected, perhaps for the last time. Because of the threat of violence, victims of stalkers endure fear and anxiety on a daily basis.

Laws related to stalking are continually evolving. Most stalkers harass their targets for long periods of time without ever breaking the law, preventing law enforcement intervention. Many state laws require that a threat of violence be made to the victim for the activity to be legally considered stalking. In 1994, the Model Anti-stalking Code was introduced, and law enforcement realized that a threat does not necessarily require words (Stalking and Harassment, 2009). Implied threats may include indirect threats with the intent to harass, annoy, or alarm another person; strikes, shoves, kicks, or following a person in public; as well as the spoken or written word. Greater numbers of workplaces and schools are getting involved with stalking issues because of the restraining orders or orders of protection issued to safeguard the victim or the

children of the victim, which could potentially include these locations. Because local, national, and international laws vary, anyone who finds themselves the target of a stalker should research their specific laws concerning this issue.

This is a crime of extreme emotional abuse, which causes the victim to experience fear and anxiety and which may escalate into threats or actual physical violence. Stalking psychodynamics range from delusional, where no actual relationship exists, to nondelusional in nature, where an historical relationship has existed with a close interpersonal association, such as marriage or common-law relationships (Campbell & Lewandowski, 1997). Although there are a variety of classifications among stalkers, the two primary categories are the nondomestic (with no domestic partnership) and the domestic stalker (with a domestic partnership, generally past). Of these, the most dangerous offender is the domestic stalker. This offender attempts to control a relationship in the stages of termination or to reestablish a previous but failed partnership. This generally occurs during a divorce or breakup of a relationship involving a former lover or husband, including nondomestic long-term relationships.

Although the offender is generally male and the victim is female, a stalker can be a female obsessed with a male in the same circumstances. Women in domestic relationships have much to be concerned with if they believe they are the target of a stalker. Too often, triggered by rejection, the man's attempt to control the situation escalates into a violent event, including kidnapping/murder/suicide as a result of the final rejection. There has generally been a history of prior abuse or conflict with the stalker, and stalking victims often describe the past relationship in terms of control issues, smothering, or domination. Others in the victim's life can also become potential victims of the stalker in their efforts to protect the victim or the victim's children, to conceal the victim's new residence or safe house, or to provide a safe working environment.

Escort Abuse: Escort Service and Prostitution-Related Offenses

Many times, criminal charges against the owners, operators, employees, and independent contractors associated with an "escort service" result from an investigation where undercover officers acting as customers are offered sexual favors for additional fees. "Johns" are typically arrested when they show up at a hotel to meet someone who they believe is a prostitute but who in fact is an officer. Charges range from prostitution to patronizing a prostitute, promoting prostitution, sex trafficking, and permitting prostitution. Related charges may include money laundering and falsifying business records. Persons who work in the escort/prostitution trade are a potentially vulnerable population and at higher risk for sexual assault. It is important for forensic nurses to embrace the cultural diversity of this high-risk population of women to accurately assess, identify, and implement forensic principles and theories to assist these women.

Violence Against Men

Little is known about the actual number of men who are in a domestic relationship in which they are abused or treated violently by women. In 100 domestic violence situations, approximately 40 cases involve violence by women against men. An estimated 400,000 women per year are abused or treated violently in the United States by their spouse or intimate partner. This means that roughly 300,000 to 400,000 men are treated violently by their wife or girlfriend (Equal Justice Foundation, 2009).

The dynamic of domestic abuse and violence is also different between men and women. The reasons, purposes, and motivations are often very different between sexes. Although the counseling and psychological communities have responded to domestic abuse and violence against women, there has been little investment in resources to address and understand the issues of domestic abuse and violence against men. In most cases, the actual physical damage inflicted by men is much greater than the actual physical harm inflected by women. The impact of domestic violence is less apparent and less likely to come to the attention of others when men are abused. For example, it is assumed that a man with a bruise or black eye was in a fight with another man or was injured on the job or playing contact sports. Even when men do report domestic abuse and violence, most people are so astonished that these men usually end up feeling like nobody believes them.

There are no absolute rules for understanding the emotional differences between men and women. There are principles and dynamics that allow the interpretation of individual situations. Domestic abuse and violence against men and women have some similarities and difference. For men or women, domestic violence includes pushing, slapping, hitting, throwing objects, forcing or slamming a door, striking the other person with an object, or using a weapon. Domestic abuse can also be mental or emotional. However, what will hurt a man mentally and emotionally can in some cases be very different from what hurts a woman. For some men, being called a coward, impotent, or a failure can have a different psychological impact than it would on a woman. Unkind and cruel words hurt, but they can hurt in different ways and linger in different ways. In most cases, men are more deeply affected by emotional abuse than they are by physical abuse.

For example, the ability to tolerate and "brush off" a physical assault by women in front of other men can in some cases reassure a man that he is strong and communicates to other men that he can live up to the code of never hitting a woman. A significant number of men are overly sensitive to emotional and psychological abuse. In some cases, humiliating a man emotionally in front of other men can be more devastating than physical abuse. Some professionals have observed that mental and emotional abuse can be an area where women are often more "brutal" than men. Men on the other hand are quicker to resort to physical abuse, and they are more capable of physical assaults that are more brutal and that can lead to homicide.

Domestic violence against men goes unrecognized for the following reasons:

- The incidence of domestic violence against men appears to be so low that it is hard to get reliable estimates.
- It has taken years of advocacy and support to encourage women to report domestic violence. Virtually nothing has been done to encourage men to report abuse.
- The idea that men could be victims of domestic abuse and violence is so unthinkable to most people that many men will not even attempt to report the situation.
- The counseling and psychological communities have responded to domestic abuse and violence against women. Not enough has been done to stop abuse against men. There has been little investment in resources to address the issues of domestic abuse and violence against men.
- In most cases, the actual physical damage inflicted by men is so much greater than the actual physical harm inflected by women. The impact of domestic violence is less apparent and less likely to come to the attention of others.
- Even when men do report domestic abuse and violence, most people are so astonished that these men usually end up feeling like nobody would believe them. It is widely assumed that a man with a bruise or black eye was in a fight with another man or was injured on the job or while playing contact sports. Women generally do not do those things.

The characteristics of men or women who are abusive fall into three categories:

- *Alcohol abuse.* Alcohol abuse is a major cause and trigger in domestic violence. People who are intoxicated have less impulse control, are easily frustrated, have greater misunderstandings, and are generally prone to resort to violence as a solution to problems. Women who abuse men are frequently alcoholics.
- *Psychological disorders.* There are certain psychological problems, primarily personality disorders, in which women are characteristically abusive and violent toward men. Borderline personality disorder is a diagnosis that is found almost exclusively with women. Approximately 1% to 2% of all women have a borderline personality disorder. At least 50% of all domestic abuse and violence against men is associated with women who have a borderline personality disorder. The disorder is also associated with suicidal behavior, severe mood swings, lying, sexual problems, and alcohol abuse.
- *Unrealistic expectations, assumptions, and conclusions.* Women who are abusive toward men usually have unrealistic expectations and make unrealistic demands of men. These women will typically experience repeated episodes of depression, anxiety, frustration, and irritability, which they attribute to a man's behavior. In fact, their mental and emotional state is the result of their own insecurities, emotional problems, trauma during childhood, or even withdrawal from alcohol. They blame men rather than admit their problems, take responsibility for how they live their lives, or do something about how they make themselves miserable. They refuse to enter treatment and may even insist the man needs treatment. Instead of helping themselves, they blame a man for how they feel and believe that a man should do something to make them feel better. They often medicate their emotions with alcohol. When men cannot make them feel better, these women become frustrated and assume that men are doing this on purpose.

Case Study **31-1**

Male Survivor

Jerry Miranda is part of a largely hidden group in domestic violence—the male victim. "It's really embarrassing," he said. "I don't want people at work to know I have these kinds of problems."

"She would give everybody the impression she was this kind-hearted, down-to-earth person. Everybody would enjoy her parties," he recalled. "But then she would come home, the door would close, and her personality would change."

H. Miranda had a fierce temper fueled by drinking, he said. She would not only abuse Jerry, but she abused their two sons as well. Jerry was afraid that if he left his wife he would lose custody of his sons. And, he said, his military status kept him from taking his children and fleeing the relationship: "That's called desertion." Jerry Miranda finally found the strength to sever ties with his wife. But on May 4, 1999, four months after he had filed for divorce, his wife broke into his house. He came home to find it ransacked. There were bullets all over the house. When police finally picked up H. Miranda, they found a fully loaded semiautomatic handgun in her pocket. She was arrested and taken to jail, but just six hours later she had posted bail and was out again. From jail she went to the Air Force Academy, where Jerry Miranda worked, and attacked him with a knife. "Then the knife comes down very hard, it gets me once in the back," he recalled. "And it kind of...luckily it hit the bone." Jerry is still constantly on guard, fearing another attack from his estranged wife. "When I leave the house, I take the gun with me," he said. "If I go in the yard, I take the gun. If I go to the mall, I take the gun." He said he will never feel safe from H. Miranda. "It'll never be over, never. This will never be over." (Personal communication with Jerry Miranda, 2009.)

Men stay in abusive and violent relationships for many different reasons, such as the following:

- *Protecting their children.* Abused men are afraid to leave their children alone with an abusive woman. They are afraid that if they leave they will never be allowed to see their children again. The man is afraid the woman will tell his children he is a bad person or that he does not love them.
- *Assuming blame (guilt prone).* Many abused men believe it is their fault or feel they deserve the treatment they receive. They assume blame for events that other people would not. They feel responsible and have an unrealistic belief that they can and should do something that will make things better.
- *Dependency (or fear of independence).* The abused man is mentally, emotionally, or financially dependent on the abusive woman. The idea of leaving the relationship creates significant feelings of depression or anxiety. They are "addicted" to each other.

Workplace Violence

Workplace violence is violence or the threat of violence against workers. It can occur at or outside the workplace and can range from threats and verbal abuse to physical assaults and homicide, one of the leading causes of job-related deaths. However it manifests itself, workplace violence is a growing concern for employers and employees nationwide.

More than 2 million American workers are victims of workplace violence each year. Workplace violence can strike anywhere, and no one is immune (Carroll & Morin, 1999). Some workers, however, are at increased risk. Among them are workers who exchange money with the public; deliver passengers, goods, or services; work alone or in small groups; work during late night or early morning hours; work in high-crime areas; or work in community settings and homes where they have extensive contact with the public. This group includes healthcare and social service workers such as visiting nurses, psychiatric evaluators, and probation officers; community workers such as gas and water utility employees, phone and cable TV installers, and letter carriers; retail workers; and taxi drivers (OSHA, www.osha.gov, 2009).

On August 20, 1986, a part-time letter carrier named Patrick H. Sherrill, facing possible dismissal after a troubled work history, walked into the Edmond, Oklahoma, post office where he worked and shot 14 people to death before killing himself. Though the most deadly, the Edmond tragedy was not the first episode of its kind in this period. In just the previous three years, four postal employees were killed by present or former coworkers in separate shootings in Johnston, South Carolina; Anniston, Alabama; and Atlanta, Georgia. The shock of the Edmond killings raised public awareness to the kind of incident now most commonly associated with the phrase "workplace violence"—murder or other violent acts by a disturbed, aggrieved employee or ex-employee against coworkers or supervisors. An early appearance of the phrase itself in Nexis, a database of articles in many major U.S. newspapers, was in August 1989, in a *Los Angeles Times* account of yet another post office shooting. As a result of this seemingly new trend, mass murders in the workplace by unstable employees have become media-intensive events. In fact, the apparent rise in these cases may have been an impression created by this increased media attention. Still, the frequency of episodes following the Edmond post office killings was startling. In Southern California alone, one summary showed that over an eight-year span, from mid-1989 to mid-1997, there were 15 workplace homicide incidents, six with multiple victims, in which 29 people were killed. In subsequent years, major workplace crimes across the country included four state lottery executives killed by a Connecticut lottery accountant (March 1998); seven coworkers killed by a Xerox technician in Honolulu (November 1999); seven slain by a software engineer at the Edgewater Technology Company in Wakefield, Massachusetts (December 2000); four killed by a 66-year-old former forklift driver at the Navistar Plant in Chicago (February 2001); three killed by an insurance executive at Empire Blue Cross and Blue Shield in New York City (September 2002); three killed by a plant worker at a manufacturing plant in Jefferson City, Missouri (July 2, 2003); and six killed by a plant worker at a Lockheed-Martin aircraft plant in Meridian, Mississippi (July 8, 2003). (The Chicago, New York, Mississippi, and Connecticut shooters killed themselves. In the Honolulu and Massachusetts cases, the shooters went to trial. Both pleaded insanity but were convicted, and both received the same sentence, life in prison without parole.) (See www.fbi.gov, 2009.)

Workplace violence is now recognized as a specific category of violent crime that calls for distinct responses from employers, law enforcement, and the community. This recognition is relatively recent. Before the Edmond shootings, the few research and preventive efforts that existed were focused on particular issues—patient assaults on healthcare workers and the high robbery and murder risks facing taxi drivers and late-night convenience store clerks.

However, contrary to popular opinion, sensational multiple homicides represent a very *small* number of workplace violence incidents. The majority of incidents that employees/managers have to deal with on a daily basis are lesser cases of assaults, domestic violence, stalking, threats, harassment (to include sexual harassment), and physical or emotional abuse that make no head-lines. Many of these incidents, in fact, are not even reported to company officials, let alone to police. Data on the exact extent of workplace violence "are scattered and sketchy," specialists acknowl-edged in a February 2001 report issued by the University of Iowa's Injury Prevention Research Center. Drawing on responses to the National Crime Victimization Survey, a Justice Department report estimated that an average of 1.7 million "violent victimizations," 95% of them simple or aggravated assaults, occurred in the work-place each year from 1993 through 1999. Estimates of the costs, from lost work time and wages, reduced productivity, medical costs, workers' compensation payments, and legal and security expenses, are even less exact but clearly run into many billions of dollars (FBI, 2009). The U. S. Department of Labor/Occupational Safety and Health Administration (OSHA) strongly recommend a worksite analysis for planning and mitigating the possibility of these violent acts.

Teacher/Mentor Student Abuse

An estimated 5 million students in United States schools have been assaulted sexually by teachers, according to a congressional report. "We have approximately 5 million children suffering and no one is calling for an investigation, for any kind of data to be collected to find out why that many children are being hurt by teachers," stated Terri Miller, who runs probably the only organi-zation in the nation that focuses specifically on assaults by edu-cators on students. In many cases, especially where the attacker is a woman and the student a male, such assaults are treated as a joke, with a hand-slap for the teacher, and some ribald locker room humor directed at the student.

Miller's volunteer group, called Stop Educator Sexual Abuse, Misconduct and Exploitation, often feels overwhelmed by the dearth of information, injuries to students, and obstacles posed by opponents such as the National Education Association.

One federal study that compiled data from previous studies showed there sometimes are no consequences, even if school administrators know about a teacher's sexual misdeeds. It found the following:

- "Educator Sexual Misconduct: A Synthesis of Existing Literature" was authored by Charol Shakeshaft, (2004) professor of educa-tional administration at Hofstra University in Hempstead, New York, and concluded that the mistreatment of those millions of students ranged from sexual comments to rape.
- Of 225 select cases of teacher sex abuse in New York; although all the accused had admitted to sexually abusing a student, not one was reported to the police and only 1% lost their license to teach.
- A 2003 study reports that 159 Washington state coaches were "reprimanded, warned, or let go in the past decade because of sexual misconduct"–and yet "at least 98 of them continued coaching or teaching afterward."
- A 2004 study reports that many school districts make confidential agreements with abusers, essentially trading a positive recommen-dation for a resignation. In one case, a Seattle educator named Luke Markishtum "had two decades of complaints of sex with students and providing alcohol and marijuana to students prior to his arrest for smuggling six tons of marijuana into the state. The district paid Markishtum the remainder of his salary that year, agreed to keep the record secret, and gave him an additional $69,000."

The 2004 study, ordered by Congress and commissioned by the U.S. Department of Education, concluded that nearly 10% of U.S. public school students have been targeted by unwanted sexual attention from school workers.

Case Study 31-2

LaFave, a teacher from the Tampa, Florida, area received no jail time despite having sex with her 14-year-old male student in a classroom and her Hillsborough County home. In another county she was accused of having sex with the boy in an SUV. LaFave claimed at a March 2006 news conference she had a bipolar disorder. The boy's father said LaFave should have received prison time in her plea deal, noting, "It's a horrible, ugly thing that she's done."

Crimes Against Homeless People

Since the late 1990s, advocates and homeless shelter workers from around the United States have seen an alarming increase in the report of homeless men, women, and even children being mur-dered, beaten, and harassed. The violent attacks and murders are often directed against people precisely because they are homeless, and thus these events constitute hate crimes.

Case Study 31-3

In May 2008, Michael, age 36, was beaten to death with sticks and logs by a group of teenagers who admitted to beating the homeless man just for fun. The autopsy report indicated Michael died of blunt-force trauma to the head and body and suffered a fractured skull, broken ribs, badly injured legs and defensive wounds on his hands. The teens returned several times to make certain the job was done.

Case Study 31-4

In September 2004, three Milwaukee teens murdered a homeless man at his forest campsite. The teens hit 49-year-old Rex B. with rocks, a flashlight, a bat and a pipe, then smeared feces on his face. They con-tinued beating Rex until they thought he was dead. One of the boys "hit the victim one last time to see if he would make a sound like in Grand Theft Auto," then cut him twice with a knife to make sure he was dead. They then covered his body with plastic and rocks, hoping animals would eat him before the body was discovered.

Sadly, these gruesome accounts are only a few of many recent assaults and murders that demonstrate the hatred, prejudice, and senseless violence faced by many of our homeless citizens. Over the six-year period from 1999–2004, the National Coalition for the Homeless (NCH) documented 156 murders and 386 violence acts against homeless individuals. The violence attacks occurred in 140 cities in 39 states in the United States (NCH, 2005).

Many of these violent acts go unpublished or unreported, mak-ing it difficult to assess the true magnitude of the problem. Often, homeless people do not report crimes committed against them because of mental health issues, substance abuse, fear of retalia-tion, or frustration with the police. Some cases were also omitted from reports like that compiled by the NCH because the victims were found beaten to death, but no suspects could be identified.

In addition, this report does not take into account the large number of sexual assaults.

There is currently no federal criminal prohibition against violent crimes directed at individuals because of their housing status, poverty, or homelessness. The NCH aims to include housing status in the Local Law Enforcement Hate Crimes Prevention Acts and future pieces of legislation. People who are forced to live and sleep on the streets for lack of an appropriate alternative are in an extremely vulnerable situation, and it is unacceptable that hate crime prevention laws do not protect them. Forensic nurses must be part of the solution by proper identification and treatment of the injuries of the homeless victims.

The National Coalition for the Homeless and the American Academy of Forensic Scientists recommend the following actions to address the rising number of hate crimes committed against homeless people:

1. A public statement by the U.S. Justice Department acknowledging that hate crimes and violence against people experiencing homelessness is a serious national trend.
2. The Justice Department would issue guidelines for local police and forensic scientists on how to investigate, treat, and work with people experiencing homelessness based on recommendation from the NCH. The Justice Department would recommend improvements to state law on how to better protect against violence directed against people experiencing homelessness, including tougher penalties.
3. A database to be maintained by the U.S. Department of Justice, in cooperation with the NCH, to track hate crimes and/or violence against people experiencing homelessness.
4. Sensitivity/awareness training at police academies and departments nationwide for trainees and police officers on how to deal effectively and humanely with people experiencing homelessness in their communities. This training will include the forensic scientists and nurses who deal with the victims of these crimes.
5. Forensic nurses take an active part in the movement to protect all victims and potential victims of crime.

Summary

With the advent of forensic nursing, a greater emphasis has been placed on the identification, documentation, and education of victims of relationship violence in developing and industrialized countries (Lynch, 1991). To shape policy in contemporary healthcare, an agenda should mandate attention to the legal, civil, and human rights of victims (female or male) of intimate partner violence (Lynch, 1993a). Forensic health science has brought a revolution in healthcare policies to help erode barriers through an interdisciplinary methodology that encompasses medicine, nursing, law, and human behaviorists (Lynch, 1993b).

The emergency/casualty department in any country is most often the first source of help for women, men, and children seeking intervention and refuge in cases of domestic violence. The forensic nurse is a vital link in the early detection of these patients and has the potential to empower victims to interrupt the cycle of abuse, providing options for safe termination of toxic relationships.

Prevention is key in addressing violence. The proactive, multidisciplinary perspective of the forensic nurse will be effective in the development of violence reduction plans. Through effective planning and problem solving, nurses can collaborate with other nurses, disciplines, and administration to enhance the future of healthcare and develop a safer world.

Resources

DOMESTIC VIOLENCE

National Domestic Violence Hotline
1-800-799SAFE (7233) / 1-800-787-3224

MALE VIOLENCE

National Organization on Male Sexual Victimization (United States)
PMB 103, 5505 Connecticut Avenue, NW, Washington, DC 20015–2601; 1-800-738-4181

National Organization on Male Sexual Victimization (Canada)
c/o BCSMSSA, 1252 Burrard Street, #202, Vancouver, B.C., V6Z 1, Canada

WORKPLACE VIOLENCE

The ANA's Workplace Violence: Can you close the door? Call (800) 274- 4ANA

Guidelines for Preventing Workplace Violence for Healthcare and Social Service Workers

U.S. Department of Labor, OSHA 3148–1996, available online. www. osha-slc. gov 80/Newinit/Workplaceviolence/index.html.

References

Ahaia, J. M., et al. (1995). *Integrative review of effects on children of witnessing domestic violence: Issues in comprehensive pediatric nursing.*

American Medical Association (AMA). (2008). www.ama-assn.org

Campbell, J. (1995). *Assessing dangerousness: Violence by sexual offenders, batters, and child abusers.* Newbury: Sage.

Campbell, J. C., & Lewandowski, L. A. (1997). Mental and physical health effects of intimate partner violence on women and children. *Psychiatric Clinics of North America, 20,* 353–374.

Carroll, V., & Morin, K. H. (1999). Workplace violence affect one-third of nurses. *The American Nurse, 15.*

Centers for Disease Control. (2008). www.cdc.gov

Colorado Domestic Violence Commission. (1991). Domestic Violence for Healthcare Providers, 3rd ed. Denver, CO.

Emergency Nurse's Association. (2009). www.ena.org

Equal Justice Foundation. (2009). Update November 1, 2009. http://www.dvmen.org/.

Federal Bureau of Investigation (FBI). (2009). http//fbi.gov

Feldhaus, K. M., Koziol-McLain, J., Amsbury, H. L., Norton, I. M., Lowenstein, S. R., & Abbott, J. T. (1997). Accuracy of 3 brief screening questions for detecting partner violence in the emergency department. *JAMA, 277*(17), 1357–1361.

Helton, A. (1986). *Protocol of Care for the Battered Woman.* Houston, TX: Houston Chapter of the March of Dimes.

Johnson, R. M. (2000). *Rural Health Response to Domestic Violence: Policy and Practice Issues Emerging Public Policy Issues and Best Practices: Federal Office of Rural Health Policy No. # 99–0545(P).* www.ruralhealth.hrsa.gov/pub/domviol.htm

Lynch, V. (1991). Forensic nursing in the emergency department: A new role for the 1990's. *Critical Care Nursing Quarterly, 14*(3).

Lynch, V. (1993a). Forensic nursing: Diversity in education and practice. *Journal of Psychosocial Nursing and Mental Health Services, 31*(11).

Lynch, V. (1993b). Forensic aspects of healthcare: New roles, new responsibilities. *Journal of Psychosocial Nursing and Mental Health Services, 31*(11).

McFarlane, J., Parker, B., Soeken, K., & Bullock, L. (1992). Assessing for abuse during pregnancy. *JAMA, 267*(3), 3176–3178.

National Coalition for the Homeless (NCH). (2009). www.nationalhomeless.org/hatecrimes/signon.

National Institutes of Health. (2005). www.nih.gov/news/pr/mar2005/nhlbi-07.htm

Nettleton, S. (2001). Losing a home through mortgage repossession: The views of children. *Children and Society, 10,* 82–94.

OSHA. (2009). www.osha.gov

Rosen, L. N., Fontaine, J., Gaskin-Laniyan, N. D., Price, C., & Bachar, K. (2008). *Violence & Victimization Research Division's Compendium of Research on Violence Against Women, 1993–2008*. www.ncjrs.gov/pdffiles1/nij/223572-.

Sampselle, C. M., Bernhard, L., Kerr, R. B., et al. (1992). Violence against women: The scope and significance of the problem. In C. M. Sampselle (Ed.), *Violence against women: Nursing research, education, and practice issues* (pp. 3–16). New York: Hemisphere.

Stalking and Harassment. (2009). www.stalkingvictims.com/stalk.htm

Stark, E., Flitcraft (1996). *Women at Risk*. Thousand Oaks, CA: Sage.

Warshaw, R. (1994). *I Never Called It Rape*. New York: Harper Collins Publishing.

Wiehe, V. R., & Richards, A. L. (1995). *Intimate Betrayal: Understanding and Responding to the Trauma of Acquaintance Rape*. Thousand Oaks, CA: Sage.

Wright, J. A., Burgess, A. G., Burgess, A. W., McCrary, G. O., & Douglas, J. E., (1995). Investigating stalking crimes. *Journal of Psychosocial Nursing and Mental Health Services, 33*(9).

CHAPTER 32 Sexual Violence: Victims and Offenders

Linda E. Ledray

One of the first researchers to systematically study the impact and needs of the sexual assault survivor was a nurse, Dr. Ann Burgess (Burgess & Holmstrom, 1974). She and her colleague, Linda Holmstrom, a social worker, identified a two-stage syndrome of response, which they referred to as rape trauma syndrome (Burgess & Holmstrom, 1974). Considerable additional research has occurred since that time, however, and has identified specific symptoms rather than a pattern of response. As a result of this more recent research, posttraumatic stress disorder (PTSD) resulting from sexual assault has become the term used to describe the symptom response following rape (American Psychiatric Association, 1994; Faigman, Kaye, & Saks et al., 1997). The American Psychiatric Association (APA) first referred to PTSD in 1980.

Nurses, including Burgess, have remained active in furthering the understanding of victim response and developing services for sexual assault survivors. The efforts of these pioneering nurses have led to the development of a new role for nurses, the forensic nurse examiner (FNE). Today, the FNE functions in a variety of roles, including clinical forensic nurse, nurse coroner, forensic investigator for the medical examiner, forensic psychiatric nurse, correctional nurse, domestic violence nurse examiner, and sexual assault nurse examiner (SANE).

This chapter focuses on the largest group of forensic nurse examiners, the SANE. It will look at the history and development of the SANE role, the impact of sexual assault, and the treatment needs of sexual assault survivors, as well as how the SANE functions today to meet these needs as a member of the sexual assault response team (SART).

SANE History and Role Development

Although men are raped too, most victims of sexual and personal violence are women. Because women are so often victims of violence, emergency department (ED) nurses have learned that whenever women present to an ED for even minor trauma, the etiology of their trauma must be thoroughly evaluated. ED staff must be aware of the types of injuries most likely resulting from violence, and the victim must be carefully questioned about the cause of the trauma to determine if it is the result of violence (Sheridan, 1993). When violence such as rape is identified, further evaluation may be necessary, including proper evidence collection and maintaining the chain of custody. Further care, beyond basic medical care, is also essential when rape is identified and will be discussed.

Only recently have our healthcare facilities begun to recognize their responsibility to have trained staff available to provide this specialized service for victims of sexual assault. Treating injuries alone is not sufficient. In 2000, a rape victim successfully sued a New York City hospital when she came to the medical facility after a sexual assault and a sexual assault evidentiary examination was not accurately performed. She was made to wait three hours before being examined, and then potentially significant evidence, her underwear and vaginal swabs, were lost. The New York Department of Health investigation also found that the hospital failed to provide complete care. It did not provide her with medication to prevent pregnancy. The authorities believed that if correct evidence collection and chain of custody had occurred, the evidence obtained may have been useful to secure a conviction against the serial sex offender charged with her rape. As a result, New York passed the Sexual Assault Reform Act requiring New York State to develop specialized sexual assault (SANE) evidence collection programs in 2001 (Chivers, 2000). Since 1992, the guidelines of The Joint Commission (TJC) has required emergency and ambulatory care facilities to have protocols on rape, sexual molestation, and domestic abuse (Bobak, 1992). By 1997 they also stated healthcare facilities should develop and train their staff to use criteria to identify possible victims of physical assault, rape, other sexual molestation, domestic abuse, and abuse or neglect of older adults and children (TJC, 1997). TJC expectations concerning hospital care of the sexually assaulted patient were once again raised in 2004 with the expectation that medical care and assessment "must be conducted within the context of the requirements of the law to preserve evidentiary materials and support future legal actions" (TJC, Standard PC 3.10.10, 2004).

At the 1996 International Association of Forensic Nurses (IAFN) meeting in Kansas City, Geri Marullo, executive director of the American Nurses' Association (ANA), predicted that within 10 years TJC would require every hospital to have a forensic nurse available (Marullo, 1996). Even though TJC still does not require a FNE or SANE to be available to do the evaluation, it is no longer optional for medical facilities to identify and provide appropriate and complete services to victims of rape and abuse. In addition, TJC survey teams have begun to ask hospitals multiple questions about sexual abuse policies and procedures and whether they have a SANE program in place to respond. This TJC emphasis has effectively set the stage for the further development of forensic nursing as an important new nursing specialty.

Many healthcare facilities have recognized that the implementation of the FNE role is an optimal way to meet this expectation of a higher level of care and that it is an effective community marketing tool for the medical facility as well. The benefits of the FNE or SANE to the victim, other ED staff, the police, and the prosecutor have been the most effective impetus to SANE role development and utilization. The availability of funding for program development has also been an important impetus.

The landmark Violence Against Women Act (VAWA) of 1994, introduced by Senator Joseph Biden of Delaware, was signed into law on September 13, 1994, as Title IV of the Violent Crime Control and Law Enforcement Act of 1994. In addition to doubling the federal penalties for repeat offenders and requiring that date rape is treated the same as stranger rape, this act made $800 million available for training and program development over a six-year period, with $32 million appropriated for the first year. This funding has had a significant impact on changing the availability of services to rape victims today. It was initially used by the existing rape crisis centers to hire paid staff and to professionalize their organizations, and more recently it has provided funding to establish SANE programs and SARTs across the United States.

The VAWA 2005 reauthorization has additional forensic compliance mandates. This reauthorization requires that states ensure all teen and adult victims do not have any out-of-pocket expenses associated with the provision of sexual assault forensic examinations and that victims are provided these forensic medical exams *without* being required to report to law enforcement, cooperate with law enforcement, or participate in the criminal justice system (42 USCA S.3796 gg-4 (d) (1)). Although many jurisdictions have been meeting these mandates for more than 20 years, under this reauthorization, states and territories were given until January 5, 2009, to certify that they are in compliance. States have several options available to meet these mandates. The evidentiary exam may be completed, the evidence collected and held by the medical facility, maintaining chain of custody, for a specific period of time, giving the victim the option of making a delayed report before the evidence is destroyed. Or the victim may be given the option of making an anonymous "Jane Doe," or blind, report in which a police report is made without disclosing the victim's identity, so the evidence can be turned over to law enforcement for storage.

DEMONSTRATING THE NEED FOR SANE PROGRAMS

The initial impetus to develop SANE and SART programs began with the individuals who were working with rape victims in hospitals, clinics, and other settings across the country. These workers primarily included nurses, other medical professionals, counselors, and advocates. It was obvious to these individuals that services to sexual assault victims were inadequate and were not being provided at the same high standard of care being given to other medical clients (Holloway & Swan, 1993; O'Brien, 1996). When rape victims came to the ED for care, they often had to wait as long as 12 hours in a busy, public area; their wounds were seen as less serious than the other trauma victims, and they competed unsuccessfully for medical staff time with the critically ill (Holloway & Swan, 1993; Sandrick, 1996; Speck & Aiken, 1995). They were often not allowed to eat, drink, or urinate while they waited, for fear of destroying evidence (Thomas & Zachritz, 1993). The medical professionals who eventually did care for them were often not sufficiently trained to do medicolegal examinations, and many were also lacking in their ability to provide expert witness testimony (Lynch, 1993).

When staff was trained, they often did not complete a sufficient number of examinations to maintain their level of proficiency (Lenehan, 1991; Tobias, 1990 Yorker; 1996). Even when the

victim's medical needs were met, his or her emotional needs all too often were overlooked (Speck & Aiken, 1995), or even worse, the survivor was not believed or the ED staff blamed the survivor for the rape (Kiffe, 1996). All too often, the rape survivor faced a time-consuming examination by a succession of healthcare professionals, some with only a few hours of orientation, many with little experience, and most not comfortable doing the examination or concerned that they would be called to testify in court.

Services were inconsistent and problematic. Often the only physician available to do the vaginal examination after the rape was male (Lenehan, 1991). Approximately half of rape victims in one study were unconcerned with the gender of the examiner, but for the other half this was extremely problematic. This study found even male victims often preferred to be examined by a woman, as they too are most often raped by a man and experienced the same generalized fear and anger toward men that female victims experienced (Ledray, 1996a).

More recently, male RNs who wanted to be SANEs have been trained and, likely as a result of their empathetic and nonjudgmental approach, victims have successfully accepted them. The forensic nurse response team in Houston, Texas, had three men on the team in 2004, and in more than 600 cases performed by the three combined, only one instance in which a patient preferred a female examiner was reported (Rooms, 2004). After having power and control over one's body ripped away by a male, having a male restore a sense of control by gaining consent before talking, touching, or examining the patient is often cited as restoring a more positive image of men in general. Men in nursing who specialize in domestic violence cases have also cited this benefit. It has been noted that the ability of the examiner to convey genuine concern, empathy, and return power and control is a more important characteristic than gender. Whether it is the responding law enforcement officer, paramedic, triage nurse, physician, or SANE, men should be encouraged to understand the psychodynamics of sexual assault and attempt to quash the myth that men have nothing to offer the sexual assault patient (Rooms, 2004).

There are also many reports of physicians being reluctant to do the examination. This reluctance was the result of many factors, which included an awareness of their lack of experience and training in forensic evidence collection and not wanting to do something they knew was extremely important and that they were concerned they would not do well (Bell, 1995; Lynch, 1993; Speck & Aiken, 1995).

The lengthy evidentiary examination takes the physician away from other medically urgent or critically ill patients in a busy ED (Frank, 1996). In addition, whenever the physician is involved in evidence collection, there is always the expectation that the doctor will later be subpoenaed and be taken away from working in the ED to testify in court and be questioned by a sometimes hostile defense attorney (Frank, 1996; Speck & Aiken, 1995; Thomas & Zachritz, 1993). All too often, such concerns resulted in evidence collection being rushed, inadequate, or incomplete. In rare instances, physicians even refused to do the examination, and the rape victim was sent home from the hospital without having an evidentiary examination completed because no physician could be found to collect the evidence (DiNitto, Martin, Yancey, et al., 1986; Kettelson, 1995). Unfortunately, many of these same problems continue today in major medical centers in the United States (Chivers, 2000).

As research with this population continued, the importance of this initial medicolegal examination for these survivors became clear, as did the need to provide the most comprehensive care possible during the initial ED visit (Gray-Eurom, Seaberg, Ledray, 2002; Lenehan, 1991). For as many as 75% of sexual assault victims, the initial ED visit was the only known contact they had with medical or professional support staff regarding the sexual assault, and it had a significant impact on their medical and psychological recovery (Ledray, 1992). Additional research confirmed that the proper collection and documentation of evidence by the ED staff had a significant impact on the successful prosecution of these cases and the lack of evidence could harm the likelihood of prosecution (Chivers, 2000; Frazier & Haney, 1996; Gray-Eurom, Seaberg, & Wears, 2002; Ledray, 2002; Tintinalli & Hoelzer, 1985). This confirmed the importance of ED physicians either being properly trained themselves to collect the evidence or supporting the development and utilization of a SANE program to provide the service for them (Gray-Eurom, et al., 2002; Wears, 2002).

SANE PROGRAM DEVELOPMENT

As a result of this identified goal to better meet the needs of this underserved population, SANE programs were established in Memphis, Tennessee, in 1976 (Speck & Aiken, 1995), Minneapolis, Minnesota, in 1977 (Ledray, 1993; Ledray & Chaignot, 1980), and Amarillo, Texas, in 1979 (Antognoli-Toland, 1985). Unfortunately, these nurses worked in isolation, unaware of the existence of similar programs until Gail Lenehan, editor of the *Journal of Emergency Nursing* (JEN), recognized the importance of this new role for nurses and published the first list of 20 SANE programs (Emergency Nurses Association, 1991). This facilitated communication, collaboration, and further SANE program development.

As a result of the collaboration fostered by the *Journal of Emergency Nursing*, 72 individuals from 31 programs across the United States and Canada came together for the first time in 1992 at a meeting hosted by the Sexual Assault Resource Service and the University of Minnesota School of Nursing in Minneapolis. It was at that meeting that the International Association of Forensic Nurses (IAFN) was formed (Ledray, 1996b). Membership in IAFN surpassed the 1000 mark in 1996 (Lynch, 1996). By January 2009, the number of members had grown to more than 3300 (personal communication with Kim Day, IAFN, February 18, 2009). Although initial SANE development was slow, with only three programs operating by the end of the 1970s, development today is progressing rapidly. In the past few years, IAFN has, however, concentrated more efforts on strengthening and sustaining the SANE programs in operation rather than developing new programs.

After years of effort on the part of SANEs and other forensic nurses, the American Nurses Association (ANA) officially recognized forensic nursing as a new specialty in 1995 (Lynch, 1996). At the October, 1996, IAFN annual meeting held in Kansas City, the SANE council voted overwhelmingly to use the title SANE, sexual assault nurse examiner, to define this new forensic nursing role. SANE is still the largest subspecialty of forensic nursing.

A SANE is a registered nurse (RN) who has advanced education in forensic examination of sexual assault victims. IAFN has recommended a 40-hour didactic SANE training program, with specified content, plus clinical experience for a nurse to function as a SANE (Ledray, 1999). At the 1996 annual meeting of IAFN, the SANE council also voted and adopted the first SANE standards of practice. The standards include goals of sexual assault nurse examiner programs, a definition of the practice area, a conceptual framework of SANE practice, evaluation, documentation, forensic examination components, and minimum SANE educational qualifications (IAFN SANE Standards, 1996). In April

2002, the first national certification examination was given to 80 nurses. Of those 80 nurses, 70 (87.5%) passed and were the first to carry the SANE-A designation after their name, for sexual assault nurse examiner—adults and adolescents. That was followed in 2007 with the designation of SANE-P for SANEs who specialize in the care of pediatric victims. Both certifications are offered through IAFN. Although SANE-A or SANE-P certification certainly identifies that the SANE has additional expertise and may be helpful in establishing credibility when testifying in court, it is not a requirement for a nurse to work as a SANE or to testify as an expert witness in court.

Sexual Assault Impact and Treatment Needs

KEY POINT The physical impact of a sexual assault on the victim includes genital and nongenital trauma as well as fear of contracting a sexually transmitted infection (STI), general health risk, fear of pregnancy, substance abuse, and all too often sexual dysfunction. The psychological impact can last for years after a sexual assault and typically includes depression, anxiety, fears, posttraumatic stress disorder (PTSD) symptoms, self-blame, and shame.

NONGENITAL PHYSICAL INJURY

Most studies indicate that significant physical injury resulting from sexual assault is rare (3% to 5% across studies, with less than 1% of victims needing hospitalization). Even minor injury usually occurs in only about one third of the reported rapes. Injuries, when they do occur, are more common in stranger rapes and rapes by someone the victim knows intimately (domestic violence) than in date rape or acquaintance rape (Kilpatrick, Edmunds, & Seymour, 1992; Ledray, 1999; Marchbanks, Lui, & Mercy, 1990; Tucker, Ledray, & Stehle Werner, 1990). Also, much like nongenital injuries, anogenital injuries include a variety of tears, bruising, scraping, irritation and redness, swelling, and cuts. These may all occur from consensual and nonconsensual sexual contact (Keller & Nelson, 2008).

In one study, the rate of physical injury for male rape victims (40%) was found to be higher than for female victims (32%). Although 25% of the men and 38% of the women in this study of 351 rape victims sought medical care after the rape for their physical injuries, only 61% of them told the treating physician they had been raped. The women expressed a strong preference for medical treatment and counseling by a woman. The male victims were less likely to express a gender preference (Petrak, Skinner, & Claydon, 1995). A more recent study of 1076 sexual assault victims, of which 96% were female, found nongenital trauma more often, 67% of the time. Physical force was, however, reported during the sexual assault in 79.6% of this population (Riggs, Houry, Long, et al., 2000).

STRANGULATION

Although we do not have statistics indicating the percentage of sexual assault victims who are strangled or smothered during the assault, we do know that in domestic violence (DV) cases, when a victim is strangled she is nine times more likely to be killed by her abuser than one who is not, and she is likely to be killed soon afterward (Battered Woman's Justice Project and the Family Justice Center, 2004; Strack et al., 2004). Because most women do not report strangulation or smothering unless they are asked, it is important that in addition to looking for signs and symptoms of strangulation, we ask all victims if anything was placed around their neck or over their nose and mouth that prevented them from breathing or speaking. Clues to look for at the time of the exam or by history would include sore throat, vocal changes such as hoarseness, neck bruising, redness, or swelling, shortness of breath, wheezing, signs of aspiration such as a cough or emesis, hyperventilation, marks on the neck or chest from a ligature or hands, scratches on the neck, petechiae to conjunctiva, mouth, face, or neck (remember, petechiae may also be in the brain and be life threatening hours or days later), bruising or petechiae behind the ears, subscleral hemorrhage, agitation, confusion, seizure, loss of bowel or bladder function, or visual changes. Whenever strangulation or smothering is suspected, additional evaluation is indicated, which may include pulse oximetry, chest or soft tissue x-ray, CT or MRI of the neck or brain, carotid Doppler ultrasound, or laryngoscopy (Adkinson, Karasov 2007; Battered Women's Justice Project and the Family Justice Center, 2004; OPDV Bulletin, 2003; Vignola, 2009).

ANOGENITAL TRAUMA

When evaluating the genital area for trauma, it is important to remember that the genital area is elastic and very vascular. As a result, it can withstand penetration without tearing, and injuries that do occur heal rapidly without scarring. Most injuries are identified in exams completed within the first 48 hours after the assault (Carter-Snell, Olson, Jensen, Cummings, & Wiebe, 2007). This is one of many reasons why the evidentiary examination should be completed as soon as possible, as anogenital injuries are seen more frequently when there is a shorter interval between the assault and examination and why it is important to remember that the absence of visual trauma does not rule out forceful, unwanted penetration (Adams, Girardin, & Faugno, 2001).

Studies indicate the likelihood of genital trauma identification without the use of a colposcope or camera equipped with a macro lens to magnify the trauma is similar to that of nongenital trauma; 1% have severe injury, and 10% to 30% have minor injury across studies. In reported studies, the injury was always accompanied by complaints of vaginal pain, discomfort, or bleeding (Cartwright, Moore, & Anderson et al., 1986; Geist, 1988; Tintinalli & Hoelzer, 1985).

In one study, Adams et al. (2001) reported that the number of genital injuries correlated greatly with the number of other nongenital injuries (p = 0.003), suggesting that some assaults are more violent in many aspects. Although they do not specifically indicate if a colposcope was used on examination, Riggs et al. (2000) found genital trauma more often, in 52% of the cases reviewed. It is uncertain if this is the result of more violence resulting in injury in their population or more careful and consistent injury evaluation by experienced examiners. Other researchers report finding more anogenital injuries in sexual assault victims who are virgins than in victims who were sexually active (Jones, Rossman, Wynn, Dunnuck, & Schwartz, 2003).

The literature also suggests that colposcopic examination is often extremely useful to visualize genital abrasions, bruises, and tears, because these injuries are often so minute they cannot be seen with the naked eye (Frank, 1996; Slaughter & Brown, 1992). These minor injuries are likely the result of tightened pelvic muscles and a lack of pelvic tilt or lubrication during the forced penetration. This minor injury usually heals completely within 48 to 72 hours. With colposcopic examination, genital trauma has been identified in up to 87% (N = 114) of sexual assault cases (Slaughter & Brown, 1992).

Another often quoted study comparing vaginal trauma in sexual assault survivors to women who had consenting sexual contact found 68% of 311 sexual assault victims had genital trauma, where as only 11% (n = 8) of the 57 women in the study who had consenting sex had genital trauma (Slaughter, Brown, Crowley, & Peck, 1997). Unfortunately, this study has not yet been replicated and is problematic, as women who recanted the sexual assault were included in the control group. The findings do not indicate if they did or did not have vaginal injuries. Although they did indicate the site of genital trauma, unfortunately they did not link the trauma to time of exam or the mechanism of injury (e.g., penile, digital, or penetration by an object). The most common sites of injury were the posterior fourchette, labia minora, hymen, fossa navicularis, and anus, followed by the cervix.

Another study looking at site of injury, but not connecting the mechanism of injury, compared 766 women ranging in age from 13 to 82. They found the most common sites of injury for the adolescents were the fossa navicularis, hymen, labia minora, and posterior fourchette. Nearly twice as many adolescents (10%) had cervical injury than did adult women. Eighty-three percent of the adolescents had anogenital injuries compared to 64% of the adult women (Jones, et al., 2003).

Both the colposcope and anoscope have been shown to improve the identification of rectal trauma; however, the colposcope may be less helpful than the anoscope. In a study of 67 male rape victims, all examined by experienced forensic examiners, 53% had genital trauma identified with the naked eye alone. This number only increased slightly, 8%, when the colposcope was used, but the positive findings increased a significant 32% when an anoscope was used. The combination of naked eye, colposcope, and anoscope resulted in total positive findings in 72% of the cases (Ernst, Green, Ferguson, et al., 2000).

We have more recently become aware of the importance of considering skin color in forensic evaluations. Unfortunately, little is known about anogenital injury prevalence and skin color. One study used experienced sexual assault examiners to evaluate 63 black and 57 white women after consensual sexual intercourse. They used colposcopes with digital imaging, and toluidine blue dye application. They found 55% of the total sample had at least one anogenital injury, with a significant difference between the groups. Injury was identified in the white women 68% of the time and only 43% of the time in the black women (p = .003). They concluded that dark skin color rather than race was a primary predictor for a decrease in injury detection (Sommers, Fargo, Baker, Fisher, Buscher, & Zink, 2009, in press).

Because rape victims often fear vaginal trauma, it is also important when they seek a medical examination that the extent of the trauma, or the lack of trauma, is explained to them after the forensic examination is completed (Ledray, 1999). When a video colposcope is available, it can be helpful to turn the screen so that the survivor can also view the genital area.

BEST PRACTICE The forensic nurse examiner should disclose and explain the nature of any physical trauma associated with the sexual assault. If there are no apparent injuries, the victim should be reassured about the absence of trauma.

The ability of the examiner to identify anogenital trauma has improved considerably with the utilization of SANEs who are better trained in trauma identification and who are more likely to use a colposcope, anoscope, or a camera with a macro lens. However, the issue has now shifted and the question raised by defense attorneys is how can one be certain that anogenital trauma is the result of a sexual assault and not "rough" consenting sexual contact. Although this has become a clearly relevant focus of study by clinical researchers, unfortunately, sufficient scientific information does not yet exist that determines if the trauma identified is the result of consenting or nonconsenting sexual contact. What is known is that anogenital trauma does not prove rape, and the absence of trauma does not prove consent (Hilden, Schei, & Sidenius, 2005; Jones, Rossman, Hartman, & Alexander, 2003; Jones, et al., 2003, Sommers & Buschur, 2004; Slaughter & Brown, 1992; Sommers, Fisher, & Karjane, 2005). There is indeed a need for additional studies that look for a pattern of injury, tied to the time from exam to penetration and the type of penetration, in consenting and nonconsenting sexual contact.

The literature suggests that a number of factors impact the likelihood of finding anogenital injuries after a reported sexual assault. These include the time between the exam and the assault, methods of examination (gross visualization, colposcopy, or the use of a digital camera), the experience and skill of the examiner, and the past sexual history of the victim. It is also important to remember that there can indeed be genital trauma from consenting sexual contact. Trauma does not result solely from nonconsenting sexual contact or sexual assault. It does, however, appear that trauma is more likely and multiple sites of trauma are more likely as a result of sexual assault than from consenting sexual contact.

KEY POINT Anogenital injury heals rapidly. Anogenital trauma can result from consenting sexual contact. Trauma does not result solely from nonconsenting sexual contact or sexual assault. Both trauma and multiple sites of trauma are more likely to occur as a result of sexual assault than from consenting sexual contact.

SEXUALLY TRANSMITTED INFECTIONS

Sexually transmitted infections (STI) and HIV concerns have been identified as a significant reason why victims seek medical care after a sexual assault. While one study found 36% of the rape victims coming to the ED stated their primary reason for coming was concern about having contracted an STI (Ledray, 1991), the actual risk is much lower. The Centers for Disease Control and Prevention (CDC) estimates the risks of rape victims getting gonorrhea is 6% to 12%, chlamydia infection is 4% to 17%, syphilis is 0.5% to 3%, and HIV is much less than 1% (CDC, 1993, 1998). The specific STI risk will, of course, vary from community to community, and it is important that the forensic examiner is aware of local rates so that this information can be provided to concerned sexual assault victims.

From a forensic and clinical perspective, treating prophylactically for STIs following the current CDC guidelines is preferable to culturing. Culturing is expensive and time consuming for the survivor who must return two or three times for additional testing, and, unfortunately, most victims do not return (Blair & Warner, 1992). In addition, STI cultures have not proved to be useful in court in adult and adolescent cases. It is still recommended in ongoing child sexual abuse cases, however, and can be useful evidence. As a result, most clinicians and forensic examiners recommend prophylactic treatment for adult and adolescent victims (American College of Emergency Physicians, 1999, CDC, 1998; Frank, 1996; Ledray, 1999; OVW, 2004).

BEST PRACTICE Prophylactic treatment for sexually transmitted diseases should be a component of all forensic examinations of adolescent and adult victims of sexual assault.

In a national study, researchers found only 58% of sexual assault victims were screened or treated for sexually transmitted infections (Amey, 2002). Fortunately, victims seen by SANE programs are more likely to have this need addressed. In a study of 61 SANE programs across the United States, 90% offered prophylactic treatment for STIs, although 54% of these programs did not offer HIV testing (Ciancone, Wilson, Collette, & Gerson, 2000).

Since the early 1980s, HIV has been a concern for rape survivors, even though the actual risk still appears to be very low with only a few published cases of HIV transmission following sexual assault (CDC, 2005). The first case in which seroconversion, from HIV negative to HIV positive, suspected to be the result of a rape occurred in 1989 (Murphy, Harris, Kitchen, & Forester, 1989). Claydon Murphy, Osborne, et al. (1991) reported four more cases in which researchers believe a rape resulted in a subsequent HIV seroconversion. Even though these numbers are extremely low considering the number of rapes that occur every year, the impact for the individual victims is, of course, extremely significant.

In a study of 412 Midwest rape victims with vaginal or rectal penetration tested for HIV in the ED at three months after rape and again at six months after rape, not one seroconverted. Because 95% of individuals who are going to seroconvert will do so by three months after exposure and 100% will do so by six months, the researchers did not recommend routine HIV testing or prophylactic care. The study also found, however, that even if the survivor did not ask about HIV in the ED, within two weeks it was a concern of theirs or their sexual partner. Based on the recommendations of the rape survivors surveyed in this study, the researchers recommend that even if the survivor does not raise the issue of HIV or AIDS in the ED, the SANE or medical professional should, in a matter-of-fact manner, provide them with information about their risk, testing, and safe sex options (Ledray, 1999).

Determining the actual risk of HIV exposure following a sexual assault is extremely difficult because of the time period and other factors that could account for any seroconversion that may occur. How to best deal with the issue of HIV is complicated and controversial (Blair & Warner, 1992). If the offender is HIV infected, the probability of a rape victim contracting HIV from a sexual assault will depend on the type of sexual contact, the presence of trauma in the involved orifice, if there was exposure to ejaculate, the viral load of the ejaculate, and the presence of other STIs (CDC, 2002). In most instances, it is impossible to determine the HIV status of the offender in a timely fashion. In the Minnesota study described earlier, two assailants told the rape victims that they were positive. However, when one was apprehended and tested for HIV, he was found to be negative (Ledray, 1999). The likely risk of an offender being HIV-infected varies from state to state, because the general rates of HIV infection vary from state to state and community to community. The forensic examiner must, of course, know the local infection rates.

The risk following a single receptive penile-anal exposure is 0.5% to 3.2%, and following receptive penile-vaginal exposure 0.05% to 0.15% (Downs & de Vincenzi, 1996; DeGruttola, Seage, Mayer & Horsburgh, 1989; Katz & Gerberding, 1998; Mastro & deVincenzi, 1996; Wiley, Herschkorn & Padian, 1989). No data are available on the risk of oral sexual transmission.

Because good data are not available on the actual risk of HIV transmission following a sexual assault, the CDC recommends postexposure antiviral prophylaxis (PEP) should be considered, or recommended, based on the risk of the rape combined with the HIV prevalence in the specific geographic area (CDC, 2005). A rape would be considered a high-risk rape if it involved rectal contact or vaginal contact with vaginal tears or existing vaginal STIs that have caused ulcerations or open sores disrupting the integrity of the vaginal mucosa. It would also be considered high risk if the victim had some reason to know or suspect that the assailant was an intravenous drug user, HIV positive, or bisexual.

As with other STIs, the risks, symptoms, and treatment options, including the impact of the HIV antiviral drug regimen, and follow-up recommendations, should be explained to the victim so he or she can make an educated decision (Ledray, 1999; US Department of Justice Office on Violence Against Women (OVW), 2004).

PREGNANCY

The risk of pregnancy from a rape is the same as the risk of pregnancy from any one-time sexual encounter, estimated to be 2% to 4% (Yuzpe, Smith, & Rademaker, 1982). Unfortunately, perhaps from a lack of education, understanding, or personal religious beliefs, many healthcare providers still do not routinely discuss emergency contraception with sexual assault victims, even though the California Court of Appeals clearly articulated in the case of *Brownfield v. Daniel Freeman Marina Hospital* that a woman who did not receive complete postrape counseling and the right to choose a postrape antipregnancy treatment has standing to sue the hospital that provided the inadequate care (Calif. State Court of Appeals, BO32109, 1989).

The National Victim Survey found only 40% of rape victims were given information about emergency contraception (EC) (National Victim Center, 1992). Similar results were found in a more recent study completed by the National Research Center for Women and Families (2006) that reported less than half of sexual assault victims seen in the ED are offered EC. However, another national survey of hospitals found as few as 20% of rape victims were given EC (Amey & Bishai, 2002). Fortunately, as with STI prophylaxis, most (97%) of SANE programs offer EC to women at risk of becoming pregnant following a sexual assault (Ciancone et al., 2000). Most rape survivors are now offered this option when they are seen within five days of the rape and have a negative pregnancy test in the ED.

One SANE program operating at a Catholic hospital went as far as to get special permission from the diocese to administer Ovral (ethinyl estradiol) (Frank, 1996). The National Conference of Catholic Bishops has agreed that "A female who has been raped should be able to defend herself against a potential conception from the sexual assault. If, after appropriate testing, there is no evidence that conception has occurred already, she may be treated with medication that would prevent ovulation, or fertilization" (National Conference of College Bishops, 1995, p. 16). Unfortunately, even with this directive only 5% of hospitals with Catholic affiliations will prescribe EC when requested (Amey & Bishai, 2002).

The importance of offering complete care to sexual assault victims, including care to prevent pregnancy when requested by the victim, was further strengthened by the successful lawsuit against the New York City hospital that did not ensure that a victim receive a full birth control prescription to prevent pregnancy (Chivers, 2000). Many states have state laws requiring all hospitals that see sexual assault victims to offer them pregnancy prevention medica-

tions. This is a significant change in responsibility. Even though as of August 24, 2006, EC is now available over the counter (U.S. Food and Drug Administration, 2006), it is still important for hospitals to provide the EC to rape victims in the ED. This is essential to avoid a delay in their getting the medication, because the longer they wait the less effective it will be in preventing a pregnancy. It is also possible that if victims are only given a prescription, they will not fill the prescription for EC because of cost, stress from the assault, or embarrassment (Womack, 2008).

Sometimes referred to as "the morning-after pill," oral contraceptives such as Ovral or Lovral were initially used for EC. The Yuzpe regimen using a combined oral contraceptive is currently the most common emergency contraceptive (Yuzpe, et al., 1982). A more recently available progestin-only contraceptive, levonorgestrel 0.75 mg (plan B), is today the EC of choice and is widely used. Plan B is slightly, but nonsignificantly, more effective in reducing the risk of pregnancy. When started within 72 hours of unprotected intercourse, 85% of pregnancies were prevented in one study, compared to 57% using the Yuzpe regimen (Task Force on Postovulatory Methods of Fertility Regulation, 1998). The effectiveness of both methods decreases as the time between the assault and the first dose increases. When given within the first 24 hours, plan B reduced the risk of pregnancy by 95%, but only by 61% when given between 48 and 72 hours after unprotected intercourse. Because there is some continued preventive efficacy for up to five days, plan B is now given for up to five days after unprotected sexual contact. An advantage of plan B was in that the only side effect, nausea and vomiting, was significantly reduced to 23.1%, from 50% with the Yuzpe method (Task Force on Postovulatory Methods of Fertility Regulation, 1998). This side effect can also be reduced by administering an antiemetic one hour before giving the pregnancy prevention. A more recent study found that it was as effective to give two tabs of levonorgestrel (75 mg) immediately, rather than as two doses (75 mg) 12 hours apart (Hertzen, Piaggio, Ding, et al., 2002).

GENERAL HEALTH RISK

More medical professionals today are aware of the convincing evidence that sexual assault can have a significant and chronic impact on the general health of a sexual assault survivor.

KEY POINT The stress resulting from rape appears to suppress the immune system and increase susceptibility to disease, and it increases the survivor's attention to subtle physical symptoms and concerns about general health (Cohen & Williamson, 1991).

Sexual assault victims interpret emotional reactions to the assault as physical disease symptoms (Koss, Woodruff, & Koss, 1990), or they may employ maladaptive coping strategies, such as an increased substance use and eating disorders that have a serious negative health impact (Felitti, 1991; Golding, 1994). Increased sexual activity with multiple partners, which also sometimes follows rape, especially in a formerly inactive adolescent, may also result in increased exposure to disease (Ledray, 1994).

Rape victims often want to avoid remembering or talking about the assault and are more comfortable seeking medical care, which they see as less stigmatizing than psychological counseling. Kimerling and Calhoun found 73% of a sample of 115 sexual assault victims sought out medical services during the first year after a sexual assault, whereas only 19% sought out mental health services during the same time period (Kimerling & Calhoun, 1994).

Poor social support was associated with higher use of medical services, and higher levels of social support were associated with better actual physical health and better health perception in this population. Koss et al. (1990) found that a statistically significant 92% of 2291 female crime victims sought medical care in the first year following the crime, and 100% sought medical care during the first two years. Those who had suffered more severe crime and victims of multiple crimes were the most likely to seek medical care. They, too, suggest that the stress of victimization may reduce resistance to disease by suppressing the immune system.

It is interesting that in their sample, Kimerling and Calhoun (1994) did not find a significant difference in the health service utilization of women who had sought out psychological services. Jones and Vischi (1980) even found a 20% decrease in medical service utilization in a sample of 87 rape victims who were in psychotherapy, stressing the importance of ensuring initial crisis intervention and follow-up counseling for victims of sexual assault.

Waigandt and Miller (1986) found that rape victims made 35% more visits to a medical doctor each year than nonvictims; however, the victims who continued to have psychological problems several years later made more visits and perceived their health as worse than the recovered victims. The recovered rape victims experienced only 12% of possible physical symptoms, and the victims with psychological problems experienced 28% of the symptoms, primarily female problems such as dysmenorrhea and incontinence. These victims also exhibited twice the number of maladaptive health behaviors such as smoking, excessive alcohol use, and overeating.

Walker, Katon, Hansom et al. (1995) found women with chronic pelvic pain were significantly more likely than women with no pelvic pain to be victims of sexual abuse, even though only 1 out of 10 were found to have an organic condition. The chronic pain groups were also more likely to be depressed and to have substance abuse problems, phobias, and sexual dysfunction. Eleven percent of the primary care visits were related to the chronic pelvic pain, at an average cost of $1816 per patient.

Rape disclosure can have a significant and positive impact on a woman's health.

Case Study 32-1

Disclosing Abuse

A 49-year-old woman experienced intermittent, severe, longstanding hypertension for which no biological cause could be identified. After a routine health visit to check her blood pressure (BP), she disclosed she had been having nightmares and was beginning to recall being raped by her sister's boyfriend when she was 14 years old. Immediately after the disclosure her BP went from 240/150 mm Hg to 150/105 mm Hg. The next morning she reported a good night's sleep, no more nightmares, and her BP was recorded at a normal 120/85 mm Hg (Mann & Delon, 1995).

Felitti (1991) compared a sample of 131 medical patients who had a history of sexual abuse to a group of matched control subjects. The majority (90%) had never before disclosed the abuse. Decades later, Felitti found the sexual assault victims to be significantly more depressed (83%) and experiencing physical symptoms of depression such as despondency, chronic fatigue, sleep disturbance, and frequent crying spells. Sixty percent had gained more than 50 pounds, and 35% had gained more than 100 pounds.

Chronic unexplained headaches were common in the victim group (45%), as were recurrent gastrointestinal disturbances (64%). Another study of 100 women concluded that women with a history of sexual abuse were 60% more likely to have unexplained pelvic pain, abnormal bleeding, and more gynecological surgery than women without a sexual assault history (Chapman, 1989). Chapman (1989) found that sexual abuse victims had five times the number of hysterectomies and three times the number of pelvic and gynecological surgeries than a nonvictim control group and cautions that unexplained pain in women with a history of sexual abuse may not be removed by a surgical procedure when pain alone is the criteria for the procedure.

Koss, Koss, and Woodruff (1991) found severity of victimization was a more effective predictor of total yearly visits to a physician and outpatient costs than was age, ethnicity, self-reported symptoms, or actual injury. They found that rape victims were twice as likely to seek the help of a physician than nonvictims, and visits increased 56% in victim groups compared to 2% in nonvictim groups.

In a study comparing sexual assault (n = 99) and life-threatening physical abuse victims (n = 68) on physical health status 10 years later, Leserman, Drossman et al. (1997) found overall poor physical health status was directly associated with sexual assault, especially with physical injury during the assault, multiple perpetrators, and the victim's life being threatened during the assault. Golding (1994) also found women with a history of sexual assault were more likely to complain of six or more medically unexplained somatic symptoms (29% versus 16% of nonrape victims) and to have a severe chronic disease such as diabetes, arthritis, difficulty in walking, paralysis, or fainting as well as having functional limitations (27% versus 16% of the nonrape victims). The increased incidence of overall explained and unexplained somatic symptoms of rape victims in this population was 60%, compared to 36% of the nonvictims.

Sexual Dysfunction

Considering the nature of sexual assault, it is not surprising that studies have found sexual dysfunction is a common reaction, and often a chronic problem, following a sexual assault. The sexual dysfunction often includes loss of sexual desire, inability to become sexually aroused, slow arousal, pelvic pain associated with sexual activity, a lack of sexual enjoyment, inability to achieve orgasm, fear of sex, avoidance of sex, intrusive thoughts of the assault during sex, or abstinence. Sexual dysfunction such as avoidance, loss of interest in sex, loss of pleasure from sex, painful intercourse, and actual fear of sex are mentioned repeatedly in the literature (Abel & Rouleau, 1995; Becker, Skinner, Abel, et al., 1986; Burgess & Holmstrom, 1979; Frazier, 2000; Kimerling & Calhoun, 1994; Koss, 1993; Ledray, 1994; Ledray, 1999). It is important to note that even though rape victims may become sexually active again within months of the assault, they may still not enjoy sex years later. Celibacy may be a coping strategy.

Substance Abuse

In one of the first large samples of 6159 college students surveyed by Koss (1988), 73% of the assailants and 55% of the victims reported using alcohol or other drugs before the sexual assault. Rape victims are clearly more vulnerable to being raped as a result of substance abuse, which leads to intoxication and an increased vulnerability. Because one study identified that 47% of the rape victims seen reported some form of sexual victimization in the past, vulnerability is clearly an issue (Ledray, 2001).

The use of alcohol and other substances prior to a sexual assault is often identified in the literature (Abbey, 2002; Kaysen, Neighbors, Martell, Fossos, & Latimer, 2006; Ledray, 1999; Logan, Walker, Cole & Leukefeld, 2002; Messman-Moore & Long, 2002). Studies indicate at least 50% to 74% of rape victims used alcohol or drugs immediately before a sexual assault (Abbey, 2002; DuMont, Miller, & Myhr, 2003; Kilpatrick, Resnick, Ruggiero, Conoscenti, & Mc Cauley, 2007; Littleton & Breitkopf, 2006; Logan, Cole, & Capillo, 2006).

It is important to remember, and it has long been recognized, that rape also can result in substance abuse, possibly as an attempt to dull the memory and avoid thinking about the rape (Goodman, Koss, & Russo, 1993; Koss, 1993; Ledray, 1994). In a national sample of 3006 survivors, both alcohol and drug use was significantly increased after a sexual assault, even for women with no prior substance use or abuse history (Kilpatrick, Acierno, Resnick, et al., 1997).

Healthcare providers have been found to be hesitant to identify and address alcohol-related problems in any patient seen in the ED (Thom, Herring, & Judd, 1999). This is true of advocates and SANEs who have historically been hesitant to discuss the role of alcohol and other drugs in sexual assault, because we do not want to appear to be blaming the victim for complicity in a crime that was perpetrated against them. This is especially true when we are treating the victim in the ED, even though, as we have already identified, at least 50% to 74% of rape victims are intoxicated at the time of the assault and in one study 90% of them reported being so intoxicated they could not have legally consented to the sex (Resnick, personal communication, February 25, 2007; Kilpatrick, Acierno, Resnick, et al., 1997). Even if the individual is not alcohol dependent, clearly binge drinking, all too common on our college campuses and with the younger populations groups most often included in sexual assault statistics, is a vulnerability issue. Because we also have previously identified that this is often our only known contact with the rape victim, perhaps it is time to reconsider the unwritten policy to not address the alcohol issue, as it clearly is not helpful to our patients (Ledray, 2008).

The National Institute of Alcohol Abuse and Alcoholism (NIAAA) recommends all medical patients be screened for unhealthy alcohol use (National Institutes of Health, NIAAA, 2005). Although we certainly need to do so in a manner that will in no way sound to the victim that we are blaming her for the assault, brief screening and intervention in the medical setting has been identified as feasible and effective in limiting unhealthy alcohol use. It has been shown effective with other ED populations, and it could result in the victim being vulnerable to another assault (D'Onofrio, Nadel, & Degutis, 2002; Gentilello, Rivara, & Donovan, et al., 1999; Spirito, Monti, & Barnett, et al., 2004). Clearly this is an opportunity for nursing to identify and address alcohol-related problems with this population and once again take the lead in providing more comprehensive care to sexual assault victims (Ledray, 2008).

PSYCHOLOGICAL IMPACT

There is considerable agreement among researchers that rape victims experience more psychological distress than do victims of other crimes. Fear, anxiety, depression, and symptoms of PTSD are the most frequently recognized and documented reactions to sexual assault (Burgess & Holmstrom, 1974; Calhoun, Atkeson, & Resick; 1982; Frazier; 2000; Kilpatrick & Veronen, 1984; Ledray, 1994; Resick & Schnicke, 1990).

Anxiety

Anxiety is also frequently recognized and documented in the literature as an immediate reaction to a sexual assault (Abel & Rouleau, 1995; Burgess & Holmstrom, 1974; Calhoun, et al., 1982; Kilpatrick & Veronen, 1984; Ledray, 1994; Littel, 2001; Resick & Schnicke, 1990). In one study, 82% of rape victims met the *Diagnostic and Statistical Manual* (DSM) criteria for generalized anxiety disorder (GAD) compared to 32% of nonvictims (Frank & Anderson, 1987). Some studies of long-term anxiety have found differences between victim and nonvictim groups (Gidycz, Coble, & Latham et al., 1993; Gidycz & Koss, 1991; Gold, Milan, & Mayall et al., 1994), and others have not (Frazier & Schauben, 1994; Riggs, Kilpatrick, & Resnick, 1992; Winfield, George, & Swartz et al., 1990). Studies also report that rape victims were more likely to meet the criteria for panic disorder several years after the rape (Burnam, Stein, & Golding et al., 1988; Winfield, et al., 1990).

Fear

Fear of death is the most common fear during the assault, and continued generalized fear after the assault is a very common response to rape (Dupre, Hampton, Morrison, et al., 1993; Ledray, 1994). Fear after a rape can be specifically related to factors associated with the sexual assault, or it can be widely generalized to include fear of all men (Ledray, 1994). Because fear is subjective, it is generally evaluated using self-report measures. Although evidence of the duration and type of fear varies, reports of long-term fear following rape is common, with up to 83% of victims reporting some type of fear following a sexual assault (Frazier, 2000; Nadelson, Notman, Zackson, et al., 1982). Girelli, Resnick, Marhoefer-Dvorak, et al. (1986) found the subjective distress of fear of injury or fear of death during rape was more significant than the actual violence as a predictor of more severe postrape fear and anxiety. It is thus important to recognize that the threat of violence alone can be psychologically devastating (Goodman, Koss, & Russo, 1993).

As might be expected, rape victims are consistently found to be generally fearful and experiencing hyperalertness to potential danger during the first year following a sexual assault. During the acute stage, up to 80% of rape victims report being generally fearful, afraid of violence, or afraid of being alone. Nearly as many, 75%, report a fear of being indoors, outdoors, or in a crowd, and 70% report a fear of death (Becker, et al., 1986). Although fear of retaliation by the assailant is a persistent and long-term result of a sexual assault, except in domestic violence rapes, retaliation by the assailant when a victim reports is, fortunately, an extremely rare occurrence (Ledray, 1994).

Depression

Depression is one of the symptoms most commonly identified following a sexual assault. Depression is easily, reliably, and quickly measured by standardized self-report measures, such as the Beck Depression Inventory (Abel & Rouleau, 1995; Atkeson, Calhoun, Resick et al., 1982; Frazier, 2000; Ledray, 1994; Kilpatrick & Veronen, 1984).

Studies that evaluate the level of depression in rape victims typically find that during the first two months, rape victims are mildly depressed (Becker, et al., 1986; Frazier & Burnett, 1994; Ledray, 1984; Gidycz, et al., 1993) to moderately depressed (Cluss, Boughton, Frank, et al., 1983; Frank & Stewart, 1984; Frazier, Harlow, Schauben, et al., 1993; Ledray, 1984; Moss, Frank, & Anderson, 1990). In studies without standardized criteria, 75% to

80% of rape victims reported feeling mildly to severely depressed six months after being raped (Kimerling & Calhoun, 1994; Norris & Feldman-Summers, 1981).

When rape victims are compared to nonvictim control groups, the results consistently show that the rape victims are more depressed during the first two months after a rape (Atkeson, et al., 1982; Kilpatrick, Veronen, & Resick, 1979; Kilpatrick, Resick, & Veronen, 1981). Rape victims are also significantly more likely to meet the DSM criteria for major depressive disorder (MDD) than are nonvictims. In one study, 38% of rape victims coming to a rape crisis center (RCC) met the MDD criteria at six months after the rape, compared with only 6% of a matched control group (Frank & Anderson, 1987). Another study reported similar results, with 33% of rape victims meeting the MDD criteria at six months, compared to 11% of the control group (Sorenson, Siegel, Golding, et al., 1991).

Nightmares are a common problem following sexual assault; researchers have found that nightmares are associated with greater general distress and lead to more anxiety (Krakow, Tandberg, Barey, et al., 1995).

At one year after the assault, rape victims continue to be mildly depressed (Koss, Dinero, Seibel, et al., 1988; Mackey, Sereika, Weissfeld, et al., 1992). When compared to nonvictim control groups, rape victims are also consistently more depressed than other victims (Frazier & Schauben, 1994) and than nonvictim groups (Burge, 1988; Cohen & Roth, 1987; Ellis, Atkeson, & Calhoun, 1981; Gidycz & Koss, 1989, 1991; Riggs, et al., 1992; Santiago, McCal-Perez, Gorcey, et al., 1985).

Suicidal Ideation

Although the completed suicide rate following a rape is considered low, suicidal ideation is a significant issue. Up to 20% may attempt suicide (Kilpatrick, et al., 1985), and many more rape victims (33% to 50%) report that they considered suicide at some point after the rape (Ellis, et al., 1981). During the immediate postrape period, rape victims are nine times more likely than nonvictims to attempt suicide (Kilpatrick, Saunders, Veronen, et al., 1987). It is thus essential that suicide risk is considered and addressed during the initial and follow-up visits. SANEs and other professionals working with this population must be aware of signs, and protocols to deal with this problem must be in place and utilized.

BEST PRACTICE SANEs and other professionals working with sexual assault victims must be aware of the potential of suicide among victims. Assessments in both initial and follow-up visits should address suicidal ideation.

Self-Blame and Shame

Self-blame is a common response in rape victims (Ledray, 1994; McFarlane & Hawley, 1993). Initially, some researchers thought some self-blame may actually be beneficial to rape victims, as it would foster a sense of future controllability and project a sense of safety from another rape, but after considerable research on internal versus external blame ascribed to victims, researchers have concluded that self-blame is associated only with past controllability, not with the perception of future controllability. All types of self-blame have been found to be associated with more depression and poor adjustment after the rape (Frazier, 1990). It is also important that forensic examiners not confuse self-blame with responsibility for the assault.

Posttraumatic Stress Disorder

Posttraumatic stress disorder (PTSD) was first recognized and defined by the American Psychiatric Association as a diagnostic criteria in the *Diagnostic and Statistical Manual III* in 1980 (American Psychiatric Association) and therefore has been considered only in studies of rape impact designed after 1980. Rape trauma syndrome (RTS), which is not a diagnosis recognized by the American Psychiatric Association, is often described as a specific type of PTSD (Frazier, 2000).

The four basic elements are included in a PTSD diagnosis:
1. Exposure to a traumatic event
2. Reexperiencing the trauma (e.g., flashbacks, intrusive memories)
3. Symptoms of avoidance and numbing (e.g., attempts to avoid thoughts or situations that remind the survivor of the traumatic event, inability to recall certain aspects of the traumatic event, feeling disconnected from others)
4. Symptoms of increased arousal (e.g., exaggerated startle response, feeling easily irritated, constant fear of danger, physiological response when exposed to similar events)

Symptoms must be present for at least one month and must cause clinically significant distress or impairment (American Psychiatric Association, 1994).

The rate of PTSD varies greatly, depending on the criteria used to define sexual assault. When sexual assault victims who have experienced less severe forms of sexual assault are included in studies, the rate for PTSD is lower, as low as 4% (Winfield, et al., 1990). Based on a more strict definition of "attacked and raped" to define sexual assault, 80% of victims met the PTSD criteria (Breslau, Davis, Andreski, et al., 1991). It can be concluded from this that more severe forms of sexual assault appear to result in more severe symptoms of distress meeting the criteria for PTSD. Women who report a sexual assault to the police or other authorities report higher PTSD rates (Rothbaum, Foa, Riggs, et al., 1992).

In an extensive review of the literature on the impact of rape, Frazier (2000) found that 75% to 94% of rape victims met the criteria for PTSD at two weeks after rape; 60% to 73% met the PTSD criteria at one to two months; 47% to 70% met the criteria at three to six months; and approximately 50% to 60% continue to meet the criteria at 12 months and beyond (Foa & Riggs, 1995; Frazier, et al., 1993; Kramer & Green, 1991; Resnick, Yehuda, Pitman, et al., 1995; Rothbaum, et al., 1992; Santello & Leitenberg, 1993). According to Freedy, Resnick, and Kilpatrick, et al. (1994), the most common symptoms at six months after rape are hypervigilance (79%) and exaggerated startle response (83%). PTSD prevalence rates for sexual assault victims several years after the rape are consistently reported to be from 12% to 17% (Frazier, 2000; Kessler, Sonnega, Bromet, et al., 1995; Kilpatrick, et al., 1987; Resnick, Kilpatrick, & Dansky et al., 1993).

SANE-SART Program Operation

The needs and care of sexual assault survivors extend far beyond their basic medical needs. For this reason, it is essential that every SANE program operate as a part of a sexual assault response team (SART). SANE programs are based on the belief that sexual assault survivors have the right to immediate, compassionate, and comprehensive medicolegal evaluation and treatment by specially trained professionals who have the experience to anticipate their needs during this time of crisis. As professionals, the SANE and other SART members have an ethical responsibility to provide victims with complete information about choices, so victims can make informed decisions about the care they want to receive.

Sexual assault survivors also have a right to report the crime of rape to law enforcement, even though not every victim may choose to report. Victims have a right to know what their options are and what to expect if they do, or do not, decide to report. Those who do report also have a right to sensitive and knowledgeable support, without bias, during this often difficult process. Those who do not report still have a right to expert, complete healthcare. Providing a higher standard of evidence collection and care cannot only, ultimately, increase the prosecution of sex offenders and hopefully reduce rape but it can also speed the victim's recovery to a higher level of functioning and prevent secondary injury or illness.

SEXUAL ASSAULT RESPONSE TEAM

The SART is the group of professionals who work together to facilitate the survivor's recovery and the investigation and prosecution of the assailant by providing information, support, and crisis intervention and by gathering evidence and facilitating the movement of the sexual assault survivor through the legal system. The SART members also work together, or individually, to improve the response to victims within their own disciplines and to educate the community they serve.

At a minimum, the SART should include the SANE or forensic examiner, law enforcement, the rape advocate, and the prosecutor. Other valuable SART members are the crime laboratory personnel who analyze the sexual assault evidence kit, the police dispatcher, emergency medical technicians, and other agencies serving sexual assault survivors such as domestic violence workers, social services personnel, and the clergy. Enlisting the support and involvement of individuals from key community agencies, before they are needed, can facilitate access to care.

HOW A SANE-SART PROGRAM TYPICALLY OPERATES

In some communities, the SART members meet and interview the sexual assault survivor together in the ED or clinic where the initial evidentiary examination is completed, but in many communities, the members function independently and coordinate their services. Although the conventional wisdom suggests that it is better to interview the sexual assault survivor only once so there is only one account of the assault and so it is less traumatic for the victim by eliminating the need for her to retell the account of the assault multiple times, no data support this approach. In fact, desensitization and exposure therapy, which involve having the survivor confront these fears and tell her story repeatedly, may be the most effective treatment identified to date (Foa, 1997; Foa & Rothbaum, 1990; Ledray, 1994; Muran & DiGiuseppe, 1994); thus, it is possible that multiple interviews may have a positive psychological benefit and may actually facilitate recovery. Research is clearly needed in this area.

A SANE is usually available on call, off premises, 24 hours a day, 7 days a week, to evaluate all male and female victims of sexual assault or abuse, and in many instances, they will also conduct suspect exams as well. Programs vary as to the age of victims they serve. The on-call SANE is paged immediately whenever a sexual assault, abuse survivor, or suspect enters the community's response system. Although most evidentiary examinations are still completed at a hospital emergency department, some SANE-SART programs also operate outside the ED, either in a clinic area located near the ED, or in a separate community-based clinic

or agency. The advantage is that because rape victims are seldom injured to the point that they require ED care, the high activity level and the expensive overhead of the ED can be avoided. The disadvantage to the SANE is that should additional medical evaluation be necessary, it may be more difficult to arrange. A plan must also be in place for medications and laboratory work to be completed (Ledray, 1999).

If the survivor was not accompanied by law enforcement or an advocate to the facility where the evidentiary examination will be performed and the protocol indicates that step, the rape advocate or law enforcement officer should also be called when the SANE is paged. In most communities, the sexual assault advocate will automatically be paged; however, law enforcement is paged only when the survivor agrees to make a police report. Remember, however, that even though the victim does not want to report to law enforcement, the VAWA 2005 Reauthorization Act clearly states that as of January 5, 2009, the sexual assault victim should be offered a sexual assault medicolegal exam and not be billed for this care (VAWA, 2005).

During the time it takes for the SANE to respond (usually no more than one hour), the ED or clinic staff will evaluate and treat any urgent or life-threatening injuries. If treatment is medically necessary, the ED staff will treat the client, always considering the forensic consequences of the lifesaving and stabilizing medical procedures. Complete documentation is essential. If the ED staff removes clothes or objects from the victim, care should be taken utilizing forensic principles for handling and storage of the physical evidence. Whenever possible, the SANE or law enforcement official should take all forensic photographs. If medical necessity dictates treatment before the arrival of the SANE, ED staff will take the photographs following established forensic procedures.

When the medical staff determines that the victim does not require immediate medical care, the survivor should be made comfortable in a private room near the ED. This area should enhance the victim's sense of safety and security and provide comfort and quiet in a soundproof room with comfortable furniture, preferably a sofa to lie down, a telephone, and a locked door. Family members who accompany the victim, with the victim's permission, should be allowed to stay with the victim while they wait. If there was no oral sex, the victim may be offered something to eat or drink. If the victim is upset and a hospital chaplain or social worker is available onsite, they may be called, with the survivor's permission, to wait with the person until the SANE or advocate arrives.

In community-based SART programs that operate outside a medical facility, the survivor may first call law enforcement, who will evaluate if there are injuries that might require treatment. Typically, fewer than 4% of rape victims will need treatment, as rape seldom involves serious injury (Tucker, Ledray, & Werner, 1990). If there are only minor injuries or no injuries are present, law enforcement will transport the survivor to the community-based SANE facility. If moderate or severe injury is suspected, the victim may be evaluated by paramedics and taken to the designated medical facility where the SANE and advocate will meet her or him. After the patient is stabilized medically, the SANE will collect the forensic evidence.

SANE RESPONSIBILITIES

Once the SANE arrives, the nurse is responsible for completing the entire sexual assault evidentiary examination, including crisis intervention, STI risk evaluation and prevention, pregnancy risk evaluation and interception, interview and the collection of forensic evidence, and referrals for additional support and care.

What the SANE will do is, however, to a great extent determined by the survivor's decision about reporting, so reporting must be addressed first.

Reporting Options

When the Victim Is Uncertain about Reporting

If the survivor has not yet decided whether to report, the SANE, in conjunction with an advocate when available, will discuss any fears and concerns and provide the information necessary for making an informed decision about reporting.

If the victim does not want to report at this time but is unsure about reporting at a future date, the SANE will make sure the victim is aware of the options and the limitations of reporting at a later date. The SANE will also offer to complete an evidentiary examination kit that can be held in a locked refrigerator, for a specified time (usually one month or according to state statutes if any exist), in case the victim chooses to report later.

The victim may also choose to make an anonymous report, referred to as a restricted report in military arenas. This option allows law enforcement, and the military commanding officer, to be made aware that a sexual assault occurred and take custody of the evidence (usually identified by a number), without disclosing the name of the victim. No further investigation of the crime will occur unless the victim decides to come forward. The victim will have a specified period of time, usually one year, to decide if he or she wants to make an official report. If so, the investigation will begin when the victim has disclosed her or his identity. It is important for the victim to understand that valuable evidence may be lost as a result of this delay.

Mandatory Reporting

It is essential that the SANE and all other medical professionals are familiar with the local mandated reporting laws and the statutory rape laws (the sexual contact between a minor and an adult, typically four or more years older). In most states, statutory rape, although against the law, is not a mandated report. In states with mandatory reporting laws, the SANE will follow established protocol regarding reporting after explaining the process and the nurse's responsibilities to the victim or the victim's family when a child is involved and a parent is present.

When the Victim Does Not Want to Report

If the rape survivor decides not to report and does not want an evidentiary exam, an evidentiary examination is not completed. The SANE can still, however, offer medications to prevent STIs, evaluate a woman's risk of pregnancy, and offer pregnancy prevention for at least up to five days postrape. The SANE will also make referrals for follow-up medical care and counseling and provide written follow-up information.

Evidentiary Examination

When a report is made or the victim indicates she or he will likely report, a complete evidentiary examination is conducted following the SANE agency protocol (Boxes 32-1 and 32-2). In most agencies, the complete examination is conducted within 72 to 120 hours of the sexual assault. After obtaining a signed consent, the SANE will conduct a complete examination.

Chain of Custody

To maintain proper chain of custody, each piece of evidence collected must be properly labeled with the victim's full name, the date

---

> **Box 32-1** Elements of a Sexual Assault Examination
>
> - Interview to guide the examination and document victim's statements
> - Collection of evidence in a sexual assault examination kit
> - Collection of clothing potentially containing evidence
> - Careful documentation of the victim's statements, evidence collected, and injuries on a sexual assault examination report (see the Sexual Assault Examination Report in Appendix C
> - Pictures of injuries
> - Prophylactic care for sexually transmitted infections
> - Evaluation of pregnancy risk and emergency contraception
> - Crisis intervention
> - Referral for follow-up medical and psychological care

> **Box 32-2** Evidence Collection
>
> The sexual assault evidence collection will vary depending on local protocol and the choice of kits. It will, however, typically include the following:
> - Collection of swabs from the orifices involved in the sexual assault to look for sperm, acid phosphatase, and, most important, the offender's DNA
> - Collection of swabs from the skin that may have body fluids of the assailant, including blood, saliva, or seminal fluid
> - Buccal swabs or blood from the survivor to identify DNA (if the victim was assaulted orally, buccal swabs should not be used, as the oral cavity may be contaminated with the suspect's DNA)
> - Collection of blood or urine for possible drug screen (especially in a suspected drug-facilitated sexual assault)
> - Pubic hair combing to look for the assailant's pubic hair
> - Collection of debris from anywhere on the victim's body or clothing

Note: Most SANE programs no longer collect pulled head hair or pubic hair, since this is seldom useful evidence, the collection is very painful, and when it is needed it can be obtained in those few cases at a later time.

and time of collection, the SANE's full name, and the identification of the evidence. It is then sealed and either given to law enforcement or placed into a locked refrigerator or cabinet with limited access. A signature record must also be kept of everyone who has possession of the evidence from the time it is collected by the SANE until it is given to law enforcement. Research comparing evidence collected in 97 cases, 24 by SANEs and 73 by non-SANEs, showed that the SANEs maintained chain of custody 100% of the time and non-SANEs only 52% of the time (Ledray & Simmelink, 1997). Similar results were found in a study of 100 kits, 41 completed by SANEs and 59 completed by non-SANEs. The SANEs maintained chain of custody in 100% of the cases, and non-SANEs 81% of the time (Griswold, 1999).

Medical Care

The purpose of the SANE examination of the sexual assault survivor is specifically to assess, document, and collect forensic evidence. In addition, the SANE provides prophylactic treatment of STIs and prevention of pregnancy following a preestablished medical protocol or with the approval of a consulting physician. Although the SANE may treat minor injuries, further evaluation and care of any major physical trauma are referred to the ED or a designated medical facility. The SANE conducts a limited medical examination, and it is important to make clear to the sexual assault survivor that routine medical care is not a part of the SANE examination. Of course, obvious pathology or suspicious findings observed are reported to the client with a suggestion for follow-up care and referral, but evaluation and diagnosis of pathology is beyond the scope of the SANE examination.

Emotional Support and Crisis Intervention

The SANE is not an advocate, and when an advocate is present, the primary role of the advocate is to provide emotional support and information about the survivor's options. The SANE, however, is also not just a technician who collects evidence. As a professional nurse, the SANE's role encompasses all aspects of the biopsychosocial needs of all patients, including the survivor of sexual assault. The SANE will always provide emotional support and crisis intervention, working as a team with the advocate and other professionals (Ledray, Faugno, & Speck, 2001). Together the SANE must also make an initial assessment of the survivor's psychological functioning sufficient to determine suicidal ideation; orientation to person, place, and time; or need of further referral for follow-up support, evaluation, or treatment. When friends or family are present, the advocate may need to spend time with them during the evidentiary examination, and thus, it may be necessary for the SANE to fill this role independently.

Discharge

If the victim is alone, the SANE or advocate will talk with him or her about whom to call and where to go from the hospital. Every effort will be made to find a place where the victim will feel safe and will not be alone. When necessary, arrangements may be made for shelter placement. If the victim is intoxicated or does not want to leave until morning, arrangements may be made to sleep in a specified area of the hospital, when this type of space is available. In many facilities, this will be an ED holding room or crisis center. If necessary, a community referral can be made to better meet long-term housing needs. Aftercare is one important component of competent care.

Testifying in Court

The SANE's role is not complete when the victim leaves the ED or clinic. An important part of the job is to testify as a witness in court, should the case be charged and prosecuted. Fortunately, more cases are closed through a guilty plea than through trial (Ledray, 1999). Although there is no research showing a direct link between a SANE examination and a guilty plea, case reports have demonstrated that when assailants are confronted with SANE evidence, they are willing to accept a guilty plea when they had denied committing any sexual abuse before seeing the evidence. One study, however, indicated 57% of a national sample of SANEs reported feeling uncomfortable when they faced intensive questioning about the credibility of the victim. This included challenges by the defense to the victim's demeanor, the veracity of the victim's history of the assault, and whether they had found evidence that corroborated the victim's history of the assault (Campbell, Townsend, Long, Kinnison, Pulley, Adames, & Wascon, 2005). This supports the need for the SANE to be properly prepared by the prosecution as to the likely issues in the case, so she or he can anticipate the line of questioning (Ledray & Barry, 1998).

When a Case Goes to Trial

The SANE may be called to testify as a factual witness or as an expert witness. When testifying as a factual witness, the SANE will simply report the facts of the examination as completed. The nurse will answer questions about what evidence she or he collected and how it was collected and will likely also testify as to what the victim told him or her about the assault and the victim's response during the examination. Because the SANE is completing a medical examination, the things the victim says are admissible in court as an exception to the hearsay rule (Ledray & Barry, 1998). The SANE may also testify as an expert witness, in which case, when qualified to do so based on experience, knowledge, and training, the SANE also will be allowed to give an opinion about what was found.

When testifying in court, the SANE should observe the following guidelines:

- Be sure to contact the attorney who subpoenaed you to review the issues in the case and get a basic understanding of what you will be asked.
- Review your records so you are familiar with the basic details of the case.
- Dress professionally and in a conservative manner; women should wear minimal makeup and jewelry.
- In court, look at the attorney when questions are asked and at the jury when answering the questions, looking them in the eye.
- Always tell the complete truth. When unsure about an answer, say you are unsure or that you do not recall. If necessary, ask to be allowed to refer to your records to refresh your memory. When you do know an answer, speak with confidence, and speak clearly and loudly, so you can be heard. Listen carefully to the questions and if they are unclear, ask to have the questions clarified.
- If either attorney raises an objection during your testimony, stop speaking immediately and wait until the judge rules. It the objection is "overruled," you may continue. If it is "sustained," wait until there is another question.
- Always remember you are an unbiased witness, not an advocate. Don't get angry; be intimidated, defensive, or evasive; or try to hide facts that may be unpleasant. If you made a mistake or left something out in your evidence collection or documentation, admit it; don't try to hide it.

Suspect Exams

Suspect exams are only completed when requested by law enforcement. These are typically of two varieties. These include evidence collection to rule out a suspect or identify the DNA of a consenting sexual partner, and the examination of a suspect under arrest by law enforcement who is indeed suspected of being the perpetrator. In both cases, a law enforcement officer should always be present in the room while the evidence is being collected. The SANE should under no circumstances be left alone with the suspect. No interview or history is obtained in either of these situations. It will be the decision of law enforcement if the suspect is left in handcuffs and or leg cuffs during the exam.

Examination to Rule Out an Individual

Often the individual in this circumstance will come in willingly to be ruled out as a suspect or because he is the consenting sexual partner of a victim and his DNA is needed by the crime laboratory. Although head and pubic hair samples may be requested, typically all that will be needed is DNA, which, depending on the preference of the jurisdiction, may be a blood, saliva, or buccal swab for DNA. Samples should be collected in an evidentiary kit, maintaining proper chain of custody. If a suspect specific kit is not available, a victim kit can be used with "victim" crossed out and "suspect" recorded both on the kit and on individual envelopes used for evidence collection. In addition, each envelope used for evidence collected should be labeled with the suspect's name, date and time collected, and the examiner's full name.

Examination of a Suspect under Arrest

Requirements for suspect exams may vary by jurisdiction. In some jurisdictions, specimens will only be collected when specifically requested by a search warrant presented to the SANE/medical staff in the ED by the investigator before the exam. This is clearly the ideal situation, because there is less likelihood that the defense will successfully challenge the admissibility of the evidence. It would certainly be appropriate for a SANE program to only collect evidence from suspects when requested by a search warrant.

However, it has been the experience of the Sexual Assault Resource Service in Minneapolis, Minnesota, that suspects are also brought to the facilities by street police who have made an arrest at or near the crime scene immediately after the reported crime. They come with no search warrant and no idea of what they want collected. Initially personnel requested a search warrant be issued and waited until that happened to conduct the exam. Recently, after more than 30 years of experience, personnel from the Sexual Assault Resource Service have met with the prosecutor and developed a new policy. The key points of this policy are as follows:

- ED staff will assess and treat any identified physical injury requiring treatment.
- As long as the suspect is under arrest, no consent is needed. However, if the suspect is not cooperative, the case is referred to the ED physician for intervention. The physician will then make the decision with law enforcement how to proceed. The SANE will not do an exam on an uncooperative suspect without a medical doctor's (MD) involvement.
- The SANE will complete a full body exam and document any identifiable marks or injuries (photographs of injuries may be taken without consent).
- Clothing will be secured and given directly to law enforcement.
- The following specimens are collected:
  - Pubic hair combing
  - Penile shaft swabs
  - Scrotum swabs
  - Fingernail swabs
  - Foreign matter
  - Blood for ETOH/drugs (the prosecutor decided that personnel should collect blood for drugs or alcohol, because the drugs and alcohol will be metabolized out of the system and the same results cannot be obtained at a later date; however, the staff does not collect blood for DNA since that will not change and can later be collected by search warrant)

Education, Training, Research, and Program Evaluation

In addition to providing direct client care and testifying in court, the SANE and other SART members need to be active in training other healthcare and community agencies to provide services to sexual assault survivors. SART programs should conduct ongoing program evaluation and periodic research to assess program impact, treatment needs, outcomes, and services. Although more research on SANE program efficacy is clearly needed, studies have shown that the practice followed by SANE programs is consistent with the empowering patient care philosophy and that the overwhelming majority of patients seen by SANEs in one study reported positive psychological well-being as a result (Campbell, Patterson, Adams, Diegel, & Coats, 2008). In another

study, 85% of the survivors reported that the SANE's listening to them was the one thing that help the most during the ED visit (Tucker, Ledray, & Stehle Werner, 1990). Other research has identified that SANEs do a significantly better job of collecting evidence and maintaining chain of custody than non-SANEs do (Ledray & Simmelink, 1997; Sievers, Murphy, & Miller, 2003). This results in reported increased rates of guilty pleas (Aiken & Speck, 1995; Ledray, 1992; Littel, 2001) and a higher rate of prosecution when the case goes to trial (Crandall & Helitzer, 2003).

The research data on SANE efficacy and system impact is still minimal. It is only through continual program evaluation and research that the services for survivors tomorrow will continue to be more effective and efficient than the services available today.

KEY POINT The members of the sexual assault response team must assume the responsibilities associated with courtroom testimony and engage in education, training, research, and program evaluation activities aimed at improving services of community agencies that assist sexual assault survivors.

Summary

The global prevalence of sexual assault is difficult to ascertain because of the high rate of nondisclosure. Available statistics show an alarmingly high rate of sexual assault across the United States and that it is an undeniable problem in every country in the world. The majority of assaults are perpetrated by acquaintances, and many women suffer repeated assaults at the hands of one perpetrator, most often their husband, boyfriend, or authority figure. Because the incidence of sexual coercion peaks at the college age of the victim, it is imperative that references are available to guide young victims to counseling centers and health clinics. The SANE plan of care for the victim of sexual assault should include a referral for counseling; if the victim desires legal action, the SANE should assist in contacting proper authorities and schedule any necessary follow-up care. Each time an aftercare appointment is met, it provides the opportunity to reevaluate the emotional status as well. Sexual assault can have devastating effects for the victim, and these effects may last for many years after the actual attack. Risk factors for sexual assault have been identified, as well as patterns of behavior commonly displayed following an assault. Barriers to both disclosure by the victim and adequate assessment by the medical/forensic examiner have been well documented in the literature. Responsibility lies with the forensic nurse examiner, who specializes in sexual assault examinations, to ensure that all patients are adequately screened for sequelae of sexual assault. SANEs are able to develop caring therapeutic relationships with patients and provide a viable foundation for the disclosure of sexual assault. Advanced practice nurses need to educate themselves regarding the risk factors and behavioral changes commonly associated with sexual assault. The challenge for the SANE must also be to put all biases aside and become comfortable with the fundamental forensic assessment guidelines used in screening patients for sexual assault. This epidemic must be brought to the forefront of the public consciousness if the stigmas and shame associated with sexual assault are to be eradicated. Unfortunately, crimes against persons, such as sexual assault, will require constant monitoring and consistent screening. These procedures by SANEs can help raise awareness and help victims identify abusive behavior.

Resources

ORGANIZATIONS

Clearinghouse on Family Violence Information
P.O. Box 1182, Washington, DC 20013; 800-394-3366

International Association of Forensic Nurses (IAFN)
1517 Ritchie Highway, Suite 208, Arnold, MD 21012-2323; (410)626-7805; http://www.iafn.org

National Coalition against Domestic Violence
Public Policy Office, 1633 Q Street, Suite 210, Washington, DC 20009; 202-745-1211, 800-799-SAFE (7233); www.ncadv.org.

National Organization on Male Sexual Victimization (United States)
Box 103, 5505 Connecticut Avenue NW, Washington, DC 20015-3201; 800-738-4181; www.malesurvivor.org

National Organization on Male Sexual Victimization (Canada)
c/o BCSMSSA, 1252 Burrard Street, #202, Vancouver, BC V6Z 1, Canada

National Sexual Violence Resource Center
123 North Enola Drive, Enola, PA 17025; 877-739-3895, 717-909-0710; www.nsvrc.org.

Office for Victims of Crime Resource Center
Office of Justice Programs, Department of Justice, 633 Indiana Avenue NW, Room 1386, Washington, DC 20531; 202-307-5983, 800-851-3420

References

Abbey, A. (2002). Alcohol-related sexual assault: A common problem among college students. *Journal of Studies on Alcohol, 63*(Suppl. 14), 118–128.

Abel, G., & Rouleau, J. (1995). Sexual abuses. *The Psychiatric Clinics of North America, 18*(1), 139–153.

Adams, J. A., Girardin, B., & Faugno, D. (2001). Adolescent Sexual Assault: Documentation of acute injuries using photo-colposcopy. *Journal of Pediatric Adolescent Gynecology, 14*(4), 175–180.

Adkinson, C., & Karasov, F. (2007). *Strangulation and Domestic Violence Medical and Legal Aspects.* Presentation sponsored by Hennepin County Medical Center, Minneapolis, MN, November.

American College of Emergency Physicians. (1999). *Evaluation and management of the sexually assaulted or sexually abused patient.* Dallas, TX: Author.

American Psychiatric Association. (1994). *Diagnostic & statistical manual of mental disorders.* (4th ed.) Washington, DC: Author.

American Psychiatric Association. (2000). DSM IV: 2000 text revision. In American Psychiatric Association, *Diagnostic & statistical manual of mental disorders.* (4th ed.) Washington, DC: Author.

Amey, B. (2002). Erratum Measuring the quality of medical care for women who experience sexual assault with data from the national hospital ambulatory medical care survey (Annals of Emergency Medicine [June 2002] [pp. 631–638]). (Journal:Erratum) *Annals of Emergency Medicine, 40*(3), 367.

Antognoli-Toland, P. (1985). Comprehensive program for examination of sexual assault victims by nurses: A hospital-based project in Texas. *Journal of Emergency Nursing: JEN, 11*(3), 132–136.

Atkeson, B., Calhoun, K. S., Resick, P. A., et al. (1982). Victims of rape: Repeated assessment of depressive symptoms. *Journal of Consulting and Clinical Psychology, 50*(1), 96–102.

Becker, J., Skinner, L., Abel, G., et al. (1986). Level of postassault sexual functioning in rape and incest. *Archives of Sexual Behavior, 15*(1), 37–49.

Bell, K. (1995). Tulsa sexual assault nurse examiners program. *The Oklahoma Nurse, 40*(3), 16.

Blair, T., & Warner, C. (1992). Sexual assault. *Topics in Emergency Medicine, 14*(4), 58–77.

Bobak, I. M., & Jensen, M. D. (1992). Violence against women. In *In Maternity & gynecologic care: The nurse and the family.* (5th ed.). St. Louis: Mosby.

Breslau, N., Davis, G., Andreski, P., et al. (1991). Traumatic events and post-traumatic stress disorder in an urban population of young adults. *Archives of General Psychiatry, 48*(3), 216–222.

Burge, S. (1988). PTSD in victims of rape. *Journal of Traumatic Stress, 1*(2), 193–210.

Burgess, A., & Holmstrom, L. (1974). Rape trauma syndrome. *The American Journal of Psychiatry, 131*(9), 981–985.

Burgess, A., & Holmstrom, L. (1979). Adaptive strategies and recovery from rape. *The American Journal of Psychiatry, 136*(10), 1278–1282.

Burnam, M. S., Stein, J. A., Golding, J. M., et al. (1988). Sexual assault and mental disorders in a community population. *Journal of Consulting and Clinical Psychology, 56*(6), 843–850.

Calhoun, K., Atkeson, B., & Resick, P. (1982). A longitudinal examination of fear reactions in victims of rape. *Journal of Consulting and Clinical Psychology, 29*(6), 655–661.

Campbell, R., Patterson, D., Adams, A. E., Diegel, R., & Coats, S. (2008). A participatory evaluation project to measure SANE nursing practice and adult sexual assault patients' psychological well-being. *Journal of Forensic Nursing, 4*(1), 19–28.

Campbell, R., Townsend, S., Long, S., Kinnison, K., Pulley, E., Adames, S., et al. (2005). Organizational characteristics of Sexual Assault Nurse Examiner programs: Results from the national survey of SANE programs. *Journal of Forensic Nursing, 1*(2), 57–64.

Carter-Snell, C., Olson, K., Jensen, L., Cummings, G., & Wiebe, N. (2007). *Women's Risk of Injures During Sexual Assault.* Paper presented at IAFN Scientific Assembly, Oct 18, 2007, Salt Lake City, UT.

Cartwright, P. S., Moore, R. A., Anderson, J. R., et al. (1986). Genital injury and implied consent to alleged rape. *The Journal of Reproductive Medicine, 31*(11), 1043–1044.

Center for Policy Alternatives. *EC for sexual assault victims. Progressive Policy Models for the States 2006.* www.stateaction.org. Accessed July 2007.

Centers for Disease Control and Prevention. (1993). Sexually transmitted diseases treatment guidelines. *MMWR, Morbidity and Mortality Weekly Report, 42*(RR-14), 1–102.

Centers for Disease Control and Prevention. (1998). Sexually transmitted diseases treatment guidelines. *MMWR, 42*(RR-14), 1–102.

Centers for Disease Control and Prevention (2002). Sexually transmitted diseases treatment guidelines. Retrieved June 2006 from www.cdc.gov/std/treatment/8-2002TG.htm

Centers for Disease Control and Prevention. (2005). Sexually transmitted diseases treatment guidelines. *MMWR: Recommendations and Reports, 54.* www.cdc.gov/mmwr/indrr_2005.html.

Chapman, D. (1989). A longitudinal study of sexuality and gynecologic health in abused women. *The Journal of the American Osteopathic Association, 89*(5), 619–624.

Chivers, C. J. (2000). In sex crimes, evidence depends on game of chance in hospitals. *The New York Times-Metropolitan Desk,* 1–6.

Ciancone, A., Wilson, C., Collette, R., & Gerson, L. (2000). Sexual Assault Nurse Examiner programs in the United States. *Annals of Emergency Medicine, 35*(4), 353–357.

Claydon, E., Murphy, S., Osborne, E., et al. (1991). Rape and HIV. *International journal of STD & AIDS, 2,* 200–201.

Cluss, P., Boughton, J., Frank, L., et al. (1983). The rape victim: Psychological correlates of participation in the legal system. *Crim Justice Behav, 10*(3), 342–357.

Cohen, L. J., & Roth, S. (1987). The psychological aftermath of rape: Long-term effects and individual differences in recovery. *J Soc Clin Psychol, 5*(4), 525–534.

Cohen, S., & Williamson, G. (1991). Stress and infectious disease in humans. *Psychological Bulletin, 109*(1), 5–24.

Crandall, C., & Helitzer, D. (2003). *Impact evaluation of a sexual assault nurse examiner (SANE) program.* (NCJ203276). Washington DC. NIJ.

DeGruttola, V., Seage, G., Mayer, K., & Horsburgh, C. (1989). Infectiousness of HIV between male homosexual partners. *Journal of Clinical Epidemiology, 42*(9), 849–856.

DiNitto, D., Martin, P., Yancey, N., et al. (1986). After rape: Who should examine rape survivors? *AJN, 86*(5), 538–540.

D'Onofrio, B., Nadel, E., Degutis, L., et al. (2002). Improving emergency medicine residents' approach to patients with alcohol problems; a controlled educational trial. *Annals of Emergency Medicine, 40*(1), 50–62.

Downs, M., & deVincezi, I. (1996). Probability of heterosexual transmission of HIV-1: Relationship to the number of unprotected sexual contacts. *Journal of Acquired Immune Deficiency Syndrome, 11*(4), 388–395.

DuMont, J., Miller, K., & Myhr, T. (2003). The Role of "Real Rape" and "Real Victim" Stereotypes in the Police Reporting Practices of Sexually Assaulted Women. *Violence Against Women, 9*(4), 466–486.

Dupre, A., Hampton, H., Morrison, H. J., et al. (1993). Sexual assault. *Obstetrical & Gynecological Survey, 28*(9), 640–648.

Ellis, E., Atkeson, B., & Calhoun, K. (1981). An assessment of long-term reactions to rape. *Journal of Abnormal Psychology, 90*(3), 323–326.

Emergency Nurses Association. (1991). Sexual assault nurse examiner resource list. *Journal of Emergency Nursing: JEN, 17*(4), 31A–35A.

Ernst, A., Green, E., Ferguson, M., et al. (2000). The utility of anoscopy and coloscopy in the evaluation of male sexual assault victims. *Annals of Emergency Medicine, 36*(5), 432–436.

Faigman, D. L., Kaye, D. H., Saks, M. J., et al. (1997). *Modern scientific evidence: The law & science of expert testimony.* St. Paul, MN: West Publishing Co.

Felitti, V. (1991). Long-term medical consequences of incest, rape, and molestation. *Southern Medical Journal, 84*(3), 328–331.

Foa, E. (1997). Trauma and women: Course, predictors, and treatment. *The Journal of Clinical Psychiatry, 58*(9), 25–28.

Foa, E., & Rothbaum, B. (1990). Rape: Can victims be helped by cognitive behavior therapy? In K. Hawton (Ed.), *Dilemmas and difficulties in the management of psychiatric patients* (pp. 197–204). New York: Oxford University Press.

Foa, E. B., & Riggs, D. S. (1995). Posttraumatic stress disorder following assault: Theoretical considerations and empirical findings. *Curr Directions, 4*(2), 61–65.

Frank, C. (1996). The new way to catch rapists. *Redbook,* 104–105, 118–120.

Frank, E., & Anderson, P. (1987). Psychiatric disorders in rape victims: Past history and current symptomatology. *Comprehensive Psychiatry, 28*(1), 77–82.

Frank, E., & Stewart, B. D. (1984). Depressive symptoms in rape victims: A revisit. *Journal of Affective Disorders, 7*(1), 77–85.

Frazier, P. (1990). Victim attributions and post-rape trauma. *Journal of Personality and Social Psychology, 59*(2), 298–304.

Frazier, P. (2000). The scientific status of research on rape trauma syndrome. In D. L. Faigman, D. H. Kay, M. J. Sakes, & J. Sanders (Eds.), *Modern scientific evidence: The law & science of expert testimony* (Vol. 1, pp. 112–126). St. Paul, MN: West Group.

Frazier, P., & Burnett, J. (1994). Immediate coping strategies among rape victims. *J Couns Dev, 72*(4), 633–639.

Frazier, P. A., & Haney, B. (1996). Sexual Assault Cases in the Legal System: Police, Prosecutor; and Victim Perspectives. *Law and Human Behavior, 20*(6), 607–628.

Frazier, P., Harlow, T., Schauben, L., et al. (1993). In *Predictors of post rape trauma.* Paper presented at the 1993 meeting of the American Psychological Association, Toronto.

Frazier, P., & Schauben, L. (1994). Causal attributions and recovery from rape and other stressful life events. *J Soc Clin Psychol, 13*(1), 1–14.

Freedy, J. R., Resnick, H. S., Kilpatrick, D. G., et al. (1994). The psychological adjustment of recent crime victims in the criminal justice system. *Journal of Interpersonal Violence, 9*(4), 450–468.

Geist, R. F. (1988). Sexually related trauma. *Emergency Medicine Clinics of North America, 6*(3), 439–466.

Gentilello, L., Rivara, F., Donovan, D., et al. (1999). Alcohol interventions in a trauma center as a means of reducing the risk of injury recurrence. *Annals of Surgery, 230*(4), 473–480.

Gidycz, C. A., Coble, C. N., Latham, L., et al. (1993). Relation of a sexual assault experience in adulthood to prior victimization experiences: A prospective analysis. *Psychol Women Q, 17*(2), 151–168.

Gidycz, C., & Koss, M. (1989). The impact of adolescent sexual victimization: Standardized measures of anxiety, depression, and behavioral deviancy. *Violence and Victims, 4*(2), 139–149.

Gidycz, C., & Koss, M. (1991). Predictors of long-term sexual assault trauma among a national sample of victimized college women. *Violence and Victims, 6*(3), 175–190.

Girelli, S., Resnick, P., Marhoefer-Dvorak, S., et al. (1986). Subjective distress and violence during rape: Their effects on long-term fear. *Violence and Victims, 1*(1), 35–46.

Gold, S., Milan, L., Mayall, A., et al. (1994). A cross-validation study of the trauma symptom checklist. *Journal of Interpersonal Violence, 9*(1), 12–32.

Golding, J. (1994). Sexual assault history and physical health in randomly selected Los Angeles women. *Health Psychology, 13*(2), 130–138.

Goodman, L., Koss, M., & Russo, N. (1993). Violence against Women: Physical, mental and health effects. In *Applied and preventive psychology.* (Chap. 2, pp. 79–89). Cambridge: Cambridge University Press.

Gray-Eurom, K., Seaberg, D., & Wears, R. (2002). The prosecution of sexual assault cases: correlation with forensic evidence. *Annals of Emergency Medicine, 39*(1), 39–46.

Griswold, C. J. (1999). *Efficacy of sexual assault nurse examiner evidence collection: A northern Michigan study.* Thesis submitted to Grand Valley State University, Kirkhof School of Nursing, Allendale, MI.

Hertzen, H., Piaggio, G., Ding, J., et al. (2002). Low dose mifepristone and two regimens of levonorgestrel for emergency contraception: A WHO multicenter randomized trial. *Lancet, 360*(9348), 1803–1810.

Hilden, M., Schei, B., & Sidenius, K. (2005). Genitoanal injury in adult female victims of sexual assault. *Forensic Science International, 154*(2–3), 200–205.

Holloway, M., & Swan, A. (1993). A & E management of sexual assault. *Nursing Standard, 7*(45), 31–35.

International Association of Forensic Nurses (IAFN). (1996). *Sexual assault nurse examiner standards of practice.* Pitman, NJ: Author.

Joint Commission on Accreditation of Health Care Organizations (JCAHO). (1997). *Comprehensive accreditation manual for hospitals: The official handbook.* Oakbrook Terrace, IL: Author.

Jones, K., & Uishi, T. (1980). Impact of alcohol, drug abuse and mental health treatment on medical care utilization: A review of the literature. *Medical Care, 17*(2), 1–82.

Jones, J., Rossman, L., Hartman, M., & Alexander, C. (2003). Anogenital injuries in adolescents after consensual sexual intercourse. *Academic Emergency Medicine, 10*(12), 1378–1383.

Jones, J., Rossman, L., Wynn, B., Dunnuck, C., & Schwartz, N. (2003). Comparative analysis of adult versus adolescent sexual assault: Epidemiology and patterns of anogenital injury. *Academic Emergency Medicine, 10*(8), 872–877.

Katz, M., & Gerberding, J. (1998). The care of persons with recent sexual exposure to HIV. *Annals of Internal Medicine, 128*(4), 306–312.

Kaysen, D., Neighbors, C., Martell, J., et al. (2006). Incapacitated rape and alcohol use: a prospective analysis. *Addictive Behaviors, 31*(10), 1820–1832.

Keller, P., & Nelson, J. (2008). Injuries to the cervix in sexual trauma. *Journal of Forensic Nursing, 4*(3), 101–146.

Kessler, R., Sonnega, A., Bromet, E., et al. (1995). Post-traumatic stress disorder in the national comorbidity survey. *Archives of General Psychiatry, 52*(12), 1048–1060.

Kettleson, D. (1995). Nurses trained to take evidence. In *Unit News/District News.* District of East Hawaii.

Kiffe, B. (1996). "Perceptions: Responsibility attributions of rape victims." Unpublished doctoral dissertation. Augsburg College MSW, Minneapolis, MN.

Kilpatrick, D., Acierno, R., Resnick, H., et al. (1997). A 2-year longitudinal analysis of the relationship between violent assault and substance use in women. *Journal of Consulting and Clinical Psychology, 65*(5), 834–847.

Kilpatrick, D., Edmunds, C., & Seymour, A. (1992). *Rape in America: A report to the Nation.* Arlington, VA: National Victim Center.

Kilpatrick, D., Resnick, R., & Veronen, L. (1981). Effects of a rape experience: A longitudinal study. *J Soc Issues, 37*(4), 1050–1121.

Kilpatrick, D., Ruggiero, K., Acierno, R., Saunders, B., Resnick, H., & Best, C. (2003). Violence and risk of PTSD, major depression, substance abuse/dependence, and comorbidity: Results from the national survey of adolescents. *Journal of Consulting and Clinical Psychology, 71*(4), 692–700.

Kilpatrick, D., Saunders, B., Veronen, L., et al. (1987). Criminal victimization: Lifetime prevalence reporting to police, and psychological impact. *Crime Delinquency*, 33(4), 479–489.

Kilpatrick, D., & Veronen, L. (1984). *Treatment of fear and anxiety in victims of rape*. (Final report, grant No. R01NG29602). Rockville, MD: National Institute of Mental Health.

Kilpatrick, D. G., Veronen, L. J., Best, C. L., et al. (1985). Factors predicting psychological distress among rape victims. In C. R. Figley (Ed.), *Trauma and its wake* (pp. 113–141). New York: Brunner/Mazel.

Kilpatrick, D. G., Veronen, L. J., & Resick, R. (1979). Assessment of the aftermath of rape: Changing patterns of fear. *J Behav Assess*, 1(2), 133–148.

Kimerling, R., & Calhoun, S. (1994). Somatic symptoms, social support, and treatment seeking among sexual assault victims. *Journal of Consulting and Clinical Psychology*, 62(2), 333–340.

Koss, M. (1988). Hidden Rape: Sexual aggression & victimization in a national sample students in higher education. In A. W. Burgess (Ed.), *Rape & Sexual Assault* (Vol. 2, pp. 3–25). New York: Garland Publishing.

Koss, M. (1993). Rape. Scope, impact, interventions, and public policy. *The American Psychologist*, 48(10), 1062–1069.

Koss, M., Dinero, T., Seibel, C., et al. (1988). Stranger and acquaintance rape: Are there differences in the victim's experience? *Psychol Women Q*, 12(1), 1–24.

Koss, M., Woodruff, W., & Koss, P. (1990). Relationship of criminal victimization to health perceptions among women medical patients. *Journal of Consulting and Clinical Psychology*, 58(2), 147–152.

Koss, M. P., Koss, P., & Woodruff, W. (1991). Deleterious effects of criminal victimization on women's health and medical utilization. *Archives of Internal Medicine*, 151(2), 342–357.

Krakow, B., Tandberg, D., Barey, M., et al. (1995). Nightmares and sleep disturbance in sexually assaulted women. *Dreaming*, 5(3), 199–206.

Kramer, T., & Green, B. (1991). Post-traumatic stress disorder as an early response to sexual assault. *Journal of Interpersonal Violence*, 6(2), 160–173.

Ledray, L. (1984). Victims of incest. *AJN*, 84(8), 1010–1014.

Ledray, L. (2002). Do All Emergency Physicians Have an Obligation to Provide Care for Victims of Sexual Assault or Is There a More Effective Alternative?. *Annals of Emergency Medicine*, 39(1), 61–64.

Ledray, L., & Chaignot, M. J. (1980). Services to sexual assault victims in Hennepin County. *Evaluation and Change, Special Issue*, 131–134.

Ledray, L., Faugno, D., & Speck, P. (2001). Sexual assault: Clinical issues. SANE: Advocate, forensic technician, nurse? *Journal of Emergency Nursing: JEN*, 27(1), 91–93.

Ledray, L. E. (1991). Sexual assault and sexually transmitted disease: The issues and concerns. In A. W. Burgess (Ed.), *Rape and sexual assault. III: A research handbook*. New York: Garland Publishing.

Ledray, L. E. (1992). The sexual assault nurse clinician: Minneapolis' 15 years experience. *Journal of Emergency Nursing: JEN*, 18(3), 217–222.

Ledray, L. E. (1993). Sexual assault nurse clinician: An emerging area of nursing expertise. In C. Linda, Andrist (Eds.), *Clinical issues in perinatal and women's health nursing* (Vol. 4, pp. 2). Philadelphia: Lippincott.

Ledray, L. E. (1994). *Recovering from rape*. (2nd ed.)New York: Henry Holt.

Ledray, L. E. (1996a). Sexual assault nurse clinician: Sexual assault nurse examiner (SANE) programs. *Journal of Emergency Nursing: JEN*, 22(5), 460–464.

Ledray, L. E. (1996b). Sexual assault: Clinical issues: Date rape drug alert. *Journal of Emergency Nursing: JEN*, 22(1), 80.

Ledray, L. E. (1999). Sexual assault: Clinical issues: Date rape drug alert. *Journal of Emergency Nursing: JEN*, 17(1), 1–2.

Ledray, L. E. (2001). Sexual Assault Nurse Examiner. In M. LeBeau, & A. Mozayani (Eds.), *Drug Facilitated Sexual Assault: A Forensic Handbook* (Chapter 11, pp. 231–252). Academic Press of London.

Ledray, L. (2008). Consent to photograph: How far should disclosure go? *Journal of Forensic Nursing (4)*, 188–189.

Ledray, L. E., & Barry, L. (1998). Sexual assault: Clinical issues: SANE expert and factual testimony. *Journal of Emergency Nursing: JEN*, 24(3), 284–287.

Ledray, L. E., & Simmelink, K. (1997). Sexual Assault: Clinical Issues. Efficacy of SANE evidence collection: A Minnesota Study. *Journal of Emergency Nursing*, 23(1).

Lenehan, G. P. (1991). A SANE way to care for rape victims. *Journal of Emergency Nursing: JEN*, 17(1), 1–2.

Leserman, J., Drossman, D., et al. (1997). Impact of sexual and physical abuse dimensions on health status: Development of an abuse severity measure. *Psychometric Med*, 59(2), 152–160.

Littel, K. (2001). Sexual assault nurse examiner programs; Improving the community response to sexual assault victims. *Office for Victims of Crime Bulletin*, 4, 1–19.

Littleton, H., & Breitkopf, C. (2006). Coping with the Experience of Rape. *Psychology of Women Quarterly*, 30(1), 106–116.

Logan, T., Cole, J., & Capillo, A. (2007). Differential characteristics of intimate partner, acquaintance, and stranger rape survivors examined by a Sexual Assault Nurse Examiner (SANE). *Journal of Interpersonal Violence*, 22(8), 1066–1076.

Logan, T., Walker, R., Cole, J., & Leukefeld, C. (2002). Victimization and substance abuse among women: Contributing factors, interventions, and implications. PsycINFO. 6(4), 325–397.

Lynch, V. A. (1993). Forensic nursing: Diversity in education and practice. *J Psychosoc Nurs*, 132(3), 7–14.

Lynch, V. A. (1996). President's report: Goals of the IAFN. In: *Fourth Annual Scientific Assembly of Forensic Nurses Conference*, Kansas City, KS.

MacFarlane, E., & Hawley, P. (1993). Sexual assault: Coping with crisis. *The Canadian Nurse*, 89(6), 21–24.

Mackey, T., Sereika, S., Weissfeld, L., et al. (1992). Factors associated with long-term depressive symptoms of sexual assault victims. *Archives of Psychiatric Nursing*, VI(1), 10–25.

Mann, S., & Delon, M. (1995). Improved hypertension control after disclosure of decades old trauma. *Psychosomatic Medicine*, 57(5), 501–505.

Marchbanks, P., Lui, K. J., & Mercy, J. (1990). Risk of injury from resisting rape. *American Journal of Epidemiology*, 132(3), 540–549.

Marullo, G. (1996). The future and the forensic nurse: New dimensions for the 21st century. In: *Fourth Annual Scientific Assembly of Forensic Nurses Conference*, Kansas City, KS.

Mastro, T., & DeVicenzi, I. (1996). Probabilities of sexual HIV-1 transmission. *AIDS*, 10, Suppl A: 575–582.

Messman-Moore, T., & Long, P. (2002). Alcohol and substance use disorders as predictors of child to adult sexual revictimization in a sample of community women. *Violence & Victims*, 17(3), 319–340.

Moss, M., Frank, E., & Anderson, B. (1990). Victims of Incest. *The American Journal of Orthopsychiatry*, 69(3), 379–391.

Muran, E., & DiGiuseppe, R. (1994). Rape. In Dattilio, Freeman (Eds.), *Cognitive behavioral strategies in crisis intervention* (pp. 161–175). New York: Guilford Press.

Murphy, S., Harris, J., Kitchen, V., & Forester, S. (1989). Rape and subsequent seroconversion to HIV. *BMJ (Clinical Research Ed.)*, 299(6701), 718.

Nadelson, C., Notman, M., Zackson, H., et al. (1982). A follow-up study of rape victims. *The American Journal of Psychiatry*, 139(10), 1326–11270.

National Conference of Catholic Bishops. (1995). *Pamphlet on ethical & religious directives for Catholic health care services*. (pp. 14–17). Washington, DC.

Norris, J., & Feldman-Summers, S. (1981). Factors related to the psychological impact of rape on the victim. *Journal of Abnormal Psychology*, 90(6), 562–567.

O'Brien, C. (1996). Sexual assault nurse examiner (SANE) program coordinator. *Journal of Emergency Nursing: JEN*, 23(5), 532–533.

Office for the Prevention of Domestic Violence (OPDV). (2003). OPDV Bulletin. Fall 2003. 15(2).

Petrak, J., Skinner, C. J., & Claydon, E. J. (1995). The prevalence of sexual assault in a genitourinary medicine clinic: Service implications. *Genitourinary Medicine*, 71(2), 98–102.

Resick, P., & Schnicke, M. (1990). Treating symptoms in adult victims of sexual assault. *Journal of Interpersonal Violence*, 5(4), 488–506.

Resnick, H., Kilpatrick, D., Dansky, B., et al. (1993). Prevalence of civilian trauma and PTSD in a representative national sample of women. *Journal of Consulting and Clinical Psychology*, 61(6), 984–991.

Resnick, H., Yehuda, R., Pitman, R., et al. (1995). Effect of previous trauma on acute plasma cortisol level following rape. *The American Journal of Psychiatry*, 152(11), 1675–1677.

Riggs, D., Kilpatrick, D., & Resnick, H. (1992). Long-term psychological distress associated with marital rape and aggravated assault: A comparison to other crime victims. *J Fam Violence, 7*(4), 283–296.

Riggs, N., Houry, D., Long, G., et al. (2000). Analysis of 1,076 cases of sexual assault. *Annals of Emergency Medicine, 35*(4), 358–362.

Rooms, R. R. (2004). Personal letter to Virginia Lynch (April 2004).

Rothbaum, B., Foa, E., Riggs, D., et al. (1992). A prospective study of PTSD in rape victims. *Journal of Traumatic Stress, 5*(3), 455–475.

Sandrick, K. J. (1996). Tightening the chain of evidence. *Hospitals & Health Networks/AHA, 70*(11), 64–66.

Santello, M., & Leitenberg, H. (1993). Sexual aggression by an acquaintance: Methods of coping and later psychological adjustment. *Violence and Victims, 8*(2), 91–104.

Santiago, J., McCal-Perez, F., Gorcey, M., et al. (1985). Long-term psychological effects of rape in 35 rape victims. *The American Journal of Psychiatry, 142*(11), 1338–1340.

Sheridan, Daniel, J. (1993). The role of the battered woman specialist. *J Psychosoc Nurs, 31*(7), 11.

Sievers, V., Murphy, S., & Miller, J. (2003). Sexual assault evidence collection more accurate when completed by sexual assault nurse examiners: Colorado's experience. *Journal of Emergency Nursing (29),* 511–514.

Slaughter, L., & Brown, C. R. (1992). Colposcopy to establish physical findings in rape victims. *American Journal of Obstetrics and Gynecology, 176*(3), 83–86.

Slaughter, L., Brown, C. R., Crowley, S., et al. (1997). Patterns of genital injury in female sexual assault victims. *American Journal of Obstetrics and Gynecology, 176*(3), 609–616.

Sommers, M., Fargo, J., Baker, R., Fisher, B., & Buschur, C., Zink, T. (in press, 2009). Health Disparities in the Forensic Sexual Assault Examination Related to Skin Color. *Journal of Forensic Nursing.*

Sommers, M., Fisher, B., & Karjane, H. (2005). Using colposcopy in the rape exam: Health care, forensics, and criminal justice issues. *Journal of Obstetric, Gynecological, and Neonatal Nursing, 1*(1), 28–34 19.

Sommers, M., & Buschur, C. (2004). Injury in women who are raped: What every critical care nurse needs to know. *Dimensions of Criticla Care Nursing, 23*(2), 62–68.

Sorenson, S., Siegel, J., Golding, J., et al. (1991). Repeated sexual victimization. *Violence and Victims, 6*(4), 299–308.

Speck, P., & Aiken, M. (1995). 20 years of community nursing service. *Tennessee Nurse/Tennessee Nurses Association, 58*(2), 5–18.

Spirito, A., Monti, P., Barnett, N., et al. (2004). A randomized clinical trial of a brief motivational intervention for alcohol-positive adolescents treated in an emergency department. *The Journal of Pediatrics, 145*(3), 396–402.

Strack, G. (2004). *Battered Women's Justice Project and the Family Justice Center. Domestic Violence and Strangulation: Coordinating dispatch, police,* *medical, prosecution, and advocacy responses* San Diego conference materials.

Task Force on Postovulatory Methods of Fertility Regulation. (1998). Randomized controlled trial levonorgestrel versus the Yuzpe regimen of combined oral contraceptives for emergency contraception. *Lancet, 53,* 4228–4333.

Thom, B., Herring, R., & Judd, A. (1999). Identifying alcohol-related harm in young drinkers: The role of accident and emergency departments. *Alcohol and Alcoholism, 34*(6), 910–915.

Thomas, M., & Zachritz, H. (1993). Tulsa sexual assault nurse examiners (SANE) program. *The Journal of the Oklahoma State Medical Association, 86*(6), 284–686.

Tintinalli, J., & Hoelzer, M. (1985). Clinical findings and legal resolution in sexual assault. *Annals of Emergency Medicine, 14*(5), 447–453.

Tobias, G. (1990). Rape examinations by GPs. *The Practitioner, 234*(1495), 874 877.

Tucker, S., Ledray, L. E., & Stehle Werner, J. (1990). Sexual assault evidence collection. *Wisconsin Med J, (7),* 3–5.

U.S. Food and Drug Administration. (2006). *FDA Approves Over-the-Counter Access for Plan B for Women 18 and Older Prescription Remains Required for Those 17 and Under.* August 24, 2006. Available at www.fda.gov.

Waigandt, C., & Miller, D. (1986). Maladaptive responses during the reorganization phase of rape trauma syndrome. *Response, 1*(2), 6–7.

Walker, E., Katon, W., Hansom, J., et al. (1995). Psychiatric diagnoses and sexual victimization in women with chronic pelvic pain. *Psychosomatics, 332*(6), 531–540.

Wiley, J., Herschkorn, S., & Padian, N. (1989). Heterogeneity in the probability of HIV transmission per sexual contact: The case of male to female transmission in penile-vaginal intercourse. *Statistics in medicine, 8*(1), 93–102.

Winfield, I., George, L. K., Swartz, M., et al. (1990). Sexual assault and psychiatric disorders among a community sample of women. *The American Journal of Psychiatry, 147*(3), 335–341.

Womack, K. (2008). Emergency Contraception to Avoid Unintended Pregnancy Following Sexual Assault. Women's Health Care: A Practical Journal for Nurse Practitioners. *Annual Conference Issue, 7*(6), 10–13.

Vignola, M. (2009). *Strangulation and Domestic Assault. Special Considerations for SANE Nurses.* SARS Meeting, February 20, 2009, Minneapolis, MN.

Yorker, B. C. (1996). Nurses in Georgia care for survivors of sexual assault. *Georgia Nursing, 56*(1), 5–6.

Yuzpe, A., Smith, R., & Rademaker, A. W. (1982). A multicenter clinical investigation employing ethinyl estradiol combined with dl-norgestrel as a postcoital contraceptive agent. *Fertility and Sterility, 37*(4), 508–513.

Pamela J. Dole

This chapter discusses the physical, emotional, and sexual consequences of sexual abuse. Consequences of sexual abuse include posttraumatic stress disorder (PTSD). PTSD also arises from all forms of violence and chronic abuse. Chronic abuse often escalates to physical violence that includes sexual violence. Other forms of intimate abuse include emotional abuse, economic abuse, destruction of pets or property, threats, and stalking.

Sexual violence affects the community on a variety of levels and spans across all socioeconomic and ethnocultural groups. These acts are committed more frequently against women than men, and laws related to prosecuting sexual violence reflect community culture and views regarding women. All aggression creates an economic burden for the community.

The forensic nurse examiner (FNE) who specializes in sexual assault intervention can have an impact on patients at all levels of healing and by knowing the possible consequences of sexual violence can better direct nursing care. In addition, much can be done at various levels by professional and nonprofessional groups from government agencies, advocacy groups, peer support groups, law enforcement, healthcare professionals, and attorneys.

KEY POINT Creating a community social consciousness that does not tolerate sexual crimes is an important role of the sexual assault nurse examiner/sexual assault forensic examiner/forensic nurse examiner (SANE/SAFE/FNE).

Social Impact of Sexual Violence

Most victims of sexual assault and childhood sexual abuse suffer lifelong effects from these acts of violence. Trauma is associated with medical, psychological, social, spiritual, and sexual health consequences and related costs. Public health concerns about trauma and its effects in the United States are reflected in the *Healthy People 2010* objectives that include decreasing interpersonal violence injuries and increasing violence prevention in an effort to reduce trauma-associated morbidity (USDHHS, 2000). The Joint Commission (TJC) guidelines call for identification, documentation, treatment and referral procedures as well as for training of appropriate staff in settings where abused or neglected patients may be encountered (TJC, PC-7, 2009). The Violence against Women Act of 1994 expresses the need for research addressing interpersonal violence. This is the first national act that addresses restructuring the philosophy, assessment, and prosecution of perpetrators while providing some privacy to the victim.

The well-known acceptance of violence in America also pervades issues of violence against women (Sigler, 1995). Reform, which began in the 1980s, was originally prompted by the feminist movement. How sexual violence is defined will affect how victims view themselves, how others view them, how the crime is reported, and what types of statistics are kept. The term *rape* is considered too narrow to adequately reflect the spectrum of acts of violence surrounding nonconsensual sexual aggression, because rape refers to actual penile penetration of the vagina and does not include oral or anal penetration. Currently, sexual aggression can be prosecuted within the context of marriage in many states, whereas it was excluded in the past.

The terms used in laws since approximately 1994 include sexual assault, sexual battery, and sexual abuse (Epstein & Langenbahn, 1994). These terms reflect the three common reforms as summarized by the National Research Council (Crowell & Burgess, 1996):
- Broadening the definition to sexual penetration of any type, including vaginal, anal, or oral penetration, whether by penis, fingers, or objects
- Focusing on the offender's behavior rather than the victim's resistance
- Restricting the use of the victim's prior sexual conduct as evidence

The concepts in this reformed language are more supportive to victims and emphasize the violence of the act itself by the perpetrator. Before 1994, because the meaning of the term *rape* was limited, perpetrators could often beat the charges by using a condom, admitting to impotence, or confining their aggression to everything short of nonconsensual coitus. It is important when reading research and reports to distinguish whether the language describing rape was presented before 1994 or after. The more recent terminology reflects an expanded concept of nonconsensual sexual aggression, thus reducing the gap in justice for these criminal acts. Some federal branches continue to use narrow definitions such as those found in the Uniform Crime Reports by the Federal Bureau of Investigation (FBI) (1993). Narrow definitions and underreporting of violence against women in partner violence, sexual assault, and stalking contribute to the paucity of research in these areas.

FBI and police agencies categorize crime by the most violent act only, often missing important facts such as sexual assault. For example, an individual who is the victim of a sexual homicide is listed as homicide. Individuals who are not legally married but living together or dating are often not adequately represented in statistics. Therefore, the accuracy of crimes involving interpersonal abuse within committed but not married relationships are often lost in statistics. This is true in cases of battered women and same-sex relationships. The FBI (1993) reported that more than 75% of violent crimes against women are committed by someone the victim knows. It is further stated that an intimate partner commits approximately 29% of those crimes and that these statistics may be underreported as a result of terminology and the categories used for reporting.

Terminology often reflects current social philosophy. Research, funding, and a comprehensive understanding of the nature of interpersonal violence against women are just beginning. Data gaps exist in areas including women of color, patterns of multiple forms of victimization, and rates of perpetration (Crowell & Burgess, 1996). Few data exist about men who have been sexually assaulted, yet they also experience consequences from sexual aggression. Until this widened knowledge base is generated, proactive prevention strategies are limited. Statistics on the prevalence of this social problem remain skewed and underestimated, especially in light of the fact that the majority of women do not report sexual assaults or seek healthcare at the time of the crime. Limited statistics are confounded by the lack of adequate screening for domestic abuse or sexual assault. Funding for research and development of interventions is inconsistent, although it appears to be gaining importance in the national agenda.

Global Issues

In postapartheid South Africa, sexual assault occurs every six minutes to infants, children, and adults. Anger from poor economic stability and the lack of role definitions have pushed black men to retaliate against women of all ages and races.

A European myth from the Middle Ages that having sex with a virgin would cure syphilis has a new deadly spin in the twenty-first century. In developing countries, prepubescent girls are being raped because of beliefs that this will cure AIDS or prevent the rapist from contracting HIV infection (Jewkes, Martin, & Penn-Kekana, 2002; Lema, 1997; Meel, 2003; Pitcher & Bowley, 2002). In 2001, virgin rape had become so pervasive that infants as young as six to nine months old were victimized in South Africa. In some third world countries, it is not uncommon for an eight-year-old girl to have already experienced multiple rapes and to have contracted numerous sexually transmitted infections (STIs) including HIV and human papillomavirus (HPV).

CHILD PROSTITUTION

Child sexual abuse in the form of child prostitution is a global concern arising from poor economic situations, gender bias, and lack of education. It is estimated that from 1 million to 10 million children are coerced or sold into the sex industry. These children have the highest rate of HIV infection (78% in China), hepatitis, tuberculosis, and STIs and generally have not received immunizations. Child prostitutes also experience malnutrition, violence, pregnancy, substance abuse, and mental illness, with suicide and PTSD rates as high as 67% (Willis & Levy, 2002).

RAPE IN WAR

For thousands of years, wars have been won without ever firing a gun. Raping the women in villages, a common war strategy, erodes families and disintegrates communities. Documentaries on the war on Yugoslavia have depicted the effects of rape by conquering soldiers. Women and families speak about the decay caused by this particular war strategy on the communities and families, especially in Bosnia, Rwanda, and Kurdistan (*AIDS Weekly Plus*, 1996). Refugees and internal displacement movements also place women and children at increased risk of sexual abuse that exceeds 60% (Amowitz, Russ, Lyons, et al., 2002; Gardner & Blackburn, 1996; Kerimova, Posner, Brown, et al., 2003). The World Health Organization (WHO), the United Nations, and advocate groups (e.g., Human Rights Watch, Amnesty International) are examples of international organizations that offer investigative assistance and emotional support to communities following the devastation of war.

Until women are viewed as equals and partners, they will remain victims of sexual assault. Social risk factors restricting a woman's autonomy contribute to sexual violence against women. Community empowerments with interventions that improve a woman's self-efficacy are needed to change current social attitudes (Gollub, 1999).

Male Victims

Men are also victims of sexual assault and molestation. Statistically, men are sexually assaulted significantly less than women; however, many similar issues, concerns, and consequences exist. Men often report increased humiliation from not being able to defend themselves against the perpetrator (McEvoy, Rollo, & Brookings, 1999; Scarce, 1997). Boys sexually abused by clergy describe rage and spiritual distress pervading their life (Fater & Mullaney, 2000). Male victims of childhood sexual assault identifying as homosexual or heterosexual orientation tend to identify with abusers and abandon their feelings as a victim (Clarke & Pearson, 2000). One study of men having sex with men who had been sexually abused by their partners experienced a 5.7% HIV seroconversion rate as a result (Relf, 2001). Male victims may be confused by traditional roles and fail to engage in self-care because of poor coping strategies. Adequate screening, research, and statistics are needed in this area.

Women in the Military

In a study of women attending the Veteran's Affairs for healthcare, civilian and military women were screened for sexual assault versus women without a history of sexual assault (Suris, Lind, Kashner, & Borman, 2007). Women experiencing sexual assault while on active duty have significantly more symptoms at all levels than civilian women. While on active duty, 25% of women report being sexually assaulted, with 43% reporting attempted rape (Donahoe, 2005; Stein, Lang, Laffaye, Satz, Lenox, & Dresselhaus, 2004; Suris et al., 2007). In both groups (civilian or military), women with a history of sexual assault had significantly more psychological symptoms including PTSD, physical and somatic symptoms, substance abuse, decreased quality of life, and increased utilization of healthcare (Suris et al., 2007). Depression and PTSD were reported a decade later and may be attributed in part to the fact that there is no downtime to process while on active duty and women often have to continue to work with the perpetrator. Survivors of sexual assault often suffer in silence to protect their careers.

Poverty-Related Sexual Assault

Individuals living in poverty are much more likely to be sexually assaulted. Persons with incomes of less than $15,000 are three times more likely to be raped, be sexually assaulted, or sustain violent injuries compared to households with annual incomes greater than $15,000 (Grisso, Schwarz, Hirschinger, et al., 1999; Von, Kilpatrick, Burgess, & Hartman, 1998). Vulnerable populations have fewer resources to cope with the consequences of sexual abuse.

Economic Impact of Interpersonal Violence

The cost of interpersonal violence is difficult to estimate. Many individuals do not report acts of violence and their effects are thus categorized in unrelated areas. The World Health Organization (WHO) and the World Bank define disability as the "incidence, duration, and severity of the morbidity and complications associated with specific conditions" (Wolfgang & Zahn, 1983). "In 1990 the assaultive violence was estimated to account for 17.5 million DALYs worldwide" (Rosenberg, Mercy, & Annest, 1998, p. 1226). DALYs refers to the measure of disability-adjusted life years lost. Intrafamilial homicide costs were calculated to be $1.7 billion annually (Straus & Gelles, 1986). The number of victims of interpersonal violence was nine times higher in households with incomes of $19,999 or less when compared to women with household incomes of $20,000 to $49,999 (CDC, 1998). Alcohol use by male partners was strongly correlated to the risk of injuries in a controlled study of domestic violence and confirmed by 67% of the female victims (Kyriacou, Anglin, Taliaferro, et al., 1999). Characteristics of assaultive partners are strongly related to the use of cocaine and past history of arrests, suggesting a pattern of violence in another study (Grisso, et al., 1999).

Sexual assault and battering also contribute to emergency department and related expenses. One study revealed that 22% of 911 (emergency telephone line) calls were related to victims of battering (Baker, Burgess, Brickman, et al., 1989). Injuries related to battering account for 12% to 35% of emergency room visits by women (Meyers, 1992). One third of battered women are also sexually assaulted by their partners. Healthcare expenses for each individual from intimate partner violence is $1775 greater per year and cost healthcare plans 92% more than a random sample of general female enrollees (Wisner, Gilmer, Saltzman, et al., 1999). The cost of domestic violence to employers for healthcare, high turnover, and lost productivity is estimated to be $3 billion to $5 billion (American Bar Association Commission on Domestic Violence, 1996; Bureau of National Affairs, 1990). Meyers (1992) calculated these same losses to be $5 billion to $10 billion per year.

Sexual assault costs are higher than for other violent crimes, costing victims $127 billion per year and $86,464 per individual (Miller, Cohen, & Weirsema, 1996). There are no statistics available on short-term disability losses or healthcare-related costs sought outside the emergency department. Nonmonetary costs to victims include fear, suffering, pain, and lost quality of life. In a controlled study, victims of sexual assault were found to increase physician visits 56% over a two-year period following their attack when compared to the nonassaulted group (Koss, Koss, & Woodruff, 1991).

Psychological, Physical, and Sexual Health Effects

Statistics represent numbers pertaining to the consequences of sexual assault and do not convey the devastation experienced by victims and the profound effects on their lives (Box 33-1). The "lived experience" of each individual varies and is experienced differently. "Understanding the meaning of violence in women's lives requires an awareness of both their life stories and the social context of the violence they have encountered" (Draucker & Madsen, 1999). The most important aspect in opening the door

to healing the effects of violence is to ask the questions of our friends, family, patients, and community. Patients presenting with discordant symptomatology are often waving a red flag and asking to be heard. Women have fewer posttraumatic problems when they possess stronger coherence and higher self-esteem (Nyamathi, 1991).

KEY POINT Trauma has an impact on the entire person. The possible consequences to sexual violence are exhibited as symptoms within the context of individual experiences. Symptoms are guideposts for intervention to reduce human suffering and to restore well-being for the individual.

POSTTRAUMATIC STRESS DISORDER

PTSD is a psychological condition often suffered by victims of violence, including sexual assault and childhood sexual abuse. This diagnosis does not capture all the symptoms experienced by victims. PTSD is defined in the *Diagnostic and Statistical Manual of Mental Disorders* (APA, 1994) and must meet the following summarized criteria:

A1. (Criterion) Witnessed a life-threatening event or serious injury

A2. (Criterion) Exposed to an unusual traumatic event that has produced intense fear, terror, horror, or helplessness

Associated symptoms that must last for at least one month include the following:

- Trauma that is reexperienced in ongoing dreams, thoughts, or perceptions (intrusive thoughts)
- Avoidance of related traumatic stimuli (physical and psychological avoidance), with a numbing of general responsiveness
- Persistent hypervigilance, exaggerated startle response, increased arousal, sleep disturbances, irritability, outbreaks of anger, and cognitive and memory disturbances (Korn, 2001)

It has been postulated that PTSD may represent a severe expression of posttrauma disturbances, and anxiety and depression represent milder manifestations of the same continuum (Fullilove, Lown, & Fullilove, 1992). It should be noted that there is disagreement among psychiatrists about whether posttraumatic stress related to sexual assault actually meets the criteria for PTSD.

The Panel on Research on Violence against Women stated that PTSD did not adequately conceptualize the experiences by victims of violence. The following four categories were listed as areas not adequately represented in the preceding definition (Crowell & Burgess, 1996, pp. 83–84):

It doesn't account for many of the symptoms manifested by victims of violence. For example, thoughts of suicide attempts, substance abuse, and sexual problems are not among the PTSD criteria.

The diagnosis better captures the psychiatric consequences of a single victimization than the consequences of chronic abusive conditions.

The description of traumatic events as outside usual human experience is not accurate in describing women's experiences with intimate violence.

The diagnosis fails to acknowledge the cognitive effects of this kind of violence. People who have been untouched often maintain beliefs (or schemas) about personal invulnerability, safety, trust, and intimacy, which are incompatible with experience of violence.

Not all victims of sexual abuse or assault develop PTSD. Contributing risk factors include gender, age, race, culture, intelligence, psychological vulnerability, and proximity to

Box 33-1 Possible Sequelae to Sexual Violence

PHYSICAL

GASTROINTESTINAL
- Irritable bowel syndrome
- Severe constipation
- Vomiting and diarrhea
- Dyspepsia

NEUROLOGICAL
- Headaches/migraines
- Postconcussion syndrome
- Hearing loss
- Detached retina
- Stroke from strangulation

MUSCULOSKELETAL
- Arthralgia
- Chronic pain
- Osteoarthritis
- Fibromyalgia

CONSTITUTIONAL
- Fatigue
- Bulimia/anorexia nervosa
- Morbid obesity
- Sleep disturbances
- Decreased concentration
- Paresis

GYNECOLOGICAL/OBSTETRICAL
- Chronic pelvic pain (often nonpathological)
- Dyspareunia
- STIs including HIV infection
- Vaginal infections
- Premenstrual syndrome
- Cystitis
- Unplanned pregnancy, especially in teens
- Bleeding during pregnancy
- Miscarriage
- Preterm labor and low-birth-weight infant
- Fetal injury and death

SEXUAL
- Dysfunction
- Decreased libido
- Decreased vaginal lubrication during intercourse
- Fear of coercion
- Decreased intimacy
- Increased casual sex

PSYCHOLOGICAL
- Posttraumatic stress disorder
- Decreased self-esteem
- Decreased self-care, including adherence to medical appointment and regimens
- Depression
- Flattened affect
- Substance abuse, including alcoholism and prescription drugs
- Increased risk-taking behavior
- Phobias
- Panic disorders
- Hypochondria
- Dissociation and multiple personality disorders
- Poor bonding with offspring
- Poor boundary setting
- Suicide

LIFESTYLE
- Unemployment
- Homelessness
- Increased risk taking
- Incarceration
- Disturbances in children

Source: Dole, P. (1996). Centering: Reducing rape trauma syndrome anxiety during a gynecologic examination. *J Psychosoc Nurs, 34*(10), 32–37; Association of Women's Health, Obstetrics and Neonatal Nurses (AWHONN). (1999). Partner & abuse violence screen. In *Universal Screening for Domestic Violence*. Washington, DC: Author.

trauma (Brunnello, Davidson, & Deahl, et al., 2001; Feeny, Zoellner, & Foa, 2002; Fullilove, et al., 1992; Kenny & McEachern, 2000; Korn, 2001; Seedat & Stein, 2000). One study reported higher levels of PTSD among Hispanic women (McFarlane, Malecha, Watson, et al., 2005). Psychological treatment is most effective when it is begun as soon after the sexual assault as possible. However, the majority of sexual assault victims never report the trauma or seek treatment, and children seldom disclose to parents (secretly feeling they themselves were bad or were to blame for the abuse). The silence provides the basis for PTSD.

When evaluating the magnitude of PTSD, it is important to keep in mind that economics, geography, and social support play an important part in the perception of trauma and subsequent recovery. Community rates of lifetime exposure to trauma range from 40% to 80%, while lifetime prevalence of PTSD is approximately 7% to 9% (Seedat & Stein, 2000). In a study of middle class Americans, only 1% reported experiencing trauma from any source (Kulka, Fairbank, Jordan, & Weiss, 1990). In a study of poor blacks in Harlem (New York City), nearly all persons reported one distressing traumatic event after another (Fullilove, Fullilove, Smith, et al., 1993). It appears that in communities experiencing high volumes of traumatic events, individuals may experience higher morbidity for risk-taking behavior, take poorer care of themselves, and suffer PTSD. This same group proposes separating violent trauma

(physical or sexual assault, mugging, witnessed murder) from all other nonviolent trauma when studying PTSD.

It should also be noted that males and females respond or define acts of trauma differently, except for natural disasters or terrorism attacks, from which 100% of the community may experience some form of PTSD. Residents of New York City have varying symptoms of PTSD following the 9/11 terrorism attacks of the World Trade Center that may increase over time (Ater, 2003). One study five to six weeks after 9/11 revealed that residents had a 9.7% increase in depression symptoms and a 7.5% increase in PTSD (Viahov & Galea, 2002). Farfel, DiGrande, Brackbill, et al. (2008) found increased rates of PTSD in 9/11 health registry enrollees two to three years later. PTSD rates were 16% and serious psychological distress was 8%, which was increased with lower income. Men frequently have PTSD after witnessing or being a victim of a violent crime similar to that experienced in combat (both military and on the streets). Women, however, additionally express homelessness and the loss of their children as traumatic events. It should be noted that much of the PTSD research to date has been done on men in the military or community disasters.

Impact during Childhood

Most victims of childhood sexual abuse experience some degree of PTSD. Multiple victimizations are a major contributing factor to PTSD in childhood sexual abuse (Jasinski, Williams, & Siegel 2000;

Polusny & Follette, 1995). PTSD is intensified when it is combined with increasing exposure to trauma, including adult sexual assault.

It is well documented that the cycle of violence generally begins in the home. Parents suffering from childhood victimization often victimize their children directly or indirectly (fail to provide a safe environment) (Hall, Sachs, & Rayens, 1998). One prospective study showed that 12% of male children sexually abused as children became pedophiles as adults. Adult abusers versus those who did not go on to abuse were more likely to have been abused by females (38% versus 17%), to witness physical abuse (81% versus 58%), to have lacked age-appropriate supervision (67% versus 40%), and to have demonstrated cruelty to animals (29% versus 5%) (Salter, McMillian, Richards, et al., 2003). Another study of men with increased risky behavior revealed that 25% had unwanted sexual activity before age 13 (Dilorio, Hartwell, & Hansen, 2002).

Previous childhood sexual trauma may interrupt the development of self-representation, contribute to the loss of self or fragmentation of self, increase concerns regarding control issues, disrupt identity issues, disrupt body-image evolution, and lower self-esteem (Hanna, 1996; Putnam, 1989). Sexual trauma is compounded if the individual is a member of a stigmatized group and is further subjected to acts of discrimination or oppression. "Stigma trauma," coined by Fullilove (1992), is often experienced by women of color in the form of gender oppression and ethnicity. Similarly, gay males may experience stigma trauma in the form of sexual orientation prejudices and bias hate crimes.

Burgess and Holmstrom (1974) coined the expression *rape trauma syndrome* (RTS) when describing the acute and long-term problems related to sexual attacks in a group of 146 victims studied four to six years later. RTS is considered a specific type of PTSD pertaining solely to consequences of trauma related to sexual assault or childhood sexual abuse and is not gender specific. RTS is broken into the acute phase or disorganization phase, which is characterized by expressive or guarded interviews following the sexual assault. Problems experienced by victims are categorized into physical, emotional, social, or sexual reactions impacting both the acute and long-term process of reorganization.

The term "rape trauma syndrome" is a nursing diagnosis for implementing recovery strategies and is not used as a diagnostic category. RTS, however, more appropriately addresses the sequel related to sexual assault, especially as experienced by women. It separates PTSD trauma experienced as a result of war or natural disaster that often happens to groups or communities and rarely involves nonconsensual invasion of the body by another individual. A wealth of research related to PTSD in nonsexual violence populations exists, but a paucity of material exists on RTS.

Recovery from sexual violence and RTS varies from person to person. One 1992 study found 94% of victims during the first week following the sexual assault had PTSD. A 1993 study found 50% of women met the criteria for PTSD one year following sexual assault (Ledray, 1994). The 1992 National Victim Center report *Rape in America: A Report to the Nation* estimated that 1.3 million women are experiencing PTSD two years after the sexual assault and that more than twice that number of women experienced PTSD at some time following the sexual assault.

Not all individuals will suffer long-term RTS. Support systems and the social environment are key factors in recovery. How the sexual assault is perceived by the individual's support system is also critical. If the sexual assault is viewed as an act of violence rather than a sexual act, recovery appears to be predictable with fewer long-term effects, provided that the individual possesses adequate coping mechanisms. Individuals who are exposed to stigma or ongoing environmental trauma appear to have increased long-term effects

represented by RTS. Draucker and Madsen (1999) found that sexually abused children experienced not only the sexual assault but may have been further traumatized by feelings of being "banished, alienated, or exiled." Sexually abused children also experienced deep-seated shame and the fear of feeling emotions producing guilt and anxiety (Zupancic & Kreidler, 1998). Individual coping mechanisms are dependent on the resolution of developmental issues and stages. Children who are victims of sexual abuse (either incest or molestation) appear to have more compromised coping mechanisms than adults of sexual abuse.

Women have twice the rate of PTSD as compared to men, especially if they were sexually abused as children (Brunnello et al., 2001; Katon, 2001; Wise, Zierler, Krieger, et al., 2001). A direct correlation between the severities of violence, the multiplicity of sexual abuse, and RTS also seems to exist (Jasinski, et al., 2000; Koss, Koss, & Woodruff, 1991; Ledray, 1990). Individuals with PTSD are 26 to 37 times more likely to develop affective illness, generalized anxiety disorder, or panic disorder (Katon, 2001).

Fear penetrates each of the categories in the acute phase and closely parallels the attack. Disturbances in sleep and eating patterns are two common occurrences caused by fear. The emotional reactions are seated in fear and phobic reactions and affect the ability to work, leave home, and relate to friends, family, and partners. Gratitude over surviving the attack is often clouded by the fear of being attacked again and possibly killed or mutilated (Hazelwood & Burgess, 1995; Koss et al., 1991). Similar to physical symptoms, emotional scars often go undetected because of poor history taking or the healthcare provider's inability or inexperience in managing or responding to acts of violence.

RTS is expressed in a complex, entangled lifestyle when an individual lacks adequate coping skills or social or medical support, or is subject to ongoing trauma in his or her environment. As time goes on, the physical, emotional, social, and sexual categories impacted by the sexual attack become less segregated and more intertwined, making the exact nature of a particular problem less obvious. Comorbidities of RTS include chemical dependence (including injecting drug use and alcoholism) in 75% of veterans with PTSD (Kulka et al., 1990), in 43% of individuals with a diagnosis of PTSD (Breslau, Davis, Andreski, et al., 1991), and in increased levels among Hispanic women (Kaukinen & Demaris, 2005). Substance abuse, especially with alcohol, cigarettes, and cocaine, is common when victims desire to numb or cope with the pain of sexual trauma. Among various drug treatment programs, 46.4% of patients had a history of sexual assault as adults and 38.2% in childhood (El-Bassel, Gilbert, Frye et al., 2004; North, 1996). In addition, 30.7% of women in a methadone maintenance treatment program (MMTP) had been sexually abused by a partner in the previous six months, and cocaine use increased this violence (El-Bassel et al., 2004). Another study found that 59% of substance abusers had symptoms consistent with PTSD, yet they were undiagnosed and at the time they were admitted for detoxification had not received any treatment (Fullilove et al., 1993). In this same study, 97% of women with PTSD reported one or more violent traumas compared to 73% of women without PTSD.

Women share a common history stating they were often revictimized in subsequent rapes or domestic violence scenarios (Coid, Petruckevitch, Feder, et al., 2001; El-Bassel et al., 2004; Fullilove et al., 1992; Johnson, Cunnington-Williams, & Cotter, 2003; Schafer, Caetano, & Cunradi, 2004; Teets, 1997; Wise, et al., 2001). Women with a history of childhood sexual abuse may use substance abuse as one of the maladaptive coping mechanisms (Blume, 1998). Subsequent substance abuse following sexual assault or incest is more common in women than in men.

KEY POINT Rape trauma syndrome is associated with risk-taking behavior, increased substance abuse, lowered self-esteem, depression and anxiety, and a wide range of physical and sexual dysfunctions.

Risk-Taking Behavior

Heightened risk-taking behavior is well documented among substance-abusing populations, placing women at an increased risk for HIV infection and other STIs. Other STIs that are commonly transmitted include hepatitis, human papillomavirus (HPV), chlamydia infection, gonorrhea, and herpes. In one study, 15% of sexually abused women had one or more STIs, and 20% had a rape-related pregnancy (McFarlane et al., 2005). Another study of African-American women showed that having a history of a STI, including HIV, placed them at an increased risk for drug use, depression, and interpersonal violence (Johnson, et al., 2003). Bitterness toward past life experiences often pushes individuals with a history of sexual abuse toward risk-taking scenarios, including multiple partners, exchanging sex for money, unsafe sexual practices, unwanted pregnancies, and revictimization by intimates (Champion, Shain, Piper, et al., 2001; Coid, Petruckevitch, Feder, et al., 2001; El-Bassel et al., 2004; Fergusen, Horwood, & Lynskey, 1997; Gonzales, Washienko, Krone, et al., 1999; Johnson et al., 2003; Manfrin-Ledet & Porche, 2003; Pitzner, McGarry-Long, & Drummond, 2000; Resnick, Acierno, & Kilpatrick, 1997; Sowell, Phillips, Seals, et al., 2002; Springs & Fredrich, 1992; Wise et al., 2001; Zierler, Feingold, Laufer, et al., 1991).

Risky sexual behavior places individuals at increased risk for acquiring HIV infection. Although risk-taking behavior is composed of many variables, the one common thread through numerous studies was a history of childhood sexual abuse in both men and women. In populations infected with HIV, between 30% and 87% of individuals had a history of childhood sexual abuse as compared to similar populations not infected with HIV (Bedimo, Kissinger, & Bessinger, 1997; Brady, Gallagher, Berger, et al., 2002; Dilorio et al., 2002; El-Bassel et al., 2001; Fullilove, 1993; Gruskin, Gange, Celentano, et al., 2002; Johnson et al., 2003; Miller, 1999; Mullings, Marquart, & Brewer, 2000; NIMH Multisite HIV Prevention Trial, 2001; O'Leary, Purcell, Remien, et al., 2003; Stevens, Zierler, Cram, et al., 1995; Thompson, Potter, Sanderson, & Maibach, 1997; Wingood & DiClemente, 1997; Wyatt, Myers, Williams, et al., 2002; Zierler et al., 1991). One contributing factor may be the increased rates of substance abuse, placing women at risk for continued poverty, incarceration, poor employment skills, and marginalization. This constellation often leaves men and women to depend on exchanging sex for money, to submit to continued partner abuse, and to neglect using condoms.

One study examining predictors of partner violence compared both male-to-female and female-to-male scenarios among African American, Hispanic, and white couples. While there were cultural differences in all groups, physical abuse in childhood by parents, impulsivity, and alcohol abuse remained the most constant predictors for intimate partner violence (Schafer, et al., 2004).

Increased Substance Abuse

Men and women with a history of sexual violence have a higher incidence of substance abuse compared to populations that do not share that history (Morrill, Kasten, Urato, et al., 2001; Wingood & DiClemente, 1997). In a study of injecting drug users, 68% of the women and 19% of the men reported histories of sexual violence (Braitstein, Li, Tyndall, et al., 2003). Women

were 4.25 times more likely to abuse substances if they had a history of sexual abuse compared with women who did not have a history of sexual abuse (Cohen, Deamont, Barkan, et al., 2000). Chaotic and marginalized minority communities may serve as persistent external oppression, providing risky sexual behavior symbolic value. Wallace et al. (1996) suggested harm-reduction community models that can build community networks and reduce sexual and substance abuse. (Wallace, Fullilove, & Flisher, 1996).

Lowered Self-Esteem

Leenerts (1999) described how abusive relationships influence self-care practices in low-income white women infected with HIV. Sexual abuse confuses self-images, damages a woman's self-image, and breaks the spirit. In this study of the abused women, 58% used drugs. Disconnecting from self-care or health-promoting behavior was the emerging theme among women with a history of sexual abuse. Other studies have also found an association between poor self-esteem and competence among women who experienced violence including verbal abuse (Hebert & Bergeron, 2007; Sowell, Seals, Moneyham, et al., 1999). Using the model that evolved from Leenerts's study (2003), forensic nurse examiners can build partnerships with victims to encourage self-care practices and build connections to self-care.

History of sexual abuse is even higher among incarcerated women, ranging from 55% to 73% (Browne, Miller, & Maguin, 1999; Dole, 1998; Harris, Sharps, Allen, et al., 2003; Leenerts, 2003; Stevens, et al., 1995). In these samples, childhood sexual abuse was reported in 30% to 59% of inmate cases. This rate reflects a significant difference from community-based studies of childhood sexual abuse reported at 18% (Finkelhor, 1994). Ethnicity and lower socioeconomic status may reflect some of the differences between incarcerated and community populations. An increased rate of suicide has been reported among women with PTSD (Lewis, 2006). Browne and colleagues (1999) reported that childhood physical or sexual victimization before age 18 appeared to predispose women to significantly more physical violence by intimates in adulthood. In this same sample, women who were molested before age 18 were twice as likely to report sexual assaults by nonintimates in their adult lives. From this study, the impact of interpersonal violence over time and generations is understood, as 82% of the women in this study had experienced "severe parental violence and/or childhood sexual abuse before reaching adulthood" (Browne et al., 1999). Browne postulated that the long-term effects of violence are the primary reasons contributing to incarceration with associations to other risk-taking behaviors, such as substance abuse and being in precarious situations.

The adoption of mandatory drug sentencing in 1987 by the U.S. Sentencing Commission was strengthened in 1996 and has resulted in increased rates of incarceration for women from 4% to 6%. Incarceration is a common consequence of substance abuse, accounting for 66% of women in federal penitentiaries and 33% of women in state prisons according to the Bureau of Justice Statistics in January 1998. These statistics have remained fairly consistent as of 2002 reports by the Department of Justice. This situation is further discussed in Chapter 38. In 2002 68% of persons jailed had used illegal drugs prior to arrest and 63% had participated in substance abuse or other programs. There have been increases in the number of persons incarcerated for arrests while using amphetamines and approximately 24% of incarcerated persons had alcohol-related crimes (DOJ, 2007). In 2005, the DOJ reported that 1,846,400 arrests were for substance abuse–related crimes.

The majority of women feel betrayed, often sparking rage, as the majority are sexually violated by someone known to them. This anger can be turned inward as well as outward. Many women on death row are there because they murdered their assailant in partner violence cases (Bureau of Justice, 2001; Greenfield, Rand, & Craven, 1998; Justice Works, 2003). Tom Mason and Dave Mercer described two repeating themes of female psychopaths: lifetime of abuse beginning in early childhood and revictimization by various institutions. PTSD with substantial Axis I and Axis II comorbidities has been documented in other works described in this chapter (Fischbach & Herbert, 1997; Heim, Newport, Heit, et al., 2000; Katon, 2001; Wise et al., 2001). Conversely, many more women return to abusive partners in the hope that their partner will change (Goss & DeJoseph, 1997).

Depression and Anxiety

Increased rates of depression and anxiety are frequently associated with sexual abuse. One study reported that 78% of women who had been physically or sexually abused had a mental illness (Leenerts, 2003). This illness can be expressed in substance abuse, as previously discussed, and in suicide and physical cutting. Childhood abuse (including sexual abuse) and household dysfunction have been highly correlated with suicide (Dube, Anda, Felitti, et al., 2001). In another study of triethnic adolescents, histories of sexual abuse, physical abuse, and environmental stresses were among five of the strong risk factors for suicide (Rew, Thomas, Horner, et al., 2001). Self-mutilation and self-injury are often cries for help from persons who have been sexually abused (Steighner, 2003).

Women sexually violated by strangers describe the devastating shifts in their relationships. Partners often feel helpless and at a loss to know what to do to support their partners. Two exceptional ABC broadcasts ("Partners of Rape," *Nightline*, March 27, 2000; "Domestic Violence," *The Oprah Winfrey Show*, September 25, 2002) presented couples searching for answers regarding sexual assault, trying to comprehend the process of violence and begin healing. Few of these marriages could survive the ordeal, and the majority of the couples interviewed were divorced.

PHYSIOLOGICAL EXPRESSION OF RAPE TRAUMA SYNDROME

Physical symptoms often parallel sites of bodily injury. Physical force and general body trauma are found in as many as 80% of sexual assault cases (Riggs, Houray, Long, et al., 2000; Slaughter & Brown, 1992; Slaughter, Brown, Crowley, & Peck, 1997). Genital injuries occur in 16% to 87% of women and in 36% of males (Biggs, Sternac, & Divinsky, 1998; Bowyer & Dalton, 1997; Cartwright, 1987; Dumont & Parnis, 2003; Riggs et al., 2000; Slaughter & Brown, 1992; Slaughter et al., 1997). Gynecological manifestations (e.g., chronic vaginal problems, changes in the menstrual cycle) may also present. Premenstrual syndrome is common in women with a history of sexual abuse (Golding, Taylor, Menard, et al., 2000). These symptoms may occur for years following the original trauma and often go undetected because history taking does not illicit questions regarding sexual trauma. RTS becomes so enmeshed in the patients over time that it is difficult to adequately assess the full impact of trauma on the human body. Only a few longitudinal studies provide answers, and few studies included control groups.

Golding, Wilsnack, and Learman (1998) found sexual assault histories to be 20% to 28% in a randomized study of the general population from two regions of the United States (n = 3131) and one national sample (n = 963). Symptoms of dysmenorrhea, menorrhagia, and sexual dysfunction were common risk indicators

for sexual assault with an increased probability for risk correlating with increasing numbers of symptoms. Symptoms were not well correlated to women over the age of 44, especially perimenopausal women. Only 4% to 5% of the study population had all three symptoms and a history of sexual assault. Few women had disclosed their sexual assault history to physicians or received mental health interventions.

During the 154th annual meeting of the American Psychiatric Association in May 2001, several studies suggested that estrogen may alter the biochemical effects of stress in women (Brady, 2001). PTSD can alter the stress-related neurotransmitter, neurohormonal, and immune functions. Continued trauma alters the normal burst response of the hypothalamic-adrenal-pituitary (HPA) glands that secrete cortisol during a stressful encounter. Increased stress or severity of the situation produces higher levels of cortisol. A person with PTSD dysregulates this response by lowering the cortisol levels. The HPA glands also appear to be influenced by the hormonal levels of the menstrual cycle. A decrease in the stress response occurs during the follicular phase. Overall, women have lower cortisol levels when compared to men irrespective of PTSD in either gender. There are no PTSD-related differences in cytokine levels between genders. Another study also found a strong association with decreased estrogen levels and increased follicle-stimulating hormone (FSH) levels, putting women into earlier menopause (Allworth, Zierler, Krieger, et al., 2001).

Another study of women with a history of childhood sexual abuse found a sixfold increase in adrenocorticotropic hormone (ACTH) response when the individual also had a major depression diagnosis (Heim et al., 2000). The findings suggest that a hyperactivity of the HPA glands and autonomic nervous system exists in women with a history of childhood sexual abuse, possibly contributing to adulthood psychopathological conditions.

Neurological impairments are common in men and women with chronic PTSD. These impairments are increased when there is a history of childhood or adult sexual abuse and are often missed. Soft neurological signs were found in 82% of persons with a history of PTSD (Gurvits, Gilbertson, Lasko, et al., 2000). Soft signs include subtle abnormalities in language and motor coordination such as motor hyperactivity, attention deficit, learning problems, or enuresis. Childhood physical abuse is associated with higher rates of migraines in adulthood (Goodwin, Hoven, Murison, et al., 2003).

Chronic abdominal pelvic pain is a common complaint of women who have a history of sexual assault and sexual abuse (Carlson, Miller, & Fowler, 1994; Golding et al., 1998; Harrop-Griffiths, Katon, & Walker, et al., 1988; Laws, 1993; Mathias, Kuppermann, Liberman, et al., 1996; Rapkin, Kames, Darke, et al., 1990; Reiter, Shakerin, Gambone, et al., 1991; Schei & Bakketeig, 1989; Walling, O'Hara, Reiter, et al., 1994; Wurtele, Kaplan, Keairnes, et al., 1990). Women with a history of childhood sexual abuse were more likely to utilize more healthcare services and to report more chronic pain symptoms (Finestone et al., 2000). For healthcare providers, evaluating this symptom is frustrating because documenting the etiology is difficult. Often a history of sexual violence is not elicited.

Studies have found that women with a history of sexual assault avoid gynecological care because the pelvic examination triggers memories of fear, loss of control, and vulnerability (Dole, 1998; Golding et al., 1998; Robohm & Buttenheim, 1996). Women with a history of sexual abuse are less likely to have routine screening such as Papanicolaou (pap) smears, placing women at increased risk for undetected cervical disease (Golding et al., 1998; Harsanyi, Mott, & Kendell, 2003) and suggesting that a history of no pap smear may represent undiagnosed PTSD. Failure to screen for sexual abuse before a pelvic examination may actually be conceptualized as revictimization (King, P., personal communication, March 7, 1999). Patients relive the sexual assault and often dissociate during the examination. Professional colleagues have witnessed such extreme dissociation and anxiety that patients have leaped off the examination table while the speculum is still in place within the vagina. Labor and delivery rooms are another source of dissociation that actually potentiates the experience of being out of control and increases pain sensitivity (Heritage, 1998).

RAPE TRAUMA SYNDROME AND SEXUAL HEALTH

Dyspareunia and urinary tract infections are common sequelae in women with sexual trauma and may represent current intimacy problems. PTSD flashbacks, decreased sexual desire, or fears of forced intercourse with a coercive intimate partner decrease vaginal lubrication, contributing to dyspareunia and urinary tract infections. In the absence of pathological findings, current sexual coercion or RTS should be considered the primary diagnosis in dyspareunia. This "cry for help" may also represent a form of testing the professional's ability to support her should she decide to disclose.

As previously mentioned, self-care is decreased in persons with a history of childhood sexual abuse and sexual assault. Past sexual abuse is a high predictor of not using condoms, increasing the risk of STIs, as previously discussed (Witte, Wada, El-Bassel, 2000). It also increases the risk for unwanted pregnancy.

Thirty percent to 40% of victims reported that their sexual functioning had not returned to normal for up to six years later (Burgess & Holmstrom, 1979; Peter & Whitehall, 1998). Pattern styles of women with a history of child sexual abuse are categorized as anger, passive, reenacting, or chaotic (Perez, Kennedy, & Fullilove, 1995). These pattern styles may shape these individuals' sexual interaction affecting choice of safe partners, adoption of safer sexual practices, and whether they promptly recognize STIs. An example of the passive style is characterized by this response: "I just lay there and you do what you got to do" (Perez et al., 1995, p. 88). The reenactment style seems to test fate and danger repeatedly in relationships, often bringing women to a new crisis or trauma. The chaotic style is particularly destructive and possibly addictive to women with a history of childhood sexual abuse. It is propelled by the need for continual crisis or trauma. The angry-styled individual is always hostile and fighting. A fragmented sense of self pervades these pattern styles, preventing healthy sexual or intimate relationships, and involves the characteristics listed in Box 33-2.

Nursing Implications

Healthcare professionals feel that they are too busy and state that histories of sexual assault or abuse are not a priority. Unfortunately, this omission often represents a missed opportunity to assist patients in beginning the healing process by telling their story. Often it simply takes "planting the seed."

Box 33-2 Barriers to Healthy Sexual Functioning

Inability to problem solve
Increased risk-taking behavior
Poor boundaries
Increased teenage pregnancy
Continuum extremes from promiscuity to lack of sexual desire
Decreased intimacy
Dyspareunia
Chronic pelvic pain

Case Study **33-1**

The Patient and Healthcare Provider Relationship

A survivor of childhood incest and domestic violence shared the importance of "planting the seed" by healthcare providers to change the situation and heal oneself. At the time she relayed this event, she had 10 years of sobriety (free from drug and alcohol use) and was employed with a publishing company. Now 34 years old, this black woman described her experience on welfare and involvement in a series of abusive relationships.

She had connected with an obstetrician in one of the clinics who had seen her on several occasions. Each time the healthcare provider had examined her, there were multiple bruises on her body, in various stages of healing. Each time, the obstetrician would comment on the bruises and ask if she was in a safe environment. There was never a lengthy discussion or a perceived judgmental attitude on behalf of the healthcare provider. During the fifth visit, a postpartum checkup, the obstetrician observed several bruises on the patient's legs and stated, "You know, you don't have to live this way."

Several weeks later, following another battering incident, the woman remembered those words. She stated she was able to pick up her baby and go to a shelter for help. She later stated that "it was the scariest yet best thing I ever did, having no money, no skills, and no support." The option to leave may not have occurred to her had the obstetrician not planted that seed. This woman added that healthcare providers do not have to "fix the situation," just raise the conscious awareness of the patient, show compassion without judgment, and support her during the process. The responsibility for reshaping her life rests with the individual.

This scenario discussed in Case Study 33-1 expresses the trust and compassion between patient and healthcare provider. The importance of such a relationship has been extensively reported in literature describing elements of adherence or harm reduction. Although few data exist evaluating follow-up programs for victims of sexual assault, perhaps drawing on related women's health literature regarding cervical disease follow-up can provide insight. In several studies, patients identified personal contact by their healthcare provider as the most important variable to future appointment adherence (Abercrombie, 2000; Segnan, Senore, Giordano, et al., 1998). A tracking system is helpful to remind patients of a forthcoming appointment and to document missed appointments (Marcus, Kaplan, Crane, et al., 1998; Paskett, Phillips, & Miller, 1995). Developing a protocol that includes phone calls and letters from the sexual assault nurse examiner/sexual assault forensic examiner/forensic nurse examiner (SANE/SAFE/FNE) may be beneficial in decreasing ongoing missed appointments (Miller, Siejak, Schroeder, et al., 1997). Consideration must be given to patients' desire to be contacted, especially with minors and individuals at risk for domestic violence. Three controlled studies found that an educational brochure available in the clinic or sent to nonadherent patients significantly reduced missed appointments (Paskett, Carter, Chu, et al., 1990; Paskett, et al., 1995; Stewart, Bucheggar, Lickrish, et al., 1993). Failure by healthcare professionals to communicate the possible consequences of sexual assault has also been found to be a primary factor in missed appointments (Lerman, Miller, Scarborough, et al., 1991).

Mental illness and childhood abuse are primary reasons for missed clinic appointments among indigent adults (Curry & Bristol, 2003; Leenerts, 2003; Pieper & DiNardo, 1998). Socioeconomic disparities in access to healthcare may contribute to undiagnosed PTSD among the poor. Mental health counseling is less available to individuals with lower income or those on Medicaid. Young, low-income mothers with or without histories of sexual abuse are generally more depressed, irrespective of race and cultural backgrounds, when compared to women with higher levels of income (Salsberry, Nickel, Polivka, et al., 1999). Given the fact that lower-income women are at increased risk for sexual assault and depression, strategies to increase adherence to follow-up appointments is a challenge for forensic nurses working with this population.

Researchers have reported that healthcare professionals fail to elicit a history of incest, molestation, or sexual abuse. One study found that older nurses were more apt to screen for abuse (Boutcher & Gallop, 1996). For this reason, patients are reluctant to make this disclosure at their first encounter with healthcare professionals (Dole, 1999; Fellitti, 1991; Golding et al., 1998). When sexual abuse was disclosed to physicians, victims stated their physician was generally not helpful. Women who failed to disclose often harbored the impression that they caused or were somehow responsible for the sexual abuse having occurred, thus perpetuating the secrecy surrounding the "social taboo."

The Joint Commission has prioritized the identification and referral of intimate partner violence including sexual assault and abuse. Education of healthcare workers at all levels and in all departments will facilitate this goal. Women who were identified stated that to share their secrets required a safe, caring, and trusting environment (Liebschutz, Battaglia, Finley, & Averbuch, 2008). Disclosure empowered the women who could then begin healing.

Victims of sexual violence have an increased utilization of medical care, especially in the emergency department (ED) and specialty areas (Felitti, 1991; Koss et al., 1991; Peter & Whitehall, 1998; Sigler, 1995). Given the underutilization of ED services by victims at the time of the traumatic event, screening for sexual violence may be the only method to unveil prior injuries and victimization. Most certainly, professionals in all areas of women's healthcare (both gynecology and obstetrics), adolescent health, and psychiatry could be trained to recognize the signs and symptoms of current and past sexual abuse. Proactive screening for sexual abuse is key to promoting healing and breaking the cycle of violence. However, curricula for medical school and extended care providers (such as physician assistants and nurse practitioners) often lack any information about the signs and symptoms of violence (Flitcraft, 1995; Koss, 1991). Graduates from these programs are not able to realize their potential to initiate services for women. Clinical medicine and psychiatric assessments fail to explore sexual histories and abuse histories regarding physical and sexual violence. It must be noted that violence is the major cause of injury to women between the ages of 15 and 44 years.

EDUCATION AND PREVENTION

A study by Moore, Zaccaro, and Parsons (1998) found that 66% of nurses had received some education about domestic violence. Most still believed that abuse was not a problem in their population and therefore did not screen for abuse. Nurses and healthcare providers often avoid using screening tools for fear that a patient will admit to being a victim of abuse, which may cause the healthcare professionals to feel inadequate to deal with it (Nieves-Khouw, 1997). Nurses who themselves were victims of abuse and violence and had not healed their own trauma were unable to fully engage in the screening questions. Unresolved abuse and trauma impacts on the physical, emotional, sexual, and spiritual well-being of the

patients and the nurse. Education is the key to empowering nurses and victims. Once verbalization begins, the FNE can begin assisting patients in creating a safer and more balanced life (Draucker & Stern, 2000).

Increasing knowledge at all levels is the best form of prevention. Utilizing the nursing process will guide nursing interventions in the hospital, community, and classroom. Curricula should include education about the myths and realities related to gender bias and unequal gender rights.

Proactive programs in secondary schools, colleges, and the workplace can facilitate decreasing the causes of interpersonal violence. Many men and women do not understand boundaries or the definitions of sexual violence (Parrot, Cummings, & Marchell, 1994; Simon & Golden, 1996; Simon & Harris, 1993a). In a longitudinal study of adolescents and college women, 88% reported at least one incident of physical or sexual victimization. In this same study, 66% of the women suffered more severe forms of sexual or physical violence (Smith, White, & Holland, 2003). Special attention is given to athletic departments and to providing education about acquaintance rape (Benedict, 1998). The following statements reflect this lack of knowledge:

- 15% to 25% of male college students have engaged in sexual aggression (Benedict, 1998; Malmutgh, Sockloskie, Koss, et al., 1991; Parrot et al., 1994).
- 27% of sexually assaulted college women did not consider themselves victims (Simon & Harris, 1993b).
- 84% of sexual assaults on campus are acquaintance rapes, and 84% of the campus men did not feel that what they did was rape (Koss, Gidycz, & Wisniewski, 1987; Simon & Harris, 1993b).

Providing clarity regarding definitions of sexual violence and acceptable sexual interactions are important components of a prevention program. Defining sexual objectification to both men and women with examples of escalation of aggression would be included. For example, understanding that telling sexist jokes or not intervening when listening to a sexist joke is a form of sexual violence progression. A myth such as submission is consent, combined with rape fantasies, can escalate to sexual violence. Forced sex was found to be a risk factor for victims of femicide. Forced sexual aggression (including during pregnancy) was found in 57% of women killed by their partners, compared to 14.9% of women who were in abusive relationships but not victims of homicide (Campbell, Webster, Koziol-McLean, et al., 2003). Program components include discussions of sexual harassment, threats, and stalking. Behavior characteristic of sexual abuse includes catcalls, peeping toms, voyeurism, obscene phone calls, sexual harassment, and exhibitionism with flashing to minors.

Sexual assault awareness on campuses would include a task force as well as a prevention program. Brown University (as did many other universities) began a sexual assault peer education (SAPE) program in response to escalating sexual assaults. Policies and procedures regarding sexual assault must be in place and require the support of all departments on a college campus.

Guiding children to reduce encounters of violence has to become a national agenda. The national broadcasting networks and the movie industry recently agreed to tighten regulations with respect to the degree of violence shown to child audiences. Revised rating systems will reflect this new philosophy with more stringent guidelines. Parents will have a better sense of the content material being viewed and can better guide their children. Parental involvement is crucial in shaping gender roles and how violence is viewed. Forensic nurses could participate in the movement to decrease violence for our children by writing reviews of movies, television programs, CDs, books, video games, and so forth for the local newspaper. Sharing the results of usage reviews on child injuries or SANE/SAFE programs can increase community involvement through increased knowledge and understanding.

SCREENING AND RISK-REDUCTION STRATEGIES

More sexual assaults are unreported (71%) when compared with the 16% to 32% of reported cases (Ciancone, Wilson, Colette, et al., 2000; Kilpatrick & Resnick, 1994). Women who are poor, are in their twenties, have PTSD, and have a prior history of sexual assault or sexual abuse are at increased risk for revictimization, especially when combined with alcohol or cocaine abuse. The 10% of women at risk for sexual assault who have a history of childhood sexual abuse, liberal sexual attitudes, higher-than-average alcohol use, and a larger number of sexual partners had a risk factor twofold higher than women without this profile (Crowell & Burgess, 1996). Another study found that the use of alcohol or drugs was reported in 20% of sexual assault victims (Brechlin & Ullman, 2002).

BEST PRACTICE It is imperative that all levels of healthcare providers identify and screen for past sexual abuse or sexual assault.

In a gynecological clinic for HIV-infected individuals, the majority of women stated that they had never been asked about past sexual victimization (Dole, 1998). It should be noted that many women were asked over several visits before they were comfortable revealing the past trauma. The time needed to assess the healthcare professional and develop a trusting rapport before disclosure may also contribute to underreporting. It is important to include sexual abuse screening with each healthcare encounter. Many healthcare professionals fail to seek the truth and remain neutral during their interviews, history taking, and assessment of patients. One study revealed that 83% of sexually abused women had never disclosed the abuse to a healthcare provider (Golding et al., 2000). Doing a gynecological examination and not asking about previous trauma or assaults can revictimize patients. Unhealed trauma fueled with environmental triggers (i.e., vaginal speculum examinations) can potentially prompt flashbacks that result in dissociation from the examination. At this point, it becomes difficult to interact with the patient to complete an examination. Indeed, it is often impossible to complete required procedures. Dole (1996) provided suggestions to reduce PTSD anxiety during a gynecological examination.

Secondary revictimization by healthcare providers, SANEs/SAFEs/FNEs, or legal or police personnel is common. Stressful situations that lack privacy and respect or blame the victim make the individual feel stigmatized or devalued. Situations that revictimize the individual include ignoring the vulnerability of the victim, discounting the trauma, patronizing the victim, and making negative or judgmental comments to the victim (Keenan & Royle, 2007; Valente, 2000). Failure to assess for sexual abuse upon admission to clinics or hospitals may also inadvertently create opportunities for secondary revictimization (Garber, Grindel, & Mitchell, 1997).

As already stated, many healthcare professionals feel inadequate to handle responses related to histories of sexual assault and abuse. Many times, however, simply acknowledging the assault can open dialogue and create opportunities for healing. When the patient is ready, she or he can be referred for psychotherapy. If the patient is disclosing after years of silence, several sessions to stabilize such

---

Box 33-3 Examples for Using the PLISSIT Model

P = permission
LI = limited information
SS = specific suggestion
IT = intensive therapy

Examples for using the elements of the PLISSIT model include the following:

P = Asking the question regarding sexual assault and abuse gives the person permission to disclose and share associated concerns.

LI = Choose the associated concern that you feel most prepared to address and make a professional statement about it. For instance, providing reassurance that many individuals experience difficult intimate relations or feel blame for the sexual assault generates a sense that they may share similar experiences with others. Patients at this point are generally feeling like they are the only ones with this concern or difficulty. Providing information specific to the concern can help the individual to feel less alone in the process and relieve guilt or shame. Perhaps the patient is experiencing dyspareunia related to psychological effects of sexual trauma (pathological etiologies have been eliminated), and you suggest that fear may decrease a woman's ability to lubricate sufficiently for sexual intercourse. Providing limited information conveys reassurance to enter into open dialogue. Those who doubt the healthcare professional's willingness to engage in the process of sorting out the consequences of the sexual assault may be relieved by this interaction.

SS = Providing a specific suggestion or task to complete before returning assures the patient that you are concerned about his or her well-being and return to health. Often asking if the patient is ready to forgive the perpetrator to promote the patient's own health provides the health professional insight as to where the patient is in the healing process and what coping mechanisms he or she may have. Asking patients to think about what they would like to accomplish and what trauma-related concerns may be holding them back will provide information about what specifically to suggest. With respect to the dyspareunia, suggesting the use of K-Y Jelly or Astroglide before penetration during sex provides individuals with a possible solution to problematic situations with their partner. Ask the patient to report back on the suggestion's effectiveness. This type of dialogue can be ongoing, contributing to the patient-provider relationship.

IT = Intensive therapy generally involves a referral to a therapist, support group, pastoral care, or whatever seems appropriate for the individual.

---

feelings may be needed with the FNE or health provider with whom the patient has an established relationship. Otherwise, the patient may be resistant to being referred. It is essential to reassure persons that they are not alone and that the nurse will continue to support them. The PLISSIT model (Box 33-3) can offer structure for anxious healthcare providers during initial interventions with individuals who may disclose sexual abuse (Annon, 1974).

Healthcare professionals in all disciplines need education included in their respective curricula to promote assessment and identification of sexual assault and sexual abuse (Box 33-4). The PLISSIT model adapted from the psychological discipline can be used by similar disciplines to provide specific guidelines and to decrease inadequate feelings regarding asking the questions listed in Box 33-4.

FNEs can make it easier for nurses and healthcare providers to use these questions by providing continuing education courses. Providing knowledge and a safe environment to practice new skills will increase the likelihood that patients are routinely asked the difficult questions about their safety and unresolved trauma. Levels of consciousness and awareness can be elevated during such classes. The success of SANE programs has shifted patients' care primarily to the FNE. EDs reported that 10% or fewer of the sexual assault cases seen require additional examination by physicians (Ciancone et al., 2000). There is an understood, basic concept that a nurse with forensic education performs the forensic

Box 33-4 Sexual Assault Screening Questions

- Have you been hit, slapped, kicked, or otherwise hurt by someone in the past year? If so, by whom?
- In your lifetime, have you ever been forced to have sex when you didn't want to?
- In your lifetime, have you ever had your private areas touched when you didn't want them touched?
- Is there a partner from a previous relationship who is making you feel unsafe now?
- Are you safe in your present relationship?
- Has a partner ever embarrassed, humiliated, or insulted you?
- Do you fear for your safety or the safety of your children from a past or present partner?
- Has a partner ever withheld money from you or your children?
- Did you seek professional assistance for this/these incidence(s) or report to the police?
- How can I assist you with these concerns?

Sources: Association of Women's Health, Obstetrics and Neonatal Nurses (AWHONN). (1999). Partner & abuse violence screen. In *Universal screening for domestic violence* (p. 12). Washington, DC: Author; Campbell, J. C. (1995). *Assessing dangerousness: Violence by sexual offenders, batterers, and child abusers* (p. 84). Thousand Oaks, CA: Sage Publications; Straus, M. A. (1979). Measuring family conflict and violence: The conflict tactics scale. *J Marriage Fam, 41*(1), 75–88; Straus, M. A. (1990). Measuring intrafamily conflict and violence: The conflict tactics scales. In M. A. Straus & R. J. Gelose (Eds.), *Physical violence in American families: Risk factors and adaptations to violence in 8,145 families* (pp. 29–47). New Brunswick, NJ: Transaction Publishers.

examination. The forensic process during an examination for child sexual abuse, sexual assault, domestic violence, or elder abuse is essentially the same, requiring the foundations of nursing and forensic science.

FOLLOW-UP CARE

The follow-up rate of sexual assault victims is low across the United States and in other countries and is rarely reported above 25% (Ciancone et al., 2000; Holmes, Resnick, & Frampton, 1998; Rambow, Atkinson, & Frost, et al., 1992). Ciancone and colleagues (2000) found that 73% of sexual assault programs could not provide information on the follow-up of their victims. This may be the result of various factors. Many victims want to forget the experience and fail to make follow-up appointments in an attempt to do so. Others may fear retribution from perpetrators (known or unknown), including those involved in partner violence. This is often the onset of a cascade of consequences that has already been described in this chapter. Statistics reveal that only 8% of sexual violence victims who present for treatment and evaluation to an ED receive immediate follow-up care. Early intervention has been shown to decrease the consequences of trauma, especially when coupled with social supports.

BEST PRACTICE The forensic nurse examiner should ensure that healthcare systems have a strong program in place to increase adherence with follow-up appointments related to sexual assault. Strict monitoring and specific remediations should be an integral component of such programs.

Other factors that may contribute to low follow-up rates include a range of possibilities. The ED is often the first contact for victims of violence. Yet the ED is not designed to do follow-up appointments. Often, there are no clear guidelines directing responsibility for missed appointments between interdepartmental referrals. Some victims refuse further contact from

the healthcare facility. Outcome measures of SANE/SAFE/FNE protocols and forensic nurse performance need to include detailed methods of follow-up and referrals. SANE/SAFE/FNE programs that exist separate from the ED have the potential to excel in the area of patient follow-up. Evaluation methods must keep the victimized patient anonymous during reviews to ensure integrity to the judicial process.

Many sexual assault programs operate through EDs. Appointments are given to return either to providers in the clinic or outside the ED. Victims are reluctant to see providers unknown to them at a time they are feeling vulnerable. The ED is often not conducive to follow-up appointments with the same provider. SANE/SAFE/FNE programs may not have strong community networks for referral and follow-up. Personnel with forensic knowledge for bridging the care between the ED and the community may not exist. This is a weakness in many of the SANE/SAFE/FNE programs.

Nurses must evaluate all patients in the same manner, regardless of whether or not they are medicolegal patients (whether or not they want to prosecute). At trial, prosecutors may reinforce this format, as it is easier for the case when there is no additional contact with the person who collected the sexual assault evidence kit. The defense attorney may try to complicate the case with advocacy issues when there is further contact from the healthcare provider. FNEs often need to educate attorneys. Nurses are more than technicians who merely document evidence and collect kits. The FNE will be challenged to listen and to assess each person to develop appropriate care for patients.

Standard of care includes follow-up for any traumatized individual irrespective of the nature of trauma. Many brochures and publications have one sentence or one paragraph referring to follow-up and referral for the treatment of infectious diseases or injuries. Neither of these national guidelines provides proactive strategies to decrease the short- and long-term sequelae of sexual assault beyond infectious diseases or injuries. If healthcare providers including forensic nurses are to diagnose, assess, treat, and refer to maximize well-being, how is this being actualized? It may be time to reexamine the guidelines and mechanisms for follow-up in all SANE/SAFE/FNE programs.

Forensic nurse examiners prepared in critical incident stress debriefing (CISD) can provide a valuable service to both patients and healthcare providers in evaluating stress related to traumatic events. It is conceivable that adding this component to SANE/SAFE/FNE curriculum would enable nurses to mobilize victims sooner and access healthcare, including keeping follow-up appointments.

Forensic nurses need to examine how they cope with stress and difficult cases to prevent burnout. Local chapters of the International Association of Forensic Nurses (IAFN) can provide education as well as support to nurses dealing with the devastation related to forensic cases. It is imperative for nurses to identify and outline a plan for coping with the ongoing stress related to forensic nursing.

CREATING A HEALING ENVIRONMENT

Creating a healing environment for both our patients and ourselves is essential to the promotion of wellness and to decrease burnout (Duquette, Kerouac, Sandhu, et al., 1994). Humor has been shown to decrease grief related stress (Moore, 2000). Using holistic and nursing frameworks such as Martha Rogers's science-based nursing practice can guide nurses' world view of their place within the total environment. Patients, too, are inclusive within the total environment. Traumatized patients bring disorganized energy patterns to this environmental field that affect the nurse as well as others in the periphery of this field. The SANE/SAFE/FNE who has just had an argument with another person and is entering the room to care for the patient brings disorganized energy patterns to the environment. However, the nurse who is "centered," well rested, and has an optimistic outlook on life brings a calm, caring, organized energy pattern to the environment. This harmonious energy pattern has the potential to defuse the traumatized disorganized field of the patient.

BEST PRACTICE A healing environment should be created for caregivers as well as victims of sexual assault.

Centering provides the nurse access to inner peace and tranquility. It also provides the nurse with a shield from the violent energy patterns of the victimized patient. Continued exposure to chaotic and violent energy can be detrimental to nurses and other healthcare providers and may contribute to burnout over time (Duquette, et al., 1994; McKivergin, Wimberly, Loversidge, et al., 1996). Centering allows the individual to access the inner self where tranquility prevails and suffering does not exist. Teaching patients to center can provide them with a tool to help heal and manage the current trauma. Asking patients what method they utilize to access calm and quiet, then assisting the patient to reach such a state, may help to empower patients during a difficult situation. Nurses who center during the forensic examination are less likely to be traumatized by the event and can potentiate a healing environment. (For more information regarding centering, see Krieger, 1997, 2002; Laurie & Tucker, 1993; and Macrae, 2001.)

Reducing the external chaotic energy of a busy ED will be beneficial to promoting calm. Earth-tone colors and classical music that is wordless and grounded but not airy can also promote a sense of calm. However, all the external finishing will not replace the power of the internal tranquility of the centered nurse. Sometimes the nurse will develop adverse associations to the colors, music, or situations that parallel those of the forensic examination room. This may be an indication that the nurse was not centered and could place the nurse at risk for burnout and PTSD (Box 33-5).

Many resources are available to meet the psychosocial needs of sexual violence victims. Nurses should not overlook even the simplest and most obvious options during follow-up appointments. At all stages of recovery, it is important to take every opportunity to empower patients. Offering patients choices as often as possible creates a mutual participatory process that is freeing and allows the individual to transform (Barrett, 1990).

Summary

FNEs can identify the needs of their community and state in caring for victims of interpersonal and sexual violence. Nightingale stated that nurses assess, treat and develop programs with patients in the community wherever they need help (Stanley, 2007). The more diverse a forensic program can be within a community, the more choices are available both to the community and to the victim. With choices, knowledge, and participation, communities and individuals feel free and empowered. Communities and victims can reduce the effects of trauma and associated PTSD when they perceive that they have power (Fig. 33-1).

Box 33-5 Signs and Symptoms of Burnout

PHYSICAL

Insomnia and fatigue
Stiff neck or shoulders
Upper-back pain
Chest or abdominal pain
Palpitations
Clammy hands
Dry mouth
Diarrhea
Anorexia or unusual hunger

EMOTIONAL

Frustration
Isolation from friends and peers
Grief, numbed to suffering of patients and loved ones
Depression
Sense of powerlessness
Fear
Anxiety
Inflexibility
Rage
Criticizing others
Self-righteousness
Hopelessness
Sense of worthlessness
Behavioral problems
Short attention span
Overactivity
Irritability
Grinding teeth
Short temper
Control or power trips
Crying easily
Blaming
Procrastination
Negative attitude
Chattering endlessly
Changes in libido
Taking risks
Driving recklessly

AT WORK

Distancing from patients
Negative self-evaluations

FNEs can pave the way by developing community friendly SANE/SAFE/FNE programs, raising the awareness of communities regarding the problems and morbidity related to sexual abuse, and developing a community initiative in all areas of the government agencies, private businesses, schools, and hospitals. Lobbying for adequate healthcare coverage and economic foundation for such programs is also crucial. Some of the current challenges for forensic nurses include enacting laws, securing sufficient funding for forensic programs, keeping the state board of nurse examiners informed, educating communities, standardizing SANE/SAFE/FNE programs and education, developing standards of care that now include certification, and conducting research while caring for victims of violence.

Nurses have caring practices that are artful, knowledgeable, and lifesaving (Benner, 2000). Morse and Penrod (1999) described the pathways of hope as a process of emerging from the trauma

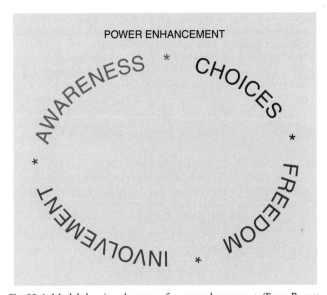

Fig. 33-1 Model showing elements of power enhancement. (From Barrett, E. A. (1998). Power enhancement. *Nurs Sci Q,* 11(3):94-96.)

to a resultant state of transcendence. Victims who endure sexual assault are often uncertain of the outcome. Suffering is a level of knowing that acknowledges the assault. FNEs can facilitate hope or acceptance of the sexual assault and provide an opportunity for victims to dream about the future again. Drawing from a holistic foundation, based on sound judgment and filled with experiential wisdom, the art of nursing is a dynamic profession able to provide creative and compassionate forensic models to care for victims of sexual abuse immediately following the assault and in the months and years following the traumatic event.

Resources

ORGANIZATIONS

International Association of Forensic Nurses (IAFN)
1517 Ritchie Highway, Suite 208, Arnold, MD 21012-2323; (410)626-7805; http://www.iafn.org/

National Organization on Male Sexual Victimization (U.S.)
Box 103, 5505 Connecticut Avenue NW, Washington, DC 20015-2601; 800-738-4181

National Organization on Male Sexual Victimization (Canada)
c/o BCSMSSA, 1252 Burrard Street, #202, Vancouver, BC V6Z 1, Canada

National Sexual Violence Resource Center
123 North Enola Drive, Enola, PA 17025; 877-739-3895, 717-909-0710; www.nsvrc.org

Nurse Healers–Professional Associates International
Box 419, Craryville, NY 12521; 877-32NHPAI; www.therapeutic-touch.org

Office for Victims of Crime Resource Center
Office of Justice Programs, Department of Justice, 633 Indiana Avenue NW, Room 1386, Washington, DC 20531; 202-307-5983, 800-851-3420

References

Abercrombie, P. R. (2000). Improving adherence to abnormal pap smear follow-up. *J Obstet Gynecol Nurs, 30*(1), 80–88.

AIDS Weekly Plus. (1996). Violence against women in war: Rape, AIDS, sex slavery (1996). *AIDS Weekly Plus,* Nov. 25–Dec. 2, 13–14.

Allworth, J. E., Zierler, S., Krieger, N., et al. (2001). Ovarian failure in late reproductive years in relation to lifetime experiences. *Epidemiology, 12*(6), 676–681.

American Bar Association Commission on Domestic Violence. (1996). *The impact of domestic violence on your legal practice.* Washington, DC: American Bar Association.

American Psychiatric Association (APA). (1994). *Diagnostic and statistical manual of mental disorders (DSM-IV-TR).* Washington, DC: Author.

Amowitz, L. L., Russ, C., Lyons, K. H., et al. (2002). Prevalence of war-related sexual assault, violence, and other human rights abuses among internally displaced persons in Sierra Leone. *JAMA, 287*(4), 513–521.

Annon, J. S. (1974). *The behavioral treatment of sexual problems.* Honolulu: Enabling Systems.

Ater, R. W. (2003). Post-traumatic stress disorder. *On the edge: The official publication of the International Association of Forensic Nurses, 9*(3), 4–7.

Baker, T. C., Burgess, A. W., Brickman, E., et al. (1989). *Report on District of Columbia police response to domestic violence.* Joint project of the D.C. Coalition Against Domestic Violence and the Women's Law Center. Washington, DC: D.C. Coalition Against Domestic Violence.

Barrett, E. A. M. (1990). Rogers' science-based nursing practice. In E. A. M. Barrett (Ed.), *Visions of Rogers' science-based nursing* (pp. 31–44). New York: National League for Nursing.

Bedimo, A. L., Kissinger, P., & Bessinger, R. (1997). History of sexual abuse among HIV-infected women. *International Journal of STD & AIDS, 8*(5), 332–335.

Benedict, J. R. (1998). *Athletes and acquaintance rape.* Thousand Oaks: Sage Publications.

Benner, P. (2000). The wisdom of our practice. *AJN, 100*(10), 99–105.

Biggs, M., Sternac, L. E., & Divinsky, M. (1998). Genital injuries following sexual assault of women with and without prior sexual intercourse experience. *CMAJ, 159*(1), 33–37.

Blume, S. B. (1998). Addictive disorders in women. In R. J. Frances, & S. I. Miller (Eds.), *Clinical textbook of addictive disorders* (2nd ed., pp. 437–452). New York: Guilford Press.

Boutcher, F., & Gallop, R. (1996). Psychiatric nurses' attitudes toward sexuality, sexual assault/rape, and incest. *Archives of Psychiatric Nursing, 10*(3), 184–191.

Bowyer, L., & Dalton, M. E. (1979). Female victims of rape and their genital injuries. *BJOG, 104*(5), 17–20.

Brady, K. (2001). Gender differences in PTSD. Retrieved on 1/6/02 from www.medscape.com/medscape/cno/2001/APACME/Story.cfm?story_id=2257

Brady, S., Gallagher, D., Berger, J., et al. (2002). Physical and sexual abuse in the lives of HIV-positive women enrolled in a primary medicine health maintenance organization. *AIDS Patient Care and STDs, 16*(3), 121–125.

Braitstein, P., Li, K., Tyndall, M., et al. (2003). Sexual violence among a cohort of injecting drug users. *Social Science & Medicine, 57*(3), 561–569.

Brechlin, L. R., & Ullman, S. E. (2002). The roles of victim and offenders alcohol use in sexual assaults: Results from the National Violence Against Women Survey. *Journal of Studies on Alcohol, 63*(1), 57–63.

Breslau, N., Davis, G. C., Andreski, P., et al. (1991). Traumatic events and post-traumatic stress disorder in an urban population of young adults. *Archives of General Psychiatry, 48*(3), 216–222.

Browne, A., Miller, B., & Maguin, E. (1999). Prevalence and severity of lifetime physical and sexual victimization among incarcerated women. *International Journal of Law Psychiatry, 22*(3–4), 301–322.

Brunnello, N., Davidson, J. R., Deahl, M., et al. (2001). Posttraumatic stress disorder: Diagnosis and epidemiology, comorbidity and social consequences, biology and treatment. *Neuropsychobiology, 43*(3), 150–162.

Bureau of Justice. (1998). *Statistics: Substance abuse among offenders.* Washington, DC: Author.

Bureau of Justice. (2001). *Crime characteristics: Violent crime-victim/offender relationship.* Washington, DC: Author. Retrieved 9/22/09 from www.ojp.gov/bjs/cvict_c

Bureau of Justice. (2001). *Crime characteristics: substance abusse.* Washington, DC: Author. Retrieved 9/22/09 from www.ojp.gov/bjs/cvict_c

Bureau of Justice Statistics. (2007). Prisoners in 2007. (Washington, DC) U.S. Department of Justice. NCJ 224280, p.1 http://www.ojp./bjs/pub/pdf/p07.pdf. Accessed January 31, 2010.

Bureau of National Affairs. (1990). *Violence and stress: The work/family connection*. Special report #32. Washington, DC: Author.

Burgess, A. W., & Holmstrom, L. L. (1974). Rape trauma syndrome. *The American Journal of Psychiatry*, *131*(9), 981–986.

Burgess, A. W., & Holmstrom, L. L. (1979). Rape: Sexual disruption and recovery. *The American Journal of Orthopsychiatry*, *49*(4), 648–657.

Campbell, J. C., Webster, D., Koziol-McLean, J., et al. (2003). Risk factors for femicide in abusive relationships: Results from a multisite case control study. *American Journal of Public Health*, *93*(7), 1089–1097.

Carlson, K. J., Miller, B. A., & Fowler, F. J. (1994). The Maine women's health study: II. Outcomes of nonsurgical management of leiomyomas, abnormal bleeding, and chronic pelvic pain. *Obstetrics and Gynecology*, *83*(4), 566–572.

Cartwright, P. S. (1987). Factors that correlate with injury sustained by survivors of sexual assault. *Obstetrics and Gynecology*, *70*(1), 44–46.

Centers for Disease Control and Prevention (CDC). (1998). Lifetime and annual incidence of intimate partner violence and resulting injuries–Georgia, 1995. *MMWR*, *47*(40), 849–853.

Champion, J. D., Shain, R. N., Piper, J., et al. (2001). Sexual abuse and sexual risk behaviors of minority women with sexually transmitted diseases. *West J Res*, *23*(3), 241–254.

Ciancone, A. C., Wilson, C., Collette, R., et al. (2000). Sexual assault nurse practitioner programs in the United States. *Annals of Emergency Medicine*, *35*(4), 353–357.

Clarke, S., & Pearson, C. (2000). Personal constructs of male survivors of childhood sexual abuse receiving cognitive analytic therapy. *The British Journal of Medical Psychology*, *73*(2), 169–177.

Cohen, M., Deamant, C., Barkan, S., et al. (2000). Domestic violence and childhood sexual abuse in HIV-infected women and women at risk for HIV. *American Journal of Public Health (AJPH)*, *90*(4), 560–565.

Coid, J., Petruckevitch, A., Feder, G., et al. (2001). Relationship between childhood sexual and physical revictimisation in women: A cross-sectional survey. *Lancet*, *358*(9280), 450–454.

Crowell, N. A., & Burgess, A. W. (Eds.), (1996). *Understanding violence against women*. Washington, DC: National Academy Press.

Curry, M., & Bristol, J. (2003). The effects of childhood abuse on adherence and health. *Focus*, *18*(5), 5–6.

Dilorio, C., Hartwell, T., & Hansen, N. (2002). Childhood sexual abuse and risk behavior among men at high risk for HIV infection. *American Journal of Public Health*, *92*(2), 214–219.

Dole, P. (1996). Centering: Reducing rape trauma syndrome anxiety during a gynecologic examination. *Journal of Psychosocial Nursing*, *34*(10), 32–37.

Dole, P. (1998). Examining sexually traumatized incarcerated women. *HEPP News (HIV Education Prison Project)*, *2*(6), 5.

Dole, P. J. (1999). *The impact of PTSS on GYN clinic adherence of paroled women with HIV disease in a New York City hospital based program.* (Abstract). American Academy of Nurse Practitioner's Annual Meeting, Atlanta, GA.

Donahoe, M. (2005). Violence against women in the military. Posted on Medscape Today, 9/14/05. Accessed January 31, 2010.

Draucker, C. B., & Madsen, C. (1999). Women dwelling with violence. *Image–The Journal of Nursing Scholarship*, *31*(4), 333–332.

Draucker, C. B., & Stern, P. N. (2000). Women's responses to sexual violence by male intimates. *Western Journal of Nursing Research*, *22*(4), 385–402.

Dube, S. R., Anda, R. F., Felitti, V. J., et al. (2001). Childhood abuse, household dysfunction, and the risk of attempted suicide. *JAMA*, *286*(24), 3089–3095.

Dumont, J., & Parnis, D. (2003). Forensic nursing in the context of sexual assault: Comparing the opinions and practices of nurse examiners and nurses. *Applied Nursing Research*, *16*(3), 173–183.

Duquette, A., Kerouac, S., Sandhu, B. K., et al. (1994). Factors related to nursing burnout: A review of empirical knowledge. *Issues in Mental Health Nursing*, *15*(4), 337–358.

El-Bassel, N., Gilbert, L., Frye, V., et al. (2004). Physical and sexual intimate partner violence among women in methadone maintenance treatment. *Psychology of Addictive Behavior*, *18*(2), 180–183.

El-Bassel, N., Witte, S. S., Wada, T., et al. (2001). Correlates of partner violence among female street-based sex workers: Substance abuse, history of childhood abuse, and HIV risks. *AIDS Patient Care STDs*, *15*(1), 41–51.

Epstein, J., & Langenbahn, S. (1994). The criminal justice and community response to rape. In *Issues and practices in criminal justice* (pp. 93–142). Washington, DC: National Institute of Justice, U.S. Department of Justice.

Farfel, M., DiGrande, L., Brackbill, R., Prann, A., Cone, J., Friedman, S., et al. (2008). An overview of 9/11 experiences and respiratoy and mental health conditions among World Trade Center Health Registry Enrollees. *Journal of Urban Health*, *85*(6), 880–909.

Fater, K., & Mullaney, J. A. (2000). The lived experience of adult male survivors who allege childhood sexual abuse by clergy. *Issues in Mental Health Nursing*, *21*(3), 281–295.

Federal Bureau of Investigation (FBI). (1993). *Uniform crime reports*. Washington, DC: U.S. Department of Justice.

Feeny, N. C., Zoellner, L. A., & Foa, E. B. (2002). Treatment outcomes for chronic PTSD among female assault victims with borderline personality characteristics: A preliminary examination. *Journal of Personality Disorders*, *16*(1), 30–40.

Felitti, V. J. (1991). Long-term medical consequences of incest, rape, and molestation. *Southern Medical Journal*, *84*(3), 328–331.

Fergusen, D. M., Horwood, L. J., & Lynskey, M. T. (1997). Childhood sexual abuse, adolescent sexual behaviors and sexual revictimization. *Child Abuse & Neglect*, *21*(8), 789–803.

Finestone, H. M., Stenn, P., Davies, F., et al. (2000). Chronic pain and health utilization in women with a history of childhood sexual abuse. *Child Abuse & Neglect*, *24*(4), 547–556.

Finkelhor, D. (1994). The international epidemiology of child sexual abuse. *Child Abuse & Neglect*, *18*(5), 409–417.

Fischbach, R. L., & Herbert, B. (1997). Domestic violence and mental health: Correlates and conundrums within and across cultures. *Social Science & Medicine*, *45*(8), 1161–1176.

Flitcraft, A. (1995). From public health to personal health: Violence against women across the lifespan. *Annals of Internal Medicine*, *123*(10), 800–801.

Fullilove, M. T., Fullilove, R. E., Smith, M., et al. (1993). Violence, trauma, and post-traumatic stress disorder among women drug users. *Journal of Traumatic Stress*, *6*(4), 533–543.

Fullilove, M. T., Lown, E. A., & Fullilove, R. E. (1992). Crack "hos and skeezers": Traumatic experiences of women crack users. *Journal of Sex Research*, *29*(2), 275–287.

Garber, A., Grindel, C., & Mitchell, D. (1997). Assessing for sexual abuse. *Journal of Psychosocial Nursing*, *35*(3), 26–30.

Gardner, R., & Blackburn, R. (1996). People who move: New reproductive health focus. *Pop Rep*, *24*(3; Series J, #45), 1–13.

Golding, J. M., Taylor, D. L., Menard, L., et al. (2000). Prevalence of sexual abuse history in a sample of women seeking treatment for premenstrual syndrome. *Journal of Psychosomatic Obstetrics and Gynaecology*, *21*(2), 69–80.

Golding, J. M., Wilsnack, S. C., & Learman, L. A. (1998). Prevalence of sexual assault history among women with common gynecologic symptoms. *American Journal of Obstetrics Gynecology*, *179*(4), 1013–1019.

Gollub, E. L. (1999). Human rights is a U.S. problem, too: The case of women and HIV. *American Journal of Public Health*, *89*(10), 1479–1482.

Gonzales, V., Washienko, K. M., Krone, M. R., et al. (1999). Sexual and drug-use risk factors for HIV and STDs: A comparison of women with and without bisexual experiences. *American Journal of Public Health*, *89*(12), 1841–1846.

Goodwin, R. D., Hoven, C. W., Murison, R., et al. (2003). Association between childhood physical abuse and gastrointestinal disorders and migraine in adulthood. *American Journal of Public Health*, *93*(7), 1065–1066.

Goss, G. L., & DeJoseph, J. (1997). Women who return to abusive relationships: A frustration for the critical care nurse. *Critical Care Nursing Clinics of North America, 9*(2), 159–165.

Greenfield, L. A., Rand, M. R., & Craven, D. (1998). *Violence by intimates: Analysis of data on crimes by current or former spouses, boyfriends, and girlfriends.* Washington, DC: U.S. Dept. of Justice.

Grisso, J. A., Schwarz, D. F., Hirschinger, N., et al. (1999). Violent injuries among women in an urban area. *The New England Journal of Medicine (NEJM), 241*(25), 1899–1905.

Gruskin, L., Gange, S. J., Celentano, D., et al. (2002). Incidence of violence against HIV-infected and uninfected women: Findings from the HIV Epidemiology Research (HER) study. *Journal of Urban Health, 79*(4), 512–524.

Gurvits, T. V., Gilbertson, M. W., Lasko, N. B., et al. (2000). Neurological soft signs in chronic posttraumatic stress disorder. *Archives of Psychiatry, 57*(2), 181–186.

Hall, L. A., Sachs, B., & Rayens, M. K. (1998). Mothers' potential for child abuse: The roles of childhood abuse and social resources. *Nursing Research, 47*(2), 87–95.

Hanna, B. (1996). Sexuality, body image, and self-esteem: The future after trauma. *Journal of Trauma Nursing, 3*(1), 13–20.

Harris, R. M., Sharps, P. W., Allen, K., et al. (2003). The interrelationship between violence, HIV/AIDS, and drug use in incarcerated women. *The Journal of the Association of Nurses in AIDS Care, 14*(1), 33–40.

Harrop-Griffiths, J., Katon, W., Walker, E., et al. (1988). The association between chronic pelvic pain, psychiatric diagnoses, and childhood sexual abuse. *Obstetrics and Gynecology, 71*(4), 589–594.

Harsanyi, A., Mott, S., & Kendell, S. (2003). The impact of a history of child sexual assault on a woman's decisions and experiences of cervical screening. *Australian Family Physician, 32*(9), 761–762.

Hazelwood, R. R., & Burgess, A. W. (1995). *Practical aspects of rape investigation: A multidisciplinary approach* (2nd ed.). Boca Raton, FL: CRC Press.

Hebert, M., & Bergeron, M. (2007). Efficacy of a group intervention for adult women survivors of sexual abuse. *Journal of Child Sexual Abuse, 16*(4), 37–61.

Heim, C., Newport, D. J., Heit, S., et al. (2000). Pituitary-adrenal and autonomic response to stress in women after sexual and physical abuse in childhood. *JAMA, 284*(5), 592–597.

Heritage, C. (1998). Working with childhood sexual abuse survivors during pregnancy, labor, and birth. *Journal of Obstetric, Gynecologic, and Neonatal Nursing, 27*(6), 671–677.

Holmes, M. M., Resnick, H. S., & Frampton, D. (1998). Follow up of sexual assault victims. *American Journal of Obstetrics and Gynecology, 179*(2), 336–342.

Jasinski, J. L., Williams, L. M., & Siegel, J. (2000). Childhood physical and sexual abuse as risk factors for heavy drinking among African-American women: A prospective study. *Child Abuse & Neglect, 24*(8), 1061–1071.

Jewkes, R., Martin, L., & Penn-Kekana, L. (2002). The virgin cleansing myth: Cases of child rape are not exotic. *Lancet, 359*(9307), 711.

Johnson, S. D., Cunnington-Williams, R. M., & Cotter, L. B. (2003). A tripartite of HIV-risk for African American women: The intersection of drug use, violence, and depression. *Drug and Alcohol Dependence, 70*(2), 169–175.

Justice Works. (2003). Mothers in prison national facts. Retrieved on 6/8/03 from www.justiceworks.org/factsheets/mip

Katon, W. (2001). Complex posttraumatic stress disorder. Retrieved 9/22/09 from www.medscape.com/Medscape/CNO/Story.cfm?story_id=2260

Kaukinen, C., & Demaris, A. (2005). Age at first sexual assault and current substance abuse and depression. *Journal of Interpersonal Violence, 20*(10), 1244–1270.

Keenan, P., & Royle, L. (2007). Vicarious trauma and first responders: A case study utilizing eye movement desensitization and reprocessing (EMDR) as the primary treatment modality. *International Journal of Emergency Mental Health, 9*(4), 291–298.

Kenny, M. C., & McEachern, A. G. (2000). Racial, ethnic, and cultural factors of a childhood sexual abuse: a selected review of the literature. *Clinical Psychology Review, 20*(7), 905–922.

Kerimova, J., Posner, S. F., Brown, Y. T., et al. (2003). High prevalence of self-reported forced sexual intercourse among internally displaced women in Azerbaijan. *American Journal of Public Health, 93*(7), 1067–1070.

Kilpatrick, D. G., & Resnick, H. S. (1994). *Rape, other violence against women, and post-traumatic stress disorder: Critical issues in assessing the adversity-stress-psychopathology relationship.* 84th Annual Meeting of the American Psychopathological Association, New York.

King, P. (Personal communication) March 7, 1999.

Korn, M. (2001). Emerging trends in understanding post-traumatic stress disorder. Retrieved from www.medscape.com/medscape/cno/2001/APACME/Story.cfm?story_id=2258. Accessed January 31, 2010.

Koss, M. P., Gidycz, C. A., & Wisniewski, N. (1987). The scope of rape: Incidence and prevalence of sexual aggression and victimization in a National Sample of Higher Education Students. *Journal of Consulting and Clinical Psychology, 55*(2), 162–170.

Koss, M. P., Koss, P. G., & Woodruff, W. J. Deleterious effects of criminal victimization on women's health and medical utilization. *Archives of Internal Medicine, 151*(2), 342–347.

Krieger, D. (1997). *Therapeutic Touch.* Santa Fe, NM: Bear & Company.

Krieger, D. (2002). *Therapeutic touch as transpersonal healing.* New York: Lantern Books.

Kulka, R. A., Fairbank, J. A., Jordan, B. K., et al. (1990). *Trauma and the Vietnam war generation.* New York: Brunner/Mazel.

Kyriacou, D. N., Anglin, D., Taliaferro, E., et al. (1999). Risk factors for injury to women from domestic violence. *The New England Journal of Medicine, 341*(25), 1892–1898.

Laurie, S. G., & Tucker, M. J. (1993). *Centering: A guide to inner growth* (2nd ed.). Rochester, VT: Destiny Books.

Laws, A. (1993). Sexual abuse history and women's medical problems. *Journal of General Internal Medicine, 8*(8), 441–443.

Ledray, L. E. (1990). Counseling rape victims: The nursing challenge. *Perspectives in Psychiatric Care, 26*(2), 21–27.

Ledray, L. E. (1994). *Recovering from rape.* New York: Henry Holt.

Leenerts, M. H. (1999). The disconnected self: Consequences of abuse in a cohort of low-income white women living with HIV/AIDS. *Health Care for Women International, 20*(4), 381–400.

Leenerts, M. H. (2003). From neglect to care: A theory to guide HIV-positive incarcerated women in self-care. *The Journal of the Association of Nurses in AIDS Care: JANAC, 14*(5), 25–38.

Lema, V. M. (1997). Sexual abuse of minors: Emerging medical and social problem in Malawi. *East African Medical Journal, 74*(11), 743–746.

Lerman, C., Miller, S. M., Scarborough, R., et al. (1991). Adverse psychological consequences of positive cytological cervical screening. *American Journal of Obstetrics and Gynecology, 165*(6), 658–662.

Lewis, C. (2006). Treating Incarcerated women: gender matters. *Psychiatric Clinics of North America, 29*(3), 773–789.

Liebschutz, J., Battaglia, T., Finley, E., & Averbuch, T. (2008). Disclosing intimate partner violence to healthcare clinicians—what a difference the setting makes: A qualitative study. *BMC Public Health.* Accessed 1/14/09 www.medscape.com

Macrae, J. A. (2001). *Nursing as a spiritual practice: A contemporary application of Florence Nightingale's views.* New York: Springer Publishing Company.

Malmutgh, N. M., Sockloskie, R. J., Koss, M. P., et al. (1991). Characteristics of aggressors against women: Testing a model using a national sample of college students. *Journal of Consulting and Clinical Psychology, 59*(5), 670–681.

Manfrin-Ledet, L., & Porche, D. J. (2003). The state of science: violence and HIV infection in women. *The Journal of the Association of Nurses in AIDS Care, 14*(6), 56–68.

Marcus, A., Kaplan, C., Crane, L., et al. (1998). Reducing loss-to-follow-up among women with abnormal pap smears. *Medical Care, 36*(3), 397–410.

Mathias, S. D., Kuppermann, M., Liberman, R. F., et al. (1996). Chronic pelvic pain: Prevalence, health related quality of life, and economic correlates. *Obstetrics and Gynecology, 87*(3), 321–327.

McEvoy, A., Rollo, D., & Brookings, J. (1999). *If he is raped: A guide for parents, partners, spouses, and friends.* Holmes Beach, FL: Learning Publications.

McFarlane, J., Malecha, A., Watson, K., Gist, J., Batten, E., Hall, I., et al. (2005). Intimate partner sexual assault against women: Frequency, health consequences, and treatment. *Obstetrics and Gynecology, 105*(1), 99–108.

McKivergin, M., Wimberly, T., Loversidge, J. M., & Fortman, R. H. (1996). Creating a work environment that supports self-care. *Holistic Nursing Practice, 10*(2), 78–88.

Meel, B. L. (2003). The myth of child rape as cure for HIV/AIDS in Transkei: A case report. *Medicine, Science, and the Law, 43*(1), 85–88.

Meyers, H. (1992). The billion-dollar epidemic. *American Medical News.* American Medical Association. Chicago, IL .

Miller, M. (1999). A model to explain the relationship between sexual abuse and HIV risk among women. *AIDS Care, 11*(1), 3–20.

Miller, S., Siejak, K., Schroeder, C., et al. (1997). Enhancing adherence following abnormal pap smears among low-income minority women: A preventive telephone counseling strategy. *Journal of the National Cancer Institute, 89*(10), 703–708.

Miller, T. M., Cohen, M. A., & Weirsema, B. (1996). *Victim costs and consequences: A new look.* Research Report NCJ 155282. Washington, DC: U.S. Department of Justice, Office of Justice Programs, and U.S. Department of Health and Human Services, Maternal and Child Health Bureau.

Moore, D. B. (2000). Make them laugh: Therapeutic humor for patients with grief-related stress or anxiety. *Advance for Nurse Practitioners, 8*(8), 34–37.

Moore, M. L., Zaccaro, D., & Parsons, L. H. (1998). Attitudes and practices of registered nurses toward women who have experienced abuse/domestic violence. *Journal of Obstetric, Gynecologic, and Neonatal Nursing, 27*(2), 175–182.

Morrill, A. C., Kasten, L., Urato, M., et al. (2001). Abuse, addiction, and depression as pathways to sexual risk in women and men with a history of substance abuse. *Journal of Substance Abuse, 13*(1–2), 169–184.

Morse, J. M., & Penrod, J. (1999). Linking concepts of enduring, uncertainty, suffering, and hope. *Image–The Journal of Nursing Scholarship, 31*(2), 145–150.

Mullings, J. L., Marquart, J. W., Brewer, V. E., & Crouch, B. M. (2000). Assessing the relationship between child sexual abuse and marginal living condition of HIV/AIDS-related risk behaviors among women prisoners. *Child Abuse and Neglect: The International Journal, 24*(5), 677–688.

Nieves-Khouw, F. C. (1997). Recognizing victims of physical and sexual abuse. *Critical Care Nursing Clinics of North America, 9*(2), 141–148.

NIMH multisite HIV prevention trial. (2001). A test of factors mediating the relationship between unwanted sexual activity during childhood and risky sexual practices among women enrolled in the NIMH multisite HIV prevention trial. *Women and Health, 33*(1–2), 163–180.

North, C. S. (1996). Alcoholism in women: More common—and serious—than you think. *Postgraduate Medicine, 100*(4), 221–224, 230, 233–232.

Nyamathi, A. M. (1991). Relationship of resources to emotional, somatic complaints, and high-risk behaviors in drug recovery and homeless minority women. *Research in Nursing & Health, 14*(4), 269–277.

O'Leary, A., Purcell, D., Remien, R. H., & Gomez, C. (2003). Childhood sexual abuse and sexual transmission risk behaviour among HIV-positive men who have sex with men. *The Journal of the Association of Nurses in AIDS Care: JANAC, 15*(1), 17–26.

Parrot, A., Cummings, N., & Marchell, T. (1994). *Rape 101: Sexual assault prevention for college athletes.* Holmes Beach, FL: Learning Publications.

Paskett, E. D., Carter, W. B., Chu, J., et al. (1990). Compliance behavior in women with abnormal pap smears, developing and testing a decision model. *Medical Care, 28*(6), 643–656.

Paskett, E. D., Phillips, K., & Miller, M. (1995). Improving compliance among women with abnormal Papanicolaou smears. *Obstetrics and Gynecology, 86*(3), 353–359.

Perez, B., Kennedy, G., & Fullilove, M. T. (1995). Childhood sexual abuse and AIDS. In A. O'Leary & L. S. Jemmott (Eds.), *Women at risk: Issues in the primary prevention of AIDS* (pp. 83–100). New York: Plenum Press.

Peter, L. M., & Whitehall, D. L. (1998). Management of female sexual assault. *American Family Physician, 58*(4), 920–926.

Pieper, B., & DiNardo, E. (1998). Reasons for missing appointments in an outpatient clinic for indigent adults. *Journal of the American Academy of Nurse Practitioners, 10*(8), 359–364.

Pitcher, G. J., & Bowley, D. M. (2002). Infant rape in So. Africa. *Lancet, 359*(9303), 274–275.

Pitzner, J. K., McGarry-Long, J., & Drummond, P. D. (2000). A history of abuse and negative life events in patients with a sexually transmitted disease and in a community sample. *Child Abuse & Neglect, 24*(5), 715–731.

Polusny, M. A., & Follette, V. M. (1995). Long-term correlates of child sexual abuse: Theory and review of the empirical literature. *Appl Prev Psychol, 4*(3), 143–166.

Putnam, F. W. (1989). *Diagnosis and treatment of multiple personality disorders.* New York: Guilford Press.

Rambow, B., Atkinson, C., Frost, T. H., et al. (1992). Female sexual assault medical and legal implications. *Annals of Emergency Medicine, 21*(6), 733–1731.

Rapkin, A., Kames, L., Darke, L., et al. (1990). History of physical and sexual abuse in women with chronic pain. *Obstetrics and Gynecology, 76*(1), 92–96.

Reiter, R. C., Shakerin, L. R., Gambone, J. C., et al. (1991). Correlation between sexual abuse and somatization in women with somatic and nonsomatic chronic pelvic pain. *American Journal of Obstetrics And Gynecology, 165*(1), 104–109.

Relf, M. (2001). Battering and HIV in men who have sex with men: A critique and synthesis of literature. *The Journal of the Association of Nurses in AIDS Care: JANAC, 12*(3), 41–48.

Resnick, H. S., Acierno, R., & Kilpatrick, D. G. (1997). Health impact of interpersonal violence 2: Medical and mental health outcomes. *Behavioral Medicine, 23*(Summer), 65–78.

Rew, L., Thomas, N., Horner, S. D., et al. (2001). Correlates of recent suicide attempts in a triethnic group of adolescents. *Journal of Nursing Scholarship, 33*(4), 361–367.

Riggs, N., Houray, D., Long, G., et al. (2000). Analysis of 1,076 cases of sexual assault. *Annals of Emergency Medicine, 35*(4), 358–362.

Robohm, J. S., & Buttenheim, M. (1996). The gynecological care experience of adult survivors of childhood sexual abuse: A preliminary investigation. *Women and Health, 24*(3), 59–75.

Rosenberg, M. L., Mercy, J. A., & Annest, J. L. (1998). The problems of violence in the United States and globally. In R. B. Wallace (Ed.), *Maxcy-Rosenau-Last: Public health & preventive medicine.* (14th ed., pp. 1223–1225). Stamford, CT: Appleton & Lange.

Salsberry, P. J., Nickel, J. T., Polivka, B. J., et al. (1999). Self-reported health status of low-income mothers. *Image–The Journal of Nursing Scholarship, 31*(4), 375–380.

Salter, D., McMillian, D., Richards, M., et al. (2003). Development of sexually abusive behavior in sexually victimized males: A longitudinal study. *Lancet, 361*(9356), 471–476.

Scarce, M. (1997). *Male on male rape: The hidden toll of stigma and shame.* New York: Insight Books–Plenum Press.

Schafer, J., Caetano, R., & Cunradi, C. (2004). A path model of risk factors for intimate partner violence among couples in the United States. *Journal of Interpersonal Violence, 19*(2), 133–142.

Schei, B., & Bakketeig, L. S. (1989). Gynaecological impact of sexual and physical abuse by spouse: A study of a random sample of Norwegian women. *BJOG, 96*(12), 1379–1383.

Seedat, S., & Stein, D. J. (2000). Trauma and post-traumatic stress disorder in women: A review. *International Clinical Psychopharmacology, 15*(Suppl. 3), S25–S33.

Segnan, N., Senore, C., Giordano, L., et al. (1998). Promoting participation in a population screening program for breast and cervical cancer:

A randomized trial of different invitation strategies. *Tumori, 84*(2), 348–353.

Sigler, R. T. (1995). The cost of tolerance for violence. *Journal of Health Care for the Poor and Underserved, 6*(2), 124–134.

Simon, T., & Golden, B. (1996). *Dating: Peer education for reducing sexual harassment and violence among secondary students.* Holmes Beach, FL: Learning Publications.

Simon, T. B., & Harris, C. A. (1993a). In *Sex without consent: Peer education training for secondary schools* (Vol. 1). Holmes Beach, FL: Learning Publications.

Simon, T. B., & Harris, C. A. (1993b). In *Peer education training for colleges and universities* (Vol. 2). Holmes Beach, FL: Learning Publications.

Slaughter, L., & Brown, C. R. (1992). Colposcopy to establish physical findings in rape victims. *American Journal of Obstetrics and Gynecology, 166*(1), 83–86.

Slaughter, L., Brown, C. R., Crowley, S., & Peck, R. (1997). Patterns of genital injury in female sexual assault victims. *American Journal of Obstetrics and Gynecology, 176*(3), 609–616.

Smith, P. H., White, J. W., & Holland, L. J. (2003). A longitudinal perspective on dating violence among adolescent and college-age women. *American Journal of Public Health, 98*(7), 1104–1109.

Sowell, R. L., Phillips, K. D., Seals, B., et al. (2002). Incidence and correlates of physical violence among HIV-infected women at risk for pregnancy in the southeastern United States. *The Journal of the Association of Nurses in AIDS Care: JANAC, 13*(2), 30–42.

Sowell, R., Seals, B., Moneyham, L., et al. (1999). Experiences of violence in HIV seropositive women in the South-eastern United States of America. *Journal of Advanced Nursing, 30*(3), 606–615.

Springs, F. E., & Friedrich, W. N. (1992). Health risk behaviors and medical sequelae of childhood sexual abuse. *Mayo Clinic Proceedings. Mayo Clinic, 57*(6), 527–532.

Stanley, D. (2007). Lights in the shadows: Florence Nightingale and others who make their mark. *Contemporary Nurse, 24*(1), 45–51.

Steighner, K. (2003). Breaking the cycle of pain. *On the Edge: The Official Publication of the International Association of Forensic Nurses, 9*(3), 4–7.

Stein, M. B., Lang, A. J., Laffaye, C., Satz, L. E., Lenox, R. J., & Dresselhaus, T. R. (2004). Relationship of sexual assault history to somatic symptoms and health anxiety in women. *General Hospital Psychiatry, 26,* 178–183.

Stevens, J., Zierler, S., Cram, V., et al. (1995). Risks for HIV infection in incarcerated women. *Journal of Women's Health, 4*(5), 569–577.

Stewart, D. E., Bucheggar, P. M., Lickrish, G. M., & Sierra, S. (1993). The effect of educational brochures on follow-up compliance in women with abnormal Papanicolaou smears. *Obstetrics and Gynecology, 81*(2), 280–282.

Straus, M. A., & Gelles, R. J. (1986). Societal change in family violence from 1975 to 1985 as revealed in two national surveys. *J Marriage Fam, 48*(3), 465–479.

Suris, A., Lind, L., Kashner, T. M., & Borman, P. D. (2007). Mental health, quality of life, and health functioning in women veterans. *Journal of Interpersonal Violence, 22*(2), 179–197.

Teets, J. M. (1997). The incidence and experience of rape among chemically dependent women. *Journal of Psychoactive Drugs, 29*(4), 331–336.

The Joint Commission. (2009). *Accreditation manual for hospitals: Core standards, and guidelines.* Oak Park IL.

Thompson, N. J., Potter, J. S., Sanderson, C. A., & Maibach, E. W. (1997). The relationship of sexual abuse and HIV risk behavior among heterosexual adult female STD patients. *Child Abuse & Neglect, 21*(2), 149–156.

U.S. Dept. of Health & Human Services (USDHHS). (2000). *Healthy People 2010 (Vols. 1 and 2).* Washington, DC: Author.

Valente, S. M. (2000). Evaluating and managing intimate partner violence. *The Nurse Practitioner, 25*(5), 18–35.

Viahov, D., & Galea, S. (2002). N.Y. study shows increase in PTSD and depression after Sept. 11. *Mental Health Weekly, 12*(13), 1.

Von, J. M., Kilpatrick, D. G., Burgess, A. W., et al. (1998). Rape and sexual assault. In R. B. Wallace (Ed.), *Maxcy-Rosenau-Last: Public Health & Preventive Medicine.* (14th ed., pp. 1238–1240). Stamford, CT: Appleton & Lange.

Von, J. M., Kilpatrick, D. G., Burgess, A. W., & Hartman, C. R. (1991). Rape and sexual assault in violence in America: A public health approach by Mark L. Rosenberg and Mary Ann Fenley (Eds) Chapter 5, pp. 95–122. Oxford University Press, New York.

Wallace, R., Fullilove, M. T., & Flisher, A. J. (1996). AIDS, violence and behavioral coding: Information theory, risk behavior and dynamic process on core-group sociogeographic networks. *Social Science & Medicine, 43*(3), 339–352.

Walling, M., O'Hara, M. W., Reiter, R., et al. (1994). Abuse history and chronic pain in women. II. A multivariate analysis of abuse and psychological morbidity. *Obstetrics and Gynecology, 84*(2), 200–206.

Willis, B. M., & Levy, B. S. (2002). Child prostitution: Global health burden, research needs, and interventions. *Lancet, 359*(20), 1417–1422.

Wingood, G. M., & DiClemente, R. J. (1997). Childhood sexual abuse, HIV sexual risk, and gender relations of African-American women. *American Journal of Preventive Medicine, 13*(5), 22–24.

Wise, L. A., Zierler, S., Krieger, N., et al. (2001). Adult onset of major depressive disorder in relation to early life violent victimization: A case-control study. *Lancet, 358*(9285), 881–887.

Wisner, C. L., Gilmer, T. P., Saltzman, L. E., et al. (1999). Intimate partner violence against women: Do victims cost health care plans more?. *The Journal of Family Practice, 48*(6), 439–443.

Witte, S. S., Wada, T., El-Bassel, N., et al. (2000). Predictors of female condom use among women exchanging street sex in New York City. *Sexually Transmitted Diseases, 27*(2), 93–100.

Wolfgang, M. E., & Zahn, M. A. (1983). Criminal homicide. In S. H. Kadish (Ed.), *Encyclopedia of crime and justice.* New York: Free Press.

Wurtele, S. K., Kaplan, G. M., & Keairnes, M. (1990). Childhood sexual abuse among chronic pain patients. *The Clinical Journal of Pain, 6*(2), 110–113.

Wyatt, G. E., Myers, H. F., Williams, J. K., et al. (2002). Does a history of trauma contribute to HIV risk of women of color? Implications for prevention and policy. *American Journal of Public Health, 92*(4), 660–665.

Zierler, S., Feingold, L., Laufer, D., et al. (1991). Adult survivors of childhood sexual abuse and subsequent risk of HIV infection. *American Journal of Public Health, 81*(5), 572–575.

Zupancic, M. K., & Kreidler, M. C. (1998). Shame and the fear of feeling. *Perspect Psychiatric Care, 34*(3), 29–34.

CHAPTER 34 Sexual Exploitation of Children and Child Pornography

Mary K. Sullivan

The forensic issue of child sexual victimization is important for all nurses. Psychiatric nurses are needed to assess and treat abused children; correctional nurses are needed to work with offenders in prison. Community health, school, and pediatric nurses are needed to help prevent victimization by knowing where to refer parents who are concerned about their child's abuse. For forensic nurse examiners (FNEs), the fact remains that skills are needed for assessment, diagnosis, evidence collection as appropriate, and expert testimony. This chapter outlines the phenomena of child and adolescent sexual abuse and the dynamics of child and adult pornography. It is intended to increase awareness of this problem as well as to highlight areas where nursing expertise is crucial, whether it be in a treatment setting or medicolegal scenario, for perpetrator or victim.

BEST PRACTICE Forensic nurses should understand that each form of sexual abuse or combination of abuses can have a profound negative impact on the physical, medical, and psychological health of a child victim. Each needs to be evaluated and addressed separately.

Child Sexual Exploitation

The study of the sexual victimization of children has primarily focused on incest or family member (intrafamilial) abuse of children. Some studies estimate that 80% to 85% of all reported cases of child sexual abuse occur by family members, by trusted friends of the parents, or by people living nearby who both the child victim and the child's parents know. This interesting phenomenon is in direct contrast to millions of parents who diligently teach their children the concept of "stranger danger" while their children are most susceptible to adults who have been given a parental stamp of trust and approval.

The sexual victimization of children ranges from one-on-one abuse within the family to multioffender/multivictim intrafamilial and extrafamilial sex rings, and from child prostitution to stranger abduction for sexual purposes. The ease of viewing child pornography has surfaced as another form of sexual exploitation that includes depicting children performing sexual acts or in nude poses that are then distributed to others for profit or pleasure. Each form of sexual abuse or combination of abuses can have a profound negative impact on the physical, medical, and psychological health of the child victim and needs to be addressed separately.

Many police departments have Crimes Against Children units that focus on the exploding crime problem of children being sexually abused. Police detectives have become on-the-job experts in dealing with child victims and child abusers as they respond to a

myriad of crimes from neglect to sexual abuse and homicide. Just within the realm of sex-related crimes, detectives investigate occurrences of inappropriate sexual contact to sexual penetration. An important by-product of child abuse is an expanding knowledge and awareness of treating victims of child abuse. Law enforcement agencies regularly maintain relationships with trained counselors and therapists and consider forensic interviews as a normal practice of their sexual abuse investigations. Schools, churches, and youth organizations go beyond the daily care of children and have policies in place for reporting suspicions of child abuse to law enforcement or to local departments to assist families and children. Healthcare professionals not only treat the immediate issues of injuries but have improved procedures for detecting child abuse and treating victims who need long-term or in-depth care. As such, nurses must distinguish their responsibilities with regard to appropriate treatment and documentation in the medical record versus collecting evidence or conducting an interview for legal purposes. Depending on the settings, forensic nurses may encounter a victim or perpetrator and must approach each without bias or judgment.

The perpetrators include every aspect of society from family members, to coaches, teachers, religious leaders, scout leaders, representatives of community-based organizations that aim to help children by mentoring to them, neighbors, and friends of the family. More often than not, when allegations of child sexual abuse become known, the parents or legal guardians of the child victim are surprised to find that the sexual abuser was able to conduct and continue the abuse for extended periods of time without their knowledge. This is partly due to the tactics of the sexual abuser—to convince the adults around the child victim that they are beyond reproach or question.

WIDESPREAD USE OF THE INTERNET

Only a small percentage of minor children are sexually abused by an adult they meet through online contact. According to the online victimization research conducted by Wolak, Mitchell, and Finkelhor (2006), approximately one in seven youth online (ages 10 to 17) received a sexual solicitation or approach over the Internet, and 4% received an aggressive sexual solicitation. Thirty-four percent had an unwanted exposure to sexual material, and 27% told a parent or guardian (Wolak et al., 2006).

As the data indicate, fewer than a third of the solicitations never get reported by the child. Some children perceive that reporting these dangerous contacts to their parents will only restrict their "freedom" of use of the Internet and result in closer supervision by their parents. Therefore, children perceive that reporting only punishes the child and not the adult.

KEY POINT The Internet predator need only find one child among millions using the Internet who is willing to take the journey with him.

In the world of the Internet, adults who want to exploit children understand this confused rationalization and use it against their victim to further convince the child to not report the contact (while pushing to extend the boundaries of the child). Children approaching puberty and sexual awareness are both curious and experimental while alternately being extremely self-conscious. They want knowledge (and experience) but are too embarrassed to go to their parents, friends, or trusted adult authority figures for advice. The Internet ideally serves their purpose by becoming the provider of knowledge while offering anonymity to the child. Conversely, the Internet provides the same sense of anonymity to those adults who realize they are overstepping societal boundaries by engaging in sexual conversations with a child. The adult offers friendship, worldly (sexual) experience, and information and asks for sexual contact in return. Adults who engage in this type of behavior, whether motivated by true pedophilic interests or by curiosity in engaging in socially bizarre behavior, have a population of more than 90 million children from which to choose actively using the Internet within the United States alone. Sexual interest in children is not an isolated incident or confined to an infinitely small percentage of our children. Child sexual abuse is a serious public health problem, and research suggests that one in four girls and one in six boys are sexually abused before they reach 18 years of age (Finkelhor, 1994) Since the mid-1990s, law enforcement has directed efforts toward combating offenders who are contacting minor victims on the Internet for the purpose of sexually exploitation. The Federal Bureau of Investigation (FBI) national initiative "Innocent Images" focuses on investigations of people using the Internet to abuse children. Currently there are 38 Innocent Images Task Forces throughout the United States with membership comprised of FBI agents and local and state law enforcement officers. The driving force of the Innocent Images Task Forces is to employ sophisticated online undercover techniques aimed at targeting people who entice children to engage in sexual activity or those who possess, distribute, or produce child pornography.

Since 1996, FBI investigations of sexual exploitation of children has steadily increased from 113 federal cases opened and 68 arrests in 1996 to 2135 federal cases opened and 1018 arrests in 2006. In this 10-year period, 17,691 federal cases have opened, and 7700 people have been arrested on federal charges pertaining to the sexual exploitation of children. In addition, every state has an Internet Crimes Against Children (ICAC) task force, funded by the Department of Justice (DOJ) Office of Juvenile Justice and Delinquency Prevention (OJJDP) with federal, state, and local law enforcement agencies working on issues of child sexual exploitation.

Since the ICAC program's inception in 1998, nearly 100,000 law enforcement officers, prosecutors, and other professionals have been trained in the United States and in 17 countries on techniques to investigate and prosecute ICAC-related cases. ICAC task forces have reviewed more than 100,000 complaints of alleged child sexual victimization during that time, resulting in the arrest of more than 13,500 individuals. In 2007, the ICAC program trained more than 20,000 law enforcement personnel and nearly 1700 prosecutors. In 2008, the number of trained law enforcement personnel increased to more than 26,500, while an additional 2219 prosecutors were trained. In 2007, ICAC investigations led to more than

10,500 forensic examinations, the identification of nearly 400 children who were victims of some form of abuse and neglect, and 2400 arrests. And in 2008, ICAC task forces resulted in the arrest of more than 3000 individuals, with more than one-third of those arrests (1109) resulting in the acceptance of a plea agreement by the defendant.

On October 23, 2002, President George W. Bush declared, "Our nation has made this commitment: Anyone who targets a child for harm will be a primary target of law enforcement. That's our commitment. Anyone who takes the life or innocence of a child will be punished to the full extent of the law." In 2006, Attorney General Alberto Gonzalez announced a new initiative called Project Safe Childhood (PSC), ordering every U.S. Attorney to designate a PSC coordinator to employ multilevel law enforcement agencies to investigate and prosecute offenders at the federal level. The Adam Walsh Child Protection and Safety Act of 2006 ("The Act") was enacted on July 27, 2006. In addition to establishing a national sex offender registry law, the act made significant changes to sexual abuse, exploitation, and transportation crimes. The act created new substantive crimes, expanded federal jurisdiction over existing crimes, and increased statutory minimum or maximum sentences.

KEY POINT The insidious nature of child pornography is that it is not "just images." It is the focal point to refine an interest to view children as sexual objects and to sexually molest a child. An image of rape is a real-life depiction of a fantasy.

Technology and Sexual Predators

A question that is often asked is whether the popularity and accessibility of the Internet has created a new classification of criminals, or is the public awareness of the threats against children more acute because of the media? Although advances in technology have made predator and prey coexist in the same arena (the Internet is the common environment), child molestation has been an undercurrent theme of mainstream civilation from the earliest ages.

Before the Internet, child molesters had to make themselves visible in an effort to interact with children. An individual child molester hung around playgrounds, schools, libraries, or amusement parks to seek out children victims. This child molester fits the traditional "strange-looking stranger" that parents warned their children about. However, a more socially competent child molester would attempt to incorporate multiple partners and sexually molest multiple child victims. These child molesters often engaged in sex ring crimes originally defined by Burgess and Grant (1988) as sexual victimization in which there are one or more adult offenders and several children who are aware of each other's participation.

Three different types of child sex rings include solo, transitional, and syndicated rings. The solo sex ring involves one or two adult perpetrators and multiple children, and the transitional ring tests children for the syndicated sex ring that involves multiple adults, multiple child victims, and a wide range of exchange of items including child pornography and sexual activities (Burgess & Grant, 1988). Sex rings existed in nurseries or childcare facilities, in religious cult environments, and isolated rural communities where a dominant personality could pervert the moral compass of others to meet their goals of sexual gratification. Although these crimes still take place, the Internet has expanded the territory of the predator exponentially.

The Internet has provided the child molester with a tool that gives him perceived anonymity while communicating with a potential victim pool of more than 90 million children actively using the Internet. They no longer have to be an engaging leader or childcare provider or work around children at all. He can now sit behind a computer and reach children instantly. His efforts can now be more focused to "groom" the child and to engage in sexual behavior with children and not "waste" his time with children who are not vulnerable. While the traditional child molester still exists, this new breed of child molester uses his skills of communication to befriend the child and to gain the child's trust in all matters.

Where do predators learn how to entice a child online? The Internet is its own source of validation and education. By engaging in chat room discussions, the novice befriends others who are more experienceed in communicating their desires. There are several chat rooms devoted to the discussion of sexual interest of children. But with just one chat room of 50 participants, the novice is emboldened with the knowledge that there are others "out there" who have the same pedophilic interests, and he realizes he is not alone. More so, the experienced "chatters" make the novice feel comfortable to be in that chat room. The common theme that is replayed over and over is that "I'm okay, you're okay, we're all okay" in our sexual interest in children.

Law enforcement working online undercover experience the same education as the novice child molester. Experienced Internet predators provide tips on how to evade law enforcement, find and groom children, places to surf and chat, and a myriad of other ideas. Law enforcement officers working online undercover investigations note that Internet child sex molesters seem to work off the same "playbook." After repeated discussion of techniques, tips, and habits, it appears as though the collective group of Internet pedophiles are, indeed, writing detailed "how-to" manuals.

Many Internet sex offenders lead a double life of being law-abiding, dedicated career professionals and responsible family members by day, yet in quiet isolation by themselves and with a computer, they can talk out their sexually deviant fantasies. This dichotomy is sometimes so extreme that even the perpetrator cannot explain how or why he was able to coexist in both worlds. One explanation is that middle-aged offenders who are relatively new consumers of the Internet have discovered the ease of use of computers. They have discovered the ease of looking at pornography. The era of point-and-click technology has made viewing formerly forbidden subjects readily accessible without the embarrassment of purchasing adult sex material from someone who might recognize them buying a magazine from the local gas station or the local adult store. Now the Pandora's box of sexual appetites is easy to explore in the privacy of their home. Combined with the privacy of computer use, many offenders initially explore all types of pornographic subjects until they realize which topics they are more interested in and which topics they are repulsed by. Those with pedophillic interests begin to filter and focus their Internet searches closer to their objects of desire until they find the magic keys to child pornography. By the time they are discovered by law enforcement, these offenders usually have already collected a variety of child pornography that suits their interests. Those who have found that they enjoy looking at child pornography achieve a dual objective—they get instant sexual gratification from looking at the images of minors engaged in sexual activities and they get to refine their sexual interests.

The advocates of child pornography would argue that viewing child pornography is the means to sexual gratification. Others would argue, however, that the sexual gratification is temporary, and the focus of their sexual interests becomes more objectified and more intense. Law enforcement officials have arrested child pornography collectors with tens of thousands of images and videos in their collections. These collectors become immunized to their early collections of child pornography images and need stronger graphic and deviant sexual images to keep their interests. Some collectors admit that merely looking at child pornography is not enough and they desire sexual activity with the child. They seek to advance their grooming techniques to find a child to engage in that sexual activity. Child pornography provides the focal point to refine an interest to view children as sexual objects and to sexually molest a child. It is a depiction of their fantasy and the picture to re-create with their own victim. This is one of the reasons that many child molesters can lead a double life as a respectable member of society while having the thoughts of a child rapist. Many offenders who are arrested for enticing a child for sexual purposes or for possession of child pornography have no prior criminal history. They have spouses or adult sexual partners who have no knowledge of their sexual interest in children.

Technology and Child Pornography

Generally speaking, child pornography is any visual depiction of a person under the age of 18 years old who is being sexually exploited either through a sexual activity or by being displayed in a "lewd and lascivious manner." *United States v. John Ashcroft* (Title 18, USC 2252A) provides a legal definition of the federal standards of child pornography. The federal standard is a person under the age of 18 years old. "Sexual activity" is generally accepted as defined by state law and includes inappropriate contact of a minor to sexual penetration. "Lewd and lascivious display" is a legal standard and generally is defined as the exhibition of the genitals or pubic area for sexual purposes. Other factors to consider in determining "lewd and lascivious display" include the level of participation of the victim, the closeness of the image, the centrality of the genitals, and the purpose of the image. An example of an image not considered a "lewd and lascivious display" would be a parent's photograph of their nude infant in a bathtub taken by the mother or father to depict an act of innocence.

With the advent of technology, a visual image may consist of images taken from traditional or digital cameras, video cameras, webcams, and cellular telephones (both images and video streams). The miniaturization of electronic equipment has created an explosion of nonconsenting images and video streams with the use of spy cameras, miniature video cameras, and cellular-based handheld equipment used on a nonsuspecting victim. The images and videos have a high demand from Internet-based websites feeding the frenzy of a populace that desires increased access to forbidden images.

An interesting dichotomy exists because of the legal definitions of the "age of majority" that exists in the United States. The federal standard for adulthood is 18 years old or older. The legal age of consent to engage in sexual activity in many states is 16 years old. So a person who is 16 or 17 years old can legally consent to sex, but a visual image of them engaging in sexual activity or displayed in a "lewd and lascivious" manner is illegal.

There are some estimates that 20,000 images of child pornography are produced around the world every week. These images are of real children engaging in sexual activity. Another way to look at it is this: child pornography is a true depiction of a crime scene, a crime of child sexual abuse. True collectors of child pornography demand more and newer images, more explicit activity, with more victims. Hardcore collectors are familiar with the hundreds of thousands of series of child pornography and demand newer product to meet their deviant sexual needs.

In a recent interview of a father who videotaped himself sexually molesting his own biological daughter from the age of 5 to 9 years old, he admitted that he first became addicted to child pornography before she was born and wanted newer material because the "old" stuff was not enough. As his daughter grew up, he instructed her in various sexual acts that he photographed to use to trade for new material. He customized sexual acts for a select few clients. As his clientele in the Internet world grew, he was able to gain access to child pornography that had not been previously distributed. His incestuous pornographic images and sexually explicit videos, known in the Internet world as the Tara Series, became one of the most widely distributed child pornographic series in the world. As a result of this investigation, he received a federal prison sentence of 70 years with no chance of parole.

KEY POINT Adults who sexually exploit children are men and women of virtually every age with varying personal characteristics, life experiences, economic status, sexual preference, and history of offending.

Types of Offenders

What kind of people seek out children for sexual pleasure? We generally think of these people as *pedophiles,* a term that has been used by many as a sexual perversion in which children are the preferred sex object. The American Psychiatric Association defines pedophilia as a disorder in which the following criteria exist:

a. Over a period of at least six months, has recurrent, intense sexually arousing fantasies, sexual urges, or behaviors involving sexual activity with a prepubescent child or children (generally age thirteen years or younger).
b. The fantasies, sexual urges, or behaviors cause clinically significant distress or impairment in social, occupational, or other important areas of functioning.
c. The person is at least age sixteen years and at least five years older than the child or children in (a). (APA, 2000).

Other terms to describe people who act on their pedophilic desires include *sexual predator* and *child molester.* However, *sexual predator* evokes an emotional image of someone who is animalistic and is stalking and consuming a *prey.* Although this is sometimes true, the term evokes fear and concern among parents who realize that their young children are the target prey that a predator desires. One of the problems with this emotionally laced term is that the associated fear clouds judgment and may elicit an irrational response to combat the fear rather than properly deal with the subject of the molestation. Law enforcement officers use the term *child molester* to describe someone who commits an illegal act of child molestation. However, the term does not apply to someone who has pedophilic desires but has not committed an illegal act of child molestation. For example, a person who is online gathering information on the most efficient way to entice and molest a child is not a child molester, nor is the person who describes his sexual interests with another person or is chatting with a potential victim but has not yet crossed the legal line of molestation.

SITUATIONAL/PREFERENTIAL CHILD MOLESTERS: A CONTINUUM

Retired FBI supervisory special agent Ken Lanning, an expert in the subject of child crimes, expanded on the concept of situational versus preferential child molesters developed by Dr. Park Dietz and created a typology for law enforcement to consider the variations of child molesters on a continuum.

The situational child molester does not have a true sexual preference for children but engages in sex with children for varied and sometimes complex reasons. Sex with children may range from a once-in-a-lifetime act to long-term pattern of behavior. Usually the situational child molester has a low self-esteem and poor coping skills; he turns to children as a sexual substitute for the preferred peer sex partner. His main victim criterion is availability, vulnerability, and opportunity. This type of molester is morally and sexually indiscriminate and molests children because the situation presents itself. He also may indulge in other deviant sexual activities to include bondage-domination-sado-masochism (BDSM), bestiality, group sex, or homosexuality. He is not fixated on any specific sexual fetishes; rather he is a sexual experimenter. He is the "try-sexual"—willing to try anything sexual. His own well-being and emotions come first. The primary goal of the situational molester is to please himself.

Preferential child molesters have a definite sexual preference for children. They are sexually attracted to and prefer children as sexual partners. Their sexual fantasies and erotic imagery is of children. They usually have age or gender preferences, which may be as narrow as a skinny seven-year-old girl with long blond hair in ponytails, blue eyes, wearing glasses, a miniskirt, and a short sleeve blouse, or it may be as wide as any boy or girl under the age of nine. Preferential child molesters have often had their pedophilic desires since adolescence and have developed a well-developed fantasy in which they are engaging in sex with their ideal loving mate who fulfills all sexual wishes. They conveniently edit out the reality that the child has a group of caretakers (parents, teachers, etc.) who may object to his presence. They edit out the reality that children are not sexual beings and are not physically or emotionally ready to handle sex nor do they have the maturity development to handle a sexual relationship. They edit out the reality that children age beyond their age preferential limits. And they edit out the reality that having sex with children is illegal, immoral, and they will be severely punished for their actions.

The preferential child molester is characterized as someone who engages children in sexual activity by seducing them with attention, affection, and gifts. Just as one adult courts another, the preferential child molester seduces children over a period of time by gradually lowering the victim's sexual inhibitions. Over time, the child is pressured to trade sex for the benefits received from the molester. The preferential child molester knows how to talk to children—but, more important, he knows how to listen to them.

According to Lanning, child molesters may not be strictly situational child molesters or strictly preferential child molesters—rather they lie somewhere on a continuum and may possess some overlapping traits (Lanning, 1992).

Most adults think they will know when they are face to face with a child molester. They think there are abnormal signs or behavioral characteristics or they will get a gut feeling that a person is perverse. Conversely, these same people think they know that a person is "good" and will go to great lengths to convince themselves or others that the person they vouch for is a "good person." Even when confronted with absolute proof of a child molester's crime, many people deny the evidence in favor of standing by the person they thought they knew. To do otherwise would reveal the failings of their own trust abilities.

In one case study, a vice president of a credit union bank was arrested for enticing a nine-year old to engage in sex. The defendant had a stable 35-year marriage, a 30-year career as a leader in the financial sector, was president of his homeowners' association, and was admired by many in his community. His best friend was a retired U.S. Secret Service agent of more than 20 years. The agent came to his defense in a court hearing and vouched for his friend's absolute law-abiding integrity. The prosecutor asked the Secret Service agent, "What would you have done if you knew of the defendant's sexual interest in children?" The agent answered that he would have taken his friend "behind the shed" and "beat the crap out of him." The federal magistrate judge astutely concluded that this is a crime so dark and so perverse that it is hidden from even the best of friends of over 20 years and a loving devoted wife of over 30 years (*United States v. Chris Becker*. Paraphrase of Federal Magistrate Judge Alan J. Baverman, March 2005, Northern District of Georgia. Assistant United States Attorney [AUSA] Aaron Danzig. Becker later pled guilty to traveling from state to state to entice a minor to engage in illicit sexual activity. The "minor" was fictional and portrayed by FBI Special Agent Michael L. Yoder in an online undercover role). The truth is that adults who sexually exploit children are men and women of virtually every age, personal characteristic, life experience, economic status, sexual preference, and history of offending. Many individuals who sexually exploit children using the Internet have the outward appearance of being normal, law-abiding citizens. It is generally accepted within the law enforcement community that no profile exists to preemptively identify a person sexually interested in children. Offenders range in age from 19 to 68 years old, are men and women involved in all types of adult relationships from single adult sex partners to long-term marriages, and they come from every social and financial strata of society. They work in menial jobs or have high-status careers from law enforcement officials to church staffers, come from business and financial sectors, are prominent leaders or are comfortably retired. Some are involved in children's groups, but not all. For those not actively around children, the common denominator is the computer and the Internet, which places them in direct contact with children and allows them the luxury of engaging in sexually explicit conversations with children without the fear of raising the suspicion of the child's adult caretakers.

MALE INTERNET PREDATORS

Indeed, the male Internet predator has the added comfort of assuming that whatever he does on the Internet comes with a veil of secrecy provided by the child. If the child reports the offensive behavior, the common response is loss of contact as the parent shuts down access. At most, a parent may respond to the predator, using the child's online identity, and will announce that he or she is the parent and that any further contact will result in a call to the local police. The predator just moves on. On the other hand, if the child maintains contact, the predator uses guilt to create a partnered bond of secrecy and further grooms the child to more explicit activity. The longer a child maintains contact, the more the child feels culpable and the more the predator gains control of his victim. The predator has many psychological tools at his disposal: sexual curiosity and experimentation, worldly knowledge, appraisal, friendship, guilt, projection of blame, rationalization, minimization of his actions, and pleasure. The predator also can use gifts, rewards, alcohol, drugs, pornography, and money to meet the child's needs. The Internet predator need only find, among millions of children using the Internet, one child willing to take the journey with him. The Internet predators offend one victim at a time but may do so for many years, engaging in sexual activity with many children.

In a study conducted at the Federal Correctional Institute in Butner, North Carolina, by Dr. Andreas Hernandez, director of the Federal Bureau of Prisons Sex Offender Treatment Program (SOTP), Hernandez collected data from 54 current and former inmates convicted of Internet sex crimes that involved possessing or distributing child pornography. Hernandez compared the number of contact sexual crimes divulged by the subjects or known by law enforcement before treatment and reported by the subjects after an intensive two-year psychological counseling program (with the understanding that any previously unknown offenses would not be punishable). Hernandez concluded that prior to treatment, the 54 subjects reported a total of 53 contact offenses. After treatment, the same study group admitted to an additional 1371 contact sex crimes that were never detected by, or reported to, the criminal justice system. In other words, these men had an average of 0.98 known victims before treatment and an average of 26.37 self-reported victims after participation in the treatment program. The other major conclusion that Dr. Hernandez revealed is that 79.6% of the subjects admitted to having prior contact sexual crimes after participation in the treatment program (Hernandez, 2000). Hernandez's study clearly shows the correlation between those who view child pornography and those who sexually molest children.

CHILD ABDUCTORS/RAPISTS

Sex offenders who abduct and rape children represent only a small fraction of sex offenders, but they capture the fears of American society. The idea of a child being raped, tortured, or even killed by a stranger is terrifying and so well reported by the media that when a "stranger abduction" occurs, the entire community becomes involved in the search for the child. However, a survey of kidnapping data conducted in 2002 for the U.S. Department of Justice revealed that of the roughly 261,000 children who are abducted each year, the majority (203,900) are taken by a family member—often in a custody dispute—and only 90 to 115 are victims of "stereotypical kidnapping"—that is, a stranger abduction (McNiff, 2009).

The sex offender who abducts and rapes a child does so, unlike their Internet counterparts, because this individual does not have the social skills to entice children to engage in sexually explicit conversations, share in secret and private activities that are sexually active, or accompany the person. Child molesters who abduct children do not have the social skills to convince a child to participate in sexual activities, and they do not have the skills to consummate their sexual activities and allow the child to go back to their normal caretakers without fearing that the child would have remorse or regret and would report their activities. Their behavior is usually more similar to that of the situational offender because they will abduct children who are victims of opportunity. These offenders are immature, have little formal education, work in lower-level unskilled jobs, have trouble getting or maintaining healthy sexual relationships with other adults, and have low self-confidence and low socialization skills. This offender may prefer the activities involving children because the offender is childlike in his behavior and he likes children for their less demanding ways. These offenders do not intend to harm the child when they plan their abductions; rather they have a fantasy that once they engage in sex with the child, that child will fall in love with them. The actual abduction is usually spontaneous. The reality of the forced rape causes the child to cry or fight back, and the offender realizes that he made a grave mistake and often only sees one recourse—to kill the child and hide the evidence.

FAMILY, FRIENDS, AND NEIGHBORS

Sexual offenders who sexually exploit children because they have easy access to children, either within their families or because of their close proximity to children, have the added burden of developing trust among the adult caretakers. Much has been written about the grooming of the child so that a child engages in sexual acts willingly and does not report the sexual activities with adults to their parents or to an authority figure. After all, the goal of most child molesters is not to act on their pedophilic interests once and then go to jail for the rest of their lives; it is to keep finding and molesting victims indefinitely. Therefore, offenders need to groom the adult caretakers who are around a child and develop levels of trust and confidence that defy suspicion. Even if the adult caretaker has a gut-level instinct to question the offender or if the child comes to the caretaker with allegations of inappropriate touching or behavior, the levels of trust are so strong that the caretaker feels impolite and will not address the issue with the offender. The caretaker used his or her own judgment to develop this relationship with the trusted friend or relative.

When the offender is a parent or close relative, the bonds of love or family loyalty also work in favor of the offender. If the offender is a close friend in a position of authority like a church leader, teacher, or coach, he is able to rely on his position to provide additional weight to his trust levels. Other parents and close neighbors also benefit from implied trust because they are viewed as "good people." In some cases, the levels of trust are so strong that when a child alleges an inappropriate act or comment directed toward them, the caretakers accuse the child of lying rather than taking his or her side. "After all," they reason, "all children lie." Besides, the moral implications of confronting a friend with an allegation such as this would be beyond any sense of political correctness and would permanently damage the friendship. Regardless, even if an offender is presented with allegations and he is able to successfully deflect the accusations (or if a child presents an allegation and is told by the caretaker to ignore it), the offender has been given carte blanche to continue the inappropriate acts or behavior toward that child with a higher degree of confidence.

FEMALE SEX OFFENDERS

Most studies show that at least 90% of child sexual abuse is committed by men (Sher, 2007) so who are the 10% women sex offenders? Most women who sexually abuse children do so against their own children. Forensic psychologist Dr. Anna C. Salter studied female sex offenders and created three categories. The first category is the incest abuser who molests her own children from a very early age, starting before the child reaches age six and sometimes continuing until the child reaches his or her teens. These women are immature, isolated, and without adult partners, and have psychotic personality defects in which they do not view themselves separate from their children. Salter termed this as "fusion" and is a psychological distortion in which mother cannot detach their children as separate entities after birth. Thus, the molestation is "masturbatory" rather than "molestation," as the child is a physical extension of the mother, more like an arm or a leg, rather than a sentient and separate human being. The second category is the teacher/lover abuser. This category captures media attention with teachers violating both the social norms of child sexual abuse and crossing the boundaries of school authority. These women are usually in their late twenties and early thirties and target middle school boys and girls who are sexually experimental and vulnerable to authority figures. The third category is the psychologically battered abusers. These women are submissive and timid; they still seek dominant male partners to control every aspect of their lives. These women may be so submissive that if combined with a dominant pedophile partner, they will acquiesce to participating in or allowing the sexual abuse of their children by the male partner. This form of female sex offender may even molest her children for the pleasure and benefit of her dominant male partners, even doing so when the male partner is not physically present.

SEX RINGS

Sex ring crime is a term that describes sexual victimization involving one or more adult offenders and several children who are aware of each other's participation. There are three different types of child sex rings.

Solo child sex rings are characterized by the involvement of multiple children in sexual activities with one adult, usually male, who recruits the victims into his illicit behavior by legitimate means. There is no exchange of photographs, nor are there sexual activities with other adults. This offender can be assessed by his methods for access to and sexual entrapment of the children, control of the children, maintaining the isolation and secrecy of the sexual activity, and by the particulars of ring activities. The events surrounding disclosure of the ring and the victims' physical and psychological symptoms are also important elements of the ring. Victims can be both male and female, and their ages can range from infancy to adolescence. The distinguishing factor is the age preference of the offender. Victims are found in nursery schools, baby-sitting and daycare services, youth groups, and camps.

By contrast, a syndicated sex ring involves multiple adults, multiple child victims, and a wide range of exchange of items including child pornography and sexual activities. At a level between these two types of rings is the transition sex ring, in which the children and pornography are exchanged between adults, often with money changing hands as well.

The transitional child sex ring involves multiple offenders as well as multiple victims. The offenders are known to each other and collect and share victims. In the transition sex ring, multiple adults are involved sexually with children, and the victims are usually pubescent. The children are tested for their role as prostitutes and thus are high risks for advancing to the syndicated level of the ring, although the organizational aspects of the syndicated ring are absent in transition rings.

It is speculated that children enter these transition rings by several routes:

1. Children may be initiated into solo sex rings by a pedophile who has lost sexual interest in the child as he or she approaches puberty and who may try, through an underground network, to move the vulnerable child into sexual activity with pederasts (those with sexual preferences for pubescent youths).
2. They may be incest victims who have run away from home and who need a peer group for identity and economic support.
3. They may be abused children who come from disorganized families in which parental bonding has been absent and multiple neglect and abuse are present.
4. They may be missing children who have been abducted or kidnapped and forced into prostitution.

A syndicated child sex ring uses a well-structured organization that involves the recruitment of children, production of pornography, delivery of sexual services, and establishment of an extensive network of customers. The syndicated ring involves multiple offenders as well as multiple victims. The syndicated child prostitution ring is a well-established commercial enterprise (Douglas, Burgess, Burgess et al., 1992).

Case Study 34-1

Transitional Child Sex Ring

A classic case example of a transitional child sex ring is more than 30 years old. From December 1977 to December 1978, described by one gay Boston newspaper as the year of the witch hunt, Boston was in the spotlight regarding a male youth prostitution ring. Earlier that year, the investigation of a solo child sex ring had led an assistant district attorney and police to uncover a second generation of rings. In the apartment of a man who had an extensive history of convictions for child molesting, investigators found numerous photos of naked youths as well as pornographic films. Sixty-three of the depicted youths were located and interviewed, and 13 agreed to testify before a grand jury. From this testimony, additional men (many with professional and business credentials) were indicted on counts of rape and abuse of a child, indecent assault, sodomy, and unnatural acts.

By December 1978, the trial of the first defendant, a physician, began. Testimony from four prosecution witnesses revealed the link between the two types of rings. According to news reports, the first witness, a man who was serving a 15- to 25-year term after pleading guilty to charges derived from the child solo ring, admitted to having sexual relations with boys as young as 10 during the 13 years he had rented the apartment. He testified that he could be considered a "master male pimp" and that he became involved in the sex-for-hire operation after meeting one of the other defendants. He said that initially no money was involved, but after a few months expenses increased, so the men were charged and the boys were given $5 to $10 for sexual services.

Newspapers reported that another prosecution witness, an assistant headmaster at a private boys' school, admitted visiting the apartment more than 40 to 50 times over a five-year period. He denied being a partner in a scheme to provide boys for hire but admitted to taking friends to the apartment with him and paying to have sex with the boys.

A prosecution witness, a 17-year-old, testified to being introduced to homosexual acts by the first witness, who had told the boys they could make all the money they wanted. "All we had to do was lay there and let them do what they wanted to us," he said.

Another victim testified that at age 12 he had met the third witness through friends. He received gifts of clothes and money for going to the man's apartment. While there, he would drink beer, smoke pot, and watch stag movies. He brought his younger brother to the apartment, and they both had sex with the man. At age 14 he was "turning tricks" and charging $10 for oral sex and $20 for anal sex. At that point he met the defendant.

The defendant, a pediatrician and psychiatrist, claimed in his defense that he went to the apartment as part of a research study, which was submitted to a journal after his indictment and subsequently published in a sex research journal.

The jury, sequestered for the 19-day trial, deliberated two and a half days before reaching a verdict of guilty. The judge sentenced the physician to five years' probation on the condition that he undergo psychiatric treatment. More than a year later, the state board of medicine revoked his license. The other defendants in the ring plea-bargained their charges, and there were no further trials.

CHILD PROSTITUTION

According to the U.S. Department of Justice, child prostitution estimates in the United States range from 300,000 to 800,000. Figures remain unaccountable because of the nature of how children become prostitutes—runaway, throw-away, and cast-off children from the foster care system are the main children who

Case Study 34-2

Syndicated Child Sex Ring

A child sex ring involved ten boys and one girl. In October 2007, information regarding the offender (Paul) was brought to the attention of a West Coast FBI office. The children involved ranged in ages from 8 to 16. Paul befriended a family with two boys and one girl; both parents worked. The parents grew to trust Paul and invited him to live in their house, renting out a bedroom to him. He drove a Cadillac equipped with a telephone, and he handed out business cards advertising a 24-hour limousine service that he provided with his Cadillac. At one point Paul made his child prostitutes wear beepers so that he could call the child he thought would best suit his customer's desires. Paul was constantly trying to recruit more children, and he would pick up runaways and use the children to recruit others.

Paul never gave any of his child prostitutes money, because he felt this would ruin them. Instead, he provided food and clothing, bought them various toys, and took them to amusement parks, sporting events, movie shows, and roller rinks.

The offender kept an apartment in a complex with a swimming pool and tennis courts. He used this apartment as a "crash pad" for many of his child prostitutes, and they used the pool and tennis courts. Paul told the older boys to keep the younger ones in line. Paul was sexually involved with several of his child prostitutes and provided Quaaludes to all the children. He also had a sizable collection of child pornography.

Because it was determined that no federal laws applied to Paul's activities, the case was turned over to local police. In November, Paul was convicted on seven felony counts (19 felony counts were dismissed), and in May he was sentenced to 13 years imprisonment and was declared a mentally disturbed sex offender.

become street kids. Left to fend for themselves, these boys and girls quickly become prey for small-time pimps and organized sex-trafficking rings. The breakdown of the family is one cause for children to run away from home. Absentee parents, marital separation, domestic violence, substance abuse, and incestuous sexual abuse are other contributing factors that force children to leave home without the means to take care of themselves. Pimps who understand this dynamic find these vulnerable children and create a pseudo-family environment by promising love, money, and affection. They then strip these children of whatever money they have and severely abuse them in order to establish dominance over them. The pimp acts as both manager and protector of the prostitutes, managing their time, money, and expenses and protecting the customers from law enforcement. Thus, adult "johns" can engage in sexual acts with a minor who is willing and experienced without fear of being reported after the act is done. Many child prostitutes who are "rescued" by law enforcement have such miniscule self-worth that they end up going back into prostitution because it is the only way they know to make a living (Whitehead, 2008).

CHILD SEX TOURISM

Another avenue for American consumers to pay for sex with children is to go to a country that is poverty-stricken or where the enforcement of sex with children is more lax or the government officials are corrupt. Although every country has laws against sex with children, many countries are known to pedophiles for the availability of children forced into prostitution. In addition, there are clandestine "sex tourism" agencies dedicated to booking the travel arrangements of Americans to come to their country and have sex with their boys and girls. Even before setting foot on foreign soil, "tourists" can find Internet websites that tell them everything they need to know about having sex with a child. These websites provide written endorsements of past "tourists," provide specific information to access a child prostitute, and even negotiate the price of the sex acts with the child. The majority of "tourists" are men from Western European countries, the United States, and Canada. In fact, North America accounts for a quarter of all child sex tourism around the world. Sex tourists seek children living in impoverished countries where they are often forced into prostitution by their own families who are desperate for money.

In the context of this discussion, children in other countries who are forced into prostitution are not an issue for healthcare professionals located in the United States. However, the men who go to other countries for this purpose often come back to the United States wanting more. For this reason, they often arrange to go overseas again or they seek children within their own communities or on the Internet. Although there are federal laws prohibiting American citizens from going to another country to engage in sexual activity with minors living outside of the United States, the ability to investigate or enforce this law is minimal, which emboldens these American citizens to continue their illegal activity (Bacon, 2007).

Compliant Victims

Many advocates of legalizing consensual sex between adults and children argue that as long as the child is willing and able, there is no harm. They assert that that the only harm is caused by the effects of societal condemnation of the behavior. Thus, children feel guilty about their involvement, suffer from "damaged goods syndrome," have low self-esteem, are depressed and suicidal, and express helpless rage because society has stigmatized sex between adults and children. The twisted logic is that if society would cease to condemn the behavior, then children could enjoy guilt-free sexual encounters with adults.

Although it is true that most adults impose their value system on children to protect them, the child molester believes he is promoting the free will of the child to choose. The fact is that the adult manipulates the "choice" and imposes the sexual behavior, which may be painful, intrusive, or overwhelming because of its novelty and sexual nature. The child has little or no knowledge of the societal or long-term personal implications of engaging in sexual acts with an adult, whereas the adult fully understands the implications. The adult may perceive that he is providing pleasure to the child when the ultimate goal is his own sexual gratification. Therefore, despite any amount of rationalization that molesters use on themselves or others, the sexual encounter is manipulative and primarily benefits the child molester.

Dr. Finkelhor described four general categories of negative effects associated with children of sexual abuse: traumatic sexualization, stigmatization, betrayal, and powerlessness. Children suffering traumatic sexualization experienced aversive feelings about sex, overvalued sex, and, subsequently, incurred sexual identity problems. Their behavioral manifestations constitute hypersexual behaviors or complete avoidance of or negative sexual encounters. Children rescued from sexual abuse suffer feelings of guilt and take responsibility for the abuse or the consequences of disclosure. Many times the adults implant the responsibility to keep "a secret" on the child, leading the child to believe that if the secret is revealed, it will be the child's fault. The child may become self-destructive and take on behaviors such as substance abuse, risk-taking acts, self-mutilation, suicidal gestures and acts, and provocative behavior to place him or herself in dangerous situations. Children who are victims of sexual abuse feel betrayed by people who should have been their protectors and nurturers. They lack fundamental trust with anyone and cannot connect emotionally with others. Thus, they display anger and borderline dysfunction. Other manifestations of their lack of trust include exploiting or manipulating others because they would rather manipulate others before they are manipulated by them. Finally, the mental age of the child becomes stymied, and the personality of the child victim remains intact as the child grows into adulthood. The "child victim" inner personality remains weak and vulnerable, while the growing person has a need to protect the inner "child victim" with an overwhelming desire to control others or prevail over any situation no matter the costs. The vulnerability effect of this powerlessness may lead to avoidant responses such as dissociation and running away, anxiety, sleep problems, elimination problems, eating problems, and revictimization (U.S. Department of Health and Human Services).

The overall argument of adult-child sex advocates focuses on the legal age of consent. *Consent* is the legal limitation, whereas *compliancy* is the emotional state of the victim. Most states currently use 16 years old as the legal age of consent to engage in sexual activity. Adult-child sex advocates want the abolishment of *any* age of consent and argue that the compliancy of the children make them *not* victims; therefore, no law is broken. In the course of his investigative experiences, the author has met and interviewed child molesters who advocate a constitutional amendment to abolish the age of consent for sexual purposes. There is a growing movement toward this goal.

Noncompliant Victims

Child victims who are brutally raped or forced to engage in sexual acts with adults have a real fear of serious injury or even death. Children are no physical match against adults who are bigger, stronger, and smarter; have more life skills and life experiences; and can outmaneuver even the most street-smart kids. The child rapist may not have the social skills to groom a child but can overwhelm a child physically. Once they engage in forced sex with a child, these rapists have little recourse to avoid punishment. They know they need to silence the child, not only during the sex act but afterward as well. Many times they resort to killing the child as a way to accomplish this goal. The unfortunate reality is that children who are abducted for the purpose of rape usually do not survive unless they can somehow convince the abductor that they will remain silent.

Grooming

Before the popularity of the Internet, child molesters seeking victims outside their immediate family, neighborhood, or sphere of influence had to create opportunities to interact with children. Some worked in occupations that put them in contact with children. Others volunteered as coaches or youth group leaders to gain the trust and confidence of potential victims and their parents. The offenders carefully "groomed" potential victims by cultivating relationships with the child and with the caretaker of the child. By making the parents feel comfortable, the molester is able to focus on the child, gradually sexualizing the relationship. After gaining access to the child victim, the molester may engage in a variety of pre-offense or grooming behaviors before actually molesting the child.

Grooming involves purposeful, calculated behavior that helps the offender perpetrate and continue the abuse and has been described as filling four basic functions. First, the offender cultivates the relationship with the child and her family to disarm them and build trust and emotional dependency. Second, the relationship gives the offender an opportunity to study and test the child while gradually overstepping boundaries such as the use of sexual jokes or discussion, affectionate touching, rough housing, "accidentally" walking in on a child in the bathroom or while the child is changing clothes, exposing themselves, or other inappropriate behaviors. If a child reacts negatively, the offender can apologize or explain away his actions without raising suspicion or fear. Third, once an offender has established himself as a "friend" and overcomes the child's resistance to being touched, the offender can advance the contact to include direct sexual touching. This may involve making the physical contact feel good, asking victims for permission to touch them, thanking them for the "special time" together, and presenting the image that the child is an equal partner.

Finally, most offenders use subtle forms of manipulation, coercion, or persuasion to maintain the child's silence. They may also resort to placing the responsibility of the sexual interest on the child or making the child feel guilty if he or she reports the abuse and gets the offender in trouble. Although this is still the most prevalent method to find victims, the public awareness of child sexual molestation makes these community contacts more difficult.

The Internet offers a way to contact children from the privacy of their homes. With the advances in computer technology, even the most computer illiterate consumers can become very knowledgeable of the Internet environment with relative ease. Sex offenders can "troll" cyberspace to meet and interact with millions of children. Child molesters regularly monitor online conversations, searching for vulnerable or sexually brazen children. They can disguise their identities to become someone else or perfect their "reality-based" identities, creating an "ideal self." It is interesting that everyone on the Internet is the ideal height and weight, has perfect skin complexion, never has any financial problems, and always know what to do. The problem is that avid Internet users may fall into the trap of believing this is real while working hard to project their idealized self on the Internet to compete with all of the other "people" on the Internet.

Novice Internet trolling child molesters quickly learn that they must "sell themselves" to children who are also on the Internet. There is fierce competition among adults vying for the attention of children—and the attention span of children is short-lived. The child molester learns ways to attract children, either through provocative sexual language or applicable topics of discussion. The adult becomes an expert on topics that children want to discuss. If a child is interested in soccer, the adult becomes an expert on soccer who is not only able to discuss the finer points of soccer play but offers to teach the child how to become better at soccer. The adult knows that children using the Internet seek to fill voids in their lives. The adult fills that void by becoming an expert in the subject matter of interest to the child as well as on how to communicate with children and gain their trust. In exchange, the molester only asks for the child's friendship and close physical contact. Later, the molester attempts to manipulate this friendship into a sexual encounter.

Child Pornography as an Industry

It is estimated that child pornography has become a $3 billion per year industry. In a study of child pornography possessors who were arrested between 2000 and 2001, 83% had images involving children under 12 years old, 39% had images of children between the ages of 3 and 5, and 19% had images of infants and toddlers. More than 20,000 new child pornography images are produced around the world every week.

Rather than focus on the dollar amounts or the numbers of images, the fact is that the distribution of child pornography remains primarily an act of addiction and sexual perversion more than a business venture. Many distributors of child pornography seek to trade images and videos for other images and videos of child pornography. The goal is sexual gratification. Also, the large amount of child pornography that is available for viewing provides rationalization to the collector. Many victims of child pornography are depicted in the images in a smiling, happy pose. If so many children are enjoying themselves by engaging in sexual acts, *it must not be so bad*, the argument goes. As more images and videos are collected, collectors not only have a steady supply of pornography for masturbation purposes but can also feel comfortable as "one of many" who enjoy child pornography. After all, they may reason, they are not the ones who are actually having sex with the children (although they wish they were). They are only vicariously enjoying an image of someone else's sexual pleasure. Therefore, they are not as bad as the adults who are molesting children.

Persons who enjoy looking at child pornography but have not yet acted on their desires may even argue that masturbating to the images satiates their desires so they do not have a need to act on their desires. Although this may be true in the short term (15 to 20 minutes after climax and ejaculation), looking at and enjoying child pornography helps to focus the desires and to perfect the fantasy-driven behavior. Over time, masturbating to images or videos may not be enough to satisfy their sexual hunger. They may progress to live video streams directing the actions of the child or directing the adult perpetrator to perform sexual acts on the child to performing actual sexual touching themselves to active sexual intercourse with a child.

One of the goals of collectors of child pornography is to collect an entire series of images—that is, every pornographic image of sexual abuse of a particular child that has captured their interest. There are bragging rights to the claim of having the entire series. Another goal is to collect the newest material or have in their possession images that others do not have, thereby trumping others in their level of collection. This demand for new material drives those who are sexually abusing children and then posting their images of abuse on the Internet to produce even more images in even more egregious sexual poses.

The child pornography collectors want to show their collections to others to justify that the enjoyment of child pornography is not just for the few but is desirable to a group that is growing in numbers. No longer does the pedophile feel alone and unable to communicate with others about his desires. Now the mass of child lovers is an emergent subset of society.

Medical Considerations

Cases involving child victims of sexual abuse need to be handled with extreme concern for the welfare of the child. Children, depending on age and circumstances, may be confused, may feel betrayed by people they thought they could trust, and may not be able to verbalize what happened to them physically or what is happening to them emotionally. The mantra of the forensic nurse examiner is that "children are not little adults"—and this applies to all professionals dedicated to serving child victims. In 1985, the first child advocacy center (CAC) established the concept of a multidisciplinary team (MDT), consisting of law enforcement, social services, prosecutors, victim services, medical professionals, and mental health professionals. The MDT is intended to reduce the trauma to an already victimized child, enhance the quality of the investigation, promote accountability, and increase the utilization of community services.

BEST PRACTICE Forensic nurses should be knowledgeable of indicators of sexual abuse, both physical and behavioral. Early recognition and intervention are keys to preventing continuing abuse and manipulation by an unknown or suspected predator.

Once a child victim is identified and rescued, careful consideration should be given to who interviews the child. Most CACs have trained forensic interviewers who are skilled in dealing with children, and many police departments train their child crimes detectives in forensic interviewing skills. Forensic interview techniques using the Rapport, Anatomy Identification, Touch Inquiry, Abuse Scenario, and Closure (RATAC) protocol has been established by organizations such as the National Association for the Prevention of Sexual Abuse of Children (NAPSAC) and the American Professional Society on the Abuse of Children (APSAC). The basic principle of forensic interviewing is that it is child friendly, nonintrusive, and uses open-ended and nonleading questions. Interviews are audiotaped and videotaped to prevent the need for repetitive interviews and to avoid repeating embarrassing disclosures to multiple strangers. If a child is ready to disclose, he or she will reveal sexual information that is more advanced than age appropriate. By contrast, however, the lack of disclosure does not mean that sexual abuse did not occur; it may simply mean that the child is not ready to disclose.

BEST PRACTICE The forensic nurse should ensure that specific actions are taken to support the child after disclosure because the child will be confused and frightened and may require protection.

Simultaneously, considerations need to be given to medically evaluate children for sexual abuse. Many times, when the medical examination is concluded there is no sign of sexual abuse. However, this does not indicate the lack of sexual abuse. Child victims often delay reporting their abuse, giving any lacerations time to heal. Pediatricians and medical professionals examining children for signs of sexual abuse need specialized training to be aware of all the normal and abnormal variations of physical trauma. The nurse examiner also needs to be familiar with an array of diseases, infections, and conditions that occur in children and are often mistaken for abuse.

BEST PRACTICE When the forensic nurse encounters child victims of pornography and sex rings, she or he should plan a support system that permits child attachment to a therapist who has expertise in child and adolescent trauma.

Every child victim of sexual abuse should be referred for a competent psychological evaluation. Understanding and verbalizing the trauma has been shown to be beneficial to the child, allowing the child to move beyond the abuse. It is also important for family members to understand the nature of the abuse so that they can adequately participate in the healing process (Taroli, 2009).

The integrated use of social services and victim services provides vital resources necessary for the child's healing.

Psychological Aspects of Being a Victim

The sexual abuse of children, as horrendous as it is, is not just one crime between a perpetrator and a child victim. Now it is a global crime. A child molester can meet and have sex with a child, take pictures of the rape, or even videotape the assault and send the images around the world in a matter of seconds. Not only do these perpetrators receive the instant physical gratification of the sexual act, they can relive the rape as they play the images and videos over and over again while receiving accolades from Internet admirers who can also enjoy the rape of a child over long distances. Some producers of child pornography will even grant directions or requests from their admirers, tailoring their rape of the child specifically to certain audiences. The child molesters can demand any number of rewards in return for "fresh" child pornography, ranging from money to gifts or favors to trade for other new child pornography of other victims. Most important, the child molester receives a position of honor among collectors of child pornography and pedophiles who enjoy viewing children as sexual objects.

Many victims of child pornography, because of their ages at the time of the sexual abuse, may not know or understand the global spread of child pornography. However, once they realize that the popularity of their images makes them pornographic "stars" of the Internet pedophile world, they are continually revictimized. The crime of sexual abuse is embarrassing, personal, and intimate beyond any scale of imagination. Broadcasting the sexual abuse by distributing images of it makes the abuse public. Some victims liken it to being raped in a crowded football stadium with the audience cheering on the abuser. Meanwhile the victim's most private and personal acts are openly displayed for the masturbatory pleasure of the audience. Victims of child pornography grow up with the knowledge that millions of strangers have enjoyed watching them being raped. They carry this knowledge with them for the rest of their lives.

Most images and videos of child pornography show children who look like they are willing participants in the sexual acts. The unfortunate truth is that this may be true. Whether the child was thoroughly groomed to accept the sexual abuse or is anticipating rewards or gifts for their compliance, the moment might contain some aspect of instant pleasure for the child. And no matter how perverse the circumstances, sexual acts may illicit a favorable physical response. This is a standard defense argument in adult rape cases in which a male being sodomized has an erection or a woman being brutally raped shows physical aspects of pleasure. It is *not* a sign of enjoyment; rather it is an involuntary physical reaction to touch. For the victims, seeing their own physical reactions elicits the feeling of shame or self-blame. The child who is compliant because he or she was manipulated or groomed by the adult must rationalize the extent of their willing involvement. What is worse for the victim, to accept blame for their willing participation or to acknowledge that they were fooled? Either option will likely lead to self-destructive behaviors. Many girls grow up with low or no self-esteem, acting inwardly to destroy themselves. Many boys grow up angry at the world, exerting violence on others and destroying others around them.

It is important for forensic psychiatric nurses to consider the fact that this history may be a factor in a patient profile and the patient may not have shared this traumatic past to avoid being revictimized or humiliated again. Careful, unbiased, and consistent communication skills are necessary to break the barriers these patients have. Trust and rapport must be developed slowly and over time, something that (inpatient) healthcare does not afford.

Moral Considerations

Small groups of militant and highly organized child molesters operate through pedophile organizations such as the North American Man-Boy Love Association (NAMBLA), the Pedophile Alert Network (PAN), and Butterfly Kisses (which promotes woman-girl love). The pedophile activists promote the idea of the adoption of "value-neutral terminology such as intergenerational intimacy and attraction" and defining a child as "one who has not achieved adulthood"; redefining the term "child sexual abuse" as "adult-child sex," in which a child has a "willing encounter with positive reactions"; promoting the idea that children can consent to sex with adults; questioning the assumption of physical or psychological harm; promoting "objective" research supporting the benefits of adult-child sex; and declassifying pedophilia as a mental illness. Child molesters are "child lovers" who are promoting the emancipation of children's freedom to choose. Organized efforts are occurring to slowly change perceptions toward pedophilic behavior. These efforts include academic discussions, legal decisions in favor of the child molester, political petitions to enact laws to abolish the age of consent or to move the age of consent lower, and opinions of pedophile advocacy groups.

The loosening of moral values in American society, while not directly linked to pro-pedophile interests, helps fuel the debate. The "Lolita effect," described as the sexual objectification of young girls, is targeting girls of increasingly younger ages. Lolita, a character in the book written by Nabokov, is a 12-year-old seductress who flaunts her sexuality and is responsible for attracting and seducing the much older Humbert, a hapless fool of a man under her "spell." Of course, the fantasy story places all of the blame on Lolita, not Humbert.

Today's young girls are told that their self-worth is based on their being "hot." Mainstream children's clothing stores market pushup bras and thong underwear with slogans like "Eye Candy" for pre-teen girls. Tesco, an enormous and popular British chain store, carried both the Peekaboo Pole Dancing Kit, a play set designed to help "unleash the sex kitten inside" and Peekaboo Strip Poker "for outrageously naughty fun" on its website in the toys and games section until pressure from consumers and outside agencies forced the company to remove the kits and redirect the sales to another part of the website. Interestingly, comments from readers submitted to the online blog carried mixed reviews about the "error" on Tesco's part. Makeup kits are designed for girls as young as four or five years old. Media and marketers give the message that girls need to be thin, glossed, and scantily clad. And, of course, they need to purchase products to help them achieve this goal. The American Psychological Association (APA) released a report that calls for the media and advertising to stop sexualizing young girls. The APA Task Force on the Sexualization of Girls studied published research on the content and effects of media (including TV, movies, music videos, lyrics, magazines, videogames, and the Internet) and found that the consequences of the sexualization of girls in media today are very real and are likely to be a negative influence on girls' healthy development.

FALSE ALLEGATIONS OF CHILD SEXUAL ABUSE

While it is important to consider the needs of a child victim, an investigator must keep the proper perspective on evaluating the significance of the victim's experiences. Since most cases of child sexual abuse are between an offender and a victim who know the identities of each other, the question becomes not "who did it?", but "what happened?" During the 1970's through the 1990's, the prevailing view was to believe the victim with absolute certainty. In child sexual abuse cases, it was believed that "children never lie about sexual abuse or exploitation. If they have details, it must have happened."[1] Interviewers of child victims would take detailed notes as children used anatomically correct dolls or gender specific drawings to point out where they were "touched" or had to touch the offender. However, children, for a variety of reasons, have been known "to fantasize, furnish false information, furnish misleading information, misperceive events, try to please adults, respond to leading questions, and respond to rewards." Children have the same faults as adults – they are human. It is up to the investigator to maintain an objective viewpoint and get to the truth. Part of the problem is that many in society have an issue with offenders who are not completely "bad" or with victims who are not completely "innocent". When an interviewer is asking a child about victimization which may have occurred multiple times over many years, which event is the interviewer asking about? It is hard to conceive that a child willingly went back for more of the same, or that a child enjoyed the sexual event. The interviewer wants to "save" the child, but the child may not want to be saved.

What about the offender? When we use terms such as "sexual predator" to describe the offender, we conjure up an emotional image that is soothing to us but is not necessarily accurate. There are child sex offenders who willingly describe themselves as boy lovers, girl lovers, child lovers, and pedophiles but will adamantly argue that they are not predators. "The label predatory conjures up an evil type of image that they're evil monsters, dirty old men in wrinkled rain coats, a wolf in sheep's clothing. Men prowling around and mean nasty people. And while there are people who fit that, a lot of these guys are pillars of the community. They go to church on Sunday and they're nice to their neighbors".[2] Many of these offenders make every effort to pull a child out of chaotic conditions and offer a better life, giving the child material things, emotional support, and attention. The child, in return, draws nearer, willingly accepting the benefits of this new provider. The price tag for the offender is sexual gratification and silence… and the child accepts this cost. Society is appalled at this concept of trading rewards for sexual favors but neglects to make a connection to similar patterns in adult behavior. If all child sex offenders are considered to be predators, the forensic community risks dismissing the actions of those who do not see themselves as predators. Furthermore the proper image may not be presented to a child victim who sees the adult benefactor as someone who is interested in them as a sexual partner. These same victims, when confronted by authorities, will be either confused by any allegations of sexual abuse or will overtly defend the offender through lies, half-truths, and deception. In the child's eyes, the authorities are the "bad guys" who will take away the child's treasure box of future gifts, continuing emotional support and attention by locking up the offender. Moreover, the child will face the guilt of being a compliant and willing partner, the scrutiny of society's moral values, and the pity of health care providers who want to help the

[1]Kenneth V. Lanning, *"Investigator's Guide to Allegations of 'Ritual' Child Abuse"*, Behavioral Science Unit, National Center for the Analysis of Violent Crime, Federal Bureau of Investigation, FBI Academy, Quantico, Virginia 22135 (1992)
[2]"Former FBI Agent Says Sex Offender Label is Problematic", http://www.waaytv.com/global/story.asp?s=8042757, March 19, 2008. Quote is from retired FBI Supervisory Special Agent Kenneth V. Lanning.

child understand. The light of discovery is truly scarier than the dark pain of sexual abuse.

Hopefully, we will learn from the hysteria of previous investigations of ritual sexual abuse which turned out to be false. The McMartin preschool trial in the 1980's featured satanic ritual abuse (SRA), hidden tunnels, killing animals, and orgies as the employees allegedly engaged in sex with the children. The McMartin preschool trial highlighted society's fear of the unknown. After seven years of criminal trials, no convictions were obtained, and all charges were dropped. Other controversial cases showed that children were giving false confessions with no corroboration, well-meaning adults were using hypnosis and other means to search for repressed memories, or other adults, with not so well-meaning intentions, were using coercion or implanting suggestions to get children to provide confessions which corroborated other children's confessions. Many of these highly publicized cases featured overzealous fanatics who looked upon children as needing to be saved from the evil sexual predators.

The objective professional investigator will evaluate all of the evidence with the goal of getting to the truth. Child abuse investigators need to equip themselves with the tools of proper forensic interviewing techniques. An investigator understanding the overall concept of forensic interviewing techniques will use every means available to preserve the integrity of the child's interview and allow the child to tell his or her story, meanwhile preventing contamination, coercion, or suggestive topics from entering into the story. The forensic interviewer understands that contamination starts even before the interview and the astute interviewer will attempt to minimize this contamination and understand how it may be reflected in the child's interview. The video and audio taping of these interviews will display the gentle and objective open-ended questioning of the interviewer and the subtle nuances of the child's answers and will minimize defense allegations of coercion, implanting, or manipulation of memories. After the interview, the investigator needs to evaluate the interview and attempt to corroborate as much as possible.

Resources

WEBSITES

Department of Justice: Office of Justice Programs
Office of Juvenile Justice and Delinquency Prevention
National Criminal Justice Reference Service. www.ojjdp.ncjrs.org
Federal Bureau of Investigation (FBI)–Crimes Against Children
www.fbi.gov/hq/cid/cac/crimesmain.htm
National Center for Missing & Exploited Children (NCMEC)
www.missingkids.com
Netsmartz
www.netsmartz.org; www.netsmartzkids.org

References

American Psychiatric Association (APA). (2000). *Diagnostic and statistical manual of mental disorders: DSM-IV-TR, Section 302.2, 256–257*, Washington, DC.

Bacon, B. (2007, July 17). Stolen innocence: Inside the shady world of child sex tourism. ABC news, http://abcnews.go.com/TheLaw/story?id=3385318&page=1&CMP=OTC-RSSFeeds0312. Accessed July 20, 2009.

Burgess, A. W., & Grant, C. (1988). *Children exploited through sex rings.* Arlington, VA: National Center for Missing & Exploited Children.

Child molesters: A behavioral analysis for law enforcement officers investigating cases of child sexual exploitation. pp. 5–9.

Douglas, J. E., Burgess, A. W., Burgess, A. G., & Ressler, R. K. (1992). *Crime classification manual.* San Francisco: Jossey-Bass.

Effects of Sexual Abuse on its Victim. www.childwelfare.gov. Accessed June 18, 2009.

Finkelhor, D. (1994). Current information on the scope and nature of child sexual abuse. *The Future of Children, 4*(2), 31, 46–48.

Enough is enough: Protecting our children online. (2005). *Child pornography.* www.enough.org/inside.php?tag=statistics. Retrieved June 2009, http://ogc.fbinet.fbi/usabook/usabook/ceos/01ceos.htm

Hernandez, A. E. Director, Federal Bureau of Prisons, Sex Offender Treatment Program. (2000). *Self-reported contact sexual crimes of federal inmates convicted of child pornography offenses.* Presented at the 19th Annual Conference Research and Treatment Conference of the Association for the Treatment of Sexual Abusers, San Diego, CA.

Lanning, K. V. Supervisory Special Agent. Federal Bureau of Investigation, Behavioral Science Unit. (1992). Child molesters: A behavioral analysis for law enforcement officers investigating cases of child sexual exploitation, pp. 5–9.

McNiff, T. (2009). *Child abductions by strangers actually rare.* Special to *The Gainesville Sun*, Florida. The survey is known as the National Incidence Studies of Missing, Abducted, Runaway and Thrownaway Children (NISMART).

National Center for Missing and Exploited Children. (2005). Child pornography possessors arrested in internet-related crimes. *National Juvenile Online Victimization Study.* Retrieved June 2009. www.unh.edu/ccrc/national_juvenile_online_victimization_publications.html

Peters, J. M. *Assistant United States Attorney.* District of Idaho, July 2001, section 1.18. The "grooming" process in the seduction of children. http://ogc.fbinet.fbi/usabook/usabook/ceos/01ceos.htm

"Pedophile organizations and activism. (2009, March 23), www.Section21.m6.net/prf-activism.php. Retrieved July 14, 2009.

Project Safe Childhood. (2006). *Protecting Children from Online Exploitation and Abuse.* Washington, DC: U.S. Department of Justice.

Salter, A. C. (2003). *Predators: Pedophiles, rapists, & other sex offenders: Who they are, how they operate, and how we can protect ourselves and our children.* New York: Basic Books.

Section 21 Tactical Corps (2009). Pedophile Organizations and Activism.

Sher, J. (2007). *Caught in the web: Inside the police hunt to rescue children from online predators.* New York: Carroll & Graf Publishers.

Statistics on pornography, sexual addiction, and online perpetrators. (2003). National Society for the Prevention of Cruelty to Children.

Taroli, A. (2009). Medical examination of sexually abused children. In *Practical aspects of rape investigation: A multidisciplinary approach.* (4th ed., pp. 289–319) Boca Raton, FL: CRC Press.

United States v. Chris Becker. Paraphrase of Federal Magistrate Judge Alan J. Baverman, March 2005. Northern District of Georgia: Assistant United States Attorney (AUSA) Aaron Danzig.

U.S. Department of Health and Human Services. *Administration for Children and Families, Children's Bureau and authored by Child Welfare Information Gateway. The Effects of Sexual Abuse on its Victim.* www.childwelfare.gov, a service of the, www.enotalone.com/article/9935.html. Accessed July 16, 2009.

U.S. Department of Justice. *Office of Juvenile Justice and Delinquency Prevention web site.* ICAC program summary. http://ojddp.ncjrs.org/programs Retrieved July 20, 2009.

Whitehead, J. W. (2008). *Children of the night: Child prostitution is America's dirty little secret.* Accessed July 20, 2009. www.huffingtonpost.com.

Wolak, K., Mitchell, K., & Finkelhor, D. (2006). *Online Victimization: 5 Years Later, (NCMEC 07–06–025).* Alexandria, VA: National Center for Missing and Exploited Children.

Cliff Akiyama

Youth gang violence has continued its upward trend nationwide, as one cannot turn on the television or radio or open the newspaper without hearing about another one of its victims. It was once thought that gangs only convened in selected areas, which left churches, schools, and hospitals as "neutral" territory. Unfortunately, this is a fallacy. Gang violence has poured into the schools, community centers, and hospitals. Throughout the country in urban, suburban, and rural communities, healthcare professionals are constantly being challenged by intramural shootings between rival gang members on a daily basis. Whether it is out in the community or in a hospital setting, as first-hand witnesses of youth gang violence, healthcare professionals represent a highly skilled community resource in the modern multiagency approach to help combat this new form of domestic terrorism. Youth gang violence has continued its upward trend nationwide according to the Department of Justice, Office of Juvenile Justice and Delinquency Prevention. Furthermore, youth gangs have been identified in every single state. Nationwide, there are 24,500 gangs with a total gang membership of more than 750,000. The ethnic composition of these gangs includes 47% Latino, 31% African American, 13% Caucasian, 7% Asian, and 2% of mixed ethnicities (OJJDP, 2008).

KEY POINT The forensic nurse serves a vital role in the suppression, intervention, and prevention of youth gangs and associated violence.

The goals of this chapter are to (1) explain the organization of youth street gangs, (2) examine the historical evolution of gangs in the United States, (3) distinguish the behavioral differences and similarities between gangs, (4) compare and contrast activities of various gangs, and (5) determine gang implications for forensic nurses.

GETTING STARTED: WHAT IS A YOUTH GANG?

To discuss implications associated with youth gangs, we must first understand the term *youth gang*. The Virginia Gang Investigators Association (VGIA) has defined the term and has outlined the essential characteristics of a gang (VGIA, 2008). Part of the problem in the youth gang debacle across the nation is determining the definition of a youth gang. There are so many variations in the definition that it is hard for law enforcement agencies at the local, state, and federal levels to agree on one uniform definition; therefore, a definition of a youth gang is *agency specific*. In response to having multiple variations of the definition and no uniformity, statewide gang investigator associations such as the VGIA in conjunction with regional gang investigator associations such as the East Coast Gang Investigators Association (ECGIA) have developed their own definition. Their formally accepted definition is used by the member agencies in court proceedings and public venues.

A **youth gang** must be ongoing (associate on a continuous or regular basis). The youth gang could be formal or informal. Moreover, the youth gang must consist of at least three members and have a name, hand sign, and symbol that is identifiable. Another important element of a youth gang is that one of the primary objectives must be criminal activity (VGIA, 2008). So that it is not confused with various social groups such as fraternities, sororities, or social clubs, what differentiates a youth gang from other groups is its criminal activity. Law enforcement must define gangs and affirmatively determine which group is a gang. The public, defense attorneys, and the judiciary continue to challenge most declarations of what is and what is not a youth gang.

Gang Member Typologies

In every gang across the nation, there are various types of gang members ranging from hardcore to wannabe members. The most plentiful type of gang member is the active/regular gang member making up between 4% and 50% of the gang (Akiyama, Comparini, & Nepomuceno, 1997; VGIA, 2008). Regular gang members admit that they are in a gang when asked. They also have gang-related tattoos, are involved in gang-related crimes, and have a past history of gang activity. Associate/affiliate gang members make up 20% to 30% of the gang (Akiyama et al., 1997; VGIA, 2008). Associate and regular gang members also use hand signs to communicate with each other and to other rival gangs. Associate and regular gang members also write gang graffiti, wear gang-related clothing (colors), associate with known gang members, and are included in gang photos. What sets associates apart from regular members is that they are able to freely come and go in and out of the gang at will, making them great informants for law enforcement. The hardcore gang members, known as "OGs" (original gangsters), make up 10% to 20% of the gang and form the primary leadership arm of the gang group (Akiyama et al., 1997; VGIA, 2008). Hardcore gang members fit into all of the criteria listed for regular and associate members, but they are also involved in narcotics distribution. Furthermore, hardcore gang members are involved in violent gang activity from assaults, shootings, and robberies, to murder. Wannabes are the last group of gang member types. Wannabes make up less than 10% of the gang; however, they are extremely dangerous (Akiyama et al., 1997; VGIA, 2008). Although other gang member types have the potential to be extremely dangerous as well, the dangerousness of the wannabes lies in their motivation to be part of the gang to begin with. The wannabes need to prove that they are "down" and have "heart" (dedication) for the gang because in the gang hierarchy, wannabes are at the bottom. To be dedicated to the gang, the wannabes are instructed by the OG to prove that they have heart for the gang by performing a gang-related crime such as killing a rival gang member or committing a robbery or property crime such as burglary (Akiyama et al., 1997; VGIA, 2008).

In determining a gang member typology, it is important to use the strongest of initial criteria to classify a suspected gang member. For example, if an individual is documented for writing gang graffiti, wears gang colors, and admits that he or she is a gang member, this individual should be classified as a gang member. To list a person as a hardcore gang member, only one of the criteria for hardcore members needs to be met. Any evidence of heavy gang involvement must be thoroughly documented.

Manifestations of Youth Gang Violence: Why Are Our Children in Gangs?

Why would someone want to join a gang? The following are just some reasons.

IDENTITY OR RECOGNITION

This allows the gang member to achieve a level or status he feels impossible outside the gang culture. Most gang members visualize themselves as warriors or soldiers protecting their neighborhood from what they perceive to be a hostile outside world.

PROTECTION

Many members join because they live in the gang area and are, therefore, subject to violence by rival gangs. Joining guarantees support in case of attack and retaliation for transgressions.

FELLOWSHIP AND BROTHERHOOD

To the majority of gang members, the gang is a substitute for a family cohesiveness lacking in the gang member's home environment. Many older brothers and relatives belong to or have belonged to the gang.

INTIMIDATION

Some members are forced into joining by their peer group. Intimidation ranges from extorting lunch money to beatings. If a particularly violent war is in progress, the recruitment tactics used by the gang can be extremely violent, even to the point of murdering someone to cause others to conform.

OTHER FACTORS

Other motivations for joining a gang include the need to make money, narcotics distribution, control over the environment, racial and cultural similarities, acceptance by peers, the loyalty and reward of just being part of the gang, recruitment, control of turf or territorial neighborhood, and common enemies. However, the most pervasive motive for joining a youth gang is a sense of finally belonging to a group that respects the individual.

BEST PRACTICE The forensic nurse must thoroughly document historical or physical evidence that confirms youth gang affiliation.

African-American Gangs

African-American gangs are probably the most well known because of the media portrayal of gangs. The primary motivation of African-American gangs is earning money and narcotics distribution (Akiyama et al., 1997; Huff, 2001; Jackson, 2000; Klein, 1997; Leet, Rush, & Smith, 2000; Schmidt & O'Reilly, 2007, Thornberry, Krohn, Lizotte, Smith, & Tobin, 2003; Valdez, 2005, 2007). African-American gangs are divided up into "sets" based on geographic location; as a result, African-American gangs are territorial, meaning

that they "claim" the neighborhood for which they often reside as belonging to that particular gang and no other gang can claim that territorial area (Egley, Maxson, Miller, & Klein, 2006; Franzese, Coivey, & Menard, 2006; Huff, 2001; Leet et al., 2000). Furthermore, in an African-American gang, the individual is important, not the entire gang group (Akiyama et al., 1997; Huff, 2001; Jackson, 2000; Klein, 1997; Leet et al., 2000; Valdez, 2005, 2007). An African-American gang member often will have a moniker or nickname, which is an arbitrary name given to a particular gang member that represents some characteristics that the individual wants to draw out (Leet et al., 2000). African-American gang members often wear identifying colors that indicate their gang affiliation, such as red clothing, shoes, and hats for Bloods and blue clothing, shoes, and hats for Crips (Akiyama et al., 1997; Huff, 2001; Jackson, 2000; Klein, 1997; Leet et al., 2000; Valdez, 2005, 2007). Since the early 1990s, the Crips and the Bloods have been two of the most popular, polarized, and often glorified African-American gang groups in the United States, due in large part to the media portrayal of these two groups.

CRIPS

The Crips were founded around 1968 by Raymond Washington from the East Side (of Interstate-110 Harbor Freeway) in South Central Los Angeles, California. "Ray Ray," as he was often known on the streets, originally formed a gang called the Baby Avenues, but after he got into a fight with another member, he decided to start his own gang called the Crips (Akiyama et al., 1997; Huff, 2001; Jackson, 2000; Klein, 1997; Leet et al., 2000; Valdez, 2005, 2007). The gang derived its name from a popular television show that Washington enjoyed, called *Tales from the Crypt*. It was also rumored that Washington's gang liked to "cripple" rival gangs (Leet et al., 2000). By 1971, Stanley "Tookie" Williams and Jamiel Barnes from the West Side of Interstate-110 Harbor Freeway joined Washington and the Crips (Huff, 2001).

The Crips identify with the color blue because Raymond Washington attended Washington High School in South Central Los Angeles, California, where the school color was navy blue (Akiyama et al., 1997; Huff, 2001; Leet et al., 2000) (Fig. 35-1). The Crips also display their colors on the left side. They also are allies

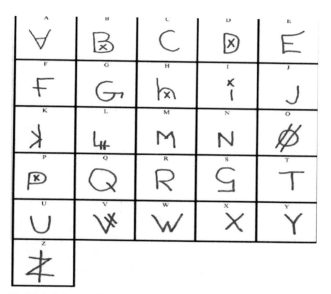

Fig. 35-1 Crip gang alphabet

with Folk Nation, an entirely separate gang located on the East Coast. It is important to note that Folk Nation is not a Crip gang, but the two are considered allies. The same is true with Bloods and People Nation. People Nation is not a Blood gang, but they too are allies. The Crips are rivals of the Bloods and People Nation, and they refer to the Bloods as "Slobs" or "Blobs" (Valdez, 2005). Graffiti is commonly referred to as the "newspaper of the streets" because of the information one can gain from reading it. Graffiti reveals the name of the gang, set, clique, and the specific members who have created it as a means to convey a message to their rivals (Akiyama et al., 1997; Huff, 2001; Jackson, 2000; Klein, 1997; Leet et al., 2000; Valdez, 2005, 2007). Crips write their alphabet in either blue or black (Leet et al., 2000).

BLOODS/PIRU

Unlike the Crips, which constitutes only one gang, there are three types of Blood gangs: (1) Los Angeles, California, affiliated, (2) independent, (3) United Blood Nation (UBN), which are most commonly found on the East Coast.

The Los Angeles–affiliated Bloods were founded around 1972 by Sylvester Scott and Vincent Owens from Centennial High School in Compton, California (Akiyama et al., 1997; Huff, 2001; Jackson, 2000; Klein, 1997; Leet et al., 2000; Valdez, 2005, 2007). Scott lived on Piru Street and fought Crip gang members who had been expanding throughout South Central Los Angeles since 1968 (Leet et al., 2000). In general, the Bloods are smaller than the Crips but are more cohesive. The Bloods identify with the color red, and whereas the Crips display their colors on the left side, the Bloods display their colors on the right side (Valdez, 2005) (Fig. 35-2). The Bloods are allies with the People Nation gang and are enemies of the Crips and Folk Nation. The Bloods refer to Crips as "Crabs" (Valdez, 2005). Bloods write their alphabet in either red, white, or green (Leet et al., 2000) (Fig. 35-3).

UNITED BLOOD NATION

The United Blood Nation (UBN) was founded in 1993, inside the prison system of New York's Rikers Island, by Leonard "Deadeye" McKenzie, known as the Godfather of the East Coast Bloods (Huff, 2001; Valdez, 2005, 2007). McKenzie started the 9-Trey, set and Omar Porter (OG Mack) started the 1–8 Trey set of the UBN (Valdez, 2005), remembering that a "set" is based on geographic location for African-American gangs. For the UBN, selected numbers have specific meanings and are very important, since one will find number sets displayed as graffiti in public places or as body

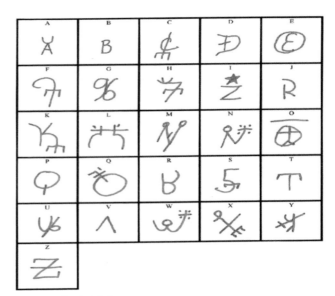

Fig. 35-3 Blood alphabet

tattoos. UBN gang members will often use 031, indicating 0 for under blood nation, 3 for the number of fingers thrown up when they form the letter "b," and 1 for one love under blood; 10/31 is also known as "Blood Day," which is also the day of Halloween. The number 021 represents the 0 for fear of nation, 2 for new life under blood, and 1 for bloods together. The numbers 9 and 3 are also important to associate with UBN because of the sets that Leonard McKenzie and OG Mack started (Valdez, 2005).

Besides using specific number sets as graffiti or body tattoos, the UBN uses the following colors in its graffiti. Green indicates the money that United Blood Nations earns and the marijuana that the members smoke. Brown represents the dirt that they bury "Crabs" or Crips under (Valdez, 2005). The United Blood Nation also uses a five-pointed star in its graffiti, tattoos, and clothing; each point of the star represents a specific ideology of the UBN. The symbolism of the five-pointed star represents being African American, unity, communication, loyalty, and an understanding of the rules and regulations of the UBN (Valdez, 2005) (Fig. 35-4). Another symbol is the red, segmented apple. When an apple falls from the tree, it splits into four segments. These four segments

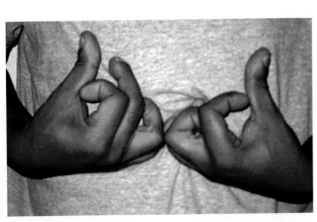

Fig. 35-2 Blood gang hand sign

Fig. 35-4 Five-pointed star of the United Blood Nation (UBN) gang on an official in-service US military high mobility multipurpose wheeled vehicle

represent the UBN's rival gangs: the Crips, the Latin Kings (a Latino gang), and the Netas (a Latino gang), with the final segment representing all that oppose the Bloods, whether rival gangs or the community at large (Valdez, 2005). A bulldog and a set of dog paws are also popular with the UBN as seen in graffiti, tattoos, and clothing. The bulldog and dog paws are to give respect to the gang's founder, Omar "OG Mack" Porter. A subtle indicator and another tribute to OG Mack is the Mack Truck logo on clothing, tattoos, or graffiti. It is often unknown to non-UBN gang members of their greeting to each other. UBN gang members greet each other by saying, "Soooo Wooooo," which is a common greeting to other UBN gang members (Valdez, 2005). UBN and other Blood gangs often use the word "Damu" in verbal and written communication. *Damu* is Swahili for "blood." UBN gang members will also spraypaint the letters "MOB" as graffiti, which means "Member of Blood" (Valdez, 2005, 2007).

FOLK NATION

The Folk Nation gang was formed in late 1960s by David Barksdale, the founder of the Black Disciples (BD) set, and Larry Hoover, the founder of the Gangster Disciples (GD) set in Chicago, Illinois (Huff, 2001; Valdez, 2005, 2007). The Folk Nation adopted the Jewish Star of David as its main symbol in honor of David Barksdale (Huff, 2001; Valdez, 2005, 2007). The symbolism of the star represents love, life, loyalty, knowledge, wisdom, and understanding (Fig. 35-5). It is common to see the Star of David as graffiti for the Folk Nation. The Folk Nation has two mottos—"All Is One" and "Folk before Family"—to illustrate its ideology (Valdez, 2005). Not to be confused with the Bloods, the Folk Nation identify to the right side. The Folk Nation also uses a pitchfork in its graffiti, and each point represents mind, body, and the soul coming together in "One Nation" (Valdez, 2005) (Figs. 35-6 and 35-7). As mentioned previously, the Folk Nation is allied with the Crips. The Folk Nation also uses specific number sets, such as 7-4-14 (for the letters GDN, as in Gangster Disciples Nation) and 2-15-19 (BOS, which stands for "Brothers of the Struggle") (Valdez, 2005).

PEOPLE NATION

The People Nation gang was formed to counter the Folk Nation alliance. It was founded by Jeff Fort, of the Black P Stone Rangers set and later the El Rukn, along with Bobby Gore, of the Vice

Fig. 35-6 Folk Nation symbols

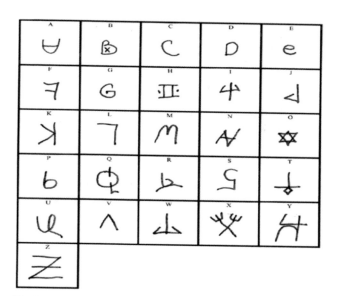

Fig. 35-7 Folk Nation alphabet

Fig. 35-5 Six-pointed Star of David of the Folk Nation/Black Disciples gang

Lords set (Huff, 2001; Valdez, 2005, 2007). The People Nation uses a five-pointed star as its main symbol of identification. Moreover, members use the number 21 to represent the 21 original sets of the gang. The People Nation is also allied with the Bloods. Some other identifying features include the number 5. The People Nation displays its colors of red/black and gold/black (Vice Lords) to the left side (Figs. 35-8 and 35-9). Lastly, the People Nation has two mottos: "All Is Well" and "All Is All" (Valdez, 2005).

Fig. 35-8 People Nation symbols

Fig. 35-9 People Nation alphabet

Latino Gangs

Latino gangs are motivated by a state of mind driven by *La Raza*, which translated means "for the race" (Akiyama et al., 1997; Huff, 2001; Jackson, 2000; Katz, & Webb, 2006; Klein, 1997; Leet et al., 2000; Schmidt & O'Reilly 2007; Thornberry et al., 2003; Valdez, 2005, 2007). It is important to note that La Raza is more of a cultural ideology than a gang-related one (Valdez, 2005, 2007). Nevertheless, Latino gangs are extremely territorial, and unlike African-American gangs, where the individual is important, for Latino gangs it is the gang as a whole that is important

and not the individual (Akiyama et al., 1997; Huff, 2001; Leet et al., 2000; Valdez, 2005, 2007). To illustrate this point, when Latino gang members go to prison, they will be controlled by one of two prison gangs, depending on the geographic location of the prison: La Eme or Nuestra Familia (Huff, 2001; Leet et al., 2000; Valdez, 2005). La Eme, otherwise known as the Mexican Mafia, is a prison gang originating in California and is considered the leadership arm of all Latino gangs in Southern California (Akiyama et al., 1997, Leet et al., 2000, and Valdez, 2005). The letter "M" in Spanish is pronounced "eme" and is the 13th letter of the alphabet. Consequently, throughout Southern California, Latino gangs will often call themselves by the city or area that they represent, followed by the number 13 to indicate "La Eme" or "Southern", thereby giving respect to the Mexican Mafia. In Northern California, the Nuestra Familia, which is translated to mean "our family," is the prison gang that controls every Latino gang north of Fresno and is often indicated by the number 14, representing the letter "N" for Nuestra and Northern (Leet et al., 2000; Valdez, 2005).

At one time in the early 1960s, La Eme and Nuestra Familia were united as one prison gang called "La Eme". It was not until the late 1960s when the two gangs began to separate to form two distinct prison gangs. This separation took place because the Latino gang members from Los Angeles in Southern California mocked fun of the predominantly migrant farm workers of Central and Northern California, thinking that the migrant factory workers in Los Angeles were better off financially and socially than the farmers of Fresno and Delano. However, these two Latino, predominantly Mexican-American prison gangs, have total control over the entire Latino street gang population throughout the state of California and Mexico—even Latino gangs who are rivals out on the street are, once incarcerated, under the control of either La Eme or Nuestra Familia, depending on geographic location (Leet et al., 2000; Valdez, 2005). Once inside the California prison system, if any gang member or gang group does not comply with the demands and orders of La Eme or Nuestra Familia, there are serious consequences, even death to that specific gang member and all members of his gang. In fact, La Eme or Nuestra Familia will issue a "hit" on that gang, and if any Latino gang member sees a member of the gang that has the "hit" on it, that person is allowed to kill those targeted gang members immediately with no questions asked (Leet et al., 2000; Valdez, 2005).

Latino gangs are very territorial and are often divided into cliques based on age, as opposed to the African-American gangs, which are divided by sets based on geographic location. An example of a Latino gang is the gang 18th Street. Membership in a Latino gang is not ethnically exclusive, especially in California. As a result, one will see other races and ethnicities in a Latino gang (Huff, 2001; Leet et al., 2000; Valdez, 2005). Membership is, however, generational for some gang members, meaning that there could conceivably be three to four generations of gang members in one gang (Valdez, 2005) (Fig. 35-10). This characteristic is unique to Latino gangs, as one will not find multiple generations in an African-American, Asian, or Caucasian gang. All Latino gang members have monikers or nicknames, which is normally based on physical appearance (Fig. 35-11). Latino gang members are also known to have tattoos that indicate their gang affiliation. Some common tattoos are the three dots meaning "Mi Vida Loca" translated to mean "My Crazy Life" (Fig. 35-12). Other examples of tattoos in Latino gangs are the "Smile Now Cry Later" tattoo (Fig. 35-13).

Fig. 35-10 Latino gang members throwing up hand signs. (Notice the multiple generations of gang members)

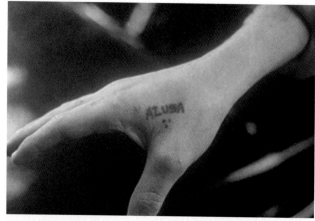

Fig. 35-12 Latino gang tattoo of the "3 dots" meaning "Mi Vida Loca" (my crazy life)

Fig. 35-11 Latino gang members throwing up hand signs. (Notice the etched picture with their monikers "Lil Joker" and "Lil Scrappy" Lil=Little)

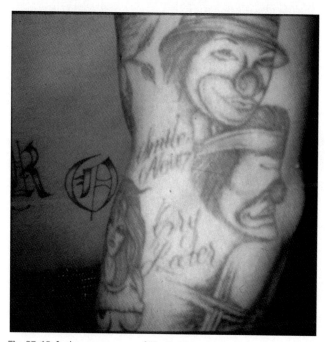

Fig. 35-13 Latino gang tattoo of "Smile Now, Cry Later"

LATIN KINGS

The Latin Kings grew out of the 1940s and 1950s Chicago gang wars that were plaguing the city (Huff, 2001; Leet et al., 2000; Schmidt & O'Reilly, 2007; Valdez, 2005, 2007). The Latin Kings are Chicago's largest gang and have been involved in numerous violent acts. Although the original members were of Puerto Rican decent, most members are now Mexican American. The gang now allows members of all races to join, yet it is mostly composed of Spanish, Caribbean, Latvian, Italian, Portuguese, Mexican, or South American members (Huff, 2001; Leet et al., 2000; Valdez, 2005).

In terms of identification, the Latin Kings use a five-pointed crown (Huff, 2001; Valdez, 2005). These five points represent love, respect, sacrifice, honor, and obedience (Huff, 2001; Valdez, 2005) (Fig. 35-14). Their graffiti may have a picture of a crown accompanied by the initials "LK" and often will have some sort of inflammatory symbolism aimed at an opposing gang. A lion or a lion wearing a crown with a variety of inscriptions may also be depicted. Latin Kings identify with the colors yellow and gold (Valdez, 2005).

The Chicago Police Department estimates that more than 25,000 Latin King gang members reside within that city alone (OJJDP, 2008). The gang also has organized chapters in numerous states across the country from Massachusetts to Florida. Among members, these gang sets are referred to as "chapters," with each reporting to a leader, OG, or veteran of the gang. The head of the entire Latin Kings gang, even all of the chapters, is known as the "Inca" (Valdez, 2005).

One of the characteristics that sets the Latin Kings apart from other gangs is that they consider themselves to be a community-based organization. The Latin Kings also preach Latino pride, "La Raza," and some Latin King chapters have formed even their own religion, called Kingdism (Valdez, 2005). During meetings, members may recite the Latin King pledge, or prayer, and continually pledge to be prepared to rise to the call for their King or Inca. Members often use meetings to discuss retaliating against other rival gangs or as a discipline session if a member breaks the rules of the gang (Valdez, 2005).

Fig. 35-14 Latin King gang member showing off his crown tattoo

When compared to most Latino street gangs, the Latin Kings are generally more structured and organized. The gang rules are strictly enforced, and some members celebrate January 6 as "King's Holy Day" and the first week in March as "King's Week" (Valdez, 2005).

MS 13

In the early 1980s, a civil war erupted in El Salvador killing an estimated 100,000 people. It is estimated that between 1 million and 2 million people immigrated to the United States as a result of the unstable environment in El Salvador (Huff, 2001; Leet et al., 2000; Valdez, 2005).

The first large population of El Salvadorian refuges settled in the Rampart (Pico Union) area of Los Angeles, California (Huff, 2001; Leet et al., 2000; Valdez, 2005). The Mexican-American population who was already residing in that area did not readily welcome this influx of immigrants looking for low-cost housing and employment. The area was already plagued with gangs and crime. These immigrant Salvadorian youth and young adults were soon were victimized by local gangs. A group of Salvadorian immigrants created a new gang called Mara Salvatrucha, also known as MS 13. It is believed the name came from combining the name of "La Mara," a violent street gang in El Salvador, with *Salvatruchas*, a term used to denote members of the Farabundo Marti National Liberation Front. This was a group of Salvadorian peasants trained as guerilla fighters. The "13" was added to pay respect to the California Latino prison gang mentioned previously,

La Eme (Mexican Mafia). The majority of MS 13 members are between 11 and 40 years old (Valdez, 2005). The colors that are important to MS 13 are blue and white, to represent the flag of El Salvador.

Members of this newly formed gang soon engaged in violent criminal acts. MS 13 quickly became known as one of the most violent gangs in the area because many of the founding members had experience and training in guerilla warfare back in their home country of El Salvador, thus giving the gang a level of sophistication that superseded its rivals. MS 13 is organized into "cliques." Some examples of these cliques include the Fulton Locos Salvatruchos (FLS), the Sailors Locos Salvatruchos Westside, the Teclas Locos Salvatruchos, and the Langley Park Salvatruchos.

Various members of MS 13 were soon arrested and deported back to El Salvador. All deportees were first housed in the Guezaltepeque Prison in Northern El Salvador. Quickly and unexpectedly, Mara Salvatrucha flourished in the prison system and recruitment began on the streets in El Salvador, while the gang continued to grow in the United States as well. With little direction and opportunities, many Central American youth admired the Mara Salvatrucha deportees and wanted to learn more about their gang. The gang soon became the largest gang in El Salvador and spread to the Honduras and Guatemala (Valdez, 2005). The gang's rival, although much smaller in number, is known as 18th Street, another Latino gang originating in Los Angeles, California, and primarily composed of members of Mexican-American decent (Leet et al., 2000; Valdez, 2005).

MS 13 members in the United States are known to be involved in all aspects of criminal activity. Some law enforcement sources have reported that because of their ties to El Salvador, MS 13 members have access to sophisticated weapons. As a result, trafficking firearms is one of MS 13's many criminal enterprises. Despite their access to weaponry, there have been many high-profile murders and assaults in which MS 13 members have used machetes to attack their victims (Valdez, 2005). MS 13 is a very dangerous and mobile gang that has connections not only in the United States but abroad as well (Figs. 35-15 and 35-16).

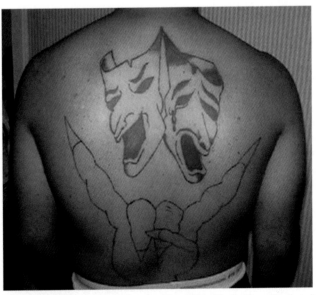

Fig. 35-15 MS 13 gang member showing off his "Smile Now, Cry Later" and "M" hand sign tattoos

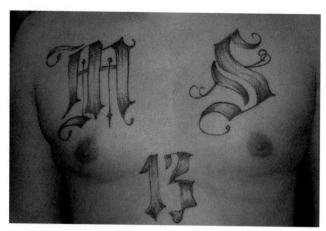

Fig. 35-16 MS 13 gang tattoo

Asian Gangs

Case Study: 35-1

In June of 2009, an Orange County, California jury recommended death for Jason Alejandro Aguirre, 33, who was convicted of first-degree murder in the 2003 shooting death of 13-year-old Minh Cong Tran.

Witnesses testified at trial that a member of the Dragon Family Junior gang eating at Alerto's alerted their leader, Jason Aguirre, that Minh Tran, his uncle, brother, and cousin were members of the Young Locs, a rival Asian gang. After Minh Tran's group finished eating, they drove away and a group of Dragon Family Junior associates gave chase in another car.

Minh Tran's uncle drove into a residential cul-de-sac to avoid detection. But the chasers quickly blocked the car. Aguirre, dressed in all-black clothing, approached on foot and fired several shots into the darkened car. Minh Tran was shot in the heart, liver, and shoulder and died from a loss of blood. His brother was shot in the stomach and his cousin was hit in the buttocks, but both recovered.

Police quickly arrested five in connection with the shooting, but Aguirre fled from the scene and disappeared. He was arrested in Tempe, Arizona several months later. He was the only one of the six co-defendants to face a death sentence in the case, in part because authorities believed he was the shooter and in part because of his history of violence as an adult. Co-defendant Quang Hal Do, 24, who was alleged to have been the driver and was 18 years old at the time of the shooting, faced a potential sentence of life without parole if convicted at a trial. The other co-defendants, including three gang members who were juveniles when the murder occurred, pleaded guilty to lesser charges (Welborn, 2009).

Case Analysis:

Jason Alejandro Aguirre was born on May 27, 1976 in San Diego, California. Aguirre's father was his mother's second husband. In 1970, Aguirre's mother married for the first time. Her first husband was her high school sweetheart. Immediately after the wedding, he was sent to Vietnam. After returning to the states, he became abusive and had numerous extramarital affairs, resulting in dissolution of the marriage. Aguirre's mother then married for the second time, to his father. Growing up was tumultuous and traumatic for Aguirre. Starting at an early age he witnessed his father inflict constant physical and emotional abuse on his mother. When Aguirre was only 18 months old, his mother divorced his father. However, Aguirre's father was awarded weekly visitation. During these visits, and in the presence of Aguirre, his father would make verbal threats to his mother that he would kidnap Aguirre and go to Mexico. As his father said these hurtful comments, Aguirre shook with fear; he cried when he had to go with his father.

Soon after her divorce from Aguirre's father, his mother remarried for a third time. The third marriage lasted eight years, but during that time the family was stable and Aguirre began to have a normal childhood. After the marriage dissolved, Aguirre's stepfather moved to Hawaii. Aguirre followed his stepfather to live with him in Honolulu.

Aguirre's time in Hawaii lasted only six months. When Aguirre's mother realized that Aguirre was sleeping on the couch, was unsupervised most of the time, and attended school sporadically, she moved him back to her home. However, his mother could not handle his aggression and defiance toward her, so for the next several years, Aguirre traveled back and forth between Honolulu and San Diego, living with various friends. In essence, his mother abandoned him at age 12.

In Honolulu he met Vietnamese youths his own age, who accepted and befriended him because he protected them from Samoan youths who were bullying them. Aguirre was known to his Vietnamese friends as a fearless fighter. On arrival back to California, Aguirre gravitated to Vietnamese friends, with whom he felt comfortable. Aguirre found himself totally immersed in the culture and community even before he joined the Dragon Family gang. The Vietnamese community embraced him as their own and made him feel loved and accepted. Finally, Aguirre had a sense of belonging.

Aguirre did not have a juvenile record. His first arrest occurred at age 19 for breaking into cars. Four months later he was arrested for auto theft and spent 30 days in the Santa Barbara County, California jail facility. Aguirre had stolen a car from the Los Angeles International Airport and was caught speeding. Three years later, in Honolulu, an arrest warrant was issued for Aguirre for stealing a moped. A year after this incident, he was arrested for attempted murder during a road rage traffic incident. In Irvine, California, at age 25, Aguirre was arrested for assault, carrying a concealed weapon, and being a gang member. This was his first arrest since joining the Dragon Family gang. His second arrest as a gang member came in November 2002 for drunk driving.

The Dragon Family including the Dragon Family Junior is a Vietnamese gang from Westminster (Orange County), California. The Dragon Family is made up of older gang members ranging in age from 17–29 years. The Dragon Family Junior is an appendage of the Dragon Family, in which gang members range in age from 7–16 years. Aguirre joined the Dragon Family gang when he was 24. He was well respected within the Dragon Family gang. His moniker (or nickname) was Slim Shady, after the Caucasian rapper Eminem. Aguirre has multiple tattoos proving his gang affiliation. Most noticeable is the Dragon Family tattooed on the inner forearms of both arms. He also has Vietnamese tattooed on his stomach, an insight into his identity perception because he received this tattoo before he joined the Dragon Family.

On the night of August 12, 2003, Aguirre received a telephone call from another member of the Dragon Family stating that their rival gang, the Young Locs, were eating at Alerto's, a Mexican restaurant in Westminster, California. The Vietnamese youths would be identified as Young Locs based on the blue color of their clothes. Six gang members went to investigate. Aguirre was a passenger in the first vehicle, which parked across the street from the restaurant. Four gang members were in the second vehicle. They waited for the group of youths to leave the restaurant.

Minh Cong Tran's uncle, aware of the car following him, pulled into a driveway in a residential cul-de-sac. The car in which Aguirre was a passenger blocked Tran's car from leaving. Terrified, the group hid inside Tran's car, hoping to trick Aguirre in to thinking they went inside the house. Aguirre approached the vehicle and fired multiple rounds into the vehicle, killing Minh Cong Tran and wounding the others.

In this case, the motive was not money but revenge for an ongoing feud between the two gangs. The tragedy was that Minh Cong Tran and his family had no gang affiliation. It was a case of mistaken identity on the part of the Dragon Family.

During the sentencing phase of the trial, the defense presented expert testimony, through CA, on Aguirre's troubled childhood, ethnic background, and risk factors for joining an Asian gang. Why would Aguirre, at 24 years of age, with a Caucasian mother and Mexican-American father join an all-Vietnamese gang? In answer to this question, the following reasons were presented to the jury.

SENSE OF BELONGING. The Vietnamese community accepted and embraced Aguirre, while making him feel safe to let his "guard down" and to be himself without anyone judging him.

SENSE OF IDENTITY. Because Aguirre was biracial, it was difficult for him to form a racial identity so he selects a third, unbiased ethnic group of Vietnamese with which to associate.

SENSE OF LOYALTY. Now being part of a "family," Aguirre feels a sense of responsibility and belonging.

SENSE OF POWER AND CONTROL. Once in the gang, Aguirre rose quickly into a leadership role. His childhood and adult background of violence was instrumental in developing his sense of entitlement, anger, and intimidation that was used to control the gang.

It took the jury 4 days to deliberate and recommended the death penalty based on the testimony that the Tran youth was not a rival gang member but an innocent victim.

Asian gangs behave very differently from African-American and some Latino gangs (Leet et al., 2000). Certain life experiences set them apart from other youths. Many of the original gang members (the "OGs") have been exposed to the violence and corruption caused by civil war in their native countries, like some gang members of MS 13 from El Salvador have seen. After immigration, they suffered the prejudices that accompany being physically different and being unable to communicate in English. Consequently, their responses to being an outsider and feeling devalued were characterized in their lifestyle and criminal activity.

Many young refugees come to the United States with little or no supervision, sometimes because of being orphaned. Adults who come over are often widowed or had to leave family members behind due to traumatic circumstances. Even when the families are intact, both parents need to work full time. The tension of the refugee experience tends to disrupt the family structure, and the Americanization of the children further erodes the traditional Asian values of "respect" for one's parents. They also discover that the public schools and laws are liberal when compared to the stricter nature of their native countries. Parents discover too late the lax nature of their child's education and the liberties afforded to them in their newly adopted country.

Consequently, the young person with little or no family structure and a distrust of authority takes this frustration to the streets, in a country that is not his native land. Seeking support, some of these youths join street gangs (Akiyama et al., 1997; Ong & Miller,

2002), only to find that there is no way out once they become members. Now part of a subculture, these young Southeast Asians quickly develop the morals and attitudes of their peers, for whom the primary motive is making money.

Under U.S. resettlement policies, many refugees were moved into low-income areas where they became easy targets for victimization by the existing African-American and Latino gangs (Akiyama & Kawasaki, 1999; Akiyama, 2008b; and Leet et al., 2000). Initially, many young Southeast Asians formed gangs for protection and survival, as noted previously. Today, they form gangs for monetary profit (Akiyama, 1999; and Leet et al., 2000).

It is imperative in understanding the Southeast Asian gang members that one first understands their philosophy regarding life and death (Akiyama, 1999). This attitude has its basis in the violence inherent in the refugee experience (Akiyama, 2008b). For many of these gang members, to commit a crime and be in jail is no problem. Death is not a problem for them, because back home many of these youths have seen violence firsthand. The gang and jail experience is like life in a country club compared to life in their homeland, a statement many of the gang members commonly express.

The ethnic characteristics of the "non-traditional" Asian street gang are different from those of other ethnic street gangs, such as the African-American or Latino gangs. The primary motive of the non-traditional Asian gang is monetary profit. Non-traditional Asian gangs tend to be extremely violent, prey on their own culture, and are extremely mobile, meaning that they move from one geographic area to another to commit crimes or evade law enforcement (Akiyama & Kawasaki, 1999; Valdez, 2007).

One group of Asian gangs is the "Pacific Islander" gang. The Pacific Islanders are made up of Filipinos, Samoans, and Chamorros, who will often follow the "traditional" patterns of gang behavior (Akiyama & Kawasaki, 1999; Leet et al., 2000) in the sense that they model themselves after Latino and African-American gangs and are territorial, wear identifying colors (much like the Crips wear blue and the Bloods wear read to indicate their gang affiliation), deface property with graffiti, develop non-verbal forms such as hand signs for communication, and affiliate themselves with a particular gang "set," which is based on age or geographic location. There tends to be racial exclusivity within the Asian gang; however, a new trend with the Filipino gangs is the inclusion of non-Asian members (African American or Latino), making gang structure harder to detect (Akiyama & Kawasaki, 1999).

As a whole, Southeast Asian gangs (i.e., Vietnamese, Laotian, and Cambodian) behave "non-traditionally," sometimes forming only to commit a single crime and then disbanding. Unlike any other gang, Southeast Asian gangs tend to prey on their own culture because many of these gangs existed on the fringes of refugee communities and the members are often shunned by their families. In some cases, parents are totally unaware of their son's or daughter's involvement in gangs. This can be attributed to a lack of supervision that sometimes results when both parents put in long hours at labor-intensive jobs. The paradox here is that the parents' intention is to improve their home life and set an example of hard work for their children. In some cases, because of the assimilation of the children, parents are unable to control the youth and do not know how to obtain help. When these parents attempt to discipline their child, the child may threaten to report the parents to the authorities. Because the parents do not want to get the authorities involved in their lives, they will not discipline their child in fear of being taken away or put in jail. Asian culture demands that family matters remain private, and the involvement of outside authority can be considered an insult to the family structure. Moreover, the gangs prey on members of their own culture, who they know are reluctant to tell the police, because back in their home country the police and the government were corrupt. When they arrive in the United States, these parents carry with them the same ideology of corruption and distrust for governmental authority. This is also why many Southeast Asians do not believe in banks, because banks too were corrupt. Therefore, families will hold their life savings in the form of cash, precious metals (gold), and jewelry, making them vulnerable to home invasion robberies by Asian gang members (Akiyama & Kawasaki, 1999). Furthermore, citizens are fearful of the gang's long-standing reputation for retaliation. Language barriers are also a problem and in some cases serve as an excuse not to call the police. Southeast Asian gang members are extremely difficult to identify because they do not adhere to the traditional gang attire, as African-American, Latino, Filipino, Samoan, or Chamorro gangs do.

Similar to the role of "respect" in Latino gangs (Valdez, 2005) is the Asian concept of "face" or "honor". The concept of face or honor can be thought of as the idea of social approval, social identity, self-respect, or social image—in other words, what we do not only reflects on us as individuals, but it is a direct reflection of our family image and name (Akiyama, 2008b). This has ramifications both for intergang rivalry and for officer safety because if an Asian gang member thinks that someone disrespected him, to save face, he will have to retaliate. If the gang member has made no effort to atone for the loss of face, the peer group will shun that member.

Generally, Asian gang members are not confrontational and are extremely polite when confronted by anyone of authority (i.e., teachers and law enforcement). They want to portray the image of being the "innocent victim" or often the "model minority" (Akiyama, 2008b). They will take full advantage of the stereotype of Asians as being law-abiding and passive citizens (Akiyama & Kawasaki, 1999). They do not fit the typical criminal profile as defined by the media and traditional law enforcement. Many gang members will stay in motels or "safe" houses to evade the police, hide stolen goods, or just to party (Akiyama & Kawasaki, 1999; Huff, 2001; Leet et al., 2000; and Valdez, 2005). When Asian gangs partake in criminal activity, the gang members will not go back to their own houses but will go to a friend's house or a motel. They will take advantage of their ability to communicate in their native language, knowing that most members of law enforcement will not be able to understand them. Law enforcement could deter this problem during a field investigation by simply separating the subjects and not allowing the gang members to speak to each other (Akiyama & Kawasaki, 1999).

For those following the more traditional structure, Asian gang graffiti resembles Latino graffiti with cross outs to mark rivals and deaths (Valdez, 2005). Vietnamese gang graffiti is usually unsigned and is found around typical hangouts such as cafés and pool halls. One unique aspect of the Asian gang is that the gang name will frequently change, depending on the success of law enforcement in making arrests in the area. However, the gang affiliation remains the same. For example, the Asian Bloods could have multiple names, from Red Scorpions to Red Lions, but the affiliation does not change (Akiyama & Kawasaki, 1999). Contrast this ideology with traditional Latino gangs, where the same name can remain for decades. Individual members often adopt monikers or

nicknames, as observed with both Latino and African-American gangs. For Asian gang members, these names could relate to a physical attribute, an ancestor, or a personality trait. Traditionally, gang members use monikers that are expressed in their native language, permitting greater anonymity from law enforcement. Gang members rarely admit to these names, although associates will freely refer to them with it. Gang investigators and emergency room personnel will recognize this trait in other gangs as well. As with any criminal gang investigation, these names could become important in the identification of suspects.

Tattoos are particularly significant, because they are usually considered reprehensible in Asian culture. The average Asian teenager is not likely to have a tattoo, so finding one may be a significant indication of gang membership (Akiyama & Kawasaki, 1999). Gang members often use their tattoos as an intimidation factor to get their way with local businesses. Some popular gang tattoos are a Chinese pictograph that means "Trust No Man"; clipper ships; animals of strength like the panther, tiger, or dragon; five dots on the hand; and, most important, cigarette burns. Cigarette burns on the back of the hand or on other parts of the body are a sure sign of gang membership (Leet et al., 2000). The cigarette burns will be organized in a pattern, and the greater the number of burns, the tougher the gang member. Those familiar with Latino gangs' initiation of "jumping in" will recognize this act of burning as a form of gang acceptance.

There are two important exceptions to Asian gang tattoos. Some Southeast Asians tattoo themselves to remember a loved one, and others may have religious tattoos. Therefore, it is imperative to be familiar with the tattoos prevalent among Southeast Asian gang members.

Weaponry is vital and used as a status symbol in the Asian gang. Southeast Asian gang members tend to carry sophisticated weapons and they practice using them, whereas Pacific Islander gangs use what they can get their hands on. The Asians take pride on their marksmanship. Their proficiency can be directly traced to their background in war-torn Vietnam, Cambodia, and Laos; it does not matter whether one was a member of the government militia or of a guerrilla movement, because each was thoroughly versed in the use and care of arms. This knowledge has been passed on to the American-born generation. The most popular guns found out in the streets are the 9-mm and 25-caliber semiautomatic handguns. However, assault rifles are very common, such as the AK-47 or the UZI (Akiyama & Kawasaki, 1999; Huff, 2001; Leet et al., 2000; Valdez, 2005). The bottom line is that Asian gangs are heavily armed with high-tech weapons and in many cases outpower the police.

Females are vital members of the Asian gang (both traditional and nontraditional). Traditionally, the females have been integrated with the guys and are used to carry the guns, hide the drugs, and act as a decoy so that other members can evade police. However, recently females have taken on an active role and in many cases have their own exclusive female gang. They are extremely violent and participate in the same crimes as their male counterparts. Risky sexual behavior has been tied to involvement in the gang culture by some Asian and Pacific Islander female youths, including Cambodians, Filipinos, Laotians, and Vietnamese. Furthermore, teen pregnancy may arise as a by-product of the gang initiation ritual for girls, often serving as the only safe way for a member to leave the gang (Fig. 35-17).

Fig. 35-17 Asian gang member throwing up a "B" for Blood, indicating he is a member of an Asian Blood gang. (Notice at the bottom of the graffiti it says "Krab Killers" Krab=Crips)

Skinhead Gangs

The Skinhead gangs originated in England in the early 1960s in an attempt to make a social or political statement and as a product of working class resentment toward immigrants during a period of economic distress. The Skinhead style was meant to symbolize tough, patriotic, anti-immigrant, working class attitudes (Gerstenfeld & Grant, 2004; Hamm, 1993; Valdez, 2005). During this time, the United Kingdom was experiencing internal turmoil; consequently, the country focused on its youth. As a result, various youth subcultures developed during this period. One of these groups adopted a mode of dress that was intended to reflect an association with the white working class. The Skinhead name was derived from the practice of shaving the head to eliminate the possibility of the hair being pulled when these individuals became involved in street fights (Gerstenfeld & Grant, 2004; Hamm, 1993; Valdez, 2005).

It took a few years before the radical influence of the Skinheads crossed over to the United States. However, before the Skinhead arrival, the fad of punk rock music set the stage. In 1978, an English punk band named Screwdriver, led by Ian Stuart, became the catalyst for the development of the Skinhead groups seen in the United States today. This band played songs that preached hatred, violence, and racism. The Skinhead message was delivered throughout England on record albums and tapes featuring music known as *Oi* ("Hey" in Cockney English–English slang). From the influence of Screwdriver, the Skinhead movement arrived in the United States around 1978–1979. Today there are approximately 3000 Skinhead gang members in the United States (Gerstenfeld & Grant, 2004; Hamm, 1993; Valdez, 2005).

Attempts have been made to organize spontaneous Skinhead gangs into a national network by older white supremacists such as Tom Metzger, former Grand Dragon of the Ku Klux Klan, and Richard Butler of the Aryan Nations. Although membership in adult hate groups has declined, recruitment of adolescents has skyrocketed, with increasing numbers of neo-Nazi and white supremacist youths involved in the Skinhead movement (Gerstenfeld & Grant, 2004; Hamm, 1993; Valdez, 2005). It is important to remember that not all Skinheads are neo-Nazis or white supremacists;

however, a large number of those in the movement are actively involved in a variety of crimes against minorities.

TYPOLOGY OF SKINHEAD GANGS

- *White Power Skinheads* cling to the white supremacy/neo-Nazi philosophy and advocate violence as a means to achieve their goals.
- *Independent Skinheads* are similar to the White Power Skinheads except that their allegiance to white supremacist-separatist ideology is not as defined and they tend to come and go within the various Skinhead gangs.
- *Nonracist Skinheads,* often called "baldies" or "two tones," considerably outnumber racist Skinheads in most areas of the United States. However, studies have shown that the distinction between the racist and the nonracist types are often blurred. Some claim that they are nonracist but believe in "white pride," a notion that is intrinsically racist (Gerstenfeld & Grant, 2004; Hamm, 1993; Valdez, 2005).

PHILOSOPHY OF THE SKINHEAD GANG

The philosophy of the Skinhead gang is that they are motivated by bigotry and view minorities as inferiors who steal jobs from the working class. They believe in the superiority of the white race (white supremacy), preventing race mixing, expounding on working class values, eliminating immigration, affinity for Nazism, belief in the Zionist Occupational Government (ZOG), where ZOG represents the Jewish culture, violence, and machismo (a macho/tough-guy ideology). They also use graffiti to deface property instead of marking territory. Slogans profess Nazism, anti-Semitism, antiminorities, and antigovernment beliefs (Gerstenfeld & Grant, 2004; Hamm, 1993; Leet et al., 2000; Valdez, 2005).

Dress characteristics of the Skinhead gang start with the individual's hair. Hair is shaved, short, cut into a Mohawk, skinned, or unevenly shaved and dyed in various colors. Skinhead gang members also wear Air Force flight jackets in green or black (Levi jackets are also acceptable, except for Neo-Nazi), Fred Perry knit polo shirts or oversized men's dress shirts, narrow suspenders (called "braces"), and Doc Marten steel-toed boots used in street fighting for kicking and stomping (Gerstenfeld & Grant, 2004; Hamm, 1993; Leet et al., 2000; Valdez, 2005).

Common Skinhead tattoos include swastikas; lightning bolts; American, Confederate, or Nazi flags; crossed hammers; spider webs; and the letters SWP (representing Supreme White Power), WP (representing White Power), WAR (representing White Aryan Resistance), and KKK (representing the Ku Klux Klan). They also have slogans or sayings such as "Boot Power." Christian crosses, hooded figures, death heads, or Viking figures are also extremely common. It is important to know that tattoos are a personal reminder to the wearer of his or her commitment to the group (Leet et al., 2000; Valdez, 2005) (Figs. 35-18 to 35-20).

As a forensic nurse, it is important to pay attention to the tattoos and understand the symbolism. For example, the lightning bolts are also called Schutzstaffel, which is German for *"Protective Squadron."* It is abbreviated by two lightning bolts (Runic) and *SS* (Latin). The Schutzstaffel was a large security and military organization of Germany's Nazi party used to guard the concentration camps. The SS was established in the 1920s as a personal guard unit for Nazi leader Adolf Hitler. The spider web tattoo, commonly seen on the elbow or on the neck, is considered to be a badge of honor to the Skinhead gangs. The symbolism carries multiple meanings—from doing prison time, to murdering a minority person, to murdering an enemy as a warning to potential

Fig. 35-18 Skinhead gang members showing various tattoos and attire. (Notice the spider web tattoo on the left elbow, various swastikas, and the confederate flag on the jackets)

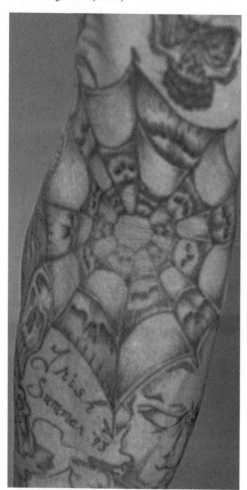

Fig. 35-19 Skinhead gang member with a spider web tattoo on his elbow indicating that he has killed a minority to earn this "badge of honor" in the Skinhead gang

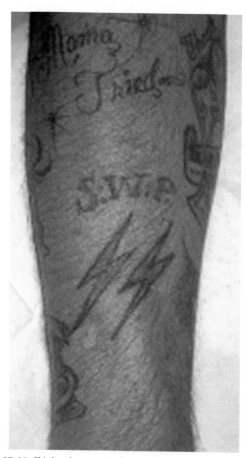

Fig. 35-20 Skinhead gang member showing tattoos of "SWP" (Supreme White Power) and "Lightning Bolts" (Schutzstaffel)

enemies—depending on the particular group. The spider web symbol originated in the late 1970s and early 1980s with the punk rock crowd who saw it on ex-cons (prison gangs) and thought it looked "cool." Aryan prison gangs ran the system in the late 1950s and early 1960s, and the spider web on the right side of the neck meant that you murdered someone while in prison (Gerstenfeld & Grant, 2004; Hamm, 1993).

Skinhead gangs, as mentioned previously, are driven by bigotry and hate, and for this reason the crimes they commit are more serious than those of any other gang. This hatred and bias toward another group is what elevates the crime to a "hate crime" (Akiyama, 2008a; Valdez, 2005). It is imperative for the forensic nurse to understand what exactly is a hate crime and bias incident and how to recognize the signs and symptoms of a hate crime.

HATE CRIMES AND BIAS INCIDENTS

A hate crime is defined as a criminal offense that is motivated, in whole or in part, by the offender's bias against a certain race, ethnicity, national origin, religion, sexual orientation, gender, or disability. It can take many forms, including physical assault, damage to property, verbal abuse, or offensive graffiti. In 2007, there were 7624 hate crime incidents and 9006 offenses; 3870 of the incidents were race-origin based (Federal Bureau of Investigation [FBI], 2008). Although all crimes are an affront to society, offenses rooted in animosity toward a victim because of these specific characteristics are especially destructive. A hate crime has great negative consequences, not only on the victim but on the community as a whole and the larger group of people targeted for that specific bias.

The victim of a hate crime experiences great traumatic psychological consequences, because the crime is a personal attack on the victim's identity. It is a devaluing act that affects the victim and the way he or she views himself or herself. Immediately after a hate crime occurs, the victim experiences shock and shows distress. For more violent acts of hate crimes, the victim may suffer from physical or even head injuries, which would increase the amount of shock experienced and may even hinder the victim from recounting the crime for a short period of time. Also, the long-term psychological responses are more intense for the victim of a hate crime. Hate crimes can also cause victims to view the world and people in it as malevolent, instilling a great sense of negativity and anger, and victims experience a reduced feeling of control. Victims of hate crimes needed as much as five years to overcome the emotional distress of the incident, compared with victims of nonbias crimes, who experienced a drop in crime-related psychological problems within two years of the crime (Perry, 2003). Consequently, victims of hate crimes experience extreme emotional distress, and results of a study conducted at the National Institute Against Prejudice and Violence (NIAPV) demonstrate this impact of hate crime victimization on its victims. The survivors of racists' hate crimes that were interviewed in the survey admitted to feeling extreme anger and fear following the incident. They further listed specific behavioral responses that included both avoidant strategies, such as relocating, as well as potential retaliatory ones, such as purchasing a firearm (Perry, 2003). Though the actual responses of hate crime victims vary, hate crime victimization in general exacts an extreme psychological toll on its victims (Akiyama, 2008a).

Hate crimes can take on many forms, including physical assault. They involve a higher level of assault than do general crimes. About 45% to 55% of hate crimes are personal assaults, whereas only 10% of overall crimes involve assaults. Additionally, hate crimes are more violent, causing physical injury in 74% of cases, whereas this occurs in only 30% of nonhate crimes; 30% of victims of hate crimes had to also be hospitalized, whereas only 7% of victims of nonhate crimes had to do so (Akiyama, 2008a). Because hate crimes are backed by such a strong force—hate—targets of these crimes are often inflicted with atrocious injuries. These offenders usually have great intent to harm or hurt, and in many instances these offenders justify this need in their minds and therefore carry through with very violent acts. Of the 7624 hate crime incidents in 2007, 4347 were crimes against persons (versus crimes against property or society); of these, nine resulted in murder or non-negligent manslaughter, two resulted in forcible rape, and 853 resulted in aggravated assault (FBI, 2008). In other words, almost 20% of hate crimes ended in a physically destructive manner, if not death.

In addition and in consequence to the psychological and physical consequences of hate crimes, victims also experience a great economic burden (Akiyama, 2008a; Perry, 2003). Victims have increased financial costs because they are more likely to seek out mental health services and other forms of assistance after a traumatic event and during the periods of distress afterward. Furthermore, because psychological health is often associated with physical health, victims may also experience more somatic problems, which then results in a greater likelihood of using physical healthcare services. This also increases the financial burden of healthcare costs (Perry, 2003). Victims of hate crimes may also not feel well enough or have the capability to perform their occupations, which may result in job loss, furthering the financial consequences of the crimes. Therefore, they face both intangible and tangible financial consequences because of hate crimes.

Most of the distress observed among hate crime survivors results from a higher sense of personal danger and vulnerability that becomes associated with their identity, because their identity is what was being attacked during the hate crime. Because of this new heightened sense of fear, victims perceive the world as more dangerous, unpredictable, and hostile. Victims often link this sense of powerlessness to their identity. Ultimately, this association is extremely psychologically harmful and is what victims need to go to therapy to undo. Hate crimes destroy the victim's self-concept, which therapy should be used to restore (Herek, 1989). In addition, the effects of a hate crime may infect the victims' relationships with other people. As of now, there are no specific treatments for hate crime victims, but professional help and talking to a therapist after such a traumatic event can do nothing but benefit the individual and lead the path to a healthy psychological recovery.

Finally, if one thinks a hate crime has occurred, he or she should ask two questions: (1) Did a crime occur? (2) Was the crime motivated by bias or hate? If the answer to both questions is yes (even if there is some doubt), then it is possible that a hate crime or at least a bias incident has occurred, and now it is time to get help immediately by calling the police and then contacting civil rights organizations that have local chapters, such as the Anti Defamation League (ADL), the Japanese American Citizens League (JACL), the Organization of Chinese Americans (OCA), the National Association for the Advancement of Colored People (NAACP), and the National Council of La Raza (NCLR). Any of these organizations can help the victim by providing legal, medical, and psychological resources to help them cope with the traumatic event. Therefore, having a list of these local organizations and their contact information can be extremely helpful.

Strategies for Reducing Youth Gang Violence in the Medical Setting

A multidisciplinary approach is imperative to help fight this epidemic and to keep everyone safe in the community, clinic, or hospital setting. A multidisciplinary approach includes communication by emergency department personnel, hospital security/police, nurses, social workers, and paramedic/fire personnel.

Here are a few recommendations that have been shown to reduce the number of gang-related incidents in the hospital. Many emergency departments, hospitals, and clinics across the country already have theses recommendations in place and in practice. This is just a friendly reminder to always keep yourself and your patients safe (Hutson, Anglin, & Mallon, 1992).

BEST PRACTICE Hospital personnel should be aware of the presence of gang members in the emergency department and should follow an established procedure for enhancing security and notifying law enforcement.

EMERGENCY DEPARTMENT

- Educate emergency department (ED) personnel regarding the identification of gang member attire, tattoos, and nonverbal clues of communication.
- Notify police or security personnel on arrival or anticipated arrival of gang members.
- Employ metal detectors in facilities that treat large number of gunshot wound victims.
- Assign "Jane Doe" or "John Doe" names to patients to prevent later hospital retaliation.
- Completely disrobe all gunshot wound victims.
- Request paramedics to transport rival gang members to separate hospitals.
- Separate rival gang members while in the ED.
- Have security personnel supervise gang members.
- Limit information and visits to immediate family members only.
- Limit the number of visitors allowed to remain in the ED waiting room.

HOSPITAL

- Educate security personnel regarding the identification of gang member attire, tattoos, and nonverbal clues of communication.
- Limit access to patients' rooms.
- Abate graffiti.

As this chapter has shown, youth gang violence is a problem that affects us all, regardless of race, gender, or socioeconomic status. We can all assist with the suppression, intervention, and prevention of gang violence. However, we first need to realize that there is a problem before we can act to resolve it. Our involvement as healthcare providers does not cease the minute the gang members leave the hospital; in fact, that is only the beginning. Most important, when dealing with these young people, it is essential to remember that they are in trouble and in pain.

References

Akiyama, C. (2008a). When you look like the enemy. *Brief Treatment and Crisis Intervention, 8*(2), 209–213.

Akiyama, C. (2008b). Bridging the gap between two cultures: An analysis on identity attitudes and attachment of Asian Americans. *Brief Treatment and Crisis Intervention, 8*(3), 251–263.

Akiyama, C., Comparini, S. O., & Nepomuceno, J. (1997). Youth gang violence: A new high risk biopsychosocial emergency. *Mind and Human Interaction, 8*(3), 186–194.

Akiyama, C., & Kawasaki, R. (1999). Southeast Asian youth gangs: A rising epidemic. *Mind and Human Interaction, 10*(4), 247–255.

Egley, A., Maxson, C. L., Miller, J., & Klein, M. W. (2006). *The modern gang reader.* Los Angeles, California: Roxbury Publishing.

Federal Bureau of Investigation. (2008). *Hate Crime Statistics.* Washington, DC: U.S. Department of Justice.

Franzese, R. J., Covey, H. C., & Menard, S. (2006). *Youth Gangs.* Springfield, IL: Charles C Thomas.

Gerstenfeld, P. B., & Grant, D. R. (2004). *Crimes of hate.* Thousand Oaks, CA: Sage.

Hamm, M. S. (1993). *American Skinheads: The criminology and control of hate crime.* Westport, CT: Praeger.

Herek, G. M. (1989). Hate crimes against lesbians and gay men: Issues for research and policy. *American Psychologist, 44*(6), 948–955.

Huff, R. C. (2001). *Gangs in America III.* Thousand Oaks, CA: Sage.

Hutson, H. R., Anglin, D., & Mallon, W. (1992). Minimizing gang violence in the emergency department. *Annals of Emergency Medicine, 21*(10), 1291–1293.

Jackson, R. K., & McBride, W. D. (2000). *Understanding street gangs.* Florence, KY: Wadsworth.

Katz, C. M., & Webb, V. J. (2006). *Policing gangs in America.* New York: Cambridge University.

Klein, M. W. (1997). *The American street gang.* New York: Oxford University.

Leet, D. A., Rush, G. E., & Smith, A. M. (2000). *Gangs, graffiti, and violence: A realistic guide to the scope and nature in gangs in America.* Incline Village, NV: Copperhouse Publishing.

Office of Juvenile Justice and Delinquency Prevention (OJJDP). (2008). *Fact sheet: Highlights of the 2005 national youth gang surveys.* Washington, DC: U.S. Department of Justice.

Ong, P., & Miller, D. (2002). *Economic needs of Asian Americans and Pacific Islanders in distressed areas: Establishing baseline information.* Los Angeles, CA: University of California, Los Angeles Press.

Perry, B. (2003). *Hate and bias crime.* New York: Routledge.

Schmidt, L. M., & O'Reilly, J. T. (2007). *Gangs and law enforcement.* Springfield, IL: Charles C Thomas.

Thornberry, T. P., Krohn, M. D., Lizotte, A. J., Smith, C. A., & Tobin, K. (2003). *Gangs and delinquency in developmental perspective.* New York: Cambridge University.

Valdez, A. (2005). *Gangs: A guide to understanding street gangs.* San Clemente, CA: Law Tech Publishing.

Valdez, A. (2007). *Gangs across America: History and sociology.* San Clemente, CA: Law Tech Publishing.

Virginia Gang Investigators Association (VGIA). (2008). *Gang specialist training fact sheet.* Chesterfield, VA.

Welborn, L. (2009). *Gang member gets death for murder of innocent 13-year-old.* The Orange County Register. August 14, 2009. Retrieved August 16, 2009 http://www.ocregister.com/articles/gang-tran-aguirre-2528986-minh-family

CHAPTER 36 Psychiatric Forensic Nursing

Tom Mason

Forensic psychiatric nursing is a dynamic profession, that has grown developmentally over many years and will likely extend its sphere of operations in both its content and its target group of patients into the future. The history of forensic psychiatric nursing shadows the other two major disciplines, forensic psychiatry and forensic psychology, but with a different developmental emergence. Whereas forensic psychiatry can trace its roots back more than 200 years and forensic psychology approximately 100 years, forensic psychiatric nursing appeared to emerge throughout the 1980s in the United Kingdom and at a similar time in the United States and Canada. This is not to say, of course, that as attendants to the psychiatric profession nurses have long been a part of the care of people detained because of their mental condition. As long as there have been asylums, there have been carers within those institutions. However, as we will see, professional nurses have a long tradition of working in secure psychiatric facilities as part of their overall caring for those with mental health problems or intellectual disabilities. Yet it is the emergence of the specialty of forensic psychiatric nursing that is, as yet, inchoate and can only claim to be in its third decade.

Notwithstanding, it is fair to say that over this relatively short period of time there has been a huge interest in examining what this psychiatric nursing specialty is and what, if any, is its unique knowledge or focus. This investigation has largely centered on the role constructs of forensic psychiatric nursing as well as on its function. Clearly delineated from working with victims of crime, the sphere of operations is on the perpetrators, whether convicted of a past offense or assessed as being potentially likely to cause harm to someone in the future because of their mental health problem or their intellectual impairment. This gives the forensic psychiatric nursing role added dimensions relating to not only caring for the perpetrators but managing the possibility of future victims through risk assessments and risk management. The role is, thus, highly complex and involves investigative elements and evaluative components.

The three pillars of this jurisprudence enterprise are the law, psychiatry, and ethics, which govern the art and science of caring for what can be a difficult patient group made up of individuals who by and large are compulsorily detained against their wishes and forced to have a treatment that they otherwise would choose not to have. This dynamic has the potential to be extremely dangerous and demanding, and it brings into stark relief the ever-present need for safe and secure professional care. Whatever the level of secure psychiatric provision, the need for safe practice remains paramount. The management of violence and aggression lies at the heart of this profession, and it is testament to their professionalism that injuries to staff and patients remain relatively few rather than many.

At a societal level, there is an increasing concern with what appears to be a rise in violence and aggression, and this is perceived to be the case on numerous fronts (this includes, for example, low-level crime such as burglary through to organized criminal activity such as protection rackets). Furthermore, societies around the world are becoming increasingly alarmed at the high levels of rape, sexual assault, and domestic violence (Keeling & Mason, 2009), not to mention the violence endemic in gang cultures, terror organizations, and certain prisoner groups. Whether or not such apparent increases in violence and aggression are real is open to debate, as some argue that the escalation of violent crime merely reflects a more effective way of collecting and communicating the incidents rather than a real increase (Marsh, 1986). Irrespective of whether or not there has been an increase, societies appear to be more concerned regarding the current levels of violence and aggression within their environments, and this is reflected in the public outcry in relation to mentally disordered offenders released into their communities who then may go on to reoffend. Therefore, the role of forensic psychiatric nurses also incorporates a public concern element to its sphere of operations.

History

The history of secure psychiatric provision in the UK is rooted in the thirteenth century at Bethlem Royal Hospital in London. However, it appears to be largely a containment philosophy grounded in the protection of the public with little, if any, treatment expectations. With the early development of psychiatry, with principles underpinning forms of intervention, albeit frequently bizarre and harmful, we can note libertarian approaches across Europe and the United States throughout the eighteenth and nineteenth centuries. All these psychiatric institutions had attendants or assistants operating in the form of carers, and these can be considered the precursors to modern-day nurses. However, forensic psychiatry appears to have emerged through the focus of the criminal act itself as a form of clinical condition (Mason & Mercer, 1998).

Michel Foucault (1978, page 1) claimed that forensic psychiatry was primarily "a pathology of the monstrous," which erupted onto the legal scene between 1799 and 1830. During this time he claims that European courts of law, judges, jurors, and legal teams began to *listen* to psychiatric testimony. Not that psychiatrists had not previously given opinion in courts, but that before this period their testimony was not viewed as a mitigation for the offender's behavior; if the person was deemed insane, then the psychiatric perspective was interesting, but the person was usually convicted anyway and often executed. However, Foucault argued that the creation of the clinical condition of *homicidal monomania* during this period allowed the psychiatrists to convince courts across

Europe that they had a specialist knowledge of this condition, that they could treat it through hospitalization in their psychiatric facilities of the time, and the "patients" would be detained indefinitely. Foucault outlined several cases in which this occurred, and all were serious, bizarre, and strange. For example, in one case a servant girl called on a neighbor of her employers and asked if she could look after their daughter for a short time. The neighbor reluctantly agreed, and when the neighbor returned for their child, the servant girl had killed the daughter, decapitated her, and thrown her head out of the window. Thus, for Foucault, forensic psychiatry was born out of a pathology of the monstrous.

Michel Foucault's interpretation of these historical beginnings is open to debate. However, a glance at any history of forensic psychiatry will attest to the "great event" that leads to changes in the legal framework, legal thinking, new laws, and psychiatric provision. In the UK in 1800, James Hadfield, a former soldier who had received head wounds, shot at King George III. At his trial, his counsel successfully argued that Hadfield was suffering from a paranoid delusion, which led to a verdict of not guilty. Although Hadfield was remanded to prison, the criminal law had no legal powers over him and the government of the day quickly passed the 1800 Act for the Safe Custody of Insane Persons Charged with Offences. This allowed the confinement of an insane person until "His Majesty's Pleasure Be Known," and although no new secure psychiatric provisions were built, these individuals were usually placed in Bethlem. This pivotal legislation was a major turning point for the treatment of offenders with mental health problems. However, the situation did not really change until Daniel McNaughtan shot and killed Edward Drummond, the private secretary to Prime Minister Sir Robert Peel, who was the intended target. At his trial in 1843, it was accepted that McNaughtan suffered from persecutory delusions, and the judge directed a verdict of not guilty by reason of insanity. Queen Victoria was outraged and claimed "insane he may have been but guilty he most assuredly was," as she herself had seen him fire the shot. This led to the establishment of a number of rules, later known as the McNaughtan rules, which involved establishing the fact that at the time of the offense the person was deemed insane or that he did not know that what he was doing was wrong.

The first asylum in Britain was established at Dundrum, near Dublin in Ireland, in 1856, and this was followed by Broadmoor, near London, in 1863. Further state asylums followed, with Rampton, near Nottingham, opening in 1912 to care for dangerous mental defectives (the Mental Deficiency Act 1913). Moss Side, near Liverpool, also for mental defectives, was opened in 1919 but had several other functions over the years until 1948, when all three state asylums came under the Ministry of Health. Park Lane Hospital, adjacent to Moss Side, was opened in 1984 but was amalgamated with Moss Side to form Ashworth Hospital. These form the High Security Psychiatric Services for the UK. Scotland has just the one state hospital, Carstairs (Blackburn, 1993).

In the United States as far back as the eighteenth century, courts were concerned about a person being able to make a well-informed plea and establishing a defense. In the Frith case of 1790, the court stated:

No man shall be called upon to make his defense at a time when his mind is in that situation as not to appear capable of so doing, for however guilty he may be, the inquiry into his guilt must be postponed to that season when by collecting together his intellects, and having them entire, he shall be able so to model his defense as to ward off the punishment of the law.

At the turn of the nineteenth century, the circuit court judge hearing a famous case involving an assault on Andrew Jackson, remarked that if a mad man is placed on trial, the judge may use discretion, discharging the jury, and sending him to jail to be tried after the recovery of his understanding. In 1899, the Sixth Circuit court held that "It is not due process of law to subject an insane person to trial upon an indictment involving liberty of life" (*Youtsey v. United States*, 1899). By the turn of the twentieth century, a test for competency was developing. The ruling in *United States v. Chisholm* (1901) alluded to the cognitive powers and communication capabilities of the defendant. Sixty years later, such capacity and skills were specifically stated in a Supreme Court ruling (*Dusky v. United States*, 1960). American law elevated the competency rule into a constitutional principle.

However, the term *forensic psychiatric nursing* did not feature in the High Security Psychiatric Services until the development of the regional secure units in the UK. These medium secure psychiatric units owe their inception to the *Report of the Committee on Mentally Abnormal Offenders* (Her Majesty's Stationary Office [HMSO], 1975), although it is fair to say that the idea was first debated in the mid-1960s (Snowden, 1990). Government money sparked the creation of these much smaller medium secure units, and there are more than 50 such facilities spread geographically across the UK. Alongside this, but someway behind, is the establishment of a third tier of secure psychiatric provision in the UK, and these are known as low secure psychiatric units. Other developments include the expansion of mental health units in prisons as well as community provision with outreach services. Therefore, the gamut of forensic psychiatric services from prisons and the three security levels of high, medium, and low through to community services is established with forensic psychiatric nurses featuring in all these facilities. It is with these developments that the term *forensic psychiatric nursing* first emerged throughout the 1980s. In the United States and Canada, the services are similar (with exceptions as outlined later) and the high security psychiatric services are usually referred to as state hospitals, which may be a part of an overall correctional facility.

At the time of writing there appears to be two general systems for secure forensic psychiatric care: (1) services that are made up only of healthcare professionals (i.e., psychiatrists, psychologists, nurses, and occupational therapists who undertake all roles pertinent to the function of the hospital, unit, or service including security functions [as in the UK]) and (2) services that are made up of healthcare personnel and separate security staff who are responsible only for the security issues (as in the United States). There are advantages and disadvantages in both systems. For example, one advantage of the UK system is that security is seen as the responsibility of all staff and they are trained to undertake these roles. One advantage of the U.S. system is that the healthcare staff can focus on health-related issues only and do not obfuscate the therapeutic relationship with the security function.

KEY POINT Histories of the development of forensic psychiatric nursing are subjective interpretations of documented facts.

Theoretical Underpinnings

There are many theories of both mental disorder and criminal behavior, and Mason and Mercer (1999) have offered a timeline of how the fusion of these theories forms the basis of contemporary forensic psychiatric nursing. They draw on psychiatric thinkers such as Szsaz, Jones, Scheff, and Laing and locate their philosophy with developments in criminology, and they consider sociological theorists such as Cloward, Goffman, Becker, Lemert, and Foucault. This fusion locates the central tenet of forensic psychiatric nursing as a psychosocial undertaking. Social scientists are continuing to attempt to make sense of the increase in both crime and mental disorder through various frameworks, and Box 36-1 describes seven major schools of thought as outlined by Ohlin and Farrington (1991).

Theories of determinism are also offered as explanations given by perpetrators who lay blame for their own actions on factors that they cannot control. For example, they may ascribe their behavior to one of three sources of determinism: (1) genetics ("It's my grandparents fault"), (2) psychological upbringing ("It's my parents fault"), and (3) environment/surroundings ("It's my partner's, boss's, culture's fault"). The forensic psychiatric nurse will factor into her or his assessment the nature of these positions and the patient's response to them.

All of these theories have some merit in secure psychiatric services and can assist the practitioner in developing a broad understanding of how the patient was functioning in society leading up to and including the circumstances of the criminal action. Forensic psychiatric nursing is psychosocial in two distinct ways:

first, it deals with the interaction between individuals, groups, and the community, and, second, it deals with the understanding of social and cultural factors that influence an offender's motivation and behavior before and during the criminal act (Coram, 2006).

KEY POINT Forensic psychiatric nursing draws on numerous theoretical disciplines and locates them in the art and science of nursing.

Role Definition and Skills/Competencies

As stated earlier, although forensic psychiatric nursing has a relatively short history, it has certainly developed at a pace over the past three decades. In the United States, forensic psychiatric nursing continues to be a dynamic area of practice, which responds to the changing patient profiles. Nurses in this area have expanded their knowledge to meet the changing needs of the individuals, groups, and communities that they serve (Coram, 2006), and forensic psychiatric nurses have increasingly been involved with patients whose chronic illnesses and behavior has led them to interface with the legal system. In the United States, jails and prisons have long used registered nurses with physical assessment skills to treat minor illnesses and injuries (American Nurses Association [ANA], 1985), and since the 1980s, changing social problems have demanded that these nurses incorporate more teaching of substance abuse, AIDS prevention, and wellness into their function. Increased substance abuse, gang involvement, easy access to weapons, and diverse social peer pressures have resulted in an explosion in the crime rates with an ever growing number of people requiring assessment and evaluation following their arrest, remand, and subsequent court appearance. Many of these had no previous contact with the mental health system at that time (Bencer, 1989).

Coram (2006) informed us that before 1993 there was no literature defining the characteristics of psychiatric nurses who also overlap into the forensic arenas. She also claimed that one could find no written work describing the expanded role of a clinical nurse specialist (CNS) who chooses to practice in an area that contains elements of physiological nursing, psychiatric nursing, correctional nursing, law enforcement, and the criminal justice system. However, early work in the United States collected data on the number of registered nurses providing forensic psychiatric nursing services. Survey forms were sent to registered nurses working in all facilities listed in the Directory of Programs and Facilities for Mentally Disordered Offenders as published by the National Institute of Mental Health (1992). Survey forms were returned from 42 states with the response rate being 45%. The data suggested that master's-prepared nurses are more likely to perform forensic functions involving assessment, consultation, or courtroom testimony. This reinforced the position that forensic psychiatric nurses viewed their intersections of practice outside their own discipline.

The study brought to light the confusion between the terms *forensic* and *correctional* nursing. Many nurses claimed identification as a forensic nurse because of the location of their work or the legal status of their patients, rather than the role functions that they were performing. For example, physiological nurses may perform their functions in psychiatric or correctional nursing facilities and refer to themselves as forensic nurses because the patients are incarcerated. However, this is different from forensic psychiatric nursing, which is not determined by the location but by the

---

Box 36-1 Seven Major Schools of Thought

1. Individual development theory predicts that conduct disorders and early delinquency lead to crime. Temperamental and developmental deficiencies are predictors of a career in crime and are disproportionately common among adolescents who continue criminal activity into adulthood.

2. Social control theory predicts that when the social constraints on antisocial behavior are weakened or absent, delinquent crime emerges. Socially acceptable behavior is more likely if the individual maintains an attachment to others, shares their values, and shares involvement in law-abiding activities.

3. Social learning theory predicts that those who persist in criminal activity continue to increase the frequency, duration, and intensity of contact with other offenders, whereas those who desist from crime decrease contact with offenders and increase contact with nonoffenders. Individuals learn how to break the law in the same way they learn other types of behavior; therefore, criminal behavior is learned. This learning is communicated in intimate groups of family and peers. The learning includes motives, attitudes, and rationalization, as well as technique.

4. Social disorganization theory predicts that crime results when community life becomes disorganized, when high mobility and a heterogeneous population cause a breakdown in conforming controls over criminal conduct. Community consensus on norms, values, and beliefs cannot develop. Residents encounter cultural conflict, loss of control, and an increase in organized illegal activities.

5. Network theory predicts that when network ties are weak, social sanctions against crime will work. People become offenders by being recruited into networks and socialized to crime.

6. Rational choice theory predicts that individuals choose crime when the benefits outweigh the costs of disobeying the law. Crime will decrease when opportunities are limited, benefits are reduced, and costs are increased. Criminal behavior is more than a response to social pressures or upbringing. It is also a choice.

7. Deterrence theory predicts that when punishment is swift and certain, incidence of crime is reduced. A study indicated that 30% of Americans believed that crime could be reduced by emphasizing punishment, and 71% supported greater use of the death penalty.

Data from Ohlin, M., & Farrington, D. (1991). *Human development and criminal behavior: New ways of advancing knowledge.* New York: Springer-Verlag.

nurse-patient relationship and the role functions that they perform. This confusion between physiological nurses being known as forensic nurses was also highlighted in a study in Canada, which focused on the competencies and skills of registered nurses working in correctional healthcare. Although the title suggested that the nurses were "working in forensic areas," none of the actual duties reported were forensic role functions (Niskala, 1986).

BEST PRACTICE The forensic psychiatric nurse must be disciplined to examine a person's motivation for a particular act in an objective, nonjudgmental fashion and be capable of personally communicating with the patient to gain the patient's perspective, which is essential for understanding the patient's actions through the patient's value system (Coram, 2006).

In the United Kingdom, there is a longstanding concern regarding the skills and competencies required by forensic psychiatric nurses working with patients with mental health problems (Ewars & Ikin, 2002), learning disabilities (Woods & Mason, 1998), and psychopathic and personality disorders (Moran & Mason, 1996; Tennant, Davies, & Tennant, 2000). However, more recent research suggests a division between role dimensions and clinical aspects. Mason, Lovell, and Coyle (2008) reported on an investigation into the skills and competencies for forensic psychiatric nurses from the perspective of three groups of healthcare professionals: (1) forensic psychiatric nurses, (2) nonforensic psychiatric nurses, and (3) professionals working in other healthcare disciplines, including psychiatrists, psychologists, social workers, and occupational therapists. From 3360 questionnaires distributed, 1172 were returned, making a response rate of 35%. The study focused on what the three groups of staff considered forensic psychiatric nursing skills and competencies to be and asked them to identify the top 10 strengths and weaknesses, required and not required skills and benefits, and finally the barriers to effective interventions. The nursing groups tended to focus on personal qualities both in relation to themselves and the patients, whereas the other disciplines focused on organizational structures both in defining the role and in the resolution of perceived deficits (Box 36-2).

In their second paper (Mason, et al., 2008), these authors focused on the clinical aspects of their research and identified the top 10 problems that forensic psychiatric nurses are likely to face, the problems that give the most difficulty, the skills best suited to overcome those problems, and the aspects of forensic psychiatric nursing care that need to be developed. The results showed a similarity between the three groups of healthcare professionals in that violence and aggression, particularly with psychopathic patients, was regarded as the main problematic area. However, there were also differences between all three groups with the greatest difference being between the forensic psychiatric nurses and the other disciplines. Further developments have recently been described by Mason, Dulson, and King (2009), who reported on research examining if differences in perceptions of forensic psychiatric nurses differed in relation to the three levels of secure psychiatric services of low, medium, and high security in the UK. The implications for these findings are that they tend to produce more negative views in the high security settings, which led to a withdrawal from therapeutic endeavors (Mason, King, & Dulson, 2009).

KEY POINT Skills and competencies of forensic psychiatric nursing are wide ranging but focus on the offender and his or her offense with the intention of evaluation, treatment, and risk assessment aimed at reducing the possibility of recidivism.

Box 36-2 Competencies and Skills for Forensic Psychiatric Nursing

MAIN STRENGTHS	MAIN WEAKNESSES
Life experience	Frustration
Empathy	Lack of knowledge
Clinical experience	Lack of assertiveness
Knowledge base	Lack of time
Listening skills	Lack of results
Patience	Lack of confidence
Communication	Frustration with aggressive patients
Fairness	Frustration with ignorant staff
Honesty	Lack of research skills
Confidence	Frustration with management/psychiatrists

SKILLS REQUIRED	SKILLS NOT REQUIRED
Skills for personality disordered patients	National vocational qualifications
Listening skills	Overconfidence
Confidence	Demanding nature
Clinical knowledge	Narrow mindedness
Communication skills	Judgmental attitude
Nonjudgmental attitude	Generic psychiatric experience
Empathy	Bad attitude
Patience	Overcontrolling nature
Knowledge of offending behavior	Lack of understanding
Multidisciplinary working skills	Poor risk assessment

MAIN BENEFITS	MAIN BARRIERS
Job satisfaction	Bureaucracy (paperwork)
Patient's progression	Lack of support from managers
Negotiation skills	Management
Patient's improvement	Medical power
Motivation	Poor support from managers
Experience	Multidisciplinary team
Insight	Medical model
Multidisciplinary working	Slow referral systems
Secure environment	Limited resources
Knowledge	Moving patients on

Role Functions

Not surprisingly, in terms of the role functions of forensic psychiatric nurses, the management of violence and aggression feature large, alongside the management of people with psychopathic/personality disorders. Mason, Coyle, and Lovell (2008) reported that the main problems identified for forensic psychiatric nurses across the three groups—(1) forensic nurses, (2) nonforensic nurses, and (3) other disciplines—involved, all agreed, aggressive patients and personality-disordered patients. Box 36-3 presents the main problems and their solutions.

Box 36-3 indicates that within the role function of forensic psychiatric nursing there is some considerable overlap of skills and competencies in which general psychiatric nurses are engaged. The added dimensions appear to be related to the relationships among the patient, the professional, and the public (as potential victims and political influences), which involves certain role developments as outlined next.

From the U.S. and Canadian perspective, the role of the forensic psychiatric nurse is slightly different. A theoretical foundation for forensic psychiatric nursing comes from King's theory for the patient-nurse relationship. She holds that the patient is a personal system within an environment, coexisting with other personal systems. The nurse and the patient perceive both one another and the situation, then they act, react, interact, and transact.

Box 36-3 Problems and Solutions for Forensic Psychiatric Nursing

	FORENSIC NURSES	NONFORENSIC NURSES	OTHER DISCIPLINES
PROBLEMS CAUSING MOST DIFFICULTY	Personality disorders	Aggressive patients	Personality disorders
	Violence	Personality disorders	Unpredictable violence
	Aggression	Manipulation by patients	Verbal threats
	Time management	Demanding patients	Lack of time
	Manipulation by patients	Lack of motivation	Lack of supervision
	Self-harm	Manic patients	Low staffing levels
	Lack of resources	System abusers	Disengagement by patients
	Extreme behavior	Complaints	Theft between patients
	Antisocial problems	Impulsivity	Upsetting other patients
	Leadership concerns	Treatment-resistance psychosis	Locking up patients
SKILLS BEST SUITED TO OVERCOME THE DIFFICULTIES	Aggression management	Relationship formation	Training in challenging behavior
	Multidisciplinary team working	Psychosocial interventions	Multidisciplinary care planning
	Violence training	Counseling skills	Counseling skills
	Consistency of approaches	Understanding	Self-reflective practice
	Team projects	Communication	Analysis skills
	Knowledge of patients	Knowledgeable staff	Client centered
	Interventions	Patience	Generic worker skills
	Boundaries	Confidence	Peer support
	Good teams	Positive reassurance	Organizational support
	Patience	Common sense	Control and restraint

King defined nursing as a process of human interactions between the nurse and patients, who communicate to set goals, explore means for achieving the goals, and then agree on the means to be used. King spoke of nursing as a discipline and an applied science, with an emphasis on the derivation of nursing knowledge from other disciplines. Systems theory from the behavioral sciences led to the development of her dynamic interacting systems, and she identified three distinct levels of operation in this system: (1) individuals, (2) groups, and (3) society (King, 1971). The patient-nurse interactions in forensic psychiatric nursing affect each level. For example, the forensic psychiatric nurse evaluates a felony defendant before a competency hearing (individual level). The expert witness testimony is given during the trial (group level), and the opinion rendered on dangerousness subsequently affects the patient's sentence (society level).

Expanded roles in nursing are defined by their practice. The Social Policy Statement of the American Nurses Association (ANA) describes scope of practice as multidimensional and characterized by four major elements: a core of professional practice common to all members of a discipline, "dimensions" or characteristics of practice, intra- and interprofessional intersections, and practice boundaries (ANA, 1980). Intersections are practice areas that interface or overlap with the professional domain of practitioners in other clinical specialty areas. A discipline's boundaries mark the outer edge of practice for which it is responsible (ANA, 1980). This demarcation is flexible and expands in response to changing societal needs (Mechanic, Weaver, & Resnick, 2003).

Forensic nursing intersections are within other disciplines, rather than other specialty areas of nursing. The forensic psychiatric nurse's scope of practice is greatly affected by the practice setting, which can vary among a crime scene, a courtroom, a forensic hospital, or a correctional facility. The dimensions of practice in forensic psychiatric nursing are affected by the nature of the patient and the patient's current involvement with the criminal justice system. The core of practice is psychiatric nursing, but the relationship between patient and nurse is affected to a greater degree by the alternative social context of the situation precipitating their interaction (Coram, 2006).

KEY POINT Forensic psychiatric nurses work alongside numerous other disciplines, and although there may be several areas of overlap, we need to forge our own identity through scientific inquiry.

DIFFERENTIATING CORRECTIONAL NURSES AND FORENSIC PSYCHIATRIC NURSES

There is much confusion around the terminology and role functions of nurses who work in secure environments. A basic distinction is physiological nurses (general nurses in the UK), who care for patients/prisoners in relation to their physical needs, and psychiatric nurses, who care for patients' mental health concerns. Within correctional environments (prisons in the UK), both groups may well operate. Unfortunately, both groups may also refer to themselves as forensic (physiological/psychiatric) nurses.

In the United States, there is a commonality between physiological forensic nurses and forensic psychiatric nurses in that the nurse-patient relationship is predicated on the possibility that a crime has been committed. The role functions performed contribute data toward answering the question of whether or not a crime has been committed. There is an investigative quality to the nursing assessment that does not exist in other areas of practice. Elsewhere, the registered nurse (RN) may be expected to describe and report findings, but not to interpret them. For example, a school nurse may observe and document the design of marks on a child's back, but the forensic child abuse specialist would take the data further and make an assessment of patterned injury that includes speculation about the type of weapon used in the suspected battering. Where a pediatric nurse treats the immediate injury, the forensic nurse sees the possibility that a crime has been committed and collects evidence that may help to determine facts of the case. Similarly, whereas the pediatric nurse without forensic training takes a history of repeated apneic spells, the forensic nurse specialist may look further for suspected Munchausen's syndrome by proxy.

Evidence collection is central to the role of all forensic nurses. One way evidence collection is performed within forensic psychiatric nursing is in the finding of intent or diminished capacity in the perpetrator's thinking at the time of the crime. This aids in determining the degree of crime and may later impact the perpetrator's sentencing. Forensic psychiatric nurses who work as competency therapists demonstrate evidence collection in another manner. They spend many hours with a defendant, and much of the dialogue related to the case is documented carefully.

Although both correctional nurses and forensic psychiatric nurses interact with the perpetrator, the nature of their relationship and the timing differentiate their roles. Correctional nurses care for the patient's present medical or mental health needs without knowing the nature of their crimes. This is a philosophy of treatment based on the premise that more objective care can be delivered when the healthcare provider is not focusing on the criminal act itself. Correctional nurses do not play a role in determining the future dangerousness of the patient. For the most part, correctional nurses care for the inmate after the charge has been adjudicated.

Role functions within correctional nursing include; (1) determining need for restraint, (2) conducting a body cavity search, (3) assessing risk for custodial suicide, and (4) collecting evidence with a sexual assault kit, among others (Coram, 2006).

A model has been developed to illustrate the differences among correctional nursing, physiological forensic nursing, and forensic psychiatric nursing, all of which overlap in the criminal justice system (Fig. 36-1).

There is a timeline that begins when an interaction between the victim and perpetrator violates a law or may be criminal in nature. The physiological forensic nurse interacts with the victim, and the nature of their relationship is based on the possibility that the interaction between victim and perpetrator was a criminal one. For this same alleged action, the future patient of the forensic psychiatric nurse is arrested. That person is detained in a correctional facility or on a forensic unit in a mental hospital. Eventually there is a hearing or trial, and the person is adjudicated. If convicted, the period in incarceration continues (most likely at a different facility than where pretrial detention took place).

Both the physiological forensic nurse who works with victims and the forensic psychiatric nurse working with the perpetrator time their nurse-patient relationship before adjudication. Correctional nurses may care for the perpetrator both before and after the trial, but the nature of their relationship differs from that of the forensic psychiatric nurses who provided part of the investigatory information

before trial. The correctional nurse deals with the perpetrator's day-to-day medical or mental health needs.

Correctional nursing is defined by the nature of the patient, an inmate. Nurses who work on long-term psychiatric units housing patients who have been acquitted by reason of insanity also define their role by the nature of the inmate. They are more accurately described as correctional mental health nurses. It is misleading for a nurse to self-identify as forensic merely because she or he works in a building with that label. Predominantly, correctional nurses do not perform forensic role behaviors. An exception would be the prison nurse who conducts a rape exam or collects a sample for DNA testing.

KEY POINT Forensic psychiatric nurses work in many settings including secure psychiatric services, prisons, courts, community settings, and legal teams.

Role Developments

Within the UK, forensic psychiatric nurses are predominantly to be found in the secure psychiatric services as outlined earlier in the chapter (i.e., the low-, medium-, and high-security services). However, they have expanded out into other arenas with some operating in court diversion schemes in which they assess the patient/prisoner suitability for referral to the psychiatric system rather than the criminal justice system. They also operate in police stations, again at the point of assessment in relation to a prisoner's mental state and suitability for a psychiatric referral. A small number operate alongside legal teams in a consultancy capacity, but these are few in number in the UK.

In the United States, successful role development must include clearly defined purposes, goals, and role responsibilities as well as mutual agreement of role expectations and both self-confidence of clinical knowledge and ability (Ball, 1990; Barrett, 1971). Forensic psychiatric nursing developments have been more specific in both the United States and Canada. A few will be briefly described.

CLINICAL NURSE SPECIALIST

The role functions of a clinical nurse specialist have been categorized in a variety of ways: clinician, educator, researcher, consultant, executive, change agent, role model, implementer, advocate, manager, and mentor. Hirst and Metcalf (1986) pointed out that it takes considerable time to integrate every role function into one's repertoire. The forensic psychiatric nurse must be highly skilled in interpersonal relations and in developing and maintaining channels of communication. Developing collegial relationships with other disciplines is central to the role because of its intersections of practice with those areas that overlap with the professional domain of other disciplines. Roles performed within forensic psychiatric nursing include forensic examiner, competency therapist, consultant to law enforcement or the criminal justice system, and so on.

In the UK, models of assessment are wide ranging with the growing number of instruments designed to evaluate a persons risk, and these fall into the two broad areas of (1) statistical or actuarial methods and (2) clinical prediction approaches. In all the various assessment tools there is a tendency to establish a cutoff point where the patient is viewed as more likely to reoffend or less likely to reoffend. However, it is not always as simple as this, and both false negatives exist as well as false positives. Predictions are notoriously poor, and we need to develop other approaches that move the focus from the legal concept of dangerousness to the decision-making concept of risk, assess on a continuum rather than as

Perpetrator is the client

Fig. 36-1 Model for nurse-patient relationship.

a simple dichotomy of yes-no, move from one-time predictions to ongoing decision making, and balance possible outcomes with probabilities of occurrence based on specific risk factors.

FORENSIC NURSE EXAMINER

In the United States, the role of the forensic examiner is to conduct an evaluation, answer specific medicolegal questions as directed by the court, and render an expert opinion. There are marked differences between the purpose, techniques, and goals of psychiatric interviews performed by mental health treatment counselors and those performed by forensic examiners. Box 36-4 highlights these differences.

The cognitive set of the forensic examiner differs from that of mental health personnel. Whereas treatment staff members strive to be supportive, accepting, and empathetic, forensic examiners strive to remain neutral, objective, and detached. A treatment intake interview is usually patient structured (nonconfronting or probing), mostly based on information from the patient and for the purpose of treatment. The purpose of the forensic evaluation is legal adjudication. The forensic examiner controls the interview, which is frequently adversarial and does more checking of the accuracy of information given by the patient. Mental health personnel advocate for the patient, whereas forensic examiners advocate for the issues or the results of the evaluation. A thorough and complete forensic evaluation must include a face-to-face interview, a review of contents of the police reports, and a thorough social/psychiatric history. The ethical forensic examiner will decline a request for an examination or expert opinion when denied access to any of the three.

The formation of an expert opinion is based on the following steps:

1. The forensic examiner collects pertinent clinical data, including observed behaviors of the patient, forensic evidence in the police reports, lab reports, psychological testing results, and a thorough social/psychiatric history.
2. The examiner processes all the information based on her or his education and training, experience, scientific/clinical knowledge, and expertise.
3. The examiner skillfully interviews the patient, noting all related clinical findings, including symptoms of mental disorder, behavior, past diagnoses, personality traits, emotions, cognitive abilities, and the psychodynamics of interpersonal relationships.
4. A mental state reconstruction will be based on both the behavior exhibited and the affect expressed. An evaluation of behavior will include evidence at the scene, witness statements of observed symptoms, a retrospective self-report of symptoms, and disclosed motivation. An assessment of the patient's affect will be based on the patient's cognitive processing and reasoning ability, presence of drugs or medical conditions, the social/interpersonal context of the crime, and any causation explanations offered by the patient.
5. The forensic examiner applies legal standards to all the assessment data. The jurisdiction's statutes and definitions of mental state/sanity/competency are compared to applicable case law and published expert legal interpretation (in law reviews, articles, books).

Traditionally, the role of forensic examiner has been only within the scope of practice of the psychiatrist or psychologist. The prerequisite to the expanded role of a forensic examiner by a forensic nurse specialist is educational preparation and experience. Nurses cannot practice in this expanded role if they hold narrow conceptualizations of the issues confronting patients or if they perceive motivation primarily within a cause-and-effect framework. Clinical role development requires not only skill in data gathering from a multisystem perspective but also critical thinking skills in interpreting and using information for problem solving (Murphy, 1986). Membership or certification in such organizations as the American Academy of Forensic Sciences or the American College of Forensic Examiners substantiates credibility in the role. The forensic nurse specialist is encouraged to seek board certification in areas previously represented only by psychiatrists or psychologists.

It is paramount that the forensic examiner verbalizes an exceptional understanding of major mental illness and personality disorders. The forensic examiner must keep abreast of theories being developed on social deviancy and interpersonal violence and must keep current on societal trends (for example, changes in drug use, growth of gang activity, participation in cults), both nationally and in the nurse's own jurisdiction.

A successful forensic examiner is able to separate personal opinion from professional opinion. Personal opinion is based on one's background, upbringing, education, and values. Professional opinion is based on scientific principle, advanced education in a specific field of endeavor, and the unbiased standards set by research in that area.

BEST PRACTICE Forensic psychiatric nurses must be able to isolate and bracket out their personal value systems in dealing with cases of criminal violence, sexual deviancy, ethnic norms, or cultural behaviors and operate as nonjudgmental professionals.

Legal Insanity

As mentioned earlier, the history of legal pleas of insanity are rooted in the McNaughton rules and survive in one form or another in Anglo-American law today. However, as Blackburn (1993, pp. 256–257) has noted:

Box 36-4 Evaluation Issues

CLINICAL ISSUE	MENTAL HEALTHCARE PROVIDER	FORENSIC EXAMINER
Person is the patient/client of:	The practitioner	The attorney
Nature of the privilege	Therapist-patient	Attorney-client or attorney-work product
Cognitive set of evaluator	Supportive, accepting, empathetic	Neutral, objective, detached
Area of expertise	Therapeutic techniques	Psycholegal evaluation standards
Standards	Diagnostic criteria/treatment	Legal criteria for adjudication
Structure of the evaluation	By patient, less structured	By evaluator, more structured
Evaluation completeness	Based on information from patient	Checked for accuracy of sources
Nature of the process	Rarely adversarial	Frequently adversarial
Advocacy of evaluator	For the patient	For issues or results of evaluation
Outcome of evaluation	To benefit the patient	To aid the legal process

They provide a very strict standard, which McNaughtan himself would not have satisfied, and have been a continual source of controversy. They focus on the assumed cognitive effects of 'disease of the mind', a legal concept which assumes defects arising from 'internal' disease, and not external factors such as voluntary ingestion of alcohol or drugs.

Furthermore, it is a requirement to establish that the "defect of reason" is due to the "disease of the mind"—a much more troublesome entity. It must be established that the person lacks the ability to understand that his or her action is legally (not morally) wrong. However, this requirement caused difficulty with volitional issues when the person knows that what he or she is doing is legally wrong but cannot control himself or herself (i.e., kleptomania). This was addressed in Alabama in 1887 through a test for "volitional control," which was subsequently adopted in other states and some British courts.

Throughout history there have been landmark cases that have changed certain aspects and terminology of legal insanity, but it has remained a thorny issue. In New Hampshire in 1870, a further test was introduced that rejected the cognitive and volitional aspects and focused on establishing that the act was a product of mental illness. This allowed the medical model of mental disease to dominate the courts for a considerable time, and some claim even to this day. Although the verdict of "not guilty by reason of insanity" (NGRI) is technically an acquittal, it still leads to compulsory admission to secure psychiatric services (Blackburn, 1993). In England the term was known as "guilty but insane."

The American Law Institute (ALI) introduced a further test during the 1980s, which states that "a person is not responsible for criminal conduct if at the time of such conduct as a result of mental disease or defect he lacks substantial capacity to appreciate the criminality of his conduct or to conform his conduct to the requirements of the law" (Blackburn, 1993, p. 257). This is now known as the ALI test and involves both cognitive and volitional elements. However, after the trial of John Hinckly, who shot at the president in 1982 and received a NGRI verdict, the public demanded reform. The result was a hastily constructed rule (the Bonnie rule), which stated that if "as a result of mental disease or defect he was unable to appreciate the wrongfulness of his conduct at the time of the offense" he should be found NGRI. However, the rider included that the mental disease should be "serious" and, thus, excluded personality disorders (Blackburn, 1983).

Legal sanity differs from clinical sanity. Legal sanity is defined as the person's ability to know right from wrong with reference to the act charged, the capacity to know the nature and quality of the act charged, and the capacity to form the intent to commit the crime. Legal sanity is determined for the specific time of the act, which may range from the split second the accused trains a weapon and fires or over a long weekend, during which several criminal acts are committed. Clinical sanity is the presence of a major mental disorder currently and at the time of the crime. In most states, a major mental disorder is a prerequisite for a finding of legal insanity. State insanity laws may have wording variations, but they will cite the presence of mental disorder or defect. The term *mental disorder* usually refers to major mental illness, whereas *mental defect* usually refers to developmental disability or some physiological condition affecting cognition (e.g., head injury, meningitis, brain tumor, dementia) (Coram, 2006).

Diminished Capacity/Responsibility

In the UK, the defense of insanity has declined since the introduction of Hospital Orders under the Mental Health Act of 1959 and the Homicide Act of 1957. Also, the abolition of capital punishment in 1965 may well have contributed to its decline as a defense. In any event, when it is used it pivots on establishing what exactly is "diminished," and the focus is on an understanding of the psychology of responsibility with, usually, psychiatrists pronouncing on their "expert" knowledge in this arena. In the case of Peter Sutcliffe (the so-called Yorkshire Ripper), who killed 13 women, both the defense and prosecution psychiatrists agreed that he suffered from paranoid schizophrenia, and the trial became a media circus with public outrage that he might receive a lenient disposal. The jury rejected the plea of diminished responsibility, and he was convicted of murder. However, his mental health soon deteriorated in prison, and he was transferred to a high-security psychiatric hospital within a relatively short space of time.

Blackburn (1993, p. 261) informed us that in the UK "diminished responsibility has been accepted in a range of cases including reactive depression, premenstrual tension and psychopathic personality as well as psychosis." However, Blackburn added that diminished responsibility does not necessarily lead to a more lenient disposal and that approximately only a third of males convicted of manslaughter receive a hospital order, reflecting the trend of psychiatrists to claim that psychopaths are untreatable.

In the United States, diminished capacity is an element of the insanity law that refers to the defendant's capacity to form the intent to commit a specific act. There are four levels of intent (purposely, knowingly, recklessly, or negligently), and a court may order an evaluation specific to one level, depending on the crime charged. The criteria for a finding of diminished capacity are based on a legal standard in each state. For example, in Washington the cause of the inability to form intent must be a mental disorder, not amounting to insanity, and not emotions like jealousy, fear, anger, or hatred. The mental disorder must be causally connected to a lack of specific intent, not just reduced perception, awareness, understanding, or overreaction. A "crime of passion" would not qualify. For example, it is not uncommon for people with drug or alcohol intoxication to initiate a defense of diminished capacity, especially if a blackout occurred. The defendant will exclaim, 'How can you hold me responsible for doing something I can't remember doing?' However, having a blackout only means one cannot remember, not that one was unable to make decisions at the time. It is true that judgment is impaired and sensibilities are deadened while intoxicated; however, some argue that altering one's own cognition voluntarily should not excuse criminal behavior. Many states have case law stipulating that voluntary consumption or intoxication precludes the defense (for example, *State v. Wicks*, 1983). On the other hand, if a person is drugged involuntarily and then, while under the influence, commits a criminal act, the behavior may be excused (Coram, 2006).

COMPETENT TO PROCEED

Another issue to be answered is whether or not the person is competent to proceed. The question of competency to stand trial is considered the most important mental health inquiry pursued within the criminal law system (Stone, 1978). An estimated 25,000 defendants are evaluated annually in the United States (Winick, 1995). Criminal insanity is a test of culpability. Competence to stand trial is an issue of "try-ability."

As far back as the eighteenth century, courts were concerned about a person being able to make a well-informed plea and establishing a defense. In the Frith case of 1790, the court stated:

> *No man shall be called upon to make his defense at a time when his mind is in that situation as not to appear capable of so doing, for however guilty he may be, the inquiry into his guilt must be postponed to that season when by collecting together his intellects, and having them entire, he shall be able so to model his defense as to ward off the punishment of the law.*

Whereas legal sanity issues are framed at the time of the alleged act, competency is in the future: "Will the defendant be competent on the day of the hearing/trial?" Competent to proceed is defined as having the capacity to assist one's attorney and to understand the proceedings. The legal standard in most jurisdictions for competence to stand trial is *Dusky v. United States*. This case brought forth the question, "Does the defendant have sufficient present ability to consult with his lawyer with a reasonable degree of rational understanding and whether he has a rational and factual understanding of the nature of the proceedings against him?" Mental retardation does not in itself result in incompetency to stand trial. Developmental disabilities occur in many varied forms and may impact the capacity of the accused to comprehend the proceedings. A disabled person may experience short attention spans, poor memory, difficulty following direction, poor reading and comprehension, and other problems. Reasoning may be deficient or illogical. One does not need to be literate to be deemed competent.

Because it is a determination of mental state in the future, a defendant's competency must be determined anew each time the defendant goes to court. A prior finding of incompetency, even when the result of a developmental disability, does not preclude a subsequent finding of competency in a later, unrelated case (*State v. Minnix*, 1991).

A number of structured interview/assessment tools address competence. These include the Competency Screening Test developed by McGarry and his colleagues (Laboratory of Community Psychiatry, 1973; Lipsett, Lelos, & McGarry, 1971), the Competency Assessment Interview, the Competency to Stand Trial Assessment Instrument (Laboratory of Community Psychiatry, 1973), the Interdisciplinary Fitness Interview (Golding, Roesch, & Schreiber, 1984), and the Georgia Court Competency Test (Wildman, Batchelor, & Thompson et al., 1980). Further studies have indicated that there is no correlation between a diagnosis of psychosis and performance on these tests. The tests can be used as an adjutant in determination, but they should not be used as the sole qualifier (Coram, 2006).

Personal Safety

In the UK, personal safety is a central theme for forensic psychiatric nurses, and it is no surprise that it has featured large in many skills, competency, and training programs (Mason & Chandley, 1999). Because of the nature of the nurse-patient relationship in forensic psychiatric nursing, the interaction is usually involuntary on the part of the patient. The patient is not seeking the services of the nurse and is not necessarily going to cooperate with any proceedings by actively participating. Although it is true that everyone is capable of committing a crime given the right circumstances and that not all criminals

are necessarily bad people, some are. In some cases it is not surprising that judges and media reports refer to the perpetrator as "evil" (Mason, 2006). In working with violent perpetrators, predators, and those who are sadistic just for the sake of continuing a lifetime of being threatening, intimidating, and harassing, it will be a natural occurrence to feel afraid—for oneself, one's family, and one's property. All may be threatened at one time or another. Acknowledging the feeling when it happens and being willing to talk about it is central to managing the negative feelings that the situation evokes. It is worrisome when individuals are not afraid, because being concerned is a response that increases alertness and is ultimately self-protective.

In the United States, the Department of Corrections provides the Victim-Witness Notification Program, which notifies participants when a violent, sex, or serious drug offender moves through the system. The forensic nurse specialist becomes eligible after being identified as a witness for the prosecution if the offender was found guilty. The forensic nurse examiner is notified when these offenders are approved for furlough from a prison or work-release facility, approved for parole, complete their sentences, transfer from prison to work release or community supervision, escape from custody, or are recaptured.

BEST PRACTICE Forensic psychiatric nurses will tenaciously guard their professional ethics and the integrity of their opinions, never sacrificing truth for the sake of persuasion (Coram, 2006). They will also constantly self-reflect on their personal and professional value systems and rigorously engage with ethical standards of conduct.

Summary

In the UK, there continues to be a growth of forensic psychiatric nurses as the system of secure services expands, and the increase in textbooks on the topic would suggest that this is likely to continue. However, the expansion of scientific inquiry appears to be a slower concern with few developments in risk assessment strategies, risk management approaches, and specific nursing interventions targeted at forensic patients. Mason and Carton (2002) have argued for a "forensic lens" model of multidisciplinary training, and they have identified a number of common areas for development. However, professional boundaries often do not allow shared education, and this continues to be difficult in the UK forensic arena.

In the United States, McGivern (1986) claimed that the expanded role is as much a way of thinking as it is a set of functions. To push the limits of one's scope of practice requires personal gumption and a commitment to the future of the profession. Nursing places a high value on its traditions. Challenge to those who push the boundaries will come as much from within the profession as from the outside. Ball (1990) pointed out that facilitation of the CNS role to its highest potential will include role acceptance by nursing, medical, and other professionals. Successful introduction of the role of the forensic psychiatric nurse specialist will set a precedent for other nurse specialists who will follow. Anyone who meets the challenge of developing a new CNS role must have justifiable confidence in one's own knowledge and ability and in one's self as an individual. One needs to have strong convictions about the value of the CNS role in which one is functioning and an appreciation of the far-reaching effects it can have on the professional practice of nursing (Barrett, 1971).

Resources

American Psychiatric Nurses Association
1555 Wilson Boulevard, Suite 602, Arlington, VA 22209
www.apna.org
Forensic Psychiatric Nurses Association (UK)
www.fnrh.freeserve.co.uk/fpna/index.html
International Association of Forensic Nurses
1517 Ritchie Highway, Suite 208, Arnold, MD 21012-2323
www.iafn.org

References

American Nurses Association (ANA). (1980). *Nursing: Social Policy Statement (Publication No. NP-68A)*. Kansas City, MO: Author.

American Nurses Association (ANA). (1985). *Standards of nursing practice in correctional facilities*. Kansas City, MO: Author.

Ball, G. (1990). Perspectives on developing, marketing, and implementing a new clinical specialist position. *Clinical Nurse Specialist CNS, 4*(1), 33–36.

Barrett, J. (1971). Administrative factors in development of new practice roles. *The Journal of Nursing Administration, 3*(2), 25–29.

Bencer, B. (1989). Caring for clients with legal charges on a voluntary psychiatric unit. *J Psychosoc Nurs, 27*(3), 16–20.

Blackburn, R. (1993). *The Psychology of Criminal Conduct: Theory, Research and Practice*. Chichester: John Wiley & Sons.

Coram, J. (2006). Psychiatric forensic nursing. In V. A. Lynch (Ed.), *Forensic Nursing*. St. Louis, MO: Elsevier Mosby.

Dusky v. U.S., 362 U.S. 402. (1960).

Ewars, P., & Ikin, P. (2002). Nursing interventions and future directions with the severely mentally ill. In A. Kettles, P. Woods, & M. Collins (Eds.), *Therapeutic Interventions for Mental Health Nurses*. London: Jessica Kingsley Publishers.

Foucault, M. (1978). About the concept of the dangerous individual in 19th century legal psychiatry. *International Journal of Law and Psychiatry, 1*(1), 1–18.

Frith, 22 Howell St. Tr. 307, 311. (1790).

Golding, G., Roesch, R., & Schreiber, J. (1984). Assessment and conceptualization of competency to stand trial. *Law and Human Behavior, 8*(14), 321–334.

Her Majesty's Stationary Office (HMSO). (1975). *Report of the Committee on Mentally Abnormal Offenders*. London: HMSO.

Hirst, S. P., & Metcalf, B. J. (1986). Learning needs of caregivers. *Journal of Gerontological Nursing, 12*(4), 24–28.

Keeling, J., & Mason, T. (2009). *Domestic Violence*. Maidenhead: Open University Press.

King, I. (1971). *Toward a theory for nursing*. New York: John Wiley & Sons.

Laboratory of Community Psychiatry, Harvard University. (1973). *Competency to stand trial and mental illness*. Department of Health, Education, and Welfare (DHEW) Pub. No. (HSM) 73-9105. Rockville, MD: National Institute of Mental Health, Center for Studies of Crime and Delinquency.

Lipsett, P., Lelos, D., & McGarry, A. (1971). Competency for trial: A screening instrument. *The American Journal of Psychiatry, 128*(1), 105–109.

Marsh, I. (1986). *Sociology in Focus: Crime*. London: Longman.

Mason, T. (2006). *Forensic Psychiatry: Influences of Evil*. Totowa, NJ: Humana Press.

Mason, T., & Carton, G. (2002). Towards a 'Forensic Lens' model of multidisciplinary training. *Journal of Psychiatric and Mental Health Nursing. 9*, 541–551.

Mason, T., & Chandley, M. (1999). *Managing Violence and Aggression: A Manual for Nurses and Health Care Workers*. Edinburgh: Churchill Livingstone.

Mason, T., Coyle, D., & Lovell, A. (2008). Forensic psychiatric nursing: skills and competencies: II clinical aspects. *Journal of Psychiatric and Mental Health Nursing, 15*(2), 131–139.

Mason, T., Dulson, J., & King, L. (2009). Binary constructs of forensic psychiatric nursing: A pilot study. *Journal of Psychiatric and Mental Health Nursing, 16*(2), 158–166.

Mason, T., King, L., & Dulson, J. (2009). Binary construct analysis of forensic psychiatric nursing in the UK: High, Medium and low security services. *International Journal of Mental Health Nursing, 18*(3), 216–224.

Mason, T., Lovell, A., & Coyle, D. (2008). Forensic psychiatric nursing: skills and competencies: I role dimensions. *Journal of Psychiatric and Mental Health Nursing, 15*(2), 118–130.

Mason, T., & Mercer, D. (1998). *Critical Perspectives in Forensic Care: Inside Out*. London: Macmillan.

Mason, T., & Mercer, D. (1999). *A Sociology of the Mentally Disordered Offender*. London: Longman.

McGivern, D. (1986). The evolution of primary care nursing. In: M. Mezney & D. McGivern (Eds.), *Nurses, nurse practioners: The evolution of primary care* (pp. 3–14). Boston: Little Brown.

Mechanic, M. B., Weaver, T. L., & Resnick, P. A. (2003). Intimate partner stalking behavior: Exploration of patterns and correlates in a sample of acutely battered women. *Violence and victims, 15*(1), 55–71.

Moran, T., & Mason, T. (1996). Revisiting the nursing management of the psychopath. *Journal of Psychiatric and Mental Health Nursing, 3*(3), 189–194.

Murphy, K. (1986). Primary care in an undergraduate curriculum. In M. D. Mezey, & D. O. McGivern (Eds.), *Nurses, nurse practitioners: The evolution of primary care* (pp. 78–85). Glenview, IL: Scott, Foreman, and Co.

National Institute of Mental Heath. (1992). *Directory of Programs and Facilities for Mentally Disorders Offenders*. Washington, DC: Dept. of Health and Human Services.

Niskala, H. (1986). Competencies and skills required by nurses working in forensic areas. *Western Journal of Nursing Research, 8*(4), 400–413.

Ohlin, M., & Farrington, D. (1991). *Human Development and Criminal Behavior: New Ways of Advancing Knowledge*. New York: Springer-Verlag.

Snowden, P. R. (1990). Regional secure units and forensic services in England and Wales. In R. Bluglass, & P. Bowden (Eds.), *Principles and Practice of Forensic Psychiatry*. London: Churchill Livingstone.

State v. Minnix (1991). 63, Wn. App 494.

State v. Wicks, (1983). 98 Wn.2d 620, 657 P.2d 781.

Stone, A. (1978). Psychiatry and the law. In A. Nichols (Ed.), *The Harvard guide to modern psychiatry*. Cambridge, MA: Harvard University Press.

Tennant, A., Davies, C., & Tennant, I. (2000). Working with the personality disordered offender. In C. Chaloner, & M. Coffey (Eds.), *Forensic mental health nursing: Current approaches*. Oxford: Blackwell.

U.S. v. Chisholm, (1901). 149 f. 284, 5th Cir Ct.

Wildman, R., Batchelor, E., Thompson, L., et al. (1980). *The Georgia competency test: An attempt to develop a rapid quantitative measure for fitness to stand trial*. Unpublished manuscript. Milledgeville, GA: Forensic Services Division, Central State Hospital.

Winick, B. (1995). The side effects of incompetency labeling and the implications for mental health law. *Psychol Public Policy Law, 1*(1), 6–42.

Woods, P., & Mason, T. (1998). Mental impairment and admission to a special hospital. *The British Journal of Developmental Disabilities, 44*(2), 119–131.

Youtsey v. U.S. (1899). 97F.937 (6th Cir).

CHAPTER 37 Suicidal Behavior and Risk Assessment

Karolina Krysinska and Paul Thomas Clements

Suicide risk continues to provide challenges for forensic nurses, especially those in psychiatric and correctional settings. There is a high probability in a variety of clinical settings that forensic nurse examiners (FNEs) will encounter a patient who may be at risk for suicide. In such circumstances, the knowledge concerning risk factors for suicidal behavior, basic tools, and methods for suicide risk assessment, as well as the role of clinical judgment, can be of great help and importance.

KEY POINT Beware of a seeming "flight into health" by victimized and traumatized patients. This apparent elevation of mood and affect is often not actually the result of an alleviation of the related intrapsychic or psychosocial stressors. Rather, it is potentially the acceptance that an overarching "solution" (i.e., a determination to commit suicide to end the problems) has been attained. The decision to commit suicide can actually bring significant relief to patients, as there is now a measurable endpoint to their distress and suffering.

Assessment of suicide risk includes identification of individuals with a potential for suicide and the assessment of an individual's intent. This implies that although it may be possible to make a clinical judgment concerning the probability of suicidal behavior in a given individual, it precludes the accurate prediction of suicide attempts or completed suicide. Although this seems to be a subtle distinction, it highlights the fact that based on current knowledge it is practically impossible to determine whether a patient will engage in suicidal behavior; it is only possible to judge the relative probability. Maris (1992) wrote, "Of course, suicidal hindsight is 20/20. But before the fact of suicide, everything is usually not so obvious . . . . One may cynically conclude that only suicide predicts suicide" (p. 3).

Suicide risk assessment can be analyzed on two levels: individual and social. Although this chapter only reviews the individual level, it should be remembered that the assessment of suicide risk in the level of the general population and specific groups (e.g., occupational, economic, ethnic) is of great importance for setting mental healthcare goals related to suicide prevention, organization of mental health systems, and healthcare budgets.

Typically, assessment of suicide risk is a first step toward prevention, intervention, and therapy for at-risk individuals. A systematic and thorough suicide risk assessment is crucial for making proper decisions concerning the type of intervention necessary in a given case: whether the patient should be referred to intensive outpatient or community-based care, whether the patient should be voluntarily or involuntarily hospitalized and treated in a psychiatric inpatient setting, whether pharmacother-

apy is indicated, or whether suicide watches or a no-suicide contract should be applied.

Assessment of suicide risk may be necessary in various settings and situations (Jacobs, Brewer, & Klein-Benheim, 1999; Maris, 1992). It may be conducted within the context of forensic or other outpatient assessment and intervention (e.g., when any suicidal ideation or behavior is noticed or whenever suicidality becomes an issue for the patient) and in the psychiatric inpatient setting (e.g., during the initial psychiatric assessment during admission and again predischarge, or before initiating or altering patient psychopharmacological regimen). The assessment of the risk for repetition of suicidal behavior by patients with previous suicide attempts who are treated in general hospitals is a basic component of postvention with this significantly vulnerable population. It is also an important tool in suicide prevention in schools and workplace settings where counselors, teachers, peers, and other gatekeepers are trained to identify and refer at-risk individuals to mental health professionals (Clements, DeRanieri, Fay-Hillier et al., 2003). Forensic nurses are also uniquely positioned to assess and identify at-risk patients.

Suicide ranks 11th among leading causes of death in the United States. It is the second leading cause of death among college students and young adults, 25-34 years of age (CDC, 2006). According to the American Association of Suicidology (AAS) (American Association of Suicidology, 2004a), since the mid-1980s the overall completed suicide rates in the United States have been relatively stable, and as recently as 2001, the national suicide rate was 10.8 per 100,000. Although there are no official statistics on attempted (nonfatal) suicide, it is estimated that there are approximately 8 to 20 attempts for each completed suicidal death. Although, from clinical and ethical perspectives, it is impossible to minimize the impact and consequences of suicidal behaviors.

According to the results of a study by Pokorny (1983), suicide risk assessment scales typically produce such large numbers of false positives (cases in which suicide was predicted but did not happen) that they cannot be distinguished from true positives (suicide correctly predicted). In the study, 4800 psychiatric patients who were monitored over a five-year period reported a significantly small number (n = 67) who died by suicide. Using the best available predictive tests, the study correctly identified 35 of 63 individuals who completed suicide (true positives) and 3435 as not being at risk of suicide (true negatives). However, of note, 1206 individuals were incorrectly identified as being at risk of suicide (false positives), and 28 patients who committed suicide were judged as being at low risk (false negatives). These results led to the conclusion that the assessment of long-term suicide risk is practically impossible, particularly because current tests or scales do not have the expected sensitivity (proportion of correctly identified positive cases) and specificity (proportion of correctly identified negative cases).

Another difficulty in suicide risk assessment stems from the basic question: What type of suicidal behaviors are being predicted and prevented—specifically, completed suicides or attempted suicides? Although the distinction between these two types is often blurred, they represent two distinct categories of direct self-destructive behaviors and subsequently require different types of assessment and intervention within different clinical settings (O'Carroll, Berman, Maris, et al., 1996).

Short-term and long-term suicide risk factors are often not identical. For example, in a study conducted by Stelmachers and Sherman (1992), it was noted that clinicians considered different sets of variables while making a judgment on short-term versus long-term suicide risk. It was also discovered that there was a low consensus among clinicians concerning the estimation of suicide potential (as well as recommended crisis management and clinical interventions). This was particularly evident in cases of long-term and low-to-moderate short-term suicide risk. This led the authors to conclude that "there is higher consistency in judgments about cases that are more emergent, critical, or extreme" (p. 263). In addition, the changeability of protective and risk factors, as well as the unpredictability of changes in an individual's life situation, may make the long-term suicide risk assessment practically impossible and lead to many false positives and negatives (Pokorny, 1983).

Ultimately, the assessment of suicide risk must be based on a thoughtful consideration of the unique and dynamic constellation and interaction of protective risk factors observed in a specific case. It is never enough to mechanically use standardized suicide screening checklists and other tools that have been created on the basis of general knowledge surrounding the characteristics of high-risk groups. The suicide risk assessment procedure should be based on clinical judgment, supported by data obtained from prediction scales, medical files, clinical history, and a thorough interview with the individual who is considered to be at risk, as well as collateral contacts such as relatives and significant others.

BEST PRACTICE The assessment of suicide risk must be based on a thoughtful consideration of the unique and dynamic constellation and interaction of protective and risk factors observed in a specific case. It is never enough for the forensic nurse to mechanically use standardized suicide screening checklists and other tools that have been created on the basis of general knowledge surrounding the characteristics of high-risk groups.

Risk Factors for Suicidal Behavior

Suicide is a complex, multidimensional phenomenon that has been associated with many correlates, antecedents, and risk factors. Although there are still some controversies among researchers and clinicians regarding predictors of suicidal behaviors, there are some risk factors that almost everyone agrees are present in most suicides (AAS, 2004b; Jacobs, et al., 1999; Maris, 1992). These are discussed next and represent risk factors identified in the populations typically seen in various mental health practice settings.

DEMOGRAPHIC CHARACTERISTICS

Demographic factors (e.g., sex, age, marital status, race, geographic location) provide a general indication of those groups in the general population that are at the highest risk of suicidal behaviors (AAS, 2004a, 2004c; Garrison, 1992). It has been identified that demographic profiles of suicide attempters and completers are different.

In the United States, males complete suicide at a rate four times that of females (in 2001: accordingly, 17.6/100,000 and 4.1/100,000). Suicide rates are the highest among the elderly (age 75 and older), the divorced, the separated, and the widowed. In regard to race and ethnicity, whites die by suicide twice as often as nonwhites, and Native Americans have the highest overall suicide rate, although there are differences between tribal groups. Blacks and Hispanics exhibit low risk of suicide; however, the suicide rate is increasing faster among African-American youths than among Caucasians. White men over the age of 85 are at the greatest risk of all demographic groups. Statistics reveal a suicide rate in this population of 15.9 per 100,000, which is almost six times the overall national suicide rate in the United States. Geographically, suicide rates are the highest in the Mountain states (in 2001: 16.2/100,000) (CDC, 2006).

Nonfatal suicidal behaviors are more frequent among the young and among females, who make three to four times as many attempts as males. African-American females are more likely to attempt suicide, but males in this ethnic group are more likely to die by suicide. Although the elderly make suicidal attempts less frequently than individuals in other age groups, their attempts are more lethal. For example, in this group, the ratio of attempted to completed suicide is 4:1, while for all ages combined the ratio is 20:1.

Although demographic factors reflect high-risk groups in the general population, there is little reliability in the predictive probability that a particular person will engage in suicidal behavior. Therefore, the consideration of other types of information is necessary to improve the sensitivity and specificity of suicide risk assessment.

MENTAL DISORDERS

Psychological autopsy studies (i.e., a postmortem examination of decedent presuicide risk factors, behaviors, and method of death) indicate that more than 90% of persons completing suicide have one or more mental disorders. These results are supported by data obtained using other methods of research (i.e., prospective follow-up studies and retrospective reviews of medical records). Suicide and nonfatal suicidal behaviors occur more frequently than expected among individuals with the diagnosis of mental disorder, and when coexisting disorders are identified, the risk is even greater (Jacobs, et al., 1999; Tanney, 1992).

Harris and Barraclough (1997) conducted a meta-analysis of 249 reports (published between 1966 and 1993) and found that 36 of 44 diagnoses (according to the DSM-III-R or ICD systems) had significantly raised standardized mortality ratios for suicide. These data led them to the conclusion that "if these results can be generalized, then virtually all mental disorders have an increased risk of suicide excepting mental retardation and possibly dementia, and agoraphobia" (p. 222). Although persons with practically any mental disorder engage in suicidal behaviors more often than individuals in the general population, the completed suicide risk is the highest among individuals diagnosed with affective disorders (major depression, bipolar disorder) and schizophrenia. The risk for nonfatal suicidal behaviors is significantly increased in case of depressive neuroses (dysthymic disorders) and personality disorders (especially Axis II diagnoses of borderline, antisocial, and narcissistic personality disorders). Many researchers and clinicians point out that comorbidity of mental disorders (e.g., panic disorder and affective disorder, schizophrenia and comorbid depressive disorder/substance abuse, co-occurrence of personality disorders and depression/schizophrenia) makes the risk of suicide even greater. The suicide risk factors in affective disorders and schizophrenia are discussed next.

Lifetime risk of suicide in affective disorders is 15%, and patients with these diagnoses constitute 50% to 70% of suicides. Among factors associated with an increased suicide risk in patients with the diagnosis of major depressive disorder are the severity of depression (the more severe clinical depression, the more acute suicide risk), increasing agitation and worsening melancholic symptoms, early course of illness before diagnosis and treatment, the recovery period and the period following hospitalization, as well as the co-occurrence of other psychiatric and substance abuse disorders.

Long-term suicide risk factors connected with the diagnosis of depressive disorders are high hopelessness, suicidal ideation, and previous suicide attempts. There is no consensus among researchers concerning increased suicide risk in delusional versus nondelusional depression (Jacobs, et al., 1999).

Significant risk factors for suicide in the manic-depressive illness include the increased severity of symptoms, family history of suicide, and history of patient's previous suicide attempt. The suicide risk is raised early in the course of the illness, in mixed states (the combination of morbid depressive thoughts with high energy and agitation), in the depressive phase, during the recovery period, and following hospitalization (Jamison, 1999).

Individuals with the diagnosis of schizophrenia account for 10% to 15% of completed suicides, and the lifetime suicide risk in this population is 10%. The risk of suicide is greater in case of comorbidity (e.g., depressive disorder or substance abuse) and in paranoid schizophrenia with numerous positive symptoms, whereas it is lower in patients with negative (deficit) subtypes of the illness. The majority of researchers point out the fact that suicide in patients with the diagnosis of schizophrenia is most often related to the painful awareness of the deterioration of their abilities and the discrepancy between the future envisioned in the past before the onset of the illness and the likely degree of chronic and incurable disability in the future (especially in young males with good intellectual functioning and good premorbid school or work progress). Additionally, the suicide risk is heightened during early stages of the illness, in periods of clinical improvement after relapse, and during periods of hopelessness and depressed mood (Jacobs, et al., 1999).

The causal relationship between the diagnosis of a mental illness and suicidal behaviors is not clear. Tanney (1992) suggested several mechanisms, ranging from direct causes or consequences (e.g., command hallucinations and depressive delusions) and indirect complications (e.g., iatrogenic toxicity of medication and hopelessness of chronic disorder) to additive and releasing effects (e.g., alcohol abuse in depression leading to psychological disinhibition) and common etiology (e.g., isolation or loneliness may lead both to suicide and depression).

SUBSTANCE ABUSE

Numerous studies have found a strong relationship between suicidal behavior and substance abuse (Jacobs, et al., 1999; Lester, 1992). There is consistent evidence of elevated suicide rate among alcoholics. Of note, approximately 18% of alcoholics commit suicide, and 21% of all suicides involve patients diagnosed with a substance abuse disorder involving alcohol. The evidence for the association between alcohol abuse and nonfatal suicidal behavior is less consistent, although some studies have found a high incidence of suicide attempts (up to 24%) in alcoholics (Lester, 1992).

Several factors have been linked to suicide in alcohol abusers. The prominent risk factors are comorbid depression, communication of suicidal intent, continued drinking (suicide in alcoholics usually is related to late stages of the addiction), serious medical illness, unemployment, living alone, and poor social support, as well as a recent loss of an important interpersonal relationship.

The pathways between suicidal behavior and alcohol abuse are numerous and variegated. For example, substance abuse can be considered a "chronic suicide" indicator, and abused substances can be used as means of suicide (e.g., cocaine and heroine overdoses, a lethal concoction of alcohol and medications). Addictions and abuse often disrupt individuals' interpersonal networks and their professional performance, which may cause isolation and social decline. Alcohol and drugs may lower restraints against suicide and impair judgment and increase impulsivity and risk taking, as well as increase an individual's self-depreciation and depression. Some people planning suicide use alcohol and other drugs to achieve such mental state to "get the courage to die." There is also a possibility that substance abuse and suicide stem from the same predisposing factors (e.g., personality disorder, mood dysregulation), and chronic alcohol abuse may directly change the brain neurochemistry through its impact on the serotonergic system. Paradoxically, in the early stages of abuse, when alcohol and other drugs are used as self-medication, they may lower the suicide risk in depression or replace direct suicidal behavior.

Much more research has been done on alcoholics than on drug abusers; however, the available data point out that individuals addicted to drugs have a higher incidence of suicide, nonfatal suicidal attempts, and suicidal ideation than do individuals in the general population. An increased suicide rate was found in narcotic and opioid addicts; for example, results of studies showed that up to 7% of cocaine abusers and 11% of methaqualone users died of suicide, and more drug abuse was noted in a sample of military trainees who attempted suicide than in the control group (Lester, 1992).

PHYSICAL ILLNESS

Medical disorders are associated with suicide in various ways (Harris & Barraclough, 1994; Kelly, Mufson, & Rogers, 1999). For example, some medical disorders may be caused by self-injury or substance abuse stemming from preexisting mental disorders, and a medical disorder and treatment (e.g., medication) may affect brain functioning, leading to personality disorders and mood disturbances. Additionally, disfigurement or disability caused by medical illness may result in mood dysregulation, and stigmatized diagnoses may contribute to social isolation and withdrawal of diseased individuals.

Numerous medical diagnoses have been related to increased suicide risk. For example, Harris and Barraclough (1994) noted that suicide risk increases with the following diagnoses (note that the number in parentheses means increased suicide risk in patients with the given diagnosis over the general population risk): HIV/AIDS (6.6), Huntington disease (2.9), malignant neoplasms (all sites, 1.8; head and neck, 11.4), multiple sclerosis (2.4), peptic ulcer (2.1), renal disease (hemodialysis, 14.5; transplantation, 3.8), spinal cord injuries (3.8), and systemic lupus erythematosus (4.3).

Suicide risk is increased in epilepsy (fivefold) and in chronic pain syndrome and traumatic brain injury, which are associated with depression and suicidal ideation (Kelly, et al., 1999).

SUICIDAL IDEATION

Suicidal thoughts range from harmless, transient fantasies that may help one to cope with life problems—as exemplified by Nietzsche's famous words: "The thought of suicide is a great consolation; by means of it one gets successfully through many a bad night" (Nietzsche & Zimmern, 1989)—to recurrent suicidal ideation and concrete plans of self-destruction (Kerkhof & Arensman, 2001; van Heeringen, 2001).

Adolescent population surveys show that considering suicide as an alternative problem solution is a rather normal and prevalent way of coping in this age group, and a study by Meehan et al. (1992) reported that 54% of college students have thought about suicide, including 26% of subjects who thought about it in the previous 12 months. Although still common, adult subjects report less suicidal ideation. Epidemiological studies have shown that the 1-year prevalence for suicidal thoughts ranges between 2.3% and 5.6%, and the lifetime prevalence is 13% to 15% (Kerkhof & Arensman, 2001).

Although suicidal ideation in the general population may be a frequent phenomenon, it should be remembered that suicidal ideation may evolve into a suicide plan, leading to self-destructive behavior that may result in death. A general population study by Kessler, Borges, and Walters (1999) showed that the transition from ideation to plan occurred in 34% of individuals who thought about suicide and further transitioned into an attempt in 72% (specifically, 26% of subjects proceeded from ideation to an impulsive attempt).

Therefore, an essential part of any suicide assessment procedure should be asking the interviewed individual about her or his suicidal ideation and plans. One of the most serious warning signs of high suicide risk, which calls for an immediate intervention, is a well thought-out and detailed suicide plan (including a place, time, and method), that is to be carried out in circumstances excluding the possibility of discovery and intervention by others. Any activities that show that an individual is preparing for death (e.g., writing a suicide note, making a will, giving away possessions) are other warning signs of suicide (Jacobs, et al., 1999).

Of course, a lack of a detailed suicide plan or denial of any suicidal ideation by a patient does not mean that there is no risk of suicide; in such cases, other means of assessment of suicide risk are recommended (e.g., the clinical judgment, risk assessment scales, and checklists).

PREVIOUS SUICIDAL BEHAVIOR

Maris (1992) has stated that "any individual with a history of one or more prior nonfatal suicide attempts is at much greater risk for suicide than most of those who have never made a suicide attempt" (p. 11). Results of his psychological autopsy study showed that 30% to 40% of suicide completers had made at least one prior nonfatal suicide attempt, and about 15% of suicide attempters eventually died by suicide.

Several factors associated with risk of suicide after attempted suicide have been identified. These include older age (only females), male gender, unemployment or retirement, marital status (widowed, divorced, or separated), living alone, poor physical health, psychiatric disorder (especially depression, alcoholism, schizophrenia, and sociopathic personality disorder), high suicidal intent in current episode, violent method in current attempt, leaving a suicide note, and previous attempt(s) (Hawton, 2000).

A history of a suicide attempt is also correlated with the risk of repetition of nonfatal suicidal behavior. A classification of suicide attempters based on the history of repetition of their behavior has been proposed by Kreitman and Casey (1988): "first evers," "minor repeaters" (lifetime history of two to four attempts), and "major/grand repeaters" (five attempts and more). A study conducted in Great Britain indicated that 48% of males with a history of nonfatal suicidal behaviors were first evers, 36% minor, and 16% grand attempters (for women, accordingly, 53%, 35%, and 12%). Factors that are associated with risk of repetition of attempted suicide have additionally been identified. These include a previous attempt, previous psychiatric treatment, personality disorder, substance abuse, unemployment, lower social class, criminal record, history of violence, age 25 to 54 years, and marital status (single, divorced, or separated) (Hawton, 2000).

Marzuk and colleagues (1997) have described a category of an "aborted suicide attempt" in which an individual has intent to kill himself or herself, changes his or her mind before making the attempt, and there is no physical injury. Their study on the prevalence of suicidal behavior among psychiatric inpatients showed that 46% of subjects made a suicide attempt, and 29% had a history of at least one aborted suicide attempt (which, in the case of almost one third of the patients, would be of high lethality, i.e., gunshot, jumping from heights). The authors concluded:

> The finding that many individuals who made aborted attempts have also made actual suicide attempts suggest that aborted attempts lie closer to the actual attempts than ideation does on the spectrum of suicidal behaviors....Some aborted suicides might have occurred before actual attempts and, in effect, served as a rehearsal....Given the high lethality of some of these aborted attempts, it is possible that aborted attempts are predictive of actual completed suicide. (p. 495)

Although Marzuk and colleagues admitted that the relationship between aborted attempts, actual attempts, and suicidal ideation is not clear, they suggested that suicide risk assessment should include inquiries about aborted attempts and reasons for abandoning the suicidal behavior.

Although the acts of self-mutilation (defined by the lack of conscious suicidal intent) are usually distinguished from suicidal behaviors, they should also be considered as suicide risk factors. Research shows that more than 50% of self-mutilators attempt suicide by a drug overdose, usually as a result of demoralization related to their inability to control self-mutilating behaviors (Favazza & Simeon, 1995).

ACCESS TO LETHAL MEANS

Although practically all methods used by individuals engaging in suicidal behaviors may lead to death or serious injuries, the statistical lethality of different means ranges from high to low risk of death (McIntosh, 1992). The likelihood of death is the highest in case of gunshot, carbon monoxide, hanging, drowning, suffocation by plastic bag, physical impact (jumping from heights, in front of a train, etc.), fire, poison, drugs, gas, and self-cutting. At least two factors contribute to the probability of death when using a particular method: the amount of time between the initiation of the suicidal act and death (e.g., drugs and poisons allow for the possibility of changing one's mind and seeking help and allow for detection and intervention by others) and availability and effectiveness of medical intervention related to the method.

The choice of means of suicide depends on several factors: availability of the method and familiarity with it, suicidal intent and motivation of the individual (although there is no direct relationship between the medical lethality of the method and the desire to die, it is mediated by the attempter's knowledge of the lethality of the method), and the cultural/ethnic factors (e.g., the gender socialization, social acceptability of suicide, the symbolic meanings of particular methods, and sites of suicide).

A specific suicide plan including an available and highly lethal means of suicide is a major risk factor of suicidal behavior and calls for a prompt and decisive intervention. Reducing access to means of suicide (e.g., legislations limiting access to firearms, careful dispensing of over-the-counter and prescription medications, detoxification or reduced toxicity of domestic gas and car exhaust, reduced access to high buildings, bridges, and legendary "suicide sites") has been proved to reduce the incidence of suicide on both individual and population levels. It has to be kept in mind that many suicidal behaviors are impulsive and involve ambivalent attitudes toward life and death; in such cases, limited access to highly lethal methods increases the probability of survival and the effectiveness of medical intervention.

FAMILY HISTORY OF PSYCHIATRIC ILLNESS AND SUICIDAL BEHAVIOR

Roy (1992) observed that "suicide, like so much else in psychiatry, tends to run in families" (p. 578). Since the mid-1980s, results of numerous studies have led to the conclusion that there may be familiar or genetic determinants of suicidal behavior. Different lines of evidence point to this possibility (Roy, 1992). For example, clinical and follow-up studies (including Amish studies) show that individuals with a diagnosis of a mental illness (mostly affective disorders, especially depression) and a history of (fatal or nonfatal) suicidal behavior and affective disorder among the first- and second-degree relatives have increased risk of engaging in suicidal behavior themselves. These data are supported by results of twin studies showing the statistically significant higher incidence of suicide and psychiatric disorder in monozygotic pairs than among dizygotic twins.

Several explanations concerning the familial vulnerability to suicide have been offered. Genetic factors related to suicide may mostly represent a genetic predisposition to psychiatric problems associated with suicide. These include affective disorders, schizophrenia, and alcoholism, as well as the inability to control impulsivity. Besides, the mechanism of social modeling may play an important role: the family member who dies by suicide may serve as a role model, pointing to suicide as the best "solution" to life problems (Krysinska, 2003).

BIOLOGICAL FACTORS IN SUICIDE

Biochemical studies of individuals with a diagnosis of depression, schizophrenia, and personality disorders show that a reduced metabolism of serotonin (5-TH; 5-hydroxytryptamine) and a lower concentration of its main metabolite, 5-hydroxyindoleacetic acid (5-HIAA), in the cerebrospinal fluid (CSF) are linked with disturbances in regulation of anxiety and inward- and outward-directed aggression (van Praag, 2001). Suicide attempters with a low CSF 5-HIAA level show an increased risk of repeated suicidal behaviors. On the basis of these results, van Praag concluded:

The association between 5-XT disturbances and states of increased aggression, suicidality and anxiety is not surprising if one takes into account, first, that in humans these affective states are highly

correlated across diagnoses, and second, that both in animals and humans serotonergic circuits play an important role in the regulation of both anxiety and depression. (pp. 59-60)

ECONOMIC FACTORS

Although suicidal behaviors are present in all occupational groups and social classes, epidemiological data show that certain economic factors are correlated with high suicide risk (Stack, 2000). Poverty increases the risk of suicide through its association with financial stress, unemployment, fear of job loss, family instability, and mental problems (e.g., alcoholism, depression, crime victimization). Sociological studies have consistently found a negative correlation between socioeconomic status and suicide rates (for example, in 1985 the U.S. suicide rate for laborers was eight times higher than the overall national rate; Stack, 2000), although there are some high-status occupations with increased suicide risk (e.g., dentists, physicians, veterinarians) stemming from high job stress and easy access to lethal medication and other means of self-destruction. Another factor connected with the increased suicide risk among the disadvantaged economic groups is the relative deprivation related to the income gap between the rich and the poor, making the latter more frustrated and suicide prone.

Unemployment has often been mentioned as a major suicide risk factor, especially among men. Although the nature of the relationship between those two phenomena has not been fully explained, many correlational or causal pathways have been described. These explore how unemployment may heighten the suicide risk directly through eroding an individual's income, economic welfare, and self-esteem, or it may affect dependent family members by lowering their financial capabilities. Psychologically disturbed persons may be at risk of both losing their jobs (and not being able to find another one) and being suicidal. High unemployment rates in the general population may lead to one's fear of losing his or her job and may be related to smaller wages and underemployment.

STRESS AND COPING POTENTIAL

Many studies have shown that individuals who attempt or commit suicide experience more stressors and negative life events than individuals in the general population. For example, in the study by Paykel, Prusoff, and Myers (1975), subjects who attempted suicide reported four times as many life events (especially negative and uncontrollable stressors) as subjects from the general population and 1.5 times as many as depressed patients, with a peak in the month preceding the suicide attempt. Among the life stressors most often found in life histories of suicidal individuals are family and relationship problems, mental and physical health problems, bereavement, unemployment, imprisonment, loss of status, abuse, and trauma (Yufit & Bongar, 1992). According to Maris (1992):

Most stress is chronic and accumulates slowly. There can be a few intense, acute, "triggering" events preceding a suicide, but without a history of stress most of us can tolerate time-limited, single, dramatic episodes of stress without resorting to suicide. Triggering events are usually not substantially different from the chronic stressors in one's life. (p. 15)

Other studies concentrate on the relationship between life events and an individual's coping potential, following the premise that "although recent (as well as long-standing) life stresses can be important catalytic events in an individual's subsequent suicide, these stressful events must be contextualized within the larger picture of the individual's personality structure and life-long characterological ability to cope with (or to be vulnerable to) stress, failure, and loss" (Yufit & Bongar, 1992, p. 557). The coping potential is usually understood as ego strengths, self-trust, problem-solving skills, sense of mastery and control, and the capacity to adjust to life changes.

An essential part of suicide risk assessment should be collecting information about the individual's past responses to stress, particularly to losses, because, as Shneidman (1996) described, the common pattern in suicide is consistency of lifelong styles:

> We must look to previous episodes of disturbance, dark times in that life, to access the individual's capacity to endure psychological pain. We need to see whether or not there is a penchant for constriction and dichotomous thinking, a tendency to throw in the towel, for earlier paradigms of escape and egression.... The repetition of tendency to capitulate, to flee, to blot it out, to escape is perhaps the most telling single clue to an ultimate suicide. (pp. 135-136)

SOCIAL ISOLATION

Isolation and the lack of social support have been related to many aspects of psychopathology, including ineffective coping with stress and life crises (Bonner, 1992). Individuals at high risk of suicide are often described as isolated and alienated from their families and communities and bereft of social support and the resources related to it (i.e., the emotional and instrumental help). Loneliness may lead to depression and emotional distress, as well as exacerbate the effects of negative stressors, as social support is often described as a buffer against life adversities. Besides, isolated and lonely individuals are at higher risk of death when they engage in suicidal behaviors, because the chances of lifesaving intervention by others are severely reduced or nonexistent.

HOPELESSNESS AND OTHER COGNITIVE FACTORS

Research by Beck and his colleagues (1985, 1990) proves that hopelessness (a state of negative expectancies concerning oneself and one's future life) is a better predictor of suicidal ideation and behavior than depression. This notion has been strongly supported by prospective studies of psychiatric inpatients and outpatients, in which individuals' self-reports as well as clinicians' ratings of hopelessness were used. According to Beck's cognitive theory of depressive schemata, in some individuals the level of hopelessness escalates during the depressive episode, later subsides with the course of the illness, and indicates the level of hopelessness during subsequent episodes. However, there is another group of individuals in whom high hopelessness seems to be a trait characteristic (e.g., individuals with personality and alcohol abuse problems) and who may be chronically prone to suicidal ideation and behavior.

Other cognitive risk factors of suicide are dysfunctional assumptions (lack of reason for life, depressiogenic attitudes, and irrational beliefs), problem-solving deficits, perfectionism, and cognitive rigidity (dichotomous "all-or-nothing" thinking) (Ellis, 1998).

OTHER RISK FACTORS

The suicide risk factors described earlier in this chapter are correlates of suicidal behaviors that are widely described in the literature and agreed on. However, other factors have been examined in the contemporary literature that may increase suicide risk in vulnerable individuals. These have not been considered to be common predictors of suicide, although there is mounting evidence to the contrary. These include a history of trauma (and a diagnosis of posttraumatic stress disorder [PTSD]) and homosexuality.

History of Childhood Trauma

Numerous studies have demonstrated that there is a relationship between an individual's history of childhood physical or sexual abuse and psychopathology (e.g., depression, substance abuse, dissociation, eating disorders, personality disorders), as well as direct and indirect self-destructiveness (Chu, 1999). For example, a study by Read and colleagues (2001) showed that the outpatients who reported at least one form of child abuse (sexual or physical) were more likely to have attempted suicide than subjects who have experienced none. Besides, current suicide risk of subjects was better predicted by past child sexual abuse than by a present diagnosis of depression. The authors concluded that "the taking of abuse histories should be a routine part of [the] assessment process so as to ensure accurate formulation and appropriate treatment planning" and added "knowledge of abuse history of adult patients will enhance the accuracy of suicide assessment" (pp. 370-371).

PTSD

Of note, an experience of adult trauma and the diagnosis of PTSD may be related to elevated suicide risk. For example, in a group of women with a history of sexual trauma (rape), almost 20% of subjects attempted suicide, and among Vietnam combat veterans, 19% reported a suicide attempt, whereas 15% of subjects were chronically thinking about suicide (Herman, 1992). Chu (1999) pointed out that suicide risk among traumatized persons may be increased as a result of trauma-related comorbidity (e.g., depressive disorders, substance abuse, anxiety, eating disorders), which should be addressed in treatment before actively working on trauma issues.

Sexual Orientation

Research on psychological and social functioning relating to sexual orientation shows that although completed suicide rates do not appear to be increased among homosexual men and women, there is a greater lifetime prevalence of nonfatal suicidal behavior in these populations (especially in gay men) when compared to heterosexuals (Catalan, 2000). Research in this field is scarce because of methodological (e.g., small samples, self-identification of sexual orientation) and cultural (e.g., published reports are limited to developed countries with liberal attitudes toward sexuality) limitations. The discussion on the relationship between homosexuality and suicidality is further complicated by association with HIV infection, which is a known suicide risk factor.

Interactions among the Risk Factors

The predictors of increased suicide risk listed and discussed here typically do not occur in mutual exclusivity. Suicide is often a result of a constant dynamic interaction and comorbidity of risk factors encompassing the entire life span of an individual ("a suicidal career"). The complexity and multidimensionality of suicide has been a serious challenge to all researchers and clinicians working in the mental health profession.

BEST PRACTICE A forensic nurse facing the challenging task of the assessment of suicide risk has to find guidelines that will help her or him conduct this procedure in a systematic and consistent manner, which will reduce the likelihood of missing important risk factors.

Protective Factors Lowering the Risk of Suicide

The assessment of an individual's suicide risk requires a careful consideration of both risk and protective factors. The following variables have been associated with reduced risk of suicide (Maris, Berman, & Maltsberger, 1992; Sanchez, 2001):
- Family and nonfamily social support
- Significant relationships (including marriage)
- Children under the age of 18 living at home
- Physical health
- Hopefulness, problem-solving and coping skills, cognitive flexibility
- Plans for the future
- Constructive use of leisure time
- Treatment and medication
- The propensity to seek treatment and maintain it when needed
- Religiosity, culture, and ethnicity
- Employment

Suicide Risk Assessment Tools

A clinician estimating a patient's level of suicide risk may use several tools. These may include both general personality tests and specific suicide risk assessment scales. However, usually these are not free from methodological flaws and never should be considered the only sources of information for the clinician, since no suicide prediction tool offers a level of accuracy that would encourage decision making on the basis of its score alone.

DIRECT ASSESSMENT OF SUICIDAL IDEATION, INTENT, AND BEHAVIOR

Numerous standardized psychological test instruments, suicide risk scales, and other estimators have been designed to assist a clinician in the difficult task of suicide risk assessment (Bongar, 1991; Rothberg & Geer-Williams, 1992).

Suicide Potential Scales

Several scales have been constructed to identify an individual's suicide potential (the likelihood that the individual will engage in suicidal behavior):
- Los Angeles Suicide Prevention Center Scale (by Beck, Brown, Berchick, et al., 1985): 65 items in 10 categories focusing on demographic and clinical characteristics of a patient; this scale along with the Suicide Potential Scale and the long and short forms of Suicidal Death Prediction Scale are popular tools used by crisis intervention centers and hot lines
- Clinical Instrument to Estimate Suicide Risk (by Motto, Heilbron, & Juster, 1985): a 15-item checklist of clinical and demographic variables
- Suicide Screening Checklist (by Yufit & Bongar, 1992): a 60-item inventory of clinical and social variables
- Index of Potential Suicide (by Zung, 1974): a self-report 69-item scale including clinical and social-demographic variables
- Suicide Risk Measure (by Plutchik, van Praag, Conte, et al., 1989): a self-report, 14-item scale
- Depression Inventory (by Beck, Ward, Mendelson, et al., 1961): a widely used and accepted 21-item inventory to measure the severity of depression in adults and adolescents
- Hopelessness Scale (by Beck, Weissman, & Lester, et al., 1974): a self-report, 20-item scale measuring the severity of the individual's negative attitudes about the future; a score of 9-plus predicts high short- and long-term suicide risk

- SAD PERSONS (by Patterson, Dohn, & Bird et al., 1983): a 10-item scale of demographic suicide risk factors: sex, age, depression, previous attempts, ethanol abuse, rational thinking loss, social supports lacking, organized plan, no spouse, sickness
- Reasons for Living Inventory (by Linehan, Goldstein, Nielson, et al., 1983): a 48-item self-report inventory, measuring protective factors

Suicide Risk Assessment in Adolescents

Some scales are designed specifically for suicide risk assessment in adolescents. They include the following:
- Hilson Adolescent Profile (by Inwald, Brobst, & Morrissey, 1987): 310 items
- Suicidal Ideation Questionnaire (by Reynolds, 1991): 15, 25, or 30 items
- Suicide Probability Scale (by Cull & Gill, 1982): a 36-item self-report measure that can be used both with adults and adolescents

Suicide Ideation Scale

The following scale can be used to measure the current levels of suicidal ideation and intent:
- Scale for Suicidal Ideation (by Beck, Kovacs, & Weisman, 1979): 19 items measuring the intensity, duration, and specificity of a patient's wish to commit suicide; a score of 10-plus indicates high short-term suicide risk

Scales for Those Who Have Attempted Suicide

A number of scales have been designed to identify individuals who attempted suicide and are at risk of completed suicide or repetition of suicidal attempt:
- Scale for Assessing Suicide Risk (by Tuckman & Youngman, 1968): a 14-item checklist of demographic variables, used to identify suicide attempters at risk of committing suicide
- Neuropsychiatric Hospital Suicide Prediction Schedule (by Farberow & McKinnon, 1974): 11 items useful to identify individuals who attempted suicide and are at high risk of subsequent suicide
- Instrument for the Evaluation of Suicide Potential (by Cohen, Motto, & Seiden, 1966): 14 items, used to predict subsequent suicides among hospitalized attempters
- Short Risk Scale (by Pallis & Sainsbury, 1976): 6 items discriminating individuals at high risk of future suicide from individuals at high risk of future suicide attempts

Scales to Evaluate Degree of Lethality of Suicide Attempt

Four scales can be used to evaluate the degree of lethality of the suicidal attempt:
- Risk-Rescue Scale (by Weisman & Worden, 1972): 10 items: 5 risk and 5 rescue factors
- Lethality of Suicide Attempt Rating Scale (by Smith, Conroy, & Ehler, 1984): an 11-point scale
- Suicide Intent Scale (by Beck, et al., 1979): 20 items
- Intent Scale (by Pierce, 1977): 12 items, combined self-report, situational and medical data

A clinician willing to use these suicide risk assessment tools should remember that they are not free from methodological flaws, and further research in this field is required. Bongar (1991) and Rothberg and Geer-Williams (1992) pointed out that in some scales there is a serious lack of detailed psychometric descriptions (no available data on their reliability, validity, specificity, and sensitivity) and their utility is not clearly defined; for example, it is not clear whether the tool can be used in any clinical context or only in a particular environment (e.g., suicide risk assessment in an emergency room versus inpatient treatment planning), if they should be used to assess acute or chronic risk, whether they are easy to use, and what amount of information can be gained from them. The considerable variation of risk estimates obtained using different tools leads to questions relating to the confidence that can be placed in their results.

Risk factors listed in the tools are rarely weighted (the noteworthy exceptions are the Los Angeles Suicide Prevention Center Scale, the Clinical Instrument to Estimate Suicide Risk, and the Suicide Screening Checklist), usually do not permit interactions between risk correlates, and exclude subtle factors that may play a decisive role in the individual case (Stelmachers & Sherman, 1992).

KEY POINT Victimization from interpersonal violence or other crime may potentially result in or increase suicidal ideation. Victimized patients should be assessed regarding their perception of the perpetrator and the related violent events. Any patient who expresses self-blame or guilt regarding his or her victimization must be assessed for self-safety and suicidal ideation, and appropriate intervention or referral should be initiated as indicated.

Case Study 37-1

Sexual Assault Victim and Suicidal Thoughts

As Betsy arrived to work the day shift at the sexual assault response clinic, she was stunned to hear that one of her patients from the previous day, "Suzy," had committed suicide by polypharmacy overdose. Betsy had been the sexual assault nurse examiner who had completed the forensic examination of Suzy after the police brought her in. Suzy, a 22-year-old student at the local college, had reported that her "date" had raped her at a frat party a few hours earlier. Suzy had consented to the forensic examination and had been quiet but cooperative throughout the evidence-collection procedure—behaviors that were not unusual within the circumstances.

It had been a long week with many complicated patients to manage. Betsy had been getting ready to leave the clinic just as Suzy arrived with the police. Betsy remembers that Suzy seemed exhausted as well, and that her answers to the examination questions were minimal and at times yielded nothing more that monosyllabic responses. Looking back, Betsy recalls that near the end of the examination, Suzy commented, "I had a friend who was date raped a few years ago. She has never been the same. I don't know how she does it....I don't think I could do it." At the time, Betsy did not think much of the comment, since Suzy was minimally responsive to the medicolegal inquiries throughout the examination. Betsy remembers thinking that the comment was likely an early attempt by Suzy to "normalize" the current situation by describing a similar situation experienced by one of her peers. However, such a comment, within the context of otherwise minimal communication, warranted additional inquiry and exploration by the forensic nurse because it more likely indicated risk for self-harm.

Suicide Risk Assessment Guidelines

A clinician facing the challenging task of the assessment of suicide risk has to find guidelines that will help him or her to conduct this procedure in a systematic mend and consistent manner, which will reduce the likelihood of missing important risk factors. In the

professional literature, many (overlapping) models of suicide risk factors have been proposed. In this chapter, three of them will be described: The Seven-step Decision Model proposed by Fremouw and colleagues (1990), the Suicide Aassessment Protocol Guidelines developed by Jacobs and colleagues (1999), and the Risk Factor Model for Suicide Assessment and Intervention by Sanchez (2001). It has to be kept in mind that the guidelines presented here have a heuristic value only, and even a strict adherence to them does not guarantee accurate estimation of an individual's suicide potential.

The Seven-Step Decision Model

This decision model provides guidance for clinicians utilizing the following seven steps (Fremouw, de Perczel, & Ellis, 1990):

1. Collection of demographic information: Identification of demographic factors associated with high suicide risk (e.g., male sex; age 65-plus; divorced, separated, or widowed marital status).

2. Examination of clinical and historical indicators: Questions about general historical-situational factors, clinical indicators and warning signs of suicide risk (i.e., having a specific plan), and psychological indicators (e.g., recent loss, hopelessness, substance abuse, change in clinical features).

3. Initial screening for risk: On the basis of the first two steps, a decision should be made if the suicide risk is elevated and further assessment is recommended. If there is no risk, the clinician should proceed in the routine fashion; in case of identification of risk factors, he or she should proceed to the next step (direct assessment of risk).

4. Direct assessment of risk: Through clinical interview (including questions about reasons for patient's suicidality) and (if suicide risk is unknown, mild, or moderate) the patient's self-report using the standardized assessment instruments (e.g., Beck Hopelessness Scale, Reasons for Living Inventory).

5. Determination of the level of risk and the implementation of a response: If direct assessment of risk leads to the conclusion that the risk is none to low or mild, the clinician should continue monitoring the patient; if the risk is moderate or high, the imminence of suicide risk should be assessed.

6. Determination of the imminence of risk: Includes questions about a specific suicide plan and availability of lethal methods; in case of imminent danger, the decision should be made whether intensified outpatient treatment will be appropriate or the option of voluntary/involuntary hospitalization should be considered.

7. Implementation of treatment strategies: On the basis of determination of risk, the outpatient treatment should be continued or contact with the hospitalized patient should be maintained and followed up. Besides, the clinician is advised to notify supervisors, document the actions taken, and indicate the rationale for his or her decisions.

Suicide Assessment Protocol Guidelines

According to this model, the following steps should be considered when assessing the patient's suicidality (Jacobs, et al., 1999):

1. Identification or detection of predisposing factors: Diagnosing the Axis I disorders (affective illness, schizophrenia, alcohol and drug abuse) and evaluating the category and course of disorder, its clinical features, and diagnostic comorbidity

2. Elucidation of potentiating factors: Gathering information about the patient's social and family environment, his or her biological vulnerability, personality disorders (especially borderline, narcissistic, and antisocial personality disorders) and traits, physical illness, life stress or crisis, and availability of lethal means
3. A specific suicide inquiry: Determining the level of the patient's suicidal ideation and intent and the history of suicidal behavior and current suicide plans
4. Determination of the level of intervention: Estimating acuteness versus chronicity of the patient's suicidality; evaluating his or her competence, impulsivity, and acting-out potential; assessing the therapeutic alliance; and planning the nature and frequency of reassessment
5. Documenting the suicide risk assessment

Risk Factor Model for Suicide Assessment and Intervention

Sanchez (2001) designed a detailed method for collecting important data from various sources. The order of inquiries depends on the specific case and available time:
1. Review record(s).
2. Conduct clinical observations.
3. Conduct clinical interview.
4. Conduct mental state evaluation.
5. Diagnose all mental disorders.
6. Assess suicidal ideation.
7. Assess suicide-homicide risk.
8. Examine prior self-injurious and suicidal behavior.
9. Request prior treatment records and collateral information.
10. Conduct psychological testing and administer rating scales.
11. Incorporate the data to develop a risk profile: identify acute and chronic suicide risk factors and temporary and permanent protective factors.

The Empirical Approach and the Clinical Approach

There are two approaches to the assessment of suicide risk: empirical and clinical (Motto, 1992). The former, which was presented earlier in this chapter, is based on the premise that an inquiry about a number of items derived from the results of epidemiological studies of individuals who committed/attempted suicide will help to identify the suicide potential of the assessed individual. The clinical approach "in pure form is a time-honored interview method that elicits detailed information about a person's life experience, character structure, and adaptive needs; when effectively carried out, it enables the examiner to recognize the circumstances under which a suicidal act is likely to occur in a given individual" (Motto, 1992, p. 626). Both have certain advantages and disadvantages. For example, the former is quicker and requires less training and experience, although it is inflexible, mechanical, and static. The latter is individualized and specific, but it is relatively time consuming and calls for an experienced and well-trained professional, as well as an undisturbed environment.

Motto (1992) pointed out that the clinical approach enables the clinician to take into consideration the protective factors and the individual's strengths, which may be overlooked while using the standardized assessment tools. It concentrates on the unique characteristics of the patient's life circumstances and personality, which sometimes may lead to paradoxical conclusions—for

example, alcohol abuse (statistically one of the major suicide risk factors) in the case of a particular individual may be a protective factor enabling him or her to cope with psychological pain and providing an escape from unbearable life circumstances. Besides, it is a valuable source of information derived from the nonverbal messages given by the patient: the tone of voice, demeanor, and subtleties of manner and speech.

Although some clinicians are highly skeptical about the usefulness of the empirical approach, the optimal and thorough assessment of suicide risk should encompass both categories. The proportion of clinical versus empirical methods used in a particular case should depend on the specific circumstances of the suicide risk assessment procedure: the amount of time available, the type of clinical setting, the patient's condition and his or her willingness to cooperate with the clinician, and the clinician's experience, training, and style.

In some cases, the clinician's judgment based on the empirical approach may contradict his or her intuitive sense—for example, when there is a discrepancy between the intuitive assessment and a score on a risk scale or the content of the patient's responses. In such circumstances, Motto (1992) advised the mental health professionals to review the situation again, but "if this does not reconcile the difference, the subjective judgment deserves precedence" (p. 628). Other suicidologists (e.g., Maris, et al., 1992) do not agree with Motto and warn that "there are also bad clinicians with poor insight and inferior training. Thus, clinical judgment is not always the answer to our suicide prediction problems" (p. 652).

Critical Points in Suicide Risk Assessment

According to Motto (1999), there are several critical points in the assessment and management of suicidal individuals that are potential sources of difficulties and mistakes made by clinicians. Eight of them pertain to the subject of this chapter and are listed here:
1. No one is invulnerable to suicide.
2. The absence of a diagnosable psychiatric disorder, especially depression, does not imply there is little or no risk of suicide.
3. Every person is unique; therefore the applicability of epidemiologically based risk factor scales is limited.
4. The use of alcohol and other drugs can be a short-term suicide preventive factor; therefore, discontinued use should be closely monitored, and the individual's support systems at such times should be strengthened.
5. Remission of a psychotic disorder (especially schizophrenia) may paradoxically increase the suicide risk, as it is the time when an individual may realize the catastrophic consequences of the illness and the relative futility of treatment, as well as be lured to discontinue taking the antipsychotic medication, which will lead to another episode of the illness.
6. Sometimes suicidal behaviors stem from chronic stress and emotional exhaustion; in such cases the identification of the triggering event ("the last straw") is practically impossible and the assessment of suicide risk is more difficult than usually.
7. Personality structure and personality disorders that temper the significance of traditional risk factors (e.g., impulsivity, need for a feeling of control) are major considerations in suicide risk assessment.
8. Protection against legal liability requires documentation of recognition, assessment, and management of suicide risk, which should follow the standards of ordinary and reasonable care to the patient.

Summary

Assessment of suicide risk continues to provide challenges for forensic nurse examiners. There is a high probability in a variety of clinical settings that forensic nurses will encounter a patient who may be at risk for suicide. In such circumstances, the knowledge concerning risk factors for suicidal behavior, basic tools, and methods for suicide risk assessment, as well as the role of clinical judgment, can be of great help and importance.

Assessment of suicide risk includes identification of individuals with a potential for suicide and the individual's intent. This implies that although it may be possible to make a clinical judgment concerning the probability of suicidal behavior in a given individual, it precludes the accurate prediction of suicide attempts or completed suicide. Although this seems to be a subtle distinction, it highlights that based on current knowledge it is practically impossible to determine whether a patient will engage in suicidal behavior; it is only possible to judge the relative probability.

Resources

ORGANIZATIONS

American Association of Suicidology
5221 Wisconsin Avenue NW, Washington, DC 20015; 202-237-2280; www.suicidology.org

American Foundation for Suicide Prevention
International Headquarters, 120 Wall Street, 22nd Floor, New York, NY 10005; 888-333-AFSP(2377), 212-363-3500; www.afsp.org

National Institute of Mental Health (NIMH)
Office of Communications, 6001 Executive Boulevard, Room 8184, MSC 9663, Bethesda, MD 20892-9663; 301-443-4513, 866-615-6464 (toll-free); www.nimh.nih.gov

National Suicide Prevention Lifeline
800-273-TALK(8255)
Provides access to trained telephone counselors, 24 hours a day, seven days a week

References

American Association of Suicidology [AAS]. (2004a). *Some facts about suicide in the U.S.A.* Retrieved October 16, 2009, from www.suicidology. org/associations/1045/files.

American Association of Suicidology [AAS]. (2004b). *Understanding and helping the suicidal person.* Retrieved October 16, 2009, from www. suicidology.org/associations/1045/files.

American Association of Suicidology [AAS]. (2004c). *U.S.A. suicide: 2001 official final data.* Retrieved October 16, 2009, from www.suicidology. org/associations/1045/files/2001datapg.pdf.

Beck, A. T., Brown, G., Berchick, R. J., et al. (1990). Relationship between hopelessness and eventual suicide: A replication with psychiatric inpatients. *The American Journal of Psychiatry, 137*(2), 190–195.

Beck, A. T., Kovacs, M., & Weissman, A. (1979). Assessment of suicidal intention: The scale for suicidal ideation. *Journal of Consulting and Clinical Psychology, 47*(2), 343–352.

Beck, A. T., Steer, R. A., Kovacs, M., et al. (1985). Hopelessness and eventual suicide: A 10-year prospective study of patients hospitalized with suicidal ideation. *The American Journal of Psychiatry, 142*(5), 559–563.

Beck, A. T., Ward, C. H., Mendelson, M., et al. (1961). An inventory for measuring depression. *Archives of General Psychiatry, 4*(6), 561–571.

Beck, A. T., Weissman, A., Lester, D., et al. (1974). The measurement of pessimism. The hopelessness scale. *Journal of Consulting and Clinical Psychology, 42*(6), 861–865.

Bongar, B. (1991). The suicidal patient. *Clinical and legal standards of care.* Washington, DC: American Psychiatric Association.

Bonner, R. L. (1992). Isolation, seclusion, and psychosocial vulnerability as risk factors for suicide behind bars. In R. W. Maris, A. L. Berman, J. T. Maltsberger, et al. (Eds.), *Assessment and prediction of suicide* (pp. 398–419). New York: Guilford Press.

Catalan, J. (2000). Sexuality, reproductive cycle and suicidal behaviour. In K. Hawton, & K. van Heeringen (Eds.). *The international handbook of suicide and attempted suicide* (pp. 293–307). Chichester: Wiley & Sons.

Centers for Disease Control and Prevention (CDC) (2006). National Center for Injury Prevention and Control (NCIPC). Atlanta, GA. National Suicide Statistics at a Glance. Accessed February 6, 2010. http://www.cdc.gov/violenceprevention/Suicide/Statistics/leading_causes.html.

Chu, J. A. (1999). Trauma and suicide. In D. G. Jacobs (Ed.), *The Harvard Medical School guide to suicide assessment and intervention* (pp. 332–354). San Francisco: Jossey-Bass.

Clements, P. T., DeRanieri, J. T., Fay-Hillier, T., et al. (2003). The benefits of community meetings for the corporate setting after the suicide of a co-worker. *Journal of Psychosocial Nursing and Mental Health Services, 41*(4), 44–49.

Cohen, E., Motto, J. A., & Seiden, R. H. (1966). An instrument for evaluating suicide potential. *The American Journal of Psychiatry, 122*(8), 886–891.

Cull, J. G., & Gill, W. S. (1982). *Suicide Probability Scale.* Los Angeles: Western Psychological Services.

Ellis, T. E. (1998). Rethinking suicide: Toward a cognitive-behavior therapy for the suicidal patient. *Behav Therapist, 21*(10), 196–201.

Farberow, N. L., & McKinnon, D. (1974). A suicide prediction schedule for neuropsychiatric patients. *Journal of Psychiatric and Mental Health Nursing, 6*(1), 9–14.

Favazza, A. R., & Simeon, D. (1995). Self-mutilation. In E. Hollander, & D. J. Stein (Eds.), *Impulsivity and aggression* (pp. 185–200). Chichester: Wiley & Sons.

Fremouw, W. J., de Perczel, M., & Ellis, T. E. (1990). *Suicide risk: Assessment and response guidelines.* New York: Pergamon Press.

Garrison, C. Z. (1992). Demographic predictors of suicide. In R. W. Maris, A. L. Berman, J. T. Maltsberger, et al. (Eds.), *Assessment and prediction of suicide* (pp. 484–498). New York: Guilford Press.

Harris, E. C., & Barraclough, B. M. (1994). Suicide as an outcome for medical disorders. *Medicine, 73*(6), 281–296.

Harris, E. C., & Barraclough, B. M. (1997). Suicide as an outcome for mental disorders. *The British Journal of Psychiatry: The Journal of Mental Science, 170*(3), 205–228.

Hawton, K. (2000). General hospital management of suicide attempters. In K. Hawton, & K. van Heeringen (Eds.), *The international handbook of suicide and attempted suicide* (pp. 519–537). Chichester: Wiley & Sons.

Herman, J. L. (1992). *Trauma and recovery.* New York: Basic Books.

Inwald, R., Brobst, K., & Morrissey, R. (1987). *Hilson Adolescent Profile.* St. Mary's University of Minnesota Minneapolis: Hilson Research.

Jacobs, D. G., Brewer, M., & Klein-Benheim, M. (1999). Suicide assessment: An overview and recommended protocol. In D. G. Jacobs (Ed.), *The Harvard Medical School guide to suicide assessment and intervention* (pp. 3–39). San Francisco: Jossey-Bass.

Jamison, K. R. (1999). Suicide and manic-depressive illness: An overview and personal account. In D. G. Jacobs (Ed.), *The Harvard Medical School guide to suicide assessment and intervention* (pp. 251–269). San Francisco: Jossey-Bass.

Kelly, M. J., Mufson, M. J., & Rogers, M. P. (1999). Medical settings and suicide. In D. G. Jacobs (Ed.), *The Harvard Medical School guide to suicide assessment and intervention* (pp. 491–519). San Francisco: Jossey-Bass.

Kerkhof, J. F., & Arensman, E. (2001). Pathways to suicide: The epidemiology of the suicidal process. In K. van Heeringen (Ed.), *Understanding suicidal behavior: The suicidal process approach to research, treatment and prevention* (pp. 15–39). Chichester: John Wiley & Sons.

Kessler, R. C., Borges, G., & Walters, E. E. (1999). Prevalence of risk factors for lifetime suicide attempts in the National Comorbidity Survey. *Archives of General Psychiatry, 56*(7), 617–626.

Kreitman, N., & Casey, P. (1988). Repetition of parasuicide: An epidemiological and clinical study. *The British Journal of Psychiatry: The Journal of Mental Science, 153*(6), 792–800.

Krysinska, K. (2003). Loss by suicide: A risk factor for suicide. *Journal of Psychosocial Nursing and Mental Health Services, 41*(7), 34–41.

Lester, D. (1992). Alcoholism and drug abuse. In R. W. Maris, A. L. Berman, J. T. Maltsberger, et al. (Eds.), *Assessment and prediction of suicide* (pp. 321–336). New York: Guilford Press.

Linehan, M. M., Goldstein, J. L., Nielson, S. L., et al. (1983). Reasons for staying alive when you are thinking of killing yourself: The reasons for living inventory. *Journal of Consulting and Clinical Psychology, 51*(2), 276–278.

Maris, R. W. (1992). Overview of the study of suicide assessment and prediction. In R. W. Maris, A. L. Berman, J. T. Maltsberger, et al. (Eds.), *Assessment and prediction of suicide* (pp. 3–22). New York: Guilford Press.

Maris, R. W., Berman, A. L., & Maltsberger, J. T. (1992). Summary and conclusions: What have we learned about suicide assessment and prediction? In R. W. Maris, A. L. Berman, & J. T. Maltsberger, et al. (Eds.), *Assessment and prediction of suicide* (pp. 640–672). New York: Guilford Press.

Marzuk, P. M., Tardiff, K., Leon, A. C., et al. (1997). The prevalence of aborted suicide attempts among psychiatric inpatients. *Acta Psychiatrica Scandinavica, 96*(6), 492–496.

McIntosh, J. L. (1992). Methods of suicide. In R. W. Maris, A. L. Berman, J. T. Maltsberger, et al. (Eds.), *Assessment and prediction of suicide* (pp. 381–397). New York: Guilford Press.

Meehan, P. J., Lamb, J. A., Saltzman, L. E., et al. (1992). Attempted suicide among young adults: Progress toward a meaningful estimate of prevalence. *The American Journal of Psychiatry, 149*(1), 41–44.

Motto, J. A. (1992). An integrated approach to estimating suicide risk. In R. W. Maris, L. Berman, J. T. Maltsberger, et al. (Eds.), *Assessment and prediction of suicide* (pp. 625–639). New York: Guilford Press.

Motto, J. A. (1999). Critical point in the assessment and management of suicide risk. In D. G. Jacobs (Ed.), *The Harvard Medical School guide to suicide assessment and intervention* (pp. 224–238). San Francisco: Jossey-Bass.

Motto, J. A., Heilbron, D. C., & Juster, R. P. (1985). Development of a clinical instrument to estimate suicide risk. *The American Journal of Psychiatry, 142*(6), 680–686.

Nietzsche, F. M., & Zimmern, H. (1989). *Beyond good and evil (Great Books in Philosophy)*. Amherst, NY: Prometheus Books.

O'Carroll, P. W., Berman, A. L., Maris, R. W., et al. (1996). Beyond the Tower of Babel: A nomenclature for suicidology. *Suicide & Life-Threatening Behavior, 26*(3), 237–252.

Pallis, D. J., & Sainsbury, P. (1976). The value of assessing intent in attempted suicide. *Psychological Medicine, 6*(3), 487–492.

Patterson, W. M., Dohn, H. H., Bird, J., et al. (1983). Evaluation of suicidal patients: The Sad Persons Scale. *Psychosomatics, 24*(4), 343–349.

Paykel, E. S., Prusoff, B. A., & Myers, J. K. (1975). Suicide attempts and recent life events. *Archives of General Psychiatry, 32*(3), 327–333.

Pierce, D. W. (1977). Pierce Suicide Attempt Scale. *The British Journal of Psychiatry: The Journal of Mental Science, 130*(4), 377–385.

Plutchik, R., van Praag, H. M., Conte, H. R., et al. (1989). Correlates of suicide and violence risk: The suicide risk measure. *Comprehensive Psychiatry, 30*(4), 296–302.

Pokorny, A. D. (1983). Prediction of suicide in psychiatric patients: Report of a prospective study. *Archives of General Psychiatry, 40*(3), 249–257.

Read, J., Agar, K., Barker-Collo, S., et al. (2001). Assessing suicidality in adults: Integrating childhood trauma as a major risk factor. *Prof Psychol Res Pr, 32*(4), 367–372.

Reynolds, W. M. (1991). *Adult Suicidal Ideation Questionnaire*. Odessa, FL: Psychological Resources.

Rothberg, J. M., & Geer-Williams, C. (1992). A comparison and review of suicide prediction scales. In R. W. Maris, A. L. Berman, & J. T. Maltsberger, et al. (Eds.), *Assessment and prediction of suicide* (pp. 202–217). New York: Guilford Press.

Roy, A. (1992). Genetics, biology, and suicide in the family. In R. W. Maris, A. L. Berman, J. T. Maltsberger, et al. (Eds.), *Assessment and prediction of suicide* (pp. 574–588). New York: Guilford Press.

Sanchez, H. G. (2001). Risk factor model for suicide assessment and intervention. *Prof Psychol Res Pr, 32*(4), 351–358.

Shneidman, E. S. (1996). *The suicidal mind*. New York: Oxford University Press.

Smith, K., Conroy, M., & Ehler, P. (1984). Lethality of suicide attempt rating scale. *Suicide & Life-Threatening Behavior, 14*(4), 215–242.

Stack, S. (2000). Suicide: A 15-year review of the sociological literature part I: Cultural and economic factors. *Suicide & Life-Threatening Behavior, 30*(2), 145–162.

Stelmachers, Z. T., & Sherman, R. E. (1992). The case vignette method of suicide assessment. In R. W. Maris, A. L. Berman, J. T. Maltsberger, et al. (Eds.), *Assessment and prediction of suicide* (pp. 255–274). New York: Guilford Press.

Tanney, B. L. (1992). Mental disorders, psychiatric patients, and suicide. In R. W. Maris, A. L. Berman, J. T. Maltsberger, et al. (Eds.), *Assessment and prediction of suicide* (pp. 277–320). New York: Guilford Press.

Tuckman, J., & Youngman, W. A. (1968). Scale for assessing suicide risk of attempted suicide. *Journal of Clinical Psychology, 24*(1), 17–19.

van Heeringen, K. (2001). The suicidal process and related concepts. In K. van Heeringen (Ed.), *Understanding suicidal behavior: The suicidal process approach to research, treatment and prevention* (pp. 3–14). Chichester: John Willey & Sons.

van Praag, H. M. (2001). About the biological interface between psychotraumatic experiences and affective dysregulation. In K. van Heeringen (Ed.), *Understanding suicidal behavior. The suicidal process approach to research, treatment and prevention* (pp. 54–75). Chichester: John Willey & Sons.

Weisman, A. D., & Worden, W. (1972). Risk rescue rating in suicide assessment. *Archives of General Psychiatry, 26*(6), 553–560.

Yufit, R. I., & Bongar, B. (1992). Suicide, stress, and coping with life cycle events. In R. W. Maris, A. L. Berman, J. T. Maltsberger, et al. (Eds.), *Assessment and prediction of suicide* (pp. 553–573). New York: Guilford Press.

Zung, W. W. (1974). Index of Potential Suicide (IPS): A rating scale for suicide prevention. In A. T. Beck, H. L. Resnick, & D. J. Lettieri (Eds.), *The prediction of suicide* (Chap. 12, pp. 206–221). Bowie, MD: Charles Press.

CHAPTER 38 Forensic Nursing in Correctional Care

Pamela J. Dole

Correctional care nursing integrates the principles of nursing, forensics, psychiatric, primary care, and public health knowledge during the care of prisoners and parolees. Violence is increasingly visible within the United States and around the world. The booming incarceration rate in the United States leads the industrialized nations, is fourth in the world, is a political and controversial topic, and is tied to complex social problems. Offenders are in need of nurses with medicolegal knowledge as well as compassion and caring, irrespective of whether we support the current social milieu regarding offenders.

Correctional nursing in this chapter refers to the job of nurses who work "behind bars" or with detained individuals. These settings may include penitentiaries, prisons, jails, detention centers, holding cells, work camps, work release programs, court programs, drug rehabilitation centers, or forensic psychiatric institutions. Individuals accused of breaking laws are confined with sanctions specific to this custody and will influence the practice of nursing. All rights are lost during confinement, and privileges must be earned. It is challenging for nurses to maintain caring and human rights under the sanctions of custody. Thus, the phrase "custody and caring" has been coined to depict this contradiction of terms (Peternelj-Taylor & Johnson, 1998).

Professional debate exists as to whether correctional care nursing and forensic nursing can be viewed in the same vein (Maeve & Vaughn, 2001). If one considers forensic nursing as being limited to the collection of medicolegal evidence, then the answer is no. However, if forensic nursing is considered within the broader context where law and medicine (nursing) intersect, then it is within this purview. Offenders have been convicted of a crime (law) and receive healthcare (medicine). Forensics provides for legal arguments that can be used to advocate for the health and well-being of offenders. Forensic nurses also comprehend the importance of detailed, unbiased documentation that protects both the institution and the offender. Correctional nursing will be viewed within the broader context of forensic nursing and as practicing within all of these institutions, both correctional and forensic psychiatry.

In 1998, the United States incarcerated a million nonviolent prisoners (Irwin, 2000). This hallmark represented a threefold increase in prison and jail populations over two decades, a direct response to escalating stringent sentencing laws culminating in 1994. These laws provide for mandatory sentencing for first-time offenses. Approximately 75% of the prison population are not violent offenders. The Rockefeller laws or the "Two Strikes" 1994 law applies to individuals who commit violent crimes a second time who are then required to serve a life sentence. Only 25% to 33% of prisoners have committed violent crimes, such as murder, rape, kidnapping, armed robbery, aggravated child molestation, aggravated sodomy, and aggravated sexual battery.

Healthcare becomes a by-product of institutional responsibilities to incarcerated individuals, because it must protect prisoners from harm. Penal and psychiatric institutions for the offender and criminally insane, respectively, are potentials for major public health problems because large aggregates of people are living together in small, confined, and overcrowded quarters. Approximately 95% of inmates will be released back into the community carrying whatever they came to prison with or acquired within prison (*Washington Times*, 2002). Minimum standards of healthcare for prisoners lack consensus among the laws governing human rights and correctional facilities, as well as among professional organizations. The issue of public health risks to incarcerated individuals and lack of consensus regarding the institutional responsibility for healthcare has a long history that has reached a pinnacle.

KEY POINT The primary objective of a correctional institution or psychiatric correctional facility is to safeguard the public by incarcerating those individuals who have committed crimes against society. The institution is responsible for its own needs and safety, as well as the safety and the needs of the prisoners and patients.

Forensic nursing has much to offer correctional facilities, which this chapter addresses in detail. In summary, forensic nurses can do the following:
- Consult and advocate on human rights issues
- Perform medicolegal examinations (not where employed)
- Teach and perform detailed, unbiased documentation
- Provide nursing care that is free of bias and judgment
- Advocate for healthcare and healthcare education
- Inspire self-care for offenders
- Assist nursing and other professionals in creating protocols with the highest ethical standards
- Assist in providing an impartial and secure environment for offenders and staff
- Develop and implement initiatives that decrease the roots of violence

While caring for offenders, nurses, as well as other healthcare providers, are often confronted with situations that raise ethical and professional dilemmas. Additionally, the issue of power and the questionable ability to consent while incarcerated demand strong moral and ethical convictions by all correctional care nurses and healthcare providers caring for offenders or the criminally insane. Advocacy, prisoner rights, health education, standards of care, and caring are often defined differently "behind bars." Forensic nurses should utilize guidelines for care developed by professional organizations. These guidelines include the following:

- Scope and Standards of Nursing Practice in Correctional Facilities, of the American Nurses Association (ANA) (1985, updated 1995)
- American Nurses Association and International Association of Forensic Nurses (ANA, 1997), Scope and Standards of Forensic Nurse Practice
- United Nations (UN, 1982), Principles of Medical Ethics and Standard Minimum Rules for the Treatment of Prisoners
- International Council of Nurses (ICN, 1989), The Nurse's Role in Safeguarding Human Rights, Nurses and Torture, and The Nurse's Role in the Care of Detainees and Prisoners
- American Correctional Health Services Association (ACHSA), Code of Ethics (1999)

Integral to correctional healthcare are many disciplines and agencies. These include nurses and other medical personnel; psychiatrists; pharmacists; social workers; nutritionists; correctional officers; parole officers; Department of Corrections (DOC) administrators; local, state, and federal officials; managed care agencies; and peer educators. Nursing is an integral component of prison life, since nurses constitute 19% of overall correctional staff. The official federal government agency is the National Institute of Law Enforcement and Criminal Justice, currently referred to as the National Institute of Justice (NIJ).

Correctional care nursing is an exciting opportunity to practice community health nursing, primary care, psychiatric nursing, and forensic nursing, to name a few specialty areas. The majority of prisoners have a history of poverty, substance abuse, and mental illness with episodic healthcare. Disenfranchised and vulnerable individuals are at increased risk for chronic illnesses (Perternelj-Taylor, 2005). Many offenders are illiterate or poor readers and often have learning disabilities. Incarceration may represent the first time an offender receives comprehensive healthcare, continuity of care, and has the opportunity to develop a relationship with the nurses and primary healthcare providers (Flanigan, 1999). Correctional facilities offer excellent opportunities for nurses to practice all their skills including the therapeutic use of the self. Correctional care nursing provides an excellent opportunity for nurses to apply the art and science of nursing and the principles of public health and forensics while providing care, health education, health promotion, injury prevention, and community health initiatives.

There have been several studies of nurses working in correctional institutions. Droes (1989) described nursing practice as acceptance of judicially mandated healthcare that requires tolerance. Tolerance is a continuum of contentious toleration, considered toleration, centered position, and acknowledged toleration. Flanagan (2006) described an inverse relationship between job satisfaction and job stress among nurses employed in correctional institutions. *Job stress was a significant predictor of job satisfaction* (p. 316). Flanagan found pay and autonomy to be major sources of job satisfaction. She also found that workload and organizational support as the highest source of stress.

The relationship between incarceration and violence is also dependent on the social and political milieu. The current climate is punitive or vindictive. It is a major public health concern and will challenge every correctional care nurse. Violence has direct and indirect costs on the healthcare system and the victims affected by it. To improve health outcomes, *Healthy People 2010* (U.S. Department of Health & Human Services, 2000) lists the reduction of violence as imperative to reduce morbidity and mortality-related injuries. Correctional care nurses will be challenged to create and initiate models that heal the mind, body, and spirit of traumatized survivors of violence.

Societal Factors Contributing to High Incarceration Rates

Most incarcerated individuals are disproportionately affected by acts of violence and are overwhelmingly from poor communities. Although many factors contribute to violence, being poor places an individual at high risk for being affected by violence and its sequel. Offenders are often members of vulnerable populations and lack access to healthcare, placing a heavy burden on correctional institutions when individuals are incarcerated.

In 2002, the World Health Organization (WHO) defined violence as follows:

> Violence is the intentional use of physical force or power, threatened or actual, against oneself, another person, or a group or community, that results in or has a high likelihood of resulting in injury, death, psychological harm, maldevelopment, or deprivation.

WHO further categorizes violence into three types, which is also used by the Centers for Disease Control (CDC). They are self-inflicted violence (suicide, mutilation), interpersonal violence, and organized violence (generally organized around political, social, or economic agendas, such as with war, gangs, or mobs).

Better crime prevention is generally related to the "War on Drugs," which was stepped up in 1994 to deflect soaring crime rates that in fact had not dropped in the preceding years. Several studies have demonstrated that increasing imprisonment does not reduce crime (Irwin, 2000). Crime rates since the late 1970s have remained relatively constant.

The 1997 annual household telephone survey conducted by the Department of Justice (DOJ) reported the following about victims:

- There were more victims with an income greater than $7,500 than with an income greater than $75,000.
- Only 37% of crimes were reported, and even fewer rapes and sexual assaults were reported.
- Victims reported 80% of automobile accidents secondary to insurance requirements.
- Half the crimes were perpetrated by known assailants, and in sexual assaults the majority of assailants were known.
- More than half the victims were between 12 to 24 years old.
- A greater number of victims were male (46% versus 33%).
- Blacks were most vulnerable (49%) compared to Hispanics (43%) and whites (38%).
- Crime was higher in urban areas.
- Crimes against the elderly are increasing.

If the statistics are carefully examined, it becomes clear that the majority of crimes occur in poor communities, disproportionately among blacks and young people. This profile has remained fairly constant according to the CDC (1997). Researchers and professionals experience the effects and affects of crime, poverty, and racial discrimination daily. Their experience is that things are getting worse. There are fewer initiatives to remedy or even to stabilize poor communities. The money is being spent on warehousing the poor behind bars rather than improving services that benefit the neighborhoods. Unfortunately, incarceration has the rippling effect of further deteriorating individuals, families, and communities who have the fewest resources.

Children arrested for a violent crime revealed a significant history of abuse (National Center on Child Abuse and Neglect, 1996). There are many public health concerns that the money would be better spent rehabilitating individuals and communities rather than incarcerating low-level crime offenders who are not rehabilitated by being incarcerated. Rehabilitation would also include universal healthcare. Change can only occur when justice is a key principle in public health and economic inequality is viewed as injustice (Drevdahl, Kneipp, Canales, et al., 2001).

Many researchers agree that vulnerable aggregates experience increased exposure to risk factors and that this greater and prolonged exposure directly impacts the higher levels of morbidity and mortality (CDC, 1997; Magura, Kang, Shapiro, et al., 1993; Wallace, Fullilove, & Flisher, 1996). Morbidity and mortality are further compounded by limited resources such as income, jobs, education, and housing; aggregates with decreased social connectedness or integration that are heightened with stigmatized discrimination and decreased social status and power; and populations with decreased environmental resources such as healthcare and quality care (Flaskerud & Winslow, 1998). Women and children are especially vulnerable and will be discussed later in this chapter.

Cohen and colleagues (2000) reported an example of compounded environmental and social influences on morbidity and mortality, which was the high correlation between neighborhood disorder and high-risk sexual behavior (which was measured by increased gonorrhea rates). This study was based on several other prevailing theories that the environment (broken windows, litter, and graffiti) contributes as much to violence as poverty by sending a message to the community that no one cares. Ellickson and McGuigan (2000) found that adolescents in middle school who had few bonds, poor grades, and deviant behavior were the same teens who later committed acts of aggression and violence in high school. These teens displayed additional risk behaviors represented by cigarette and marijuana use.

Health outcomes must be expanded to encompass the environment and social needs of the individual and their aggregates. Researchers at Columbia University stated that risk-taking behavior is reflective of an interwoven social network in low socioeconomic communities and that community initiatives must be comprehensive:

We suggest that violent acts in particular may emerge as key behavioral symbols for "sending a message" in socially disorganized communities, implying that school-based or other individual-oriented harm reduction strategies for violence prevention, in the absence of a comprehensive, multifactorial reform program, cannot significantly reverse the effects of continuing economic and social constraints or of public policies of planned shrinkage and benign neglect, factors primarily responsible for the disorganization of urban minority communities within the United States. (Wallace, Fullilove, & Flisher, 1996, p. 533)

Initiatives must be holistic and include all needs related to disorganized and disenfranchised communities. In addition to access to quality healthcare, initiatives must include employment (with income that will provide power, housing, and educational opportunities) as well as violence prevention initiatives at all levels that include decreasing racism, gender bias, cultural indifference, and lack of respect.

Researchers of disorganized communities, many social and religious leaders, as well as ghetto survivors support public health initiatives within communities and not "behind bars."

Recommendations by these groups are for alternatives to incarceration for first-time nonviolent crime offenders, especially women with children. Their philosophy is that warehousing the poor without rehabilitation only further disorganizes the communities and families they have come from. There are individuals who do commit horrific crimes and need to be separated from society. Several decades ago the majority of prisoners fell into these categories. Distinction must be made between the violent offender and the nonviolent offenders. Drug law reforms are emerging in the form of legislative laws supported by voters in various states. Twenty-five states enacted new mandatory minimum sentencing laws in 2003 as a response to pressure from social justice groups (Drug Policy Alliance, 2003). Although the Rockefeller Drug Laws have not been repealed, Michigan, Washington, Kansas, Texas, and New York have significantly reduced the harshness of these laws. State prisons in California, Texas, Kansas, and Indiana have instituted drug treatment in place of prison for nonviolent offenses related to substance abuse, and governors of other states are considering plans for similar programs (VonZielbauer, 2003b). Federal penitentiaries have not instituted such programs, and, in fact, former Attorney General John Ashcroft gave federal prosecutors orders to reduce plea bargaining and tighten prosecution for serious crimes. The forensic nurse should apply critical thinking when a simple solution or theory is offered for this immensely complex public health concern.

Who Is Incarcerated?

There are 2.1 million prisoners in the U.S. jails and prisons (Bureau of Justice Statistics, 2006). The faces behind bars have always been disproportionately from minority, poor, vulnerable, and disenfranchised populations. Minority groups within the prison population have risen significantly since the late 1990s. Of black (non-Hispanic) males age 25 to 29, 13.1% were in prison or jail. In the same age group, only 4.1% of Hispanic males and 1.7% of white males were jailed. Male inmates make up 88.6% of local jail populations (Beck & Karlberg, 2001).

Female prisoners have doubled since 1990 and now account for 6.7% of jailed prisoners (Beck & Harrison, 2001; Beck & Karlberg, 2001). Among incarcerated females in 2000, black (non-Hispanic) women were three times more likely than Hispanic females and six times more likely than white women to be in jails or prisons. For black women, the highest rate of incarceration was among those 30 to 34 years old.

The highest number of arrests in the United States (21.9%) occurred in the 15-to-19-year-old age group (Department Justice–FBI, 1999). The 20-to-39-year-old age group followed in the most numbers of arrests with rates decreasing with age (Department Justice–FBI, 1999).

More minority youth were also incarcerated in the late 1990s and early twenty-first century. The majority of juvenile offenders were male (86.5%) and black (40%) (Office of Juvenile Justice and Delinquency Prevention [OJJDP], 1999). The balance for racial/cultural breakdown of youth offenders includes 37.5% white, 18.5% Hispanic, 1.5% American Indians, 1.8% Asian Americans, and 0.3% Pacific Islanders (OJJDP, 1999). Private facilities (nongovernmental organizations) provided 27.8% of the assigned beds, as compared to 5.6% for adult incarcerations (Beck & Harrison, 2001; OJJDP, 1999). Serious personal or property offenses constituted 42.4% of crimes. This breaks down into 25% aggravated assault, a kidnapping, or a robbery; 20% serious property offenses including arson, auto theft, and burglary; and 2% were charged or adjudicated for homicide or murder. Another 6.5% of status offenses included running away, underage drinking, truancy, curfew violations, and other offenses that would not be classified as offenses for adults (OJJDP, 1999).

Federal prisoners sentenced for violent crimes declined from 17% to 11% (Beck & Harrison, 2001). Robberies, however, had increased 81% with a 21% decrease in other offenses such as assault and sex offenses (Beck & Harrison, 2001). In the federal penitentiaries, 92.5% of offenders are male. Within penitentiaries, men who committed violent crimes constitute 60% of the population, and 58.4% are incarcerated for drug offenses. Women have similar drug offense crimes rates in federal prison; however, only 25% to 33% are violent offenders. There are gender differences among homicides: men murder strangers, whereas two thirds of the homicides committed by women involve a family member or significant other. Women are more apt to commit filicide or the killing of a child. Each year approximately 500 children are killed by parents (Lewis, 2006). By the end of 2000, all state and federal prisons were operating above capacity, 15% and 31%, respectively (Beck & Harrison, 2001).

Rockefeller drug laws have contributed to the 6% annual increase in state and federal prisons. Jail populations have grown at a slightly faster rate. In 1999, 61% of federal prisoners had drug-related offenses (Beck & Harrison, 2001); 71% of prisoners were tested for drugs in 1998, and only 25% of prisons were testing prisoners in 2000. Fifty-one percent of prisoners were using alcohol or drugs when they committed their offense, and 57% were using drugs in the month before their offense; 83% of prisoners reported past substance abuse. Only 25% of offenders in federal prison and 33% of offenders in state prison had participated in substance abuse programs since admission (Mumola, 1999). For offenders who had used substance during the month before committing the offense, only one in seven had received treatment. Another 33% had enrolled in other drug abuse programs such as Alcoholics Anonymous (AA) or peer education programs.

Since the late 1990s and early twenty-first century, offenders have reported increased use of alcohol while committing offenses. These rates have increased from 10% to 20%. State and federal prisons had treated 14% of these offenders. A third of these offenders had enrolled in other alcohol programs such as AA or peer education programs. Arrests for drinking while intoxicated (DWI) decreased 18%, whereas applicants for driver's licenses increased 15% (Mumola, 1999).

Lack of social and environmental attainments combined with physical impairments and poor access to care contribute to increased risks for incarceration (Flaskerud & Winslow, 1998). Approximately 10.7% of offenders have learning disabilities, two fifths of inner city youth read at a fifth grade level or less, and most offenders have not completed high school (Persersilia, 2000). Another 4% to 10% of offenders are mentally challenged. Seventh graders who got into trouble in school were significantly more violent five years later. Predictors of adolescent violence included poor grades, poor self-esteem, rebelliousness, early tobacco and marijuana abuse, moving frequently and not being bonded to the school, and attending schools that were located in poor socioeconomic communities (Ellickson & McGuigan, 2000). Approximately 10% of the jail populations are supervised in alternative programs (Beck & Karlberg, 2001). Many activist groups believe that treating substance abuse and alcoholism would be a better alternative for nonviolent offenders.

Historically, sheriffs and correctional officers have underrepresented minority populations. This has been problematic for other departments who care for offenders, including departments of nursing and medicine. Since the late 1990s and early twenty-first century, employment of sheriffs and correctional officers has risen, as has the representation of racial and ethnic minorities within correctional departments. In sheriffs departments, 19% of full-time officers were minorities compared to 13.4% in 1987 (Bureau of Justice Statistics [BJS], 2000). Increasing minority representation at all levels of employment may have the benefit of decreasing racial disparities and tensions behind bars.

History of Prison Care

Prisons and jails have historically gone between the philosophies of punishment and rehabilitation. During the earlier periods of punitive philosophies, poor diets, hygiene, sanitation, and healthcare placed prisoners at risk for plagues, tuberculosis, typhus, sexually transmitted infections (STIs), gangrene, and scurvy. Prison reform has impacted the living conditions and healthcare of prisoners.

Following numerous typhus outbreaks in 1775, prisons began delousing prisoners on arrival to prison and began issuing clean clothing. Prisoners started receiving examinations by a physician, and moral and medical crusades urged improved diets.

In the 1800s, Louis René Villerme of France was the first to do epidemiological studies in institutions (King, 1998). Reform issues began to include rehabilitation of prisoners and with it came education, exercise, reduced crowding, increased lighting and ventilation, green vegetables, work, and fair treatment of inmates. Making these reforms was thought to improve the mental outlook of prisoners and contribute to their rehabilitation.

It was also Villerme and others who began to question the role of the physician in correctional care. Should physicians be independent of the institution or employees of the institution? As independent practitioners, they would be unbiased; however, the prisoners would not have the continuity and physical presence of a doctor within the institution. If employees of the institution, who would they report to and what would they be responsible for? These questions persist.

Physicians during this time period began seeing prisoners with more regularity. This effort included reexamining inmates before their release, a practice that has continued, although it has become more of a medicolegal issue taken to protect the institution from lawsuits from the prisoner.

The Walnut Street Jail was the first detention center in the United States, opening in 1776 in Philadelphia (May, 2000). The Quaker belief in redemption through penitence was a revolutionary departure from European institutions and embraced the new "nationalistic" philosophy of the founders of the U.S. government. Unfortunately, reading the Bible in isolation did little to rehabilitate prisoners who were not ready to be saved.

By the 1800s, redemption would again be replaced by a philosophy of punishment. Inmate labor became a popular method to redeem inmates. In 1851, a Texas prison constructed a cotton mill within the prison walls and offenders were used as laborers. Chain gangs in the Texan and southern prisons resembled slavery, as 75% of the inmates were black and the guards were primarily white (Edgardo, 1995). Imbalance of ethnic diversity among prison staff continues to plague the penal system. In the later part of the 1800s, prisoners were employed to build railroads, public utilities, iron mines, and foundries.

Today incarceration is viewed as punitive with little rehabilitation offered. Even if the social milieu were more favorable, it is doubtful that many rehabilitation efforts will be realized due to the incredible prison growth occurring since the mid-1990s. Most penal facilities find it challenging enough to keep up with standard healthcare. Prisoners have few rights, no privacy, and sometimes endure maltreatment. They have limited exercise and only basic hygiene.

In 1929, the United States published two reports that would not be acted on for nearly five decades. The first was a report of the National Society on Penal Information, which gave rise to correctional care as it is known today. President Herbert Hoover appointed the National Commission on Law Observance and Enforcement (also known as the Wickersham Commission), which published 14 reports endorsing parole, probation, and incarceration treatment to be individualized for prisoners. The Wickersham Commission reports were the first national and comprehensive survey of the American criminal justice system. These two sources of reports laid the foundation for significant future correctional care reform.

In 1975, the National Institute of Law Enforcement and Criminal Justice published another report. The Prescriptive Package: Health Care in Correctional Institutions, authored by Edward Brecher and Richard Della Penna, was a historic landmark with several original foundations laid for correctional healthcare as it is practiced today. The authors called for social and medical reform in what they viewed as "the typical chaos of healthcare delivery in most prisons and jails at that time" (King, 1998, p. 8). The Prescriptive Package, as it came to be known, provided guidance on organizing medical services within prisons and jails. It endorsed the following topics:

- Utilization of outside healthcare agencies to provide medical care to inmates as an effort to increase the variety of services needed, decrease the isolation of medical personnel within correctional care, and make prison care affordable
- Community liaisons and collaboration in all aspects of healthcare
- Locked secure units in community hospitals
- Designing a system of care that offered consistently good healthcare was the antidote for the numerous class-action suits plaguing prison administration, which the authors noted as being a highly effective method in this instance for change
- Utilization of physician assistants to decrease staffing problems
- Improved medical record systems
- In the areas of quality of care and issues of recidivism among healthcare workers, the community ties were again addressed (increase compensation and support staff; increase ties to professional organizations, continuing education, academic faculty appointments, and relationships with schools of medicine and nursing) (Brecher & Della Penna, 1975)

In retrospect, the Prescriptive Package has significantly influenced healthcare reform since the 1970s. The end result has been improved and more humane care for prisoners with increases in contractual medical arrangements. Although a for-profit agency and some private managed care agencies specializing in correctional healthcare have been under attack for their profit margin, they have provided increased autonomy to healthcare providers within correctional healthcare that is viewed as an advantage for prisoners. The 1975 Prescriptive Package has been criticized for its lack of rehabilitative and mental health issues that were found in the earlier 1929 reports.

Correctional healthcare continues to improve. The relationship between healthcare providers and respective correctional institutions is often poorly defined. The federal courts have articulated some questions. Correctional institutions and professional organizations continue to improve and standardize care. Prisoners lose their rights for public healthcare through Medicaid and Medicare and are not subject to the healthcare standards set forth by these two government agencies. The custody and healthcare of offenders is the financial responsibility of local communities and state and federal budgets. The doubling and tripling of offenders nationally since the mid-1980s, with increasing numbers of HIV-infected prisoners, has heightened the financial, healthcare, and public health concerns once again. The "one strike and you're out" law is responsible for the current rise in correctional populations, and of those incarcerated as a result of this law, the numbers are disproportionately higher among blacks and Hispanics, especially women. Increased numbers of HIV-infected prisoners have added costly healthcare visits and medications. At no other point is the health education of prisoners and correctional staff, including guards, so necessary to reduce mortality, morbidity, and escalating financial costs.

The current attitude toward prisoners and their advocates is less than positive and is reflected in the Violent Crime Control and Law Enforcement Act of 1994 (refined from the 1987). In 1987, the United States responded to the frustration of citizens and law enforcement by enacting stiffer prison sentences as part of the questionable "War on Drugs." These laws are commonly referred to as the War on Drugs laws, the Rockefeller laws, or the 1994 crime bill. Under the state and federal drug laws, crack possession carries a mandatory prison sentence for a first-time offense. This law was strengthened with the 1994 federal crime bill after financial incentives were added to state budgets when certain offenders served 85% of their sentence. Unfortunately, this law has barely affected high-level drug dealers. Many states have since reformed these laws in favor of substance abuse treatment programs.

The 1994 crime bill law also added Title 42, U.S. Code, Section 14141, which empowers the Department of Justice (DOJ) to enforce the constitutional rights of incarcerated individuals through civil suit. Built on the 1980 Civil Rights of Institutionalized Persons Act (CRIPA), it enabled the U.S. government to investigate and bring legal action against state institutions when there is a question of civil rights (constitutional) violations. CRIPA will be important when prisoner abuse and medical issues are examined.

The 1994 crime bill was weakened two years later when Congress passed the 1996 Prison Litigation Reform Act (PLRA) as part of the Balanced Budget Down Payment Act II of 1996. This law significantly decreases the ability to intervene in class-action suits pertaining to medical and prison conditions (including abuse) by the federal courts, nongovernmental organizations, or individuals. This law provides some check and balance for prisoners requiring correctional institutions to be responsible for the quality of healthcare and healthcare providers.

The Violence against Women Act passed by Congress in 1994 was a long-waited bill to increase prosecutions of perpetrators, to provide organizations with startup and educational money, to reduce some of the humiliation and embarrassment for women by shielding their past during courtroom proceedings, and to prompt research (Crowell & Burgess, 1996). This act has slightly increased the number of people (primarily men) serving longer sentences for domestic violence, stalking, and sexual assault.

Prison Life and Organization

Most correctional facilities are organized utilizing a military or police force model. The warden or superintendent is the highest position, followed by captains, lieutenants, sergeants, and correctional/custody officers. Until recently these have been male-dominated organizations.

Employment reflected gender-based dualism, and men were employed as correctional officers for both men and women. Integration of women into the workforce was afforded under the 1972 amendments to Title VII of the Civil Rights Act of 1964. However, not until *Dothard v. Rawlinson* in 1977 did integration of women into the workforce of correctional institutions actually occur. The amendment carried height and weight restrictions, and women correctional officers were restricted to female prisons and were not allowed to have contact with offenders. In 1979, *Gunther v. Iowa State Men's Reformatory* ruled that women could not be excluded from training and contact with offenders. It also marked the beginning of the divide regarding privacy rights accorded to male and female offenders.

Fourth Amendment rights for reasonable privacy were upheld only if they did not jeopardize the security of the institution. Reasonable cell searches were clarified in 1979 by *Bell v. Wolfish* and 1981 by *Hudson v. Palmer*. *Turner v. Safely* clarified reasonable body cavity searches in 1987.

The viewing of naked female bodies by male correctional officers was perceived as a violation of elemental self-respect and personal dignity. Female prisoners have a right to privacy in their housing units, in showers, and during other periods of surveillance. *York v. Story* in 1968 and *Forts v. Ward*, restricting male correctional officers from areas where women undress, upheld these conditions.

Even the handling and viewing of the clothed female body during cross-gender searches or patdowns came under question. In 1991 with *Ellison v. Brady* and in 1992 with *Jordan v. Gardner*, courts upheld the right of female prisoners for same-gender searches, thus protecting women from inappropriate touching by male corrections officers.

Maintaining Human Rights during Incarceration

Forensic nurses in the area of correctional care are not well organized in a collective manner through professional institutions. Therefore, a unified voice in the areas of healthcare, ethics, and advocacy for human rights is often lacking. The nursing profession lacks or has limited position statements in many areas related to caring for detained individuals. The majority of the available position statements have been listed throughout this chapter.

Human rights issues have become an even greater concern for nurses and healthcare professionals employed by correctional facilities. Understanding these rights requires some familiarity with the Constitution and its interpretation, knowledge that forensic nurses should possess on a limited basis. The Office of the Attorney General on both state and federal levels can guide questions about interpretation. Prisoners are afforded human rights even when their freedom has been taken away. In fact, healthcare is the right of an incarcerated person, whereas members of the general population, including the underinsured, have no entitlements to healthcare.

ISSUES RELATED TO INCARCERATING PRISONERS

In 1966, the American Correctional Association (ACA) developed guidelines for the minimum conditions of confinement. These conditions included minimum access to outdoor exercise, adequate clothing, and minimum square footage of space per prisoner. Acceptable levels of violence were also defined. *Jeldness v. Pearce* (1994) provided the equal protection theory. Programs and services available to male prisoners such as education must also be available to female prisoners.

The Fourth Amendment of the U.S. Constitution provides protection against sexual abuse while incarcerated. It states, "The right of the people to be secure in their persons ... against unreasonable searches and seizures, shall not be violated." This raises issues with respect to body searches and bodily privacy while showering and toileting. Whereas sexual misconduct between prisoner and prison guards is expressly prohibited within the federal system, states are not bound to this law. Many states have enacted laws that prohibit sexual abuse and misconduct during incarceration; however, 23 states still have no such laws (Human Rights Watch, 1996).

Human rights for detained people are also guided by global history. In 1998, the United Nations (UN) celebrated the 50th anniversary of the adoption of the Universal Declaration of Human Rights. It was the belief that the adoption of this proclamation by all UN member countries (including the United States) would preserve and define human rights and freedoms. The action followed the post–World War II Nuremberg Nazi war crime trials, which had produced the Nuremberg Code stating that "the voluntary consent of human subjects is absolutely essential" for medical research. Other international standards are guided by the International Covenant on Civil and Political Rights (ICCPR); the Convention against Torture and Other Cruel, Inhumane, or Degrading Treatment or Punishment (Convention against Torture, or CAT); the Convention on the Elimination of All Forms of Discrimination against Women (CEDAW); and the International Convention on the Elimination of All Forms of Racial Discrimination (CERD). All of these standards seek respectful, reasonable, and compassionate interactions between facilities that detain individuals and the incarcerated individual. Women and ethnic minorities generally carry a disproportionate burden of abuse and incarceration (see the sections on substance abuse and violence), further complicated by the fact that the United States has ratified and abides by ICCPR, CERD, and CAT but has failed to ratify CEDAW, which might assist in decreasing crimes against women, especially while incarcerated. Many of these rights were challenged in the post-9/11 detainment of 5000 foreigners (Eviatar, 2003).

Many of the aforementioned international standards have their foundations in the First United Nations Congress on the Prevention of Crime and the Treatment of Offenders adopted in 1955 and updated in 1977. This document outlines the standards for minimum rules for the treatment of prisoners (United Nations, 1982). It includes guidelines on accommodations, personal hygiene, clothing and bedding, food, exercise and sport, medical services, discipline and punishment, instruments of restraint, handling complaints of prisoners, contact with the outside world, books, religion, retention of prisoners' property, notification of death, illness and transfers to families, removal of prisoners, behavior of institutional personnel, inspection of the prison, separation of prisoners by offenses, privileges, work, education and recreation, social relations and aftercare, treatment of insane and mentally abnormal prisoners, treatment of prisoners under arrest or awaiting trial, treatment of civil prisoners, and treatment of people arrested or detained without charge. The fundamental thread throughout this document is humanity and dignity for all prisoners or detainees regardless of race, religion, color, creed, gender, or economics.

During this same period, federal courts were hearing *Ruiz et al. v. Estelle*. In 1980, the courts found that widespread "pernicious conditions" were serious enough to be unconstitutional. The major issues that came out of this ruling included deficient health-care, sanitation, access to courts, employee brutality, vague and unconstitutional disciplinary procedures, overcrowding, other general conditions of confinement, and correctional guards who "build tenders", i.e. (solicit inmates to assist them).

In 1978, Human Rights Watch began to monitor human right abuses internationally, especially in three categories: arms transfers, children's rights, and women's rights (www.hrw.org). Other nongovernmental organizations such as Amnesty International have similar goals. Box 38-1 highlights organizations that monitor human rights internationally and nationally, as well as humanitarian and social justice organizations.

Human rights within correctional institutions have come to the forefront as jail and prison overcrowding has reached its highest point to date. In March 1999, Amnesty International released its report "Not Part of My Sentence" as part of its human rights violations campaign on the custody of female offenders. Numerous examples of misuse of power, humiliation, sexual assault, and inappropriate conduct of male guards with female prisoner during patdowns and body searches were reported. The findings were so appalling that ABCs *Nightline* featured a six-part series titled "Crime & Punishment: Women in Prison," which aired beginning October 29, 1999 (Koppel, 1999). CNN also featured correctional care stories in February 2000. Twenty-seven percent of incarcerated women and 20% of incarcerated men reported sexual abuse. The Prison Rape Reduction Act was introduced to the U.S. Senate and House with the goal of establishing a national commission to set standards that would reduce and eliminate prison rape (*Washington Times*, 2002).

Nurses can advocate for offenders when they suspect improprieties. However, they must be careful not to be labeled a "snitch" by offenders or a troublemaker by prison or jail authorities. Nurses must also understand that advocacy and empowerment are not highly valued behind bars and must be offered with care to provide for the safety of the entire facility. Institutions fear that prisoners will become agitated and create safety issues such as riots or other behavior problems.

RESTRAINT AND SECLUSION

There are two primary guidelines for the use of restraint and seclusion in correctional facilities. These are the American Psychiatric Association's Resource Document on the Use of Restraint and Seclusion in Correctional Mental Health Care (RD) (Metzner, Tardiff, Lion, et al., 2007) and the National Commission on Correctional Health Care (NCCHC), which provides standards for health

---

Box 38-1 Professional Organizations Contributing to Correctional Healthcare Standards

- American Correctional Health Care Services Association (ACHSA)—position statement available
- American Medical Association—Standards for Health Services in Prisons
- American Nurses Association (ANA)—position statement
- American Public Health Association's (APHA), Jail and Prison Health Council—position statement available
- Association of Nurses in AIDS Care (ANAC)
- National Commission on Correctional Health Care (NCCHC)
- Society of Correctional Physicians (SCP)
- World Health Organization (WHO)

---

services in correctional facilities. Like The Joint Commission (TJC), the American Correctional Association (ACA) and the Commission on Accreditation for Corrections (CAC) provide accreditation for adult and juvenile correctional institutions. Initially, the Health Care Financing Administration for the Center of Medicaid and Medicare (CMS) defined rules for the use of seclusion and restraint in facilities participating in Medicaid and Medicare; however, the majority of correctional institutions do not receive Medicaid or Medicare (Metzner, Tardiff, Lion, et al., 2007). CMS impacted community practice after it was revised in July, 1999. Applying community standards behind bars has it's own challenges and differences from the community as it is dealing with not only mental health issues but violent offenders. The primary mission of correctional facilities is to protect the public from offenders and has a punitive component (Metzner et al., 2007). Thus, there is both a custodial and clinical purpose in the use of seclusion and restraints behind bars.

Definitions

- *Restraint.* Any manual method, physical or mechanical device, material, or equipment that immobilizes or reduces the ability of a patient to move his or her arms, legs, body, or head freely; or a drug or medication when it is used to restrict the patient's behavior or freedom of movement and is not a standard treatment or dosage for the patient's condition (CMS, 2006).
- *Custody restraint.* Use of steel handcuffs, leg irons, waist restraints, and chair restraints to control an inmate's assaultive behavior. An inmate in maximum security when outside the cell will typically have wrist, waist, and leg restraints and is accompanied by a security guard (Champion, 2007).
- *Seclusion.* Involuntary confinement of the patient alone in a room or an area where the patient is physically prevented from leaving; a situation where a patient is restricted to a room or area alone and staff members physically intervene to prevent the patient from leaving is also considered seclusion (CMS, 2006).
- *Segregation.* Disciplinary segregation is used as punishment for an institutional infraction. Administrative segregation is imposed for what an inmate might do (Metzner & Dvoskin, 2006). Segregation is instituted for the following three groups (Metzner & Dvoskin, 2006):
  ○ Inmates who do not follow the rules
  ○ Leaders of gangs or organized crimes or "shot-callers"
  ○ Inmates who are unable to follow prison rules because of mental illness or intellectual limitations

The American Psychiatric Nurses Association (APNA) (Stokowski, 2007) has suggested alternative guidelines for the use of restraint and seclusion addressing safety concerns, such as learning effective de-escalation techniques to employ when individuals are in crisis. Prevention can reduce use of restraint and seclusion by careful patient assessment that includes trauma, abuse history, prior seclusions or restraints, and identifying triggers for violence. Anger or frustration combined with fear may lead to violence. Seclusion is less restrictive and safer for patients who may be obese or unable to control impulses and may present a danger to others.

Restraints require more one-on-one personnel and may not be appropriate with reduced staffing. There are two types of restraints: mechanical or chemical. Mechanical restraints should not be appropriate for offenders with a history of sexual abuse or trauma and place individuals at risk for positional asphyxia or cardiac arrest. Chemical restraints may help individuals to manage themselves, although caution regarding overmedicating is of concern (Stokowski, 2007).

The Four S Model is one alternative to reduce the use of seclusion and restraint developed by Delaney, Pitula, and Perraud (Stokowski, 2007). These are safety (both physical and emotional), support (listening and talking), structure techniques (limit setting), and symptom management (stress and relaxation measures).

Restraints behind bars are used for both custodial and clinical purposes (Champion, 2007). Custody restraints are used to control inmates with assaultive behavior and as maximum security during security escorts or transfers to other facilities. They include steel handcuffs, leg irons, waist restraints, and occasionally chair restraint. Whether an inmate is in restraints or seclusion, it is important for the healthcare provider to monitor for physical and emotional decompensation especially with mentally ill inmates. It is also important to monitor for aspiration, positional asphyxia, dehydration, and restrictive circulation leading to pulmonary embolism. Suicides attempts and self-injurious behavior increase during seclusion.

The American Psychological Association (APA) recommends that a physician does a face-to-face assessment within 4 hours of restraint or seclusion, and every 12 hours thereafter, that restraint or seclusion not be longer than 12 hours, that documented 15-minute checks by health professionals occur, and that range-of-motion exercises occur every two hours (Champion, 2007).

It is important to identify mentally ill inmates and initiate proper medication management as well as group and individual therapy (Vlach & Daniel, 2007). This may include directly observed medication therapy (DOT) to reduce the need for restraints or seclusion with psychotic or depressed inmates. Prisons are nontherapeutic environments, and when mental health emergencies occur, inmates should be stabilized and transferred to psychiatric institutions (Appelbaum, 2007).

ISSUES RELATED TO THE HEALTHCARE OF PRISONERS

The Eighth Amendment of the Constitution provides the right of prisoners to a safe and humane environment. The *Spicer v. Williams* Supreme Court case (191 N.C. 487) in 1926 stated that the public must care for prisoners who, because they are deprived of their liberties, cannot care for themselves. This ruling fell short of recognizing the prisoners' constitutional rights under the Eighth Amendment. Many correctional healthcare practices originated from the 1975 Prescriptive Package that incorporated Eighth Amendment considerations. The 1976 U.S. Supreme Court Estelle decision further clarified that correctional facilities could not deliberately show indifference to serious medical needs, upholding the Eighth and Fourteenth amendments of the U.S. Constitution (*Estelle v. Gamble*, 429 U.S. 97, 1976; McNally, 1998). This decision initiates rights of prisoners to healthcare and begins to set minimum standards of healthcare for prisoners. In 1975 and 1976, community standards for healthcare were applied within the correctional institutions. In 1983 (*Revere v. Massachusetts Gen. Hospital*, 463 U.S. 239, 244), pretrial detainees under the Fourteenth Amendment were also provided legal rights to healthcare. More and more lawsuits, legal decisions, and professional organizations are applying community standards to correctional healthcare. In lawsuits, prisoners must prove that correctional facilities purposefully intended to provide inadequate treatment (*Wilson v. Seiter*, 111 S. Ct. 2321, 1991). A 1994 ruling (*Farmer v. Brennan*, 511 U.S. 825) stated that prison officials must ensure that prisoners receive "adequate" food, clothing, shelter, and medical care but that "deliberate indifference" requires a culpable state of mind.

The consequence of these decisions, however, is disproportionate to the rights of those in the general public, to whom the government is not required to pay for healthcare. Correctional facilities were not prepared for escalating populations that are sicker than in the past and aging prisoners who develop chronic illnesses sooner than those their age in the general population. HIV issues are costly and complex, and when the disease is managed with appropriate antiretroviral therapy (ART), costs of medications are less than the costs of opportunistic diseases and their sequelae (Bozzette, Joyce, McCaffrey, Leibowitz, et al., 2001; DeGroot, 2000). Costs for healthcare within correctional facilities have skyrocketed. These costs are the subject of many debates.

Box 38-2 highlights examples of professional organizations that contribute to correctional healthcare standards.

ETHICAL ISSUES

The forensic nurse can be beneficial within correctional facilities by assisting nurses and staff in developing guidelines and protocols regarding ethical issues. The principle of justice is the area where issues of ethics and human rights intersect. Forensic nurses must deliver care that is distributed fairly and equitably. It should be free of discrimination with rules enforced equally, be free of exploitation, and be free of derogatory statements about others. Nursing care should be consistent among all prisoners; social action should increase the availability and access to care for all prisoners and protect human rights through education, allowing for informed choices (ANA, Ethics and Human Rights Position Statement, 1991; International Council of Nurses, 2006). Many nurses and healthcare providers choose to not know the particulars of an individual offender's conviction in an effort to remain unbiased. This is easier to accomplish for healthcare providers who are subcontracted by the correctional institution for specific work.

The correctional care nurse must define the relationship with offenders with respect to advocacy, confidentiality, care and special needs of disabled inmates, codes of ethics as they relate to informed consent, the right to refuse care, the right to die, participation in executions, the use of pharmaceuticals to restrain prisoners, and hunger strikes. These may be dictated by the employment arrangement. If a healthcare professional is an employee of the institution, then often nonmedical professionals such as the warden significantly affect medical ethics. Nurses and other healthcare professionals must often rely on the judgments of correctional officers (COs), who have no medical knowledge yet are with offenders most of the time, to suggest that a prisoner attend sick call when there is a medical problem. Nurses must be proactive and should not expect COs to assess prisoners or disburse medications.

Box 38-2 Human Rights, Humanitarian, and Social Justice Organizations

ORGANIZATIONS THAT MONITOR HUMAN RIGHTS INTERNATIONALLY AND NATIONALLY

- Amnesty USA and International—Rights for All Campaign
- Critical Resistance Organizing Committee
- Human Rights Watch—Women's Rights Project
- Humanitarian and Social Justice Organizations
- National Prison Project—American Civil Liberties Union
- Justice Policy Institute
- Justice Works (interfaith efforts by community churches, citizens, ex-offenders, and attorneys on a local and national basis)
- United Nations

Correctional care nurses often get caught between the needs of the institution and ethics with respect to safety and security, including body cavity searches, patdowns, collecting forensic evidence, use of restraints and force, writing up offenders, and segregation. Most professional organizations including the ANA prohibit healthcare professionals from participating in executions, which presents a catch-22. Who will ensure compassion and appropriate doses of medications, and who will certify the death? Presently, 39 states have death penalties, including the U.S. government and the military, and more than 1100 deaths by execution have occurred since the late 1970s. Fifteen of those states have women on death row, and four women have been executed since the death penalty was reinstated in 1976. Present DNA technology is becoming more available to inmates, especially those on death row, which will help to decrease wrongful executions (Clines, 2000). Nurses can advocate for the use of DNA to reduce prosecution errors. Both the International Council of Nurses and the American Nurses Association have position statements that maintain that participating in the taking of a life is a breach in the ethical code of nursing (American Correctional Health Services Association, 1999; American Nurses Association, 1994; International Council of Nurses, 1998).

BEST PRACTICE The forensic nurse should ensure that medicolegal examinations of prisoners are done in accordance with strict protocols to avoid breaching Fourth Amendment rights.

The skills and knowledge of forensic sciences can assist in the proper collection of forensic evidence. When body searches are required, the forensic nurse can be instrumental in developing relationships with consultant forensic nurses who can be called to do such examinations, thereby maintaining the relationship with offenders and their facility nurses. Forensic nurses must insist that during patdowns and body cavity searches, women offenders are examined by women professionals to avoid breaching Fourth Amendment rights. Developing protocols that use an independent forensic nurse for medicolegal examinations would provide one solution to this conflict.

In 1997, the National Commission on Correctional Health Care (NCCHC) clarified the issue of nurses and healthcare providers collecting medicolegal evidence. It called for written policy and procedures for the collection of medicolegal evidence and prohibited facility-employed healthcare providers from doing the collection (NCCHC, 1997). This policy benefits both the nurses and the offenders. Impartial medicolegal evidence collection can benefit offenders who are wrongly accused or who are trying to document an assault that occurred while being incarcerated. The caring and trusted relationship between nurses and offenders can be preserved.

Debate regarding clinical research/trials in correctional institutions goes in and out of favor. During the 1960s and 1970s, prisoners tested over 90% of FDA drugs, which brought significant financial rewards to the prison (DeGroot, Bick, & Thomas, et al., 2001). Coercion of prisoners to participate in research studies and several deaths prompted the development of the Belmont Report (National Commission for the Protection of Human Subjects, 1978). This was followed by the code of federal regulations in correctional care that stipulates that only the following types of research can be conducted (HHS Regulations 45 CFR 46, 45 CFR 46.306, 45 CFR 46.306):

1. Low-risk studies of "the possible causes, effects, and processes of incarceration, and of criminal behavior"
2. Low-risk studies of "prisoners as institutional structures" or of "prisoners as incarcerated persons"
3. Research on conditions particularly affecting prisoners as a class (e.g., vaccine trials and other research on hepatitis, which is much more prevalent in prisons than elsewhere)
4. Research that demonstrates "the intent and reasonable probability of improving the health or well-being of the subject" (U.S. Department of Health and Human Services, 1978)

Access to clinical trials for HIV drugs has raised the issues of inmate rights to standard healthcare afforded under the Eighth and Fourteenth U.S. amendments. With the increase in the number of HIV-infected individuals behind bars, shouldn't inmates be able to access HIV medications available to HIV-infected individuals in the community? This is especially critical for offenders who are resistant to many of the HIV medications. Clinical trials and research in correctional institutions were banned because of coercion and the inability of inmates to freely consent. Some prisons have begun to allow HIV clinical trials back into their systems to provide medications that are available in the community.

Privacy

For safety reasons, privacy in correctional facilities does not exist. Hiring more female correctional officers would reduce the humility and embarrassment associated with daily dressing and showering, menstrual care, and during required isolation. Before 1975, few female COs were employed in prison facilities. It is the belief of many human rights groups that increasing the number of female COs would decrease violations of the Fourth and Eighth Amendments.

Confidentiality

Confidentiality is another difficult issue, as privacy virtually does not exist within a prison or jail. However, nurses are responsible for being careful as to where and when they speak about confidential issues. For example, specialists often provide HIV care in a specialty clinic, and everyone knows who attends the clinic; however, the nurse cannot reveal in front of other offenders the fact that an offender attends an HIV specialty clinic. The Health Insurance Portability and Accountability Act of 1996 (HIPAA) regulations further strengthen this issue of confidentiality.

Informed Consent

Prisoners are unable to give informed consent because they lack true freedom of choice. This raises many ethical considerations related to sexual activity, participation in research protocols, and healthcare. It is generally accepted that the inmates most at risk for coercion are those with the fewest resources both economically and socially. This is especially true for women who often participate in sexual activity or other activities to buy favors or status. Forensic nurses can establish proactive support groups that empower these women and decrease the risk of damage to their self-esteem.

Advocacy

Advocacy for offenders is often a delicate matter behind bars. If the forensic nurse is an employee or consultant to the correctional facility, safety of all prisoners must be the first concern. Empowering prisoners is sometimes viewed by administration as a threat to security. Assisting prisoners to heal their emotional wounds requires empowerment during the process. This process must be well thought out and planned so as not to encourage aggression or create agitation. "You are a guest in the warden/supervisors' house" is a phrase that reminds all employees, visitors, and offenders who enter a facility who has the last word. Communication with all levels of staff is important to the success of implemented programs. Human rights violations are serious and need solutions that provide for the safety and compassion of all concerned.

SCOPE OF PRACTICE

Since the 1970s, prison reform has improved standards of community life and healthcare within correctional facilities. The NCCHC is now the national accrediting agency. Standards of care are beginning to emerge after the court ruling mandating that community standards are met behind bars (NCCHC, 2003). The prison environment is a minisociety complete with healthcare; however, it is not a free society. It is important to set boundaries for the safety of all. Failure to do so can jeopardize lives and human rights.

In 1991, the American Nurses Association (ANA) developed the Scope and Standards of Nursing Practice in Correctional Facilities. This document includes all the generic scope and standards found in its basic nursing document that defines both nurses and advance practice nursing. The beliefs and philosophy of these standards are equivalent to community standards and regulations. There are some additional issues found within this document. As a specialty it describes the isolation of the profession working in this environment. Nurses must also balance professional performance with maintenance of safety and security for themselves and the institution:

Nurses practicing in correctional facilities provide health care services as their sole responsibility, and matters of nurse's judgment are solely their province. Therefore, it is inappropriate for nurses to be involved in the security aspects of the facility and registered nurses would not participate in procedures performed solely for correctional purposes. It is also inappropriate for nurses to participate in disciplinary decisions or committees or to participate directly or indirectly in executions by lethal injection. However, security regulations applicable to facility personnel also apply to health personnel. (Scope and Standards of Nursing Practice in Correctional Facilities ANA, p. 2)

As previously mentioned, nurses should not be involved in capital punishment. These ethics are guided by the code for nurses and related ANA position statement including the Position Statement on Nurses' Participation in Capital Punishment (Scope and Standards of Nursing Practice in Correctional Facilities, ANA).

KEY POINT Professional conduct with appropriate behavior and the ability to set boundaries are essential when working with forensic and incarcerated individuals.

Professional dress codes and interpersonal relationships must be respectful and therapeutic. Mental illness and disease often present as antisocial, manipulative, aggressive, impulsive, or angry behavior requiring nurses to exercise restraint and caution. Destructive manipulation is oriented for the sole purpose of the individual with no regard for the feelings of others, and others are often treated as dehumanized objects. Correctional nurses must be careful not to be manipulated into providing personal information, granting favors for specific offenders, or participating in sexual or erotic interpersonal relationships (Love, 2001).

Individuals who find themselves in hostage situations often exhibit the Stockholm syndrome as a survival mechanism. This bizarre syndrome, characterized by emotional bonding between captors and captives, was first documented in 1973. Hostages fearing for their lives who perceive some act of kindness from their captor, defend the captor and refuse to prosecute after the situation is resolved. Conditions that must be met for the Stockholm syndrome to occur include the following (Trigiani, 1999):

1. A perceived threat to survival with the belief that the captor will act on it
2. Within the context of terror, a perceived act of kindness from the captor
3. Isolation that restricts the hostage's perceptions to that of the captor
4. Perceived inability to escape

The hostage-captor bond phenomenon exists in other scenarios as well. Other victims of this phenomenon include concentration camp prisoners, prisoners of war, cult members, pimp-procured prostitutes, incest victims, physically or emotionally abused children, battered women, and victims of hijackings. This codependency is manipulated for the captor's advantage. The captives deny the stress, terror, and anger related to the incident. Often, self-destructive behavior follows. For women, recovery from the Stockholm syndrome includes developing strong friendships and political alliances with feminist women (Trigiani, 1999). Given the high level of lifetime victimization, including sexual and emotional abuse, experienced by individuals behind bars, offenders are at high risk for manipulation and may already suffer from the Stockholm syndrome. Correctional nurses must be aware of these phenomena in the event they also find themselves in hostage situations.

Nurses account for 19% of all correctional staff and have the same types of professional responsibilities within correctional facilities with the added concern of safety. Learning to be caring while being cautious is often a challenge. All equipment, supplies, and pharmaceuticals must be locked. Used needles, instruments, gloves, and other materials can be used as contraband and must be accounted for. There are no newspapers, magazines, and other such material to read on breaks. There are no beepers or cell phones. Health education material must be evaluated for appropriateness before it can be dispensed.

Nursing personnel must develop working relationships with correctional officers who have their own issues and responsibilities for the safety of the institution. It is imperative to understand and work within their policies and procedures regarding security. Lockdowns, counts, passes, and the like often interfere with the flow of nursing care. However, these impositions are necessary to protect the integrity of the institution.

Healthcare professionals approve many privileges for prisoners. These include work restrictions, shoe passes, slow eating passes, air conditioning, lower bunk status, special diets, sunglasses, special soaps, blankets, and special clothing. Offenders often try to manipulate this perceived power.

Some facilities have complete medical accommodations including hospitals, radiology departments, and laboratories, and some facilities provide essential surgery. Other facilities will have a physician several hours per day and a small infirmary. Work release programs may offer no healthcare, expecting prisoners to seek care in the community. In most facilities, sick call requests are answered within 24 hours.

Correctional care nurses suffer from isolation on several levels. Prisons are often located in geographically undesirable places outside of mainstream society. This often precludes nurses from attending local professional meetings or from pursuing continuing education. Presently this problem has been remedied by telemedicine conferences, Internet conferences, or public health initiatives designed to bridge this gap by affiliating with colleges and universities. There is stigma associated with being employed by a correctional facility, decreasing available applicants. Failure to meet competitive salaries has also decreased the diversity and availability of the working pool.

Applying the art and science of nursing itself can be utilized to develop areas of offender advocacy that benefit everyone. Correctional care facilities can be a nurse's paradise if the individual enjoys health education. Many offenders have never had an opportunity to develop a relationship with any healthcare provider. Basic anatomy and physiology, self-care strategies, anger management, parenting, pharmacology, health promotion, and health prevention are all potential teaching opportunities behind bars. Health education in these areas empowers offenders and improves health outcomes that are beneficial to the offender and the institution. Educating offenders about the medication system and sick call procedures is also valuable. Many institutions require prisoners to notify the medication nurse when they are low on medications and need refills (for "on person" medications). Refills often take a week, because they go to an outside vendor. Creating charts and calling offenders to sick call at times when medications should be running low would provide an opportunity for health education, evaluation of adherence, and mutual participation in creating a plan of care. Teaching offenders to follow self-care practices, to appropriately utilize healthcare, and to journal concerns (including symptoms) benefits both offenders and correctional healthcare providers.

Stress and anxiety increases for most offenders during incarceration. Any method to decrease stress would contribute to the overall well-being of the offender. Some facilities offer poetry or writing programs, meditation, music, and art therapy as means to manage stress. Stress reduction methods learned and practiced during incarceration will also benefit offenders when they are released back into the community.

Overall education for correctional officers on issues of universal precautions, reporting changes in the conditions of offenders, not withholding medications or sick calls as punishment, and general health education are also beneficial to the prisoners and the institution. This education is particularly necessary for informing all of those within the correctional facility about the transmission of communicable disease including hepatitis, tuberculosis, and HIV. Basic anatomy and physiology as well as women's health including reproductive issues, vaginal and sexual health, and mental health issues including depression and suicide are useful topics. Dispelling myths and providing accurate information is beneficial for everyone.

Nurses have an opportunity to apply *Healthy People 2010* behind bars. In addition to topics already mentioned, programs in the following areas are needed and would benefit offenders:

- Violence prevention
- Anger management
- Parenting skills
- Coping strategies
- Skills building and social support enhancement
- Injury prevention
- Smoking prevention
- Substance abuse rehabilitation
- Reduction of the harm resulting from sexually transmitted diseases
- Increased literacy and assistance in obtaining a general equivalency diploma (GED)
- Increased social skills
- Job training

Nurses can play a key role by assessing offenders for functional (low) illiteracy and learning disabilities, which are pervasive among incarcerated populations. Failure to adequately screen and identify illiteracy results in offenders not understanding prison protocols, medical regimens, informed consent, and ultimately the inability to perform self-care practices (American Medical Association [AMA], 1999; Perdue, Degazon, & Lunney, 1999). Low literacy can also result when English is not an offender's first language (Collins, Gullette, & Schnepf, 2005). Many offenders with low literacy have learned to compensate and hide it very well (Doak, Doak, & Root, 1996; Schultz, 2002). Nurses must be alert to offenders who only use visual cues and demonstrate difficulty adhering to medical regimens.

Illiterate youth and adults are also at risk for future incarceration if they are not identified early. Sixty-five percent of offenders in state prisons have not completed high school (Health Resources and Services Administration, 2000). Incarcerated people must be supported in the hope that they are worthwhile and can accomplish their goals. Providing the desire to overcome illiteracy combined with a program to do so requires educators who are gentle, have a positive outlook, are forgiving of offenders' shortcomings and their own, and interact with unconditional caring (Carrera, 1996). Until incarcerated individuals are helped to attain skills to overcome low literacy (and other deficits), they will remain at risk for recidivism and marginalization as they generally lack employable skills or a high school diploma. Box 38-3 highlights additional references that address issues related to literacy and learning disabilities.

Nurses in Cascade County, Montana created the first correctional healthcare service, which opened in January 1998 and is run by the Montana State University–Bozeman College of Nursing at Great Falls. Nurse practitioners (NP) on the faculty provide 95% of the healthcare to offenders, thereby reducing transportation and overall costs to Cascade County (Boswell, 2000). In addition to the two nurse practitioners, there are three full-time nurses, an administrative assistant, a medical records assistant, and nursing students. The nurses contract physician services. Early reports from jail administrators, offenders, and nurses have been positive. The program received awards from the National Organization of Nurse Practitioner Faculty (NONPF).

Box 38-3 Resources Related to Literacy and Learning Disabilities

- Hayes M. Social skills: The bottom line for adult LD success; www.ldonline.org/ld_indepth/social_skills/social-1.html.
- "Improving Patient Education for Poor Readers"; http://nsweb.nursing-spectrum.com/ce/ce195.htm.
- Literacy behind Prison Walls. (1994). National Center for Education Statistics.
- Literacy Volunteers of America, www.literacyvolunteers.org.
- Parker, R. M., Baker, D. W., Williams, M. V., et al. (1995). The test of functional health literacy in adults: A new instrument for measuring patients' literacy skills. *Journal of General Internal Medicine*, 36 (5).
- Schultz, M. (2002). Low literacy skills needn't hinder care. *Registered Nurse*, 65(4), 45–48.

Box 38-4 Non-Nursing Creative Programs to Empower and Heal Offenders

- *Cell Block Art* (Princeton Publishers, 2001) by Joyce is a collection of work done by offenders. This art therapy program is designed to empower the human spirit through art, thus providing the mind with the freedom to escape the pain.
- Girl Scouts behind Bars brings mothers and daughters together to develop service, values, and healing.
- "Jesus Hopped the 'A' Train," written by Stephen Adly Giurgis as part of the Hospital Audiences, Inc. (HAI), Violence Prevention Program, is a play about two inmates, religious cults, and life in prison. Shown to offenders at Ryker's Island, the play provided dialogue between actors, correctional officers, and offenders. The play moved to a London theater after receiving "Fringe" Edinburgh Festival awards.
- Training Seeing Eye Dog Program in New York State. Offenders earn the right to evolve responsibility and improve self-esteem.
- The Wild Animal Rescue Project at the Maryville Prison in Ohio affords women inmates the opportunity to develop self-worth by caring for injured animals until the animals can be released back into nature.

Box 38-4 displays some examples of other non-nursing creative programs designed to empower and heal offenders.

Nurses can create healing environments within the chaos of prison life. Nursing leader Martha Rogers supported holistic nursing practice where individuals work, play, and live. Campbell (1992) stated that nursing education in the area of interpersonal violence would be more beneficial if it were rooted in "ways of knowing" rather than pathology and taught "advocacy, mutuality, critique, and transformation" as tools of empowerment for both practitioners and patients. Both of these nursing leaders recognize the power of nursing to affect their environment and patients. It is important to not revictimize offenders by being critical and judgmental. Compassion, caring, and programs that empower and educate are needed behind bars.

Health Problems of Inmates
GENERAL HEALTH STATUS OF INMATES

Escalated morbidity and mortality rates are secondary to earlier lives in poverty and poor access to healthcare prior to incarceration (Hammett, Harmon, & Rhodes, 2002; McLaughlin & Stokes, 2002). Minority groups, especially African Americans, are overrepresented within the prison systems and generally enter the prison system in the poorest of health secondary to disparity in healthcare while in the community (Davis, Liu, & Gibbons, 2003; Nelson, 2002). Twenty percent of offenders report health concerns other than injuries at the time of admission. Approximately 5% to 7% of offenders have more than one medical impairment or mental condition. Another 26% to 28% of offenders in state and federal prisons report injuries secondary to accidents or fights while incarcerated (Maruschak & Beck, 2001). Injuries increase with time served and double after 72 months of incarceration. The likelihood that inmates will require surgery also increases with length of time incarcerated from 2.5% of offenders confined less than 6 months to 21% of offenders confined 120 months or greater.

Table 38-1 highlights common medical problems of state and federal inmates. It should be noted that some physical and mental impairments are three times higher in prison than in the general populations. These include learning and speech impairments and mental impairments. Box 38-5 highlights the types and number of deaths in state prisons.

Table 38-1 Medical Problems

CONDITION	STATE%	FEDERAL%
Learning (including dyslexia and attention deficit disorder)	9.9	5.1
Speech (including lisp/stutter)	3.7	2.2
Hearing	5.7	5.6
Vision	8.3	7.6
Mental impairment	10.0	4.8
Physical impairment	11.9	11.1
Mental illness	16	7
Significant psychiatric problems	12.5	Combined
Colds/flu/virus	19.0	21.9
Medical conditions	21.4	21.7
HIV infection	7.5, Northeast (especially New York and Florida), 1.1, Midwest, 0.8 West	5

Data from Maruschak, L. M., & Beck, A. J. (2001). Medical problems of inmates, 1997. U.S. Department of Justice, Bureau of Justice Statistics, January, NCJ 181644. www.ojp.usdoj.gov/bjs (accessed October 16, 2009); Health Resources and Services Administration (HRSA). (2000). Incarcerated people and HIV/AIDS. U.S. Department of Health and Human Services, Washington, DC: Author, August/September, www.hrsa.gov/hab (accessed October 16, 2009); Hammett, T. M., Harmon, P., & Maruschak, L. M. (1997). 1996–1997 Update: HIV/AIDS, STDs, and TB in Correctional Facilities. Washington, DC: U.S. Department of Justice, NCJ 176344, July; Ditton, P. M. (1999, July). Mental health and treatment of inmates and probationers, Bureau of Justice Statistics Special Report, NCJ U.S. Department of Justice, 1–12.

Box 38-5 Types and Number of Deaths in State Prisons

Total = 3095
Natural (not HIV/AIDS) = 55%
AIDS = 29% (slightly Ø over the past several years secondary to HAART, except in women)
Suicide = 5%
Accident = 1.3%
Execution = 1.3%
By another person = 1.95%
Other/unspecified = 5.19%

Data from Bureau of Justice Statistics (BJS); National Prisoner Statistics, 1996; and CDC. (1999). Decrease in AIDS-Related Mortality in a State Correctional System. New York, 1995–1998. *MMWR*, 47(51), 1115–1117.

HEALTHCARE COSTS FOR INMATES

Offenders lose federal- and state-funded medical care benefits such as Medicaid and Medicare. Healthcare for offenders is therefore passed on to taxpayers through DOC budgets. Costs for healthcare are often escalated if medical charts are not electronic. This occurs during transfers to hospital locked wards for care or more often when offenders are transferred to other correctional facilities. Transfers to other correctional facilities occur frequently for a variety of security and medical reasons. For security reasons, transports generally occur in the middle of the night and are on a need-to-know basis, generally leaving medical personnel out of the loop. This is problematic for offenders who may wait days or weeks for medical records to follow without needed medications. Approximately 18 to 20 state and federal institutions have electronic medical records that can easily follow offenders, thereby reducing the chance for missed medications, repeated procedures, or the need for additional laboratory tests and healthcare provider visits. Table 38-2 highlights approximate incarceration costs per offender each year.

Table 38-2 Approximate Incarceration Costs per Offender Each Year*

TYPE OF OFFENDER	YEARLY COST
Average offender	$38,500
Geriatric offenders	$69,000
HIV-infected offenders	$80,000–$106,600

*Costs vary from location to location.
Data from Health Resources and Services Administration (HRSA). (2000). *Incarcerated people and HIV/AIDS. U.S. Department of Health and Human Services.* Washington, DC: Author; August/September, www.hrsa.gov/hab (accessed October 16, 2009); and Pelosi, A. (1997, May 5). Age of innocence: A glut of geriatric jailbirds. *The New Republic*, 216, 15–18.

With healthcare costs soaring and as many as 90% of offenders abusing tobacco, applying *Healthy People 2010* can reduce morbidity and mortality behind bars. Smoking cessation programs can benefit correctional institutions by reducing healthcare expenditures related to smoking. Fraser Regional Maximum-Security Prison in British Columbia was the first of six correctional institutions in Canada to require a smoke-free environment (*Edmonton Sun*, 2000). Legal battles between offender rights and employees being exposed to secondhand smoke ensued. It is reasonable to expect smoking regulations to increase in prison systems.

Healthcare costs, as previously mentioned, come out of public health budgets that are designated for the department of corrections on local, state, and federal levels. Private healthcare companies specializing in correctional healthcare often participate in healthcare delivery to prisoners at various levels. This may involve providing physicians, nurse practitioners, or physician assistants to provide most of the healthcare within a facility, or it may be limited to specific specialties such as gynecology or infectious disease/HIV care. Perhaps several facilities share a pharmacist or contract those duties out to a private agency. Some hospitals contract to provide HIV care to correctional institutions in the area. The advantage of private agencies is that highly specialized areas like HIV care is furnished by healthcare providers with that expertise. The downside is that offenders may not see the same person from visit to visit, further contributing to fragmented care and preventing offenders from developing lasting or trusting relationships. For the institution, the use of private agencies reduces transfers to outside medical facilities, a costly and potentially unsafe venture. Correctional care nurses can benefit by being intellectually stimulated by outside healthcare providers. Offenders often prefer or take joy in the fact that their "doc" is from the "outside." There are several keys to successful and cost-effective correctional healthcare (Kendig, 2004; Raimer & Stobo, 2004). A direct collaboration with a university provides access to subspecialites, evidence-based medicine, and more structured healthcare (Kendig, 2004), which was a recommendation of the Prescriptive Package in 1975. A comprehensive correctional healthcare program should include standardized disease management guidelines, a common pharmaceutical formulary, clinician education, and electronic records (Raimer & Stobo, 2004).

Increased utilization of telemedicine behind bars has been identified as another key to successful and cost-effective healthcare (Fox, Somes, & Waters, 2007; Kendig, 2004; Raimer & Stobo, 2004). Prisoners can sit and speak with an outside specialist in the presence of a correctional physician or nurse practitioner who has already performed an examination. This method of healthcare delivery is especially suited for specialty areas such as dermatology, urology, otolaryngology, orthopedics, general surgery, and the treatment of infectious diseases. It also is helpful in states with rural correctional facilities. Initiated in the late 1990s, telemedicine has become a viable system in many states including Texas, Florida, California, Iowa, and New York, to name a few. Telemedicine decreases the need to transport a prisoner outside of the facility, which decreases cost and increases security/safety. Eliminating the need to transport a prisoner in shackles and chains reduces the humiliation many offenders experienced during clinic appointments.

GERIATRIC OFFENDERS

Nineteen percent of the incarcerated population is over the age of 45, representing 250,000 prisoners (Stojkovic, 2007). One state reported that among offenders over the age of 60, two thirds were incarcerated between 1996 and 2001 for violent or sexual offenses. These offenders did not grow old behind bars from youthful offenses but rather had committed crimes as elders.

The primary problems with aging offenders include elder abuse and reduced housing safety, increased chronic illness and health needs, increased costs to the department of corrections (DOC), and end-of-life issues. Offenders over age 45 reported having medical problems other than common colds or injuries since admission. In federal penitentiaries, rates for older offenders were approximately 48%, and in state prisons approximately 40% of those incarcerated entered prison with medical problems (Maruschak & Beck, 2001). This is two times higher than for younger offenders.

Seventy-five percent of elder offenders (50 years old or older) have chronic illness suffering from hypertension (40%), myocardial infarctions (19%), emphysema (18%), and gross physical functional impairment (42%) including missing teeth (Colsher, Wallace, Loeffelholz, et al., 1992). They suffer from Alzheimer's disease as well as hearing and visual impairments that decrease their quality of life and place them at higher risk for elder abuse from other offenders (Stojkovic, 2007). They require skilled nursing care, physical therapy, special diets, and increased pharmacy needs. Some will require surgery including cardiovascular interventions.

The needs of aging offenders are more complex within correctional institutions. Accessibility and safety issues are often difficult to accommodate. Doors in prisons may not be the required 3 feet wide to accommodate wheelchair access; doors may be very heavy, sometimes more than 5 pounds; and there may be insufficient space for ramps or handrails (Carroll, 2001). Frail elders may not be able to defend themselves and are therefore vulnerable to physical abuse and may lose commodities including food.

Many offenders will face dying behind bars without the support of family and friends. End-of-life issues must be met with compassion and caring, qualities not always fostered behind bars for fear of institutional security. Whether or not to release older offenders with life-threatening illnesses continues to be debated. Several states have dealt with this dilemma by developing special needs facilities for those offenders that would never qualify for release such as first- and second-degree murderers. In some states, offenders over age 50 who have served at least the average time for their crime and are terminally ill may be released under various programs to halfway houses or other postrelease housing arrangements. Project for Older Prisoners (POPS) has been one such program releasing half of those who qualify to relatives and others to church-run low-cost apartments (Himelstein, 1993). The National Institute of Justice provides program guidelines for the release of offenders with chronic diseases. Canadian correctional programs parallel guidelines used in the United States for release of older offenders. Risk of recidivism does decrease with age, an argument often used to encourage compassionate release programs.

Correctional institutions will then have to decide what the policy is for those not eligible for release. Is it plausible to adapt a hospice program behind bars? Many correctional nurses and administrators have negative attitudes toward offenders, and this is exhibited by professional inattention that must first be addressed (Cohn, 1999). The National Prison Hospice Association provides guidance for implementing such programs without sacrificing the safety of the institution. Using other offenders as hospice volunteers can be done with discretion, careful planning, and good organization with a multidisciplinary team of physicians, nurses, social workers, chaplains, correctional officers, and offenders (Rold, 2002). Coordinators generally choose from offenders in good standing with no infractions in the previous 6 months. They attend educational sessions and ongoing meetings.

Offenders often have mixed feelings about utilizing hospice programs. Many individuals are in denial about their illness, whereas others fear being vulnerable and exploited if they are in a hospice program. Some offenders refuse palliative care including pain medication for fear of being out of control and therefore vulnerable to other inmates. Offenders who utilize the hospice program have the opportunity to experience community, compassion, and dignity behind bars (Beck, 1999; Linder & Meyers, 2007; Mahon, 1999).

COMMUNICABLE DISEASES

Offenders have all of the same medical concerns as the general population. At the time of incarceration, they often have undiagnosed or poorly managed chronic diseases, sexually transmitted infections (STIs) including human immunodeficiency disease (HIV), pregnancy, and mental illness secondary to the social conditions previously mentioned. As offenders age, increased rates of cancer and chronic disease require increased medical services and nursing care.

After the issue of safety, public health issues pose the most significant problem to correctional facilities. Confined space with overcrowding, poor ventilation, and increased community rates of tuberculosis (TB) and HIV have set the stage for several outbreaks of tuberculosis (TB) that peaked in 1991 (New York), again in 2000 (South Carolina) (Maddow, Vernon, & Pozsik, 2001), and again in 2004 (Florida) (Ashkin, Malecki, & Thomas, 2005). TB remains the single most communicable disease behind bars and occurs five times more frequently than in the general population (Hammett, Harmon, & Maruschak, 1999; Hoskins, 2004; Maddow, et al., 2001). The initial outbreak prompted mandatory TB testing in 73% of all correctional facilities with slightly higher rates of mandatory testing in state prisons and lower rates of required testing in jails. TB prevalence is 7% to 10% of correctional facilities with the highest rate seen in local jails where offenders often enter the correctional system. The CDC recommends initial TB screening of all inmates and detainees on entry and periodic follow-up screening to prevent and control TB (MMWR, 2006). Correctional facilities account for one third of all cases of TB in the United States (Nicodemus & Paris, 2001). Multidrug-resistant TB (mTB) is especially problematic behind bars where higher rates of HIV exist as well. The nurse can play an important role by developing proactive screening programs and policies that increase awareness of all communicable diseases.

Other communicable diseases are also higher among offenders. Concern about confidentiality, combined with fear and denial,

often affect whether an offender seeks care. Substance abusers often report not seeking care before their incarceration and are at the highest risk for STIs. Rates of communicable diseases are difficult to estimate without routine testing policies.

Hepatitis was found in 155,000 offenders (Bureau of Justice Statistics, 2000). Compared to the general population, hepatitis B (HBV)/hepatitis C (HCV) is the second communicable disease that disproportionately affects incarcerated individuals at higher rates. Vaccinating offenders who do not test positive would reduce healthcare costs in the long run. Hepatitis C when co-infected with HIV is more difficult to treat, and each infection increases progression of the other disease (Baillargeon, Paar, Wu, et al., 2008). Co-infected inmates have substantially more psychiatric illnesses and the treatment of hepatitis C augments depression. Treatment for hepatitis C may not be readily available behind bars and remains controversial. The cost of treatment may still outweigh the limited outcomes from treatment. In an effort to reduce viral hepatitis, the National Commission on Correctional Health Care (NCCHC) has produced a CD titled "The ABC Hepatitis Education" as a resource for both inmates and prison staff (888-4-HEP-CDC).

An estimated 558,000 offenders had syphilis in 1999 (Bureau of Justice Statistics, 2000). Alabama experienced an outbreak of syphilis in three male prisons during 1999. New York City reported a 25% syphilis rate among incarcerated women (Nicodemus & Paris, 2001). This is alarming given the decreasing syphilis rates in the general population. Outbreaks of syphilis in prisons have been linked to mixing of offenders with unscreened jail prisoners, transfer of infected offenders to other prisons, and multiple concurrent sexual partners (Wolfe, Xu, Patel, et al., 2001).

Chlamydia rates among offenders are approximately 13%, and gonorrhea rates are 9%; 1% have both diseases (Bureau of Justice Statistics, 2000; Centers for Disease Control, 1999). Not unsurprisingly, chlamydia rates were higher among juveniles, with females having a 22.2% rate of infection and males having an 8.7% rate in several Texas juvenile detention centers.

Incarcerated individuals also acquire sexually transmitted infections (STIs) while behind bars. Sexual relations are prohibited in correctional facilities, considered a felony in many states and federal prisons, and therefore not widely discussed. Rape and HIV in prison are reported to be 8 to 10 times that of the general population (*Washington Times*, 2002). Harm reduction strategies such as distributing bleach kits, condoms, sterile needles, and methadone can reduce transmission of STIs (Gaiter, Jurgens, Mayer, et al., 2000). Condoms are considered contraband, and bleach is not available to clean syringes. In addition to sexual acquisition of communicable diseases, shared needles for tattooing, body piercing, and injecting drugs also contribute to the spread of disease. Only seven correctional facilities distribute condoms: the New York City jail, Los Angeles County jail, Philadelphia jail, San Francisco jail, Washington jail, Vermont prison, and Mississippi prison (Nerenberg, 2002; Sallot, 2002). In some of these facilities, the offender must self-proclaim to be homosexual to receive condoms. This does not help men who have sex with men (MSM) who do not identify as gay. This practice has raised civil liberties questions.

Condoms have been widely available in correctional institutions outside the United States. As of 1997, 81% of European prison systems distributed condoms (Nerenberg, 2002). Since the 1990s, Canadians have provided condoms to incarcerated individuals. Ralf Jürgens, who represents the Canadian HIV/AIDS Legal Network, stated that researchers had found that 82% of correctional facilities had not found problems related to safety or security since the distribution of condoms (Nerenberg, 2002). The 18% reporting problems stated that their concerns were related not to safety or security but to using too many. The experience of other industrialized nations poses questions as to why U.S. policies have not been updated.

HIV-INFECTED OFFENDERS

The World Health Organization (WHO) reported that the United States was one of four industrialized nations lacking a national policy regarding correctional care for the HIV-infected inmate (Harding & Schaller, 1992). The rate of HIV within prison is seven times higher than that found in the general population. HIV, substance abuse, and mental illness are the leading medical conditions within prison.

HIV rates differ geographically and between genders behind bars (see Table 38-1). In Northeast areas, 30% to 40% of incarcerated women are HIV infected–nearly double that of men in the same area. The majority of women learn their HIV status while incarcerated or during pregnancy.

Often, incarcerated individuals have not had continuous healthcare when they enter prison, so viral loads (HIV-1 RNA) are frequently high and these individuals are generally sicker. Offenders not on highly active antiretroviral therapy (HAART) with elevated viral loads are more susceptible to opportunistic infections (OI), including tuberculosis, and experience reduced treatment outcomes with a higher risk for end-of-life complications. Offenders with high viral loads are potentially more contagious and pose a safety threat to others during sex, needle exchange, or altercations (including biting). HIV-infected offenders present a multitude of challenges for prison administrators ranging from housing, medical care delivery, administration of medications (including special dietary requirements), and increased economic burdens in an already constricted financial picture.

Maintaining confidentiality behind bars is complicated by several issues. Offenders often fill roles where they either hear or handle information related to healthcare. Word of mouth behind bars is a highly efficient means of transmitting information among prisoners. This often places offenders at risk for not disclosing a health concern, because they fear stigmatization and subsequent abuse. Fear of stigmatization may include choosing not to be tested for HIV. HIV-infected offenders who enter prison knowing their status may choose to defer treatment so as not to be identified. Many prisons contract out for specialty care such as infectious disease and HIV care. Care may occur in special clinics inside or outside the prison. Attending these special clinics also labels the prisoner. Choosing to "take care of yourself" in prison is not always a simple choice.

As in the general population, offenders seek to interact with professionals who can provide competent, trusting, and respectful services (Abercrombie, 2001; Altice, 1998; Flanigan, 1999; Parker & Paine, 1999; Stone, 1999). Confidentiality is a component of this therapeutic relationship as well. Healthcare provider relationships, as previously mentioned, are somewhat dictated by the administration and safety boundaries that cannot be broken. There is an overriding distrustful paranoia in prison that is increased by a number of factors, such as the power structures, mental illness and substance abuse issues, the history of prisons, the history of medical research inside prison (including the Tuskegee experiments in Georgia), disenfranchised communities of origin, and the discrepancies ethnically with respect to who is incarcerated and who has the power. Healthcare professionals have a responsibility to provide information for informed consent and to reduce refusal for treatment. These issues have medicolegal repercussions.

Many prisons do not have mandatory testing or optimal voluntary testing, so the HIV rates reflected are low. Only 16 states in the United States have mandatory HIV testing at admission. Developing nations in particular often omit testing unless requested by offenders. If the HIV status of an offender is unknown, healthcare costs are reduced.

HIV testing is an important component to diagnosis and treatment. Providing voluntary testing that has the support and confidence of the inmates is imperative to a good program and strongly recommended by the CDC (Lyons, Lindsell, Fichtenbaum, & Camargo, 2007). One study showed rapid HIV testing was feasible and highly accepted by jail detainees (Beckwith, Atunah-Jay, Cohen, et al., 2007). Sufficient education and counseling is required to prevent increased anxiety and possible suicide, increase hope, replace myths with facts, and establish a plan of action that adequately addresses treatment options. The issue of partner notification must be explored as well. It is important to understand before the results are back whether inmates fear retribution from partners or family members or have economic concerns that make dealing with this issue sensitive. Women are at increased risk for abandonment upon returning to the community, and they risk domestic violence when partners have been notified of their HIV status (Rothenberg & Paskey, 1995). Incarcerated women may also fear for their children if those children remain in the care of violent partners. Most public health departments have anonymous mechanisms for notifying individuals of risk from exposures to STIs, including HIV, without linking the exposure to a specific person.

Disclosing HIV results is an opportunity for education. The inmate needs to hear about the hope surrounding HIV and that it is not a death sentence but considered a chronic disease. Discussing the natural disease of HIV can dispel myths and provide a basis for assessing a prisoner's readiness to commit to the rigorous medication regime. It is important not to start individuals on medications until they have had time to internalize the information and make a reasonable decision. Stopping and starting HIV medication is a worse scenario than waiting to start medication, as it can contribute to ART resistance. The correctional care nurse is invaluable in this role, which can be expanded to include HIV peer educators.

The majority of prisons are in a difficult position with respect to drugs and sex, neither of which is supposed to occur. Yet it is widely known that both sex and substance abuse occur behind bars. Unfortunately, this dualistic problem is a major health concern. If sex is prohibited, then possessing condoms or using oral contraceptives is prohibited, which is the policy of most prisons. That policy is under review because of the rising number of HIV cases in prison. Clean needles and bleach policies for injection drug use (IDU) lag even further behind and reflect not only the positions of prison officials but the philosophical debate in the United States regarding needle exchange policies (Burris, Lurie, Abrahamson, et al., 2000). Conservative estimates are that approximately 3.2% of offenders are becoming HIV infected from sex and IDU during incarceration (Health Resources and Services Administration, 2000; Taylor, Goldberg, Emslie, et al., 1995). One ex-prisoner in New York City said that he and 50 other known prisoners who were part of an inmate "drug-shooting" circle and shared one needle had become infected while incarcerated in a state prison. The correctional care nurse can routinely teach about modes of HIV transmission, universal precautions, safer sex, and how to clean a needle properly. Postexposure protocols (PEP) should be in place for altercations between individuals and needle sticks that pose the threat of HIV infection.

Increasingly, the treatment of HIV infection has become more complex. It is the belief of many professional organizations that HIV care should be left to those healthcare providers who specialize in treating HIV-infected individuals (DeGroot, Hammett, & Scheib, 1996). This has been a challenge for prisons, with safety the primary concern. Many larger state institutions utilize telemedicine to bring state-of-the-art treatment to inmates infected with HIV.

In other states such as Alabama, Mississippi, Georgia, and South Carolina, HIV populations are housed in one facility, creating a much-debated human rights issue. Offenders complain that they are being stigmatized; prison officials state this is the only way they can provide quality healthcare in a cost-effective manner and keep non-HIV-infected prisons safe from HIV transmission. It should be noted that aggregate HIV housing was shown to contribute to TB outbreaks (Nicodemus & Paris, 2001). Prison policy to segregate HIV-infected inmates from the rest of the prison population was upheld by the U.S. Supreme Court on January 18, 1990, when the court stated that the policy did not violate the Rehabilitation Act of 1973. The ruling further denounced that this policy discriminated against offenders testing positive for HIV. Prisoners who were assigned to segregated prison housing for HIV-infected offenders are then identified by association.

Specific laws related to HIV/AIDS have evolved since the 1990s. Circuit courts applying Eighth Amendment rights to HIV-infected individuals have been divided in their rulings, leaving HIV management to healthcare providers in the various correctional facilities (Sylla & Thomas, 2000). Most rulings to "deliberate indifference" have failed to set HIV standards of care to which offenders are entitled. Box 38-6 highlights key cases related to HIV/AIDS in correctional facilities.

The second most problematic area in the treatment of HIV-infected offenders is medications. HIV is a complex disease with a high resistance. Drug resistance can occur in a number of ways and combinations. The first combination of medications used to treat newly diagnosed HIV cases is the most important step. If not carefully chosen, a number of treatment options are lost when resistance to them develops. Triple combination ART is the recommended therapy for HIV, and other therapies such as monotherapy are considered substandard and may contribute to drug resistance. Resistance can develop via sexual intercourse where the resistance of one person is transferred to the other person via body fluids. Missing doses or not taking medications properly also increases the likelihood that resistance to medications will develop. This is the single most perplexing problem for those who care for HIV-infected people. Inmates and staff need education on resistance, preferably before they begin therapy. Medication adherence is further complicated in prisons by the food/no food restrictions that many of the HIV medications carry. Some prisons find it difficult to allocate the extra foods necessary for medications or to treat associated disease states.

Medication resistance with HIV is further complicated while a person is incarcerated. There is a multitude of situations that may leave the offender without medications for days and weeks at a time. Diminishing missed HIV medication doses is the primary goal of healthcare providers and an area where correctional nurses can take a leading role. Educating prison administration and correctional officers regarding the importance of this policy is imperative in the fight against HIV. Correctional officers often possess the least amount of knowledge regarding HIV disease and express the most negative attitudes about HIV-infected people (Kantor, 1998).

The areas that remain problematic are transferring offenders for healthcare appointments, paroling and releasing inmates from prison, refilling medications in a timely manner, lockdowns and searches, and safety transfers to other facilities that occur in the middle of the night with no notice to healthcare professionals and without medications. Unfortunately, on arrival at the second institution, a transferred inmate has no medications and must wait to see a physician. When seeing the healthcare provider, the offender must often wait from one to two weeks to receive the medications since most facilities contract out to management and pharmaceutical companies.

On a day-to-day basis, the lack of adherence to medications and the withholding of medications as a form of punishment are ongoing challenges, and community health nurses can best address these issues through education at a variety of levels. Whether to allow prisoners to hold medications "on person" or to require directly observed therapy (DOT) is often determined by prison policy, and both options have their strengths and weaknesses (Babudieri, Aceti, D'Offizi, et al., 2000; Lucas, Flexner, & Moore, 2002). Triple combination therapy and the advent of protease inhibitors have significantly reduced AIDS-related mortalities in prisons (Wright & Smith, 1999). A study in Florida compared DOT with on-person therapy with respect to viral suppression. The findings revealed that 85% of the DOT and only 50% of the matched self-administered group had a viral suppression (plasma HIV RNA) of less than 50 copies/mL at week 48 (Fischl, Rodriguez, Sceppella, et al., 2000). This study may greatly affect the decisions of correctional facilities regarding medication administration and the reintroduction of clinical trials behind bars. The primary objection by offenders regarding DOT is that it labels them as HIV-infected because no other chronic disease has the number and frequency of doses that HIV carries. With newer improvements to decrease the number and frequency of doses, HIV medications may begin to resemble medication patterns similar to those of other diseases.

Box 38-6 Key Cases Related to HIV/AIDS in Correctional Facilities

1997—*Nolley v. Johnson* (U.S. Dist. LEXIS 17651. S.D.N.Y.) ruled that the prison did not show "deliberate indifference" when an inmate was off HIV medication for a week during transport between facilities. This was of concern to healthcare providers because of the high resistance patterns that occur when there is not a 95% adherence rate (missing one dose a week).

1999—*Perkins v. Kansas Dept. of Corrections* (165 F.3d 803) upheld correctional facilities' decision to treat HIV with two (no protease inhibitor) rather than three antiretroviral medications even though three medication regimens had been the community standard of care for several years. The ruling stated that the offender had received care and there was no "deliberate indifference."

2000—*Sullivan v. County of Pierce* (U.S. App. LEXIS 8251) upheld the complaint of "deliberate indifference" when the offender's protease inhibitor was withheld because the prison did not stock it. The court felt that this was far from the medical norm.

2000—*Leon v. Johnson* (96 F. Supp. 2d 244. WDNY) upheld that the prison did not show "deliberate indifference" when a Spanish-speaking-only offender missed picking up medications because directions were written in English, even though his condition worsened.

2000—*Edwards v. Alabama Dept. of Corrections* (81 F. Supp. 2d 1242) upheld that the prison was not liable for damages resulting from delivering HIV medication three to four days late, basing its decision on the fact that Alabama was poor and care did not differ from that in the community.

Adherence to medications is generally related to a number of factors including knowledge of the medications and HIV together with a good rapport with healthcare providers. Because adherence is vital to decrease resistance to HIV medications, it is important that institutions examine treatment outcomes. Research has shown that adherence and acceptance of medications depend on three factors: trust in the medication, trust in the healthcare system, and good interpersonal relationships with providers and peers (Abercrombie, 2001; Altice & Buitrago, 1998; Holzemer, Corless, Nokes, et al., 1999; Mostashari, Riley, Selwyn, et al. 1998; Roberts, 2002). Additional barriers in medication administration behind bars include frequency of dosing, being asymptomatic, mental illness, stigmatization, correctional issues related to safety and administration, and fear of side effects. A study reported that institutions find accommodating HIV medication regimes difficult; nurses are often not knowledgeable about all the food-related timing issues required and the drug-to-drug interactions; and observation about the overall needs of the facility and staff must be examined when trying to increase adherence (Finlay & Jones, 2000; Frank, 1999; Miller & Rundio, 1999). A suggested tool to improve medication ordering, administration, and delivery is to do periodic, retrospective chart reviews (Ungvarski & Rottner, 1997). Nurses can collectively develop a process for addressing these issues that will in the long run help offenders to be more successful in the medication regime. For recommendations regarding treatment options, a number of publications are available including two that are specific to correctional care and HIV.

Nurses can foster a caring attitude within the prison system. This can be a motivating factor in prisoners choosing to be tested for HIV, receiving adequate healthcare, being receptive to learning about HIV and their medications, adhering to HIV medications, and decreasing stereotypes and myths about HIV. An onsite weekly or daily HIV nurse practitioner can contribute to continuity of care, education, and adherence of complex HIV medications (Miller & Rundio, 1999). Educating correctional officers, prison administrators, and other offenders about HIV is the first step in empowering inmates to take care of themselves as well as decreasing tension by debunking myths. As noted earlier, several studies report correctional officers as possessing the most negative attitudes toward HIV-infected inmates, as well as being the least informed about HIV transmission and prevention (Allard, April, & Martin, 1992).

Educational opportunities within prison are limitless. One study showed education was the single most important element for improving the quality of life for HIV offenders (Hammett, Harmon, & Maruschak, 1999). Prisons and jails have significantly increased HIV rates. However, only 10% of state/federal prison systems and 5% of jail systems have comprehensive programs. A comprehensive program includes the following elements:

- Orientation
- Peer education
- Community-based prevention and education
- Individual prevention and education, on request
- Written and audiovisual materials
- Prevention and education in prerelease, day reporting, and pretrial populations
- Gender-specific programs at facilities housing women
- Expansion of HIV curriculums to cover other communicable diseases
- Programs and materials in Spanish and English (Hammett, et al., 1999, p. 27)

In order of the most prevalent, the following methods have been utilized to promote education in prisons and jails: pre-/posttest counseling, written material, inviting lecturers to do educational programs, use of audiovisual materials, peer-led education, and health fairs. A comparison of the 1994 to 1997 National Institute of Justice/Centers for Disease Control surveys shows that educational programs about HIV have increased from half the federal and state prisons surveyed in 1994 to 61% in 1997 (CDC, 1996; Hammett, et al., 1999). In the 1997 survey, jails reported that approximately 66% had educational programs. It should be pointed out that having an educational program does not mean that offenders attend or utilize the program.

GENDER DIFFERENCES IN CORRECTIONS

The natural question would be why is the population of women in prison growing in such large numbers? Women in general have the least amount of power, which is often represented by a lack of economic power or gender inequality. Most single parents, generally women, live in poverty. Economic power buys better legal advice, which translates into reduced sentences for crimes. Women for the most part lack high-level knowledge about their crimes. Lack of knowledge results in little information to trade for reduced sentences. Women of color often lack respect among their peers and society in general, so they may be viewed as castaways or incidentals. Women may lack political power in general and are often underrepresented by their elected officials. This lack of power means more severe sentences than their male counterparts.

This lack of power extends to the correctional facilities. Studies have indicated that one of the most stressful problems for women related to incarceration is their lack of power with prison guards, the majority of whom are men. Studies have shown that anxiety and depression escalate during incarceration by this lack of power combined with fear of retribution, including sexual assault.

Sexual assaults and harassment were found in 50 states in America, reported Congresswoman Eleanor Norton (Geraldo Rivera special, "Women in Prison: Nowhere to Hide," September 10, 1999). The code among prisoners is to keep their mouths shut and submit to sexual assault or shakedowns. Shakedowns or patdowns are often viewed as authority to "feel up" prisoners. Sexual assault is often termed "consensual sex with intimidation" or viewed as "trading favors." Offenders may be "traded" to other prisoners or to correctional staff for sex (Human Rights Watch, 1996). The power imbalance while incarcerated makes consent between prisoner and guards impossible, and it is also illegal in federal prisons. There are prisoners, especially women, who lack family and social support and find themselves in a position of swapping favors as their only means for attaining money. Here again is the imbalance of power from an economic and psychological perspective. Offenders who have access to money can negotiate more favorable conditions for themselves while incarcerated. Prison staff and guards retaliate by placing feces in the offenders' food, urinating on the person, forced hanging, and refusing medical care. Offenders in isolation or "segs" are often more vulnerable to sexual misconduct. A federal judge found the progressive, prolonged, and prurient observation in dressing areas is considered sexual misconduct.

Most women enter prison with a long history of victimization resulting in anxiety, depression, and posttraumatic stress disorder (PTSD). One study reported that in the year before incarceration, women experienced 10 stressful life events, and 90% of women suffered from severe anxiety and depression (Keaveny & Zauszieski, 1999). Researchers have estimated that 75% of incarcerated women have a history of childhood or adult sexual abuse (Browne, Miller, & Maguin, 1999; Haney & Kristiansen, 1998; Harris, Sharps, & Allen et al., 2003; Health Resources and Service Administration, 2000; Maeve, 1999). The majority of women (90%) have come from homes where there was violence in the form of hitting, striking, and slapping (Bond & Semaan, 1996; Browne, et al., 1999; Fogel, 1993). Forty-four percent of women behind bars were beaten by one or both parents (Bond & Semaan, 1996). Many women have seen violence in their environment on a daily basis, which contributes significantly to PTSD (Wallace, et al., 1996). Although men in the impoverished areas also experience daily violence, their rates of PTSD are not as high. Researchers postulate that it is the long history of victimization (secondary to power inequities) that occurs in conjunction with physical and sexual abuse that contributes to the higher rates of PTSD in incarcerated women. Another compounding factor to the increased rates of PTSD is the fact that approximately 50% of prisoners have some form of mental illness and that the combined effect of mental illness with PTSD contributes to the criminal behavior leading to the incarceration of women (Jordan, Schlenger, Fairbank, et al., 1996). Additionally, PTSD is associated with increased risky behavior and increased risk for suicide (Lewis, 2006).

PTSD and the related anxiety and depression also contribute to the inability of female offenders to cope, both before incarceration and during incarceration (Kupers, 1999). A high correlation exists between alcohol and substance abuse following sexual abuse, either as a child or as an adult (Blume, 1998). Although not all women who are victims of sexual abuse rely on substances to numb their feelings, it is more prevalent among women who have fewer family and social resources. Additionally, women who have been beaten about the head during interpersonal violence may suffer from postconcussion syndrome (PCS), placing them at risk for poor decisions and the inability to multitask, thereby placing them at risk for further abuse (Fullilove, Fullilove, Smith, et al., 1993). Leenerts (1999, 2003) reported that the experience of abuse significantly decreased the offender's self-care practices. The constellation of PTSD, substance abuse, and possible postconcussion syndrome places women at risk for overall poor decisions and at risk for behavior that contributes to their arrest.

Physical and sexual abuse are problematic within prisons and are further complicated by the poor state of mental health described earlier. Female inmates often develop PTSD. Women with PTSD are unable to return and reintegrate into their communities and as mothers. They become paralyzed by their state of mental distress.

Correctional nurses can assist prisoners and facilities in developing confidential anonymous reporting systems for offenders to disclose sexual misconduct and sexual assaults. Georgia and California have either confidential anonymous hot lines or reporting boxes. Georgia prison reform now requires that 85% of guards in female prisons are women and forbids male correctional officers to do patdowns, strip searches, or frisks. Nurses must be able to identify symptoms of anxiety, depression, and PTSD in prisoners and provide intervention strategies.

Women enter prison in overall poor health, both physically and psychologically. Up to 21% of women in prison are HIV infected, and those who are not infected are at significant risk for acquiring HIV (DeGroot, 2000). Those women who are HIV infected were less likely than men to have accessed healthcare with any regularity and entered prison with more advanced stages of HIV disease than men. HIV is highest among black women who were less likely to have accessed healthcare (Lynch & Pugh, 2000). Nearly half of the incarcerated women were sexually active with a drug-injecting partner. Few practiced any form of safe sex. The combined effects of substance abuse, mental illness including PTSD, few socioeconomic resources, and increased risk-taking behavior place women at a very high risk for acquiring HIV (DeGroot, Hammett, & Scheib, 1996; El-Bassel, Ivanoff, Schilling, et al., 1995; Wyatt, Myers, Williams, et al., 2002). Many studies have shown a high correlation between domestic violence/childhood sexual abuse and the risk of acquiring HIV (Dilorio, Hartwell, Hansen, et al., 2002; Flitcraft, 1995; Fogel & Belyea, 2001; Hartwell et al., 2002; Magura, et al., 1993; Manfrin-Ledet & Porche, 2003; Mullings, Marquart, & Brewer, 2000; Schwab-Stone, Chen, Greenberger, et al., 1999; Stevens, Zierler, Dean, et al., 1995).

Prison therefore presents a unique opportunity for HIV prevention. Subgroups of detainees at greatest risk for acquiring HIV include injecting drug users, people whose arrests were associated with drug charges (either misdemeanors or felonies), people who had several prior arrests for less serious charges especially related to drug charges, and people with severe mental illness (McClelland, Teplin, Abram, et al., 2002). Providing substance abuse rehabilitation is an important aspect of HIV prevention. Teaching condom use is not especially helpful in this population because of fears of retribution from their partners (Bond & Semaan, 1996; Manfrin-Ledet & Porche, 2003). Female condom education, however, has proved to be more accepted by some women (VanDevanter, Gonzalez, Mertel, et al., 2002; Witte, Wada, El-Bassel, et al., 2000). Teaching empowerment skills may reduce risk-taking behavior. Many women released from prison felt this type of risk reduction was not met while they were incarcerated (Fickenscher, Lapidus, Silk-Walker, et al., 2001; Young, 2000).

REPRODUCTIVE AND SEXUAL HEALTH ISSUES

Many women currently in prison are incarcerated for the first time. Eighty-five percent are mothers, and three quarters of their children are under the age of 18. It should be noted, however, that only one third of these children were living with them at the time of the arrest. Many children had been removed from the home because of problems related to previous substance abuse. Some children live with relatives, whereas others are in foster care or have been adopted. Other incarcerated women leave children behind and are concerned about their safety and who is taking care of them. Family members or the father (who may have been abusive) often watch these children. Mothers who do not keep in touch with their children often lose them to adoption. It is therefore important for incarcerated mothers to write regularly to their children. Nurses can assist offenders in this process.

Women generally suffer from empty nest syndrome. Many women have already lost their children because of substance abuse issues that have forced placement of their children in foster care or because of a lack of continued contact with children in foster care. A number of HIV-infected inmates may have lost children who were also infected. Children visit their mothers less frequently than they do fathers who are incarcerated, with only 50% of women ever seeing their children (Maeve, 1999). Prisons are often a distance geographically from families, and the families may be unable to travel because of economic constraints. Many women spend the long hours being locked up thinking about their children and longing for improved scenarios. Many women are guilty and ashamed that they were not better mothers. Many women are angry at the bureaucratic system for the mess they are in. As most women are in their reproductive years when incarcerated, many think about starting new families upon release.

The correctional care nurse can do much in this area. Many women do not understand basic anatomy and physiology and would benefit from education in this area, as well as being taught basic fertility awareness and being provided with contraception information. Parenting classes are very important. Women would benefit from support groups that allow them to express their feelings regarding their children and offering some healing for this deep wound. It is not until women can heal from these emotions, including the guilt and shame, that they can begin to set healthy plans for their release. Offering suggestions as to how to begin to heal the pain of their loss and supporting them as they reach out to children they have harmed are necessary steps that will help to prevent these women from repeating old patterns.

Few prison systems have provisions for children to accompany their mothers while incarcerated; those that do have long waiting lists. Fragmenting families has become a social and economical issue as more women are being incarcerated for nonviolent crimes. Most pastoral groups are calling for alternatives to incarceration that promote family unity rather than further destroying already fragile family units. They argue that these alternatives are cheaper than the current system. Some states have also begun to introduce special programs, such as Girl Scout programs at prison, to promote interaction among mothers and daughters. Such programs typically transport the children to prison and conduct structured family programs.

Approximately 6% to 10% of women entering prison are pregnant (Hoskins, 2004). Some women may not have known that they were pregnant and may choose a pro-choice option if they can afford it. Some correctional facilities may not offer therapeutic abortions. Other women choose to continue their pregnancies, with approximately 1300 live births per year (Richardson, 1998). This is often a more difficult choice for prisons that find it problematic to provide additional nutritional food. Transporting shackled offenders to and from prenatal appointments and for delivery of the baby has been the source of much criticism nationally. Stories of women delivering while shackled to the bed have raised numerous issues ranging from human rights to medical complications (Siegal, 1998). The end result for the offender has been generally little time with her newborn infant, who will typically be shuttled off to foster care.

New York State's Bedford Hills is one of a few model programs offering comprehensive services to offenders and allowing mothers to keep their babies following delivery. Federal prisons have the Mothers and Infants Together (MINT) program for women who qualify. These offenders are placed in halfway houses three months before delivery and for two months after delivery.

These programs offer an opportunity for mother-child bonding. Parenting classes offer an opportunity for offenders to build relationships with each other. Nursing staff reports that women with PTSD often have difficulty bonding with their infants. Being touched and touching are often associated with abuse, and women with PTSD have fears related to physical touch and intimacy. Women often avoid breast-feeding, rocking, or cuddling their babies. The correctional nurse who is aware of these possibilities could utilize prenatal visits to explore these concerns and issues with mothers and provide educational and emotional support. Appropriate psychiatric counseling would be beneficial in altering old patterns of childcare that have their roots in past traumatic events and violence.

It is also important to remember that pregnancy may not have occurred within the framework of a loving relationship. One lesbian woman said that her only heterosexual coitus occurred as the result of being raped. At the same time she became pregnant for the first time, she also became HIV-positive and was exposed to human papillomavirus (HPV) and Neisseria gonorrhea, which resulted in pelvic inflammatory disease (PID) and continual abdominal discomfort. Eventually she also developed cervical disease from the HPV, which could progress to cervical cancer. In addition to the medical complications of this assault, she suffered emotionally with PTSD, issues related to her body image, and sexual orientation identity issues related to being a lesbian and being pregnant. Her mother agreed to care for her child until the woman was emotionally able to bond with the child. Portions of this scenario were common to many incarcerated women.

Many people might ask, what benefit is having family-oriented programs in prison if women are not bonding with their children? Case Study 38-1 demonstrates the importance and raises the issue of whose standards are being used to measure program success. This example stresses the amount of education and support women often require when they are arrested for a drug-related charge. Studies have shown that women lacking social support and who come from families where physical and emotional abuse were present are more likely to then abuse their own children (Hall, Sachs, & Rayens, 1998). Bedford Hills and the MINT programs provide an opportunity to break the cycles of violence by providing education and counseling to mothers and babies. Without this intervention, the women would be at risk for continuing in the same lifestyle.

Case Study 38-1

Breaking the Cycle

An inmate and mother of two delivered her third baby at Bedford Hills in New York. Both of her other children were in foster care and slated for adoption. The inmate had a long history of substance abuse and stated that this was the first delivery she had experienced while not high on crack cocaine. She appreciated the opportunity to turn her life around and begin a new life with supervision. On release, she moved to a halfway house with her newborn where emotional support and parenting skills were provided. She eventually went back to using drugs but stated that she was able to place the baby in responsible hands before doing so. She would have just abandoned the baby in the past. She was also able to get back on track within a few weeks rather than being incarcerated again.

Women with a history of sexual abuse and who experience PTSD find childbirth and gynecological exams, including colposcopy, extremely difficult. These medical exams trigger memories of sexual abuse and cause these women to dissociate from the examination. Dissociation may become out-of-control behavior and extreme anxiety. It is important to screen for sexual abuse histories so care can be taken to guide women through the process. This may be the first time that someone has made the association with them—between exams, anxiety, and sexual abuse—and the new awareness often generates many tears. Many women will not disclose sexual abuse the first time they are asked but will wait until they feel there is respect and trust between themselves and the healthcare provider. Admission gynecological screening for concealed contraband or weapons may revictimize women with a history of sexual abuse.

An inmate experiencing difficulty with a gynecological exam could receive a digital exam only, which would satisfy prison staff that nothing is concealed within the vagina. At this point, the gynecological examination could be broken into smaller steps to allow the inmate to begin dealing with her anxiety surrounding the vulnerability of this process. This gentle stepped process of providing gynecological care to traumatized inmates is described elsewhere (Dole, 1996, 1999). A stepped process is especially helpful with women who have HIV and HPV diseases that require colposcopy and gynecological examinations every six months. Approximately half the women offenders who have HIV also have cervical disease, which is a rate approximately double that of women not incarcerated (DeGroot, 2000; Dole, 1999). Non-HIV-infected offenders have much lower rates of HPV infection; however, the rates are still considerably higher for this population compared to nonincarcerated women.

Taking the additional time with inmates who experience difficulty with gynecological examinations is imperative if healing the painful wounds of sexual abuse is to occur. Prison affords healthcare providers this opportunity, since many inmates are incarcerated for several years. Not taking the time to assist inmates with this concern further victimizes and traumatizes these women. The correctional nurse can do much in this area to identify women who may suffer from PTSD and alert healthcare providers of the problem. Whenever possible, sensitive female providers should examine offenders with PTSD who are anxious about gynecological exams. As many as 50% to 75% of female offenders may suffer from PTSD. Support groups and education would benefit this population. Offenders suffering from PTSD may repeatedly seek excuses or refuse to have a gynecological examination. Another tip to PTSD is chronic abdominal pain or dysmenorrhea without apparent pathology (Golding, Wilsnack, & Learman, 1998; Keamy, 1998). Lifestyle and high-risk behavior before incarceration place women at higher risk for STIs including cervical disease, making pap smears an essential component of incarcerated women's healthcare.

Nurses working in corrections also have the unique opportunity to affect change through education and policies related to female products carried in the commissary. Many women douche regularly, feeling that this is required for cleanliness. Data suggest that douching can actually facilitate pelvic inflammatory disease (PID) by pushing bacteria further up the reproductive track, and douching may facilitate the acquisition of STIs including HIV (Koblin, Mayer, Mwatha, et al., 2002; Vermund, Sarr, Murphy, et al., 2001; Visser, Moorman, Irwin, et al., 1995). Offenders require information about the relationship between various vaginal secretions and the menstrual cycle. Education about vaginal cleanliness and debunking the douching myth would reduce gynecological complications and benefit offenders by saving money for the institutions while empowering the inmates with knowledge.

Education is also beneficial with respect to sexual health. Many women prisoners have traded sex for money or drugs and possess little knowledge about sexuality or their bodies. Feminine hygiene products (including douches), deodorant, sanitary napkins and tampons, perfumed powders, and the relationship between these products and contact dermatitis and ovarian cancer risks needs to be taught (Cook, Kamb, & Weiss, 1997). This topic also provides the healthcare provider with an excellent opportunity to discuss human sexuality issues, the menstrual cycle, reproduction, and the human sexual response cycle. This discussion often leads to disclosures of dyspareunia and lack of sexual fulfillment. Decreased sexual functioning is sometimes associated with PTSD, providing nurses with an opportunity to further explore these concerns. Male offenders would also benefit from similar discussions, which would offer healthcare providers the opportunity to substitute

myths with facts. Knowledge is power and the foundation for change.

For HIV-positive inmates who are considering pregnancy, nurses may also discuss how these women can protect their babies from HIV and neural tube deficiencies (folate acid education). Education can alleviate fears and dispel myths that many women hold regarding use of zidovudine (AZT), the CDC-recommended medication to reduce horizontal transmission (Vitiello & Smeltzer, 1999). Education about not breast-feeding with HIV infection is also helpful. These discussions of pregnancy and infant care may also present the opportunity for nurses to discuss smoking cessation before pregnancy and the impact of smoke on the mother's health and the health of her baby. Men should also understand this relationship and how secondhand smoke increases a child's risk for asthma.

Women also need assistance in redefining their sexuality, as the majority have been sexually abused and have used their bodies to acquire money or drugs. For many of these women, love often equaled sex, whereas intimacy and empowered relationships were unknown. While incarcerated, 80% of women will participate in sexual relationships with other women, including half the women who self-identified as heterosexual (Maeve, 1999). Women seek relationships that provide love, caring, and support.

BEST PRACTICE Nurses can assist in redefining concepts of sexuality by being nonjudgmental about this behavior and using relationships to explore definitions of loving relationships.

Mental Illness

Poor mental health is a significant contribution to incarceration rates. Mental illness, including serious psychiatric conditions, substance abuse, physical and sexual abuse, and poor coping skills, contributes to high-risk behavior and poor decision making. Offenders with mental illness were more likely to be incarcerated for a violent crime, were more likely to have used alcohol or drugs during the offense, and were twice as likely to have been homeless before their arrest (Ditton, 1999). Low literacy, poor social skills, and being mentally challenged also contribute to poor mental health and increased risk for incarceration. Mental illness also contributes to higher rates of recidivism and longer sentences. Approximately 60% of offenders with mental illness receive psychiatric services while incarcerated. One study found the majority of the mentally ill were in local jails (Cox, Banks, & Stone, 2000).

It should be noted that psychopathy or antisocial behavior is the extreme end of the serious mental disease continuum. Offenders have lifelong patterns of exploitive behavior, including manipulation (see "Scope of Practice"). Psychopathic offenders are devoid of anxiety or depression, which differentiates them from people suffering from other mental illnesses. As many as 50% of sexual offenders (especially rapists) may be psychopaths as measured by the Hare Psychopathy Checklist, Revised (Hare, 1998; Hare, Cox, & Hart, 1994). Interventions are rarely successful with individuals who lack a conscience and are unable to be compassionate.

It is clear from the literature that there is a strong link between the cycles of violence, poverty (poor access to care), and mental illness, although there is no consensus on the interrelationship. Seventy-eight percent of female offenders and 30% of male offenders have experienced physical and sexual abuse (Health Resources and Services Administration, 2000). Physical and sexual abuse are often given as the reasons youths have run away, placing them in unsafe places and often leading to incarceration. Correlations have shown increased alcohol and substance abuse among individuals who are abused, especially among women (Singer, Bussey, Song, et al., 1995). As previously addressed, higher rates of depression are related to PTSD and its related sequel of sexual abuse. Is it possible that the victims of crime have now become the incarcerated?

Over half of the individuals incarcerated stated that they had used illegal drugs in the month before they were arrested. However, the majority of offenders had used illegal drugs at some time in their past: 73% of federal offenders, 83% of state offenders, and 66% of people in jail (CDC, 2001b). Substance abuse places individuals at increased risk for incarceration. Substance abuse also places individuals at increased risk for health-related problems, such as HIV (especially for IDUs), hepatitis, STIs, acquired brain injury, renal impairment, cardiovascular complications, poor nutrition, and poor self-care.

The CAGE diagnostic instrument is an easy screening tool for alcoholism based on the responses to four factors:

- Cut down on drinking (Have you ever felt you should cut down on your drinking?)
- Annoyed by criticism about drinking habits
- Guilty feelings about drinking
- Eye opener drink needed in the morning

Based on CAGE screening, one third of the mentally ill also have a history of alcohol dependence. Untreated alcoholism contributes to incarceration despite the fact that 22% of mentally ill offenders and 11% of other offenders had been in a detoxification unit at some time before their arrest. Most offenders admit to negative consequences of drinking before arrests such as lost jobs and scrapes with law enforcement. Alcoholics Anonymous (AA) is available in most correctional facilities, offering a peer program for recovery. AA has been the most successful program overall for individuals who are no longer in denial about their alcoholism. Society has failed to develop adequate strategies for reducing denial. Many offenders often admit years later that incarceration forced them to deal with their substance abuse denial, allowing for successful rehabilitation.

Treatment for substance abuse (including alcoholism) behind bars is available. In addition to AA, Narcotics Anonymous (NA) provides self-help and recovery for substance abusers. Additional interventions available to offenders include the following (CDC, 2001a):

- Detoxification when needed upon admission
- Education and counseling
- Therapeutic communities (TC) (long-term, highly structured residential treatment programs have been shown to reduce recidivism)
- Methadone maintenance offered in some correctional facilities
- Diversion programs (including drug courts): sentences are reduced if the individual successfully completes treatment
- Intermediate sanctions: short incarceration with mandated substance abuse program
- Coerced abstinence: mandatory frequent drug testing during probation

Despite available treatment for substance abuse, it is clear that more offenders need treatment. Many community advocates, such as Justice Works (an interfaith organization), support increasing community programs and decreasing incarceration for substance abuse in nonviolent offenses. Some of the innovative programs that are beginning to address this problem include the following (CDC, 2001a):

- *California's Proposition 36.* Requires substance abuse treatment, not jail, for drug possession or use.
- *The National Compendium of Local and State Interventions for Substance-Abusing Persons Involved with the Justice System.* A federal collaborative program that will provide online information for the most promising public health and criminal justice programs.
- *The Residential Substance Abuse Treatment for State Prisoners Formula Grant Program (RSAT).* Funding from the Department of Justice (DOJ) for correctional residential facilities operated by state and local agencies.
- *Breaking the Cycle.* Demonstration project from the DOJ for early identification and evaluation of offenders for substance abuse; provides early individualized treatment with intensive supervision, and strong judicial oversight may reduce crime.
- *Treatment Accountability for Safer Communities (TASC).* A program that integrates the criminal justice and substance abuse treatment programs to increase effective criminal processing, correctional supervision, and aftercare.

Healthcare professionals also have a significant role to play in community efforts to screen and identify alcoholism and substance abuse, and to refer individuals for treatment. This is difficult to accomplish with inadequate mental health insurance and detoxification programs. Untreated mental illness or continuing treatment for those who are diagnosed is also problematic. Community and family support are vital. It is essential for healthcare professionals to screen and identify substance abuse, including alcoholism. Ongoing missed opportunities contribute to the larger problem of untreated mental illness and increasing incarceration rates (Lovell & Jemelka, 1998). One study showed a high association with marijuana use before incarceration (Braithwaite, 2004). Substance abuse is often viewed as a psychosocial problem and therefore omitted as a priority during healthcare appointments.

Ninety percent of offenders with schizophrenia, bipolar disorder, and antisocial personality disorder were also found to have addictive disorders, often in the form of alcohol or substance abuse. In one study, 2% to 4.3% of offenders were found to have bipolar disorder, and another 2.3% to 3.9% of offenders have schizophrenia (Greifinger, 1999).

Inmates displaying psychotic, suicidal, or violent behavior are housed in forensic psychiatric units (Moran & Mason, 1996). Nurses must be astute to crisis intervention, good history, and assessment skills while developing therapeutic relationships. Offenders must be closely supervised for self-mutilation, suicidal attempts, anger outbursts, and swallowing contraband including sharps. Providing patient-centered care to these prisoners while maintaining a secure environment can be a challenge. Nurses have an opportunity to offer individual counseling, lead therapeutic groups that include assistance with anger management, and teach coping and problem-solving strategies (Melia, Moran, & Mason, 1996; Perez & Batong, 2003). Nurses can model and foster self-esteem, hope, and positive outlets.

It is important to distinguish between depression (previously discussed) and neurocognitive disorders that are particularly prevalent in patients with AIDS, as well as those who have Parkinson's disease and Huntington disease. Distinguishing between subcortical signs (HIV) and cortical signs (depression) will aid in the differential diagnosis. Screening tools that test subcortical signs include the Johns Hopkins HIV Dementia Scale or the Center for Epidemiologic Studies-Depression Test (CES-D) for patients who display symptoms such as being irritable, forgetful, disorganized, apathetic and slow, and distractible (Herfkens, 2001).

Bridge Programs with the Community

The role of the correctional nurse is vital in this area of correctional care. Few model programs at this time use nurses in their discharge or release plans. Yet recidivism is highest in the first 24 hours and first days on release. Many release plans lack proper coordination to ensure success. The primary resources needed are housing, a job, and continuity in medical care (CDC, 2001a). One exemplar program is the Doe Fund in New York City's Harlem, which provides released prisoners with shelter and a job while building self-sufficiency (Richardson, 2003; VonZielbauer, 2003a). Providing these necessities actually decreases public costs by decreasing substance abuse and poor access to healthcare. The benefit of comprehensive prerelease programs is that they decrease recidivism by half (Flanigan, Kim, Zierler, et al., 1996; Freudenberg, Willets, Greene, et al., 1998). Recidivism rates vary but are approximately 35%.

Four types of prevention programs have been shown to be effective in reducing transmission, morbidity, and mortality related to HIV. They include peer education, discharge planning, transitional case management, and technical assistance outreach models (AIDSAction, 2001). These models can also be applied to other medical problems. HIV education and prevention is important because approximately 25% of all HIV cases pass through jails and prisons at some time (Spaulding, Stephensen, Macalino, et al., 2002). HIV prevention in prison should include mandatory HIV testing (including oral tests), continuity of care for HIV-infected inmates, and access by community-based groups to provide AIDS-based education and prevention programs (Braithwaite & Arriola, 2003). Organizations that have received grants to implement such programs are being evaluated by the Corrections Demonstration Project of the Centers for Disease Control and Prevention (Arriola, Kennedy, Coltharp, et al., 2002; Bauserman, Ward, Eldred, et al., 2001).

Few correctional facilities utilize peer education programs (7% prisons, 3% jails, and 3% penitentiaries) to provide offenders with information that will help them to develop skills that can be applied on the outside (Hammett et al., 1999). The Bedford Hills ACE (AIDS Counseling and Education) program is probably one of the original models to be implemented nationally on a limited basis (Dubik-Unruh, 1999; Members of the ACE Program at Bedford Hills Correctional Facility, 1998). New York has expanded the program to the other state prisons under the name PACE (Prisoners AIDS Counseling and Education). The curriculum tenets outlined by ACE (1998) include the following as well as the suggested comprehensive components outlined previously:
- Harm reduction through intention to engage in safer behavior
- The examination of life situations that create stressors, gender-based imbalance, or aggression
- The concept of taking care of oneself first
- Groups of at least three sessions
- Advisory boards to include inmate planning
- HIV knowledge
- HIV prevention
  - Female and male condom utilization (O'Leary, Jemmott, Goodhart, et al., 1996)
  - Issues of love and cultural consideration
  - Issues of abuse and condom utilization (Amaro & Hardy-Fanta, 1995)
- HIV transmission
  - Relationship to viral load (Lurie, Miller, Hecht, et al., 1998)
  - Sexual
  - IDU
  - Perinatal and breast milk

- Occupational and incarceration altercations
- Confounding belief systems
- African American concerns
- Tuskegee backlash
- HIV origination in chimpanzees of west central Africa
- Duesberg theory: HIV-is-not-the-cause-of-AIDS theory

HIV peer education programs may increase voluntary testing for HIV and adherence to HIV medications (Fink, Walker, Dole, et al., 2001). Most offenders preferred peer-led groups to groups led by professionals (Grinstead et al., 1997, 1999).

Release programs use a systematic approach to release and network with community organizations and halfway houses to maximize a successful transition back into the community. The two oldest programs are found in Rhode Island (Project Bridge) and New York (ETHICS, founded 1967) (Flanigan, Kim, Zierler, et al., 1997). These programs as well as nine others were funded by Ryan White CARE Act federal funds (Health Resources and Services Administration, 2000). Connecticut has also added a program. The program objectives are to provide continuing comprehensive care to HIV-infected inmates on release. In New York these programs network with others designed for released prisoners including the Fortune Society and ETHICS (Empowerment through HIV Information). Both New York programs are run and operated by ex-offenders. Common to these programs are substance abuse treatment, mental healthcare, and comprehensive medical care including HIV care, social support with constructive ties to the community, job readiness training, and court advocacy. Several comprehensive residential programs are being evaluated for recidivism and successful reentry back into the community. Study findings from Healthlink, a research demonstration grant at Hunter College that networks with Fortune Society and other community programs, support this type of comprehensive residential model.

Building community partnerships by developing a personal link with healthcare providers is imperative for the success of any program (Rich, Holmes, Salas, et al., 2001). Healthcare providers who will come into the prisons and assist prisons with first appointments help to promote ideal situations. Most offenders have difficulty maneuvering the healthcare system, and this allows offenders to make contact with their providers before their release (Mitty, Holmes, Spaulding, et al., 1998). It is helpful to schedule a drop-in policy for offenders initially and to schedule an appointment for the second week postrelease. This time can be used to familiarize offenders with the clinic, and it gives them a sense that their transition is being carefully managed by a staff that cares about them and their successful transition. Providing a business card and encouraging offenders to call for help with any problem increases their confidence and provides them with a safety net as well as social and medical support. Offenders are anxious on release, because they must now deal with many life stressors concurrently. Having a safe place to visit may often mean the difference between success and reincarceration. Box 38-7 provides additional resources for information on HIV in correctional facilities.

Summary

Caring for offenders involves many important forensic issues. Among the roles and responsibilities of correctional nurses are advocacy and protection of the offender's human rights. Unbiased documentation is vital for both the facility and its incarcerated population. The healthcare of prisoners is a critical element that requires an understanding of major public heath problems and

---

Box 38-7 Additional Resources on HIV in Correctional Facilities

PUBLICATIONS

- Albany Medical College HIV educational series for corrections in Spanish and English; includes special tapes on women's issues; 518-262-6864, santosm@mail.amc.edu
- Cell Wars by Bristol-Meyers Squibb is distributed free; in comic book format appropriate for low literacy; basic HIV information
- Get Tested (video geared toward correctional populations—Glaxco Welcome)
- Infectious Diseases in Corrections Report, formerly Hepp (HIV Education Prison Project), distributed by Brown University AIDS Program for Corrections and HIV Health Care Providers; www.idcronline.org
- HIV Inside, distributed free for healthcare providers
- HIV Invading T-cell Model—Merck
- HIV Medication Guide—Glaxco Welcome of Canada (can be downloaded from www.jag.on.ca)
- My Gramma Has HIV—Agouron

WEBSITES

amfAR Global Link: HIV information source
www.amfar.org/td
Association of Nurses in AIDS Care (ANAC)
www.anacnet.org
HIV InSite: information on HIV/AIDS treatment, prevention, and policy
http://hivinsite.ucsf.edu
Kaisernetwork.org: Daily HIV/AIDS report
www.report.kff.org/aidshiv
Medscape: HIV
www.hiv.medscape.com

---

their management within a confined population. The correctional nurse must possess knowledge, skills, and attitudes consistent with advocacy, health education, and prisoner rights as outlined in key documents of federal and state agencies as well as professional nursing organizations.

Resources

BOOKS

Scope and standards of nursing practice in correctional facilities. (2007). Silver Spring, MD: American Nurses Publishing.

ORGANIZATIONS

Academy of Correctional Health Professionals (ACHP)
PO Box 11117, Chicago, IL 60611; 877-549-ACHP (2247); www.correctional-health.org
American Correctional Association
4380 Forbes Boulevard, Lanham, MD 20706-4322; 800-ACA-JOIN (800-222-5646), 301-918-1800; www.aca.org
American Correctional Health Services Association
250 Gatsby Place, Alpharetta, GA 30022-6161; 877-918-1842; www.achsa.com
Correctional News Online
1241 Andersen Drive, Suite N, San Rafael, CA 94901; 415-460-6185; www.correctionalnews.com
Corrections Connection Network
159 Burgin Parkway, Quincy, MA 02169; 617-471-4445; www.corrections.com
Criminal Justice Institute, Inc. (CJI)
213 Court Street, Suite 606, Middletown, CT 06457; 860-704-6400; www.cji-inc.com
National Commission on Correctional Health
1145 West Diversey Parkway, Chicago, IL 60614; 773-880-1460; www.ncchc.org

References

Abercrombie, P. D. (2001). Improving adherence to abnormal pap smear follow-up. *JOGN Nursing; Journal of Obstetric, Gynecologic, and Neonatal Nursing, 30*(1), 80–88.

AIDSAction. (2001). *What works in HIV prevention for incarcerated populations.* Washington, DC: Author. www.aidsaction.org Retrieved from Accessed October 16, 2009.

AIDS Counseling and Education Program (ACE). (1998). *Breaking the walls of silence: AIDS and women in a New York state maximum security prison.* New York: Overlook Press.

Allard, F., April, N., & Martin, G. (1992). Knowledge and attitudes of correctional staff towards HIV and HBV-infections. In: Program and Abstracts of the VIII International Conference on AIDS Amsterdam. Abstract PUD 3003.

Altice, F. L. (1998). Overview of HIV care. In M. Puisis (Ed.), *Clinical practice in correctional medicine* (pp. 141–163). St. Louis: Mosby.

Altice, F. L., & Buitrago, M. I. (1998). Adherence to antiretroviral therapy in correctional settings. *J Correctional Health Care, 5*(2), 179–200.

Amaro, H., & Hardy-Fanta, C. (1995). Gender relations in addiction & recovery. *Journal of Psychoactive Drugs, 27*(4), 325–337.

American Correctional Health Services Association's (ACHSA). (1999). *ACHSA Code of Ethics.*

American Medical Association (AMA). (1999). Health literacy, report of the Council on Scientific Affairs. *JAMA: The Journal of the American Medical Association, 281*(6), 552–557.

American Nurses Association (ANA). (1991). *Ethics and Human Rights Position Statement.*

American Nurses Association (ANA). (1991). *Scope and Standards of Nursing Practice in Correctional Facilities.*

American Nurses Association (ANA). (1994). *ANA's Nurses' Participation in Capital Punishment.*

American Nurses Association (ANA) and the International Association of Forensic Nurses (IAFN). (1997). *Scope and standards of forensic nursing practice.* Waldorf, MD: American Nurses Publishing.

Appelbaum, K. L. (2007). Commentary: The use of restraint and seclusion in correctional mental health. *J Am Academy Psychiatry Law, 35*(4), 431–435.

Arriola, K. R. J., Kennedy, S. S., Coltharp, J. C., et al. (2002). Development and implementation of the cross-site evaluation of the CDC/HRSA Corrections Demonstration Project. *AIDS Education & Prevention, 14*(Suppl. A), 107–118.

Ashkin, D., Malecki, J., & Thomas, D. (2005). TB outbreaks among staff in correctional facilities, Florida, 2001–2004: lessons re-learned. *Infectious Diseases in Corrections Report, 8*(2), 1–7.

Babudieri, S., Aceti, A., D'Offizi, G. P., et al. (2000). Directly observed therapy to treat HIV infection in prisoners. *JAMA: The Journal of the American Medical Association, 284*(2), 179–180.

Baillargeon, J. G., Paar, D. P., Wu, H., Giordano, T. P., Murray, O., Raimer, B. G., et al. (2008). Psychiatric disorders, HIV infection and HIV/hepatitis co-infection in the correctional setting. *AIDS Care, 20*(1), 124–129.

Bauserman, R. L., Ward, M. A., Eldred, L., et al. (2001). Increasing voluntary HIV testing by offering oral tests in incarcerated populations. *American Journal of Public Health, 91*(8), 1226–1229.

Beck, J. A. (1999). Compassionate release from New York state prisons: Why are so few getting out?. *J Law, Med Ethics, 27*(3), 216–233.

Beck, A. J., & Harrison, P. M. (2001). *Prisoners in 2000.* Washington, DC: U.S. Department of Justice, Bureau of Justice Statistics.

Beck, A. J., & Karlberg, J. C. (2001). *Prison and jail inmates at midyear 2000.* Washington, DC: U.S. Department of Justice, Bureau of Justice Statistics.

Beckwith, C. G., Atunah-Jay, S., Cohen, J., Macalino, G., Poshkus, M., Rich, J. D., et al. (2007). Feasibility and acceptability of rapid HIV testing in jail. *AIDS Patient Care and STDs, 21*(1), 41–47.

Blume, S. B. (1998). Addictive disorders in women. In R. J. Frances, & S. I. Miller (Eds.), *Clinical textbook of addictive disorders.* (2nd ed., pp. 413–429). New York: Guilford.

Bond, L., & Semaan, S. (1996). At risk for HIV infection: Incarcerated women in a county jail in Philadelphia. *Women and Health, 24*(4), 27–45.

Boswell, E. (2000). *Nurses in jail keep inmates in prison. Montana State University Communications Services.* Retrieved on June 26, 2000, from www.montana.edu/wwwpb/univ/jailone.

Bozzette, S. A., Joyce, G., McCaffrey, D. F., Leibowitz, A. A., Morton, S. C., et al. (2001). Expenditures for the care of HIV-infected patients in the era of highly active antiretroviral therapy. *The New England Journal of Medicine, 344*(11), 817–823.

Braithwaite, R. L., & Arriola, K. R. J. (2003). Male prisoners and HIV prevention: A call for action ignored. *American Journal of Public Health, 93*(5), 759–763.

Braithwaite, R., Stephens, T., Conerly, R. C., et al. (2004). The relationship among marijuana use, prior incarceration, and inmates' self-reported HIV/AIDS risk behaviors. *Addictive Behaviors, 29*(5), 995–999.

Brecher, E. M., & Della Penna, R. D. (1975). *Health care in correctional institutions.* Washington, DC: National Institute of Law Enforcement and Criminal Justice, U.S. Department of Justice.

Browne, A., Miller, B., & Maguin, E. (1999). Prevalence and severity of lifetime physical and sexual victimization among incarcerated women. *International Journal of Law and Psychiatry, 22*(2–3), 301–322.

Bureau of Justice Statistics (BJS). (1998). *Sheriffs' departments, 1997.* Washington, DC: U.S. Department of Justice.

Bureau of Justice Statistics (BJS). (2000). *HIV in Prisons and Jails, 1999.* Washington, DC: U.S. Department of Justice.

Bureau of Justice Statistics. (2006). *Prison and jail inmates at midyear 2005.* Washington, DC: Department of Justice.

Buris, S., Lurie, P., Abrahamson, J. D., et al. (2000). Physician prescribing of sterile injection equipment to prevent HIV infection: Time for action. *Annals of Internal Medicine, 133*(3), 218–226.

Campbell, J. (1992). Violence demands nursing solutions. *The American Nurse, 24*(4), 4.

Carrera, M. A. (1996). *Lessons for lifeguards: Working with teens when the topic is hope.* New York: Donkey Press.

Carroll, L. A. (2001). *Geriatrics in the prison system. York College of Pennsylvania.* Retrieved from www.ycp.edu/besc/Journal2001/Article_1.htm Accessed October 16, 2009.

Centers for Disease Control and Prevention (CDC). (1996). HIV/AIDS education and prevention programs for adults in prisons and jails and juveniles in confinement facilities. *Morbidity and Mortality Weekly Report, 45*(13), 268–1227.

Centers for Disease Control and Prevention. (1997). Mortality patterns-preliminary data US, 1996. *Morbidity and Mortality Weekly Report, 46*(40), 941–944.

Centers for Disease Control and Prevention. (1999). High prevalence of Chlamydial and gonococcal infection in women entering jails and juvenile detention centers–Chicago, Birmingham, and San Francisco, 1998. *Morbidity and Mortality Weekly Report, 48*(36), 793–796.

Centers for Disease Control and Prevention. (2001a). *Helping inmates return to the community.* Washington, DC: Author, Retrieved from www.cdc.gov/idu/facts/cj-transition Accessed October 16, 2009.

Centers for Disease Control and Prevention. (2001b). *Substance abuse treatment for drug users in the criminal justice system.* Atlanta, GA: Divisions of HIV/AIDS Prevention.

Centers for Disease Control and Prevention. (2006). Prevention and control of tuberculosis in correctional and detention facilities: Recommendations for CDC. *MMWR. Recommendations and Reports: Morbidity and Mortality Weekly Report, 55*(RR-9), 1–44.

Centers for Medicare and Medicaid Services (CMS). (2006). http://www.cms.hhsgov/apps/media/press/release.asp?counter = 2057. Accessed February 1, 2010.

Champion, M. K. (2007). Commentary: Seclusion and restraint in corrections–a time for change. *The Journal of the American Academy of Psychiatry and the Law, 35*(4), 426–439.

Clines, F. X. (2000). *Access by inmates to tests for DNA gains ground.* New York Times, A22.

Cohen, M., Deamant, C., Barkan, S., et al. (2000). Domestic violence and childhood sexual abuse in HIV-infected women and women at risk for HIV. *American Journal of Public Health, 90*(4), 560–565.

Cohn, F. (1999). The ethics of end-of-life care for prison inmates. *The Journal of Law, Medicine & Ethics: A Journal of the American Society of Law, Medicine & Ethics, 27*(3), 252–259.

Collins, A. S., Gullette, D., & Schnepf, M. (2005). Break through language barriers. *Advance Practice Nurses, 30*(Suppl. 1), 19–20.

Colsher, P. L., Wallace, R. B., Loeffelholz, P. L., & Sales, M. (1992). Health status of older male prisoners: A comprehensive survey. *American Journal of Public Health, 82*(6), 881–895.

Cook, L. S., Kamb, M. L., & Weiss, N. S. (1997). Perineal powder exposure and the risk of ovarian cancer. *American Journal of Epidemiology, 145*(5), 459–465.

Cox, J. F., Banks, S., & Stone, J. L. (2000). Counting the mentally ill in jails and prisons. *Psychiatric Services (Washington, D. C.), 51*(4), 533.

Crowell, N. A., & Burgess, A. W. (Eds.), (1996). *Understanding violence against women.* Washington, DC: National Academy Press.

Davis, S. K., Liu, Y., & Gibbons, G. H. (2003). Disparities in trends of hospitalization for potentially preventable chronic conditions among African Americans during 1990s: Implications and benchmarks. *American Journal of Public Health, 93*(3), 447–455.

DeGroot, A. S. (2000). HIV infection among incarcerated women: Epidemic behind bars. *AIDS Reader, 10*(5), 287–295.

DeGroot, A. S., Bick, J., Thomas, D., et al. (2001). HIV clinical trials in correctional settings: Right or retrogression. *AIDS Reader, 11*(1), 34–40.

DeGroot, A. S., Hammett, T. S., & Scheib, R. G. (1996). Barriers to care of HIV-infected inmates: A public health concern. *AIDS Reader, 6*(3), 78–87.

Department of Justice. (1997). *Criminal victimization.* Washington DC: Author.

Department of Justice–FBI. (1999). *Crime in the United States.* Washington DC: Author.

Dilorio, C., Hartwell, T., Hansen, N., et al. (2002). Childhood sexual abuse and risk behaviors among men at high risk for HIV infection. *American Journal of Public Health, 92*(2), 214–219.

Ditton, P. M. (1999). In *Mental health and treatment of inmates and probationers.* Bureau of Justice Statistics Special Report, NCJ US Department of Justice, pp. 1–12.

Doak, C. C., Doak, L. G., & Root, J. H. (1996). *Teaching patients with low literacy skills* (2nd ed.). Philadelphia: J.B. Lippincott.

Dole, P. J. (1996). Centering: Reducing rape trauma syndrome anxiety during a gynecologic examination. *J Psychosoc Nurs, 34*(10), 32–37.

Dole, P. J. (1999). Examining sexually traumatized incarcerated women. *HEPPNews, 2*(6), 3.

Drevdahl, D., Kneipp, S. M., Canales, M. K., et al. (2001). Reinvesting in social justice: A capital idea for public health nursing?. *Advances in Nursing Science, 24*(2), 19–31.

Droes, N. S. (1989). *An exploration of the nature and problems of nursing practice in correctional settings.* San Francisco: University of California, doctoral dissertation.

Drug Policy Alliance Organization. (2003). http://www.drugpolicy.org/docuploads/DPA_10_yearreview.pdf. Accessed February 1, 2010.

Drummond, T. (1999). Cellblock seniors: they have grown old and frail in prison: Must they still be locked up? *Time, 153,* 60.

Dubik-Unruh, S. (1999). Peer education programs in corrections: Curriculum, implementation, and nursing interventions. *J Am Nurses AIDS Care, 10*(6), 53–62.

Edmonton Sun. (2000). Edmonton, Alberta, Canada, March 2, p. 3.

Edgardo, R. (1995). The failure of reform. In N. Morris, & D. Rothman (Eds.), *The Oxford history of the prison: The practice of punishment in Western Society* (pp. 151–177). New York: Oxford University Press.

El-Bassel, N., Ivanoff, A., Schilling, R. F., et al. (1995). Preventing HIV/AIDS in drug-abusing incarcerated women through skills building and social support enhancement: Preliminary outcomes. *So Work Res, 19*(3), 129–192.

Ellickson, P. L., & McGuigan, K. A. (2000). Early predictors of adolescent violence. *American Journal of Public Health, 90*(4), 566–572.

Eviatar, D. (2003). Foreigners' rights in the post 9/11 era: A matter of justice. *New York Times,* Arts & Ideas, B7, B9.

Families against Mandatory Minimums (FAMM). (2003). *Positive Trends in State-Level Sentencing and Corrections Policy.* www.smartoncrime.org Accessed October 16, 2009.

Fickenscher, A., Lapidus, J., Silk-Walker, P., et al. (2001). Women behind bars: Health needs of inmates in a county jail. *Public Health Reports, 116*(3), 191–196.

Fink, M. J., Walker, S., Dole, P., et al. (2001). Educational videotapes for incarcerated women: Using focus groups to learn and teach. Paper presented at the 25th National Conference Correctional Health Care, and the Academy of Correctional Health Care Professionals, Albuquerque, New Mexico.

Finlay, I. G., & Jones, N. K. (2000). Unresolved grief in young offenders in prison. *The British Journal of General Practice: The Journal of the Royal College of General Practitioners, 50*(456), 569–570.

Fischl, M., Rodriguez, A., Sceppella, E., et al. (2000). Impact of directly observed therapy on outcomes in HIV clinical trials. *Programs and Abstracts of the Seventh Conference on Retroviruses and Opportunistic Infections* (abstract 7).

Flanigan, T. P. (1999). *HIV behind bars: The challenge of providing comprehensive care.* Women and HIV Conference, Los Angeles, CA. October 12.

Flanigan, T. P., Kim, J. Y., Zierler, S., et al. (1996). A prison release program for HIV positive women: Linking them to health services and community follow-up. *American Journal of Public Health, 86*(6), 886–887.

Flanigan, T. P., Kim, J. Y., Zierler, S., et al. (1997). A prison release program for HIV-positive women: Linking them to health services and community follow-up. *J Correctional Health Care, 4*(2), 1–9.

Flanagan, N. A. (2006). Testing the relationship between job stress and satisfaction in correctional nurses. *Nursing Research, 55*(5), 316–327.

Flaskerud, J. H., & Winslow, B. J. (1998). Conceptualizing vulnerable populations health-related research. *Nursing Research, 4*(2), 69–78.

Flitcraft, A. (1995). From public health to personal health: Violence against women across the lifespan. *Annals of Internal Medicine, 123*(9), 800–801.

Fogel, C. I. (1993). Hard time: The stressful nature of incarceration for women. *Issues in Mental Health Nursing, 14*(4), 367–377.

Fogel, C. I., & Belyea, M. (2001). Psychological risk factors in pregnant inmates. *Am J Matern Child Nurs, 26*(1), 10–16.

Fortinash, K. M., & Holoday-Worret, P. A. (1996). *Psychiatric mental health nursing.* St. Louis, MO: Mosby–Year Book.

Fox, K. C., Somes, G., Waters, T. (2005). Telemedicine as an alternative to improving health care services to youth in state custody. Abstract no. 3182. Academy Health Meeting, Boston, MA.

Frank, L. (1999). Prisons and public health: Emerging issues in HIV treatment adherence. *The Journal of the Association of Nurses in AIDS Care: JANAC, 10*(6), 25–31.

Freudenberg, N., Wilets, I., Greene, M. B., et al. (1998). Linking women in jail to community services: Factors associated with rearrest and retention of drug-using women following release from jail. *Journal of the American Medical Women's Association, 53*(2), 89–93.

Fullilove, M. T., Fullilove, R. E., Smith, M., et al. (1993). Violence, trauma, and post-traumatic stress disorder among women drug users. *Journal of Traumatic Stress, 6*(4), 533–543.

Gaiter, J., Jurgens, R., Mayer, K., et al. (2000). Harm reduction inside and out: Controlling HIV in and out of correctional institutions. *AIDS Reader, 10*(1), 45–52.

Golding, J. M., Wilsnack, S. C., & Learman, L. A. (1998). Prevalence of sexual assault history among women with common gynecologic symptoms. *American Journal of Obstetrics and Gynecology, 179*(4), 1013–1019.

Greifinger, R. (1999). An interview. *HEPPNews, 2*(12), 4.

Grinstead, O., Faigeles, B., & Zack, B. (1997). The effectiveness of peer HIV education for male inmates entering state prison. *J Health Educ, 28*(1), s31–s37.

Grinstead, O. A., Zack, B., & Faigles, B. (1999). Collaborative research to prevent HIV among male prison inmates and their female partners. *Health Education & Behavior: The Official Publication of the Society for Public Health Education, 26*(2), 225–238.

Hall, L. A., Sachs, B., & Rayens, M. K. (1998). Mothers' potential for child abuse: Roles of childhood abuse and social resources. *Nursing Research, 47*(2), 87–95.

Hammett, T. M., Harmon, P., & Maruschak, L. M. (1999). *1996–1997 update: HIV/AIDS, STDs, and TB in correctional facilities.* Washington, DC: U.S. Department of Justice, NCJ 176344, July.

Hammett, T. M., Harmon, P., & Rhodes, W. (2002). The burden of infectious disease among inmates of and release from US correctional facilities, 1997. *American Journal of Public Health, 92*(11), 1789–1794.

Haney, J., & Kristiansen, C. (1998). An analysis of the impact of prison on women survivors of childhood sexual abuse. In J. Harden & M. Hill (Eds.), *Breaking the rules: Women in prison and feminist therapy.* New York: Harrington Park Press.

Harding, T. W., & Schaller, G. (1992). *HIV/AIDS and prisons: Updating and policy review. A survey in 31 countries.* Geneva: University Institute of Legal Medicine for the WHO Global Programme on AIDS.

Hare, R. (1998). Psychopaths and their nature: Implications for the mental health and criminal justice systems. In T. Millon, E. Simonsen, M. Birket-Smith, & R. D. Davis (Eds.), *Psychopathy: Antisocial, criminal and violent behavior* (pp. 188–214). New York: The Guilford Press.

Hare, R. D., Cox, D. N., & Hart, S. D. (1994). *Manual for the psychopathy check-list: Screening version.* Toronto, Ontario: Multi Health Systems.

Harris, R. M., Sharps, P. W., Allen, K., et al. (2003). The interrelationship between violence, HIV/AIDS, and drug use in incarcerated women. *Journal of American Nurses AIDS Care, 14*(1), 27–31.

Hartwell, T., Hansen, N., NIMH Multisite HIV Prevention Trial Group. (2002). Childhood sexual abuse and risk factors among men at high risk for HIV infection. *American Journal of Public Health, 92*(2), 214–219.

Health and Human Services Regulations. (1978). Sections 45 CFR 46.305 and 45 CFR 46.306. Additional DHHS Protections Pertaining to Biomedical and Behavioral Research Involving Prisoners as Subjects. National Institutes of Health, Office for Protection from Research Risks, Part 46. Washington, DC: Protection of Human Subjects.

Health Resources and Services Administration (HRSA). (2000). *Incarcerated people and HIV/AIDS.* Washington, DC: U.S. Department of Health and Human Services. Retrieved from www.hrsa.gov/hab. Accessed October 16, 2009.

Herfkens, K. M. (2001). Depression, neurocognitive disorders and HIV in prisons. *HEPPNews, 4*(1), 1–9. Retrieved from www.hivcorrections.org Accessed October 16, 2009.

Himelstein, L. (1993). The case for not letting 'em rot: Freeing old cons may make sense. *Business Week,* 89.

Holzemer, W. L., Corless, I. B., Nokes, K. M., et al. (1999). Predictors of self-reported adherence in persons living with HIV disease. *AIDS Patient Care and STDs, 13,* 185–197.

Hoskins, I. A. (2004). Women's health care in correctional facilities: A lost colony. *Obstetrical & Gynecological Survey, 59*(4), 234–236.

Human Rights Watch. (1996). Sexual abuse of women in U.S. state prisons. December 6, 1996. New York, NY.

International Council of Nurses (ICN). (2006). *Death Penalty and Participation by Nurses in Executions.* Geneva, Switzerland: Author.

Irwin, J. (2000). *America's one million nonviolent prisoners.* Justice Policy Institute. 2/26. Retrieved from www.cjcj.org/jti/one million Accessed October 16, 2009.

Jeldness v. Pearce. (1994). 30F. 3d 1220 (9th circ).

Jordan, K., Schlenger, W. E., Fairbank, J. A., et al. (1996). Prevalence of psychiatric disorders among incarcerated women. *Archives of General Psychiatry, 53*(6), 513–519.

Joyce, B. (2001). *Cell block art.* Princeton, NJ: Princeton Publishers. Aired on AMC, We Entertainment, Cool Women, November 4.

Kantor, E. (1998). AIDS and HIV Infections in Prisoners. *The AIDS Knowledge Base,* HIV InSite. Retrieved from www.hivinsite.ucsf.edu Accessed October 16, 2009.

Keamy, L. (1998). Women's health care in the incarcerated setting. In M. Puisis (Ed.), *Clinical practice in correctional medicine* (pp. 188–205). St. Louis, MO: Mosby.

Keaveney, M. E., & Zausznieski, J. A. (1999). Life events and psychological well-being in women sentenced to prison. *Issues in Mental Health Nursing, 20*(1), 73–89.

Kendig, N. E. (2004). Correctional health care systems and collboration with academic medicine. *JAMA: The Journal of the American Medical Association, 292*(4), 501–503.

King, L. N. (1998). Doctors, patients, and history of correctional medicine. In M. Puisis (Ed.), *Clinical practice in correctional medicine* (pp. 3–11). St. Louis, MO: Mosby.

Koblin, B. A., Mayer, K., Mwatha, A., et al. (2002). Douching practices among women at high risk of HIV infection in the U.S.: Implications for microbicide testing and use. *Sexually Transmitted Diseases, 29*(7), 406–412.

Koppel, T. (1999). Crime & punishment: Women in prison (six-part series). *Nightline ABC*, October 29. ABCNewsstore.com or 1-800-CALL-ABC for transcripts.

Kupers, T. A. (1999). *Prison madness: The mental health crisis behind bars and what we must do about it.* San Francisco: Jossey-Bass.

Leenerts, M. H. (1999). The disconnected self: consequences of abuse in a cohort of low-income white women living with HIV/AIDS. *Health Care for Women International, 20*(4), 381–400.

Leenerts, M. H. (2003). From neglect to care: A theory to guide HIV-positive incarcerated women in self-care. *The Journal of the Association of Nurses in AIDS Care: JANAC, 14*(5), 25–38.

Lewis, C. (2006). Treating incarcerated women: gender matters. *Psychiatric Clinics of North American, 29*(3), 773–789.

Linder, J. F., & Meyers, F. J. (2007). Palliative care for prison inmates: don't let me die in prison. *JAMA: The Journal of the American Medical Association, 298*(8), 894–901.

Love, C. C. (2001). Staff-patient erotic boundary violations. *On the Edge, 7*(4), 4–8.

Lovell, D., & Jemelka, R. (1998). Coping with mental illness in prisons. *Family & Community Health, 21*(3), 54–66.

Lucas, G. M., Flexner, C. W., & Moore, R. D. (2002). Directly administered antiretroviral therapy in the treatment of HIV infection: Benefit or burden? *AIDS Patient Care and STDs, 16*(11), 527–535.

Lurie, P., Miller, S., Hecht, F., et al. (1998). Post-exposure prophylaxis after non-occupational HIV exposure: Clinical, ethical, and policy considerations. *JAMA: The Journal of the American Medical Association, 280*(20), 1769–1773.

Lyons, M. S., Lindsell, C. J., Fichtenbaum, C. J., & Camargo, C. A. (2007). Interpreting and implementing the 2006 CDC recommendations for HIV testing in health-care settings. *Public Health Reports, 122*(5), 579–583.

Lynch, M., & Pugh, K. (2000). Uneven ground: HIV in women of color. *Advance for Nurse Practitioners, 8*(1), 45–50.

Maddow, R., Vernon, A., & Pozsik, J. (2001). TB and the HIV-positive prisoner. *HEPP News*, Retrieved on March 2001 from www.hivcorrections.org.

Maeve, M. K. (1999). The social construction of love and sexuality in a women's prison. *Advances in Nursing Science, 21*(3), 46–65.

Maeve, M. K., & Vaughn, M. S. (2001). Nursing with prisoners: the practice of caring, forensic nursing or penal harm nursing. *Advances in Nursing Science, 24*(2), 47–64.

Magura, S., Kang, S. Y., Shapiro, J., et al. (1993). HIV risk among women injecting drug users who are in jail. *Addiction (Abingdon, England), 88*(10), 1351–1360.

Mahon, N. B. (1999). Death and dying behind bars–cross-cutting themes and policy imperatives. *The Journal of Law, Medicine & Ethics: A Journal of the American Society of Law, Medicine & Ethics, 27*(3), 213–215.

Manfrin-Ledet, L., & Porche, D. J. (2003). The state of science: Violence and HIV infection in women. *J Am Nurses AIDS Care, 14*(6), 56–68.

Maruschak, L. M., & Beck, A. J. (2001). *Medical problems of inmates, 1997.* Washington, DC: U.S. Department of Justice, Bureau of Justice Statistics. January, NCJ 181644. Retrieved from www.ojp.usdoj.gov/bjs. Accessed October 16, 2009.

May, J. P. (2000). *Building violence.* Thousand Oaks, CA: Sage.

McClelland, G. M., Teplin, L. A., Abram, K. M., et al. (2002). HIV and AIDS risk behaviors among female jail detainees: Implications for public health policy. *American Journal of Public Health, 92*(5), 818–825.

McLaughlin, D. K., & Stokes, C. S. (2002). Income inequality and mortality in U.S. counties: Does minority racial concentration matter? *American Journal of Public Health, 92*(1), 99–104.

McNally, P. (1998). Offenders who have a learning disability. *British Journal of Nursing (Mark Allen Publishing), 5*(13), 805–809.

Melia, P., Moran, T., & Mason, T. (1996). Triumvirate nursing for personality disordered patients: Crossing the boundaries safely. *Journal of Psychiatric and Mental Health Nursing, 6*(1), 15–20.

Members of the ACE Program at Bedford Hills Correctional Facility. (1998). *Breaking the walls of silence.* New York: Overlook Press.

Metzner, J., & Dvoskin, J. (2006). An overview of correctional psychiatry. *Psychiatric Clinics of North America, 29*(3), 761–772.

Metzner, J. L., Tardiff, K., Lion, J., Reid, W. H., Recupero, P. R., Schetky, D. H., et al. (2007). Resource document on the use of restraint and seclusion in correctional mental health care. *The Journal of the American Academy of Psychiatry and the Law, 35*(4), 417–425.

Miller, S. K., & Rundio, A. (1999). Identifying barriers to the administration of HIV medications to county correctional facility inmates. *Clinical Excellence for Nurse Practitioners: The International Journal of NPACE, 3*(5), 286–290.

Mitty, J. A., Holmes, L., Spaulding, A., et al. (1998). Transitioning HIV-infected women after release from incarceration: Two models for bridging the gaps. *Journal of Correctional Health Care, 5*(2), 239–251.

Moran, T., & Mason, T. (1996). Revisiting the nursing management of the psychopath. *Journal of Psychiatric and Mental Health Nursing, 3*(3), 189–194.

Mostashari, F., Riley, E., Selwyn, P. A., et al. (1998). Acceptance and adherence with antiretroviral therapy among HIV-infected women in a correctional facility. *Journal of Acquired Immune Deficiency Syndromes and Human Retrovirology, 18*(4), 341–348.

Mullings, J. L., Marquart, J. W., & Brewer, V. E. (2000). Assessing the relationship between child sexual abuse and marginal living conditions on HIV/AIDS-related risk behavior among women prisoners. *Child Abuse & Neglect, 24*(5), 677–688.

Mumola, C. J. (1999). *Substance abuse and treatment, state and federal prisoners, 1997.* Washington, DC: U.S. Department of Justice.

Naegle, M. A., Richardson, H., & Morton, K. (2004). Rehab instead of prison. *The American Journal of Nursing, 104*(6), 58–61.

National Center on Child Abuse and Neglect. (1996). *Third national incidence study of child abuse and neglect.* Washington, DC: U.S. Government Printing Office.

National Commission for the Protection of Human Subjects. (1978). *The Belmont report: Ethical principles and guidelines for the protection of human subjects of research.* Washington, DC: Author.

National Commission on Correctional Health Care (NCCHC). (1997). *Standards for health services in prison.* Chicago: Author.

National Commission on Correctional Health Care (NCCHC). (2003). *Standards for health services in prison.* Chicago: Author.

Neeley, L. C., Addison, L., & Moreland-Craig, D. (1997). Addressing the needs of elderly offenders. *Corrections Today, Corrections Today, 59*(5), 120–124.

Nelson, A. (2002). Unequal treatment: confronting racial and ethnic disparities in health care. *Journal of the National Medical Association, 94*(8), 666–668.

Nerenberg, R. (2002). Condoms in correctional settings. *HEPPNews, 5*(1), 1–9.

Nicodemus, M., & Paris, J. (2001). Bridging the communicable disease gap: Identifying, treating and counseling high-risk inmates. *HEPPNews, 4*(8 & 9). Retrieved from www.hivcorrections.org. Accessed October 16, 2009.

Office of Juvenile Justice and Delinquency Prevention (OJJDP). (1999). *Fact Sheet #96.* Washington, DC: National Institute of Justice.

O'Leary, A., Jemmott, L. S., Goodhart, F., et al. (1996). Effects of an institutional AIDS prevention intervention: Moderation by gender. *AIDS Education and Prevention: Official Publication of the International Society for AIDS Education, 8*(6), 516–528.

Parker, F. R., & Paine, C. J. (1999). Informed consent and the refusal of medical treatment in the correctional setting. *The Journal of Law, Medicine & Ethics: A Journal of the American Society of Law, Medicine & Ethics, 27*(3), 240–251.

Perdue, B. J., Degazon, C., & Lunney, M. (1999). Diagnoses and interventions with low literacy. *Nursing Diagnosis: ND: The Official Journal of the North American Nursing Diagnosis Association, 10*(1), 36–39.

Perez, J. C., & Batong, J. (2003). Patients and prisoners. *Advance for Nurses, 3*(19), 14.

Persersilia, J. (2000). When prisoners return to the community: Political, economic, and social consequences. *Sentencing & Corrections: Issues for the 21st Century.* Washington, DC: U.S. Department of Justice, National Institute of Justice.

Peternelj–Taylor, C. (2005). Conceptualizing nursing research with offenders: Another look at vulnerability. *International Journal of Law and Psychiatry, 28*(4), 348–359.

Peternelj-Taylor, C. A., & Johnson, R. (1998). *Custody & caring: A challenge for nursing. (Video documentary).* Saskatchewan: University of Saskatoon.

Raimer, B. G., & Stobo, J. D. (2004). Health care delivery in the Texas prison system. *JAMA: The Journal of the American Medical Association, 292*(4), 485–489.

Rich, J. D., Holmes, L., Salas, C., et al. (2001). Successful linkage of medical care and community services for HIV-positive offenders being released from prison. *Journal of Urban Health: Bulletin of the New York Academy of Medicine, 78*(2), 279–289.

Richardson, L. (2003). A blue jumpsuit and a path to self-sufficiency. *New York Times,* Section B, 2.

Richardson, S. Z. (1998). Preferred care of the pregnant inmate. In M. Puisis (Ed.), *Clinical practice in correctional medicine* (pp. 181–187). St. Louis, MO: Mosby.

Rivera, G. (1999). *Women in prison: Nowhere to hide.* NBC. Aired on September 10.

Roberts, K. J. (2002). Physician-patient relationships, patient satisfaction, and antiretroviral medication adherence among HIV-infected adults attending a public health clinic. *AIDS Patient Care & STDs, 16*(1), 43–50.

Rothenberg, K. H., & Paskey, S. J. (1995). The risk of domestic violence and women with HIV infection: Implications for partner notification, public policy, and the law. *American Journal of Public Health, 85*(11), 1569–1575.

Rold, W. (2002). End of life care. *CorrectCare, 16*(3), 1–21.

Sallot, J. (2002). You can have the right to remain safe: Las Correct HELP goes behind bars to save lives. *Positive Living (Los Angeles, Calif.), 11*(1), 24–28.

Schultz, M. (2002). Low literacy skills needn't hinder care. *Registered Nurse (Toronto, Ont.), 65*(4), 45–48.

Schwab-Stone, M., Chen, C., Greenberger, E., et al. (1999). No safe haven II: The effects of violence on urban youth. *Journal of the American Academy of Child and Adolescent Psychiatry, 38*(4), 359–367.

Scope and Standards of Nursing Practice in Correctional Facilities. (2007). Silver Spring, MD: American Nurses Publishing.

Siegal, N. (1998). *Women in prison.* MS, pp. 64–73.

Singer, M. I., Bussey, J., Song, L. Y., et al. (1995). The psychological issues of women serving time in jail. *Social Work, 40*(1), 103–113.

Spaulding, A., Stephensen, B., Macalino, G., et al. (2002). Human immunodeficiency virus in correctional facilities: A review. *Clinical Infectious Diseases: An Official Publication of the Infectious Diseases Society of America, 35*(3), 305–312.

Stevens, J., Zierler, S., Dean, D., et al. (1995). Prevalence of prior sexual abuse and HIV risk-taking behaviors in incarcerated women in Massachusetts. *Journal of Correctional Health Care, 2*(2), 137–149.

Stojkovic, S. (2007). Elderly prisoners: A growing and forgotten group within correctional systems vulnerable to elder abuse. *Journal of Elder Abuse & Neglect, 19*(3/4), 97–117.

Stokowski, L. (2007). *Alternatives to restraint and seclusion in mental health settings.* Accessed 1/10/09 at www.medscape.com/viewarticle/555686

Stone, V. (1999). Considerations for special populations with HIV infection. *HIV Physicians Strategic Treatment Initiative–Medscape,* December, program 5. Retrieved from www://hiv.medscape.com. Accessed October 16, 2009.

Sylla, M., & Thomas, D. (2000). The rules: Law and AIDS in corrections. *HEPPNews,* 1–2.

Taylor, A., Goldberg, D., Emslie, J., et al. (1995). Outbreak of HIV infection in a Scottish prison. *Br J Med, 310*(4 February), 289–292.

Trigiani, K. (1999). Societal Stockholm syndrome. *Women's Web Ring,* Retrieved from http://web2.airmail.net/ktrig246/out_of_cave/sss.html Accessed October 16, 2009.

Ungvarski, P. J., & Rottner, J. E. (1997). Errors in prescribing HIV-1 protease inhibitors. *The Journal of the Association of Nurses in AIDS Care: JANAC, 8*(4), 55–61.

United Nations (UN). (1982). *Principles of medical ethics and standard minimum rules of the treatment of prisoners.* Washington, DC: United Nations General Assembly.

U.S. Department of Health & Human Services. (1978). *Code of federal regulations.* Title 45, part 46. Washington, DC: Author.

U.S. Department of Health and Human Services. (2000). *Healthy People 2010.* 2 volumes (November 2000) Retrieved from Washington, DC: Authors. www.health.gov/healthpeople. Accessed October 16, 2009.

VanDevanter, N., Gonzales, V., Mertel, C., et al. (2002). Effect of an STD/HIV behavioral intervention on women's use of the female condom. *American Journal of Public Health, 92*(1), 109–115.

Vermund, S. H., Sarr, M., Murphy, D. A., et al. (2001). Douching practices among HIV infected and uninfected adolescents in the United States. *The Journal of Adolescent Health, 29*(3S), 8–86.

Visser, E., Moorman, A. C., Irwin, K., et al. (1995). The influence of douching on the severity and microbiology of acute pelvic inflammatory disease. *Women's Health Weekly,* pp. 13–17.

Vitiello, M. A., & Smeltzer, S. C. (1999). HIV, pregnancy, and zidovudine: What women know? *The Journal of the Association of Nurses in AIDS Care: JANAC, 10*(4), 41–47.

Vlach, D. L., & Daniel, A. E. (2007). Commentary: evolving toward equivalency in correctional mental health care: a view from the maximum security trenches. *The Journal of the American Academy of Psychiatry and the Law, 35*(4), 436–438.

VonZielbauer, P. (2003a). City creates post-jail plan for inmates. *New York Times,* Metro section, B1–B2.

VonZielbauer, P. (2003b). Rethinking the key thrown away. *New York Times,* Metro section, pp. 41–42.

Wallace, R., Fullilove, M. T., & Flisher, A. J. (1996). AIDS, violence and behavioral coding: Information theory, risk behavior and dynamic process on core-group sociogeographic networks. *Social Science & Medicine, 43*(3), 339–352.

Washington Times. (2002). Prison rapes spreading deadly diseases. Available online CDC News Updates, HIV/AIDS Sexually Transmitted Diseases, and Tuberculosis Prevention News Update.

Witte, S., Wada, T., El-Bassel, N., et al. (2000). Predictors of female condom use among women exchanging street sex in New York City. *Sexually Transmitted Diseases, 27*(2), 93–100.

Wolfe, M. I., Xu, F., Patel, P., et al. (2001). An outbreak of syphilis in Alabama prisons: Correctional health policy and communicable disease control. *American Journal of Public Health, 91*(8), 1220–1225.

Wright, L. N., & Smith, P. F. (1999). Decrease in AIDS mortality in a state correction system: New York State 1995–1998. *MMWR, 47*(51–2), 1115–1117.

Wyatt, G. E., Myers, H. F., Williams, J. K., et al. (2002). Does a history of trauma contribute to HIV risk for women of color? Implications for prevention and policy. *American Journal of Public Health, 92*(4), 660–665.

Young, D. S. (2000). Women's perceptions of health care in prison. *Health Care Women International, 21*(3), 219–234.

CHAPTER 39 Sudden Death During Restraint: Excited Delirium Syndrome

Theresa G. Di Maio and Vincent J. M. Di Maio

The sudden, unexplained death of an individual in custody presents a difficult challenge to the medicolegal community, especially if the individual dies during or immediately after a violent struggle, and a complete autopsy fails to reveal either an anatomical cause of death or evidence of sufficient trauma to explain death. Typically the struggle ends with employment of physical restraint. Most such deaths occur in conjunction with the use of illegal stimulants such as cocaine or methamphetamine or involve individuals with a history of intrinsic mental disease, usually schizophrenia. Similar deaths occur in emergency rooms and in mental health facilities where the individuals employing the restraint are medical personnel. A review of these cases reveals that the reason either police or medical personnel intervened was that the individuals in custody were in a state of excited delirium.

Delirium is characterized by an acute (minutes to hours), transient disturbance in consciousness and cognition. There is disorganized and inconsistent thought processes, disorientation, inability to distinguish reality from hallucinations, disturbances in speech, and disorientation to time and place. When the delirium involves combative or violent behavior, it is termed excited delirium (Di Maio & Di Maio, 2006). Most cases of delirium are due to natural disease and occur in the hospital setting. The cases we are interested in, however, are those that occur when police or medical personnel attempt to restrain an individual so as to protect the individual or the public from harm.

Deaths Associated with EDS

Excited delirium syndrome (EDS) involves the sudden death of an individual, during or following an episode of excited delirium in which an autopsy fails to reveal evidence of sufficient trauma or natural disease to explain the death. In virtually all such cases, the episode of excited delirium is terminated by a struggle with police or medical personnel and the use of physical restraint (Di Maio & Di Maio, 2006). The individual may go into cardiopulmonary arrest during or within minutes following cessation of the struggle. Attempts at resuscitation are usually unsuccessful. If a cardiac monitor is available at the time of the arrest, the rhythm noted is usually bradycardia, pulseless electrical activity (PET) or asystole. If resuscitation is "successful," the individual is found to have suffered irreversible hypoxic encephalopathy and death usually occurs in a matter of days.

The concept of death as a result of "excited delirium" was introduced in 1849 by Dr. Luther Bell of the McLeon Asylum for the Insane in Somerville, Massachusetts (Bell, 1849). According to Bell, the patient was agitated and anxious, with increasing confusion that appeared suddenly. Any attempt to approach the patient resulted in a violent struggle regardless of the number who tried to restrain him or her. The physical and mental state of the patient continued to deteriorate over the course of weeks resulting in death. This entity became known as "Bell's mania." Deaths resulting from Bell's mania continued to be reported in the medical literature until the early 1950s when they abruptly disappeared with the introduction of phenothiazines for treatment of mental illness (Cancro, 2000; Lieberman et al., 2000). Although all of Bell's patients had mental disease and their symptoms progressed over days to weeks before death, deaths seen today in association with excited delirium principally involve abusers of stimulants (e.g., cocaine or methamphetamine), with symptoms present for only hours. Deaths do still occur in patients suffering from mental illness, usually in individuals with schizophrenia and occasionally bipolar disease and usually outside medical facilities. In individuals with intrinsic mental disease, death usually occurs following the use of restraint because of an acute psychotic episode.

MECHANISMS OF DEATH AND USE OF RESTRAINT

The mechanism of death in emergency departments has been obscured by erroneous experiments and assumptions that appear superficially logical and correct but are wrong. Because such deaths almost always occur after restraint is either instituted or attempted, the cause of death has typically been attributed to "restraint/positional asphyxia," even when there is neither testimonial nor physical evidence of this condition. Because of the circumstances surrounding deaths resulting from excited delirium, there are often charges of police or medical misconduct. In some cases, allegations of murder are made.

In 1988, Reay et al. conducted a series of experiments to determine the effects on peripheral oxygen saturation and heart rate when an individual is hog-tied and placed prone following exercise (Reay et al., 1988). They concluded that hog-tie restraint prolongs recovery from exercise as determined by changes in peripheral oxygen saturation and heart rate. In an article published in 1993 by O'Halloran and Lewman on the association of restraint and asphyxiation, hog-tying and death were codified in the concept of "restraint asphyxia" or "positional asphyxia" (O'Halloran & Lewman, 1993). Even with the elimination of hog-tying, however, the number of deaths due to EDS continued, if not increased. Almost immediately after the concept of positional/restraint asphyxia was offered, the concept was expanded such that whenever anyone is restrained and dies, positional or restraint asphyxia is said to be the cause of death whatever the position of the deceased, the method of restraint, or the presence of drugs.

In 1997, Chan et al. published a study on restraint asphyxia (Chan et al., 1997). They repeated the experiments of Reay et al. (1988) using a more systematic approach and more sophisticated technology. Pulmonary function testing (forced vital capacity; forced expiratory volume in one second and maximal voluntary ventilation) was performed on individuals in the sitting, supine, prone, and restraint position (hog-tying). The subjects were then subjected to two exercise periods and two rest periods. During the rest periods, determinations of arterial blood gas, pulse rate, oxygen saturation by CO-oximetry and pulse oximetry, and pulmonary function testing (PFT) were performed. Determinations at the rest periods were made with the subject alternatively in the sitting position and restraint position. Placing individuals in the restraint position after exercise resulted in restrictive pulmonary functioning as measured by PFT. However, the PFT changes, although statistically significant, were not clinically relevant. Based on arterial PO_2 and CO-oximetry, oxygenation of blood increased with exercise, what one would expect and in contrast to Reay et al.'s findings. Most important was the fact that there was no evidence of hypoxia in the restraint position after exercise with no evidence of hypercapnia either during exercise or in restraint. Chan et al. concluded that there was no evidence that body position, while in the "hog-tie" or "hobble" restraint position, in and of itself causes hypoventilation or asphyxiation.

In an attempt to counter Chan et al.'s work, some individuals now claim that the death is due to compromise in ventilation occurring when an officer/medical worker applies body weight to the upper torso of an individual in an attempt to restrain the individual or prevent further struggle. This is usually accomplished by lying across an individual's back or applying pressure on the back with a knee or hands. Because of this allegation, Michalewicz et al. (2007) conducted a series of experiments. They investigated ventilatory and metabolic demands in healthy adults when placed in the prone maximal restraint position (PMRP) (e.g., hog-tie restraint). Maximal voluntary ventilation (MVV) was measured in seated subjects, in the PMRP, and when prone with 90.1 to 102.3 kg (198 to 225 lb) of weight on the back. Subjects were then placed in the PMRP and struggled vigorously for 60 seconds. The authors found no clinically important restriction of ventilatory reserve when subjects were placed in the PMRP or when prone with up to 90.2 or 102.3 kg of weight on their back. Likewise, when subjects were maximally struggling for 60 seconds while in the PMRP, there were no clinically important limitations of metabolic or ventilatory functions. They stated: "Based on these findings, as well as previously published studies, we suggest that factors other than ventilatory failure associated with the restraining process may be responsible for the sudden unexpected deaths of restrained individuals" (Michalewicz, et al., 2007, p. 174).

PHYSIOLOGICAL EFFECTS

The question then arises as to what is actually causing these deaths. It is the conclusion of the authors that sudden death from excited delirium is due to the effects of the normal physiological changes seen in a struggle, combined with, depending on the case, the use of illicit drugs, cardiotoxic medications, and natural disease. In some individuals, polymorphism of cardiac adrenoreceptors with resultant exacerbation of the normal responses to violent physical activity may also play a role. In fatal cases of excited delirium, death usually occurs immediately after the individual is restrained

and struggling ceases. This poststruggle period corresponds to the time of "postexercise peril" defined by Dimsdale et al. (1984), a time where an individual is susceptible to developing a fatal cardiac arrhythmia. An understanding of the physiological changes that lead to postexercise peril is important in understanding EDS. These changes, resulting in cardiac dysfunction and arrest, are due to the physiological effects of the catecholamines, epinephrine, and norepinephrine, as well as potassium, on the heart.

Dimsdale et al. (1984) found that in the three minutes immediately following cessation of strenuous exercise, epinephrine and norepinephrine continue to rise with norepinephrine at more than 10-fold baseline levels. Norepinephrine's action on the heart is stimulation of alpha-1 and beta-1 receptors (McCance, 1994). Stimulation of beta-1 receptors increases heart rate, contractility, and velocity of conduction. Alpha-1 receptors are found in the coronary arteries. Norepinephrine interacting with alpha-1 receptors causes vasoconstriction, thus decreasing the amount of oxygenated blood being supplied to the myocardium at a time when an increased amount is needed because of greater demand being put on the heart resulting from the stimulation of the beta-1 receptors.

Excessive levels of catecholamines, especially norepinephrine, can be cardiotoxic, resulting in catecholamine (norepinephrine) cardiomyopathy with impairment of myocardial contractility (Powers et al., 1994). Cardiac injury from excessive norepinephrine may be permanent. The lesions seen in catecholamine cardiomyopathy are myofibrillar degeneration, leukocyte infiltration, and focal necrosis. The pathogenesis of catecholamine-induced cardiomyopathy is disruption of myocardial calcium transport with resultant high levels of intracellular calcium. This results in a decreased rate of ventricular relaxation and an increased rate of diastolic tension, with resultant left ventricular dysfunction. Both diastolic and systolic functions are acutely impaired. Systolic function improves within 48 hours, whereas diastolic function remains depressed.

The effects of catecholamines and their role in sudden lethal cardiac arrhythmias were further expanded on by Young et al. (1992). They investigated not only the relationship between stress and catecholamine levels but potassium levels as well. Like Dimsdale et al. (1984), Young et al. found that the highest levels of plasma catecholamines occurred during the three minutes postexercise. In addition, they found that during strenuous exercise, potassium increases dramatically. Postexercise, while norepinephrine continues to rise, potassium levels fell at a maximum rate for one to two minutes to hypokalemic or near-hypokalemic levels.

Blood potassium concentrations have a narrow range of safety. Fatal cardiac arrhythmias are associated with both hyperkalemia and hypokalemia. If sudden death occurs with increased levels of potassium, the question then arises as to why a fatal arrhythmia does not occur during the rising phase of potassium during exercise rather than postexercise. Paterson et al. found that exercise-induced increases in circulating catecholamines have a cardioprotective effect to the rapidly rising potassium levels (Paterson et al., 1993). This cardioprotective effect is not known to occur for falling potassium levels.

Thus, changes in catecholamine and potassium levels, independent of each other, are potentially lethal. Poststruggle, however, the lethal potential of these changes converge, increasing the possibility of sudden cardiac death. The low incidence of cardiac death among the exercising population, or even in individuals in excited delirium, indicate that in most instances changes in catecholamine and potassium levels poststruggle, in and of themselves, rarely cause fatal cardiac arrhythmias. For death to occur in the postexercise period, there must be either the presence of medications or drugs that potentiate the action of the catecholamines; cardiotoxic medications, including typical and atypical antipsychotic drugs (Ray, 2009); mental disease such as schizophrenia, which may be associated with elevated levels of catecholamines (Yamamoto & Hornykiewicz, 2004); or polymorphism of the alpha and beta receptors that result in abnormally high levels of norepinephrine (Small et al., 2002). These factors produce a cascade of biochemical actions that set a lethal course resulting in sudden cardiac death (Fig. 39-1).

Taser Use Wrongly Linked to EDS Deaths

In a number of deaths resulting from excited delirium, a Taser has been used. In some cases, the cause of death has been attributed to the Taser. Tasers are handheld devices that fire two fishhook-like barbed darts attached to wires, simultaneously, up to a distance of 21 feet (Kroll & Tchou, 2007). The darts are propelled by a cartridge of compressed nitrogen. The wires are copper-clad steel wires with an insulated coating. At the end of each wire is a barb similar to a fishhook. The darts are designed to penetrate skin or lodge in clothing. On lodging in an individual or the individual's clothing, a circuit is achieved and the Taser provides a series of electrical pulses for five seconds. When the dart strikes bare skin, it penetrates until the full flange on the dart stops it. Penetration of skin is not necessary because the electric pulse it delivers can penetrate up to 2 inches of clothing. A high-voltage (50,000 volt), low-amperage current is delivered down the wires to the target. Each time the trigger is pulled, a five-second pulse is delivered. The Taser is designed to produce electromuscular disruption (EMD) (i.e., muscular contractions) via externally applied electric fields, with uncontrollable contraction of the muscles and immediate collapse. The shocks can be repeated. The Taser records the exact number of seconds pulses are delivered and the time delivered.

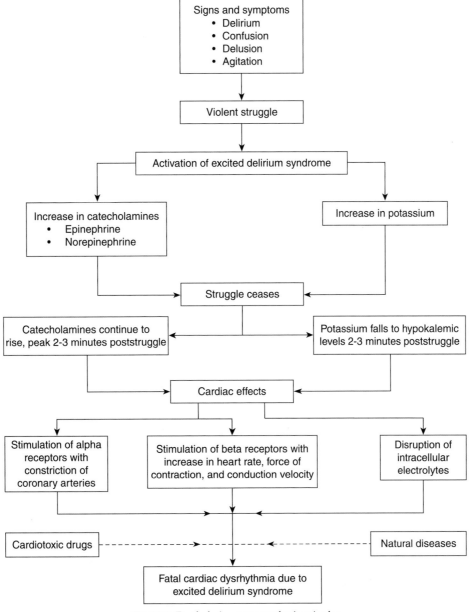

Fig. 39-1 Death during acute psychotic episodes.

One pull of the trigger generates five seconds of pulses. There are approximately 19 pulses per second. Each pulse is 2.1 milliamps and 0.36 Joules per pulse. For comparison, a bathroom ground fault circuit interrupter trips with 5 milliamps of current; household electrocutions require 75 to 100 milliamps.

There is no evidence that use of a Taser causes death. A Taser can be employed two ways. The most common way is as an EMD that causes neuromuscular incapacitation or strong muscle contractions through the involuntary stimulation of nerves. In the drive-stun mode, it is a pain compliance device. The second way is the drive-stun mode which does not incapacitate a subject but may assist in taking a subject into custody because of the induced pain. In neither mode does it interfere with respiration, as human experimentation has demonstrated. It has been estimated that approximately 750,000 law enforcement individuals have been voluntarily tasered with no deaths or fatal arrhythmias. There is no evidence that multiple use of the Taser in the EMD mode causes death.

The only way a Taser could theoretically cause death directly would be by producing a fatal cardiac arrhythmia (i.e., by electrocution), and then only when employed as an EMD. The arrhythmia produced would have to be ventricular fibrillation, the arrhythmia produced by electrocution. The arrhythmia would have to occur at the time the individual was last tasered in the EMD mode, as electricity does not accumulate in the body. Ventricular fibrillation would result in loss of consciousness in 5 to 15 seconds (Di Maio & Di Maio, 2001). Respiration may continue for about 1 minute. If the individual does not go unconscious within 5 to 15 seconds after being tasered, then one can dismiss the Taser as the cause of death.

Some individuals have contended that the Taser can produce a fatal arrhythmia, especially if the barbs impact adjacent to the heart. This is based on a few studies using pigs and a lot of speculation and is not generally accepted in the medical community. The problem with this contention is that the electrical circuitry of the pig heart is not similar to that of humans (Kroll et al., 2008). In addition, the experiments with the pigs involved artificial conditions.

In an interim report on EMDs (also known as conducted energy devices [CEDs]) and death issued by the National Institute of Justice in June 2008, it was concluded that there is currently no medical evidence that CEDs pose a significant risk for induced cardiac dysrhythmia when deployed reasonably and there is no medical evidence to suggest that exposure to a CED produces metabolic or physiological effects substantial enough to produce abnormal cardiac rhythms in normal, healthy adults (NIJ, 2008).

Assessment and Prevention of Deaths by Medical Personnel

Forensic nurse examiners can make a unique contribution to death prevention in individuals presenting to or patients in medical facilities who have symptoms of excited delirium or who are predisposed to develop it. Forensic nursing is not only involved in the medicolegal aspects of a death but its impact on families and the community as a whole. Forensic nurse examiners can educate healthcare providers and law enforcement officers (both of whom encounter this entity) about this syndrome to prevent such deaths.

KEY POINT Of critical importance in the prevention of death from excited delirium is the early identification of high-risk patients.

Key behavioral and cognitive identifying indicators for excited delirium include the following:
- Bizarre behavior
- Agitation and restlessness
- Incoherent and rambling speech
- Hallucinations
- Delusions with paranoid features
- Disorganized thought content
- Combativeness
- Violence

As a tool for patient care, accurate nursing diagnoses have always been of fundamental importance. Assessment for prevention of sudden death as a result of EDS can now be another measure of patient care. Thus, a nursing diagnosis might be *"potential for sudden death due to excited delirium syndrome, as evidenced by a history of endogenous mental disease with past violent behavior"* (Di Maio, & Di Maio, 2006, p. 117). Assessing characteristics for high-risk patients are as follows:
- A prior episode of excited delirium
- Violent and aggressive behavior
- Use of medication that increases the release or blocks reuptake of norepinephrine
- Cardiac disease
- Asthma or any pulmonary disease involving restriction of airway
- Epilepsy
- Use of stimulants such as cocaine and methamphetamine
- History of schizophrenia

Age is not an identifying factor, as these deaths can occur in the young as well as the old.

Early identification of behaviors predictive of violent activity requires immediate intervention measures to reduce escalating anger and aggression (Rawlins et al., 1993). Behavior characteristics for violence include the following:
- Verbal threats of violence
- Screaming, swearing, shouting at others
- Breaking or throwing objects
- Motor agitation, rigid/taut body expressions with poor concentration
- Projecting angry emotions onto another (e.g., blaming)
- Nonverbal behavior of rejecting others
- Pacing, restlessness, inability to sleep or eat, hyperactivity
- History of violent behavior with need for physical restraint
- Delusions and confusion of mental state
- Defiance
- Bullying others
- Using stimulants (e.g., cocaine, methamphetamine)
- Paranoid behavior with auditory hallucinations

KEY POINT The most critical time during excited delirium syndrome occurs when the staff engages in physically restraining the patient. It is the struggle between patient and staff that initiates catecholamine/potassium actions. Consequently, it is of extreme importance to prevent a struggle and the use of physical restraint.

When an individual's internal mechanisms for control are lost because of an acute psychotic episode, the person has lost his or her ability to perceive reality. These episodes are often extremely frightening to individuals having to care for such patients and require immediate attention to prevent violence to self or others.

Acute psychotic breaks can also occur from endogenous disease processes. MEND-A-MIND is a mnemonic for disorders that can cause an acute psychotic episode (Farrell et al., 1998):

- M – Metabolic disorder
- E – Electrical (convulsive) disorder
- N – Neoplastic disease
- D – Degenerative (chronic) brain disease
- A – Arterial (cerebrovascular) disease
- M – Mechanical disease (actual physical structures of the brain)
- I – Infectious disease
- N – Nutritional disease
- D – Drug toxicity

Regardless of the cause of a psychotic break, prevention of violence and maintenance of the safety of the patient and staff are of direct importance.

Use of Physical Restraint

The standard of care in behavioral emergencies is nonphysical and based on initial and ongoing assessment. This includes knowledge of communicative techniques, verbal and nonverbal; the patient's and family's direct participation in care planning; and the reduction of environmental stimulants that may trigger the escalation of violent behavior.

BEST PRACTICE Prevent a struggle during the use of physical restraint by reducing environmental stimulation that may trigger or escalate violent behavior.

More restrictive measures (for example, physical restraint) should be used only in extreme behavioral emergencies. The use of physical restraint must be determined to outweigh the risk associated with it. Physical restraint should only be used when all other less restrictive measures have been used and failed to prevent the patient from harming self or others. The therapeutic benefit as well as the moral treatment of physically restraining patients have been debated frequently in the literature. Although the elimination of physical restraint may not be possible in all situations, the least amount of time and the fewest points of restraint should be used to prevent the patient from harming self or others (American Psychiatric Nurses Association [APNA], 2000). If physical restraint must be used, it should be rapid, with overwhelming force (i.e., a minimum of five to six individuals), to reduce the length of the struggle.

Management of Violence

Many theories have been written on the management of violence and aggression in mentally ill and violent patients. Planning to manage potentially violent situations before they occur should be the first component in providing care for the patient as well as the staff. Teaching medical, emergency, and police personnel to identify excited delirium and methods used to prevent death must be incorporated in training programs to prevent death from excited delirium.

BEST PRACTICE If the need for physical restraint becomes unavoidable, releasing the patient quickly and allowing the patient to pace or walk off anger will help prevent critical fluctuations of catecholamines and potassium levels during the poststruggle period.

Studies on treatment modules that may influence the success of reducing the need for restraint indicate that the training of staff in early assessment and intervention of alternative methods to defuse and de-escalate aggression and violence can reduce the requirement for physical restraint (Mercer et al., 2000).

In cases of excited delirium when de-escalation is unsuccessful, the following steps can be taken to prevent death:
- Apply rapid restraint using overwhelming force to prevent prolonged struggling with the associated increase in levels of norepinephrine and epinephrine. The recommended number of personnel is six.
- Monitor vital signs continuously.
- Instigate cooling to prevent elevated body temperature, which can lead to rhabdomyolysis and acute renal failure. Markedly elevated body temperature is an ominous sign that death may ensue rapidly.
- Provide additional oxygen.
- Sedate immediately with a benzodiazepine-related compound. The recommended route of administration is either intravenously or intranasally. In a struggling individual, the intranasal route is more practical. Lorazepam can be administered intranasally. Another possibility is intranasal fentanyl. The use of antipsychotic medications, either typical or atypical, for sedation is not recommended at this time as they predispose to cardiac arrhythmias and sudden death (Ray, 2009). This includes Haldol.
- In cases outside a medical institution, immediately transport the individual to a hospital, as excited delirium is a medical emergency.

Summary

Sudden death as a result of EDS in individuals with acute psychotic episodes is not caused by positional asphyxia, hog-tie restraint, or the physical restraint of patients in general. Death is due to a number of effects, cascading together, culminating in a lethal cardiac arrest. The clinical forensic nurse examiner who specializes in forensic mental health is in a key position to prevent death from this particular syndrome. Prevention involves knowledge of the mechanism of death for the early initial identification of high-risk patients. Successful prevention requires alternative methods, other than physical restraint, to reduce aggression and violence. This information is also essential for the forensic nurse death investigator (FNDI) or forensic nurse coroner/deputy coroner during the evaluation of a fatal episode. Mandatory teaching of these methods should be a standard of care for all individuals encountering aggressive and violent patients.

Case Study 39-1

Sudden Death in a Schizophrenic Patient

The patient was a 25-year-old white male with a well-documented history of schizophrenia who was transported to a hospital for a medical examination prior to being transported to a psychiatric facility. He was seen in the emergency department (ED) where he was hallucinating. In the ED, the patient became aggressive, and a violent struggle ensued between him and law enforcement personnel escorting him. As they struggled, a nurse gave him an intramuscular injection of Haldol. Almost immediately, he seemed to become calm. At this time, he was noted to be cyanotic without pulse or respiration. An electrocardiogram showed asystole. Resuscitation was instituted, but the patient died. The autopsy, including toxicology, was negative except for some minor abrasions and contusions.

Case Study **39-2**

Sudden Death in an Apparently Healthy Teenager

The deceased was a 16-year-old black female with a history of recurrent depression. At the time of her death, she was a patient in a mental institution. She saw another patient being restrained and went to the patient's aid. She was described as extremely violent. The staff responded, placed her in a basket hold, and took her to the floor. She was given a 50-mg IM injection of Thorazine. Approximately 10 minutes later, she stopped struggling. She was carried to her room. When checked several minutes later, she was found unresponsive. At autopsy, there were no injuries. Her heart was slightly enlarged, weighing 330 g (the mean heart weight in individuals 15 to 19 years old is 232 g with a standard deviation of 43 g). A complete toxicology screen was negative for any drugs or medications, including Thorazine. A subsequent investigation revealed that her father had died of Wolfe-Parkinson-White syndrome at age 31.

In this case, the deceased had slight enlargement of the heart and a family history of a potentially fatal cardiac condition. In Wolfe-Parkinson-White syndrome, there are congenital conduction abnormalities of the heart that produce arrhythmias. Occasionally, the arrhythmias are fatal. This condition may have been present in the patient, as there is a hereditary tendency, and may have been a contributory factor in her death.

Case Study **39-3**

Sudden Death of a Child on Prescribed Medication

The deceased was a 9-year-old white male with bipolar disease and attention deficit disorder who suddenly became violent while in a mental facility. He was brought to the floor and held there with a basket-hold method of restraint for 20 minutes. He appeared to calm down and then was noted to be unresponsive. Emergency medical services personnel were summoned, and he was transported to a hospital. He survived approximately 21 hours in the hospital. At autopsy, there were minor abrasions and contusions. Toxicology on blood obtained at autopsy revealed blood levels of: 0.61 mg/L venlafaxine and 0.20 mg/L amphetamine. Both are high therapeutic levels (Baselt, 2000). These numbers represent levels at the time of death—21 hours plus after arrest. The blood levels at the time of cardiac arrest would have been significantly higher.

Venlafaxine, like cocaine, is a potent inhibitor of norepinephrine reuptake (*Physician's Desk Reference* [PDR], 2004). Amphetamine causes release of norepinephrine from sympathetic fibers. Increased quantities of norepinephrine increase the heart rate, force of contraction, and conduction velocity while at the same time causing coronary artery constriction with resultant decreased perfusion of the myocardium (McCance & Huether, 1994). Thus, in this case, the elevated levels of the two medications present were felt to be cardiotoxic and contributory to the death.

Case Study **39-4**

Sudden Death of a Prisoner in Association with Use of a TASER®

The patient was a 25-year-old male with a history of schizophrenia who had been in jail for approximately three weeks when he became agitated and began to act bizarrely. It was decided to administer medications for his psychiatric symptoms. In consultation with a physician, the jail nurse obtained haloperidol and lorazepam for intramuscular

administration. The nurse and four guards entered the cell to give him medications, whereupon a violent struggle ensued. The guards tasered the prisoner a number of times with no effect. The struggle continued for a number of minutes until the guards were finally able to apply handcuffs. The nurse then injected the medications. The prisoner was placed in a restraint chair. Almost immediately, he was noted to be without pulse or respiration. A defibrillator placed on his chest indicated asystole. Resuscitation was instituted but the patient died after transport to the hospital. The autopsy was negative except for mild enlargement of the heart. Use of the Taser was not felt to be a cause of death because of the time interval between being tasered and the cardiopulmonary arrest.

Resources

BOOKS/ARTICLES

Di Maio, T. G., & Di Maio, V. J. M. (2006). *Excited delirium syndrome.* Boca Raton, FL: CRC Press Inc.

Grant, J. R., Southall, P. E., Mealey, J., Scott, S. R., & Fowler, D. R. (2009). Excited delirium in custody: Past and present. *The American Journal of Forensic Medicine and Pathology, 30*(1), 1–5.

ORGANIZATIONS

National Association of Medical Examiners
430 Pryor Street SW, Atlanta, GA 30312, 404-730-4781; http://thename. org

References

American Psychiatric Nurses Association (APNA). (2000). *Seclusion and restraints task force.* Arlington, VA: Position statement on the use of seclusion and restraint, Author.

Baselt, R. C. (2000). Disposition of toxic drugs and chemicals in man. (5th ed.). Chemical Toxicology Institute. Foster City, CA.

Bell, L. V. (1849). On a form of disease resembling some advanced stages of mania and fever, but so contradistinguished from any ordinarily observed or described combination of symptoms, as to render it probably that it may be an overlooked and hitherto unrecorded malady. *American Journal of Insanity, 6*(2), 97–127.

Cancro, R. (2000). The introduction of neuroleptics: A psychiatric revolution. *Psychiatric Services, 51*(3).

Chan, T. C., Vilke, G. N., Neuman, T., et al. (1997). Restraint position and positional asphyxia. *Annals of Emergency Medicine, 30*(5), 578–586.

Di Maio, T. G., & Di Maio, V. J. M. (2006). *Excited Delirium Syndrome.* Boca Raton, FL: CRC Press Inc.

Di Maio, V. J. M., & Di Maio, D. (2001). *Forensic pathology* (2nd ed.). Boca Raton, FL: CRC Press Inc.

Dimsdale, J. E., Hartley, G. T., Ruskin, J. N., et al. (1984). Post-exercise peril: Plasma catecholamines and exercise. *JAMA: The Journal of the American Medical Association, 251*(5), 630–632.

Farrell, S. P., Harmon, R. B., & Hastings, S. (1998). Nursing management of acute psychotic episodes. *The Nursing Clinics of North America, 33*(1), 187–200.

Kroll, M. W., & Tchou, P. (2007). How a Taser Works. IEEE Spectrum, published December 2007, www.spectrum.ieee.org/dec07/5731: Accessed November 18, 2009.

Kroll, M. W., Calkins, H., Luceri, R. M., Graham, M. A., & Heegaard, W. G. (2008). Taser Safety (Letter). *CMAJ: Canadian Medical Association Journal, 179*(7), 677–678.

Lieberman, J. A., Golden, R., Stroup, S., & McEnvoy, J. (2000). Drugs of the psychopharmacological revolution in clinical psychiatry. *Psychiatric Services, 51*(10), 1524–1528.

McCance, K. L., & Huether, S. E. (1994). *Pathophysiology: The biologic basis for diseases in adults and children* (2nd ed.). St. Louis: Mosby.

Mercer, D., Mason, T., & McKeown, M., et al. (Eds.) (2000). *Forensic mental health care: A case study approach*. London: Churchill Livingstone.

Michalewicz, B. A., Chan, T. C., Vilke, G. M., et al. (2007). Ventilatory and metabolic demands during aggressive physical restraint in healthy adults. *Journal of Forensic Sciences, 52*(1), 171–175.

National Institute of Justice. (2008). *Study of Deaths Following Electro Muscular Disruption: Interim Report*. June.

O'Halloran, R. L., & Lewman, L. V. (1993). Restraint asphyxiation in excited delirium. *The American Journal of Forensic Medicine and Pathology, 14*(4), 289–295.

Paterson, D. J., Rogers, J., Powell, T., et al. (1993). Effects of catecholamines on the ventricular myocyte action potential in raised extracellular potassium. *Acta Physiologica Scandinavica, 148*(2), 177–186.

Physician's Desk Reference (PDR) (59th ed.). (2004). Montvale, NJ: Thomson Healthcare.

Powers, F. M., Pifarre, R., & Thomas, J. X. (1994). Ventricular dysfunction in norepinephrine-induced cardiomyopathy. *Circulatory Shock, 43*(3), 122–129.

Rawlins, R. P., Williams, S. R., & Beck, C. K. (Eds.). (1993). *Mental health–psychiatric nursing: A holistic life-cycle approach* (3rd ed.). St. Louis: Mosby.

Ray, W. A. (2009). Atypical antipsychotic drugs and the risk of sudden cardiac death. *The New England Journal of Medicine, 360*, 225–235.

Reay, D. T., Howard, J. D., Fligner, C. L., & Ward, R. J. (1988). Effects of positional restraint on oxygen saturation and heart rate following exercise. *The American Journal of Forensic Medicine and Pathology, 9*(1), 16–18.

Small, K. M., Wagoner, L. E., Levin, A. M., Kardia, S. L. R., & Liggett, S. B. (2002). Synergistic polymorphisms of B_1 and alpha $_{2c}$ adrenergic receptors and the risk of congestive heart failure. *The New England Journal of Medicine, 347*(15), 1135–1142.

Yamamoto, K., & Hornykiewicz, O. (2004). Proposal for a nonadrenaline hypothesis of schizophrenia. *Progress In Neuro-Psychopharmacology & Biological Psychiatry, 28*(5), 913–922.

Young, D. B., Srivastava, T. N., Fitzovich, D. E., et al. (1992). Potassium and catecholamine concentrations in the immediate post exercise period. *The American Journal of Medical Sciences, 304*, 150–153.

CHAPTER 40 Sociocultural Crimes: A Forensic Approach

Rakesh K. Gorea

The world is becoming a global village as people migrate between countries to seek newer avenues for jobs and prosperity. With the migration of people of different social and cultural beliefs, crimes based on these values are also spreading to the host countries. Sociocultural crimes will not be limited to a particular country but will become omnipresent. There is an urgent need to become familiar with sociocultural crimes so that they can be identified, assessed, and investigated and so that the perpetrators of sociocultural crimes can be prosecuted according to the law of the host land. Once forensic nurse examiners (FNEs) become aware of these crimes, it will become less complicated for the forensic nurse examiner to understand the psychology responsible for the social and cultural values behind them. It will also become less complicated for the nurse to identify the underlying causes and manage the victims and assailants. Knowledge of sociocultural crimes will also help the investigating agencies to reduce and prevent future crimes. There are various theories and concepts for the root cause and frequency of occurrence of sociocultural crimes. These crimes may be explained on the basis of the psychological, biological, behavioral, economic, social, and cultural conditions of a society. The origin of sociocultural crime is usually limited to one region, state, or country according to its social and cultural beliefs. Some sociocultural crimes are rampant in adjoining countries because these countries have been formed by partition of one parent country and they inherit the same sociocultural beliefs.

Gender-Based Crimes

Gender-based discrimination, wife battering, dowry deaths, criminal abortions, female feticide, female infanticide, sati pratha, honor killings, geriatric battering, child marriages, witchcraft and tantriks, custodial torture, ragging, corporal punishment in schools, rights of passage to adulthood, religious and therapeutic injury and death for both males and females constitute the sociocultural crimes that are practiced to different extents in diverse areas of the world.

DOWRY DEATH

This sociocultural crime, also known as bride burning, is rampant in India, particularly in Hindu and Sikh families. In-laws often kill brides for bringing insufficient dowry into the marriage. In addition, brides are often brutalized, tortured, and punished for bringing inadequate money or unsatisfactory gifts in dowry. They are tormented to such an extent that these women often commit suicide by drowning, hanging, or burning themselves or ingesting

lethal poisons. Dowry death has been defined by Indian law as death occurring within seven years of marriage or death occurring before a woman attains the age of 30 years. The most common method employed in India is either death by poison or death by conflagration (throwing kerosene on a woman and igniting it). The most common perpetrator in such crimes is the mother-in-law.

Dowry deaths are now more effectively prosecuted in India under Section 302/304-B IPC. The government has also increased the punishment for those responsible for dowry deaths. To prevent undue public influence on the forensic physician in such cases, a board of doctors provides postmortem examinations. In spite of these laws, the rate of dowry deaths has not shown any decline; rather it has shown an alarming increase since the early 2000s. Reported cases of dowry deaths included the following: in 2003, 6208 cases; in 2004, 7026 cases; in 2005, 6787 cases; in 2006, 7618 cases; and in 2007, 8093 cases (National Crime Records Bureau [NCRB], 2007a). Dowry deaths are considered a bane in Indian society, but they continue despite the effort of the government and various nongovernmental organizations. This malevolence is compounded by the poor conviction rate in India. Although 92.8% of dowry deaths were charged, there were convictions in merely 33% of 8093 cases in 2007 (NCRB, 2007b) (Fig. 40-1).

FEMALE FETICIDE

Female feticide is the crime of aborting a fetus after sex determination has identified the fetus as female. One of the most heinous crimes is to prevent the birth of female babies. With the advent of ultrasound sex determination, such tests are performed with impunity because of the greed of doctors and the societal pressure on women to have male children. As a result of this mass elimination of the female fetus, the male-to-female sex ratio is being disturbed in various states for a variety of reasons. The practice of female feticide is more common in areas where a mania exists for having a son instead of a daughter, particularly in the Hindi-speaking area of North India.

FEMALE INFANTICIDE

Infanticide is covered under Section 302 IPC and Section 315 IPC and is defined as a crime against a newborn to 1 year of age as opposed to feticide (a crime against a fetus), which is covered under Sections 315 and 316 IPC. This practice is ingrained to such an extent that even male fetuses wrongly diagnosed as female are often aborted, resulting in serious anguish and pain for the mothers. In one instance, a wife sued her husband for demanding the abortion of a male fetus when it was wrongly diagnosed as female (*Hindustan Times*, 2008a). The root causes of this obsession for

Fig. 40-1 Conflagration punishment of a bride with an inadequate dowry; young woman was splashed with kerosene and ignited.

male children are superstitions, poverty, illiteracy, and the dowry system. There are also religious rites that add to this problem. For example, only sons can perform the last rites at the cremation of the deceased father or mother (Gorea, 2004a). In the absence of a son, a brother, father, uncle, or nephew is called on to ignite the funeral pyre. If a daughter is the only child of the decedent and the daughter is married, her husband may be allowed to light the first flames of the funeral pyre. To curb the practice of female infanticide, the government of India has promulgated the 2002 Pre Natal Diagnostic Techniques Act and the Regulation and Prevention of Misuse Amendment 14 of 2003.

BEST PRACTICE When investigating cases of female feticide, it is imperative for the forensic nurse to establish (1) that the fetus is female and (2) that it belongs to a particular woman in order to establish the DNA profile of both the fetus and the mother as required by law.

The greatest problem in such cases is that there is no complainant. Neither mothers nor indulging doctors complain about this crime, and the fetus cannot speak for itself. Only social vigilance and change of societal mindset will provide a solution to this historical problem. Because of sustained efforts by government and nongovernmental organizations (NGOs), this situation has now changed in seven villages of the Mansa district of Punjab. Currently there are more girls than boys, in contrast to 2001 when there were 784 girls to 1000 boys. This difference is due to increased awareness, stringent laws, and a changed state of mind (Sidhu, 2009). Female babies born in certain male-dominant societies of the world are not welcome and become unwanted family members. Failure to provide stringent laws, funding, or facilities for the female infant will result in an act of infanticide by those who do not want female children. The dowry system is mainly responsible for female infanticide, in addition to other social causes. In Punjab, unwanted newborn girls are not properly nursed or nourished. Punjabis fail to take proper care of the girl child after birth, which results in a higher death rate of girls in the age group of 0 to 5 years (Dainik Jagran, 2009). The girl child may also be deprived of education, both in India and in Pakistan, which has resulted in illiteracy and the inability for many women to provide a better life for themselves and their daughters. In the Northwest Swat Valley of Pakistan, the Taliban has demanded that girls should not go to school. If this order was violated after a certain date, the Taliban threatened to start killing the girls (*Hindustan Times*, 2008b). In spite of the stated evidence, a segment of society has realized,

"It is unfortunate, for one reason or the other, that the practice of female infanticide still prevails despite the fact that the gentle touch and the voice of a daughter has a soothing effect on their parents" (National Commission for Women, 2008).

FEMALE GENITAL MUTILATION

The intentional cutting of female genital organs without valid medical reasons is known as female genital mutilation (FGM) or female circumcision and is carried out in different parts of the world including some areas of Australia, Europe, South America, Mexico, and Asia. As evidence of the gravity of this problem, it is believed that 100-140 million women worldwide are living with the negative effects of FGM. In some African tribes, the tradition of female genital mutilation is common, with some 3 million girls considered at risk. This procedure is carried out primarily on girls from infancy to 15 years of age (World Health Organization, 2009). Cutting is performed by traditional circumcisers, but different methods are applied. The labia majora, labia minora, and clitoris are partially or completely excised, or only the clitoris may be removed. Sometimes only narrowing of the vagina may be done, or cautery or incision of the genital organs may be performed. FGM reduces or eliminates the woman's pleasure during sexual intercourse. In the final statement of a conference on FGM held on November 24, 2006, by the Target Group of Germany, it was emphasized that this unconscionable tradition is an assault on women and should be considered criminal (religioustolerance.org, 2009).

This practice commonly leads to infections, hemorrhage, shock, and scarring, which in turn often leads to difficult childbirth and infertility. It also causes painful sexual intercourse and nervousness, as well as urinary and menstrual problems. Sudan, Somalia, Kenya, Ethiopia, and Mali are more affected by the practice of infibulation or pharaonic circumcision, the most extensive and serious cutting category of FGM (Hosken, 2009). According to a study by the United Nations International Children Emergency Fund (UNICEF), infants, girls, and women suffering from FGM face irreversible lifelong health risks. "FGM/C (female genital mutilation/cutting) is a fundamental violation of the rights of the girl child. It is discriminatory and violates the rights to equal opportunities, health, and freedom from violence, injury, abuse, torture, cruel or inhuman and degrading treatment, protection from harmful traditional practices, and to make decisions concerning reproduction" (UNICEF, 2009). International law protects the rights to equal opportunities, thus female genital mutilation is a violation of basic human rights as outlined in the United Nations Universal Declaration of Human Rights (UNUDHR). Various reasons underlie the perpetuation of this practice, and these must be understood in a way that does not undermine their complexity. Despite this necessity, cultural sensitivity must be informed by basic rights and the ways in which they are violated, avoiding cultural and legal pluralism. Education and program development are essential characteristics of eradication efforts (unicef.org, 2009). (See Chapter 42 on female genital mutilation.)

Criminal Abortion

Among the most emotive cultural and legal issues worldwide are those regarding the termination of unwanted pregnancies. Public health workers believe that sexual abuse is an often neglected, widespread problem in many countries. Abortion procedures of underage girls in Brazil primarily involve those who have survived sexual abuse. One of Brazil's women's health clinics, which specializes in care for victims of sexual abuse, has stated that nearly half of its 15 daily cases involves children younger than 12 years of age (*New York Times*, March 28, 2009).

These children are primarily victims of sexual abuse and rape. The perpetrators are primarily family members. In 80% of the cases, fathers or stepfathers committed the sexual abuse. Jefferson Drezett, a gynecologist and coordinator of sexual abuse services at the hospital, said, "A part of Brazilian society still doesn't want to stop treating women like they are property: This has to change" (newyorktimes.com). Brazil's Ministry of Health reports the number of legal abortions performed on girls ages 10 to 14 has more than doubled from 22 procedures in 2007 to 49 in 2008. Considering all Latin American countries, only Chile, El Salvador, and Nicaragua—all of which ban abortion for any reason—have stricter abortion laws than Brazil (*New York Times*, March 28, 2009).

Case Study 40-1

Abortion in Latin American

Physicians in Brazil performed an abortion on a 9-year-old girl who reportedly had been raped by her stepfather and was 15 weeks pregnant with twins. Abortion is illegal in Brazil except in cases of rape or when the woman's life is in danger. Both exceptions seem applicable to this 9-year-old girl's case. However, the Brazilian archbishop excommunicated the physicians who performed the abortion and the girl's mother who permitted the procedure. The stepfather, however, was excommunicated. The case has ignited debates about reproductive rights in Brazil and has "brought to light other instances of young girls being raped and impregnated by family members." (*New York Times*, March 28, 2009).

INDIA

The 1971 Medical Termination of Pregnancy Act of India states that any abortion performed against the provisions of this act becomes an illegal or criminal abortion. Most pregnancies in unmarried females are aborted against the provision of this act because of the social shame factor. Married females may also resort to criminal abortion when the sex of the child is determined unacceptable, when the number of children is unfavorable to the mother's health, or if pregnancy is due to an illicit relation, that is not sanctioned by Indian society. Because of the low cost of illegal abortions performed by untrained persons, the practice of criminal abortion is increasing. If the ultrasonogram test for sex determination during pregnancy indicates that the fetus is female, most are aborted. Such abortions are not carried out at centers that permit abortion but at other facilities, often jeopardizing the health and life of the pregnant woman.

CHINA

Conversely, the Chinese government's one-child policy first implemented in 1978 sanctions widespread, forced abortions and sterilizations for essentially the same reason as that presented in India: a boy child is preferred. Although the policy was initially introduced to curb overpopulation, it is the female child that is dispensable. Because of the one-child policy, there are 60 million more Chinese boys than girls. Brutally coercive population control in rural areas is a reminder that Beijing's one-child policy remains in effect despite calls for reform by human rights organizations and Chinese demographers. The success of this policy has checked China's population growth to the extent that the country now

confronts the rapid aging of its total population in the next two decades. Critics point out that India has achieved broadly similar declines in fertility without government coercion or occasional brutality (www.time.com/time/world/article/0,8599,1615936,00.html).

Case Study 40-2

Forced Abortion in China

In China, pregnancy outside of marriage is illegal. On September 7, 2000, family-planning officials arrested 20-year-old Jin Yani, an expectant mother who was in her ninth month of pregnancy. Her crime was to become pregnant by her fiance five months prior to her reaching her 20th birthday, the minimum legal age for marriage under Chinese law. She was full-term and her membranes had already ruptured by the time she was being taken to a local abortion center. There, the unborn baby girl was injected with a lethal medication, and two days later removed from the mother's body with forceps. Jin Yani had massive hemorrhaging and was hospitalized for 44 days. She is now infertile due to the abortion. The couple decided to sue governmental agencies for medical costs, psychological distress, and the medical fiasco, which resulted in the couple's inability to conceive (Hoyden, 2008).

UNITED STATES

Abortion in the United States is one of the most controversial and politically charged issues in U.S. Supreme Court history. The case of *Roe v. Wade*, addressed in 1973 by the U.S. Supreme Court, challenged the constitutionality of a state's criminal abortion laws, which proscribed procuring or attempting an abortion except on medical advice for the purpose of saving the mother's life. This case resulted in a landmark decision leading to a federal law that allowed independent states to determine the outcome regarding abortion and reshaped national politics. At that time, the decision overturned all state and federal statutes outlawing or restricting abortions that were inconsistent with the findings of the issues presented. The *Roe v. Wade* decision prompted a national debate that continues today and has divided the nation into pro-choice and pro-life campaigns. The current judicial interpretation of the U.S. Constitution regarding abortion and subsequent companion decisions is that abortion is legal but may be restricted by the states to varying degrees. States have passed laws to restrict late-term abortions, require parental notification for minors, and mandate the disclosure of abortion risk information to patients before the procedure is performed (Touro Law Center, 1995).

IRELAND

Strict abortion laws in Ireland have a controversial history that remains a disputed subject today. The 1861 Offences against the Person Act, which was introduced by Britain, maintained all abortions to be illegal and subject to "penal servitude for life." As the twentieth century brought liberalized laws across Europe, a predominantly Catholic Ireland remained implacably opposed to abortion. In 1967, after 100 years, Britain allowed the termination of pregnancies. The legalization of abortion has resulted in an annual increase in the number of Irish women traveling to the United Kingdom to obtain an abortion. Although legal in the Republic of Ireland and in Northern Ireland, restrictions exist regarding the endangerment of the woman's life through continuance of the pregnancy (Blush Response, 2001).

Domestic Terrorism

WIFE BATTERING

Violence against women and gender-based violence infects every society. Wife battering refers to violent acts–psychological, sexual, or physical assault–by an assailant against his wife or partner made with the intent of controlling the partner by inducing fear and pain (http://legal-dictionary.thefreedictionary.com/Wife-beating). Wife battering is observed on different pretexts in Indian society. In a social and historical context, wife beating is common in some cultures to such an extent that it is considered a routine family affair, particularly in strata with low socioeconomic status. Such cases are not reported to the police, even in extreme situations. Only when the act may result in death is it is reported to the authorities. These are not just isolated cases in India but are common across different countries. A White Ribbon Campaign in India represents the efforts to reduce and prevent wife battering and other forms of violence against women. Places of sanctuary are needed where a woman can take her children when violence is out of control. (See Chapter 31.)

BABY BATTERING

Battering babies is not uncommon in many countries. It goes on without impunity in different forms. A child who does not behave according to the wishes of parents or guardians is often cursed and beaten to make the child fall in line with the wishes of the batterer. Gracia and Herrero (2008) have studied the crime of child abuse, which often occurs because of different beliefs in these societies. According to this research, 56.13% of respondents believed in the necessity of punishment to children; 59.2% of women believed in the necessity of corporal punishment, compared to 40.8% of men. With a new age of social responsibility, some countries are reviewing antiquated perspectives on physical punishment. (See also Chapter 29.)

GERIATRIC BATTERING

In many countries it is the government that assumes the responsibility of caring for the old people in their society. In some countries, the elderly are dependent on their children who may not be able or willing to provide the basic necessities for their parents. Poverty is believed to be one of the primary reasons for this negligence. It has also been observed in these societies that the elderly are beaten by the very children who are supposed to provide for them. Battery also occurs because of disputes about the inheritance of property. Could this be related to the corporal punishment these children received from their parents in early childhood? Social scientists have posed this question since the 1970s, and many have indicated that violence is learned behavior. (See Chapter 30.)

Antiquated Cultural Crimes

CHILD MARRIAGE

According to a report issued by the United Nations, early marriages violate the young woman's basic human rights by putting her into a life of isolation and service where she may have to contend with a lack of education, health problems, and abuse. UNICEF stated, "because marriage under the age of 18 may threaten a child's human rights (including the right to education, leisure, good health, freedom of expression, and freedom from discrimination), the best way to ensure the pro-

tection of children's rights is to set a minimum age limit of 18 for marriage" (About.com, 2009) This issue has both cultural and religious aspects. The views on child marriage in four major countries are addressed and compared in the following sections.

India

Child marriages were common in India in past centuries. But now, because of the expansion of education and the Child Marriage Restraint Act of 1929, child marriages are on the decline. However, illegal child marriages are still reported and prosecuted in India. Statistics indicate that 125 cases were reported in 2005; 99 cases in 2006 and 96 cases in 2007 were prosecuted. The statistics in India's Andhra Pradesh documented 21 cases (21.9% of the total cases reported in India), followed by Gujarat (14 cases, 14.6%), and West Bengal (9 cases, 9.4%) (NCRB, 2007c). Child marriages are often performed in India, and sometimes more than one girl child in the family might be married on the same day. About 15,000 child marriages occur annually (Taboo, 2008a). The practice of child marriage is not limited to India but is commonly accepted practice in many other Asian countries.

Saudi Arabia

There are no laws in Saudi Arabia that define the minimum age for marriage. Though a woman's consent is legally required, some marriage officials do not seek it. For example, a father can marry off a 1-year-old girl as long as sex is delayed until she reaches puberty, said one marriage official, Ahmad al-Muabi. In Saudi Arabia a 58-year-old man married an 8-year-old girl. In a case filed by her mother, the girl was not granted a divorce, as divorce can be granted only after the girl reaches puberty (*Hindustan Times*, 2008c). In Riyadh, it has been reported that the law allows for marriages of 10-year-old girls.

Case Study **40-3**

Marriage and the Death Penalty in Saudi Arabia

A death row inmate, Muhammad Ali al-Zahrani arranged for the marriage of his 15-year-old daughter to a prison cellmate, who also had been sentenced to death by beheading. The wedding took place in prison in the presence of prison officials. After the wedding, the groom, Awad al-Harbi, and his teenage bride were permitted to spend two nights together in special prison quarters. The couple's wedding pictures appeared in several newspapers, and the media reported on the ceremony. Al-Harbi later told the newspaper, *Al-Madina*, that his wife was pregnant. (*Hindustan Times*, 2009a).

Ethiopia

Underage marriage is typically illegal worldwide, but in rural areas such as Ethiopia it is difficult to maintain an awareness of these illegal, but cultural, events. "Child marriages are prevalent in rural regions; Amhara, where Yinsa is located, has the highest rate in Ethiopia. About 40 percent of the girls are married by 15 or younger" (Wilson, 2007). The cultural belief in Ethiopia is that "early marriage ensures that a girl hasn't had sex before marriage with a boy or man who does not meet the family's approval. Once a girl loses her virginity, it is virtually impossible to find a man who will marry her" (Wilson, 2007). A woman who is sexually active before marriage is seen as unclean and unwanted. Though the reason given for underage marriages may seem harmless and relevant to the Ethiopian cultural belief of sexual purity, early marriage undercuts a young woman's possibilities in life. It introduces her early on to heavy workloads in the fields and at home, and to bearing children at an age when complications are more likely. "Girls who marry early are more likely to be abused and, these days, to be infected with HIV" (Wilson, 2007). Overworked children, women who are abused, and those who are infected with HIV all tend to be at a higher risk to die earlier than the average person.

United States

A prime example of religion used to inflict abuse was an incident that raised awareness about early forced marriage and the sexual abuse of young girls in the United States. In a high-profile case, authorities rescued numerous children from a polygamist sect of the Fundamentalist Church of Jesus Christ of Latter Day Saints (FLDS). The FLDS, a separatist body of the Mormon religion, was founded in 1935 when the practice of polygamy among members ended; yet members of the FLDS still practice plural marriages. In April 2008, Child Protective Services removed 52 girls, ages 6 months to 17 years, from a secretive religious retreat built by polygamist members. The investigation resulted from a complaint by a 16-year-old girl in which she reported physical abuse and forced marriage to a 50-year-old man. Although the Mormon Church renounced polygamy in 1890, it has continued to be practiced in secret. Charges filed against the leader of this sect included four counts of incest, sexual conduct with a minor, and serving as an accomplice in the rape of minor teenage girls by older men. Parents neglected more than 250 other children by failing to protect them from becoming future victims (Quest. Live. com/News4/5/2008). Warren Jeffs, one-time leader and self-proclaimed prophet of the group that created its own branch of religion from the mainstream FLDS, explained, "The church currently practices 'The Law of Placement' under which all marriages are assigned by the prophet of the church." Jeffs claimed to receive revelations from God "to put a woman with a particular man." However, these girls weren't yet women at all. Jeffs has been known to perform weddings in which girls as young as 14 were married to much older men. Because polygamy is illegal in the United States, marriages with underage persons are identified as sexual assault. To get around the requirement to register multiple marriages with the state and to therefore keep the plural marriage practice legal, "Typically, the husband will have only his first marriage registered with the state. Subsequent wives receive only a religious marriage that is not registered." Because consent cannot be given by underage girls, forced marriages are not legal, even for the religious purposes of 'multiplying and replenishing.' (op.cit.)

SATI PRATHA

Historically practiced, sati, also known as "widow burning," is the Hindu tradition whereby a widow immolates herself on her husband's funeral pyre. Women were expected to sit on the burning funeral pyre of their dead husband during cremation ceremonies. The meaning of the word *sati* is "virtuous women." As remarriages were not common in Hindu society (in fact, they were implicitly forbidden), some women preferred dying to remaining widowed. Some women who were deeply in love with their husbands also considered killing themselves at the time of their husband's death as a way to symbolize their love. A large number of women committed *sati* in a group in the aftermath of the Johar war in Rajasthan. These women died to protect their honor and to keep from being raped by the invading enemies after their men had perished on the battlefield (kamat.com, 2008). Sati is now rarely if ever practiced. If sati pratha should occur, it is attributed to the pressure of the dead husband's relatives. One case reported in 1987 in Rajasthan involved a well-educated young woman, 18-year-old Roop Kanwar. She was witnessed to have voluntarily, without "cries or shrieks," died on her husband's pyre, although they had only been married eight months (christianaggression. org, 2008). Another case was reported as recently as 2005 (NCRB, 2007a), and the latest was reported in 2006. Although practiced as early as the fourth century B.C., sati pratha was condemned by the British and declared illegal in 1829. The movement against sati pratha was headed by Raja Ram Mohan Rai and led to the ban on this tradition by the Commission of Sati (Prevention) Act in 1987 (inanswers.yahoo.com, 2008).

HONOR KILLING

The concept of honor and dignity are closely tied to the reputation of a man and his family. The victims of honor killing are, by and large, female. This is a murder sanctioned by social and cultural norms. It most often occurs when a woman of a particular community or religion marries a person of a different community or religion. The couple generally elopes to avoid the terror of nonconsenting parents, relatives, or the village folk of their community. When these couples are caught, they are usually brutally beaten or killed to prevent disgrace to the honor of their families. Many times these couples are unlawfully confined to keep them from meeting with each other. After the young woman is apprehended, she is often forced to marry a person from her own community. If she does not agree, she is assaulted and may be killed. Caste factors also play a large role. When people of the same castes are members of the police force, the investigating officer is of a different mindset to deal with such crimes. Numerous examples of honor killing can be found in many countries, including India, Pakistan, and Indonesia. In one incident, a 17-year-old girl who was forbidden to marry the boy of her choice eloped in another country. When the couple returned to their village, the girl's father, Nirmal Singh, would not accept the affair. In a fit of rage, he shot his daughter in the name of honor killing (*Hindustan Times*, 2009b). In a different incident, two girls were late returning home, and when they did return they were escorted by two boys. The family was outraged to the extent that the girls were beaten with sticks and ax handles. Realizing that the girls were near death, the family cremated them as the whole village watched. Although this incident occurred on October 28, 2008, no case was registered until November 11, 2008, as no one had complained to the police (*Hindustan Times*, 2008d). Similarly, two other girls were fatally shot by a male cousin in the city of Noida for attempting to meet their boyfriends. The cousin who killed the girls had become enraged when he discovered their plan (*Hindustan Times*, 2008e).

SIRI

The concept of one's honor and dignity and that of the family's reputation is known as *ripakasiri*, commonly referred to as *siri* in Indonesia. If someone causes the loss of siri (loss of honor or dignity), the victim is considered useless or worthless if he does not redeem his siri against the person responsible. According to customary law (adat), that person and his family are obliged to restore their siri through execution by violent means. Usually the person does this by killing the opponent. This type of crime is prevalent among the Buginese-Makassarese society in Sulawesi, Indonesia. Ripakasiri is a socially accepted form of revenge for the elopement of a girl with a boy, rape, sexual harassment, or homicide. In the Mandarese community, touching the head of another person may amount to one's loss of siri and may result in criminal violence against the offender (Mustofa, 2008).

Blind Superstition, Rampant Illiteracy
TANTRIKS AND WITCHCRAFT

In Asia, a tantrik is a man who is usually associated with black magic and practices of the occult. These men are known for their superstitious rituals. *Tantriks* are often called on to free a person who is "possessed." They are similar to "exorcists" in the Western culture. According to Aderinto and Akinwale (2008), anthropologists have discovered many different traditions involving three entities thought to be used in controlling the world: religion (the supernatural), magic (the unnatural), and science (the natural). When these entities become commingled, their complete separation seems impossible. Many incurable diseases are thought to be the result of a number of false beliefs, including the existence of ghosts and bad souls. Certain cultures believe that the root cause of every bad event is a ghost. Although tantriks and witches claim to cure the evil effects of ghosts, they often inflict severe physical damage or death in the process. Furthermore, they give false hope of bringing the dead back to life (Dainik Jagran, 2009) (Fig. 40-2).

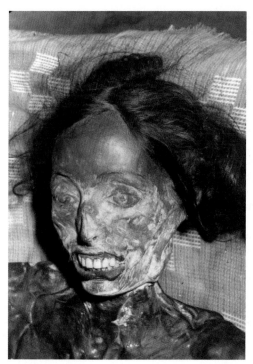

Fig. 40-2 Mummification with well preserved features leading family to believe that the woman was not actually dead.

Case Study 40-4

Spiritual Coma

Gorea (2008) reported a case in which a woman died as a result of gastroenteritis and was declared dead. Relatives were not satisfied regarding the cause of death, since the doctor was young and looked inexperienced. They took the body to a private doctor who was not a qualified professional but a nonregistered practitioner. This practitioner said that the decedent was not dead but rather was in a spiritual coma. He advised them to take her to a tantrik, who gave them a bottle of water and advised them to give her a teaspoonful of this water every 12 hours and she would recover. Placing the body in a well-ventilated room with heaters around it, relatives followed the instructions. With the disappearance of rigor mortis, some water went inside the decedent's mouth and the relatives thought the water was showing good effects. Because of the excessive heat and good ventilation, the body mummified and features were well preserved. People in the area learned of this event and came to see the mummified body, considering it a miracle. They began offering prayers, money, and other articles to the family. This continued for two years until there was a dispute among the family members over sharing the decedent's money. At that point, a member of the family complained to the police and the incident came to light. Only at the time of the postmortem examination was it explained to the relatives that the decedent's body had been mummified and that the event was not a miracle. This is one more example of how tantriks manipulate the emotions of the people who believe in them.

Witchcraft is illegal in Saudi Arabia. Fawza Falih, an illiterate woman, was detained by Saudi religious police in 2006 and allegedly beaten and forced to fingerprint a confession that she could not read. The woman was tried for the undefined crime of witchcraft and was found guilty and sentenced to death. Beheading is the customary method of execution. Her conviction was based on the written statements of witnesses who said that she had bewitched them. Her accuser was a man who alleged she made him impotent. The United States–based Human Rights Watch group described the trial and conviction as a miscarriage of justice, stating that Falih had exhausted all chances of appealing against her death sentence and could only be saved if King Abdullah intervened. The Saudi ruler, King Abdulla, has been asked to void Falih's conviction and to bring charges against the religious police who detained her and are alleged to have mistreated her. Human Rights Watch said that the trial failed to meet the safeguards in the Saudi justice system. The confession that the defendant was forced to fingerprint was not even read out to her, the group said. Also, Falih and her representatives were not allowed to attend most of the hearings. When an appeals court decided she should not be executed, the law courts imposed the death sentence again, arguing that it would be in the public interest (BBC News, February 14, 2008). As of January 2009, Fawza Falih's status and whereabouts are unknown.

Religious and Therapy-Related Death
FAITH AND MEDICINE COLLIDE
Faith Healing

The term "faith healing" refers to the healing that occurs supernaturally—as the result of prayer rather than the use of medicine or involvement of physicians or other healthcare. Although some healings occur, the teachings of some churches, movements and individuals amount to spiritual abuse. Other legitimate churches do not consider use of drugs or proper medical attention with unbelief, insufficient faith or sin against God. (ReligionNewsBlog.com) (Item 20974, March 27, 2008)

The unacceptable cost of religious superstition is not limited to Asia and the Middle East. It is estimated that every month between one and five children die alone in the United States because of the religious superstitions of their parents or guardians. Concerned legislators are trying to change the laws that allow this assault on children and are calling for an end to the religious exemptions that promote this type of deadly superstition. Do healthcare professionals have a responsibility to protect children from this category of irreversible catastrophes brought on by superstition and religion? Who is responsible? Cases exemplifying the rationale for legislative changes include the death of Harrison Johnson in September of 1998. Harrison was stung by more than 430 yellow jackets. His parents, who believed in faith healing, prayed for him for seven hours before calling for medical help. Harrison died. His parents' actions are legal in the state of Florida where this occurred and are also legal in 45 other states. The only states that do not permit lack of medical treatment for religious reasons are Hawaii, Maryland, Massachusetts, and South Dakota. Amy Hermanson from Sarasota, Florida, had diabetes and was visibly sick for a period of four weeks. Amy's mother, a practitioner of faith healing, took Amy to visit a neighbor who encouraged her to take Amy to a doctor. She refused. Amy died a few days later. In a different incident, Ian Lundman from Minnesota also suffered from both diabetes and faith healing. Minnesota is one of the 46 states where it legal for religious beliefs to embrace faith healing. Caleb Tribble was only four months old when he became a casualty of religious ignorance in New Zealand (www.deism.com/harrison.htm).

Case Study 40-5

"Children Don't Often Die Like This in the U.S." (Omar Ali, 2008)

In Weston, Wisconsin 11-year-old Madeline Kara Neumann died of diabetic ketoacidosis, a treatable though serious condition of type 1 diabetes. The parents didn't take her to a doctor. They prayed for healing. The common course of medical treatment for the disease involves injections of insulin and intravenous fluids, said Omar Ali, assistant professor of pediatric endocrinology at the Medical College of Wisconsin in Wauwatosa. "A fatal outcome would be unusual these days in the United States," Ali said. The death of the girl has raised profound moral and legal questions over when medicine should trump faith, especially when the life of a child is at stake. Parents told the Associated Press that the family does not belong to any organized religion or faith but believes in the Bible and said that healing comes from God. For religious reasons, the family would not take the child to the hospital. During an interview with detectives, the parents mentioned that they believed that with enough faith and prayer that God would heal her.

A report noted that the parents said it was the course of action they would take again. "They firmly believe even if they had taken her to a doctor, if this was the time God had chosen for her to die, she would die regardless of medical interference" (*Milwaukee Journal-Sentinel*, March 26, 2008).

Parents Dale and Leilani Neumann were each charged with reckless homicide in connection with the death of Madeline Kara Neumann on March 23, 2008. Prosecutors say the Neumanns chose to pray for their daughter's recovery rather than treat her diabetes. The Neumanns have argued that their right to religious freedom means they cannot be prosecuted under current state law (Starck, *J. Wausau Daily Herald*, March 21, 2009).

These deaths pose difficult issues about the relationship of religious beliefs and medical intervention and the role of parents in assuming responsibility for the health and welfare of their children. Police and courts have grappled with such issues for decades.

Therapy for the Soul

A report of death regarding a case of paralysis involved a poor villager in India. In this case, a tantrik claimed to have special powers of healing and said he could cure the paralysis. In order for him to be treated, the family members were instructed to bring the patient to the home of the tantrik on a Thursday night. After arrival, the patient was laid on the floor of the house, and amidst prayers the tantrik started beating the patient with a rod. During this torture, the tantrik's son and another tantrik follower held the patient's arms and legs. When the patient's son asked the tantrik to stop, he was also beaten for interfering in the works of the God. Escaping, the patient's son informed other villagers. When the villagers came to the tantrik's house, they observed that the patient had died (Dainik Jagran, 2009). Tantriks claim that to cure the disease, they must beat the *bad soul* residing inside the body (the cause of the disease) and ask the bad soul to leave. Thus, the pain and torture is inflicted on the bad soul and not on the patient. Unfortunately, the patient was now dead.

Attachment Therapy

Comparable to the previous case are the reported cases in the United States of religious exorcism practices. In one case a psychotherapist, using a method know as *rebirthing*, wrapped a victim tightly in a sheet for this purpose; the victim later died from asphyxia. On August 22, 2003, an autistic 8-year-old boy in Milwaukee was bound in sheets and held down by church members during a prayer service to exorcise the evil spirits they blamed for his condition. An autopsy found extensive bruising on the back of the child's neck and concluded that he died of asphyxiation. Since the late 1990s, there have been at least four other exorcism-related deaths in the United States alone, and two of the victims were children. Then there are several tragic cases like that of Texas mother Andrea Yates, who drowned three of her five children in 2001 to exorcise the devil from herself. More recently, a South African couple was arrested for keeping their 15-month-old daughter caged, unfed, and tied up because they believed the child was possessed.

Rebirthing

In 2000, the death of a North Carolina girl, Candace Newmaker, during a "two-week intensive" in attachment therapy (AT), was a result of "rebirthing." She was sent to Colorado on the advice of attachment therapists operating in North Carolina. The 10-year-old girl died from asphyxiation during a "rebirthing" session during which she pleaded for her life, but the five adults in the room, including her adoptive mother, a pediatric nurse at Duke University in Durham, disregarded her screams. There is a dearth of scientific evidence that AT is effective in any way for positive change in the behavior of children. Many professional organizations around the United States, however, deem its procedures—irrespective of rebirthing—as abusive to the children forced to endure it. The use of restraint in rebirthing is considered dangerous. Activists working to ban restraint as psychotherapy in Utah and elsewhere have a website (www.kidscomefirst.info) that now includes a film clip demonstration of "holding therapy" (Science in the News, 2003).

Socially Unacceptable Behavior

CORPORAL PUNISHMENT

Corporal punishment refers to the use of physical punishment to correct behavior. The term derives from the Latin *corpus*, meaning "body." In educational institutions throughout the Asian subcontinent, particularly in India, there has long been a trend whereby students are physically punished if they do not conform to set social behavior or do not do their homework properly. The punishment varies from physical abuse to psychological abuse. Because of the uncontrollable anger of some teachers, this practice has often resulted in injuries and death. Children even younger than 3 years old are not immune to corporal punishment. One head teacher beat a small child for weeping over something the child did not like (Amar Ujala, 2007a). Sometimes children cannot tolerate these actions and try to commit suicide. In one case, a girl jumped into a river in an attempt to kill herself (Amar Ujala, 2007b).

Numerous cases of sexual harassment of girl students by teachers have been reported. In one school, many girls alleged that a particular drawing teacher was sexually harassing them, and they refused to go to school (*The Tribune*, 2007a). One girl accused a teacher of raping her (*The Tribune*, 2007b). Gorea et al. (2002) have maintained that teachers punish erring students both physically and mentally for personal satisfaction stemming from issues of control. In described injuries in two cases of corporal punishment in schools, the researchers discovered another six cases of punishment in their school study area. They are of the opinion that these actions must be stopped to let the youth of India mature to adulthood without excessive pressure and punishment from educators. As Gorea and colleagues continued to raise their voices against corporal punishment in schools through newspapers and conferences, their efforts have successfully resulted in a ban on corporal punishment in schools by the high court in India (*The Tribune*, 2000). Schoolteachers have been suspended or dismissed from service for beating students since the ban was enacted. In Haryana, one of the Indian states, eight teachers were suspended after being charged with sexually harassing girl students (Haryana Bureau, 2007). In India, many people have often considered corporal punishment as part of life. Parents have even asked teachers to be stern and to discipline their children by slapping them if they did not behave properly or do their work (Singh, 2007). According to the Raghvan committee, corporal punishment in schools was a contributory factor in the development of bullying tactics and ragging tendencies among students as per the observation of the Supreme Court of India (*The Tribune*, 2007c).

The National Commission for Protection of Child Rights (NCPCR) has included slapping, beating with a ruler, pinching, locking a student alone in a room, making a student sit like a chair or kneeling down, and making a child run in the school as means of corporal punishment. This national ban has given a warning to teachers and forbids them from inflicting these practices (*The Tribune*, 2007d). According to Gracia and Herrero (2008), we will have to challenge the beliefs that led to the corporal punishment of children. Forensic nurse examiners can diagnose the problem and make the public aware of the maltreatment of children in schools. They can also contribute by educating the public about this problem.

Case Study 40-7

School Crimes

Rinki Kaushik, a 15-year-old class X student, was hit on the head by her teacher; as a result, she slipped into a coma that lasted more than a month. The girl had attended this school for three years; the teacher, Dhirendra Dinkar, the son of the school principal, had initiated tutoring classes during free periods for a fee. The girl had enrolled in these classes to improve her ability to do well on board exams. However, she discontinued a few days later, complaining that the tutor was not explaining basic concepts. Instead, she enrolled in a tutoring center but complained of severe pain in her head. After the pain became worse and was interfering with her eyesight, Rinki told how a teacher had struck her on the head several times with a stick in retaliation for having dropped out of his classes. Rinki had fainted after the thrashing and as she regained consciousness, Dinkar threatened her with dire consequences if she related the incident to anyone. Rinki was first taken to a private hospital and later was moved to a public hospital because her parents could not afford private healthcare. As her condition steadily deteriorated she slipped into a coma and died. (*Times of India*, 2008).

Discipline in Europe

The infliction of physical pain as an official means of punishment is as old as human history. As an officially administered or sanctioned method of enforcing discipline, corporal punishment is virtually declining. Despite persistent enthusiasm for physical chastisement among significant sections of the population, social scientists are virtually unanimous in arguing that corporal punishment has more negative than positive effects. The issue of corporal punishment must now be considered in light of the Human Rights Act 1998 and the European Convention on Human Rights, particularly Article 3 on protection against torture, inhuman or degrading treatment or punishment. The provisions of the Convention of the Rights of the Child 1989 is also important in relation to child punishment; as Article 19 states: "Parties shall take all appropriate legislative, administrative, social and educational measures to protect the child from all forms of physical or mental violence, injury or abuse, neglect or negligent treatment, maltreatment or exploitation." Corporal punishment remains legal when used by parents. Since 1860, parents have been permitted to use "reasonable chastisement" on their children, and this remains the case today, except in Scotland, which has legislated to ban parental corporal punishment. In 1995, the Committee on the Rights of the Child, after examining the United Kingdom's first report under the UN Convention on the Rights of the Child, recommended that corporal punishment in the family should be prohibited and criticized the existence of the defense of "reasonable chastisement." Following the 1997 case of *A v. UK* (United Kingdom) in the European Court of Human Rights, which found that the defense of "reasonable chastisement" did not provide sufficient protection for the rights of the child, the government promised a review. Despite persistent public enthusiasm for corporal punishment, no mainstream political party in the United Kingdom appears intent on reversing the trend of the past 50 years. In the United Kingdom, legislation prohibiting corporal punishment does not apply to the home or to some alternative care settings. It was not until 1998 that corporal punishment was outlawed for the few remaining independent schools that retained the practice.

Sex Discrimination

Early moves to ban teachers from "giving girls the belt" at school were thwarted by sex discrimination laws, newly released government papers reveal. National Archives of Scotland documents also show that Scottish education officials feared a move to ban the belt altogether would be met with "violent opposition" from teachers. The documents, dating from the late 1970s–10 years before the belt was banned–were kept secret for 30 years and reveal that sex discrimination laws of the time prevented a reprieve from corporal punishment for girls. Although it was eventually banned in 1987, early moves to outlaw the punishment more than a decade earlier met with massive opposition from government officials. A possible ban was proposed in a House of Lords private members' bill. However, despite the fact that the then Secretary of State for Scotland, Bruce Millan, believed it was not an appropriate punishment for girls, new sex discrimination legislation of the time prevented ministers from changing the law. Scotland's secretary of state did not agree with corporal punishment for girls but could not say so because of the sex discrimination. A letter from the Scottish Education Department dated July 8, 1977, explained the problem:

> Education authorities must comply with the Sex Discrimination Act 1975. Any rules which provide that boys should receive corporal punishment where girls do not would be illegal. Government ministers did not want to have the subject of corporal punishment in schools raised in debate and therefore decided that rules relating to the corporal punishment of children should not be exempted. The Secretary of State for Scotland did not agree with corporal punishment for girls but could not say so because of the Sex Discrimination Act. The Secretary of State felt strongly that girls of any age should not receive corporal punishment.

An earlier memo from the Scottish Education Department, dated November 19, 1973, states the government's view on corporal punishment in general, "There does not appear to be any good reason for a switch of policy in this matter. The desirability of eventually eliminating corporal punishment is generally accepted and there has been a gradual reduction in its use." However, there is no evidence of a widespread demand among education authorities, parents, or others that it should be summarily stopped.

Rights of the Child

Numerous human rights bodies, including the UN Committee on the Rights of the Child, have made it clear that corporal punishment of children breaches children's fundamental human rights to respect for their dignity and physical integrity. This reality provides an immediate imperative for ending the practice. While speaking at the launch of the Council of Europe's initiative against corporal punishment, Mieke Schuurman, secretary general of the European Children's Network said, "Much work still needs to be done to make Europe a corporal punishment free zone for children. Research into the harmful physical and psychological effects of corporal punishment, into the relative significance of links with other forms of violence, in childhood and later life, add further compelling arguments for condemning and ending the practice, suggesting that it is an essential strategy for reducing all forms of violence, in childhood and later life" (Politics.co.uk, 2008). The issue of corporal punishment must now be considered in light of the Human Rights Act 1998 and the European Convention of Human Rights, particularly Article 3 on protection against torture, inhuman or degrading treatment or punishment. The provisions of the Convention of the Rights of the Child 1989 is also important for child punishment; as Article 19 states: "Parties shall take all appropriate legislative, administrative, social and educational measures to protect the child from all forms of physical or mental violence, injury or abuse, neglect or negligent treatment, maltreatment or exploitation." Fortunately, as an officially administered or sanctioned method of enforcing discipline, corporal punishment is in virtually terminal decline. States with full prohibition of corporal punishment in legislation, where it is prohibited in the home, in schools, in alternative care settings, and in the penal system both as a sentence for crime and as a disciplinary measure, are Austria, Bulgaria, Chile, Croatia, Cyprus, Denmark, Finland, Germany, Greece, Hungary, Iceland, Israel, Latvia, Netherlands, New Zealand, Norway, Portugal, and Romania.

Hazing

Any activity expected of someone joining a group (or to maintain full status in a group) that humiliates, degrades, or risks emotional or physical harm, regardless of the person's willingness to participate, is referred to as hazing. Activities generally involve a school, sports team, military unit, or organization. Hazing is illegal. Three categories of hazing have been recognized: subtle hazing, harassment hazing, and violent hazing. However, hazing behavior that is degrading, embarrassing, or causes an injury is illegal. Military hazing is defined as any conduct whereby a military member (or members), regardless of service or rank, without proper authority, causes another member to suffer or be exposed to any activity that is cruel, abusive, humiliating, oppressive, demeaning, or harmful. Soliciting or coercing another to perpetrate such activity is considered hazing. It need not involve physical contact among military members; it can be verbal or psychological in nature. Actual or implied consent to acts of hazing does not eliminate the culpability of the perpetrator. Because of the number of injuries and deaths that have resulted from hazing behavior, 42 U.S. states have outlawed hazing (www.stophazing.org/definition.html, 2009). U.S. federal attention has recognized the problems associated with hazing, and the judiciary committee is reviewing drafts that would criminalize hazing and put mandates on universities. These laws are being tested in the courts, and litigations have jolted the financial foundation of national fraternities, resulting in an insurance crisis. Subservience, ridicule, verbal abuse, intimidation, sleep deprivation, forced calisthenics, and unfair tests are all forms of hazing and should be reported. No one should have to compromise his or her dignity to belong to any group. If you are allowing yourself to be hazed, or looking the other way when someone else is being hazed, you are enabling this ugly practice to continue and jeopardizing the emotional and physical well-being of others. The media continues to report the hard truth, abuses, indignities, injuries, and fatalities, 80 in the past decade) associated with hazing. Even seemingly harmless activities have led to problem situations. Most reported hazing incidents involve alcohol.

Ragging

Another form of hazing known as ragging has been an accepted norm for new entrants in Indian schools and colleges for many decades. Students have been asked to act out odd behaviors such as singing, acting, and doing menial jobs. They have even been asked to appear naked in front of others. This also included sexual harassment of the girl and boy students. Those students who failed to perform this nonsense were beaten. Some students who could not bear the humiliation have committed suicide. To reduce the menace of ragging, the Supreme Court of India issued an order making institutional authorities responsible for failing to take action against students indulging in ragging (*The Tribune*, 2007c). Because most cases of hazing/ragging take place on educational campuses or on military bases, forensic nurse examiners are in a position to recognize, document, and report injuries or resulting deaths to the proper authorities. Prevention education programs and explanations of laws should be included in all orientation programs involving any groups at risk for these illegal activities.

Circulating Indecent Multimedia Messaging Services

Multimedia messaging service (MMS) has changed the way society communicates through the world of advancing technology. However, MMS has also provided another way to abuse women. With the advent of photo-capable mobile phones, it has been reported that an increasing number of men are using this technology to sexually harass women. Females are lured into compromising sexual situations by young men who take insulting photographs without permission and then pass them on to other men via MMS circulation. The resulting humiliation has caused victims to experience severe anguish, sometimes resulting in suicides. In one case, a fellow student who had promised marriage raped his female classmate after she had consumed a cup of tea laced with drugs and became unconscious. This rape was recorded via MMS and posted on the Internet. When the girl became aware of what had happened, she jumped from the roof of a high building, dying from the injuries (Bhaskar, 2008). In a different case, Singh (2009) reported that another schoolgirl was lured into indecent sexual acts by a boy she loved who also made MMS photos. Later, he circulated them to the girl's classmates when she refused his overtures for sexual favors again. Teenagers who send indecent photographs of themselves electronically—often called "sexting" if it is done via cell phone—are often under the impression that the photos will remain private. Recent distribution of such photographs taken and sent with cell phones in the United States has created a serious criminal charge, against both those sending and receiving the photos. Some prosecutors have begun charging teens that send and receive such images with child pornography and other serious felonies ("Sexting," 2009).

Case Study 40-8

"Sexting" or Child Porn?

A 14-year-old girl in New Jersey has been accused of child pornography and distribution after posting almost 30 explicit nude photos of herself on MySpace.com. The case results from a nationwide effort of prosecutors to pursue child pornography cases involving kids who have sent nude photos over cell phones and e-mail. Legal experts cannot recall a case of child porn that resulted from a teen posting to a social networking site. If convicted of distribution, she would be forced to register with the state as a sex offender under Megan's law and could face from 1 to 7 years in jail. Some observers and legislators have criticized the trend of prosecuting teens who send sexually explicit text messages or post illicit photos of themselves, stating that these teens need help such as counseling and intervention, not legal trouble (*National News*, March 26, 2009.aol.com).

Circulating Indecent SNS

Social networking sites (SNS) such as MySpace and Facebook have reported similar incidents ranging from photographs to blatant lies. In the United States, social networking sites have been blamed for numerous offenses, fairly and unfairly, but in public opinion, the worst offense has been their indirect involvement in suicides. Many factors are responsible in each case, but there does seem to be links between social networking and a rash of suicides, including the tragic case of Megan Meier, who killed herself after a classmate's mom impersonated a teen boy and harassed her over MySpace. The company has a team to review its network for inappropriate images and content. The teenage habit of "sexting" by cell phone is a nationwide problem that has confounded parents, school administrators, and law enforcers. In one case, Anthony

Stanci, an 18-year-old high school student from Wisconsin, allegedly posed as a girl online in order to fool at least 31 male classmates into sending him naked photos or videos of themselves. Authorities stated he used the images to blackmail some of them in exchange for sex acts. Prosecutors in Pennsylvania, Connecticut, North Dakota, Ohio, Utah, Vermont, Virginia, and Wisconsin have tried to stop such consequences by charging teens who send and receive these photos. "Unfortunately, youths do not have the same judgment as adults and often, adults don't have the same technical savvy as youths," according to Attorney General Milgram of New Jersey (AOL News, March 28, 2009).

Custodial Torture

The interrogation of individuals accused of a crime often constitutes torture. The state police, often an arm of the government, do not use scientific methods. They use means of torture to evoke the desired confessions from the accused. Forced confession by torture is not uncommon in India. Custodial torture is considered to be an assault on a person, though it is not qualified as a specific crime under the current domestic legislations in India. In May of 2008, newspapers reported acts of torture against three minors in Surat who were arrested for allegedly stealing money. The police officials responsible were later suspended, however (Saiyed, 2009). In September 2005, an individual who was arrested for causing a disturbance in a public place while drinking complained that he was beaten by three police officials who used a wooden stick, belt, and patta to beat him (timesofindia, 2009). The People Vigilance Committee on Human Rights have documented 800 cases of police torture in six districts of the Upper Pradish of India alone (mynews.in, 2009). Abichandani, a court justice in India (2009) believes that torture is an attack on human dignity. He is of the view that that there should be custodial dignity without custodial cruelty. Abichandani has documented seven cases of custodial torture, out of which five individuals died as a result of custodial torture or custodial negligence. According to Basu (1997), custodial torture is a grievous violation of an individual's human dignity and a degradation that, to a large extent, destroys the human personality.

In 1975, the International Council of Nurses (ICN) adopted a resolution on the "Role of the Nurse in the care of Detainees and Prisoners." This document provides an ethical framework for nurses who work in custodial settings.

KEY POINT Forensic nurses fill an important role in combating acts of custodial torture by effectively documenting all injuries when they recognize such cases.

Reports of abuse or misconduct should be made to a higher authority than the investigating agencies that have inflicted these injuries. For forensic nurse examiners (FNEs), documentation must remain independent and unbiased. The FNE documenting the injuries must know what constitutes torture by legal definition; regulations on methods of interrogation for detainees or prisoners at risk; and the characteristic of torture-related trauma. FNEs documenting these injuries must not be swayed by their emotions or accept explanations of the custodial agency without suspicion (Gorea, 2000). Gorea further described the role of FNEs as protectors of human rights by detecting the violations in unannounced visits to centers of detention such as police stations, jails, and prisons. As sexual assault nurse examiners are experts in detecting and documenting sexual violence, they are able to perform forensic examinations that will provide vital evidence, in cases of sexual assault involving victims in custody.

Societal Discrimination

COMMUNAL RIOTS

Because of differences in religious beliefs and political thoughts, people become intolerant of religious practices other than their own and instigate minor or major provocations that result in conflict and rioting. Communal riots are the product of incentives at the state and the local level; political or sociological factors increase the likelihood of violence. Often electoral competition is most intense when it involves "parties that represent elites within ethnic groups." These parties may use antiminority protests, demonstrations, and physical attacks that precipitate riots to "encourage members of their wider ethnic category to identify with their party and the 'majority' identity rather than a party that is identified with economic redistribution or some ideological agenda" (Wilkinson, 2005). The suburbs of Paris, France, have been ravaged with rioting by, for the most part, Muslim youth, causing the government to impose curfews. During the violence, more than 5000 vehicles were torched, 77 police officers were injured, and 1285 people were arrested. Police departments mobilized 9500 officers, and concerns have been raised about police and community relations. Emergency law imposed curfews in the "Cites," as the suburban housing projects are called; once a godsend, these areas have fallen into disrepair, adding to the racial tensions and unemployment of the mostly immigrant populations that live there. Members of the Muslim group *Tabligh* have been fanning out across the suburbs of Paris at night, calming violent youth. The violent riots by young people highlight a problem with the integration of Muslim immigrants, which is also apparent in the United Kingdom as well as Germany. In Kerala, India, clashes between two communities (Hindus and Muslims) erupted over the question of eve teasing, a form of sexual harassment. The whole region was gripped in violence. In another case, religious conflicts caused a mosque near Ambedkar Chowk to be damaged by a rampaging mob that pulled down portions of another mosque. A house belonging to a cleric behind the mosque was set on fire (www.sacw.net/2002/EngineerJan03.html, January 28, 2009).

CASTE CONFLICTS AND SEGREGATION

The caste system has historically existed in the Indian society. Some castes consider themselves superior to others. Conflicts between different castes occur for a variety of reasons. If a boy of lower caste marries a girl of higher caste, it becomes unacceptable to the upper caste family. In this process, they will attack members of other communities, frequently causing serious injuries and deaths. When members of different races mutually prefer to associate and do business with members of their own race, it is usually described as *separation* or *de facto separation* of the races rather than segregation. The influence of the caste system in India is now weakening since it "officially" ended with Indian independence. As a product of the Aryan migration of 1500 B.C.E., it was utilized to control the indigenous population. Society was divided into five groups, and it was a tenet of Hinduism that the only way to advance to a higher group was to live an exemplary life, following the rules of the caste into which you were born. Perhaps, in your next incarnation, you may experience rebirth into a higher caste. At the top of the system were the Brahmins. These were the priests and scholars. Next down the social scale were the Kshatriyas, the rulers and warriors, followed by merchants and tradesmen, called Vaishyas. Lower on the ladder were the Shudras, the peasants. The lowest of society were the "out-castes," those without a caste, also known as the "untouchables." Built into the Hindu religion was the belief that you simply did not associate with people of a lower caste. Vaishyas stood aside on the road whenever a Brahmin walked by, not even letting their shadows get in the way of the person of higher caste.

United States

Western knowledge of the caste system was prevalent enough that in New England the term "Boston Brahmin" became synonymous with wealthy, upper-class society. Although modern Westerners are amazed at such beliefs, it must be remembered that in pre-Civil War America, religion was used to enforce a similar pattern of social behavior between people of different races. As Westerners first discovered its existence, during British colonial expansion, there seemed to be a direct correlation between skin color and caste ranking—"the lighter the skin, the higher the caste". It is hard not to infer that it represented a system of domination by people of white skin who used religion to enforce imposed racism. In the United States, racism remains an unresolved issue in spite of the legal end of racial segregation. Before the civil rights movement, segregation referred to the separation of different racial groups, commonly applied in situations such as eating in a restaurant, drinking from a water fountain, using a restroom, attending school, being admitted to hospitals, going to the movies, or renting or purchasing a home. Segregation was mandated by law and social norms. Segregation in hiring practices contributes to economic imbalance between the races. However, segregation allowed a person of one race to work as a servant for a member of another race. Segregation was maintained by means of discrimination in hiring and in the rental and sale of housing to certain races. It was also enforced with vigilante violence (such as lynchings). In the United States, legal segregation was required in some states, and it came with antimiscegenation laws (prohibitions against interracial marriage, also prohibited in the apartheid era of South Africa). There were laws passed against segregation in the United States in the 1960s.

South Africa

Certainly, during the era of apartheid in South Africa, the indigenous people of origin were categorized as white, colored (mixed although primarily Indian), or black. Apartheid is identified as a crime by international law. The 2002 Rome Statute of the International Criminal Court (which established the International Criminal Court) defined the crime of apartheid as inhumane acts of a character similar to other crimes against humanity "committed in the context of an institutionalized regime of systematic oppression and domination by one racial group over any other racial group or groups and committed with the intention of maintaining that regime." It lists such crimes as murder, enslavement, deprivation of physical liberty, forced relocation, sexual violence, and collective persecution (United Nations, 2002). On November 30, 1973, the United Nations General Assembly opened for signature and ratification the International Convention on the Suppression and Punishment of the Crime of Apartheid (ICSPCA) (United Nations, 2006). It defined the crime of apartheid as "inhuman acts committed for the purpose of establishing and maintaining domination by one racial group of persons over any other racial group of persons and systematically oppressing them."

REGIONAL CONFLICTS

People from one region sometimes grow intolerant of people from other regions because they believe that the others are they taking away their chances of obtaining jobs. Many times politicians run systematic hate campaigns that result in clashes and death. The

Supreme Court of India took *suo motto* notice of such hate campaigns and asked the government of Maharashtra to take action after one north Indian was killed in the train station and another person was fatally shot. Shortly after this incident, two Indian doctors were also killed by a hate-angered mob (*Hindustan Times*, 2008g). Riots and civil unrest are common in many countries for similar reasons. New York City, Los Angeles, and Miami have experienced severe riots related to race, religion, and political conflicts.

CRIMES OF THE RICH AND POWERFUL

It has been observed that individuals who are wealthy or have political influence often gain special status and are difficult to prosecute. This may be due to intricate weaknesses in the social system. When investigating officers come from the same social strata as the wealthy, justice becomes difficult for both witnesses and victims. One example of this form of injustice involves a German mother who requested that charges against two men accused of assaulting her daughter be withdrawn. These men were the son and nephew of Goa government ministers who were very rich. The mother believed she would never be able to get justice for her daughter and complained that her life had become hell after filing the complaint (*Hindustan Times*, 2008g, 2008h). The mother of a victim of gang rape experienced the same difficulties with the accused, who were closely associated with a local member of the Haryana legislative assembly (*Hindustan Times*, 2008i). Another example concerns the alleged killing of an engineer by a local Member of Legislative Assembly (MLA) of the Uttar Pradesh (UP) state in India. The MLA demanded 5 million rupees as a gift for the chief minister's birthday party, which the engineer refused. He was severely beaten and later died as a result of the 32 sharp injuries to his body, as well as being subjected to electric shocks. The postmortem examination indicated the cause of death was brain hemorrhage resulting from the injuries (*Hindustan Times*, 2008j). Although the United States does not recognize the now illegal system of caste as India does, there appears to be a system of discrimination and classism in the United States that would rival that of the subcontinent. However, caste—although outlawed by the British over a hundred years ago and condemned by Gandhi in this past century—still exists. Perhaps it is a less dramatic classism that pits the wealthy against the poor in America, but it remains a crime against those in poverty or those who are unfortunate enough to be caught between the wealthy and the poor.

Forbidden Behavior
HUMAN SACRIFICE (NARBALI)

Sacrifices are carried out to please particular gods or a deity of a certain sect and to seek favor or blessings for a desired goal. Usually the objects of sacrifices are animals, but on occasion a human being may be sacrificed for the god's blessing or to please the soul of a dead person. Human sacrifice was common during the days when kings ruled and offered money or land to the family of the person who volunteered to be sacrificed. Human sacrifice, once thought to be eliminated, still occurs. Police may come across a crime scene where circumstances suggest that human sacrifice has been performed, although the scene may suggest otherwise. Dan McDougall (2006) reported other examples involving blind superstitions and rampant illiteracy. According to police in Khurja, India, dozens of sacrifices had been reported over a six-month period. In a case that occurred in a village near Barha, a woman killed and dismembered her neighbor's 3-year-old child after a tantrik promised her unlimited riches. In another case, a couple who had no son kidnapped a 6-year-old boy and mutilated him amid the chanting of mantras by a tantrik (the

practitioner of certain ancient religions) who told them they would then gain a son. The ritual was completed by washing in the child's blood. According to an unofficial tally by the local newspaper, 28 human sacrifices in western Uttar Pradesh were reported during those six months. To curb such practices, four tantrik priests were jailed and scores of others forced to flee. John Lancaster, in an article on human sacrifice (*Hindustan Times*, 2003), mentioned that there have been 25 human sacrifices in western Uttar Pradesh in six months alone and police have cracked down against tantriks, jailing four and forcing scores of others to close their practices and to stop advertising in newspapers and on television. These killings focused renewed attention on *tantrism*, which is an amalgam of mysticism practices.

Milton Blahyi, a former feared rebel commander in Liberia's brutal civil war, admitted to taking part in human sacrifices that included killing a child and taking out the child's heart to eat it after dividing it among all present as a part of traditional ceremonies intended to ensure victory in battle (Paye-layleh, 2008). In Ireland, the decomposing remains of Paiche Unyolo Onyemaechi, daughter of Leonard Unyolo, Malawi's justice minister and a leading African politician, were found next to a stream close to the sleepy village of Piltown, Co Kilkenny. However, her head was not found with the remains, causing detectives to consider the possibility that this was a case of a human sacrifice in Ireland's first ritual or "muti" killing. Killing a person and consuming the body parts is not a common crime, but it is not unheard of. In 2008, many children were kidnapped and killed in the Indian city of Noida. Based on the circumstances of the crime scene, it appeared that the perpetrator sadistically enjoyed these killings (*Hindustan Times*, 2008f). After raping and killing the victims, he later returned to mutilate and eat certain body parts (breasts). The act was considered to be linked to human sacrifices (deccanherald.com, 2008).

MUTI MURDER

The sangoma or traditional healer (witchdoctor) in certain areas of Southern Africa prey on the superstition of ignorant villagers by selling a potion, or medicine (muti) that may require human flesh from a living victim for the customer to assume the good qualities of the murdered victim, most often a child. The customer may be required to produce the body parts or the sangoma may arrange for the recovery of specific materials. This practice is occasionally seen in present-day India, in sub-Saharan Africa, and in the immigrant African Diaspora (Jewish communities living outside the Holy Land) in Europe. Certain ethnic groups (Aztec) of Mexico also practiced human sacrifices (en.wikipedia.org, 2008). In an article titled "A Horrendous Trade, *The Economist* reported, "According to the Tanzanian Albino Society, at least 35 albinos were murdered in Tanzania last year, to supply witch doctors with limbs, organs, and hair for their potions." The article also noted that the murders have spread to nearby countries, including Kenya, Uganda, and Burundi. The witchdoctors have largely evaded punishment by using bribery or the threats of spells to avoid even being put on trial for their crimes. The story contains virtually everything wrong with humanity: superstition, hatred, and baseless fear compounded with savage violence and greed (Fig. 40-3 AB).

MEN AND HIV

Sexually-transmitted infections among Pakistani men have been responsible for indirectly encouraging homosexuality (*Indian Asian News Service*, July 22, 2009). Social taboos, which are also compounding the problem of controlling a raging HIV epidemic in Pakistan, are explored by Syed Ali and colleagues from Aga

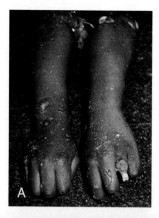

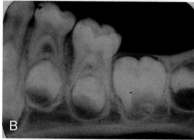

Fig. 40-3 *A,* Forearms of young child that were amputated for the purpose of creating muti. *B,* Dental X-ray indicating the presence of unerupted permanent teeth, suggesting that the child muti victim was 4-6 years of age.

Khan University, Karachi. According to this report, "in Pakistan, seven times more men are reported to be infected with HIV than women.... If unconfirmed reports are to be believed, the prevalence of HIV among homosexual and bisexual Pakistani men is reaching alarming proportions." Ali further asserted that for the most part, the sexual transmission of HIV has resulted from the failure to practice "safe sex" among heterosexual couples; homosexual and bisexual contact represents serious methods of transmission. Under Islamic tenets, sex of any kind, other that between husband and wife, is strictly forbidden. Homosexual behavior is stigmatized, discriminated against, ostracized, and can even be prosecuted (Indi-Asian News Service [AIMS], 2006). Most Pakistanis believe that HIV transmission through illicit sexual activity cannot be a problem in the Muslim world, yet statistics contradict this notion. Islam forbids all extramarital sex, particularly illicit sex among men who have *sex with men* (MSM), which serves to drive the behavior underground in a Muslim state. Education promoting safe sex is viewed as the equivalent of promoting sex and makes the MSM HIV epidemic even more difficult to control, especially among prisoners, migrants, truck drivers, and pederasts/pedophiles. These authors acknowledge that even relatively conservative countries such as India and Bangladesh have begun to address the HIV prevention more openly. "In Pakistan, however, sociocultural and religious taboos hamper recognition of HIV/AIDS as a sexually transmitted disease and limit discussion on sexual health," the authors concluded. This study appeared in the August edition of *The Lancet Journal of Infectious Diseases,* a special edition devoted to HIV on the eve of the forthcoming world HIV conference in Mexico. With government or privately funded sexual assault clinics, such as in South Africa where forensic nurses are employed, confidential treatment and education could significantly reduce the spread of HIV and AIDS.

Superstitions and Negative Myths
SOCIAL TABOOS

Shocking and bizarre customs are practiced throughout the world ("Taboos," 2008b). Whereas some traditional rituals and behaviors are acceptable in some cultures, they are illegal, forbidden, or reviled in others. We examine some of these social taboos in the following sections.

IN THE NAME OF GOD

Certain individuals possess the capacity to experience serious pain and suffering based on religious beliefs. Their suffering is endured specifically to please certain gods as these individuals hope to receive something in return, for the community or for themselves. Historically, this willingness to suffer in the name of God has been observed in a number of countries. Thai worshippers pierce their cheeks with iron rods, pins, swords, and other metallic objects to inflict pain for this reason. The community gathers to watch in amazement as these people experience great agony ("Taboos," 2008c). In Papua, New Guinea, young men of the Yamok Village cut the skin on their body with sharp blades in spite of the pain and suffering so that upon healing their skin will resemble that of a crocodile. The pattern of crocodile skin on the front and back of the body symbolizes adulthood and masculinity. This practice is usually performed by a group of maturing boys so that they emerge as men ("Taboos," 2008d).

MYTHS

Mind-altering drugs constitute one of the few taboo customs widely practiced yet fiercely contested. Most societies ban mind-altering drugs by law. However, in certain regions of the world these drugs are not taboo when used in cultural or religious rituals, although medical science and most governments argue that their use leads to addiction and antisocial behavior. In the heart of Australia, in the city of Canberra deep in the bushland, there are tribal cultures where these drugs are sanctioned and even encouraged. The drugs are used as part of religious rituals or for traditional healing practices. When people use drugs that allow them to enter an altered state of consciousness, they risk severe health consequences ("Taboo," 2008f).

In the Australian bushland, men suffer great pain to become respected in their society. A man must experience a physically torturous ritual to become the spiritual leader known as a *shaman.* The rites that confer the title of shaman include taking a hallucinogenic drug and suffering painful spasms from the stings and bites of ants. If he can tolerate the pain, he becomes a shaman, believed to have special powers of prophecy and the ability to heal ("Taboo," 2008e). Similarly, a ritual of womanhood at the time of puberty requires the girl's faces to be tattooed, using a thorn and a mixture of blood and ash, which is also borne with stoicism ("Taboo," 2008f).

Summary

These customs have been accepted by some societies for centuries. They believe that bearing intense pain and suffering indicates a special power in the person who chooses to undergo these rituals. Wider societies question such practices as harmful to health and believe they are misleading to unsophisticated people who may become controlled and manipulated by so-called spiritual leaders. Although cultural beliefs, inhumane traditions, and religious dogmas are often accepted by one society or another, are they acceptable to the victims? What must be done in the twenty-first century to eradicate the unacceptable practices that inflict harm, cause infectious diseases, and often kill? Global societies must determine if such rituals are to be allowed to continue, and those same global societies must provide solutions. As healthcare professionals we must ask, are we lifting ancient traditions to a new consciousness of a gentler social order, or are we interfering with a way of life best left alone?

KEY POINT In the United States, forensic nurse examiners and other social networks designed to protect children have concluded that harmful practices brought by immigrants from their country of origin are not acceptable.

However, intent, as one element of crime, must be considered. If the parent's intent is to provide healthcare but he or she causes harm instead, we have a responsibility to teach new healthcare methods. How does one investigate suspected child abuse when a parent's perspective is formed from a lifelong traditional practice or religious belief? Forensic nurses, as clinical investigators, are responsible for familiarizing themselves with known practices of the immigrant population most likely to be treated in local hospitals or public clinics. Certain categories of immigrants tend to populate specific regions where they have access to others from their geographical area. Individuals who migrate from Asia, India, or Russia to somewhere else generally form communities in which individuals share a common language, religion, beliefs, and values. Culturally competent care begins with understanding their beliefs and values, educating them regarding current laws and standards of healthcare, explaining legal concepts of abuse, and offering new information for better approaches to child rearing.

BEST PRACTICE The forensic nurse examiner must be aware of the crime, the circumstances, and the laws pertaining to feticide and infanticide if she or he practices in an area where this sociocultural crime is a common occurrence.

Many sociocultural crimes are accepted as a normal way of life until they are committed to such an extent that they hamper the very existence of the society. When the affected people or nongovernment human rights groups raise a cry, the ruling governments then work to counter the effect of harmful practices, which laws alone do not stop. Rather, it is through a change of social mindset within a culture, an awareness of the ill effects of these practices, and strict implementation of existing laws that we begin to witness a decrease such crimes. Acceptance of sociocultural crimes, to various extents, depends on the tolerance of a society—that is, until these crimes begin to create havoc with public life. Identifying the root causes of sociocultural crimes is essential to initiate preventive interventions. With changing times we must change the social values that are becoming social evils. A concerted effort must be made to inform societies of the threats that have become unacceptable and to orient the people to new values and utility for their way of life. What is needed more than the stricter laws is social planning. As the science of forensic nursing is integrated into health and justice systems worldwide, nurses will become one more significant resource among existing social and legal scientists who will influence the mindset of society, because they are an influential and respected part of humanity. Changing society's state of mind is the only true measure of social change.

References

Abichandani, R. K. (2009). Custodial Dignity. Viewed at http://cestat.gov.in/Articles%20by%20President/Custodial%20Dignity.doc on Jan. 1, 2009.

About.com. (2009). (www.webcrawler.com) (marriage.about.com/od/arrangedmarriages/a/childb) on Jan 29, 2009. http://marriage.about.com/od/arrangedmarriages/a/?once=true& Viewed on January 29, 2009.

Aderinto, A., & Akinwale, A. (2008). Viewed at www.cbaac77.com/pdf/Dr_Aderinto.pdf on Oct. 12, 2008.

Amar Ujala. (2007a). Jalandhar. *5*(124), 3.

Amar Ujala. (2007b). Jalandhar. *5*(122), 1.

BBC, News. (February 14, 2008). Viewed at http://news.bbc.co.uk/2/hi/middle_east/7244579.stm on February 7, 1990.

Basu, D. K. (1997). Supreme Court in D.K.Basu V. State of W.B. 1 SCC: 416

Bhaskar, Danik. (2008). Patiala Ed. *1*(328), 3.

Blush Response. (2001).

censusindia.gov.in. (2008a). Viewed at http://censusindia.gov.in/Census_Data_2001/India_at_glance/fsex.aspx on Dec. 26, 2008.

censusindia.gov.in. (2008b). Sex ratio of selected countries. Viewed at http://censusindia.gov.in/Data_Products/Library/Provisional_Population_Total_link/PDF_Links/chapter6.pdf on Dec. 26, 2008.

China forced abortions. Viewed at (www.time.com/time/world/article/0,8599,1615936,00.html). On February 22, 2009.

christianaggression.org. (2008). Viewed at www.christianaggression.org/item_display.php?id=1143494697&type=articles on Dec. 29, 2008.

Dainik Jagran. (2009).

Dainik Jagran. *2*(20): 2. Larkio ki parvarish me kotahi karte hain Punjabi. www.timesonline.co.uk/tol/news/world/article468989.ece on Dec. 29, 2008.

deccanherald.com. (2008). Viewed at www.deccanherald.com/CONTENT/Nov42008/national2008110398711.asp on Dec. 29, 2008.

en.wikipedia.org. (2008). Viewed at http://en.wikipedia.org/wiki/Human_sacrifice_in_Aztec_culture on Dec. 29, 2008.

Glauber, B. (2008, Mar. 26). *Milwaukee Journal-Sentinel*.

Gorea, L., Gorea, R. K., & Garg, S. P. (2002). Child rights violations in schools. *International Journal of Medical Toxicology and Legal Medicine*, *5*(1), 20–21.

Gorea, R. K. (2000). Forensic medicine and human rights. *Journal of Forensic Medicine and Toxicology*, *17*(2), 20–22.

Gorea, R. K. (2004a). Editorial. *Journal of Indian Academy of Forensic Medicine*, *26*(3), 91.

Gorea, R. K. (2004b). Bringing Hope to India. *The Edge*, *10*(3), 3–5, 16.

Gorea, R. K. (2008). A case of mummification reported as spiritual coma. In K. Vij (Ed.), *Textbook of Forensic Medicine and Toxicology–Principles and Practice*. (4th ed., p. 130). New Delhi: Elsevier.

Gracia, E., Herrero, J. (2008). Beliefs in the necessity of corporal punishment of children and public perceptions of child physical abuse as a social problem. *Journal of Child Abuse and Neglect*, *32*(11), 1058–1062.

Haryana Bureau. (2007). *8 Teachers dismissed since' 2005: Mullana* (p. 5). Chandigarh: Hindustan Times, March 13, 2007.

Hindustan Times. (2003). Lancaster, John. (2003). *In India, case links mysticism, murder* . Washington Post, 11/29/2003.

Hindustan Times. (2008a). Punjab Metro. Dec. 29, 2008: p. 2.

Hindustan Times. (2008b). Taliban threatens to kill schoolgirls in Pakistan. Hindustan Times. New Delhi: Punjab Metro, Dec. 26, 2008: p. 11.

Hindustan Times. (2008c). No divorce for 8-year-old married to 58-years-old. Hindustan Times, New Delhi: Punjab Metro, Dec, 24, 2008: p. 11.

Hindustan Times. (2008d). *No FIR in Diwali Honour killing*. Hindustan Times, Chandigarh, New Delhi: Punjab Nov 11, 2008: p. 5.

Hindustan Times. (2008e). Chandigarh, New Delhi: Punjab Metro. Nov 10, 2008: p. 8.

Hindustan Times. (2008f). Punjab Metro, Dec. 29, 2008: p4-W

Hindustan Times. (2008g). New Delhi: Punjab Nov 10, 2008: p. 1.

Hindustan Times. (2008g). *SC Notice to Maharashtra over hate campaign* (p. 7). Chandigarh, New Delhi: Punjab metro, Nov 11, 2008.

Hindustan Times. (2008h). *My daughter may meet the Scarlette's fate: German* (p. 9). New Delhi: Punjab metro, Chandigarh, Nov 11, 2008.

Hindustan Times. (2008i). *Panchkula gangrape: HC Notice to Haryana* (p. 1). Chandigarh Live: Nov 11, 2008.

Hindustan Times. (2008j). *Torture marks on slain engineer's body: Maya defends local MLA* (p. 6). New Delhi: Punjab Metro, Dec 26, 2008.

Hindustan Times. (2009a). *OK for 10-yr-old girls to marry* (p. 1). New Delhi: Punjab Metro, Jan. 15, 2009.

Hindustan Times. (2009b). *Honour killing accused in custody*. New Delhi.

Hosken, F. P. (2009). Female Genital Mutilation (FGM). Viewed at www.feminist.com/resources/artspeech/inter/fgm.htm, on Jan. 1, 2009.

Hoyden in the News. (2008). *Olympics Special: Forced Abortion in China Lauredhel*. August 8, http://viv.id.au/blog/?p=2062. Viewed January 28, 2009.

Indian Asian News Service. (2009, July 22). Viewed at www.ians.in on January 29, 2009.

Indi-Asian News Service Homosexuals prosecuted [AIMS]. (2006). Viewed on January 29, 2009.

in.answers.yahoo.com. (2008). Viewed at http://in.answers.yahoo.com/question/index?qid=20081217042857AA62e7o on Dec. 29, 2008.

kamat.com. (2008). Viewed at www.kamat.com/kalranga/hindu/sati.html on Dec. 29, 2008.

KIDS. (www.kidscomefirst.info), January 28, 2009.

McDougall, D. (2006). The Observer, in Khurja, India, Sunday March 5, 2006 (Indian cult kills children for goddess: Holy men blamed for inciting dozens of deaths).

Mustofa, M. (2008). The sociocultural approach in controlling violent crime: a case study of "siri" phenomenon in buginesemakassarese community, South Sulawesi, Indonesia. Viewed at www.aic.gov.au_publications_proceedings_12_mustofa.pdf on Sept. 12, 2008.

mynews.in (2009). Peoples' Tribunal on Custodial Torture to be held in Varanasi. viewed at www.mynews.in/fullstory.aspx?storyid=4248 on Jan. 1, 2009.

Nationalatlas.gov. (2009). Gender in the United States. Viewed at www.nationalatlas.gov/articles/people/a_gender.html on Jan. 22, 2009.

North Carolina General Assembly. (2003). (www.ncga.state.nc.us/html2003/bills/currentversion/ratified/senate/sbil0251.full.html). January 28, 2009.

National Crime Records Bureau. (2007a). Crime against women. Viewed at http://ncrb.nic.in/cii2007/cii-2007/CHAP5.pdf on Dec 20, 2008.

National Crime Records Bureau. (2007b). Figres at a glance-2007. Viewed at http://ncrb.nic.in/cii2007/cii-2007/FIGURES_2007.pdf on Dec 20, 2008.

National Crime Records Bureau. (2007c). Crime against children. Viewed at http://ncrb.nic.in/cii2007/cii-2007/CHAP6.pdf on Dec 20, 2008.

National Commission for Women. (2008). Viewed at http://ncw.nic.in/PNDT%20conference.pdf on Dec 27, 2008.

New York Times Examines Abortion Procedures among Underage Girls iIn Brazil. Article Date: March 31, Mar 2009.

Paye-layleh, J. (2008). I ate children's hearts, Ex-rebel says. Viewed at http://news.bbc.co.uk/2/hi/africa/7200101.stm on Dec. 29, 2008.

Politics.co.uk. (2008). Viewed at www.politics.co.uk/briefings-guides/issue-briefs/education/corporal-punishment-$366656.htm on January 29, 2009

(Quest.Live.com/News4/5/2008). On January 14, 2009.

religioustolerance.org. (2009). Debates about FGM in Africa, the Middle East & Far East. Viewed at www.religioustolerance.org/fem_cirm.htm on Jan. 1, 2009.

Saiyed, K. (2009). Custodial torture': 3 cops suspended. Viewed at www.expressindia.com/latest-news/custodial-torture-3-cops-suspended/304864/ on Jan. 1, 2009.

Science in the news. (2003). www.kidscomefirst.info, and www.kidscomefirst.info/48Hours1.mpg, Viewed January 28, 2009, at www.ncga.state.nc.us/html2003/bills/currentversion/ratified/senate/sbil0251.full.html

Sex discrimination in Scotland: Viewed at news.scotsman.com/scotland/Sex-discrimination-la on January 29, 2009.

Sexting. Viewed at www.dailymail.com/News NationandWorld/200902042505 on February 20, 2009.

Sidhu, H. (2009). *7 Mansa villages have more girls than boys* (p. 2). Hindustan Times. New Delhi: Punjab Metro, Jan 9, 2009.

Singh, P. (2009). Premika ka ashlil MMS banakar dosto ko bheja. Dainik Bhaskar, Patiala Ed, Ludhiana; 2(21), 1.

Singh, R. (2007). Disciplining the child. The Tribune, Late City Ed., Aug. 14, 2007; 127(224), 14.

Taboo. (2008a). viewed at http://channel.nationalgeographic.com/series/taboo#tab-Videos/05411_00 on Dec. 27, 2008.

Taboo. (2008b). Viewed at http://channel.nationalgeographic.com/series/taboo#tab-Overview on Dec. 27, 2008.

Taboo. (2008c). Viewed at http://channel.nationalgeographic.com/series/taboo#tab-Videos/03004_04 on Dec. 27, 2008.

Taboo. (2008d). Viewed at http://channel.nationalgeographic.com/series/taboo#tab-Videos/02802_04 on Dec. 27, 2008.

Taboo. (2008e). Viewed at http://channel.nationalgeographic.com/series/taboo#tab-Videos/05915_00 on Dec. 27, 2008.

Taboo. (2008f). Viewed at http://channel.nationalgeographic.com/series/taboo#tab-Videos/06140_00 on Dec. 27, 2008.

The Tribune. (2000). HC bans corporal punishment for school children. Chandigarh, City Ed: The Tribune, 120(333), 1.

The Tribune. (2007a). 127(85) late city edition, Chandigarh, March 28, 2007: p. 9

The Tribune. (2007b). 127(85) late city edition, Chandigarh, March 28, 2007: p. 7.

The Tribune. (2007c). File Criminal cases in Ragging Incidents: SC. 127(135) Chandigarh, late city Ed. May 17, 2007: p. 1.

The Tribune. (2007d). 127(224) Late City Ed, Aug. 14, 2007: p. 14.

timesofindia.indiatimes.com. (2009). ASI accused of custodial torture. Viewed at http://timesofindia.indiatimes.com/articleshow/1225322.cms on Jan. 1, 2009.

Touro Law Center. (2009). Row v Wade, www.tourolaw.edu/Patch/Roe. Viewed on Jan, 2.

unicef.org. (2009). Child Protection from Violence, Exploitation and Abuse, Female Genital Mutilation/Cutting. Viewed at www.unicef.org/protection/index_genitalmutilation.html on Jan. 1, 2009.

United Nations. (2002). "Rome Statute of the International Criminal Court, Part 2, Article 5," www.un.org/law/icc/statute/99_corr/2.htm#art.5. Retrieved July 21, 2007.

United Nations. (2006, November 30). International Convention on the Suppression and Punishment of the Crime of Apartheid. www.unhchr.ch/html/menu3/b/11.htm. Retrieved on October 8, 2006.

World Health Organization. who.int (2009). Female Genital Mutilation. Viewed at www.who.int/mediacentre/factsheets/fs241/en/ on Jan. 1, 2009.

Wilkinson, S. I. (2005). Communal Riots in India, The Economic and Political Weekly. October 29, 2005.

Wilson, B. Rural Ethiopia Ignores Law Against Child Bride, NPR. 15 January 2007. http://www.npr.org/templates/story/story.php?storyId=6560441&from=mobile. Accessed October 2, 2009.

CHAPTER 41 Sexual Deviant Behavior and Crimes

Anil Aggrawal

Forensic nurses, especially those working in the psychiatric field, will continue to work with sexual offenders and deviants. This chapter highlights some salient features of sexual offenders and how forensic nurses can best cooperate with medical and legal personnel for the psychiatric assessment and evaluation, treatment, and legal commitments relating to these offenders.

Who Is a Sexual Offender?

Contrary to popular belief, sexual offenses and deviant behaviors are not a product of modern civilization. Both sexual offenses and deviant behaviors have been mentioned in ancient books such as the Holy Bible (Aggrawal, 2009b). **Sexual offender** is a term that is still in search of a universally acceptable definition. Plainly put, a sex offender is one who offends sexually. However, sexual behaviors within a group or community are greatly influenced by prevailing sociocultural norms. A behavior that may offend one person, group, or culture may not offend another, because it may be the norm in that culture. For instance, in some cultures, shaking hands with a female might be regarded as grossly inappropriate behavior, if not a downright sexual offense. In other cultures, shaking hands—even social kissing—may be considered quite appropriate. A sexually explicit behavior is also not necessarily a product of advanced civilization. In some primitive tribes of Africa, going topless for females is a norm, whereas if a woman walked topless on the streets of New Delhi or New York, she would almost certainly be arrested as a sexual offender (Aggrawal, 2009a). In addition, norms within a particular community may change over time.

One would imagine that sexual acts that are construed almost universally as loathsome or harmful behaviors may be agreed on as sexual offenses by all societies, but even this is not true. The case of rape—forcible sexual intercourse against the will of the other party—illustrates this point. Among the *Hmong* tribe of Laos, where marriage by bride capture is a continuing cultural practice, rape under certain circumstances is perfectly legal. This practice continues even among Hmong communities that have migrated to the United States and has even given them the so-called "cultural defense" against allegations of rape.

Marriage by bride capture is a practice whereby a man abducts a woman he likes and holds her captive for three days. During this time, he repeatedly rapes her. After the third day, the girl is freed and given a choice to either reject or marry him. In practice, however, the girl always ends up marrying her abductor, either willingly or under her parents' pressure. Rape, at least under these circumstances, thus is a perfectly legal activity among the Hmongs. In one highly publicized case (1985), Kong Moua,

a male member of the Hmong community in America, kidnapped Seng Xiong, a female member of his own community, and had repeated sexual intercourse with her. Moua genuinely believed he was following Hmong customary marriage practices. After she was set free, Xiong not only rejected the marriage-by-capture tradition but filed kidnapping and rape charges against Moua. Moua sought "cultural defense." Allowing the defense, the judge asked Moua to plead guilty to one misdemeanor count of false imprisonment and sentenced him to just 120 days in jail and a mere $1000 fine (Aggrawal, 2007).

Sex crime, sexual offense, and *sexual offender* are terms that have no universal meanings. In broad and general terms, however, a sex crime is a sexually explicit behavior that is illegal in a given jurisdiction. It has been determined to be a criminal act because it exploits, caters to, makes possible, or is dependent on explicit sexual behavior (MacNamara & Sagarin, 1977). A useful definition of sex offenders was offered in 1965 by the Kinsey group: "A sex offender is a person who has been legally convicted as a result of an overt act, committed by him for his own immediate sexual gratification, which is contrary to the prevailing sexual mores of the society in which he lives and/or is legally punishable" (Gebhard, Pomeroy, & Christenson 1967). Definitions provided by most workers are similar or simple modifications of this one. Some authors include specific crimes, such as pedophilia or incest, within this general definition, signifying, perhaps, a personal weight given by them to a specific sex crime. Glass (2004), for instance, includes pedophilia in the previous definition, and in her modified definition states that a sex offender is "someone who has committed or attempted to commit any type of illegal or nonconsensual sexual act and/or any sexual behavior involving children under the legal age of consent, based upon the laws governing the location where the sexual behavior occurred (p. 222)."

Another term that appears frequently in discussions of sexual offenses is sexual violence. **Sexual violence**, according to the World Health Organization (WHO), refers to "any sexual act, attempt to obtain a sexual act, unwanted sexual comments or advances, or acts to traffic, or otherwise directed, against a person's sexuality using coercion (i.e., psychological intimidation, physical force, or threats of harm), by any person regardless of their relationship to the victim, in any setting, including but not limited to home and work" (NSVRC, 2004, p. 4).

Sexual offenses have been committed in virtually every condition and setting. More recently, sexual offenses in a military environment, the so-called *military sexual trauma* (MST), has been making headlines both in the lay press and in academic publications (David, Simpson, et al., 2006; Himmelfarb, Yaeger, et al., 2006; Kelly, Vogt, et al., 2008; Kimerling, Gima, et al., 2007;

Kimerling, Street, et al., 2008; O'Brien, Gaher, et al., 2008; Regan, Wilhoite, et al., 2007; Valente & Wight, 2007; Suris & Lind, 2008; Yaeger, Himmelfarb, et al., 2006)

What Is Deviant Behavior?

Sexually deviant behaviors are more commonly known among medical parlance as *paraphilias*. Just as there can be no universal definition of a sexual offender, there cannot be a universally accepted definition of *sexually deviant behavior*. The case of homosexuality perhaps demonstrates this best. Homosexuality, even between two consenting adults, is considered a sexually deviant behavior in many societies. But in several other societies, it is legally acceptable. Even within the same communities, the behavior has been viewed differently at different times. In Ancient Greece, homosexual behavior was not considered abnormal and was even considered to be more elevated and spiritual than heterosexual relationships. As time passed, however, it gradually began to be considered a sexual perversion and even a criminal behavior. Until 1968, homosexuality was listed as a sexual deviation in the *Diagnostic and Statistical Manual of Mental Disorder*s (American Psychiatric Association, 1968). However, during the next decade, it began to be considered normal sexual behavior and finally in 1980, it was removed from DSM-III (Lamberg, 1998). It is, however, not considered an exalted form of sexual relationship yet.

Other sexual behaviors, such as fellatio, cunnilingus, anal sex, prostitution, and some categories of visual and literary erotica and pornography, which were once considered sexually deviant behaviors, have been decriminalized in many societies and are tolerated relatively better than in other societies. Sexually deviant behavior, or paraphilia, may thus be conceived more as a social rather than a medical concept. There is, however, a core of extremely deviant behavior (say lust murder) that has always been, and perhaps always will be, considered abnormal.

From a biomedical point of view, paraphilias have been defined explicitly in the *Diagnostic and Statistical Manual*, fourth edition, revised (*DSM-IV-TR*) (American Psychiatric Association, 2000). It specifically mentions 15 paraphilias by name. Of these, eight have been allotted specific diagnostic codes (Table 41-1).

Seven other paraphilias—telephone scatologia (obscene phone calls), necrophilia (sexual attraction to corpses), partialism (exclusive focus on part of body), zoophilia (sexual attraction to animals), coprophilia (erotic attraction to feces), klismaphilia (erotic attraction to enemas), and urophilia (erotic attraction to urine)—are grouped in the category "Paraphilia not otherwise specified." It is specifically stated that these are examples, but this category is not limited to these.

Table 41-1 DSM-IV-TR Codes for Paraphilias

302.2	Pedophilia
302.3	Transvestic fetishism
302.4	Exhibitionism
302.81	Fetishism
302.82	Voyeurism
302.83	Sexual masochism
302.84	Sexual sadism
302.89	Frotteurism
302.9	Paraphilia not otherwise specified

Etiology of Sexually Deviant Behavior

Several theories have been advanced regarding the etiology of sexually deviant behavior. Some of the most common ones are discussed next.

PSYCHODYNAMIC THEORY

According to the psychodynamic theory of the mind, human psyche is composed of three primary elements: the id, which is guided by the pleasure principle; the superego, the rational component of human psyche, which controls the id to a great extent; and the ego. Sexual deviancy occurs when the id is overactive. This theory appears to have a strong clinical foundation as well, especially as successful treatments have been based on this theory (Lohse & Hauch, 1983).

BIOLOGICAL THEORY

According to this theory, sexually deviant behavior can be explained by abnormal sex hormone levels (Saleh & Berlin, 2003), testosterone levels (Studer, Aylwin, et al., 2005), and even chromosomal makeup (Wiedeking, Lake, et al., 1977). This theory also has a sound clinical basis, especially as antiandrogens (e.g., leuprolide acetate) seem to have a corrective effect on sexually deviant behavior (Bancroft, Tennent, et al., 1974; Berlin, 1988; Briken, Berner, et al., 2000; Buvat, Lemaire, et al., 1996; Cooper, 1986; Cooper, Ismail, et al., 1972; Gagne, 1981; Kravitz, Haywood, et al., 1995, 1996; Krueger & Kaplan, 2001; Rosler & Witztum, 1998; Rousseau, Couture, et al., 1990; Thibaut, Cordier, et al., 1993, 1996; Thibaut, Kuhn, et al., 1998).

FEMINIST THEORY

Feminists tend to explain sexually deviant behavior, especially rape, from a cultural, historical, and even political context. Rape is explained as men's tendency to oppress women. According to this theory, psychodynamic and biological factors do not play a part in sexual offending. Sexual offending results merely from men's desire to suppress women (Drieschner & Lange, 1999).

ATTACHMENT THEORY

According to this theory, all humans love to establish strong emotional bonds with others. An individual who has experienced some loss or emotional distress may act out abnormally because of loneliness and isolation.

BEHAVIORAL THEORY

Initially developed by Pavlov, behavioral theory tends to explain all behaviors in terms of rewards or punishments. A behavior that is rewarded tends to become a habit, whereas a behavior that is punished becomes extinct. Sexually deviant behavior is rewarded by the sexual pleasure that the culprit enjoys. If the behavior is not punished (say, if the culprit is not apprehended), it is not extinguished. Thus, a sexual deviant who remains free will tend to repeat the sexual behavior. Behavioral theory, on its own, is unable to completely explain such complex behavior as sexual deviancy.

COGNITIVE-BEHAVIORAL THEORY

This theory takes into account cognitive factors too. If the offender does not have feelings of guilt or shame or rationalizes them through excuses and justifications, the sexually offending behavior is enforced.

PSYCHOSOCIAL THEORY

Psychosocial theory, initially propounded by Erikson, conceived child development occurring as a series of fixed, predetermined stages. This model extends Freud's psychoanalytical theory by focusing on the child's emotional development. According to this theory, deviant sexual behavior may be viewed as a response to external social factors.

INTEGRATED THEORY

This theory tends to integrate all previous theories. It takes into account elements such as motivations to offend, rationalization of behavior, diminishing of internal barriers, and various external social factors.

Cycle of Sexual Offending

The term *cycle* is used in two senses in the literature on sexual exploitation. The first sense refers to the theory of *generational cycle*, whereby some people who are sexually abused as children go on to become abusers themselves. This theory has been challenged because, whereas clinical evidence supports the view that some abusers were abused themselves as children, it cannot account for the gender imbalance in female victims and male perpetrators. There are far more female victims than female perpetrators of sexual crimes, and if all or even most of the female victims were to become sexual offenders, the gender imbalance would not be as much. The second sense of the term *cycle* refers to a *behavioral cycle*, sometimes also known as *Wolf's cycle of offending* (Wolf, 1984). This cycle refers to a self-reinforcing sequence of sex offender behavior (Fig. 41-1).

Wolf's model was initially applied to pedophile offending and later was developed for work with adolescents. Sexual offenders are often people whose self-esteem is low and who expect rejection from others. Often they have poor social skills. Some may have experienced some kind of emotional trauma in their lives, such as a divorce, a bereavement, or a redundancy, which may leave them feeling bad about themselves. As a result, these people can withdraw from others, thus becoming emotionally isolated.

Not all people from this group become sexual offenders. Those who are likely to offend sexually tend to compensate for their isolation, low esteem, and personal unhappiness by developing relationships with children, which may lead to sexual offending.

KEY POINT Before sexual culprits can offend, they must overcome their inhibitions and convince themselves that their deviant acts will do no harm.

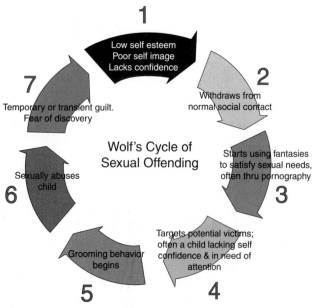

Fig. 41-1 Wolf's cycle of sexual offending.

For sexual offending to take place, the potential culprits have to first overcome their "internal inhibitions." They have to convince themselves that what they want to do is not wrong. They must quiet their conscience and persuade themselves that no harm will be done if they engage in the sexually offending behavior. This occurs through a process called *cognitive distortion*.

The next stage consists of identifying a target child. Often, the child will be vulnerable in some way. For instance, the child may have a low self-esteem and may be looking for attention. Initial fantasies about the child may be reinforced by using pornography, perhaps using the Internet. Internet chat rooms may also be used to find a child.

Now the stage comes to overcome the *external inhibitions*. These include the child's parents, the society, and the child's own resistance. To break the child's resistance, the perpetrator engages in the *grooming process*, a way of gaining the child's trust (Table 41-2). The perpetrator may lure the child with chocolates, toys, or by simply paying attention to him or her to make the child feel special (Lang & Frenzel, 1988). The child thrives on this attention and becomes attracted to the perpetrator.

The perpetrator may now tell the child that sexual activity is a way for them to show their love for each other. If the child is aroused, the perpetrator may say that the child must want the activity to continue and may suggest that the child will enjoy the sexual relationship.

Following the abuse, the child often feels confused, guilty, ashamed, betrayed, lost, and afraid. The perpetrator may quiet the child with bribery or threats. Any initial guilt a perpetrator experiences will lead to further lowering of self-esteem and the cycle starts all over again.

An understanding of this cycle is vital for law enforcement authorities and for personnel engaged in treating sexual offenders. The cycle has to be broken by increasing the self-esteem of perpetrators. Law enforcement authorities may look with suspicion at any person who is a loner and whose house is full of chocolates, candies, and toys.

Female Sexual Offenders

The term *female sexual offender* may sound like an oxymoron to many, especially as females, usually considered the weaker sex, are seen as victims rather than as perpetrators of sexual abuse.

Table 41-2 Some Examples of "Grooming" Behavior
Be nice to the child.
Take the child for rides on motorcycle or snowmobile.
Give the child money.
Get into playful horseplay and wrestling around.
Take off their clothes during horseplay.
Play Nintendo together.
Sleep in the same room and climb on top of the child's body and act as if asleep.
Play house.
Buy toys and candy.
Sleep with the child.
Give the child piggyback rides or invite lap-sitting.
Appear to be hugging, but thinking sexual thoughts.
Pretend to be interested in toys of the child.
Be kind and then become more than a friend.
Spend free time with the child and discover their special interests.
Exhibit porn magazines to the child.

However, recent crime reports and academic papers are fairly consistent in showing that the number of females who commit sexual offenses is not trivial (Oliver, 2007). According to a 1999 Bureau of Justice Statistics report, between 1993 and 1997, 2.2% of offenders arrested for forcible rape each year were female. This amounts to roughly 10,000 female sexual offenders being arrested each year in the United States alone (Greenfeld, Snell, et al., 1999).

Among the female sex offenders, mothers are also involved. By interviewing them in depth, Denov (2004) derived data from a small sample of 14 adult victims (7 men, 7 women) of child sexual abuse by females. Most respondents reported severe sexual abuse by their mothers. It might also intuitively appear that female-perpetrated sexual abuse may be relatively harmless as compared to sexual abuse by men. However, in Denov's study, a vast majority of victims reported that the experience of female-perpetrated sexual abuse was harmful and damaging. Both male and female victims reported long-term difficulties with substance abuse, self-injury, suicide, depression, rage, strained relationships with women, self-concept and identity issues, and a discomfort with sex.

> **BEST PRACTICE** When assessing children who have been victims of sexual abuse, forensic nurses should consider the mother as a suspect or potential offender.

More recently, Peter has compared male- and female-perpetrated sexual abuse in terms of victim and abuser characteristics, type of abuse, family structure, and worker information, and has shown a prevalence rate of 10.7% for female-perpetrated sexual abuse (Peter, 2008). According to this study, girls were more likely to be victimized for both male- and female-perpetrated sexual violence. Also females tended to abuse younger children. The majority of children came from families with lower socioeconomic status although one in five victims of female-perpetrated sexual abuse came from middle-class homes. Also, when females abused, referrals to child welfare agencies were more likely to be made by nonprofessionals.

Assessment of Sexual Offenders

The assessment of risk for *criminal recidivism* (reoffending) among sex offenders is a task of great concern to the judicial system, the correctional services, and society at large. Data from the United States Bureau of Justice Statistics (Langan, Schmitt, et al., 2003) show that 5% of about 10,000 sex offenders who were released from prison in 1994 were rearrested for a sex crime within three years. More recently, a review of 61 studies (n = 23,393) demonstrated that the sexual offense recidivism rate was 13.4% (Hanson & Bussiere, 1998). There were, however, subgroups of offenders who recidivated at higher rates. Sexual recidivism rates of up to 42% have been reported (Hagan, Anderson, et al., 2008).

The assessments of sexual offenders aid in making several crucial decisions about these individuals. These include sentencing, prison classification, parole, and whether these individuals should be restrained (in some kind of treatment facilities) after their sentences are over (conditional release).

The enactment of "sexual predator" laws with regard to the long-term incapacitation of high-risk sex offenders after serving their criminal sentences have further increased the need for such assessments. Furthermore, limited monetary and professional resources have created a need for assessment tools that are simple in nature and sound with regard to their accuracy in identifying offenders with risk of reoffending.

There is now a legal necessity of such assessments too. Case law and legislation, on a number of occasions (*Tarasoff v. Regents of the University of California, 1976; Macintosh v. Milano, 1979*), have charged mental health professionals with the responsibility of identifying potentially violent patients and protecting the public from them. Several jurisdictions have codified such clinician responsibility (Weinberger, Sreenivasan, et al., 1998).

> **KEY POINT** Sexual offender assessments are essential for judicial decisions about correctional care and for determining the risks for recidivism.

RISK FACTORS

Several key variables—the *risk factors*—are known to increase the likelihood of committing an offense. These variables are subdivided into *static* and *dynamic* factors. Static factors are historical and unchangeable, whereas dynamic factors are current and changeable. Static factors include age at first offense, history of prior convictions, gender, type of victim, and motivation for committing past crimes. Dynamic factors include present economic situation, marital status, attitudes supportive of crime, faulty cognitions, sexually deviant preference, family condition, leisure activities, criminal friends, substance abuse, and employment status. Most assessment tools seek to uncover and quantify these risk factors.

TOOLS FOR ASSESSMENT

> **BEST PRACTICE** The forensic clinical team should employ actuarial methods, rather than unstructured clinical decision making, to predict the future behaviors of sexual offenders.

Predicting how an individual will behave in the future is a difficult—if not impossible—task. Yet clinicians entrusted with the assessment of sexual offenders must make this prediction fairly accurately. It is now known that sexual offense recidivism can be predicted to a certain extent by measures of sexual deviancy (e.g., deviant sexual preferences, prior sexual offenses) and, to a lesser extent, by general criminological factors (e.g., age, total prior offenses).

A variety of tools for the assessment of sex offender recidivism risk have been devised. The three main tools are (1) unstructured clinical decision making, (2) actuarial decision making, and (3) structured professional judgment (SPJ) approach (Hall, 2008). The three tools have been likened to the three legs of a stool, the top of which represents public safety from sexual offenders (Fig. 41-2).

UNSTRUCTURED CLINICAL DECISION-MAKING

Clinical decision making, the traditional approach, relies on clinical examination of the sex offender and is heavily dependent on the competence and acuity of the assessor. Because of this drawback, this approach is inherently unreliable. It may, however, be more suited to "on-the-fly" assessments, where speed and cost are more of an issue than accuracy and reliability. Noted authorities have described such approaches as informal, 'in the head,' impressionistic, or subjective conclusions reached somehow by a human clinical judge (Douglas and Ogloff, 2003; Grove and Meehl, 1996). Some have referred to it as "little more than the best intuitive guess on the part of the clinician" (Monahan, 1996, p. 107).

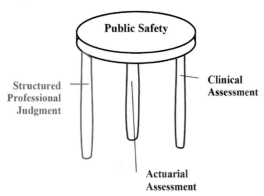

Fig. 41-2 The three assessment tools—clinical assessment, actuarial assessment, and structured professional judgment—may best be visualized as three legs of a stool on which public safety from sex offenders rests.

Actuarial Methods

Actuarial methods are more rigorous. They rely on *known* statistical correlations between certain "risk factors" and occurrence of future sexual violence. For instance, a person who has committed a greater number of sex offenses previously is likely to reoffend more often. Similarly, a person who is a drug and alcohol addict is more likely to display sexual violence than a person who is not. A number of such risk factors are taken and weighted according to their known correlations with the existence of future sexual violence. A final score is then calculated, which predicts the rate of future sexual violence.

This approach can perhaps best be understood by an analogy. When setting premium costs, a medical insurance company needs to have some indication as to which groups of individuals are likely to be at an increased risk of having a heart attack in the future (so they can charge more premium from them). Known risk factors of heart attack are obesity, cigarette smoking, hypertension, and high levels of cholesterol. Statistical correlations exist between these risk factors and the occurrence of heart attack. Insurance companies can use these data to set up premium amounts for individuals.

Based on this approach, different individuals and groups have devised different actuarial instruments or tests. Those used most commonly for risk assessment among sex offenders are (1) the *Violence Risk Appraisal Guide* (VRAG) (Harris, Rice, & Quinsey, 1993), (2) *Sex Offender Risk Appraisal Guide* (SORAG) (Ducro & Pham, 2006), (3) *Rapid Risk Assessment for Sexual Offense Recidivism* (RRASOR) (Hanson, 1997; Sjostedt & Langstrom 2001), (4) *Static-99* (Ducro & Pham, 2006; Nunes, Firestone, et al., 2002; Sjostedt & Langstrom, 2001), (5) *Minnesota Sex Offender Screening Tool* (Revised) or MnSOST-R (Epperson, et al., 1998), and (6) *Colorado Sex Offender Risk Scale* (English, Retzlaff, et al., 2002).

Each of these tests takes into account a fixed number of risk factors, "loads" them according to the known risk of reoffending associated with them, and arrives at a score. For instance, RRASOR rates an individual based on either the presence or absence of four identifiable risk factors: (1) the number of sex offenses for which the individual has previously been either charged or convicted, (2) the individual's current age, (3) the gender of the individual's former victims, and (4) the nature of the individual's relationship to them (intra- or extrafamilial). Predictions are made according to a scoring guide. Individuals scoring 1 on RRASOR have a 2.4% and 6.5% risk of recidivism at 5 and 10 years, respectively; those with a score of 3 have a 21.8% and a 36.9% risk of recidivism at 5 and 10 years, respectively; and that those with a score of 5 have

a 49.8% and 73.1% risk of recidivism at 5 and 10 years, respectively. Similarly, The Minnesota Sex Offender Screening Tool–Revised (the MnSOST-R) is a 16-item actuarial tool. Scoring is as below (Table 41-3). Based on this scoring method, an MnSOST-R score of 8 or higher is considered suggestive of a high risk of recidivism.

Structured Professional Judgment

Actuarial tools offer little scope for any subjective interpretation. Thus, while unstructured clinical decision making is overly subjective, actuarial tools are strictly objective. Structured professional judgment (SPJ) tools are third-generation tools, which judiciously mix elements from both of the previous tools and may be the best approach to predict recidivism. Major SPJ tools in use today are the Sex Offender Need Assessment Rating (SONAR) (Hanson & Harris, 2001), Psychopathy Checklist Revised (PCL-R) (Bolt, Hare, et al., 2007; Pereira, Huband, et al., 2008; Urbaniok, Noll, et al., 2007), Historical, Clinical, Risk Management-20 (HCR-20) (Dietiker, Dittmann, et al., 2007; Gray, Taylor, et al., 2008), Level of Service Inventory-Revised (LSI-R) (Dahle, 2006; Manchak, Skeem, et al., 2008), and Structured Assessment for Violence Risk among Youth (SAVRY) (Lodewijks, Doreleijers, et al., 2008). Each takes into account a fixed number of items that are scored. The clinician's judgment is also factored in.

The forensic psychiatric nurse (FPN) has a great role to play in the assessment of sexual offenders. A forensic psychiatric evaluation of risk performed by an FPN can influence conviction, sentencing, and course of treatment, thereby preventing violence or recidivism (Patterson & Campbell, 2009).

Management and Supervision of Sex Offenders in the Community

Treatment and management of sex offenders has been a contentious issue. Opinions have varied from treating sex offenders like any other psychiatric patient to giving them antiandrogens and even castrating them.

One of the central goals in the treatment of sex offenders is the reduction of recidivism. Studies have shown that offenders who fail to complete treatment are at higher risk for reoffending than those who complete treatment (Hanson & Bussiere, 1998).

During sex offender treatment programs (SOTPs), the therapists aim at certain objectives. Among these are (1) patient honesty with therapists, group members, family, and other important people; (2) patient compliance with treatment procedures; and (3) patient compliance with supervision conditions (Kokish, 2003). There has been an increasing belief that with the use of the polygraph (lie detector) during such treatment programs, the ability of the therapists to attain these objectives is significantly enhanced (Kokish, Levenson, et al., 2005). American clinicians have even argued that polygraph testing in the treatment of sex offenders is akin to urine analysis in the treatment of drug addiction (Meijer, Verschuere, et al., 2008). This is now widely known as Post Conviction Sex Offender (polygraph) Testing (PCSOT).

PROBATION AND PAROLE

Sex offenders are a unique population to manage. Most convicted sex offenders at some point in time would be under the supervision of either a probation officer or a parole officer, with approximately 60% of sex offenders receiving probation sentences (Terry, 2006).

Table 41-3 Scoring Method for MnSOST-R

S. NO	RISK FACTOR	SCORING
1.	Number of sex/sex-related convictions (including current conviction)	Score 0 for one previous conviction and +2 for two or more previous convictions
2.	Length of sex offending history	If history is less than one year, score –1; if 1–6 years, score +3 and if >6 years, score 0
3.	Was the offender under any form of supervision when they committed any sex offense for which they were eventually charged or convicted?	No (0); yes (+2)
4.	Was any sex offense (charged or convicted) committed in a public place?	No (0); yes (+2)
5.	Was force or the threat of force ever used to achieve compliance in any sex offense (charged or convicted)?	No force in any offense (–3); force present in at least one offense (0)
6.	Has any sex offense (charged or convicted) involved multiple acts on a single victim within any single contact event?	No (–1); probable but not fully documented (0); yes (+1)
7.	Number of different age groups victimized across all sex/sex-related offenses (charged or convicted): Age group of victims: (check all that apply) __ Age 6 or younger __ Age 7 to 12 years __ Age 13 to 15 and the offender is more than 5 years older than the victim __ Age 16 or older	No age groups or only one age group checked (0); two or more age groups checked (+3)
8.	Offended against a 13- to 15-year-old victim and the offender was more than 5 years older than the victim at the time of the offense (charged or convicted)	No (0); yes (+2)
9.	Was the victim of any sex/sex-related offense (charged or convicted) a stranger?	No victims were strangers (–1); at least one victim was a stranger (+3); neither of the above can be confirmed, because of missing data (0)
10.	Is there evidence of adolescent antisocial behavior in the file?	No indication (–1); some relatively isolated antisocial acts (0); persistent, repetitive pattern (+2)
11.	Pattern of substantial drug or alcohol abuse during the most recent 12 months in the community (generally, this will be the 12 months before the arrest for the instant sex offense, but in some cases offenders will have been in the community for 12 or more months before being returned on a revocation or a new nonsex conviction)	No (–1); yes (+1)
12.	Employment history during the most recent 12 months in the community (generally, this will be the 12 months before the arrest for the instant sex offense, but in some cases offenders will have been in the community for 12 or more months before being returned on a revocation or a new non-sex conviction)	Stable employment for one year or longer prior to arrest (–2); homemaker, retired, full-time student, or disabled/unable to work (–2); part-time, seasonal, unstable employment (0); unemployed or significant history of unemployment (+1); file contains no information about employment history (0)
13.	Discipline history while incarcerated (does not include discipline for failure to follow directives to complete treatment successfully)	No major discipline reports or infractions (0); one or more major discipline reports (+1)
14.	Chemical dependency treatment while incarcerated	Treatment recommended and successfully completed or in program at time of release (–2); no treatment recommended/not enough time/no opportunity (0); treatment recommended but offender refused, quit, or did not pursue (+1); treatment recommended but terminated (+4)
15.	Sex offender treatment while incarcerated	Treatment recommended and successfully completed or in program at time of release (–1); no treatment recommended/not enough time/no opportunity (0); treatment recommended but offender refused, quit, or did not pursue (0); treatment recommended but terminated (+3)
16.	Age at release from institution	Age 30 or younger (+1); age 31 or older (–1)

Civil Commitment of Sexual Offenders

Unlike other criminal offenders, sex offenders who have done time do not always regain their liberty. Many jurisdictions around the world, including many U.S. states, now use the legal term **sexually violent predator** or *SVP*, which refers to any person who has been convicted of or charged with a crime of sexual violence and who suffers from a mental abnormality or personality disorder that makes the person likely to engage in predatory acts of sexual violence again, if not confined in a secure facility. These jurisdictions have laws that treat SVPs strictly, allowing them to

be held in state-run, in-custody mental institutions *after* their sentence is complete if they are considered to be a risk to the public (civil commitment).

The first sexually violent predator law in the U.S. was the Community Protection Act of 1990, passed in the state of Washington. As of now, 16 other states have passed similar laws. These programs have been fiercely debated at many forums, not only because they are considered a severe drain on public exchequer but also because they are thought to be inhumane. However, the justification of these programs has often been cited as recidivism, which among sex offenders poses a serious problem (as noted earlier). Civil commitment laws have been challenged time and again, but the U.S. Supreme Court, in *Kansas v. Hendricks 521 U.S. 346* (1997), has upheld their constitutionality (Box 41-1) (Grudzinskas & Henry, 1997).

Registration and Community Notification Laws Regarding Sexual Offenders

Sex offender registration is a system in place in a number of jurisdictions designed to allow governmental authorities to keep track of the residence and activities of sex offenders, including those who have completed their criminal sentences. In some jurisdictions—especially in the United States—information in the registry is made available to the general public via a website or other means (community notification). In many jurisdictions, registered sex offenders are subject to additional restrictions, including housing. Those on parole or probation may be subject to restrictions that do not apply to other parolees or probationers. Sometimes these include restrictions on being in the presence of minors, living in proximity to a school or daycare center, or owning toys or other items of interest to minors.

Box 41-1 *Kansas v. Hendricks*—Upholding the Constitutionality of Civil Commitment of Sexual Offenders

Under the Kansas *Sexually Violent Predator Act*, any person who, because of "mental abnormality" or "personality disorder," is likely to engage in "predatory acts of sexual violence" can be indefinitely confined. Leroy Hendricks and Tim Quinn had an extensive history of sexually molesting children. When they were due to be released from prison, Kansas filed a petition under the act in state court to involuntarily commit Hendricks and Quinn. Hendricks and Quinn challenged the constitutionality of the act on several grounds: (1) it was a case of *double jeopardy* (i.e., they were being tried twice for the same crime; double jeopardy is prohibited by the Fifth Amendment); (2) *ex post facto application* of a law (i.e., they were being punished for a law that was enacted *after* the crime was committed); (3) they were being detained *without due process of law*, something that is ensured by the Fourteenth Amendment; and, finally, (4) it was a *cruel and unusual punishment* unconstitutional under the Eighth Amendment.

A trial by jury was requested, which the court granted. Hendricks and Quinn testified during the trial that they agreed with the diagnosis by the state psychiatrist that Hendricks and Quinn suffer from pedophilia and admitted that they continued to experience uncontrollable sexual desires for children when they are under extreme stress. The jury decided that they qualified as *sexually violent predators*. Because pedophilia is defined as a mental abnormality under the act, the court ordered that Hendricks be civilly committed. Hendricks appealed the validity of his commitment in the State Supreme Court. The court ruled in favor of Hendricks, declaring that the act was invalid. Finally the case reached the U.S. Supreme Court.

The Supreme Court ruled against Hendricks in a 5-4 decision. It agreed with the act's procedures and the definition of a "mental abnormality" as a "congenital or acquired condition affecting the emotional or volitional capacity which predisposes the person to commit sexually violent offenses to the degree that such person is a menace to the health and safety of others." It agreed with Kansas that the act limits persons eligible for confinement to persons who are not able to control their dangerousness. Further, the court decided the act does not violate the Constitution's *double jeopardy* prohibition nor the ban on *ex post facto law* because the act does not establish criminal proceedings and therefore *involuntary confinement under it is not punishment*. Because the act is civil, Hendricks's confinement under the act is not a second prosecution nor is it double jeopardy. In other words, *the confinement is civil rather than criminal* (please note the phrase "civil commitment of sexual offenders").

Hendricks's other contentions were also dismissed on similar grounds.

Summary

With the rise of the incidence of sexually deviant behavior, forensic nurse practitioners are going to witness an increasing number of such cases in the course of their practice. By understanding the sexual offending behavior in all its aforementioned dimensions, the forensic nurse can meaningfully help and assist in the management of sexual offenders.

References

Aggrawal, A. (2007). Bride Capture. D. S. Clark (Ed.), *Encyclopedia of Law And Society: American And Global Perspectives* Vol. 1. (pp. 134–135). Thousand Oaks, London: Sage Publications.

Aggrawal, A. (2009a). *Forensic and medico-legal aspects of sexual crimes and unusual sexual practices.* Boca Raton, FL; London: CRC Press.

Aggrawal, A. (2009b). References to the paraphilias and sexual crimes in the Bible. *J Forensic Leg Med, 16*(3), 109–114.

American Psychiatric Association. (1968). *Diagnostic and statistical manual of mental disorders.* Washington, DC: American Psychiatric Association.

American Psychiatric Association. (2000). *Diagnostic and statistical manual of mental disorders: DSM-IV-TR.* Washington, DC: American Psychiatric Association.

Bancroft, J., Tennant, G., Loucas, K., et al. (1974). The control of deviant behaviour by drugs. *British Journal of Psychiatry, 125*(3), 310–315.

Berlin, F. S. (1988). Issues in the exploration of biological factors contributing to the etiology of the "sex offender," plus some ethical considerations. *Annals of the New York Academy of Sciences, 528*(3), 183–192.

Bolt, D. M., Hare, R. D., et al. (2007). Score Metric Equivalence of the Psychopathy Checklist-Revised (PCL-R) across criminal offenders in North America and the United Kingdom: A critique of Cooke, Michie, Hart, and Clark (2005) and new analyses. *Assessment, 14*(1), 44–56.

Briken, P., Berner, W., et al. (2000). [Treatment of paraphilia and sexually aggressive impulsive behavior with the LHRH-agonist leuprolide acetate]. *Der Nervenarzt, 71*(5), 380–385.

Buvat, J., Lemaire, A., et al. (1996). [Role of hormones in sexual dysfunctions, homosexuality, transsexualism and deviant sexual behavior: Diagnostic and therapeutic consequences]. *Contraception, Fertilite, Sexualite (1992), 24*(11), 834–846.

Cooper, A. J. (1986). Progestogens in the treatment of male sex offenders: A review. *Canadian Journal of Psychiatry. Revue Canadienne De Psychiatrie, 31*(1), 73–79.

Cooper, A. J., Ismail, A. A., et al. (1972). Antiandrogen (cyproterone acetate) therapy in deviant hypersexuality. *The British Journal of Psychiatry: The Journal of Mental Science, 120*(554), 59–63.

Dahle, K. P. (2006). Strengths and limitations of actuarial prediction of criminal reoffence in a German prison sample: A comparative study of LSI-R, HCR-20 and PCL-R. *International Journal of Law and Psychiatry, 29*(5), 431–442.

David, W. S., Simpson, T. L., et al. (2006). Taking charge: A pilot curriculum of self-defense and personal safety training for female veterans with PTSD because of military sexual trauma. *Journal of Interpersonal Violence, 21*(4), 555–565.

Denov, M. S. (2004). The long-term effects of child sexual abuse by female perpetrators: A qualitative study of male and female victims. *Journal of Interpersonal Violence, 19*(10), 1137–1156.

Dietiker, J., Dittmann, V., et al. (2007). [Risk assessment of sex offenders in a German-speaking sample: Applicability of PCL-SV, HCR-20+3, and SVR-20]. *Der Nervenarzt, 78*(1), 53–61.

Douglas, K. S., & Ogloff, J. R. (2003). The impact of confidence on the accuracy of structured professional and actuarial violence risk judgments in a sample of forensic psychiatric patients. *Law and Human Behavior, 27*(6), 573–587.

Drieschner, K., & Lange, A. (1999). A review of cognitive factors in the etiology of rape: Theories, empirical studies, and implications. *Clinical Psychology Review, 19*(1), 57–77.

Ducro, C., & Pham, T. (2006). Evaluation of the SORAG and the Static-99 on Belgian sex offenders committed to a forensic facility. *Sexual Abuse: A Journal of Research and Treatment, 18*(1), 15–26.

English, K., Retzlaff, P., et al. (2002). The Colorado Sex Offender Risk Scale. *Journal of Child Sexual Abuse, 11*(2), 77–96.

Epperson, D., Kaul, J. D., Huot, S. J., Hesselton, D., Alexander, W., & Goldman, R. (1998). *Minnesota Sex Offender Screening Tool-Revised (MnSOST-R).* St. Paul, Minnesota: Department of Corrections.

Gagne, P. (1981). Treatment of sex offenders with medroxyprogesterone acetate. *The American Journal of Psychiatry, 138*(5), 644–646.

Gebhard, P. H., Gagnon, I. H., Pomeroy, W. B., & Christenson, C. V. (1967). *Sex Offenders: An Analysis of Types.* New York: Bantam.

Glass, B. J. (2004). Sex offenders. In M. D. Smith (Ed.), *Encyclopedia of Rape* (pp. 222–224). Westport, CT: Greenwood Press.

Gray, N. S., Taylor, J., et al. (2008). Predicting violent reconvictions using the HCR-20. *The British Journal of Psychiatry: The Journal of Mental Science, 192*(5), 384–387.

Greenfeld, L. A., Snell, T. L., et al. (1999). *Women offenders.* Washington, DC: U.S. Dept. of Justice, Office of Justice Programs, Bureau of Justice Statistics.

Grove, W. M., & Meehl, P. E. (1996). Comparative efficiency of informal (subjective, impressionistic) and formal (mechanical, algorithmic) prediction procedures: The clinical-statistical controversy. *Psychology, Public Policy, and Law, 115*(2), 293–323.

Grudzinskas, A. J., Jr., & Henry, M. G. (1997). Kansas v. Hendricks. *The Journal of the American Academy of Psychiatry and the Law, 25*(4), 607–612.

Hagan, M. P., Anderson, D. L., Caldwell, M. S., & Kemper, T. S. (2008). Five-year accuracy of assessments of high risk for sexual recidivism of adolescents. *International Journal of Offender Therapy and Comparative Criminology, 52*(5), 495–498.

Hall, H. V. (2008). *Forensic psychology and neuropsychology for criminal and civil cases.* Boca Raton, FL; London: CRC.

Hanson, R. K. (1997). *The development of a brief actuarial risk scale for sexual offense recidivism.* Ottawa, Ontario: Public Works and Government Services Canada.

Hanson, R. K., & Bussiere, M. T. (1998). Predicting relapse: A meta-analysis of sexual offender recidivism studies. *Journal of Consulting and Clinical Psychology, 66*(2), 348–362.

Hanson, R. K., & Harris, A. J. (2001). A structured approach to evaluating change among sexual offenders. *Sexual Abuse: A Journal of Research and Treatment, 13*(2), 105–122.

Harris, G., Rice, M. E., & Quinsey, V. L. (1993). Violent recidivism of mentally disordered offenders: The development of a statistical prediction instrument. *Criminal Justice Behaviour, 20*(4), 315–335.

Himmelfarb, N., Yaeger, D., et al. (2006). Posttraumatic stress disorder in female veterans with military and civilian sexual trauma. *Journal of Traumatic Stress, 19*(6), 837–846.

Kelly, M. M., Vogt, D. S., et al. (2008). Effects of military trauma exposure on women veterans' use and perceptions of Veterans Health Administration care. *Journal of General Internal Medicine: Official Journal of the Society for Research and Education in Primary Care Internal Medicine, 23*(6), 741–747.

Kimerling, R., Gima, K., et al. (2007). The Veterans Health Administration and military sexual trauma. *American Journal of Public Health, 97*(12), 2160–2166.

Kimerling, R., Street, A. E., et al. (2008). Evaluation of universal screening for military-related sexual trauma. *Psychiatric Services (Washington, DC), 59*(6), 635–640.

Kokish, R. (2003). The current role of post-conviction sex offender polygraph testing in sex offender treatment. *Journal of Child Sexual Abuse, 12*(3–4), 175–194.

Kokish, R., Levenson, J. S., et al. (2005). Post-conviction sex offender polygraph examination: Client-reported perceptions of utility and accuracy. *Sexual Abuse: A Journal of Research and Treatment, 17*(2), 211–221.

Kravitz, H. M., Haywood, T. W., et al. (1996). Medroxyprogesterone and paraphiles: Do testosterone levels matter? *The Bulletin of the American Academy of Psychiatry and the Law, 24*(1), 73–83.

Kravitz, H. M., Haywood, T. W., et al. (1995). Medroxyprogesterone treatment for paraphiliacs. *The Bulletin of the American Academy of Psychiatry and the Law, 23*(1), 19–33.

Krueger, R. B., & Kaplan, M. S. (2001). Depot-leuprolide acetate for treatment of paraphilias: A report of twelve cases. *Archives of Sexual Behavior, 30*(4), 409–422.

Lamberg, L. (1998). Gay is okay with APA–forum honors landmark 1973 events. American Psychiatric Association. *JAMA: The Journal of the American Medical Association, 280*(6), 497–499.

Lang, R. A., & Frenzel, R. R. (1988). How sex offenders lure children. *Sexual Abuse: A Journal of Research and Treatment, 1*(2), 303–317.

Langan, P. A., Schmitt, E. L., et al. (2003). *Recidivism of sex offenders released from prison in 1994.* Washington, DC: U.S. Dept. of Justice, Office of Justice Programs, Bureau of Justice Statistics: iv, 40 p.

Lodewijks, H. P., Doreleijers, T. A., et al. (2008). Predictive validity of the Structured Assessment of Violence Risk in Youth (SAVRY) during residential treatment. *International Journal of Law and Psychiatry, 31*(3), 263–271.

Lohse, H., & Hauch, M. (1983). Ambulatory psychotherapy of sex offenses. *Psychiatrische Praxis, 10*(5), 147–152.

MacNamara, D., & Sagarin, E. (1977). *Sex, crime, and the law.* New York: Free Press.

Manchak, S. M., Skeem, J. L., et al. (2008). Utility of the Revised Level of Service Inventory (LSI-R) in predicting recidivism after long-term incarceration. *Law and Human Behavior, 32*(6), 477–488.

Meijer, E. H., Verschuere, B., et al. (2008). Sex offender management using the polygraph: A critical review. *International Journal of Law and Psychiatry, 31*(5), 423–429.

Monahan, J. (1996). The past twenty and the next twenty years. *Criminal Justice Behaviour, 23*(1), 107–120.

National Sexual Violence Resource Center (NSVRC). (2004). Global Perspectives on Sexual Violence: Findings from the World Report on Violence and Health. (Abstracted from Krug, E. G., et al. (Eds.), *World Report on Violence and Health.* Geneva: World Health Organization 2002.

Nunes, K. L., Firestone, P., et al. (2002). A comparison of modified versions of the Static-99 and the Sex Offender Risk Appraisal Guide. *Sexual Abuse: A Journal of Research and Treatment, 14*(3), 253–269.

O'Brien, C., Gaher, R. M., et al. (2008). Difficulty identifying feelings predicts the persistence of trauma symptoms in a sample of veterans who experienced military sexual trauma. *The Journal of Nervous and Mental Disease, 196*(3), 252–255.

Oliver, B. E. (2007). Preventing female-perpetrated sexual abuse. *Trauma, Violence & Abuse, 8*(1), 19–32.

Patterson, D., & Campbell, R. (2009). A comparative study of the prosecution of childhood sexual abuse cases: The contributory role of pediatric forensic nurse examiner (FNE) programs. *Journal of Forensic Nursing, 5*(1), 38–45.

Pereira, N., Huband, N., et al. (2008). Psychopathy and personality. An investigation of the relationship between the NEO-Five Factor Inventory (NEO-FFI) and the Psychopathy Checklist-Revised (PCL-R) in a hospitalized sample of male offenders with personality disorder. *Criminal Behaviour and Mental Health: CBMH, 18*(4), 216–223.

Peter, T. (2008). Exploring taboos: Comparing male- and female-perpetrated child sexual abuse. *Journal of Interpersonal Violence, 24*(7), 1111–1128.

Regan, J., Wilhoite, K., et al. (2007). Military sexual trauma. *Tennessee Medicine: Journal of the Tennessee Medical Association, 100*(2), 41–42.

Rosler, A., & Witztum, E. (1998). Treatment of men with paraphilia with a long-acting analogue of gonadotropin-releasing hormone. *The New England Journal of Medicine, 338*(7), 416–422.

Rousseau, L., Couture, M., et al. (1990). Effect of combined androgen blockade with an LHRH agonist and flutamide in one severe case of male exhibitionism. *Canadian Journal of Psychiatry. Revue Canadienne De Psychiatrie, 35*(4), 338–341.

Saleh, F. M., & Berlin, F. S. (2003). Sex hormones, neurotransmitters, and psychopharmacological treatments in men with paraphilic disorders. *Journal of Child Sexual Abuse, 12*(3–4), 233–253.

Sjostedt, G., & Langstrom, N. (2001). Actuarial assessment of sex offender recidivism risk: A cross-validation of the RRASOR and the Static-99 in Sweden. *Law and Human Behavior, 25*(6), 629–645.

Studer, L. H., Aylwin, A. S., et al. (2005). Testosterone, sexual offense recidivism, and treatment effect among adult male sex offenders. *Sexual Abuse: A Journal of Research and Treatment, 17*(2), 171–181.

Suris, A., & Lind, L. (2008). Military sexual trauma: A review of prevalence and associated health consequences in veterans. *Trauma, Violence & Abuse, 9*(4), 250–269.

Terry, K. J. (2006). *Sexual offenses and offenders: Theory, practice, and policy.* Belmont, CA; London: Thomson Learning/Wadsworth.

Thibaut, F., Cordier, B., et al. (1993). Effect of a long-lasting gonadotrophin hormone-releasing hormone agonist in six cases of severe male paraphilia. *Acta Psychiatrica Scandinavica, 87*(6), 445–450.

Thibaut, F., Cordier, B., et al. (1996). Gonadotrophin hormone releasing hormone agonist in cases of severe paraphilia: A lifetime treatment? *Psychoneuroendocrinology, 21*(4), 411–419.

Thibaut, F., Kuhn, J. M., et al. (1998). Hormone treatment of sex offenses. *L'Encephale, 24*(2), 132–137.

Urbaniok, F., Noll, T., et al. (2007). The predictive quality of the Psychopathy Checklist-Revised (PCL-R) for violent and sex offenders in Switzerland. A validation study. *Fortschritte der Neurologie-Psychiatrie, 75*(3), 155–159.

Valente, S., & Wight, C. (2007). Military sexual trauma: violence and sexual abuse. *Military Medicine, 172*(3), 259–265.

Weinberger, L. E., Sreenivasan, S., et al. (1998). Extended civil commitment for dangerous psychiatric patients. *The Journal of the American Academy of Psychiatry and the Law, 26*(1), 75–87.

Wiedeking, C., Lake, C. R., et al. (1977). Plasma noradrenalin and dopamine-beta-hydroxylase during behavioral testine of sexually deviant XYY and XXY males. *Human Genetics, 37*(2), 243–247.

Wolf, S. C. (1984). *A multifactor model of deviant sexuality.* Lisbon: Third International Conference on Victimology.

Yaeger, D., Himmelfarb, N., et al. (2006). DSM-IV diagnosed posttraumatic stress disorder in women veterans with and without military sexual trauma. *Journal of General Internal Medicine: Official Journal of the Society for Research and Education in Primary Care Internal Medicine, 21*(Suppl 3), S65–S69.

CHAPTER 42 Female Genital Mutilation

Patricia A. Crane

Denouncing the practice of female genital mutilation (FGM) can make some countries feel superior and self-righteous, but it certainly does not solve the problem. Our purpose should not be to criticize and condemn. Nor can we remain passive, in the name of some bland version of multiculturalism. We know that the practice of genital mutilation is painful and can have dire consequences on the health of the baby girl and, later on, of the woman. But we must always work from the assumption that human behaviors and cultural values, however senseless or destructive they may appear to us from our particular personal and cultural standpoints, have meaning and fulfill a function for those who practice them. People will change their behavior only when they themselves perceive the new practices proposed as meaningful and functional as the old ones. Therefore, what we must aim for is to convince people, including women, that they can give up a specific practice without giving up meaningful aspects of their own cultures.

—Statement of the Director General to the World Health Organization's Global Commission on Women's Health (WHO, 1996)

The clinical forensic role is found applicable in many professional positions where the nurse faces intersecting ethical challenges, cultural issues, and legal matters affecting the provision of healthcare. One of the newest crimes of interpersonal violence to confront nursing, female genital mutilation or female circumcision (FGM/FC), is achieving great international notoriety in political, human rights, and women's reproductive health research in the United States, Canada, and other countries to which women migrate. In the face of unfamiliar and often inhumane acts that may be confronted on a daily basis, the forensic responsibility must be integrated into the nursing process. Integral to professional practice is the ability to honor individual human rights and to maintain professional and legal objectivity, as well as cultural sensitivity and respect for patients.

KEY POINT The forensic nurse must understand the social, cultural, and ethical practices which negatively impact women's health and violate their human rights.

An overview of the history of FGM/FC, its psychological and physical health consequences, and the possible legal ramifications will provide a background for the development of appropriate assessment, diagnosis, and intervention. Case studies support the need for cultural competence and patient education, while accessible resources are available throughout the nursing process for follow-up and referral of patients and families for evaluation. With the combination of cultural competence and forensic knowledge to the application of the nursing process, enhanced patient outcomes are assured.

Significance of the Issue

Worldwide, more than 130 million women and ultimately their families are affected by the practice of FGM/FC. The World Health Organization (WHO, 2000) admittedly underestimates that nearly 2 million more are subjected to the ritual annually with prevalence rates ranging from 18% (Tanzania) to 97% (Egypt) in African countries (Muteshi & Sass, 2005). The age at which a young woman undergoes FGM/FC varies greatly but may be from sometime in the first year of life up to 18 years old. In villages and communities with limited access, the person performing the ritual procedure may travel through the area every four to five years, so girls in a wide age range are expected and often forced by peers and parents to undergo the procedure. According to the Program for Appropriate Technology in Health (PATH, 1997), the rural population is not as likely to support FGM as are the employed and educated women. In larger cities, a ritual practitioner may be available for hire on a daily basis. For others, a celebration and feast takes place after a season of superfluous crops and is associated with fertility. The village elder decides which group of marriageable girls will participate in an associated FGM ritual (Hosken, 1981), and it has been reported that the younger the girls are, the better. Smaller girls are easier to restrain when cut and are less likely to remember the pain and terror. Girls may be more verbally and physically rebellious as they get older and have more education regarding the FGM practice and the harm it may cause.

Large university surveys of students in Khartoum, Sudan, report that more than half are mutilated. It seems promising for the future generations that 88% of the women and 78% of the men want the practice to be abolished (Herieka & Dhar, 2003).

Early estimates stated that more than 168,000 people from countries where FGM is practiced had entered the United States by 1997, either as immigrants or as refugees. Within this group, those who may be at risk for FGM/FC are under the age of 18 and number more than 60,000 (E. T. Ortiz, personal communication, January 30, 1997). Bringing the tradition with them, indigenes are leaving their countries of origin for new opportunities in various countries throughout Europe, Canada, and South America. In the United States, large pockets of FGM/FC-practicing populations are settling together in communities in major metropolitan areas such as Los Angeles, Washington, D.C., Dallas, Denver, New York, and Boston. Hence, health personnel and educators who face the issue on a daily basis may have little or no knowledge of how to initiate conversation regarding the problem or how to control their reaction when it comes up in a medical interview or examination. Recent data assessing the healthcare professionals' awareness classifications and definitions of FGM/FC showed that almost all had experience with examining women and knew the definition of FGM/FC. However, they knew little about the laws and could not classify the type of FGM/FC, and only half of them had the necessary knowledge for medical management (Zaidi, Khalil, Roberts, & Browne, 2007).

Girls are subjected to the inhumane tradition of FGM/FC across all continents. Although the practice is not mandatory or supported by Islam, Christian, or Judaic law, it is found to be performed and encouraged at various times in history by members of all religions. Hosken's (1981) extensive investigation on worldwide genital cutting resulted in reports, with few actual medical studies, of such ancient practices being found in South America, Mexico, Europe, Australia, Asia, India, and primarily in Africa. Genital mutilation is not unknown in the United States. In the 1950s, such procedures were documented as a treatment for control of women with hysteria and sexual problems. Medical reports and statistics indicate that FGM/FC is utilized, with varying degrees of severity, primarily across the central belt of Africa in more than 28 countries (Fig. 42-1) and a few isolated groups in Asia and the Middle East (WHO, 2000). They follow local indigenous religious customs and Islamic law. However, Muslim leaders are adamantly opposed to references to FGM/FC as a religious practice. In fact, they are sought out and used in the movement to eradicate FGM/FC in Africa and in the United States because of their highly influential roles as teacher and authority.

Criminalization of FGM/FC

Congress amended the U.S. Code as part of the Illegal Immigration and Reform and Immigrant Responsibility Act of 1996, by adding "whoever knowingly circumcises, excises, or infibulates the whole or any part of the labia majora or labia minora or clitoris of another person who has not attained the age of 18 years shall be fined under this title or imprisoned not more than 5 years, or both." The Immigration and Naturalization Services (INS) in cooperation with the

Department of State is required to inform aliens who are issued visas when they enter the United States of the severe harm of FGM. The information must be presented in a manner that is limited to the practice and respectul of the cultural values of the societies that practice FGM. Most importantly the information must explain that there are legal consequences for performing or subjecting a child to FGM under the criminal or child protection statutes or as a form of child abuse (Center for Reproductive Rights, 2004). The Center for Reproductive Law & Policy (1997) claims that no one has been convicted based on the laws but cases based on the statutes have been brought before the courts.

Sixteen states in the United States have developed laws criminalizing the practice of FGM addressing the issue in a manner similar to the federal legislation, by prohibiting the practice of FGM and instituting criminal sanctions (Center for Reproductive Rights, 2004). Other states consider child abuse law adequate to guarantee protection of individual human rights of a child.

KEY POINT The criminalization of FGM in the United States requires that forensic nurses be prepared to deal with its associated issues with immigration groups and experts in immigration law, as well as the courts, to protect the human rights of the patients who have been victimized by the practice.

Criminalizing the offense in the United States can have drastic effects on noncitizens depending on the judge, the skill of the attorney, and the extent of their knowledge of immigration law (Brady & Tooby, 1997). For many authorities, little is known about the practice of FGM and its health implications, despite its emergence in the United States. Adverse consequences, such as deportation even without a conviction, are possible, with no consideration for the person's length of residency. Persons participating in the perpetration of the crime in the United States can be faced with fines and jail sentences but must also consider their personal value of keeping the family together and the survival outcomes for the family members who may be left behind should deportation or incarceration occur. Brady and Tooby also strongly advise contacting an immigration organization and experts in immigration law to best meet the needs of clients who are not citizens.

Hundreds of young women, after being educated and given the choice, seek to escape their country of origin and inhumane rituals, often seeking asylum in Europe, Canada, or the United States. The asylum standard in the United States requires three elements: (1) persecution, (2) a well-founded fear, and (3) an act of persecution that was based on the grounds of race, religion, nationality, or membership in a particular social group. Despite the need for education, ultimately a decision on the matter would rest with the asylum officer or immigration judge. Asylum law is in need of reform and may not offer much in the way of protection for a woman (Stern, 1997). There may be detrimental effects on a woman's physical and psychological health, yet being granted asylum may be impossible or take years. However, case summaries of gender asylum clearly show that increasing numbers of immigrant women from many different countries are succeeding in being granted asylum.

On a global perspective, the international health community has addressed the practice through many forums for at least half a century. The Universal Declaration of Human Rights in 1948, the United Nations (UN) Convention on the Rights of the Child in 1959, the African Charter on the Rights and Welfare of the

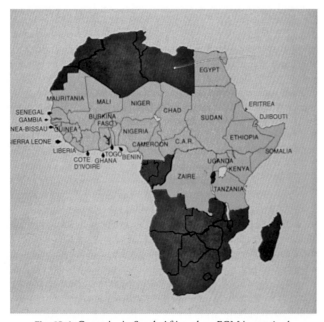
Fig. 42-1 Countries in South Africa where FGM is practiced.

Child in 1990, the UN Declaration on Violence Against Women in 1993, the UN High Commission on Refugees Statement Against Gender-Based Violence in 1996, to name a few, express opposition to the practice and strongly encourage enforcement of the law in countries where it is forbidden. The International Council of Nurses' position statement (1992) advises that nurses pay particular attention to protecting children from all forms of abuse so they can grow up in health and dignity. Human rights are essential to quality of life, regardless of ethnicity or sex. Many feel that outlawing FGM/FC in other countries was a move to please the advocates in the Western world whose voice and money have influence. Family or community decisions to cease a ritual practice that is deeply rooted and of incalculable value are not likely to be made based on foreign policy alone, although this may carry weight in the long run. Laws in the European Community and Canada have resulted in arrests that have gained international notoriety but resulted in little change in FGM-practicing countries. In Egypt there is evidence that the practice of FGM/FC appears to be in decline following passage of the prohibition laws six years ago, but the decline is thought to be related to multimedia education and publicized deaths of young women (Hassanin, Saleh, Bedaiwy, Peterson, & Badaiwy, 2008). The shift in public opinion, public denouncement of the practice, and its decline will continue as parents see that other parents have stopped the practice.

Educational awareness of the health complications and educational programs appear to be effective prevention in Kenya with a noteworthy decline in FGM/FC. The law passed in 2001, and although this is a positive step, it may deter women from seeking medical assistance for complications from FGM/FC (Livermore, Monteiro & Rymer, 2007). Researchers in Nigeria, following a health education intervention, documented a statistically significant increase in the number of adults who wanted to stop FGM/FC and in those who do not want their daughters mutilated. It is not known if the intervenion and postive attitude changes will lead to actual behavioral changes (Asekun-Olarinmoye & Amusan, 2008). Placing FGM elimination within a comprehensive development strategy that envelops reproductive and gender issues may be most effective. Also the health education must be accompanied by skill building if behavior changes are desired when complex cultural issues are deep rooted (Asekun-Olarinmoye & Amusan, 2008).

In the United States, as with other crimes of violence, many feel that making the act illegal could drive it underground where it will flourish, shrouded in secrecy. There are reports from immigrant groups in California that circumcision is being surreptitiously performed on immigrant girls. In personal conversations with young African immigrant working mothers, they relay fears that family members or babysitters, perceiving that the practice is still of social value and a necessary cultural tradition, may locate an individual with little medical training to perform circumcisions. Returning from work to find the baby mutilated is a constant fear. As documented in the University of California Hastings gender asylum case summaries (2000), the fear that young daughters will be taken and circumcised is prevalent in mothers who try to leave this ritual behind. On the other hand, wealthy families may send their daughters on "holiday" to be circumcised (Reichert, 1998).

Historical Basis

Ritual ceremonies that involve the cutting of women's genitalia are rooted in tradition thousands of years old. As with many cultural practices, the original rationale is recondite. Documented history is lacking with much of women's health behavior, such as birthing and circumcision rituals. However, the reasons most often given for FGM/FC were of a psychosexual, sociological, or hygienic nature (Gibeau, 1998). Passed down through generations of oral history, there is no foundation for rationalizing such practices today.

Some say eliminating a woman's sexual desire reduces any undue sexual demands of her husband, who may have several wives to enhance his progeny and wealth. In addition, destruction of the clitoral nerve endings would prevent her from seeking sexual pleasure with other men. The clitoris was also seen as masculinizing and the rumor was that it would grow very large and turn a woman into a man unless it was removed when she was young. To others the clitoris is thought to be poisonous to the man or to the newborn, and those who were to touch it would die.

Hygienic reasons required that the clitoris and labia be removed to make the woman clean and beautiful. Closing the vagina ensures virginity and a high bride price, critical issues in an area where families may depend on the price of daughters and cattle to keep the family subsistent. Not only can the surgery keep her virginal before marriage, if the man is away for long periods of time hunting, trading, and protecting herds of grazing animals, a woman may have the vagina resutured, reinfibulation, to assure her virtue in his absence and prevent rape.

If originally instituted for any or all of these stated reasons, the most often quoted reason for FGM/FC in recent times is that it is simply the tradition. Previously, no man would think of marrying a woman who had not been cut (Hosken, 1993). Female relatives consider that it is something they must do to maintain their daughters' marriageability, family status, and honor. It is not felt to be mutilation.

Naming the Ritual

What to call the procedure varies from international conferences to meetings of policy makers. Unequivocally, in healthcare and policy settings, the WHO terminology of female genital mutilation is accepted. Admittedly, the reason the surgery takes place is not to mutilate one's daughter. To insinuate the idea is insulting to the ancestors and sets up an impenetrable barrier in communication between patient and provider. However, mutilation is often the end result. In the country of origin, those who practice the procedure may refer to it as being made clean, being cut, or excision. Others refer to it as circumcision, and it is linked with premarital celebrations and coming-of-age rituals at the time of adolescence. In reality, there is little resemblance to the circumcision of males, which refers to the foreskin of the penis being removed. An Arabic word, sunna, meaning tradition, is the only word known for FGM/FC in some countries. In personal communication, a physician said that if she used any other word the women would not know what she was saying. The WHO has developed descriptions of four categories of FGM/FC: Type I, Type II, Type III, and Type IV (WHO, 2000).

TYPE I

Type I may include removal of the prepuce or hood of the clitoris and partial or total removal of the clitoris. This is typically the procedure known as sunna.

TYPE II

Type II may be known as excision and includes removal of the clitoris and labia minora. The vagina is typically not covered, but copious scar tissue and adhesions may obliterate the vaginal introitus over time.

TYPE III

Type III, also known as infibulation or pharaonic circumcision, includes removal of the clitoris, labia minora, and part of the labia majora. The two sides of the remaining vulvar tissue are closed over the vagina in a crude fashion, often with suture or acacia thorns. A small hollow reed from a local plant may be left in place while the injury is healing. This allows for a small opening to be left for the passage of urine and menstrual flow. The girls' legs may be bound together for several weeks. It is not uncommon for the incision to require opening at the time of marriage or childbirth. Many women request that they be resutured afterward, as local practice and the woman's family may dictate.

TYPE IV

Type IV is an unclassified grouping of all other mutilations of the female genital area such as pricking, piercing, cutting, and scraping of vaginal tissue, incisions to the clitoris and vagina, and burning, scarring, or cauterizing of tissue. (See Figs. 42-2, 42-3, and 42-4.)

Physical Consequences

Despite often noted horrific outcomes, many variables influence the severity of scarring and damage to the genital area after cutting, backed by little scientific evidence (Morison, Scherf, Ekpo, et al., 2001). In areas where the trend is toward medicalization, the educated, trained professionals perform procedures with proper surgical technique using up-to-date sterile equipment so there is less risk. Medicalization is not the norm, and FGM/FC is still against the law and a punishable criminal act. As the severity of cutting increases, so do the gynecological and obstetrical problems (Jones, Diop, Askew, et al., 1999).

Data-based research is emerging and is more powerful than anecdotal cases. One study in Egypt (n = 264) was comprised of 75% circumcised rural women and the rest were urban, educated, noncircumcised women (Elnashar & Abdelhady, 2007). The researchers noted statisically significant greater amounts of dysmenorrhea, dyspareunia, loss of libido, failure of orgasm, husband disatisfaction, vaginal tears with childbirth, episiotomy, and distressed babies with circumcised women. Mental problems such as somatization, anxiety, and phobia were significant in circumcised women as well (Elnashar & Abdelhady, 2007).

Often the village midwife, traditional birth attendant (TBA), local barber, or a male or female circumciser performs the procedure. Routinely, these are not highly educated people, and they have little or no knowledge of anatomy, asepsis, disinfectant, or

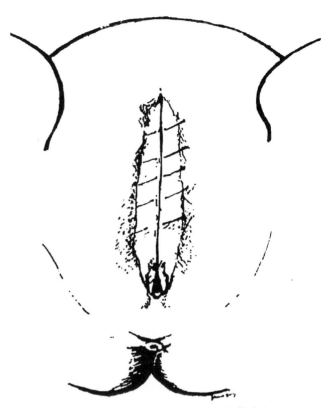

Fig. 42-3 Illustration of thorns used for infibulation.

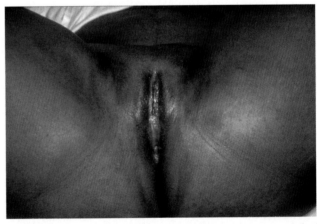

Fig. 42-4 Adult FGM victim deinfibulation. Note extensive scarring and disfigurement.

medications and rarely use anesthesia. They may have a reputation throughout the region and have learned to earn a living in this manner through several generations of women. Local educators often provide circumcisers with less primitive equipment as well as education on asepsis in an attempt to curb some of the problems.

Despite the use of applications of local herbs, animal products, and primitive closure of the vagina with thorns, hemostasis may not be accomplished, resulting in hemorrhage as well as an irreversible state of anemia. Immediate physical problems include shock, not only from hemorrhage but also from severe pain resulting from the tragic degree of sensory nerve damage, an irreversible condition. If the circumciser is using items such as a rusty razor, sharp stone, shell, piece of glass, machete, or scissors, it is not difficult to comprehend frequent and widespread infections. Tetanus

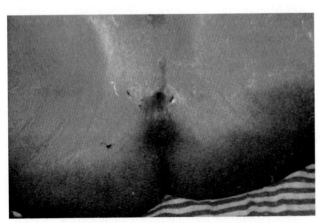

Fig. 42-2 Seven-year-old victim of FGM.

may be fatal in many cases and risks of exposure to human immunodeficiency virus (HIV), various forms of hepatitis, and other pathogens are greater when instruments are used on a group of girls without cleaning, which is often the case. Damage to surrounding organs and lack of knowledge of nerves and arteries in the genital area end in tragic results, including gangrene. Urinary retention can occur with the blockage of the urinary opening with eventual irreversible kidney damage. Urinary tract infections can be immediate or occur more frequently the rest of a woman's life. Over the long term, damage to the urethra from the cutting, frequent infections, and growth of scar tissue undoubtedly cause chronic pain, urinary hesitancy, and incontinence. Women and girls often report that it takes 10 to 15 minutes to complete urination. The bartholin gland openings near the vaginal introitus may be covered with scar tissue, a blockage that can lead to cysts, abscesses, and tumors in the vulvar area up to 10 cm in diameter.

Childbirth itself is a risk because scar tissue reduces the elasticity of the birth canal and limits the local tissue response to hormones designed to make this natural process occur with minimal discomfort. Hence, the women undergo more pain and tissue damage. Laceration and fistula formations between the vagina and rectum or vagina and urethra are not uncommon. An obstructed birth canal can prolong second stage labor and increase the likelihood of stillbirth or irreversible brain damage to the newborn (Morgan, 1997). Hosken (1993) stated that infant and maternal morbidity and mortality rates are highest in communities where FGM/FC is the norm.

In the United States, healthcare providers are often called on to to manage the devastating effects of the primitive surgeries. Additional incisions anterior and posterior to the vaginal opening may be necessary at the time of childbirth (Lightfoot-Klein & Shaw, 1991). Healthcare providers may be asked to resuture the women postpartum in a manner that leaves the vaginal opening as small as it was before delivery. An inspection by the husband, an older woman, or a midwife is not unusual to confirm that the vagina was sutured enough. Women report that marital problems arise if resuturing the vagina after childbirth is not done properly (Hosken, 1993). Some healthcare providers may justify a few extra sutures in an episiotomy postpartum to satisfy a woman and her family. Healthcare providers desire to do the best for their patients and return them home in the same condition as when they came to the hospital, without breaking the law. The illegal act of performing FGM on a child or unnecessary surgery on an adult female would not be medically prudent however. While providing information about laws in the United States to immigrants is the responsibility of INS and the State Department, the ethical responsibility for a healthcare provider is to inform patients that the law requires healthcare providers to make reports to legal authorities if patients are in danger of being subjected to abusive acts like FGM, or other types of abuse. If a child is involved, a report should be made to Child Protective Services, because FGM is a crime in the United States. Menstrual problems are quite common following FGM/FC. The sutured and scarred tissue may block menstrual flow, leading to the inappropriate drainage of blood backward into the peritoneal cavity. With the retention of menstrual blood, there is abdominal distention and pain as it is resorbed, as well as the increased risk of infection and scarring of internal reproductive organs. Social problems abound when there is no evidence of monthly menstrual flow, which leads others to misinterpret symptoms and assume a young unmarried woman is pregnant. This brings dishonor on the family and leads to negative repercussions and ostracism. Extreme pain with menses is

common following genital tract infections. Abscesses, keloids, and hypertrophic scarring add to the physical agony and contribute to infertility. In a culture where children increase a family's wealth, infertility is a cause of disrespect, diminishing a woman's worth, and is likely to lead to her rejection by the family or community. Ironically, many who practice it think FGM increases a woman's fertility.

Psychosexual Problems

Damage to vulval nerve endings, neuromas, and scarring may be causes for lifelong intractable pain and limit the blood flow to the rich body of sensitive tissue responsible for the initiation and completion of the human sexual response cycle. Lack of scientific studies and lack of open discussion regarding women's sexuality in their cultural context have been the norm until recently, and Hosken's surveys (1993) provide limited knowledge on acts of intercourse that provide no pleasure to circumcised women.

Einstein (2008) stated that there is no acknowledgement in the medical literature of any neurobiological consequences of FGM/FC other than the neuromas. Cutting of the sensory and motor nervous system and interruption of neural networks in the skin and muscle in gynecological surgeries performed under anesthesia are known to produce neurological outcomes and vulvodynia.

Catania and colleagues (2007) claimed that sexuality must be considered in the context of the environment. Some studies on sexual function following FGM/FC have been conducted in the countries of origin. Other research occurred after women migrated, and sexuality education may have influenced their attitudes. Women with FGM/FC that did not suffer grave long-term complications, may have healthy satisfying sexual relations. That is not to deny that women with sexual dysfunction deserve counseling and therapy directed toward healthy sexuality.

Einstein (2008) quoted Abusharaf's 2001 interview with a woman who claimed the infibulation did not eliminate the desire for sex, even at an advanced age. "If the tongue is removed do you stop feeling hunger?" (p. 90) she questioned. If the woman has a good husband, she explains, sex can be good even after circumcision, just as the sex can be bad with a selfish bad husband with women who have not been cut. Some women will say they have no feelings at all for sex. Diverse accounts may be related to the instrumentation, type of procedure, depth of cutting, effective healing of tissue, and the individual differences of neuronal pathways in women's bodies. In addition, women have deep internal clitoral innervation as well as various neural pathways to orgasm, which would allow for sexual pleasure to continue despite circumcision. Einstein addressed the outcomes of cutting that destroys neurobiological pathways and large nerve bundles and stressed the repercussions of cutting on the entire CNS, viscera, spinal cord, and brain.

Obermeyer's (2005) systematic review represents some of the highest-level evidence on health and sexuality following FGM/FC and reported many conceptual and methodological problems with the 35 articles reviewed. Available evidence does not support the hypothetical global statement that sexual function or pleasure is destroyed with cutting of the female genitalia. The majority of studies reported no significant differences in sexual enjoyment and pleasure between circumcised and uncircumcised women.

Women may harbor deep psychological fears, losing trust and confidence in women and caregivers in general. Chronic depression and anxiety are commonly confounded by psychotic episodes. Deep-seated behavioral problems and marital conflict result

(WHO, 2000). Oddly, healthcare providers are confronted with the disconcerting challenges associated with individuals who are choosing not to carry on the practice as well as those who have endured it in their past. Eliminating a practice thousands of years old is causing upheaval in highly regarded family values. With little support, women and their families may suffer physically and mentally if they maintain the practice illegally and in secret or if they seek to put an end to it.

Medicalization

In many countries, there are movements to medicalize the procedure to maintain asepsis and curb the mortality rate. Physicians claim to have been taught the "right" way to do it (sterile with less severe cutting), while in medical school and in many areas this continues. Healthcare providers have also promoted the use of Type I, supposedly to incur less tissue damage, in their local communities in an attempt to help mitigate the serious health risks associated with the routinely practiced infibulation. To satisfy the family and community demand for the ritual, it was felt that progress was made if the practice could be reduced to a simple clitoridectomy.

However, WHO (2000) claimed that the inequitable position of women is seen as a threat to their health and development as well as social and economic development as a whole. Hence, the movement to eradicate the dangerous and life-threatening practices in any form must be the priority. Negative repercussions are advised for those who perform FGM in any of its forms or profit from it in any way. The human rights approach for children and women is suggested as the best approach. In the United States, with the recognition of the practice being perpetuated in secret and requested of physicians, the consensus is that adamant refusal of any form of sexual mutilation of females must be maintained.

Some see the cessation of FGM/FC as the main priority for survival of women affected by it, although the women themselves may not see it that way (WHO, 2000). Those outside the ethnic or cultural group must realize that they may never understand such practices. Even within a single country, the tribal, sexual, and genetic differences vary greatly. In the Gambia, for instance, FGM is nearly universal in one ethnic group, the Mandinkas, but it is rare in the Wollofs (Morison, et al., 2001). In three Nigerian tribes, the Igbo, Yoruba, and Hausa, women's meanings, beliefs, and practices varied also, according to religion, education, and occupation. Researchers caution that importing foreign values will promote resistance and drive the practice further underground (Anuforo, Oyedele, & Pacquiao, 2004).

Families who move to the United States in general seek to improve their lives and health and that of their children by letting go of old ways that are harmful while appreciating the new opportunities available to them. Indeed, across African countries as well, data show that generation to generation there is a reduction in the number of girls circumcised in some countries. Reproductive Health Outlook (2004) quoted development experts as recommending numerous small steps rather than grand solutions.

The need to adhere to the value-laden societal norm encourages populations to continue to self-enforce a tradition that has long lost its origins. Mackie (1996) compared FGM/FC to the outdated practice of foot binding in China. Methods of eliminating an outdated practice initially involve educating the population at risk about the physiological facts regarding the practice.

This has been going on for close to a century in Africa, with health workers in the communities and civic leaders providing supportive education to the young and old alike, particularly in refugee camps. Information regarding the laws in other countries is explained to emigrants with special focus on matters such as FGM being a crime that could result in jail and deportation. The second point Mackie made is that an international attitude regarding the issue must be conveyed. This is evident in the international denunciation of FGM by the health councils, organizations concerned with world health, and laws passed in European and North American countries making FGM illegal. Finally, all those concerned, from international organizations to the individual healthcare workers, must exhibit tact and respect for the enduring and motivating fact that families love and value their children and want what is best for them. Critical to the elimination of dangerous practices is that individuals at all levels in the at-risk group must commit to change.

The Nurse's Role

Congress passed legislation in 1996 delineating the responsibility of the healthcare community through the Department of Health and Human Services (DHHS), which was to compile data on the number of women who may be affected by FGM/FC, specifically those under the age of 18. The DHHS also was required to identify communities that practice the ritual and develop and implement outreach activities in collaboration with the ethnic groups. Third, the DHHS was to develop and distribute information on FGM/FC and its complications to educators and students in medical training. These steps can be viewed as the assessment of the range of need, the development of a care plan, and patient education when viewing the community as client in the nursing process (Lundy & Barton, 1995). Traditional nursing courses and nursing textbooks do not teach these issues as a role responsibility of the general nurse, however. The subject of FGM, the United States federal laws regarding FGM, and the responsibilities of the healthcare provider are not adequately addressed, with the exception of courses in forensic or transcultural nursing, or human rights issues.

Lynch (1993) clarified that "the application of forensic principles and standards represents a new perspective in the holistic approach to the treatment of victims and perpetrators of criminal acts." Furthermore, Lynch added that "forensic science is relevant to contemporary curricula and will ensure that clinicians are prepared to identify and report" all manner of abuse and suspicious trauma. The discipline of healthcare unites with law enforcement and forensic science in their common concern for human acts of violence. Goals articulating the full spectrum of knowledge are necessary to address the safety and public health issue of FGM/FC.

Despite the fact that opinion and policy oppose FGM/FC, being politically correct is not always culturally sensitive. The more culturally competent the provider, the more likely he or she is to stimulate changes in healthcare behaviors and attitudes, whether one is choosing patient care, advocacy, or the activist role outside the clinical arena. It is imperative that the clinician confront her or his own prejudice just as those affected by FGM/FC will need to confront the issue for themselves. Overt prejudice exhibited by the provider may be experienced as another violation of the patient's rights, the right to sensitive and respectful healthcare despite ethnic and cultural differences (Black & Matassarin-Jacobs, 1997).

Incorporating cultural competency, the nursing process enhances the logical, holistic approach to problem solving. Preliminary to the initial assessment, nurses must examine their own prejudices and convey respect for the values, beliefs, and customs of the patient. Sensitivity to their culture must be perceived, and focusing on finding similarities will produce familiarity while reducing prejudice. Nursing care focused on differences is threatening. Attention must be given to the unique positive features of each culture. The Foundation for Women's Health, Research, and Development (FORWARD) produced a guide for health professionals listing such positive attributes as strong family support, improved parenting strategies such as breastfeeding and close contact of mothers and babies, and community involvement in child rearing (Adamson, no date available).

Initial assessment with acceptable communication style will build rapport. Information offered about the health effects of a practice one wishes to discourage will be more likely accepted and viable replacement alternatives considered. Alternative ceremonies instituted in 1996 by Maendeleo Ya Wanawake Organization (MYWO) included a week-long rite-of-passage ceremony with the ritual singing, flowers, and gifts for girls, leaving out the mutilation of the genitals. The women were given accurate health information along with the expectations inherent in the role of wife and mother. Individual families are also being encouraged to have their own parties in the girls' honor (Chege, Askew, & Liku, 2001). Utilizing successful approaches, such as these new rituals, are also promoted in the United States as part of the education campaign that includes videotapes of the celebrations.

BEST PRACTICE Nurses who do physical assessments or who perform procedures on female patients should be alert to the anatomical, physiological, and psychological changes that may accompany female circumcision or associated ritualistic procedures of certain cultures. They must anticipate changes in medical or surgical procedures involving female genital anatomy.

Intervention and management plans for patients may be multifaceted, taking into account the medical concerns for which the woman has sought care as well as the possible need for a referral for mental health counseling (Box 42-1). When initial contact with a woman who has been subjected to FGM in the past is in the labor and delivery suite or emergent care setting, marshaling all resources as quickly as possible may be necessary. Medical risks of childbirth, language barriers, the sex of the healthcare provider, and the fact that the provider may never have seen a patient who has undergone FGM add to the challenge of assessment and management in these situations (Reichert, 1998). Stories abound concerning the gasps of shock and amazement when, unknowingly, a nurse or physician unfamiliar with FGM first views the infibulated vagina. Prevention of such a response can be best managed by educating healthcare providers about FGM and being aware of local resources.

Healthcare professionals must have accessible educational material, colleagues sensitive to the issue, awareness of the prevalence of FGM in a given community, and knowledge of their forensic responsibility.

BEST PRACTICE Hospitals accredited by The Joint Commission (TJC) must develop and use criteria to identify possible victims of physical assault, rape, or other sexual molestation, domestic abuse, and abuse or neglect of older adults and children, and they must educate and train all personnel to use interview and physical assessment skills to detect abuse and to initiate appropriate referrals to other healthcare providers or agencies for follow-up care.

Box 42-1 Selected Nursing Diagnoses for FGM/FC Patients

Low self-esteem because of abuse from family or a coworker
Pain related to tissue, nerve, or vessel disruption from penetrating trauma
Risk for infection because of the loss of skin integrity
Sexual dysfunction related to injury
Fear related to perceived inability to the control situation

Documentation of the initial assessment is critical as well as the patient's expectations after delivery. A proactive stance is to provide patient education on the fact that reinfibulation is not legal, nor is the perpetuation of FGM on female infants. Because of its value in some ethnic groups, significant family members and influential elders should be involved in preventive education efforts.

Opportunities for counseling on psychosocial and physical problems associated with FGM must be in place for use with patients in the ambulatory and inpatient settings. Options for surgical intervention or deinfibulation that are not associated with childbirth should be included. It is standard practice in discussion of a procedure that the patients provide informed consent. Barstow (1999) explained that consent must be voluntary. Second, the patients must have the mental capacity to make a decision. Third, patients must receive information on the pros and cons of the procedure in a language they understand. Last, patients must not be coerced physically or emotionally. Most healthcare providers are familiar with informed consent as a universal process in patient education. Barstow has claimed that women who have undergone FGM procedures and request them for themselves or their daughters are not able to give informed consent. Because FGM is a relatively new forensic issue in the United States, there remain many questions to be answered and much to be learned about how to handle families that desire to have the ritual performed on the minor child or themselves. In addition to assessment of risk and education, involving law enforcement may be considered a choice, as with other forensic or medicolegal challenges such as domestic violence, sexual assault, and other forms of child abuse. Having a protocol in place for such situations, with counselor and adjunct support staff on hand, is critical.

Participants in a focus group in California working on interventions for possible recurring FGM discussed corrective surgeries that had been done at no charge to the women requesting it. The possibility of reconstructing vulvar and urethral tissue to some semblance of normalcy, providing nerve blocks for intractable pain, removal of scar tissue that entraps nerve bundles, and fistula repair are invasive, specialized, and expensive management for the results of FGM. What is the likelihood of surgery being available through local gynecologists or through private or federally funded health insurance plans? Coding the diagnosis and potential surgical treatments remain unresolved issues. There are clinics and physicians who specialize in treating patients suffering from the long-term health effects of FGM and offer surgical solutions. However, they are not the norm and are seen in few communities such as Boston and Washington, D.C., where the political and legal climate helps to generate financial support for the agencies. In the United Kingdom, where FGM has long been illegal, specialists routinely perform reconstructive surgery at specific clinics and can be contacted for consultation if the need arises.

Law and justice professionals and educators are in need of education and support, as well as are healthcare providers. Few are sensitized to the issue, and most have little knowledge of what to do if it is reported (Zaidi, et al., 2007). Kmietowicz (2000) surveyed 16 international health and welfare agencies and found that fewer than half were aware of the legal position on FGM. To test the responses of local authorities, several practitioners in California made anonymous phone calls to child protection agencies and law enforcement regarding cases of FGM in the local area. The reports were rebuffed with claims of ignorance regarding California law, knowledge of FGM, and what they needed to do.

Evaluation of the success of nursing interventions must be ongoing. This may include phone calls and follow-up visits in conjunction with all health professionals involved in the initial treatment plan. As yet, there are limited protocols for evaluation. Results of mental and physical health treatments must be documented, including a review of the law and its repercussions, particularly if there are plans to subject the children to FGM. Advocacy and support agencies with counselors of the same ethnicity may be the most effective support for the practitioner, and a concerted effort must be made for ongoing communication between the agencies involved.

Health workers in the front lines will most likely be the initial contact for patients at risk. It is essential that information be presented to professionals and the public in general about the denouncement of inhumane acts and the progress being made in the human rights arena with laws and community movements. Hosken (1993) has strongly encouraged those in opposition to support in any way they can the grassroots organizations that have implemented eradication movements in Africa. She has explained that no matter what is done in Western countries, the real changes must take place with the millions of people in Africa carrying on the tradition. However, with the legislation criminalizing FGM/FC and its initial discovery is likely to occur in the healthcare setting, it is incumbent on all healthcare providers in the United States to play a more active role.

KEY POINT A culturally valued tradition of an extremely personal nature that is illegal in the United States and laden with controversy demands a sensitive approach. From a holistic forensic healthcare perspective, it is imperative that all involved understand it to be a violation of human rights.

The scientific implications that may be intepreted from studies at high levels of evidence may or may not have any significant ramifications to the FGM/FC-practicing individuals in communities across the globe. Further replication of studies such as Hassanin and colleagues (2008), Livermore and colleagues (2007), and Asekun-Olarinmoye and Oluwatayin (2008) adhering to research method criteria will further confirm that interventions are effective for prevention with attitude and behavior changes.

Gender Asylum Case Summaries

It is inaccurate and illegal to justify the continuance of FGM on the grounds of necessity. More appropriately, it involves child abuse and violence against women (Morison, et al., 2001). Respect for the lives at risk must take precedence over a cultural tradition antithetical to professional ethics and

the law. Legal mandates, resources, and knowledge of its health implications allow nurses to confront FGM with the forensic responsibility inherent to their role. These gender asylum cases amplify the problems associated with immigration laws and practice.

Case Study 42-1

Nigerian Applicant

A Nigerian woman with two young daughters, fled to the United States and applied for asylum to protect her daughters from being subjected to FMG/FC. She is Catholic and strongly opposed to these cultural practices.

At the time of her marriage, the fact that she had not been subjected to FGM was not disclosed to the husband's family. The husband's mother is a village elder who performs FGM on the village girls and put pressure on the woman to have the daughters cut. The applicant hid the girls 24 hours a day in fear of the relatives taking them.

Because of her refusal to submit, her husband began to beat her. She was locked in the home, raped, and psychologically abused. Often she was beaten into unconsciousness, and once she was hospitalized. Her family members reported the situation to the police, who interviewed the husband but refused to intervene because it was a marital matter. Once, after threatening the woman with a loaded gun, the husband managed to bribe the police, succeeding in getting them to drop the matter.

The government was unwilling to take action to prevent enforcement of the traditions supporting abusive treatment of women and girls, doing less than other African countries to protect her.

Although living in the United States, the woman continued to receive threatening letters for her refusal to allow the daughters to undergo FGM. The husband blamed her for the death of another child she left in Africa and for his poor health. If deported, the daughters would be forced to undergo FGM, and the mother would suffer violence at the hands of her husband.

Based on the circumstances, the immigration judge granted her asylum.

Case Study 42-2

Malian Applicant

The applicant is a Malian woman with a young daughter and son who were both born in the United States. The father of the children, her husband, is a Malian citizen living in the United States.

The woman suffered the persecution of FGM herself as a child and strongly opposes the practice for her daughter. She fears that the husband's family will subject her daughter to FGM if they are forced to return to Mali, and she can do nothing to prevent this mutilation. She will endure violence and be ostracized by both of their families.

She is violating a deep-rooted family and cultural tradition. Over 95% of the women are subjected to FGM in her hometown, and no laws in Mali prohibit it.

Although the application for asylum was made in 1996, the immigration judge did not grant asylum until May of 1999.

Case Study **42-3**

Ethiopian Applicant

The applicant is of the Harari ethnic group in Ethiopia, of which close to 100% of the women are subjected to FGM in early childhood. Her daughter is a U.S. citizen, and the applicant fears her daughter will be tortured in the same manner if returned to Ethiopia.

Although Ethiopian officials are aware of the prevalence of FGM, they have passed no law specifically outlawing it. The woman feels sure that her family will force the daughter to be mutilated and anything else necessary to bring her in line with the traditions of the group. As an unmarried mother with a child of mixed heritage, she will face extreme scrutiny and be ostracized.

The immigration judge denied asylum, but withholding removal was granted.

Case Study **42-4**

Guinean Applicant

The applicant was considered to be a person with no one to protect her rights when her monogamous father died in Guinea. Her mother became the fourth wife of an uncle. She was forced to undergo the torture of FGM at age 5 and was mistreated in the household.

Later the applicant fell in love and had a child by a man whom the uncle refused to let her marry. The uncle beat her often, causing her to lose a subsequent pregnancy. Eventually he had the father of her children imprisoned and beaten, then forced her to marry a 60-year-old man with three other wives.

She was beaten, abused, raped, drugged, and threatened with death. Escape attempts were followed by beatings. Eventually she managed to enter the United States with a friend's help and a false passport.

She fears that her daughter will be forced to endure FGM as the family has threatened. She will be an outcast if she is returned, or she will be killed.

The immigration judge granted her asylum in February 1998.

Resources

ORGANIZATIONS

Equality Now USA
PO Box 20646, Columbus Circle Station, New York, NY 10023; www.equalitynow.org.

FORWARD International (Foundation for Women's Health, Research, and Development)
Unit K, 765–767 Harrow Road, London, England NW10 5NY; www.forwarduk.org.uk.

Immigrant Legal Resource Center
1663 Mission Street, Suite 602, San Francisco, CA 94103; www.ilrc.org.

National Immigrant Law Center
3435 Wilshire Boulevard, Suite 2850, Los Angeles, CA 90010; www.nilc.org.

PATH (Program for Appropriate Technology in Health)
1455 NW Leary Way, Seattle, WA 98017; www.path.org.

WIN News (Women's International Networks News)
187 Grant Street, Lexington, MA 02420; www.feminist.com/win.htm.

References

Adamson, F. (undated). *Female genital mutilation: A counseling guide for professionals.* London: Forward.

Anuforo, P. O., Oyedele, L., & Pacquiao, D. F. (2004). Comparative study of meanings, beliefs, and practices of female circumcision among three Nigerian tribes in the United States and Nigeria. *Journal of Transcultural Nursing, 15*(2), 103–113.

Asekun-Olarinmoye, E. O., & Amusan, O. A. (2008). The impact of health education on attitudes towards female genital mutilation (FGM) in a rural Nigerian community. *European Journal of Contraception and Reproductive Health Care, 13*(3), 289–297.

Barstow, D. G. (1999). Female genital mutilation: The penultimate gender abuse. *Child Abuse & Neglect, 23*(5), 501–510.

Black, J. M., & Matassarin-Jacobs, E. (1997). *Medical-surgical nursing: Clinical management for continuity of care* (5th ed.). Chicago: Saunders.

Brady, K., & Tooby, N. (1997). Protecting defendants from immigration consequences. *Crime Crim Justice, 24*(3), 54.

Catania, L., Abdulcadir, O., Vincenzo, P., Verde, J., Abdulcadir, J., & Abdulcadir, D. (2007). Pleasure and orgasm in women with female genital mutilation/cutting (FGM/C). *Journal of Sexual Medicine, 4*(6), 1666–1768.

Center for Reproductive Law and Policy. (1997). *Legislation on female genital mutilation in the United States.* New York: Author.

Center for Reproductive Rights. (2004). *Legislation on female genital mutilation in the United States.* New York: Author. Accessed October 10, 2009 at http://reproductiverights.org/en/document/legislation-on-female-genital-mutilation-in-the-united-states.

Chege, J., Askew, I., & Liku, J. (2001). *An assessment of the alternative rites approach for encouraging abandonment of female genital mutilation in Kenya.* Nairobi: Population Council.

Einstein, G. (2008). From body to brain: considering the neurobiological effects of genital cutting. *Perspectives in Biology and Medicine, 51*(1), 84–97.

Elnashar, A., & Abdelhady, R. (2007). The impact of female genital cutting on health of newly married women. *International Journal of Gynecology and Obstetrics, 97*(3), 238–244.

Gibeau, A. M. (1998). Female genital mutilation: When a cultural practice generates clinical and ethical dilemmas. *JOGN Nursing; Journal of Obstetric, Gynecologic, and Neonatal Nursing, 27*(1), 85–91.

Hassanin, I., Saleh, R., Bedaiwy, A. A., Peterson, R. S., & Bedaiwy, M. A. (2008). Prevalence of female genital cutting in upper Egypt: 6 years after enforcement of prohibition law. *Ethics, Bioscience and Life, 3*(1), 27–31.

Herieka, E., & Dhar, J. (2003). Female genital mutilation in the Sudan: Survey of the attitude of Khartoum University students towards this practice. *Sexually Transmitted Infections, 79*(3), 220–223.

Hosken, F. P. (1981). Female genital mutilation in the world today: A global review. *International Journal of Health Science, 11*(3), 415–430.

Hosken, F. P. (1993). *The Hosken report.* (4th ed.). Lexington, KY: Women's International Network News.

International Council of Nurses. (1992). *Resolution: Elimination of female genital mutilation.* Geneva, Switzerland: Author.

Jones, H., Diop, N., Askew, I., et al. (1999). Female genital cutting practices in Burkino Faso and Mali and their negative health outcomes. *Studies in Family Planning, 30*(3), 219–230.

Kmietowicz, Z. (2000). MPs recommend tightening the law on female circumcision. *British Medical Journal, 321*(7273), 1365.

Lightfoot-Klein, H., & Shaw, E. (1991). Special needs of ritually circumcised women patients. *JOGN Nursing; Journal of Obstetric, Gynecologic, and Neonatal Nursing, 20*(2), 102–107.

Livermore, L., Monteiro, R., & Rymer, J. (2007). Attitudes and awareness of female genital mutilation: A questionnaire-based study in a Kenyan hospital. *Journal of Obstetrics and Gynaecology, 27*(8), 816–818.

Lundy, K. P., & Barton, J. A. (1995). Assessment: Data collection of the community as client. In P. J. Christensen, & J. W. Kenney (Eds.), *Nursing process: Application of conceptual models.* (4th ed., pp. 102–119). St. Louis: Mosby.

Lynch, V. (1993). Forensic aspects of health care: New roles, new responsibilities. *Journal of Psychosocial Nursing and Mental Health Services, 31*(11), 5–6.

Mackie, G. (1996). Ending footbinding and infibulation: A convention account. *American Sociological Review, 61*(6), 999–1017.

Morgan, M. A. (1997). Female genital mutilation: An issue on the doorstep of the American medical community. *The Journal of Legal Medicine, 18*(1), 93–115.

Morison, L., Scherf, C., Ekpo, G., et al. (2001). The long-term reproductive health consequences of female genital cutting in rural Gambia: A community-based survey. *Tropical Medicine & International Health: TM & IH, 6*(8), 643–653.

Muteshi, J., & Sass, J. (2005). *Female genital mutilation in Africa: An analysis of current abandonment approaches.* Nairobi: PATH, 2005).

Obermeyer, C. M. (2005). The consequences of female circumcision on health and sexuality: An update on the evidence. *Cultural Health and Sexual, 7*(5), 443–461.

Program for Appropriate Technology in Health (PATH). (1997). *Female circumcision/female genital mutilation: The facts.* Washington, DC: Author.

Reichert, G. A. (1998). Female circumcision: What you need to know about genital mutilation. *AWHONN lifelines/Association of Women's Health, Obstetric and Neonatal Nurses, 2*(3), 29–34.

Reproductive Health Outlook. (2004). Harmful traditional health practices. Retrieved from www.rho.org/html/hthps_overview.htm.

Stern, A. (1997). Female genital mutilation: United States asylum laws are in need of reform. *Journal of Gender Law, 6,* 89–109.

Center for Gender and Refugee Studies. University of California Hastings. (2000). *Gender asylum case summaries.* Accessed October 10, 2009 from http://cgrs.uchastings.edu/law/detail.php.

World Health Organization. (1996). H.R. Doc. 104-863, 104th Cong., 2nd Sess.

World Health Organization. (2000). Female genital mutilation information pack. Retrieved from www.who.int/frh-whd/FGM/infopack/English/fgm_infopack.htm.

Zaidi, N., Khalil, A., Roberts, C., & Browne, M. (2007). Knowledge of female genital mutilation among healthcare professionals. *Journal of Obstetrics and Gynaecology, 27*(2), 161–164.

CHAPTER 43 Human Trafficking

Nancy B. Cabelus

Human trafficking, a form of modern-day slavery, is a violation of human rights that imposes serious threats to the health, safety, and well-being of its victims. Research sponsored by the U.S. government estimates that approximately 800,000 persons are trafficked across national borders each year, which does not include millions of persons trafficked within their own countries. Approximately 80% of the victims are women and girls, and up to half of them are children (U.S. Department of State, 2008). The Department of State estimates that nearly 20,000 persons are trafficked into the United States. According to reports of "the International Labor Organization (ILO), the United Nations agency responsible for addressing labor standards, employment, and social protection issues, there are an estimated 12.3 million people in forced labor, bonded labor, forced child labor, and sexual servitude at any given time" (U.S. Department of State, 2008).

While some trafficked persons may be hidden away as domestic servants or sex slaves, others are referred to as "hiding in plain sight" (Herman, 2003; Hughes, 2003) because they may be the persons in mainstream society who work at unskilled jobs in relatively visible venues such as farms, hotels, or street prostitution. Poor social and economic conditions often set the stage for the first encounter between the trafficker and the victim. Sheer desperation may be the cause for a vulnerable victim to get caught in the ruse of a trafficker's promises for a good salary, education, or a better way of life. Victims sometimes leave their homes and families to voluntarily go with the trafficker only later to learn that they are caught in the trap and unable to get out for fear of the threatened consequences. Others may travel to foreign countries seeking employment opportunities as laborers, domestic servants, or nannies. According to one trafficking survivor who had responded to an advertisement for domestic help, she arrived to her destination country only to be held in captivity by her employer who would beat her and treat her cruelly. After a considerable amount of time and anguish, this survivor crafted a plan to escape and jumped from a balcony, four stories high (Fernando, 2005).

Many victims are not able to escape. According to Kevin Bales (1999), the world's leading expert on contemporary slavery and founder of the not-for-profit organization Free the Slaves, "every case of slavery involves many crimes—fraud, kidnap, assault, rape and sometimes murder" (Bales, 1999, p. 48). Bales has stated that these crimes are deliberate and systematic and are repeated in brothels thousands of times each month.

Although poverty and inequality make some more vulnerable to being trafficked than others, the Polaris Project warns that these are not the primary causes of trafficking. Forerunners in human trafficking research, outreach, and victim identification, the Polaris Project has described human trafficking as "a criminal industry driven by 1) the ability to make large profits due to high demand, and 2) negligible-to-low risk of prosecution. As long as demand is unchecked and the risks for traffickers are low, trafficking will exist regardless of other contributing factors" (Polaris Project, 2009).

Following trafficking of narcotics, human trafficking is one of the most predominant forms of organized crime—an enterprise that grosses $9.5 billion per year (U.S. Department of State [DOS], 2006).

Awareness of Human Trafficking

HUMAN TRAFFICKING DEFINED

The United Nations approves the global definition of trafficking in persons as follows:

> *The recruitment, transportation, transfer, harbouring or receipt of persons, by means of a threat or use of force or other forms of coercion, of abduction, of fraud, of deception, of the abuse of power or of a position of vulnerability or of the giving or receiving of payments or benefits to achieve the consent of a person having control over another person, for the purpose of exploitation. Exploitation shall include, at a minimum, the exploitation of the prostitution of others or other forms of sexual exploitation, forced labour or services, slavery or practices similar to slavery, servitude or the removal of organs. (United Nations, 2008)*

The United Nations Global Initiative to Fight Human Trafficking (UNGIFT) has developed a comprehensive toolkit to guide individuals, with best practices for individuals who work with trafficking victims. The toolkit offers a protocol to prevent and combat trafficking, to protect and assist its victims, and to promote international cooperation. Further, the toolkit defines trafficking as a human rights violation and clearly identifies the differences between human trafficking and smuggling.

Smuggling is different from trafficking as it is the intent of the subject to be transported from one country to another. "Smuggling of migrants shall mean the procurement, in order to obtain, directly or indirectly, a financial or other material benefit, of the illegal entry of a person into a State Party of which the person is not a national or a permanent resident" (United Nations Office on Drugs and Crime [UNODC], 2008). The Human Smuggling and Trafficking Center (2005) clarified that the "key components that will always distinguish trafficking from smuggling are the elements of fraud, force, or coercion." The majority of people who are illegally assisted to enter the United States each year are smuggled rather than trafficked. A situation of smuggling may become a case of trafficking as soon as the person is deceived, forced, or coerced into circumstances he or she has not agreed to.

Trafficking Victims Protection Act

Originally signed into United States law in 2000, the Trafficking Victims Protection Act (TVPA) sets the global standard for anti-trafficking law. The TVPA is intended to combat severe forms of trafficking through prevention, protection of victims, and prosecution of offenders. The TVPA also encourages a victim-centered response to trafficking that would include rescue, rehabilitation, and reintegration into society for trafficking survivors (DOS, 2006; TVPA, 2009). Human trafficking, also called trafficking in persons, is defined by the TVPA as follows:

1. Sex trafficking in which a commercial sex act is induced by force, fraud, or coercion, or in which the person induced to perform such an act has not attained 18 years of age; or
2. The recruitment, harboring, transportation, provision, or obtaining of a person for labor or services, through the use of force, fraud, or coercion for the purpose of subjection to **involuntary servitude, peonage, debt bondage**, or slavery (DOS, 2008).

Similarly, the key terms defined by the United Nations of force, fraud, and coercion are also the elements within the TVPA. Although the victims may have voluntarily sought out employment or opportunity with the trafficker, once they are captured, they are not free to leave for fear of threats of harm to their loved ones, serious injury, or death. There are also incidents of trafficking known as debt bondage when people give themselves into slavery as security against a loan or when they inherit a debt of a relative (Bales, 1999). Peonage is holding someone against his or her will to pay off a debt (Hughes, 2003). Rarely will traffickers release those enslaved, whether or not the debt is paid.

Each year in June, the State Department releases its Trafficking in Persons (TIP) report. Within the report, the United States ranks countries according to compliance with the TVPA and attempts to reduce human trafficking through prevention, protection of victims, and prosecution of traffickers. The three-tier placement ranking takes the following into consideration:

1. The extent to which the country is a country of origin, transit, or destination for severe forms of trafficking
2. The extent to which the government of the country does not comply with the TVPA's minimum standards including, in particular, the extent of the government's trafficking-related corruption
3. The resources and capabilities of the government to address and eliminate severe forms of trafficking in persons (DOS, 2008)

Countries may be ranked on a different tier each year based on performance for the year evaluated. Those ranked at tier 1 are in full compliance with minimum standards to prevent trafficking, protect victims, and prosecute cases. Tier 2 countries are those that have made some efforts to combat trafficking but have not met the required standards. The tier 2 watch list is for countries that are meeting minimum standards to comply with TVPA requirements but there are a large number of severe forms of trafficking cases, there are few prosecutions of cases, and there is little evidence that efforts have been made by way of prevention. Tier 3 countries are those that not only have not met the basic standards but also have not indicated an attempt to do so (DOS, 2008).

Forms of Trafficking

The most commonly known forms of trafficking are labor trafficking and forced prostitution. Involuntary servitude requires that laborers work for long hours in often deplorable conditions for little or no pay. They may be deprived of food, water, or sleep (Barrows & Finger, 2008). They are under constant supervision, not free to leave, and most female victims of labor trafficking are subjected to sexual abuse (Bales, 1999, DOS, 2008). Forms of sexual exploitation could include forced prostitution, exotic dancing, stripping, or pornography (Hughes, 2003). Research by Spear (2004) informs that in 1995, Snakeheads—an Asian crime syndicate, smuggled more than 1000 Asian women into the United States. The women were regularly traded between local and out-of-state brothels to avoid detection and because customers got tired of the same women. The women lived in brothels described as prison compounds and suffered beatings, forced abortions, and isolation. One girl was kept in a closet for 15 days for trying to escape (Spear, 2004).

An unhappy customer may result in beatings and torture by the customer and also by the pimp. Bales (1999) recounted the story of a woman who tried to escape from a brothel in Thailand.

The pimp beat her and then took her into the viewing room; with two helpers he beat her again in front of all the girls in the brothel. She was locked in a room for three days without food or water. When she was released she was immediately put to work. For most girls it becomes clear that they can never escape. (Bales, 1999, p. 58)

Traffickers sometimes use advertisements to recruit women to work as waitresses, household help, nannies, or even mail-order brides. Popular areas from which to traffic brides are poor regions of China's inland provinces, where poverty causes women to become more vulnerable to trafficking (DOS, 2008). As China's economic development has soared, some experts believe that the kidnapping and sale of women has increased and that such trafficking may account for 30% to 90% of marriages in some villages (DOS, 2008).

Children are some of the most vulnerable and are therefore the easiest prey for traffickers. Some forms of labor require small hands or bodies to perform skills proficiently. Children have been used as camel jockeys, brick makers, and laborers working on farms and fishing docks, as means to financially support their families (DOS, 2006). In underdeveloped countries, desperate parents too poor to support their families may sell their children in exchange for a nominal amount of money or sell a daughter to a would-be husband in trade for a few sheep or a goat. Parents may not be aware they are selling a child into slavery or that they may never see their child again. Once the child belongs to the trafficker, the child is forced into involuntary servitude and is placed at high risk for sexual abuse and exploitation.

Child sex tourism involves people who travel from their own country to another and engage in commercial sex acts with children (DOS, 2008). Some customers, especially Chinese or Thais, will pay up to $2000 to have sex with a virgin because they believe their sexual virility will reawaken and life will be prolonged (Bales, 1999). Some men prefer sex with virgins because they believe the risk of acquiring HIV would be very low. Other customers, positive for HIV, believe that having sex with a virgin child cures the disease (Bales, 1999). DOS estimates that 2 million children worldwide are engaged in the transnational sex trade.

Another form of child trafficking is the increasing use of children by armies, militias, and rebels in global conflict zones (Beyrer, 2004). DOS reports that the majority of child soldiers range between 15 and 18 years of age, but some may be as young as 7 or 8. Children are especially vulnerable for recruitment into informal paramilitary groups and "have been used for nightmarish tasks that include the clearing of landmines, use as porters and servants, and for sexual services" (Beyrer, 2004, p.16).

Children become more vulnerable when displaced by war and civil conflict, isolated by natural disasters, or orphaned by the death of parents or guardians (Beyrer, 2004; Farley et al., 2003). "Those familiar with data on the AIDS pandemic know that HIV/AIDS has generated more than 14 million new orphans—having lost one or both parents to AIDS" (Beyrer, 2004, p. 17). It is estimated that 90% of these orphaned children live in developing countries of sub-Saharan Africa, and because they may have to work to survive, they become highly susceptible to exploitation, trafficking, and HIV (Beyrer, 2004; IOM, 2008).

Not only children in developing countries are at risk to be trafficked. Through use of the Internet, children can be lured by traffickers who pose online as child peers. Children may innocently engage in e-mails or chats with child predators who entice children to disclose where they live or attend school or coax a child into meeting them in a discreet location.

Happy trafficking is a term for victim turned trafficker (DOS, 2008). Women are commonly used as recruiters of young persons and operators of brothels. Criminal organizations employ female traffickers because governments frequently exhibit leniency toward female criminals. In some Eurasian countries, female traffickers are released from serving prison time when they are pregnant or mothers of young children and receive lighter sentences than men (DOS, 2008).

Case Study 43-1

Smuggling or Trafficking?

A young woman is enticed by an offer of employment as household help so she can save for her education. Beyond working long hours and not being free to leave the employer's residence, she is forced to perform sexual favors for her employer or she will not get paid for her work.

A boy leaves his village so he can seek money and food for his family. He is hired to work as a laborer at a coastal resort in Sri Lanka. He is refused food and water. He must work day and night and suffers beatings when he does not work hard enough.

A Somali man pays his life savings to a businessman in exchange for assistance to bring him to the United Kingdom with expectations for a better life. The businessman gives the Somali man a fake identification, passport, and a plane ticket to London. Upon arriving in London, he gets a job under his new assumed name.

An Israeli couple pays someone to help them flee the country to escape civil conflict. The couple is secreted in a cargo container on a train. Upon arrival to their destination, someone opens the container and allows them to go free.

BIO-PSYCHO-SOCIAL IMPACT

Trafficking victims are exposed to several serious health risks that could impact global health. They may be exposed to violence such as rape and torture, dangerous working conditions, communicable and sexually transmitted diseases such as HIV/AIDS, poor nutrition, and drug and alcohol addiction (DOS, 2008; Spear, 2004). Victims trafficked for sexual exploitation face physical and emotional damage from violent sexual activity, and some may suffer permanent damage to their reproductive organs (DOS, 2008). Some are beaten or drugged into compliance and may become drug addicted when they use drugs as a way to cope with the trauma. Physical injuries associated with trafficking could include signs of beatings, burns, broken bones and teeth, complications

associated with pregnancy or illegal abortion, and even permanent disability. "No brothel wants to take on the responsibility of a sick or dying girl. It is more cost-effective to discard her and replace her with someone fresh" (Bales, 1999).

KEY POINT The highest priority for a trafficking survivor is safety. This is precedent over the many and complex other human needs.

When victims are trafficked to a location where they cannot speak or understand the language, feelings of isolation and domination may only compound the psychological trauma inflicted by the traffickers (DOS, 2006). Trafficking victims suffer with layers of fear and mental anguish and may have feelings of being trapped with no way out. Under the trafficker's control, the trafficked are often residing in a country illegally and unfamiliar to them. Most often, the traffickers have taken away any legal documents the victims may have possessed. Victims may be terrified of law enforcement and have little knowledge of their rights or legal options (U.S. Department of Health and Human Services [DHHS], 2008a). They may fear incarceration or deportation. Victims often fear for their lives and for the lives of their loved ones left behind. If the trafficker should discover that a victim has attempted to make contact with the police, the victim could face serious beatings or torture and the victim's family could be placed at risk for harm or death.

The bio-psycho-social needs of trafficking survivors are many and complex, but nurses must keep in mind that the highest priority of the trafficking survivor is safety. On the surface they may present with some of the same indicators as domestic violence survivors: vague in telling what has happened, fearful that someone may find out they sought medical help, showing physical signs of injury such as bruises or lacerations, and in need of a safe place to go. Beneath the surface, however, there is much more.

The Department of Health and Human Services identifies several health issues observed in victims of human trafficking:

- Health issues that were not treated in the early stages but tend to fester until they become critical, even life-endangering
- Infections or mutilations caused by unsanitary and dangerous medical procedures performed by the trafficker's so-called doctor
- Chronic back, hearing, cardiovascular, or respiratory problems from endless days toiling in dangerous agriculture, sweatshop, or construction conditions
- Weak eyes and other eye problems from working in dimly lit sweatshops
- Psychological trauma from daily mental abuse and torture, including depression, stress-related disorders, disorientation, confusion, phobias, and panic attacks
- Feelings of helplessness, shame, humiliation, shock, denial, or disbelief
- Cultural shock from finding themselves in a strange country (DHHS, 2008b)

Forensic nurses who are involved in the clinical care of trafficking survivors must be aware of the bio-psycho-social impact of trafficking and understand that the survivor may not want to notify the police of the situation. After long periods of trauma and abuse, survivors may not know who they can trust. Trafficking victims may break their own cycle of violence by disclosing information to persons perceived as least threatening.

Box 43-1 Persons Likely to Detect Victims of Human Trafficking	
Members of clergy	Good samaritans
Business owners	Consulate or embassy
Other trafficked persons/witnesses	Shelters
Law enforcement	Private attorneys
Customers/clients of the trafficked person	Forensic nurses
Mental health service providers	School nurses or teachers

Persons most likely to detect a trafficking victim are members of clergy, medical personnel, shelter workers, police officers, and good samaritans (Box 43-1).

Resources to Guide Forensic Nursing Practice

According to Wahed and Bhuiy (2007), health providers are typically reluctant to ask women about experiences of abuse in fear of either offending the victims or getting involved in issues too deep to handle. Some providers may feel that they do not have the knowledge nor skill to address the problem at hand (Wahed & Bhuiy, 2007). Nurses may lack knowledge of national antitrafficking legislation and available referral services for trafficking survivors.

As part of their professional role, forensic nurses must be aware of available resources for protecting trafficking victims and when appropriate, collaborate with law enforcement agencies and immigration services. Culturally sensitive questioning by the nurse may afford the victim an opportunity to speak out and be rescued (Moynihan, 2006).

The U.S. Department of Health and Human Services has indicated that it is important to talk to a potential victim in a safe and confidential environment. When the victim is accompanied by someone who seems controlling, it is important to separate the victim from that individual who could be the trafficker or someone working for the trafficker (DHHS, 2008a). When possible, seek the help of a staff member who speaks the patient's language and understands the patient's culture. Screening of translators to ensure that the translator and victim do not know each other is highly recommended (DHHS, 2008a; Zimmerman & Watts, 2003). Interpreter services such as those provided by ATT Language Line are resourceful when a translator is not available (DHHS, 2008a) (Box 43-2).

BEST PRACTICE Forensic nurses must think globally and act domestically in the prevention of human trafficking. When trafficking is suspected and the forensic nurse is unsure what to do, it is best practice call the National Human Trafficking Resource Center Hotline for assistance: 1-888-373-7888.

Zimmerman and Watts (2003), authors of the "World Health Organization's Ethical and Safety Recommendations for Interviewing Trafficked Women," suggest adherence to the following 10 principles:

1. Do no harm.
2. Know your subject and assess the risks.
3. Prepare referral information without making promises that you cannot meet.
4. Adequately select and prepare interpreters.
5. Ensure anonymity and confidentiality.
6. Get informed consent.
7. Listen to and respect each woman's assessment of her situation and risk to her safety.
8. Do not retraumatize.
9. Be prepared for emergency intervention.
10. Put information to good use.

Box 43-2 Contact Telephone Numbers
National Human Trafficking Hotline: 1-888-373-7888
U.S. Immigrations and Customs Enforcement: 1-866-347-2423
ATT Language Line: 1-800-752-6096

The National Human Trafficking Resource Center (NHTRC) Hotline, operated by the Polaris Project, responded to approximately 6000 calls in 2008, the highest annual call volume on the hotline to date. Calls received include victim calls, reports of potential trafficking situations, and requests for training, services, and general information about human trafficking. The NHTRC is equipped to handle calls from all regions of the United States from a wide range of callers including, but not limited to, potential trafficking victims, community members, law enforcement, medical professionals, legal professionals, service providers, researchers, students, and policy makers (Polaris Project, 2008).

The NHTRC may be able to offer contact information for service providers when the forensic nurse is unaware of local resources or when dealing with an emergency after normal business hours. The forensic nurse may recognize that the survivor will need referrals to services such as free health services, social services, safe shelter locations, women's groups, and faith-based support (Zimmerman & Watts, 2003).

Trafficking victims who are willing to testify in court against their captors may be eligible for certification under the Victims Trafficking Protection Act (TVPA, 2000). Under this act, certified victims may be afforded witness protection privileges and issued a T-visa that allows them temporary residency in the United States while a court case is pending or when it may be too dangerous to return to their originating country. Although it is important for the forensic nurse to be aware of these legal options, not all victims are eligible for certification and it is not the role of the nurse to offer it to them. It is important for the nurse to remember not to make promises to the victims that may not be fulfilled.

BEST PRACTICE The forensic nurse should be aware of legal options for the trafficking survivor, but should be aware that offering legal options is not within their purview.

Public awareness campaigns such as public service announcements and advertisements are common approaches to primary prevention (Wahed & Bhuiya, 2007). The United Nations Global Initiative to Fight Human Trafficking (UNGIFT) has released online videos and televised public service announcements that depict chilling images of the various forms of human trafficking that occur in our world today. Links to these websites can be found in the reference list at the end of this chapter.

Human traffickers should be considered dangerous criminals. For the sake of public safety, members of the general public who may be alerted by unusual activity that appears to be human trafficking should immediately contact local law enforcement authorities and never attempt to follow or intervene with suspicious persons.

Summary

Forensic nurses could play a significant role in all three prongs of antitrafficking legislation: prevention, protection, and prosecution. Primary prevention, through education and awareness, is critical for forensic nurses to effectively identify trafficking victims and for understanding what to do when a victim discloses critical information in a clinical setting. The forensic nurse has a duty to protect patients from further harm and could prevent a bad situation from becoming worse. Being aware of community resources for trafficking victims could be instrumental in channeling a survivor to safety. Further, a forensic nurse may testify in court to evidence gathered in the scope of clinical care of the trafficking survivor. This evidence could make a difference in the successful prosecution against persons accused of this global crime of violence against humanity.

KEY TERMS used in the Trafficking Victims Protection Act (TVPA)

Child sex tourism involves people who travel from their own country to another and engage in commercial sex acts with children.

Coercion means (1) threats of serious harm to or physical restraint against any person; (2) any scheme, plan, or pattern intended to cause a person to believe that failure to perform an act would result in serious harm to or physical restraint against any person; or (3) the abuse or threatened abuse of the legal process.

Happy trafficking is a term for victim turned trafficker.

Human smuggling is the facilitation, transportation, attempted transportation, or illegal entry of a person(s) across an international border, in violation of one or more countries' laws, either clandestinely or through deception, such as the use of fraudulent documents.

Involuntary servitude includes a condition of servitude induced by means of (1) any scheme, plan, or pattern intended to cause a person to believe that, if the person did not enter into or continue in such condition, that person or another person would suffer serious harm or physical restraint or (2) the abuse or threatened abuse of the legal process.

References

Bales, K. (1999). *Free the slaves.* Los Angeles: The Regents of the University of California.

Barrows, J., & Finger, R. (2008). *Human trafficking and the healthcare professional.* Retrieved on January 21, 2009, from www.sma.org/pdfs/objecttypes/smj/EDDFFC7C-1109-A387-6032CDB488512CB8/521.

Beyrer, C. (2004). Global child trafficking. *Lancet, 364,* 16–17.

Farley, M., Cotton, A., Lynne, J., Zumbeck, S., Spiwak, F., Reyes, M., et al. (2003). Prostitution and trafficking in nine countries. In M. Farley (Ed.), *Prostitution, trafficking and traumatic stress* (pp. 77–79). Binghamton, NY: The Hawthorne Maltreatment & Trauma Press.

Fernando, B. (2005). *In contempt of fate.* Merrimac, MA: BeaRo Publishing.

Herman, J. (2003). Introduction: Hiding in plain sight: Clinical observation on prostitution. In M. Farley (Ed.), *Prostitution, trafficking and traumatic stress* (pp. 1–13). Binghamton, NY: The Hawthorne Maltreatment & Trauma Press.

Hughes, D. (2003). *Hiding in plain sight. A practical guide to identifying victims of trafficking in the U.S.* Retrieved December 19, 2005, from www.acf.hhs.gov/trafficking/resources/plain_site.html.

Human Smuggling and Trafficking Center. (2005). *Fact Sheet: Distinctions between human trafficking and smuggling.* Retrieved March 6, 2006, from www.state.gov/g/tip/rls/fs/2005/57345.htm.

International Organization for Migration (IOM). (2008). *Human trafficking in eastern Africa.* Geneva: Author.

Moynihan, B. (2006). The high cost of human trafficking. *Journal of Forensic Nursing, 2*(2), 100–101.

Polaris Project. (2009). Retrieved on December 30, 2008, from www.polarisproject.org/index.php?option=com_content&task=view&id=26&Itemid=86

Spear, D. (2004). Human trafficking: A health care perspective. *AWHONN Association of Women's Helath, Obstetric and Neonatal Nurses, 4*(8), 314–321.

Trafficking Victims Protections Act of 2000. (2009). Retrieved February 5, 2009, from www.state.gov/documents/organization/10492.pdf.

United Nations Global Initiative to Fight Human Trafficking. (2009). Retrieved February 2, 2009, from www.ungift.org/ungift/en/multimedia/video.html

United Nations Global Initiative to Fight Human Trafficking. (2009).

United Nations Office on Drugs and Crime (UNODC). (2008). *Toolkit to combat trafficking in persons.* Retrieved February 2, 2009, from www.ungift.org/docs/ungift/pdf/knowledge/UNODC_toolkit_Oct_2008.pdf

U.S. Department of Health and Human Services (DHHS). (2008a). *Campaign to rescue and restore victims of human trafficking.* Retrieved February 4, 2009, from www.acf.hhs.gov/trafficking/campaign_kits/tool_kit_health/identify_victims.html.

U.S. Department of Health and Human Services. (2008b). *Common health issues seen in victims of human trafficking.* Retrieved February 4, 2008, from www.acf.hhs.gov/trafficking/campaign_kits/tool_kit_health/health_problems.html.

U. S. Department of State (DOS). (2006). Trafficking in persons report. Retrieved July 2, 2007, from www.state.gov/g/tip/rls/tiprpt/2006.

U.S. Department of State (DOS). (2008). Trafficking in persons report. Retrieved January 5, 2009, from www.state.gov/documents/organization/105655.pdf.

Wahed, T., & Bhuiy, A. (2007). Battered bodies & shattered minds: Violence against women in Bangladesh. *Indian Journal of Medical Research, 126*(4), 341–354.

Zimmerman, C., & Watts, C. (2003). WHO Ethical and safety recommendations for interviewing trafficked women. World Health Organization. Retrieved September 15, 2007, from www.who.int/gender/documents/en/final%20recommendations%2023%20oct.pdf.

CHAPTER 44 Legal and Ethical Issues in Forensic Nursing Roles

Susan Chasson

One of the many challenges for the forensic nurse is learning how to bridge between the healthcare system and the criminal justice system. To function in this dual role, it is essential for the nurse to understand the legal foundation for nursing practice. It is also important for the nurse to be aware of the sources of law and how they apply to forensic practice. This chapter discusses state, federal, and international laws and how they impact the role of the forensic nurse. The chapter also examines the application of agency regulations and case law. Forensic nurses need to comprehend how the law affects decision making in forensic practice and how to protect the legal rights of the patients they serve.

Every day, new laws and new interpretations of existing laws are created. Forensic nurses must understand where to find the current sources of laws and how to apply those laws to their forensic practice. Because the law is constantly changing, a textbook should be used only as a reference source for legal information. When nurses require specific legal advice, they should consult with an attorney who is familiar with that area of the law. The laws of each state may deal differently with the same issue or question. Federal laws may also be interpreted and applied differently in some states.

Sources of Law

Forensic nursing practice is regulated and influenced by state and federal laws. Each level of government can create laws through the legislative process. Laws passed by state legislatures or the U.S. Congress are called statutes. Most nurses are familiar with the process of legislative lawmaking, but they may be unaware of the process government agencies use to create law. The purpose of legislation is to provide a framework for the government to create standards for regulating a subject. But many areas of government regulation require detailed descriptions of what and how an area of subject matter will be legally controlled.

Because elected officials often do not have the technical expertise to write regulations for a specific subject matter, they often delegate this task to governmental agencies. The process government agencies use to make rules and regulations is called administrative rule making. In most states and within the federal government, administrative rule making follows strict procedures. These procedures protect the rights of citizens, because once these rules are made and approved, they become enforceable law. When an agency wants to create a new regulation, it usually publishes a draft of the proposed rule. After the publication of a proposed rule, the public is usually allowed to comment in writing. Sometimes the agency will open a public hearing to allow interested groups and individuals to make comments. Once the public has been given an opportunity to comment on the proposed rule, then a final rule is published and a date of enforcement is announced. This is a very simplified explanation of what, at times, can be a very complex process. If certain groups or individuals believe a rule or regulation is not properly promulgated, they may be able to challenge the agency in court to prevent enforcement of the rule.

Rules and regulations often govern details that may need to be modified or changed frequently. For example, the Nevada Nurse Practice Act gives the Nevada Board of Nursing the power to "adopt regulations establishing reasonable standards ... of professional conduct for the practice of nursing" (Nev. Rev. Stat. § 632.120(1)(a)(2), 1985). Using this legislative mandate to regulate the professional conduct of nurses, the Nevada Board of Nursing can create regulations to control nursing practice as new practice areas develop. In 1996 the Nevada Board passed a regulation that determines how nurses will identify themselves to a client or patient when practicing telenursing (Nev. Admin. Code § 632.248, 1996). Because the Board has been granted the power to create rules, change can occur without involving the legislative process. This two-tiered approach to creating laws to regulate a practice or subject matter area allows the elected officials to create broad policies for regulating a field, while the details of the regulations are left to professionals with expertise in that area.

The federal government uses legislation and administrative rule making when there is a need for the uniform application of standards across the nation. For example, Medicare is a national health insurance program for the elderly and disabled. The Social Security Act describes who qualifies for Medicare, but there are many pages of regulations that describe the details concerning what kind of care is covered and how healthcare providers must bill for their services. The law of the United States is found in the U.S. Code Annotated (U.S.C.A.), and federal regulations are recorded in the Code of Federal Regulations (C.F.R.).

In addition to laws created by legislators and rules and regulations created by agencies, the state and federal courts can interpret existing law and create case law by making decisions in appellate cases. Both state and federal case law can have an impact on nursing practice. For example, in 1991 Richard Heinecke argued before the Utah Court of Appeals that having sexual relations with a patient was not unprofessional conduct and therefore was not a violation of the Utah Nurse Practice Act that should result in revocation of his license (*Heinecke v. Department of Commerce,* 1991). In this case, the court interpreted the Utah Nurse Practice Act to prohibit sexual relations with a patient by looking at the clause that stated that a nurse can be charged with unprofessional conduct if he or she is "guilty of immoral, unethical, or unprofessional conduct as it relates to the practice of nursing" (Utah Code Ann. §58-31-14(1)(b), 1990). When a judge makes a decision in an appellate case, that decision becomes appellate case law. It is important to understand that attorneys may use case law to argue for a desired interpretation of the law in other legal cases.

For a judge to rule that a previous decision in a court case is the legal rule for another situation, the facts need to be similar. The Utah Board of Nursing did not want a different judge to decide that a different fact situation might allow a nurse to have sexual relations with a patient. As a result of this concern, in 1998 language was added to the Utah Nurse Practice Act to specify when sexual relations with a patient or former patient would be considered unprofessional conduct (Utah Code Ann. §58-31b-502, 1998).

State laws are the source of regulation for most areas of health and safety for state residents. State laws that are important to forensic nursing practice include the practice acts for each healthcare profession, including both nurse and physician practice acts. A forensic nurse should also be familiar with state laws that regulate the licensing of healthcare facilities, laws that protect public health, and mandatory reporting laws for child or elder abuse.

Each state is also responsible for creating criminal codes. Criminal codes specify which acts are considered crimes and what the punishment will be if a person is convicted of a crime. Because a criminal conviction can result in the loss of an individual's liberty, these laws must be written in a manner that specifies what types of behavior are prohibited. Forensic nurses need to understand that criminal codes may define the same unlawful act differently in different states. Legal activity in one state may be illegal in another. For example, the age of consent for sexual intercourse varies from age 12 to age 18 in different U.S. states (Sutherland, 2003). The federal government also creates criminal statutes. These laws deal with crimes that occur on federal property or deal with criminal activity that crosses state borders. Federal criminal laws also deal with areas of the law that are enforced by federal agencies. For example, the U.S. Security and Exchange Commission (SEC) regulates the trading of stocks and bonds. When a person illegally trades stocks or bonds, these criminal violations are prosecuted under federal law.

As standards for nursing become more global, there is also a need to appreciate the importance of international law. International law is created through treaties signed by two or more countries and through decisions made by international courts. The United Nations is the source of many international treaties that protect human rights and have potential application to nursing practice. The Universal Declaration of Human Rights (UDHR) is the document that provides the legal foundation for the protection of human rights throughout the world. On December 10, 1948, 48 of the 56 member nations of the United Nations General Assembly ratified this document that states in Article I, "All human beings are born free and equal in dignity and rights. They are endowed with reason and with conscience and should act towards one another in a spirit of brotherhood" (UDHR, 1948).

The Declaration goes on to state what rights are basic to both women and men, such as freedom to own property and the right to a standard of living that is adequate for health and well-being (UDHR, 1948). The Declaration also prohibits practices that deprive individuals of human rights, such as torture and slavery (UDHR, 1948). When looking at treaties as sources of international law, it is important to see if a nation that signs a treaty has created a reservation to a particular part of the document.

A reservation allows a nation to opt out of any part of a treaty that it does not want to support or enforce. For example, the U.S. has adopted the International Covenant on Civil and Political Rights but has reserved the right to not enforce Article 6, which prohibits the execution of persons who committed capital crimes prior to the age of 18 (International Covenant on Civil and Political Rights, 1966).

In recent years, there has been an increased use of international courts to investigate and prosecute war crimes and violations of human rights. Forensic nurses with training in death investigation and injury identification are in a unique position to assist with these international proceedings (Weaver & Lynch, 1998).

KEY POINT The passage of new laws and the interpretations of existing laws are part of the constantly changing body of knowledge required in forensic practice. Creating a list of legal resources to update critical changes in regulations and case law interpretation is an important aspect of maintaining competence.

Two excellent sources of legal information are professional organizations and state bar associations. Professional organizations often publish newsletters and create online services informing members of the changes in the laws that apply to a specific area of practice.

The state bar associations are professional organizations for the attorneys of each state. The American Bar Association provides continuing education and updates about changes in state laws for attorneys. Information about continuing education offerings for attorneys is often accessible online and available to the public. When the forensic nurse needs to research a specific topic, most state government websites provide online access to state statutes and case law. Several Internet websites are dedicated to providing sources of legal information. Law libraries and their staffs can also offer valuable assistance in locating legal materials. Being able to locate statutes, regulations, and case law is a fundamental part of forensic nursing.

Forensic Nursing and the Nurse Practice Act

Nurses should begin practice with a thorough understanding of their state's nurse practice act. This state statute determines the scope of practice for nurses in each state. In many states, forensic nursing is a relatively new area of practice. Nurses should examine their state's act to make sure that they can document that they are functioning within the scope of a registered nurse.

BEST PRACTICE Forensic nurses should possess a thorough understanding of their nurse practice acts to ensure that they are functioning within an acceptable scope and standard of practice for a registered nurse or an advanced practice registered nurse in the state.

The Alabama Nurse Practice Act states, "Additional acts requiring appropriate education and training designed to maintain access to a level of healthcare for the consumer may be performed under emergency or other conditions which are recognized by the nursing and medical professions as proper to be performed by a registered nurse" (Alabama Nurse Practice Act §34-21-1(3)(a)). In Utah, the practice of nursing includes "performing delegated procedures only within the education, knowledge, judgment and skill of the licensee" (Utah Code Ann. §58-31b-102(12)(f)). These clauses allow for the expansion of nursing practice into new areas without redefining the role of nursing in the nurse practice act.

Nurses can request a ruling from their board of nursing to determine whether they are functioning within their scope of practice. In Florida, sexual assault nurse examiners (SANEs) went before the Board of Nursing to discuss their forensic practice. The SANEs petitioned the Board to obtain a determination about whether performing evidence collection on adult and adolescent sexual battery patients was within a registered nurse's scope of practice. After examining national standards for the education and practice of SANEs, the Board voted to affirm that the role of the SANE was within the scope of practice of the registered nurse (Florida Board of Nursing Minutes, 2003).

Challenges to the expansion of nursing practice can come from nursing or other healthcare professions. In Missouri, two nurses who worked for a family planning clinic were charged with the unauthorized practice of medicine (*Sermchief v. Gonzales,* 1983). In their jobs they performed pelvic examinations and provided contraception under standing protocols from the clinic's physicians. Many organizations and individuals felt these nurses were functioning beyond the scope of the Missouri Nurse Practice Act, and the nurses were charged with the unlawful practice of medicine. The Supreme Court of Missouri examined the trend both nationally and within the state of Missouri to change nurse practice acts to allow for the expansion of responsibilities for professional nurses. The court determined that if the nurses had postgraduate training to perform family planning services and were using written standing orders and protocols, the nurses were well within the definition of professional nursing (*Sermchief v. Gonzales,* 1983).

Nurses who want to expand their scope of practice should maintain comprehensive records of education and training (*Hoffson v. Orentreich, M.D.,* 1989). They should also work closely with their professional organizations to create and follow standards of practice for their specialty area. In 1995, the American Nurses Association recognized forensic nursing as a specialty and in collaboration with the International Association of Forensic Nurses (IAFN) published the *Scope and Standards of Forensic Nursing Practice* (McHugh & Leake, 1997). The 2009 edition of the *Scope and Standards of Forensic Nursing Practice* (ANA and IAFN, 2009), identifies for the first time standards for both the basic forensic registered nurse and the advanced practice registered nurse. Collaborative relationships with other professionals in the field who value and support an expansion of forensic nursing practice is another way to demonstrate the need for a change in nursing practice.

It is important for the expansion of forensic nursing practice to be evidence based. By collecting practice data, nurses can demonstrate increased access to care and the increased quality of care. Nurses should understand how to evaluate forensic programs and forensic practice. Documenting the outcomes of forensic practice will help forensic nurses continue to be pioneers in the field of providing care and improving the lives of victims of interpersonal violence.

In addition to understanding the general nursing practice for the purpose of legally expanding forensic nursing practice, nurses need make sure that they are not violating the nurse practice act when they collaborate with other professionals who are not healthcare providers. Nurses are often placed in challenging situations when requests are made by other professionals such as law enforcement or prosecutors to alter their nursing practice. For example, a nurse may be requested to limit documentation about a patient's mental health status or previous history of drug abuse to prevent this potentially damaging information to be available to a defense attorney. It is important that the nurse be able to justify his or her forensic nursing practice based on the healthcare needs of the patient, not the prosecutorial needs of the criminal justice system. Failure to document findings that may affect a patient's healthcare may be a direct violation of the nurse practice act. In the state of Alaska, "failing to maintain a record for each client which accurately reflects the nursing problems and interventions for the client" is considered to be unprofessional practice (Alaska Administrative Code, Chapter 12, §44.770.10).

As nurses seek employment with attorneys and law enforcement agencies, they need to make sure they know the difference between using nursing knowledge in a non-nursing role and practicing as a nurse. They should ask themselves the following questions:

1. Is there a nurse-patient relationship?
2. Would a reasonable person assume there is a nurse-patient relationship?
3. Does a non-nurse or someone who is not recognized under the Nurse Practice Act supervise my nursing practice?
4. In my job, do I need to carry nursing malpractice insurance?

If there is a nurse-patient relationship, either actual or assumed by the client, then the nurse's practice should comply with the nurse practice act. If you are practicing as a nurse and someone who is not a nurse is supervising your nursing practice, you may be in violation of your nurse practice act. If a nurse sees a patient at the request of another professional, she or he should give informed consent to the patient about the purpose of the evaluation and the limitations of the nurse-patient relationship in this situation. As nurses expand their forensic practice outside of the heathcare settings, they need to make sure they are either not practicing nursing or that their role does not violate the nurse practice act.

Patient Confidentiality and the Forensic Nurse

The duty of confidentiality is a basic concept of ethical nursing practice. In the realm of forensic nursing, patient confidentially must be balanced with public and individual safety concerns. Both state and federal laws dictate how confidential patient information will be handled. Nurses who breach patient confidentiality can be sued for malpractice and lose their professional license. Under new federal privacy laws, a nurse may face fines and possible prison sentences for breaching confidentiality. It is important for a nurse to know where to look for privacy information, because different rules may apply in different states.

Each nurse should first look at the state's nurse practice act. Breach of confidentiality is usually considered an unprofessional practice. State laws may create other privacy standards for patient information. State laws will also dictate specific circumstances when a nurse may be required to breach confidentiality.

The forensic nurse examiner will often be required to breach confidentiality as a result of mandatory reporting laws. All 50 states have mandatory reporting laws for both child and elder abuse. Under the elder abuse statutes of most states, the abuse of disabled adults is usually included. In addition to reporting elder and child abuse, 42 states require that healthcare providers report injuries that are the results of weapons, 23 states require the reporting of injuries that are the result of any crime, and 7 states specifically require the reporting of injuries that are the result of domestic violence (Houry, Sachs, Feldhaus, et al., 2002).

The nurse should know who can make a report, what needs to be reported, and where reports should be made. By following the requirements of the mandatory reporting laws, the healthcare provider usually receives immunity from any liability that results from making a report. It is important to understand the extent of the immunity granted by law, because in each state that protection from liability may be interpreted differently. In California, immunity is extended to both "required" and "authorized" reports of abuse (California Penal Code §§11172, 11172 (a)). Once a report is made, if a mandated reporter continues to provide information requested by an investigator of the abuse, those statements may also receive immunity (*Ferraro v. Chadwick, M.D.*, 1990). In Illinois, an initial report made by a provider is protected by statutory immunity. If a provider gives negligent care after a report is made, then the provider may be held liable for malpractice (*Doe v. Winny*, 2002).

Failure to follow mandatory reporting laws is usually considered a misdemeanor criminal offense. Some states have refused to define failure to report as a cause of action for malpractice, and other states are allowing families or the legal representatives of patients to sue providers if an injury occurs after a provider should have reported suspected abuse (*First Commercial Trust v. Rank*, 1996). In Florida, the courts do not allow victims of elder or child abuse to claim malpractice against a provider who fails to report suspected abuse (*J.B. v. Department of Health and Rehab. Servs.*, 1991; *Mora v. South Broward Hospital District*, 1998). However, in Maryland, the courts have taken the duty to report one step further, by stating that compliance with a reporting statute does not necessarily preclude a finding of negligence if a reasonable person would take precautions beyond the statutorily required measure (*Bently v. Carroll, M.D.*, 1998).

In addition to laws that require the reporting of abuse or injuries, most states also have public health laws that require the reporting of communicable diseases such as tuberculosis or gonorrhea. The purpose of these laws is to provide public health officials with information about patients who could be spreading infectious diseases. When a patient with a communicable disease is identified, the public health worker contacts the patient. The public health worker then determines if there are other people at risk for infection who need to be notified, tested, or treated. It is important to remember that laws that require reporting of infectious diseases apply to all patients. For example, if the nurse is providing care to a sexual assault victim who is known to be HIV positive, a report needs to be made to the appropriate public health authorities. If possible, the suspect can then be contacted and notified of his or her exposure to an infectious disease.

In some states, other diseases and health problems are reported to track and study other public health risks. Many states keep a record of patients with cancer to look for patterns that might indicate an environmental cause of the disease. In the state of Washington, there is a mandatory reporting law for pesticide exposure (Washington Statutes 70.104.055). Nurses must be aware of the kinds of healthcare problems that are reportable in their community.

A nurse may also breach confidentiality when there is a direct threat to a specific person. On October 27, 1969, Prosenjit Poddar killed his former girlfriend. Two months earlier, Poddar had informed his psychologist about his plans to kill Tatiana Tarasoff. Tarasoff's parents sued the psychologist and his employers for failure to warn (*Tarasoff v. Regents of the University of California*, 1976). This case established a duty to breach confidentiality when a healthcare provider is made aware of a specific threat to a specific individual. Since the *Tarasoff* decision (1976), many states have imposed a duty to warn either by statute or case law (Furrow, Greaney, Johnson, et al., 2001). At this time only Virginia and Texas have upheld the duty of confidentiality when the life of another person is threatened (*Nasser v. Parker, M.D.*, 1995; *Thapar, M.D. v. Zezulka*, 1999).

Until recently, privacy laws and regulations have been controlled by state statutes and state case law. In 1996, Congress passed the Health Insurance Portability and Accountability Act (HIPAA). Part of this law included a mandate from Congress to create privacy regulations for personal health information. As more individual health information is being placed into computers, there exists a real concern that private health information can be made readily accessible to the public. Incidents that reinforced this fear included the following: a Michigan-based health system accidentally posted the medical information of thousands of patients on the Internet, a truck in Connecticut dropped thousands of health insurance claims on the road on the way to the dump, and a patient in a Boston-area hospital discovered her medical record had been read by more than 200 of the hospital's employees (65 F.R. 82462, 82467). In an attempt to prevent future and more extensive disclosures of personal health information, on April 14, 2003, several hundred pages of new federal privacy regulations became effective (65 F.R. 82462). Under the new privacy regulation, an unintentional disclosure can result in civil penalties of $100 per violation with a maximum fine of $25,000 in one calendar year. Intentional disclosure can result in fines of $50,000 to $100,000 and up to 10 years in prison.

It is important for the nurse to recognize when HIPAA regulations apply to forensic practice. If a nurse is either employed by a covered entity or signs a written agreement to maintain HIPAA standards with a covered entity, then the rules and regulations of HIPAA apply. Under HIPAA, three types of groups or individuals are classified as "covered entities." Covered entities include healthcare plans, healthcare clearinghouses, and healthcare providers. Law enforcement officers are not considered to be covered entities under HIPAA (Podrid, 2003). Although HIPAA does impact how law enforcement can access healthcare information, police officers do not have to follow any of the HIPAA privacy regulations once they have obtained the personal health information of a patient.

If a forensic nurse is employed by a healthcare entity or provides healthcare as any part of the forensic role, then the privacy regulations apply to his or her forensic practice. Under HIPAA, all patients are required to receive a written copy of their privacy rights. The patient is also entitled to a copy of all of his or her personal medical information, which may include the forensic record if it is created during the course of providing healthcare and includes personal health information. If a patient seeks care from a health provider, it is assumed under HIPAA that consent is given to the provider to share personal health information for the purpose of treatment, billing, and operating the business aspects of the provider's practice. This means that a forensic nurse may share a patient's confidential health information to consult with another healthcare professional about the patient's treatment.

If a forensic nurse needs to release personal health information to a non-healthcare provider, such as law enforcement or a prosecutor, the patient must first give written authorization. This authorization must give details about the type of information to be released and who will receive this information. The authorization should also include a disclaimer to the patient stating that once this information is released, it no longer carries any federal protection of privacy. The patient can revoke this authorization at any time, but the forensic nurse is not responsible for any release of information that occurs before the revocation. This revocation must be given in writing. The nurse is responsible for keeping a record of all disclosures so that a patient will know exactly who has received the personal health information. Forensic evidence that might be considered personal health information includes blood, urine, trace evidence swabs, photographs of injury, and any written records.

There are specific exceptions to HIPAA that deal with both victims and suspects of crime. HIPAA does not void any mandatory state reporting laws for the reporting of abuse, injuries, or communicable diseases (45 C.F.R. 164.512). Any state privacy laws that require stricter privacy standards than HIPAA override the federal regulations. Law enforcement may obtain personal health information from healthcare providers without the consent of the patient for the purpose of identifying and locating a suspect, fugitive, material witness, or missing person. Information that can be given to law enforcement includes name, address, social security number, date of birth, place of birth, type of injury, description of distinguishing physical characteristics, ABO blood type, Rh factor, and date and time of treatment (45 C.F.R. 164.512(f)(i)). Healthcare providers cannot release DNA, DNA analysis, dental records, or samples of body fluid or tissues without consent of the suspect or a court order (45 C.F.R. 164.512(f)(ii)).

Once a patient is deceased, his or her personal health information is still protected, except under the following circumstances. Covered entities may disclose information to coroners and medical examiners for the purpose of identifying a body or determining the cause of death (45 C.F.R. 164.512(g)(1)). State laws that require additional reporting when a death occurs are still enforceable under HIPAA. Forensic nurses can play an important role by understanding HIPAA and facilitating the release of information deemed permissible under the new privacy regulations.

Breach of confidentiality can be a complicated issue when working with adolescent patients. Forensic nurses need to be aware of any state or federal laws that entitle adolescents to confidential care. In many states, adolescents may access confidential healthcare for reproductive health problems, drug and alcohol treatment, and mental healthcare. These laws vary from state to state, and in some cases state laws determine which institutions can provide confidential care. For example, in Utah, adolescents can receive confidential information about contraception unless they access healthcare at a state-funded facility (Utah Code Ann. §76-7-322, 1988). In some states, confidential reproductive healthcare can be received only at federally funded clinics.

Under HIPAA, if a state law requires confidential care for an adolescent, then the adolescent must authorize any release of personal health information. In forensic practice, an adolescent may

be entitled to confidential care, but a nurse cannot guarantee that parents will not be made aware of what has happened to the child. Privacy laws prevent the nurse from contacting the parents without the child's consent. Yet once information is released to law enforcement, under mandatory reporting laws, the police may contact parents.

To maintain confidentiality, forensic nurses should create procedures that prevent the unauthorized release of information. Patients should be asked how they want the nurse to contact them. Permission should be obtained to leave messages. Phone calls from an agency should not be identifiable by caller identification devices. Medical records should be kept in a secure area, and computerized information should be protected from unauthorized access.

Informed Consent

It is essential for a forensic nurse examiner to recognize the right of the patient to be given informed consent before providing care to a patient. The concept of informed consent is based on the right of the individual to make choices about what will happen to his or her body. This right of bodily self-determination was first acknowledged by Justice Benjamin Cardozo in 1914 when he stated, "Every human being of adult years and sound mind has a right to determine what shall be done with his own body" (*Schloendorff v. Society of N.Y. Hosp.*, 1914). For a patient to have control over what happens to his or her body, informed consent must be given before any treatment or procedure.

Informed consent comprises four parts. First, the risks of the procedure or treatment must be explained. Second, the patient should be told about the benefits. Third, the patient should be informed of any alternatives to the recommended treatment. Finally, the patient needs to be told the consequences if the treatment or procedure is not performed.

Informed consent is an important part of any forensic examination and is particularly important when examining a victim of a crime. Most victims of crime perceive the crime as a loss of control and an invasion of their privacy. Informed consent allows the patient to regain control over the situation by explicitly permitting access to his or her body. Evidence collection usually consists of collecting specimens from different parts of the body. Although a patient may have given consent for the entire examination, the patient should be given an opportunity to consent during each new step of the examination.

If a victim of a crime is unconscious, the collection of forensic evidence may need to be delayed until the patient can give consent. When a patient is unconscious, there is implied consent for any emergency or lifesaving procedures. Forensic evidence can be collected if it is part of any required emergency care. For example, a woman arrives at the emergency department with unexplained loss of consciousness. Under these circumstances, it is a routine part of the medical care to collect urine and blood for a toxicology screen. The primary purpose for collecting these specimens is to determine why the patient is unresponsive, but the specimens may be collected in a manner that preserves their value as evidence.

When deciding to collect evidence from an unconscious patient, the forensic nurse should consider two issues. First, will evidence be lost if the patient is allowed to regain consciousness before the evidence collection? Second, could the collection of evidence be considered an assault and battery by a patient who later becomes conscious and decides against having that evidence collected? Nurses who collect evidence in emergency departments and critical care areas should create protocols for the collection of evidence in the unconscious patient. The development of protocols should include input from hospital legal counsel and ethics committees. It may be beneficial to have the policy reviewed by the state board of nursing (Pierce-Weeks & Campbell, 2008). In Maine, the legislature has created statutory protections for nurses who collect sexual assault evidence. Nurses may collect sexual assault evidence on an unconscious victim if "a reasonable person would conclude that exigent circumstances justify conducting a forensic examination" (State of Maine Revised Statute, Title 24, Chapter 21 §5, 2005). If a nurse believes that critical evidence will be lost before a patient regains consciousness and an appropriate protocol does not exist, the prosecutor in charge of the case should be consulted. If the prosecutor wants the evidence collected, a court order can be obtained from a judge.

The care of children and adolescents creates unique concerns with informed consent. Before providing care to a child, the informed consent of a parent or guardian is required. In cases of child abuse, often the state will take temporary custody of the child and provide consent for the examination. In some states, if abuse is suspected, a healthcare provider may be able to provide care without parental consent. Even if a child cannot give legal consent, the child's assent should be obtained before collecting forensic evidence.

Assent is the process of explaining a procedure to a child and requesting the child's cooperation. Even though a child is usually not capable of understanding the risks and benefits of a procedure, the child should be allowed to give permission, in order to obtain cooperation, before having a procedure performed. In forensic practice, it is important to obtain the cooperation of the child. First, giving the child control will prevent further physical and psychological damage (Lynch & Faust, 1998). Second, a child who has been traumatized by a forensic examination may not be able to differentiate between the abuse and the medical examination when asked to testify at trial.

Adolescents may be allowed to give informed consent under several circumstances. As mentioned earlier, in certain situations adolescents are entitled to confidential care. If an adolescent can receive confidential care, he or she can also consent to that care. In some states, adolescents can be granted the rights of an adult, depending on their legal status. Some states consider minors to be emancipated and have the rights of adult if they are married or pregnant. Other states require a court order to establish that a child is emancipated (Office of Technology Assessment, 1991).

Nurses must also be aware that if an adolescent can consent to care, then he or she can also refuse care. Even when a child has a life-threatening illness or condition, some states recognize a mature minor exception. This exception allows a child to refuse lifesaving medical care if a court determines that the child is mature enough to understand the risks and benefits of refusing treatment. Nurses need to realize that they often hold the unique position of patient advocate. Informed consent should be an integral part of every forensic practice. Ultimately, the rights of patients need to be respected to enable them to make decisions about their healthcare.

When Should a Forensic Nurse Consult an Attorney?

The field of forensics requires the nurse to have a working knowledge of several areas of the law. Keeping informed of changes in state and federal laws and regulations is an essential part of forensic practice. Although the Internet provides an incredible ability for nurses to research legal issues online, the forensic nurse should know when it is important to seek the advice of an attorney.

There are several places to access legal advice. Nurses who work for the state or local government agencies can seek advice through city or county attorneys or their state attorney general's office. State and local governments usually employ both civil and criminal attorneys. Hospitals often have a risk manager or in-house counsel who can access or provide legal assistance for the nursing staff. The state board of nursing will usually be able to provide the forensic nurse with legal interpretations of the nurse practice act and other nursing regulations. The state bar association can make referrals to local attorneys, and sometimes state nurses' associations maintain a list of attorneys who are familiar with nursing issues and practice.

When a change in a law or regulation impacts forensic practice, a hospital or agency may need to change policies. An attorney who is familiar with that area of the law should review any changes in the policy and make sure they are appropriate and consistent with the new regulation. If a forensic nurse is dealing with a situation outside the standard procedures and protocols for collecting evidence or is in a conflict about evidence collection with a law enforcement agency, most jurisdictions have a prosecutor on call who can answer any questions or concerns. A nurse who is considering setting up a private practice should consult a lawyer to review any contracts. Corporate lawyers can also provide consultation on tax issues and how to structure a business relationship.

Case Study **44-1**

Patient Confidentiality

Karen Smith is a sexual assault nurse examiner (SANE). She has completed her second examination of the day and has gone into the examination bathroom to clean and restock. The toilet will not stop running, so she lifts the lid and in the back of the toilet is a plastic bag containing what appears to be a dried green leafy substance. Karen calls security to come and get the bag. Security notifies local law enforcement. The police determine that the bag contains marijuana, and they want Karen to give them the names of all the patients who have received an examination during the past month. Karen is not sure what she needs to do to protect patient confidentiality. She contacts the hospital risk manager and the hospital's HIPAA privacy officer. The HIPAA privacy officer is the person designated by the hospital to train hospital employees about HIPAA and help the hospital enforce the federal privacy standards. After reviewing hospital policy and HIPAA regulations, Karen and the risk manager inform the police department that the patients' names cannot be released unless the patients agree to authorize the release of information or unless the police obtain a court order signed by the judge.

Summary

Forensic nursing is the intersection of nursing practice and the law. Nurses must maintain a working knowledge of the laws that apply to their specific area of practice. Updating this aspect of a practitioner's knowledge base should be a regular part of continuing education in order for the nurse to maintain competency in practice. The forensic nurse should not hesitate to seek legal advice when a situation requires a comprehension or interpretation of the law that might best be provided by an attorney.

Resources
ORGANIZATIONS
American Association of Legal Nurse Consultants (AALNC)
401 North Michigan Avenue, Chicago, IL 60611; 877-402-2562; www.aalnc.org
A nonprofit organization dedicated to the professional enhancement of registered nurses practicing in a consulting capacity in the legal field.

American Bar Association
321 North Clark Street, Chicago, IL 60610; 312-988-5000; www.abanet.org

American Nurses Association (ANA)
8515 Georgia Avenue, Suite 400, Silver Spring, MD 20910; 800-274-4ANA; www.nursingworld.net

International Association of Forensic Nurses (IAFN)
1517 Ritchie Highway, Suite 208, Arnold, MD, 21012; 410-626-7805; www.IAFN.org

References

Alabama Nurse Practice Act §34-21–1(3)a.

Alaska Administrative Code Chapter 12 § 44.770.10

Bently v. Carroll, M.D., 734 A.2d 697 (Md. 1998).

California Penal Code §§11172,11172(a).

Code of Federal Regulations. U.S. Government Printing Office, Washington, DC.

Doe v. Winny, 764 N.E.2d 143 (Ill. 2002).

Ferraro v. Chadwick, M.D., 221 Cal. App. 3d 86 (Cal. 1990).

First Commercial Trust v. Rank, 915 S.W.2d 262 (Ark. 1996).

Florida Board of Nursing. (Dec. 3-5, 2003). Minutes of meeting (p. 6).

Furrow, B.R, Greaney, T. L., Johnson, S. H., et al. (2001). *Health law cases and materials*. (p. 336). St. Paul, MN: West Group.

Health Insurance Portability and Accountability Act of 1996. 42 U.S.C. §§201, et seq.

Heinecke v. Department of Commerce, 810 P.2d 459 (Utah 1991).

Hoffson v. Orentreich, M.D., 543 N.Y.S.2d 242 (N.Y. 1989).

Houry, D., Sachs, S. J., Feldhaus, K. M., et al. (2002). Violence-inflicted injuries: Reporting laws in fifty states. *Annals of Emergency Medicine*, *39*(1), 56–60.

International Association of Forensic Nursing. (2009). Forensic nursing: scope and standards of practice. Silver Spring, Maryland: American Nurses Association.

International Covenant on Civil and Political Rights. (December 16, 1966). 999 U.N.T.S.171.

J. B. v. Department of Health and Rehab. Servs., 591 So.2d 317 (Fla. 1991).

Lynch, L., & Faust, J. (1998). Reduction of stress in children undergoing sexual abuse medical examination. *The Journal of Pediatrics*, *133*(2), 296–299.

McHugh, J., & Leake, D. (Eds.), (1997). *Scope and standards of forensic nursing practice*. Washington, DC: American Nurses Publishing.

Mora v. South Broward Hospital District, 710 So.2d 633 (Fla. 1998).

Nasser v. Parker, M.D., 455 S.E.2d 502 (Va. 1995).

Nev. Admin. Code §632.248 (1996).

Nev. Rev. Stat.§632.120(1)(a)(2) (1985).

Office of Technology Assessment. (1991). Adolescent Health Volume III Crosscutting Issues in the Delivery of Health and Related Services. Chapter 17 Consent and Confidentiality in Adolescent Health Care Decisionmaking. Washington, DC: U.S. Congress.

Pierce-Weeks, J., & Campbell, P. (2008). The challenges forensic nurses face when their patient is comatose: Adressing the needs of our most vulnerable patient population. *Journal of Forensic Nursing*, *4*(3), 104–108.

Podrid, A. (2003). HIPAA–Exceptions providing law enforcement officials and social service providers access to protected health information. *Am Prosecutors Res Inst Update*, *16*(4), 4.

Schloendorff v. Society of N.Y. Hosp., 105 N.E. 93 (N.Y. 1914).

Sermchief v. Gonzales, 660 S.W.2d 683 (Mo. 1983).

State of Maine Revised Statute Title 24 Chapter 21 § 5, 2005.

Sutherland, K. (2003). From jailbird to jailbait: Age of consent laws and the construction of teenage sexualities. *William & Mary J Women Law*, *9*, 313–339.

Tarasoff v. Regents of the University of California, 551 P.2d 334 (Cal. 1976).

Thapar, M.D. v. Zezulka, 994 S.W.2d 635 (Tex. 1999).

United States Code Annotated. (2000). Washington, DC: U.S. Government Printing Office.

Universal Declaration of Human Rights (UDHR). (Dec. 10, 1948). U.N.G.A. Res. 217 III.

Utah Code Ann. §58-31-14(1)(b) (1990).

Utah Code Ann. §58-31b-102(12)(f).

Utah Code Ann. §58-31b-502 (1998).

Utah Code Ann. §76-7-322 (1988).

Washington Statutes 70.104.055.

45 C.F.R. 164.512.

45 C.F.R. 164.512(f)(i).

45 C.F.R. 164.512(f)(ii).

45 C.F.R. 164.512(g)(1).

65 F.R. 82462, 82467.

65 F.R. 82462.

Weaver, J. D., & Lynch, V. (1998). Forensic nursing: Unique contributions to international law. *Journal of Nursing Law*, *5*(4), 23–34.

CHAPTER 45 Testifying as a Forensic Nurse

Cari Caruso

PART I: CRIMINAL CASES

Testifying in court can be very exciting. The anticipation of sitting before a judge and jury, being questioned by attorneys, can also produce considerable anxiety and stress, especially if it is a new experience. For a nurse who has never been in court, the local district attorney (DA) can usually arrange for the observation of a trial. Generally, this involves calling the DA's office and introducing oneself as a forensic nurse examiner and explaining that it would be beneficial to see some court proceedings. The DA will usually be receptive to the request because if there is a chance that, in the future, the nurse may have a case that goes to trial, the DA would like to be assured that the nurse has some prior knowledge of how the court system works. Such an observation will also afford the nurse an opportunity to see the way the courtroom is set up, where witnesses will be seated, and where the jury, prosecutor, and the defense attorneys will be located. Forensic nurses should arrange to attend courtroom observations during a trial that has pertinent elements of their practice specialty. If that is not possible, any criminal proceeding will provide insight to the justice system. The day of the visit, the DA will ask the judge for permission to admit an observer for the proceedings; typically, the judge will give approval if it can be ascertained that the observer has no connections with the case. Typically, trials are open to the public but on occasion, depending on the kind of case being tried, the courtroom may be closed to the public.

Normally, for a trial, a testifying witness may not be allowed in the courtroom to hear anyone else's testimony (Federal Rules of Evidence, 2000). Sometimes defense witnesses may listen to prosecution witnesses to prepare for rebuttal. Witnesses should expect to be seated on the hard benches in the hallway or other adjacent area or anteroom. Although pleasantries may be exchanged with others, it is inappropriate for a witness to speak to anyone about the case. There may be jurors, family members, or other witnesses in the area. It is a good idea for the nurse witness to bring a neutral kind of book or other activity to pass the time. If your phone or handheld computer has games, they will help pass the time until it is time for the nurse to testify.

If the nurse has conducted the forensic examination in the case being tried, she or he will be built in to the prosecution's case so the dealings will be done with the prosecutor or the deputy district attorney. The DA will attempt to schedule a witness as close as possible to the anticipated time that the nurse will go on the stand. However, it is likely that the estimate of the time for testimony will go awry, and the nurse should always expect that there may be waiting involved. Many times circumstances prevent the nurse from even testifying that day, and she or he must come back the next day or another time when testimony continues.

Witnesses who may be anxious or have had little experience with public speaking should keep in mind certain techniques that may help them to appear relaxed and comfortable while on the witness stand. It is recommended that a witness analyze her or his own demeanor to pinpoint some basic areas for improvement. For example, an individual who has a tendency to fidget while sitting may make a conscious effort to control this behavior. A witness who appears at ease will likely have optimal impact with the jury. Soft, timid voices may convey a lack of confidence and possibly detract from credibility. Additionally, it complicates proceedings if the court needs to request the witness to speak up or to repeat testimony. Practicing is an effective way to improve performance during testimony. For example, merely relating a story or event in front of friends or family members and requesting their critique may be valuable. It may be helpful for a witness to ask someone to record such sessions so that she or he can study the effectiveness of delivery, presence, and style. Was the event related accurately? Was the speech enunciated and distinct, or was there mumbling, stuttering, hesitation, or stumbling over certain words? Was the pace of speaking too slow or too fast? Remember that a court reporter must be able to understand the words and enter the testimony into the record. Was eye contact maintained with the audience? Were there meaningless phrases, such as "you know" or "um"? Did the speaker maintain the audience's attention throughout the presentation? Some guidelines that may help the witness to convey a positive impression are outlined in Box 45-1.

Even though a witness may have limited experience in the forensic nursing field, he or she will typically have considerable experience as a nurse. These skills will serve the expert well during the testifying process, in which the major task is to educate the jury. Medical and nursing professionals employ their body of knowledge and clinical information to explain certain dynamics to a body of the public that must make sense of it in order to come to a reasonable conclusion. The lay public has little knowledge of medical terminology or physiology, so everything that is stated on the witness stand must be simplified and put into lay terms that can be readily understood. Nothing should be taken for granted in this arena. When most sexual assault nurses speak about the external genitalia, they mean parts anterior to the hymen. However, the layperson may think that the reference is to the pubic area. The terms *external* and *internal* should be explained. Technical terms can be used if they have been thoroughly defined. Things that may seem second nature to a nurse may not have the same meaning to the jury, so it essential for the witness to assume the role of a teacher to ensure that the listeners adequately understand the information.

It may be strange, to a novice, that before the courtroom session begins, the prosecutor and defense attorney may be making plans for a golf game or amiably chatting about a recent sports event. They may not be rivals outside the court milieu; however, each has a job to do and they must maintain their professional facade during the proceedings.

Box 45-1 Guidelines for Effective Testimony

- Dress professionally. A professional appearance shows the jury that nurses take themselves and the proceedings seriously.
- Remember to breathe. When under stress, people tend to take shallow breaths. When getting tense, take a few deep breaths. Take normal breaths before speaking so that your voice will stay at a good level.
- Walk into the courtroom with authority. Before arriving at the witness box, turn to the clerk, who will ask you to raise your right hand and recite, "Do you swear to tell the truth ...." Say, "I do" in a clear and audible tone. Then sit in the witness box. It may be good to start by smiling and saying, "Good morning" to the judge and jury.
- Sit up straight and look attentive. Do not fidget.
- Speak clearly and audibly.
- Make eye contact with those speaking, especially when replying to a question.
- Exude confidence.

Role of the Forensic Nurse Examiner

Forensic nurse examiners who have conducted forensic examinations in that jurisdiction are called by the prosecution to testify because they have provided an important service that contributed to a particular body of evidence. They are more or less incorporated into the prosecution case. It is, however, extremely important to understand that they do not work for the prosecutor and must remain independently objective and not feel responsible to tell anything but the truth. Whether the individual functions as a sexual assault nurse examiner (SANE), a death investigator, or any type of forensic nurse, he or she may have collected and evaluated information that will contribute to a larger body of information.

The forensic nurse is an educator and interpreter of the type of work we do and its protocols, standards, and procedures. By the time of the trial, the district attorney has determined that the case has merit and viability because of evidence of one kind or another. The forensic nurse should have an opinion about whether findings from the forensic examination could be consistent with the history provided by the patient, remembering that the history is only the patient's version of the events, as told to us, and be honest enough to acknowledge that the findings could be equally consistent with something else, such as consensual sexual contact, a nonspecific finding, or a medical condition. The SANE cannot substantiate force or determine consent versus nonconsent, so the nurse must maintain total neutrality. The forensic nurse can never cross over into the providence of the jury by stating that a sexual assault occurred. Only the jury can make that determination. The forensic nurse examiner has been given a particular history, regarding an event, but has no idea whether that history is accurate. This is why the forensic nurse's objectivity is paramount. The nurse should be unbiased and truthful to establish her or his credibility.

The SANE's testimony will not usually be the single hinge on which the verdict decision rests. It will be a supporting part, in a large body of evidence, but not necessarily the only consideration. Each witness is a cog in the wheel. The role of the forensic nurse examiner is to tell the unbiased truth. The nurse was not present at the scene and did not witness the event firsthand; therefore, the intention of the nurse is to relay her or his findings in the documentation and photography, to ensure that each is a fair and accurate representation of the examination, and to reflect this in the testimony without editorializing. Although the forensic nurse does not want a guilty person to go free or a person who

is not guilty to go to prison, the nurse should not even entertain the idea that she or he can be the judge or jury of any case. The nurse examiner should not be tempted have a stake in the case. To appear to be siding with one party or another will expose the nurse to be biased and taint the testimony, so the nurse should avoid disparaging comments on the witness stand about the defendant or the patient. The nurse may be competent at identifying findings and injuries, but the nurse cannot verify causation. The nurse may have opinions, but it is inappropriate for the forensic nurse examiner to declare that a sexual assault occurred, and the nurse could be disqualified for such a statement. Determining whether a sexual assault occurred is not the role of the testifying nurse. The forensic nurse should attempt to impress the court with professionalism, objectivity, and knowledgeable explanations of her or his exam findings. The nurse's unbiased testimony, in combination with the other testimony offered in trial, will provide the clear information jurors need to reach a satisfactory decision. Testimony should be based in current literature and the training and experience of the examiner, because a peer, in the role of an opposing expert, may be challenging the nurse's explanations.

KEY POINT The forensic nurse is a registered nurse who is an objective, nonbiased, skilled professional who has additional education and training in a forensic specialty.

A forensic nurse examiner may be called as a prosecution witness or a defense witness. However, most often the nurse will appear as part of the prosecution's case if she or he has conducted the examination. As mentioned before, the SANE is "built in" to the prosecution's case simply by the fact that she or he has conducted the forensic examination. That, however, does not mean that she or he must say only things that will benefit the prosecution. In essence, the forensic nurse examiner is testifying about the condition of the patient, the evidence that was collected, and the facts that the findings reveal. The opposition will often attempt to discredit the forensic nurse examiner and raise questions about the nurse's credentials, making it appear that the nurse is biased for the prosecution. However, that is the job of the opposing side in our adversarial system, and the nurse should not take it personally. Despite a sound education and outstanding credentials, the opposing attorney may bring the credibility of forensic nurses into question because the nurse's honest testimony will more than likely be damaging to one side or the other. It also could be beneficial to one or both sides. Some forensic nurse examiners/SANEs act as consultants for defense counsel. That shows definitive objectivity.

KEY POINT The forensic nurse examiner's objective is to relay the information about the evidentiary findings and to educate the court as to what those findings mean.

Curriculum Vitae

A curriculum vitae (CV) is an organized summary of employment and educational history. It functions like an extended résumé. It also may help to validate the credibility of the nurse witness. It should include the nurse's legal name and contact information along with details regarding academic achievements, organizational affiliations, professional presentations, publications, and relevant work experiences.

There are many ways to design a CV, and some nurses choose to have a professional assist them in developing an exemplary record for use in the legal arena. It should be constructed to serve as a formal document that illustrates the education, training, and experience that contribute to the nurse's expertise. It should always be kept current and completely truthful.

The forensic nurse examiner will be asked to furnish a CV to the prosecutor. It should include any classes, seminars, and conferences attended that may demonstrate expertise, including dates and the names of the speakers. This will illustrate specific study topics along with venerable lecturers who taught them.

Many nurses prepare both a comprehensive and an abbreviated CV. The shorter version would contain the elements from the full CV that are most important for the court to hear. It is advisable for the nurse to look over the brief form before going into the courtroom to ensure that all pertinent information can be relayed without hesitation, because it is easy to overlook elements of education and experience when sitting in the witness chair. Credentials should be listed first, followed by a work history, specialized training, other achievements, and publications. Pay special attention to true credentials, certifications, designations, and certificates of completion. If there are numerous training sessions or conferences, the nurse may report, "I have attended all required annual training sessions at my employing institution and certain specific scientific assemblies for six consecutive years." Copies of the CV should be readily available upon request.

The CV will not be read in court, so what is said in the court regarding the nurse's qualifications may bear weight on whether the court will accept the nurse as an expert. The forensic nurse examiner should not allow her or his credentials to be stipulated. It is important for the jury to hear about the forensic nurse examiner's qualifications. Most likely, the prosecutor will have shared the CV with defense counsel to ensure the counsel's awareness of the individual's qualifications to serve as an expert. However, the CV may also be used to attempt to disqualify an expert who is perceived to be a powerful tool against the opposition. The CV could also damage the nurse's credibility if the listings are not entirely truthful. Be sure to check the accuracy of the CV and that the corresponding dates correlate to the correct activities.

Subpoena

When the forensic nurse receives a subpoena, she or he should note certain details right away, such as the date of the trial. In many jurisdictions, the subpoena comes shortly before the trial or preliminary hearing. Subpoenas usually list the name of the defendant and not the name of the victim. If the work was primarily with the victim, the nurse may not know the name of the defendant. Look for the contact number of the witness coordinator's officer and make contact promptly. The witness coordinator may be the source of communication regarding the trial appearance and continuations. The nurse should state that she or he is the forensic nurse who conducted the evidentiary examination and has received a subpoena. The nurse will be asked to provide the case number, which may be found in a prominent site on the subpoena along with the name of the prosecuting attorney. The witness coordinator will confirm who the prosecutor will be and verify the identity of the victim. Ordinarily the coordinator will establish the nurse's availability for testifying within a certain time span and will ask whether the nurse will be on vacation or unavailable at certain times. The nurse should confirm the name and number of the prosecutor and make contact as soon as the chart and other materials from the case have been located. The prosecutor may only have the forensic exam report and might not be aware that the file contains consents, nurse's notes, medication records, photographs, and other documents related to the patient. Make sure the prosecutor has a copy of all documents related to the case.

Generally a subpoena includes two checkboxes that refer to the courtroom appearance: (1) be in court, and (2) be on call. The nurse should request to be placed, "on call." If, "be in court," has been checked, the nurse should contact the DA and the witness coordinator and request be switched to "on call." This way, the witness will not have to be in court until needed and will avoid hours of waiting in the hall. The prosecutor will provide an estimated time for the nurse's appearance.

A subpoena may be issued for the preliminary hearing. Most of the time, the forensic nurse will not be expected to appear at a preliminary hearing; however, there are exceptions, so make sure you communicate with the DA. The preliminary hearing determines whether there was probable cause for the suspect's arrest and if there is enough evidence for an indictment. There is no jury at this time. If an indictment is filed, then the matter goes to trial.

A pretrial conference may be held between the preliminary hearing and the trial. A subpoena may be received for that, too. A pretrial conference is used to review evidentiary issues before trial, but again, the forensic nurse may not be required to be present.

When the forensic nurse receives a subpoena for the actual trial, he or she should contact the prosecutor and the witness coordinator, keeping in mind that trials may be continued and continued and continued. Maintain ongoing and consistent communication so there is no ambiguity about what is happening. It is possible that, somewhere along the line, the defendant will plead and there will be no trial at all. When this occurs, the information should be filed with nurse's other case records for subsequent reference.

Again, the on-call trial date status should be verified. The first day of the trial as listed on the subpoena will not necessarily be for testimony but the beginning of procedures. The first steps will be for motions and for jury selection. This may take a day or more, so the nurse's testimony will most likely not be on that day but days later. Once the jury has been selected, the DA will have a better idea when the nurse will appear.

BEST PRACTICE Any potential expert should make sure that the DA and witness coordinator have all the pertinent contact information to facilitate communication regarding the date and time of appearance.

There is always a chance that the presence of the forensic nurse examiner may not be required. Photos and documentation will have been entered into evidence, and perhaps no further explanations or a court appearance will be necessary.

Potential witnesses should bring their subpoena to court on the prescribed day of appearance (it may even grant parking privileges in a restricted area or at no cost). Even after the trial is over, the witness should maintain the subpoena and file it with the chart. It is a useful document for recording the outcome of the case, including the details of sentencing.

Fact Witness versus Expert Witness

Different types of witnesses may testify in a trial. The two types that most often involve the nurse are *fact witness* and *expert witness*. In either case, it is most important for the nurse to be nonbiased, objective, and scientific. The forensic nurse must be a witness, not an advocate. The role of a fact witness, as defined by Webster's Revised Unabridged Dictionary (1998), is "To see or know by personal presence; to have direct cognizance of." These witnesses have firsthand knowledge of a particular event. That role may apply to nurses who are testifying regarding the observations and direct contact with the patient. A fact witness may testify to things that she or he heard, seen, touched, tasted, or smelled and may give an opinion related to those things perceived by his or her senses.

The expert witness, as defined by Barron's Law Dictionary (Giftis, 1996), is

> *a witness having special knowledge of the subject about which he is about to testify; that knowledge must generally be such as is not normally possessed by the average person. This expertise may derive from either study and education or from experience and observation. An expert witness must be qualified by the court to testify as such ... but the court must be satisfied that the testimony presented is of a kind which in fact requires special knowledge, skill or experience.*

Fact witnesses only testify to what they saw, collected, and observed. Expert witnesses deliver this type of testimony as well, but they may also contribute opinions and provide additional information regarding their area of expertise. They may not, however, make any statements or declarations that are within the providence of the jury. The experienced forensic nurse examiner will likely appear as an expert witness.

BEST PRACTICE The forensic nurse should maintain an up-to-date curriculum vitae that outlines education, experience, and credentials, including licensure and certification.

FRYE RULE

Forensic nurses should become familiar with the term *Kelly-Frye,* also called the *Frye Rule,* from *United States v. Frye* (1923). This case established, in the rules of evidence, that the results of scientific tests or procedures are admissible as evidence only when the tests or procedures have gained general acceptance in the particular field to which they belong. It clarified that an expert witness with knowledge, skill, experience, training, or education may offer an opinion in his or her area of expertise that is relevant to the case and will assist the court with its understanding of the matter at hand.

DAUBERT TEST

Another important term is the *Daubert test.* Under *Daubert* (*Daubert v. Merrell Dow Pharmaceuticals,* 1993) and *Kumho* (*Kumho Tire Company v. Patrick Carmichael,* 1999), which establishes the important legal principle that the opinion of experts must be based on reliable methodology or analysis and not subjective belief or unsupported speculation. Furthermore, the reliability of expert testimony is deemed to be as important as the relevance of the expert testimony. The Daubert decision caused much controversy because the scientific world had grown in leaps and bounds and some felt that the Frye rule was too weak, that because a proclaimed expert had made studies and observations and had come to a conclusion, even if it had gained acceptance in that field, if it was not supported by standardized scientific methodology and stringent controls, it

could be challenged. All evidence can be challenged in court, but the Daubert decision made the criteria more rigorous. States have chosen to opt for either the Frye rule or Daubert test as their criteria, and other states have chosen methods of their own.

In 1993, the U.S. Supreme Court replaced the Frye test with the Daubert test (*Daubert v. Merrell Dow Pharmaceuticals*). The Court clarified this decision in 1999 in *Kumho Tire Company, Ltd. v. Patrick Carmichael.* The Daubert test is now the standard for the admissibility of opinion testimony in federal courts. The criteria applied under Daubert and subsequent cases, as decided by lower federal courts, include the following:

> *The specific factors explicated by the Daubert Court are (1) whether the expert's technique or theory can be or has been tested—that is, whether the expert's theory can be challenged in some objective sense, or whether it is instead simply a subjective, conclusory approach that cannot reasonably be assessed for reliability; (2) whether the technique or theory has been subject to peer review and publication; (3) the known or potential rate of error of the technique or theory when applied; (4) the existence and maintenance of standards and controls; and (5) whether the technique or theory has been generally accepted in the scientific community.*

Still, the reliability of some issues thought to be valid under *Daubert* is wavering as a result of continuing controversies over techniques and new innovations in technology.

HEARSAY RULE

Hearsay is a statement other than one made by the declarant while testifying at the trial or hearing, offered in evidence to prove the truth of the matter asserted (Federal Rules of Evidence, 2000). This means that the nurse may not testify to something that someone else told her or him. In other words, if the victim or suspect tells the nurse something during an interview or examination, it is considered hearsay.

There are many exceptions to the hearsay rule. For the most part, the exceptions are related to "trustworthiness" and "necessity." The Federal Rules of Evidence and the individual state evidence codes all have similar statutes, so it is advisable for the nurse to research the rules of hearsay exceptions for that state.

According to the California Evidence Code Section 1200:

> *(a) "Hearsay evidence" is evidence of a statement that was made other than by a witness while testifying at the hearing and that is offered to prove the truth of the matter stated.*
> *(b) Except as provided by law, hearsay evidence is inadmissible.*
> *(c) This section shall be known and may be cited as the hearsay rule.*

Whether or not the rules of evidence in a state allow the nurse an exception to the hearsay rule, it is still up to the court and the judge to decide if those statements will be admissible.

Uniform Rules of Evidence Hearsay Exception, Rule 803(6)
Records in any form are admissible in evidence, if they are the following:
- Records of act or event
- Made at or near the time of the event
- By or from a person with knowledge
- Kept in the course of regularly conducted business activity

One exception is a deathbed confession. It is presumed that people do not lie when they are about to die. According to the California Evidence Code:

1243. Evidence of a statement made by a dying person respecting the cause and circumstances of his death is not made inadmissible by the hearsay rule if the statement was made upon his personal knowledge and under a sense of immediately impending death.

Another exception refers to spontaneous utterances.

California Evidence Code:
1240. Evidence of a statement is not made inadmissible by the hearsay rule if the statement:
(a) Purports to narrate, describe, or explain an act, condition, or event perceived by the declarant; and
(b) Was made spontaneously while the declarant was under the stress of excitement caused by such perception.

Federal Rules of Evidence Rule 803, Section 4
Yet another exception refers to purposes of medical history:

(4) Statements for purposes of medical diagnosis or treatment. Statements made for purposes of medical diagnosis or treatment and describing medical history, or past or present symptoms, pain, or sensations, or the inception or general character of the cause or external source thereof insofar as reasonably pertinent to diagnosis or treatment.

The following rule, in the California Evidence Code, states that it only applies to victims under the age of 12, describing any act or attempted act of abuse or neglect:

1226. Evidence of a statement by a minor child is not made inadmissible by the hearsay rule if offered against the plaintiff in an action brought under Section 376 of the Code of Civil Procedure for injury to such minor child.
1228. Notwithstanding any other provision of law, for the purpose of establishing the elements of the crime in order to admit as evidence the confession of a person accused of violating Section 261, 264.1, 285, 286, 288, 288a, 289, or 647a of the Penal Code, a court, in its discretion, may determine that a statement of the complaining witness is not made inadmissible by the hearsay rule if it finds all of the following:
(a) The statement was made by a minor child under the age of 12, and the contents of the statement were included in a written report of a law enforcement official or an employee of a county welfare department.
(b) The statement describes the minor child as a victim of sexual abuse.
(c) The statement was made prior to the defendant's confession. The court shall view with caution the testimony of a person recounting hearsay where there is evidence of personal bias or prejudice.
(d) There are no circumstances, such as significant inconsistencies between the confession and the statement concerning material facts establishing any element of the crime or the identification of the defendant, that would render the statement unreliable.
(e) The minor child is found to be unavailable pursuant to paragraph (2) or (3) of subdivision (a) of Section 240 or refuses to testify.
(f) The confession was memorialized in a trustworthy fashion by a law enforcement official.

If the prosecution intends to offer a statement of the complaining witness pursuant to this section, the prosecution shall serve a written notice upon the defendant at least 10 days prior to the hearing or trial at which the prosecution intends to offer the statement.
If the statement is offered during trial, the court's determination shall be made out of the presence of the jury. If the statement is found to be admissible pursuant to this section, it shall be admitted out of the presence of the jury and solely for the purpose of determining the admissibility of the confession of the defendant.
1360. (a) In a criminal prosecution where the victim is a minor, a statement made by the victim when under the age of 12 describing any act of child abuse or neglect performed with or on the child by another, or describing any attempted act of child abuse or neglect with or on the child by another, is not made inadmissible by the hearsay rule if all of the following apply:
(1) The statement is not otherwise admissible by statute or court rule.
(2) The court finds, in a hearing conducted outside the presence of the jury, that the time, content, and circumstances of the statement provide sufficient indicia of reliability.
(3) The child either:
(A) Testifies at the proceedings.
(B) Is unavailable as a witness, in which case the statement may be admitted only if there is evidence of the child abuse or neglect that corroborates the statement made by the child.
(b) A statement may not be admitted under this section unless the proponent of the statement makes known to the adverse party the intention to offer the statement and the particulars of the statement sufficiently in advance of the proceedings in order to provide the adverse party with a fair opportunity to prepare to meet the statement.
(c) For purposes of this section, "child abuse" means an act proscribed by Section 273a, 273d, or 288.5 of the Penal Code, or any of the acts described in Section 11165.1 of the Penal Code, and "child neglect" means any of the acts described in Section 11165.2 of the Penal Code.

The hearsay rules may vary from state to state and even from trial to trial, so the court decides whether the nurse may quote a patient's statement during testimony. A patient's statement may be on a form or document that has been entered into evidence. That may stand, or a part of the document could be construed as hearsay. For example, if a SANE has documented an injury on a reporting form that indicates a purple bruise to the left arm, this is permissible because the nurse examiner witnessed, firsthand, the injury and its characteristics. If the nurse examiner states that the victim told her the injury was sustained by the suspect punching her, there may be an objection, citing hearsay. Even though the form may say, "Purple bruise to left arm. Patient states, 'He punched me,'" the fact that the victim told the nurse how it happened may be considered hearsay. On the witness stand, the nurse will be able to state that there was a bruise to the patient's left arm but may not be allowed to say, "The patient said, 'He punched me.'" The nurse should be prepared to comply with whatever the ruling is. The jury will be able to examine documents so they may be able to see those entries during deliberation.

There is a phrase that states: "You can't unring a bell." It refers to something said in court that may be stricken from the record, but the jurors have already heard it. It may be spoken unintentionally or intentionally. The jurors will be instructed to disregard the statement, but once the bell is rung, can it be unrung? Let's use the preceding example: If the prosecutor asks the nurse what injury she or he observed on the patient's left arm, suppose the nurse answers, "A purple bruise where the defendant punched her." The defense may then object and ask that the statement be stricken from the record, citing hearsay. If the objection is sustained, the court will ask the nurse to only answer to what she observed. The prosecutor will ask the question again, and the nurse's answer should be, "A purple bruise." However, the jury may not easily forget the nurse's prior statement that the defendant caused the injury–that is, the bell that cannot be unrung. In this case, the nurse may not have known that such a statement would be stricken due to hearsay, but in some cases litigators may use this as a tactic in their strategy. In other cases, the nurse's statement would be appropriate; it depends on what the court will accept in terms of hearsay.

Preparation for Trial

Preparation for trial should be done reasonably close to the actual time of trial. If preparation is done too early, the nurse may forget the details and even may confuse one case for another.

The first step is to obtain the documentation that was prepared at the time of the nurse's encounter with the patient. Then have any photographs that relate to the case copied onto a disc. If the nurse has received a separate subpoena for records and photographs, these items should be prepared and delivered in response to the subpoena. These records may also be supplied to the DA in a manner that is customary in the local region. The forensic nurse may want to make some notes about the case but should remember that everything recorded, even brief notes, may be discoverable, meaning that it may be submitted as evidence to the court. That is not to say that the nurse should not make notes, only that he or she should be prepared to hand them over to the court. Notes should be written with the mindset that they are not for the writer's eyes only.

The forensic nurse should study all documentation thoroughly, almost memorizing it. Although records may be accessed in courtrooms, it is preferred that witnesses know all of the details before testifying. The focus should be on significant information, and the witness should be able to retrieve it promptly if a question about it arises during the testimony. Certain questions will surely be asked in nearly every case, such as questions regarding when the examination was conducted, what evidence was collected, and what injuries were observed.

The nurse should not make notes on the actual documents to be submitted. For example, if an error is noted on the sexual assault documentation form, do not write "Uh-oh, problem" in the margin. In fact, no unofficial commentary should ever be written anywhere on a document. If the defense happens to ask to see a copy of the document or, even worse, a notation has been made on the document that will be duplicated for evidence, the nurse witness would have supplied great ammunition for the testimony to be attacked by the opposition. Although forensic nurses do not have a bias toward one party or the other, they must be aware of their role in the process. If an error has been made in documentation, the nurse should bring it to the DA's attention as soon as possible. Errors can be addressed in a manner that avoids accusing someone of being deceptive, misleading, or untruthful. Once the DA knows that an error was made, she or he can rehabilitate the issue. For instance, if something was improperly labeled (right versus left arm, for example), the DA will have that information and will not be surprised if it comes up later. It may or may not

be addressed in court, depending on how significant it is. The exchange could go like this:

Q: Ms. C., on diagram A you drew an injury to Ms. J.'s left arm; is this correct?

A: Yes.

Q: In your notes, you wrote, "Injury to right arm." Is this correct?

A: Yes.

Q: If you recall, Ms. C., was the injury to the right arm or to the left arm?

A: I do recall. The injury was to the left arm. Apparently, that was a clerical error.

Notes may contain pertinent bits of information that are always useful but located on several different pages of an existing document. If the nurse summarizes notes for these references on one page, it will prevent the need to rifle through many pages during testimony. Keep in mind, though, everything may be discoverable. At times, referring to the original document will be unavoidable. When witnesses must refer to written documents, they should ask the court's permission. Before starting a search, say, "Your Honor, may I refer to the document?"

Although it is difficult to predict what questions the prosecutor or the defense will ask a witness, certain questions are generally included among the interrogatives. If the examiner has conducted the forensic examination, she or he will likely appear for the district attorney. Before the trial, it is helpful to prepare a series of questions for the DA to ask the forensic nurse. As knowledgeable as the DA may be about certain issues, the DA's field is not the nurse's field and the DA must be educated about what the forensic nurse does so that he or she will have a clearer picture of the expert witness's work. This information will educate the jury as well. Often, in court, a witness will wait for the DA to ask a pertinent question so that she or he can expound on a point or support a statement. The DA may have no idea to ask that particular question, leaving the witness frustrated about not being able to bring out an important issue regarding the case. As an expert in the field, the forensic nurse should assist the DA in making the testimony demonstrable and illustrative.

Nurse witnesses should stress how important it will be to have an hour or so to meet with the DA before the court appearance. This is when the CV can be reviewed and the DA can be presented with the questions the nurse has prepared for him or her to ask. This meeting is not a rehearsal for testimony. Counsel should not tell a witness what to say on the stand; however, there is always a strategy involved in a trial, and it is important to know what that strategy is. The DA will have a plan of action and will want to focus on certain elements of the case, which may not be immediately evident to the expert. If the nurse witness knows where the DA is going with those characteristics, the parties will be able to communicate more effectively. The nurse should ascertain the identity of any opposing expert and about what that expert will be testifying. It is also important to determine the strengths and weaknesses of the case and what barriers, if any, might be present from the prosecutor's perspective. The prosecutor may have unrealistic expectations about what the forensic nurse examiner can say. If the prosecutor and the forensic nurse examiner discuss the issues, then the relationship will be more productive.

A witness may, and should, speak to defense counsel, if asked. However, the DA should be informed about this action. When a witness avoids speaking with the defense, it appears that he or she is being uncooperative or hostile. Although as an expert, the nurse is appearing as a neutral participant, testifying to the findings; the nurse should remain guarded about what kind of information that is disclosed to the opposition. Even though the conversation may seem informal, nothing is off the record. It would be improper to give strategic information to the defense that the prosecutor intends to use in trial to prove the case; and vice versa, if the expert is working for defense counsel, she or he should be willing to speak with the DA, keeping in mind that defense counsel also has a strategy to protect. Nevertheless, the truth is still the truth. Most often, the defense will request information regarding the meaning of medical terminology that was written on forms or questions about anatomy. Any given witness will not know everything about the case or what the devices are for either side, so staying conservative is a good approach. Rather, the witness should allow defense counsel to ask questions and not offer information that was not solicited.

Court Appearance

After being sworn in, a witness will be asked to state and spell his or her name. The prosecutor will then begin the direct examination, followed by cross-examination by defense counsel.

Direct examination is the first direct questioning of a witness by the person who called the witness. *Cross-examination* is the questioning of a witness by someone other than the party who called the witness. *Redirect* is when the direct examiner asks questions after the cross-examination. *Recross-examination* is questioning after the redirect examination. This continues, back and forth, until the questioning has been completed. At that time, the nurse witness will be excused; however, there may be the potential for recall. This means that even though there are no more questions at the time, a witness may be asked to return at a later time for more questioning.

There will be questions about the nurse's credentials and qualifications as well as questions about the case that are certain to be asked (Box 45-2). There may be exhibits to describe. The prosecutor

---

The forensic nurse may be asked for the following information:
- Describe your current position and background as a nurse. How long have you been a registered nurse and in what areas have you practiced?
- How long have you been working as a forensic nurse? What education have you had to prepare for this specialty?
- What continuing education have you had in your specialty?
- What professional organizations do you belong to?
- Are you certified in your field?
- Have you published any material in your field?
- Please describe what you do as a forensic nurse.
- How does a forensic nurse conduct an examination (step by step)?

Note that a sexual assault nurse examiner (SANE) may be asked to describe the sexual assault response team (SART) and its members.
- How many examinations have you done?
- What equipment is used, how does it work, and why is it used?
- How do you spell the name of the equipment and supplies that you use?
- Please describe other technical and procedural aspects of forensic work.
- Have you appeared as an expert witness in court before?
- How many times have you testified?
- Have you ever been disqualified as an expert witness?

The defense may ask, in cross-examination, whether the nurse always appears for the prosecution. If asked this question, you should remind the court that you are appearing neither for the prosecution nor for the defense but as a witness for the truth and that a nurse may most often be called by the prosecution because of the nature of the work.

If you have ever worked for defense counsel, as a consultant, let that be known in court. It will further your credibility as a nonbiased, objective participant.

---

may have parts of a report, photographs, or diagrams enlarged and may request that the nurse describe certain details. There will be markers, pointers, and other tools to enhance the visual presentation. When asking a question that refers to the diagram, the prosecutor will direct the nurse to the easel. At this point, the witness should step down from the stand, go to the easel, and take a moment to look over the diagram. The nurse witness should always wait for a question to be asked and should not skip ahead and talk about things that are currently not being queried.

The nurse should be aware of leading questions. *Leading questions* are those that suggest the answer sought by the questioner. They may be intended to elicit an answer that the nurse would not otherwise give or to guide the witness to a specific answer. The forensic nurse examiner must be careful when interviewing patients, especially children, to not ask them leading questions; the nurse, as an expert witness, should be just as aware when leading questions are asked of the nurse. An example of a leading question would be, "Did he steal your $10,000 diamond ring?" The nurse witness would want to establish who "he" was and whether the ring was actually worth $10,000. "He" may have taken the ring, but it may not have been worth $10,000. Questions need to be clear and specific to be answered accurately. A better question would be, "What items did the robber take from you?" or "What items did you find to be missing?" in the case of a burglary as opposed to a robbery.

According to the California Rules of Evidence 767,

(a) Except under special circumstances where the interests of justice otherwise require:
(1) A leading question may not be asked of a witness on direct or redirect examination.
(2) A leading question may be asked of a witness on cross-examination or recross-examination.
(b) The court may in the interests of justice permit a leading question to be asked of a child under 10 years of age in a case involving a prosecution under Section 273a, 273d, 288, or 288.5 of the Penal Code.

Box 45-3 offers some important points that will maximize the impact of testimony and prevent mistakes from being made.

It may be wise to keep in mind that each attorney has an agenda. The nurse is a cog in the wheel of the attorney's plan but may not be privy to it. Witnesses should not think that the prosecutor will protect them from tough questioning or shield them from embarrassment and humiliation. In fact, there may be times that a witness feels totally alienated and vulnerable. These bad experiences, as well as the good ones, are sources of important learning. Bad experiences may teach the witness more than the good ones ever will!

After the trial has concluded, a nurse witness should call the prosecutor and ask what the outcome was. As an objective participant, this will not be to see if anyone "won" or because we should not see trials in this manner, but it could be beneficial to evaluate our testimony and our skills as a witness and a method to implement improvement. The jury is often interviewed after the trial is over to see how conclusions were reached. It is important to ask what the strongest evidence appeared to be and what was the weakest. What helped the case the most, and what helped the least? Were there any shortcomings that failed to make the point? If the defendant was found guilty, what was the most compelling evidence for the jury? The sentencing will take place days or a few weeks after the conclusion of the trial, so the nurse should call and find out the results of the sentencing. If the defendant was found not guilty, what motivated the jury to acquit? What factors were lacking to convict?

Box 45-3 Case-Related Interrogatives

The forensic nurse may be asked the following questions:

- Do you recall the case on the date specified?
- Describe the demeanor of the subject.
- Describe the procedures that were conducted, how they were conducted, and who was present during those procedures.
- Describe specific aspects of evidence collection, such as how the evidence was packaged and preserved and what happened to the evidence after its collection.
- Were photographs taken? If so, describe their disposition.
- Describe the findings of your examination.
- What injuries were observed? What could have been the cause of said injuries? What was the age of the injuries?
- What are your opinions regarding the findings, and how did you come to have those opinions?

Questions that further refine the possibilities:

- "Isn't it possible … ?" questions.

The following gives other pointers that may help the nurse:

- Pause before giving an answer to a question so that the attorney has a chance to object.
- Answer only the question that is asked. Do not elaborate unnecessarily.
- Do not answer until the question has been completely stated; do not interrupt to give an answer.
- If you don't understand a question, ask that it be restated.
- Be sure to answer only the question asked.
- If you do not know an answer to a question, say that you do not know. Do not guess at answers.
- If there is silence after the answer is finished, do not fill the void with more talk or say, "That's it."
- If you don't remember something, do not guess. State that you do not recall.
- Keep the answers brief. Many questions cannot be answered by a simple yes or no. If you must elaborate on an answer, ask permission by saying, "Your honor, may I explain?"
- Beware of multifaceted or compound questions. For example, consider the question, "Did Ms. J. tell you that she was walking on Ninth Street at 12 o'clock?" Perhaps Ms. J. told you that she was walking on Ninth Street, but it was at 9 o'clock. The answer to that question cannot be yes because some of the information is incorrect. Ask the attorney to restate the question or answer the question with the statement, "Ms. J. told me that she was walking on Ninth Street at 9 o'clock."
- Beware of rapid-fire questions, one right after another. Ask that the questions be asked one at a time.
- Avoid using medical terminology. Try to translate the medical words to simple terms that the jury can understand. Remember, the nurse witness is the jury's teacher.

- Do not show anger or frustration at the questions asked, no matter how elementary or how many times the same question is asked.
- Hypothetical questions may be asked. These questions are not based in the context of this particular case. They may take a variety of forms. They are often meant for the nurse witness to contradict herself. For example:

  "Is it possible that … ?"
  "Isn't it true …?"
  "In your opinion could … ?"

- Always answer truthfully, saying, "In this case …," or follow the answer by saying, "But in this case …." An attempt to answer may be struck down as unresponsive, but at least you tried to clarify. Perhaps the prosecutor will be aware that you had a point to make and address it on redirect.
- Never testify beyond your own scope of practice. If asked about a technique or process that is not within your field, even if you have some basic knowledge of it, do not attempt to answer. For example, if asked whether you collected samples for DNA analysis, answer that you did so, but if asked how the samples are analyzed, simply state that that is beyond your scope of practice and that you do not analyze the samples; they are sent to the crime lab. Let the person from the crime lab answer how the analysis is done.
- Be cautious about bringing articles into court. You may be interested in citing a particular point from an article, but the defense role is to try and make you look foolish by exposing that you have not memorized every word of the article and may even ask you to discuss the authors in the bibliography. Rather, answers should be based on your experience and knowledge. If asked whether you are familiar with a study or an article, either you are or you are not. Occasionally, you may be asked to take an article home, read it, and come back to give an opinion.
- If asked whether you are familiar with certain studies, answer; but studies have been done on certain subject matter that may be indicative of a particular region, population, or practice area, or they may be outdated and out of context.
- Never attempt do the jury's job. It is the jury's responsibility to pass judgment on the case. Although you may be asked, do not fall into the trap of stating whether someone is guilty or not guilty or stating that you can tell if something was consensual or nonconsensual. You may state whether something is "consistent with" something or "not consistent with" something, but you must not mislead the court.
- The defense may take a "shot" by declaring that you are "only a nurse" or may say, "You are not a doctor, are you?" You should gracefully reply that you are a medical professional and a very good nurse.
- Be confident with things you know. Information does not always have to come from a book. Your experience as a nurse and a forensic examiner is valuable in and of itself.

Again, the forensic nurse is not there to "help" anyone. More correctly, the forensic nurse has information that may benefit the prosecution or the defense. A wise attorney will listen to what the forensic nurse can and cannot say. The forensic nurse should not be tempted to say things to make a party happy that could compromise her or his ethics. Sometimes it is beneficial for the forensic nurse to ask the attorney what information she or he wants to garner from the forensic examination.

Every time a witness testifies, it is expected that there will be increased proficiency for anticipating the needs of the system. As comfort levels rise and stress levels fall, nurses may eventually look forward to court appearances. Good advice is to make every experience a learning experience, and one will understand more and more about the workings of the court and the role of the attorneys. The justice system has its own intricacies, and many complex elements are employed that should not be taken

personally but accepted as part of legal strategies. Over time, attorneys will have confidence in the adeptness of certain nurses and may even look to them for advice and guidance regarding other cases.

Consulting for the Defense

The defense attorney may ask a forensic nurse to consult on a case. Generally, this is most often done outside one's own immediate jurisdiction. It may seem contrary to be working for "the other side," but as was discussed earlier, the nurse doesn't have a side, and in the name of justice can assist in any effort to get to that truth.

As a consultant, the nurse will be privy to aspects of the case that she or he normally would not be aware of while directly involved as a participant in the forensic examination. The nurse will be an outside surveyor and will have a unique overview of the event; she or he will be more or less peer reviewing the opposition's work. The nurse will be supplied with materials, such as police reports; victim statements, suspect statements, and witness statements; photographs of the scene, the victim, and the suspect; reports of analyzed evidence and medical reports; and possibly transcripts of the preliminary hearing. The task will be to evaluate the materials available and use experience and education to make deductions regarding the findings. The nurse should try to look at the big picture. Opinions may be based on the information that is available and information that is blatantly absent. There may be evidence that was collected but not analyzed and questions about potential evidence that, perhaps, should have been but was not collected at all. Was the evidence collected and packaged correctly? Were the standards of forensic nursing practice followed? Were there any breaks in the chain of custody? Was there a chance of evidence contamination? Are the reports consistent with the statements? Are the statements consistent with previous statements? Are there any medical or psychological circumstances that may account for inconsistencies? Because the nurse is the expert in that particular field, she or he should be aware of any procedural or technical breaches in the methods used.

The nurse will not be singling out any particular entity to criticize; the nurse examiner's work and the work of the police officers or detectives (unless it is obviously lacking) will be fitting together the pieces of a puzzle to see if the picture has continuity and cohesion. Have the standards of care been met? Any red flags that are spotted will come into play when the findings are relayed to the attorney.

Make notes of impressions as the material is read. Keep in mind, as with any written material, that it may be discoverable, particularly if this is a civil case. Civil cases are more guarded. Attorneys make writings that are referred to as "work product," which refers to an attorney's notes, statements, theories, tactics, and strategy that are anticipated to be used in trial. The attorney's work product is generally not discoverable. However, the nurse's work for the attorney may be discoverable if the status changes. A consultant's confidential work product may become discoverable if the witness is designated as a testifying witness. Regardless, all writings should be formal with the idea that they may end up as evidence in court.

According to California Evidence Code Section 911-920 (1999):

915. (a) Subject to subdivision (b), the presiding officer may not require disclosure of information claimed to be privileged under this division or attorney work product under subdivision (c) of Section 2018 of the Code of Civil Procedure in order to rule on the claim of privilege; provided, however, that in any hearing conducted pursuant to subdivision (c) of Section 1524 of the Penal Code in which a claim of privilege is made and the court determines that there is no other feasible means to rule on the validity of the claim other than to require disclosure, the court shall proceed in accordance with subdivision (b).

(b) When a court is ruling on a claim of privilege under Article 9 (commencing with Section 1040) of Chapter 4 (official information and identity of informer) or under Section 1060 (trade secret) or under subdivision (b) of Section 2018 of the Code of Civil Procedure (attorney work product) and is unable to do so without requiring disclosure of the information claimed to be privileged, the court may require the person from whom disclo-

sure is sought or the person authorized to claim the privilege, or both, to disclose the information in chambers out of the presence and hearing of all persons except the person authorized to claim the privilege and any other persons as the person authorized to claim the privilege is willing to have present. If the judge determines that the information is privileged, neither the judge nor any other person may ever disclose, without the consent of a person authorized to permit disclosure, what was disclosed in the course of the proceedings in chambers.

The first contact with the attorney, after the nurse's review of the case, should not contain any written material. Instead, the nurse should relay opinions and comments verbally. If written material is required, it can be supplied later in a determined format. Most often, questions will come up while reading the material. Prepare questions and discuss them with counsel. For example, a complainant has accused the defendant of sexually assaulting her, without a condom, and ejaculating into her vagina, yet the crime lab reports no semen or sperm was found during analysis. Although there may be several explanations for this, one of them being that there was no sexual contact, consider asking counsel if he or she knows whether the client has had a vasectomy. This may be a point to consider to account for absence of sperm. She still must explain to the attorney that the expert cannot state whether penetration did or did not occur because no sperm was found.

Create a timeline of the case to help map the events in order of their occurrence. The statements of witnesses and subjects will be in narrative form and can be compared while reading through each statement. Graphing who was present and when, and times things occurred, can help the consultant to reconstruct the scenario with better clarity and can also reveal inconsistencies.

The first step when consulting on a case is to negotiate the fee. The nurse may want to see what the going rate is for specific types of consulting services in her or his area. Forensic nurses should not sell themselves short but also should not set too high a fee. Set rates according to experience as a consultant in the forensic field. Fees do not have to be etched in stone. As a nurse progresses and grows as a consultant, she or he may want to adjust the rates on an annual basis. As a rule, one may want to set an initial fee for reviewing the documents and providing a verbal summary. Then charge hourly for any additional work. Some consultants have complicated fee schedules that have different fees for every step of the process. Some law firms and public defenders will negotiate an offer for a fee with a limit on the number of hours so they can predict the budget. If more hours are needed, the nurse contacts the attorney. Because some of the work may take the nurse out of town, she or he may also want to create a fee schedule that outlines a daily fee for travel plus expenses, accommodations, and miscellaneous charges. This writer's fee schedule is simple with one fee for reviewing, research, and writing, and one daily fee for travel. The client pays for accommodations and any travel arrangements such as airfare, with input from me, to plan the trip. While traveling out of town, the nurse may have to pay for some reimbursable expenses up front, such as car rental. Keep meticulous records of meals, gas, and miscellaneous expenses so they can be itemized on the invoice sent to the client. Of course, keep records of time spent on work for that client.

After reviewing the case, the nurse may conclude that the examining nurse did a stellar job and there do not seem to be omissions or inconsistencies That is perfectly fine. The nurse was hired to evaluate the case, not to manufacture something that may not exist to help to exonerate the defendant. Defense counsel will appreciate the expert's honest evaluation and be armed with that information. Many times the defense counsel is required to hire an expert to review the case, although these individuals do not necessarily have to be testifying experts. Defense attorneys are not always delighted with their clients. It is not the nurse's responsibility to manufacture loopholes to acquit the defendant. Remember that we are but a cog in the wheel. The defense attorney has the obligation to provide the best defense possible for the client. The expert's client is the attorney, not the defendant. The truth is the truth. When the case is finished, send an invoice and offer your services in the future.

The nurse is first hired as a consultant and expert witness to the defense counsel. Whether the nurse actually testifies as an expert witness depends on many factors. For example, the nurse may be needed to oppose the prosecution's expert. That need may depend on what the opposing expert will be testifying. If the opposing expert is going to testify that an injury can be sustained only in a certain manner and the nurse knows of other ways that the injury can occur, the nurse may be asked to take the stand to give that perspective.

As the consultant, the nurse may want to suggest other experts for the defense to secure for the trial. If the nurse has discovered, through review of the documents, that there are scientific evidence reports that may require explanation, the nurse may suggest that defense counsel find an analyst who is an expert in that field to explain the findings. The nurse may see that the DNA samples of the defendant did not match those found at the crime scene. However, because the nurse is not a DNA analyst, he or she should not testify to those findings because the natural follow-up of questioning would be to explain how the analyst performed the testing and came to that conclusion. It would not be appropriate for the nurse to offer testimony not in the nurse's area of expertise or scope of practice.

The job of a consultant is to give opinions, clarify the facts, and guide counsel toward a logical understanding of the forensic nurse examiner's work that will contribute to her or his defense strategy. The forensic nurse is in an excellent position for this task because his or her experience as a prosecution witness has exposed the nurse to the types of issues that will come into play.

Generally, the nurse will be doing most of the work long distance. Often the nurse will communicate with the defender's assistants through paralegals or investigators. Once most of the information has been organized, the nurse will speak directly to counsel and relay the findings and discuss the options. The defender will let the nurse know if it will be necessary for them to meet in person or for the nurse to appear as a witness in the trial. Sometimes that will not be known until the last minute. The examining nurse may say all the right things and satisfy the needs of both tables. The defendant may decide to take a plea. There may be many reasons a case concludes.

The nurse should follow up, later, to learn the outcome of the trial and the verdict. Again, this will be to determine if the nurse can learn anything to improve her overall performance on the case. The nurse should ask whether the jury was interviewed or polled after the trial and how they perceived the case. If the client was found not guilty, ask what issues brought the jurors to that conclusion and gave them reasonable doubt. If the client was found guilty, ask what the specific weak spots were and what evidence was the strongest that precipitated their conviction.

If the client is found guilty, the sentencing will take place a few days to several weeks after the trial. The nurse should ask what sentence the client received and then document that information is his or her records.

Working for the defense will enhance the nurse's overall competency in being of service to the courts. It will increase her or his credibility as an objective, nonbiased witness when called by the prosecution, and it will give the nurse a more balanced impression of the workings of the system.

Case Study **45-1**

Sexual Assault of a Homeless Woman

In August 2000, a 37-year-old woman (W.M.) was brought in for a forensic sexual assault examination. She had a history of insulin-dependent diabetes, gallstones, and cesarean sections. She was gravida 5, para 5. At this time, W.M. was homeless and staying in a shelter. She was compliant with her insulin medication, alert, oriented, and cooperative. She was tearful at times while recollecting the events of the previous six days. A 41-year-old male, whom W.M. met at the homeless shelter, offered her a shower, food, cigarettes, and a place to sleep if she wanted to go with him. After she arrived at his apartment, she took a shower and had some food. She slept there that night and when she thanked the man and told him it was time to leave, he refused to let her go. He told her he would kill her, and he showed her a gun and threatened her with a knife. Over the next six days he held her hostage, hit her in the face (left cheek) with the handle of a knife, sexually assaulted and sodomized her multiple times, and threatened her with the gun and the knife. On the sixth day she told him that she badly needed her diabetes medicine and begged him to let her go to the clinic at the rescue mission. He went with her to the rescue mission to get her medication, but he threatened to kill her if she told anyone that he was keeping her against her will. At the rescue mission she told a security guard what was happening and the police were called.

The forensic evidentiary examination revealed evidence of a healing abrasion to the left cheek. There were no external vaginal injuries, but minor internal vaginal injuries (petechiae to the cervix) were found. There were anal injuries (abrasions and tears with positive toluidine blue dye uptake). Those findings were documented and photographed.

The case went to trial in January 2003. The forensic nurse examiner appeared by subpoena on the prosecution's witness list. After being qualified as an expert by the court, the sexual assault nurse examiner described the injuries that the patient had sustained and testified that the absence of injury to the external vaginal area is not directly related to whether or not there was forced intercourse. She further stated that compliance does not necessarily imply consent in that the subject was threatened with harm if she did not cooperate. Because the assailant had already hit her and caused her injury and pain, the subject was fearful that if she resisted the sexual assaults, he would hurt her more or even kill her. The nurse examiner stated that although the injuries appeared minor, they could be consistent with the history given by the subject. When asked if the injuries could also be consistent with consensual sex, the nurse examiner stated that they could. The nurse was asked about the demeanor of the subject and replied that the subject was cooperative and anxious, verbalizing fear of retaliation from the assailant. The nurse examiner stated that the subject relayed the history of the event in a concise, straightforward manner.

The defendant was found guilty and sentenced to several years in prison.

Ethics of Testifying and Malpractice Issues

The nurse's own personal and professional ethics should dictate the integrity and veracity in which one should approach testifying in court. The authenticity of everything from the validity of the nurse's credentials, experience, and knowledge to whether the testimony is completely truthful may come under scrutiny, which is one reason it is important for the nurse expert to realize objectivity. It is not the nurse's role to believe or not to believe the patient but to do their work methodically and scientifically.

Expert witnesses were generally thought of as hard-working professionals who have taken time from their busy schedules to assist the court by shedding light on technical matters in which they have expertise. However, some people have found that they can make a comfortable living by becoming professional witnesses. Physicians have left their practices behind to sell themselves exclusively as "hired guns." There should not be anything wrong with that choice, except some unscrupulous characters have discarded their principles and will say anything, for a fee, to discredit the opposition's expert witness. This kind of behavior is frequently seen through, but it could mean trouble if there are issues of professional misconduct. If a person is found to have lied about his or her credentials or strayed from acceptable parameters, there could be serious consequences, including professional malpractice. Nurse witnesses are accountable for their testimony, and the facts that are presented are subject to peer review and standards of care in that profession. Medical malpractice is based on the fact that there are accepted methods of appropriate treatment. Testimony in legal proceedings is readily available to other litigators, and testifying experts will lose credibility if their testimony varies radically about the same issue. Consistency with honesty is the best policy. One does not need to have a good memory when one tells the truth.

One's professional organization would be the body to establish standards of practice and determine whether those standards have been violated. Each state has a board of registered nursing that defines nursing practice in that state. Most nurses carry their own professional liability insurance. They know that they will be covered only if they abide by their scope and standards of practice. The International Association of Forensic Nurses (IAFN), with the support and recognition of the American Nurses Association (ANA) (1995), has created and published the Scope and Standards of Forensic Nursing Practice (IAFN and ANA, first in 1997). The ANA Standards of Clinical Nursing Practice governs the fundamental practice of nursing. The IAFN Scope and Standards defines the role of the forensic nurse in this unique and independent specialty. It dictates the standards of care and the standards of professional performance. To deviate from these standards violates the trust and responsibility that is expected of all forensic nurses. Although forensic nursing is an ever-evolving specialty that is constantly progressing with the advances of technology and innovations of science, the forensic nurse must demonstrate competency and exercise excellent judgment in her or his ability to deliver services that are based on the fundamental nursing process. It is essential that the forensic nurse keep up with the science, technology, and current practice of the specialty. Forensic nurses that quote old and retired theories can be held accountable for their lack of contemporary knowledge.

The expert witness was thought to have complete immunity from liability dating back to English common law. If witnesses could be held liable for their testimony, they would be less willing to testify. But now, in some states, the expert witnesses may be held liable if they are negligent in forming their expert opinions, knowingly misleading the court, or lying under oath. It was the advent of the "hired gun" witness that caused this to be true. Experts could get up on the stand and say anything without worrying about repercussions. Things have now changed, and these witnesses may be held liable.

Expert witnesses can be held liable for testimony that deviates from the standard of care appropriate for their profession. The court often needs assistance with identifying inappropriate expert witnessing, and it may depend on others in the same specialty to bring it to light. It is common for the prosecution and the defense to each have experts testify on the same subject. It may be up to one of those experts to report any improper testimony by the other to the professional organization to which he or she belongs.

A case in point is the ruling of the Seventh Circuit Court of Appeals, Chicago, Illinois, on June 2001, which allowed persons to be disciplined by their professional organizations when their testimony did not reflect the standards of those organizations. The case revolved around a 1995 malpractice suit against a neurosurgeon (Dr. D), a member of the American Association of Neurological Surgeons (AANS), who performed an anterior cervical fusion; the patient subsequently developed complications that led to the need for a tracheostomy. The neurosurgeon had performed more than 700 such operations, and this was his first adverse outcome. A second neurosurgeon (Dr. A), for opposing counsel, who also was a member of the AANS, testified that the majority of neurosurgeons would agree that the only way such complications could arise would be if there was negligence and the doctor had been careless. Dr. A had performed approximately 25 to 30 of the same procedures in 30 years of practice. His testimony was based on two articles that he brought into court that outlined procedures for avoiding complications with the surgery. However, neither article supported his testimony. Although rare (0.07%), this complication was a well-known risk of the surgery.

Dr. D reported Dr. A's testimony to the AANS, and the AANS suspended Dr. A in 1997 for six months for irresponsible testimony, not conferring with other medical professionals in this matter, and having no basis for testifying as an expert. The AANS contended that the testimony in court did not reflect the view of the majority of neurosurgeons and violated provisions of the AANS's ethical code. It stated further that testimony that is one's personal opinion should be identified as personal opinion and not the consensus of the organization.

In 1998, Dr. A attempted to sue the AANS for lost profits as an expert witness, stating that the organization was punishing him for testifying against another AANS member and that by suspending him the AANS had caused his income to drop from $220,000 to $77,000. The ruling went against Dr. A because his membership in the prestigious organization was voluntary. He still had his regular practice, which afforded him adequate income, and his expert witness work was a side job. His testimony was ruled irresponsible and may have damaged Dr. D's reputation.

Dr. A resigned from the AANS. He appealed his case in 2001, but the judge dismissed it. The AANS was praised for upholding the standards of its organization and its peer review system. Because this was the first case of its kind, it set the precedent for this type of action. Now, most states acknowledge that absolute immunity cannot be granted to expert witnesses.

The issue of malpractice may confront the forensic nurse if the scope and standards of nursing practice and forensic nursing practice are not met. Additionally, if the standards of the professional organization are not met, the organization can take action if the its ethics were not upheld or if the behavior of the subject was not representative of the organization's integrity.

For perspective on an early case in which a forensic nurse was involved, consider *Commonwealth v. Johnston,* Supreme Court of Virginia, which occurred in 2000. The positive milestone was that a sexual assault nurse examiner was accepted as an expert witness. The nurse cited Masters and Johnson, some early literature by Laura Slaughter, and an article by Mark Norvell, among others, in stating that the human sexual response protects consenting females from injury and that certain injuries, visible by gross visualization, without magnification, are determined to be nonconsensual. She opined that the sexual contact was not consensual. It is improper for the nurse examiner to come to such a conclusion, and the medical literature does not support the nurse's determination. This declaration is beyond the nurse examiner's scope and invades the providence of the jury. To be clear, and fair, there were things that were taught in the early 1990s that we now know are not accurate. Actually, by the mid-1990s and certainly by the year 2000 we knew that we could not differentiate between findings in consensual and nonconsensual sexual contact and we were no longer using the human sexual response as a valid reference to explain why a female may or may not sustain injuries during sexual intercourse. In the *Johnston* case, the court limited the nurse's testimony and permitted her to testify about the injuries she observed and her opinion of what might be consistent with sexual intercourse or penetration, but it did not allow her to testify to consent.

Although unbelievable, the 1966 Masters and Johnson study on the human sexual response, Slaughter's early studies, and Norvell's study from 1984, clearly outdated, still come up in court. They are studies that helped build the foundation for further research and proved the need for future studies in the sexual assault arena. They are respected and valued for what they were in their time, but they have been surpassed and hold little acceptance today. This is great example of why it is important for nurse witnesses to continue their education and keep current.

Summary

Always tell the truth. Forensic nurses represent not only themselves when testifying in court, but also forensic nursing as a whole, along with their professional organizations. The nurse must abide by the standards set forth by his or her profession and the scientific standards that govern the practice. Approach the task by picturing yourself on the witness stand and being able to justify everything you do with pride. That means not cutting corners on even the most menial of undertakings. Do the best work possible–always. The nurse should develop organizational skills and routines so that when asked whether something was done, the nurse can confidently answer, "Yes, I always do that" or can state that something was not done because the occasion did not warrant it. The idea of having to tell the court that something was not done because the nurse was in a rush to get to the next case or to a meeting can be devastating on the stand. Inconsistency is the spark that fans the flames to bring a case to court in the first place, so it would be unwise to furnish fuel for the fire.

Every time the forensic nurse goes to court, her or his performance will improve. The nurse know what to expect and will be better at preparing for the trial. There are no shortcuts to excellence, but the path is exciting and rewarding. After all, this is what forensic nursing is about by its very definition–connecting the nursing process to the law. Going to court is the ultimate responsibility, and the nurse may even learn to like it.

PART II: CIVIL DEPOSITIONS

Contributing Author: Belinda Manning Howell

Civil adjudication is another aspect of the justice system. The goal is to financially repair what has been damaged with an eye toward preventing further damage. In the criminal system, those found to be guilty of a crime are punished by a loss of liberty, by imprisonment for a period of days to years. On the other hand, if found by a judge or jury to be liable, civil defendants are required to compensate the injured person, the plaintiff, by paying that person specific sums of money. Nurses may be involved in criminal actions by virtue of their contact with victims of crimes in a healthcare setting, or in civil actions through personal involvement with a patient who brings a lawsuit against another individual. In either situation, a nurse may be asked to tell the relevant facts, to provide important pieces of the puzzle that must be reconstructed for a judge or jury. Typically, that fact finding will be done by way of a formal deposition, often making it unnecessary for the nurse to appear in the courtroom during the trial.

Purpose of Depositions

In preparing to file a civil lawsuit, an attorney must consider the questions that ultimately will be posed to a jury relevant to the plaintiff's claims. Relevant factual information and the opinions of experts must be gathered. To accomplish that objective, the parties' attorneys will engage in the process of *pretrial discovery,* a stage of the lawsuit that allows the story to unfold and gives the parties the tools to carve the most concise presentation of the facts and their relationship to applicable law. Depositions may be obtained from both involved parties and experts consulting in the suit.

KEY POINT The information obtained in a deposition constitutes evidence for attorneys who are either prosecuting or defending a client.

One critical step toward preparing an effective presentation of the events, related to the plaintiff's claims in a civil matter, is the taking of depositions. The purpose of a deposition is to elicit and preserve sworn testimony to rely on at all stages of the litigation (O'Keefe, 2001).

BEST PRACTICE A witness involved or named in a lawsuit should seek legal counsel before complying with requests to furnish tangible items for use in an oral deposition. An expert should be aware that everything created by the expert is discoverable, so caution should be taken before putting statements into writing.

A party's attorney can discover information pertinent to a legal claim or relative factual issue through this formal question-and-answer process, which, because the witness is under oath, is identical to the process of eliciting testimony in the courtroom. The opposing attorney will structure questions for the witness to determine their value to the case and to elicit the witness's position on key points. This pretrial deposition permits a preview of the witness's testimony and allows ample time for the opposition to engineer an effective rebuttal.

KEY POINT The testimony provided in an oral pretrial deposition, and given later in the courtroom, must be highly consistent if the witness is to be perceived as credible.

A person who brings a civil lawsuit must retain an attorney. The process is very different from criminal cases where it is the "state" or the "people" against an individual or individuals; in criminal cases, the "people" are represented by the prosecutor or the district attorney's office, and the defendant is represented by a public defender or a private attorney. Once a case commences, information must be gathered. This process involves documents, witnesses, and other elements vital to the issue.

To initiate the deposition process, either party will serve a notice or subpoena to a witness to appear at a certain time and place to answer questions related to the issues of the case. The notice may include a list of documents or tangible items the witness is to bring, relevant to the subject matter of the action and within the witness's possession or control. Materials may include anything that would amplify testimony. A witness should consult with counsel before complying with such requests for documents or tangible items.

Oral Deposition

Various types of depositions exist, including written and electronic depositions; however, standard oral depositions are the most common. An oral deposition consists of a series of questions posed by attorneys for the plaintiff and the defendant. Ordinarily, this type of deposition is accomplished in an attorney's office or conference space that will permit the formality and privacy required for the proceeding. In addition to the attorneys and the witness, a deposition officer, usually a court reporter, will attend to assure that every question, answer, objection, and statement made "on the record" is recorded verbatim.

The parties, spouses of parties, and employees of counsel may choose to attend the depositions, and, with reasonable notice and by agreement, other individuals may be allowed to attend. If either party chooses to have a videographer present, a video recording is made, giving the attorneys the option of having the judge and jury see the witness during the trial, without the witness having to make another appearance. Recording will also be useful in the event of inconsistencies in the testimony of parties to the suit or other witnesses who typically appear in person in the courtroom. The written record of testimony from a deposition may be read at trial instead of showing a video to the judge and jury, again saving a witness the inconvenience of making a second appearance.

PREPARATION

Generally, a witness will spend some time with one of the attorneys in the suit, to be given an idea of the kind of questions to expect and an opportunity to ask questions about the process. Whether an attorney will meet with a witness before his or her deposition and which attorney will meet with the witness depend on the role of the witness. If the witness is a party to the lawsuit, the attorney representing that party will prepare the witness. With expert witnesses, the party seeking that witness's services will spend time discussing the case with the witness revealing their opinions about the case. The expert will be reviewing the case file and suggesting the kinds of questions the expert might be asked. An expert might be composing questions for the attorney to ask the expert and the other parties, so that pertinent information will be addressed and essential information will not be passed over. However, when a witness is an individual with knowledge of relevant facts but not subject to the control of a party (for example, with an employer-employee relationship), either party's attorney may offer the witness an idea of what matters and what will be discussed at the deposition.

WITNESS REPRESENTATION BY COUNSEL

All deponents are free to bring an attorney to the deposition to represent them. Certainly, if the witness is a party or is retained by a party, as in the case of an expert witness, the party's attorney and the opposing party's attorney will attend the deposition and represent their respective clients' interests. Fact witnesses may choose to bring their own counsel, depending on the potential for a conflict of interest or incrimination.

PROFESSIONAL INSURANCE CARRIER SUPPORT

In the case of a nurse whose employer is a defendant or a potential defendant, the nurse should clarify with his or her professional liability insurance carrier that a lawsuit is pending and that there is counsel available for her or him through the carrier; and if the carrier is the same as his or her employer's carrier, the nurse is well advised to request different counsel. This verification should take place well before any interviews or depositions, as sometimes the nurse's interests and the employer's interests do not coincide. It has always been the best practice for every nurse to have her or his own professional liability policy, separate from the employer's, regardless of the nurse's specialty area.

Although nurses encounter ongoing stress in their daily work, the stressors associated with legal proceedings are considerably different. The experience is typically intimidating and removes the nurse from a "comfort zone." The ordeal can be fatiguing because of its length and the intensity of the questioning process.

LENGTH OF DEPOSITION

Rules vary by state and jurisdiction in regard to the length of the deposition. The attorneys should be able to give a witness a fair estimate of the time expected to obtain the deposition as well as an explanation of any rule limiting the time allowed for a deposition. A witness should receive a precise answer as to whether or not she or he may be required to appear each day until the deposition is complete. The deposition officer, generally the court reporter, is the timekeeper.

Interrogatives

The attorney who initiated or filed notice for the deposition will most likely begin questioning the witness or deponent. At the completion of that direct examination, there may be further examination from attorneys representing other parties to the lawsuit.

Cross-examination may or may not take place, but when necessary it is generally reserved for the courtroom.

FOCUS OF QUESTIONING

During depositions, the attorney may query the witness about anything as long as the question is reasonable and has been designed to lead to the disclosure of admissible evidence (Required Disclosures: Methods to Discover Additional Matter, 1998). The expert deponent should expect a series of questions about education, experience, credentials, and work experience (O'Keefe, 2001). The layperson or involved party can expect questions about anything that may contribute to the gathering of information relating to the case or anything that will contribute to the credibility of the witness. This may mean delving into the witness's personal life. The majority of interrogatives, however, will be about the case or incident that is the subject of the lawsuit. A witness should expect both redundant and repetitive lines of questions that are extremely detailed. This is a tedious process, and the deponent must consciously guard against frustration that is often felt during this part of the deposition. The witness should answer each question carefully and precisely without undue elaboration, which might reveal even the slightest of inconsistencies in the testimony. It is imperative for nurses to be prepared to answer precise questions about the state's nurse practice act, hospital policies and procedures, and nursing standards of practice that would impact the case (O'Keefe, 2001).

COMPOSING ANSWERS

In short, questions should always be answered truthfully. A witness should not answer until, and unless, she or he understands the question in its entirety. If there is any hesitation caused by a possible misunderstanding, the witness should address this issue before responding to the question. Once understood, a question should be answered clearly, but concisely. Avoid being forced into giving a yes or no answer when a qualified answer is required. The deponent may ask for the questions to be restated or "broken down" if the question is confusing or contains more than one question. A deponent has the right to explain or qualify an answer (Lanros & Barber, 1997). It is not wise to offer information that has not been asked about, as is commonly done in conversations; the examiner should carry the responsibility of asking the questions. And remember that the truth includes, "I don't know," and, "I don't remember." A deponent should not feel pressured to come up with an answer or speculate on what would be most helpful to either party. The deponent should not guess. Witnesses should remember that they have taken an oath to tell the complete truth, exactly as they would in a court of law. The deponent should guard against gamesmanship or attempts to outwit the questioning attorney. Not only are most trial lawyers very skilled at oral jousting, but it is the witness who will lose face and risk not being allowed to testify if inconsistencies or incompleteness are attempted. There is no skill involved in truth telling.

SUPPORTING DOCUMENTATION

It is important to remember that typically each individual called to testify will be required by the court to produce any relevant documents or notes in the custody of the testifying individual. Emotional reactions and opinions should be omitted if making personal notes following an incident. Nothing takes the place of meticulous documentation at the time care is rendered to make a nurse's actions clear. This alone can eliminate lawsuits. If the nurse is a party to the lawsuit, the documentation will play a significant role. There may be an earlier investigation by the hospital's counsel in anticipation of litigation by the family or by a peer review committee, and factual notes may be useful in preparing for those meetings. A witness may choose to bring copies of documents to the deposition; however, the originals must be available for inspection. The court reporter can make copies of documents for attachment to the deposition and return originals to the witness.

BEST PRACTICE When making notes about unusual occurrences or sentinel events, the nurse should record only objective details, avoiding opinions and any reference to emotions surrounding the event. The forensic nurse should remember that science has no emotion.

OBJECTIONS TO QUESTIONS

There is no judge in attendance at the deposition, so no one is authorized to rule on objections to questions. Generally, all questions asked must be answered if they are understood. In some instances, however, an attorney objecting to a question may be in a position to seek a ruling from the judge before allowing the witness to answer or to produce a particular document. It may be possible to get the judge's ruling immediately by telephone; but more often, the witness may be advised not to respond to that particular question, and the deposition will continue until a hearing before the judge may be scheduled. The question may be "held" or the opposing attorney may object, for the record.

It is safe to say that judges are not patient with attorneys or witnesses who attempt to restrict testimony, so most questions must be answered at the time of the deposition. Although opposing counsel has an interest in avoiding disclosure of information that is privileged, unless an objection is made, the question must be answered. Whether the testimony will be admissible at trial is determined at a later date.

Completion of the deposition in the face of inappropriate questioning is not required. A question may be asked that puts the witness at risk of self-incrimination or appears to violate basic rights to privacy. In that event, a witness is wise to stop the questioning and request that the deposition be completed at a later date. Because the attorneys attending the deposition are representing their respective clients and not representing the witness, the witness should seek advice from an independent attorney before the scheduled date for completion of the deposition.

BEST PRACTICE A deponent has the right to read and correct any errors in a deposition before presentation at trial. This right should not be waived (Aiken, 2004).

POSTDEPOSITION PROCEDURES

After the examination process is complete, the deponent is usually given an opportunity to review the deposition in its written form, make minor corrections, and sign it. If answers are changed, such that the substance of an answer is revised, the witness will likely be recalled for a second deposition to address that issue. Witnesses who are nonparties, and not aligned with any party, whose depositions are not signed and returned, will have effectively "waived" the signing; the deposition may still be used at trial, or it may be suppressed.

Testifying Expert

In any trial, the role of the judge is to rule on issues of law; in a "nonjury" trial, the judge will also serve as the trier of fact. However, when a case is tried to a jury, it is the jury's role to determine the facts. To assist the jury in understanding the evidence or in determining a vital fact issue, an individual with knowledge or experience who can assist the jury with fact finding is retained to be an "expert." An expert is not a party to the circumstances and is an independent person retained by an attorney to evaluate and advise regarding elements of the case. The expert may be designated as a consultant or one who will testify at trial and can count on being deposed in advance of trial. Questions will be focused on determining bias and weakening the expert's credibility. Attempts will be made to bolster the examining lawyer's own expert's opinions, for instance, by exposing flaws in the analysis utilized by the expert. The examining attorney must ascertain what the expert intends to say at trial and whether that testimony needs to be challenged for reliability in advance of allowing the fact finder(s) to hear the expert's testimony. Both attorneys may retain experts.

The expert is generally asked to review documents and, if named as a "testifying expert," to provide a written report describing opinions formed upon review of materials. Written materials should never be created until the attorney asks for them. That expert will be deposed so that the opposing party, or parties, may have an opportunity to ask questions about those opinions and the reliability of the bases for those opinions. The opposing party may assert that a particular expert should not be allowed to testify and may request that the court hold a hearing to review certain reliability criteria.

The greatest disservice a nurse expert can provide is to agree to consult or testify in a situation in which the nurse is not actually qualified or is professing to hold opinions or beliefs that the attorney wants to hear. As a rule, all opinions should be evidence based, current, and supported by literature, training, and experience.

Jury Access to Oral Depositions

Specific question-and-answer segments of the deposition testimony may be presented at trial. Similarly, if a witness is called to testify live, the questions will be narrowed to present the evidence as briefly as possible. Much of the material that can be covered in a deposition may not be admissible in the courtroom for various reasons, including lack of relevance or a claim of privilege.

In the case of a lawsuit filed because of the death of a patient, the family of the deceased patient will, most likely, be the party bringing the suit (plaintiff) and will have their own attorney(s) to represent them. This case will be against the personnel named in the event and the hospital. It is likely that each nurse and the hospital will be named separately rather than collectively and will be represented by their own individual attorneys. It may be worth mentioning, again, that nurses have their own, personal professional liability insurance.

There will be nurses that will be named as involved parties, in the lawsuit, and there may also be nurses who will act as consultants and experts, in that specific field of nursing, for the attorneys. The hospital will have its own law firm and may retain its own experts, and the defense firm will retain its own experts.

Anticipation of Testimony

When an unusual occurrence or sentinel event takes place, nurses involved in the case should immediately take steps to prepare for later legal proceedings that may follow. It is important to remember that courts typically require each individual called to testify to produce any relevant documents or notes that are in his or her custody. Emotional reactions and opinions should always be omitted if making personal notes following an incident. Merely recording facts that may be relative—such as the staff-to-patient ratio in the unit, the request by the lab technician to assist with lab work, the time of the admission, and the charge nurses' duties other than patient care—may be helpful to the nurse if litigation commences weeks, months, or even years later. There may be an earlier investigation by the hospital's counsel in anticipation of litigation by the family or by a peer review committee, and factual notes may be useful in preparation for those meetings.

When nurses are involved in an unusual occurrence or sentinel event, it is imperative that they make prompt notification up the chain of command and to their personal liability insurance carrier. At this time, they will be advised about how to prepare for subsequent internal investigations or legal proceedings. For example, they will discuss with counsel whether or not to prepare written documentation and what should be precisely recorded for later reference. No documentation should be prepared without advisement of counsel. All documentation can be discoverable. Nurses should communicate details of the event only to the attorney assigned by their insurance carrier and to the hospital's attorney. No discussion of the matter should take place with other individuals such as the patient's family, the other staff members, or any other attorney without consultation with the hospital attorney or the attorney assigned to the case by a personal insurance carrier.

All individuals who are involved in an unusual occurrence or sentinel event are potential fact witnesses (i.e., those with knowledge of relevant facts by virtue of having been present in the unit and seen or heard something related to the incident). There may be subsequent involvement of an expert witness, as previously discussed, who possesses expertise in a specific area (e.g., relevant nursing standards of practice or hospital policies). These experts may be asked to testify by either the plaintiff's attorneys or the defendant's attorneys, depending on who has retained them, to shed light on issues unfamiliar to attorneys or the layperson. It is common after unusual occurrences or sentinel events for the hospital's attorneys to meet with each staff person involved to ascertain who has relevant knowledge about the incident or the situation leading up to it. Each staff member will be asked to bring any notes made and retained. Additionally, each individual will be reminded not to discuss the facts, both for reasons of confidentiality and to avoid coloring the testimony of others. Fact witnesses often recall facts differently, but gathering and organizing the facts are the responsibilities of the attorneys, not the witnesses.

Witnesses in the Courtroom

It is not unusual to feel uneasy in a courtroom, and a bit out of one's own element, as there is a certain formality to the venue. "All rise!" is heard as the judge enters or leaves the courtroom. Everyone stands while the jury is entering and exiting the courtroom. The judge is always addressed as "Your Honor." Those wishing to speak may do so only with the court's permission when court is in session and on the record. The jury flows in and out as a group and only at the direction of the judge. Because the judge has complete control of the steady movement of the trial process, all participants in the courtroom are to give full attention to the judge and to assist in the orderly progression of the litigation.

Individuals, whether involved as a party or nonparty, must observe and adhere to the rules of the courtroom regarding dress and demeanor. Most judges disallow beverages, food, newspapers, and chewing gum in the courtroom. Clothing should be conservative: dark suits for men, suits or conservative attire for women. Dress that could be described as "revealing" should be avoided; judges have been known to halt a proceeding to ask an individual to leave the courtroom and return in clothing that is more appropriate to the setting and the occasion. Various locales may have different standards according to what they will allow, but the witness should know those standards.

The outside world is all but forgotten when court is in session, as the trial proceeds toward completion and resolution. Attorneys, jurors, parties, and witnesses may be requested to remain in the courtroom into the evening to avoid the disruption of testimony or arguments. The length of a trial is typically estimated beforehand, but it is more typical for those estimates to go out the window because of the length of testimony and unexpected circumstances that prevent adherence to predicted schedules. Although judges will attempt to accommodate any serious scheduling needs of jurors or witnesses, an individual who has been called to testify as a fact or expert witness is well advised to consider the impact on all the participants in a trial before requesting any special considerations.

Summary

Providing testimony during trial, whether in an oral deposition or from the witness stand, is a valuable investment in the judicial system. The individual who is deposed should carefully prepare for the deposition by reviewing all pertinent documentation related to the case. The attorney representing the deponent should provide essential counsel regarding the expected line of questioning from the opposing attorney and offer advice on strategies appropriate to the deposition process.

During the deposition, the witness must carefully consider each question before answering it, seeking clarification when necessary. The witness may even want to pause to give the attorneys a chance to object. The witness should keep her or his answers brief, direct, and without elaboration, because witnesses who do not do this may reveal information that otherwise might not have been elicited. If certain information is requested and the facts are vague or unknown, the witness should avoid speculation. Above all, a witness should always be truthful, regardless of the impact it might have on the case.

There is a big difference between the nurse who is a party to a civil action and the nurse who is retained as an expert for counsel. There is also a big difference between civil and criminal cases. Legal nurse consultants (LNCs) are suited to review records and act as consultants or testifying witnesses. These nurses are specialists in organizing records and citing inconsistencies, commissions, and omissions in events related to medical issues.

Besides LNCs, there are other specialties of nursing that lend themselves well to being consultants and expert witnesses in their specific fields. They may do different things with a different focus, but once expertise is gained in a particular field, it may well be sought after.

Resources

ORGANIZATIONS

American Association of Legal Nurse Consultants
AALNC Headquarters, 401 North Michigan Avenue, Chicago, IL 60611; 877-402-2562; www.aalnc.org
Nonprofit organization dedicated to the professional enhancement of registered nurses practicing in a consulting capacity in the legal field.

American Bar Association
321 North Clark Street, Chicago, IL 60610; 312-988-5000; www.abanet.org

American Nurses Association (ANA)
8515 Georgia Avenue, Suite 400, Silver Spring, MD 20910; 800-274-4ANA; www.nursingworld.com

WEBSITES

American Association of Nurse Attorneys
www.taana.org

American Society for Healthcare Risk Management
www.hospitalconnect.com/DesktopServlet

JOURNALS

Journal of Nursing Law
PESI HealthCare, L.L.C., 200 Spring Street, P.O. Box 1000, Eau Claire, WI 54702-1428; Tel: 800-846-7763

References

Daubert v. Merrell Dow Pharmaceuticals, Inc. 509 U.S. 579 (1993).

Federal Rules of Evidence. (2000). Washington DC: U.S. Department of Justice, U.S. Government Printing Office.

Giftis, S. H. (1996). *Law dictionary (Barron's Educational Series)*. New York: Barron's International Association of Forensic Nurses and American Nurses' Association. (1997). *Scope and standards of forensic nursing practice*. Washington, DC: American Nurses Association.

http://www.devineconnell.com/pdfs/johnston.pdf

Laura Slaughter, M. D. and Carl R. V. Brown, PhD. (1992). Colposcopy to Establish Physical Findings in Rape Victims, 166 *Am. J. Obstet. Gynecol.* 83.

Laura Slaughter, M. D., Carl R. V. Brown, PhD, Sharon Crowley, MN and Roxy Peck, PhD. (1997). Patterns of Genital Injury in Female Sexual Assault Victims, 176 *Am. J. Obstet. Gynecol.* 609.

Mark K., Norvell, M. D., Guy I. Benrubi, M. D. and Robert J. Thompson, M. D. (1984). Investigation of microtrauma after sexual intercourse. *J. of Reprod. Med.* 29(4): 269–271.

Kumho Tire Company v. Patrick Carmichael, 526 U.S. 137. (1999).

State of California. (1999). *California Evidence Code*. State of California: Department of Justice.

United States v. Frye, 293 F. 1013. (1923).

ADDITIONAL REFERENCES

Aiken, T. D. (2004). *Legal, ethical and political issues in nursing*. (2nd ed.). Philadelphia: F. A. Davis.

Lanros, N. E., & Barber, J. M. (1997). Legal and forensic considerations. In *Emergency nursing*. (4th ed., pp. 559–575). Stamford, CT: Appleton & Lange.

O'Keefe, M. E. (2001). *Nursing practice and the law: Avoiding malpractice and other legal risks*. Philadelphia: F. A. Davis.

Required disclosures: Methods to discover additional matter. (1998). Federal Rule of Civil Procedure 26(a), 30(b)(1)'

CHAPTER 46 Malpractice and Negligence

Alice C. Murr and Mary Frances Moorhouse

Nursing is a dynamic profession that continually evolves in response to changing needs, demands, and resources of society. The complexity of the healthcare delivery system today is such that the roles and responsibilities of the nurse are constantly expanding. Increased responsibility and independence are accompanied by increased accountability for nursing decisions and practice. Furthermore, Internet sites and television advertisements help shape expectations of healthcare recipients and may impact decisions to litigate. In a litigious society, an increasing number of nurses are being named in malpractice lawsuits by patients turned plaintiffs (Sharpe, 1999). For their own protection, and certainly for that of their patients, nurses must be aware of their legal rights and responsibilities.

Laws provide a basis for nursing intervention in the provision of patient care, they distinguish the roles and responsibilities of the nurse from those of other healthcare providers, and they define the boundaries of dependent or autonomous practice in various roles and clinical settings.

Standards of Care

When a nurse is sued for malpractice, he or she is being sued for *negligence*, broadly defined as "the failure to use ordinary or reasonable care" (Garner, 2004). Being held to a "reasonable standard" dictates that the nurse practices within professional standards of care.

Nursing practice is based on the understanding and use of a body of knowledge, some of which is borrowed from other disciplines, some of which is unique to nursing. The American Nurses Association (ANA) defines "standard" as the "authoritative statements by which the nursing profession describes the responsibilities for which its practitioners are accountable....written in measurable terms, standards also define the nursing profession's accountability to the public and the client outcomes for which nurses are responsible." (ANA, 1991)

The term *standard of care* is defined in tort law as "that average acceptable degree of skill, care, or diligence that a reasonable and prudent person in the same profession, would, or should, exercise under the same or similar circumstances" (Sharpe, 1999). This broad definition is further refined by various means. It is established through regulatory agencies, such as state boards of nursing, as well as by healthcare facility policies, procedures, and protocols; practice guidelines published by policy and accrediting agencies (e.g., The Agency for Healthcare Research and Quality [AHRQ], or The Joint Commission [TJC]); and by professional and clinical specialty organizations, (e.g., ANA, American Association of Critical-Care Nurses [AACN], Association of Operating Nurses [AORN]).

Standards of care are published in professional journals, nursing textbooks, and practice guidelines (e.g., care maps/clinical pathways, algorithms, protocols, technical bulletins). Standards

may be implied in the advertising of any agency (e.g., "neonatologist on staff 24 hours a day" or "XYZ Hospital provides the best care in the Midwest") making a claim that can be held as a standard of care, particularly when a legal action is considered (Harvey, 2004).

KEY POINT Forensic nurses must be familiar with several sources of standards that influence their professional practice, including those of professional organizations, state boards of nursing, and other regulatory bodies.

Although all nurses at all practice levels are held to a standard of care, that standard of care varies somewhat according to geographical locale and practice setting (e.g., intensive care unit; inner city health clinic; industrial, educational and corrections facilities; legal and investigative arenas), and type of practice (e.g., advance nurse practitioner, staff nurse in hospital or community clinic, facility administrator, medical examiner, legal consultant).

Standards of care, arise from the following:

- *Regulations based on state and federal statutes.* The clinician has an obligation to adhere to federal laws and her or his state's nurse practice act and scope of practice guidelines. State boards of nursing set the standards for entry into nursing practice, regulate licensure, enact regulations and standards, and adjudicate cases involving violations of professional standards or rules. Nurse practice acts contain general statements of appropriate professional nursing actions. They define nursing, set standards for the nursing profession, and give guidance regarding scope of practice issues. As such, a state's nurse practice act is the single most important piece of legislation affecting nursing practice. The nurse must incorporate the nurse practice act with her or his educational background, previous work experience, institutional policies, certification requirements, and technological advancements. The nurse must demonstrate competence through the elements of a professional knowledge base, awareness and use of appropriate practice standards, decision-making and communication skills, and experience. Performance may be quantified periodically through continuing education, peer review, and clinical area certifications. Violating any statute or regulation of the state automatically makes the nurse and her or his employing facility negligent.
- *Professional practice guidelines.* In the ANA Code of Ethics, provisions are listed that state the ethical obligations and duties of professional nurses. The elements describe the nurse's fundamental commitment and values, boundaries of duty and loyalty, aspects of duties related to advancing the profession, and collaborative efforts with other healthcare professions to shape policy and meet the health needs of society (ANA, 2004). Professional practice is also guided by protocols and guidelines

written for specific practice areas that are drafted in a general way so as to apply to nursing care in a variety of settings.

- *Facility policies and procedures.* Required by law and accrediting agencies, policies and procedures are used in court to establish standards of care. It is expected that the nurse's practice is consistent with these policies and procedures, and when a lawsuit has been brought, they are most likely the first documents examined when evaluating whether or not a standard of care was met. Failure to follow policy does not mean that the nurse is automatically negligent, but it can mean that it will be up to a jury to decide whether or not the nurse was negligent.

Nursing Malpractice and Negligence

The term *malpractice* is used to define professional negligence; as such, it is a subset of negligence, although in general the terms are used interchangeably. Specifically, malpractice is negligence committed by a person in a professional capacity and differs from simple negligence in that it involves specialized skills and training not possessed by the average person.

KEY POINT The most common legal charge brought against nurses is for an act of negligence that represents a deviation from a standard of care.

Although there are numerous legal claims that may be brought against a nurse, the most prevalent claim is negligence. Simply stated, nursing negligence is deviation from the standard of care. If the nurse acts in a way that a reasonably prudent nurse would not act, or fails to take action in a way that a reasonably prudent nurse would act, the nurse's actions (or omissions) are negligent. The law touches on a wide range of possible nursing conduct that falls under the legal heading of negligence (including failure to render care or failure to rescue), that meets applicable standards, or that indicates the nurse acted in a manner that was intentionally harmful to the patient (Sharpe, 1999).

Even when a nurse's actions are not intended to bring harm to the patient, the patient or representative can bring a negligence suit against the nurse. Negligence per se is a situation in which expert testimony is not required to establish the applicable standard of care, if the defendant's conduct violates a law that is designed to protect the class of persons of which the plaintiff is a member. For example, liability existed without citing standard of care when a student nurse administered anesthesia, in violation of a state statute, and injured the patient (*Central Anesthesia Assoc., P.C. v. Worthy,* 1985, cited in *Brown v. Belinfante,* et al., 2001).

Expert witnesses are used by both prosecuting and defense attorneys to establish standards of care. The expert's role is to explain to the jury the standard of care based on her or his particular expertise. The question of who can testify to standards of care may depend on specific statutory or case law in any jurisdiction, but in general, a testifying expert must possess sufficient training, experience, and knowledge (as a result of practice or teaching in the clinical setting or specialty area where the incident occurred) as to satisfy the court that she or he is familiar with the accepted standard of care (Harvey, 2004). Although physicians have testified regarding nursing practice, it is being recognized that medicine and nursing have different philosophies and approaches, and physicians are not educated in nursing. Nurses should testify regarding nursing practice and should not testify as a medical expert linking a breach of the nursing standard of care to medical

complications suffered by the plaintiff (*Echard v. Barnes-Jewish Hosp.,* 2002). In the end, the jury will interpret the opinions of the expert witnesses and determine if negligence has occurred.

Elements of Negligence

In order for a plaintiff to prevail in a suit against a nurse for negligence, the plaintiff must prove all four elements of the cause of action: duty, breach of duty, causation, and damages.

DUTY

Duty is defined as acts or interactions required after the presumption of a relationship between the provider and a patient. Duty is established when the nurse (1) provides direct care to an individual, (2) observes an unattended person in need of care, or (3) observes or is aware of another provider performing care in a manner that may cause harm (Brent, 2001; O'Keefe, 2001).

BREACH OF DUTY

A breach of duty is defined as neglect or failure to fulfill, in an appropriate and proper manner, the duties of a job (Ashley, 2004; O'Keefe, 2001). To determine whether or not a duty was violated, it is necessary to delineate the standard of care of a particular circumstance. It must be determined if the nurse (1) met the standard of care, (2) did not do the right thing (misfeasance), (3) did nothing/did not act (nonfeasance), or (4) did the right thing in the wrong way (malfeasance) (Murr & Moorhouse, 2001).

CAUSATION

The proximate cause (causation) is often the most difficult element to prove. The difficulty lies in the fact that the cause of an injury often cannot be easily identified. A nurse's negligence may be one of several possibilities. Foreseeability is a causation concept that can apply, stating that the nurse has a responsibility to anticipate harm and eliminate risk. For example, if a drug book states that wrong dosage of a certain seizure medication may cause injury, the element of forseeability of causation of harm exists. If a wrong dosage is administered and the patient suffers a seizure as a result, a direct relationship could be proved between the patient's injury and the nurse's action (Marquis & Huston, 2008).

Another element called *res ipsa loquitur* (the thing speaks for itself) can apply to causation, if four conditions have been met:

1. The act that caused the injury was exclusively in the nurse's control.
2. The injury would not have happened but for the nurse's negligence.
3. No negligence on the patient's part contributed to the injury.
4. Evidence of the truth as to what happened is unavailable (Iyer & Aiken, 2001).

A simple example of res ipsa loquitur might include this: a patient emerges from the operating room with a burn on his right posterior thigh that was not present before surgery. The surgical table equipment was under the nurse's control, and the patient had no part in the injury because he was unconscious. Therefore, the causation for injury would be considered as applying to the nurse.

DAMAGES

Damages are defined as monetary compensation that may be recovered in court if the plaintiff shows that the act or omission damaged or harmed him or her in some way. Actual or compensatory damages are losses sustained by the injured person and include relevant medical expenses, lost earnings, impairment of future earnings, and past and future pain and suffering. Punitive damages are designed to punish defendants. The character of negligence necessary to sustain an award of punitive damages must be of "a gross and flagrant character, evincing reckless disregard of human life, or of the safety of persons" (Brent, 2001, p. 88). For example, a patient admitted to an extended care center for rehabilitation was left restrained in a bed or chair for extended periods of time until advanced pressure ulcers developed, ultimately leading to his death (Doherty, 1993).

Criminal versus Civil Law

Laws can be classified in a number of ways, based on whether they are substantive, procedural, civil, or criminal. All types of law are intermingled in various ways and in different areas of litigation and practice. Civil law recognizes and enforces the rights of individuals and organizations. Criminal law defines crimes and the punishment an individual can incur, including loss of freedom (Aiken, 2004).

When it comes to guilt, the scales of justice are balanced in a civil trial, but weighted for the defendant in a criminal case. In a criminal case, the defendant is presumed innocent until proved guilty. The winner in a civil trial need only move the scale a "feather's weight" (to 51%) to prevail, whereas in a criminal case, guilt must be proved beyond a reasonable doubt (Murr & Moorhouse, 2004).

One of the two areas of civil law is tort law. A tort is a wrong that harms. The three types of torts include intentional torts, negligence (nonintentional torts), and strict liability. These wrongful acts, whether arising from intentional or negligent conduct, have as their common principle the idea that injuries are to be compensated. Differences between intentional and nonintentional torts can be characterized as differences in intent, injury, duty, and consent (Aiken, 2004).

Although negligence can occur without harmful intent, an intentional tort is an action requiring a specific state of mind, usually an intention to do a wrongful act. In intentional tort actions, plaintiffs do not have to prove that any actual injury occurred, as the harm is in the invasion of a person's rights. Potential consequences of intentional torts include loss of reputation and esteem, exposure to criminal liability, loss of professional license, loss of insurance, and punitive damages (Murr & Moorhouse, 2001; ANA Clinical Standards of Care, 2004).

BEST PRACTICE The forensic nurse must monitor direct nursing care measures to ensure that they do not constitute intentional torts, such as assault, battery, and false imprisonment.

Intentional Torts

These actions include acts that violate another person's rights or property. In the medical arena, this includes assault, battery, and false imprisonment (Harvey, 2004; O'Keefe, 2001).

ASSAULT

Assault is an act that is designed to make a person fearful or in apprehension of bodily harm. Assault does not require touching; it can be a threatening statement, such as, "If you don't stay in that chair, I am going to tie you down."

BATTERY

Battery is the unlawful or offensive touching of another without consent. Examples of battery committed by a nurse are inserting an intravenous (IV) line after the patient revokes permission or inserting a feeding tube in a terminal patient who is refusing care.

FALSE IMPRISONMENT

False imprisonment is defined as unlawful, intentional, and unjustifiable detention of a person against his or her will within fixed boundaries so that the person is conscious of or harmed by the confinement. An example of false imprisonment could be the use of direct physical or chemical restraints or detaining the person in a care setting against his or her will or desire for treatment.

QUASI-INTENTIONAL TORTS

These actions include such elements as defamation, slander, invasion of privacy, and breach of confidentiality. The latter two have more implications in the healthcare environment of today (Harvey, 2004; Morrison, 2000).

- Invasion of privacy can occur in any medical setting where a patient's name or medical information is viewed or obtained by unauthorized individuals; these actions can involve public exposure of private facts, intrusion on the seclusion or private concerns of the person, or the patient's name or picture being used without express written consent.
- Breach of confidentiality is a legal and ethical concern for healthcare providers, especially in this day of electronic record keeping and transmission of medical information through various means, such as e-mail, the Internet, and facsimile (fax). For example, information can be left on a computer screen, faxes can be sent to providers, or payers can be viewed by many persons, and sensitive information can be unintentionally given to unauthorized individuals.

Liability Issues in Healthcare

Common sources of nursing liability include failure to notify the physician, making assumptions about following questionable orders, inadequate monitoring, failure to follow policies and procedures, medication errors, failure to safeguard against falls and other preventable injuries, use of unsafe equipment or failure to use equipment correctly, and breach of confidentiality. Each will be discussed briefly here.

FAILURE TO NOTIFY THE PHYSICIAN

The nurse must communicate thorough, accurate, and timely information about the patient's condition to the physician and others as appropriate (e.g., other caregivers, family [if patient allows], and chain of command in nursing/facility staff). Some malpractice cases have hinged on whether the nurse was persistent enough in attempting to notify the physician or in convincing the physician of the seriousness of a patient's condition. Courts are likely to recognize that after-the-fact communication is no communication.

MAKING ASSUMPTIONS AND FOLLOWING ORDERS

Assumptions cannot be defended in court, and neither can a nurse's assertion that she or he was "just following orders." The standard of care requires that nurses question and clarify orders, especially when orders seem inappropriate, written orders are illegible, or the patient's life or safety is at stake. As a general rule, verbal and phone orders are acceptable only under acute or emergency circumstances when a doctor cannot promptly attend to the patient. Standing orders or protocols must be individualized and reviewed from time to time for accuracy and efficacy (Marden, 2000).

INADEQUATE MONITORING

Inadequate monitoring includes failure to adequately observe, especially when a patient's condition is undergoing change, or if the patient possesses self-destructive tendencies, or if appropriate monitoring would have detected the complication or change in condition. One of the greatest responsibilities of a nurse is to assess, monitor, and report to other healthcare providers, including the physician. In *Harrington v. Rush Presbyterian, St Luke's Hospital*, a patient who was admitted for drug dependency began to suffer headaches and finally fainted. The nurses returned the patient to her bed. They did not contact a physician. Progress notes between 11 p.m. and 7 a.m. were not written. The patient died of drug toxicity. The verdict was $4 million awarded to the plaintiff's estate (Tammelleo, 1991).

An additional concern in this area is failure to intervene when monitoring has revealed a problem with the patient. The nurse has an independent duty to act for the safety of the patient. Both failure to intervene and inappropriate interventions can result in liability.

FAILURE TO FOLLOW POLICIES AND PROCEDURES

Facility documents are intended to guide their employee's patient care to comply with accreditation standards and to educate staff in the facility's expectations for employee conduct. Often, not having a policy or failing to follow an established policy can have legal consequences (Marden, 2000). However, a defendant being unaware of a policy is not deemed an excuse for failure to follow the standard.

MEDICATION ERRORS

This problem encompasses the largest group of errors resulting in legal action. The major categories include the following:
- Not knowing or being unfamiliar with the drug that is ordered. Unless the order is questionable, the law expects the drug to be administered as ordered.
- Not administering what is ordered (which can encompass deviating from the "five rights": right patient, right drug, right route, right dose, right time) is cause for nursing negligence. Some facilities have added a sixth right, namely "the right to refuse" any medication (Timby, 2009) and in this age of delegation, one might add a seventh right as well: "the right unlicensed delagatee," as the professional nurse is responsible for that delagatee.
- Not documenting what is administered. Poor record keeping is a common cause of duplicate and omitted medication doses. Not documenting what is administered is considered as failing to give the medication. Likewise, documenting a medication as given when it was not given, is a liable action on the part of the nurse (ANA & NCSBN, 2006).
- Lack of awareness or documentation of allergies, or disregard for at-risk populations (e.g., the young, elderly, mentally ill, developmentally delayed persons with limited or compromised communication). Ask and record client's response to allergies and adverse reactions. Be sensitive to contraindications with regard to special populations.

FAILURE TO PROVIDE SAFEGUARDS

The rapid expansion of complex and specialized nursing practice, along with enhanced access to medical information and use of technology, increases the healthcare consumers expectations for favorable outcomes as a result of treatment received. Reliance on technology to capture and convey patient information has increased the scope of nurse-related malpractice risks. Lawsuits may arise from many sources including proper patient identification, timely reporting of critical lab tests, complying with reportable injuries, or potential abuse.

Failure to provide safeguards may include anything from failure to appropriately monitor client to failure to follow safeguards already in place. Examples are multiple and variable, and they might include such occurrences as divulging patient information to a third party, failing to communicate observations or changes in client's condition, failing to disclose abuse of vulnerable adult; a patient slip and fall incident, a medication error related to a verbal or transcribed order, or failure to follow in-place procedures when collecting or preserving physical evidence specimens in a suspected sexual assault or attempted murder.

In one public health hearing regarding failure to provide safeguards, findings concluded:

> The nursing staff failed to implement the facility policy regarding prompt intervention of a patient with an emergency medical condition by placing patient back into the waiting room for over an hour without being monitored, and failed to notify the physician of a critical high blood glucose level. In addition, the hospital failed to develop a policy and procedure that provided direction to staff regarding where to place patients needing prompt medical intervention when the emergency treatment areas were full. (California Health and Human Services, 2008)

Although this event is reported as findings of a public health agency (not a verdict of malpractice), it could be typical of events that could result in malpractice lawsuits associated with providing safeguards.

EQUIPMENT FAILURES OR USER ERRORS

Equipment may be a central or peripheral issue in litigations. Malfunctioning devices as well as user errors must be considered in this category. For example, nurses may fail to set up or monitor equipment; they may also fail to note and correct a problem that causes harm to the patient (e.g., the patient could be burned from hot-pack therapy or may receive too much or too little fluid or medication through an IV pump).

BREACH OF CONFIDENTIALITY

This area has recently become a popular ground for lawsuits because people are increasingly reluctant to reveal their health status and because of the ease of access to medical data. Health information is typically considered confidential and privileged and cannot be disclosed without authorization or as otherwise provided by law (Marden, 2000). This is supported by the ANA Code of Ethics (2004) and by other documents, including the Health Insurance Portability and Accountability Act of 1996 (HIPAA Overview, 2004).

Reducing Risks of Malpractice

Perhaps the best defense against malpractice lies in the ethical practice of nursing. The profession founded on caring cannot afford to forget that patients are people. People generally do not sue people they like. So treat patients better than they expect to be treated. Value them. Listen to their concerns. Bear in mind that attorneys report that people frequently complain to them that healthcare providers could not or would not answer their questions.

Keep well informed. Continuing one's education, training, and certifications is key to keeping abreast of the knowledge and skills required to provide nursing care that falls well within standards of care. Although not all states require continuing education for relicensure, most nursing specialties have certification requirements to ensure that nurses are kept up-to-date on the latest healthcare information. When it comes to patient care, recognize the importance of accurate clinical assessment data (and its absence). Identify actual and potential complications. Obtain additional data when not at ease about a patient's condition. Anticipate staffing needs and secure adequate resources to assure safe patient care and document the patient's clinical status as well as provider actions and responses.

Value the nursing task of doing complete and accurate documentation in the patient's record. It has been said that "the best defense against lawsuits is a good documentation offense" (Wetter, 2004). Documentation forms the framework for all nursing activities, and documentation standards establish specific regulatory guidelines and policies (Aiken, 2004). Nurses have been heard to say, "How could you possibly want to chart, let alone enjoy it, when it keeps you from giving direct patient care?" In reality, documenting is patient care. Certainly, the old saying, "if it's not documented, it was not done" has never been timelier as state and federal governments continue to enact legislation to protect healthcare consumers. Effective documentation is factual, accurate, complete, and timely (FACT). Failure to document or faulty or unfactual documentation is risky behavior that should be avoided (Aiken, 2004).

In this day of nursing shortage and pressure associated with providing care for too many patients with too few resources, issues of quality are constantly arising. "It's not my job" reflects the view that raising issues of quality (e.g., inadequate staffing to do the job, operating obsolete or unsafe equipment) is simply too time consuming and must be left to others with the energy and desire to pursue them. However, if the nurse fails to raise the issue with those who can effect change, and a patient sues for damages sustained as a result of the problem (e.g., inadequate staffing), the nurse as well as the facility could be found liable (DeWitt, 2001).

Another major issue relates to delegation of nursing tasks, and who is responsible for what. The nurse is directly responsible for her or his own actions, assignments, and supervision. The nurse has the right to rely on other staff to competently carry out tasks within the scope of their employment. This is true for licensed and nonlicensed personnel. Each individual has certain responsibilities and will be held accountable for carrying out those responsibilities competently (Marden, 2000). There are, however, guidelines for what cannot be delegated by a nurse to an unlicensed person. These duties include assessments, formulating care plans, tasks to be done only by licensed individuals, patient teaching, and administration of medications (this last duty is not firmly decided yet and is being reviewed in a number of states as it relates to medication administration in certain care facilities) (Reinhard, Young, Kane, & Quinn, 2006). It is vital for nurses to know their facility's job description for various categories of workers, as well as the state board's practice acts and limitations for licensed and unlicensed workers who might be under their supervision. All nurses should understand who can delegate and what tasks can be delegated and to whom and under what circumstances. All nurses

should exercise their rights (e.g., right task, right person, right circumstances, right direction, and right supervision) (Joint Position Statement, ANA, & National Council of State Boards of Nursing [NCSBN], 2005).

Common Malpractice Defenses

A specific time limit is allowed for bringing litigation. This is known as the "statute of limitations." In many states, the time period in which a malpractice suit can be filed has been set at two to three years. However, the statute of limitations may be extended if the individual does not know he or she was injured until after the statute has run, if fraud has been perpetrated, or if the individual was a minor (as defined by state law) at the time the injury occurred (Brent, 2001). For example, an individual injured at birth (a bad obstetrical outcome) may have until his or her 18th or 21st birthday to file suit.

In some states, a defendant nurse can also file counterclaims. These counterclaims include (1) contributory negligence (by an injured plaintiff), (2) comparative negligence (when negligence is measured in a certain percentage against the defendant nurse and a certain percentage against the plaintiff), and (3) assumption of risk (e.g., a patient signs out of the hospital against medical advice) (HIPAA Overview, 2004).

BEST PRACTICE Although employers may provide some insurance for nurses, forensic nurses should maintain their personal insurance coverage for professional liability.

Malpractice insurance is also considered a type of defense against malpractice, in that it can protect a nurse or employer by paying all or a portion of assessed damages when the court finds for the plaintiff. Although most facilities cover their nurses with malpractice insurance, there is a growing recognition of the importance of nurses carrying their own professional liability insurance. Reasons for this include (1) expanding functions and practice arenas of nurses, (2) increasing responsibility for supervising subordinate staff with delegated tasks, (3) employer insurance coverages that are lower than potential judgments, and (4) failure of some employers to initiate an adequate defense for nurses (Cherry & Jacob, 2005).

Case Study **46-1**

Complications and Negligence Involving an Intravenous Line

A patient came to the hospital with complaints of abdominal pain and was evaluated in the emergency department. The physician's orders included intravenous (IV) medications, for which a line needed to be inserted. The nurse assigned to the patient had difficulty finding veins in the woman's arms. He attempted to start a line in her hand and was successful on the third attempt. For the remainder of the patient's treatment in the hospital, it was documented that the patient complained of discomfort at the IV site and tolerated it poorly.

Although there was no indication that other symptoms of complication existed, there was also no indication that placement of another line was offered to, or refused by, the patient. Following her discharge, the patient filed a suit alleging negligence on the part of the nurse and the hospital. Specifically she claimed a poorly performed catheter insertion caused her to develop reflex sympathetic dystrophy (RSD) in her right hand, a condition characterized by severe burning pain, pathological changes in bone and skin, excessive sweating, tissue swelling, and extreme sensitivity to touch.

CRITICAL THINKING QUESTIONS

1. What are the critical factors to be considered in determining the need for replacement of the IV?
   Potential answers/thoughts for discussion:
   • Type(s) of solution, additives, and rate of infusion
   • Type of reaction and expected duration of the infusion
2. Did the nurse adhere to the standard of care regarding IV starts?
   Potential answers/thoughts for discussion:
   • What is the standard?
   • Who determines the standard?
   • Who determines the standard in your locale and practice setting?
3. Who should be included in the decision-making process concerning the patient's problem with the IV?
   Potential answers/thoughts for discussion:
   • The patient, nursing colleagues/supervisor, and physician. For example, the patient might have decided to leave the IV in if only one more dose of antibiotic was to be administered.
   • Or if an additive, such as potassium, was infusing, would dose or infusion rate change alter the discomfort?
   • Did follow-up nursing assessments document a growing problem?
   • Did the physician know what was occurring?
4. What documentation is prudent regarding this incident and the appropriate standard of care?
   Potential answers/thoughts for discussion:
   • Documentation of patient reports about the problem, nurses' observations, plans, and actions, including consultation with the physician.

AND WHAT HAPPENED AFTERWARD?

Eventually the case went to trial, during which the chart was reviewed and expert testimony was presented in the courtroom. No deficiencies in technique could be found in the placement of the catheter. By his employment record and training, the nurse was fully qualified to place IV lines as part of his scope of practice as a registered nurse.

It was noted that the hospital's standards of care were breached as they allowed for a maximum of two attempts before calling for assistance. However, further review revealed that the "community" standard (which was the measure used in the case) allowed for four insertion attempts. By this standard of care, the nurse was within reasonable limits by trying three times.

Expert testimony addressed the issue of causation of the RSD. No direct causative links could be established between the starting of an IV and a diagnosis of RSD. In this case, summary judgment was entered for the hospital, finding that no negligence was evident. The client appealed, and the appeals court affirmed the judgment of the lower court (*Coleman v. East Jefferson General Hosp.*, 747 S.2d 1047-LA [1999]).

Case Study 46-2

Leg Injury, Missed Diagnosis, and Nurse Advocacy

A minor child (teen) [referred to here as Mr. R] lost control of his motorcycle while participating in a motocross event. During the crash, the motorcycle tumbled onto the teen's left leg, injuring his knee. He was transported by ambulance to the emergency room.

The patient arrived at the hospital at approximately 4:05 PM., where emergency room nurses examined his left leg. Over the course of the next 2½ hours, the nurses made extensive notes in the patient's file. The notes indicate that the patient complained of severe pain in his left knee and numbness in his foot. The nurses were repeatedly unable to find a pulse in the patient's lower left leg and foot either by palpitation or with the assistance of a portable Doppler ultrasound device.

The patient was also examined by an emergency room physician, who noted tenderness and swelling in the left knee and lower left leg, and he had difficulty finding—but claimed he did find—a pulse in the patient's lower leg and foot. A nurse stated that she told the doctor that she was unable to detect a pulse in the patient's foot and that she asked the doctor why she was not getting a pulse. The doctor stated he did not know.

X-rays showed fragments of bone in the patient's knee joint. The doctor noted in the patient file that Mr. R had a "severe sprain, [left] knee." [Review of documents for this case do not indicate whether the doctor saw the x-ray results.]

The patient was discharged at 6:20 PM. to be taken home by his mother. He was given instructions to elevate his left leg and apply ice to the knee. The nurses informed the [parents] that they could not find a pulse in his lower leg, but that the swelling probably caused this condition and that a pulse would return when the swelling went down. He was instructed to make an appointment with an orthopedist several days later and was told that in the meanwhile, if his pain continued or became worse, he should return to the emergency room.

That night, the teen's knee and leg continued to swell, and the pain intensified. His parents called several physicians by phone, and one agreed to see him 10:00 AM. the next morning at a different emergency room. An examination revealed that the patient had a dislocated knee and a lacerated popliteal artery, an artery that passes behind the knee joint and provides circulation to the lower leg.

Because of the loss of blood flow, the physician contemplated amputation of the lower left leg. However, after extensive surgery to repair the knee and artery, to relieve pressure on the leg and to remove dead tissue, the lower leg was saved. The patient was hospitalized for 35 days and currently has significant impairment to the use of his left leg.

CRITICAL THINKING QUESTIONS

1. Did the nursing staff do enough to see that the patient's potential injuries were properly assessed and treated?
   Potential answers/thoughts for discussion:
   • It appears the documentation of their assessment findings were appropriate, as were their assessment actions.
   • If the nurses failed, where was that failure?
   • Did they tell their supervisor that their findings conflicted with those of the physician, and did they advocate for further assessment of the pulselessness?
2. Could the nurse have done more to elicit further evaluation by the physician?
   Potential answers/thoughts for discussion:
   • Records do not indicate that the nurse said, "show me where you felt the pulse" so the area could be marked and evaluated again in that area. Maybe the nurse could have handed the physician the Doppler and asked him to listen in the area where he said he felt a pulse.
   • Was more than one person available to support the nurse's findings and question the doctor?
3. What standard(s) of care might have been breached?
   Potential answers/ thoughts for discussion:
   • What is the hospital's policy regarding questioning a potential missed or incorrect diagnosis?
4. Where does the nurse's allegiance lie when it appears that the system may be failing the patient?
   Potential answers/ thoughts for discussion:
   • Why do you think the parents were told that the nurses could not find a pulse? Was this a veiled reference to the fact that the nurse

disagreed with the physician? Because the parents were told to bring the patient back to the emergency department if he worsened, should the nurses have indicated "or take him to another hospital of your choosing for more evaluation" or something to that effect?

- would thus be ethical?
- What would you do differently in the same circumstance?

AND WHAT HAPPENED AFTERWARD?

Mr. R subsequently brought a lawsuit against the doctor and against [hospital 1] for negligence. After 8 years of litigation, the patient settled his cause of action against the doctor and the case proceeded to trial against the hospital alone.

At trial, it was asserted [hospital 1] nurses had breached the standard of care by not adequately advocating his interests when he was discharged with unexplained and unaddressed symptoms.

Evidence was presented that [hospital 1's] policy—and the guiding standard of care for all emergency room nurses—was that when a nurse "believe[d] that appropriate care [was] not being administered to a patient by a physician," the nurse was to report the situation to a supervisor who would discuss it with the doctor. If that did not alleviate the problem, the matter was to be referred up the chain of command so that another doctor could evaluate the problem.

As the plaintiff's expert stated:

[T]he nurses at [hospital 1] failed to advocate for [the patient] in the sense that they knew that he had compromised circulation to his left leg. He had no pulse. He was not able to move his foot. He had no sensation in his foot…. [T]he nurses did not intervene with the physician and try to influence his care so that he would have gotten further medical care to address those serious problems. ([*Patient*] v. *Sisters of Pallottine Missionary Society*, 2001, WL i585453 s.e.2e)

A jury returned a verdict against [hospital 1].

Adapted from case report available online at the Nursefriendly, Inc., website. Written permission granted by Andrew Lopez, site manager, on January 16, 2009.

Summary

The highly charged emotional and technical arenas in which forensic nurses practice compel them to be extremely accountable for their activities. In fact, the definition of forensic nursing alone would imply that members of the discipline should have a high regard for the principles, standards, laws, and other regulatory guidance pertinent to the specialty. In addition to comprehension of the scope and standards of forensic nursing, it is imperative that practitioners be knowledgeable about their state's nurse practice act.

The immense responsibilities of independent forensic nursing demand a thorough understanding of nursing malpractice and negligence. In order for a plaintiff to prevail in a suit against a nurse for negligence, the plaintiff must prove all four elements of the cause of action: duty, breach of duty, causation, and damages. Forensic nurses should have no ambivalence about what constitutes their roles and responsibilities to individuals and the community they serve. Exemplary documentation and supportive patient and family interactions are vital to a sound offense within the practice arena.

Resources

ORGANIZATIONS

American Association of Legal Nurse Consultants
AALNC Headquarters, 4700 West Lake Avenue, Glenview, IL 60025; 877-402-2562; www.aalnc.org

American Bar Association
321 North Clark Street, Chicago, IL 60610; 312-988-5000; www.abanet.org
American Nurses Association (ANA)
8515 Georgia Avenue, Suite 400, Silver Spring, MD, 20910; 800-274-4ANA; www.nursingworld.org

References

Aiken, T. D. (2004). *Legal, ethical, and political issues in nursing* (2nd ed.). Philadelphia: F. A. Davis.

American Nurses Association (ANA). (1991). *Standards of clinical practice*, p. 1, Kansas City: MO.

American Nurses Association (ANA). (2004). *Code of ethics with interpretive statements*. Retrieved December 2008 from www.nursingworld.org

American Nurses Association (ANA) and the National Council of State Boards of Nursing (NCSBN). (2006). *Joint statement on delegation*. Available at www.ncsbn.org/Joint_statement.pdf.

Ashley, R. C. (2004). The third element of negligence. *Crit Care Nurse*, *24*(3), 65–66.

Brent, N. J. (2001). *Nurses and the law: A guide to principles and applications* (2nd ed.). Philadelphia: Saunders.

Bellinfante, Brown, et al. A01A1339. (252 Ga. App. 856)(557 SE2d 399). (2001). *Citation of use of original case law re Central Anesthesia Assoc. v. Worthy*. Retrieved January 2009. From www.lawskills.com/case/ga/id/20063/#note23.

California Health and Human Services Agency Department of Public Health. Results of Hearing (03/21/2008). Retrieved January 2009. From www.cdph.ca.gov/certlic/facilities/Documents/HospitalAdministrativePenalties-2567Forms-LNC/2567KaiserFoundationHospital-SanJose-Event-45EC11.pdf.

Central Anesthesia Assoc., PC, et al. v. Worthy. 333 S.E.2d 829 (1985) 254 (Ga.) 728.

Cherry, B., & Jacob, S. R. (2005). *Contemporary nursing* (3rd ed., p. 165). St. Louis: Elsevier Mosby.

DeWitt, A. L. (2001). The top 10 things you can do to get sued. Retrieved March 2004 from Advance for Nurses website: www.advancefornurses.com.

Doherty, 619 So.2d 367, Fla. 3d DCA (1993). Case available for review in January 2009 on website of Perenich, Carroll, Perenich. Cauldwell, A case that truly shows "Reckless Indifference" to the rights of a nursing home resident. Retrieved January 2009 from www.usalaw.com/articles.

Echard v. Barnes-Jewish Hosp., S.W.3d (WL 1902103). August 20, 2002. *Legal Eagle Eye Newsletter for the Nursing Profession*, October 2002, p. 7.

Garner, B. A. (Ed.), (2004). *Black's Law Dictionary*. (8th ed.). New York: West Group.

Harrington v. Rush Presbyterian, St Luke's Hospital. (1989). In *Medical Malpractice Verdicts*. (Vol. 5, No. 2), February 1989. Chicago: American Bar Association.

Harvey, C. J. (2004). *"Malpractice: What every nurse should know."* Course for Nurses in Colorado Springs, CO. Outline published by HTA Consulting, Inc.

Health Insurance Portability and Accountability Act (HIPAA). Overview. Your health information privacy rights. Public information pamphlet. Washington, DC: Department of Health. Retrieved December 2008 from www.hhs.gov/ocr/hipaa/consumer_rights.pdf.

Iyer, P. W., & Aiken, T. D. (2001). *Nursing Malpractice* (2nd ed.). Tucson, AZ: Lawyers and Judges Publishing Company, Inc.

Legal and Legislative Issues. In B. L. Marquis, & C. J. Huston (Eds.), *Leadership Roles and Management Functions in Nursing* (6th ed.) (2008). Wolters Kluwer: Lippincott, Williams & Wilkens.

Marden, C. (2000). *Nursing law update*. Houston, TX: Southwest Seminars Association.

Morrison, C. A. (2000). *Nursing malpractice, liability & your license*. Altoona, WI: Medical Educational Services.

Murr, A. C., & Moorhouse, M. F. (May 24, 2001). *Legal nurse consulting: You, too, can do it. Guest lecture, forensic program*. Colorado Springs: University of Colorado.

O'Keefe, M. E. (2001). *Nursing practice and the law: Avoiding malpractice and other legal risks*. Philadelphia: F. A. Davis.

Reinhard, S. C., Young, H. M., Kane, R. A., & Quinn, W. V. (2006). Nurse delegation of medication administration for older adults in assisted living. *Nursing Outlook, 54*(2), 74–80.

Sharpe, C. C. (1999). *Nursing malpractice: Liablity and risk management*. Westport, CT: Auburn House.

Tammelleo, A. D. (1991). Failure to monitor patient: deplorable nursing care. Case in point: *Harrington v. Rush-Presbyterian-St. Luke's* (569 N.E. 2d 15–IL (1990). *Regan Rep Nurs Law, 32*(1), 2.

Timby, B. K. (2009). In *Fundamental Nursing Skills and Concepts* (9th ed., p. 771). Philadelphia: Wolters Kluwer Health Lippincott, Williams & Wilkins.

Wetter, D. (2004). *The best defense is a good documentation offense*. Online course. Washington, DC: Corexecel: Linking learning to performance.

CHAPTER 47

Ethics and Ethical Decision Making in Forensic Nursing

Zug G. Standing Bear

The Challenge of Interdisciplinary Ethics

The study of ethics rests squarely within the academic discipline of philosophy. However, virtually every occupation fields a set of behavioral rules or code of ethics for its members. Many, if not most, organizations (associations, corporations, governmental agencies, etc.) structure their set of ethical rules on laws, regulations, or even those things that have caused them problems in the past. Some sets of rules are complex and occupy many pages of "dos and don'ts," such those advanced by the American Psychological Association (American Psychological Association, 2002) where others are perfunctory and involve only a few terse sentences, as the code espoused by the American Academy of Forensic Sciences (AAFS, 1986). Regardless of this wide variation of prescriptions and the dire warnings proffered within each organization, the study of ethics requires an incisive, reflective, and educated look at the entire spectrum of this demanding and complex discipline. Accordingly, there is no convenient shortcut to understand and make informed decisions based on the trying and often troubling situations with which one may be faced in forensic nursing.

One immediate challenge facing the forensic nurse is the disparity of disciplines within which the forensic nurse operates. In many, if not most, areas of nursing, the nurse remains true to nursing ethics, which is a subset of the field known as biomedical ethics. However, once traveling out into the "forensic" aspect of social activity, the nurse finds that other rules of deportment come into play, such as legal ethics, criminal justice ethics, as well as a subset of rules known as police ethics. If those variances were not enough, one may factor in the continually evolving changes within the various professions. For example, is it now ethical to permit "waterboarding" (or other forms of torture) at Guantanamo Bay in the interests of "justice" or "national security"?

In an organized and deliberate way using time tested and established approaches, this chapter provides suggestions and guidelines concerning ethical conduct for forensic nurses.

Always a Nurse!

First, an individual needs to provide a primary identification and reference point from which that person may operate in a profession. With the emergence of forensic nursing over time, several allied disciplines (law enforcement, death investigation) have attempted to co-opt nurses into a different primary professional identification. Nurses have fought this co-optation over the years, and justifiably so. An honorable and time-tested profession that need take no secondary role to any other, nursing requires long-term dedication and study, examination, and licensure. It is, therefore, illogical that any nurse entering the field of forensic science, criminal justice, or law enforcement abandons or subordinates the primary obligations and role of the nurse to any other field or profession. It is the skill that the nurse brings to these allied fields that provides the richness and quality to make a genuine difference (Bandman, 2002). Duplicating the skills and efforts of those already present in a field does not appear to be a wise alternative.

BEST PRACTICE The forensic nurse brings the respected and licensed profession of nursing to other disciplines engaged in forensic practice and should always remain true to the profession of nursing.

Ethics and Its Place in Philosophy

Ethics is one of five major fields that makes up the discipline of philosophy. From the Greek term *ethos,* meaning manners, custom, disposition, *ethics* has come to mean the analysis of concepts such as ought, should, duty, moral rules, right, wrong, obligation, and responsibility. Ethics involves the inquiry into the nature of morality or moral acts. Professions, crafts, trades, and even minimally skilled vocations, as well as individual organizations, create and enforce ethical standards, codes, and rules for what is, in their view, correct deportment.

Ethics does not, however, exist as an island onto itself. It is inextricably bound to the other four philosophical disciplines, and this condition must be recognized and accepted from the outset.

METAPHYSICS

Of all the areas of philosophy, *metaphysics* is certainly the most complex and esoteric. The prefix *meta* implies the notion of after or beyond the suffix of the term—hence, *beyond the physics*. Metaphysical questions, therefore, address such imponderables as what is after forever, the meaning of life, the nature of the universe, the infinite and the infinitesimal. Many of these metaphysical questions are answered through attention to interpretations of introspection, nature, or the revelations of others. Regardless of the methods of trying to understand these monumental concepts, the majority of humans adopt some form of metaphysical understanding, an understanding generally defined as faith or religion. These adopted concepts, usually learned from childhood, invariably define the individual's concepts of right and wrong.

LOGIC

The term *logic*, also derived from Greek *(logikos)*, pertains to intelligent speech that is ordered and systematized (*Note:* Are you getting the drift that this is all derived from the Greek? Perhaps this gives new meaning to the oft-used expression, "It's all Greek to me"). Logic involves the study of the rules of exact reasoning and of the forms of sound or valid thought. Without studying logic, one cannot make much sense of the other areas of philosophy, including ethics.

EPISTEMOLOGY

Epistemology is a term (from the Greek *epistome*, meaning knowledge) that is frequently misunderstood. It is the study of the origins, nature, presuppositions, extent, and veracity of knowledge. This discipline asks, essentially, "How do we know what we think we know?" Of all of the disciplines of philosophy, often epistemology is the most intimidating because it questions the basic roots of our rationale for asserting what it is we think we know.

AESTHETICS

Finally, *aesthetics* (Greek, *aesthetikos*, which means one who is perceptive of things through sensations, feelings, intuitions), is the study of beauty and related concepts such as the sublime, tragic, ugly, humorous, drab, and pretty. This discipline involves the analysis of values, tastes, attitudes, and standards involved in experiences and judgments made about things made by humans or found in nature. Where epistemology is potentially the most daunting of the disciplines of philosophy, aesthetics is often the most ignored or misunderstood. Yet aesthetics influences everything we do in life where, because of our socialization, we are attracted or repelled by the appearances of things around us. Moreover, "appearances" include not only the visual but all of the senses, including sound, touch, taste, and scent. Numerous studies about reactions to aesthetic issues, including *first impressions*, abound in the literature in an astonishing array of contexts (Bateman & Mawby, 2004; Fiore, 1992; Fiore & Kim, 1997; Kazumi, Takafumi, & Kenji, 2001). The forensic nurse in daily practice is inundated continually with all manners of "appearances," a fact that requires the practitioner to pay close attention to her or his preferences when interacting with those that are involved as patient, victim, suspect, witness, family, acquaintance, colleague, or in some other related capacity. How any of these individuals look, dress, speak, walk, and even smell will form an impression that may dictate how they are treated or given credibility.

KEY POINT One of the five major fields of the discipline of philosophy, ethics does not exist in a vacuum and must always be considered in relation to the other philosophical disciplines of metaphysics, logic, epistemology, and aesthetics.

Universality—Ethical Frameworks

A great challenge is often an attempt to define the seemingly simplest of terms, such as the word *good*. After all, the pursuit of ethics is nothing more than the study of what is *good*. Dictionaries are of little help, where the best definition of *good* often uses the word

to define itself or reads: "Something that conforms to the moral order of the universe." All of the terms in that definition were plausibly understandable except one *(moral)* and maybe another *(universe)*. Because we, as humans, cannot presume knowledge of "the universe," we must make do with the widest parameters we can know about, and for right now it seems to be the planet earth. The word *moral* effectively brings us back to the original word *good*, except with this definition we now include the *universe* of our planet. To do this, the subject may be explored using a series of frameworks, in this case defining the term *framework* as frames of reference that move from narrow (as in individual preferences) to broad (the planet), or vice versa.

Universality addresses the viability of using the widest possible ethical framework when considering dilemmas. This is not problematic as long as there is no conflict between narrower and broader frameworks. However, when there is conflict, then it could be argued that the broader ethical framework takes precedence. Six ethical frameworks appear next, from the broad to the most narrow.

METAETHICS

Metaethics is the study of the nature of ethics, the reasoning used to arrive and justify moral knowledge and decisions. Like metaphysics, metaethics refers to broad and often imponderable questions such as "What is moral?" This framework transcends all other levels of ethics and, accordingly, poses the most difficult questions.

GLOBAL ETHICS

Although not often included as an ethical framework, for the purposes of this discussion, this category is included to differentiate it from the next category, normative ethics, because it appears that there are ethical values that transcend those of a particular society, and that those values, by and large, would be recognized and honored by most people on the planet. In some societies and in certain times, such as in Nazi Germany, extermination of millions of people was carried out by the state, and in the normative ethic of the "master race," such killing was considered ethical from a normative point of view. A global ethic, however (i.e., the view of most of the peoples of the earth), would condemn such practices as unethical. In contemporary times, certain countries consider it to be normal to perform female genital mutilation as a rite of cultural passage. This practice is considered unethical by a majority of people, and well-respected international organizations, such as the World Health Organization and the International Council of Nurses, condemn the practice.

NORMATIVE ETHICS

In a general sense, normative ethics provide the moral philosophy that gives members of a society the rules for living a good (ethical) life by defining what is right and wrong and what should be pursued in life. As societies differ widely, so do normative ethics from society to society (hence the need for the wider *global ethics*). As a discrete entity, normative ethics may encompass a large population, such as the 300 million or so living in the United States of America or a small extended family living on the Kalahari Desert in Africa.

DESCRIPTIVE ETHICS

Descriptive ethics operationalizes normative ethics to a certain degree and seeks to describe what ethical rules are common to achieve the normative ethical ideal. Some descriptive ethical applications of normative ethical principles in the United States, as espoused by its people and government, for example, are such notions as "equal justice for all" and "freedom of speech." Although such descriptive notions may generally personify the wider normative ethical field, they may be limiting in application. For example, "freedom of speech" may exemplify a descriptive ethical principle in the United States, but wider normative ethical rules are deemed as unethical, such as yelling "fire" in a crowded theater if no fire is present, or in issuing libelous statements.

PROFESSIONAL ETHICS

Professional ethics espouses codes or standards for a particular work group or profession. These include the Hippocratic oath for physicians, bar association canons or rules, and police codes of ethics. Professional codes of ethics are more narrowly framed than descriptive ethics, which pertains to the wider society as a whole. Generally, professional ethics embrace most of the ethical principles found in wider frameworks, such as descriptive or normative ethics, but not always. In these cases of conflict, ethical dilemmas often occur, and it is left to debate (and consequences) as to what would dictate which ethical framework would prevail in the case of dispute. For example, in the legal profession it is considered ethical for an attorney to take a case on a contingency fee basis (the attorney gets a percentage of a court award as compensation), where in forensic science, it is generally considered unethical for an expert to accept this form of compensation.

APPLIED ETHICS

This involves the study of codes or standards of behavior for a particular organization. This narrow framework attempts to derive an ethical code from all of the preceding categories and seeks to fashion an acceptable ethical code for an organization. Often such efforts simply mimic applicable laws and regulations or endeavor to "cover bases" where an organization has had difficulties in the past.

KEY POINT In the event of conflicts between the ethical values of different agencies, which are common in interdisciplinary activities, turning to a broader ethical framework may provide a solution.

Survival

When considering ethical decision making, the notion of survival is, perhaps, the most difficult to understand and describe. This notion acknowledges that survival is a basic human (and other animal) need. Accordingly, it is advanced that a model for ethical human behavior must take this into consideration, even though it may cause us to wrestle with difficult problems. We may harken back to early British law, where the crew of a sunken ship, now on life rafts, contemplated their survival based on the killing of their weakest member (or one of their members by drawing straws) so the others may dine upon the crewmember's flesh and live. In the final judicial decision, cannibalism was not allowed, no matter how desperate the situation. Few of us are faced with genuine life-or-death situations, but many

must confront lesser survival questions that ring with practical ethical conflicts. Let us go from the most obvious to the more subtle, so as to get a feel for the range of issues in this contentious arena.

The most obvious cases of *survival* cover those recently investigated situations of the killing of many people by Serbian soldiers. It is similar, in some ways, to the Nazi excuses at the Nuremberg trials of "just following orders." One soldier, who had been ordered to shoot dozens of unarmed civilians, supposedly balked at doing so. He reported that he was informed by his commanding officer, "Well, if you feel so sorry for these people, you can join them." The soldier carried out the orders, and killed the civilians. Later, however, he reported his actions and those of his superiors. Should the outcome of his trial for murder be significantly different from that of Nazi General Field Marshal Wilhelm Keitel, ordered to hang at Nuremberg, who also alleged he was "just following orders?"

It may be that the solution to this sort of complex ethical dilemma rests with an incisive investigation of the motives and actions of the actor. Each case must be investigated on its own merits. What, for example, did the Serb soldier do once the atrocities were accomplished? Did he, for example, desert his unit and seek refuge or asylum? At the very least, did he do *something* that attempted to "right" this wrong? If this man is then brought before an international court and tried for genocidal crimes, what defense has he? It seems to look a lot better for the man if he, after killing the victims, fled his military unit, escaped across an international border, and agreed to testify to the atrocities. It looks far bleaker if this soldier is picked out of a lineup of Serbian troops who committed the executions, identified by a chance survivor. His objections to the killings now ring hollow as he tries to save his own neck.

The ordinary citizen seldom has to confront such life-or-death matters. But the concept embracing the dilemma of the Serbian soldier may be used in less serious ethical conflicts. Interestingly enough, what may be a minor matter for a forensic scientist (testifying in court) may, indeed, be a life-or-death matter for a criminal defendant. Many in the criminal justice field have witnessed police investigators and commanders, as well as prosecutors hell-bent to convict a defendant, regardless of evidence to the contrary. In a case in which the author was personally involved, a medical examiner casually tossed out an incredibly outrageous "finding" supposedly (the author could not determine a malicious motive) to either accommodate police or get them off his back. This "finding" that a high-powered rifle had been fired from a distance of 3 to 5 feet from the face of the decedent, was enough evidence to have the decedent's husband jailed in pretrial confinement for a year on a charge of murder. He was later acquitted. This semiliterate indigent man was not represented by any legal dream team but rather by a young court-appointed attorney recently out of law school. This young attorney asked for advice from a former forensic science professor. His subsequent investigation literally blew apart the prosecution's case *and* caused the state medical examiner to agree on the stand with the defense expert witnesses. Throughout this drama, the prosecution had complete discovery of the correspondence from the forensic scientists participating on the part of the defense. Perhaps it is part of the survival instinct of the prosecutor that she or he "never give up," even in the face of evidence. This attitude is unconscionable and not ethically supportable, even in the light of the *survival* business of keeping one's job as a prosecutor.

The following case study allows a look at a situation that is more subtle and closer to the practice arena of a forensic nurse.

Case Study **47-1**

You are a sexual assault nurse examiner under contract with a public hospital to be on call to conduct sexual assault examinations, and you are paid by the case. You learn that a person reporting she had been raped had been treated at the hospital emergency department and released, but that you had not been notified to examine the complainant. Upon your inquiry about the non-notification, you are informed that the emergency department director and the police investigator agreed not to call you in on the case because the person reporting the incident was a prostitute, continuously intoxicated on drugs, reported rape nearly every week, and was especially prone to report rape when one of her johns failed to pay her what she demanded for sexual services. What would be your action, if any, in this matter?

This case is more complex than it initially appears. Let's explore some of the alternatives for the contract nurse examiner. First, the matter could be dropped, as you agree with the emergency department director and the police investigator that this "revolving door" case does not require the continuous services of a specialist in sexual assault investigation. Second, you could drop the matter because your notification in instances of this type is a management decision of the hospital administration that engages your services. Third, you could insist on notification of *all* sexual assault cases because it is called for in the contract. However, this may not bode well for your continued employment as a contractor with this hospital. Fourth, you could insist on being paid for *all* reported sexual assault cases, whether or not you are notified, because the agreement stipulates you will be on call for services and the availability factor interferes with your personal life and, therefore, part of the compensation must take into account this inconvenience. Fifth, you could insist on being notified in *all* reported sexual assault cases, as the occupation or personal problems of the victim should not determine the level of care.

Ethically, which answer seems most correct? Certain populations are more at risk for crime victimization and false allegations. Should *all* reports be investigated equally? The second and third choices are framed solely in monetary/compensation terms. Should these considerations be driving ethical decisions? Should the standard of healthcare (and police services as well as medical emergency services) reach all citizens, regardless of their station?

KEY POINT *Survival* is a multifaceted and multilevel challenge that should be studied in detail when faced with making decisions that have ethical implications.

When the ramifications of the preceding case were discussed with a philosopher, he replied, "This is an easy case for you since there is at least some implied duty of caring for patients inherent to the profession of nursing. What about other fields such as law enforcement, psychiatry, or toxicology?" His question posed an interesting dimension, especially in light of the fact that this author had authored an article on nurses engaged in the field of death investigation warning against the dangers of being co-opted into the police subculture (Standing Bear, 1995). Although the police have a professed public service role, especially more recently with the movement toward the concept of community policing,

the obligation toward problematic members of the population remains a point of contention. Even in the well-intentioned field of victim advocacy, victim-witness assistance programs are oriented toward a narrowly defined group of victims, such as female victims of sexual assault, paying sparse attention to the bulk of crime victims—young males of color.

When raising these same questions to a group of emergency department nurses, several veteran nurses complained that these "revolving door" cases put a strain on the department's resources and consisted of people that were "exploiting the system." But are these cases not the very ones that truly test the mettle of scientific integrity coupled with the lofty ideals of a civilized society? Does the forensic nurse not have an obligation to speak out, using the knowledge provided by the multitude of disciplines that make up a complete education bringing together nursing, justice, and law? If so, can or should that same individual become suddenly unemployed because of their position? The question of *survival* is a difficult one and has many levels of importance. However, in any discussion of ethics, it is a question that must be considered.

Criminologists know that the poor generally receive the worst treatment in the criminal justice system. So how do we assure that all citizens achieve equal justice under law? A good start is to adopt a standard of care that treats all individuals as equals, regardless of their circumstances. Several professional organizations, such as the American Chemical Society, take serious account of their obligations to society in their professional codes. The original code of ethics of the International Association of Forensic Nurses (IAFN, 2004) (which served the organization from 1994 until November, 2008) made specific note of disenfranchised populations. However, a new "vision" of ethics was approved by IAFN in November 2008 (IAFN, 2008). See box 47-1.

Case Study **47-2**

A forensic nurse delivered an impressive scientific presentation at an international meeting of a professional organization. However, several members of the audience recognized that the nurse had used the core content and case illustrations of a colleague without any attribution or acknowledgment. (The content and case studies also had been published in a journal, as well as presented at a previous scientific meeting of another organization.) Assuming that the individual belonged to both the International Association of Forensic Nurses and the American Academy of Forensic Sciences, compare and contrast how these organizations might respond to a formal complaint involving this incident of ethical misconduct. (See Boxes 47-1 and 47-2).

Theoretical Considerations

No discussion of ethics would be complete without recognition of the various ideas and explanations that have driven ethical thought for hundreds of years. We call these "theories" because they purport to provide answers to ethical questions. In mainstream ethical thought as it pertains to forensic nursing, seven prescriptive theories are prominent. Briefly stated, they are as follows:

1. *Religious ethics.* Ethical, moral, or good behavior as dictated by a religious code.
2. *Ethical formalism.* The ethical notion that defines good or moral behavior in terms of duty, intent, and appeal to higher reason. The focus is on intent and action (the deontological or *means* approach) rather than the results (the teleological or *ends* approach).

Box 47-1 International Association of Forensic Nurses Vision of Ethical Practice, 2008-Present

INTRODUCTION

The International Association of Forensic Nurses expects its members to aspire to the highest standards of ethical nursing practice. This vision of ethics is a framework for approaching professional decisions and stimulating ethical dialogue based on the ideals of our organization.

Forensic nurses acknowledge the importance of membership in a global society. This includes providing forensic nursing care in a manner that respects the uniqueness of the patient or client. Forensic nurses collaborate with nurses, healthcare providers, and other professionals throughout the world to promote ethically informed and culturally competent practices.

When faced with ethical choices, forensic nurses should use recognized ethical frameworks for decision making. The guiding principles of ethical decision making are autonomy, justice, beneficence and non-malfeasance. Forensic nurses should consult and collaborate with appropriate ethical resources.

SCOPE

Fidelity to Patients and Clients

Forensic nurses serve patients and clients faithfully and incorruptibly. Forensic nurses respect confidentiality and advise patients and clients about the limits of confidentiality as determined by their practice setting.

Responsibility to the Public

Forensic nurses have a professional responsibility to serve the public welfare. Forensic nurses should be actively concerned with the health and welfare of the global community. Forensic nurses should recognize their role in preventing violence that includes understanding the societal factors, such as oppression that promote violence. Forensic nurses acknowledge the value and dignity of all human beings and strive to create a world where violence is not accepted.

Obligation to Science

Forensic nurses should seek to advance nursing and forensic science, understand the limits of their knowledge, and respect the truth. Forensic nurses should ensure that their research and scientific contributions are thorough, accurate and unbiased in design and presentation. Forensic nurses should incorporate evidence based knowledge in practice decisions.

Conflicts of interest should be disclosed. Scientific misconduct, such as fabrication, falsification, slander, libel, and plagiarism are incompatible with this Vision of Ethical Practice. Public comments regarding scientific matters should be made with care and precision, devoid of unsubstantiated claims, exaggeration, and/or premature conclusions.

Dedication to Colleagues

Forensic nurses perform work honestly and competently, fulfill obligations, and safeguard proprietary information. Forensic nurses should regard the tutelage of students as a trust conferred by society for the promotion of the student's learning and professional development. Forensic nurses should treat colleagues with respect, share ideas honestly, and give credit for their contributions.

The Vision of Ethical Practice was revised by the IAFN Ethics Committee, reviewed by members, and approved by IAFN Board in November of 2008.

Box 47-2 American Academy of Forensic Sciences

(ARTICLE II.)   CODE OF ETHICS AND CONDUCT

SECTION 1 - THE CODE: As a means to promote the highest quality of professional and personal conduct of its members and affiliates, the following constitutes the Code of Ethics and Conduct which is endorsed by all members and affiliates of the American Academy of Forensic Sciences:

a. Every member and affiliate of the Academy shall refrain from exercising professional or personal conduct adverse to the best interests and objectives of the Academy. The objectives stated in the Preamble to these bylaws include: promoting education for and research in the forensic sciences, encouraging the study, improving the practice, elevating the standards and advancing the cause of the forensic sciences.

b. No member or affiliate of the Academy shall materially misrepresent his or her education, training, experience, area of expertise, or membership status within the Academy.

c. No member or affiliate of the Academy shall materially misrepresent data or scientific principles upon which his or her conclusion or professional opinion is based.

d. No member or affiliate of the Academy shall issue public statements that appear to represent the position of the Academy without specific authority first obtained from the Board of Directors.

SECTION 2 - MEMBER AND AFFILIATE LIABILITY: Any member or affiliate of the Academy who has violated any of the provisions of the Code of Ethics (Article II, Section 1) may be liable to censure, suspension or expulsion by action of the Board of Directors, as provided in Section 5h below.

SECTION 3 - INVESTIGATIVE BODY: There shall be constituted a standing Ethics Committee (see Article V for composition), the primary function of which shall be:

a. To order and/or conduct investigations and, as necessary, to serve as a hearing body concerning conduct of individual members or affiliates which may constitute a violation of the provisions of Article II, Section 1.

b. To act as an advisory body, rendering opinions on contemplated actions by individual members or affiliates in terms of the provisions of Article II, Section 1.

SECTION 4 - INVESTIGATION INITIATING ACTION: The following are the principal forms by which the Ethics Committee may initiate investigative action:

a. A member or affiliate of the Academy may submit a written complaint alleging violation(s) of Article II, Section 1 by a member or affiliate to the Academy Office (see Article II, Section 5, Rules and Procedures, below) or to the Chair of the Ethics Committee. Such a complaint should be made in a timely manner.

b. The Ethics Committee may institute an inquiry based on any evidence that may come to its attention from any source which in its opinion indicates the need for further query or action under the provisions of these bylaws.

SECTION 5 - RULES AND PROCEDURES: The following procedures shall apply to any allegation of unethical conduct against a member or affiliate of the Academy:

a. Allegations of unethical conduct against a member or affiliate received by the Academy shall be transmitted promptly to the Chair of the Ethics Committee.

b. The Ethics Committee shall determine whether the alleged unethical conduct falls within its jurisdiction and whether there is probable cause to believe that the allegation is well founded.

c. If the Ethics Committee, in its preliminary determination, finds that it does not have jurisdiction or that there is a lack of probable cause to believe that the allegation is well founded, it shall close the case. It shall issue a report of such determination to the Board of Directors, setting forth the basic facts but omitting the names of the parties, and stating the reasons for its decision to close the case. Notice of the allegation, including the source, and its disposition, shall be given to the accused. Notice of the disposition shall also be given to the complainant(s).

d. If the Ethics Committee finds that it has jurisdiction and that there is probable cause to believe that the allegation is well founded, it shall give notice of the filing of the allegation and its sources to the accused. In accordance with Rules and Procedures formulated by the Ethics Committee and approved by the Board of Directors, the Committee shall assemble such information from both the accused and the complainant(s) which shall permit it to determine whether the allegation requires further action.

Box 47-2 American Academy of Forensic Sciences—cont'd

e. The Ethics Committee may appoint an Academy Fellow or Fellows to investigate the allegation and/or to present the evidence to the Committee.

f. If, based on the results of an investigation, the Ethics Committee decides to dismiss the allegation without a formal hearing, it may do so. It shall notify the accused and the complainant(s) of its decision and shall issue a report to the Board of Directors setting forth the basic facts and stating the reason(s) for its decision, but omitting the names of the accused and complainant(s).

g. If the Ethics Committee decides to formally hear the case, it shall give the accused a reasonable opportunity to attend and be heard. The complainant(s) shall also be given a reasonable opportunity to be heard. Following the hearing, the Committee shall notify the accused and the complainant(s) of its decision. The Ethics Committee shall also submit a report on its decision to the Board of Directors. If the Committee finds unethical conduct, the report shall include the reasons for its decision, and any recommendations for further action by the Board. The accused may also submit to the Board of Directors a written statement regarding what sanctions, if any, should be imposed.

h. If the Ethics Committee's decision is that unethical conduct on the part of the accused member or affiliate has occurred, the Board of Directors shall review the report, and ratify or overturn the decision, or remand the case to the Committee for further action. If the Board of Directors ratifies the Committee's decision, it shall also review any written submission provided by the member or affiliate found to be in violation of the Code. The member or affiliate may then, upon a vote of three-fourths of the members of the Board present and voting, be censured, suspended or expelled. The nature and conditions of any sanction must be provided to the member or affiliate. A suspended member or affiliate may only be reinstated by the procedure set forth in Article II, Section 6.

i. A member or affiliate who has been found in violation of the Code of Ethics has the right to appeal the actions of the Board of Directors to the membership of the Academy. To initiate an appeal, the member or affiliate must file a brief written notice of the appeal, together with a written statement, with the Academy Secretary not less than one hundred twenty days prior to the next Annual Meeting of the Academy.

j. The Board of Directors shall then prepare a written statement of the reasons for its actions and file the same with the Academy Secretary not less than forty days prior to the next annual meeting.

k. Within twenty days thereafter, the Academy Secretary shall mail to each voting member of the Academy a copy of the appellant's notice of appeal and supporting statement, and a copy of the Board of Directors' statement.

l. A vote of three-fourths of the members present and voting at the Academy's annual business meeting shall be required to overrule the action of the Board of Directors in regard to censure, suspension or expulsion of a member or affiliate.

m. No member of the Board of Directors who is the subject of an Ethics Committee investigation, or who has any other conflict of interest, shall participate in any matter before the Board concerning ethics.

n. The Ethics Committee shall formulate internal Rules and Procedures designed to facilitate the expeditious, fair, discreet, and impartial handling of all matters it considers. The Rules and Procedures shall be subject to the approval of the Board of Directors.

SECTION 6 - SUSPENSION OF MEMBERS AND AFFILIATES: Members or affiliates who have been suspended may apply to the Board of Directors for reinstatement once the period of suspension is completed. A suspended member or affiliate shall not be required to pay dues during the period of suspension. If reinstated, the required dues payment shall be the annual dues less the pro-rated amount for the period of suspension.

Reprinted with permission of the American Academy of Forensic Sciences, Colorado Springs, CO.

3. *Utilitarianism.* The ethical theory that defines ethical behavior as those acts that assure the greatest possible good (benefits or pleasure) for the greatest number of individuals.

4. *Egoism.* The notion that what is good for one's survival and personal happiness is moral.

5. *Ethical relativism.* The contention that what is good or right is cultural and individual and that there are no universal laws.

6. *Caring.* The definition of goodness and moral behavior as defined by the level of kindness and caring toward others (which also may include animals, plants, and the environment).

7. *Connectedness.* The notion that ethical behavior must take into the account the effect that the behavior will have on others (other people, other societies, even other planets or universes).

It seems that the seven contemporary theoretical arguments fall into three categories for the modern caregiver and scientist: acceptable arguments, contentions, and accommodations. Experience may show that there are two acceptable arguments (utilitarianism and ethical formalism), three contentions (religious ethics, egoism, and relativism), and two accommodations (caring and connectedness).

The major arguments made for utilitarianism versus ethical formalism (ends versus means) are controversial, and rightfully so, as frequently the arguments have singular, yet opposing merits. Let us say, for example, that the police search every automobile leaving a parking garage where a child has been kidnapped. Most would argue that the ethical ends of rescuing the kidnapped child outweighs the ethical means of protecting a person's right to privacy, even though 300 innocent people were forced to submit to the vehicle search.

On the other hand, it has long been a tradition in the United States to afford a great deal of due process to most accused offenders. The rationale has been to advocate the release of ten guilty persons than to imprison one that is innocent. The controversies fill volumes, so let it suffice here to simply raise the issue.

The contentious arguments are those dealing with theories based on religion, egoism, or relativism. Egoism may be rejected most easily because of its focus on hedonistic self-centeredness. Religious ethics vary widely in terms of their prescriptive directives. One religious code (Christian Bible), for example, requires that homosexuals be executed, while another (Native American–Lakota) identifies homosexuals as persons with exceptional insight and highly valued as counselors. Finally, ethical relativism has been discussed and wrestled with at great length and may be best considered by the newly introduced ethical framework of "global ethics."

The two accommodating ethical theories, caring and connectedness, may blend with all other theories because they do not threaten other theories. Indeed, most other theories embrace various notions of caring and connectedness within their own prescriptions. For example, the connectedness notion in Eastern thought embraces the Golden Rule (Do unto others as you would have them do unto you) and appeared in the Buddhist Tripitaka more than 4000 years ago. This notion is repeated in far more modern religious texts, such as the Christian Bible. Caring ethics, although a focal point of feminist perspectives and a foundation of the profession of nursing, finds itself as an integral part of other ethical theories (Tschudin, 2003).

Taking all of these things into consideration, a model for ethical decision making must have a *heart*, or a *soul*–the center of its existence. Adjusting for the frameworks and considering the treacherous arena of self-preservation are necessary measures, but they are merely preparation for the essence of an ethical decision-making model. As noted earlier, ethical theories do not provide concise answers and often, when considered side by side, may offer more questions than answers. Perhaps the notion of an ethical decision-making model needs to be simplified down to a very basic view, possibly distilled to simply two dimensions: wisdom and kindness. The concept is not original and is based on the writings of two well-known philosophers, Bertrand Russell and the Dalai Lama.

Wisdom

Wisdom is required to make good decisions. Human beings must realize that they will never be completely wise, or knowing, in any and all given situations. However, it is an ethical duty to become as wise as possible, especially in an individual's area of specialty and responsibility, and to act accordingly. This notion is well fitted to Neil Trautman's set of ethical decision-making questions in criminal justice, where a person applying wisdom to an ethical decision therefore discounts actions based on anger, greed, or lust (the author adds prejudice to this list) (Trautman, 1988). A forensic pathologist or toxicologist who does not stay current in the research literature in her or his field is short-changing the responsibility to be wise and therefore is committing an ethical breach. A criminologist who manipulates crime statistics to demonstrate what some agency wants to promote in the interests of obtaining a research grant, especially when there are conflicting data, is doing so out of prejudice and greed rather than wisdom and is therefore behaving unethically. The forensic scientist who "extends" his or her knowledge on the witness stand so as to make a stronger case for the side that arranged for the testimony is unwise in that unsupportable claims are being made.

Several years ago, this author had the occasion to observe the testimony of a medical examiner in a murder trial. A major point of contention in the case was whether a bruise found on the body submerged in water had occurred before or after death. The medical examiner who performed the autopsy and was engaged by the prosecution contended that the bruise was antemortem in origin and he had determined this as a result of his experience. (*Note:* The bruise was *not* examined microscopically.) He could not, however, cite any sources or research for his conclusion, other than to repeatedly say he knew so because of *experience*. The defense brought in another medical examiner (from a different jurisdiction) who testified that the bruise was a postmortem artifact because the bruise did not appear in a crime scene photograph. However, the single crime scene photograph of the area of the body where the bruise occurred was overexposed, and the body had been found submerged in water. Both medical examiners had extended their knowledge unwisely and therefore committed unethical acts.

One of the most vexing parts of the consideration of wisdom as an essential ingredient for ethical behavior is the notion of truth. As an academic pursuit (the word *veritas* appears as the sole word on the shield of one of this country's most prestigious universities), truth equates perfectly with wisdom. In the forensic sciences, truth and wisdom *should* be in agreement. Problems occur, however, in the wider realm of criminal justice, especially in the investigative phases of criminal cases. Whereas lying on the witness stand (perjury) by police is generally condemned, deception when conducting investigations is an accepted part of skillful police work and is, indeed, taught in police investigative courses. Many defend this practice by arguing that to seek justice, incapacitate the guilty, and

vindicate the victim is a noble and ethical pursuit and therefore it is wise to lie to a suspect from time to time to elicit a confession or otherwise further an investigation. Hugo Grotius (Dutch philosopher of the early 1600s) bolsters this argument by asserting that truthfulness is not owed to thieves. The complex interaction between truth and wisdom cannot be adequately explored in this small space, but it merits considerable further attention. Sissela Bok has authored three excellent books on the nature of lying, deception, and secrets, which have been published in paperback by Vintage Books (Bok, 1989a, 1989b, 1999).

Kindness

Kindness, as an admirable trait of interaction between a human and her or his environment, has been espoused by philosophical leaders throughout the world and down through history. It is seen as an essential part of integrity and ethical behavior. In modern medical and nursing practice, the term *beneficence* is often used, meaning "the doing of good, active goodness, or kindness, charity." However, although essential, kindness must be combined with the preceding actions in order to be reasonable and logical. For example, to release a serial killer such as Ted Bundy may be viewed as *kind* by the killer himself, but it would be considered completely unwise as well as unkind to the society as a whole. If a police officer is being physically attacked, wisdom would dictate that the officer should use whatever self-defense skills at her or his disposal to neutralize the attack, which can also be seen as an act of kindness toward a victim being defended as well as the officer's family. However, once the attacker is neutralized, it would be considered ethical to show kindness (nonviolence) toward the attacker (as the officer is transporting the attacker to the station for booking). Having many years of experience in criminal investigation, this author has always treated suspects with respect and kindness. A side benefit has been that even though responsible for sending some offenders away to prison for a very long time, there was no worry about retaliation (the film *Cape Fear* illustrates this point well).

BEST PRACTICE After all other considerations are made from philosophical, universal, survival, and theoretical points of view, the ethical decision comes down to the application of wisdom and kindness.

Whistle-Blowing

The term *"whistle-blowing"* has come to mean a situation where a member of an organization reports improprieties concerning other organizational members. The term originated with early London police officers ("Bobbies"), who would blow their whistles upon noticing the commission of a crime so as to alert other police officers and the public. A key element in the nature of whistle-blowing is that the whistle-blower usually faces reprisal. For the forensic nurse, because of the interdisciplinary and interorganizational nature of forensic nursing work, that reprisal may come from various organizations with which the forensic nurse works. Even though the forensic nurse may not be directly employed by a particular agency, political and operational pressure may be brought to bear by allied agencies if the whistle-blowing report involves misfeasance, nonfeasance, or malfeasance by the personnel of that agency. Adding to the complexities of this issue is the fact that the field of forensic sciences in general has been the subject of harsh scrutiny in recent times culminating with the publication of the National Academy of Sciences report (2009).

Whistle-blowing was addressed in the nursing ethics work by Perrin and McGhee (2001) where the authors urged readers to seriously consider the potential repercussions of whistle-blowing by asking themselves the following questions:

1. Do I have a legitimate concern? If uncorrected, will it result in grave danger to healthcare providers, patients, or the community?
2. Why am I involved in this situation? Do I need to be?
3. Have I reported my concerns along appropriate channels?
4. Have I exhausted my avenues for redress within the institution?
5. What do I envision will be the result of my action? Is it a worthwhile goal?
6. Am I likely to accomplish my purpose?
7. What are my motivations for going to outside authority?
8. Are there any reasons someone may distrust the purity of my motives?
9. What are the likely personal consequences?

These questions provide a logical set of inquiries for self-examination of the necessity for whistle-blowing, although a negative answer to any of the questions may still provide just cause to move forward with the whistle-blowing activity. Because of the interdisciplinary nature of forensic nursing, however, question 2 takes on special meaning, where it may be that the activities of others may be considered "none of your business." Consider the following case.

Case Study 47-3

You are a nurse death investigator employed by a district medical examiner. In a case where a man was found dead of an apparent gunshot wound to the head in his home, you come across a report of gunshot residue extraction from the hands of a suspect prepared by a police investigator. Several items in the report are not only incomplete but also led you to believe that the samples were improperly gathered and may lead to a false conclusion in laboratory analysis. You telephone the police investigator who took the samples and you are told, "Look I've been doing this for years and this is the way it's done. So why don't you just butt out and mind your own business?" Your concern is that, because the samples were collected in this way, the laboratory may report a false positive reading.

Summary

The four major points of this chapter (universality, survival, wisdom, and kindness) are reasonable and objective strategies by which to analyze and interpret acts as ethical or unethical. They are always used in consort with one another, and their principles can be learned. These points are separate and apart from *ethical theories*, which may or may not hold up under this model. Several

theories, such as religious ethics and egoism, for example, are only coincidentally accommodated by this model. Situational ethics is partly accommodated by this process but generally fails because of a lack of the structured objectivity and logic that the model provides. The most serious ethical theories (which are often in conflict with one another), ethical formalism (Kantian ethics, deontological ethics, etc.) and utilitarianism (the ethics of Bentham, teleological ethics, etc.), are accommodated or negated on a case-by-case basis in this model. Finally, ethical theories newly entertained in the West, such as caring ethics (feminist ethics, nursing theory, etc.) and the ethics of connectedness (Buddhist philosophy, etc.), are most easily accommodated, in large part because these theories do not require a repudiation of other theories to be considered, and they also accommodate well the notion concerning kindness.

References

American Academy of Forensic Sciences. *Code of ethics and conduct, Article II, Bylaws*, February 12, 1986, as amended. Colorado Springs, Colorado.

American Psychological Association. (2002). *Ethical principles of psychologists and code of conduct* (effective June 1, 2003). Washington, DC.

Bandman, E., & Bandman, M. (2002). *Nursing ethics through the life span.* (4th ed.). Upper Saddle River, NJ: Pearson.

Bateman, I. J., & Mawby, J. (2004). First impressions count: Interviewer appearance and information effects in stated preference studies, *Ecological Economics*, 49(1), 47–55. Elsevier Science, B. V. Shannon, Ireland.

Bok, S. (1989a). *Secrets: On the ethics of concealment and revelation.* New York: Knopf Doubleday Publishing Group.

Bok, S. (1989b). *Strategy for peace: Human values and the threat of war.* New York: Knopf Doubleday Publishing Group.

Bok, S. (1999). *Lying: Moral choices in public and private life.* New York: Knopf Publishing Group.

Fiore, A. (1992). Effect of composition of olfactory cues on impressions of personality. *Social Behavior and Personality: An International Journal*, 20(3), 149–161.

Fiore, A., & Kim, S. (1997). Olfactory cues of appearance affecting impressions of professional image of women. *Journal of Career Development*, 23(4), 247–263.

International Association of Forensic Nurses. (2004). *Forensic Nurses Code of Ethics.* Arnold, MD.

International Association of Forensic Nurses. (2008). *Forensic Nurses Vision of Ethical Practice.* Arnold, MD.

Kazumi, K., Takafumi, M., & Kenji, O. (2001). An analytical study on impressions and determinants of appearance of the industrialized houses. *Bulletin of Nagoya Institute of Technology*, 52, 55–63.

National Academy of Sciences. (2009). *Strengthening Forensic Science in the United States: A path forward.* Washington, DC: The National Academies Press.

Perrin, K. O., & McGhee, J. (2001). *Ethics and conflict (Nursing Concept Series).* Thorofare, NJ: Slack Incorporated.

Standing Bear, Z. G. (1995). Forensic nursing and death investigation: Will the vision be co-opted? *Journal of Psychosocial Nursing and Mental Health Services*, SLACK, Inc., 33(9), 59–64.

Trautman, Neal. (1988). *Law Enforcement - The making of a profession: A comprehensive guide for the police to achieve and sustain professionalism.* Springfield, MO: Charles C Thomas, Publisher.

Tschudin, V. (2003). *Ethics in nursing: The caring relationship* (3rd ed.). New York: Butterworth Heinemann.

Gordon D. MacFarlane

Research is an essential component of evidence-based practice. Current Good Clinical Practice Guidelines (International Conference on Harmonisation [ICH], 1996) are designed to protect research subjects, assure the quality of the collected data, and provide transparency for the generation, gathering, processing, and evaluation of research data.

Current Ethical Framework

Contemporary protections for clinical subjects are derived from both the Nuremberg trials following World War II and reactions to various research abuses. Human experimentation by physicians of the Third Reich on prisoners included studies of hypothermia, infectious diseases such as malaria and spotted fever, and drug reactions. The Tuskegee Syphilis Study, which ran from 1932 to 1972, examined the natural history and progression of syphilis in a population of educationally and economically disadvantaged African-American men (Jones, 1993). Subjects who contracted syphilis were not provided treatment for the disease, even after the introduction of penicillin in the general population, a known effective therapy for syphilis. The Willowbrook School hepatitis study, which ran from 1966 to 1969, infected institutionalized mentally disabled children with hepatitis to study treatment regimens (Rothman and Rothman, 2005). In 1963, elderly subjects at Jewish Chronic Disease Hospital in New York were injected with live cancer cells without their consent (Katz, 1972). The subjects were not informed of the content of the injections.

Each of these studies involved vulnerable populations that were unable to protect themselves from either intentional or inadvertent harm. The Nuremberg Code (U.S. Government Printing Office, 1949), issued in 1949, the Declaration of Helsinki (World Medical Association, 2000), originally issued in 1964, and the Belmont Report (National Commission for the Protection of Human Subjects, 1983), issued in 1979, form the current ethical framework for human subjects research.

THE NUREMBERG CODE

As the Nuremberg trials progressed, it became clear that no accepted guidelines for human experimentation existed to define what was or was not legal or ethical. The resulting Nuremberg Code (U.S. Government Printing Office, 1949) described 10 directives for human experimentation. Voluntary consent by the subject of the experimentation was considered essential. Voluntary consent means the subject (or legal representative) not only has the legal capacity to consent, but also has sufficient information upon which to make an informed choice. The design of the study should provide results for the good of society that cannot be obtained by other means. The study design should incorporate the previous knowledge of the disease or research question at hand, such that the clinical study is justified by the state of the knowledge. The experiments should be designed and conducted to avoid unnecessary suffering or injury to the subject. Death or

disabling injury as an expected outcome should not be allowed. The degree of risk should be balanced by the benefit to society from the information gained. Subjects should be protected from anticipatable injury, disability, or death. The experiments should only be conducted by qualified individuals. The subject must have the option of voluntary withdrawal from the study at any time or for any or no reason. Finally, researchers must be prepared to terminate the study if they have cause to believe that continuation of the study is likely to result in injury, disability, or death to the subjects.

DECLARATION OF HELSINKI

The Declaration of Helsinki was issued in 1964 by the World Medical Association and has undergone seven revisions (World Medical Association, 2000). It expanded on the Nuremberg Code, particularly in regard to vulnerable populations (children, mentally disabled, temporarily incapacitated). It included two additional concepts as well.

The first concept was that the interests and protection of the individual subject was to always take precedence over the interest of society. The World Medical Association has focused heavily on the role of the physician to safeguard the health of the subject in any medical research. The second concept was that every subject was to receive the best known therapy during the course of the study. This concept is a restatement of the concept of equipoise. Equipoise requires that the investigator honestly not know if the experimental therapy or intervention is better than the control therapy or intervention. Once a therapy or intervention has been demonstrated to be effective for a given disease condition, the use of an inactive or nontherapeutic control or placebo is no longer ethical. Because of the comparison with an active control rather than a placebo, the resulting effect sizes, or difference in outcome measure between the experimental and control groups, may be much smaller.

THE BELMONT REPORT

The National Commission for the Protection of Human Subjects of Biomedical and Behavioral Research was formed as a result of the National Research Act in 1974. This commission put forth the Belmont Report in 1979 (National Commission for the Protection of Human Subjects, 1983). The Belmont Report outlined three guiding ethical principles: the respect for persons, beneficence, and justice.

The respect for a person's ethics incorporates several aspects we see in current regulations. This principle requires not only the recognition of individuals as autonomous, but also that those with diminished autonomy are entitled to protection. Respect for the individual's autonomy is reflected in informed consent requirements. An individual cannot make an autonomous decision in the absence of information regarding the risks and benefits of that decision. Critical illness, mental disability, or circumstances that severely restrict liberty may limit an individual's autonomy and thus entitles the individual to specific protections. Applied to prisoners, this principle would require that prisoners be given the opportunity to volunteer to participate in research, while being protected from coercion or undue influence to participate in research in which they would not otherwise volunteer to participate.

The second principle is beneficence. This is expressed both as do no harm and maximize possible benefits and minimize possible harms. This principle can be viewed both in terms of the individual and society. Research into treatment methods for childhood diseases, for example, may provide societal benefits that justify the research, even though the individual subjects may not benefit directly. With vulnerable subjects, research that presents greater than minimal risk but does not present immediate and direct benefit to the subject involved requires continuous oversight.

The third principle is justice. This principle applies to who assumes the risks and who accrues the benefits. The selection of research subjects needs to be based on the research question rather than the ease of availability, compromised ability, or manipulability of the subject. As an example, the Tuskegee Syphilis Study risks were assumed by a disadvantaged minority, whereas the benefits applied to the much wider society.

These principles require that research that would benefit groups that we have typically considered vulnerable should include those groups as study subjects while ensuring adequate protection for their participation. Before the 1970s, vulnerable groups, if they were protected, were generally protected by exclusion from the study (Schwenzer, 2008). This has led to the situation whereby a large proportion of drugs developed for use in children have not been studied in children (Choonara, 2000; Impicciatore & Choonara, 1999; Pandolfini & Bonati, 2005). With the recognition that vulnerable groups were underrepresented in clinical research in general, additional protections were instituted along with an effort to include these groups. In the United Sates, clinical trials can be conducted under the auspices of 16 governmental agencies, among them the Department of Agriculture, Department of Defense, and the Department of Health and Human Services, each of which had its own set of rules protecting human subjects. The core requirements from these various agencies were consolidated into the Common Rule (45 CFR Part 46) in 1991. The Department of Health and Human Services added guidelines to deal with vulnerable subjects (pregnant women, fetuses, children, and prisoners), which were not in the Common Rule. These additional guidelines deal primarily with the selection, informed consent, and special considerations for these populations. The concept of who represents a vulnerable subject continues to evolve and now generally includes the groups described in Box 48-1.

Box 48-1 Vulnerable Subjects in Clinical Research

Children
Prisoners
Pregnant women and/or fetuses
Mentally disabled or cognitively impaired
Educationally disadvantaged
Economically disadvantaged
Wards of the state
Students
Employees
Elderly

Institutional Review Board Oversight

The National Research Act of 1974 also established the initial framework for the approval and oversight of research with human subjects by establishing the modern institutional review board (IRB) system in place today. Under federal regulations, with only a limited set of exclusions, all research with human subjects must be reviewed and approved by an IRB.

COMPOSITION

The composition of the IRB is mandated by federal policy and must have at least five members. The IRB must have a representative whose credentials are nonscientific as well as a lay member who is not otherwise affiliated with the institution. The IRB must also have a clinically licensed practitioner. The IRB must reflect a diversity of professions and backgrounds and is expected to reflect the cultural diversity relevant to the institution. In practice, most IRBs will require more than five members to accomplish their mandated diversity. Additional representation is required when reviewing studies involving specific vulnerable groups (Penslar & Porter, 1993). For example, for studies involving prisoners, the IRB must have a prisoner or prisoner representative as a member.

RESPONSIBILITIES

The primary responsibility of the IRB is to protect the health and welfare of study subjects and to assess the risk/benefit balance of the proposed study. To accomplish these goals, the IRB reviews and approves study procedures, informed consent, subject recruitment methods, and adverse event reporting. The IRB has the authority to modify protocols before the start of a study or to terminate a study if it believes the welfare of the subjects is at risk. Risk and benefit are especially important with respect to research conducted in children. The IRB must determine the level of risk and the potential benefit to both the individual child and society. The risk/benefit balance for the child then determines not only if the research is permissible, but what level of consent, who needs to provide consent, and what level of continuing oversight is required.

Research Protections for Vulnerable Subjects
INFORMED CONSENT

Informed consent is an essential element of ethical and responsible research. Informed consent requires that the potential subject, or the subject's legal representative, be informed of the purpose, procedures, duration, risks, benefits, confidentiality of records, and available alternative treatment options before participation in the study (Smith-Tyler, 2007). The information must be presented in a language that is understandable to the subject (usually interpreted as the subject's native language) at a reading level appropriate to the subject's understanding. This may require multiple translations of the consent documents, and the IRB must approve each translation of the informed consent. The informed consent document may not contain any language that waives or appears to waive any of the subject's rights resulting from negligence on the part of the investigator, institution, or sponsor (Smith-Tyler, 2007). Most IRBs will have boilerplate templates with preapproved language for major sections of the informed consent. In some situations, informed consent can be given orally, provided a witnessed written summary of the consent is also obtained.

Informed consent is normally to be provided by the subject in the absence of time pressures. The subject must have sufficient time to review and understand the information and formulate and ask any questions. Vulnerable subjects are often vulnerable because of their inability to provide informed consent because of cognitive or physical limitations. The types of research eligible for surrogate consent and who can provide such consent varies by state and national jurisdiction. The hierarchy of who can provide consent may also vary by jurisdiction and by age of the subject. A common hierarchy is guardian, parent (for children), person with power of attorney for healthcare, spouse, adult children, parent (for adults), and adult siblings (Neff, 2008). Because the highest person in the hierarchy has the final decision, researchers should be aware of requirements in their jurisdiction.

Children/Assent

Children, fetuses, and the cognitively impaired are unable to provide consent. In studies involving children that present only minimal risk, or greater than minimal risk but could benefit the individual child, informed consent may be provided by one parent. Minimal risk is specifically defined as the "probability and magnitude of harm or discomfort anticipated in the research are not greater in and of themselves than those ordinarily encountered in daily life or during the performance of routine physical or psychological exams or tests" (U.S. Department of Health and Human Services [USDHHS], 2001). For studies involving greater than minimal risk in children, both parents must provide consent, unless one parent is deceased, incarcerated, or one parent has sole legal custody of the child. If the legal custody of the child changes during the course of the study, the new legal guardian must also provide informed consent for the child to continue in the study. If the research involves the parent or legal guardian providing information about themselves in relation to the child or answering questions about the child, then the parent must provide informed consent for themselves as well as the child.

In addition to the informed consent of the parent, most situations also require the child to provide assent to participate. Assent is similar to consent, in that it is the child's affirmative agreement to participate. A failure to object to participation is not considered assent. The IRB may waive consent for very young children, usually younger than 6 years of age, or for children whose cognitive or emotional impairment makes assent impossible.

Cognitively Impaired

There has been renewed interest in the informed consent issues confronted in research with the cognitively impaired, particularly as it pertains to emergency and critical care medicine. Cognitive impairment may result from congenital defect, injury, medication, or sedation. In cases where the legal guardian is the state or someone who could otherwise provide surrogate consent is not likely to be available, as in emergency situations, a public notification process may be employed as part of the exemption from informed consent. The IRB must document, before approving the study, that the protocol was disclosed to the community in which the study is to take place and that the community has had the opportunity to provide feedback on the protocol. It is also the responsibility of the IRB to ensure that community feedback has been appropriately incorporated into the research procedures. To approve this type of study, a licensed physician must be an IRB member, and the IRB minutes must show that the physician concurred with the IRB approval (USDHHS, 2006).

CONFIDENTIALITY AND PRIVACY

The overall research process for studies with vulnerable subjects is not that different than the overall research process. Although there are additional steps to be completed, it should be kept in mind that study subject protection is a primary responsibility in all studies. The process starts with the development of the clinical protocol. Protocol development is a somewhat iterative process, with the number of iterations depending on the number of entities involved in the development. When working with vulnerable populations, there are areas of protocol development that warrant additional attention.

Subject confidentiality and data privacy are extremely important. Only one list correlating study subject numbers to subjects' identities should exist, and that list needs to be kept by the principle investigator in a secure locked location. Protected health information, or any information that links health status, provision of healthcare, or payment to an individual, should not appear in any clinical study record without a corresponding waiver signed by the subject.

HEALTH INSURANCE PORTABILITY AND ACCOUNTABILITY ACT AND EUROPEAN PRIVACY LAWS: PROTECTED HEALTH INFORMATION

As a general guiding principle, if specific identifying information is not necessary, researchers should not collect it. Box 48-2 lists individually identifying information that falls under the U.S. Health Insurance Portability and Accountability Act (HIPAA) as protected health information. Researchers should also keep in mind that identifying data may be situational. If the researcher is studying obesity in children, the child's weight may be identifiable, particularly if the child is the only 500-pound subject.

Situational Information

The confidentiality of subject data needs to be fully explored during protocol development. Depending on the type of study, these issues may be more difficult and thus need to be worked out in advance. Studies that involve sensitive information, such as

---

Box 48-2 Protected Health Information

- Names
- Geographical subdivisions smaller than a state, including street address, city, county, precinct, zip code and equivalent geocodes, except for the initial three digits of a zip code if the geographic unit formed by combining all zip codes with the same three initial digits contains more than 20,000 people
- All elements of dates (except year) for dates directly related to an individual, including birth date, admission date, discharge date, date of death, and all ages over 89
- Telephone numbers
- Fax numbers
- Electronic mail addresses
- Social Security numbers
- Medical record numbers
- Health plan beneficiary numbers
- Account numbers
- Certificate/license numbers
- Vehicle identifiers and serial numbers, including license plate numbers
- Device identifiers and serial numbers
- Web uniform resource locator (URL)
- Biometric identifiers, including fingerprints or voiceprints
- Full-face photographs or any comparable images
- Internet protocol addresses/numbers
- Any other unique identifying number, characteristic, or code

sexual behavior in adolescents, illegal drug usage, or child abuse, for example, may collect information that is included in mandatory reporting laws. How sensitive data or information will be handled should be carefully specified in the protocol and reviewed at length with the research team before the IRB review. These procedures need to be fully disclosed and discussed at the time of informed consent (Box 48-3).

Certificates of Confidentiality

Researchers working with sensitive information may further protect subject data by applying for a certificate of confidentiality. Certificates of confidentiality are issued by the National Institutes of Health and prevent the researcher from being compelled to release names or identifying characteristics in any local, state, or federal criminal, civil, administrative, or legislative proceeding (Public Health Service Act 301(d), 42 U.S.C. 241(d) (U.S. DHHS, 2003). Certificates of confidentiality do not prevent voluntary disclosures of identifying information. The Department of Health and Human Services has clearly stated that certificates of confidentiality were never intended to circumvent state mandatory reporting laws for certain diseases and conditions (U.S. DHHS, 1991). In general, a certificate of confidentiality will only be issued if the researcher assures compliance with these local reporting statues. These are issues that not only need to be fully disclosed and discussed as part of informed consent but also need to be thoroughly reviewed by the research team as part of protocol development.

Privacy in Data Collection

Privacy and confidentiality may include where and how data are collected. This is of particular importance when dealing with subjects who may face physical or psychological harm as a result of their participation, such as victims of domestic abuse or child abuse. Data collection procedures need to be reviewed with attention to not only the data but also to sight lines, sound barriers, and room configurations. The protocol should specifically outline how data collection procedures will be protected. If the research is funded with federal dollars, the study data are public record, and confidential information could be inadvertently released as part of a freedom of information (FOIA) request. At the present time, most raw data are not required to be disclosed under an FOIA request. However, this may change as the public tries to curb research abuses with greater transparency and scrutiny. Structuring case report forms and data collection instruments so that uniquely identifying data can be easily separated and awareness of what identifying data are truly necessary is perhaps the best approach to preventing inadvertent disclosure.

Subject Selection

Subject selection, or the inclusion/exclusion criterion, is an important issue in all trials. If there is legitimate rationale for the exclusion of pregnant women or women of childbearing potential, then the inclusion criteria must include a pregnancy test. If the study involves an investigational drug, reproductive toxicity testing must be completed before women of childbearing potential are enrolled. Procedures for dealing with subjects who become pregnant during the study period (as well as the disposition of their data) need to be established in the protocol. For drug studies, this usually means the subject immediately exits the study.

PREGNANT WOMEN AND WOMEN OF CHILDBEARING POTENTIAL

Pregnant women are generally actively excluded from a study that represents greater than minimal risk. As with women of childbearing potential, drug studies involving pregnant women need to have reproductive toxicity testing completed before enrolling pregnant women. Pregnant women are also to be excluded if there is no potential benefit to the woman and there is potential risk to the fetus.

Subjects Vulnerable Because of Coercion

Prisoners, employees, and students are vulnerable subjects because of the potential that their situations create for coercion to participate (Bach-y-Rita, 1974).

Box 48-3 Required Elements of Informed Consent

A statement that the study involves research—this includes as a minimum:
- The purpose of the research
- Descriptions of all procedures to be followed and identification of those procedures that are experimental
- The expected duration of subject participation
- That participation is voluntary with no penalty for lack of participation or withdrawal from participation

A description of foreseeable risks or discomforts to the subject

A description of foreseeable benefits to either the subject or others to be expected from the research

A description of alternative treatments or options that may be of benefit to the subject

A description of how confidentiality of records will be maintained, including a notation that the FDA may inspect-clinical trial records

Contact information if the subject has questions about the research, his or her rights, and who to contact in the event of a research-related injury to the subject

For studies involving more than minimal risk, a description of any available compensation and whether medical treatments are available in the event of subject injury, including what those treatments consist of and where further information may be obtained

When appropriate the following additional elements may also be required:
- A statement that particular procedures may involve risks to the subject that are unforeseeable (if pregnant or may become pregnant, may also include the fetus)
- Additional costs to the subject as a result of study participation
- Anticipatable situations where the investigator may terminate the subject's participation without regard to the subject's consent
- Consequences of and procedures for subject withdrawal from the study
- A statement that study results which may influence the subject's willingness to continue will be provided to the subject
- The approximate total number of study subjects

PRISONERS

Before the 1970s, the majority of pharmaceutical and cosmetic products were tested on prisoners. Prisoners have suffered significant research abuses in studies such as the MKULTRA project run by the Central Intelligence Agency, in which prisoners were given hallucinogenic drugs as mind-control agents (Schwenzer, 2008). Current federal regulations require that only research that has potential to benefit the prisoner is permissible. Coercion and inducements must be carefully scrutinized in this population. Methods, procedures, and financial incentives that may not be improper in other populations may be coercive or improper inducements in an incarcerated population. A nominal payment for participation has a different meaning in this population. Study participation, or lack of participation, may not be a consideration in parole or other official decisions. Recruitment procedures need to be fair and equitable for all potential prisoner participants.

STUDENTS AND EMPLOYEES

The situation of students or employees is one of unequal power. The student or employee may view participation as a condition of continued employment. An investigator should not recruit his or her students or employees. Potential participants should be recruited by general media methods such as posted flyers rather than direct requests from the investigator. The subject should be required to actively seek out participation to prevent coercion. Particular care must be taken to ensure the privacy and confidentiality of the subject's data.

Data Safety Monitoring Boards

Studies that are funded by the National Institutes of Health require that the protocol include a plan to monitor and protect both subjects and their data. For studies that present more than minimal risk, a separate data safety monitoring board (DSMB) may be required. DSMBs serve as independent assessors of the safety of the study and will review the study data according to a plan specified in the protocol. As a separate entity, the DSMB can review unblinded interim data without compromising or biasing the investigator's review of the data.

Research conducted in vulnerable populations requires attention to details. The regulatory and ethical issues in clinical trial management are continually evolving. As horrific as the reported abuses have been, abuse in a research setting is an uncommon event. This is due in large part to the public's increasing requirements for clinical trial transparency. The public's need to have transparency in how studies are conducted as well as the public safety needs regarding access to all clinical trial data, both positive and negative, require well thought out protocols and strict adherence to regulatory procedures to ensure subject privacy and confidentiality.

Resources

WEBSITES

The Collaborative IRB Training Initiative (CITI)
www.miami.edu/UMH/CDA/UMH_Main_Printable/1,2153,6460-300.html
National Institutes of Health/Bioethics Resources on the Web
http://bioethics.od.nih.gov
National Institutes of Health/National Cancer Institute Training Course: Clinical Trials Education Series: Protecting Human Research Participants
http://phrp.nihtraining.com/users/login/php

National Institutes of Health/Office of Human Subjects Research; Regulations and Ethical Guidelines
http://ohsr.od.nih.gov/guidelines/index.html
United States Department of Health and Human Services: IRB Guidebook
www.hhs.gov/ohrp/irb/irb_guidebook.htm
United States Food and Drug Administration: Good Clinical Practice in FDA-Regulated Clinical Trials
www.fda.gov/oc/gcp/default.htm

References

Bach-y-Rita, G. (1974). The prisoner as an experimental subject. *JAMA: The Journal of the American Medical Association, 229*(1), 45–46.

Choonara, I. (2000). Clinical trials of medicines in children. *British Medical Journal, 321*(7269), 1093–1094.

Impicciatore, P., & Choonara, I. (1999). Status of new medicines approved by the European Medicines Evaluation Agency regarding paediatric use. *British Journal of Clinical Pharmacology, 48*(1), 15–18.

International Conference on Harmonisation of Technical Requirements for Registration of Pharmaceuticals for Human Use (ICH). (1996). E6(R1) Good clinical practice: Consolidated guideline. www.ich.org/LOB/media/MEDIA482.pdf, accessed 10 Mar 09.

Jones, J. (1993). *Bad blood: the Tuskegee syphilis experiments* (2nd ed.). New York: Free Press.

Katz, J. (1972). *Experimentation with human beings.* New York: Russell Sage Foundation.

National Commission for the Protection of Human Subjects of Biomedical and Behavioral Research. (1983). *The Belmont Report.* Washington, DC: Office of Policy, Planning, and Research (OPPR), U.S. Government Printing Office.

Neff, M. J. (2008). Informed consent: What is it? Who can give it? How do we improve it? *Respiratory Care, 53*(10), 1337–1341.

Pandolfini, C., & Bonati, M. (2005). A literature review on off-label drug use in children. *European Journal of Pediatrics, 164*(9), 552–558.

Penslar, R. L., & Porter, J. P. (1993). *IRB Guidebook.* Office for Human Research Protections, United States Department of Health and Human Services. www.hhs.gov/ohrp/irb/irb_guidebook.htm, accessed 10 Mar 09.

Rothman, D. J., & Rothman, S. M. (2005). *The Willowbrook war.* Piscataway, NJ: Transaction Publishers.

Schwenzer, K. J. (2008). Protecting vulnerable subjects in clinical research: Children, pregnant women, prisoners, and employees. *Respiratory Care, 53*(10), 1342–1349.

Silverman, H. (2007). Ethical issues during the conduct of clinical trials. *Proceedings of the American Thoracic Society, 4*(2), 180–184.

Smith-Tyler, J. (2007). Informed consent, confidentiality, and subject rights in clinical trials. *Proceedings of the American Thoracic Society, 4*(2), 189–193.

United States Department of Health and Human Services. (2006). *Guidance for institutional review boards, clinical investigators, and sponsors: Exemption from informed consent requirements for emergency research.* www.fda.gov/cder/guidance/index.htm, accessed 10 Mar 09.

United States Department of Health and Human Services. (1991). *Notifiable disease reporting with certificates of confidentiality.* www.cdc.gov/od/science/regs/disease.htm, accessed 10 Mar 09.

United States Department of Health and Human Services (May 2001). Protections for children in research, a report to Congress. *Section 1003, Public Law,* pp. 106–310.

United States Department of Health and Human Services. (2003). Office for Human Research Protections. Guidance on certificates of confidentiality. http://hhs.gov/ohrp/humansubjects/guidance/certconf.htm, accessed 10 Mar 09.

United States Government Printing Office. (1949). Trials of war criminals before the Nuremberg Military Tribunals under control council law No. 10, *2,* 181–182.

World Medical Association. (2000). Declaration of Helsinki: Ethical principles for medical research involving human subjects. *JAMA: The Journal of the American Medical Association, 284*(23), 3043–3045.

CHAPTER 49 Organ Donation and Tissue Transplantation

Teresa J. Shafer

Other than a few papers in medical journals during the 1970s and early 1980s (after cadaver kidney recovery became more commonplace), little has been published concerning the effect of a medical examiner/coroner (ME/C) on organ retrieval efforts since kidney transplantation began in the United States in the late 1950s. Only since the early 1990s and the decade that followed has the issue of ME/C cooperation and its effect on organ donation been examined with a critical eye. Organ donation and transplantation has changed substantially since the late 1970s. Before the 1980s when transplantation became more successful, commonplace, and organized, bodies were transported to the medical examiner's office following death and the autopsy was conducted unencumbered by requests for organs. This practice quickly became antiquated as organs became immediately and desperately needed for the thousands of people in communities throughout the United States waiting for organ transplants. Currently, nearly 18% of those waiting for a heart and 14% of those waiting for a liver will die before an organ becomes available. A person dies every two hours in the United States waiting for an organ (United Network for Organ Sharing [UNOS], 2009).

Nationwide, more than 100,000 people are waiting for lifesaving or life-enhancing organ transplants, yet only approximately 25,000 organs from 7500 organ donors have been available each year (UNOS, 2009). The organ donor shortage is the foremost challenge faced by the transplant community. Until 2003, organ recovery had not significantly increased in recent decades. In 2003, the U.S. Department of Health and Human Services (USDHHS) launched the Organ Donation Breakthrough Collaborative (ODBC). Organ donation increased a cumulative 22.5% from October 2003 to October 2006 (Organ Procurement and Transplantation Network [OPTN] and Scientific Registry of Transplant Recipients [SRTR], 2004; Shafer et al., 2006, 2008). This nationwide effort resulted in broad sharing of identified Best Practices and process improvements in organ procurement organization (OPO) and across the largest donor hospitals in the country. Because of this nationwide effort, donation increased as stated previously, and the number of organ donors has remained above the precollaborative (pre-2003) levels.

Many past and continuing efforts in addition to the ODBC have been made to maximize organ donation, most with small to modest success. They include the following:

1. Studying methods to increase public acceptance of organ donation (Ganikos, McNeil, Braslow, et al., 1994)

2. Understanding and implementing Best Practices to increase family consent for donation (Ehrle, Shafer, & Nelson, 1999; Siminoff et al., 2001, 2006)
3. Understanding and implementing methods to increase consent rates and donation within the minority populations (Shafer, Wood, Van Buren, et al., 1997)
4. Focusing on and improving organ procurement organization and hospital processes and collaboration to increase donation (Beasley, Capossela, Brigham, et al., 1997)
5. Studying healthcare professionals' attitudes and their effects on organ donation (Siminoff, Arnold, & Caplan, 1995)
6. Exploring the possibility of using financial incentives to increase organ donation (Council of Ethical and Judicial Affairs, 1995)
7. Implementing required request legislation (U.S. Code Annotated, Title 42, 1987)
8. Exploring public policy initiatives such as presumed consent and mandated choice (Council of Ethical and Judicial Affairs, 1994)
9. Studying, proposing, or implementing other major legislative, regulatory, and policy initiatives (Siminoff, Arnold, Caplan, et al., 1995)
10. Increasing the use of "marginal" or older donors and expanding donor medical suitability criteria, including the use of organs from non–heart-beating donors (Kauffman, Bennett, McBride, et al., 1997)
11. Standardizing hospital requirements for donation programs (The Joint Commission, 2009)

Before 2003, compared to the growth in the waiting list each year, the number of organ donors had remained relatively flat since 1986 (UNOS, 2004). In fact, the growth in organ donors averaged only 3.5% per year (Table 49-1). In contrast, the recipient waiting list grew at 10 times that rate, significantly and steadily increasing during the same time (Fig. 49-1). Put simply, the number of organ donors continues to lag far behind the number of people waiting for a lifesaving organ.

Despite numerous local public education activities, legislative actions–such as request and contractual requirements between hospitals and OPOs mandated by federal law, involvement of the Surgeon General and the U.S. General Accounting Office USDHHS, 1991; U.S. General Accounting Office [GAO], 1993)–and nationwide public awareness campaign themes, there were no significant increases in organ donation in the 1990s.

Medical professionals sometimes mistakenly believe that only young, healthy individuals can be organ donors. While the ideal organ donor has an irreparable brain injury, is relatively young, is a trauma victim, is otherwise medically well, and has excellent multiorgan function, donors dying under these circumstances are becoming more and more uncommon because of demographic changes regarding age in the country's population (Morrissey &

Special thanks to the United Network for Organ Sharing, particularly for the excerpts from *Donation and transplantation: Medical school curriculum.* Richmond, VA: United Network for Organ Sharing, LCCN: 92-60708.

Table 49-1 Organ Donors, Waiting List, and Cadaveric Organ Transplants in the United States

YEAR	PERSONS ON WAITING LIST	PERCENTAGE INCREASE IN PATIENTS ON WAITING LIST	CADAVERIC ORGAN DONORS	PERCENTAGE INCREASE IN ORGAN DONORS	CADAVERIC ORGAN TRANSPLANTS	PERCENTAGE INCREASE IN ORGAN TRANSPLANTS
1980	5072*	—	5038†		NA	
1981	NA	—	5041†	0.1	NA	
1982	NA	—	2300†	7.4	NA	
1983	NA	—	2705†	17.6	NA	
1984	NA	—	3290†	50.6	NA	
1985	NA	—	3637†	10.6	NA	
1986	NA	—	3990†	9.7	NA	
1987	13,115	159	4000†	.3	NA	
1988	16,034	22.3	4084	2.1	10.783	
1989	19,169	19.6	4019	−1.6	11,208	3.9
1990	50,914	14.3	4509	12.2	12,858	14.7
1991	23,901	9.1	4526	0.4	13,318	3.6
1992	28,987	50.3	4520	−0.1	13,471	1.1
1993	33,181	14.5	4861	7.5	14,635	8.6
1994	37,365	12.6	5100	4.9	15,083	3.1
1995	43,333	16.0	5360	5.1	15,780	4.6
1996	49,445	14.1	5418	1.1	15,784	0
1997	55,751	12.8	5479	1.1	15,044	−4.7
1998	62,740	12.5	5798	5.8	16,748	11.3
1999	69,054	10.1	5810	0.50	16,810	0.4
2000	76,115	10.2	5985	3.0	17,081	1.6
2001	84,798	11.4	6081	1.6	17,591	3.0
2002	80,790	1.6	6190	1.8	18,290	3.7
2003	83,731	3.6	6457	4.3	18,665	2.1
2004	87,146	4.1	7150	10.7	20,044	7.4
2005	90,526	3.9	7593	6.2	50,501	5.8
2006	94,441	4.3	8020	5.6	22,196	4.6
2007	97,980	3.7	8086	0.9	22,049	−0.7
2008	108,200	2.9	7312	−9.6	20,048	−9.3

All data are from the United Network for Organ Sharing (UNOS) unless otherwise indicated. U.S. Scientific Registry of Transplant Recipients and the Organ Procurement Transplant Network: Transplant Data 1989-2000. (2001, February 16). Rockville, MD and Richmond, VA: HHS/HRSA/OSP/DOT and UNOS.
*From Southeastern Organ Procurement Foundation, Richmond, VA.
†1980-1987. From Evans, R. W. (1992, June). The National Cooperative Transplant Study. United Network for Organ Sharing/Health Care Financing Administration. Health and Population Research Center, Battelle-Seattle Research Center, Seattle, WA. BHARC-100-91-020, Control Number 01.
NA: not applicable.

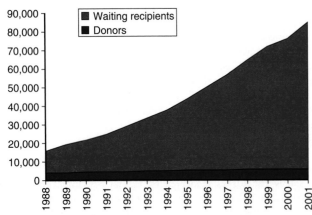

Fig. 49-1 Organ donors waiting for potential recipients, 1988-2001.

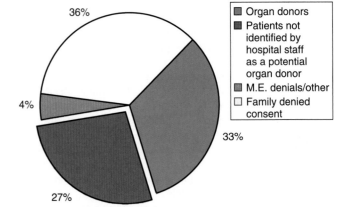

Fig. 49-2 Outcome of total U.S. potential donor pool: medical examiner and nonmedical examiner cases, 1998.

Monaco, 1997). Transplantation professionals look at all brain-dead patients, regardless of age or current medical condition, as potential organ donors. Nonetheless, the shortfall of organ donors has continued, despite the fact that donor criteria have been greatly relaxed in order to recover more organs for those who wait. Given this shortage of organs, every suitable donor from whom organs are not recovered results in the loss of lives.

Actual recovery of organ donors falls far short of the potential donor pool for a number of reasons, chief among them being (1) denied consent from families for organ donation when asked to donate and (2) nonreferral of the potential donor by the hospital to the OPO (Fig. 49-2). Additionally, to some extent, downward trends in motor vehicle accidents, gunshot wounds, and other

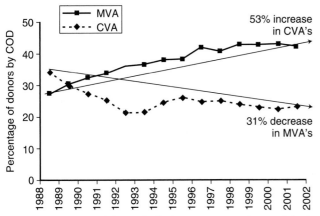

Fig. 49-3 Percentage of donor deaths by circumstances/cause of death: motor vehicle accident versus cerebrovascular accidents.

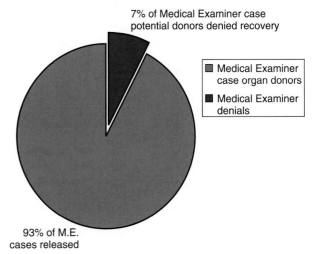

Fig. 49-4 Percentage of medical examiner cases released/denied organ recovery, 1994-2001.

traumatic brain injuries play a role (Sosin, Sniezek, & Waxweiler, 1995). Decreased speed limits as well as helmet and seat belt laws have greatly decreased the number of motor vehicle accidents, with a concomitant decrease in organ donors who have died under these circumstances. Organ donors whose circumstance of death was a motor vehicle accident decreased 31%, from 34.3% in 1988 to 23.5% in 2002. Over the same period, organ donors with the diagnosis of cerebrovascular death rose 53%, from 27.7% to 42% of all deaths (Fig. 49-3).

KEY POINT Healthcare personnel should view all brain-dead patients, regardless of age or current medical condition, as potential organ donors.

Further, with age being greater in the population of individuals dying of cerebrovascular accidents (CVAs), along with the relaxed restrictions on donor criteria, recovery of organs from donors older than 65 grew an astounding 900% for the same period, from 0.9% in 1988 to 9% of all donors in 1999 (UNOS, 2002). In fact, maintaining recovery levels along with the minor increases in donors has only been achieved through the recovery of older, more marginal donors.

Impact of the Medical Examiner on Organ Donation

Another reason for the organ shortage lies directly in the sphere of forensic death investigation. Despite widespread attention in 1994 to organ donor losses resulting from medical examiner denials, many areas of the country still needlessly lose significant numbers of organ donors because a local medical examiner refuses to release the organs of potential donors. In this chapter, the term *medical examiner* will be considered in the legal sense, the same as coroner and justice of the peace. Medical examiners are the physicians who are trained to do autopsies. Coroners and justices of the peace may have a background in law enforcement. In counties that do not have medical examiners, coroners or justices of the peace may give authorization for organ and tissue recovery. In some instances, the justice of the peace or a coroner may possess the legal authority to release such organs, so this information on organ recovery also applies to these officials except when a reference is made to specific medical duties such as performing an autopsy (see Chapter 16, 2nd edition; "Medical Examiners," 1994; "Organ Releases," 1994; Shafer, Schkade, Warner, et al., 1994;

"Study Finds," 1994; Voelker, 1994). The most recent study on this issue indicates that the loss of transplantable organs because of medical examiner refusals remains close to the 1992 level, about 7% (Shafer, Schkade, Evans, et al., 2004) (Fig. 49-4).

This is particularly a problem with potential pediatric organ donors who have died because of suspected child abuse or sudden infant death syndrome (SIDS). Nonrecovery of organs in this age group is a significant contributing reason for the pediatric death rate on the waiting list for a liver transplant in children age five and under. In 1990-1992, 22% of all ME/C denials were from child abuse cases, compared with 25% in 2000-2001. In 1990-1992, 73% of child abuse potential organ donors were denied, compared with 44% in 2000-2001. In one report of loss of pediatric organs for transplantation because of ME/C denials, 20.1% of all ME/C denials involved children younger than one year old increasing to 41% of all denials involving children age 10 and younger. Because only 183 actual organ donors in 2000-2001 were younger than one year old, it followed that nearly one third (31.1%) of these potential donors were denied recovery (Shafer, Schkade, Evans et al., 2004). Denials associated with pediatric potential organ donors remain a serious issue.

Medical examiners play a vital role in organ transplantation and could significantly increase organ recovery in the United States if cases falling under their jurisdiction, after appropriate examination, were routinely and expeditiously released for organ recovery and transplantation. Because litigation in general has increased over the years, the development of protocols detailing procedures used in recovering evidence before organ recovery might assist ME/Cs in releasing cases for organ donation. If such protocols, as well as firm public policy requiring organ release in ME/C cases, were put into place throughout the United States, a truly significant increase in organ donors would be accomplished. Such firm public policy would mandate that medical examiners and transplant professionals collaborate to satisfy mutual needs.

Therefore, medical examiners and forensic nurse examiners (FNEs) have a key role in the U.S. public health system when working with the dead—and the living—in a number of ways. The role of the FNE in death investigation puts him or her in an ideal position to affect the lives of patients throughout the United States waiting for an organ that will give them a second chance at life. The FNE works directly with medical examiners and organ procurement specialists to ensure that all forensic evidence is collected and that all medically suitable organs are recovered. With close cooperation between the FNE and OPO, the expectation should be that in cases in which the family has consented to donate and the potential donor is medically suitable, organs for transplantation will be recovered 100% of the time.

The FNE role in tissue donation will be discussed separately in this chapter, following the discussion on organ donation.

BEST PRACTICE The forensic nurse examiner should work directly with medical examiners and procurement specialists to ensure that all forensic evidence is collected and that all medically suitable organs are recovered 100% of the time when the family has consented to donate.

Impact of the Forensic Nurse on Organ Donation

As a public policy issue, it is crucial that the supply of organs and tissues for transplantation be maximized. Congress acknowledged this public policy goal by mandating hospital protocols that offered organ donation as an option in appropriate cases and, in 1997, by mandating by regulation that all U.S. hospitals participating in the Medicare and Medicaid Program refer every death occurring within the hospital to an OPO [42 U.S.C.§273(b)(2)(k)]. One source of donated organs that can be tapped immediately is the group of organs lost from ME/C denials of organ recovery. Because of this issue, nurses practicing in the emergent field of forensic nursing are in an ideal position to assume a leadership role in improving the public health crisis in the United States resulting from the desperate shortage of organs.

Nurses have longed served the public through the many roles they have assumed, and the roles they have been asked to assume, throughout the history of nursing. No other healthcare professional so touches the basic human needs of people. Nurses are accustomed to dealing with a variety of clients, including patients, their families, and the communities in which they live; nurses do this while juggling many priorities and tasks. It is cliché to attribute this quality to a feminine nature, but, nonetheless, this cooperative and sometimes "nurturing" quality can be attributed to nurses—male or female—who have historically demonstrated, through practice, the caregiving role in the greatest sense of the word. Historically, when entering specialty-nursing roles, nurses have not given up their nurturing, caring side; they have not become more circumscribed, elevated, and less accessible to their patients and community. Nurses never abandoned their generalist, their Nightingale image. The ability to see the larger picture is what enables FNEs to look beyond the important but unidimensional need of death investigation and see the waiting recipients, the potential donors and their families, and the community at large. The FNE, by keeping the big picture in view, ensures that organ donation is accomplished in all cases simultaneously with competent death investigations, a primary responsibility of the FNE.

It is reasonable and appropriate to expect a FNE to ensure that the forensic investigations are grounded, thorough, and expedient, and that they work in harmony with the recovery of lifesaving organs intended for transplantation. Such a holistic approach of care to a variety of individuals (waiting potential transplant recipients, donor, donor family crime victim, crime victim's family, police, attorneys, transplant team, and community members from both the donor's and the recipient's respective communities) involved in the organ donation and forensic examination process is certainly not foreign to the nursing profession. It is here where the FNE can excel—in investigating the death of the potential donor using the highest possible standards of forensic death investigation, ensuring the transplantation of the potential donor's organs, and resolving any conflicts between the two in the process.

The resolution of any perceived conflicts between organ recovery and death investigation has been referred to as a win-win situation in that forensic evidence is collected and organs are recovered. The term *win-win* is certainly an oversimplified description of the interdisciplinary process through which an FNE works to ensure, in a holistic approach to care, that the community is served.

National System

The National Organ Transplant Act (1984) mandated the establishment of both the national OPTN and the national SRTR. The OPTN and SRTR were to be administered by a private, nonprofit entity through contracts with the U.S. Department of Health and Human Services. The UNOS administers the OPTN, and the University Renal Research and Education Association (URREA) administers the SRTR. UNOS is responsible for promoting, facilitating, and scientifically advancing organ procurement and transplantation throughout the United States while administering a national organ allocation system based on scientific and medical factors and practices. URREA is responsible for the ongoing evaluation of the scientific and clinical status of transplanted organs and OPO performance for recovery of organs for transplantation.

Policies governing the transplant community are developed by the OPTN membership through a series of regional meetings, national committee deliberations, a public comment period, and final approval by a board of directors that includes both physicians and nonphysicians. The OPTN has adopted policies to ensure equitable organ allocation to patients on the national waiting list. These policies forbid favoritism based on political influence, race, sex, or financial status; they rely, instead, on medical and scientific criteria (Bowers & Servino, 1992).

Procurement Organizations

Organ procurement organizations (OPOs) are nonprofit, government-certified agencies that facilitate organ recovery services in designated areas of the United States. OPOs are the link between the organ donor and the transplant center and recipient. Highly specialized and trained OPO staff members, who normally come from nursing backgrounds, provide these major services:
• Assist hospitals with procedures and education on donation
• Receive all organ and tissue donor referrals
• Evaluate potential donors
• Discuss and obtain consent for donation from families
• Medically manage patient for organ preservation
• Coordinate surgical organ and tissue recovery
• Allocate organs
• Transport organs to transplant centers
• Arrange importing/receiving/procuring of distant organ (imports)
• Enter and maintain recipient waiting lists
• Provide professional education for nurses, physicians, and other healthcare professionals

- Provide public education about donation and increase public awareness of the need for organ donation
- Provide public policy advice and assist in public policy formulation
- Maintain an extensive database on organ donation and provide data to UNOS and other governmental agencies

OPOs can also facilitate tissue recovery either directly or indirectly by referring the potential donor to a tissue, skin, or eye bank. OPO and tissue personnel are available 24 hours a day, 365 days a year, to assist physicians, nurses, and families as needed (Bowers & Servino, 1992).

Donation and Death Investigation Process

The organ donation process is complex. Box 49-1 provides a general overview of the steps involved during the donation process. The major steps always occur, but the sequence and timeframe between events vary depending on the individual circumstances. Once the family consents to organ or tissue donation, the timeframe for this process will vary from a few hours up to 20 or more hours. Coordinated teamwork between the physicians, nurses, hospital staff, surgical recovery teams, and the procurement coordinator are critical for assuring the viability of the transplant graft. Four major steps generally define the donation process: potential donor identification and referral, consent, donor evaluation and maintenance, and organ and tissue recovery (Seem & Skelley, 1992).

DONOR CRITERIA

More than 20 different organs and tissues can be transplanted or used in research. Each potential donor's options for organ and tissue donation is assessed by a procurement specialist. Criteria have expanded, so it is essential that an organ or tissue procurement organization be referred to every single hospital death for evaluation as a potential donor.

Box 49-1 Process of Organ Donation

1. The patient
   - is admitted to hospital.
   - does not respond to efforts made to save the patient's life.
   - has sustained head injuries, bleeds, or anoxic events severe enough that patient will not recover.
   - is pronounced brain dead after evaluation, testing, and documentation.
2. Referral is made to the organ procurement organization (OPO) to evaluate the patient as an organ/tissue donor.
3. The patient is evaluated by the OPO, and the family is approached about donation.
4. Consent for donation is requested to initiate the recovery process.
5. The medical examiner's (ME's) cases need the ME's authorization to proceed with donation.
6. The donor is maintained on a ventilator, stabilized with fluids and drugs, and undergoes numerous laboratory and diagnostic tests.
7. Recipients are identified for the placement of organs.
8. Surgical teams are mobilized and coordinated to arrive at donor hospital for removal of organs and tissues.
9. The donor is brought to the operating room on the ventilator once the surgical teams have arrived at the local hospital where the donor is located.
10. Multiple organ recovery is performed with organs being preserved through special solutions and cold packaging. Ventilator support is discontinued following cross-clamping of the aorta.
11. Tissue donation occurs once the vascular organ donation is completed.
12. The donor's body is reconstructed and surgically closed.
13. The donor's body is released to the funeral home.

Note: Confidentiality is maintained for the donor family and recipients.

Organ donors are previously healthy individuals who suffer irreversible and catastrophic brain injury resulting in brain death with sustained cardiac function (heartbeat). To sustain cardiac function, they are maintained on a ventilator and clinically managed with appropriate fluids and medications until the organs are removed. Transplantable organs include heart, kidney, liver, lung, pancreas, and small bowel. Some physicians accept non–heart-beating donors as organ donors.

Tissue donors, on the other hand, are non–heart-beating. That is, tissue is most commonly obtained from a person who has died of cardiopulmonary arrest or from a solid-organ donor after removal of transplantable organs. Transplantable tissues include dura, eyes, corneas, skin, fascia, cartilage, tendons, ligaments, bones (e.g., ribs, femurs, tibias, fibulas, and ilium), saphenous veins, and heart valves. Tissues are recovered within 24 hours after death if the donor's body has been refrigerated (6 hours or sooner is preferable for eyes) (Seem & Skelley, 1992).

BRAIN DEATH

Brain death is a medically and legally valid declaration of death and is defined as the complete and irreversible loss of brain and brain stem functions. Brain death is determined by considering the following factors:

- There is a known etiology for the brain death.
- Reversible conditions, such as hypothermia, drug intoxication, or metabolic abnormalities, must be excluded.
- The patient must be clinically examined to demonstrate (1) absence of cerebral function, (2) no spontaneous movements, (3) no response to stimulation, (4) no brain stem reflexes, and (5) apnea.
- Diagnostic tests, such as CT scans, electroencephalograms (EEGs), and cerebral blood flow (CBF) studies, may be performed in conjunction with a clinical exam.
- CBF studies may be used as a confirmatory test for the diagnosis of brain death.
- Brain death can be diagnosed in full-term newborns older than seven days, provided that confirmatory tests are employed.
- When brain death is diagnosed, the patient is declared dead and appropriate documentation is made in the patient's record.
- If the brain-dead patient is to be an organ donor, organ donor management interventions must be continued until the time of organ recovery.
- If the patient is not to be an organ donor, mechanical support of the body functions can be terminated (Seem & Skelley, 1992).

DONOR IDENTIFICATION AND REFERRAL

First, the hospital staff identifies a potential donor and makes a referral to the local OPO. An attending or consulting physician, a staff nurse, or designated hospital staff may complete this function. Organs are recovered from individuals declared dead on the basis of brain death criteria (98% of all U.S. organ donors) or individuals who have sustained a severe neurological injury, the family chooses to withdraw life support, and cardiac death occurs in such a manner that organ recovery can proceed immediately (5 to 10 minutes) after cessation of cardiac function (less than 5% of U.S. organ donors) (UNOS, 2004).

The physician determines death according to neurological criteria and informs family members of the patient's death. The decedent's family members in most cases are not approached about donation until it has been determined that they understand that "brain death" is death. Family members often raise the issue of donation themselves before this time, and hospital or OPO staff may make a premention of donation as the futility of care becomes evident to all involved. The OPO procurement coordinator is able to provide specific information about donation to the family in a way that ensures informed consent is accomplished and the benefits of donation for both the donor family and the waiting recipients are fully explained. If the family wishes to donate, a consent form, supplied by the hospital or OPO coordinator, is completed and signed (Seem & Skelley, 1992).

Up until this point, the medical examiner's office has usually not been contacted. It is normally only after the official declaration of death that the medical examiner is notified. However, the OPO coordinator is normally on the scene much earlier than this point and ensures that the medical examiner is notified immediately following pronouncement of death. At this time, the FNE might join the OPO coordinator at the hospital, whether in the emergency department or in the intensive care unit, and begin collecting forensic evidence.

Table 49-2 lists items that may be provided to the medical examiner's office by the hospital or OPO staff. In some circumstances, the FNE might facilitate collection of such evidence by going directly to the hospital in which the potential organ donor is located and speaking directly with the OPO and hospital staff. This provides for enhanced communication between the medical examiner's office and hospital/OPO staff serving not only the purposes of collection of evidence and establishment of chain of custody, but also the reinforcement of the role of the FNE in the healthcare community. Additionally, it allows the FNE to examine the body in the hospital, soon after death, so that an exam by a trained forensic examiner is conducted before organ recovery, and that, in addition to organ recovery in all situations in which there are one or more organs suitable for transplant in a brain-dead patient, more tissues (bone, skin, eyes) might be released for donation. The FNE's role is to collaborate with medical examiners, hospital staff, and organ procurement professionals.

FAMILY CONSENT

Acute care hospitals are legally obligated to offer families of potential organ donors the option of organ and tissue donation. Approaching a grieving family about donation can be difficult. But research reveals that when the conversation is sincere and sensitive, the majority of families experience important short- and long-term benefits whether or not they choose to donate. In fact, families can become angry and frustrated when denied the opportunity to donate. Research on public attitudes and family experience of donation repeatedly have come to the same conclusion: the manner in which the donation request is made is the main factor in a family's ultimate decision, regardless of preexisting attitudes.

Approaching a family about donation requires coordinated efforts among the physician, hospital staff, and the OPO coordinator. The physician has the responsibility to inform the family of their relative's death. Time must be allowed for the family to accept the reality of death before raising the question of donation. The person who is most comfortable and knowledgeable about donation should discuss donation with the family, and that individual is usually the OPO coordinator. OPO coordinators bring knowledge, experience, and a confidence in their ability to handle all aspects of the donation process. They know firsthand the benefits that the process offers the family (Ehrle, Shafer, & Nelson, 1999). Donation is a process. Obtaining consent does not consist of simply asking the family if they wish to donate, in essence, "popping the question." Informed consent takes time; OPO staff members have the time that busy physicians and nurses do not have. OPO staff members spend significant time, often many hours, with families during the donation process (Shafer, Schkade, Evans, et al., 2004). An investment of the time of bedside nurses and physicians is not possible in today's environment of limited healthcare resources.

Table 49-2 Items That May Be Provided to Medical Examiner's/Coroner's Office by Hospital/OPO Staff*	
ITEM	COMMENT
Two red-top tubes of blood	Labeled with the donor's name, medical examiner case number, date and time of collection, and initials of the collecting party. All should be sealed inside of a protective container with evidence tape. (Whenever possible, a pretransfusion serum sample, so labeled, should be provided.)
Urine sample	Labeled with the donor's name, medical examiner case number, date and time of collection, and initials of the collecting party. All should be sealed inside of a protective container with evidence tape and admission. (Whenever possible, an admission urine sample, so labeled, should be provided.)
A copy of the OPO medical record	To be placed in a plastic bag.
Polaroid photos of the body	To be taken before any preoperative procedures, with the date and medical examiner case number written in black on a white sheet of paper, which is to be displayed in the foreground of the photo. (The medical examiner is responsible for training OPO staff in the appropriate techniques for obtaining such photographs.)
Additional photos of the body will be taken preoperatively, using a 35-mm camera and with the medical examiner case number and date displayed as above	Each roll of film is to contain photos of only one donor. No photos of any other subject will be included on the roll. The roll of film will be placed in a film-processing envelope provided by the medical examiner, labeled with the date and medical examiner case number, and delivered by OPO staff to the medical examiner's office.
An operative note dictated by one of the transplant surgeons in attendance noting all operative findings	Delivered to the medical examiner in a timely manner.
Written reports of any organ biopsies performed by OPO or transplant centers	To be submitted upon request of the medical examiner's office.
X-rays or reports of x-rays	In child abuse cases, a computed tomography (CT) or magnetic resonance imaging (MRI) of the head may be useful.

*Each office and OPO is different and has its own arrangement. This is a list of those items that may prove useful to the medical examiner in certain circumstances.

The family should be provided sufficient information to make an informed decision about whether or not they wish to donate organs or tissues. The positive benefits of donation help families cope with their loss by helping to save the life of someone else, by having their loved one live on in a sense, and by fulfilling the implicit and explicit wish of their loved one.

Concerns of the family should be anticipated and addressed in a forthright manner. A person's reluctance to donate is most often rooted in misinformation or a lack of information. Before beginning the donation discussion, OPO coordinators assess families as to their knowledge and acceptance of brain death as death. Families are informed that (1) the OPO pays all costs involved with donation, (2) there is no disfigurement of the body and that an open-casket funeral is possible, (3) their loved one will feel no pain because their loved one is dead and the brain has no ability to sense or convey pain, and (4) all major religions and religious traditions allow organ donation. Some families have questions about how the organs are distributed and to whom they are given. They are informed that there is a national OPTN that monitors and regulates organ distribution to assure fairness. Buying and selling of organs is illegal (Seem & Skelley, 1992).

Once the OPO coordinator has obtained consent for donation, the FNE can confer with the family and answer any questions they might have regarding the process that will occur following donation with the autopsy. Families often have questions about the autopsy process, which, by default, nurses and OPO coordinators answer because no representative of the medical examiner's office is present. This is another role the FNE could fill in a more informed manner than hospital or OPO staff.

DONOR EVALUATION

Evaluation begins at the time of referral. The referring physician or nurse provides specific information about the donor, such as age, sex, race, date and time of admission, diagnosis, and vital signs (admission and current). The donor's hemodynamic stability is maintained through mechanical ventilation until the time of organ removal. Individuals who have died from cardiopulmonary arrest may be acceptable donors of corneas, skin, bone, heart valves, and other tissue. Other initial criteria for donor suitability include age limits specific to each organ and tissue and an absence of metastatic cancer or unresolved systemic infections.

Once the procurement coordinator arrives at the donor hospital, he or she begins with a thorough chart review. A review of the emergency department admission record and the emergency medical services run report is essential. Information regarding the cause of admission, including details such as a cardiac or respiratory arrest, ejection from a vehicle, and submersion in water, is vital to the multiorgan donor workup. Knowledge of such events may indicate whether the organs have suffered significant damage. A review of physician and nursing notes provides an overall picture of the patient's status. A complete assessment of blood pressure and temperature curves, use of vasoactive drugs, and episodes of hypotension, hypertension, bradycardia, and tachycardia are noted. Progress notes should provide documentation of the patient's brain death determination. Brain death laws vary from state to state, as do determination and criteria policies from hospital to hospital.

The coordinator conducts a thorough assessment of the social and medical history of the donor. The social profile includes occupational history, sexual habits and preferences, marital and family status, and substance use or abuse. History of foreign service or travel of the donor in the previous 12 to 18 months may need to be reviewed with the donor's family because of possible exposure of the donor to malaria, typhoid fever, acquired immune deficiency syndrome, or other serious illnesses. Past medical history includes recent and past illnesses, previous operations, and blood transfusions. The donor's family usually can answer the social and past medical history questions.

The laboratory studies from admission are important in the establishment of a baseline of individual organ systems and in preparation for donor management. Blood samples for cytomegalovirus, HIV I/II, HTLV I/II, hepatitis B and C, and syphilis (VDRL) are tested. Box 49-2 includes laboratory and other diagnostic tests that are normally performed in a donor evaluation (Mendez & Phillips, 1992). The FNE can collect all of these findings and put them together in the assessment of this individual's life and death.

Box 49-2 Laboratory and Diagnostic Tests Done on Organ Donors

CHEMISTRY PROFILE
Chem 7, Chem 6
Electrolytes
Na
K
Cl
CO_2
Ca
Serum osmo
Cr
BUN
Glu
Amylase
Lipase
Bili-tot
Bili-direct
Bili-direct/indir
Liver profile
ALT
AST
GGT
Tot protein
Albumin
LDH
Alk phosphatase
CK
CK-isoenzymes or MB
ABG
Mg
PO_4
Drug screen (i.e., pentobarbital)

HEMATOLOGY
CBC/platelets
Diff
H/H
PT
PTT
Fibrinogen
Fibrin split products

MICROBIOLOGY
Blood culture
Urine culture
Sputum culture
Urinalysis
Gram stain
Microsensitivity (Kirby-Bauer)

DONOR MANAGEMENT AND ORGAN PLACEMENT

Donor management should be considered the beginning of organ preservation for transplantation. The ultimate survival of the transplanted organs depends heavily on the pre- and intraprocurement management of the cadaveric organ donor, as well as organ preservation after removal. Ideally, medical management should begin as soon as death is pronounced. Irreversible cardiac arrest usually ensues within 48 to 72 hours of brain death in adults, despite all efforts to maintain hemodynamic stability.

After death has been declared by neurological criteria and proper consent has been obtained from the family, the procurement team needs to maximize the function of the various organs being considered for transplantation. Teamwork and coordination between the intensive care, surgical, and anesthesia staffs are paramount in assuring graft function following transplantation.

An OPO coordinator manages the donor medically with the assistance of the nurse caring for the patient. The coordinator, under the guidance of the OPO medical director, usually writes hospital orders for donor management. Donor management is aimed at maximizing the function of organs before surgical removal. Hemodynamic and oxygenation status is monitored and laboratory studies initiated.

Hemodynamic instability begins before the diagnosis of brain death. Intracranial hypertension secondary to the brain becoming ischemic and necrotic results in severe system hypertension. A low cardiac output state secondary to ventricular dysfunction characterizes the brain-dead patient. Associated pulmonary changes, as a result of hemodynamic instability, might contribute to the frequent acute failure of lung function following lung transplantation.

Following the diagnosis of brain death, the most important cause of hemodynamic instability is hypovolemia. Cerebral resuscitative measures before the declaration of brain death generally incorporate diuresis and dehydration. Marked increases in serum osmolality occur in the majority of brain-dead patients. This increase occurs in spite of accurate central venous pressure (CVP) monitoring of fluid balance and attempts at replacement therapy with vasopressin for diabetes insipidus.

Subsequently, other factors compound the tendency toward hypotension. Extremely rapid fluctuations in blood pressure may occur in brain-dead patients because of instability of the brain stem vasomotor center. Complete brain stem herniation can occur at any time, even after the diagnosis of brain death. Pontine and medullary structures are destroyed, leading to a breakdown of all central regulatory mechanisms and resulting in the loss of spontaneous respiration and circulatory regulation, as well as hypothermia.

Electrolyte status at the initiation of donor management dictates fluid replacement. Donors frequently become hypernatremic, hypokalemic, and hypomagnesemic secondary to free-water loss from both diabetes insipidus (DI) and diuretics. Hypocalcemia and hypophosphatemia can also occur and, when severe, cause myocardial depression.

An important determinant of organ viability is the maintenance of an adequate systemic perfusion pressure. Volume expansion and replacement of urinary losses stabilize the hemodynamic status of many brain-dead patients. CVP monitoring facilitates volume repletion and is recommended by many transplant centers for all organ donors. Arterial lines are also strongly recommended for moment-to-moment vigilance of blood pressure and the effects of agents employed to normalize hemodynamic function. Pulmonary artery catheters in certain donors prove useful.

The ideal hematocrit for a multiorgan donor ranges from 25% to 35%; if necessary, transfusion is required to obtain this level. Fluid resuscitation to a CVP of 15 mm Hg may be all that is needed to normalize hemodynamic status in many initially unstable kidney donors. However, for multiple organ donors, institution of dopamine when the CVP is greater than 10 mm Hg and the systolic pressure remains below 100 mm Hg may be required. Low-dose dopamine increases systemic pressure while dilating the renal vasculature increasing renal blood flow. The mesenteric and coronary vessels are also dilated with doses below 5 mcg/kg/minute.

All donors are maintained on mechanical ventilators. Management of pulmonary status varies little from the living patient in that arterial blood gases determine ventilator settings. Positive-end expiratory pressure (PEEP) of 5 cm H_2O helps prevent atelectasis, as does tidal volume of 15 ml/kg. To ensure cardiovascular stability, the donor's core temperature should be maintained above 34°C.

UNOS maintains the list of patients throughout the United States who are waiting for an organ. The UNOS computer must be accessed to obtain a national donor identification number and to identify potential recipients for extrarenal (heart, liver, lungs, pancreas) organs. The procurement coordinator contacts prospective extrarenal transplant teams and relays donor information. This information includes the donor's medical status, including past medical and social history.

While awaiting the transplant surgical teams, the procurement coordinator manages donor care. Following the diagnosis of death, hypovolemia is the most frequent cause of hemodynamic instability resulting from the following (Boyd, Diethelm, & Phillips, 1992):

- Cerebral resuscitative measures
- Instability of the brain stem vasomotor center
- Nonfunction of the sympathetic nervous system
- Diabetes insipidus (77% to 98% develop diabetes insipidus)

SURGICAL RECOVERY OF ORGANS

Once all recipients are identified, the coordinator schedules the operating room for organ and tissue removal. The procurement coordinator arranges the arrival and departure times of the surgical teams for removing extrarenal organs. Local surgical teams remove kidneys. The teams typically consist of transplant surgeons, their assistants, and organ procurement or preservation coordinators. When the surgical teams arrive, the donor is taken to the operating room. Vital signs are monitored en route to the operating room, usually by portable monitor. The operating room is staffed by the donor hospital surgery staff and consists of scrub nurses, circulating nurses, and anesthesia. An anesthesiologist or nurse anesthetist is present to assist in donor ventilation, monitor hemodynamic status, and administer fluids and medications (Mendez & Phillips, 1992).

The medical examiner may, in selected cases, attend the donation surgery to view the organ recovery. This affords the medical examiner physician a direct view of the organs in the oxygenated and perfused state, an opportunity obviously not available on the vast majority of his or her cases. Because time constraints rarely allow for the medical examiner to do this, attending surgery is reserved for the most unusual cases in which the physician feels that his or her attendance in the operating room might allow for observation of something that the transplant surgeon might miss. The medical examiner might also feel that, on selected cases, attendance in the operating room would leave little room for questions from a future defense attorney about the thoroughness of the autopsy. However, the medical examiner's attendance in surgery occurs rarely to never in most jurisdictions, primarily because it is not needed, even in homicide and other high-profile cases, to obtain the required forensic evidence. The medical examiner or the FNE would more likely view the patient in the intensive care unit in the hospital. This is more convenient because it can be done any time before the surgical recovery of the organs.

In most situations, the medical examiner simply requests a copy of the operative notes or an organ donor operative assessment sheet, the structure of which has been agreed on in advance by both the medical examiner's office and the OPO. OPOs and medical examiners' offices routinely work out such procedures to assure that the mutual goals of organ recovery and collection of forensic evidence are met. An example of such a donor operative assessment sheet is included on the evolve website. Forms such as these can be used to document the condition of the organs intraoperatively. (This is information the medical examiner would not obtain in the vast majority of cases because they are not organ donors.) Additionally, the FNE will already have documented through notes as well as photography the outward appearance of the body.

Before the actual removal of the organs, the aorta is cross-clamped and mechanical ventilation as well as monitoring devices are discontinued. Tissue recovery occurs after organ recovery is completed (if permission for tissue recovery was obtained). Eye banks and tissue banks do not always require the operating room for tissue recovery. Once tissue recovery is completed, the body is reconstructed and surgically closed. Disposition of the body takes place according to hospital guidelines. An open-casket funeral is possible, as the decedent should have a normal appearance after organ and tissue donation.

The recovery teams return to their transplant hospitals with the organs maintained hypothermically in special preservation solutions. The recipients are taken to surgery and the organ transplants are performed. Recovered corneas are processed and transplanted within days following recovery. Other tissues, such as bone segments and heart valves, may be stored for many years, depending on preservation techniques (Mendez & Phillips, 1992).

FOLLOW-UP OF TRANSPLANTED ORGANS

The OPO coordinator follows up with the healthcare professionals involved in the donor case by writing a letter regarding the disposition of the organs. This normally includes information such as whether or not the organ was transplanted and, if not, the reason it was not transplanted, as well as the general location of the recipient and the initial function of the organ following transplantation. Patient identifiers are omitted. Medical examiners have found this information useful in the past when testifying as to the cause of death in a trial. Should the defense attorney bring up the heart, for example, as possibly involved in the cause of death (instead of the gunshot wound to the victim's head), the medical examiner can refer to and enter into evidence the letter from the OPO documenting the medical condition of the heart and its function in the recipient.

Child Abuse Cases: Special Attention

In 1992, roughly 30% of the cases that were denied were child abuse cases. For every child abuse or suspected child abuse case released by the medical examiner for organ recovery, approximately two cases were denied. This is the most frequently denied circumstance of death in medical examiner cases that are potential organ donors. This is especially unfortunate for two reasons: first, pediatric organs are in critically short supply and are essential

for needed transplants in young recipients where size is crucial; second, nonfatal child abuse cases are routinely prosecuted with evidence that can be gathered through external physical examination, lab results, x-rays, CT scans, and so on. In the case of organ donation, all this medical data can still be provided; in addition, direct examination and photography of internal organs and tissues can be offered as further evidence (Shafer, Schkade, Warner, et al., 1994).

The FNE can be instrumental in interfacing with the pediatric intensivist, the child's physician, and nursing staff to ensure that photographs are taken early during the hospitalization before death. If the child is hospitalized for some time, some crucial evidence may be lost that may have proven useful. OPO staff will become involved in the case after it has been determined that the child has had a devastating head injury but well before the declaration of death. The OPO can work with the FNE to ensure that the appropriate specimens are obtained and may actually facilitate doing some needed diagnostic tests before organ removal and cessation of circulation. Such documentation is more likely to occur when the OPO is evaluating the cases for organ donation than when the child does not have the potential to become an organ donor. This is another reason for the medical examiner to cooperate with organ recovery from child abuse cases: he or she will obtain more diagnostic information about the nature of the child's injuries, which can be invaluable in the death investigation.

Therefore, there is a greater chance for more information to be collected, which may prove useful to the medical examiner if the child becomes an organ donor, not vice versa. Actual visualization of the organs in vivo is accomplished, whereas this would not be the case if the child were not an organ donor. The FNE could either take such information in the form of a written report from the transplant surgeon (see Chapter 16, 2nd edition) or request that the medical examiner attend surgery to view the actual operative recovery, noting the condition of the organs at the time of surgery. Biopsy specimens, if needed, could easily be obtained for the ME/C.

Case Law Related to Organ Donation

Theoretically, a criminal investigation or prosecution could be impaired by evidence that is lost, damaged, or altered by virtue of the removal of the crime victim's organs for donation. There has been no case in which a state was unable to adequately investigate a crime or prosecute a criminal defendant because necessary evidence had been impaired by organ donation. Further, no reported case was found that demonstrated that the removal of organs for donation rendered a subsequent autopsy so deficient that the cause of death could not be determined (Strama, Burling-Hatcher, & Shafer, 1994). To the contrary, several cases demonstrate that an autopsy performed after organ donation was sufficient to determine the cause or time of death (*People v. Bonilla*, 1983; *People v. Eulo*, 1984; *People v. Wilbourn*, 1978; *State v. Morrison*, 1989).

KEY POINT Case review to determine whether any reported case demonstrated that a criminal investigation or prosecution has been impaired or adversely affected by organ donation reveals that no such incident has ever occurred.

Although no reported cases indicated that a criminal investigation or prosecution was impaired or adversely affected by organ donation, the removal of a crime victim's organs has been asserted as a defense by defendants. Penal laws define homicide in terms of conduct that causes the death of another person. Therefore,

Case Study 49-1

People v. Bonilla and People v. Lai

In *People v. Bonilla* (1983), the court addressed the question of whether a defendant who inflicted a mortal wound on another person can escape a homicide conviction because of the acts of physicians in removing the victim's organs for transplant and thereafter disconnecting life support systems. The defendant, who had been convicted of manslaughter, alleged on appeal that because the victim's organs had been donated, the state had not proven beyond a reasonable doubt that the defendant had caused the death of the victim. The defendant contended that, therefore, he could not be found guilty of murdering the victim because organ retrieval was an intervening cause of death.

The court expressly rejected defendant's assertion, finding that "the bullet wound to the brain was the proximate cause of death and the homicide was properly attributed to the defendant" (*People v. Bonilla*, at 608-809, 1983). Thus, although the defendant alleged that the declaration of brain death and the removal of organs were intervening causes of the victim's death, the court rejected the argument and affirmed the guilty verdict. This same claim was unsuccessful in *People v. Lai* (1987) when the defendant's conviction for murder was affirmed despite the defendant's assertion that the victim's death was not caused by the gunshot wound inflicted by the defendant but was caused by surgery to remove the victim's organs for transplantation and the subsequent disconnection of the respirator (*People v. Lai*, 1987).

Case Study 49-2

State v. Matthews

In *State v. Matthews* (1986), the defendant was convicted of the murder of a 16-year-old girl. The victim's kidneys were donated after she had been pronounced dead. On appeal, the defendant asserted that the doctors prematurely declared the victim dead and that the removal of her kidneys created a superseding cause of death that relieved the defendant of liability for murder. The court rejected defendant's assertion. South Carolina law provided that negligent medical treatment by a physician would not relieve a defendant from liability. The court held that the decision to declare a patient dead and to harvest organs for transplantation is clearly part of the care or duty that a doctor is responsible for providing. Therefore, the physician's actions were not a superseding cause of the victim's death.

Case Study 49-3

People v. Wilbourn

In *People v. Wilbourn* (1978), the defendant appealed his conviction for murder. The defendant asserted that the decedent/victim had died as a result of cardiac arrest following the removal of his kidneys on the day of his death and that therefore the operation to remove decedent's kidneys was the cause of death, supervening the effect of the gunshot wound delivered by the defendant. The court disagreed, finding that the evidence in the case demonstrated beyond a reasonable doubt that the gunshot wound to decedent's head was the cause of death.

Case Study 49-4

People v. Eulo and State v. Shaffer

In *People v. Eulo* (1984), a homicide defendant asserted that his conduct did not cause the victim's death where the victim's respirator was turned off after the victim's vital organs were removed. In assessing the defendant's criminal responsibility, the court stated that if a victim's death is prematurely pronounced because of a doctor's negligence, the subsequent procedures may have been a cause of death, but that negligence would not constitute a superseding cause of death relieving the defendant of liability. The court in Eulo found that there was sufficient evidence for a rational juror to have concluded beyond a reasonable doubt that the defendant's conduct caused the victim's death and that the medical procedures were not superseding causes of death.

Similarly, in *State v. Shaffer* (1977), the court affirmed the defendant's appeal from a conviction for first-degree murder. After the victim was pronounced dead, his kidneys were removed and the respirator was turned off. In affirming the defendant's conviction, the court stated that "[w]here a person inflicts upon another a wound which is calculated to endanger or destroy life, it is not a defense to a charge of homicide that the alleged victim's death was contributed to or caused by the negligence of the attending physicians or surgeons."

Although the fact that the victims' organs were donated did provide the defendants in the cases presented in this chapter with an additional defense, in none of the cases was the defense found to be valid. Therefore, these cases do not support an assertion that organ donation has adversely affected the investigation or prosecution of a criminal case.

to convict a defendant for murder or manslaughter, a state must prove beyond a reasonable doubt that the defendant's conduct caused the victim's death. Accordingly, defendants in homicide cases have asserted that the removal of the victim's organs or the termination of life support systems was the cause of the victim's death, not the defendant's actions (Strama, Burling-Hatcher, & Shafer, 1994).

LEGAL CASES INVOLVING REMOVAL OF LIFE SUPPORT

Although there have not been many cases in which a defendant has asserted that the donation of his victim's organs was a supervening cause of death relieving the defendant of liability, there have been numerous cases in which defendants have asserted that the removal of a victim from life support systems constituted an intervening cause, relieving the defendant of criminal responsibility. The defendants have been equally unsuccessful in such cases (Strama, Burling-Hatcher, & Shafer, 1994).

For example, in *State v. Velarde*, the defendant was convicted of second-degree murder. On appeal, the defendant asserted that the termination of decedent's life support systems was the cause of victim's death, not the injuries inflicted on the victim by the defendant. The court rejected this assertion, stating that the victim was brain dead before the respirator was removed. The court stated that the head injuries inflicted by the defendant were the cause of the victim's death, not the removal of the respirator. The court noted that even if the support systems were removed prematurely, the defendant still would be responsible for the victim's death because intervening medical error is not a defense to a defendant who has inflicted a mortal wound upon another (*State v. Velarde*, 1986).

Similarly, in *State v. Meints,* the court affirmed the defendant's conviction for vehicular homicide. The court held that the trial court properly instructed the jury that the withdrawal of life support from the victim was not an intervening cause of death. The court found that the fact that some other agency combined with the act of the defendant to cause the victim's death is not a defense unless the other agency is an efficient intervening cause. The court held that proof of brain death is sufficient as proof of the victim's death in a homicide case, and removal of life support systems is not an efficient intervening cause of death in such cases (*State v. Meints,* 1982). Numerous other cases have reached the same conclusion (*Commonwealth v. Golston,* 1977; *Commonwealth v. Kostra,* 1985; *People v. Saldana,* 1975; *People v. Vaughn,* 1991; *State v. Brown,* 1971; *State v. Fierro,* 1979; *State v. Inger,* 1980; *State v. Olson,* 1989; *State v. Watson,* 1983; Strama, Burling-Hatcher, & Shafer, 1994).

EVIDENTIARY ISSUES PRESENTED BY ORGAN DONATION

Defendants in criminal cases also have attempted to use the removal of the victim's organs to preclude the admission of photographs into evidence. For example, in *Green v. State,* the defendant was found guilty of murder. On appeal, the defendant alleged that the trial court erred in admitting into evidence a photograph of the victim taken after several of his organs had been removed for transplantation. The court rejected the defendant's assertion, stating that the gruesome nature of the photo was not grounds to exclude it if it shed light on the issue being tried (*Green v. State,* 1991). Similarly, in *State v. Bock,* the appellate court rejected the defendant's assertion that photographs of the victim taken after his organs had been removed for donation had been admitted into evidence improperly. The court found that although the admission of the photographs may have been prejudicial, such error was harmless (*State v. Bock,* 1992; Strama, Burling-Hatcher, & Shafer, 1994).

IMMUNITY FROM LIABILITY

All 50 states have enacted a statute governing anatomical gifts. These state acts are based largely on the Uniform Anatomical Gift Act (UAGA), which provides immunity for those participating in organ donation. The UAGA insulates from civil and criminal liability those involved in the organ donation process who act in good faith. Section 11 of the UAGA provides that a person who acts in accordance with the UAGA, or with the applicable anatomical gift law of another state (or a foreign country), or attempts in good faith to do so is not liable for that act in a civil action or criminal proceeding. Thus, it is likely that the anatomical gift acts in individual states contain provisions that provide immunity to those who participate in the organ donation process in good faith, including hospitals, physicians, and medical examiners (Strama, Burling-Hatcher, & Shafer, 1994). "Good faith" is defined as an "honest belief, the absence of malice and the absence of design to defraud or to seek an unconscionable advantage" (Black's Law Dictionary, 1979). In one case, the court held that the eye bank acted in good faith in removing eyes from the decedent because it relied on a facially valid permission form and did not have actual knowledge that the woman who signed the form was not formally married to decedent (*Nicoletta v. Rochester Eye & Human Parts Bank, Inc.,* 1992).

Some states have expanded on the liability provisions of the UAGA. For example, the Texas statute pertaining to declared donors pursuant to a driver's license signification of donation provides the following:

> *A person who carries out this section is not civilly or criminally liable. The legislature recognizes that because swiftness of action is required in organ and tissue donation situations, good-faith*

errors are preferable to delay as a matter of public policy. Medical examiners are encouraged to permit organ and tissue removal at the earliest possible time consistent with their duties regarding the cause and manner of death. (Strama, Burling-Hatcher, & Shafer, 1994, p. 50)

SUMMARY OF CASE LAW DISCUSSION

Although case law on legal issues related to organ donation is relatively scarce, the cases that have been reported generally give great deference to the encouragement of organ donation procedures and uphold the immunity provisions of the UAGA. Good faith decisions with respect to organ procurement should not subject OPOs, physicians, or medical examiners to civil or criminal liability (Strama, Burling-Hatcher, & Shafer, 1994). (See Box 49-3 for legal notes.)

Box 49-3 Legal Notes

Commonwealth v. Golston, 366 N.E.2d 744, 750 (Mass. 1977), cert. denied, 434 U.S. 1039 (1978). In affirming the defendant's conviction for murder, the court found that the physician's disconnecting the respirator was not a superseding act that was the sole cause of the victim's death.

Commonwealth v. Kostra, 502 A.2d 1287 (Pa. Super. Ct. 1985). In affirming the defendant's conviction for homicide by motor vehicle, the court rejected the defendant's argument that the direct cause of the decedent's death was not the car accident but the removal of life support systems.

People v. Bonilla, 467 N.Y.S.2d 599, 602 (N.Y. App. Div. 1983), aff'd sub nom.

People v. Eulo, 482 N.Y.S.2d 436 (1984) (superseded by statute). The medical examiner performed an autopsy the day after the victim's organs were removed and determined the cause of the victim's death.

People v. Saldana, 150 Cal. Rptr. 243 (Ct. App. 1975). In affirming the defendant's murder conviction, the court rejected the defendant's assertion that the removal of the victim from a respirator removed the defendant's criminal responsibility for the victim's death; rather, the court concluded that the victim was already dead when he reached the hospital and when the artificial life support systems were removed.

People v. Vaughn, 579 N.Y.S.2d 839 (Sup. Ct. 1991). The defendant is not relieved of criminal liability, even if the victim's life support system was turned off by an unauthorized act of a third party.

People v. Wilbourn, 372 N.E.2d 874 (Ill. Ct. App. 1978). Based on postmortem examination, the medical examiner testified as to cause of decedent's death.

State v. Brown, 491 P.2d 1193 (Or. Ct. App. 1971). In affirming the defendant's conviction for murder, the court rejected the defendant's assertion that disconnecting the victim's respirator was the act that terminated the victim's life, not the bullet wound delivered by the defendant.

State v. Fierro, 603 P.2d 74, 77 (Ariz. 1979). In affirming a conviction for murder, the court stated that the removal of life support systems did not alter the natural progression of the victim's physical condition (from the gunshot wounds in the head) to his death.

State v. Inger, 292 N.W.2d 119, 124-125 (Iowa 1980). Even if the victim's respirator was stopped prematurely, the defendant remains liable because intervening medical error is not a defense to a defendant who inflicts a mortal wound upon another.

State v. Morrison, 437 N.W.2d 422 (Minn. Ct. App. 1989). An autopsy was performed the day after a child abuse victim's organs were donated, and the coroner testified about the condition of the child's internal organs and injuries.

State v. Olson, 435 N.W.2d 530, 534 (Minn. 1989). The doctor's conduct in removing the infant from life support was not a superseding, intervening cause; rather, the medical intervention was a normal, foreseeable consequence of the defendant's shaking the child, and removal of life support did not produce a death that would not otherwise have occurred.

State v. Watson, 467 A.2d 590 (N.J. Super. Ct. App. Div. 1983). Death resulted not from turning off the victim's respirator but from the acts of defendant, which undeniably caused the victim's brain to die.

State Legislation

Two states have legislation requiring a medical examiner's release on organ donors: New York and Tennessee. Three other states require a medical examiner's release unless the medical examiner or his or her designee is physically present in surgery, viewing the organ in question: New Jersey, Texas, and California (Boxes 49-4 and 49-5). In December 1993, the New Jersey Assembly and the Senate voted unanimously to allow the medical examiner to deny organ recovery only if the medical examiner or his or her designee attended the surgical procedure. Similarly, in 1995, the Texas legislature also unanimously passed legislation requiring the medical examiner's release of organs unless the medical examiner was present in surgery, viewing the organ in question, and then denied the recovery because of concerns (Tex. Rev. Civ. Stat. Ann. art. 6687b). Finally, in 2003, California passed essentially the same legislation. These laws prevent the denial of an organ recovery without doing everything possible to gather the information that the medical examiner needs. They allow the medical examiner to make a decision relative to the release or nonrelease of organs after viewing the organ in its undisturbed state during surgery, which might prove helpful in child abuse cases. This can be done by

personally attending the surgical recovery of the organs or having another do so. Colorado attempted unsuccessfully in 2000 to pass the Texas and New Jersey medical examiner laws, while California, in 2003, passed the legislation through both houses (California State Leg AB 777, 2003; Vaughn, 2000).

On November 19, 2002, the Advisory Committee on Organ Transplantation, appointed by Tommy G. Thompson, Department of Health and Human Services, unanimously agreed on a series of recommendations concerning various aspects of organ donation and transplantation. One of the recommendations directs the secretary to use his good standing with the National Governor's Association, the National Association of State Legislatures, the Uniform Commissioners of State Laws, or with individual states to amend the Uniform Anatomical Gift Act (UAGA) to add a new subsection that mirrors the Texas and New Jersey laws. The amendment, which would appear at the end of Section 4 of the act, would insert language nearly identical to that of the Texas medical examiner law. Further, the secretary has been asked to encourage individual states to adopt state laws to the same or similar effect (Department of Health and Human Services, 2003).

Box 49-4 Autopsy and Tissue Organ Analysis

State of New Jersey
Introduced March 15, 1993, by Senator Bassano
An ACT concerning autopsy and tissue or organ analysis and supplementing Title 52 of the Revised Statutes. BE IT ENACTED by the Senate and General Assembly of the State of New Jersey:

1. Notwithstanding any provision of law to the contrary, if a deceased person whose death is under investigation pursuant to section 9 of P.L. 1967, c.234 (C.52:17B-86) is a donor of all or part of his body as evidenced by an advance directive, will, card or other document, or as otherwise provided in the "Uniform Anatomical Gift Act," P.L. 1969, c.161 (C.26:6-57 et seq.), the state medical examiner or the county medical examiner, or his designee, who has notice of the donation shall perform an examination, autopsy, or analysis of tissues or organs only in a manner and within a time period compatible with their preservation for the purposes of transplantation.

2. A healthcare professional authorized to remove an anatomical gift from a donor whose death is under investigation pursuant to section 9 of P.L. 1967, c.234 (C.52:17B-86) may remove the donated part from the donor's body for acceptance by a person authorized to become a donee after giving notice to the state medical examiner or the county medical examiner or his designee, if the examination, autopsy, or analysis has not been undertaken in the manner and within the time provided in section 1 of this act. The state medical examiner or the county medical examiner or his designee shall be present during the removal of the anatomical gift if in his judgment those tissues or organs may be involved in the cause of death. In that case, the state medical examiner or the county medical examiner or his designee may request a biopsy of those tissues or organs or deny removal of the anatomical gift. The state medical examiner or the county medical examiner or his designee shall explain in writing his reasons for determining that those tissues or organs may be involved in the cause of death and shall include the explanation in the records maintained pursuant to section 15 of P.L. 1967, c.234 (C.52:17B-92).

3. The healthcare professional performing a transplant from a donor whose death is under investigation pursuant to section 9 of P.L. 1967, c.234 (C.52:17B-86) shall file with the state medical examiner a report detailing the condition of the part of the body that is the anatomical gift and its relationship to the cause of death. If appropriate, the report shall include a biopsy or medically approved sample from the anatomical gift. The report shall become part of the medical examiner's report.

4. This act shall take effect immediately.

Box 49-5 Texas Legislation Regarding Organ Donation and Medical Examiner Cases

Introduced January 27, 1995, by Senator Moncrief
AN ACT relating to clarifying procedures for the removal of organs or tissues from decedents when an inquest is required.
   693.002. Removal of Body Part or Tissue from Decedent Who Died under Circumstances Requiring an Inquest

(1) On request from a qualified organ procurement organization, as defined in Section 692.002, the medical examiner may permit the removal of organs from a decedent who died under circumstances requiring an inquest by the medical examiner if consent if obtained pursuant to Section 693.003.

(2) If no autopsy is required, the organs to be transplanted shall be released in a timely manner to the qualified organ procurement organization, as defined in Section 692.002, for removal and transplantation.

(3) If an autopsy is required and the medical examiner determines that the removal of the organs will not interfere with the subsequent course of an investigation or autopsy, the organs shall be released in a timely manner for removal and transplantation. The autopsy will be performed in a timely manner following the removal of the organs.

(4) If the medical examiner is considering withholding one or more organs of a potential donor for any reason, the medical examiner shall be present during the removal of the organs or during the procedure to remove the organs. In such case, the medical examiner may request a biopsy of those organs or deny removal of the anatomical gift. If the medical examiner denies removal of the anatomical gift, the medical examiner shall explain in writing the reasons for the denial and shall provide the explanation to the qualified organ procurement organization.

(5) If, in performing the duties required by this subsection, the medical examiner is required to be present at the hospital to examine the decedent prior to removal of the organs or during the procedure to remove the organs, the qualified organ procurement organization shall on request reimburse the county of the entity designated by the county for the actual costs incurred in performing such duties, not to exceed $1,000. Such reimbursements shall be deposited in the general fund of the county. The payment shall be applied to the additional costs incurred by the medical examiner's office in performing such duties, including the cost of providing coverage beyond the regular business hours of the medical examiner's office. The payment shall be used to facilitate the timely procurement of organs in a manner consistent with the preservation of the organs for the purposes of transplantation.

(6) At the medical examiner's request, the healthcare professional removing organs from a decedent who died under circumstances requiring an inquest shall file with the medical examiner a report detailing the condition of the organs removed and their relationship, if any, to the cause of death.

Organ Procurement and the Medical Examiner

Approximately 7% of organs were denied recovery in 1992, and Shafer et al. (2003) documented that 7% of medical examiner cases were denied each year in 2000-2001 in this country. Best estimates based on this study revealed that likely 1451 individuals did not receive a second chance at life during 2000-2001 because of medical examiner denials. There are, however, many areas of the country, including large metropolitan areas, where there are no, or zero, medical examiner denials of organ recovery.

The issue of nonrelease of organs for recovery and transplantation from medical examiner cases has become increasingly controversial ("Medical Examiners," 1994; "Organ Releases," 1994; "Study Finds," 1994; Vaughn, 2000; Voelker, 1994) as the number of deaths on the transplant waiting list has increased.

RELEASE/NONRELEASE PATTERNS

Trends have appeared from the data. In 1992, 29.3% of all the cases that were denied were child abuse cases, and 22.8% of the cases involved a gunshot wound to the head. Seventy-one percent of all denied cases were possible homicide cases. In 1992, as noted earlier, for every child abuse case that was released for organ donation, two were denied; for every SIDS case that was released, one was denied. Other than these obvious trends, this study reported no other common threads to medical examiner denials (Shafer, Schkade, Warner, et al., 1994). In the narrative comments received during the 1992 study, several respondents noted that release for organ donation could depend on which examiner is on call, whether or not the request was made during daylight hours, and whether or not the case was a homicide or high-profile case.

SUCCESSFUL COLLABORATIONS AMONG MEDICAL PROFESSIONALS

It is clear that numerous models exist throughout the United States where death investigation and organ transplantation occur in harmony. Most of the strategies reported by organ recovery professionals that are used in assisting release of donors from the medical examiner's office are strategies designed to protect the collection of forensic evidence, provide more clinical data for the medical examiner's investigation, and foster positive communication. The forensic nurse examiner is in an ideal position to figure prominently in making these strategies successful in accomplishing both goals of collection of forensic evidence and recovery of lifesaving organs.

These strategies include the following:

- Obtaining blood, urine, and other specimens for the medical examiner at or before the time of organ recovery and locating admission specimens in the hospital
- Inviting the medical examiner or his or her designee to attend the surgical procedure
- Obtaining additional exams that the medical examiner would not be able to obtain, such as CAT scans, MRIs, echocardiograms, cardiac catheterizations, and other diagnostic and laboratory tests
- Videotaping the operative recovery of the organs
- Providing follow-up to the ME/C on the organs recovered and the progress of the recipients; additionally, transplant surgeons may offer to provide testimony at any later trial as to the condition of the internal organs at the time of organ recovery

It is the responsibility of the organ procurement and transplant community to represent the potential recipient, just as it is the responsibility of the medical examiner to represent the community in successfully concluding death investigations. It is their joint responsibility to the community to do them together—saving lives. Even one life lost is tragic; FNEs can play a pivotal role in the health of the communities in which they work, if they help resolve these situations where duties overlap.

There is a balance between protecting forensic evidence and protecting recipients and potential donor families. Medical examiners routinely release donors in some areas of the country, so it can be done. Medical examiners have often changed their ruling and allowed donation to proceed after someone, usually a transplant or organ procurement professional, has questioned the decision and personally conferred with the medical examiner. The FNE can provide this communication early in the organ donation process so that organ recoveries are not delayed.

ME/C denials vary by geographical area. During 2000-2001, in New York, Houston, and Philadelphia—three of the five largest cities in the United States—and in four states, there were no (0) potential organ donor denials by ME/Cs (Shafer et al., 2003). The absence of any donor denials in these large cities and states begs the questions: (1) Shouldn't we work toward zero donor denials in all areas of the country? (2) Should potential recipients, those people waiting on the national waiting list, be dependent on the good working relationships between medical examiners' offices and organ recovery organizations? (3) Should there be appropriate state and federal statutes that ensure that organs are recovered whenever family consent is obtained, while ensuring that steps are taken to preserve valuable forensic evidence for the medical examiner so he or she may fulfill all legal obligations? (4) Finally, how best can the FNE serve the community in fulfilling his or her role in death investigation while working with organ and tissue donation healthcare professionals?

Dr. Edmund Donoghue, chief medical examiner of the Office of the Medical Examiner of Cook County in Chicago, during his year as president of the National Association of Medical Examiners (NAME), presented an abstract at the annual NAME meeting in 1999, noting:

Medical Examiners may have a conflict of interest between their duty to criminal justice in prosecuting homicide cases and their duty to public health in making organs available for transplantation. Difficulties arise when they weight their duty to one sector more heavily than another. First comes the recognition that multiple obligations exist. Next come solutions that allow forensic pathology, criminal justice, and public health to each fulfill their responsibilities.

Events in Illinois have led us to review policies for organ transplantation in Cook County. Recently, a coroner in another part of the state imposed a ban on organ transplantation in all homicide cases. Based on our experience in Cook County, this clearly seemed unreasonable.

When we examined our own denials, we realized that they might not be entirely reasonable. We found that refusals were based on irrational fear and the false belief that organ transplantation might interfere with the prosecution of homicide cases. Thirty years' experience with organ transplantation in the U.S. offers absolutely no evidence that this is true.

A 1994 JAMA study of regional organ procurement organizations revealed ten areas of the country with no donor denials and five other areas with only one donor denial. Areas cited for outstanding performance included St. Louis, MO; New York City;

Tennessee; North Carolina; Hawaii; Hartford, CT; Long Island, NY; Fort Worth, TX; and Indiana.

If colleagues in other areas could do this without difficulty, we began to wonder whether we might match their performance. As a result, we are making changes in policy that will attempt to make Cook County a no denial area. We would be very pleased if our remaining colleagues would examine their policies and see if they might also attempt to become no denial areas. (Donoghue & Lifschultz, 1999)

Forensic nursing examiners and medical examiners play a vital role in organ transplantation and therefore play a vital role in the public health. They are involved in 50% to 60% of all organ donor cases. If situations such as those seen in New York City, Houston, Texas, and other successful cities in which organ donation and death investigation occur in tandem could be replicated, this would undeniably result in the largest overall increase in organ donation in the past several years. The donor pool has not been maximized, and there is room for improvement. Medical examiners, coroners, and forensic nurse examiners may be the sole group with the ability to increase organ donation.

Tissue Donation

An estimated 450,000 Americans receive tissue transplants each year, ranging from sight-saving corneas to hip replacements and bone repair to heart valves. The availability of donated bone, tendon, and ligament tissue for transplant has revolutionized the practice of sports medicine—and extended the playing careers of athletes from sandlot to Olympic stadium.

But the average American can be forgiven for not knowing about the benefits of tissue transplantation. Although 25 tissue transplants are performed for every organ transplant, the lion's share of attention has been garnered by the inherent drama of organ transplantation. When a celebrity receives an organ transplant, it is headline news. When an equally popular public figure receives a tissue transplant, the action receives little attention. Patients and their families may not even realize that donated tissue made their recovery possible.

With the exception of blood and bone marrow, virtually all allograft tissue (a transplant from one individual to another) is donated after death. As with organs, the need for donated tissue is growing at a much faster rate than donation. In part, this supply-demand problem is due to rapid advances in the science and practice of transplant medicine and the increase in medical applications for tissue. Population shifts also contribute to demand, especially the maturing of the baby boom generation and the improving health and longevity of older Americans. The availability of donated tissue helps Americans of all ages to recover from a growing list of debilitating conditions.

Many healthcare professionals know little or nothing about tissue donation. Whereas the donation of solid organs—the heart, lungs, kidneys, pancreas, and liver—can occur only when a patient is declared brain dead and dies in a hospital where mechanical support/ventilation is available to keep the organs viable, tissue donation can occur in a much wider range of circumstances.

Transplantable tissue does not require a blood supply, so brain death and artificial support are not essential criteria (although organ donors can donate tissues as well). This means that individuals who die of cardiac (heart) failure or who die away from a hospital can be tissue donors. Even when an autopsy is required, as for homicides and some accident victims, tissue donation is a realistic possibility. Because tissue can be donated under such varying conditions, the potential pool of tissue donors is significantly larger than for organ donors.

Another important distinction between tissue and organ donation is that most tissue, after it is processed, can be stored for later use. Organs, on the other hand, must normally be transplanted within 48 hours of donation. Donated tissues are subjected to rigorous testing and processing procedures before they are made available to transplant surgeons by bone banks, eye banks, and skin banks. There is no single national waiting list for tissue comparable to the United Network for Organ Sharing (UNOS), the nonprofit body contracted by the federal government to manage the matching and allocation of organs. The nation's tissue banks are, however, regulated by the Federal Food and Drug Administration.

Tissue donation affects so many lives. A single tissue donor, depending on the extent of the donation, can provide tissue for as many as 50 people. From the child with the congenital heart-valve defect to the cancer victim facing loss of a limb, from the promising athlete with a potentially career-ending injury to the older citizen with crippling arthritis, from the burn patient to the visually impaired—the gift of just one tissue donor holds the promise of faster healing, improved function, restored mobility, and the return to healthy and productive living ("Tissue Donation," 2000).

The recovery of tissues should begin as soon as possible once the evaluation and consent process is completed to minimize the overgrowth of skin organisms. If retrieval must be delayed, it is imperative that the body of the donor be refrigerated at 4°C. Both the American Association of Tissue Banks (AATB) and the Southeastern Organ Procurement Foundation (SEOPF) standards require that tissue must be retrieved within 24 hours of death, provided that the body of the donor has been refrigerated. Otherwise, the maximum postmortem period for safe tissue recovery is 12 hours (Leslie & Bottenfield, 1989).

Surgical recovery of tissue may be performed in a standard operating room environment using routine sterile technique or in a clean environment using nonsterile technique. It should be noted that all tissues recovered by the latter method will require some means of terminal sterilization. Most large tissue banks have teams available at all times to travel throughout their region to perform tissue recovery. Teams generally consist of two to three technicians or nurses who are specially trained in operative procedures and techniques specific to tissue recovery. The recovery teams are self-contained, providing all supplies, packs, and instruments necessary to recover donated tissues in a sterile manner. The donor hospital operating room staff is not usually required to assist. These procedures are not deemed to be emergency in nature and can be scheduled so as not to interfere with normal operating room cases.

The donor is brought to the operating room, shaved, prepped, and draped in standard surgical fashion. Because of the extent of the incisions to be made, additional bactericidal solution may be left on the skin for additional protection from contamination by normal skin flora. The extent of the prep will be determined by the specific tissues donated. If vascular organs are also being donated, tissue recovery will follow excision of the organs. In this case, the donor will be reprepped and draped before the initiation of tissue recovery (Leslie & Bottenfield, 1989). See Box 49-6.

Box 49-6 Process for Tissue Donation Only

1. The patient dies from a cardiac arrest.
2. A referral is made; local organ or tissue banks are notified.
3. An evaluation for tissue donation is made (i.e., eyes, skin, bone).
4. The family is approached regarding donation.
5. The consent for donation triggers several activities.
6. The medical examiner's (ME's) cases need the ME's authorization to proceed with donation.
7. Extensive chart reviews and laboratory testing are done for communicable diseases and infection.
8. Tissue recovery is performed in the operating room, morgue, or ME's office.
9. The donor's body is reconstructed as needed and surgically closed.
10. An autopsy is performed when required or requested.
11. The donor's body is released to the funeral home.

Note: Confidentiality is maintained for the donor family and recipients.

BONE RECOVERY

The actual excision technique for each tissue will vary somewhat according to individual tissue bank procedures. In general, with bone recovery, long incisions are made along the lateral aspect of the legs with the long bones and ilia removed. Occasionally a rib or ribs will be removed, which obviously requires a chest incision. Also, occasionally, the humerus and humeral heads are removed from the arms, requiring a long incision on the lateral aspect of the upper arm and shoulder. Mandibles are also occasionally removed in bodies that are scheduled for cremation.

Crucial to the recovery process is an attitude of respect for the donor. After all donated tissues are removed, the donor's body is carefully reconstructed to restore natural form and appearance. Prosthetic devices are placed in the surgical incisions to restore form where large bones have been removed. Finally, the incisions are tightly closed using heavy silk suture. It is important for the OPO or tissue bank to develop close working relationships with the funeral home professionals in their area to avoid any interference with funeral arrangements because of tissue donation.

The bone may be used with little processing (simple hypothermia or fresh frozen) or it may be processed and sterilized using chemical (ethylene oxide) or physical (radiation) methods. It may be stored using, again, simple hypothermia, deep freezing, cryopreservation, or lyophilization (freeze-drying). Care is taken to maintain the biological integrity of the allograft.

SKIN RECOVERY

Using a dermatome, skin is removed from the front and back of the torso and the front and back of the upper legs. It is removed in strips .015 to .030 inch thick. After removal, the body might look as if the cadaver had sunburn. A body suit is put on the body following recovery to prevent seepage of serous fluid following recovery. Procured skin is placed in a sterile solution to be transported to the tissue bank, where it will either be stored fresh (unfrozen), frozen and stored at −70°, frozen and stored at −170°, or freeze-dried. The length of time skin can be stored varies greatly from seven days for fresh skin to an indefinite time period for fresh frozen skin. Next to autografts, allogeneic skin continues to be the most effective coverage for the burn wound. Because of this and a growing number of other uses for dermal grafts, skin donation remains insufficient to meet increasing clinical needs (Alexander, Plessinger, & Robb, 1992).

HEART VALVE DONATION

Cryopreserved allograft valves have been shown to have impressive long-term durability and low reoperation rates, lasting up to 10 to 12 years. It is also known from past experience that they have low thromboembolic, hemorrhagic, and infectious complication rates, which allow these valves to compare favorably with mechanical valves and porcine bioprostheses.

The heart itself is removed without clamping the aorta and with the entire arch, part of the descending aorta, and the main branches of the pulmonary artery included. Caval and pulmonary veins are divided at their entry to the heart. In contrast to hearts retrieved for immediate transplantation, those used for valve donation do not require the use of cardioplegia solutions. In fact, it is important to avoid needle punctures in the aorta of hearts recovered for valves.

Once removed from the donor, the heart is placed in cold saline solution, double-covered in sterile plastic bags, packaged in ice, and sent to the processing lab. Explanted hearts must arrive for processing within 16 hours of recovery. They are immediately dissected to salvage pulmonary and aortic valves and the accompanying valved conduits—the arterial stems. In over 70% of cases, both valves are usable. The valves are incubated for 8 to 24 hours in an antibiotic-containing medium and, following incubation, placed in a tissue culture medium with 10% dimethyl sulphoxide (DMSO) solution and frozen at a regulated rate in a microprocessor-controlled liquid nitrogen freezer (Miller & Moreno-Cabral, 1992).

EYE OR CORNEAL DONATION

The cornea is the 12-mm "clear window" in the front part of the eye. Corneal transplantation, such as penetrating keratoplasty, penetrating corneal transplant, and penetrating corneal graft, is a surgical procedure in which abnormal, full-thickness corneal tissue is removed from a patient and substituted with full-thickness donor corneal tissue.

Two methods are used to obtain donor cornea. One method involves whole-eye enucleation. The eyes are placed in a sterile, moist chamber in a cool transporting box and transported to the eye bank. There, the eyes are placed in a storage-viewing chamber containing preservation media. The enucleated eyes are then examined carefully with a slit-lamp microscope to identify any abnormal endothelial cells that would make the cornea tissue unsuitable for corneal transplantation. The second method of tissue recovery entails removing the cornea with a rim of sclera (in situ) and placing the tissue directly into preservation media. The corneal tissue also is examined with a slit lamp by the eye bank in the storage containers. Eye caps are placed in the eye socket of the donor following the recovery of the eyes or corneas (Shapiro, 1992).

OPOs who recover tissue as well as freestanding tissue and eye banks also work closely with the ME/C in requesting consent for release of tissue in cases falling under the jurisdiction of the medical examiner. For obvious reasons, tissue donors are far more numerous than organ donors. For this reason as well as the fact that tissue transplantation is not lifesaving (in most instances), there are more circumstances in which tissue donation is not authorized by the medical examiner than organ donation, particularly in homicide cases, child abuse or SIDS cases, and occasionally accidental deaths or apparent suicide cases. The FNE could greatly aid in increasing release of tissue donors in these ME/C cases as the medical examiner or coroner's concerns largely rest with fear that the evidence may be altered with the recovery of tissue. In most cases, the medical examiner's concerns could be allayed if the FNE examined the body and documented her or his findings before the actual tissue recovery. Particularly with eye donors, if the medical examiner is not looking for retinal bleeding as is seen with some deaths, and because eyes should be recovered within six hours after the heartbeat ceases, the FNE could travel to the hospital or morgue within six hours of death and, as part of the initial examination, examine the condition of the head, face, and neck and review the cause of death. More likely, the FNE could do the examination in the medical examiner's/coroner's office when the body arrives, allowing for eyes to be removed in a timely manner.

If the cause of death fell within certain protocols, the FNE could examine the condition of the eyes and eyelids and then, after conferring with the medical examiner, authorize eye donation. Three broad categories in which the FNE could assist would include: (1) deaths from homicide or suspicion of homicide; (2) asphyxial deaths, a broad category including death by manual or ligature strangulation, hanging, overlays (heavy object on chest), drowning, noxious fumes, and so on; and (3) deaths from unknown causes. In all cases, the nurse could document that condition of the eyes by looking for and photodocumenting any subconjunctival hemorrhage. The protocols might exclude authorization of eye donation in cases where retinal hemorrhage needs to be documented. For example, in situations such as shaken baby syndrome, in which the pediatrician may already have documented these hemorrhages, the medical examiner will section the eye and further document them.

Summary

The FNE can serve as a bridge between families of the bereaved and the medical examiner. Time spent with grieving families, helping them to cope with the events surrounding the death of their loved one, is certainly a role in which the FNE, as a nurse, would excel. Organ and tissue donation are often the only comfort that a family gains in an otherwise tragic situation. The FNE works closely with the organ recovery coordinator by coordinating information in donation situations, and she or he works jointly with other healthcare professionals by assisting families in moving forward through their loss.

The FNE plays a vital role in organ and tissue donation and transplantation and, therefore, in the health and welfare of the community. The FNE is a catalyst in forging positive and lasting relationships among the medical examiner, healthcare professionals (including OPO staff), and the community, ensuring that death investigations and organ donation proceed in harmony. His or her background is ideal for such a role. In more ways than one, the FNE plays a lifesaving role in the community. The FNE, who often conducts the preliminary death investigation, serves as a bridge between the medical examiners' offices, law enforcement agencies, OPOs, and tissue and eye banks. Collaborative practice between the FNE and organ recovery coordinators offers the greatest opportunity and reward, both for the professionals involved and the community. It is a lifesaving and life-honoring collaboration.

Resources

ORGANIZATIONS

American Society of Transplant Surgeons
1020 North Fairfax Street, Suite 200, Alexandria, VA 22314; 888-990-2787; www.asts.org

National Kidney Foundation
30 East 33rd Street, Suite 1100, New York, NY 10016; 800-622-9010, 502-889-2500; www.kidney.org

North American Transplant Coordinators Organization
8310 Nieman Road, Lenexa, KS 66504; 913-492-3600; www.natco1.org

United Network for Organ Sharing
700 North 4th Street, Richmond, VA 23509; 804-782-4800; www.unos.org

World Kidney Fund
National Kidney Foundation, Singapore, 81 Kim Keat Road, Singapore 328836; +65 251-7555; www.worldkidneyfund.org.

WEBSITES

Organ Donation
www.organdonor.gov
Umbrella government site for organ and tissue donation issues. Lists all U.S. organ procurement organizations and provides contact information.

Transweb.org
www.transweb.org
Map of organ procurement locations and contact information for the United States.

U.S. Department of Health and Human Services, Division of Transplantation
www.hrsa.gov/osp/dot/dotmain.htm

References

Alexander, J. W., Plessinger, R. T., & Robb, E. C. (1992). Skin transplantation. *Donation and transplantation: Medical school curriculum.* Richmond, VA: United Network for Organ Sharing.

Beasley, C. L., Capossela, C. L., Brigham, L. E., et al. (1997). The impact of a comprehensive, hospital-focused intervention to increase organ donation. *Journal of Transplant Coordination, 7*(1), 6–13.

Black's Law Dictionary. (7th ed.). (1999), 623.

Bowers, V. D., & Servino, E. M. (1992). An overview of organ and tissue donation. *Donation and transplantation: Medical school curriculum.* Richmond, VA: United Network for Organ Sharing.

Boyd, G. L., Diethelm, A. G., & Phillips, M. G. (1992). Donor management. *Donation and transplantation: Medical school curriculum.* Richmond, VA: United Network for Organ Sharing.

California State Legislature. (2004). Concurrence in Senate Amendments AB 777 (Dutton). As amended July 15, 2003. As passed ASM floor May 29, 2003, Senate July 50, 2003.

Commonwealth v. Golston. (1977). 366 N.E.2d 744, 750 (Mass.).

Commonwealth v. Kostra. (1985). 502 A.2d 1287 (Pa. Super. Ct.).

Coroners and transplant. (1977). Letter: From our legal correspondent. *British Medical Journal, 1*, 1418.

Council on Ethical and Judicial Affairs, American Medical Association. (1994). Strategies for cadaveric organ procurement: Mandated choice and presumed consent. *JAMA: The Journal of the American Medical Association, 272*(10), 809–812.

Council on Ethical and Judicial Affairs, American Medical Association. (1995). Financial incentives for organ procurement: Ethical aspects of future contracts for cadaveric organ donors. *Archives of Internal Medicine, 155*(6), 581–589.

Davis, J. H., & Wright, R. K. (1977). Influence of the medical examiner on cadaver organ procurement. *Journal of Forensic Sciences, 22*(4), 824–826.

Department of Health and Human Services. (2003). *Secretary's advisory committee on organ transplantation (ACOT) interim report, recommendations and appendices.* ACOT authorized by section 150.12 of the amended final rule of the Organ Procurement and Transplantation Network (OPTN) (42 CFR Part 150).

Donoghue, E. R., & Lifschultz, B. D. (1999, October 20). *"Every organ, every time" Could we do it? Special session–organ and tissue donation and effective death investigations: Tensions and resolutions.* Minneapolis, MN: Abstract presented at the annual meeting of the National Association of Medical Examiners.

Ehrle, R. N., Shafer, T. J., & Nelson, K. R. (1999). Determination and referral of potential organ donors and consent for organ donation: Best practices–A blueprint for success. *Critical Care Nurse, 19*(2), 50–133.

Ganikos, M. L., McNeil, C., Braslow, J. B., et al. (1994). A case study in planning for public health education: The organ and tissue donation experience. *Public Health Reports, 109*(5), 3256–3257.

Green v. State (1991). 591 So. 2d 576 (Ala. Crim. App.).

Kauffman, H. M., Bennett, L. E., McBride, M. A., et al. (1997). The expanded donor. *Transplantation Reviews, 11*(4), 165–199.

Leslie, H., & Bottenfield, S. (1989). Donation, banking, and transplantation of allograft tissues: Organ and tissue transplantation. *The Nursing Clinics of North America, 24*(4), 891–905.

Mendez, R., & Phillips, M. G. (1992). *Donor evaluation. Donation and transplantation: Medical school curriculum.* Richmond, VA: United Network for Organ Sharing.

Miller, D. C., & Moreno-Cabral, C. D. (1992). Heart-valve allografts. *Donation and transplantation: Medical school curriculum.* Richmond, VA: United Network for Organ Sharing.

Morrissey, P. E., & Monaco, A. P. (1997). A comprehensive approach to organ donation. *Hospital Practice, 32*(8), 181–196.

Nicoletta v. Rochester Eye & Human Parts Bank, Inc (1992). 519 N.Y.S.2d 928 (Sup. Ct.).

Organ Donation Breakthrough Collaborative. Best Practices Final Report. HRSA Knowledge Gateway. U.S. Department of Health and Human Services; Health Resources and Services Administration. Office of Special Programs, Division of Transplantation. Contract 240-94-0037. Task Order Number 12, September 2003. www.healthdisparities.net/hdc/hdcsearch/isysquery/4b37ac9d-bba2-47fb-ab13-3334fdb45c8d/1/doc.

Organ Procurement and Transplantation Network (OPTN) and Scientific Registry of Transplant Recipients (SRTR) Annual Report. *Chapter 3: Organ Donation and Utilization in the U.S., 2004. Table III:1. Eligible, Actual and Additional Donors, 2002–2003.* Richmond, VA: United Network for Organ Sharing, www.optn.org/AR2004/Chapter_III_AR_CD.htm?cp=4. Accessed February 24, 2009.

Organ releases needlessly delayed. (1994, November 23). *San Francisco Examiner.*

People v. Bonilla. (1983). 467 N.Y.S.2d 599, 602 (N.Y. App. Div.).

People v. Eulo. (1984). 482 N.Y.S.2d 436.

People v. Lai. (1987). 516 N.Y.S.2d 300 (App. Div.).

People v. Saldana. (1975). 150 Cal. Rptr. 243 (Ct. App.).

People v. Vaughn. (1991). 579 N.Y.S.2d 839 (Sup. Ct.).

People v. Wilbourn. (1978). 372 N.E.2d 874 (Ill. Ct. App.).

Seem, D. L., & Skelley, L. (1992). *The donation process. Donation and transplantation: Medical school curriculum.* Richmond, VA: United Network for Organ Sharing.

Shafer, T. (1995). In Reply. *JAMA: The Journal of the American Medical Association, 273*(20), 1579.

Shafer, T. J., Schkade, L. L., Evans, R. W., et al. (2004). The vital role of medical examiners and coroners in organ transplantation. *American Journal of Transplantation, 4*(2), 160–168.

Shafer, T. J., Schkade, L. L., Warner, H. E., et al. (1994). The impact of medical examiner/coroner practices on organ recovery in the United States. *JAMA: The Journal of the American Medical Association, 272*(20), 1607–1613.

Shafer, T. J., Wagner, D., Chessare, J., Schall, M. W., McBride, V., Zampiello, F., et al. (2008). Organ donation breakthrough collaborative increases organ donation. *Critical Care Nurse Quarterly, 51*(3), 190–500.

Shafer, T. J., Wagner, D., Chessare, J., Zampiello, F. A., McBride, V., & Perdue, J. (2006). Organ donation breakthrough collaborative: Increasing organ donation through system redesign. *Critical Care Nurse, 26*(2), 33–52.

Shafer, T. J., Wood, R. P., Van Buren, C. T., et al. (1997). A success story in minority donation: The LifeGift/BenTaub General Hospital in-house coordinator program. *Transplantation Proceedings, 29*(8), 3753–3755.

Shapiro, M. B. (1992). Cornea transplantation *Donation and transplantation: Medical school curriculum.* Richmond, VA: United Network for Organ Sharing.

Siminoff, L. A., Gordon, N., Hewlett, J., & Arnold, R. M. (2001). Factors influencing families' consent for donation of solid organs for transplantation. *JAMA: The Journal of the American Medical Association, 286*(1), 71–77.

Siminoff, L. A., Arnold, R. M., & Caplan, A. L. (1995). Health care professional attitudes toward donation: Effect on practice and procurement. *The Journal of Trauma, 39*(3), 553–559.

Siminoff, L. A., Arnold, R. M., Caplan, A. L., et al. (1995). Public policy governing organ and tissue procurement in the United States: Results from the National Organ and Tissue Procurement Study. *Annals of Internal Medicine, 123*(1), 10–17.

Siminoff, L. A., Kean, A., Shafer, T. J., Teagarden, R., Wertlieb, S., Wylie, M., et al. (2006). Requesting organ donation: Effective Communication. In L. Ohler, T. J. Shafer, D. L. Rudow, D. LaPointe-Rudow, L. Ohler, & T. J. Shafer, (Eds.), *A Clinician's Guide to Donation and Transplantation* (pp. 791–804). Lenexa, KS: Applied Measurement Professionals, Inc Publishers.

Sosin, D. M., Sniezek, J. E., & Waxweiler, R. J. (1995, June 14). Trends in death associated with traumatic brain injury, 1979–1992. *JAMA: The Journal of the American Medical Association, 273*(22), 1778–1780.

State v. Bock. (1992). 490 N.W.2d 116, 123 (Minn. Ct. App.).

State v. Brown. (1971). 491 P.2d 1193 (Or. Ct. App.).

State v. Fierro. (1979). 603 P.2d 74, 77 (Ariz.).

State v. Inger (1980). 292 N.W.2d 119, 124-125 (Iowa).

State v. Matthews. (1986). 353 S.E.2d 444 (S.C.).

State v. Meints. (1982). 322 N.W.2d 809 (Neb.).

State v. Morrison. (1989). 437 N.W.2d 422 (Minn. Ct. App.).

State v. Olson. (1989). 435 N.W.2d 530, 534 (Minn.).

State v. Shaffer. (1977). 574 P.2d 205 (Kan.).

State v. Velarde. (1986). 734 P.2d 449 (Utah).

State v. Watson. (1983). 467 A.2d 590 (N.J. Super. Ct. App. Div.).

Strama, B. T., Burling-Hatcher, S., & Shafer, T. J. (1994, Summer). Criminal investigations and prosecutions not adversely affected by organ donation: A case law review. *Newsletter of Medicine and Law Committee,* Tort and Insurance Practice Section, American Bar Association, 15–50.

The Joint Commission. (2009). Transplant Safety. *Comprehensive Accreditation Manual for Hospitals: The Official Handbook.* Joint Commission Resources.

U.S. Code Annotated. (1997, December 22). Title 42: The public health and welfare 273: Organ procurement organizations and organ procurement and transplantation network [42 U.S.C.§ 273(b)(2)(k)].

U.S. Department of Health and Human Services: Public Health Service. (1991, July 8-10). The Surgeon General's workshop on increasing organ donation. Proceedings report.

U.S. General Accounting Office. (1993, April). *Organ transplants: Increased effort needed to boost supply and ensure equitable distribution of organs.* Washington, DC: U.S. General Accounting Office, Publication GAO/HRD-93-56.

United Network for Organ Sharing. (2009). Death Removals by Region by Year. Richmond, VA www.optn.org/latestData/rptData.asp. Accessed February 24, 2009.

Voelker, R. (1994). Can forensic medicine and organ donation coexist for the public good? *JAMA: The Journal of the American Medical Association, 271*(12), 891–892.

CHAPTER 50 International Law and the Forensic Nurse Examiner

Jane Weaver Diedrich and Alden Fahy

Relevance of International Law to Forensic Nursing

Forensic practitioners are well aware of the partnership between law and forensic science that their profession entails. Usually, U.S. forensic clinicians are enforcing municipal (local) ordinances or state laws, although the 14th Amendment to the U.S. Constitution also applies. If a federal crime is being prosecuted, then federal statutes and the U.S. Constitution are involved. It has also long been recognized that by harming a citizen of another nation, a country indirectly injures that nation as well because a nation state has an interest in protecting its citizens wherever in the world they may be or wherever in the world a crime is committed against them. These latter two ideas extend certain legal rights and privileges, as well as the rule of national laws, beyond national boundaries. U.S. jurisprudence, for instance, authorizes prosecution in the United States for certain crimes committed abroad. In 2008, Mexico extradited more than 95 suspects, mostly Mexican members of drug cartels, to face prosecution in the United States in the wake of drug smuggling to the United States and related murders surpassing 5300 in 2008 alone (Associated Press Mexico, 2008).

U.S. civil courts also allow causes of action to recover damages for wrongs alleged to have occurred abroad, often obtaining jurisdiction over non-U.S. citizens and ordering them to pay monetary awards. For example, in *Massie et al. v. The Government of the Democratic People's Republic of Korea*, three U.S. servicemen, the USS *Pueblo* captain's spouse, and one civilian oceanographer were awarded $65 million for being taken hostage in 1968 from international waters and then tortured while held in captivity for 11 months, causing permanent injuries. North Korea never responded to the lawsuit filed in the U.S. District Court for the District of Columbia.

Increasingly frequently, however, for both U.S. and overseas forensic practitioners, an entirely separate body of law–international law–may be involved.

KEY POINT International law involves agreements between two or more countries, formal bilateral or multilateral treaties, decisions of international courts, and universal norms as actually and consistently practiced from a sense of legal obligation by the majority of civilized nations (known as customary international law).

Although traditionally international law encompassed relations between countries or treatment of groups vis-à-vis nation-states, since the founding of the United Nations (UN), the individual has become a primary concern of international law. Indeed, the Preamble and Articles 55, 56, and 68 of the UN Charter indicate that the protection of human rights was to be one of the UN's highest priorities (Buergenthal & Shelton, 1995; Hannum & Fischer, 1993). Some examples follow. A "domestic" legal case might involve a forensic nurse giving evidence in a hearing regarding the granting of asylum status by the United States based on persecution by the applicant's home country under rules of the U.S. Customs and Immigration Service. That same forensic nurse asked to testify before a regional international human rights body (such as the European Court of Human Rights) or to submit a statement to the Human Rights Council of the UN might be operating under international law originating outside the United States.

Forensic testimony as to the cause of kidney stones in children drinking Chinese-manufactured milk could be strictly a Chinese matter. Indeed, recently a Chinese dairy supplier and dairy manager were sentenced to death under Chinese criminal law for adding melamine, which like protein is rich in nitrogen, to watered-down milk to fool for protein content. Their actions resulted in kidney stones, thousands of ill children, and several children's deaths (Associated Press Beijing, 2009). However, where importation of tainted milk or lead-containing Chinese toys is alleged to have harmed U.S. children, international trade law becomes involved (Cortez, 2008). Two final examples are the use of Tasers on handcuffed suspects/arrestees or waterboarding possible terrorist detainees. The first has been determined to be excessive force under the U.S. Constitution (*Orem v. Rephann,* No. 07-1696, Fourth Circuit, April 28, 2008), and either might be ruled "torture" under the Covenant against Torture and Other Cruel, Unusual or Degrading Punishment (CAT), which the United States ratified in 1994. In the USS *Pueblo* case, besides finding North Korea liable for state tort claims such as intentional infliction of emotional distress, Judge Kennedy awarded damages for violations of the International Convention against the Taking of Hostages (1979; United States ratified in 1984).

Sources of International Law

International law emanates from a variety of sources. Two of the easiest to understand are treaties and laws or administrative regulations that originate in the international bodies such as the African Union or the Parliament of the European Union, as such entities parallel the legislative bodies found in most countries. A third source of international law, actually the oldest but perhaps the hardest to understand conceptually, is customary international law.

TREATIES

Treaties are formal written agreements between two or more countries' governments intended to be legally binding by having the status of at least national law and national law enforcement behind them. Most international agreements and treaties into which the United States entered before World War II are bilateral (between two countries) as compared to trilateral (among three countries) or multilateral. Bilateral agreements can be conceived of and entered into force within a week, whereas multilateral treaties can take years of drafting, or months of debate within the international organization(s) involved, and even decades to obtain enough countries' ratifications for them to finally enter into force. The Supremacy Clause of the U.S. Constitution, Article VI, clause 2, states:

... and all Treaties made.... under the Authority of the United States, shall be the supreme Law of the Land; and the Judges in every state shall be bound thereby, any Thing in the Constitution or laws of any state to the Contrary notwithstanding.

Even though a country has supported a multinational treaty through the arduous drafting process, it does not mean it will then become a party to it. For instance, despite its often claimed leading role in advocating for human rights, by 1994 the United States had become a party to only four major post–World War II human rights treaties (Box 50-1). Specifically, the United States helped negotiate and draft the International Covenant on Economic, Social, and Cultural Rights, which President Carter signed and sent to the Senate, but it still remains pending (Article 12 recognizes the right of everyone to the enjoyment of the highest attainable standard of physical and mental health). The United States was also instrumental in calling for the global improvement of the status of children and women worldwide, which led to the Convention on the Rights of the Child (CRC, 1989) and the Convention on the Elimination of All Forms of Discrimination against Women (CEDAW, or the women's convention of 1979). The first has now been ratified by 192 countries (virtually every recognized country in the world save Somalia and the United States), the latter by at least 186 countries (National Committee for CEDAW, 2009).

The United States President signed CEDAW in 1980 and sent it to the Senate where it languished in committee. President Clinton sent a letter to a Democratic-majority Senate requesting ratification. However, even with significant reservations, understandings, and interpretations added by the U.S. Department of State designed to meet critics' objections, the Senate still failed to vote on CEDAW. The children's convention (CRC) has yet to even be sent to the Senate for ratification, ostensibly over parental rights issues. Because the U.S. Senate has not given its advise and consent to either of these two treaties, the United States has ratified neither.

A well-organized U.S. National Committee for Ratification of CEDAW, with support from both the American Nurses and American Bar Associations, would certainly welcome forensic practitioners' support as well. Indeed, grassroots efforts to support the women's convention, without waiting for Congress to act, have resulted in many states and towns enacting legislation adopting the treaty within their own geographical jurisdictions. (See Box 50-2.)

A treaty that is self-executing takes effect immediately. If a treaty is not self-executing, each country/state intending to be legally bound must enact further domestic laws to see that the treaty is given full effect and enforced. The Geneva Convention of 1864 is an example of a self-executing international treaty. Thus, as soon as the United States ratified the treaty (thanks to the efforts of Clara Barton), meaning that the U.S. President had signed it and the U.S. Senate had given its advise and consent, its terms became the supreme law of the land (U.S. Constitution, Article VI). On the other hand, the International Covenant on Civil and Political Rights (ICCPR, 1966), a multilateral treaty promulgated by the UN General Assembly in the mid-1960s and ratified by the United States in 1992, is not considered by the U.S. executive or judicial branch to be self-executing. Therefore, it requires the U.S. Congress and/or individual states/municipalities to pass further domestic laws before the treaty is given full force and effect by U.S. courts. When such further internal legislation has been enacted, U.S. tribunals are more likely to grant individuals

---

Box 50-1 Key Treaties the United States Has Ratified: Human Rights versus Humanitarian* Lraw

The following list presents key human rights conventions. The first date indicates the adoption, or opening, for signature of the treaty; the second indicates when the United States ratified.

- Convention on the Prevention and Punishment of the Crime of Genocide (1948/1988)
- International Convention on the Elimination of All Forms of Racial Discrimination (1965/1994)
- International Covenant on Civil and Political Rights (ICCPR, 1966/1992). Held not self-executing
- Convention against Torture and Other Cruel, Inhumane, or Degrading Treatment or punishment (CAT, 1984/1994). When Congress passed the Antiterrorism and Effective Death Penalty Act of 1996, the United States retroactively lifted the immunity of foreign states officially designated as state sponsors of terror, as well as the immunity of their officials who participated in terrorist activities.

*In 1872, after five years of political lobbying and advocacy by Clara Barton, the United States ratified one of the first multilateral treaties: the Geneva Convention (humanitarian law as deals with armed conflict). In 1949, the United States ratified two additional Geneva Conventions, but it has not ratified further Geneva Conventions (circa 1967) that deal with situations such as the Vietnam War (civilian clothes by day, combatants at night) or treatment of armed conflict created refugees.

Box 50-2 Women's Convention Effective 1981 (But Still Not in the United States)

The UN's Convention on the Elimination of All Forms of Discrimination against Women was the fastest modern multilateral treaty to be ratified by a sufficient number of countries to go into effect. The method that its 186 parties use to measure progress is through initial and then staggered periodic self-assessment reports (each 70 to 100 pages long) concerning every article of the convention. Countries are urged to involve NGOs (such as IAFN) in preparing their reports. Rapporteurs assist the UN CEDAW Committee to raise issues and make country-specific recommendations based on discussion of the reports, which are available on the website of the Office of the UN High Commissioner for Human Rights. Additionally, to address issues common to many countries, the Committee has adopted at least 25 general recommendations, including one on violence against women (No. 19) and one on access to healthcare (No. 24).

In 1999, an optional protocol was adopted allowing individual women to bring communications to the Committee's attention for possible inquiry. To date, more than 11 communications have been received and several inquiries initiated. While Senators, both Joseph Biden and Barack Obama pledged support for U.S. ratification of the "Women's Treaty." In January 2008, the Secretariat of CEDAW was transferred to the office of the High Commissioner for Human Rights in Geneva.

Source: National Committee, 2008; Working Group on Ratification of the U.N. Convention on the Elimination of All Forms of Discrimination Against Women (195 U.S. NGOs engaged in outreach and education to achieve ratification by the United States of the treaty for the rights of women), (www.womenstreaty.org, accessed 09/29/2009).

their treaty rights. The U.S. Supreme Court ruled recently that even detainees from the "war on terror" at Guantanamo have recognized Constitutional rights. Yet, in 2008 the same Supreme Court refused to make Texas remedy its international law violations of foreign nationals' treaty rights to contact their embassies upon arrest in the United States. The United States ratified the Vienna Convention on Consular Relations (VCCR) in 1969, which requires such notification. The difference can be explained by the Supreme Court's ruling that the VCCR is not self-executing, despite then President George W. Bush's requests/direction to states to abide by U.S. treaty obligations (*Medellin v. Texas*, 128 S. Ct. 1346 (2008)). Apparently, within our federal republic, concurrent consensus by all three branches of the federal government is the determining factor in whether the United States behaves as if a treaty is self-executing. What this local nonrecognition and enforcement of treaty law in individual communities of the United States means, however, is that when U.S. citizens are arrested abroad, the U.S. Embassy or U.S. consular officials may not be notified.

Because there are an increasing number of treaties governing almost every aspect of human behavior, from oceanic disposal of medical waste to creation of an international criminal court, the scope and origin of laws, rules, and regulations that forensic practitioners will practice under will increasingly originate from international law. Although this may take more time in the United States than elsewhere, the process is well under way. One example involves the definition of *refugee* in deportation proceedings. In the case of *INS v. Cardoza-Fonseca*, 510 U.S. 421, 441 (1987), the Supreme Court recognized that in writing legislation on refugees, Congress purposefully incorporated the definition from the UN Protocol on the Status of Refugees, which the United States ratified in 1968. Other terms, such as *torture* and *genocide*, continue to carry different meanings even within our own branches of government, let alone around the world (Albrecht, Apt, Frazier, et al., 2005). To understand treaty law as currently applied to forensics in the United States then, forensic practitioners must know whether a treaty is considered self-executing or has been implemented by parallel U.S. federal or state laws, and what the legal definitions of the treaty's terms are.

INTERNATIONAL LAW ORIGINATING IN INTERNATIONAL BODIES

This source of international law includes both laws passed by regional governmental organizations, such as the European Union, or by international bodies such as the International Labor Organization (ILO) founded in 1919. The ILO typifies many other specialty international bodies whose members have developed a considerable body of international law, as well as an effective global monitoring system (Mission of Inquiry, 1990). With some 200 international labor conventions now in operation, plus the Convention on the Rights of Migrant Workers (1990), international law even concerns the working conditions, living standards, and equitable treatment of forensic practitioners (Associated Press, 2007). (See Box 50-3.)

CUSTOMARY INTERNATIONAL LAW

As certain truths, practices, or fundamental rules become recognized authority universally or generally and consistently practiced as behavioral standards across a majority of territories and borders, they attain status as customary international law. Such laws are said to be "of custom" as opposed to being decreed or written by particular authorities. One example is the right of all nations'

Box 50-3 Hostage, Prisoner, and Detainee Protection

The following sources give the international legal standards on hostage, prisoner, and detainee treatment, as well as U.S. congressional legislation interpreting these international obligations. Since 2004, as many as 62 detainees have died in U.S. immigration custody, largely because of untimely or inadequate medical care (Neeley, 2008).

- Standard Minimum Rules for the Treatment of Prisoners (Sales No. E 1956 IV. 4, annex I.A). United Nations (1956). New York: United Nations Secretariat.
- Vienna Convention of Consular Relations 1967 (see Article 36).
- Principles of medical ethics relevant to the role of health personnel, particularly physicians, in the protection of prisoners and detainees against torture and other cruel, inhuman, or degrading treatment or punishment. Res 37/194 (December 18, 1982). New York: United Nations General Assembly.
- International Convention Against the Taking of Hostages (1979; United States ratified in 1984).
- United Nations Convention Against Torture and Other Cruel, Inhuman, or Degrading Treatment or Punishment, UN Document A/39/51 (1984, entered into force June 26, 1987).
- Torture, Death Penalty and Participation by Nurses in Executions (2006). Geneva: ICN

---

ships to sail the high seas, free from piracy. Although not initially written down as a legal decree, legal scholars have historically recognized this right as customary international law since at least the 1700s, and since that time the majority of civilized nations have actually consistently pursued and prosecuted pirates. Lip service to "universal" morality or norms is insufficient to confer status as customary international law; only actual consistent behavior resulting from a sense of legal obligation by the majority of civilized nations meets the criteria.

As the world becomes more interdependent, the body of customary international law will be expanded and refined. For example, in 2008, a U.S. appellate court upheld the right of sexual abuse victims to sue U.S. archbishops, bishops, and priests who, following a 1962 Holy See "secrecy policy," refused to report cleric child abusers to police. The U.S. federal court held that such behavior violated the customary law of human rights (O'Bryan et al., 2008).

KEY POINT Customary international law refers to minimum standards *as actually practiced* from a sense of legal obligation governing relations between governments, between governments and certain citizens, and among human beings in general. In many societies, notions of universal justice or natural law support the concept of customary international law.

Human Rights Under International Law

Critics have claimed that some standards identified by legal scholars to be customary international law emanated too predominantly from Western cultural perspectives or that the values of Western cultures and religions did not encompass the full range of human rights. However, such criticism has subsided since 1948 when the UN General Assembly adopted the Universal Declaration of Human Rights (UDHR). After President Roosevelt's death, President Truman asked Eleanor Roosevelt to be U.S. representative to the UN, where she chaired the committee that developed the UDHR; copies are available at www.udhr.org. A declaration is not intended to be legally binding and therefore is not the same as a treaty. However, the UDHR is cited not only as evidence that nations representing numerous cultures and all the major religions recognize certain minimum standards or "inalienable" human

Josephine Ensign, an associate professor of psychosocial and community health nursing at the University of Washington, Seattle, described her experiences with homeless teenagers in Thailand since 1993:

Things about my work there certainly inform my work [in the United States]. It has spurred me to be bolder in doing things here. Thai people who work with issues relating to street children use an international human rights framework to guide their work, such as the UN's Convention on the Rights of the Child. Their example has made it clear to me what a necessary framework this is for my work with homeless young people here in the United States—and how important more equitable access to basic education and healthcare [is] to our young people (Unrau, 2007).

rights, but also as evidence of what those international standards encompass. Such universally recognized rights include certain rights to life and the humane treatment of prisoners. Having stood the test of 60 years' time within the 186+ nation forum of the UN, the UDHR is now considered by some to constitute customary international law.

Since 1951, many detailed declarations, agreements, conventions, and numerous treaties to flesh out the human rights enumerated in the UDHR have been negotiated and come into force. This development, often referred to as the modern human rights movement, does impact nurses. (See Box 50-4.)

One way devised to address philosophical, religious, and cultural differences when it comes to codifying human rights into enforceable international law is the reservations, declarations, and understandings mechanism. This allows nations becoming a party to a treaty to file certain legal interpretations and reserve aspects of domestic law, even while ratifying a treaty. For instance, more than 185 countries have ratified the Convention on the Elimination of All Forms of Discrimination against Women. However, most of those signatory parties also filed reservations, some of which have been criticized as so extensive and so incongruent with the intent and spirit of the treaty as to effectively nullify the country's obligations to comply. The United States often files an "understanding" that the U.S. Constitution will prevail if there appears to be any conflict between it and a treaty. As nations file reservations to written international laws being created by multilateral entities like the UN, as international courts render decisions interpreting written treaties, and as sovereign nations comply with the findings and orders of international judicial forums by paying damages or changing certain behaviors, the body of customary international law is clarified and grows. For instance, war crimes tribunals (beginning with Tokyo) have firmly established that rape, when used systematically against a civilian population or as a strategy toward ethnic decimation, constitutes a war crime under humanitarian law (de Brouwer, 2005). Human rights forums have established that rape can also be a crime against humanity.

Responsibility to Protect: A New Concept for Forensic Practitioners

In Cambodia (1970s), Rwanda (1994), and Srebrenica (1995), horrific mass murder occurred; the international community failed to respond in a timely and effective manner. The latter two instances actually proceeded under the watch of UN peacekeepers. By 1998 and 1999, ethnic cleansing in Kosovo spurred UN debate by

squarely framing the issue as a political will choice to either stand by or exercise the political will to intervene militarily, as had or did happen in Somalia and Kosovo (Luck, 2008).

Early in the 1990s, Francis Deng and colleagues at The Brookings Institute were developing the concept of sovereignty as responsibility (Luck, 2008). In 2000, the Constitutive Act of the African Union asserted the right of the African Union to intervene in a member state experiencing war crimes, genocide, or crimes against humanity. Also in 2000, the Canadian government launched an independent International Commission on Intervention and State Sovereignty, which coined the phrase "responsibility to protect." This concept combines measures of prevention, reaction, and rebuilding when genocide, war crimes, crimes against humanity, and ethnic cleansing, or their incitement occurs. Although crimes against humanity remain largely uncodified and ethnic cleansing is not a crime in its own right, there is now a substantial and growing body of case law from the various international courts and tribunals elaborating their nature and content (Luck, 2008).

Some of the Canadian's commission's key recommendations were incorporated by then UN Secretary General Kofi Annan's High Level Panel on Threats, Challenges and Change (2004), and Kofi Annan's 2005 "In Larger Freedom" report. Finally, at the 2005 World Summit, the largest gathering of heads of state in history to date (which included leaders from a number of countries that were not yet parties to the major human rights, humanitarian, or refugee conventions), a major step forward in protecting fundamental human rights was taken with the adoption of an outcome document endorsing the responsibility to protect (Luck, 2008).

The responsibility to protect (R2P, or RtoP) concept rests on three pillars:

1. The responsibility of the sovereign state to protect its population from genocide, war crimes, ethnic cleansing, crimes against humanity, and their incitement
2. The commitment of the international community to assist states in meeting these obligations
3. The responsibility of states to respond in a timely and decisive manner when another state is manifestly failing to provide its population such protection

Unlike humanitarian intervention, R2P puts relatively little weight on military or coercive responses (Luck, 2008). For example, UN Peacebuilding Commission work in Burundi and Sierra Leone intentionally focused only on reducing the risk of recurrence of violence. Pope Benedict XVI embraced the moral principles of R2P in his 2008 address to the UN; Kofi Annan said he saw the Kenyan post-election crisis of 2008 through the R2P prism.

The new UN Secretary General, Ban Ki-Moon, has pledged to operationalize R2P and seek debate of his related proposals in the 2009 UN General Assembly. The new Asian-Pacific Centre for the Responsibility to Protect in Bangkok is publishing the first international journal in R2P, *The Global Responsibility to Protect.* Another global center for R2P exists at the City University of New York, which published a R2P primer in 2008. The World Federalist Movement's Institution for Global Policy is organizing a worldwide network of R2P groups and organizations to build a global public constituency for R2P. R2P acts politically to amplify demands for accountability, whether through International Criminal Court (ICC) prosecution, regional tribunals, or other appropriate forums of redress. Operationalizing R2P will enhance efforts to protect women, children, minorities, internally displaced persons, and refugees suffering from the five listed violations (Luck, 2008). The International Association of Forensic Nurses (IAFN) should

Box 50-5 The Responsibility to Protect (RtoP or R2P)

THE THREE PILLARS OF THE RESPONSIBILITY TO PROTECT

1. The responsibility of the state to protect its population from genocide, war crimes, ethnic cleansing, crimes against humanity, and their incitement
2. The commitment of the international community to assist states in meeting their obligations
3. The responsibility of states to respond in a timely and decisive manner when a state is manifestly failing to provide such protection

THREE R2P IMPLEMENTATION STRATEGIES

1. *To prevent* the five situations listed in item 1 above
2. *To react* in a timely and decisive manner (using all means short of military intervention whenever possible)
3. *To rebuild,* focusing on healing, capacity building for conflict resolution, and avoidance of a recurrence of mass violence (Luck, 2008)

Source: Davis, R., Majekodunmi, B., & Smith-Hohn, J. (2008). Prevention of genocide and mass atrocities and the responsibility to protect: Challenges for the UN and the international community in the 21st century. *Occasional Paper Series.* New York: International Peace Institute.

recognize/adopt the concept of R2P and consider joining this new global movement and network. (See Box 50-5.)

More Global Opportunities for Forensic Nurses

As professional associations adopt ethics codes and promulgate position statements recognizing globally accepted standards within that profession, those documents become supporting evidence for customary international law. The International Council of Nurses (ICN), founded in 1899, is the world's first and widest reaching international organization for health professionals (ICN, 1995). The ICN has promulgated numerous position statements on human rights and nurses' roles in relation to violence. Kenneth Hoffman, Esq., an authority on humanitarian law (the branch of international law governing armed conflict), has stated that certain position statements accepted by the 134 national nurses' associations members currently making up the ICN (representing between 5 million and 6 million of the world's professional nurses) are evidence that certain universal human rights exist. Because the ICN position statements actually impact professional nursing practice, such standards actually help clarify customary international law (Hoffman, 1997).

Another important contribution of forensic nurses should be strengthening national capacities to collect morbidity and mortality data in UN priority areas such as violence against women and children, human trafficking, and child prostitution and pornography (United Nations Non-Governmental Liaison Service, 1998a, 1998b).

KEY POINT Forensic nurses have a responsibility to possess a sound foundation in international law. They should assist in the enforcement of universal human right laws, participate in the investigation and prosecution of related violations, and assist in the delineation of global ethical standards for forensic practice.

Even though international law may not be as easy to understand or interpret as local, domestic, or national law, this difficulty cannot be an excuse for forensic nurse practitioners to avoid becoming familiar with it. By working in concert with forensic, law, nursing, and health colleagues across borders in efforts to prevent, react, and

rebuild following violence, forensic nurses are actually contributing to the formation and rule of international law. This results from helping to investigate and prosecute violations of international law, by assisting in the enforcement of universal human rights laws, including those regarding prisoners, and by further delineating the ethical standards for clinical forensic practice and the role of forensic practitioners globally.

Most significantly, with the creation in 2002 of the now 110-member ICC, demand for forensic clinicians in prosecuting the most egregious international crimes should increase. The 1997 Treaty of Rome authorizes ICC jurisdiction over genocide, crimes against humanity, and war crimes committed in both international or internal armed conflicts, *but only if* national judicial systems are unwilling or unable to prosecute accused individuals (Box 50-6). Just as demand in most countries for domestic rape services is growing, with continued armed conflict, the global demand for forensic nurses to treat rape victims from civil wars and refugee situations is expected to increase. Unfortunately, even UN peace-keepers and aid workers have been involved in sexual misconduct (Busari, 2008; Lynch, 2005). If the U.S. and Canadian experience with increased chances of successful domestic rape prosecution via forensic nursing (Weaver & Lynch, 1999) is combined with a global reduction in impunity for war criminals, including certain systematic rapists, because of the new ICC, forensic practitioners can deter even more potential perpetrators. Although President Clinton signed the Rome Treaty creating the ICC, before the Senate proceeded with ratification, President Bush "un-signed" the United States following 9-11 with the entry of U.S. troops into Afghanistan and Iraq (Kime, 2009).

Although the United States is investigating and prosecuting members of U.S. armed forces accused of committing possible crimes while on duty, under the U.S. Uniformed Code of Military Justice, no senior U.S. officials who gave the orders to intervene abroad or who drafted detention and interrogation policies have been charged. This contrasts with the ICC's focus on bringing those "most responsible" to trial and holding leaders accountable (SaCouta & Cleary, 2008). With President Obama's executive order to close Guantanamo and the "admission" of the new U.S. attorney general that waterboarding is torture (Meyer, 2009), some are

Box 50-6 The Only Five Crimes the International Criminal Court Prosecutes

Jurisdiction of the International Criminal Court created in 2002 is limited by:
• Gravity threshold
• A focus on the individuals with the greatest responsibility
• Situations where nations do not, or cannot, prosecute themselves

1. **Genocide**
   Examples: Nazi exterminations in WWII, Cambodia, Rwanda, Bosnia murdering Muslims, Burundi, Democratic Republic of the Congo, ?Darfur (not yet international consensus here)
2. **Crimes against humanity—when part of a widespread or systematic practice.**
   Examples: Slavery, massacres
3. **War crimes**
   Example: See U.N. Report on Gaza (2009)*
4. **Crimes of aggression**
   Example: Hitler in World War II invading neighboring countries
5. **Incitement of above**
   Example: Radio broadcasts in Rwanda urging genocide against a certain tribe

*Report of the United Nations Fact Finding Mission on the Gaza Conflict available from www2.ohchr.org/english/bodies/hrcouncil/specialsession/9/docs/UNFFMGC_Report.pdf accessed 10/01/2009.

predicting that other countries and some released "war on terror" detainees will sue the United States and high-ranking U.S. officials for war crimes, crimes against humanity, or any torture they endured (Dean, 2009). Indeed, one such suit against former U.S. Attorney General Gonzalez and other senior G. W. Bush officials has been proceeding in Spain (Haven, 2009).

Forensic nurses should prepare for their increasing role in the rule of international law by studying the various regional and multilateral human rights legal instruments (most can be found on the Internet), by attending meetings about international human rights, and by reading about international human rights law (search Findlaw on the Internet, the U.S. Department of State's annual human rights reports for every country, and the Wikipedia "war rape" site). Once better prepared, volunteer with international nongovernment organizations (NGOs) working abroad in the health, human rights, or legal arenas. Anne Marie de Brouwer did just that as part of her dissertation research, resulting in a book on war tribunals' treatment of sexual violence since World War II. Much of her book is on the Internet; full copies sell for more than $100. Finally, experienced forensic nurses could contact international law or human rights attorneys for potential roles as expert witnesses in cases involving sexual violence, torture, cruel or inhumane treatment of detainees or prisoners, and human trafficking.

Forensic nurses should seek professional contacts and form professional networks to advance forensic practice city by city, state by state, nation by nation, global region by region. It is also advisable to apply for grants to conduct international forensic research, to develop robust forensic programs incorporating international law, and to publish the results, thus elevating the body of forensic knowledge. Key issues include why people chose not to fight, incentives related to peacekeeping, and the role of peace entrepreneurs (Goodhand, 2006). Do not those who work with both perpetrators and victims of violence have something to contribute on reconciliation?

Grants may also be used to introduce formal forensic nursing courses in collegiate nursing or continuing education offerings or to add international law content to U.S. forensic curriculums. Finally, grant and government agency funds may be sought to support the attendance of international law experts, ICC staff or justices, international criminal tribunals (Yugoslavia, Rwanda) staff, or human rights judges at forensic meetings.

BEST PRACTICE Forensic nurses should maintain contacts with international organizations and be prepared through education and training to assume roles in supporting human rights. This can be done by preventing violence, by distinguishing human-inflicted wounds from naturally caused injuries, by protecting detainees, and by training developing countries' nurses and police in forensic skills (See Will, 2004).

Forensic nurses, individually or through the IAFN, should also collaborate with international professional associations or NGOs that have the potential to add forensic services to their projects (see U.S. Department of State, 2008)–examples might be Interpol, World Vision, World Council of Churches, Amnesty International, Planned Parenthood, and Seeds of Hope–Inform them about forensic issues relevant to their work, and ideally offer to help them accomplish their stated aims. When seeing where a connection might have been made but does not appear to have been, the forensic nurse might disperse a letter or e-mail or send some literature on the many forensic nursing roles and how a forensic nurse might be able to contribute. Keep the communications and networking robust, living the axiom: "Success is the meeting of preparation and opportunity."

In regard to helping governments or organizations in countries with endemic or crises of violence, former U.S. Ambassador to Afghanistan (2005-07) Ronald Neumann has called for mastery of the art of multinational implementation, as opposed to enhanced policy formulation. He reminds us of Aesop's fable in which mice called a council to protect themselves from the cat. Consensus on the strategy to hang a bell on the cat was reached. However, the policy proved useless, as no one could "bell the cat." In Afghanistan, Neumann noted the need for a qualified Afghan citizenry to assess possible strategies and work with local governors to shore up government authority and delivery of services. Opinion polls confirm that Afghans welcome projects that deliver them from violence and misgovernment, but only when the approach is to help them build their own state. A key lesson regarding policy, even when reached through consensus, is that cooperation often breaks down over technical disagreements over how to implement the policy. A great deal of time and education is needed to solve underlying problems of lack of qualified Afghan staff

---

Case Study 50-1

Nwaokolo v. Immigration and Naturalization Service

After a Nigerian woman lost her original deportation proceeding, she filed again in July 1999, seeking protection under the Convention Against Torture (CAT) as implemented through 8 C.F.R. Section 208.16(c). She argued that both she and her 13-year-old American daughter would face female genital mutilation (FGM) if deported to Nigeria. Relief was denied on grounds that she offered no evidence she would be tortured upon return to Nigeria.

In 2002, the woman filed again on grounds of changed circumstances, namely the birth of another daughter, only 4 years old, whom she claimed would also be tortured, subjected to FGM, and suffer irreparable injury if she was deported to Nigeria (*Nwaokolo v. Immigration and Naturalization Service*, No. 02-2964 7th Cir. 2002). Citing new legal protections and remedies under the CAT, she presented evidence, using U.S. Department of State documents, describing the serious physical and psychological injuries from FGM. The Board of Immigration Appeals issued another denial without addressing the risk to her American minor-aged daughters.

Upon appeal, the Seventh Circuit held that the board abused its discretion in failing to consider the hardship to the U.S. children. The court took judicial notice of U.S. government reports that 60% to 90% of the female population of Nigeria undergo FGM. The court also cited World Health Organization and UN documents concluding that FGM has serious effects on health including infection or hemorrhage, which can cause death, permanent disfigurement, and increased chance of death during childbirth. The court noted that previous board rulings recognized the prevalence and brutality of FGM in Nigeria and had allowed the threat of FGM as a basis for asylum (*In re Kasinger*, 21 I.N. Dec. 357, 361-62) (BIA, 1996).

Finally, the federal appeals court ruled that a stay of deportation would promote the U.S. public's compelling interest in ensuring that U.S. citizens are not forced into exile to be tortured. The court ordered the board to give a full airing on its duty to consider notifying responsible state authorities of the departure of these minor American girls to Nigeria, a country where they would be in immediate danger of significant harm.

(Neumann, 2008). Possibly, the IAFN could collaborate with the Stanley Foundation, with United States Agency for International Development (USAID), with the UN Inter-Agency Standing Committee, or with professional or training organizations, such as the Academy for Educational Development (AED) or the ICN, to assist Afghan nurses and police build forensic capacities, possibly beginning with the creation of all-female domestic violence, rape, and forced marriage intervention units.

Testifying in International Forums

Be sure to know the legal framework of the forum and case (what is the governing law?), the exact nature of the proceeding (civil or criminal, fact finding or adjudicatory, damage assessment or sentencing), and the standards for evidence (Pitts, 2001). Will the forum ask about the forensic expert's training or experience, how evidence was collected, the science behind analysis of the evidence? Are scientific articles, documents regarding credentials, or equipment needed/allowed in court? What language will be used? How can one verify what a translator is saying? Is it possible to import and export cameras, equipment, or graphic photographs into and out of another country without problems? What are the forum's rules on patient confidentiality? If allowed to accept compensation for work, how are work permits and taxes handled? If one follows the suggestions in the preceding section (i.e., the forensic nurse has connected with speakers from international tribunals at professional meetings and networked to establish and maintain contacts with staff or justices of such forums), it is hoped that one will be better prepared to assist internationally. The de Brouwer book on the prosecution of sexual violence contains great detail about how the International Criminal Court, the International Criminal Tribunal-Yugoslavia (ICT-Y), and the International Criminal Tribunal-Rwanda (ICT-R) have functioned and reached decisions. Once opportunities to practice internationally are found, be prepared and professional; know both ICN (ICN, 1995) and IAFN standards. After testifying, nurses should record and share their experiences with colleagues and offer to serve as a mentor.

Summary

The role of the forensic nurse examiner domestically has been a success in strengthening the health of the individual crime victim, as well as the initially accused who benefit from better evidence collection and preservation. In addition, forensic nurse examiners within jails and prisons or as advocates for the application of international law regarding detention have contributed to improvements for the unjustly incarcerated, for actual perpetrators, and for those who desire rehabilitation. Physicians and other providers, such as nurses, working for the United States have been accused as well, though, of violating international law in regard to detainees of the "war on terror" (Singh, 2003). In late 2008, an army medic was sentenced to life in prison (but with the possibility of parole) for murder for the summary execution of four bound and blindfolded Iraqi prisoners who had been ordered released (AFP, 2009). Eventually, better and more humane justice systems can lessen or prevent crime and thus improve the public health. Prevention of the most egregious humanitarian and rights violations will allow for exponential increases of more constructively used human energy. Thus, forensic practitioners have a major contribution to make by weaving the tapestry integrating domestic and international laws to produce a new global order of justice (Weaver & Lynch, 1999). Forensic nurses can help create a global future with less violence, less human suffering, and greater solidarity and achievement. In short, forensic nurses have a tremendous role to fulfill in the "big picture" concerning the health of the human family by contributing both healthcare and legal system expertise.

In his reflections on the April 1963 Birmingham campaign, Dr. Martin Luther King stated, "The ultimate tragedy is not the brutality of the bad people but the silence of the good. Pessimism is a chronic disease. It destroys the red corpuscles of hope and slows down the powerful heartbeat of positive action." Forensic nurses need to involve themselves with international issues, speak out, use, and help operationalize international law as a progressive tool. By taking positive action sooner rather than later, forensic nurses can enhance global civil society, as well as more rapidly develop international justice systems based on universal human rights.

Case Study **50-2**

The "Benghazi Six"

In 1998, Libyan authorities arrested numerous medical personnel, primarily foreign nurses, and accused them of spreading, either intentionally or grossly negligently, the HIV virus to more than 425 children, thereby killing Libyan citizens and threatening national security. Over the course of the next eight years, the nurses were held without bail, denied regular access to counsel, subjected to excessive judicial delays, and tortured. One torture technique the nurses described was electric shock to their breast and genital areas; another was *falaqa,* or beating the soles of the feet with electric cables. Release efforts by their governments, the International Red Cross and Red Crescent Societies, and the International Council of Nurses were only partially successful, although Libyan, Polish, Hungarian, and Filipino workers were released. The 108th U.S. Congress passed a resolution condemning the trial delays.

At trial, several local medical personnel testified that they believed the HIV disease had spread because of the reuse of syringes. Forensic DNA results verified the strain of HIV virus involved came from West Africa and was spreading in Libya before the Bulgarian nurses, with Libyan permission, entered the country to work.

Eventually, the Bulgarian nurses confessed, which they claim they did to stop being tortured, and in December 2006, the Libyan Court condemned them and a Palestinian physician to death by firing squad (Kreisel, 2007). After stepped-up international pressure and diplomatic negotiation, early in 2007, the nurses were deported. Although there has been speculation the Bulgarian nurses could seek legal redress under international law, to date the authors are unaware of any such claims.

Case Study **50-3**

False Positives in Colombia

When you hear the term *false positives,* you probably think in terms of medical exams, but in Colombia the term has acquired a much more insidious meaning. Specifically, it has been confirmed that the army was taking poor people, often young men who were unemployed, transporting them to another part of the country, and then presenting them as guerilla fighters who had been killed in battle. As the details of this horror were made public in 2008, a number of highly placed army officials were dismissed. A human rights organization had pointed out the impossible numbers of guerrilla fighters the government claimed to have eliminated, far more than all those thought to belong to the different guerilla groups combined (Winters, 2008).

References

Agence France- Presse. (2009, March 30). *U.S. Sergeant convicted for murder of Iraq prisoners.* www.france24.com/en/20090330-usa-iraq-sergeant-mayo-convicted-murder-iraq-prisoners-murder. Accessed 4/3/09.

Albrecht, L., Apt, F., Frazier, M., et al. (2005, Summer). International Human Rights. In *39 The International Lawyer 2* (pp. 517–553). Chicago: American Bar Association.

Associated Press. (2009, January 2). *"Chinese Police Detain Tainted Milk Activist."* Beijing, China: AP.

Associated Press. (2007, October 24). *"Job Search Made Easier for EU Citizens as Degrees, Skills Recognized Across the Bloc".* Strasbourg, France: AP.

Associated Press. (2008, December 31). *"Mexico Extradites 10 Drug Cartel Suspects to US".* Mexico City, Mexico: AP.

Buergenthal, T., & Shelton, D. (Eds.), (1995). *Protecting human rights in the Americas: Cases and materials.* (4th ed.) Arlington, VA: N. P. Engle.

Busari, S. (2008, May). *"Charity: Aid workers raping, abusing children."* London: CNN.

Cortez, E. (2008). Total recall on chinese imports: Pursuing an end to unsafe health and safety standards through Article XX of GATT. *Am U Int'l L. Rev, 23*(5), 915–942.

Davis, R., Majekodunmi, B., & Smith-Hohn, J. (2008). Prevention of genocide and mass atrocities and the responsibility to protect: Challenges for the UN and the international community in the 21st century. In *Occasional Paper Series.* New York: International Peace Institute.

Dean, J. (2009, January 23). Legal jeopardy for American torturers here and abroad? A Q & A Session with an Expert on the Issue, Phillipe Sands. http://writ.news.findlaw.com/dean/20090123.html. Accessed 9/23/2009.

de Brouwer, A. (2005). *Supranational criminal prosecution of sexual violence: The ICC and practice of the ICTY and ICTR.* Tilberg: School of Human Rights Research, (published online ISBN 9050955339).

Goodhand, J. (2006). *Aiding peace? The role of NGOs in armed conflict.* New York: Lynne Rienner Publishers.

Hannum, H., & Fischer, D. (Eds.). (1993). *United States ratification of the international covenants on human rights* (p. 7). New York: Transnational Publishers.

Haven, P. (2009, March 30). *Lawyer, ex-US officials must face torture charges.* Madrid: AP.

Hoffman, K. (1997). International humanitarian law. *Global Migration.* Washington, DC: American Academy of Nursing.

International Council of Nurses (ICN). (1995–Present). "Position Statements" *e.g., Nurses and Human Rights 2006.*" Geneva: ICN www.icn.ch. Accessed 9/23/2009.

Kime, A. O. (2009, March). *International criminal court.* www.matrixbookstore.biz/icc.htm. Accessed 4/3/09.

Kreisel, J. (2007). The 'Benghazi Six' and International medical neutrality in times of war and peace. *Health Policy and Law, 2*(1), 42–50.

Luck, E. (2008, August). *"The United Nations and the Responsibility to Protect."* Muscatine, IA: The Stanley Foundation.

Lynch, C. (2005, March 13). *UN faces more accusations of sexual misconduct.* The Washington Post, A22.

Massie et al. v. The Government of the Democratic Peoples' Republic of Korea, 592 F. Supp. 2d 57 (D.D.C. 2008).

Medellin, v. (2008). Texas 128 S. Ct. 1346.

Meyer, J. (2009, January 16). *Eric Holder: Waterboarding is torture; Attorney General nominee vows review of [G.W.] Bush Administration's practices.* Chicago: AP (archives chicagotribune.com. Accessed 4/3/09.

Mission of Inquiry, American Association for the Advancement of Science. (1990). *"Apartheid Medicine: Health and Human Rights in South Africa: A Report to the American Association for the Advancement of Science, American Psychiatric Association, American Public Health Association, Institute of Medicine of the National Academy of Sciences".* Washington, DC: American Association for the Advancement of Science.

National Committee on CEDAW, the UN Convention on the Elimination of All Forms of Discrimination Against Women. (1980-Present) 520 North Camden, Beverly Hills, California.

Neeley, S. (2008, Summer). Immigration detention: The inaction of the Bureau of Immigration and Customs Enforcement. In *60 Admin L. Rev 3* (pp. 729–748). Washington, DC: Washington College of Law, American University.

Neumann, R. (2008, April). *Implementation: A new approach to multinational coordination in Afghanistan.* Muscatine, Iowa: The Stanley Foundation.

O'Bryan et al. v. Holy See, 556 F. 3d 361 (6th Cir. 2009).

Pitts, L. (January, 2001). Beyond rhetoric: A civil rights approach to protecting children's due process rights. In *Trial Briefs* (p. 3). North Carolina Trial Lawyers Association.

SaCouta, S., & Cleary, K. (2008). The gravity threshold of the International Criminal Court. In *23 Am U. Int'l L. Rev. 5* (pp. 807–854). Washington, DC: Washington College of Law, American University.

Singh, J. (2003). American physicians and dual loyalty obligations in the war on terror. *BMC Medical Ethics, 4,* 4–12. www.biomedcentral.com/1472-6939/4/4. Accessed 4/3/09.

Unrau, L. (Fall, 2007). The hidden homeless. In *18 Connections 2* (pp. 8–9). Seattle: University of Washington School of Nursing.

United Nations Non-Governmental Liaison Service. (April, 1998a). 31st Session of the Commission on Population and Development. In *NGLS Round-Up* (p. 1). Washington, DC: Author.

United Nations Non-Governmental Liaison Service. (April, 1998b). 42nd Session of the Commission on the Status of Women. In *NGLS Round-Up* (p. 2). Washington, DC: Author.

U.S. Department of State. (2008). Celebrating 60 years of human rights: The Universal Declaration of Human Rights 1948–2008. www.america.gov/publications/ejournalusa/1108.html. Accessed 4/3/09.

Weaver, J., & Lynch, V. (1999). Forensic nursing: A unique contribution to international law. *J Nurs Law, 5*(4), 23–34.

Working Group on Ratification of the U.N. Convention on the Elimination of All Forms of Discrimination Against Women (195 U.S. NGOs engaged in outreach and education to achieve ratification by US of the treaty for the rights of women). *www.womenstreaty.org.* Accessed 4/3/09.

Will, C. N. (2004, January 19). Sticks and stones: Nurses can play a key role to prevent childhood bullying. *Advance for Nurses,* 37.

Winters, A. (2008, December). Christmas Letter. p. 2. Available from author Jane Diedrich, Esquire contact JDOffices@comcast.net.

ADDITIONAL REFERENCES

Andrews, K., & Holt, V. (2007, August). *United Nations-African Union Coordination on Peace and Security in Africa," Issue Brief, The Future of Peace Operations Programs.* Washington, DC: The Henry L. Stimson Center.

Associated Press. (2008, December 4). *"European Court Makes Landmark DNA-Sample Ruling."* London, England: AP.

Basch, P. (1999). The organization of international health since 1900. In *Textbook of international health.* New York: Oxford University Press.

Bouchet-Saulnier, F. (2002). *The practical guide to humanitarian law.* New York: Rowman & Littlefield Publishers.

Gill, W. (2001). Global cooperation in international public health. In M. Merson, R. Black, and A. Mills (Eds.), *International public health: Diseases, programs, systems, and policies* (pp. 667–698). Sudbury, MA: Jones and Bartlett Publishers.

Human Rights Brief & Human Rights Brief Blog. www.wcl.american.edu/hrbrief. Accessed 4/3/09 www.wcl.american.edu/blog/hrbrief. Accessed 9/23/2009.

Inter-Agency Standing Committee (IASC). New York: United Nations. www.humanitarianinfo.org/iasc. Accessed 4/3/09.

Kickbusch, I., & Buse, K. (2001). Global influences and global responses: International health at the turn of the twenty-first century. In M. Merson, R. Black, & A. Mills (Eds.), *International public health: Diseases, programs, systems, and policies* (pp. 701–737). Sudbury, MA: Jones and Bartlett Publishers.

Kraig, M. (Fall, 2008). Protection Needed. In *Courier*. Muscatine, Iowa: The Stanley Foundation.

Moir, L. (2001). *The law of internal armed conflict*. Cambridge, UK: Cambridge University Press.

Oulton, J. (2002). Nursing in the International community. In D. Mason, J. Leavitt, & M. Chaffee (Eds.), *Policy and politics in nursing and health care*. (4th ed, pp. 711–722). Philadelphia: W. B. Saunders.

Rome Statute for the International Criminal Court. http://untreaty.un.org/cod/icc/statute/romefra.htm. Accessed 9/23/2009.

Todres, J., & Marcogliese, P. (2005, Summer). International Health Law. In *39 The International Lawyer 2* (pp. 503–516). Chicago: American Bar Association.

U.S. Department of State Notice. (2008, December 29). 2008 Paul Wellstone Anti-Slavery Ambassador of the Year. Available from author Jane Diedrich, Esquire contact JDOffices@comcast.net.

Weaver, J. (1998). Nursing, health, and healthcare in the international community. In D. Mason, & J. Leavitt (Eds.), *Policy and politics for nurses* (3rd ed.). Philadelphia: W. B. Saunders.

White, V. (2007). *"Peacemaking in a Violent World."* Louisville, Kentucky: Presbyterian Peacemaking Programs.

Zwi, A. (2001). Complex humanitarian emergencies. In M. Merson, R. Black, & A. Mills (Eds.), *International public health: Diseases, programs, systems, and policies* (pp. 439–513). Sudbury, MA: Jones and Bartlett Publishers.

CHAPTER 51 Credential Development for Forensic Nurses

Susan B. Patton

Credentialing within forensic nursing, as with all new professional specialties, has become an increasingly important issue. Different types of credentials pertain to nursing–both within the discipline and without. Although all nurses should have an understanding of credentialing and the implications and responsibilities that accompany such a designation, it is uniquely important for forensic nurses who maintain close relationships to both the medical and the legal communities. Forensic nurses provide care when health and the law intersect and must therefore have credentials that speak to their unique qualifications to give that specialized care. In addition, forensic nurses must have a clear understanding of the benefits as well as the limitations of specific credentials in order to become informed consumers of the credentialing industry.

Purpose and Value of Credentialing

Credentials are used in a number of ways depending on the organization granting the credential and the individual(s) who are granted the designation. *Credentialing* is "the umbrella term that includes the concepts of accreditation, licensure, registration, and professional certification"...; (it) grants formal recognition to, or records the recognition status of individuals, organizations, institutions, programs, processes, services, or products that meet predetermined and standardized criteria" (Durley, 2005, p. 5). Emanating from this broad definition are the purposes of credentialing, which are equally as broad. The purposes of professional nurse credentialing include protection of the public; assurance to consumers that professionals have met standards of practice developed for the profession; identification of individual(s) and, to a certain degree, organizations possessing the desired knowledge, skills, abilities, and personal attributes; and promotion of a sense of pride and professional accomplishment as nurses demonstrate a commitment to nursing and to life-long learning.

The value of credentialing, whether required or voluntary, lies with the consumer. If a regulatory agency, on behalf of the consumer public, mandates a credential before a product or service can be utilized, then the credential is more highly valued by all. If the credential is voluntary, expensive, but makes little difference in the consumer's perception of quality, then the credential will be less utilized. In general, credentialing agencies and the boards that oversee the credentialing process make every effort to ensure the reputation of the credential as a good indicator of the qualifications it purports to represent so consumers and candidates alike will respect the designation.

Standards of credentialing have been developed in response to the need for consumer confidence in assurance of quality care or services–particularly healthcare credentialing. Internationally, organizations have developed standards for credentialing in healthcare. For example, the World Health Organization (WHO) Collaborating Centre, dedicated exclusively to patient safety solutions, is a joint partnership between the World Health Organization, The Joint Commission, and Joint Commission International (JCI). JCI has been working with healthcare organizations, ministries of health, and global organizations in more than 80 countries to provide accreditation of more than 220 public and private healthcare organizations such as hospitals, ambulatory care facilities, clinical laboratories, care continuum services, medical transport organizations, and primary care services in 33 countries since 1994 (Joint Commission International, n.d.). The United States Congress in 1977 created the National Commission for Health Certifying Agencies (NCHCA). Its mission was to develop standards for quality certification in the allied health fields and to accredit organizations that met those standards. As credentialing standards developed for healthcare, there was a realization that credentialing of all industries was beneficial. Subsequently, the NCHCA was restructured and became the National Organization for Competency Assurance (NOCA), which accredits not only health-related boards but a wide variety of industries requiring credentialing (National Association of Competency Assurance, 2009). In other words, NOCA sets standards for and accredits those organizations that offer credentials. Among the membership boards is the American Board of Nursing Specialties, which represents 30 nursing specialty boards and testing agencies.

Types of Credentials

Several types of credentials are granted to and by healthcare providers, academic centers of health, professional organizations, and healthcare facilities. These include accreditation, academic degrees, regulatory licensure, membership in a professional organization, clinical privileges, and certification. Each type of credential carries its own privilege as well as responsibility.

ACCREDITATION

The American Board of Nursing Specialties (ABNS) broadly defines accreditation as "a voluntary, self-regulatory process by which governmental, nongovernmental, voluntary associations, or other statutory bodies grant federal recognition to programs or institutions that meet stated quality criteria" (American Board of Nursing Specialties, n.d.). Each type of accreditation is based on the service provided. For example, NOCA's credentialing body, the National Commission for Certifying Agencies, has accredited the American Nurses Credentialing Center (ANCC) as a certifying body of professional nursing. ANCC accredits universities and professional nursing organizations that offer continuing education contact hours. University schools and colleges of nursing are also accredited by the Commission on Credentialing of Nursing Education (CCNE). One university may be approved and accredited by multiple credentialing organizations examining different functions or standards.

ACADEMIC DEGREES

Academic degrees, such as the baccalaureate, master's, and doctoral degree, are yet another credential awarded for successful completion of a formal educational degree program. When educational measures of a college, such as the curriculum and testing methods, are evaluated by an accreditation body and approved for preparation of nurses, the public has some assurance that its graduates have met reasonable standards for safe practice. In addition, the development of core curriculum for levels of education and specialties of practice committees, such as those developed for advanced practice forensic nurses, promotes program consistency across colleges and helps to facilitate the development of common or standard competencies that can be measured for that specialty. Therefore, academic degree programs teach and promote standards of practice and are subsequently informed by the standards of practice set by nursing organizations.

REGULATION OF PRACTICE

Regulation is "the mandatory process government agencies grant time-limited permission to an individual to engage in a given profession, after verifying the individual has met predetermined and standardized criteria (experience, education, and examination)" (Durley, 2005, p. 7). Generally permission or license to practice is afforded by the regulatory agency, such as a board of nursing, when a nurse has graduated from an accredited academic program and passed a mandatory written test. The test measures entry level competencies, whether in generalist or advanced practice, to ensure the minimum-essential level for safety and effectiveness using rigorous testing practices for "high stakes" summative evaluation (Epstein, 2007, p. 389). The successful candidate's name is placed on a registry, which is continuously updated for past and current status. Licensure, which is title protected, is generally renewed at regular periods of time according to legislative directive (National Organization of Competency Assurance, 2006).

MEMBERSHIP IN A PROFESSIONAL ORGANIZATION

Professionals who are granted membership, by application or nomination, into an organization or "academy," often receive credentials. The membership qualifications range from successful passage of a certifying exam or evidence of extraordinary professional skills, accomplishments, or expertise. The candidate is then entitled membership or in some cases the title of "fellow." Maintenance of membership is generally contingent upon continued observance of the high standards and expectations of the professional organization.

CLINICAL PRIVILEGING

Clinical privileging, sometimes referred to as credentialing, is used within a healthcare organization or facility to denote a process of procuring, verifying, and analyzing the eligibility and qualifications of the clinician to execute healthcare services. Privileges are also extended to perform (order) specific diagnostic or therapeutic services in providing specific care within well-defined limits within that organization. Privileges are usually based on state practice acts, agency regulations, license, education, training, experience, competence, health status, and judgment (Smolenski, 2005).

CERTIFICATION

Certification is a formal recognition of the specialized knowledge, skills, experience, and, in some cases, personal attributes valued as critical standards of the profession and demonstrated by an individual. Certification is generally voluntary and awarded by nongovernmental entities that grant time-limited recognition and award credentials. Standards for certification should include competency testing, which is "psychometrically sound and legally defensible," to afford the certificant the greatest professional credibility (Goudreau & Smolenski, 2008). Certification programs include standards, policies, procedures, assessment instruments, and activities identified as necessary by the certification board of directors of that agency. They are also tasked with other decision making, including governance and terms for withdrawal of credentials (National Organization of Competency Assurance, 2006).

Certification and certificates should be differentiated. Certification attests to competence. A certificate can be awarded on completion of a nondegree attendance or curriculum-based educational offering. A certificate is not an academic degree or professional credential. The recipients are not required to demonstrate competence, but the certificate may be used to meet eligibility for certification depending on the criteria set by the certifying body. The National Organization of Competency Assurance has recently published the first standards for certificate programs, which specify the essential requirements for certificate programs and define the ingredient for a high-quality program (National Organization of Competency Assurance, 2009).

Assessment of Competence

The assessment of competence is integral to credential granting. Although they are often used synonymously, *competence* and *competencies* are not the same. Competence has been referred to as "an individual's intention or aptitude to engage in clinical activity—and competency—behavioral performance during episodes of practice" (Cassidy, 2009, p. 40). Competencies, on the other hand, are generally viewed as the demonstrated skill to perform an actual task that one is capable (or competent) of performing. Benner (1982) simplistically defined competence within nursing as "the ability to perform a task with desirable outcomes under varied circumstances in the real world" (p. 304). This is reflective of a behavioral model of competence that focuses on skills instead of a holistic integration of skills and more nontraditional dimensions of competence such as contextual, relationship, and affective/moral dimensions (Cowin et al., 2008; Epstein & Hundert, 2002). More recently, a broader understanding of competence, which is in line with our understanding of nursing, has been offered by Epstein (2007) in discussing medical competence. He wrote that competence includes "the habitual and judicious use of communication, knowledge, technical skills, clinical reasoning, emotions, values, and reflection in daily practice for the benefit of individuals and communities being served" (p. 387). In addition, Epstein and Hundert (2002) have observed that some of the more important domains of professional medical practice that we believe are valuable to nursing, such as interpersonal skills, lifelong learning, and professionalism, are often omitted from definitions of competence. Based on this understanding, Cassidy (2009) and McKinley et al. (2008) recommended a more "holistic assessment" method that would be multiprofessional, multilevel, multimodal to evaluate clinical skills that are needed to provide care in unpredictable care situations. The challenge is to design a method (or methods) that are psychometrically sound enough for national "high stakes," entry-level credentialing as well as recognition of expert levels of practice.

Organizations that offer credentialing should clearly delineate the expected levels of competencies for the novice (or advanced beginner) and the expert nurse (Benner, 1984). Measures should have a defined level of practice and education; they should differentiate between the nurse who is at an acceptable level of care standard and the nurse that is demonstrating "innovative excellence in clinical practice" (Cassidy, 2009, p. 41). Currently, entry-level certification examinations are based on role delineation studies conducted with individuals who have been in that role for a period of 3 to 5 years. Descriptions of practice during this period reflect entry level. Conversely, experts who have been in practice for many more years possess unique, elaborated, and well-organized bodies of knowledge that are often revealed only when they are triggered by characteristic clinical patterns. [This] "implies the practical wisdom to manage ambiguous and unstructured problems, balance competing explanations, avoid premature closure, note exceptions to rules and principles, and—even when under stress—choose one of the several courses of action that are acceptable but imperfect" (Epstein, 2007, p. 394). Therefore, analysis of practice, used to establish a criterion for standards through which performance is measured and individuals are accredited, must be conducted and set at the appropriate level of expectation (Smith, 1996).

FACTORS IN SELECTING MEASURES OF COMPETENCE

In selecting the appropriate tool to measure and predict competence, several factors should be considered. First, credentialing organizations consider the type of assessment to be conducted: formative, summative, or both. Each has a defined level of practice and education. Formative evaluation of an individual generally occurs during the education phase. It provides a snapshot of the student's current level of understanding and performance and may guide future learning or instructional design. To use it to the fullest advantage, formative assessment methods should provide for an opportunity to adequately appraise the student of their progress while "instilling motivations for continued learning" (Epstein, 2007, p. 388). Summative evaluation generally occurs at the conclusion of the education phase. It makes a more overall judgment of the student's competence or qualification to advance to higher levels of responsibility or education. Tools for summative assessment must possess high levels of rigor to appropriately determine an individual's readiness to graduate, enter into professional practice, or become certified in an advanced practice specialty.

Cary and Smolenski (2005) have delineated other questions to ask when selecting a competency measure (Table 51-1).

Finally, strength of the measurement instrument should be considered when making a selection. In determining the strength of a tool, the main factors are reliability, validity, the preparation provided to assessors administering or performing the assessment, and the impact of the instrument on future learning and practice. Reliability is the degree to which the method is stable in measuring the same competency with repeat administration by numerous assessors or, in the case of a written test, with similar forms of administration such as rewording the same question with the same meaning. Two alternate methods for increasing the reliability of an assessment tool are to either limit the number of assessors over an extended period of time or use a large number of assessors over a short period of time then allow enough time between subsequent use of the tool for reevaluation (Cary & Smolenski, 2005, p. 10). Because the degree to which a method of assessment measures what it is intended to measure may vary, establishing the validity of an instrument involves clearly defining what attributes are to be tested. Resources used to establish validity in professional organizations include practice standards, role delineation studies that narrow competency priorities, content experts who validate the application of content and theory, and early test takers who provide feedback on the test experience. In addition, Miller's pyramid of competence is one attempt to establish a framework for conceptualizing the essential facets of clinical competency and selection of methods that are most valid for measurement. The facets include the knowledge component (knows), applied knowledge (knows how), performance in simulated situations (shows how), and actual performance (does) (Wass, VanderVleuten, Shatzer, & Jones, 2001). In application, the pyramid points the assessor to the appropriate tool for the phase of skill development and gives direction to the learning that needs to occur in moving toward the goal of competent practice (performance). The feedback that candidates receive regarding their current level of competence may positively or negatively affect their future learning and practice, so criteria for selection of measurement items that are shared and validated by test takers can inform future competence building and further validate the instrument. The criterion and standards should also be reviewed in detail with the assessors. The strength

---

Table 51-1 Cary and Smolenski's Questions to Address When Selecting Competency Measures

- What current methodologies and techniques assess and document continuing professional competence?
- Should licensees be permitted to demonstrate their continuing competence by a variety of approved methods and techniques, or should licensing boards specify a particular approach?
- How frequently should licensees be required to demonstrate their competence?
- Should all licensees be required to demonstrate their continuing competence periodically, or should this requirement apply only to those licensees whose performance causes the licensing board to question their competence?
- How should state legislatures take into account the relationship between the continuing competence requirements of licensing boards and those of specialty certification boards?
- Should current board certification satisfy a licensing board that a licensee has again demonstrated his or her competence?
- How should state legislatures address the relationships between licensing board continuing competence requirements and those of hospitals and other provider institutions?
- Who should pay the costs of recertification? Licensees? The state?
- What should be the legal status of a licensee who cannot meet relicensure or recertification standards? What rules of confidentiality, if any, should apply to this information?
- What information should be given to the public concerning a healthcare provider's continuing competence?

Source: Smolenski, M. C. (2005). Credentialing, certification, and competence: Issues for new and seasoned nurse practitioners. *Journal of the American Academy of Nurse Practitioners,* 17(6), 201-204.

of measurement methods, particularly methods that are viewed as qualitative and subjective, will be improved by the development and use of clear grading guidelines and assessors thoroughly trained on the administration and measurement process.

Measures of Competence

Measures of competence have application to specific groups of people, under specific conditions, based on their construction and unique characteristics. Six commonly acknowledged methods of assessment will be discussed here: testing, continuing education, performance-based evaluation, anecdotal subjective evaluation, case studies, and portfolio.

TESTING

Testing (formerly written examination) evaluates knowledge and the ability to solve problems. Once considered the gold standard of evaluation, questions have been raised regarding its ability to assess attitudes such as ethical treatment of patients or cultural competence, as well as abilities and behaviors in the clinical setting. Currently, testing's greatest contribution is in the summative high-stakes evaluation such as academic progression, licensing, and certification. This is due to the inherent ability to assess multiple content areas and the ability to use a computer to score a large number of tests in a short period of time with high reliability. The main limitations of testing result from the fact that many tests are "context poor" (Epstein, 2007, p. 390). It is difficult and time consuming to write complex questions in multiple choice, short answer, and matching formats that measure competencies and the ability to transfer that understanding to other clinical situations. Structured essays are well suited for formative or summative evaluation because they allow for more complexity of thought process including demonstration of synthesis of information and integration of assigned literature. Essays can also eliminate the problem of cueing the student found in other item formats. But structured essays take time to grade and like oral examinations depend on clear grading guidelines for validity as well as reliability (Cary & Smolenski, 2005).

CONTINUING EDUCATION

Continuing education requirements are found in all arenas of credentialing. It is a commonly held belief that with increased knowledge comes increased levels of performance. And certainly participation in educational opportunities is a demonstration of a professional's dedication to learning. Therefore, more exposure to new knowledge should create a better understanding of the scientific principles that undergird practice, and it should also promote professionalism overall. However, that is not necessarily true. Although formal educational offerings that feature a testing element have proven to increase knowledge and subsequent performance, there is no strong evidence that knowledge obtained from either attendance at a lecture, electronic offering, or other didactic continuing education offerings results in a change of behavior. However, when content is offered in conjunction with in vivo simulation or hands-on participation, it has a strong correlation with improved competency and is more closely predictive of actual practice.

PERFORMANCE-BASED EVALUATION

Observation of clinical behaviors that constitute competent practice can occur directly in simulated or actual patient care settings. There are advantages and disadvantages to both methods of evaluation. Both are prone to error because assessment findings are dependent on a subjective interpretation of one or more assessors. However, both can be used as powerful tools for instruction and development of student capabilities.

Simulation is one form of performance-based evaluation that is growing in popularity and use despite the financial and time expenditures. It asks participants to imagine an actual clinical situation–often created by clinical laboratory settings with real equipment–and then respond to that situation with interventions that demonstrate in vivo competencies. It is perceived to be a valuable formative as well as summative evaluation instrument as long as, in the case of a formative evaluation setting, time is allotted for appropriate feedback. Checklists of target behaviors and multiple raters across multiple cases are all strategies used to increase reliability. Sufficient time for development of the case is considered essential.

The same principles apply when standardized patients are used in "simulated" patient care assessment. Standardized patients are individuals employed to interact with clinicians and facilitate their instruction in performing patient assessment and procedures of care. They are an exceptional resource who, when well prepared with an understanding of the behaviors to be evaluated as well as the standard for success, can participate in the instruction and the evaluation of students. Then, a series of stations can be set up to teach or test clinical competencies. This is known as objective structured clinical examinations (OSCE) and can be used in the same manner for education and evaluation.

Computer and video simulation eliminates the need for synchronous evaluation by multiple assessors. This in turn can greatly reduce the cost of simulated testing. Fero, Witsberger, Wesmiller, Zullo, and Hoffman (2009) demonstrated the use of 10 videotaped vignettes that simulated change in patient status to develop critical thinking skills in 2144 newly hired nurses using the Performance-Based Development System Assessment tool. The research was conducted using Benner's Novice to Expert Model and results indicated that years of experience was the greatest predictor of competence but that nurses with experience and higher degrees performed the best. Results were used to plan learning experiences to develop critical thinking for the new hires.

Clinicians know that assessment of potential or actual clinical practice skill is complex and behaviors that constitute competent practice are difficult to isolate, especially in actual patient care settings. More than one method of performance-based evaluation is often required. The predominant use of multisource measurement tools in healthcare occurs most often within medical residency programs. Multisource measurements, also known as 360-degree assessment, have increased measurement validity when applied to testing of competencies identified as core by the American College of Graduate Medical Education (ACGME) (Smith, 1996). For example, Brown University's residency program evaluates each physician using methods most amenable to the ACGME framework. The 360-degree assessment program utilizes evaluation by student peers and nurses working with residents, in combination with a portfolio that includes quality assurance projects, research projects, community service projects, and a compilation of materials germane to the educational instruction (Brown Medical School Residency Program in Emergency Medicine, n.d.). Like many of the new applications of multisource measurement, there is no definitive research on the efficacy of this application. Although nurses have participated as assessors of physician performance or as participants in a multidisciplinary team evaluation, there is little experience with 360-degree evaluation in nursing.

ANECDOTAL SUBJECTIVE EVALUATION

Anecdotal recall of clinical skills by participants in evaluation situations can be valuable when shared in the appropriate manner. Participants may include peers, clients who are the recipients of care, incognito standardized patients, supervisors, and finally the candidates themselves. Tools for assessment vary from detailed procedure-specific forms (Miller, 2007) to more holistic tools that make use of larger competency categories that are applied generically to all patient situations and clinical settings for a variety of practice disciplines (McKinley et al., 2008). Peers seem willing to offer criticism and perform consistently well regardless of the manner in which they are selected. Their observations are valuable and valued by the candidate as long as their observations are kept confidential and the information is presented by a supportive adviser. Client observations have a tendency to be inflated but may be used to determine global competencies such as the ability to instill trust, achieve patient satisfaction, and use effective communication. Insurers have used this form of assessment as a summative method of evaluation to determine who may participate in their program and which clinicians to bonus for exceptional performance. Assessment by a supervisor takes on an equally unique perspective. Supervisors along with patients, incognito and otherwise, are in a position to judge actual practice habits, especially those considered competencies of professionalism such as communications patterns, teamwork, presentation skills, organizational skills, and work habits.

Self-assessment is a necessary skill for all competent clinicians. The desire to improve judgment and abilities combined with a willingness to evaluate practice patterns that need improvement are characteristics that foster the development of professionals who are lifelong learners. However, individuals have an intrinsic limitation in their ability to know themselves and to see performance objectively. In fact, the ability to rate themselves on past clinical performance does not necessarily carry over to the ability to make that assessment in real time in new patient situations. More work is needed to develop methods of self-assessment that not only provide data for decisions on competency but will link reflective practice to self-learning and career development (Cowin et al., 2008).

CASE STUDIES

Case studies have been used in a number of settings as an instructional, as well as an evaluative, tool. Case studies allow for a complexity of thought and decision making that can be offered as a whole for illustration of salient points or learning objectives. Or the information can be presented in segments, prompting the student to respond to given data. The interaction between candidate and assessor may be presented as synchronous or asynchronous. For example, online courses often utilize case studies to illustrate the application of modular didactic content as a first step toward incorporating the principles into clinical practice. Oral exams often use case studies that evaluate the ability of the candidate to assess a situation, gather critical data, and make appropriate decisions based on the data at hand. The medium of case study presentations can be in hard copy or computer script, utilizing graphs, video, and photography. In nursing, staging with standardized patients promotes authenticity for the candidate. Conversely, students and candidates for credentialing may be asked to write a case study that demonstrates their understanding of patient care guidelines. The case study may be fictional, or in the case of more high-stakes credentialing, the case should be an authentic one in which

the participants are the primary providers of care. Currently, the case study is commonly used as a summative evaluation component of doctor of nursing programs. But determination of competency based on evaluation of a case study is the most subjective of the methods discussed. Efforts to increase the reliability of this method include the use of well-developed measurement criteria based on accepted standards of practice. In addition, assessors should be educated regarding best practice in evaluation and opportunities to discuss initial evaluation efforts to understand discrepancies in ratings. The scores of each evaluator may be compared using statistical tests to determine inter-rater reliability. In addition, because of the wide variety of case study formats, candidates should receive information on developing a case study and suggested templates as a structure for inclusion of required data. With these efforts, a case study that is rich in context can provide an opportunity for candidates to demonstrate the type of knowledge, critical thinking, and decision making that is representative of their actual practice.

PORTFOLIO

The portfolio method of evaluation is similar to and can be used as a component of 360-degree multisource evaluation. It combines many of the assessments heretofore discussed into one tool with criteria based on the nature of the data (or evidence piece collected). Because no one measurement tool has proven adequate to evaluate all professional competencies across the spectrum of knowledge, skills, behaviors, and attitude, it is postulated that the combination of methods allows the limitations of one instrument to be compensated for by the strength of another method. Driessen and colleagues, in a 2007 review of some 1990 sources on portfolio, collated data against the research question, number of subjects, design, setting, findings, and limitations, purpose and content, mentoring, and assessment. In addition, impact was analyzed using a modified version of Kirkpatrick's hierarchy. The authors concluded that successful use of the portfolio, particularly in the academic setting, is contingent on "clearly communicated goals and procedures; integration with curriculum and assessment; flexible structure; support through mentoring, and measures to heighten feasibility and reduce required time. Moderately good inter-rater reliability was reported and global criteria and discussions among raters were beneficial. Integration of the portfolio into curriculum including periodic review were recommendations for increasing the validity of the instrument" (Driessen, van Tartwuk, van der Vleuten, & Wass, 2007, p. 1224). Despite the favorable use of portfolio in the educational setting, there is currently no conclusive evidence that portfolios are a consistent method of measuring competence in entry-level and practicing professionals. And because of the variety of research designs used to test the efficacy of the portfolio, no meta-analysis is possible now. But that has not swayed proponents. Epstein (2007) has compared the combination of assessment methods in the portfolio to the art of diagnosis requiring the clinician to create an overall picture based on available data.

Nurses have used portfolio as a tool to demonstrate in the academic arena since the 1980s. Then in the 1990s, healthcare and professional organizations started to use portfolio as a tool of self-reflection on practice measured against current standards of practice (Dennison, 2005). More recently, portfolios are used to make a determination on individual promotions in the United Kingdom, as well as an indicator of the overall quality of care such as the Magnet Hospital Program Accreditation Program (Dion, n.d.). Regulatory bodies have utilized the portfolio for licensure evaluation in Ontario and the United Kingdom but only to a limited extent in the United States. The National Council of State Boards of Nursing (2005) developed a model portfolio called the Continued Competency Accountability Profile in 1998. However, Nebraska is currently the only state to require a portfolio for relicensure (Law, 2006). The Credentialing Committee of the International Society of Genetics in Nursing (ISOGN) also began work in 1998 to establish the first initial certification effort for nurses utilizing a portfolio method. In cooperation with the American Nurses' Credentialing Center's Commission on Accreditation (ANCCCA), ISOGN utilized the Genetics Nurse Scope and Standards as the framework for evaluation criteria. A small ad hoc committee of genetics experts developed a tool that delineated well-defined criteria of observable behaviors that demonstrate professional competency in six standards or areas of care in a multisource document using Neural Net, which purports the ability to compile scores based on not only a predetermined standard score but against a criterion that evolves with increasing numbers of portfolio evaluated (Cook, Kase, Middleton, & Monsen, 2003). In 2007, after several years of conversation with ISOGN and ANCCA, the International Association of Forensic Nurses (IAFN) initiated a similar process to institute use of the portfolio method to assess competencies based on practice standards for the advanced practice forensic nurse. Those efforts are expected to come to fruition in 2009 when the first candidates will be recognized by the American Nurses Credentialing Center.

Application of the Credentialing Process in Forensic Nursing

The demonstration of competence has become a key regulatory requirement and performance indicator for nurses. The ability to evaluate and predict the competence of nurses is key to safe, quality patient outcomes. Competency measurement may also be a unit-based activity, where it is incorporated in a quality assurance or evidence-based practice surveillance program for individuals or organizations. Miller (2007) recommended utilization of del Bueno's Dimensions of Competent Performance, as an assessment model for unit-based evaluation, based on three dimensions of competencies: technical skills, interpersonal skills, and critical thinking skills. Early work to establish a correlation between domains and practice outcomes is limited but promising (Cowin et al., 2008).

Environmental Influences on Forensic Nursing Credentials

New specialties in nursing as well as forensic science are continually developing. Nurses coming to forensic nursing emerge from a number of educational and experiential backgrounds. Therefore, credentials are varied. A forensic nurse who is trained by *Finding Words* to interview child victims of violence may be a certified forensic interviewer. A forensic nurse with a master's degree in forensic science may be employed to conduct investigations for a police department. Nurses who focus on their career in forensic practice may become fellows in the American Academy of Forensic Science. All of these are examples of forensic nurses who are credentialed. Additional credentials can define their specialized focus to others, including the judicial system. During a Daubert hearing, qualifications of the forensic nurse may come into question when expert testimony is challenged. Credentials may be required for regulation of practice limited by a state through boards of nursing. Politically, the credentials may be needed when other disciplines attempt to limit the practice or reimbursement for care by nurses in a forensic setting.

National and International Credentialing for Forensic Nurses

The majority of registered nurses across the globe are graduates of an educational program, licensed by their regulatory body, but are not certified in their area of practice. Certification is used as a marker of mastery of a specialty, but it is not a regulatory requirement for entry into a generalist practice such as a licensure exam. Advanced practice nurses require national board certification to receive state licensure to practice and in most cases prescribe medications. National certification is available to forensic nurses, at both the generalist and advanced practice level, from a variety of certification programs, to demonstrate competency in subspecialty areas (including sexual assault, death investigation, legal consulting, and corrections) as well as a broad generalist forensic nursing practice. Competencies, eligibility criteria, method of assessment, process, and requirements for continued competence are largely addressed by nurses in the practice area and the parent organizations or certification bodies.

SEXUAL ASSAULT EXAMINATION

The Forensic Nurse Certification Board was established in 2002, and later that year, the sexual assault nurse examiner–adult/adolescent (SANE A) certification exam was developed. The examination is based on analysis of the forensic nursing care of adults and adolescents, conducted by a panel of practicing content experts to develop the defining characteristics of competent practice for content and face validity. Appropriate tests to determine content validity and reliability were used in both development and refinement of the test, ensuring that the exam is a psychometrically sound and legally defensible instrument. Revisions of the certification exam were conducted in 2005 and 2008. In 2007, the sexual assault nurse examiner–pediatric examination was developed using the same process to establish validity as well as reliability; pass rates for both examinations have been consistent over test sites from year to year. In 2009, there are more than 1000 board-certified SANE As internationally; the majority practice in the United States and Canada. The majority of IAFN members identify themselves as SANEs, but there are no statistical data on the number of forensic nurses or SANEs internationally (see Tables 51-2 and 51-3).

DEATH INVESTIGATION

The American Board of Medical Legal Death Investigators (ABMDI) certifies individuals who have the proven knowledge and skills necessary to perform medicolegal death investigations as set forth in the National Institutes of Justice 1999 publication, "Death Investigation: A Guide for the Scene Investigator." The ABMDI offers certification at two levels: board registered (basic) and board certified (advanced). Forensic nurses are eligible in both categories depending on their experiential qualifications and member recommendation. The credential assists the courts and public in evaluating competence of the certified individual. In 2005, the ABMDI was accredited by the Forensic Specialties Accreditation Board.

Table 51-2 Eligibility Criteria for SANE A

To become a board-certified sexual assault nurse examiner (SANE A), a candidate must meet the following qualifications:

- Hold a current, full, and unrestricted license as a registered nurse (RN) in the United States or its territories, or a license as a first-level general nurse in the country/jurisdiction of current practice. If the candidate is not licensed in the United States or its territories, the candidate must have successfully completed a postsecondary (as defined by the country) nursing education program that included classroom instruction and clinical practice in the five major areas of nursing: medical, surgical, obstetric, pediatric, and psychiatric.
- Have a minimum of two full years of practice as a registered nurse in the United States or as a first-level general nurse in the country of licensure.
- Have successfully completed an adult/adolescent SANE education program that includes either (1) a minimum of 40 continuing-education contact hours of didactic (classroom) instruction or (2) three semester hours (or the equivalent) of academic credit in an accredited school of nursing.
- Have had supervised clinical practice until determined competent in SANE practice. Current SANE competency in the care of adults and adolescents must be validated by an appropriate clinical authority (e.g., nursing supervisor, formal peer review), as outlined in the adult section of the IAFN's SANE education guidelines (1998).

Table 51-3 Eligibility Criteria for SANE P

To become a board certified sexual assault nurse examiner (SANE P), a candidate must meet the following qualifications:

- Hold a current, full, and unrestricted license as a registered nurse (RN) in the United States or its territories or a license as a first-level general nurse in the country/jurisdiction of current practice. If the candidate is not licensed in the United States or its territories, the candidate must have successfully completed a postsecondary (as defined by the country) nursing education program that included classroom instruction and clinical practice in the five major areas of nursing: medical, surgical, obstetric, pediatric, and psychiatric. A transcript documenting nursing education may be requested from the candidate's nursing education program for validation.
- Have a minimum of three years of practice as a registered nurse in the United States or as a first-level general nurse in the country of licensure, with a minimum of one year (or academic equivalent) of clinical experience conducting pediatric medical/forensic sexual abuse evaluations in the past three years. The clinical activities are those described in the clinical competencies.
- Have completed a pediatric-specific SANE didactic and clinical coursework consistent with the most recently published IAFN *Sexual Assault Nurse Examiner Adult/Adolescent* and *Pediatric Education Guidelines.*
- Have completed adolescent-specific SANE didactic and clinical coursework consistent with the most recently published IAFN *Sexual Assault Nurse Examiner Adult/Adolescent* and *Pediatric Education Guidelines.*
- Have validation of current clinical competence in the performance of pediatric medical/forensic examinations, signed by a practicing healthcare provider in the area of child sexual assault, as outlined in the document, IAFN *SANE Pediatric Clinical Competency Objectives.**
- Have validation of current clinical competence in the performance of adolescent medical/forensic examinations, signed by a practicing healthcare provider in the area of adolescent sexual assault† or proof of IAFN SANE A certification.

*Validation must include the pediatric clinical skills areas listed in the Required Clinical Preceptorship section of IAFN's *Sexual Assault Nurse Examiner Adult/Adolescent and Pediatric Education Guidelines.*
†Validation must include the adolescent clinical skills areas listed in the Clinical Preceptorship section of the IAFN's *Sexual Assault Nurse Examiner Adult/Adolescent and Pediatric Education Guidelines.*

LEGAL NURSE CONSULTATION

The legal nurse consultant is a licensed, registered nurse who performs a critical analysis of clinical and administrative nursing practice, healthcare facts and issues, and their outcomes for the legal profession, healthcare professions, consumers of healthcare and legal services, and others as appropriate. With a strong educational and experiential foundation, the legal nurse consultant is qualified to assess adherence to standards and guidelines of healthcare practice as it applies to the nursing and healthcare professions. Founded in 1989, the American Association of Legal Nurse Consultants (AALNC, www.aalnc.org) is a not-for-profit membership organization dedicated to the professional enhancement and growth of registered nurses practicing in the specialty of legal nurse consulting and to advancing this nursing specialty. The AALNC is the preeminent resource for professionals with an interest in the legal nurse consulting arena, including novice and veteran legal nurse consultants. The AALNC provides networking opportunities, educational advancement, and professional development, and it supports certification through the American Legal Nurse Consultant Certification Board (ALNCCB).

CORRECTIONS

The Correctional Certification Program is the certification arm of the American Corrections Association. The association offers testing for the certified corrections nurse (CCN) and the certified corrections nurse manager (CCN/M). This category includes individuals who work with both staff and offenders in a correctional setting. It includes nurses who are responsible for implementing agency procedures but do not supervise or evaluate personnel. It is based on performance-based Standards for the correctional healthcare and corrections nurse: Scope and Standards of Practice (ANA). Distinctions between the two levels are educational preparation and length of employment and responsibility of supervising other personnel. Recertification requirements are contact hours, active practice in corrections, and satisfactory performance evaluations.

CERTIFIED FORENSIC NURSE

The American Board of Forensic Nurses functions through the American Board of Forensic Examiners, which is the certification board associated with the American College of Forensic Examiners International. Eligibility criteria for the certified forensic nurse (CFN) include the following: must hold a current, full, and unrestricted license as a registered nurse (RN) in the United States or its territories or hold a license as a first-level general nurse in the country/jurisdiction of current practice; must have practiced for a minimum of 5 years as a registered nurse in the United States, or as a first-level general nurse in the country of licensure; must have successfully completed a formal didactic educational program in forensic nursing including a three-hour undergraduate,

graduate, or postgraduate course (or an equivalent hour-based educational course), including a minimum of 40 contact hours in the core areas of forensic nursing; must be an American College of Forensic Examiners (ACFE member in good standing; must validate his or her current forensic nurse competency by providing supporting documentation (a clinical experience validation form) signed by an appropriate clinical authority, such as a forensic mentor, employer, or nursing supervisor; and must provide two professional references on the CFN application.

ADVANCED FORENSIC NURSE RECOGNITION

The international definition of an advanced practice nurse (APN) is "a registered nurse who has acquired expert knowledge base, complex decision-making skills and clinical competencies for expanded practice, the characteristics of which are shaped by the context and/or country in which s/he is credentialed to practice. A master's degree is recommended for entry level" (Schober & Affara, 2006, p. 12). Although the definition is uniform, the title is not. Nurses serving in the APN role are generally recognized as nurse midwives (CNMs), clinical nurse specialists (CNSs), nurse practitioners (NPs), or nurse anesthetists (CRNAs). Advanced nursing practice—now differentiated from advanced practice nursing—includes nurse administrators and public health nurses prepared at the graduate level (Doctor of Nursing Practice Essentials). The minimum educational preparation ranges from undergraduate to graduate preparation at the doctoral level. Several professional organizations offer certification, including the American Nurses Credentialing Center, the National Board on Certification and Recertification of Nurse Anesthetists, the American Midwifery Certification Board, and the American Academy of Nurse Practitioners.

Advanced practice forensic nurses (AFNs) are advanced practice nurses who have further specialized preparation in forensic nursing. Certification is often used as a qualification for entry into advanced practice or as proof that the nurse has mastered a specialty of advanced practice. Regulatory agencies (such as those within the government) may use certification as requirement for title protection and legal authorization to practice. Qualifications for the recognition of one's AFN status include a graduate education and advanced forensic nursing experience and competencies. The required graduate preparation is initially inclusive of any graduate degree with practice focus in forensic nursing. Subsequent to two years, the credential will be offered to graduate preparation in programs specific to nursing. By definition, APNs are board certified, and they are title protected in the several countries. Recognition of AFNs is based on competencies outlined by the IAFN and the American Nurses Association (ANA) and consistent with competencies for APNs in other countries such as Canada.

The portfolio method of measurement was selected for credentialing because of the complexity and flexibility of the method as previously outlined. Because the IAFN is an international professional organization, the portfolio will allow nurses from all countries to submit their data in the language of choice. Additionally, the portfolio method is supported by the National Council of State Boards of Nursing (NCSBN) (National Council of State Boards of Nursing, 2005).

The only degree programs that specialize in educating the forensic nurse are at the graduate level; there remains a relatively fewer number of AFNs than generalists in the IAFN (Table 51-4). Additionally, the position outlined by the National Council of State Boards of Nursing regarding limitations of new certifi-

Table 51-4 Competencies of an Advanced Practice Forensic Nurse Addressed in the ANCC Portfolio Recognition Based on Forensic Nurses Scope and Standards of Practice

- **Education.** Lifelong learning to maintain currency and expand knowledge
- **Scientific process.** Provides developmentally appropriate, culturally sensitive, and nondiscriminatory client-centered care
- **Collegiality, collaboration, and ethics.** Behaviors that support professional practice as part of the interdisciplinary team
- **Research, QI, and quality of practice.** Uses findings of sound methods of inquiry to systematically improve the quality of client care
- **Professional practice evaluation.** Seeks feedback to identify strengths and areas for improvement
- **Resource utilization and leadership.** Leads efforts to utilize a range of resources, evaluate innovative care options, and teach others

cation examinations accepted for state licensure of APNs did not support the development of a certification exam (National Council of State Boards of Nursing, 2002). In the future, development of an examination will be informed by data from the portfolio.

Controversies on Credentialing of Forensic Nurses

EFFORTS OF PROFESSIONAL GROUPS OUTSIDE OF NURSING TO REGULATE PRACTICE

Some professional organizations outside of nursing have recently attempted to regulate or constrain the trade of nurses. Internationally, physicians have opposed expansion of nursing practice and limited the ability of nurses to care for victims of injury and perpetrators of crime. The American Medical Association has taken the position that APNs are not qualified to practice independently despite evidence to the contrary (Coddington & Sands, 2008; Sekula, 2005). The American Academy of Pediatrics has published a position paper that states that generalist nurses should not conduct evidentiary exams without physician supervision (Pediatrics, 1999). It is, however, the purview of a discipline to define what constitutes a safe and effective scope of practice. The ability to accurately define competence and the validity of current measures create confidence in the ability of nurses to self-regulate (Cowin et al., 2008).

CLINICAL NURSE SPECIALIST SCOPE OF PRACTICE

Currently, there is no specialty certification for a clinical nurse specialist in several clinical focus areas, including forensic nursing. This lack of specialty certifications prevents credentials to practice by regulatory agencies in some states. When certification and subsequent authority to practice is a requirement for reimbursement, it limits care and constrains trade (Goudreau & Smolenski, 2008). Prescribing and other individual patient care competencies have not been stressed in the preparation of the clinical nurse specialist. In some programs, pharmacology was not a required course. The NCSBN has taken the position that while academic preparation of the clinical nurse specialist occurs in the graduate setting, the academic preparation does not consistently prepare the graduate for a new scope of practice and the certification examination is geared toward increased content in specialties but not a new level of responsibilities. The NCSBN is moving toward a more limited credentialing of APNs, focused on the traditional roles and across the life span groups of patients (Goudreau & Smolenski, 2008; National Council of State Boards of Nursing, 2002).

There is also an Advanced Practice Compact (APRN) covering all four categories of advanced practice—NPs, CNSs, certified nurse midwives, and CRNAs—which was introduced in 2004. Utah and Iowa are the only two states that have joined the compact for APRNs as of October 2007 and only for the purpose of recognizing NPs and CNSs.

CERTIFICATION ARENAS

Currently the Forensic Nurse Certification Board (FNCB) does not certify non-nurses. Every year the FNCB receives requests from non-nurses, usually physician assistants, for changes to the eligibility criteria. After years of successful certification of nurses worldwide in the care of sexual assault patients, there is concern as to how the change would affect not only the quality of the care, but the applicability of care standards within other disciplines and the influence other disciplines will have on the certification board. Proponents point to the National Protocol for Sexual Assault Medical Forensic Examinations, which acknowledges that more than one discipline is qualified to conduct evidentiary examinations (Office on Violence Against Women, 2004). Related is the issue of nurses such as death investigators certifying with organizations outside of nursing. Can organizations outside of nursing hold the same values that guide nursing practice or represent nurses in the marketplace? Therein lays the motivation to develop new credentials for forensic nurses.

New Credentials on the Horizon
RECOGNITION OF ADVANCED PRACTICE NURSES

Recognition of the advanced forensic nurse by the American Nurses Credential Commission took place in 2009. While the credential will represent a specialty focus for the AFN, it is not anticipated to represent an avenue for initial or entry-level certification. It is anticipated that CNS will first seek certification from the Core Certification Exam for the CNS specialty. The exam addresses care across the life span regardless of specialization (Goudreau & Smolenski, 2008) www.nursecredentialing.org/NurseSpecialties/CNSCoreExam.aspx). It was launched in 2009. The 150-question exam covers the core competencies identified for the CNS through a role analysis (American Nurses Credentialing Center, 2008). The majority of graduate forensic nursing programs prepare forensic nurses in a curriculum described as focusing on or utilizing a framework for CNSs. It is uncertain how many states will accept this credential for APN practice privileges and licensure qualifications.

International Association of Forensic Nurses Generalist Certification

The IAFN is in the process of selecting an organization to begin development of a certification exam for the entry-level generalist nurse working in a forensic setting. Development will begin with a nationally conducted role analysis because of the diversity of forensic clients and practice settings. The *Scope and Standards of Practice* will provide a framework for the designation of competencies.

Forensic Nurse Death Investigation

Several nurses who practice in death investigation are certified by the American Board of Medical Legal Death Investigators. Early research in role delineation for forensic nurse death investigator by Mitchell (2006) began the first attempt to demonstrate a difference in the perspective of nurses and non-nurse investigators. Further research is needed to examine the intricacies of the role. Forensic nurse death investigation education guidelines as well as Scope and Standards of Practice are currently under development. These documents will be necessary before a certification can be considered.

Summary

As practicing nurses describe current practice and roles are defined, there is a better understanding of the knowledge, skills, abilities, and attitudes necessary to practice in a particular discipline or specialty. Differentiation of similar roles within and outside of nursing is possible when competencies are well delineated. Then, best practice can be tested and standards of care recognized. Finally, evaluation of competencies can become the basis for a number of different types of credentials recognized by the public as an indication of safe and, in some cases, expert care. Forensic nurses who have a good understanding of credentialing and the standards of appropriate competency measurement will be able to make informed decisions regarding the credentials desired for their own career advancement.

Websites

American Association of Legal Nurse Consultants
www.aalnc.org
American Board of Forensic Nurses
www.acfei.com/forensic_certifications/cfn
American Board of Medical Legal Death Investigation (ABMDI)
http://medschool.slu.edu/abmdi/index.php
American Board of Nursing Specialties, Research Bibliography
www.nursingcertification.org
American Corrections Association
www.aca.org/certification/ccn.asp
International Council of Nurses Registry for Credentialing Research (ICNRCR)
www.icn.gq.nu
Professional Portfolio
http://decisioncritical.com/products_portfolio.asp

References

American Board of Nursing Specialties. (n.d.). *Accreditation standards [Electronic Version]*. Retrieved April 1, 2009 from http://www.nursingcertification.org/pdf/ac_standards_short.pdf.

American Nurses Credentialing Center. (2008). *Clinical nurse specialist core exam board certification test content outline*. Retrieved March 1, 2009, from http://www.nursecredentialing.org/Documents/Certification/TestContentOutlines/CNSCoreExamTCO.aspx.

Benner, P. (1982). Issues in competency-based testing. *Nursing Outlook*, 30(5), 303–309.

Benner, P. (1984). *From novice to expert: Excellence and power in clinical nursing practice*. Menlo Park, California: Addison-Wesley.

Brown Medical School Residency Program in Emergency Medicine. (n.d.). *Introduction to the 360 degree evaluation process*. Retrieved April 20, 2009, from http://www.brown.edu/Administration/Emergency_Medicine/emr/pages/Eval_360_Intro.pdf.

Cary, A. H., & Smolenski, M. C. (2005). Overview of competency and the methods for evaluating continued competence. In R. B. Monsen (Ed.), *Nursing portfolios* (pp. 1–10). Silver Springs, MD: nursesbooks.org: The Publishing Program of ANA.

Cassidy, S. (2009). Interpretation of competence in student assessment. *Nursing Standard*, 23(18), 39–46.

Coddington, J. A., & Sands, L. P. (2008). Cost of health care and quality outcomes of patients at nurse-managed clinics. *Nursing Economics, 26*(2), 75–83.

Cook, S. S., Kase, R., Middleton, L., & Monsen, R. B. (2003). Portfolio evaluation for professional competence: Credentialing in genetics for nurses. *Journal of Professional Nursing, 19*(2), 85–90.

Cowin, L. S., Hengstberger-Sims, C., Eagar, S. C., Gregory, L., Andrew, S., & Rolley, J. (2008). Competence measurements: Testing convergent validity for two measures. *Journal of Advanced Nursing, 64*(3), 272–277.

Dennison, R. D. (2005). Portfolios: Current uses. In R. B. Monsen (Ed.), *Genetics nursing portfolios: A new model for the profession* (pp. 25–36). Silver Springs, MA: nursesbooks.org: American Nurses Association.

Dion, K. (n.d.). *Critical portfolio.* Retrieved May 1, 2009, from http://decisioncritical.com/products_portfolio.asp.

Driessen, E., van Tartwuk, J., van der Vleuten, C., & Wass, V. (2007). Portfolios in medical education: Why do they meet with mixed success? A systematic review [Electronic Version]. *Medical Education, 41*, 1224–1233.

Durley, C. (2005). *The NOCA guide to understanding credentialing concepts.* Washington, DC: National Organization of Competency Assurance.

Epstein, R. M. (2007). Assessment in medical education. *The New England Journal of Medicine, 356*(4), 387–396.

Epstein, R. M., & Hundert, E. M. (2002). Defining and assessing professional competence. *Journal of the American Medical Association, 287*(2), 226–235.

Fero, L. J., Witsberger, C. M., Wesmiller, S. W., Zullo, T. G., & Hoffman, L. A. (2009). Critical thinking ability of new graduate and experienced nurses. *Journal of Advanced Nursing, 65*(1), 139–148.

Goudreau, K. A., & Smolenski, M. C. (2008). Credentialing and certification issues: Issues for clinical nurse specialists [Electronic Version]. *Clinical Nurse Specialist, 22*, 245–246.

Joint Commission International. (n.d.). *About joint commission international.* Retrieved May 1, 2009, from http://www.jointcommissioninternational.org/about-jci/.

Law, E. (2006). State-by-state guide for RN license renewal requirements [Electronic Version]. *Nursing, 36*, 30–33. Retrieved May 1, 2009 from http://www.nursingcenter.com/library/JournalArticle.asp?Article_ID=636579.

McKinley, R. K., Strand, J., Gray, T., Schuwirth, L., Alun-Jones, T., & MIller, H. (2008). Development of a tool to support holistic generic assessment of clinical procedure skills. *Medical Education, 42*(6), 916–1617.

Miller, P. J. (2007). Enhancing effectiveness in assessing forensic nursing staff competency. *Journal of Forensic Nursing, 3*(2), 72–76, 86.

Mitchell, S. A. (2006). *Program evaluation of the forensic nurse death investigator program at the Harris County medical examiner's office.* Unpublished dissertation. University of Tennessee Health Science Center.

National Association of Competency Assurance. (2009). *National Association of Competency Assurance (home page).* Retrieved May 16, 2009, from http://www.noca.org/.

National Council of State Boards of Nursing. (2002). *Regulation of advanced practice nursing.* National Council of State Boards of Nursing, Inc. Retrieved from https://www.ncsbn.org/index.htm. Accessed March 24, 2010.

National Council of State Boards of Nursing. (2005). *Meeting the ongoing challenge of continued competence.* Chicago, IL.

National Organization of Competency Assurance. (2006). *NOCA's basic guide to credentialing terminology.* Retrieved May 16, 2006, from http://www.noca.org/portals/0/nocasbasicguidetocredentialingterminology.pdf.

National Organization of Competency Assurance. (2009). *NOCA 1100-quality standard for assessment-based certificate programs,* from http://www.noca.org/PublicationsandResources/Publications/tabid/77/Default.aspx.

Office on Violence Against Women. (2004). *A national protocol for sexual assault medical forensicd examinations - adults/adolescents.* Washington, DC: U.S. Department of Justice.

Pediatrics, A. A. O. (1999). Guidelines for the evaluation of sexual abuse abuse of children. *Pedatrics, 103*(1), 186–190.

Schober, M., & Affara, F. (2006). *International council of nurses: Advanced nursing practice.* Oxford, UK: Blackwell Publishing, Ltd.

Sekula, K. L. (2005). The advance practice forensic nurse in the emergency department. *Topic in Emergency Medicine, 27*(1), 5–14.

Smith, M. K. (1996). *Competence and competency.* Retrieved April 1, 2009, from http://www.infed.org/biblio/b-comp.htm.

Smolenski, M. C. (2005). Credentialing, certification, and competence: Issues for new and seasoned nurse practitioners. *Jounal of the American Academy of Nurse Practitioners, 17*(6), 201–204.

Wass, V., VanderVleuten, C., Shatzer, J., & Jones, R. (2001). Assessment of clinical competence. *The Lancet, 357*, 945–949.

CHAPTER 52 Global Expansion and Future Perspectives

Virginia A. Lynch

Global advances in forensic science and technology; united with dramatic economic, political, societal, and environmental changes, have created unprecedented opportunities for an international focus on the science of forensic nursing. Considering that nurses comprise the largest group of healthcare workers worldwide, forensic nurse examiners represent a previously untapped resource to universal healthcare and are the ideal group to advance international considerations in health and justice.

Although specific legal concerns within the healthcare communities vary from country to country, all nations struggle with issues of public health and safety. Quality forensic services have been inadequate to deal with victims of sexual violence, domestic abuse, cultural and religious rituals, ethnic cleansing, and other atrocities that accompany armed conflict.

Nurses throughout the world, despite wide cultural variations, share the basic goal of providing care to the people of their country. These issues have been addressed by the International Council of Nurses (ICN), the American Nurses Association, and the World Health Assembly. Forensic nurses have become integral partners in the new medicolegal systems of the world. Their unique contributions assist in substantiating prosecutor's claims, exonerating suspects who are falsely accused, and aiding both victims and defendants in difficult and perhaps emotionally charged legal battles.

The International Association of Forensic Nurses (IAFN) is the designated specialty organization that facilitates nurses coming together to examine issues related to forensic healthcare. This organization was founded in 1992 and is headquartered in the United States. The IAFN maintains membership across North America and in several other countries, including alliances with organizations in the United Kingdom, Sweden, Italy, India, Portugal, and Africa. In 1995, the IAFN fulfilled its requirement for special recognition with the acceptance and publication of *Scope and Standards of Forensic Nursing Practice* (IAFN and the American Nurses Association [ANA], 1997). This document was updated and approved by the ANA and the IAFN in 2009 to prevent the effects of becoming static. Since its founding, the IAFN has conducted an annual scientific assembly for its membership of more than 3000 nurses from 20 countries. The IAFN's official peer-reviewed publication is the *Journal of Forensic Nursing*. The quarterly online issues provide a forum for scientific papers and research designed to advance the science of forensic nursing.

Frontiers of Forensic Nursing

In addition to the United States, several other countries have emerging initiatives in the science of forensic nursing. With the prevalent issues of interpersonal violence, crime, and violations of human rights, multiple driving forces for the development of forensic nursing have emerged.

However, according to Lambe (2007), many countries continue to severely restrict their nurse's scope of practice and hinder the development of expanded roles. In some, because of the financial restraints of a healthcare system based primarily on principles of socialized medicine, most physicians are opposed to delegating more responsibilities to nurses and are afraid of position and power loss within their profession. Such views restrict nurses from becoming involved with clinical forensic nursing as well as the scientific investigation of death (Lambe & Gage-Linder, 2007).

International Evolution

It is vital to understand the social, cultural, and political issues in selected countries throughout the world that have created both barriers and opportunities that influence the development of forensic nursing. If forensic nursing is expected to flourish in the international community, both economic and human resources must be committed to its advancement.

The United States has led the advancement of forensic nursing science as it continues to expand in both developed and developing areas of the world. The discipline of forensic nursing has become well established in North America. Canada and Great Britain have employed nurses for decades in different forensic capacities as well. Forensic nursing is moving forward at a rapid pace in South Africa, Italy, Ireland, Sweden, and England. However, in some other places such as Scotland, Singapore, Switzerland, Israel, Panama, Japan, and the Caribbean, there has been reluctance to expand into certain sub-specialties.

Strong foundations in nursing science, forensic science, and criminal justice are responsible for the advanced progress of forensic nursing as a scientific discipline in the United States. Significant to this development are the multilevel education and training programs offered in colleges and universities at graduate, postgraduate, and doctoral levels for advanced practice roles and faculty positions in undergraduate and certificate programs. Other countries are exploring funding and available resources necessary to establish educational programs and job opportunities for nurses who have completed state and national requirements for practice in this field. Obstacles are not limited to funding. Success also depends on their ability to convince the courts and law enforcement agencies regarding the values of forensic nursing science and to persuade faculties in schools of nursing and medicine to establish pilot programs and evaluate their outcomes.

COMMONWEALTH OF AUSTRALIA

Trends and patterns in crime and criminal justice have historically impacted vulnerable populations affected by social violence and violations of human rights; among them are the aboriginal tribes indigenous to Australia as well as those who have immigrated throughout centuries. Victimization rates for human abuse and sexual assault continue to rise, but even with the diligent work of forensic nurses, many interpersonal crimes are not being reported (Australian Institute of Criminology, 2009).

Australia has been a world leader in forensic nursing education. There are several key programs throughout Australia for educating forensic nurses at both the undergraduate and graduate levels. Flinders, Perth, and Victoria have developed certificate courses and degree programs in basic and advanced education as well as implemented roles within the healthcare and legal community. Australia hosted the southern hemisphere's first forensic nursing scientific meeting in 2000. This meeting brought together nurses from nearby countries as well as from North America. Those of prominence include Flinders University in Adelaide, the University of Notre Dame in Perth, and the Institute of Forensic Medicine in Victoria. Queensland is also investing in the training of forensic nurse examiners (FNEs).

In 2010 a new clinical forensic nursing role is to be piloted in South Australia. Flinders University, in collaboration with the South Australian Police Department, has been working to establish a role for registered nurses to collect forensic evidence from arrested suspects within associated legal frameworks. This is a new initiative to Australia that will complement the newly established SANE role in the eastern states. This move has led to a review and redevelopment of the curriculum with a more practical approach that includes skill acquisition in evidence collection, court procedures, and witness examination to support this new role.

AFRICA

Crime is a prominent issue in twenty-first-century South Africa, identified in 2002 as the most dangerous country in the world not at war (news.bbc.org). However, by 2009, South Africa's status as perhaps the world's most dangerous country had been challenged by Somalia, the Democratic Republic of the Congo, Pakistan, Israel, and Sudan. Crime, often cultural and superstition based, remained at an alarming rate in the immediate postapartheid era and continues to intimidate a country struggling to resolve conflict without violence. Dangers include bombing, looting, murder, rape, farm attacks, carjacking, and armed incited fear and increased victimization during decades of apartheid violence. The media speculates that much of the violence is regarded as a means for dissidents to avenge social inequalities among the people. Feelings of inadequacy are believed to contribute to hopelessness and acts of anger. The long-standing apartheid, of course, is also a major factor in the ongoing unrest among Africa's people.

In 1996, South Africa adopted a National Crime Prevention Strategy, which aimed to reduce and prevent violent crime by reinforcing community structures. This historic document included the Proposal for Reconstruction of Forensic Services in South Africa, drafted by Dr. J. E. Els, Kimberley's forensic medical officer (FMO). He envisioned the role of the forensic nurse as one step forward in the reduction and prevention of crime during these early endeavors and established the Northern Cape Institute in Forensic Studies in Nursing (NCIFS). Students of the NCIFS were challenged to address issues of homicide, rape, domestic violence, and alcohol abuse as a primary focus. Graduates received diplomas as FNEs and were employed in the newly developed Thuthuzela Care Centres (TCC) for forensic patients and

in medicolegal death investigation (Duma, 2006; Lynch, 1999; National Prosecution Authority pamphlet, undated). Since that time, numerous programs have spread across Southern Africa and adjacent countries.

Zimbabwe became the second African country to address forensic nursing as an emerging specialty. The first FNE training program became operational in 2001 in Harare, the nation's capitol. IAFN member Emilia Hlatywayo, an FNE and graduate of the first training program in South Africa, was employed by Amani Trust to provide forensic care and evidence collection for the survivors of torture in Zimbabwe's political unrest. The Amani Trust is a Zimbabwean nonprofit, nongovernmental organization dedicated to preventing organized violence and torture, advocating for the rights of victims, and rehabilitating victims through community-based care. Hlatywayo was instrumental in bringing a U.S. team of forensic nurses to Zimbabwe to teach the 24 registered nurses who graduated as FNEs (Amnesty International, 2003) (www.amnesty.org/en/library/info/AFR46/015/2003).

Kenya, an East Africa country with a long history of sexual and gender-based violence, has more than a million children who have been orphaned by AIDS (www.UNICEFUSA.org). In 2009, Nancy Cabelus (DNP, RN), a U.S. FNE, established residency in Nairobi as an employee of the U.S. Department of Justice. Cabelus's designated project spans law enforcement, nursing, and forensic development. Cabelus works with the Jordan Foundation in an effort to improve forensic laboratory facilities for Kenya. She has provided valuable assistance to the U.S. Embassy in Nairobi in compiling information for its annual report on trafficking in persons. Much of Cabelus's work relates to a pilot program to combat sexual/gender-based violence. An enthusiastic response indicates that Kenyans are eager to learn about the ways that forensic science can aid their citizens and improve conditions within their communities. The University of Nairobi, School of Nursing has requested that Dr. Cabelus assist in the development of a master's degree and postmaster's certificate in forensic nursing.

Nonhlanhla Dlamini, a member of Parliament (MP) from Ludzeludze Constituency in Manzini, Swaziland, Africa, became the first FNE in Swaziland. She has been a strong advocate for the rights of women and children and a member of Swaziland Action Group against Abuse (SWAGAA), an organization that works to incorporate men in the fight against gender-based violence. SWAGAA provides several types of educational programs and has trained 25 FNEs to provide services to victims of rape. Dr. Dlamini has been a strong advocate for including forensic nursing as a curricular component in schools of nursing in the southern regions of Africa. She has affirmed that she will use her influence in Parliament to campaign for the successful adoption of this proposal (Phakathi, 2008).

CANADA

In July 2007, the Canadian Nurses Association (CNA) recognized the Forensic Nurses Society of Canada (FNSC) as an emerging special interest group, according to Sheila Early, a prominent FNE in Surrey, British Columbia. This is an initial step to achieving specialty recognition. The FNSC was developed as a Canadian organization for forensic nurses.

Although the Canadian forensic nurse death investigator (FNDI) was the first in North America to be identified as a forensic role as early as 1975, other subspecialties of forensic nursing science have expanded the scope and practice of the discipline.

Sexual assault nurse examiner (SANE) programs were initiated in 1993 at two locations. Currently there are 46 programs throughout Canada. The University of Saskatoon (Saskatchewan) is the center for forensic psychiatric and forensic corrections nursing, which has long filled a vital role in national forensic services. Legal nurse consultants (LNCs) are also emerging from within the general forensic nursing framework and becoming established in independent practice throughout Canada. This is a significant trend, as 10 years ago, very little was known about legal nurse consulting in Canada.

Major issues that have become barriers to the evolution and expansion of forensic nursing practice within Canada include limited educational opportunities and public acceptance. It remains difficult to establish any kind of program for sexual assault outside of larger centers. For example, five sites in British Columbia have expressed interest in specialized programs but are unable to secure funding from their health regions or other sources, due in part to the lack of physician support for forensic nursing. Fortunately, however, the established programs appear to have enthusiastic support from the medical community.

The Ontario Coroner's Service for Death Investigation has yet to accept registered nurses as coroners based on provincial law, which requires all coroners to be medical doctors; however, in British Columbia, Saskatchewan, and the Yukon Territory, nurses frequently hold this position. The provinces with a medical examiner service, such as Alberta and Manitoba, were first to employ registered nurses as investigators. However, Ontario leads Canada with a network of 35 sexual assault/domestic violence treatment centers that care for forensic patients of sexual assault, domestic violence, elder abuse, and child maltreatment. This network is by far the most advanced in the country and can serve as a role model for the rest of the provinces and territories if developmental and support funds can be obtained. Healthcare is a provincial and territorial matter, and the federal government does not mandate the destiny of funds given to each province/territory.

A major initiative is the development of a national sexual assault evidence recovery kit by the Royal Canadian Mounted Police (RCMP), soon to be available for FNE services. In spite of the benefits of an official evidence recovery kit, Ontario and Quebec will not be included, as they have forensic centers outside the RCMP mandate. This means that the protocols for forensic evidence collection and the supplies used will be standardized for eight provinces and three territories. In the greater Vancouver, British Columbia area, Surrey Memorial Hospital in Surrey is now in the process of adding the care of human trafficking victims to its mandate. This is a newly established process that is now evolving under the direction of the Office to Combat Trafficking in People (OCTIP), which was established in British Columbia in 2007.

CENTRAL AND SOUTH AMERICA

Larger cities in Central America have begun initiatives in forensic nursing. Several hospitals and community agencies have established special programs related to sexual assault, domestic violence, and child/elder abuse screening. Because there is a lack of a qualified forensic nursing faculty, they have relied heavily on the United States for education and training resources. Physicians and nurses are routinely receiving basic forensic indoctrination within their basic and graduate curricula in the healthcare professions. The Roman Catholic churches throughout the country are also active in providing domiciliary care and victim services.

Dr. Juan Geraldo Ugalde Lobo, Presidente Asociacionde Derecho Medico de Costa Rica, became the first in Latin America to recognize the significance of a forensic specialist in nursing and the need to bring this new concept in forensic services to Costa Rica. The First Latin American Congress on Forensic Medicine and Science (Association Latinoibero Americana Del Derecho a La Salud) was held in San Jose, Costa Rica, in 1998. At the meeting, a delegation of U.S. forensic nurses introduced the role of forensic nursing and assisted in the founding of the organization *Forensic Nurses of the Americas*. The following year, a 40-hour forensic nursing training program was offered in El Salvador, and indoctrination was provided for law enforcement officers, prosecutors, and defense attorneys. Jamie Ferrell, an FNE employed by the Texas Office of the Attorney General, presented an extensive educational offering designed to provide Salvadorian justice officials with a contemporary perspective on sexual assault. Other initiatives of El Salvadorian forensic physicians and nurses include identifying the remains of thousands of "missing" children who were extricated from their families during the civil wars that persisted from 1980 through 1992. The organization U.S. Physicians for Human Rights has also participated in this effort, as well as the quest to reunite missing children with their families (PHR Update, 2008).

Honduras, like other countries in Central America, experiences high incidents of interpersonal violence, especially since the 1990s when wars in neighboring countries raged, fueling the proliferation of military weapons, police corruption, and political unrest. The country continues to be challenged by human rights abuses, high homicide rates, substance abuse, human trafficking, and conflicts between criminal bands (NotiCen Publication, August 31, 2000). These concerns were a great burden to the chief medical examiner of Honduras as he attended the FNE training program at the Department of Legal Medicine in El Salvador in 1998. Although initially doubtful of the value of a forensic nurse, he became a convert and invited the U.S. team to present this program in Tegucigalpa for his medical staff and a number of nurses in 1999. In the interim, a hurricane demolished the entire forensic facility in Tegucigalpa and the program was relocated to San Pedro Sula. With support from U.S. forensic pathologists and the American Academy of Forensic Sciences, forensic services in the Honduran capital were eventually restored and revitalized.

In 2008 the International Justice Mission (IJM) contracted with forensic nurse examiner Ruth Downing, MSN RN CNP SANE-A, to establish the role of the forensic nurse in sexual assault examination in Peru. The IJM is a human right agency that works in Peru with partner organization Paz y Esperanza (Peace and Hope) to provide investigative, legal and aftercare services to victims of sexual assault. After time working in the field, the IJM found a lack of forensic capacity among local law enforcement and medical practitioners to be a regular obstacle to securing perpetrator convictions. Downing provided education in evidence collection for sexual assault patients to law enforcement, lawyers, forensic physicians, nurses, teachers and social workers in Huánuco, Peru. This central providence is located in the Andes Mountains, one of the poorest regions, with a high rate of sexual abuse. In 2009, Downing returned to Huánuco with a team of professionals from The River Church Community in San Jose, California, to continue education and support for Paz y Esperanza. This faith-based mission continues to be well received by the local community, and in 2009 the District Attorney, local law enforcement and Paz y Esperanza agreed to form a sexual assault response team to increase collaboration as they continue to address child sexual abuse in their community. Since 2003, when IJM and Paz y Esperanza began their work in Huánuco, the forensic community has greatly increased their response to child sexual abuse. Currently, the health and justice partners share the highest prosecution rate in Peru, and are committed to their mission to bring justice to victims despite frequent threats on their lives and numerous struggles in dealing with government corruption and lack of resources.

Since International Justice Mission began their work in 2003 in Huánuco, Peru, the community has greatly increased their response to child sexual abuse. Future plans include a collaborative partnership between the Hermilio Valdizan National University in Huánuco and the University of Tennessee Health Science Center, College of Nursing for the purpose of training and education to forensic physicians and other professionals in the areas of sexual assault. Patricia M. Speck DNSc, APN, FNP-BC, SANE-A, SANE-P, DF-IAFN, FAAFS, FAAN and Margaret T. Hartig, PhD, APN, FNP-BC, FAANP will be developing curriculum and SAFE classes. This initiative will create opportunities for telehealth and provide distance education through the Doctorate in Nursing Practice (DNP) located at the University of Tennessee Health Science Center in the College of Nursing.

UNITED KINGDOM AND EUROPE

There is a misconception in England that forensic nursing refers only to mental health/psychiatric nursing within institutional care units and prisons. This is not the case. In fact, women have been practicing forensic type services as early as the fourteenth century when they were involved in examinations to confirm the virginity of women who were marrying royalty or to evaluate sexual assault victims. Nevertheless, in the 1990s FNEs expanded their roles, not only within the mental health arena, but as custody nurses (nurses working in police stations), SANEs, and nurses working in accident and emergency units.

Forensic nursing science within England is a rapidly developing new subspecialty for the profession. Custody nursing, for example, was developed, piloted, and implemented with the Kent Police Constabulary in 2000 and is now being practiced in many other police forces. The SANE role was developed in 2001 and is currently practiced in Greater Manchester, Lancashire, and London. Despite these tentative and innovative developments, few members of other professions allied to the medicolegal system, including nursing at present, acknowledge these roles or analyze its benefits to any great extent. Forensic nursing services, with the exception of forensic psychiatric nursing, remain somewhat unrecognized in the United Kingdom. This, however, is beginning to change.

The United Kingdom Association of Forensic Nurses (UKAFN) was founded in March 2007 at King's College Hospital, an NHS Foundation Trust in London. Support from Scotland Yard and the Metropolitan Police has been the major driving force in the development of forensic nursing in the United Kingdom. Jo Delaforce, chair of the UKAFN, is a forensic clinical nurse specialist (FCNS) in London and has been instrumental in developing a designated *Centre of Excellence* for the care of victims of sexual violence. The UK's first Custody Nurse and Sexual Assault Nurses Conference was held in May 2009 in Liverpool, and it was attended by nurses, forensic medical examiners, physicians, law enforcement officers, and other forensic personnel (www.ukafn.org).

Academia in England is rapidly gaining momentum in the education of forensic nursing. Professor Jane Rutty, PhD, designed and developed a curriculum module for postregistration nurses entitled "Medico-legal Healthcare and Safeguarding People." This offering focuses on the care of vulnerable populations and managing the associated forensic cases. As part of a European Commission grant, Professor Rutty has been designated to assume a leading role in strategic mass casualty and forensic planning associated with the XXX Olympiad.

Scotland has recognized the need to address forensic nurse specialists in light of a United Nations report that has labeled it as the most violent country in the developed world. There are considerable opportunities for FNEs within death investigation, sexual assault services, and child abuse evaluations in the wake of political and religious violence. Considering the fact that Scottish law often requires corroboration of findings by two examiners, forensic nurses could assist in meeting the need for quality forensic resources, as they could assume the role of one of these two examiners.

Northern Ireland also experiences social issues that have prompted interest in improving its forensic services. The recent release of an investigative report outlined the extent of pedophilia and child abuse within Northern Ireland (Peel, 2009). Amnesty International and other groups have been critical of its lack of services to support victims of rape and domestic violence. As part of the End Violence against Women Coalition, the state of mind in Ireland is changing. There is concern for intimate partner and sexual violence that was illuminated in the results of a 2008 survey of young adults, which shed light on disturbing attitudes indicating a general acceptance of aggression against women (Amnesty International, 2008). This report was in part responsible for the development of the first FNE program in Dublin (news.bbc.org, 2008). In January 2009, the first eight nurses in Ireland completed the year-long pilot program and obtained the Higher Diploma Nursing in Sexual Assault Forensic Examination. These nurses are registered as clinical nurse specialists in sexual assault forensic examination and are employed in a new Sexual Assault Treatment Unit (SATU) in Mullingar County, Westmeath, and the other seven nurses are based in different SATUs throughout Ireland. According to leading nurse educators, the main concern in Ireland is to have well-established programs for sexual assault forensic examiners. They believe that there will be advancement into areas such as child sexual abuse and other subspecialties when a cohort of expertise is firmly in place. In 2008, the *Journal of the Irish Nurses Organization* published an article regarding the development of the original eight nurses who were sponsored to undertake the Higher Diploma in Nursing in Sexual Assault Forensic Examination. This, along with reports in other publications, is expected to stimulate interest in forensic nursing within Ireland.

In Germany, great concern for the lack of forensic nursing services remains an active debate. In 2007, Andrea Lambe, a nurse at the Institute of Legal Medicine and Nancy Gage-Linder, Esq. Section Head of Violence Prevention and Intervention, challenged the German healthcare and legal system to develop an innovative, cost-efficient, and competent plan of forensic nursing practice based on the World Health Organization's proposal (2002). Since the new plan has been in place, the German Federal Law Enforcement Agency has identified and recorded many acts of violent crimes that would have previously not been noted, including homicide, manslaughter, sexual assault, rape, aggravated assault, and robbery, as well as lesser charges of assault with intent to harm (Lambe & Gage-Linder, 2007).

Exemplary federal laws and adequate resources were developed in 2001 to the ensure safety and well-being of victims of interpersonal crimes. However, mandatory reporting of child abuse does not exist in Germany. Screenings for interpersonal and domestic violence are also not mandatory, and many cases go unnoticed within the country's healthcare system. Although it is recognized that FNEs could provide a valuable resource in these cases, the German judicial system prefers the opinions of forensic medical examiners (FMEs) as the standard for legal recognition and reporting of crimes. Currently, Germany and other European countries are in the process of adapting their current nursing educational model to that of the United States, perhaps paving the way for the integration of forensic nursing science into the curricula (Lambe & Gage-Linder, 2007).

Turkey has been positively impacted by forensic nursing practice since the 1990s, and the need for advancing both education and practice for these specialty roles has been recognized. The Institute of Legal Medicine and Forensic Sciences (LEMFOS) of the Istanbul University teaches graduates of diverse disciplines the forensic aspects of their field. LEMFOS is the only institution in the field of forensic science available to graduates of various disciplines to enroll nurses in 1995 as a general education and public service project. The focus of this program is to address the reduction and prevention of sexual violence. The lack of experience and insensitivity to victims was associated with physicians who were reluctant to conduct the examination. This reaction often occurs because specific education in sexual assault evaluation is typically not provided for general practitioners. Victims wait several hours for an examination, and in some regions, they have to travel to another city to find a hospital where the examination can be accomplished. After making a legal statement, the victims are sent to the Council of Forensic Medicine to have another examination by court order (Lynch, 2006). In 2006, LEMFOS introduced the Section of Sexual Assaults (SSA) to ensure a more timely, thorough, and precise collection of forensic evidence. In the process, the SSA developed procedures for the physical examination and collection of evidence, as well as a variety of report forms. Educational literature was also written covering topics such pregnancy and cessation, sexually transmitted diseases, and suggestions for providing support to the victim. This program was developed and directed by the faculty of the Istanbul University and the Public Health Department, the Ministry of Justice, and the Ministry of the Interior and was lauched within the College of Nursing at Istanbul University during the 1997-1998 academic year. Currently, forensic nurses are trained as specialists who will apply their dual expertise in nursing and forensic sciences to assist in the administration of justice to complete complex forensic investigations (Gorea, Jasuja, Lynch, et al., 2003). Through the work of forensic nursing specialists and the support received from the forensic physicians, scientists, police, and attorneys, FNEs have secured their place within the forensic science community in Turkey.

In Eastern Europe, the sequelae of war-related violence resulting from the Bosnian/Serb War in 1992-1995 included the atrocities of Muslim mass murders and incarcerating women in rape camps for the purpose of ethnic cleansing (sexual genocide). In the southern Serbian province of Kosovo, sexual violence and trafficking of persons continues to be a serious concern. In the past, women seldom voluntarily reported rape, and historically this war crime has gone unpunished. However, international tribunals have now declared it to be a crime of war, stemming from the Bosnian civil war and the Rwanda genocide. This action has effectively paved the way for involvement of the FNE in international bodies such as the United Nations and the International Committee of the Red Cross, who identify such atrocities and provide care and treatment of the victims.

In 2002, the Kosovo Department of Justice and the Office on Missing Persons and Forensics implemented an initial SANE training program for the adult and child victim. Venera Mehmeti and Valbona Keqekolla started to work in January 2003 at the Office of Missing Persons and Forensics in the Office of the Medical Examiner and Department of Justice as FNEs. In addition to sexual assault case management, initial duties include assisting the forensic physician and forensic technician during autopsies of the recently dead and assisting the forensic anthropologists during the autopsy on the remains of the war dead. When requested, the FNEs respond to the scene of a crime as representatives of the Office of the Medical Examiner and work with the police officers to document and collect evidence (Mehmeti, V., personal correspondence, 2009).

Northern Europe is struggling to develop a forensic nurse specialist role in the Netherlands. In spite of many difficulties, Piet Machielse, who studied forensic nursing science in the United States in 2005, has brought this issue to the forefront. Machielse, a highly experienced emergency department nurse at the University Hospital of Rotterdam, used his acumen to introduce the science of forensic nursing and to bring attention to its contribution to healthcare. He presented a paper at the Dutch Forensic Institute in an endeavor to promote the need for forensic nursing services in the Netherlands. "Yet, as in Germany, there is no existing policy related to forensic evidence collection in Rotterdam or elsewhere in the Netherlands healthcare systems while a growing number of patients continue to present as a result of forensic scenarios," acknowledged Machielse (IAFN, 2008).

The southern region of Europe has taken the lead in the development of forensic nursing in Puglia, Italy under the direction of Dr. Giancarlo Di Vella, a prominent forensic pathologist. In 2007, the University of Bari awarded master's degrees to 42 nurses who completed requirements of its rigorous curricula in forensic nursing. Forensic nurses from the United States supplemented their faculty resources, teaching selected subject matter in forensic nursing and providing academic advice to the Bari faculty, and assisting in career mentoring for the students. In addition to gaining clinical experiences within Puglia, selected students also had a unique opportunity to participate in extensive forensic nursing initiatives of the Harris County (Houston, Texas) Medical Examiner's Office to better understand the several roles of the forensic nurse in the United States. Such cooperative international endeavors are characteristic of the collaboration required to maximize scarce educational resources required for basic and advanced nursing education. In 2010, the University of Bari expects to also award doctorates in this specialty.

To illustrate the unique contributions of the professional nurse in death investigation, Michele Stallone, a graduate of the master's program in forensic nursing at the University of Bari, presented his work at the 2009 American Academy of Forensic Sciences meeting in Denver, Colorado. Stallone demonstrated how nurses are utilized within the Office of the Medical Examiner in Bari as on-scene investigators. He stated that the use of forensic nurses has positively impacted the forensic science community by demonstrating the unique contributions of the professional nurse in solving cases (AAFS Proceedings, 2009). The University of Bari has chosen to give major emphasis to forensic nursing in the advanced education degree (magisterial bachelor degree). The educational program addresses forensic topics such as elder abuse and child abuse, domestic violence, mass disasters, evidence collection and preservation, and death investigation. A master's program on postmortem findings and crime scene investigation provides additional information and advanced clinical training in the field.

The first postgraduate program in forensic nursing science in Portugal has been established at the University of Autonoma in Lisbon. This program, a one-year postgraduate course, was developed and implemented in 2009 by Albino Gomes, who holds a master of science degree in legal medicine and is the president of the recently established Portuguese Association of Forensic Nursing Science. He lectures throughout the country and has stimulated a great interest in this specialty (Gomes-Lynch, personal communication, 2009). Dr. Duarte Nuno Vieria, professor of forensic medicine at the University of Coimbra, is president of the Portuguese National Institute of Legal Medicine and has supported the development of forensic roles for nurses. Dr. Vieria delegates various forensic tasks and responsibilities to a small number of nurses under his direction and believes that the future of forensic nursing is promising within Portugal (Vieria-Lynch, personal communication, 2009).

Although forensic nursing as a discrete discipline in Spain has not been formally recognized, it is offered as a postgraduate optional study in nursing. This program is a one-year course that introduces students to the forensic aspects of healthcare through a wide range of medicolegal topics. The University of Spain's National Distance Education (UNED) also offers courses through its online network. The potential for forensic nurses in Spain obviously exists, but because of limited opportunities for employment in the specialty, progress is slow and laborious for both education and practice.

MIDDLE EAST

The Islamic Republic of Iran introduced the concept of a forensic specialist in nursing at the First International Islamic Congress on Crime Scene Investigation in Tehran in 2009. This opportunity represents openness to the advancement of forensic services in a country with considerable sociocultural dissonance. The academic centers for forensic medicine include the Universities of Medical Sciences and the Legal Medicine Organization (LMO). The LMO is an official body of the judiciary situated in Tehran and has medicolegal centers located throughout the provinces. Forensic nursing science has the potential to serve as one such medium of knowledge and technology transfer regarding medicolegal management in the investigation of crime-related trauma and death. Dr. Nahid Khodaramy, nursing professor at Shahid Beheshti Medical University, was the first to express the need for nurses in Iran to become skilled in the concepts of forensic nursing science. Khodaramy has worked to introduce this specialty to the nurse/midwifery school faculty and others who are interested in this field. Dr. Akram Sanagu, associate professor of nursing in Gorgam (Northern Iran), directs student research and has encouraged students to replicate certain concepts identified in Virginia Lynch's thesis, "Clinical Forensic Nursing: Role Development" (Lynch, 1990). The future of forensic nursing education will require a great deal of clarification and direction as FNEs move toward qualification and credentials in this field. Study results reveal that nursing students and registered nurses are essentially unaware of the roles of a forensic nurse and their potential contributions to healthcare and social justice (Khodakarami, N., personal correspondence, 2003).

Israel is a small country with a large issue of violence according to official forensic-related statistics deposited in the Ministry of Health in Jerusalem. War and political-related trauma is a constant concern. Domestic violence and sexual assault throughout the country is often not reported. Honor killings still occur in the Bedouin communities and Arab towns in the north and south of the country. Although the level of forensic medicine is viewed as optimal in the central urban areas of Israel, the concept of forensic nursing associates has not been embraced. Physicians manage forensic cases within healthcare settings and participate in associated legal proceedings. They are reluctant to accept the fact that nurses could function in such a role and augment their resources, which are in short supply, especially outside the major urban areas. One IAFN member, Shoshanna Melech-Shalom, is the only nurse in a health clinic in a rural community setting near Beer Sheva. She provides nursing care for a broad range of patients and coordinates the care of medicolegal cases with a social service provider. She reports that forensic patients seen in the hospital are very different from those seen in community clinics. The patients admitted to the hospital emergency department are victims of more serious violent incidents and in need of immediate care or resuscitation. Forensic patients seen in community clinics are those with the early or more subtle signs of abuse, involving family violence and abuse such as incest or rape. There are some glimmers of change, however.

Recently the Association of Rape Crisis Centers in Israel (ARCCI) launched a social awareness campaign called "Men Can Stop Rape," which is designed to advance the notion that sexual violence is a social problem rather than a women's issue. Orli Grinstein-Cohen, PhD, also a member of IAFN and the faculty of nursing at Ben Gurion University, is an advocate for making the science of forensic nursing a reality in Israel. She developed enthusiasm for this specialty during her doctoral studies as she worked with crime victims. There are efforts to open forensic examination centers with nurses participating in case management. Dr. Nissa Lang has established a model in Tiberius that has been replicated in other areas of Israel. Zafrir Goren, a police chief in Jerusalem, has indicated that in spite of a definite need, the vision of forensic nursing in Israel is dim.

ASIA

India is a country where the social, cultural, and religious violations of women have been practiced and often accepted for over a millennium. However, with the foundations of forensic nursing now established, the victimization of women will be brought to the courts in a new and efficient manner. Since 2003, Dr. R. K. Gorea, professor of forensic medicine at Gian Sagar Medical College in the Punjab, and forensic physicians across India have endeavored to bring this new discipline to the forefront in forensic services. With these concerted efforts, forensic nursing is now an accepted discipline among forensic pathologists and police officials in India, which has a unique set of longstanding sociocultural crimes. Among these are dowry deaths, female infanticide, honor killing, acid attacks, antiquated sociocultural superstitions, oppressions, and fear. Forensic nurses from the United States have served as resources for the development of forensic nursing in India, providing lectures, workshops, and serving as mentors to both educators and practitioners.

In direct contrast to the New India, recognized as a center of progress in education, technology, and employment opportunities in the global market, there remains a backlash against women who attempt to define new cultural perspectives in an ancient society. Marital violence remains symptomatic of the general oppression of women in any patriarchal society. Should a woman lash out against her oppressors in word or action, she becomes an outcast in a male-dominated society. In India like many other countries, a sizable number of crimes against women go unreported because of the attached social stigma. Violence against women remains one of the most intractable violations of women's human rights (Ahluwala, 2002).

In 2009, a course introducing forensic nursing science was initiated in Gian Sagar Nursing School and is now a required course of study for all second-year graduate nursing students. Concerted efforts are needed to persuade the Nursing Council of India and various universities to also initiate postgraduate courses in forensic nursing and to integrate key concepts and principles throughout nursing curricula (Gorea, 2002, 2004, 2005). Dr. Gorea, the moving force to establish the science of forensic nursing in India, was recognized for his continued efforts when he was granted the prestigious Vision Award by the membership of the International Association of Forensic Nurses in 2007 at the 15th Annual Scientific Assembly in Salt Lake City, Utah, in the United States (*On the Edge*, 2008).

In Pakistan, organized crime includes drug trafficking, money laundering, forged Indian currency printing, extortion, murder for hire, fraud, human trafficking, corruption, black marketeering, political violence, terrorism, and abduction. Socio-cultural-religious values and beliefs impact the treatment of women and impunity of offenders in spite of the laws against physical and sexual violence. Attaining gender parity and universal female literacy remains a challenge because of large regional variations and low female enrollment and retention in rural areas. There have been some impressive gains in the empowerment of women in recent years, with reserved representation in federal, provincial, and local elected bodies. Sweeping changes in the medicolegal system are gravely needed, and there is a role for forensic nursing. However, change comes slow to countries that have longstanding social and cultural values that impede fundamental changes, especially in domestic crimes and violence against women.

Historically in Japan, healthcare, law enforcement, and the public have not acknowledged interpersonal violence. Forensic psychiatric nurse Nanako Yoneyama explained that crimes against women have not been recognized as a violation of human rights; therefore, it is not surprising that women seldom ask for help. Although some Asian countries have well-established domestic violence laws, Japan has only now recognized violence against women as an interpersonal crime. In 1997, a program for battered women was established at a private clinic at the Institute of Family Function (IFF) in Tokyo (Lynch, 2000; Yoneyama, 2006). However, because of the stigma related to domestic violence and the lack of legal recourse, few women sought protection and the center closed. New interest was awakened with the Shelter-Net Conference in Tokyo in 2000, a national symposium on domestic violence and women's shelters. The attendance of a cadre of nurses indicated a greater interest and commitment to this vulnerable population. In 2002, the Law for the Prevention of Spousal Violence and the Protection of Victims was established into legislation. With Japan's recent focus on public health and social welfare services, nurses in Japan believe that forensic nursing is an obvious resource for its victims of violence. However, the characteristics of Japanese culture must be thoroughly understood before successful programs can be established.

Taiwan is faced with various issues on the care for new immigrants' children and the aged, the heightened public awareness of human rights and personal interests, and the implementation of the new Criminal Procedure Code and cross-examination system. It has also been these issues that, in turn, prompted Taiwan's nursing community to pay more attention to forensic nursing. Chen-Kuan Huang is pioneering forensic nursing science in Taiwan's

Cardinal Tien College of Healthcare and Management in Taipei where she has integrated concepts and principles of this discipline into a new course. Currently there are no credit-based forensic nursing programs in the country. However, there are two nursing professionals enrolled on the Central Police University's doctorate program in crime prevention with a specialization in forensic nursing, which also features training in criminal investigation and forensic science. There are also other initiatives in forensic nursing education at the undergraduate level in Taiwan's universities. However, within clinical practice areas such as the emergency department, there are no dedicated nursing resources devoted to forensic care componenets. Injury examination and evidence collection are typically conducted by doctors or nurses with relevant continuing educational training in collecting evidence.

Thailand's tsunami in 2005 provided an excellent illustration of why there is a need for more skilled forensic clinicians and investigators of death. Although forensic nursing was introduced in Bangkok in 2000, it was not followed by any specific actions to develop educational or clinical programs. However, now there are plans to incorporate various forensic nursing roles and responsibilities in mass disaster planning as well as the clinical environment within healthcare.

Singapore, an independent island, was the first Asian country to employ FNEs as investigators in the medical examiner system at the Institute of Legal Medicine and Forensic Sciences. Although Singapore was the first among Asian countries to send nurses to the United States to study the expanded role of forensic nursing and have long employed forensic psychiatric nurses, the implementation of clinical forensic practice in emergency trauma departments or sexual assault care has been slow to develop (Lynch, 1999). On the other hand, even though the concept of a forensic nurse in clinical practice is new to this area of Asia, it appears to be progressing with an acceptance not found in other Asian countries. The need, nonetheless, is greater in these countries than in many other areas of the world, and with perseverance and support from government and nongovernment agencies, forensic nursing will no doubt become an important component of healthcare services in Asia and neighboring eastern countries.

Forensic Nursing in the U.S. Military Services

Members of the United States military services are subject to multiple stressors in their living conditions and their duty assignments, especially during times of armed conflict. Frequent changes in assignments, overseas deployments which disrupt family life, financial problems, fear of being wounded or killed in combat, sleep deprivation and chain-of-command conflicts have been identified among the precursors that lead to loss of self-control and acts of impulsive behavior and violence. These include physical assaults, homicides, suicide, and more. Consequently, there are both offenders and victims involved, and the military services must assume responsibility for both.

Although today's military forensic nurses are well educated in a variety of specialty areas of forensic science, most achieved their earliest indoctrination as sexual assault nurses examiners or "SANEs". However, today, they represent several other forensic specialty areas including human abuse and neglect, death investigation, intimate partner violence, and healthcare risk management. When considering all branches of the military, there are reported examples of forensic nursing roles active within the hospital emergency departments, clinics, security police forces, mortuary services, family advocacy and other social services, Office of Special Investigations and hospital risk management. Although, all services have SANEs, at least in the larger facilities and overseas, few installations currently have the resources to permit any nurse to function in a full-time role as a forensic nurse examiner. There are encouraging reports, however, that nurses are enrolling in courses and are completing required training in various aspects of the forensic sciences, and military leadership is engaged in strategic planning to ensure that its members have the benefits and protection afforded by the various forensic sciences, including nursing. Military nurses, themselves, have been tenacious in their determination to provide the highest quality of forensic services for those affected by violence, both victims and offenders.

In order to understand the military's current views and attitudes towards active duty FNEs and its transition towards recognition as a profession, it is necessary to review recent historical events that have allowed this specialty to become increasingly accepted within the military.

HISTORICAL BACKGROUND

In the past, the United States Congress, and civilian advocacy groups such as the Miles Foundation, have frequently voiced their concerns about the ability of the U.S. military to follow national standards of sexual assault care for military patients and questioned their ability to collect quality forensic evidence. In 2004, as a result of an increased focus on sexual assault issues in the military, Secretary of Defense Donald Rumsfeld commissioned a task force to inquire into the overall care being provided to victims of sexual assault in the military. Based on the recommendations of the Care for Victims Task Force, Secretary Rumsfeld formed the Joint Task Force for Sexual Assault Prevention and Response (JTF-SAPR) to serve as the military's single point of accountability for sexual assault prevention and response policy (DOD, 2004). After the establishment of this office, the JTF-SAPR developed a comprehensive sexual assault policy for the DOD, and collaborated closely with other military departments and services to construct and provide implementation processes for its program.

It was due to recommendations made by the Care for Victims Task Force that policy makers carefully scrutinized the military's medical responses to sexual assault patients. Because of supportive research that demonstrated the benefit and efficacy of utilizing SANEs in sexual assault evidence collection, the 2004 Task Force Care for Victims of Sexual Assault report specifically identified a need for the military to integrate the use of SANE nurses in their medical programs (Ferguson, 2008). Specifically the Task Force recommended that the military "develop DOD-wide medical standards of care and clinical practice guidelines for treatment and care of victims of sexual assault" and also recommended that it "establish a health care integrated process team" to consider how to better incorporate SANEs within the military health system in both the active and reserve component force structure, and/or through contract support (DOD, 2004).

On June 23, 2006, in response to the 2004 Care for Victims report and the work done by the DOD JTF-SAPR, the new permanent DOD Sexual Assault Prevention and Response (SAPR) office released the first DOD Instruction titled DOD Instruction 6495.02–Sexual Assault Prevention and Response Program Procedures. This instruction, available on the DOD SAPR website (www.sapr.mil), identified key personnel to be considered for training in performing sexual assault examinations. It also mandated that the military services provide: (1) training for sexual assault responders; (2) options for confidential reporting, and (3) standardized avenues for individuals who have suffered a sexual assault to access needed services through Sexual Assault Response Coordinators (SARCs) and Victim Advocates (DOD, 2006).

While SANEs were specifically recommended in the DOD Care for Victims Task Force report as critical in providing quality care to sexual assault victims within the Armed Forces, the military community recognized its own requirement for increased versatility within its ranks regarding various levels of providers to provide sexual assault care (DOD, 2006). This was particularly true in remote areas of operation, where medical clinics were staffed with limited personnel and provided minimal resources.

One factor that has complicated the issue of providing care to military sexual assault patients has been the increasing number of state nursing board requirements for advanced practice nursing certification in the area of sexual assault and/or forensic nursing. For example, the state of Maryland requires that all nurses who perform sexual assault examinations be licensed as FNEs and further divides the forensic nursing specialization into adult and/or pediatric patient populations (Ferguson, 2008). Other states such as New Jersey and Nevada require that nurses pass the SANE IAFN exam before being allowed to perform sexual assault examinations (New Jersey Division of Consumer Affairs, 2004; Nevada State Board of Nursing, 2004). Changes such as this may significantly impact forensic services at military treatment facilities in the future, as nurses who perform sexual assault examinations are required to demonstrate competency and/or possess advanced practice certification under their independent state licensure.

TRAINING AND EDUCATION

Although the United States military employs several healthcare providers who have been trained in the technique of performing a sexual assault forensic examination, to date there are only 15 military nurses who have become certified as SANEs through the IAFN (Ferguson, 2008). Many other U.S. military physicians, nurse practitioners, and nurses have attended SANE or SAFE courses, but have not achieved official certification (Ferguson, 2008).

The maintenance of sexual assault examiner competency has been a concern voiced by both military and civilian communities. This is because some facilities receive few sexual assault cases per year. In some instances, military facilities have contracted with civilian clinics and nursing personnel to perform sexual assault exams for these patients because of concern that their own military nurses could not maintain sexual assault examination competency. Transporting victims, in these cases, has often resulted in a two- to three-hour delay in obtaining vital forensic evidence, to include blood and urine toxicology, as well as contributed to a loss or contamination of existing evidence. In addition, removing the ability of military nurses to perform sexual assault examinations while in CONUS dramatically reduces the number of adequately trained personnel available to perform this procedure in the operational theatre. In deployment arenas there are limited, if not an absence of, facilities to transfer patients for a properly conducted forensic exam. What facilities need to understand is that competencies of forensic nurses can be maintained by providing simulation training and case scenario drills.

One of the most comprehensive DOD sexual assault training programs provided by the Armed Forces in the past has been the Sexual Assault Response Team (SART) training course, hosted by the Armed Forces Institute of Pathology (AFIP) Office of the Medical Examiner. This 40-hour course was planned, developed and organized by military nurse corps officers from the U.S. Air Force and the U.S. Navy, Col. Susan Hanshaw and LCDR, Cynthia Ferguson. These two nurses utilized their subject matter expertise and experience in forensic nursing and sexual assault care, as well as the guidance and advice of other forensic professionals, to organize this program, as well as instruct many aspects of the course. Since 2005, this course has trained over 500 joint military and civilian personnel on the military management of sexual assault, legal, investigative, and psycho-social issues. It also included laboratory sessions to introduce sexual assault forensic examination techniques, forensic photography, documentation of injuries and physical evidence collection to participants. Its program continues to be the gold standard of sexual assault examiner training in the Armed Forces, and the program design will continue to serve as a model for future related joint service trainings.

Providing multiple options for training, education, and maintenance of skills in the sexual assault examination are essential to provide military personnel with the tools they need to optimally perform these exams. Military medical professionals administering medicolegal care to sexual assault patients are required to be trained in how to perform sexual assault examinations and forensic evidence collection, as stated in the DOD Instruction 6495.02. In these cases, it would be highly useful to develop a means for identifying military personnel with existing skills in sexual assault examination and forensic collection. Military medical providers should have ready means to maintain their competencies and skills in sexual assault medical and forensic care, particularly in cases of deployment overseas. Providers should also be afforded the opportunity to develop a valuable and lasting partnership within the civilian communities.

Many changes have occurred to improve sexual assault prevention and response in the military, but there is still much to be done. The violence of sexual assault needs to be seen as a part of the larger public health problem of violence issues in communities. Often, it is improperly considered solely a women's issue, which reduces the scope and effectiveness of addressing the problem. Sexual assault affects populations of men, children, the mentally and physically disabled, and the elderly, as well as the female population. Addressing its root causes requires a public health preventative approach as well as a carefully planned community response. Military services might consider basing their sexual assault programs under a larger umbrella of violence prevention and response, and placing that umbrella over the purview of their Armed Forces Public Health divisions.

Despite advancements in policy in the area of sexual assault care in the U.S. military, there is currently no designated military nursing specialty of FNE or SAFE in the military services. Recognizing the need for expertise, and adhering to training requirements, the U.S. military services frequently provides increased training opportunities for physicians, nurse practitioners/midwives, physicians' assistants, and RNs in the areas of sexual assault examination and forensic evidence collection (Ferguson, 2008). Military nurses interested in certification as a SANE via the IAFN are often encouraged by medical leadership to pursue this educational venue. However, the certification is not currently required for Armed Forces medical personnel because of the large training burden that it would place on the military services (Ferguson, 2008).

Many problems concerning the ability for the military to provide adequate sexual assault medical and forensic care in the deployed arena have yet to be completely solved. In the future, operational platforms could benefit from assigning a healthcare provider who is known to be qualified in the procedure of sexual assault examination and forensic evidence collection, to a deploying unit. These providers with specialty skills in forensic and sexual assault care could then ensure proper care of patients who reported assault and requested collection of forensic evidence. Military services may discover that there is even a benefit to creating a specialty role for "Forensic Nurse Examiner" or "Forensic Clinical Nurse Specialist" among certain healthcare providers and RNs. This would allow for tracking forensic expertise of medical professionals in the field to utilize their specialty skills on deployments or other needed areas. In addition, the development of an FNE nursing specialty within all of the military Services would allow for the provision of a greater standard of care for patients and an increased quality of collected medical forensic evidence.

The development of the specialty of forensic nursing within the military, and the benefits it could provide the DOD, would not only allow for a higher standard of care in this area but would also promote a more comprehensive integration of other violence prevention and response programs in the U.S. military. In addition, military forensic nurses would be able to provide the Department of Defense with a medical cadre of in-house experts who are prepared to care for all manner of victims of violence, and would be able to utilize their expertise to develop, implement, and evaluate prevention and response programs related to medical violence. Other areas of prevention and response that military forensic nurses could lend their expertise towards are issues of suicide, homicide, forensic processing of mass graves, terrorism, disaster management, military gang violence, workplace violence, military and civilian physical assaults, domestic violence and child abuse/assault. Forensic nurses in the military also possess the expertise to serve as expert witnesses in criminal cases related to their background knowledge and experience, and to provide medicolegal chart reviews.

The unique and diverse settings in which military nurses serve are fertile ground for the development and growing recognition of forensic nurses as a specialty in uniform. For the shipboard sailor, the Marine on the Horn of Africa, the soldier overseas, and the Airman in the Middle East, timely access to quality forensic care can be a logistical challenge. However, this patient population is no less likely to be victimized than any other, and is deserving of the same caliber and effective standards of care afforded to civilian populations in the United States (Ortiz, 2008).

MORTUARY AFFAIRS AND FORENSIC PATHOLOGY

A distinguished Air Force Reserve Nurse Corps officer, Col. Susan Hanshaw served in a unique capacity at the Charles C. Carson Center for Mortuary Affairs, located at Dover Air Force Base in Delaware. The facility is a world-renowned state-of-the art morgue facility whose staff cares for fallen heroes of the American military and processes their human remains.

Three words, "*Dignity, Honor, and Respect*" inscribed on the wall of the reception area is a continual reminder of the center's core values. The mission of the center is twofold—positive/conclusive identification of all fallen service members (conducted by the Office of the Armed Forces Medical Examiner [OAFME]), and preparation and transportation of decedents to their final place of interment. When the remains of service members arrive at Port Mortuary they are in a "believed to be" status until their positive or conclusive identification (ID) is confirmed.

Transfer cases carrying remains of fallen service members are off-loaded from aircraft arriving at Dover AFB and are transported to the loading dock of Port Mortuary. Under OAFME jurisdiction, all remains are put through an eight-step identification process before being released to the preparation side of the house for embalming, wrapping, dressing, and transportation to their final place of interment:

Step 1. The first step in the identification process is assignment of a medical examiner number. After a medical examiner number has been assigned, the decedent moves to *Step 2* of the process—the explosive ordnance disposal (EOD) section. EOD is housed with two cement bunkers each approximately 12 inches thick, with a ½-inch stainless steel outer casing, built to withstand a 60-mm mortar blast. The decedent is placed through an automated fluoroscopy machine where trained EOD technicians look for unexploded ordnances. Once the decedent is cleared through EOD the body goes to *Step 3,* forensic photography. Here the human remains pouch will be digitally photographed both fully zipped and unzipped, creating a permanent digital record. Following forensic photography, the decedent is moved to *Step 4* to receive a bar-coded band that is scanned during each of the various processes within the Mortuary Operations Management System [MOMS]. Administrative personnel can promptly locate any while housed at the center. *Step 5* of the process is FBI fingerprinting. OAFME has a memorandum of understanding with the FBI latent fingerprint section to conduct fingerprint exams on all decedents coming through Port Mortuary. Positive identification is made 97% of the time via fingerprints. Postmortem prints are taken, compared to ante-mortem records and verified by two latent print examiners. After fingerprinting, the decedent is transported to step six of the process—full body digital x-ray. *Step 6*: Digital x-rays are taken and stored on a mainframe system where the images are sent to computer terminals at each autopsy station, and stored on CDs. In January 2004, Port Mortuary started using virtual autopsy performed Multidetector Computed Tomography (MDCT), through the auspices of a Defense Advanced Research Projects Agency (DARPA) grant. The overall aim of assessing virtual autopsy is to improve survivability on the battlefield. Since its inception, over 4000 casualties have been scanned with MDCT. Multidetector CT has aided in the prediction of lethal wounds, location of metallic fragments, reassociation of disassociated body portions, and supported the diagnosis of drowning when other causes of death have been excluded by means of limited autopsy. *Step 7* of the process is postmortem dental x-ray/exam. Postmortem dental exams and digital radiographs are performed by members of the Armed Forces Institute of Pathology's (AFIP) forensic odontology team augmented by staff at the Dover AFB dental clinic. After dental, the decedent is transported to *Step 8* in the process—autopsy. The autopsy suite is equipped with ten stations, each with its own computer terminal where radiologic digital images can be viewed. Once scientific identification of the decedent is confirmed, it is turned over to the preparation side of Port Mortuary where embalming, wrapping, dressing, and transportation to a final resting place takes place. The Port Mortuary is the largest in the Department of Defense and plays a vital role as a place of honor where the remains of DOD personnel killed overseas are received.

Along with other duties at the center, Col. Hanshaw has trained hundreds of joint military mortuary affairs specialists from the U.S. Army Quartermaster Center and School at Fort Lee, VA. In 2006, the office of the Air Force Surgeon General mandated the development of medical forensic sustainment support teams. Col. Hanshaw developed the curricula and trained five teams creating a mission support capability to augment the work at Port Mortuary. In addition, she has worked diligently with the Department of Defense and tri-service teams to improve the standards and quality of forensic medical care in the U.S. military, and has served as a primary consultant on forensic nursing issues within the military.

Forensic nurses in the military have demonstrated that they possess unique training and skills that may be applied in many ways within the Armed Services, both to improve the lives of its members and to enhance judicial processes. The question is whether or not they will be afforded the opportunities. Given the wide scope of the responsibilities associated with being a military officer, and their infinite dedication to service, it seems certain that forensic nursing is destined to flourish within the U.S. Armed Forces.

Boundaries in Practice

Traditional boundaries between nursing and medicine over recent years have become a fusion of roles and responsibilities. As a consequence, traditional roles performed by doctors within the medicolegal sphere are becoming available to nurse practitioners. Dr. Guy N. Rutty, head of the Department of Pathology at the University of Leicester, United Kingdom, wrote:

> *I suppose one of the problems may be the old school opinion of doctors that the only people who can undertake this work is a doctor. The same resistance was met with the development of the advanced nurse practitioner. I am sure that if we went back 20 years the thought that nurses would be undertaking their own clinics, prescribing drugs or undertaking surgical procedures then one might of considered one a heretic, a dreamer, or a mad man. But this is medicine today.*

Boundaries between forensic disciplines are often vague, despite federal or state statutes, institutional policies or regulations, licensure, role definition, or job descriptions. Much is determined by the personalities involved and whether or not there is collegiality and mutual respect for one another's contributions. In recent years, forensic nurses have been added to the mix of law enforcement, medical, and legal disciplines and at times have been viewed as trespassers. However, roles and relationships are slowly being more clearly defined, and coordinated procedures are resulting in improved delivery of forensic services.

Boundaries and relationships are often forged during multidisciplinary team investigations of large-scale incidents or mass disasters. Yet the scene could be as simplistic as interface with the police accompanying a victim to the emergency department or transferring a prisoner from the jail for evidence collection or emergency treatment. Each discipline must understand its unique duties and stand ready to appreciate those of others. Law enforcement agencies control the crime scene, who and when one is allowed to enter, and what activities they are allowed to perform. At the same time, the police must recognize the duly authorized presence of the FNE or FNDI regulated by law or executive request to take charge of a decedent's body and recover medical evidence under the auspices of the officiator of death. Forensic nurses must bring their maturity, professionalism, and restraint to the scene to avoid the need to engage in conflict management, which is often embarrassing, time consuming, and counterproductive. Less stressful opportunities should be planned to achieve a clear understanding of one another's contributions to forensic science. These include educational programs, social situations, and encounters within one another's work settings when urgent issues are not on the agenda. Outcomes are sometimes referred to as *transdisciplinary* where a perspective is sought that recognizes, accepts, and works

Box 52-1 National Academy of Sciences Recommendations

Recommendation 1: As soon as reasonably practicable, a validation investigation must be launched by a scientific organization with the highest credentials into each forensic science practice for which serious challenges regarding its scientific foundation exist or are raised in the future. If the validation investigation concludes that this scientific foundation is lacking, that organization or its equivalent must determine the research needed to validate the forensic science practice.

Recommendation 2: All public and private forensic science laboratories, at a minimum, must be compliant with the laboratory-accreditation requirements set by ASCLD/LAB or an equivalent accrediting organization.

Recommendation 3: Forensic science laboratory accreditation requirements established by ASCLD/LAB and equivalent accrediting organizations should be strengthened to include a mandate that all laboratory personnel designated by their units to testify in criminal prosecutions be board-certified in their respective fields.

Recommendation 4: It is essential that forensic science methodologies and terminology be standardized and that the definitions of the terminology be readily accessible to the public.

Recommendation 5: All professional forensic science organizations should establish, and provide the resources to enforce, Codes of Ethics imposing on their members, under penalty of expulsion or other serious sanction, the obligation to conduct investigations and provide testimony with the highest integrity.

Recommendation 6: Any federal forensic science oversight agency should incorporate into any mandatory system of accreditation, certification, and/or validation those independent professional entities already engaged in the accreditation and certification tasks, such as the Forensic Specialties Accreditation Board, ASCLD/LAB, the Medical Specialties Accreditation Board, and the Forensic Science Education Programs Accreditation Commission.

Recommendation 7: The knowledge of attorneys and judges with respect to forensic science and scientific evidence must be improved. The responsibility for this improvement properly falls on forensic science practitioners and attorneys. A curriculum covering all forensic science disciplines, with entries at varying levels of proficiency, should be developed through the cooperative efforts of professional organizations of forensic practitioners and attorneys such as the American Academy of Forensic Sciences, the International Association for Identification, the National Association of Criminal Defense Lawyers, the National District Attorneys Association, and the National Center for State Courts and government agencies such as the Federal Judicial Center and the National Institute of Justice.

Source: *Strengthening Forensic Science in the United States: A Path Forward*, Committee on Identifying the Needs of the Forensic Sciences Community: Committee on Applied and Theoretical Statistics, National Research Council, National Academy of Sciences, 2009.

with the differences in values and perspectives. It is not just the solution that is being explored but the means of achieving this solution (www.lhds.bcu.ac.uk/strategicdevelopment/exploring-boundaries).

A clear understanding of what is and what is not nursing is essential knowledge. Forensic nurses practice strictly within the nurse practice act, which is defined by state laws that govern nursing practice and, in some cases, nursing education, protecting the safety and welfare of the public. Many states have already revised their nurse practice acts and licensure provisions to include specific guidance for those engaged in certain general and advanced practice roles such as forensic nursing.

PUBLIC EXPECTATIONS

Public expectations of forensic science have been fueled by the media and citizens expecting rapid resolution of crimes, but governmental agencies have not funded the facilities and human resources required to reap the benefits of the proven forensic sciences. In 2009, the National Academy of Sciences released its report *Strengthening Forensic Science in the United States: A Path Forward*, which exposed the shortcomings of today's forensic science initiatives, including those associated with the output of crime laboratories. In response, during the 61st American Academy of Forensic Sciences (AAFS) meeting in Denver, President Thomas L. Bohan recognized the strengths of forensic sciences in the United States and praised those who work in the forensic sciences, but he expressed serious concern over the report's findings that crime laboratories were characterized by serious deficiencies. He appointed a panel of experts to examine issues within the forensic sciences and to prepare a set of recommendations aimed at strengthening the integrity of the profession (Box 52-1). A formal position statement followed, which established the Academy's expectations of the forensic science community. This includes forensic nursing (Box 52-2).

Box 52-2 AAFS Position Statement on Strengthening Forensic Science in the United States

The American Academy of Forensic Sciences supports the recommendations of the National Academy of Sciences report Strengthening Forensic Science in the United States: A Path Forward (NAS Report, 2009). From among the various views and recommendations espoused, we particularly emphasize, endorse, and promote the following principles:

1. All forensic science disciplines must have a strong scientific foundation.
2. All forensic science laboratories should be accredited.
3. All forensic scientists should be certified.
4. Forensic science terminology should be standardized.
5. Forensic scientists should be assiduously held to Codes of Ethics.
6. Existing forensic science professional entities should participate in governmental oversight of the field.
7. Attorneys and judges who work with forensic scientists and forensic science evidence should have a strong awareness and knowledge of the scientific method and forensic science disciplines.

Source: AAFS News Release to Members, August 9, 2009.

HORIZONS FOR THE FORENSIC NURSE

Increasingly, the United States and other countries are turning to FNEs to fill a void where there is a serious deficiency in the numbers of physicians who are engaged in the forensic sciences. Former deficiencies have resulted in loss of evidence, long delays in response times, inadequate prosecution, and the loss of human lives. Forensic nursing services can assist law enforcement and emergency physicians in meeting the expectations of victims and their families through accessible and cost-effective programs (Lynch, 2006, p. 383). Roles once limited to physicians, politicians, police, or attorneys have now become available to forensic nursing personnel. Such roles are recognized to provide critical thinking and forensic assessments involving rape, torture, and custodial abuse. Forensic nurses are now accomplishing investigations that were once strictly within the purview of other agents. These roles include pronouncement of death, forensic assessments of refugees for the immigration courts, clinical forensic investigations of clustered deaths in hospitals, sexual assault examinations, and digital evidence recovery (Bogart, 1998).

Innovations in Forensic Nursing Service Delivery

Memorial Hermann Hospital is world renown in healthcare, especially for its level one trauma center where forensic nurses have been providing specialized care for victims of sexual assault since 1993. Forensic services were expanded to additional interpersonal violence victims in 2003, including child and elder abuse, intimate partner violence, and other individuals with healthcare-related forensic issues. In the same year, the *Forensic Nurse Response Team* was formalized to provide this specialized care throughout the Memorial Hermann Healthcare System which encompasses 10 hospitals, including a children's hospital. To serve this extended network, a mobile forensic unit was outfitted with over $20,000 of equipment donated by its hospital voluneers. During that first month of its operation, forensic nurses only saw 10 patients, but in 2009, the team averaged over 110 patients per month.

Over 50 law enforcement agencies from six countries in the Houston metropolitan area utilize the *Forensic Nurse Response Team* to provide forensic services for victims and suspects. Law enforcement, victim advocacy, and district attorneys are members of an associated multi-disciplinary team working to improve the response to vicitms as well as to assure fair treatment for those suspected or convicted of committing crimes.

Best practices for forensic nursing cannot be achieved in a vacuum, and the success of Memorial Hermann's programs attest to this. The Houston model illustrates the value of forensic nursing services, and confirms the benefits of collaborate practice with other disciplines. Informal meetings, case reviews, and problem-solving sessions allow opportunities for members to appreciate one another's role in the medicolegal processes. Justice can be best served when law enforcement ensures victim safety and an efficient investigation of the crime, when the courts are provided essential scientific evidence, and when the victim has been adequately supported to withstand courtroom proceedings.

The forensic nurse is a significant resource for victims of a domestic and international terrorism that results from a society's culture, tradition, and religious beliefs. With the rapid sociocultural transformation of modern urban societies, perspectives about crime and criminality are changing. These new perspectives require stronger education, more extensive experience, credentials, the development of new roles, and the acceptance of nurses as partners in health and justice systems worldwide.

Summary

Forensic nursing leadership continues the quest to develop new and innovative roles and deliver forensic nursing care in settings as diverse as the countries in which they practice. Problems associated with human rights violation, crimes against children and the elderly, and human trafficking have no geographical or cultural boundaries. The FNE educated at an advanced level has unlimited potential in the global healthcare market to fill essential roles in government and nongovernment (NGO) positions (Fagin, 1990).

The United Nations (UN) and the International Committee of the Red Cross (ICRC) have designated missions to address issues of human rights, especially during the times of armed conflict or during episodes of ethnic cleansing. These organizations are developing improved strategies to reduce crimes against women and children, especially during armed conflict when these individuals become easy targets for physical exploitation and sexual abuse. The ICRC has a permanent mandate under international law to impartially care for prisoners, the wounded and sick, and civilians affected by conflict. Within the UN and the ICRC, there are many opportunities for infusing the knowledge and skills of the forensic nurse. The FNE can provide a range of services appropriate and appealing to the agencies that respond to disasters such as in the Thai tsunami tragedy, the investigation of social and gender crimes in South Africa, and now in wartime, support the military's forensic medical services.

THE FUTURE

Among forensic nurses, there is great enthusiasm for expanding the field and for advancing the specialty an extant component of nursing education and practice. However, there are limitations imposed by financial and human resources that impede program development and role evolutions. Along with other worthwhile initiatives in healthcare and social justice, forensic nursing must establish the required credentials and prove its credibility, awaiting the chance to fully emerge and flourish.

References

Ahluwala, A. (2002). *Domestic violence against women in India: A socio-legal study. Master's of law dissertation.* Patiala, Punjab: Punjabi University.
AIDS Orphans of East Africa. (www.UNICEFUSA.org). Viewed April 14, 2009.
American Academy of Forensic Sciences. (2009). Proceedings, Vol. 15, (D26), Denver, CO. February 16–21, 2009. pp. 193.
American Academy of Forensic Sciences. President's message to members. August 9, 2009, Colorado Springs, CO: 2009.
Amnesty International. (April 2003). *Zimbabwe: Rights under siege: State intimidation of Human Rights NGO Amani Trust.* Index Number: AFR 46/015/2003. www.amnesty.org/en/library/info/AFR46/015/2003. Viewed May 20, 2009.
Australian Institute of Criminology. (2008). *Australian crime: Facts and figures.* Canberra. www.aic.gov.au/en/publications/current%20series/facts/1-20/2008.aspx. Viewed April 20, 2009.
Bogart, J. B. (1998). *Legal Nurse Consulting: Principles and Practices.* Houston,TX: American Association of Legal Nurse Consultants.
Crime in Ireland: A Growing Concern. News.bbc.org. February 10, 2007. http://goireland.about.com/b/2007/02/10/crime-in-ireland-a-growing-concern.htm. Viewed May 20, 2009.
Department of Defense (DOD). (2004). *Task force report on care for victims of sexual assault.* April 2004.
Department of Defense (DOD). (2006a). *DOD Instruction 6495.02 – Sexual assault prevention and response program procedures.* Retrieved on June 27, 2008 from www.sapr.mil.
Department of Defense (DOD). (2006b). *DOD Instruction 6495.02 - Sexual assault prevention and response program procedures.* Retrieved on June 27, 2008 from www.sapr.mil.
Department of Defense (DOD). (2006c). *DOD Instruction 6495.02 - Sexual assault prevention and response program procedures.* Retrieved on June 27, 2008 from www.sapr.mil.
Diamond Fields Advertiser. Forensic Detective for the Northern Cape. July 2, 1999. pg. 3.
Duma, S. (2006). Women's journey of recovery from sexual assault trauma. Doctoral dissertation. Kimberley, South Africa: University of Cape Town.

Fagin, C. (1990). Nursing's values prove itself. *American Journal of Nursing, 90*(10), 17–30.

Ferguson, C. (2008). Caring for sexual assault patients in the military. *Journal of Forensic Nursing, 4*(4), 190–198.

Flinders University. www.flinders.edu.au/courses/postgrad/ng-for/. Accessed online, May 20, 2009.

Forensic Medicine in Israel. http://lib.bioinfo.pl/medid:58910. Accessed online, April 28, 2009.

Gorea, R. K. (2004). Bringing hope to India. *On the Edge, 10*(3).

Gorea, R. K. (2005). Development of forensic nursing in India: Step by step. *Journal of Indian Academy of Forensic Medicine, 27*(4), 207.

Gorea, R. K., Jasuja, O. P., Lynch, V., & Singh, K. (2002). Forensic nursing in India: Need of the hour. *Journal of Punjab Academy of Forensic Medicine and Toxicology, 2,* (1): 49.

Honduras: Police undergoing purge as crime rate soars. Thursday, August 31, 2000. www.alibusiness.com/central-america/623747-1.hmtl. Viewed April 30, 2009.

Honduras Crime, (NotiCen Publication, August 31, 2000). (2009). Viewed April 30, 2009. http://findarticles.com/p/articles/mi_go1655/is_2000_August_31/ai_n28789094/.

International Association of Forensic Nurses and American Nurses Association. (2009). *Scope and Standards of Forensic Nursing Practice.* Silver Spring, MD: American Nurses Publishing.

International Association of Forensic Nurses in 2007 at the 15th Annual Scientific Assembly in Salt Lake City, Utah, USA (*On the Edge*, p. 450, 2008).

Israel rape and sexual assault against minors on the rise in Israel. 27 July 2008. http://lib.bioinfo.pl/medid:58910. Viewed May 10, 2009.

Lynch, V. (1990). Clinical forensic nursing: Role development. Thesis. University of Texas at Arlington, TX.

Lynch, V. (2006). *Forensic nursing.* St. Louis. MO: Elsevier.

Lynch, V. (2007). *Global update. UK Association of Forensic Nursing. On the Edge.* IAFN Newsletter. Volume 13, Number 3 - Fall 2007.

Machielse, P. (2008). Forensic emergency nursing - Role integration. *On The Edge – Fall 2008.* www.iafn.org/displaycommon.cfm?an=1&subarticlenbr=244. Viewed May 2, 2009.

National Academy of Sciences. (2009). *Strengthening Forensic Science in the United States: A Path Forward, Committee on Identifying the Needs of the Forensic Sciences Community.* Committee on Applied and Theoretical Statistics, National Research Council, National Academy of Sciences.

Nevada State Board of Nursing. (2004). *Nurse Practice Act.* Retrieved on August 27, 2008 from: www.nursingboard.state.nv.us/pinf/pracdecs.htm#sexual%20assault%20nurse%20examiner.

New Jersey Division of Consumer Affairs. (2004). *New Jersey Register Volume 36, Number 6 Monday, March 15, 2004 Rule Adoption: Law and Public Safety Division of Consumer Affairs: State Board of Nursing Sexual Assault Nurse Examiner Program.* Retrieved August 27, 2008 from http://www.state.nj.us/lps/ca/adoption/nurado31504.htm.

Njogu, A. *Kenya: The War on Kenyan Women. Pambazuka News Weekly Forum for Social Justice in Africa.* 30 January 2009 (All Africa.com). Viewed May 24, 2009.

Notre Dame University, Perth Australia. www.studyinaustralia.gov.au/Sia/ko/CourseSearch/courselist.htm?Sectors=HIGHER-EDUCATION&Provider=01032F&PrintMode=true&FoS=16&Course=nursing&States=ACT%2CNSW%2CNT%2CQLD%2CSA%2CTAS%2CVIC%2CWA. Accessed October 17, 2009.

Ortiz, M. (2008). Standing by, ready to serve: The case for forensic nurses in uniform. *Military Medicine, 173*(1), 42–45.

Peterson, C. (2000). Nursing International. *American Journal of Nursing,* ANA Issues Update. January, *100*(1), 65–66.

Phakathi, M. *Politics in Swaziland: New lawmaker arrives with female view.* Mbabane, Swaziland: IPS/GIN. (October 24, 2008).

Radio Free Europe, Radio Liberty. (August, 2009). *Bosnian Serbs arrested on Wartime Massacre.* www.rferl.org/content/Two_Bosnian_Serbs_Arrested_On_Wartime_Massacre_Charges/1808824.html Charges. Viewed August 6, 2009.

Rawoot, I: Mail and Guardian Online. (2009). *Grammar of violence.* Johannesburg, SA. www.mg.co.za/article/2009-08-27-grammar-of-violence. Viewed Sept. 6, 2009.

Thuthuzela Care Centres (TCC). National Prosecution Authority pamphlet, (undated) Cape Town, South Africa.

United Kingdom Association of Forensic Nurses. (www.ukafn.org). Viewed April 14, 2009.

Victoria Institute of Forensic Medicine. www.vifm.org/gc_nursing.html. Viewed April 14, 2009.

World Health Organization. (2007). Lynch, V. The forensic nurse examiner: New strategies in pediatric sexual assault examination. Conference Proceedings. Johannesburg, South Africa: 1st International Congress on Sexual Abuse of the African Child.

World Health Report on Violence and Health. (2002). whr@who.int. Viewed May16, 2009.

Yacoub, S. Arellando, S., & Padgett-Moncada, D. (2006). Violence related injuries, deaths and disabilities in the capital of Honduras. *Journal of Clinical Forensic Medicine, 37*(5), 428–434.

International Association of Forensic Nurses Vision of Ethical Practice*

Used by permission of the International Association of Forensic Nurses

The International Association of Forensic Nurses expects its members to aspire to the highest standards of ethical nursing practice. This vision of ethics is a framework for approaching professional decisions and stimulating ethical dialogue based on the ideas of our organization.

Forensic nurses acknowledge the importance of membership in a global society. This includes providing forensic nursing care in a manner that respects the uniqueness of the patient or client. Forensic nurses collaborate with nurses, health care providers, and other professionals throughout the world to promote ethically informed and culturally competent practices.

When faced with ethical choices, forensic nurses should use recognized ethical frameworks for decision making. The guiding principles of ethical decision making are autonomy, justice, beneficence, and non-malfeasance. Forensic nurses should consult and collaborate with appropriate ethical resources.

Scope

FIDELITY TO PATIENTS AND CLIENTS

Forensic nurses serve patients and clients faithfully and incorruptibly. Forensic nurses respect confidentiality and advise patients and clients about the limits of confidentiality as determined by their practice setting.

RESPONSIBILITY TO THE PUBLIC

Forensic nurses have a professional responsibility to serve the public welfare. Forensic nurses should be actively concerned with the health and welfare of the global community. Forensic nurses should recognize their role in preventing violence that includes understanding the societal factors, such as oppression that promote violence. Forensic nurses acknowledge the value and dignity of all human beings and strive to create a world where violence is not accepted.

OBLIGATION TO SCIENCE

Forensic nurses should seek to advance nursing and forensic science, understand the limits of their knowledge, and respect the truth. Forensic nurses should ensure that their research and scientific contributions are thorough, accurate, and unbiased in design and presentation. Forensic nurses should incorporate evidence-based knowledge in practice decisions.

Conflicts of interest should be disclosed. Scientific misconduct, such as fabrication, falsification, slander, libel, and plagiarism are incompatible with this Vision of Ethical Practice. Public comments regarding scientific matters should be made with care and precision, devoid of unsubstantiated claims, exaggeration, and/or premature conclusions.

DEDICATION TO COLLEAGUES

Forensic nurses perform work honestly and competently, fulfill obligations, and safeguard proprietary information. Forensic nurses should regard the tutelage of students as a trust conferred by society for the promotion of the student's learning and professional development. Forensic nurses should treat colleagues with respect, share ideas honestly, and give credit for their contributions.

*The Vision of Ethical Practice was revised by the IAFN Ethics Committee in 2008, reviewed by Members and approved by the IAFN Board in November of 2008.

Nursing Diagnoses for Forensic Nursing Problems and Issues*

Cris Finn

Victim Management: Psychological and Emotional

- Fear related to perceived inability to control situation
- Ineffective individual or family coping skills
- Anxiety related to situational crisis
- Body image disturbance
- Potential for violence—self-directed or directed at others
- Disturbance in self-concept related to self-esteem, body image, and personal identity
- Social isolation related to situational depression
- Disturbance related to self-esteem
- Fear related to perceived retaliation or physical harm (fear of blame for activity, fear of punishment, fear of threats)
- Fear related to cognitive confusion
- Disturbance in sleep pattern related to manifestations of anxiety
- Anxiety related to prognosis and feelings of helplessness
- Anxiety related to discussion of intimate information, diagnosis, and concerns for partner and/or children
- Disturbance in self-concept related to loss of control
- Ineffective coping related to inability to manage situational crisis
- Anxiety related to pain, treatment methods, and lifestyle implications
- Alteration in thought process, perception
- Body image disturbance related to lifestyle changes necessitated by treatment
- Anxiety related to loss of self-control
- Altered thought process related to depression
- Potential disturbance in self-concept as a result of abuse from caregiver

Victim Management: Physical Injuries and Disabilities Associated with Violence

- Risk of infection as a result of interruption in integrity of skin barrier
- Knowledge deficit related to prevention of injury
- Knowledge deficit related to diagnosis and therapeutic procedures

- Potential for injury related to helplessness
- Pain related to tissue, nerve, or vessel disruption from penetrating, blunt, or extremity trauma
- Pain related to swelling and dislocation
- Potential for infection related to unsafe sexual exposure
- Alteration in comfort because of pain
- Risk of injury because of altered state of consciousness and neurological defects
- Ineffective breathing pattern related to altered ventilator mechanisms
- Ineffective airway clearance related to mechanical obstruction (asphyxia)
- Fluid volume deficit—actual or potential—related to blood loss
- Impaired physical mobility related to injury and pain
- Alteration in tissue perfusion related to hypovolemia (impaired blood supply) or vascular compromise from fractures
- Risk of altered body temperature as a result of loss of skin integrity and environmental heat losses
- Anxiety related to hemorrhage and uncertainty of treatment
- Knowledge deficit related to cause of bleeding
- Potential for activity intolerance related to weakness
- Potential for secondary infection
- Alteration in skin integrity as a result of animal or human bite
- Altered thought process related to cerebral hypoxia
- Potential for self-care deficit related to visual impairment
- Anxiety related to prognosis
- Potential for infection secondary to immunocompetence
- Ineffective bowel elimination as a result of inflammation, obstruction, or ileus
- Ineffective breathing pattern related to hyperventilation
- Alteration in thought processes as a result of delirium or coma
- Sensory-perceptual alteration—visual, auditory, kinesthetic
- Knowledge deficit related to discharge instructions
- Impaired or ineffective verbal communication
- Alteration in health maintenance
- Potential for injury related to hopelessness (elder)
- Anxiety related to discomfort, procedures, surgery, prognosis, loss of function, and alteration of body image
- Sensory-perceptual alteration regarding self and situation
- Disturbance in sleep pattern related to manifestations of anxiety

*Partial List

631

Procedures for Sexual Assault Examination for Male Victims

Sheila D. Early

General Guidelines

- Male patients presenting for sexual assault medical forensic examination are more likely than female patients to have suffered physical trauma and genital injuries.
- Male patients are at greater risk of secondary traumatization by caregivers because of the lack of experience and expertise of the examiner in situations of male assault.
- Male patients are more likely to show symptoms of behavioral disorders than female patients on first presentation.

Process

A signed consent for care is needed before commencing the sexual assault medical forensic examination and forensic evidence collection protocol. The patient's options for care and the procedure for examination need to be thoroughly explained and discussed. The examiner will do the following:

- Obtain an accurate medical and event history.
- Provide a medical forensic examination.
- Collect forensic evidence according to facility protocols and local forensic lab procedures.
- Document the medical and forensic findings.
- Initiate and maintain chain of custody for forensic evidence.
- Provide or arrange for treatment of physical injuries, sexually transmitted infection prophylaxis, and referrals for aftercare resources.
- Provide a legal report of medical forensic examination.
- Testify in court as a neutral, objective witness.

Procedure

1. Explain all procedures and the forensic evidence collection process to the patient.
2. Obtain a history of the event from the patient and law enforcement officer if present:
   - Date and time of the event
   - Location of the event—geographical area as well as physical location, such as house, park, or car (may correlate history with findings)
   - Nature of injuries and any use of weapons, force, threats, or restraints (may correlate with physical findings)
   - Nature of events:
     ○ Oral-penile
     ○ Penile-rectal
     ○ Digital-rectal
   - Penetrations or attempted penetrations
   - Condom usage
   - Ejaculation occurrence
   - History of foreign object(s); include site and object
   - Loss of consciousness and, if occurred, for how long
   - Ingestion of drugs, medications, or alcohol before or after the presenting event

3. Obtain a history of postevent behaviors including bathing, showering, urinating, defecating, changing clothes, eating or drinking, brushing teeth, gargling, chewing gum. These activities may result in loss of forensic evidence.
4. Obtain a pertinent personal history including last consensual coitus, whether oral-penile, penile-anal, or penile-vaginal as appropriate (within 72 hours is an accepted guideline). Include date and time if possible.

Personal History

- Medical problems or conditions (e.g., diabetes; cardiac, renal, hepatic conditions; history of thrombus or pulmonary embolism; blood disorders; carcinomas; surgical procedures on genital organs)
- Pertinent anal/rectal history (e.g., hemorrhoids, surgery, fistulas, fissures, carcinoma, bleeding)
- Medications, including antiepileptic medication, antidepressant and antipsychotic medication, and nonprescription medication (especially antihistamines and antacids); this information is needed for possible drug interactions with medications to be administered
- Allergies to drugs
- Tetanus/diphtheria and hepatitis B immunization status
- HIV status if known by patient

Body Evidence

- Use powder-free gloves for all specimen collections.
- With the patient standing on two sheets of paper, have him remove all items of clothing separately and place each article in a separate paper bag. As clothing is removed, examiner labels each bag and lists contents on appropriate program or agency documentation.
- Retain top sheet of paper, bundle, and place in a paper bag. Label with patient's personal data and forensic evidence label, and initial it. Discard bottom sheet of paper.
- Document any stains, tears, cuts, or foreign material that may be present on clothing.
- Inspect for any area of staining on patient's body. Use alternate light source or ultraviolet light to identify area of stains. Remove sample with a swab moistened with sterile water. Document location swab is taken from on appropriate documentation forms. Repeat for every area of staining.
- Inspect entire body for T.E.A.R.S.:
  T = tears or tenderness
  E = ecchymosis (bruises are different from ecchymosis and are documented as bruises)
  A = abrasions
  R = redness
  S = swelling or signs of physical injury
  Document each finding on appropriate body diagrams.

- Query bite marks are swabbed for DNA in the following manner:
  - With a sterile swab moistened with sterile water, swab the entire inside and edges of the query bite mark.
  - With a second sterile swab, remove all moisture from the inside and edges of the query bite mark left by previous swabbing. Both swabs can usually be submitted as one sample with the location from which swabs were taken clearly identified.
  - Each query bite mark area needs to be swabbed and identified separately.
- Check for broken fingernails on patient's hands. Fingernails should be clipped with either scissors or clippers and collected from each hand separately.
- Debris under patient's fingernails can be collected by using a sterile nail pick or by using a sterile swab moistened with sterile water to swab under the fingernails, using a separate swab for each hand.

Oral Examination

- Inspect mouth, tongue, buccal surfaces, uvula, hard and soft palate, and upper and lower lips for signs of trauma. If patient wears orthodontic appliances, inspect for intactness of appliances.
- Semen may be collected in the areas where gums meet the teeth if oral penetration and ejaculation has occurred. Collect oral swab from these areas.
- Obtain medical specimen swabs for gonorrhea if oral penetration has occurred.

Anal/Rectal Examination

- Inspect for T.E.A.R.S., blood, signs of semen, lubricant, or any other foreign substance. Spread buttocks with thumb and index finger. Lacerations or other injuries may occur at 6 and 12 o'clock positions.
- Patient may be examined in chest-knee position (sigmoid position) or left lateral position.

- If there is a history of penetration with foreign objects or any concern regarding rectal trauma, examiner or physician will examine anal/rectal area using anoscope.
- Obtain anal swab from anal sphincter.
- Obtain rectal swab. In chest-knee position it will take approximately two to three minutes for anal sphincter to dilate.
- Collect medical specimen swab for gonorrhea if rectal penetration has occurred.

Medical Laboratory Examinations

Collect medical samples according to facility procedures.

Securing the Evidence

- When the examiner is collecting evidence for the police, he or she must collect and identify each specimen separately, noting the date and in some cases the time, and initialing the labels. Each item is identified by patient data and forensic evidence label.
- When evidence collection has commenced, evidence must never leave the sight of the examiner until it is either transferred to law enforcement or secured as per facility protocols. This maintains a chain of evidence, and the examiner may have to testify in court proceedings that this chain was never broken.
- Forensic evidence is collected and given to the law enforcement officer for all cases when the patient has reported to law enforcement. Documentation is completed as per facility protocols.
- The receiving officer's name and badge number and the case file number are documented.

Baseline Status and Prophylaxis

The patient should be offered protection or prevention for tetanus/diphtheria, hepatitis B, sexually transmitted infections (including gonorrhea, chlamydia, and others depending on local protocols), and HIV postexposure prophylaxis as per facility protocols.

Index

Note: Page Numbers followed by *b* indicate boxes; *f* figures; *t* tables.

A

AAFS (American Academy of Forensic Sciences), 2
  on future of forensic science, 627, 627*b*
AALNC (American Association of Legal Nurse
  Consultants), 613
AAS (Abuse Assessment Screen), 372
AATB (American Association of Tissue Banks),
  594
Abduction, of children, 418
ABFO (American Board of Forensic Odontology)
  No. 2 reference scale, 73, 73*f*
  for bite mark injuries, 320*f*
ABFO (American Board of Forensic Odontology)
  ruler, 55
ABMDI (American Board of Medical Legal Death
  Investigators), 612
ABNS (American Board of Nursing Specialties),
  607–608
Abortion, 498–499
  in China, 499, 499*b*
  by female prisoner, 480
  in India, 499
  in Ireland, 499
  in Latin America, 499, 499*b*
  in United States, 499
Abrasion(s), 292–293, 297
  due to air bag deployment, 276, 277*f*, 278*f*
  appearance of, 292–293, 292*f*, 293*f*
  classification of, 293
  direction of force with, 292–293, 293*f*
  due to elder abuse, 359
  first response to, 126
  graze, 126, 293
  patterned, 292*f*
Abrasion margin, 303
Abrasion ring, 303
Absorption, of drugs, 107–109, 108*t*, 109*t*
Abuse Assessment Screen (AAS), 372
Abusive head trauma, 346–347
ACA (American Correctional Association),
  467, 468
Academic degrees, 608
Acceleration, 271, 272–273
Acceleration injuries, 272
Accidental death, 189
Accidental overlay, due to co-sleeping, 220, 328
Accountability, in forensic nursing, 6, 16
Accreditation, 607–608
ACE (AIDS Counseling and Education)
  Program, 483
ACFE (American College of Forensic Examiners),
  613–614
ACGME (American College of Graduate Medical
  Education), 610
Acquaintance rape. *See* Acquaintance violence.
Acquaintance violence, 372–374
  aspects of, 373
  defined, 372

Acquaintance violence *(Continued)*
  drugs used in, 373
  historical background of, 372
  myth *vs.* reality of, 374*t*
  prevention of, 373–374
  scope of problem of, 373
  screening and assessment for, 373
  statistics on, 372, 373
Acquired immunodeficiency syndrome (AIDS).
  See Human immunodeficiency virus (HIV).
ACTH (adrenocorticotropic hormone),
  posttraumatic stress disorder and, 403
Active gang members, 426
Actual damages, 561–562
Actuarial methods, for assessment of sexual
  offenders, 516, 517*t*
Adam Walsh Child Protection and Safety Act, 415
Adelson, Lester, 184
ADFAA (Aviation Disaster Family Assistance Act), 171
Adipocere, 187, 267–268
Administrative rule making, 537
Administrators, influence on forensic nursing
  education of, 27
Admissable evidence, in emergency department, 163
Admission, crime scene security concerning, 49
Adolescents
  confidentiality with, 541
  informed consent of, 542
  suicidal ideation in, 454
  suicide risk assessment in, 457
Adrenocorticotropic hormone (ACTH),
  posttraumatic stress disorder and, 403
Adult protective services (APS), 355, 357, 364
Adult-child sex, 424
Adulterants, of urine specimens, 114, 114*t*
Advanced Practice Compact, 615
Advanced practice forensic nurses (AFNs), 614,
  614*t*, 615
Advanced practice nurse (APN), 614, 614*t*, 615
Advanced Practice Registered Nurses (APRNs), 615
Advocacy, of prisoners, 470–471, 472
Aerial photography, in taphonomy, 258, 258*f*,
  262, 264
Aesthetics, ethics and, 569
Affective disorders, as suicide risk factors, 453
Affiliate gang members, 426
AFIP (Armed Forces Institute of Pathology),
  624–625
AFNs (advanced practice forensic nurses), 614,
  614*t*, 615
Africa
  female genital mutilation in, 498, 522, 522*f*
  forensic nursing in, 618
African-American gang(s), 427–429
  Bloods as, 428, 428*f*
  Crips as, 427–428, 427*f*
  Folk Nation as, 429, 429*f*
  People Nation as, 429, 430*f*
  United Blood Nation as, 428–429, 428*f*

Age
  drug overdose deaths by, 36–37, 37*t*
  of homicide victims, 40, 41*t*
  natural deaths by, 35, 35*f*
Agencies, identification of, in crime scene
  processing, 47–48
Aging prisoners, 474–475
Aguirre, Jason Alejandro, 433*b*
AIDS. *See* Human immunodeficiency virus (HIV).
AIDS Counseling and Education (ACE) Program,
  483
Air bags, 275, 283
  deployment of
    deaths due to, 275, 276*f*
    injuries related to, 275–278, 277*f*, 278*f*, 283
    mechanism of, 275, 283
  design of, 275, 283
  efficacy of, 275
  functions of, 283
  history of, 275
  injuries from module cover of, 275, 276*f*, 277*f*
  seat belts and, 275
Airway injuries, due to air bag deployment,
  275–276
Alcohol abuse
  case study on, 120*b*
  and domestic violence, 375
  in drug-facilitated sexual assault, 117, 117*f*
  and incarceration
    epidemiology of, 482
    with mental illness, 482
    screening for, 482
    treatment for, 482
  and sexual assault, 386–387, 401, 402
  as suicide risk factor, 453
Algor mortis, 267
ALI (American Law Institute), on legal insanity,
  448
Ali, Omar, 503
Ali, Syed, 508–509
Alibek, Ken, 33
Allograft tissue, 594
Alprazolam, half-life of, 119*t*
Alternative light source (ALS)
  in emergency department, 158
  for sexual assault examination, 147
Alzheimer's disease, sexual abuse with, 362
Amani Trust, 618
American Academy of Forensic Sciences
  (AAFS), 2
  on future of forensic science, 627, 627*b*
American Association of Legal Nurse Consultants
  (AALNC), 613
American Association of Tissue Banks (AATB),
  594
American Bar Association, 538
American Board of Forensic Odontology (ABFO)
  No. 2 reference scale, 73, 73*f*
  for bite mark injuries, 320*f*